Oxford Essential Portuguese Dictionary

SECOND EDITION

Portuguese–English
English–Portuguese

OXFORD
UNIVERSITY PRESS

OXFORD

UNIVERSITY PRESS

Great Clarendon Street, Oxford, OX2 6DP,
United Kingdom

Oxford University Press is a department of the University of Oxford.
It furthers the University's objective of excellence in research, scholarship,
and education by publishing worldwide. Oxford is a registered trade mark of
Oxford University Press in the UK and in certain other countries

First published as the Oxford Portuguese Mini Dictionary in 2006
First Edition published in 2009
Second Edition published in 2012

British Library Cataloguing in Publication Data
Data available

Library of Congress Cataloguing in Publication Data
Data available

ISBN 978-0-19-964097-3

Printed and bound in Great Britain by Clays Ltd, Elcograf S.p.A.

Contents/Índice

Proprietary terms/Nomes comerciais   iv

Contributors/Colaboradores   v

Introduction/Introdução   vi

Portuguese pronunciation/Pronúncia portuguesa   x

Portuguese spelling reform/Acordo ortográfico   xiv

English pronunciation/Pronúncia inglesa   xvi

Abbreviations/Abreviaturas   xviii

Portuguese–English/Português–Inglês   **1–212**

English–Portuguese/Inglês–Português   **213–474**

Portuguese verbs/Verbos portugueses   475

Verbos irregulares ingleses/English irregular verbs   483

Proprietary terms

This dictionary includes some words which are, or are asserted to be, proprietary names or trade marks. Their inclusion does not imply that they have acquired for legal purposes a non-proprietary or general significance, nor is any other judgement implied concerning their legal status. In cases where the editor has some evidence that a word is used as a proprietary name or trade mark this is indicated by the symbol ®, but no judgement concerning the legal status of such words is made or implied thereby.

Nomes comerciais

Este dicionário inclui algumas palavras que são, ou acredita-se ser, nomes comerciais ou marcas registadas. A sua inclusão no dicionário não implica que elas tenham adquirido para fins legais um significado geral ou não-comercial, assim como não afeta em nenhum dos conceitos implícitos o seu status legal. Nos casos em que o editor tenha prova suficiente de que uma palavra seja usada como um nome comercial ou marca registada, este emprego é indicado pelo símbolo ®, mas nenhuma apreciação relativa ao status legal de tais palavras é feita ou sugerida por esta indicação.

Contributors/Colaboradores

Portuguese-English *compiled by John Whitlam*
English–Portuguese *compiled by Lia Correia Raitt*
Revisions for the second edition: *Vanda Meneses Santos, Teresa Barbosa, Daniel Grassi, Helen Newstead, Catarina Fouto, Alison Aiken, Mike Harland, Sarah Bailey, Mariana Cunha, Susana Valdez*

Thanks are due to/Agradecimentos a: Dr John Sykes, Prof. A. W. Raitt, Comandante Virgílio Correia, Marcelo Affonso, Eng. Pedro Carvalho, Eng. Vasco Carvalho, Dr Iva Correia, Dr Ida Reis de Carvalho, Eng. J. Reis de Carvalho, Prof. A. Falcão, Bispo Manuel Falcão, Dr M. Luísa Falcão, Prof. J. Ferraz, Prof. M. de Lourdes Ferraz, Drs Ana e Jorge Fonseca, Mr Robert Howes, Eng. Hugo Pires, Prof. M. Laura Pires, Dr M. Alexandre Pires, Embaixador L. Pazos Alonso, Dr Teresa Pinto Pereira, Dr Isabel Tully, Carlos Wallenstein, e Dr H. Martins e os membros de sua Mesa Lusófona do St Anthony's College, em Oxford.

Introduction

This new edition of the *Oxford Essential Portuguese Dictionary* is designed as a practical reference tool for tourists, students and business people alike, and it includes a host of new features to help the user get the most out of the dictionary.

The wordlist has been updated to include the latest words and meanings in both languages (e.g. *blogger, carbon footprint, social networking; avatar, ciberespeculador, mídia social*), and all the Portuguese text has been revised in line with the latest spelling reform (see also page xiv). This new edition also includes notes on life and culture in the United Kingdom and the United States (e.g. *Congress, Edinburgh Festival, gap year*), as well as special treatment of complex grammatical words in both languages, such as *do, have; de, estar*. These expanded entries are presented in boxes to help the user find them more easily, and contain language notes to warn of possible pitfalls.

The dictionary has an easy-to-use, streamlined layout. Bullets separate parts of speech within an entry, and different meanings are signposted using indicators or typical collocates with which the headword frequently occurs. The swung dash (~) is used to replace a headword, or that part of a headword preceding the vertical bar (|).

In both English and Portuguese, only irregular plural forms are given. Plural forms of Portuguese nouns and adjectives ending in a single vowel are formed by adding an s (e.g. *livro, livros*). Those ending in *n, r, s* where the stress falls on the final syllable, and *z*, add *es* (e.g. *mulher, mulheres, falaz, falazes*). Nouns and adjectives ending in *m* change the final *m* to *ns* (e.g. *homem, homens, bom, bons*); those ending in *ol* change their ending to *óis* (e.g. *lençol, lençois*); and nouns ending in *al* change their ending to *ais* (e.g. *casal, casais*). Most of those ending in *ão* change their ending to *ões* (e.g. *estação, estações*).

Portuguese nouns and adjectives ending in an unstressed *o* form the feminine by changing the *o* to *a* (e.g. *belo, bela*). Those ending in *or* become *ora* (e.g. *trabalhador, trabalhadora*). All other masculine–feminine changes are shown at the main headword.

English and Portuguese pronunciation is given by means of the International Phonetic Alphabet. It is shown for all headwords, and for those derived words whose pronunciation is not easily deduced from that of a headword.

Portuguese verb tables will be found in the appendix.

Introdução

Esta nova edição do *Oxford Essential Portuguese Dictionary* foi concebida como uma ferramenta de referência prática para turistas, estudantes e profissionais, e inclui uma série de novos recursos para ajudar o utilizador a tirar o máximo proveito do dicionário.

A lista de vocábulos foi atualizada de modo a incluir palavras e significados mais recentes em ambas as línguas (ex. *blogger, carbon footprint, social networking*; *avatar, ciberespeculador, mídia social*) e todo o português foi revisto à luz do Acordo Ortográfico. Esta nova edição também inclui notas culturais sobre o Reino Unido e os Estados Unidos (ex. *Congress, Edinburgh Festival, gap year*), bem como um tratamento especial a palavras gramaticais complexas em português e inglês, tais como *do, have*; *de, estar*. Estes verbetes mais detalhados encontram-se destacados dentro de caixas, de modo a facilitar a sua identificação, e contêm anotações linguísticas alertando o utilizador para possíveis armadilhas.

O dicionário possui uma apresentação visual simplificada e fácil de usar. Em cada verbete, as categorias gramaticais estão separadas por itens e os significados distintos encontram-se sinalizados através de indicadores ou colocações típicas utilizadas no contexto em que a palavra frequentemente ocorre. O sinal (~) é usado para substituir o verbete, ou parte deste precedendo a barra vertical (|).

Tanto em inglês como em português, somente as formas irregulares do plural são dadas. As formas regulares do plural dos substantivos ingleses recebem um *s* (ex. *teacher, teachers*), ou *es* quando terminarem em *ch, sh, s, ss, us, x* ou *z* (ex. *sash, sashes*). Os substantivos terminados em *y* e precedidos por uma consoante, mudam no plural para *ies* (ex. *baby, babies*).

O passado e o particípio passado dos verbos regulares ingleses são formados pelo acréscimo de *ed* à forma infinitiva (ex. *last, lasted*). Os verbos terminados em *e* recebem *d* (ex. *move, moved*). Aqueles terminados em *y* têm o *y* substituído por *ied* (*carry, carried*). As formas irregulares dos verbos aparecem no dicionário por ordem alfabética, remetidas à forma infinitiva, e também na lista de verbos no apêndice.

As pronúncias inglesa e portuguesa são dadas em acordo com o Alfabeto Fonético Internacional. A pronúncia é dada para todos os verbetes, assim como para aquelas palavras derivadas cuja pronúncia não seja facilmente deduzida a partir do verbete.

Portuguese Pronunciation

The phonetics shown in this dictionary are for Brazilian Portuguese. The main differences in the pronunciation of European Portuguese are shown at the end of this section.

Vowels and Diphthongs

a, à, á, â	/ã/	chamam, ambos, antes	1) before *m* at the end of a word, or before *m* or *n* and another consonant, is nasalized
	/a/	aba, à, acolá, desânimo	2) in other positions is like *a* in English *rather*
ã	/ã/	irmã	is nasalized
e	/ẽ/	sem, venda	1) before *m* at the end of a word, or before *m* or *n* and another consonant, is nasalized
	/i/	arte	2) at the end of a word is like *y* in English *happy*
	/e/	menas	3) in other positions is like *e* in English *they*
é	/ɛ/	artéria	is like *e* in English *get*
ê	/e/	fêmur	is like *e* in English *they*
i	/ĩ/	sim, vindo	1) before *m* at the end of a word, or before *m* or *n* and another consonant, is nasalized
	/i/	fila	2) in other positions is like *ee* in English *see*
o	/õ/	com, sombra, onda	1) before *m* at the end of a word, or before *m* or *n* and another consonant, is nasalized
	/u/	muito	2) at the end of a word, unstressed, is like *u* in English *rule*
	/o/	comover	3) in other positions, unstressed, is like *o* in English *pole*
	/o/	bobo	4) stressed, is like *o* in
	/ɔ/	loja	English *pole* or *o* in *shop*
ó	/o/	ópera	is like *o* in English *shop*
ô	/o/	tônica	is like *o* in English *pole*

u, ú		guerra, guisado, que, quilo	1) is usually silent in *gue*, *gui*, *que*, and *qui* but is sometimes pronounced /w/, as in tranqu*i*lo, cinqu*e*nta, ung*ue*nto
	/u/	mula, púrpura	2) in other positions is like *u* in English r*u*le
ãe	/ãj/	mãe, pães, alemães	is like *y* in English b*y*, but nasalized
ai	/aj/	vai, pai, sai, caixa	is like *y* in English b*y*
ao, au	/aw/	aos, autodefesa	is like *ow* in English h*ow*
ão	/ãw/	não	is like *ow* in English h*ow*, but nasalized
ei	/ej/	lei	is like *ey* in English th*ey*
eu	/ew/	deus, fleugma	both vowels pronounced separately
õe	/õj/	eleições	is like *oi* in English c*oi*n, but nasalized
oi	/oj/	noite	is like *oi* in English c*oi*n
ou	/o/	pouco	is like *o* in English p*o*le

Consonants

b		banho	is like *b* in English *b*all
c	/s/	cinza, cem	1) before *e* or *i* is like *s* in English *s*it
	/k/	casa	2) in other positions is like *c* in English *c*at
ç	/s/	estação	is like *s* in English *s*it
ch	/ʃ/	chá	is like *sh* in English *sh*out
d	/dʒ/	dizer, donde	1) before *i* or final unstressed *e* is like *j* in English *j*oin
	/d/	dar	2) in other positions is like *d* in English *d*og
f	/f/	falar	is like *f* in English *f*all
g	/ʒ/	agente, giro	1) before *e* or *i* is like *s* in English vi*s*ion
	/g/	gato	2) in other positions is like *g* in English *g*et
h		haver	is silent in Portuguese, but see *ch*, *lh*, *nh*
j	/ʒ/	junta	is like *s* in English vi*s*ion
k	/k/	kit	is like *k* in English *k*ey
l	/w/	falta	1) between a vowel and a consonant, or following a vowel at the end of a word, is like *w* in English *w*ater
	/l/	lata	2) in other positions is like *l* in English *l*ike
l	/ʎ/	calhar	is like *lli* in English mi*lli*on
m		ambas/ãbuʃ/ com/kõ/	1) between a vowel and a consonant, or after a vowel at the end of a word, *m* nasalizes the preceding vowel
	/m/	mato, mão	2) in other positions is like *m* in English *m*other

. . . .

n		cinza/'sĩza/	1) between a vowel and a consonant, n nasalizes the preceding vowel
	/n/	benigno	2) in other positions is like n in English near
nh	/ɲ/	banho	is like ni in English opinion
p	/p/	paz	is like p in English poor
q	/k/	que, inquieto	1) qu before e or i is like English k
	/kw/	quase, quórum	2) qu before a or o, or qü before e or i, is like qu in English queen
r	/ɾ/	aparato, gordo	1) between two vowels, or between a vowel and a consonant, is trilled
	/x/	rato, garra, melro, genro, Israel	2) at the beginning of a word, or in rr, or after l, n, or s, is like ch in Scottish loch
s	/ʃ/	depois	1) at the end of a word is like sh in English shoot
	/z/	asa, desde, abismo, Israel	2) between two vowels, or before b, d, g, l, m, n, r, v, is like z in English zebra
	/s/	suave	3) in other positions is like s in English sit
t	/tʃ/	tio, antes	1) before i or final unstressed e is like ch in English cheese
	/tʃi/	kit	2) at the end of a word is like chy in English itchy
	/t/	atar	3) in other positions is like t in English tap
v	/v/	luva	is like v in English vain
w	/u/	watt	is shorter than English w
x	/z/	exato, exemplo	1) in the prefix ex before a vowel, is pronounced like z in zero
	/ʃ/	xícara, baixo, peixe, frouxo	2) at the beginning of a word or after ai, ei or ou, is pronounced like sh in show
	/s/	explodir, auxiliar	3) is like s in English sit
	/ks/	axila, fixo	4) is like x in English exit
			5) in the combination xce, xci, x is not pronounced in Portuguese e.g. excelente, excitar
z	/s/	falaz	1) at the end of a word, is like s in English sit
	/z/	dizer	2) in other positions, is like English z

• •

European Portuguese Pronunciation

The main differences in pronunciation are:

d	/d/	dar, dizer, balde, donde	1) at the beginning of a word, or after *l*, or *n*, is like *d* in English *dog*
	/ð/	cidade, medroso	2) in other positions is a sound between *d* in English *dog* and *th* in English *this*
e	/ə/	arte	at the end of a word, is like *e* in English *quarrel*
r	/rr/	rato, garra, melro, genro, Israel, guelra, tenro, israelense	at the beginning of a word, or in *rr*, or after *l*, *n*, or *s*, is strongly trilled
s	/ʃ/	depois, asco, raspar, costura	1) at the end of a word, or before *c*, *f*, *p*, *qu*, or *t*, is like English *sh*
	/ʒ/	desde, Islã, abismo, Israel	2) before *b*, *d*, *g*, *l*, *m*, *n*, *r*, or *u* is like *s* in English *vision*
t	/t/	atar, antes, tio	is like *t* in English *tap*
z	/ʃ/	falaz	at the end of a word, is like *sh* in English *shake*

. . . .

Portuguese spelling reform

. . . .

Brazil and Portugal are in the process of implementing a new spelling reform, which was agreed between all Portuguese-speaking countries in 1990. The aim of the Portuguese spelling reform is to standardize spellings across all Portuguese-speaking countries, and many of the spelling differences that used to exist between Brazilian and European Portuguese have been eliminated. Brazil and Portugal introduced the new spellings in 2009 and 2008 respectively, but there will be a transition period of four years (in Brazil) and six years (in Portugal) in which both spellings will be accepted.

All the spellings in this dictionary have been updated in line with the new reform. Here follows a summary of the main changes:

– Silent consonants -c- and -p- are omitted in words in which the consonants are not pronounced, e.g.

Pre-spelling reform	Post-spelling reform
Br ator, *Port* actor	ator
Br correto, *Port* correcto	correto
Br ótimo, *Port* óptimo	ótimo

Note, however, that the consonant remains in cases where the pronunciation differs between the two countries, e.g. *Br* fato, *Port* facto; *Br* súdito, *Port* súbdito.

– Accents are suppressed in the diphthongs -éi- and -ói- in penultimate syllables:

Pre-spelling reform	Post-spelling reform
Br/Port bóia	boia
Br idéia, *Port* ideia	ideia

– Words ending in -êem and -ôo lose their accents:

Pre-spelling reform	Post-spelling reform
Br/Port vêem	veem
Br vôo, *Port* voo	voo

– Accents used to differentiate homographs, such as *pára* (verb) and *para* (preposition) have been removed. An important exception is *pôr* (verb) and *por* (preposition), which have not been harmonized.

– The diaeresis is no longer present in -güe-, -güi-, and -qüe-, -qüi-:

• •

Pre-spelling reform   **Post-spelling reform**
Br agüentar, *Port* aguentar   aguentar
Br cinqüenta, *Port* cinquenta   cinquenta

– Certain hyphenated compounds lose their hyphens:

Pre-spelling reform   **Post-spelling reform**
Br/Port auto-escola   autoescola
Br/Port mini-saia   minissaia

However, a few differences between European Portuguese and Brazilian spellings still remain, mostly to reflect how the words are pronounced. An important difference to remember is when a written accent is required on *o* or *e* before *m* and *n*, Brazilian Portuguese uses a circumflex, whereas European Portuguese uses an acute accent, e.g. *econômico* (Br), *económico* (Port); *gêmeo* (Br), *gémeo* (Port); *tênis* (Br), *ténis* (Port). Due to the size of the dictionary, it has not been possible to show all European Portuguese spelling variants in the entries. However, the most common European Portuguese lexical variants are included (e.g. *chávena*, *comboio*, *pequeno-almoço*, *telemóvel*).

Pronúncia inglesa

Vogais e Ditongos

/iː/	see, tea	como *i* em *giro*
/ɪ/	sit, happy	é um som mais breve do que *i* em *li*
/e/	set	como *e* em *tépido*
/æ/	hat	é um som mais breve do que *a* em *amor*
/ɑː/	arm, calm	como *a* em *cartaz*
/ɒ/	got	como *o* em *exótico*
/ɔː/	saw, more	como *o* em *corte*
/ʊ/	put, look	como *u* em *murro*
/uː/	too, due	como *u* em *duro*
/ʌ/	cup, some	como *a* em *pano*
/ɜː/	firm, fur	como *e* em *enxerto*
/ə/	ago, weather	como *e* no português europeu *parte*
/eɪ/	page, pain, pay	como *ei* em *leite*
/əʊ/	home, roam	é um som mais longo do que *o* em *coma*
/aɪ/	fine, by, guy	como *ai* em *sai*
/aɪə/	fire, tyre	como *ai* em *sai* seguido por /ə/
/aʊ/	now, shout	como *au* em *aula*
/aʊə/	hour, flower	como *au* em *aula* seguido por /ə/
/ɔɪ/	join, boy	como *oi* em *dói*
/ɪə/	dear, here, beer	como *ia* em *dia*
/eə/	hair, care, bear, there	como *e* em *etéreo*
/ʊə/	poor, during	como *ua* em *sua*

Consoantes

/p/	snap	como *p* em *pato*
/b/	bath	como *b* em *bala*
/t/	tap	como *t* em *tela*
/d/	dip	como *d* em *dar*
/k/	cat, kite, stomach, pique	como *c* em *casa*
/ks/	exercise	como *x* em *axila*
/g/	got	como *g* em *gato*
/tʃ/	chin	como *t* em *tio*
/dʒ/	June, general, judge	como *d* em *dizer*
/f/	fall	como *f* em *faca*

....

/v/	vine, of	como v em vaca
/θ/	thin, moth	não tem equivalente, soa como um s entre os dentes
/ð/	this	não tem equivalente, soa com um z entre os dentes
/s/	so, voice	como s em suave
/z/	zoo, rose	como z em fazer
/ʃ/	she, lunch	como ch em chegar
/ʒ/	measure, vision	como j em jamais
/h/	how	h aspirado
/m/	man	como m em mala
/n/	none	como n em nada
/ŋ/	sing	como n em cinto
/l/	leg	como l em luva
/r/	red, write	como r em cara
/j/	yes, yoke	como i em ioga
/w/	weather, switch	como u em égua

ˈ indica a sílaba tônica, e.g. abusar /abuˈzar/

Abbreviations/Abreviaturas

adjective	*a*	adjetivo
abbreviation	*abbr/abr*	abreviatura
adverb	*adv*	advérbio
article	*art*	artigo
American (English)	*Amer*	(inglês) americano
anatomy	*anat*	anatomia
architecture	*arquit*	arquitetura
astrology	*astr/astrol*	astrologia
motoring	*auto*	automobilismo
aviation	*aviat*	aviação
biology	*biol*	biologia
botany	*bot*	botânica
Brazilian Portuguese	*Br*	português do Brasil
cinema	*cine*	cinema
colloquial	*colloq*	coloquial
commerce	*comm/com*	comércio
computing	*comput*	computação
conjunction	*conj*	conjunção
cookery	*culin*	cozinha
electricity	*electr/eletr*	eletricidade
feminine	*f*	feminina
familiar	*fam*	familiar
figurative	*fig*	figurativo
geography	*geog*	geografia
grammar	*gramm/gram*	gramática
infinitive	*inf*	infinitivo
interjection	*int*	interjeição
interrogative	*interr*	interrogativo
invariable	*invar*	invariável
legal, law	*jur/jurid*	jurídico
language	*lang*	linguagem
literal	*lit*	literal
masculine	*m*	masculino
mathematics	*mat*	matemática
mechanics	*mech*	mecânica

• •

medicine	*med*	medicina
military	*mil*	militar
music	*mus*	música
noun	*n*	substantivo
nautical	*naut*	náutico
negative	*neg*	negativo
oneself	*o.s.*	se, si mesmo
European Portuguese	*P*	português de Portugal
pejorative	*pej*	pejorativo
philosophy	*phil*	filosofia
plural	*pl*	plural
politics	*pol*	política
European Portuguese	*Port*	português de Portugal
past participle	*pp*	particípio passado
prefix	*pref*	prefixo
preposition	*prep*	preposição
present	*pres*	presente
present participle	*pres p*	particípio presente
pronoun	*pron*	pronome
psychology	*psych/psic*	psicologia
past tense	*pt*	pretérito
relative	*rel*	relativo
religion	*relig*	religião
somebody	*sb*	alguém
singular	*sing*	singular
slang	*sl*	gíria
something	*sth*	algo
subjunctive	*subj*	subjuntivo
technology	*techn/tecn*	tecnologia
theatre	*theat/teat*	teatro
television	*TV*	televisão
United Kingdom	*UK*	Reino Unido
United States	*US*	Estados Unidos
university	*univ*	universidade
auxiliary verb	*v aux*	verbo auxiliar
intransitive verb	*vi*	verbo intransitivo
pronominal verb	*vpr*	verbo pronominal
transitive verb	*vt*	verbo transitivo
transitive & intransitive verb	*vt/i*	verbo transitivo e intransitivo

Aa

a /a/ ● *artigo*

····▶ the; ~ **casa** the house; ~ **Maria ainda não chegou** Maria hasn't arrived yet

❗ O artigo é omitido em inglês com nomes próprios, ou com parentes: **a vovó já chegou** *grandma has arrived*; **onde está a Joana?** *where's Joana?*

····▶ (*com partes do corpo, roupa*) **ela quebrou ~ perna** she broke her leg; ~ **sua camisa está do lado contrário** your shirt is back to front

❗ Em português, utiliza-se em geral o artigo para se referir a partes do corpo, enquanto no inglês usa-se o pronome possessivo.

● *pron*

····▶ (*mulher*) her

····▶ (*coisa*) it

····▶ (*você*) you

● *prep*

····▶ (*direção*) to; **vou ~ São Paulo** I am going to São Paulo

····▶ (*posição*) **à esquerda** on the left; **ao meu lado** by my side

····▶ (*distância*) ~ **dez quilómetros daqui** ten kilometres from here

····▶ (*frequência*) **uma vez ao ano** once a year; **tenho aulas de dança às sextas** I have dance classes on Fridays

····▶ (*esporte*) **ganharam de 2 ~ zero** they won 2 nil

····▶ (*modo, meio*) **ir ~ pé** go on foot; **lavar à mão** handwash; **escrever (ao computador)** type

····▶ (*com preço, medida*) **cinco libras ~ hora** five pounds an hour; **às centenas** by the hundreds; **vender às dúzias** sell by the dozen

····▶ (*com tempo, idade, parte do dia*) **às onze** at eleven; **aos cinquenta anos** at (the age of) 50; **à noite** at night

····▶ (*com velocidade*) **estão ~ 100 quilómetros por hora** they're going at 100 kilometres per hour

····▶ (*seguido de infinitivo*) **fomos os primeiros ~ chegar** we were the first to arrive

····▶ (*complemento indireto*) to; **dê isto à sua tia** give this to your aunt

····▶ (*em expressões*) **provar por ~ mais b** prove beyond doubt

à /a/ = **a** *prep*

aba /'aba/ *f* (*de chapéu*) brim; (*de camisa*) tail; (*de mesa*) flap

abacate /aba'katʃi/ *m* avocado (pear)

abacaxi /abaka'ʃi/ *m* pineapple; 🄸 (*problema*) pain, headache

aba|de /a'badʒi/ *m* abbot. ~**dia** *f* abbey

aba|fado /aba'fadu/ *a* (*tempo*) humid, close; (*quarto*) stuffy. ~**far** *vt* (*asfixiar*) stifle; muffle (*som*); smother (*fogo*); suppress (*informação*); cover up (*escândalo, assunto*)

abagunçar /abagũ'sar/ *vt* mess up

abaixar /aba'ʃar/ *vt* lower; turn down (*som, rádio*). ~**se** *vpr* bend down

abaixo /a'baʃu/ *adv* down; ~ **de** below; **mais ~** further down. ~**assinado** *m* petition

abajur /aba'ʒur/ *m* (*quebra-luz*) lampshade; (*lâmpada*) (table) lamp

aba|lar /aba'lar/ *vt* shake; *fig* shock. ~**lar-se** *vpr* be shocked, be shaken. ~**lo** *m* shock

abanar /aba'nar/ *vt* shake, wave; wag (*rabo*); (*com leque*) fan

abando|nar /abãdo'nar/ *vt* abandon; (*deixar*) leave. ~**no** /o/ *m* abandonment; (*estado*) neglect

abarcar /abar'kar/ *vt* comprise, cover

abarro|tado /abaxo'tadu/ *a* crammed full; (*lotado*) crowded, packed. ~**tar** *vt* cram full, stuff

abastado /abas'tadu/ *a* wealthy

abaste|cer /abaste'ser/ *vt* supply; fuel (*motor*); fill up (with petrol) (*carro*); refuel (*avião*). ~**cimento** *m* supply; (*de carro, avião*) refuelling

aba|ter /aba'ter/ *vt* knock down; cut down, fell (*árvore*); shoot down (*avião, ave*); slaughter (*gado*); knock down, cut (*preço*); ~**ter alguém** (*trabalho*) get sb down; wear sb out; (*má notícia*) sadden sb; (*doença*) lay sb low, knock the stuffing out of sb. ~**tido** *a* dispirited, dejected; (*cara*) haggard, worn. **~timento** m dejection; (de preço) reduction

abaulado /abaw'ladu/ a convex; ‹estrada› cambered

abcesso /ab'sɛsu/ m Port ▶ ABSCESSO

abdi|cação /abidʒika'sãw/ f abdication. **~car** vt/i abdicate

abdômen /abi'domẽ/ m abdomen

abecedário /abese'dariu/ m alphabet, ABC

abeirar-se /abe'rarsi/ vr draw near

abe|lha /a'beʎa/ f bee. **~lhudo** a inquisitive, nosy

abençoar /abẽso'ar/ vt bless

aber|to /a'bɛrtu/ pp de ▶ ABRIR ● a open; ‹céu› clear; ‹gás, torneira› on; ‹sinal› green. **~tura** f opening; Foto aperture; Pol liberalization

abeto /a'betu/ m fir (tree)

abis|mado /abiz'madu/ a astonished. **~mo** m abyss

abjeto /abi'ʒetu/ a abject

abóbada /a'bɔbada/ f vault

abobalhado /aboba'ʎadu/ a silly

abóbora /a'bɔbora/ f pumpkin

abobrinha /abo'briɲa/ f courgette, Amer zucchini

abo|lição /aboli'sãw/ f abolition. **~lir** vt abolish

abomi|nação /abomina'sãw/ f abomination. **~nável** (pl **~náveis**) a abominable

abo|nar /abo'nar/ vt guarantee ‹dívida›; give a bonus to ‹empregado›. **~no** /o/ m guarantee; (no salário) bonus; (subsídio) allowance, benefit; (reforço) endorsement

abordar /abor'dar/ vt approach ‹pessoa›; broach, tackle ‹assunto›; Naut board

aborre|cer /aboxe'ser/ vt (irritar) annoy; (entediar) bore. **~cer-se** vpr get annoyed; get bored. **~cido** a annoyed; bored. **~cimento** m annoyance; boredom

abor|tar /abor'tar/ vi miscarry, have a miscarriage ● vt abort. **~to** /o/ m abortion; (natural) miscarriage

aboto|adura /abotoa'dura/ f cufflink. **~ar** vt button (up) ● vi bud

abra|çar /abra'sar/ vt hug, embrace; embrace ‹causa›. **~ço** m hug, embrace

abrandar /abrã'dar/ vt ease ‹dor›; temper ‹calor, frio›; mollify, appease, placate ‹povo›; tone down, smooth over ‹escândalo› ● vi ‹dor› ease; ‹calor, frio›

become less extreme; ‹tempestade› die down

abranger /abrã'ʒer/ vt cover; (entender) take in, grasp; **~ a** extend to

abrasileirar /abrazile'rar/ vt Brazilianize

abre-|garrafas /abriga'xafas/ m invar Port bottle opener. **~latas** m invar Port can opener

abreugrafia /abrewgra'fia/ f X-ray

abrevi|ar /abrevi'ar/ vt abbreviate ‹palavra›; abridge ‹livro›. **~atura** f abbreviation

abridor /abri'dor/ m **~ (de lata)** can opener; **~ de garrafa** bottle opener

abri|gar /abri'gar/ vt shelter; house ‹sem-teto›. **~gar-se** vpr (take) shelter. **~go** m shelter

abril /a'briw/ m April

abrir /a'brir/ vt open; (a chave) unlock; turn on ‹gás, torneira›; make ‹buraco, exceção› ● vi open; ‹céu, tempo› clear (up); ‹sinal› turn green. **~se** vpr open; (desabafar) open up

abrupto /a'bruptu/ a abrupt

abrutalhado /abruta'ʎadu/ a ‹sapato› heavy; ‹pessoa› coarse

abscesso /abi'sɛsu/ m abscess

absolu|tamente /abisoluta'mẽtʃi/ adv absolutely; (não) not at all. **~to** a absolute; **em ~to** not at all, absolutely not

absol|ver /abisow'ver/ vt absolve; Jurid acquit. **~vição** f absolution; Jurid acquittal

absor|ção /abisor'sãw/ f absorption. **~to** a absorbed. **~vente** a ‹tecido› absorbent; ‹livro› absorbing. **~ver** vt absorb. **~ver-se** vpr get absorbed

abs|têmio /abis'temiu/ a abstemious; (de álcool) teetotal ● m teetotaller. **~tenção** f abstention. **~tencionista** a abstaining ● m/f abstainer. **~ter-se** vpr abstain; **~ter-se de** refrain from. **~tinência** f abstinence; síndrome de **~tinência** withdrawal symptoms pl

abstra|ção /abistra'sãw/ f abstraction; (mental) distraction. **~ir** vt separate. **~to** a abstract

absurdo /abi'surdu/ a absurd ● m nonsense

abun|dância /abũ'dãsia/ f abundance. **~dante** a abundant. **~dar** vi abound

abu|sar /abu'zar/ vi go too far; **~sar de** abuse; (aproveitar-se) take advantage of. **~so** m abuse

abutre /a'butri/ *m* vulture

aca|bado /aka'badu/ *a* finished; (*exausto*) exhausted; (*velho*) decrepit. **~bamento** *m* finish. **~bar** *vt* finish ● *vi* finish, end; (*esgotar-se*) run out; **~bar com** put an end to, end; (*abolir, matar*) do away with; split up with ‹*namorado*›; wipe out ‹*adversário*›; **~bou de chegar** he has just arrived; **~bar fazendo** ou **por fazer** end up doing. **~bar-se** *vpr* end, be over; (*esgotar-se*) run out

acabrunhado /akabru'ɲadu/ *a* dejected

aca|demia /akade'mia/ *f* academy; (*de ginástica etc*) gym. **~dêmico** *a* & *m* academic

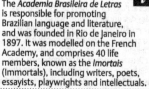

Academia Brasileira de Letras
The *Academia Brasileira de Letras* is responsible for promoting Brazilian language and literature, and was founded in Rio de Janeiro in 1897. It was modelled on the French Academy, and comprises 40 life members, known as the *Imortais* (Immortals), including writers, poets, essayists, playwrights and intellectuals.

açafrão /asa'frãw/ *m* saffron

acalentar /akalẽ'tar/ *vt* lull to sleep ‹*bebê*›; cherish ‹*esperanças*›; have in mind ‹*planos*›

acalmar /akaw'mar/ *vt* calm (down) ● *vi* ‹*vento*› drop; ‹*mar*› grow calm. **~se** *vpr* calm down

acam|pamento /akãpa'mẽtu/ *m* camp; (*ato*) camping. **~par** *vi* camp

aca|nhado /aka'ɲadu/ *a* shy. **~nhamento** *m* shyness. **~nhar-se** *vpr* be shy

ação /a'sãw/ *f* action; *Jurid* lawsuit; *Com* share

acariciar /akarisi'ar/ *vt* (*com a mão*) caress, stroke; (*adular*) make a fuss of; cherish ‹*esperanças*›

acarretar /akaxe'tar/ *vt* bring, cause

acasalar /akaza'lar/ *vt* mate. **~se** *vpr* mate

acaso /a'kazu/ *m* chance; **ao ~** at random; **por ~** by chance

aca|tamento /akata'mẽtu/ *m* respect, deference. **~tar** *vt* respect, defer to ‹*pessoa, opinião*›; obey, abide by ‹*leis, ordens*›; take in ‹*criança*›

acautelar-se /akawte'larsi/ *vpr* be cautious

acei|tação /asejta'sãw/ *f* acceptance. **~tar** *vt* accept. **~tável** (*pl* **~táveis**)

a acceptable

acele|ração /aselera'sãw/ *f* acceleration. **~rador** *m* accelerator. **~rar** *vi* accelerate ● *vt* speed up

acenar /ase'nar/ *vi* signal; (*saudando*) wave; **~ com** promise, offer

acender /asẽ'der/ *vt* light ‹*cigarro, fogo, vela*›; switch on ‹*luz*›; heat up ‹*debate*›

aceno /a'senu/ *m* signal; (*de saudação*) wave

acen|to /a'sẽtu/ *m* accent. **~tuar** *vt* accentuate; accent ‹*letra*›

acepção /asep'sãw/ *f* sense

acepipes /ase'pipʃ/ *m pl* Port cocktail snacks

acerca /a'serka/ **~ de** *prep* about, concerning

acercar-se /aser'karsi/ *vpr* **~ de** approach

acertar /aser'tar/ *vt* find ‹(*com o*) *caminho, (a) casa*›; put right, set ‹*relógio*›; get right ‹*pergunta*›; guess (correctly) ‹*solução*›; hit ‹*alvo*›; make ‹*acordo, negócio*›; fix, arrange ‹*encontro*› ● *vi* (*ter razão*) be right; (*atingir o alvo*) hit the mark; **~ com** find, happen upon; **~ em** hit

acervo /a'servu/ *m* collection; *Jurid* estate

aceso /a'sezu/ *pp de* ▶ ACENDER ● *a* ‹*luz*› on; ‹*fogo*› alight

aces|sar /ase'sar/ *vt* access. **~sível** (*pl* **~síveis**) *a* accessible; affordable ‹*preço*›. **~so** /ɛ/ *m* access; (*de raiva, tosse*) fit; (*de febre*) attack. **~sório** *a* & *m* accessory

acetona /ase'tona/ *f* (*para unhas*) nail varnish remover

achado /a'ʃadu/ *m* find

achaque /a'ʃaki/ *m* ailment

achar /a'ʃar/ *vt* find; (*pensar*) think. **~se** *vpr* (*estar*) be; (*considerar-se*) think that one is; **acho que sim/não** I think so/ I don't think so

achatar /aʃa'tar/ *vt* flatten; cut ‹*salário*›

aciden|tado /asidẽ'tadu/ *a* rough ‹*terreno*›; bumpy ‹*estrada*›; eventful ‹*viagem, vida*›; injured ‹*pessoa*›. **~tal** (*pl* **~tais**) *a* accidental. **~te** *m* accident

acidez /asi'des/ *f* acidity

ácido /'asidu/ *a* & *m* acid

acima /a'sima/ *adv* above; **~ de** above; **mais ~** higher up

acio|nar /asio'nar/ *vt* operate; *Jurid* sue. **~nista** *m/f* shareholder

acirrado /asi'xadu/ *a* stiff, tough

acla|mação /aklama'sãw/ f acclaim; (de rei) acclamation. **~mar** vt acclaim

aclarar /akla'rar/ vt clarify, clear up ● vi clear up. **~se** vpr become clear

aclimatar /aklima'tar/ vt acclimatize, Amer acclimate. **~se** vpr get acclimatized, Amer get acclimated

aço /'asu/ m steel; **~ inoxidável** stainless steel

acocorar-se /akoko'rarsi/ vpr squat (down)

acolá /ako'la/ adv over there

acolcho|ado /akowʃo'adu/ m quilt. **~ar** vt quilt; upholster ‹móveis›

aco|lhedor /akoλe'dor/ a welcoming. **~lher** vt welcome ‹hóspede›; take in ‹criança, refugiado›; accept ‹decisão, convite›; respond to ‹pedido›. **~lhida** f, **~lhimento** m welcome; (abrigo) refuge

acomodar /akomo'dar/ vt accommodate; (ordenar) arrange; (tornar cômodo) make comfortable. **~se** vpr make o.s. comfortable

acompa|nhamento /akõpaɲa'mẽtu/ m Mus accompaniment; (prato) side dish; (comitiva) escort. **~nhante** m/f companion; Mus accompanist. **~nhar** vt accompany, go with; watch ‹jogo, progresso›; keep up with ‹eventos, caso›; keep up with, follow ‹aula, conversa›; share ‹política, opinião›; Mus accompany; **a estrada ~nha o rio** the road runs alongside the river

aconche|gante /akõʃe'gãtʃi/ a cosy, Amer cozy. **~gar** vt (chegar a si) cuddle; (agasalhar) wrap up; (na cama) tuck up; (tornar cômodo) make comfortable. **~gar-se** vpr ensconce o.s.; **~gar-se com** snuggle up to. **~go** /e/ m cosiness, Amer coziness; (abraço) cuddle

acondicionar /akõdʒisio'nar/ vt condition; pack, package ‹mercadoria›

aconse|lhar /akõse'λar/ vt advise; **~lhar alguém a** advise sb to; **~lhar algo a alguém** recommend sth to sb. **~lhar-se** vpr consult. **~lhável** (pl **~lháveis**) a advisable

aconte|cer /akõte'ser/ vi happen. **~cimento** m event

acordar /akor'dar/ vt/i wake up

acorde /a'kɔrdʒi/ m chord

acordeão /akordʒi'ãw/ m accordion

acordo /a'kordu/ m agreement; **de ~ com** in agreement with ‹pessoa›; in accordance with ‹lei etc›; **estar de ~** agree

Açores /a'soris/ m pl Azores

açoriano /asori'anu/ a & m Azorean

acorrentar /akoxẽ'tar/ vt chain (up)

acossar /ako'sar/ vt hound, badger

acos|tamento /akosta'mẽtu/ m hard shoulder, Amer berm. **~tar-se** vpr lean back

acostu|mado /akostu'madu/ a usual, customary; **estar ~mado a** be used to. **~mar** vt accustom; **~mar-se a** get used to

acotovelar /akotove'lar/ vt (empurrar) jostle; (para avisar) nudge

açou|gue /a'sogi/ m butcher's (shop). **~gueiro** m butcher

acovardar /akovar'dar/ vt cow, intimidate

acre /'akri/ a ‹gosto› bitter; ‹aroma› acrid, pungent; ‹tom› harsh

acredi|tar /akredʒi'tar/ vt believe; accredit ‹representante›; **~tar em** believe ‹pessoa, história›; believe in ‹Deus, fantasmas›; (ter confiança) have faith in. **~tável** (pl **~táveis**) a believable

acre-doce /akri'dosi/ a sweet and sour

acrescentar /akresẽ'tar/ vt add

acres|cer /akre'ser/ vt (juntar) add; (aumentar) increase ● vi increase; **~cido de** with the addition of; **~ce que** add to that the fact that

acréscimo /a'kresimu/ m addition; (aumento) increase

acriançado /akriã'sadu/ a childish

acrílico /a'kriliku/ a acrylic

acroba|cia /akroba'sia/ f acrobatics. **~ta** m/f acrobat

acuar /aku'ar/ vt corner

açúcar /a'sukar/ m sugar

açuca|rar /asuka'rar/ vt sweeten; sugar ‹café, chá›. **~reiro** m sugar bowl

açude /a'sudʒi/ m dam

acudir /aku'dʒir/ vt/i **~ (a)** come to the rescue (of)

acumular /akumu'lar/ vt accumulate; combine ‹cargos›

acupuntura /akupũ'tura/ f acupuncture

acu|sação /akuza'sãw/ f accusation. **~sar** vt accuse; Jurid charge; (revelar) reveal, show up; acknowledge ‹recebimento›

acústi|ca /a'kustʃika/ f acoustics. **~co** a acoustic

adap|tação /adapta'sãw/ f adaptation. **~tado** a ‹criança› well-adjusted. **~tar** vt adapt; (*para encaixar*) tailor. **~tar-se** *vpr* adapt. **~tável** (*pl* **~táveis**) *a* adaptable

adega /a'dɛga/ *f* wine cellar

adentro /a'dẽtru/ *adv* inside; **selva ~** into the jungle

adepto /a'dɛptu/ *m* follower; *Port* (*de equipa*) supporter

ade|quado /ade'kwadu/ *a* appropriate, suitable. **~quar** *vt* adapt, tailor

adereços /ade'resus/ *m pl* props

ade|rente /ade'rẽtʃi/ *m/f* follower. **~rir** *vi* (*colar*) stick; join ‹*a partido, causa*›; follow ‹*a moda*›. **~são** *f* adhesion; (*apoio*) support. **~sivo** *a* sticky, adhesive ● *m* sticker

ades|trado /ades'tradu/ *a* skilled. **~trador** *m* trainer. **~trar** *vt* train; break in ‹*cavalo*›

adeus /a'dews/ *int* goodbye ● *m* goodbye, farewell

adian|tado /adʒiã'tadu/ *a* advanced; ‹*relógio*› fast; **chegar ~tado** be early. **~tamento** *m* progress; (*pagamento*) advance. **~tar** *vt* advance ‹*dinheiro*›; put forward ‹*relógio*›; bring forward ‹*data, reunião*›; get ahead with ‹*trabalho*› ● *vi* ‹*relógio*› gain; (*ter efeito*) be of use; **não ~ta (fazer)** it's no use (doing). **~tar-se** *vpr* progress, get ahead. **~te** *adv* ahead

adi|ar /adʒi'ar/ *vt* postpone; adjourn ‹*sessão*›. **~amento** *m* postponement, adjournment

adi|ção /adʒi'sãw/ *f* addition. **~cionar** *vt* add. **~do** *m* attaché

adivi|nhação /adʒiviɲa'sãw/ *f* guesswork; (*por adivinho*) fortune telling. **~nhar** *vt* guess; tell ‹*futuro, sorte*›; read ‹*pensamento*›. **~nho** *m* fortune teller

adjetivo /adʒe'tʃivu/ *m* adjective

adminis|tração /adʒiministra-'sãw/ *f* administration; (*de empresas*) management. **~trador** *m* administrator; manager. **~trar** *vt* administer; manage ‹*empresa*›

admi|ração /adʒimira'sãw/ *f* admiration; (*assombro*) wonder(ment). **~rado** *a* admired; (*surpreso*) amazed, surprised. **~rador** *m* admirer ● *a* admiring. **~rar** *vt* admire; (*assombrar*) amaze. **~rar-se** *vpr* be amazed. **~rável** (*pl* **~ráveis**) *a* admirable; (*assombroso*) amazing

admis|são /adʒimi'sãw/ *f* admission; (*de escola*) intake. **~sível** (*pl* **~síveis**) *a* admissible

admitir /adʒimi'tʃir/ *vt* admit; (*permitir*) permit, allow; (*contratar*) take on

adoçante /ado'sãtʃi/ *m* sweetener

adoção /ado'sãw/ *f* adoption

ado|çar /ado'sar/ *vt* sweeten. **~cicado** *a* slightly sweet

adoecer /adoe'ser/ *vi* fall ill ● *vt* make ill

adoles|cência /adole'sẽsia/ *f* adolescence. **~cente** *a* & *mf* adolescent

adorar /ado'rar/ *vt* (*amar*) adore; worship ‹*deus*›; 🄸 (*gostar de*) love

adorme|cer /adorme'ser/ *vi* fall asleep; ‹*perna*› go to sleep, go numb. **~cido** *a* sleeping; ‹*perna*› numb

ador|nar /ador'nar/ *vt* adorn. **~no** /o/ *m* adornment

ado|tar /ado'tar/ *vt* adopt. **~tivo** *a* adopted

adquirir /adʒiki'rir/ *vt* acquire

adu|bar /adu'bar/ *vt* fertilize. **~bo** *m* fertilizer

adu|lação /adula'sãw/ *f* flattery; (*do público*) adulation. **~lar** *vt* make a fuss of; (*com palavras*) flatter

adulterar /aduwte'rar/ *vt* adulterate; cook, doctor ‹*contas*› ● *vi* commit adultery

adul|tério /aduw'tɛriu/ *m* adultery. **~to** *a* & *m* adult

adúltero /a'duwteru/ *m* adulterer (*f*-ess) ● *a* adulterous

advento /adʒi'vẽtu/ *m* advent

advérbio /adʒi'vɛrbiu/ *m* adverb

adver|sário /adʒiver'sariu/ *m* opponent; (*inimigo*) adversary. **~sidade** *f* adversity. **~so** *a* adverse; (*adversário*) opposed

adver|tência /adʒiver'tẽsia/ *f* warning. **~tir** *vt* warn

advo|cacia /adʒivoka'sia/ *f* legal practice. **~gado** *m* lawyer. **~gar** *vt* advocate; *jurid* plead ● *vi* practise law

aéreo /a'ɛriu/ *a* air

aeróbica /'aɛ'rɔbika/ *f* aerobics

ae|rodinâmica /aerodʒi'namika/ *f* aerodynamics. **~rodinâmico** *a* aerodynamic. **~ródromo** *m* airfield. **~romoça** /o/ *f* air hostess. **~ronauta** *m* airman (*f*-woman). **~ronáutica** *f* (*força*) air force; (*ciência*) aeronautics. **~ronave** *f* aircraft. **~roporto** /o/ *m* airport

aeros|sol /aero'sɔw/ (*pl* **~sóis**) *m* aerosol

afabilidade /afabili'dadʒi/ *f* friendliness, kindness

afagar /afa'gar/ vt stroke

afamado /afa'madu/ a renowned, famed

afas|tado /afas'tadu/ a remote; ‹parente› distant; ~tado de (far) away from. ~tamento m removal; (distância) distance; (de candidato) rejection. ~tar vt move away; (tirar) remove; ward off ‹perigo, ameaça›; put out of one's mind ‹ideia›. ~tar-se vpr move away; (distanciar-se) distance o.s.; (de cargo) step down

afá|vel /a'favew/ a (pl ~veis) a friendly, genial

afazeres /afa'zeris/ m pl business; ~ domésticos (household) chores

Afeganistão /afeganis'tãw/ m Afghanistan

afe|gão /afe'gãw/ a & m (f ~gã) Afghan

afeição /afej'sãw/ f affection, fondness

afeiçoado /afejsu'adu/ a (devoto) devoted; (amoroso) fond

afeminado /afemi'nadu/ a effeminate

aferir /afe'rir/ vt check, inspect ‹pesos, medidas›; (avaliar) assess; (cotejar) compare

aferrar /afe'xar/ vt grasp; ~se a cling to

afe|tação /afeta'sãw/ f affectation. ~tado a affected. ~tar vt affect. ~tivo a (carinhoso) affectionate; (sentimental) emotional. ~to /ɛ/ m affection. ~tuoso /o/ a affectionate

afi|ado /afi'adu/ a sharp; skilled ‹pessoa›. ~ar vt sharpen

aficionado /afisio'nadu/ m enthusiast

afilhado /afi'ʎadu/ m godson (f-daughter)

afili|ação /afilia'sãw/ f affiliation. ~ada f affiliate. ~ar vt affiliate

afim /a'fĩ/ a related, similar

afinado /afi'nadu/ a in tune

afinal /afi'naw/ adv ~ (de contas) (por fim) in the end; (pensando bem) after all

afinar /afi'nar/ vt tune ● vi taper

afinco /a'fĩku/ m perseverance, determination

afinidade /afini'dadʒi/ f affinity

afir|mação /afirma'sãw/ f assertion. ~mar vt claim, assert. ~mativo a affirmative

afivelar /afive'lar/ vt buckle

afixar /afik'sar/ vt stick, post

afli|ção /afli'sãw/ f (física) affliction; (cuidado) anxiety. ~gir vt ‹doença› afflict; (inquietar) trouble. ~gir-se vpr worry. ~to a troubled, worried

afluente /aflu'ẽtʃi/ m tributary

afo|bação /afoba'sãw/ f fluster, flap. ~bado a in a flap, flustered. ~bar vt fluster. ~bar-se vpr get flustered, get in a flap

afo|gado /afo'gadu/ a drowned; morrer ~gado drown. ~gador m choke. ~gar vt/i drown; Auto flood. ~gar-se vpr (matar-se) drown o.s.

afoito /a'fojtu/ a bold, daring

afora /a'fɔra/ adv pelo mundo ~ throughout the world

afortunado /afortu'nadu/ a fortunate

afresco /a'fresku/ m fresco

África /'afrika/ f Africa; ~ do Sul South Africa

africano /afri'kanu/ a & m African

afrodisíaco /afrodʒi'ziaku/ a & m aphrodisiac

afron|ta /a'frõta/ f affront, insult. ~tar vt affront, insult

afrouxar /afro'ʃar/ vt/i loosen; (de rapidez) slow down; (de disciplina) relax

afta /'afta/ f (mouth) ulcer

afugentar /afuʒẽ'tar/ vt drive away; rout ‹inimigo›

afundar /afũ'dar/ vt sink. ~se vpr sink

agachar /aga'ʃar/ vi, ~se vpr bend down

agarrar /aga'xar/ vt grab, snatch. ~se vpr ~se a cling to, hold on to

agasa|lhar /agaza'ʎar/ vt, ~lhar-se vpr wrap up (warmly). ~lho m (casaco) coat; (suéter) sweater

agência /a'ʒẽsia/ f agency; ~ de correio post office; ~ de viagens travel agency

agenda /a'ʒẽda/ f diary

agente /a'ʒẽtʃi/ m/f agent

ágil /'aʒiw/ a (pl ágeis) a ‹pessoa› agile; ‹serviço› quick, efficient

agili|dade /aʒili'dadʒi/ f agility; (rapidez) speed. ~zar vt speed up, streamline

ágio /'aʒiu/ m premium

agiota /aʒi'ɔta/ m/f loan shark

agir /a'ʒir/ vi act

agi|tado /aʒi'tadu/ a agitated; ‹mar› rough. ~tar vt wave ‹braços›; wag ‹rabo›; shake ‹garrafa›; (perturbar) agitate. ~tar-se vpr get agitated; ‹mar› get rough

aglome|ração /aglomera'sãw/ f collection; (*de pessoas*) crowd; **~rar** vt collect. **~rar-se** vpr gather

agonia /ago'nia/ f anguish; (*da morte*) death throes

agora /a'gɔra/ adv now; (*há pouco*) just now; **~ mesmo** right now; **de ~ em diante** from now on; **até ~** so far, up till now

agosto /a'gostu/ m August

agouro /a'goru/ m omen

agraciar /agrasi'ar/ vt decorate

agra|dar /agra'dar/ vt please; (*fazer agrados*) be nice to, fuss over ● vi be pleasing, please; (*cair no gosto*) go down well. **~dável** (*pl* **~dáveis**) a pleasant

agrade|cer /agrade'ser/ vt **~cer algo a alguém**, **~cer a alguém por algo** thank sb for sth ● vi say thank you. **~cido** a grateful. **~cimento** m gratitude; *pl* thanks

agrado /a'gradu/ m **fazer ~s a** be nice to, make a fuss of

agra|far /agra'far/ vt Port staple. **~fador** m stapler

agrário /a'grariu/ a land, agrarian

agra|vante /agra'vãtʃi/ a aggravating ● f aggravating circumstance. **~var** vt aggravate, make worse. **~var-se** vpr get worse

agredir /agre'dʒir/ vt attack

agregado /agre'gadu/ m (*em casa*) lodger

agres|são /agre'sãw/ f aggression; (*ataque*) assault. **~sivo** a aggressive. **~sor** m aggressor

agreste /a'grestʃi/ a rural

agrião /agri'ãw/ m watercress

agrícola /a'grikola/ a agricultural

agricul|tor /agrikuw'tor/ m farmer. **~tura** f agriculture, farming

agridoce /agri'dosi/ a bittersweet

agropecuá|ria /agropeku'aria/ f farming. **~rio** a agricultural

agru|pamento /agrupa'mẽtu/ m grouping. **~par** vt group. **~par-se** vpr group (together)

água /'agwa/ f water; **dar ~ na boca** be mouth-watering; **ir por ~ abaixo** go down the drain; **~ benta** holy water; **~ de coco** coconut water; **~ doce** fresh water; **~ mineral** mineral water; **~ salgada** salt water; **~ sanitária** household bleach

aguaceiro /agwa'seru/ m downpour

água-colônia f eau de cologne

aguado /a'gwadu/ a watery

aguardar /agwar'dar/ vt wait for, await ● vi wait

aguardente /agwar'dẽtʃi/ f spirit

aguarrás /agwa'xas/ m turpentine

água-viva /agwa'viva/ f jellyfish

agu|çado /agu'sadu/ a pointed; <*sentidos*> acute. **~çar** vt sharpen. **~deza** f sharpness; (*mental*) perceptiveness. **~do** a sharp; <*som*> shrill; *fig* acute

aguentar /agwẽ'tar/ vt stand, put up with; hold <*peso*> ● vi <*pessoa*> hold out; <*suporte*> hold

águia /'agia/ f eagle

agulha /a'guʎa/ f needle

ai /aj/ m sigh; (*de dor*) groan ● int ah!; (*de dor*) ouch!

aí /a'i/ adv there; (*então*) then

aidético /aj'detʃiku/ a suffering from Aids ● m Aids sufferer

AIDS /'ajdʒis/ f Aids; **vírus da ~** AIDS virus

ainda /a'ĩda/ adv still; **melhor ~** even better; **não ... ~** not ... yet; **~ assim** even so; **~ bem** just as well; **~ por cima** moreover, in addition; **~ que** even if

aipim /aj'pĩ/ m cassava

aipo /'ajpu/ m celery

ajeitar /aʒej'tar/ vt (*arrumar*) sort out; (*arranjar*) arrange; (*ajustar*) adjust. **~se** vpr adapt; (*dar certo*) turn out right, sort o.s. out

ajoe|lhado /aʒoe'ʎadu/ a kneeling (down). **~lhar** vi, **~lhar-se** vpr kneel (down)

aju|da /a'ʒuda/ f help. **~dante** m/f helper. **~dar** vt help

ajuizado /aʒui'zadu/ a sensible

ajus|tar /aʒus'tar/ vt adjust; settle <*disputa*>; take in <*roupa*>. **~tar-se** vpr conform. **~tável** (*pl* **~táveis**) a adjustable. **~te** m adjustment; (*acordo*) settlement

ala /'ala/ f wing

ala|gação /alaga'sãw/ f flooding. **~gadiço** a marshy ● m marsh. **~gar** vt flood

alameda /ala'meda/ f avenue

álamo /'alamu/ m poplar (tree)

alarde /a'lardʒi/ m **fazer ~ de** flaunt; **make a big thing of** <*notícia*>. **~ar** vt/i flaunt

alargar /alar'gar/ vt widen; *fig* broaden; let out <*roupa*>

alarido /ala'ridu/ m outcry

a

alar|ma /a'larma/ *m* alarm. **~mante** *a*
alarming. **~mar** *vt* alarm. **~me** *m* alarm.
~mista *a* & *m* alarmist

alastrar /alas'trar/ *vt* scatter;
(*disseminar*) spread ● *vi* spread

alavanca /ala'vãka/ *f* lever; **~ de**
mudanças gear lever

alba|nês /awba'nes/ *a* & *m* (*f* **~nesa**)
Albanian

Albânia /aw'bania/ *f* Albania

albergue /aw'bεrgi/ *m* hostel

álbum /'awbũ/ *m* album

alça /'awsa/ *f* handle; (*de roupa*) strap;
(*de fusil*) sight

alcachofra /awka'ʃofra/ *f* artichoke

alçada /aw'sada/ *f* competence, power

Alcaida /aw'kaida/ *f Port* ▶ **AL-QAEDA**

álcali /'awkali/ *m* alkali

alcan|çar /awkã'sar/ *vt* reach;
(*conseguir*) attain; (*compreender*)
understand ● *vi* reach. **~çável**
(*pl* **~çáveis**) *a* reachable; attainable. **~ce**
m reach; (*de tiro*) range; (*importância*)
consequence; (*compreensão*)
understanding

alcaparra /awka'paxa/ *f* caper

alcatra /aw'katra/ *f* rump steak

alcatrão /awka'trãw/ *m* tar

álcool /'awkɔw/ *m* alcohol

alcoó|latra /awko'ɔlatra/ *m/f* alcoholic.
~lico *a* & *m* alcoholic

alcunha /aw'kuɲa/ *f* nickname

aldeia /aw'deja/ *f* village

aleatório /alia'tɔriu/ *a* random,
arbitrary

alecrim /ale'krĩ/ *m* rosemary

ale|gação /alega'sãw/ *f* allegation.
~gar *vt* allege

ale|goria /alego'ria/ *f* allegory.
~górico *a* allegorical

ale|grar /ale'grar/ *vt* cheer up; brighten
up ‹*casa*›. **~grar-se** *vpr* cheer up. **~gre**
/ε/ *a* cheerful; ‹*cores*› bright. **~gria** *f* joy

alei|jado /alei'ʒadu/ *a* crippled ● *m*
cripple. **~jar** *vt* cripple

alei|tamento /alejta'mẽtu/ *m*
breastfeeding. **~tar** *vt* breastfeed

além /a'lẽj/ *adv* beyond; **~ de** (*ao
lado de lá de*) beyond; (*mais de*) over;
(*ademais de*) apart from

Alemanha /ale'maɲa/ *f* Germany

ale|mão /ale'mãw/ (*pl* **~mães**) *a* & *m*
(*f* **~mã**) German

alen|tador /alẽta'dor/ *a* encouraging.
~tar *vt* encourage. **~tar-se** *vpr* cheer up.

~to *m* courage; (*fôlego*) breath

alergia /aler'ʒia/ *f* allergy

alérgico /a'lerʒiku/ *a* allergic (**a** to)

aler|ta /a'lerta/ *a* & *m* alert ● *adv* on the
alert. **~tar** *vt* alert

alfa|bético /awfa'bεtʃiku/ *a*
alphabetical. **~betização** *f* literacy.
~betizar *vt* teach to read and write.
~beto *m* alphabet

alface /aw'fasi/ *f* lettuce

alfaiate /awfaj'atʃi/ *m* tailor

al|fândega /aw'fãdʒiga/ *f* customs.
~fandegário *a* customs ● *m* customs
officer

alfine|tada /awfine'tada/ *f* prick; (*dor*)
stabbing pain; *fig* dig. **~te** /e/ *m* pin; **~te
de segurança** safety pin

alforreca /alfo'xeka/ *f Port* jellyfish

alga /'awga/ *f* seaweed

algarismo /awga'rizmu/ *m* numeral

algazarra /awga'zaxa/ *f* uproar, racket

alge|mar /awʒe'mar/ *vt* handcuff.
~mas /e/ *f pl* handcuffs

algibeira /alʒi'bejra/ *f Port* pocket

algo /'awgu/ *pron* something; (*numa
pergunta*) anything ● *adv* somewhat

algodão /awgo'dãw/ *m* cotton;
~(-doce) candy floss, *Amer* cotton
candy; **~ (hidrófilo)** cotton wool, *Amer*
absorbent cotton

alguém /aw'gẽj/ *pron* somebody,
someone; (*numa pergunta*) anybody,
anyone

al|gum /aw'gũ/ (*f* **~guma**) *a* some;
(*numa pergunta*) any; (*nenhum*) no,
not one ● *pron pl* some; **~guma coisa**
something

algures /aw'guris/ *adv* somewhere

alheio /a'ʎeju/ *a* (*de outra pessoa*)
someone else's; (*de outras pessoas*) other
people's; **~ a** foreign to; (*impróprio*)
irrelevant to; (*desatento*) unaware of;
~ de removed from

alho /'aʎu/ *m* garlic. **~-poró** *m* leek

ali /a'li/ *adv* (over) there

ali|ado /ali'adu/ *a* allied ● *m* ally. **~ança**
f alliance; (*anel*) wedding ring. **~ar** *vt*,
~ar-se *vpr* ally

aliás /a'ljaʃ/ *adv* (*além disso*) what's
more, furthermore; (*no entanto*)
however; (*diga-se de passagem*) by the
way, incidentally; (*senão*) otherwise

álibi /'alibi/ *m* alibi

alicate /ali'katʃi/ *m* pliers; **~ de unhas**
nail clippers

alicerce /ali'sɛrsi/ *m* foundation; *fig* basis

alie|nado /alie'nadu/ *a* alienated; (*demente*) insane. **~nar** *vt* alienate; transfer <*bens*>. **~nígena** *a* & *m/f* alien

alimen|tação /alimẽta'sãw/ *f* (*ato*) feeding; (*comida*) food; *Tecn* supply. **~tar** *a* food; <*hábitos*> eating ● *vt* feed; *fig* nurture; **~tar-se de** live on. **~tício** *a* gêneros **~tícios** foodstuffs. **~to** *m* food

ali|nhado /ali'ɲadu/ *a* aligned; <*pessoa*> smart, *Amer* sharp. **~nhar** *vt* align

alíquota /a'likwota/ *f* (*de imposto*) bracket

alisar /ali'zar/ *vt* smooth (out); straighten <*cabelo*>

alistar /alis'tar/ *vt* recruit. **~se** *vpr* enlist

aliviar /alivi'ar/ *vt* relieve

alívio /a'liviu/ *m* relief

alma /'awma/ *f* soul

almanaque /awma'naki/ *m* yearbook

almejar /awme'ʒar/ *vt* long for

almirante /awmi'rãtʃi/ *m* admiral

almo|çar /awmo'sar/ *vi* have lunch ● *vt* have for lunch. **~ço** /o/ *m* lunch

almofada /awmo'fada/ *f* cushion; *Port* (*de cama*) pillow

almôndega /aw'mõdʒiga/ *f* meatball

almoxarifado /awmoʃari'fadu/ *m* storeroom

alô /a'lo/ *int* hallo

alocar /alo'kar/ *vt* allocate

alo|jamento /aloʒa'mẽtu/ *m* accommodation, *Amer* accommodations; (*habitação*) housing. **~jar** *vt* accommodate; house <*sem-teto*>. **~jar-se** *vpr* stay

alongar /alõ'gar/ *vt* lengthen; extend, stretch out <*braço*>

alpendre /aw'pẽdri/ *m* shed; (*pórtico*) porch

Alpes /'awpis/ *m pl* Alps

alpinis|mo /awpi'nizmu/ *m* mountaineering. **~ta** *m/f* mountaineer

Al-Qaeda /aw'kaida/ *f BR* Al-Qaeda

alqueire /aw'keri/ *m*: = 4.84 hectares; (*in São Paulo*) = 2.42 hectares

alquimi|a /awki'mia/ *f* alchemy. **~sta** *mf* alchemist

alta /'awta/ *f* rise; **dar ~ a** discharge; **ter ~** be discharged

altar /aw'tar/ *m* altar

alterar /awte'rar/ *vt* alter; (*falsificar*) falsify. **~se** *vpr* change; (*zangar-se*) get angry

alter|nado /awter'nadu/ *a* alternate. **~nar** *vt/i*, **~nar-se** *vpr* alternate. **~nativa** *f* alternative. **~nativo** *a* alternative; <*corrente*> alternating

al|teza /aw'teza/ *f* highness. **~titude** *f* altitude

altifalante /awtʃifa'lãtʃi/ *m Port* ▶ **ALTO-FALANTE**

alti|vez /awtʃi'ves/ *f* arrogance. **~vo** *a* arrogant; (*elevado*) majestic

alto /'awtu/ *a* high; <*pessoa*> tall; <*barulho*> loud ● *adv* high; <*falar*> loud(ly); <*ler*> aloud ● *m* top; **os ~s e baixos** the ups and downs ● *int* halt!. **~falante** *m* loudspeaker

altura /aw'tura/ *f* height; (*momento*) moment; **ser à ~ de** be up to

aluci|nação /alusina'sãw/ *f* hallucination. **~nante** *a* mind-boggling, crazy

aludir /alu'dʒir/ *vi* allude (**a** to)

alu|gar /alu'gar/ *vt* rent <*casa*>; hire, rent <*carro*>; <*locador*> let, rent out, hire out. **~guel**, *Port* **~guer** /ɛ/ *m* rent; (*ato*) renting

alumiar /alumi'ar/ *vt* light (up)

alumínio /alu'miniu/ *m* aluminium, *Amer* aluminum

aluno /a'lunu/ *m* pupil

alusão /alu'zãw/ *f* allusion (**a** to)

alvará /awva'ra/ *m* permit, licence

alve|jante /awve'ʒãtʃi/ *m* bleach. **~jar** *vt* bleach; (*visar*) aim at

alvenaria /awvena'ria/ *f* masonry

alvo /'awvu/ *m* target

alvorada /awvo'rada/ *f* dawn

alvoro|çar /awvoro'sar/ *vt* stir up, agitate; (*entusiasmar*) excite. **~ço** /o/ *m* (*tumulto*) uproar; (*entusiasmo*) excitement

amabilidade /amabili'dadʒi/ *f* kindness

amaci|ante /amasi'ãtʃi/ *m* (*de roupa*) (fabric) conditioner. **~ar** *vt* soften; run in <*carro*>

amador /ama'dor/ *a* & *m* amateur. **~ismo** *m* amateurism. **~ístico** *a* amateurish

amadurecer /amadure'ser/ *vt/i* <*fruta*> ripen; *fig* mature

âmago /'amagu/ *m* heart, core; (*da questão*) crux

amaldiçoar /amawdʒiso'ar/ *vt* curse

a

amamentar /amamẽ'tar/ vt
breastfeed

amanhã /ama'ɲã/ m & adv tomorrow;
depois de ~ the day after tomorrow

amanhecer /amaɲe'ser/ vi & m dawn

amansar /amã'sar/ vt tame; fig placate
‹pessoa›

a|mante /a'mãtʃi/ m/f lover. **~mar** vt/i
love

amarelo /ama'rɛlu/ a & m yellow

amar|go /a'margu/ a bitter. **~gura** f
bitterness. **~gurar** vt embitter; (sofrer)
endure

amarrar /ama'xar/ vt tie (up); Naut
moor; **~ a cara** frown, scowl

amarrotar /amaxo'tar/ vt crease

amassar /ama'sar/ vt crush, squash;
screw up ‹papel›; crease ‹roupa›; dent
‹carro›; knead ‹pão›; mash ‹batatas›

amá|vel /a'mavew/ (pl **~veis**) a kind

Ama|zonas /ama'zonas/ m Amazon.
~zônia f Amazonia

Amazônia The Amazon region
is home to the world's largest
rainforest, covering 7 million square
kilometres, half of which is in Brazilian
territory. It is made up of the Amazon
Basin, which has the highest flow of
river water in the world, and the
Amazon Rainforest, and is home to vast
biodiversity, including more than sixty
thousand types of trees.

âmbar /'ãbar/ m amber

ambi|ção /ãbi'sãw/ f ambition.
~cionar vt aspire to. **~cioso** /o/ a
ambitious

ambien|tal /ãbiẽ'taw/ (pl **~tais**) a
environmental. **~tar** vt set ‹filme, livro›;
set up ‹casa›. **~tar-se** vpr settle in. **~te**
m environment; (atmosfera) atmosphere

am|biguidade /ãbigwi'dadʒi/ f
ambiguity. **~bíguo** a ambiguous

âmbito /'ãbitu/ m scope, range

ambos /'ãbus/ a & pron both

ambu|lância /ãbu'lãsia/ f ambulance.
~lante a (que anda) walking; ‹músico›
wandering; ‹venda› mobile. **~latório** m
outpatient clinic

amea|ça /ami'asa/ f threat. **~çador** a
threatening. **~çar** vt threaten

ameba /a'mɛba/ f amoeba

amedrontar /amedrõ'tar/ vt scare.
~se vpr get scared

ameixa /a'mejʃa/ f plum; (passa) prune

amém /a'mẽj/ int amen ● m agreement;
dizer ~ a go along with

amêndoa /a'mẽdoa/ f almond

amendoim /amẽdo'ĩ/ m peanut

ame|nidade /ameni'dadʒi/ f
pleasantness; pleasantries, small talk.
~nizar vt ease; calm ‹ânimos›; settle
‹disputa›; tone down ‹repreensão›. **~no**
/e/ a pleasant; mild ‹clima›

América /a'mɛrika/ f America; **~ do
Norte/Sul** North/South America

america|nizar /amerikani'zar/ vt
Americanize. **~no** a & m American

amestrar /ames'trar/ vt train

ametista /ame'tʃista/ f amethyst

amianto /ami'ãtu/ m asbestos

ami|gar-se /ami'garsi/ vpr make
friends. **~gável** (pl **~gáveis**) a amicable

amígdala /a'migdala/ f tonsil

amigdalite /amigda'litʃi/ f tonsillitis

amigo /a'migu/ a friendly ● m friend;
~ da onça false friend

amistoso /amis'tozu/ a & m friendly

amiúde /ami'udʒi/ adv often

amizade /ami'zadʒi/ f friendship

amnésia /ami'nɛzia/ f amnesia

amnistia /amnis'tia/ f Port ▶ ANISTIA

amo|lação /amola'sãw/ f annoyance.
~lante a annoying. **~lar** vt annoy,
bother; sharpen ‹faca›. **~lar-se** vpr get
annoyed

amolecer /amole'ser/ vt/i soften

amol|gadura /amowga'dura/ f dent.
~gar vt dent

amoníaco /amo'niaku/ m ammonia

amontoar /amõto'ar/ vt pile up;
amass ‹riquezas›. **~se** vpr pile up

amor /a'mor/ m love

amora /a'mɔra/ f **~ preta**, Port
~ silvestre blackberry

amordaçar /amorda'sar/ vt gag

amoroso /amo'rozu/ a loving

amor-perfeito /amorper'fejtu/ m
pansy

amor-próprio /amor'propriu/ m
self-esteem

amorte|cedor /amortese'dor/ m
shock absorber. **~cer** vt deaden; absorb
‹impacto›; break ‹queda› ● vi fade

amostra /a'mɔstra/ f sample

ampa|rar /ãpa'rar/ vt support;
protect. **~rar-se** vpr lean. **~ro** m (apoio)
support; (proteção) protection; (ajuda)
aid

ampere /ãˈpɛri/ m amp(ere)
ampli|ação /ãplia'sãw/ f (de foto) enlargement; (de casa) extension. **~ar** vt enlarge ‹foto›; extend ‹casa›; broaden ‹conhecimentos›
amplifi|cador /ãplifika'dor/ m amplifier. **~car** vt amplify
amplo /'ãplu/ a ‹sala› spacious; ‹roupa› full; ‹sentido, conhecimento› broad
ampola /ã'pola/ f ampoule
amputar /ãpu'tar/ vt amputate
Amsterdã /amister'dã/ f, Port **Amsterdão** /amiʃter'dãw/ m Amsterdam
amu|ado /amu'adu/ a in a sulk, sulky. **~ar** vi sulk
amuleto /amu'letu/ m charm
amuo /a'muu/ m sulk
ana|crônico /ana'kroniku/ a anachronistic. **~cronismo** m anachronism
anais /a'najs/ m pl annals
analfabeto /anawfa'betu/ a & m illiterate
analgésico /anaw'ʒeziku/ m painkiller
analisar /anali'zar/ vt analyse
análise /a'nalizi/ f analysis
ana|lista /ana'lista/ m/f analyst. **~lítico** a analytical
analogia /analo'ʒia/ f analogy
análogo /a'nalogu/ a analogous
ananás /ana'naʃ/ m invar Port pineapple
anão /a'nãw/ a & m (f **anã**) dwarf
anarquia /anar'kia/ f anarchy; fig chaos
anárquico /a'narkiku/ a anarchic
anarquista /anar'kista/ m/f anarchist
ana|tomia /anato'mia/ f anatomy. **~tômico** a anatomical
anca /'ãka/ f (de pessoa) hip; (de animal) rump
anchova /ã'ʃova/ f anchovy
ancinho /ã'siɲu/ m rake
âncora /'ãkora/ f anchor
anco|radouro /ãkora'doru/ m anchorage. **~rar** vt/i anchor
andaime /ã'dajmi/ m scaffolding
an|damento /ãda'mẽtu/ m (progresso) progress; (rumo) course; dar **~damento a** set in motion. **~dar** m (jeito de andar) gait, walk; (de prédio) floor; Port (apartamento) flat, Amer apartment ● vi (ir a pé) walk; (de trem, ônibus) travel;

(a cavalo, de bicicleta) ride; (funcionar, progredir) go; **ele ~da deprimido** he's been depressed lately
Andes /'ãdʒis/ m pl Andes
andorinha /ãdo'riɲa/ f swallow
anedota /ane'dɔta/ f anecdote
anel /a'nɛw/ (pl **anéis**) m ring; (no cabelo) curl; **~ viário** ring road
anelado /ane'ladu/ a curly
anemia /ane'mia/ f anaemia
anêmico /a'nemiku/ a anaemic
anes|tesia /aneste'zia/ f anaesthesia; (droga) anaesthetic. **~tesiar** vt anaesthetize. **~tésico** a & m anaesthetic. **~tesista** m/f anaesthetist
ane|xar /anek'sar/ vt annex ‹terras›; (em carta) enclose; (juntar) attach. **~xo** /a'nɛksu/ a attached; (em carta) enclosed ● m annexe; (em carta) enclosure; Comput attachment
anfetamina /ãfeta'mina/ f amphetamine
anfíbio /ã'fibiu/ a amphibious ● m amphibian
anfiteatro /ãfiti'atru/ m amphitheatre; (no teatro) dress circle
anfi|trião /ãfitri'ãw/ m (f **~triã**) host (f-ess)
angariar /ãgari'ar/ vt raise ‹fundos›; canvass for ‹votos›; win ‹adeptos, simpatia›
angli|cano /ãgli'kanu/ a & m Anglican. **~cismo** m Anglicism
anglo-saxônico /ãglusak'soniku/ a Anglo-Saxon
Angola /ã'gɔla/ f Angola
angolano /ãgo'lanu/ a & m Angolan
angra /'ãgra/ f inlet, cove
angular /ãgu'lar/ a angular
ângulo /'ãgulu/ m angle
angústia /ã'gustʃia/ f anguish, anxiety
angustiante /ãgustʃi'ãtʃi/ a distressing; ‹momento› anxious
ani|mado /ani'madu/ a (vivo) lively; (alegre) cheerful; (entusiasmado) enthusiastic. **~mador** a encouraging ● m presenter. **~mal** (pl **~mais**) a & m animal. **~mar** vt encourage; liven up ‹festa›. **~mar-se** vpr cheer up; ‹festa› liven up
ânimo /'animu/ m courage, spirit; tempers
animosidade /animozi'dadʒi/ f animosity

aniquilar /aniki'lar/ vt destroy; (prostrar) shatter

anis /a'nis/ m aniseed

anistia /anis'tʃia/ f amnesty

aniver|sariante /aniversari'ãtʃi/ m/f birthday boy (f girl). **~sário** m birthday; (de casamento etc) anniversary

anjo /'ãʒu/ m angel

ano /'anu/ m year; **fazer ~s** have a birthday; **~ bissexto** leap year; **~ letivo** academic year. **~bom** m New Year

anoite|cer /anojte'ser/ m nightfall ● vi **~ceu** night fell

anomalia /anoma'lia/ f anomaly

anonimato /anoni'matu/ m anonymity

anônimo /a'nonimu/ a anonymous

anorexia /anorek'sia/ f anorexia

anoréxico /ano'rɛksiku/ a & m anorexic

anor|mal /anor'maw/ (pl **~mais**) a abnormal

ano|tação /anota'sãw/ f note. **~tar** vt note down, write down

ânsia /'ãsia/ f anxiety; (desejo) longing; **~s de vômito** nausea

ansi|ar /ãsi'ar/ vi **~ por** long for. **~edade** f anxiety; (desejo) eagerness. **~oso** /o/ a anxious

antártico /ã'tartʃiku/ a & m Antarctic

antebraço /ãtʃi'brasu/ m forearm

antece|dência /ãtese'dẽsia/ f **com ~dência** in advance. **~dente** a preceding. **~dentes** m pl record, past

antecessor /ãtese'sor/ m (f **~a**) predecessor

anteci|pação /ãtʃisipa'sãw/ f anticipation; **com ~pação** in advance. **~padamente** adv in advance. **~pado** a advance. **~par** vt anticipate, forestall; (adiantar) bring forward. **~par-se** vpr be previous

antena /ã'tena/ f aerial, Amer antenna; (de inseto) feeler

anteontem /ãtʃi'õtẽ/ adv the day before yesterday

antepassado /ãtʃipa'sadu/ m ancestor

anterior /ãteri'or/ a previous; (dianteiro) front

antes /'ãtʃis/ adv before; (ao contrário) rather; **~ de/que** before

antessala /ãtʃi'sala/ f anteroom

anti|biótico /ãtʃibi'ɔtʃiku/ a & m antibiotic. **~caspa** a anti-dandruff.

~concepcional (pl **~concepcionais**) a & m contraceptive. **~congelante** m antifreeze. **~corpo** m antibody

antídoto /ã'tʃidotu/ m antidote

antiético /ãtʃi'ɛtʃiku/ a unethical

antigamente /ãtʃiga'mẽtʃi/ adv formerly

anti|go /ã'tʃigu/ a old; (da antiguidade) ancient; ‹móveis etc› antique; (anterior) former. **~guidade** f antiquity; (numa firma) seniority; (monumentos) antiquities; (móveis etc) antiques

anti-|higiênico /ãtʃiʒi'eniku/ a unhygienic. **~histamínico** a & m antihistamine. **~horário** a anticlockwise

antilhano /ãtʃi'ʎanu/ a & m West Indian

Antilhas /ã'tʃiʎas/ f pl West Indies

anti|patia /ãtʃipa'tʃia/ f dislike. **~pático** a unpleasant, unfriendly

antiquado /ãtʃi'kwadu/ a antiquated, outdated

antis|semitismo /ãtʃisemi-'tʃizmu/ m anti-Semitism. **~séptico** a & m antiseptic. **~social** (pl **~sociais**) a antisocial

antítese /ã'tʃitezi/ f antithesis

antologia /ãtolo'ʒia/ f anthology

antônimo /ã'tonimu/ m antonym

antro /'ãtru/ m cavern; (de animal) lair; (de ladrões) den

antro|pófago /ãtro'pɔfagu/ a man-eating. **~pologia** f anthropology. **~pólogo** m anthropologist

anu|al /anu'aw/ (pl **~ais**) a annual, yearly

anu|lação /anula'sãw/ f cancellation. **~lar** vt cancel; annul ‹casamento›; (compensar) cancel out ● m ring finger

anunciar /anũsi'ar/ vt announce; advertise ‹produto›

anúncio /a'nũsiu/ m announcement; (propaganda, classificado) advert(isement); (cartaz) notice

ânus /'anus/ m invar anus

an|zol /ã'zɔw/ (pl **~zóis**) m fish hook

aonde /a'õdʒi/ adv where

apadrinhar /apadri'ɲar/ vt be godfather to ‹afilhado›; be best man for ‹noivo›; (proteger) protect; (patrocinar) support

apa|gado /apa'gadu/ a ‹fogo› out; ‹luz, TV› off; (indistinto) faint; ‹pessoa› dull. **~gar** vt put out ‹cigarro, fogo›; blow out ‹vela›; switch off ‹luz, TV›; rub out ‹erro›; clean ‹quadro-negro›.

~gar-se vpr ‹fogo, luz› go out; ‹lembrança› fade; (desmaiar) pass out; Ⓟ (dormir) nod off

apaixo|nado /apaʃoˈnadu/ a in love (por with). **~nar-se** vpr fall in love (por with)

apalpar /apawˈpar/ vt touch, feel; ‹médico› examine

apanhar /apaˈɲar/ vt catch; (do chão) pick up; pick ‹flores, frutas›; (ir buscar) pick up; (alcançar) catch up ● vi be beaten

aparafusar /aparafuˈzar/ vt screw

apa|ra-lápis /aparaˈlapiʃ/ m invar Port pencil sharpener. **~rar** vt catch ‹bola›; parry ‹golpe›; trim ‹cabelo›; sharpen ‹lápis›

aparato /apaˈratu/ m pomp, ceremony

apare|cer /apareˈser/ vi appear; **~çal** do drop in!. **~cimento** m appearance

apare|lhagem /apareˈʎaʒẽ/ f equipment. **~lhar** vt equip. **~lho** /e/ m apparatus; (máquina) machine; (de chá) set, service; (fone) phone

aparência /apaˈrẽsia/ f appearance; **na ~** apparently

aparen|tado /aparẽˈtadu/ a related. **~tar** vt show; (fingir) feign. **~te** a apparent

apartado /aparˈtadu/ m Port PO Box

apar|tamento /apartaˈmẽtu/ m flat, Amer apartment. **~tar** vt, **~tar-se** vpr separate. **~te** m aside

apatia /apaˈtʃia/ f apathy

apático /aˈpatʃiku/ a apathetic

apavo|rante /apavoˈrãtʃi/ a terrifying. **~rar** vt terrify. **~rar-se** vpr be terrified

apaziguar /apaziˈgwar/ vt appease

apear-se /apiˈarsi/ vpr (de cavalo) dismount; (de ônibus) alight

ape|gar-se /apeˈgarsi/ vpr become attached (a to). **~go** /e/ m attachment

ape|lação /apelaˈsãw/ f appeal; fig exhibitionism. **~lar** vi appeal (de against); **~lar para** appeal to; fig resort to

apeli|dar /apeliˈdar/ vt nickname. **~do** m nickname

apelo /aˈpelu/ m appeal

apenas /aˈpenas/ adv only

apêndice /aˈpẽdʒisi/ m appendix

apendicite /apẽdʒiˈsitʃi/ f appendicitis

aperceber-se /aperseˈbersi/ vpr **~ (de)** notice, realize

aperfeiçoar /aperfejsoˈar/ vt perfect

aperitivo /aperiˈtʃivu/ m aperitif

aper|tado /aperˈtadu/ a tight; (sem dinheiro) hard-up. **~tar** vt (segurar) hold tight; tighten ‹cinto›; press ‹botão›; squeeze ‹esponja›; take in ‹vestido›; fasten ‹cinto de segurança›; step up ‹vigilância›; cut down on ‹despesas›; break ‹coração›; fig pressurize ‹pessoa›; **~tar a mão de alguém** shake hands with sb ● vi ‹sapato› pinch; ‹chuva, frio› get worse; ‹estrada› narrow. **~tar-se** vpr (gastar menos) tighten one's belt; (não ter dinheiro) feel the pinch. **~to** /e/ m pressure; (de botão) press; (dificuldade) tight spot, jam; **~to de mãos** handshake

apesar /apeˈzar/ **~ de** prep in spite of

apeti|te /apeˈtʃitʃi/ m appetite. **~toso** /o/ a appetizing

apetrechos /apeˈtreʃus/ m pl gear; (de pesca) tackle

apimentado /apimẽˈtadu/ a spicy, hot

apinhar /apiˈɲar/ vt crowd, pack. **~se** vpr crowd

api|tar /apiˈtar/ vi whistle ● vt referee ‹jogo›. **~to** m whistle

aplanar /aplaˈnar/ vt level ‹terreno›; fig smooth ‹caminho›; smooth over ‹problema›

aplau|dir /aplawˈdʒir/ vt applaud. **~so(s)** m(pl) applause

apli|cação /aplikaˈsãw/ f application; (de dinheiro) investment; (de lei) enforcement. **~car** vt apply; invest ‹dinheiro›; enforce ‹lei›. **~car-se** vpr apply (a to); (ao estudo etc) apply o.s. (a to). **~que** m hairpiece

apoderar-se /apodeˈrarsi/ vpr **~ de** take possession of; ‹raiva› take hold of

apodrecer /apodreˈser/ vt/i rot

apoi|ar /apojˈar/ vt lean; fig support; (basear) base. **~ar-se** vpr **~ar-se em** lean on; fig be based on, rest on. **~o** m support

apólice /aˈpɔlisi/ f policy; (ação) bond

apon|tador /apõtaˈdor/ m pencil sharpener. **~tar** vt (com o dedo) point at, point to; point out ‹erro, caso interessante›; aim ‹arma›; name ‹nomes›; put forward ‹razão› ● vi ‹sol, planta› come up; (com o dedo) point (para to)

apoquentar /apokẽˈtar/ vt annoy

aporrinhar /apoxiˈɲar/ vt annoy

após /aˈpɔs/ adv after; **loção ~barba** aftershave (lotion)

aposen|tado /apozẽ'tadu/ a retired ● m pensioner. **~tadoria** f retirement; (*pensão*) pension. **~tar** vt, **~tar-se** vpr retire. **~to** m room

após-guerra /apoz'gexa/ m post-war period

apos|ta /a'pɔsta/ f bet. **~tar** vt bet (**em** on); *fig* have faith (**em** in)

apostila /apos'tʃila/ f revision aid, book of key facts

apóstolo /a'pɔstolu/ m apostle

apóstrofo /a'pɔstrofu/ m apostrophe

apre|ciação /apresia'sãw/ f appreciation. **~ciar** vt appreciate; think highly of <*pessoa*>. **~ciativo** a appreciative. **~ciável** (pl **~ciáveis**) a appreciable. **~ço** /e/ m regard

apreen|der /apriẽ'der/ vt seize <*contrabando*>; apprehend <*criminoso*>; grasp <*sentido*>. **~são** f apprehension; (*de contrabando*) seizure. **~sivo** a apprehensive

apregoar /aprego'ar/ vt proclaim; cry <*mercadoria*>

apren|der /aprẽ'der/ vt/i learn. **~diz** m/f (*de ofício*) apprentice; (*de direção*) learner. **~dizado** m, **~dizagem** f (*de ofício*) apprenticeship; (*de profissão*) training; (*escolar*) learning

apresen|tação /aprezẽta'sãw/ f presentation; (*teatral etc*) performance; (*de pessoas*) introduction. **~tador** m presenter. **~tar** vt present; introduce <*pessoa*>. **~tar-se** vpr (*identificar-se*) introduce o.s.; <*ocasião, problema*> present o.s., arise; **~tar-se a** report to <*polícia etc*>; go in for <*exame*>; stand for <*eleição*>. **~tável** (pl **~táveis**) a presentable

apres|sado /apre'sadu/ a hurried. **~sar** vt hurry. **~sar-se** vpr hurry (up)

aprimorar /aprimo'rar/ vt perfect, refine

aprofundar /aprofũ'dar/ vt deepen; study carefully <*questão*>. **~-se** vpr get deeper; **~-se em** go deeper into

aprontar /aprõ'tar/ vt get ready; pick <*briga*> ● vi act up. **~-se** vpr get ready

apropriado /apropri'adu/ a appropriate, suitable

apro|vação /aprova'sãw/ f approval; (*num exame*) pass. **~var** vt approve of; approve <*lei*> ● vi make the grade; **ser ~vado** (*num exame*) pass

aprovei|tador /aprovejta'dor/ m opportunist. **~tamento** m utilization. **~tar** vt take advantage of; take <*ocasião*>; (*utilizar*) use ● vi make the most of it; *Port* (*adiantar*) be of use. **~tar-se** vpr take advantage (**de** of); **~tei** (*divirta-se*) have a good time!

aproxi|mação /aprosima'sãw/ f (*chegada*) approach; (*estimativa*) approximation. **~mado** a <*valor*> approximate. **~mar** vt move nearer; (*aliar*) bring together. **~mar-se** vpr approach, get nearer (**de** to)

ap|tidão /aptʃi'dãw/ f aptitude, suitability. **~to** a suitable

apunhalar /apuɲa'lar/ vt stab

apu|rado /apu'radu/ a refined. **~rar** vt (*aprimorar*) refine; (*descobrir*) ascertain; investigate <*caso*>; collect <*dinheiro*>; count <*votos*>. **~rar-se** vpr (*com a roupa*) dress smartly. **~ro** m refinement; (*no vestir*) elegance; (*dificuldade*) difficulty; pl trouble

aquarela /akwa'rɛla/ f watercolour

aquariano /akwari'anu/ a & m Aquarian

aquário /a'kwariu/ m aquarium; **Aquário** Aquarius

aquartelar /akwarte'lar/ vt billet

aquático /a'kwatʃiku/ a aquatic, water

aque|cedor /akese'dor/ m heater. **~cer** vt heat ● vi, **~cer-se** vpr heat up. **~cimento** /akesi'mẽtu/ m heating; **~cimento global** global warming

aqueduto /ake'dutu/ m aqueduct

aquele /a'keli/ a that; those ● pron that one; those; **~ que** the one that

àquele =A + AQUELE

aqui /a'ki/ adv here

aquilo /a'kilu/ pron that

àquilo =A + AQUILO

aquisi|ção /akizi'sãw/ f acquisition. **~tivo** a **poder ~tivo** purchasing power

ar /ar/ m air; (*aspecto*) look, air; *Port* (*no carro*) choke; **ao ~ livre** in the open air; **no ~** *fig* up in the air; *TV* on air; **~ condicionado** air conditioning

árabe /'arabi/ a & m Arab; *Lang* Arabic

Arábia /a'rabia/ f Arabia; **~ Saudita** Saudi Arabia

arado /a'radu/ m plough, *Amer* plow

aragem /a'raʒẽ/ f breeze

arame /a'rami/ m wire; **~ farpado** barbed wire

aranha /a'raɲa/ f spider

arar /a'rar/ vt plough, *Amer* plow

arara /a'rara/ f parrot

arbi|trar /arbi'trar/ *vt/i* referee ‹jogo›; arbitrate ‹disputa›. **~trário** *a* arbitrary

arbítrio /ar'bitriu/ *m* judgement; **livre ~** free will

árbitro /'arbitru/ *m* arbiter ‹da moda etc›; *Jurid* arbitrator; (de futebol) referee; (de tênis) umpire

arborizado /arbori'zadu/ *a* wooded, green; ‹rua› tree-lined

arbusto /ar'bustu/ *m* shrub

ar|ca /'arka/ *f* **~ca de Noé** Noah's Ark. **~cada** *f* (galeria) arcade; (arco) arch

arcaico /ar'kajku/ *a* archaic

arcar /ar'kar/ *vt* **~ com** deal with

arcebispo /arse'bispu/ *m* archbishop

arco /'arku/ *m* *Arquit* arch; (arma, Mus) bow; *Eletr, Mat arc.* **~da-velha** *m* **coisa do ~da-velha** amazing thing; **~íris** *m invar* rainbow

ar|dente /ar'dẽtʃi/ *a* burning; *fig* ardent. **~der** *vi* burn; ‹olhos, ferida› sting

ar|dil /ar'dʒiw/ (*pl* **~dis**) *m* trick, ruse

ardor /ar'dor/ *m* heat; *fig* ardour; **com ~** ardently

árduo /'arduu/ *a* strenuous, arduous

área /'aria/ *f* area; **(grande) ~** penalty area; **~ (de serviço)** yard

arear /ari'ar/ *vt* scour ‹panela›

areia /a'reja/ *f* sand

arejar /are'ʒar/ *vt* air ● *vi*, **~se** *vpr* get some air; (descansar) have a breather

are|na /a'rena/ *f* arena. **~noso** /o/ *a* sandy

arenque /a'rẽki/ *m* herring

argamassa /arga'masa/ *f* mortar

Argélia /ar'ʒɛlia/ *f* Algeria

argelino /arʒe'linu/ *a & m* Algerian

Argentina /arʒẽ'tʃina/ *f* Argentina

argentino /arʒẽ'tʃinu/ *a & m* Argentinian

argila /ar'ʒila/ *f* clay

argola /ar'gɔla/ *f* ring

arguido /ar'gwidu/ *m* defendant

argumen|tar /argumẽ'tar/ *vt/i* argue. **~to** *m* argument; (de filme etc) subject matter

ariano /ari'anu/ *a & m* (do signo Aries) Arian

árido /'aridu/ *a* arid; barren ‹deserto›; *fig* dull, dry

Áries /'aris/ *m* Aries

arisco /a'risku/ *a* timid

aristo|cracia /aristokra'sia/ *f* aristocracy. **~crata** *m/f* aristocrat. **~crático** *a* aristocratic

aritmética /aritʃ'metʃika/ *f* arithmetic

arma /'arma/ *f* weapon; arms; **~ de fogo** firearm

ar|mação /arma'sãw/ *f* frame; (de óculos) frames; *Naut* rigging. **~madilha** *f* trap. **~madura** *f* suit of armour; (armação) framework. **~mar** *vt* (dar armas a) arm; (montar) put up, assemble; set up ‹máquina›; set, lay ‹armadilha›; fit out ‹navio›; hatch ‹plano, complô›; cause ‹briga›. **~mar-se** *vpr* arm o.s.

armarinho /arma'riɲu/ *m* haberdashery, *Amer* notions

armário /ar'mariu/ *m* cupboard; (de roupa) wardrobe

arma|zém /arma'zẽj/ *m* warehouse; (loja) general store; (depósito) storeroom. **~zenagem** *f*, **~zenamento** *m* storage. **~zenar** *vt* store

Armênia /ar'menia/ *f* Armenia

armênio /ar'meniu/ *a & m* Armenian

aro /'aru/ *m* (de roda, óculos) rim; (de porta) frame

aro|ma /a'roma/ *m* aroma; (perfume) fragrance. **~mático** *a* aromatic; fragrant

ar|pão /ar'pãw/ *m* harpoon. **~poar** *vt* harpoon

arquear /arki'ar/ *vt* arch. **~se** *vpr* bend, bow

arque|ologia /arkiolo'ʒia/ *f* archaeology. **~ológico** *a* archaeological. **~ólogo** *m* archaeologist

arquétipo /ar'ketʃipu/ *m* archetype

arquibancada /arkibã'kada/ *f* terraces, *Amer* bleachers

arquipélago /arki'pelagu/ *m* archipelago

arquite|tar /arkite'tar/ *vt* think up. **~to** /ɛ/ *m* architect. **~tônico** *a* architectural. **~tura** *f* architecture

arqui|var /arki'var/ *vt* file ‹papéis›; shelve ‹plano, processo›. **~vista** *m/f* archivist. **~vo** *m* file; (conjunto) files; (móvel) filing cabinet; (do Estado etc) archives

arran|cada /axã'kada/ *f* lurch; (de atleta) *fig* spurt. **~car** *vt* pull out ‹cabelo etc›; pull off ‹botão etc›; pull up ‹erva daninha etc›; take out ‹dente›; (das mãos de alguém) wrench, snatch; extract ‹confissão, dinheiro› ● *vi* ‹carro› roar off; ‹pessoa› take off; (dar solavanco)

lurch forward. **~car-se** *vpr* take off. **~co**
m pull, tug

arranha-céu /axaɲa'sɛw/ *m*
skyscraper

arra|nhadura /axaɲa'dura/ *f* scratch.
~nhão *m* scratch. **~nhar** *vt* scratch; have
a smattering of ‹*língua*›

arran|jar /axã'ʒar/ *vt* arrange; (*achar*)
get, find; (*resolver*) settle, sort out.
~jar-se *vpr* manage. **~jo** *m* arrangement

arrasar /axa'zar/ *vt* devastate; raze,
flatten ‹*casa, cidade*›. **~se** *vpr* be
devastated

arrastar /axas'tar/ *vt* drag; ‹*corrente,
avalancha*› sweep away; (*atrair*) draw
● *vi* trail. **~se** *vpr* crawl; ‹*tempo*› drag;
‹*processo*› drag out

arreba|tador /axebata'dor/ *a*
entrancing; shocking ‹*notícia*›. **~tar** *vt*
(*enlevar*) entrance, send; (*chocar*) shock

arreben|tação /axebẽta'sãw/ *f* surf.
~tar *vi* ‹*bomba*› explode; ‹*corda*› snap,
break; ‹*balão, pessoa*› burst; ‹*onda*›
break; ‹*guerra, incêndio*› break out ● *vt*
snap, break ‹*corda*›; burst ‹*balão*›;
break down ‹*porta*›

arrebitar /axebi'tar/ *vt* turn up ‹*nariz*›;
prick up ‹*orelhas*›

arreca|dação /axekada'sãw/ *f*
(*dinheiro*) tax revenue. **~dar** *vt* collect

arredar /axe'dar/ *vt* **não ~ pé** stand
one's ground

arredio /axe'dʒiu/ *a* withdrawn

arredondar /axedõ'dar/ *vt* round up
‹*quantia*›; round off ‹*ângulo*›

arredores /axe'dɔris/ *m pl*
surroundings; (*de cidade*) outskirts

arrefecer /axefe'ser/ *vt/i* cool

arregaçar /axega'sar/ *vt* roll up

arrega|lado /axega'ladu/ *a* ‹*olhos*›
wide. **~lar** *vt* **~lar os olhos** be wide-
eyed with amazement

arreganhar /axega'ɲar/ *vt* bare
‹*dentes*›. **~se** *vpr* grin

arrema|tar /axema'tar/ *vt* finish off;
(*no tricô*) cast off. **~te** *m* conclusion;
(*na costura*) finishing off; (*no futebol*)
finishing

arremes|sar /axeme'sar/ *vt* hurl. **~so**
/e/ *m* throw

arrendar /axẽ'dar/ *vt* rent

arrepen|der-se /axepẽ'dersi/ *vpr*
be sorry; ‹*pecador*› repent; **~der-se
de** regret. **~dido** *a* sorry; ‹*pecador*›
repentant. **~dimento** *m* regret; (*de
pecado, crime*) repentance

arrepi|ado /axepi'adu/ *a* ‹*cabelo*›
standing on end; ‹*pele, pessoa*› covered
in goose pimples. **~ar** *vt* (*dar calafrios*)
make shudder; make stand on end
‹*cabelo*›; **me ~a (a pele)** it gives me
goose pimples. **~ar-se** *vpr* (*estremecer*)
shudder; ‹*cabelo*› stand on end; (*na
pele*) get goose pimples. **~o** *m* shudder;
me dá ~os it makes me shudder

arris|cado /axis'kadu/ *a* risky. **~car** *vt*
risk. **~car-se** *vpr* take a risk, risk it

arroba /a'xoba/ *m Comput* @, at sign

arro|char /axo'ʃar/ *vt* tighten up ● *vi*
be tough. **~cho** /o/ *m* squeeze

arro|gância /axo'gãsia/ *f* arrogance.
~gante *a* arrogant

arro|jado /axo'ʒadu/ *a* bold. **~jar** *vt*
throw

arrombar /axõ'bar/ *vt* break down
‹*porta*›; break into ‹*casa*›; crack ‹*cofre*›

arro|tar /axo'tar/ *vi* burp, belch. **~to**
/o/ *m* burp

arroz /a'xoz/ *m* rice; **~ doce** rice
pudding. **~al** (*pl* **~ais**) *m* rice field

arrua|ça /axu'asa/ *f* riot. **~ceiro** *m*
rioter

arruela /axu'ɛla/ *f* washer

arruinar /axui'nar/ *vt* ruin. **~se** *vpr*
be ruined

arru|madeira /axuma'dera/ *f* (*de
hotel*) chambermaid. **~mar** *vt* tidy (up)
‹*casa*›; sort out ‹*papéis, vida*›; pack
‹*mala*›; (*achar*) find, get; make up
‹*desculpa*›; (*vestir*) dress up. **~mar-se**
vpr (*aprontar-se*) get ready; (*na vida*) sort
o.s. out

arse|nal /arse'naw/ (*pl* **~nais**) *m* arsenal

arsênio /ar'seniu/ *m* arsenic

arte /'artʃi/ *f* art; **fazer ~** ‹*criança*› get
up to mischief. **~fato** *m* product, article

arteiro /ar'teru/ *a* mischievous

artéria /ar'tɛria/ *f* artery

artesa|nal /arteza'naw/ (*pl* **~nais**) *a*
craft. **~nato** *m* craftwork

arte|são /arte'zãw/ (*pl* **~s**) *m* (*f* **~sã**)
artisan, craftsman (*f*-woman)

ártico /'artʃiku/ *a & m* arctic

articu|lação /artʃikula'sãw/ *f*
articulation; *Anat, Tecn* joint. **~lar** *vt*
articulate

arti|ficial /artʃifisi'aw/ (*pl* **~ficiais**) *a*
artificial. **~ficio** *m* trick

artigo /ar'tʃigu/ *m* article; *Com* item

arti|lharia /artʃiʎa'ria/ *f* artillery.
~lheiro *m Mil* gunner; (*no futebol*) striker

artimanha /artʃi'maɲa/ f trick; (*método*) clever way

ar|tista /ar'tʃista/ m/f artist. **~tístico** a artistic

artrite /ar'tritʃi/ f arthritis

árvore /'arvori/ f tree

arvoredo /arvo'redu/ m grove

ás /as/ m ace

às ▶ A

asa /'aza/ f wing; (*de xícara*) handle. **~delta** f hang-glider

ascen|dência /asẽ'dẽsia/ f ancestry; (*superioridade*) ascendancy. **~dente** a rising. **~der** vi rise; ascend ‹ao trono›. **~são** f rise; *Relig* Ascension; **em ~são** rising; fig up and coming. **~sor** m lift, *Amer* elevator. **~sorista** m/f lift operator

asco /'asku/ m revulsion, disgust; **dar ~** be revolting

asfalto /as'fawtu/ m asphalt

asfixiar /asfiksi'ar/ vt/i asphyxiate

Ásia /'azia/ f Asia

asiático /azi'atʃiku/ a & m Asian

asilo /a'zilu/ m (*refúgio*) asylum; (*de velhos, crianças*) home

as|ma /'azma/ f asthma. **~mático** a & m asthmatic

asneira /az'nera/ f stupidity; (*uma*) stupid thing

aspargo /as'pargu/ m asparagus

aspas /'aspas/ f pl inverted commas

aspecto /as'pektu/ m appearance, look; (*de um problema*) aspect

aspereza /aspe'reza/ f roughness; (*do clima, de um som*) harshness; fig rudeness

áspero /'asperu/ a rough; ‹clima, som› harsh; fig rude

aspi|ração /aspira'sãw/ f aspiration; *Med* inhalation. **~rador** m vacuum cleaner. **~rar** vt inhale, breathe in ‹ar, fumaça›; suck up ‹líquido›; **~rar a** aspire to

aspirina /aspi'rina/ f aspirin

asqueroso /aske'rozu/ a revolting, disgusting

assa|do /a'sadu/ a & m roast. **~dura** f (*na pele*) sore patch

assalariado /asalari'adu/ a salaried ● m salaried worker

assal|tante /asaw'tãtʃi/ m/f robber; (*na rua*) mugger; (*de casa*) burglar. **~tar** vt rob; burgle, *Amer* burglarize ‹casa›. **~to** m (*roubo*) robbery; (*a uma casa*)

burglary; (*ataque*) assault; (*no boxe*) round

assanhado /asa'ɲadu/ a worked up; ‹criança› excitable; (*erótico*) amorous

assar /a'sar/ vt roast

assassi|nar /asasi'nar/ vt murder; *Pol* assassinate. **~nato** m murder; *Pol* assassination. **~no** m murderer; *Pol* assassin

asseado /asi'adu/ a well-groomed

as|sediar /asedʒi'ar/ vt besiege ‹cidade›; fig harass. **~sédio** m siege; fig pestering; **~sédio sexual** sexual harassment

assegurar /asegu'rar/ vt (*tornar seguro*) secure; (*afirmar*) guarantee; **~ a alguém algo/que** assure s.o. of sth/ that; **~se de/que** make sure of/that

assembleia /asẽ'bleja/ f *Pol* assembly; *Com* meeting

Assembleia da República The Portuguese Assembly of the Republic, located in the Palácio de São Bento, Lisbon, is the Portuguese parliament. The Assembly's 230 seats are allocated by proportional representation, and the members collectively represent the country's twenty-two constituencies and the two autonomous regions, Madeira and the Azores.

assemelhar /aseme'ʎar/ vt liken. **~se** vpr be alike; **~se a** resemble, be like

assen|tar /asẽ'tar/ vt (*estabelecer*) establish, define; settle ‹povo›; lay ‹tijolo›; **~tar com** go with; **~tar a** ‹roupa› suit ● vi ‹pó› settle. **~tar-se** vpr settle down. **~to** m seat; fig basis; **tomar ~to** take a seat; ‹pó› settle

assen|tir /asẽ'tʃir/ vi agree. **~timento** m agreement

assertivo /aser'tʃivu/ a assertive

assessor /ase'sor/ m adviser. **~ar** vt advise

assexuado /aseksu'adu/ a asexual

assiduidade /asidui'dadʒi/ f (*à escola*) regular attendance; (*diligência*) diligence

assíduo /a'siduu/ a (*que frequenta*) regular; (*diligente*) assiduous

assim /a'sĩ/ adv like this, like that; (*portanto*) therefore; **e ~ por diante** and so on; **~ como** as well as; **~ que** as soon as

assimétrico /asi'metriku/ a asymmetrical

a

assimilar /asimi'lar/ vt assimilate. ~**se** vpr be assimilated

assinalar /asina'lar/ vt (marcar) mark; (distinguir) distinguish; (apontar) point out

assi|nante /asi'nãtʃi/ m/f subscriber. ~**nar** vt sign. ~**natura** f (nome) signature; (de revista) subscription

assis|tência /asis'tẽsia/ f assistance; (presença) attendance; (público) audience. ~**tente** a assistant ● m/f assistant; ~**tente social** social worker. ~**tir (a)** vt/i (ver) watch; (presenciar) attend; assist ‹doente›

assoalho /aso'aʎu/ m floor

assoar /aso'ar/ vt ~ **o nariz**, Port ~**se** blow one's nose

assobi|ar /asobi'ar/ vt/i whistle. ~**o** m whistle

associ|ação /asosia'sãw/ f association. ~**ado** a & m associate. ~**ar** vt associate (a with). ~**ar-se** vpr associate; Com go into partnership (a with)

assolar /aso'lar/ vt devastate

assom|bração /asõbra'sãw/ f ghost. ~**brar** vt astonish, amaze. ~**brar-se** vpr be amazed. ~**bro** m amazement, astonishment; (coisa) marvel. ~**broso** /o/ a astonishing, amazing

assoprar /aso'prar/ vi blow ● vt blow; blow out ‹vela›

assoviar etc ▶ ASSOBIAR etc

assu|mido /asu'midu/ a (confesso) confirmed, self-confessed. ~**mir** vt assume, take on; accept, admit ‹defeito› ● vi take office

assunto /a'sũtu/ m subject; (negócio) matter

assus|tador /asusta'dor/ a frightening. ~**tar** vt frighten, scare. ~**tar-se** vpr get frightened, get scared

asterisco /aste'risku/ m asterisk

as|tral /as'traw/ (pl ~**trais**) m Ⅰ state of mind. ~**tro** m star. ~**trologia** f astrology. ~**trólogo** m astrologer. ~**tronauta** m/f astronaut. ~**tronave** f spaceship. ~**tronomia** f astronomy. ~**tronômico** a astronomical. ~**trônomo** m astronomer

as|túcia /as'tusia/ f cunning. ~**tuto** a cunning; ‹comerciante› astute

ata /'ata/ f minutes

ataca|dista /ataka'dʒista/ m/f wholesaler. ~**do** m por ~**do** wholesale

ata|cante /ata'kãtʃi/ a attacking ● m/f attacker. ~**car** vt attack; tackle ‹problema›

atadura /ata'dura/ f bandage

ata|lhar /ata'ʎar/ vi take a shortcut. ~**lho** m shortcut

ataque /a'taki/ m attack; (de raiva, riso) fit; ~ **aéreo** air strike

atar /a'tar/ vt tie

atarantado /atarã'tadu/ a flustered, in a flap

atarefado /atare'fadu/ a busy

atarracado /ataxa'kadu/ a stocky

atarraxar /ataxa'ʃar/ vt screw

até /a'tɛ/ prep (up) to, as far as; (tempo) until ● adv even; ~ **logo** goodbye; ~ **que** until

ateia /a'teja/ a & f ▶ ATEU

ateliê /ateli'e/ m studio

atemorizar /atemori'zar/ vt frighten

Atenas /a'tenas/ f Athens

aten|ção /atẽ'sãw/ f attention; pl (bondade) thoughtfulness; **com ~ção** attentively. ~**cioso** a thoughtful, considerate

aten|der /atẽ'der/ ~**der (a)** vt/i answer ‹telefone, porta›; answer to ‹nome›; serve ‹freguês›; see ‹paciente, visitante›; grant, meet ‹pedido›; heed ‹conselho›. ~**dimento** m service; (de médico etc) consultation

aten|tado /atẽ'tadu/ m murder attempt; Pol assassination attempt; (ataque) attack (contra on). ~**tar** vi ~**tar contra** make an attempt on

atento /a'tẽtu/ a attentive; ~ **a** mindful of

aterrador /atexa'dor/ a terrifying

ater|ragem /ate'xaʒẽ/ f Port landing. ~**rar** vi Port land

aterris|sagem /atexi'saʒẽ/ f landing. ~**sar** vi land

aterro /a'texu/ m ~ **(sanitário)** landfill

ater-se /a'tersi/ vpr ~ **a** keep to, go by

ates|tado /ates'tadu/ m certificate. ~**tar** vt attest (to)

ateu /a'tew/ a & m (f **ateia**) atheist

atiçar /atʃi'sar/ vt poke ‹fogo›; stir up ‹ódio, discórdia›; arouse ‹pessoa›

atinar /atʃi'nar/ vt work out, guess; ~ **com** find; ~ **em** notice

atingir /atʃĩ'ʒir/ vt reach; hit ‹alvo›; (conseguir) attain; (afetar) affect

atirar /atʃi'rar/ vt throw ● vi shoot; ~ **em** fire at

atitude /atʃi'tudʒi/ f attitude; **tomar uma ~** take action

ati|va /a'tʃiva/ f active service. **~var** vt activate. **~vidade** f activity. **~vo** a active ● m Com assets

Atlântico /at'lãtʃiku/ m Atlantic

atlas /'atlas/ m atlas

at|leta /at'lɛta/ m/f athlete. **~lético** a athletic. **~letismo** m athletics

atmosfera /atʃmos'fera/ f atmosphere

ato /'atu/ m act; (ação) action; **no ~** on the spot

ato|lar /ato'lar/ vt bog down. **~lar-se** vpr get bogged down. **~leiro** m bog; fig fix, spot of trouble

atômico /a'tomiku/ a atomic

atomizador /atomiza'dor/ m atomizer spray

átomo /'atomu/ m atom

atônito /a'tonitu/ a astonished, stunned

ator /a'tor/ m actor

atordoar /atordo'ar/ vt ‹golpe, notícia› stun; ‹som› deafen; (alucinar) bewilder

atormentar /atormẽ'tar/ vt plague, torment

atração /atra'sãw/ f attraction

atracar /atra'kar/ vt/i Naut moor. **~se** vpr grapple; 🄸 neck

atraente /atra'ẽtʃi/ a attractive

atraiçoar /atrajso'ar/ vt betray

atrair /atra'ir/ vt attract

atrapalhar /atrapa'ʎar/ vt/i (confundir) confuse; (estorvar) hinder; (perturbar) disturb. **~se** vpr get mixed up

atrás /a'traʃ/ adv behind; (no fundo) at the back; **~ de** behind; (depois de, no encalço de) after; **um mês ~** a month ago; **ficar ~** be left behind

atra|sado /atra'zadu/ a late; ‹país, criança› backward; ‹relógio› slow; ‹pagamento› overdue; ‹ideias› old-fashioned. **~sar** vt delay; put back ‹relógio› ● vi be late; ‹relógio› lose. **~sar-se** vpr be late; (num trabalho) get behind; (no pagar) get into arrears. **~so** m delay; (de país etc) backwardness; pl Com arrears; **com ~so** late

atrativo /atra'tʃivu/ m attraction

através /atra'vɛs/ **~ de** prep through; (de um lado ao outro) across

atravessado /atrave'sadu/ a ‹espinha› stuck; **estar com alguém ~ na garganta** be fed up with sb

atravessar /atrave'sar/ vt go through; cross ‹rua, rio›

atre|ver-se /atre'versi/ vpr dare; **~ver-se a** dare to. **~vido** a daring; (insolente) impudent. **~vimento** m daring, boldness; (insolência) impudence

atribu|ir /atribu'ir/ vt attribute (**a** to); confer ‹prêmio, poderes› (**a** on); attach ‹importância› (**a** to). **~to** m attribute

atrito /a'tritu/ m friction; (desavença) disagreement

atriz /a'tris/ f actress

atrocidade /atrosi'dadʒi/ f atrocity

atrope|lar /atrope'lar/ vt run over, knock down ‹pedestre›; (empurrar) jostle; mix up ‹palavras›; **~lamento** m (de pedestre) running over. **~lo** /e/ m scramble

atroz /a'tros/ a awful, terrible; heinous ‹crime›; cruel ‹pessoa›

atuação /atua'sãw/ f (ação) action; (desempenho) performance

atu|al /atu'aw/ a (pl **~ais**) a current, present; ‹assunto, interesse› topical; ‹pessoa, carro› up-to-date. **~alidade** f (presente) present (time); (de um livro) topicality; pl current affairs. **~alizado** a up-to-date. **~alizar** vt update. **~alizar-se** vpr bring o.s. up to date. **~almente** adv at present, currently

atum /a'tũ/ m tuna

aturdir /atur'dʒir/ vt ▶ ATORDOAR

audácia /aw'dasia/ f boldness; (insolência) audacity

audi|ção /awdʒi'sãw/ f hearing; (concerto) recital. **~ência** f audience; Jurid hearing

audiovisu|al /awdʒiovizu'aw/ (pl **~ais**) a audiovisual

auditório /awdʒi'tɔriu/ m auditorium; **programa de ~** variety show

auge /'awʒi/ m peak, height

aula /'awla/ f class, lesson; **dar ~** teach

aumen|tar /awmẽ'tar/ vt increase; raise ‹preço, salário›; extend ‹casa›; (com lente) magnify; (acrescentar) add ● vi increase; ‹preço, salário› go up. **~to** m increase; (de salário) rise, Amer raise

au|sência /aw'zẽsia/ f absence. **~sente** a absent ● m/f absentee

aus|pícios /aws'pisius/ m pl auspices. **~picioso** /o/ a auspicious

auste|ridade /awsteri'dadʒi/ f austerity. **~ro** /ɛ/ a austere

Austrália /aws'tralia/ f Australia

australiano /awstrali'anu/ a & m Australian

Áustria /'awstria/ f Austria

austríaco /aws'triaku/ *a & m* Austrian

autarquia /awtar'kia/ *f* public authority

autêntico /aw'tẽtʃiku/ *a* authentic; genuine ‹pessoa›; true ‹fato›

autobio|grafia /awtobiogra'fia/ *f* autobiography. **~gráfico** *a* autobiographical

autocarro /awto'kaxu/ *m Port* bus

autocrata /awto'krata/ *a* autocratic

autodefesa /awtode'feza/ *f* self-defence

autodidata /awtodʒi'data/ *a & m/f* self-taught (person)

autódromo /aw'tɔdromu/ *m* race track

autoescola /awtois'kɔla/ *f* driving school

autoestrada /awtois'trada/ *f* motorway, *Amer* expressway

autógrafo /aw'tɔgrafu/ *m* autograph

auto|mação /awtoma'sãw/ *f* automation. **~mático** *a* automatic. **~matizar** *vt* automate

auto|mobilismo /awtomobi-'lizmu/ *m* motoring; (*esporte*) motor racing. **~móvel** (*pl* **~móveis**) *m* motor car, *Amer* automobile

automutilação /awtomutʃila'sãw/ *f* self-harm

au|tonomia /awtono'mia/ *f* autonomy. **~tônomo** *a* autonomous; ‹trabalhador› self-employed

autopeça /awto'pesa/ *f* car spare

autópsia /aw'tɔpsia/ *f* autopsy

autor /aw'tor/ *m* (*f* **~a**) author; (*de crime*) perpetrator; *Jurid* plaintiff

autoria /awto'ria/ *f* authorship; (*de crime*) responsibility (**de** for)

autori|dade /awtori'dadʒi/ *f* authority. **~zação** *f* authorization. **~zar** *vt* authorize

autorretrato /awtoxe'tratu/ *m* self-portrait

autuar /awtu'ar/ *vt* sue

au|xiliar /awsili'ar/ *a* auxiliary ● *m/f* assistant ● *vt* assist. **~xílio** *m* assistance, aid

aval /a'vaw/ (*pl* **avais**) *m* endorsement; *Com* guarantee

avali|ação /avalia'sãw/ *f* (*de preço*) valuation; *fig* evaluation. **~ar** *vt* value ‹quadro etc› (**em** at); assess ‹danos, riscos›; *fig* evaluate

avan|çar /avã'sar/ *vt* move forward ● *vi* move forward; *Mil fig* advance; **~çar a** (*montar*) amount to. **~ço** *m* advance

avar|eza /ava'reza/ *f* meanness. **~ento** *a* mean

ava|ria /ava'ria/ *f* damage; (*de máquina*) breakdown. **~riado** *a* damaged; ‹máquina› out of order; ‹carro› broken down. **~riar** *vt* damage ● *vi* be damaged; ‹máquina› break down

avatar /ava'tar/ *m* avatar

ave /'avi/ *f* bird; **~ de rapina** bird of prey

aveia /a'veja/ *f* oats

avelã /ave'lã/ *f* hazelnut

avenida /ave'nida/ *f* avenue

aven|tal /avẽ'taw/ (*pl* **~tais**) *m* apron

aventu|ra /avẽ'tura/ *f* adventure; (*amorosa*) fling. **~rar** *vt* venture. **~rar-se** *vpr* venture (**a** to). **~reiro** *a* adventurous ● *m* adventurer

averiguar /averi'gwar/ *vt* check (out)

avermelhado /averme'ʎadu/ *a* reddish

aver|são /aver'sãw/ *f* aversion. **~so** *a* averse (**a** to)

aves|sas /a'vesas/ **às ~sas** the wrong way round; (*de cabeça para baixo*) upside down. **~so** /e/ *m* **ao ~so** inside out

avestruz /aves'trus/ *m* ostrich

avi|ação /avia'sãw/ *f* aviation. **~ão** *m* (aero)plane, *Amer* (air)plane; **~ão a jato** jet

avi|dez /avi'des/ *f* (*cobiça*) greediness

ávido /'avidu/ *a* greedy

avi|sar /avi'zar/ *vt* (*informar*) tell, let know; (*advertir*) warn. **~so** *m* notice; (*advertência*) warning

avistar /avis'tar/ *vt* catch sight of

avo /'avu/ *m* **um doze ~s** one twelfth

avó /a'vɔ/ *f* grandmother. **~s** *m pl* grandparents

avô /a'vo/ *m* grandfather

avoado /avo'adu/ *a* dizzy, scatterbrained

avulso /a'vuwsu/ *a* loose, odd

avultado /avuw'tadu/ *a* bulky

axila /ak'sila/ *f* armpit

azaléia /aza'leja/ *f* azalea

azar /a'zar/ *m* bad luck; **ter ~** be unlucky. **~ado**, **~ento** *a* unlucky

aze|dar /aze'dar/ *vt* sour ● *vi* go sour. **~do** /e/ *a* sour

azei|te /a'zejtʃi/ *m* oil. **~tona** /o/ *f* olive

azevinho /aze'viɲu/ m holly

azia /a'zia/ f heartburn

azucrinar /azukri'nar/ vt annoy

azul /a'zuw/ (pl **azuis**) a blue

azulejo /azu'leʒu/ m (ceramic) tile

azul-marinho /azuwma'riɲu/ a invar navy blue

. . . .

Bb

. . . .

babá /ba'ba/ f nanny; **~ eletrônica** baby alarm

ba|bado /ba'badu/ m frill. **~bador** m bib. **~bar** vt/i, **~bar-se** vpr drool (**por** over); ‹bebê› dribble. **~beiro** Port m bib

baby-sitter /bejbi'siter/ (pl **~s**) m/f babysitter

bacalhau /baka'ʎaw/ m cod

> **bacalhau** *Bacalhau* is the   *i*
> Portuguese word for 'cod',
> although it is most commonly used to
> refer to salt (or dried) cod. Salt cod
> originated during the time of the
> Portuguese discoveries, when people
> needed a way to preserve fish before
> the advent of refrigeration. It's a hugely
> popular food, so much so that it's
> commonly said there are 365 ways to
> cook *bacalhau*, one for each day of the
> year, but in reality, there are many
> more.

bacana /ba'kana/ a 🔲 great

bacha|rel /baʃa'rɛw/ (pl **~réis**) m bachelor. **~relado** m bachelor's degree. **~relar-se** vpr graduate

bacia /ba'sia/ f basin; (da privada) bowl; Anat pelvis

backup /be'kap/ m Port Comput backup

baço /'basu/ m spleen

bacon /'bejkõ/ m bacon

bactéria /bak'tɛria/ f bacterium; pl bacteria

bada|lado /bada'ladu/ a 🔲 talked about. **~lar** vt ring ‹sino› ● vi ring; 🔲 go out and about. **~lativo** a 🔲 fun-loving

badejo /ba'deʒu/ m sea bass

baderna /ba'dɛrna/ f (tumulto) commotion; (desordem) mess

badulaque /badu'laki/ m trinket

bafafá /bafa'fa/ m 🔲 to-do, kerfuffle

ba|fo /'bafu/ m bad breath. **~fômetro** m Breathalyser. **~forada** f puff

bagaço /ba'gasu/ m pulp; Port (aguardente) brandy

baga|geiro /baga'ʒeru/ m (de carro) roof rack; (homem) porter. **~gem** f luggage; (cultural etc) baggage

bagatela /baga'tɛla/ f trifle

Bagdá /bagi'da/ f Baghdad

bago /'bagu/ m berry; (de chumbo) pellet

bagulho /ba'guʎu/ m piece of junk; pl junk; **ele é um ~** he's as ugly as sin

bagun|ça /ba'gũsa/ f mess. **~çar** vt mess up. **~ceiro** a messy

baia /ba'ia/ f bay

baiano /ba'janu/ a & m Bahian

baila /'bajla/ f **trazer/vir à ~** bring/ come up

bai|lar /baj'lar/ vt/i dance. **~larino** m ballet dancer. **~le** m dance; (de gala) ball

bainha /ba'iɲa/ f (de vestido) hem; (de arma) sheath

baioneta /bajo'nɛta/ f bayonet

bairro /'bajxu/ m neighbourhood, area

baixa /'baʃa/ f drop, fall; (de guerra) casualty; (dispensa) discharge. **~mar** f low tide

baixar /ba'ʃar/ vt lower; issue ‹ordem›; pass ‹lei›; Comput download ● vi drop, fall; 🔲 (pintar) turn up

baixaria /baʃa'ria/ f sordidness; (uma) sordid thing

baixela /ba'ʃɛla/ f set of cutlery

baixeza /ba'ʃeza/ f baseness

baixo /'baʃu/ a low; ‹pessoa› short; ‹som, voz› quiet, soft; ‹cabeça, olhos› lowered; (vil) sordid ● adv low; ‹falar› softly, quietly ● m bass; **em ~** underneath; (em casa) downstairs; **em ~ de** under; **para ~** down; (em casa) downstairs; **por ~ de** under(neath)

baju|lador /baʒula'dor/ a obsequious ● m sycophant. **~lar** vt fawn on

bala /'bala/ f (de revólver) bullet; (doce) sweet

balada /ba'lada/ f ballad

balaio /ba'laju/ m linen basket

balan|ça /ba'lãsa/ f scales; **Balança** (signo) Libra; **~ça de pagamentos** balance of payments. **~çar** vt/i (no ar) swing; (numa cadeira etc) rock; ‹carro, avião› shake; ‹navio› roll. **~çar-se** vpr swing. **~cete** /e/ m trial balance. **~ço** m Com balance sheet; (brinquedo) swing; (movimento no ar) swinging; (de carro, *avião)* shaking; *(de navio)* rolling; *(de cadeira)* rocking; **fazer um ~ço de** *fig* take stock of

balangandã /balãgã'dã/ *m* bauble

balão /ba'lãw/ *m* balloon; **soltar um ~ de ensaio** *fig* put out feelers

balar /ba'lar/ *vi* bleat

balbu|ciar /bawbusi'ar/ *vt/i* babble. **~cio** *m* babble, babbling

balbúrdia /baw'burdʒia/ *f* hubbub

bal|cão /baw'kãw/ *m* (em loja) counter; *(de informações, bilhetes)* desk; *(de cozinha)* worktop, *Amer* counter; *(no teatro)* circle. **~conista** *m/f* shop assistant

balde /'bawdʒi/ *m* bucket

baldeação /bawdʒia'sãw/ *f* **fazer ~** change (trains)

baldio /baw'dʒiu/ *a* fallow; **terreno ~** (piece of) waste ground

balé /ba'lɛ/ *m* ballet

balear /bali'ar/ *vt* shoot

baleia /ba'leja/ *f* whale

balido /ba'lidu/ *m* bleat, bleating

balísti|ca /ba'listʃika/ *f* ballistics. **~co** *a* ballistic

bali|za /ba'liza/ *f* marker; *(luminosa)* beacon. **~zar** *vt* mark out

balneário /bawni'ariu/ *m* seaside resort

balofo /ba'lofu/ *a* fat, tubby

baloiço, balouço /ba'lojsu, ba'losu/ *Port m (de criança)* swing

balsa /'bawsa/ *f (de madeira etc)* raft; *(que vai e vem)* ferry

bálsamo /'bawsamu/ *m* balm

báltico /'bawtʃiku/ *a & m* Baltic

baluarte /balu'artʃi/ *m* bulwark

bambo /'bãbu/ *a* loose, slack; ‹pernas› limp; ‹mesa› wobbly

bambo|lê /bãbo'le/ *m* hula hoop. **~lear** *vi ‹pessoa›* sway, totter; ‹coisa› wobble

bambu /bã'bu/ *m* bamboo

ba|nal /ba'naw/ *(pl ~nais) a* banal. **~nalidade** *f* banality

bana|na /ba'nana/ *f* banana ● *m/f* 🖪 wimp. **~nada** *f* banana fudge. **~neira** *f* banana tree; **plantar ~neira** do a handstand

banca /'bãka/ *f (de trabalho)* bench; *(de jornais)* news stand; **~ examinadora** examining board. **~da** *f Pol* bench

bancar /bã'kar/ *vt (custear)* finance; *(fazer papel de)* play; *(fingir)* pretend

bancário /bã'kariu/ *a* bank ● *m* bank employee

bancarrota /bãka'xota/ *f* bankruptcy; **ir à ~** go bankrupt

banco /'bãku/ *m Com* bank; *(no parque)* bench; *(na cozinha, num bar)* stool; *(de bicicleta)* saddle; *(de carro)* seat; **~ de areia** sandbank; **~ de dados** database

banda /'bãda/ *f* band; *(lado)* side; **de ~** sideways on; **nestas ~s** in these parts; **~ desenhada** *Port* cartoon; **~ larga** broadband

bandei|ra /bã'dera/ *f* flag; *(divisa)* banner; **dar ~ra** 🖪 give o.s. away. **~rante** *m/f* pioneer ● *f* girl guide. **~rinha** *m* linesman

bandeja /bã'deʒa/ *f* tray

bandido /bã'dʒidu/ *m* bandit

bando /'bãdu/ *m (de pessoas)* band; *(de pássaros)* flock

bandolim /bãdo'lĩ/ *m* mandolin

bangalô /bãga'lo/ *m* bungalow

Bangcoc /bã'koki/ *f* Bangkok

bangue-bangue /bãgi'bãgi/ *m* 🖪 western

banguela /bã'gela/ *a* toothless

banha /'bana/ *f* lard; *pl (no corpo)* flab

banhar /ba'nar/ *vt (molhar)* bathe; *(lavar)* bath. **~se** *vpr* bathe

banhei|ra /ba'nera/ *f* bath, *Amer* bathtub. **~ro** *m* bathroom; *Port* lifeguard

banhista /ba'nista/ *m/f* bather

banho /'banu/ *m* bath; *(no mar)* bathe, dip; **tomar ~** have a bath; *(no chuveiro)* have a shower; **tomar um ~ de loja/cultura** go on a shopping/cultural spree; **~ de espuma** bubble bath; **~ de sol** sunbathing. **~maria** *(pl ~s-maria) m* bain-marie

ba|nimento /bani'mẽtu/ *m* banishment. **~nir** *vt* banish

banjo /'bãʒu/ *m* banjo

banqueiro /bã'keru/ *m* banker

banqueta /bã'keta/ *f* footstool

banque|te /bã'ketʃi/ *m* banquet. **~teiro** *m* caterer

banzé /bã'zɛ/ *m* 🖪 commotion, uproar

baque /'baki/ *m* thud, crash; *(revés)* blow. **~ar** *vi* topple over ● *vt* hit hard, knock for six

bar /bar/ *m* bar

barafunda /bara'fũda/ *f* jumble; *(barulho)* racket

bara|lhada /bara'ʎada/ *f* jumble. **~lho** *m* pack of cards, *Amer* deck of cards

barão /ba'rãw/ m baron

barata /ba'rata/ f cockroach

bara|tear /barat∫i'ar/ vt cheapen. **~teiro** a cheap

baratinar /barat∫i'nar/ vt fluster; (*transtornar*) rattle, shake up

barato /ba'ratu/ a cheap ● adv cheaply ● m 🄸 um **~** great; que **~l** that's brilliant!

barba /'barba/ f beard; pl (*de gato etc*) whiskers; fazer a **~** shave. **~da** f walkover; (*cavalo*) favourite. **~do** a bearded

barbante /bar'bãt∫i/ m string

bar|baridade /barbari'dadʒi/ f barbarity; 🄸 (*muito dinheiro*) fortune. **~bárie** f, **~barismo** m barbarism

bárbaro /'barbaru/ m barbarian ● a barbaric; 🄸 (*forte, bom*) terrific

barbatana /barba'tana/ f fin

bar|beador /barbia'dor/ m shaver. **~bear** vt shave. **~bear-se** vpr shave. **~bearia** f barber's shop. **~beiragem** f 🄸 bit of bad driving. **~beiro** m barber; 🄸 (*motorista*) bad driver

bar|ca /'barka/ f barge; (*balsa*) ferry. **~caça** f barge. **~co** m boat; **~co a motor** motor boat; **~co a remo/vela** rowing/sailing boat, Amer rowboat/sailboat

barga|nha /bar'gaɲa/ f bargain. **~nhar** vt/i bargain

barítono /ba'ritonu/ m baritone

barômetro /ba'rometru/ m barometer

baronesa /baro'neza/ f baroness

barra /'baxa/ f bar; (*sinal gráfico*) slash, stroke; 🄸 (*situação*) situation; segurar a **~** hold out; forçar a **~** force the issue

barra|ca /ba'xaka/ f (*de acampar*) tent; (*na feira*) stall; (*casinha*) hut; (*guarda-sol*) sunshade. **~cão** m shed. **~co** m shack, shanty

barragem /ba'xaʒẽ/ f (*represa*) dam

barra-pesada /baxape'zada/ a invar 🄸 <*bairro*> rough; <*pessoa*> shady; (*difícil*) tough

bar|rar /ba'xar/ vt bar. **~reira** f barrier; (*em corrida*) hurdle; (*em futebol*) wall

barrento /ba'xẽtu/ a muddy

barricada /baxi'kada/ f barricade

barri|ga /ba'xiga/ f stomach, Amer belly; **~ga da perna** calf. **~gudo** a pot-bellied

bar|ril /ba'xiw/ (pl **~ris**) m barrel

barro /'baxu/ m (*argila*) clay; (*lama*) mud

barroco /ba'xoku/ a & m baroque

barrote /ba'xɔt∫i/ m beam, joist

baru|lheira /baru'ʎera/ f racket, din. **~lhento** a noisy. **~lho** m noise

base /'bazi/ f base; fig (*fundamento*) basis; com **~** em on the basis of; na **~** de based on. **~ado** a based; (*firme*) well-founded ● m 🄸 joint. **~ar** vt base; **~ar-se em** be based on

básico /'baziku/ a basic

basquete /bas'ket∫i/ m, **basquetebol** /basket∫i'bɔw/ m basketball

bas|ta /'basta/ m dar um **~ta em** call a halt to. **~tante** a (*muito*) quite a lot of; (*suficiente*) enough ● adv (*com adjetivo, advérbio*) quite; (*com verbo*) quite a lot; (*suficientemente*) enough

bastão /bas'tãw/ m stick; (*num revezamento, de comando*) baton

bastar /bas'tar/ vi be enough

bastidores /bast∫i'doris/ m pl (*no teatro*) wings; **nos ~** fig behind the scenes

bata /'bata/ f (*de mulher*) smock; (*de médico etc*) overall

bata|lha /ba'taʎa/ f battle. **~lhador** a plucky, feisty ● m fighter. **~lhão** m battalion. **~lhar** vi battle; (*esforçar-se*) fight hard ● vt fight hard to get

batata /ba'tata/ f potato; **~ doce** sweet potato; **~ frita** chips, Amer French fries; (*salgadinhos*) crisps, Amer potato chips

bate-boca /bat∫i'boka/ m row, argument

bate|deira /bate'dera/ f whisk; (*de manteiga*) churn. **~dor** m (*policial etc*) outrider; (*no criquete*) batsman; (*no beisebol*) batter; (*de caça*) beater; **~dor de carteiras** pickpocket

batelada /bate'lada/ f batch; **~s de** heaps of

batente /ba'tẽt∫i/ m (*de porta*) doorway; **para o/no ~** 🄸 (*ao trabalho*) to/at work

bate-papo /bat∫i'papu/ m chat

bater /ba'ter/ vt beat; stamp <*pé*>; slam <*porta*>; strike <*horas*>; take <*foto*>; flap <*asas*>; (*datilografar*) type; (*lavar*) wash; (*usar muito*) wear a lot <*roupa*>; 🄸 pinch <*carteira*>; **~ à máquina** type; **~ à ou na porta** knock at the door; **~ em** hit; harp on <*assunto*>; **~ com o carro** crash one's car, have a crash; **~ com a cabeça** bang one's head; **ele batia os dentes de frio** his teeth were chattering with cold; **ele não bate bem** 🄸 he's not all there ● vi <*coração*> beat; <*porta*> slam; <*janela*>

bang; ‹horas› strike; ‹sino› ring; (à porta) knock; (com o carro) crash; ‹luz, sol› shine on. **~se** vpr (lutar) fight

bate|ria /bate'ria/ f Eletr battery; Mus drums; **~ria de cozinha** kitchen utensils. **~rista** m/f drummer

bati|da /ba'tʃida/ f beat; (à porta) knock; (no carro) crash; (policial) raid; (bebida) cocktail of rum, sugar and fruit juice. **~do** a beaten; ‹roupa› well worn; ‹assunto› hackneyed ● m **~do de leite** Port milkshake

batina /ba'tʃina/ f cassock

ba|tismo /ba'tʃizmu/ m baptism. **~tizado** m christening. **~tizar** vt baptize; (pôr nome) christen

batom /ba'tõ/ m lipstick

batu|cada /batu'kada/ f samba percussion group. **~car** vt/i drum in a samba rhythm. **~que** m samba rhythm

batuta /ba'tuta/ f baton; **sob a ~ de** under the direction of

baú /ba'u/ m trunk

baunilha /baw'niʎa/ f vanilla

bazar /ba'zar/ m bazaar; (loja) stationery and haberdashery shop

bê-a-bá /bea'ba/ m ABC

bea|titude /beatʃi'tudʒi/ f (felicidade) bliss; (devoção) piety, devoutness. **~to** a (devoto) pious, devout; (feliz) blissful

bêbado /'bebadu/ a & m drunk

bebê /be'be/ m baby; **~ de proveta** test-tube baby

bebe|deira /bebe'dera/ f (estado) drunkenness; (ato) drinking bout. **~dor** m drinker. **~douro** m drinking fountain

beber /be'ber/ vt/i drink

bebericar /beberi'kar/ vt/i sip

bebida /be'bida/ f drink

beca /'bɛka/ f gown

beça /'bɛsa/ f **à ~** 🄸 (com substantivo) loads of; (com adjetivo) really; (com verbo) a lot

becape /be'kap/ m Comput backup

beco /'beku/ m alley; **~ sem saída** dead end

bedelho /be'deʎu/ m **meter o ~ (em)** stick one's oar in(to)

bege /'bɛʒi/ a invar beige

bei|cinho /bej'siɲu/ m **fazer ~cinho** pout. **~ço** m lip. **~çudo** a thick-lipped

beija-flor /bejʒa'flor/ m hummingbird

bei|jar /be'ʒar/ vt kiss. **~jo** m kiss. **~joca** /ɔ/ f peck

bei|ra /'bera/ f edge; fig (do desastre etc) verge, brink; **à ~ra de** at the edge of; fig on the verge of. **~rada** f edge. **~ra-mar** f seaside. **~rar** vt (ficar) border (on); (andar) skirt; fig border on, verge on; **ele está ~rando os 30 anos** he's nearing thirty

beisebol /bejzi'bɔw/ m baseball

belas-artes /belaʃ'artʃiʃ/ f pl fine arts

beldade /bew'dadʒi/ f, **beleza** /be'leza/ f beauty

belga /'bewga/ a & m Belgian

Bélgica /'bewʒika/ f Belgium

beliche /be'liʃi/ m bunk

bélico /'bɛliku/ a war

belicoso /beli'kozu/ a warlike

belis|cão /belis'kãw/ m pinch. **~car** vt pinch; nibble ‹comida›

Belize /be'lizi/ m Belize

belo /'bɛlu/ a beautiful

beltrano /bew'tranu/ m such-and-such

bem /bẽj/ adv well; (bastante) quite; (muito) very ● m (pl **bens**) good; pl goods, property; **está ~** (it's) fine, OK; **fazer ~ a** be good for; **tudo ~?** 🄸 how's things?; **se ~ que** even though; **~ feito (por você)** 🄸 it serves you right; **muito ~!** well done!; **de ~ com alguém** on good terms with sb; **~ como** as well as

bem|-apessoado /bẽjapeso'adu/ a nice-looking. **~comportado** a well-behaved; **~disposto** a keen, willing; **~estar** m well-being; **~humorado** a good-humoured; **~intencionado** a well-intentioned; **~passado** a ‹carne› well-done; **~sucedido** a successful; **~vindo** a welcome; **~visto** a well thought of

bênção /'bẽsãw/ (pl **~s**) f blessing

bendito /bẽ'dʒitu/ a blessed

benefi|cência /benefi'sẽsia/ f (bondade) goodness, kindness; (caridade) charity. **~cente** a ‹associação› charitable; ‹concerto, feira› charity. **~ciado** m beneficiary. **~ciar** vt benefit. **~ciar-se** vpr benefit (de from)

benefício /bene'fisiu/ m benefit; **em ~ de** in aid of

benéfico /be'nɛfiku/ a beneficial (a to)

benevolência /benevo'lẽsia/ f benevolence

benévolo /be'nevolu/ a benevolent

benfeitor /bẽfej'tor/ m benefactor

bengala /bẽ'gala/ f walking stick; (pão) French stick

benigno /be'niginu/ a benign

ben|to /'bẽtu/ a blessed; ‹*água*› holy. **~zer** vt bless. **~zer-se** vpr cross o.s.

berço /'bersu/ m (*de embalar*) cradle; (*caminha*) cot; *fig* birthplace; **ter ~** be from a good family

berimbau /berĩ'baw/ m: Brazilian percussion instrument shaped like a bow

berinjela /berĩ'ʒela/ f aubergine, *Amer* eggplant

Berlim /ber'lĩ/ f Berlin

berma /'berma/ f *Port* hard shoulder, *Amer* berm

bermuda /ber'muda/ f Bermuda shorts

Berna /'berna/ f Berne

ber|rante /be'xãtʃi/ a loud, flashy. **~rar** vi ‹*pessoa*› shout; ‹*criança*› bawl; ‹*boi*› bellow. **~reiro** m (*gritaria*) yelling, shouting; (*choro*) crying, bawling. **~ro** /ɛ/ m yell, shout; (*de boi*) bellow; **aos ~ros** shouting

besouro /be'zoru/ m beetle

bes|ta /'besta/ a (*idiota*) stupid; (*cheio de si*) full of o.s.; (*pedante*) pretentious ● f (*pessoa*) dimwit, numbskull; **ficar ~ta** 🇧🇷 be taken aback. **~teira** f stupidity; (*uma*) stupid thing; **falar ~teira** talk rubbish. **~tial** (*pl* **~tiais**) a bestial. **~tificar** vt astound, dumbfound

besuntar /bezũ'tar/ vt coat; (*sujar*) smear

betão /be'tãw/ *Port* m concrete

beterraba /bete'xaba/ f beetroot

betoneira /beto'nera/ f cement mixer

bexiga /be'ʃiga/ f bladder

bezerro /be'zeru/ m calf

bibelô /bibe'lo/ m ornament

Bíblia /'biblia/ f Bible

bíblico /'bibliku/ a biblical

biblio|grafia /bibliogra'fia/ f bibliography. **~teca** /ɛ/ f library. **~tecário** m librarian ● a library

bica /'bika/ f tap; *Port* (*cafezinho*) espresso; **suar em ~s** drip with sweat

bicama /bi'kama/ f truckle bed

bicar /bi'kar/ vt peck

bíceps /'biseps/ m invar biceps

bicha /'biʃa/ f 🇧🇷 queer, fairy; *Port* (*fila*) queue

bicheiro /bi'ʃeru/ m organizer of illegal numbers game, racketeer

bicho /'biʃu/ m animal; (*inseto*) insect, *Amer* bug; **que ~ te mordeu?** what's got into you? **~-da-seda** (*pl* **~s-da-seda**) m silkworm; **~ de sete cabeças** m 🇧🇷

big deal, big thing; **~ do mato** (*pl* **~s do mato**) m very shy person

bicho-papão /'biʃupa'pãw/ m (*pl* **bichos-papões**) bogeyman

bicicleta /bisi'kleta/ f bicycle, bike

bico /'biku/ m (*de ave*) beak; (*de faca*) point; (*de sapato*) toe; (*de bule*) spout; (*de caneta*) nib; (*do seio*) nipple; (*de gás*) jet; 🇧🇷 (*emprego*) odd job, sideline; (*boca*) mouth

bidê /bi'de/ m bidet

bidimensio|nal /bidʒimẽsio'naw/ (*pl* **~nais**) a two-dimensional

biela /bi'ela/ f connecting rod

Bielo-Rússia /bielo'xusia/ f Byelorussia

bielo-russo /bielo'xusu/ a & m Byelorussian

bie|nal /bie'naw/ (*pl* **~nais**) a biennial ● f biennial art exhibition

bife /'bifi/ m steak

bifo|cal /bifo'kaw/ (*pl* **~cais**) a bifocal

bifur|cação /bifurka'sãw/ f fork. **~car-se** vpr fork

bigamia /biga'mia/ f bigamy

bígamo /'bigamu/ a bigamous ● m bigamist

bigo|de /bi'gɔdʒi/ m moustache. **~dudo** a with a big moustache

bigorna /bi'gɔrna/ f anvil

bijuteria /biʒute'ria/ f costume jewellery

bila|teral /bilate'raw/ (*pl* **~rais**) a bilateral

bilhão /bi'ʎãw/ m thousand million, *Amer* billion

bilhar /bi'ʎar/ m pool, billiards

bilhe|te /bi'ʎetʃi/ m ticket; (*recado*) note; **~te de ida e volta** return ticket, *Amer* round-trip ticket; **~te de identidade** *Port* identity card; **o ~te azul** 🇧🇷 the sack. **~teria** f, *Port* **~teira** f (*no cinema, teatro*) box office; (*na estação*) ticket office

bilíngue /bi'lĩgwi/ a bilingual

bilionário /bilio'nariu/ a & m billionaire

bílis /'bilis/ f bile

binário /bi'nariu/ a binary

bingo /'bĩgu/ m bingo

binóculo /bi'nɔkulu/ m binoculars

biocombustível /biokõbus'tʃivew/ m biofuel

biodegradá|vel /biodegra'davew/ (*pl* **~veis**) a biodegradable

b

biodiesel /bio'dʒizew/ m biodiesel

biodiversidade /biodʒiversi'dadʒi/ f biodiversity

bio|grafia /biogra'fia/ f biography. **~gráfico** a biographical

biógrafo /bi'ɔgrafu/ m biographer

bio|logia /biolo'ʒia/ f biology. **~lógico** a biological

biólogo /bi'ɔlogu/ m biologist

biombo /bi'õbu/ m screen

biônico /bi'oniku/ a bionic; *Pol* unelected

biópsia /bi'ɔpsia/ f biopsy

bioquími|ca /bio'kimika/ f biochemistry. **~co** a biochemical ● m biochemist

biquíni /bi'kini/ m bikini

birma|nês /birma'nes/ a & m (f **~nesa**) Burmese

Birmânia /bir'mania/ f Burma

birô /bi'ro/ m bureau

bir|ra /'bixa/ f wilfulness; **fazer ~ra** have a tantrum. **~rento** a wilful

biruta /bi'ruta/ 🔟 a crazy ● f windsock

bis /bis/ *int* encore!, more! ● m *invar* encore

bisa|vó /biza'vɔ/ f great-grandmother. **~vós** m pl great-grandparents. **~vô** m great-grandfather

bisbilho|tar /bizbiʎo'tar/ vt pry into ● vi pry. **~teiro** a prying ● m busybody. **~tice** f prying

bisca|te /bis'katʃi/ m odd job. **~teiro** m odd-job man

biscoito /bis'kojtu/ m biscuit, *Amer* cookie

bisnaga /biz'naga/ f (*pão*) bridge roll; (*tubo*) tube

bisne|ta /biz'neta/ f great-granddaughter. **~to** /e/ m great-grandson; pl great-grandchildren

bis|pado /bis'padu/ m bishopric. **~po** m bishop

bissexto /bi'sestu/ a occasional; **ano ~** leap year

bissexu|al /biseksu'aw/ (pl **~ais**) a & m/f bisexual

bisturi /bistu'ri/ m scalpel

bito|la /bi'tɔla/ f gauge. **~lado** a narrow-minded

bizarro /bi'zaxu/ a bizarre

blablablá /blabla'bla/ m 🔟 chit-chat

black /'blɛki/ m black market. **~tie** m evening dress

blas|femar /blasfe'mar/ vi blaspheme. **~fêmia** f blasphemy. **~femo** /e/ a blasphemous ● m blasphemer

blecaute /ble'kawtʃi/ m power cut

ble|far /ble'far/ vi bluff. **~fe** /ɛ/ m bluff

blin|dado /blĩ'dadu/ a armoured. **~dagem** f armour plating

blitz /blits/ f invar police spot check (on vehicles)

blo|co /'blɔku/ m block; *Pol* bloc; (*de papel*) pad; (*no carnaval*) section. **blogar** /blo'gar/ vi blog

blogue /'blɔgi/ m blog

blogueiro /blo'gejru/ m, *Port* **bloguista** /blo'gista/ m/f blogger

blo|quear /blo'kjar/ vt block; *Mil* blockade. **~queio** m blockage; *Psic* mental block; *Mil* blockade

blusa /'bluza/ f shirt; (*de mulher*) blouse; (*de lã*) sweater

blusão /blu'zãw/ m jacket

boa /'boa/ f de ▶ **BOM** ● **numa ~** 🔟 well; (*sem problemas*) easily; **estar numa ~** 🔟 be doing fine. **~gente** a invar 🔟 nice; **~nova** (pl **~s-novas**) f good news. **~pinta** (pl **~s-pintas**) a 🔟 nice-looking; **~praça** (pl **~s-praças**) a 🔟 friendly, sociable

boate /bo'atʃi/ f nightclub

boato /bo'atu/ m rumour

boa|-vida /boa'vida/ (pl **~s-vidas**) m/f good-for-nothing, waster. **~zinha** a sweet, kind

bo|bagem /bo'baʒẽ/ f silliness; (*uma*) silly thing. **~beada** f slip-up. **~bear** vi slip up. **~beira** f ▶ **BOBAGEM**

bobe /'bɔbi/ m curler, roller

bobina /bo'bina/ f reel; *Eletr* coil

bobo /'bobu/ a silly ● m fool; (*da corte*) jester. **~ca** /ɔ/ a 🔟 stupid ● m/f 🔟 twit

bo|ca /'boka/ f mouth; (*no fogão*) ring; **~ca da noite** nightfall. **~cado** m (*na boca*) mouthful; (*pedaço*) piece, bit. **~cal** (pl **~cais**) m mouthpiece

boce|jar /bose'ʒar/ vi yawn. **~jo** /e/ m yawn

boche|cha /bo'ʃeʃa/ f cheek. **~char** vi rinse one's mouth. **~cho** /e/ m mouthwash. **~chudo** a with puffy cheeks

bodas /'bodas/ f pl wedding anniversary; **~ de prata/ouro** silver/golden wedding

bode /'bɔdʒi/ m (billy) goat; **~ expiatório** scapegoat

bodega /bo'dega/ f (de bebidas) off-licence, Amer liquor store; (de secos e molhados) grocer's shop, corner shop

boêmio /bo'emiu/ a & m Bohemian

bofe|tada /bofe'tada/ f, **bofetão** /bofe'tãw/ m slap. **~tear** vt slap

boi /boj/ m bullock, Amer steer

bói /bɔj/ m office boy

boia /'bɔja/ f (de balizamento) buoy; (de cortiça, isopor etc) float; (câmara de borracha) rubber ring; (de braço) armband, water wing; (na caixa-d'água) ballcock; ⚀ (comida) grub; **~ salva-vidas** lifebelt. **~fria** (pl **~s-frias**) m/f itinerant farm labourer

bolar /bo'lar/ vt/i float; ⚀ be lost

boico|tar /bojko'tar/ vt boycott. **~te** /ɔ/ m boycott

boiler /'bojler/ (pl **~s**) m boiler

boina /'bojna/ f beret

bo|jo /'boʒu/ m bulge. **~judo** a (cheio) bulging; (arredondado) bulbous

bola /'bɔla/ f ball; **dar ~ para** ⚀ give attention to ‹pessoa›; care about ‹coisa›; **~ de gude** marble; **~ de neve** snowball

bolacha /bo'laʃa/ f (biscoito) biscuit, Amer cookie; (descanso) beer mat; ⚀ (tapa) slap

bo|lada /bo'lada/ f large sum of money. **~lar** vt think up, devise

boleia /bo'leja/ f cab; Port (carona) lift

boletim /bole'tʃĩ/ m bulletin; (escolar) report

bolha /'boʎa/ f bubble; (na pele) blister ● m/f ⚀ pain

boliche /bo'liʃi/ m skittles

Bolívia /bo'livia/ f Bolivia

boliviano /bolivi'anu/ a & m Bolivian

bolo /'bolu/ m cake

bo|lor /bo'lor/ m mould, mildew. **~lorento** a mouldy

bolo rei A ring-shaped fruit bread, covered in crystallized fruit and nuts, and eaten at Christmas time. Traditionally, a lucky coin or trinket and a *fava* (bean) would be hidden in the cake. In Portugal, whoever found the *fava* would be entitled to make a wish.

bolota /bo'lɔta/ f (glande) acorn; (bolinha) little ball

bol|sa /'bowsa/ f bag; **~sa (de estudo)** scholarship; **~sa (de valores)** stock exchange. **~sista** m/f, Port **~seiro** m scholarship student. **~so** /o/ m pocket

bom /bõ/ a (f **boa**) good; (de saúde) well; ‹comida› nice; **está ~** that's fine

bomba¹ /'bõba/ f (explosiva) bomb; (doce) eclair; fig bombshell; **levar ~** ⚀ fail

bomba² /'bõba/ f (de bombear) pump; **~ de gasolina** Port petrol pump

Bombaim /bõba'ĩ/ f Bombay

bombar|dear /bõbardʒi'ar/ vt bombard; (do ar) bomb. **~deio** m bombardment; (do ar) bombing

bomba-relógio /bõbaxe'lɔʒiu/ (pl **~s-relógio**) f time bomb

bom|bear /bõbi'ar/ vt pump. **~beiro** m fireman; (encanador) plumber

bombom /bõ'bõ/ m chocolate

bombordo /bõ'bɔrdu/ m port

bondade /bõ'dadʒi/ f goodness

bonde /'bõdʒi/ m tram; (teleférico) cable car

bondoso /bõ'dozu/ a good(-hearted)

boné /bo'nɛ/ m cap

bone|ca /bo'nɛka/ f doll. **~co** /ɛ/ m dummy

bonificação /bonifika'sãw/ f bonus

bonito /bo'nitu/ a ‹mulher› pretty; ‹homem› handsome; ‹tempo, casa etc› lovely

bônus /'bonus/ m invar bonus

boqui|aberto /bokia'bertu/ a open-mouthed, flabbergasted. **~nha** f snack

borboleta /borbo'leta/ f butterfly; (roleta) turnstile

borbotão /borbo'tãw/ m spurt

borbu|lha /bor'buʎa/ f bubble. **~lhar** vi bubble

borda /'bɔrda/ f edge. **~do** a edged; (à linha) embroidered ● m embroidery

bordão /bor'dãw/ m (frase) catchphrase

bordar /bor'dar/ vt (à linha) embroider

bor|del /bor'dɛw/ (pl **~déis**) m brothel

bordo /'bɔrdu/ m a **~** aboard

borra /'boxa/ f dregs; (de café) grounds

borra|cha /bo'xaʃa/ f rubber. **~cheiro** m tyre fitter

bor|rão /bo'xãw/ m (de tinta) blot; (rascunho) rough draft. **~rar** vt (sujar) blot; (riscar) cross out; (pintar) daub

borrasca /bo'xaska/ f squall

borri|far /boxi'far/ vt sprinkle. **~fo** m sprinkling

bosque /'bɔski/ m wood

bosta /'bɔsta/ f (de animal) dung; (chulo) crap

bota /'bɔta/ f boot

botâni|**ca** /bo'tanika/ f botany. **~co** a botanical ● m botanist

bo|**tão** /bo'tãw/ m button; (de flor) bud; **falar com os seus ~tões** say to o.s.

botar /bo'tar/ vt put; put on ‹roupa›; set ‹mesa, despertador›; lay ‹ovo›; find ‹defeito›

bote[1] /'bɔtʃi/ m (barco) dinghy; **~ salva-vidas** lifeboat; (de borracha) life raft

bote[2] /'bɔtʃi/ m (de animal etc) lunge

botequim /butʃi'ki/ m bar

botoeira /boto'era/ f buttonhole

boxe /'bɔksi/ m boxing. **~ador** m boxer

brabo /'brabu/ a ‹animal› ferocious; ‹calor, sol› fierce; ‹doença› bad; ‹prova, experiência› tough; ‹zangado› angry

bra|**çada** /bra'sada/ f armful; (em natação) stroke. **~çadeira** f (faixa) armband; (ferragem) bracket; (de atleta) sweatband. **~çal** (pl **~çais**) a manual. **~celete** /e/ m bracelet. **~ço** m arm; **~ço direito** fig (pessoa) right-hand man

bra|**dar** /bra'dar/ vt/i shout. **~do** m shout

braguilha /bra'giʎa/ f fly, flies

braile /'brajli/ m Braille

bra|**mido** /bra'midu/ m roar. **~mir** vi roar

branco /'brãku/ a white ● m (homem) white man; (espaço) blank; **em ~** ‹cheque etc› blank; **noite em ~** sleepless night

bran|**do** /'brãdu/ a gentle; ‹doença› mild; (indulgente) lenient, soft. **~dura** f gentleness; (indulgência) softness, leniency

brasa /'braza/ f **em ~** red-hot; **mandar ~** 🆒 go to town

brasão /bra'zãw/ m coat of arms

braseiro /bra'zeru/ m brazier

Brasil /bra'ziw/ m Brazil

brasi|**leiro** /brazi'leru/ a & m Brazilian. **~liense** a & m/f (person) from Brasília

bra|**vata** /bra'vata/ f bravado. **~vio** a wild; ‹mar› rough. **~vo** a (corajoso) brave; ‹zangado› angry; ‹mar› rough. **~vura** f bravery

breca /'brɛka/ f **levado da ~** very naughty

brecar /bre'kar/ vt stop ‹carro›; fig curb ● vi brake

brecha /'brɛʃa/ f gap; (na lei) loophole

bre|**ga** /'brɛga/ a 🆒 tacky, naff. **~guice** f 🆒 tack, tackiness

brejo /'brɛʒu/ m marsh; **ir para o ~** fig go down the drain

brenha /'brɛɲa/ f thicket

breque /'brɛki/ m brake

breu /brew/ m tar, pitch

bre|**ve** /'brɛvi/ a short, brief; **em ~ve** soon, shortly. **~vidade** f shortness, brevity

briga /'briga/ f fight; (bate-boca) argument

briga|**da** /bri'gada/ f brigade. **~deiro** m brigadier; (doce) chocolate truffle

bri|**gão** /bri'gãw/ a (f **~gona**) belligerent; (na fala) argumentative ● m (f **~gona**) troublemaker. **~gar** vi fight; (com palavras) argue; ‹cores› clash

bri|**lhante** /bri'ʎãtʃi/ a (reluzente) shiny; fig brilliant. **~lhar** vi shine. **~lho** m (de sapatos etc) shine; (dos olhos, de metais) gleam; (das estrelas) brightness; (de uma cor) brilliance; fig (esplendor) splendour

brin|**cadeira** /brĩka'dera/ f (piada) joke; (brinquedo, jogo) game; **de ~cadeira** for fun. **~calhão** (f **~calhona**) a playful ● m joker. **~car** vi (divertir-se) play; (gracejar) joke

brinco /'brĩku/ m earring

brin|**dar** /brĩ'dar/ vt (saudar) toast, drink to; (presentear) give a gift to; **~dar alguém com algo** afford sb sth; (de presente) give sb sth as a gift. **~de** m (saudação) toast; (presente) free gift

brinquedo /brĩ'kedu/ m toy

brio /'briu/ m self-esteem, character. **~so** /o/ a self-confident

brisa /'briza/ f breeze

britadeira /brita'dera/ f pneumatic drill

britânico /bri'taniku/ a British ● m Briton; **os ~s** the British

broca /'brɔka/ f drill

broche /'brɔʃi/ m brooch

brochura /bro'ʃura/ f **livro de ~** paperback

brócolis /'brɔkulis/ m pl, Port **brócolos** /'brɔkolos/ m pl broccoli

bron|**ca** /'brɔka/ f 🆒 telling-off; **dar uma ~ca em alguém** tell sb off. **~co** a coarse, rough

bronquite /brõ'kitʃi/ f bronchitis

bronze /'brõzi/ m bronze. **~ado** a tanned, brown ● m (sun)tan. **~ador** a tanning ● *m* suntan lotion. **~amento** *m* tanning. **~ar** *vt* tan. **~ar-se** *vpr* go brown, tan

bro|tar /bro'tar/ *vt* sprout ‹folhas, flores›; spout ‹lágrimas, palavras› ● *vi* ‹planta› sprout; ‹água› spout; ‹ideias› pop up. **~tinho** *m* 🇵 youngster. **~to** /o/ *m* shoot; 🇵 youngster

broxa /ˈbrɔʃa/ *f* (large) paint brush ● *a* 🇧 impotent

bruços /ˈbrusus/ **de ~** face down

bru|ma /ˈbruma/ *f* mist. **~moso** /o/ *a* misty

brusco /ˈbrusku/ *a* brusque, abrupt

bru|tal /bru'taw/ (*pl* **~tais**) *a* brutal. **~talidade** *f* brutality. **~to** *a* ‹feições› coarse; ‹homem› brutish; ‹tom, comentário› aggressive; ‹petróleo› crude; ‹peso, lucro, salário› gross ● *m* brute

bruxa /ˈbruʃa/ *f* witch; (feia) hag. **~ria** *f* witchcraft

Bruxelas /bruˈʃelas/ *f* Brussels

bruxo /ˈbruʃu/ *m* wizard

bruxulear /bruʃuliˈar/ *vi* flicker

bucha /ˈbuʃa/ *f* (tampão) bung; (para paredes) Rawlplug®; **acertar na ~** 🇧 hit the nail on the head

bucho /ˈbuʃu/ *m* gut; **~ de boi** tripe

budis|mo /buˈdʒizmu/ *m* Buddhism. **~ta** *a* & *m/f* Buddhist

bueiro /buˈeru/ *m* storm drain

búfalo /ˈbufalu/ *m* buffalo

bu|fante /buˈfãtʃi/ *a* full, puffed. **~far** *vi* snort; (reclamar) grumble, moan

bufê /buˈfe/ *m* (refeição) buffet; (serviço) catering service; (móvel) sideboard

bugiganga /buʒiˈgãga/ *f* knick-knack

bujão /buˈʒãw/ *m* **~ de gás** gas cylinder

bula /ˈbula/ *f* (de remédio) directions; (do Papa) bull

bulbo /ˈbuwbu/ *m* bulb

bule /ˈbuli/ *m* (de chá) teapot; (de café etc) pot

Bulgária /buwˈgaria/ *f* Bulgaria

búlgaro /ˈbuwgaru/ *a* & *m* Bulgarian

bulhufas /buˈʎufas/ *pron* 🇵 nothing

bulício /buˈlisiu/ *m* bustle

bulimia /buliˈmia/ *f* bulimia

bullying /ˈbʊliɳ/ *m* bullying

bumbum /bũˈbũ/ *m* 🇧 bottom, bum

bunda /ˈbũda/ *f* bottom

buquê /buˈke/ *m* bouquet

buraco /buˈraku/ *m* hole; (de agulha) eye; (jogo de cartas) rummy; **~ da fechadura** keyhole

burburinho /burbuˈriɲu/ *m* (de vozes) hubbub

burca /ˈburka/ *f* burka

bur|guês /burˈges/ *a* & *m* (*f* **~guesa**) bourgeois. **~guesia** *f* bourgeoisie

burlar /burˈlar/ *vt* get round ‹lei›; get past ‹defesas, vigilância›

buro|cracia /burokraˈsia/ *f* bureaucracy. **~crata** *m/f* bureaucrat. **~crático** *a* bureaucratic. **~cratizar** *vt* make bureaucratic

bur|rice /buˈxisi/ *f* stupidity; (uma) stupid thing. **~ro** *a* stupid; (ignorante) dim ● *m* (animal) donkey; (pessoa) halfwit, dunce; **~ro de carga** *fig* workhorse

bus|ca /ˈbuska/ *f* search; **dar ~ca em** search. **~ca-pé** *m* banger. **~car** *vt* fetch; (de carro) pick up; **mandar ~car** send for

bússola /ˈbusola/ *f* compass; *fig* guide

busto /ˈbustu/ *m* bust

butique /buˈtʃiki/ *f* boutique

buzi|na /buˈzina/ *f* horn. **~nada** *f* toot (of the horn). **~nar** *vi* sound the horn, toot the horn

....

Cc

....

cá /ka/ *adv* here; **o lado de ~** this side; **para ~** here; **de ~ para lá** back and forth; **de lá para ~** since then; **~ entre nós** between you and me

ca|bal /kaˈbaw/ (*pl* **~bais**) *a* complete, full; ‹prova› conclusive

cabana /kaˈbana/ *f* hut; (casinha no campo) cottage

cabeça /kaˈbesa/ *f* head; (de lista) top; (inteligência) mind ● *m/f* (chefe) ringleader; (pessoa inteligente) brains; **de ~** off the top of one's head; **de ~ para baixo** upside down; **deu-lhe na ~ de** he took it into his head to; **esquentar a ~** 🇧 get worked up; **fazer a ~ de alguém** convince sb; **quebrar a ~** rack one's brains; **subir à ~** go to sb's head; **ter a ~ no lugar** have one's head screwed on. **~da** *f* (no futebol) header; (pancada) head butt; **dar uma ~da no teto** bang one's head on the ceiling. **~ de porco** *f* tenement; **~ de vento** *m/f* scatterbrain, airhead. **~lho** *m* heading

cabe|cear /kabesi'ar/ vt head <bola>. **~ceira** f head. **~cudo** a pig-headed

cabe|dal /kabe'daw/ (pl **~dais**) m wealth

cabelei|ra /kabe'lera/ f head of hair; (peruca) wig. **~reiro** m hairdresser

cabe|lo /ka'belu/ m hair; **cortar o ~lo** have one's hair cut. **~ludo** a hairy; (difícil) complicated; <palavra, piada> dirty

caber /ka'ber/ vi fit; (ter cabimento) be fitting; **~ a** <mérito, parte> be due to; <tarefa> fall to; **cabe a você ir** it is up to you to go; **~ em alguém** fit sb

cabide /ka'bidʒi/ m (peça de madeira, arame etc) hanger; (móvel) hat stand; (na parede) coat rack

cabimento /kabi'mẽtu/ m **ter ~** be fitting, be appropriate; **não ter ~** be out of the question

cabine /ka'bini/ f cabin; (de avião) cockpit; (de loja) changing room; **~ telefônica** phone box, Amer phone booth

cabisbaixo /kabiz'baʃu/ a crestfallen

cabi|vel /ka'bivew/ (pl **~veis**) a appropriate, fitting

cabo[1] /'kabu/ m (militar) corporal; **ao ~ de** after; **levar a ~** carry out; **~ eleitoral** campaign worker

cabo[2] /'kabu/ m (fio) cable; (de panela etc) handle; **TV por ~** cable TV; **~ de extensão** extension lead; **~ de força** tug of war

caboclo /ka'boklu/ a & m mestizo

ca|bra /'kabra/ f goat. **~brito** m kid

ca|ça /'kasa/ f (atividade) hunting; (caçada) hunt; (animais) game ● m (avião) fighter; **à ~ça de** in pursuit of; **~ça das bruxas** f witch hunt. **~cador** m hunter. **~ça-minas** m invar minesweeper; **~ça-níqueis** m invar slot machine. **~car** vt hunt <animais, criminoso etc>; (procurar) hunt for ● vi hunt

cacareco /kaka'rɛku/ m piece of junk; pl junk

cacare|jar /kakare'ʒar/ vi cluck. **~jo** /e/ m clucking

caçarola /kasa'rɔla/ f saucepan

cacau /ka'kaw/ m cocoa

cace|tada /kase'tada/ f blow with a club; fig annoyance. **~te** /e/ m club ● int 🆃 damn

cachaça /ka'ʃasa/ f white rum

cachê /ka'ʃe/ m fee

cache|col /kaʃe'kɔw/ (pl **~cóis**) m scarf

cachimbo /ka'ʃĩbu/ m pipe

cacho /'kaʃu/ m (de banana, uva) bunch; (de cabelo) lock; 🆃 (caso) affair

cachoeira /kaʃo'era/ f waterfall

cachor|rinho /kaʃo'xiɲu/ m (nado) doggy paddle. **~ro** /o/ m dog; Port puppy; (pessoa) scoundrel. **~ro-quente** (pl **~ros-quentes**) m hot dog

cacife /ka'sifi/ m fig pull

caci|que /ka'siki/ m (índio) chief; (político) boss. **~quia** f leadership

caco /'kaku/ m shard; (pessoa) old crock

cacto /'kaktu/ m cactus

caçula /ka'sula/ m/f youngest child ● a youngest

cada /'kada/ a each; **~ duas horas** every two hours; **custam £5 ~ (um)** they cost £5 each; **~ vez mais** more and more; **~ vez mais fácil** easier and easier; **ele fala ~ coisa** 🆃 he says the most amazing things

cadafalso /kada'fawsu/ m gallows

cadarço /ka'darsu/ m shoelace

cadas|trar /kadas'trar/ vt register. **~tro** m register; (ato) registration; (policial, bancário) records, files; (imobiliário) land register

ca|dáver /ka'daver/ m (dead) body, corpse. **~davérico** a cadaverous, corpse-like; <exame> post-mortem

cadê /ka'de/ adv 🆃 where is/are...?

cadeado /kadʒi'adu/ m padlock

cadeia /ka'deja/ f (de eventos, lojas etc) chain; (prisão) prison; (rádio, TV) network

cadeira /ka'dera/ f (móvel) chair; (no teatro) stall; (de político) seat; (função de professor) chair; (matéria) subject; pl Anat hips; **~ de balanço** rocking chair; **~ de rodas** wheelchair; **~ elétrica** electric chair

ca|dência /ka'dẽsia/ f Mus (da voz) cadence; (compasso) rhythm.

~denciado a rhythmic; ‹*passos*› measured

cader|neta /kader'neta/ f notebook; (*de professor*) register; (*de banco*) passbook; **~neta de poupança** savings account. **~no** /ε/ m exercise book; (*pequeno*) notebook; (*no jornal*) section

cadete /ka'detʃi/ m cadet

cadu|car /kadu'kar/ vi ‹*pessoa*› become senile; ‹*contrato*› lapse. **~co** a ‹*pessoa*› senile; ‹*contrato*› lapsed. **~quice** f senility

cafajeste /kafa'ʒestʃi/ m swine

ca|fé /ka'fε/ m coffee; (*estabelecimento*) cafe; **~fé da manhã** breakfast; **tomar ~fé** have breakfast. **~fé-com-leite** a invar coffee-coloured, light brown ● m white coffee. **~feeiro** a ● m coffee plant. **~feicultura** f coffee-growing. **~feína** f caffein(e)

cafetã /kafe'tã/ m caftan

cafetão /kafe'tãw/ m pimp

cafe|teira /kafe'tera/ f coffee pot; **~ de pistão** cafetière. **~zal** (*pl* **~zais**) m coffee plantation. **~zinho** m small black coffee

cafo|na /ka'fɔna/ a 🔟 naff, tacky. **~nice** f tackiness; (*coisa*) tacky thing

cágado /'kagadu/ m turtle

calar /ka'jar/ vt whitewash

câibra /'kãjbra/ f cramp

cai|da /ka'ida/ f fall; ▶ **QUEDA**. **~do** a ‹*árvore etc*› fallen; ‹*beiços etc*› drooping; (*deprimido*) dejected; (*apaixonado*) smitten

caimento /kaj'mẽtu/ m fall

caipi|ra /kaj'pira/ a ‹*pessoa*› countrified; ‹*festa, música*› country; ‹*sotaque*› rural ● m/f country person; (*depreciativo*) country bumpkin. **~rinha** f cachaça with limes, sugar and ice

cair /ka'ir/ vi fall; ‹*dente, cabelo*› fall out; ‹*botão etc*› fall off; ‹*comércio, trânsito etc*› fall off; ‹*tecido, cortina*› hang; **~ bem/mal** ‹*roupa*› go well/badly; ‹*ato, dito*› go down well/badly; **estou caindo de sono** I'm really sleepy

cais /kajs/ m quay; *Port* (*na estação*) platform

caixa /'kaʃa/ f box; (*de loja etc*) cash desk ● m/f cashier; **~ de correio** letter box; **~ de entrada** *Comput* inbox; **~ de mudanças**, *Port* **~ de velocidades** gear box; **~ postal** post office box, PO Box; **~ de saída** *Comput* outbox. **~-d'água** (*pl* **~s-d'água**) f water tank; **~-forte** (*pl* **~s-fortes**) f vault

cai|xão /ka'ʃãw/ m coffin. **~xeiro** m (*em loja*) assistant; salesman. **~xilho** m frame. **~xote** /ɔ/ m crate

caju /ka'ʒu/ m cashew fruit. **~eiro** m cashew tree

cal /kaw/ f lime

calado /ka'ladu/ a quiet

calafrio /kala'friu/ m shudder, shiver

calami|dade /kalami'dadʒi/ f calamity. **~toso** /o/ a calamitous

calar /ka'lar/ vi be quiet ● vt keep quiet about ‹*segredo, sentimento*›; silence ‹*pessoa*›. **~se** vpr go quiet

calça /'kawsa/ f trousers, *Amer* pants

calça|da /kaw'sada/ f pavement, *Amer* sidewalk; *Port* (*rua*) roadway. **~dão** m pedestrian precinct. **~deira** f shoehorn. **~do** a paved ● m shoe; *pl* footwear

calcanhar /kawka'ɲar/ m heel

calção /kaw'sãw/ m shorts; **~ de banho** swimming trunks

calcar /kaw'kar/ vt (*pisar*) trample; (*comprimir*) press; **~ algo em** *fig* base sth on, model sth on

calçar /kaw'sar/ vt put on ‹*sapatos, luvas*›; take ‹*número*›; pave ‹*rua*›; (*com calço*) wedge ● vi ‹*sapato*› fit. **~se** vpr put one's shoes on

calcário /kaw'kariu/ m limestone ● a ‹*água*› hard

calças /'kawsas/ f pl ▶ **CALÇA**

calcinha /kaw'siɲa/ f knickers, *Amer* panties

cálcio /'kawsiu/ m calcium

calço /'kawsu/ m wedge

calcu|ladora /kawkula'dora/ f calculator. **~lar** vt/i calculate. **~lista** a calculating ● m/f opportunist

cálculo /'kawkulu/ m calculation; (*diferencial*) calculus; *Med* stone

cal|da /'kawda/ f syrup; *pl* hot springs. **~deira** f boiler. **~deirão** m cauldron. **~do** m (*sopa*) broth; (*suco*) juice; **~do de carne/galinha** beef/chicken stock

calefação /kalefa'sãw/ f heating

caleidoscópio /kalejdos'kɔpiu/ m kaleidoscope

calejado /kale'ʒadu/ a ‹*mãos*› calloused; ‹*pessoa*› experienced

calendário /kalẽ'dariu/ m calendar

calha /'kaʎa/ f (*no telhado*) gutter; (*sulco*) gulley

calhamaço /kaʎa'masu/ m tome

calhambeque /kaʎã'bεki/ m 🔟 banger

calhar /ka'ʎar/ vi **calhou que** it so happened that; **calhou pegarem o mesmo trem** they happened to get the same train; **~ de** happen to; **vir a ~** come at the right time

cali|brado /kali'bradu/ a (bêbado) tipsy. **~brar** vt calibrate; check (the pressure of) <pneu>. **~bre** m calibre; **coisas desse ~bre** things of this order

cálice /'kalisi/ m (copo) liqueur glass; (na missa) chalice

caligrafia /kaligra'fia/ f (letra) handwriting; (arte) calligraphy

calista /ka'lista/ m/f chiropodist, Amer podiatrist

cal|ma /'kawma/ f calm. **com ~ma** int calm down. **~mante** m tranquilizer. **~mo** a calm

calo /'kalu/ m (na mão) callus; (no pé) corn

calombo /ka'lõbu/ m bump

calor /ka'lor/ m heat; (agradável) fig warmth; **estar com ~** be hot

calo|rento /kalo'rẽtu/ a <pessoa> sensitive to heat; <lugar> hot. **~ria** f calorie. **~roso** /o/ a warm; <protesto> lively

calota /ka'lɔta/ f hubcap

calo|te /ka'lɔtʃi/ m bad debt. **~teiro** m bad risk

calouro /ka'loru/ m (na faculdade) freshman; (em outros ramos) novice

ca|lúnia /ka'lunia/ f slander. **~luniar** vt slander. **~lunioso** /o/ a slanderous

cal|vície /kaw'visi/ f baldness. **~vo** a bald

cama /'kama/ f bed; **~ de casal/ solteiro** double/single bed. **~-beliche** (pl **~s-beliches**) f bunk bed

camada /ka'mada/ f layer; (de tinta) coat

câmara /'kamara/ f chamber; (fotográfica) camera; **em ~ lenta** in slow motion; **~ de ar** inner tube; **~ digital** digital camera; **~ municipal** town council; Port town hall

camarada /kama'rada/ a friendly ● m/f comrade. **~gem** f comradeship; (convivência agradável) camaraderie

camarão /kama'rãw/ m shrimp; (maior) prawn

cama|reira /kama'rera/ f chambermaid. **~rim** m dressing room. **~rote** /ɔ/ m (no teatro) box; (num navio) cabin

cambada /kã'bada/ f gang, horde

cambalacho /kãba'laʃu/ m scam

camba|lear /kãbali'ar/ vi stagger. **~lhota** f somersault

cambi|al /kãbi'aw/ (pl **~ais**) a exchange. **~ante** m shade. **~ar** vt change

câmbio /'kãbiu/ m exchange; (taxa) rate of exchange; **~ oficial/paralelo** official/black market exchange rate

cambista /kã'bista/ m/f (de entradas) ticket tout, Amer scalper; (de dinheiro) money changer

Camboja /kã'bɔʒa/ m Cambodia

cambojano /kãbo'ʒanu/ a & m Cambodian

camburão /kãbu'rãw/ m police van

camelo /ka'melu/ m camel

camelô /kame'lo/ m street vendor

camião /kami'ãw/ Port m ▶ CAMINHÃO

caminhada /kami'nada/ f walk

caminhão /kami'nãw/ m lorry, Amer truck

cami|nhar /kami'nar/ vi walk; fig advance, progress. **~nho** m way; (estrada) road; (trilho) path; **a ~nho** on the way; **a meio ~nho** halfway; **~nho de ferro** Port railway, Amer railroad

caminho|neiro /kamino'neru/ m lorry driver, Amer truck driver. **~nete** /ɛ/ m van

camio|neta /kamio'neta/ f van. **~nista** Port m/f ▶ CAMINHONEIRO

cami|sa /ka'miza/ f shirt. **~sa de força** straitjacket; **~sa de vênus** condom. **~seta** /e/ f T-shirt; (de baixo) vest. **~sinha** f 🆔 condom. **~sola** /ɔ/ f nightdress; Port sweater

camomila /kamo'mila/ f camomile

campainha /kãpa'ina/ f bell; (da porta) doorbell

campanário /kãpa'nariu/ m belfry

campanha /kã'pana/ f campaign

campe|ão /kãpi'ãw/ m (f **~ã**) champion. **~onato** m championship

cam|pestre /kã'pɛstri/ a rural. **~pina** f grassland

cam|ping /'kãpĩ/ m camping; (lugar) campsite. **~pismo** Port m camping

campo /'kãpu/ m field; (interior) country; (de futebol) pitch; (de golfe) course; **~ de concentração** concentration camp. **~nês** m (f **~nesa**) peasant

camu|flagem /kamu'flaʒẽ/ f camouflage. **~flar** vt camouflage

camundongo /kamũ'dõgu/ m mouse

cana /'kana/ f cane; **~ de açúcar** sugar cane

Canadá /kana'da/ m Canada

canadense /kana'dẽsi/ a & m Canadian

ca|nal /ka'naw/ (pl **~nais**) m channel; (hidrovia) canal; **~ de televisão a cabo** cable channel

canalha /ka'naʎa/ m/f scoundrel

canali|zação /kanaliza'sãw/ f piping. **~zador** Port m plumber. **~zar** vt channel ‹líquido, esforço, recursos›; canalize ‹rio›; pipe for water and drainage ‹cidade›

canário /ka'nariu/ m canary

canastrão /kanas'trãw/ m (f **~trona**) ham actor, (f actress)

canavi|al /kanavi'aw/ (pl **~ais**) m cane field. **~eiro** a sugar cane

canção /kã'sãw/ f song

cance|lamento /kãsela'mẽtu/ m cancellation. **~lar** vt cancel; (riscar) cross out

câncer /'kãser/ m cancer; **C~** (signo) Cancer

cance|riano /kãseri'anu/ a & m Cancerian. **~rígeno** a carcinogenic. **~roso** /o/ a cancerous ● m person with cancer

cancro /'kãkru/ m Port (câncer) cancer; fig canker

candango /kã'dãgu/ m person from Brasilia

cande|eiro /kãdʒi'eru/ m (oil) lamp. **~labro** m candelabra

candida|tar-se /kãdʒida'tarsi/ vpr (a vaga) apply (**a** for); (à presidência etc) stand, Amer run (**a** for). **~to** m candidate (**a** for); (a vaga) applicant (**a** for). **~tura** f candidature; (a vaga) application (**a** for)

cândido /'kãdʒidu/ a innocent

candomblé /kãdõ'blɛ/ m Afro-Brazilian cult; (reunião) candomble meeting

candomblé *Candomblé* is one of the principally Afro-Brazilian religions that worship the gods of Western Africa, known as *orixás*. The ceremonies take place in *terreiros* to the sound of percussion, and can include animal sacrifices and the consumption of alcoholic drinks in a bid to 'raise the spirit'. The main festival is the *Festa de Iemanjá*, the Queen of the Ocean, on the 2nd of February.

candura /kã'dura/ f innocence

cane|ca /ka'nɛka/ f mug. **~co** /ɛ/ m tankard

canela¹ /ka'nɛla/ f (condimento) cinnamon

canela² /ka'nɛla/ f (da perna) shin. **~da** f **dar uma ~da em alguém** kick sb in the shins; **dar uma ~da em algo** hit one's shins on sth

cane|ta /ka'neta/ f pen; **~ esferográfica** ballpoint pen. **~ta-tinteiro** (pl **~tas-tinteiro**) f fountain pen

cangote /kã'gɔtʃi/ m nape of the neck

canguru /kãgu'ru/ m kangaroo

canhão /ka'ɲãw/ m (arma) cannon; (vale) canyon

canhoto /ka'ɲotu/ a left-handed ● m (talão) stub

cani|bal /kani'baw/ (pl **~bais**) m/f cannibal. **~balismo** m cannibalism

caniço /ka'nisu/ m reed; (pessoa) skinny person

canícula /ka'nikula/ f heat wave

ca|nil /ka'niw/ (pl **~nis**) m kennel

canivete /kani'vetʃi/ m penknife

canja /'kãʒa/ f chicken soup; **▯** piece of cake

canjica /kã'ʒika/ f corn porridge

cano /'kanu/ m pipe; (de bota) top; (de arma de fogo) barrel

cano|a /ka'noa/ f canoe. **~agem** f canoeing. **~ista** m/f canoeist

canonizar /kanoni'zar/ vt canonize

can|saço /kã'sasu/ m tiredness. **~sado** a tired. **~sar** vt tire; (aborrecer) bore ● vi, **~sar-se** vpr get tired. **~sativo** a tiring; (aborrecido) boring. **~seira** f tiredness; (lida) toil

can|tada /kã'tada/ f **▯** chat-up. **~tar** vt/i sing; **▯** chat up

cântaro /'kãtaru/ m **chover a ~s** pour down, bucket down

cantarolar /kãtaro'lar/ vt/i hum

cantei|ra /kã'tera/ f quarry. **~ro** m (de flores) flower bed; (artífice) stonemason; **~ro de obras** site office

cantiga /kã'tʃiga/ f ballad

can|til /kã'tʃiw/ (pl **~tis**) m canteen. **~tina** f canteen

canto¹ /'kãtu/ m (ângulo) corner

can|to² /'kãtu/ m (cantar) singing. **~tor** m singer. **~toria** f singing

canudo /ka'nudu/ m (de beber) straw; (tubo) tube; **▯** (diploma) diploma

cão /kãw/ (pl **cães**) m dog

caolho /ka'oʎu/ a one-eyed

ca|os /kaws/ m chaos. **~ótico** a chaotic

capa /'kapa/ f (de livro, revista) cover; (roupa sem mangas) cape; **~ de chuva** raincoat

capacete /kapa'setʃi/ m helmet

capacho /ka'paʃu/ m doormat

capaci|dade /kapasi'dadʒi/ f capacity; (aptidão) ability. **~tar** vt enable; (convencer) convince

capataz /kapa'tas/ m foreman

capaz /ka'pas/ a capable (de of); **ser ~ de** (poder) be able to; (ser provável) be likely to

cape|la /ka'pɛla/ f chapel. **~lão** (pl **~lães**) m chaplain

capen|ga /ka'pẽga/ a doddery. **~gar** vi dodder

capeta /ka'peta/ m (diabo) devil; (criança) little devil

capilar /kapi'lar/ a hair

ca|pim /ka'pĩ/ m grass. **~pinar** vt/i weed

capi|tal /kapi'taw/ (pl **~tais**) a & m/f capital. **~talismo** m capitalism. **~talista** a & m/f capitalist. **~talizar** vt Com capitalize; (aproveitar) capitalize on

capi|tanear /kapitani'ar/ vt captain ‹navio›; fig lead. **~tania** f captaincy; **~tania do porto** port authority. **~tão** (pl **~tães**) m captain

capitulação /kapitula'sãw/ f capitulation, surrender

capítulo /ka'pitulu/ m chapter; (de telenovela) episode

capô /ka'po/ m bonnet, Amer hood

capoeira /kapo'era/ f Brazilian kick-boxing

capoeira Capoeira was created as a form of self-defence by the descendants of African slaves during the colonial period. When the practice was banned by the colonizers, it developed into a gentle and graceful art form, in which participants are not allowed to touch each other. Capoeira originated in the state of Bahia, and is 'played' in pairs to the sound of percussion instruments, such as the berimbau.

capo|ta /ka'pɔta/ f roof. **~tar** vi overturn

capote /ka'pɔtʃi/ m overcoat

capri|char /kapri'ʃar/ vi excel o.s.. **~cho** m (esmero) care; (desejo) whim; (teimosia) contrariness. **~choso** /o/ a (cheio de caprichos) capricious; (com esmero) painstaking, meticulous

capricorniano /kaprikorni'anu/ a & m Capricorn

Capricórnio /kapri'kɔrniu/ m Capricorn

cápsula /'kapsula/ f capsule

cap|tar /kap'tar/ vt pick up ‹emissão, sinais›; tap ‹água›; catch, grasp ‹sentido›; win ‹simpatia, admiração›. **~tura** f capture. **~turar** vt capture

capuz /ka'pus/ m hood

caquético /ka'kɛtʃiku/ a broken-down, on one's last legs

caqui /ka'ki/ m persimmon

cáqui /'kaki/ a invar & m khaki

cara /'kara/ f face; (aparência) look; (ousadia) cheek ● m 🄸 guy; **~ a ~** face to face; **de ~** straightaway; **dar de ~ com** run into; **está na ~** it's obvious; **fechar a ~** frown; **~ de pau** 🄸 sheepish look

cara|col /kara'kɔw/ (pl **~cóis**) m snail

caracte|re /karak'teri/ m character. **~rística** f characteristic, feature. **~rístico** a characteristic. **~rizar** vt characterize. **~rizar-se** vpr be characterized

caramba /ka'rãba/ int (de espanto) wow; (de desagrado) damn

caramelo /kara'mɛlu/ m caramel; (bala) toffee

caramujo /kara'muʒu/ m water snail

caranguejo /karã'geʒu/ m crab

caratê /kara'te/ m karate

caráter /ka'rater/ m character

caravana /kara'vana/ f caravan

car|boidrato /karboi'dratu/ m carbohydrate. **~bono** /kar'bonu/ m carbon; **de ~bono neutro** carbon-neutral ‹produtos, programa›

carbu|rador /karbura'dor/ m carburettor, Amer carburator. **~rante** m fuel

carcaça /kar'kasa/ f carcass; (de navio etc) frame

cárcere /'karseri/ m jail

carcereiro /karse'reru/ m jailer, warder

carcomido /karko'midu/ a worm-eaten; ‹rosto› pockmarked

cardápio /kar'dapiu/ m menu

carde|al /kardʒi'aw/ (pl ~ais) a cardinal
cardíaco /kar'dʒiaku/ a cardiac; **ataque ~** heart attack
cardinal /kardʒi'naw/ a cardinal; **tecla ~** hash key
cardio|lógico /kardʒio'lɔʒiku/ a heart. **~logista** m/f heart specialist, cardiologist
cardume /kar'dumi/ m shoal
careca /ka'rɛka/ a bald ● f bald patch
ca|recer /kare'ser/ vt **~ de** lack. **~rência** f lack; (social) deprivation; (afetiva) lack of affection. **~rente** a lacking; (socialmente) deprived; (afetivamente) in need of affection
carestia /kares'tʃia/ f high cost; (geral) high cost of living; (escassez) shortage
careta /ka'reta/ f grimace ● a 🅸 straight, square
car|ga /'karga/ f load; (mercadorias) cargo; (elétrica) charge; (de cavalaria) charge; (de caneta) refill; fig burden; **~ga horária** workload. **~go** m (função) post, job; **a ~go de** in the charge of. **~gueiro** m (navio) cargo ship, freighter
cariar /kari'ar/ vi decay
Caribe /ka'ribi/ m Caribbean
caricatu|ra /karika'tura/ f caricature. **~rar** vt caricature. **~rista** m/f caricaturist
carícia /ka'risia/ f (com a mão) stroke, caress; (carinho) affection
cari|dade /kari'dadʒi/ f charity; **obra de ~dade** charity. **~doso** /o/ a charitable
cárie /'kari/ f tooth decay
carim|bar /karĩ'bar/ vt stamp; postmark ‹carta›. **~bo** m stamp; (do correio) postmark
cari|nho /ka'riɲu/ m affection; (um) caress. **~nhoso** /o/ a affectionate
carioca /kari'ɔka/ a from Rio de Janeiro ● m/f person from Rio de Janeiro ● Port m weak coffee
caris|ma /ka'rizma/ m charisma. **~mático** a charismatic
carna|val /karna'vaw/ (pl ~vais) m carnival. **~valesco** /e/ a carnival; ‹roupa› over the top, overdone ● m carnival organizer

car|ne /'karni/ f (humana etc) flesh; (comida) meat. **~neiro** m sheep; (macho) ram; (como comida) mutton. **~niça** f carrion. **~nificina** f slaughter. **~nívoro** a carnivorous ● m carnivore. **~nudo** a fleshy
caro /'karu/ a expensive; (querido) dear ● adv ‹custar, cobrar› a lot; ‹comprar, vender› at a high price; **pagar ~** pay a high price (for)
caroço /ka'rosu/ m (de pêssego etc) stone; (de maçã) core; (em sopa, molho etc) lump
carona /ka'rona/ f lift
carpete /kar'petʃi/ m fitted carpet
carpin|taria /karpĩta'ria/ f carpentry. **~teiro** m carpenter
carran|ca /ka'xãka/ f scowl. **~cudo** a ‹cara› scowling; ‹pessoa› sullen
carrapato /kaxa'patu/ m (animal) tick; fig hanger-on
carrasco /ka'xasku/ m executioner; fig butcher
carre|gado /kaxe'gadu/ a ‹céu› dark, black; ‹cor› dark; ‹ambiente› tense. **~gador** /kaxega'dor/ m (de celular, computador) charger; (profissão) porter; **~ de pilhas** battery charger. **~gamento** m loading; (carga) load. **~gar** vt load ‹navio, arma, máquina fotográfica›; (levar) carry; charge ‹bateria, pilha›; **~gar em** overdo; pronounce strongly ‹letra›; Port press
carreira /ka'xera/ f career
carre|tel /kaxe'tew/ (pl ~téis) m reel
car|ril /ka'xiw/ (pl ~ris) Port m rail
carrinho /ka'xiɲu/ m (para bagagem, compras) trolley; (de criança) pram; **~ de mão** wheelbarrow
carro /'kaxu/ m car; (de bois) cart; **~ alegórico** float; **~ esporte** sports car; **~ fúnebre** hearse. **~ça** /ɔ/ f cart. **~ceria** f bodywork. **~chefe** (pl ~s-chefes) m (no carnaval) main float; fig centrepiece; **~forte** (pl ~s-fortes) m security van
carros|sel /kaxo'sew/ (pl ~séis) m merry-go-round
carruagem /kaxu'aʒẽ/ f carriage

carta /'karta/ f letter; (mapa) chart; (do baralho) card; ~ **branca** fig carte blanche; ~ **de condução** Port driving licence, Amer driver's license. ~**bomba** (pl ~**s-bomba**) f letter bomb. ~**da** f fig move

cartão /kar'tãw/ m card; Port (papelão) cardboard; ~ **de cidadão** Port identity card; ~ **de crédito** credit card; ~ **de visita** visiting card; ~ **magnético** swipe card; ~ **pré-pago** top-up card; ~ **SIM** SIM (card); ~ **telefônico** phonecard. ~**postal** (pl cartões-postais) m postcard

cartão de cidadão All Portuguese citizens above the age of ten are required to carry an identity card. It can be used instead of a passport for travel within the European Union. The older bilhete de identidade (identity card) is gradually being phased out in favour of an electronic cartão de cidadão, which combines the identity card together with various social security and electoral documents.

car|taz /kar'tas/ m poster, Amer bill; **em ~** showing, Amer playing. ~**teira** f (para dinheiro) wallet; (cartão) card; (mesa) desk; ~**teira de identidade** identity card; ~**teira de motorista** driving licence, Amer driver's license. ~**teiro** m postman

carteira de identidade Carteira de identidade, cédula de identidade or registro geral (RG) are all names for the identity card that is used throughout Brazil. This contains the holder's name, date of birth, parents' names, signature and the issue date, as well as the bearer's right thumb print.

car|tel /kar'tɛw/ m (pl ~**téis**) m cartel
cárter /'karter/ m sump
carto|la /kar'tɔla/ f top hat ● m director. ~**lina** f card. ~**mante** m/f tarot reader, fortune teller
cartório /kar'tɔriu/ m registry office
cartucho /kar'tuʃu/ m cartridge; (de dinamite) stick; (de amendoim etc) bag
car|tum /kar'tũ/ m cartoon. ~**tunista** m/f cartoonist
caruncho /ka'rũʃu/ m woodworm
carvalho /kar'vaʎu/ m oak
car|vão /kar'vãw/ m coal; (de desenho) charcoal. ~**voeiro** a coal
casa /'kaza/ f house; (comercial) firm; (de tabuleiro) square; (de botão) hole; **em ~** at home; **para ~** home; **na ~ dos 30 anos** in one's thirties; ~ **da moeda** mint; ~ **de banho** Port bathroom; ~ **de campo** country house; ~ **de saúde** private hospital; ~ **decimal** decimal place; ~ **popular** council house
casaco /ka'zaku/ m (sobretudo) coat; (paletó) jacket; (de lã) pullover
ca|sal /ka'zaw/ (pl ~**sais**) m couple. ~**samento** m marriage; (cerimônia) wedding. ~**sar** vt marry; fig combine ● vi get married; fig go together. ~**sar-se** vpr get married; fig combine; ~**sar-se com** marry
casarão /kaza'rãw/ m mansion
casca /'kaska/ f (de árvore) bark; (de laranja, limão) peel; (de banana) skin; (de noz, ovo) shell; (de milho) husk; (de pão) crust; (de ferida) scab
cascalho /kas'kaʎu/ m gravel
cascata /kas'kata/ f waterfall; 🔟 fib
casca|vel /kaska'vɛw/ (pl ~**véis**) f (cobra) rattlesnake; (mulher) shrew
casco /'kasku/ m (de cavalo etc) hoof; (de navio) hull; (garrafa vazia) empty
ca|sebre /ka'zɛbri/ m hovel, shack. ~**seiro** a (comida) home-made; ‹pessoa› home-loving; ‹vida› home ● m housekeeper
caserna /ka'zɛrna/ f barracks
casmurro /kaz'muxu/ a sullen
caso /'kazu/ m case; (amoroso) affair; (conto) story ● conj in case; **em todo ou qualquer ~** in any case; **fazer ~ de** take notice of; **vir ao ~** be relevant; ~ **contrário** otherwise
casório /ka'zɔriu/ m 🔟 wedding
caspa /'kaspa/ f dandruff
casquinha /kas'kiɲa/ f (de sorvete) cone, cornet
cassar /ka'sar/ vt revoke, withdraw ‹direitos, autorização›; ban ‹político›
cassete /ka'sɛtʃi/ m cassette
cassetete /kase'tɛtʃi/ m truncheon, Amer nightstick
cassino /ka'sinu/ m casino; ~ **de oficiais** officers' mess
casta|nha /kas'taɲa/ f chestnut; ~**nha de caju** cashew nut. ~**nha-do-pará** (pl ~**nhas-do-pará**) f Brazil nut. ~**nheiro** m chestnut tree. ~**nho** a chestnut(-coloured). ~**nholas** /ɔ/ f pl castanets
castelhano /kaste'ʎanu/ a & m Castilian
castelo /kas'tɛlu/ m castle

casti|çal /kastʃi'saw/ (pl ~çais) m candlestick

cas|tidade /kastʃi'dadʒi/ f chastity. **~tigar** vt punish. **~tigo** m punishment. **~to** a chaste

castor /kas'tor/ m beaver

castrar /kas'trar/ vt castrate

casu|al /kazu'aw/ (pl ~ais) a chance; (fortuito) fortuitous. **~alidade** f chance

casulo /ka'zulu/ m (de larva) cocoon

cata /'kata/ f à ~ de in search of

cata|lão /kata'lãw/ (pl ~lães) a & m (f ~lã) Catalan

catalisador /kataliza'dor/ m catalyst; (de carro) catalytic convertor

catalogar /katalo'gar/ vt catalogue

catálogo /ka'talogu/ m catalogue; (de telefones) phone book

Catalunha /kata'luɲa/ f Catalonia

catapora /kata'pɔra/ f chicken pox

catar /ka'tar/ vt (procurar) search for; (recolher) gather; (do chão) pick up; sort ‹arroz, café›

catarata /kata'rata/ f waterfall; (no olho) cataract

catarro /ka'taxu/ m catarrh

catástrofe /ka'tastrofi/ f catastrophe

catastrófico /katas'trɔfiku/ a catastrophic

catecismo /kate'sizmu/ m catechism

cátedra /'katedra/ f chair

cate|dral /kate'draw/ (pl ~drais) f cathedral. **~drático** m professor

cate|goria /katego'ria/ f category; (social) class; (qualidade) quality. **~górico** a categorical. **~gorizar** vt categorize

catinga /ka'tʃĩga/ f body odour, stink

cati|vante /katʃi'vãtʃi/ a captivating. **~var** vt captivate. **~veiro** m captivity. **~vo** a & m captive

catolicismo /katoli'sizmu/ m Catholicism

católico /ka'tɔliku/ a & m Catholic

catorze /ka'torzi/ a & m fourteen

cau|da /'kawda/ f tail. **~dal** (pl ~dais) m torrent

caule /'kawli/ m stem

cau|sa /'kawza/ f cause; Jurid case; por ~sa de because of; ~sa fraturante divisive issue. **~sar** vt cause

caute|la /kaw'tela/ f caution; (documento) ticket. **~loso** /o/ a cautious, careful

cava /'kava/ f armhole

cava|do /ka'vadu/ a ‹vestido› low-cut; ‹olhos› deep-set. **~dor** a hard-working ● m hard worker

cava|laria /kavala'ria/ f cavalry. **~lariça** f stable. **~leiro** m horseman; (na Idade Média) knight

cavalete /kava'letʃi/ m easel

caval|gadura /kavawga'dura/ f mount. **~gar** vt/i ride; sit astride ‹muro, banco›; (saltar) jump

cavalhei|resco /kavaʎe'resku/ a gallant, gentlemanly. **~ro** m gentleman ● a gallant, gentlemanly

cavalo /ka'valu/ m horse; a ~ on horseback; **~vapor** (pl ~s-vapor) horsepower

cavanhaque /kava'ɲaki/ m goatee

cavaquinho /kava'kiɲu/ m ukulele

cavar /ka'var/ vt dig; fig go all out for ● vi dig; fig go all out; ~ em (vasculhar) delve into; ~ a vida make a living

caveira /ka'vera/ f skull

caverna /ka'verna/ f cavern

caviar /kavi'ar/ m caviar

cavidade /kavi'dadʒi/ f cavity

cavilha /ka'viʎa/ f peg

cavo /'kavu/ a hollow

cavoucar /kavo'kar/ vt excavate

caxemira /kaʃe'mira/ f cashmere

caxumba /ka'ʃũba/ f mumps

Cc /'sese/ abr (= cópia carbono) Cc

Cco /'seseo/ abr (= com cópia oculta) Bcc

cear /si'ar/ vt have for supper ● vi have supper

cebo|la /se'bola/ f onion. **~linha** f spring onion

ceder /se'der/ vt give up; (dar) give; (emprestar) lend ● vi (não resistir) give way; ~ a yield to

cedilha /se'dʒiʎa/ f cedilla

cedo /'sedu/ adv early; mais ~ ou mais tarde sooner or later

cedro /'sedru/ m cedar

cédula /'sedula/ f (de banco) note, Amer bill; (eleitoral) ballot paper

ce|gar /se'gar/ vt blind; blunt ‹faca›; às ~gas blindly. **~go** /ɛ/ a blind; ‹faca› blunt ● m blind man

cegonha /se'goɲa/ f stork

cegueira /se'gera/ f blindness

ceia /'seja/ f supper

cei|fa /'sejfa/ f harvest; (*massacre*) slaughter. **~far** vt reap; claim ‹*vidas*›; (*matar*) mow down

cela /'sela/ f cell

cele|bração /selebra'sãw/ f celebration. **~brar** vt celebrate

célebre /'sɛlebri/ a celebrated

celebridade /selebri'dadʒi/ f celebrity

celeiro /se'leru/ m granary

célere /'sɛleri/ a swift, fast

celeste /se'lɛstʃi/ a celestial

celeuma /se'lewma/ f pandemonium

celibato /seli'batu/ m celibacy

celofane /selo'fani/ m cellophane®

celta /'sɛwta/ a Celtic ● m/f Celt ● m (*língua*) Celtic

célula /'sɛlula/ f cell; **~ estaminal** Port stem cell

celu|lar /selu'lar/ a cellular ● m mobile, Amer cell phone. **~lite** f cellulite. **~lose** /ɔ/ f cellulose

célula-tronco /'sɛlula'trõku/ f (*pl* células-tronco) stem cell

cem /sẽj/ a & m hundred

cemitério /semi'tɛriu/ m cemetery; *fig* graveyard

cena /'sena/ f scene; (*palco*) stage; **em ~** on stage

cenário /se'nariu/ m scenery; (*de crime etc*) scene

cênico /'seniku/ a stage

cenoura /se'nora/ f carrot

cen|so /'sẽsu/ m census. **~sor** m censor. **~sura** f (*de jornais etc*) censorship; (*órgão*) censor(s); (*condenação*) censure. **~surar** vt censor ‹*jornal, filme etc*›; (*condenar*) censure

centavo /sẽ'tavu/ m cent

centeio /sẽ'teju/ m rye

centelha /sẽ'teʎa/ f spark; *fig* (*de gênio etc*) flash

cente|na /sẽ'tena/ f hundred; **uma ~na de** about a hundred; **às ~nas** in their hundreds. **~nário** m centenary

centésimo /sẽ'tɛzimu/ a hundredth

cen|tigrado /sẽ'tʃigradu/ m centigrade. **~tilitro** m centilitre. **~tímetro** m centimetre

cento /'sẽtu/ a & m hundred; **por ~** per cent

cen|tral /sẽ'traw/ (*pl* **~trais**) a central ● f switchboard; **~tral eólica** wind farm. **~tralizar** vt centralize. **~trar** vt centre. **~tro** m centre

cera /'sera/ f wax; **fazer ~** waste time, faff about

cerâmi|ca /se'ramika/ f ceramics, pottery. **~co** a ceramic

cer|ca /'serka/ f fence; **~ca viva** hedge. **~ca de** adv around, about. **~cado** m enclosure; (*para criança*) playpen. **~car** vt surround; (*com muro, cerca*) enclose; (*assediar*) besiege

cercear /sersi'ar/ vt *fig* curtail, restrict

cerco /'serku/ m Mil siege; (*policial*) dragnet

cere|al /seri'aw/ (*pl* **~ais**) m cereal

cere|bral /sere'braw/ (*pl* **~brais**) a cerebral

cérebro /'serebru/ m brain; (*inteligência*) intellect

cere|ja /se'reʒa/ f cherry. **~jeira** f cherry tree

cerimônia /seri'monia/ f ceremony; **sem ~** unceremoniously; **fazer ~** stand on ceremony

cerimoni|al /serimoni'aw/ (*pl* **~ais**) a & m ceremonial. **~oso** /o/ a ceremonious

cer|rado /se'xadu/ a ‹*barba, mata*› thick; ‹*punho, dentes*› clenched ● m scrubland. **~rar** vt close. **~rar-se** vpr close; ‹*noites, trevas*› close in

certeiro /ser'teru/ a well-aimed, accurate

certeza /ser'teza/ f certainty; **com ~** certainly; **ter ~** be sure (**de** of **de que** that)

certidão /sertʃi'dãw/ f certificate; **~ de nascimento** birth certificate

certifi|cado /sertʃifi'kadu/ m certificate; **~car-se de** make sure of. **~car** vt certify

certo /'sertu/ a (*correto*) right; (*seguro*) certain; (*algum*) a certain ● adv right; **dar ~** work

cerveja /ser'veʒa/ f beer. **~ria** f brewery; (*bar*) pub

cervo /'servu/ m deer

cer|zidura /serzi'dura/ f darning. **~zir** vt darn

cesariana /sezari'ana/ f Caesarian

césio /'sɛziu/ m caesium

cessar /se'sar/ vt/i cease

ces|ta /'sesta/ f basket; (*de comida*) hamper; **~ta de lixo** waste-paper basket. **~to** /e/ m basket

ceticismo /setʃi'sizmu/ m scepticism

cético /'sɛtʃiku/ a sceptical ● m sceptic

cetim /se'tʃĩ/ m satin

céu /sεw/ m sky; (na religião) heaven; ~ **da boca** roof of the mouth

cevada /se'vada/ f barley

chá /ʃa/ m tea; ~ **de bar** bachelor party, Amer stag night; ~ **de panela** hen night, Amer wedding shower

cha|cal /ʃa'kaw/ (pl ~**cais**) m jackal

chácara /'ʃakara/ f smallholding; (casa) country cottage

chaci|na /ʃa'sina/ f slaughter. ~**nar** vt slaughter

chafariz /ʃafa'ris/ m fountain

chaga /'ʃaga/ f sore

chaleira /ʃa'lera/ f kettle

chama /'ʃama/ f flame

cha|mada /ʃa'mada/ f call; (dos presentes) roll call; (dos alunos) register. ~**mado** m call ● a (depois do substantivo) called; (antes do substantivo) so-called. ~**mar** vt call; (para sair etc) ask, invite; attract ‹atenção› ● vi call; ‹telefone› ring. ~**mar-se** vpr be called. ~**mariz** m decoy. ~**mativo** a showy, flashy

chamejar /ʃame'ʒar/ vi flare

chaminé /ʃami'nε/ f (de casa, fábrica) chimney; (de navio, trem) funnel

champanhe /ʃã'paɲi/ m champagne

champu /ʃã'pu/ Port m shampoo

chamuscar /ʃamus'kar/ vt singe, scorch

chance /'ʃãsi/ f chance

chanceler /ʃãse'ler/ m chancellor

chanchada /ʃã'ʃada/ f (peça) second-rate play; (filme) B movie

chanta|gear /ʃãtaʒi'ar/ vt blackmail. ~**gem** f blackmail. ~**gista** m/f blackmailer

chão /ʃãw/ (pl ~**s**) m ground; (dentro de casa etc) floor

chapa /'ʃapa/ f sheet; (foto) plate; ~ **eleitoral** electoral list; ~ **de matrícula** Port number plate, Amer license plate ● m Ⅱ mate

chapéu /ʃa'pεw/ m hat

charada /ʃa'rada/ f riddle

char|ge /'ʃarʒi/ f (political) cartoon. ~**gista** m/f cartoonist

charla|tanismo /ʃarlata'nizmu/ m charlatanism. ~**tão** (pl ~**tães**) m (f ~**tona**) charlatan

char|me /'ʃarmi/ m charm; **fazer ~me** turn on the charm. ~**moso** /o/ a charming

charneca /ʃar'nεka/ f moor

charuto /ʃa'rutu/ m cigar

chassi /ʃa'si/ m chassis

chat /'ʃat/ m (na internet) chat; **sala de ~** chatroom

chata /'ʃata/ f (barca) barge

chate|ação /ʃatʃia'sãw/ f annoyance. ~**ar** vt annoy. ~**ar-se** vpr get annoyed

cha|tice /ʃa'tʃisi/ f nuisance. ~**to** a (tedioso) boring; (irritante) annoying; (mal-educado) rude; (plano) flat

chauvinis|mo /ʃovi'nizmu/ m chauvinism. ~**ta** m/f chauvinist ● a chauvinistic

chavão /ʃa'vãw/ m cliché

cha|ve /'ʃavi/ f key; (ferramenta) spanner. ~**ve de fenda** screwdriver; ~**ve inglesa** wrench; ~**veiro** m (aro) key ring; (pessoa) locksmith

chávena /'ʃavena/ f soup bowl; Port (xícara) cup

checar /ʃe'kar/ vt check

check-up /ʃe'kap/ m Med check-up; **fazer um ~** to have a checkup

che|fe /'ʃεfi/ m/f (patrão) boss; (gerente) manager; (dirigente) leader. ~**fia** f leadership; (de empresa) management; (sede) headquarters. ~**fiar** vt lead; be in charge of ‹trabalho›

che|gada /ʃe'gada/ f arrival. ~**gado** a ‹amigo, relação› close. ~**gar** vi arrive; (deslocar-se) move up; (ser suficiente) be enough ● vt bring up ‹prato, cadeira›; ~**gar a fazer** go as far as doing; **aonde você quer ~gar?** what are you driving at?; ~**gar lá** fig make it

cheia /'ʃeja/ f flood

cheio /'ʃeju/ a full; Ⅱ (farto) fed up

chei|rar /ʃe'rar/ vt/i smell (a of). ~**roso** /o/ a scented

cheque /'ʃεki/ m cheque, Amer check; ~ **de viagem** traveller's cheque; ~ **em branco** blank cheque

chi|ado /ʃi'adu/ m (de pneus, freios) screech; (de porta) squeak; (de vapor, numa fita) hiss. ~**ar** vi ‹porta› squeak; ‹pneus, freios› screech; ‹vapor, fita› hiss; ‹fritura› sizzle; Ⅱ (reclamar) grumble, moan

chiclete /ʃi'kletʃi/ m chewing gum; ~ **de bola** bubble gum

chico|tada /ʃiko'tada/ f lash. ~**te** /ɔ/ m whip. ~**tear** vt whip

chi|frar /ʃi'frar/ vt Ⅱ cheat on ‹marido, esposa›; two-time ‹namorado, namorada›. ~**fre** m horn. ~**frudo** a horned; Ⅱ cuckolded ● m cuckold

Chile /'ʃili/ m Chile

chileno /ʃi'lenu/ a & m Chilean

chilique /ʃi'liki/ 🔲 m funny turn

chil|rear /ʃiwxi'ar/ vi chirp, twitter.
~**reio** m chirping, twittering

chimarrão /ʃima'xãw/ m
unsweetened maté tea

chimpanzé /ʃĩpã'zɛ/ m chimpanzee

China /'ʃina/ f China

chinelo /ʃi'nɛlu/ m slipper

chi|nês /ʃi'nes/ a & m (f ~**nesa**) Chinese

chinfrim /ʃĩ'frĩ/ a tatty, shoddy

chio /'ʃiu/ m squeak; (de pneus) screech;
(de vapor) hiss

chique /'ʃiki/ a ‹pessoa, aparência,
roupa› smart, Amer sharp; ‹hotel, bairro,
loja etc› smart, upmarket, posh

chiqueiro /ʃi'keru/ m pigsty

chis|pa /'ʃispa/ f flash. ~**pada** f dash.
~**par** vi (soltar chispas) flash; (correr)
dash

choca|lhar /ʃoka'ʎar/ vt/i rattle. ~**lho**
m rattle

cho|cante /ʃo'kãtʃi/ a shocking;
🔲 incredible. ~**car** vt/i hatch ‹ovos›;
(ultrajar) shock. ~**car-se** vpr ‹carros etc›
crash; ‹teorias etc› clash

chocho /'ʃoʃu/ a dull, insipid

chocolate /ʃoko'latʃi/ m chocolate

chofer /ʃo'fɛr/ m chauffeur

chope /'ʃopi/ m draught lager

choque /'ʃɔki/ m shock; (colisão)
collision; (conflito) clash

cho|radeira /ʃora'dera/ f fit of crying.
~**ramingar** vi whine. ~**ramingas** m/f
invar whiner. ~**rão** m (salgueiro) weeping
willow ● a (f ~**rona**) tearful. ~**rar** vi cry.
~**ro** /o/ m crying. ~**roso** /o/ a tearful

chouriço /ʃo'risu/ m black pudding;
Port sausage

chover /ʃo'ver/ vi rain

chuchu /ʃu'ʃu/ m chayote

chucrute /ʃu'krutʃi/ m sauerkraut

chumaço /ʃu'masu/ m wad

chum|bado /ʃũ'badu/ a 🔲 knocked
out. ~**bar** Port vt fill ‹dente›; fail ‹aluno›
● vi ‹aluno› fail. ~**bo** m lead; Port
(obturação) filling

chu|par /ʃu'par/ vt suck; ‹esponja› suck
up. ~**peta** /e/ f dummy, Amer pacifier

churras|caria /ʃuxaska'ria/ f
barbecue restaurant. ~**co** m barbecue.
~**queira** f barbecue. ~**quinho** m kebab

chu|tar /ʃu'tar/ vt/i kick; 🔲 (adivinhar)
guess. ~**te** m kick. ~**teira** f football boot

chu|va /'ʃuva/ f rain; ~**va de pedra** hail.
~**varada** f torrential rainstorm. ~**veiro**
m shower. ~**viscar** vi drizzle. ~**visco** m
drizzle. ~**voso** /o/ a rainy

ciberespaço /siberis'pasu/ m
cyberspace

ciberespeculador
/siberispekula'dor/ m cybersquatter

ciberterrorismo /sibertexo'rizmu/
m cyberterrorism

cica|triz /sika'tris/ f scar. ~**trizar** vt scar
● vi ‹ferida› heal

ci|clismo /si'klizmu/ m cycling. ~**clista**
m/f cyclist. ~**clo** m cycle. ~**clone** /o/ m
cyclone. ~**clovia** f cycle lane

cida|dania /sidada'nia/ f citizenship.
~**dão** (pl ~**dãos**) m (f ~**dã**) citizen. ~**de** f
town; (grande) city. ~**dela** /ɛ/ f citadel

ciência /si'ẽsia/ f science

cien|te /si'ẽtʃi/ a aware. ~**tífico** a
scientific. ~**tista** m/f scientist

ci|fra /'sifra/ f figure; (código) cipher.
~**frão** m dollar sign. ~**frar** vt encode

cigano /si'ganu/ a & m gypsy

cigarra /si'gaxa/ f cicada; (dispositivo)
buzzer

cigar|reira /siga'xera/ f cigarette case.
~**ro** m cigarette

cilada /si'lada/ f trap; (estratagema)
trick

cilindrada /silĩ'drada/ f (engine)
capacity

cilíndrico /si'lĩdriku/ a cylindrical

cilindro /si'lĩdru/ m cylinder; (rolo)
roller

cílio /'siliu/ m eyelash

cima /'sima/ f em ~ on top; (na casa)
upstairs; **em** ~ **de** on, on top of; **para**
~ up; (na casa) upstairs; **por** ~ over the
top; **por** ~ **de** over; **de** ~ from above;
ainda por ~ moreover

címbalo /'sĩbalu/ m cymbal

cimeira /si'mera/ f crest; Port (cúpula)
summit

cimen|tar /simẽ'tar/ vt cement. ~**to**
m cement

cinco /'sĩku/ a & m five

cine|asta /sini'asta/ m/f film-maker.
~**ma** /e/ m cinema

cínico /'siniku/ a cynical ● m cynic

cinismo /si'nizmu/ m cynicism

cinquen|ta /sĩ'kwẽta/ a & m fifty. ~**tão**
a & m (f ~**tona**) fifty-year-old

cinti|lante /sĩtʃi'lãtʃi/ a glittering. ~**lar**
vi glitter

cin|to /'sĩtu/ m belt; **~to de segurança** seat belt. **~tura** f waist. **~turão** m belt

cin|za /'sĩza/ f ash ● a invar grey. **~zeiro** m ashtray

cin|zel /sĩ'zɛw/ (pl **~zéis**) m chisel. **~zelar** vt carve

cinzento /sĩ'zẽtu/ a grey

ci|pó /si'pɔ/ m vine, liana. **~poal** (pl **~poais**) m jungle

cipreste /si'prɛstʃi/ m cypress

cipriota /sipri'ɔta/ a & m Cypriot

ciranda /si'rãda/ f fig merry-go-round

cir|cense /sir'sẽsi/ a circus. **~co** m circus

circu|ito /sir'kuitu/ m circuit. **~lação** f circulation. **~lar** a & f circular ● vt circulate ● vi ‹dinheiro, sangue› circulate; ‹carro› drive; ‹ônibus› run; ‹trânsito› move; ‹pessoa› go round

círculo /'sirkulu/ m circle

circunci|dar /sirkũsi'dar/ vt circumcise. **~são** f circumcision

circun|dar /sirkũ'dar/ vt surround. **~ferência** f circumference. **~flexo** /ɛks/ a & m circumflex. **~scrição** f district; **~scrição eleitoral** constituency. **~specto** /ɛ/ a circumspect. **~stância** f circumstance. **~stanciado** a detailed. **~stancial** (pl **~stanciais**) a circumstantial. **~stante** m/f bystander

cirrose /si'xɔzi/ f cirrhosis

cirur|gia /sirur'ʒia/ f surgery. **~gião** m (f **~giã**) surgeon

cirúrgico /si'rurʒiku/ a surgical

cisão /si'zãw/ f split, division

cisco /'sisku/ m speck

cisma¹ /'sizma/ m schism

cis|ma² /'sizma/ f (mania) fixation; (devaneio) imagining, daydream; (prevenção) irrational dislike; (de criança) whim. **~mar** vt/i be lost in thought; ‹criança› be insistent; **~mar em** brood over; **~mar de ou em fazer** insist on doing; **~mar que** insist on thinking that; **~mar com alguém** take a dislike to sb

cisne /'sizni/ m swan

cistite /sis'tʃitʃi/ f cystitis

ci|tação /sita'sãw/ f quotation; Jurid summons. **~tar** vt quote; Jurid summon

ciúme /si'umi/ m jealousy; **ter ~s de** be jealous of

ciu|meira /siu'mera/ f fit of jealousy. **~mento** a jealous

cívico /'siviku/ a civic

ci|vil /si'viw/ (pl **~vis**) a civil ● m civilian. **~vilidade** f civility

civili|zação /siviliza'sãw/ f civilization. **~zado** a civilized. **~zar** vt civilize

civismo /si'vizmu/ m public spirit

cla|mar /kla'mar/ vt/i cry out, clamour (por for). **~mor** m outcry. **~moroso** /o/ a ‹protesto› loud, noisy; ‹erro, injustiça› blatant

clandestino /klãdes'tʃinu/ a clandestine

cla|ra /'klara/ f egg white. **~raboia** f skylight. **~rão** m flash. **~rear** vt brighten; clarify ‹questão› ● vi brighten up; (fazer-se dia) become light. **~reira** f clearing. **~reza** /e/ f clarity. **~ridade** f brightness; (do dia) daylight

cla|rim /kla'rĩ/ m bugle. **~rinete** /e/ m clarinet

clarividente /klarivi'dẽtʃi/ m/f clairvoyant

claro /'klaru/ a clear; ‹luz› bright; ‹cor› light ● adv clearly ● int of course; **~ que sim/não** of course/of course not; **às claras** openly; **noite em ~** sleepless night; **já é dia ~** it's already daylight

classe /'klasi/ f class; **~ média** middle class

clássico /'klasiku/ a classical; (famoso, exemplar) classic ● m classic

classifi|cação /klasifika'sãw/ f classification; (numa competição esportiva) placing, place. **~cado** a classified; ‹candidato› successful; ‹esportista, time› qualified. **~car** vt classify; (considerar) describe (de as). **~car-se** vpr ‹candidato, esportista› qualify; (chamar-se) describe o.s. (de as). **~catório** a qualifying

classudo /kla'sudu/ a Ⅱ classy

claustro|fobia /klawstrofo'bia/ f claustrophobia. **~fóbico** a claustrophobic

cláusula /'klawzula/ f clause

cla|ve /'klavi/ f clef. **~vícula** f collar bone

cle|mência /kle'mẽsia/ f clemency. **~mente** a ‹pessoa› lenient; ‹tempo› clement

cleptomaníaco /kleptoma'niaku/ m kleptomaniac

clérigo /'klɛrigu/ m cleric, clergyman

clero /'klɛru/ m clergy

clicar /kli'kar/ vi Comput click

cliché /kli'ʃe/ m cliché

clien|te /kli'ẽtʃi/ *m/f* (*de loja*) customer; (*de advogado, empresa*) client. **~tela** /ɛ/ *f* (*de loja*) customers; (*de restaurante, empresa*) clientele

cli|ma /'klima/ *m* climate. **~mático** /kli'matʃiku/ *a* climatic; **alterações ~máticas** climate change

clímax /'klimaks/ *m invar* climax

clíni|ca /'klinika/ *f* clinic; **~ca geral** general practice. **~co** *a* clinical ● *m* **~co geral** general practitioner, GP

clipe /'klipi/ *m* clip; (*para papéis*) paper clip

clonar /klo'nar/ *vt* clone

clone /'kloni/ *m* clone

cloro /'klɔru/ *m* chlorine

close /'klɔzi/ *m* close-up

clube /'klubi/ *m* club

coação /koa'sãw/ *f* coercion

coadjuvante /koadʒu'vãtʃi/ *a* ‹ator› supporting ● *m/f* (*em peça, filme*) co-star; (*em crime*) accomplice

coador /koa'dor/ *m* strainer; (*de legumes*) colander; (*de café*) filter bag

coadunar /koadu'nar/ *vt* combine

coagir /koa'ʒir/ *vt* compel

coagular /koagu'lar/ *vt/i* clot. **~se** *vpr* clot

coágulo /ko'agulu/ *m* clot

coalhar /koa'ʎar/ *vt/i* curdle. **~se** *vpr* curdle

coalizão /koali'zãw/ *f* coalition

coar /ko'ar/ *vt* strain

coaxar /koa'ʃar/ *vi* croak ● *m* croaking

cobaia /ko'baja/ *f* guinea pig

cober|ta /ko'bɛrta/ *f* (*de cama*) bedcover; (*de navio*) deck. **~to** /ɛ/ *a* covered ● *pp de* ▶ **COBRIR**. **~tor** *m* blanket. **~tura** *f* (*revestimento*) covering; (*reportagem*) coverage; (*seguro*) cover; (*apartamento*) penthouse

cobi|ça /ko'bisa/ *f* greed, covetousness. **~çar** *vt* covet. **~çoso** /o/ *a* covetous

cobra /'kɔbra/ *f* snake

co|brador /kobra'dor/ *m* (*no ônibus*) conductor. **~brança** *f* (*de dívida*) collection; (*de preço*) charging. **~brança de pênalti/falta** penalty (kick)/free kick. **~brar** *vt* collect ‹dívida›; ask for ‹coisa prometida›; take ‹pênalti›; **~brar algo a alguém** (*em dinheiro*) charge sb for sth; *fig* make sb pay for sth; **~brar uma falta** (*no futebol*) take a free kick

cobre /'kɔbri/ *m* copper

cobrir /ko'brir/ *vt* cover. **~se** *vpr* ‹pessoa› cover o.s. up; ‹coisa› be covered

cocaína /koka'ina/ *f* cocaine

coçar /ko'sar/ *vt* scratch ● *vi* (*esfregar-se*) scratch; (*comichar*) itch. **~se** *vpr* scratch o.s.

cócegas /'kɔsegas/ *f pl* **fazer ~ em** tickle; **sentir ~** be ticklish

coceira /ko'sera/ *f* itch

cochi|char /koʃi'ʃar/ *vt/i* whisper. **~cho** *m* whisper

cochi|lada /koʃi'lada/ *f* doze. **~lar** *vi* doze. **~lo** *m* snooze

coco /'koku/ *m* coconut

cócoras /'kɔkoras/ *f pl* **de ~** squatting; **ficar de ~** squat

côdea /'kodʒia/ *f* crust

codificar /kodʒifi'kar/ *vt* encode ‹mensagem›; codify ‹leis›

código /'kɔdʒigu/ *m* code; **~ de barras** bar code

codinome /kodʒi'nomi/ *m* code name

coeficiente /koefisi'ẽtʃi/ *m* coefficient; *fig* (*fator*) factor

coelho /ko'eʎu/ *m* rabbit

coentro /ko'ẽtru/ *m* coriander

coerção /koer'sãw/ *f* coercion

coe|rência /koe'rẽsia/ *f* (*lógica*) coherence; (*consequência*) consistency. **~rente** *a* (*lógico*) coherent; (*consequente*) consistent

coexis|tência /koezis'tẽsia/ *f* coexistence. **~tir** *vi* coexist

cofre /'kɔfri/ *m* safe; (*de dinheiro público*) coffer

cogi|tação /koʒita'sãw/ *f* contemplation; **fora de ~tação** out of the question. **~tar** *vt/i* contemplate

cogumelo /kogu'mɛlu/ *m* mushroom

coibir /koi'bir/ *vt* restrict; **~se de** keep o.s. from

coice /'kojsi/ *m* kick

coinci|dência /koĩsi'dẽsia/ *f* coincidence. **~dir** *vi* coincide

coisa /'kojza/ *f* thing

coitado /koj'tadu/ *m* poor thing; **~ do pai** poor father

cola /'kɔla/ *f* glue; (*cópia*) crib

colabo|ração /kolabora'sãw/ *f* collaboration; (*de escritor etc*) contribution. **~rador** *m* collaborator; (*em jornal, livro*) contributor. **~rar** *vi* collaborate; (*em jornal, livro*) contribute (*em* to)

colagem /ko'laʒẽ/ f collage

colágeno /ko'laʒenu/ m collagen

colapso /ko'lapsu/ m collapse

colar[1] /ko'lar/ m necklace

colar[2] /ko'lar/ vt (grudar) stick; (copiar) crib ● vi stick; (copiar) crib; ‹desculpa etc› stand up, stick

colarinho /kola'riɲu/ m collar; (de cerveja) head

colate|ral /kolate'raw/ (pl ~**rais**) a efeito ~**ral** side effect

col|cha /'kowʃa/ f bedspread. ~**chão** m mattress

colchete /kow'ʃetʃi/ m fastener; (sinal de pontuação) square bracket; ~ **de pressão** press stud, popper

colchonete /kowʃo'netʃi/ m (foldaway) mattress

coldre /'kowdri/ m holster

cole|ção /kole'sãw/ f collection. ~**cionador** m collector. ~**cionar** vt collect

colega /ko'lɛga/ m/f (amigo) friend; (de trabalho) colleague

colegi|al /koleʒi'aw/ (pl ~**ais**) a school ● m/f schoolboy (f -girl)

colégio /ko'lɛʒiu/ m secondary school, Amer high school

coleira /ko'lera/ f collar

cólera /'kɔlera/ f (doença) cholera; (raiva) fury

colérico /ko'lɛriku/ a (furioso) furious ● m (doente) cholera victim

colesterol /koleste'rɔw/ m cholesterol

cole|ta /ko'lɛta/ f collection. ~**tânea** f collection. ~**tar** vt collect

colete /ko'letʃi/ m waistcoat, Amer vest; ~ **salva-vidas** life jacket, Amer life preserver

coletivo /kole'tʃivu/ a collective; ‹transporte› public ● m bus

colheita /ko'ʎejta/ f harvest; (produtos colhidos) crop

colher[1] /ko'ʎer/ f spoon

colher[2] /ko'ʎer/ vt pick ‹flores, frutos›; gather ‹informações›

colherada /koʎe'rada/ f spoonful

colibri /koli'bri/ m hummingbird

cólica /'kɔlika/ f colic

colidir /koli'dʒir/ vi collide

coli|gação /koliga'sãw/ f Pol coalition. ~**gado** m Pol coalition partner. ~**gar** vt bring together. ~**gar-se** vpr join forces; Pol form a coalition

colina /ko'lina/ f hill

colírio /ko'liriu/ m eyewash

colisão /koli'zãw/ f collision

collant /ko'lã/ (pl ~**s**) m body; (de ginástica) leotard

colmeia /kow'meja/ f beehive

colo /'kɔlu/ f (regaço) lap; (pescoço) neck

colo|cação /koloka'sãw/ f placing; (emprego) position; (exposição de fatos) statement; (de aparelho, pneus, carpete etc) fitting; ~**car** put; fit ‹aparelho, pneus, carpete etc›; put forward, state ‹opinião, ideias›; (empregar) get a job for. ~**cado** a placed; **o primeiro** ~**cado** (em ranking) person in first place. ~**cador** m fitter

Colômbia /ko'lõbia/ f Colombia

colombiano /kolõbi'anu/ a & m Colombian

cólon /'kɔlõ/ m colon

colônia[1] /ko'lonia/ f (colonos) colony

colônia[2] /ko'lonia/ f (perfume) cologne

coloni|al /koloni'aw/ (pl ~**ais**) a colonial. ~**alismo** m colonialism. ~**alista** a & m/f colonialist. ~**zar** vt colonize

colono /ko'lonu/ m settler, colonist; (lavrador) tenant farmer

coloqui|al /koloki'aw/ (pl ~**ais**) a colloquial

colóquio /ko'lɔkiu/ m (conversa) conversation; (congresso) conference

colo|rido /kolo'ridu/ a colourful ● m colouring. ~**rir** vt colour

colu|na /ko'luna/ f column; (vertebral) spine. ~**nável** (pl ~**náveis**) a famous ● m/f celebrity. ~**nista** m/f columnist

com /kõ/ prep with; **o comentário foi comigo** the comment was meant for me; **você está ~ a chave?** have you got the key?; ~ **seis anos de idade** at six years of age

coma /'koma/ f coma

comadre /ko'madri/ f (madrinha) godmother of one's child; (mãe do afilhado) mother of one's godchild; (urinol) bedpan

coman|dante /komã'dãtʃi/ m commander. ~**dar** vt lead; (ordenar) command; (elevar-se acima de) dominate. ~**do** m command; (grupo) commando group

comba|te /kõ'batʃi/ m combat; (a drogas, doença etc) fight (a against). ~**ter** vt/i fight. ~**ter-se** vpr fight

combi|nação /kõbina'sãw/ f combination; (acordo) arrangement; (plano) scheme; (roupa) petticoat. ~**nar**

vt (*juntar*) combine; (*ajustar*) arrange ● vi go together, match. **~nar com** go with, match; **~nar de sair** arrange to go out; **~nar-se** vpr (*juntar-se*) combine; (*harmonizar-se*) go together, match

comboio /kõ'boju/ m convoy; Port (*trem*) train

combustí|vel /kõbus'tʃivew/ (pl **~veis**) m fuel

come|çar /kome'sar/ vt/i start, begin. **~ço** /e/ m beginning, start

comédia /ko'mɛdʒia/ f comedy

comediante /komedʒi'ãtʃi/ m/f comedian (f comedienne)

comemo|ração /komemora'sãw/ f (*celebração*) celebration; (*lembrança*) commemoration. **~rar** vt (*festejar*) celebrate; (*lembrar*) commemorate

comen|tar /komẽ'tar/ vt comment on; (*falar mal de*) make comments about. **~tário** m comment; (*de texto, na TV etc*) commentary; **sem ~tários** no comment. **~tarista** m/f commentator

comer /ko'mer/ vt eat; ‹ferrugem etc› eat away; take ‹peça de xadrez›; **dar de ~** a feed ● vi eat. **~se** vpr (*de raiva etc*) be consumed (**de** with)

comerci|al /komersi'aw/ (pl **~ais**) a & m commercial. **~alizar** vt market. **~ante** m/f trader. **~ar** vi do business, trade. **~ário** m shopworker

comércio /ko'mɛrsiu/ m (*atividade*) trade; (*loja etc*) business; (*lojas*) shops; **~ eletrônico** e-commerce; **~ justo** fair trade

comes /'komis/ m pl **~ e bebes** 🄸 food and drink. **~tíveis** m pl foods, food. **~tível** (pl **~tíveis**) a edible

cometa /ko'meta/ m comet

cometer /kome'ter/ vt commit ‹crime›; make ‹erro›

comichão /komi'ʃãw/ f itch

comício /ko'misiu/ m rally

cômico /'komiku/ a (*de comédia*) comic; (*engraçado*) comical

comida /ko'mida/ f food; (*uma*) meal

comigo = com + mim

comi|lão /komi'lãw/ a (f **~lona**) greedy ● m (f **~lona**) glutton

cominho /ko'miɲu/ m cummin

comiserar-se /komize'rarsi/ vpr commiserate (**de** with)

comis|são /komi'sãw/ f commission. **~sário** m commissioner; **~sário de bordo** (*aéreo*) steward; (*de navio*) purser. **~sionar** vt commission

comi|tê /komi'te/ m committee. **~tiva** f group; (*de uma pessoa*) retinue

como /'komu/ adv (*na condição de*) as; (*da mesma forma que*) like; (*de que maneira*) how ● conj as; **~?** (*pedindo repetição*) pardon?; **~ se** as if; **assim ~** as well as

cômoda /'komoda/ f chest of drawers, Amer bureau

como|didade /komodʒi'dadʒi/ f comfort; (*conveniência*) convenience. **~dismo** m complacency. **~dista** a complacent

cômodo /'komodu/ a comfortable; (*conveniente*) convenient ● m (*aposento*) room

como|vente /komo'vẽtʃi/ a moving. **~ver** vt move ● vi be moving. **~ver-se** vpr be moved

compacto /kõ'paktu/ a compact ● m single

compadecer-se /kõpade'sersi/ vpr feel pity (**de** for)

compadre /kõ'padri/ m (*padrinho*) godfather of one's child; (*pai do afilhado*) father of one's godchild

compaixão /kõpaj'ʃãw/ f compassion

companhei|rismo /kõpaɲe'rizmu/ m companionship. **~ro** m (*de viagem etc*) companion; (*amigo*) friend, mate

companhia /kõpa'ɲia/ f company; **fazer ~ a alguém** keep sb company

compa|ração /kõpara'sãw/ f comparison. **~rar** vt compare. **~rativo** a comparative. **~rável** (pl **~ráveis**) a comparable

compare|cer /kõpare'ser/ vi appear; **~cer a** attend. **~cimento** m attendance

comparsa /kõ'parsa/ m/f (*ator*) bit player; (*cúmplice*) sidekick

comparti|lhar /kõpartʃi'ʎar/ vt/i share (**de** in). **~mento** m compartment

compassado /kõpa'sadu/ a (*medido*) measured; (*ritmado*) regular

compassivo /kõpa'sivu/ a compassionate

compasso /kõ'pasu/ m Mus beat, time; (*instrumento*) compass, pair of compasses

compatí|vel /kõpa'tʃivew/ (pl **~veis**) a compatible

compatriota /kõpatri'ɔta/ m/f compatriot, fellow countryman (f -woman)

compelir /kõpe'lir/ vt compel

compene|tração /kõpenetra'sãw/ f
conviction. **~trar** vt convince. **~trar-se**
vpr convince o.s.

compen|sação /kõpẽsa'sãw/ f
compensation; (de cheques) clearing;
~sação de carbono carbon offsetting.
~sar vt make up for ‹defeitos, danos›;
offset ‹peso, gastos›; clear ‹cheques› ● vi
‹crime› pay

compe|tência /kõpe'tẽsia/ f
competence. **~tente** a competent

compe|tição /kõpetʃi'sãw/ f
competition. **~tidor** m competitor. **~tir**
vi compete; **~tir a** be up to. **~tividade** f
competitiveness. **~titivo** a competitive

compla|cência /kõpla'sẽsia/ f
complaisance. **~cente** a obliging

complemen|tar /kõplemẽ'tar/ vt
complement ● a complementary. **~to** m
complement

comple|tar /kõple'tar/ vt complete;
top up ‹copo, tanque etc›; **~tar 20 anos**
turn 20. **~to** /ɛ/ a complete; (cheio) full
up; **por ~to** completely; **escrever por
~to** write out in full

comple|xado /kõplek'sadu/ a with a
complex. **~xidade** f complexity. **~xo** /ɛ/
a & m complex

compli|cação /kõplika'sãw/ f
complication. **~cado** a complicated.
~car vt complicate. **~car-se** vpr get
complicated

complô /kõ'plo/ m conspiracy, plot

com|ponente /kõpo'nẽtʃi/ a & m
component. **~por** vt/i compose. **~por-se**
vpr (controlar-se) compose o.s.; **~por-se
de** be composed of

compor|tamento /kõporta'mẽtu/
m behaviour. **~tar** vt hold; bear ‹dor,
prejuízo›. **~tar-se** vpr behave

composi|ção /kõpozi'sãw/ f
composition; (acordo) conciliation.
~tor m (de música) composer; (gráfico)
compositor

compos|to /kõ'postu/ pp de ▶ COMPOR
● a compound; ‹pessoa› level-headed
● m compound; **~to de** made up of.
~tura f composure

compota /kõ'pɔta/ f fruit in syrup

com|pra /'kõpra/ f purchase; pl
shopping; **fazer ~pras** go shopping.
~prador m buyer. **~prar** vt buy; bribe
‹oficial, juiz›; pick ‹briga›

compreen|der /kõpriẽ'der/ vt (conter
em si) contain; (estender-se a) cover,
take in; (entender) understand. **~são**
f understanding. **~sível** (pl **~síveis**) a

understandable. **~sivo** a understanding

compres|sa /kõ'presa/ f compress.
~são f compression. **~sor** m
compressor; **rolo ~sor** steamroller

compri|do /kõ'pridu/ a long. **~mento**
m length

compri|mido /kõpri'midu/ m pill,
tablet ● a ‹ar› compressed. **~mir** vt
(apertar) press; (reduzir o volume de)
compress

comprome|tedor /kõpromete'dor/
a compromising. **~ter** vt (envolver)
involve; (prejudicar) compromise; **~ter
alguém a fazer** commit sb to doing.
~ter-se vpr (obrigar-se) commit o.s.;
(prejudicar-se) compromise o.s.. **~tido** a
(ocupado) busy; (noivo) spoken for

compromisso /kõpro'misu/ m
commitment; (encontro marcado)
appointment; **sem ~** without obligation

compro|vação /kõprova'sãw/ f
proof. **~vante** m receipt. **~var** vt prove

compul|são /kõpuw'sãw/ f
compulsion. **~sivo** a compulsive. **~sório**
a compulsory

compu|tação /kõputa'sãw/
f computation; (matéria, ramo)
computing; **~ na nuvem** cloud
computing. **~tador** m computer.
~tadorizar vt computerize. **~tar** vt
compute

comum /ko'mũ/ a common; (não
especial) ordinary; **fora do ~** out of the
ordinary; **em ~** ‹trabalho› joint; ‹atuar›
jointly; **ter muito em ~** have a lot in
common

comungar /komũ'gar/ vi take
communion

comunhão /komu'ɲãw/ f
communion; Relig (Holy) Communion

comuni|cação /komunika'sãw/ f
communication; **~cação social/visual**
media studies/ graphic design. **~cado**
m notice; Pol communiqué. **~car** vt
communicate; (unir) connect ● vi,
~car-se vpr communicate. **~cativo**
a communicative

comu|nidade /komuni'dadʒi/ f
community. **~nismo** m communism.
~nista a & m/f communist. **~nitário** a
(da comunidade) community; (para todos
juntos) communal

côncavo /'kõkavu/ a concave

conce|ber /kõse'ber/ vt conceive;
(imaginar) conceive of ● vi conceive.
~bível (pl **~bíveis**) a conceivable

conceder /kõse'der/ vt grant; ~ **em** accede to

concei|to /kõ'sejtu/ m concept; (opinião) opinion; (fama) reputation. ~**tuado** a highly thought of. ~**tuar** vt (imaginar) conceptualize; (avaliar) assess

concen|tração /kõsẽtra'sãw/ f concentration; (de jogadores) training camp. ~**trar** vt concentrate. ~**trar-se** vpr concentrate

concepção /kõsep'sãw/ f conception; (opinião) view

concernir /kõser'nir/ vt ~ **a** concern

concerto /kõ'sertu/ m concert

conces|são /kõse'sãw/ f concession. ~**sionária** f dealership. ~**sionário** m dealer

concha /'kõʃa/ f (de molusco) shell; (colher) ladle

concili|ação /kõsilia'sãw/ f conciliation. ~**ador** a conciliatory. ~**ar** vt reconcile

concílio /kõ'siliu/ m council

conci|são /kõsi'zãw/ f conciseness. ~**so** a concise

conclamar /kõkla'mar/ vt call ‹eleição, greve›; call upon ‹pessoa›

conclu|dente /kõklu'dẽtʃi/ a conclusive. ~**ir** vt/i conclude. ~**são** f conclusion. ~**sivo** a concluding

concor|dância /kõkor'dãsia/ f agreement. ~**dante** a consistent. ~**dar** vi agree (em to) ● vt bring into line. ~**data** f abrir ~**data** go into liquidation

concórdia /kõ'kɔrdʒia/ f concord

concor|rência /kõko'xẽsia/ f competition (a for). ~**rente** a competing. ~**rer** vi compete (a for); ~**rer para** contribute to. ~**rido** a popular

concre|tizar /kõkretʃi'zar/ vt realize. ~**tizar-se** vpr be realized. ~**to** /ɛ/ a & m concrete

concurso /kõ'kursu/ m contest; (prova) competition

con|dado /kõ'dadu/ m county. ~**de** m count

condeco|ração /kõdekora'sãw/ f decoration. ~**rar** vt decorate

conde|nação /kõdena'sãw/ f condemnation; Jurid conviction. ~**nar** vt condemn; Jurid convict

conden|sação /kõdẽsa'sãw/ f condensation. ~**sar** vt condense. ~**sar-se** vpr condense

condescen|dência /kõdesẽ'dẽsia/ f acquiescence. ~**dente** a acquiescent. ~**der** vi acquiesce; ~**der a** comply with ‹pedido, desejo›; ~**der a ir** condescend to go

condessa /kõ'desa/ f countess

condi|ção /kõdʒi'sãw/ f condition; (qualidade) capacity; **ter ~ção ou ~ções para** be able to; **em boas ~ções** in good condition. ~**cionado** a conditioned. ~**cional** (pl ~**cionais**) a conditional. ~**cionamento** m conditioning

condimen|tar /kõdʒimẽ'tar/ vt season. ~**to** m seasoning

condoer-se /kõdo'ersi/ vpr ~ **de** feel sorry for

condolência /kõdo'lẽsia/ f sympathy; pl condolences

condomínio /kõdo'miniu/ m (taxa) service charge

condu|ção /kõdu'sãw/ f (de carro etc) driving; (transporte) transport. ~**cente** a conducive (a to). ~**ta** f conduct. ~**to** m conduit. ~**tor** m (de carro) driver; Eletr conductor. ~**zir** vt lead; drive ‹carro›; Eletr conduct ● vi (de carro) drive; (levar) lead (a to)

cone /'koni/ m cone

conec|tar /konek'tar/ vt connect. ~**tado** a connected; Comput online

conectividade /konektʃivi'dadʒi/ f connectivity

cone|xão /konek'sãw/ f connection. ~**xo** /ɛ/ a connected

confec|ção /kõfek'sãw/ f (roupa) off-the-peg outfit; (loja) clothes shop, boutique; (fábrica) clothes manufacturer. ~**cionar** vt make

confederação /kõfedera'sãw/ f confederation

confei|tar /kõfej'tar/ vt ice. ~**taria** f cake shop. ~**teiro** m confectioner

confe|rência /kõfe'rẽsia/ f conference; (palestra) lecture. ~**rencista** m/f speaker

conferir /kõfe'rir/ vt check (**com** against); (conceder) confer (**a** on) ● vi (controlar) check; (estar exato) tally

confes|sar /kõfe'sar/ vt/i confess. ~**sar-se** vpr confess. ~**sionário** m confessional. ~**sor** m confessor

confete /kõ'fetʃi/ m confetti

confi|ança /kõfi'ãsa/ f (convicção) confidence; (fé) trust. ~**ante** a confident (**em** of). ~**ar** vt/i (dar) entrust; ~**ar em** trust. ~**ável** (pl ~**áveis**) a reliable. ~**dência** f confidence. ~**dencial**

(*pl* ~**denciais**) *a* confidential. ~**denciar** *vt* tell in confidence. ~**dente** *m/f* confidant (*f* confidante)

configu|ração /kõfigura'sãw/ *f* configuration. ~**rar** *vt* (*representar*) represent; (*formar*) shape; *Comput* configure

con|finar /kõfi'nar/ *vi* ~**finar com** border on. ~**fins** *m pl* borders

confir|mação /kõfirma'sãw/ *f* confirmation. ~**mar** *vt* confirm. ~**mar-se** *vpr* be confirmed

confis|car /kõfis'kar/ *vt* confiscate. ~**co** *m* confiscation

confissão /kõfi'sãw/ *f* confession

confla|gração /kõflagra'sãw/ *f* conflagration. ~**grar** *vt* set alight; *fig* throw into turmoil

confli|tante /kõfli'tãtʃi/ *a* conflicting. ~**to** *m* conflict

confor|mação /kõforma'sãw/ *f* resignation. ~**mado** *a* resigned (**com** to). ~**mar** *vt* adapt (**a** to); ~**mar-se com** conform to ‹*regra, política*›; resign o.s. to, come to terms with ‹*destino, evento*›. ~**me** /ɔ/ *prep* according to ● *conj* depending on; ~**me** it depends. ~**midade** *f* conformity. ~**mismo** *m* conformism. ~**mista** *a & m/f* conformist

confor|tar /kõfor'tar/ *vt* comfort. ~**tável** (*pl* ~**táveis**) *a* comfortable. ~**to** /o/ *m* comfort; **comida de** ~**to** comfort eating; **zona de** ~**to** comfort zone

confraternizar /kõfraterni'zar/ *vi* fraternize

confron|tação /kõfrõta'sãw/ *f* confrontation. ~**tar** *vt* confront; (*comparar*) compare. ~**to** *m* confrontation; (*comparação*) comparison

con|fundir /kõfũ'dʒir/ *vt* confuse. ~**fundir-se** *vpr* get confused. ~**fusão** *f* confusion; (*desordem*) mess; (*tumulto*) commotion. ~**fuso** *a* (*confundido*) confused; (*que confunde*) confusing

conge|lador /kõʒela'dor/ *m* freezer. ~**lamento** *m* (*de preços etc*) freeze. ~**lar** *vt* freeze. ~**lar-se** *vpr* freeze

congênito /kõ'ʒenitu/ *a* congenital

congestão /kõʒes'tãw/ *f* congestion

congestio|nado /kõʒestʃio'nadu/ *a* ‹*rua, cidade*› congested; ‹*pessoa, rosto*› flushed; ‹*olhos*› bloodshot. ~**namento** *m* (*de trânsito*) traffic jam. ~**nar** *vt* congest. ~**nar-se** *vpr* ‹*rua*› get congested; ‹*rosto*› flush

conglomerado /kõglome'radu/ *m* conglomerate

congratular /kõgratu'lar/ *vt* congratulate (**por** on)

congre|gação /kõgrega'sãw/ *f* (*na igreja*) congregation; (*reunião*) gathering. ~**gar** *vt* bring together. ~**gar-se** *vpr* congregate

congresso /kõ'gresu/ *m* congress

conhaque /ko'naki/ *m* brandy

conhe|cedor /kone'se'dor/ *a* knowing ● *m* connoisseur. ~**cer** *vt* know; (*ser apresentado a*) get to know; (*visitar*) go to, visit. ~**cido** *a* known; (*famoso*) well-known ● *m* acquaintance. ~**cimento** *m* knowledge; **tomar** ~**cimento de** learn of; **travar** ~**cimento com alguém** make sb's acquaintance, become acquainted with sb

cônico /'koniku/ *a* conical

coni|vência /koni'vẽsia/ *f* connivance. ~**vente** *a* conniving (**em** at)

conjetu|ra /kõʒe'tura/ *f* conjecture. ~**rar** *vt/i* conjecture

conju|gação /kõʒuga'sãw/ *f Ling* conjugation. ~**gar** *vt* conjugate ‹*verbo*›

cônjuge /'kõʒuʒi/ *m/f* spouse

conjun|ção /kõʒũ'sãw/ *f* conjunction. ~**tivo** *a & m* subjunctive. ~**to** *a* joint ● *m* set; (*roupa*) outfit; (*musical*) group; **o** ~**to de** the body of; **em** ~**to** jointly. ~**tura** *f* state of affairs; (*econômica*) state of the economy

conosco = **com** + **nós**

cono|tação /konota'sãw/ *f* connotation. ~**tar** *vt* connote

conquanto /kõ'kwãtu/ *conj* although, even though

conquis|ta /kõ'kista/ *f* conquest; (*proeza*) achievement. ~**tador** *m* conqueror ● *a* conquering. ~**tar** *vt* conquer ‹*terra, país*›; win ‹*riqueza, independência*›; win over ‹*pessoa*›

consa|gração /kõsagra'sãw/ *f* (*de uma igreja*) consecration; (*dedicação*) dedication. ~**grado** *a* ‹*artista, expressão*› established. ~**grar** *vt* consecrate ‹*igreja*›; establish ‹*artista, estilo*›; (*dedicar*) dedicate (**a** to); ~**grar-se** *a* dedicate o.s. to

consci|ência /kõsi'ẽsia/ *f* (*moralidade*) conscience; (*sentidos*) consciousness; (*no trabalho*) conscientiousness; (*de um fato etc*) awareness. ~**encioso** /o/ *a* conscientious. ~**ente** *a* conscious. ~**entizar** *vt* make aware (**de** of). ~**entizar-se** *vpr* become aware (**de** of)

consecutivo /kõseku'tʃivu/ *a* consecutive

C

conse|guinte /kõse'gĩtʃi/ *a* por ~guinte consequently. ~guir *vt* get; ~guir fazer manage to do ● *vi* succeed

conse|lheiro /kõse'ʎeru/ *m* counsellor, adviser. ~lho /e/ *m* piece of advice ● *pl* advice; (*órgão*) council

consen|so /kõ'sẽsu/ *m* consensus. ~timento *m* consent. ~tir *vt* allow ● *vi* consent (em to)

conse|quência /kõse'kwẽsia/ *f* consequence; por ~quência consequently. ~quente *a* consequent; (*coerente*) consistent

conser|tar /kõser'tar/ *vt* repair. ~to /e/ *m* repair

conser|va /kõ'serva/ *f* (em vidro) preserve; (em lata) tinned food. ~vação *f* preservation. ~vador *a & m* conservative. ~vadorismo *m* conservatism. ~vante *a & m* preservative. ~var *vt* preserve; (manter, guardar) keep. ~var-se *vpr* keep. ~vatório *m* conservatory

conside|ração /kõsidera'sãw/ *f* consideration; (estima) esteem; levar em ~ração take into consideration. ~rar *vt* consider; (estimar) think highly of ● *vi* consider. ~rar-se *vpr* consider o.s.. ~rável (pl ~ráveis) *a* considerable

consig|nação /kõsigna'sãw/ *f* consignment. ~nar *vt* consign

consigo = com + si

consis|tência /kõsis'tẽsia/ *f* consistency. ~tente *a* firm. ~tir *vi* consist (em in)

consoante /kõso'ãtʃi/ *f* consonant

conso|lação /kõsola'sãw/ *f* consolation. ~lador *a* consoling. ~lar *vt* console. ~lar-se *vpr* console o.s.

consolidar /kõsoli'dar/ *vt* consolidate; mend ‹fratura›

consolo /kõ'solu/ *m* consolation

consórcio /kõ'sɔrsiu/ *m* consortium

consorte /kõ'sɔrtʃi/ *m/f* consort

conspícuo /kõs'pikuu/ *a* conspicuous

conspi|ração /kõspira'sãw/ *f* conspiracy; teoria da ~ração conspiracy theory. ~rador *m* conspirator. ~rar *vi* conspire

cons|tância /kõs'tãsia/ *f* constancy. ~tante *a & f* constant. ~tar *vi* (em lista etc) appear; não me ~ta I am not aware; ~ta que it is said that; ~tar de consist of

consta|tação /kõstata'sãw/ *f* observation. ~tar *vt* note, notice; certify ‹óbito›

conste|lação /kõstela'sãw/ *f* constellation. ~lado *a* star-studded

conster|nação /kõsterna'sãw/ *f* consternation. ~nar *vt* dismay

consti|pação /kõstʃipa'sãw/ *f* Port (resfriado) cold. ~pado *a* (resfriado) with a cold; (no intestino) constipated. ~par-se *vpr* Port (resfriar-se) get a cold

constitu|cional /kõstʃitusio'naw/ (pl ~cionais) *a* constitutional. ~ição *f* constitution. ~inte *a* constituent ● *f* Constituinte Constituent Assembly. ~ir *vt* form ‹governo, sociedade›; (representar) constitute; (nomear) appoint

constran|gedor /kõstrãʒe'dor/ *a* embarrassing. ~ger *vt* embarrass; (coagir) constrain. ~ger-se *vpr* get embarrassed. ~gimento *m* (embaraço) embarrassment; (coação) constraint

constru|ção /kõstru'sãw/ *f* construction; (terreno) building site. ~ir *vt* build ‹casa, prédio›; fig construct. ~tivo *a* constructive. ~tor *m* builder. ~tora *f* building firm

cônsul /'kõsuw/ (pl ~es) *m* consul

consulado /kõsu'ladu/ *m* consulate

consul|ta /kõ'suwta/ *f* consultation. ~tar *vt* consult. ~tor *m* consultant. ~toria *f* consultancy. ~tório *m* (médico) surgery, Amer office

consu|mação /kõsuma'sãw/ *f* (taxa) minimum charge. ~mado *a* fato ~mado fait accompli. ~mar *vt* accomplish ‹projeto›; carry out ‹crime, sacrifício›; consummate ‹casamento›

consu|midor /kõsumi'dor/ *a & m* consumer. ~mir *vt* consume; take up ‹tempo›. ~mismo *m* consumerism. ~mista *a & m/f* consumerist. ~mo *m* consumption

conta /'kõta/ *f* (a pagar) bill; (bancária) account; (contagem) count; (de vidro etc) bead; pl Com accounts; em ~ economical; por ~ de on account of; por ~ própria on one's own account; ajustar ~s settle up; dar ~ de fig be up to; dar ~ do recado 🄳 deliver the goods; dar-se ~ de realize; fazer de ~ pretend; ficar por ~ de be left to; levar ou ter em ~ take into account; prestar ~s de account for; tomar ~ de take care of; ~ bancária bank account; ~ corrente current account

contabi|lidade /kõtabili'dadʒi/ *f* accountancy; (contas) accounts; (seção) accounts department. ~lista Port *m/f* accountant. ~lizar *vt* write up ‹quantia›;

fig notch up
contact- *Port* ▶ contat-
conta|dor /kõta'dor/ *m* (*pessoa*) accountant; (*de luz etc*) meter. **~gem** *f* counting; (*de pontos num jogo*) scoring; **~gem regressiva** countdown
contagi|ante /kõtaʒi'ãtʃi/ *a* infectious. **~ar** *vt* infect. **~ar-se** *vpr* become infected
contágio /kõ'taʒiu/ *m* infection
contagioso /kõtaʒi'ozu/ *a* contagious
contami|nação /kõtamina'sãw/ *f* contamination. **~nar** *vt* contaminate
contanto /kõ'tãtu/ *adv* **~ que** provided that
contar /kõ'tar/ *vt/i* count; (*narrar*) tell; **~ com** count on
conta|tar /kõta'tar/ *vt* contact. **~to** *m* contact; **entrar em ~to com** get in touch with; **tomar ~to com** come into contact with
contem|plação /kõtẽpla'sãw/ *f* contemplation. **~plar** *vt* (*considerar*) contemplate; (*dizer respeito a*) concern; **~plar alguém com** treat sb to ● *vi* ponder. **~plativo** *a* contemplative
contemporâneo /kõtẽpo'raniu/ *a & m* contemporary
contenção /kõtẽ'sãw/ *f* containment
conten|cioso /kõtẽsi'ozu/ *a* contentious. **~da** *f* dispute
conten|tamento /kõtẽta'mẽtu/ *m* contentment. **~tar** *vt* satisfy. **~tar-se** *vpr* be content. **~te** *a* (*feliz*) happy; (*satisfeito*) content. **~to** *m a* **~to** satisfactorily
conter /kõ'ter/ *vt* contain. **~se** *vpr* contain o.s.
conterrâneo /kõte'xaniu/ *m* fellow countryman (*f*-woman)
contestar /kõtes'tar/ *vt* question; *Jurid* contest
conteúdo /kõte'udu/ *m* (*de recipiente*) contents; *fig* (*de carta etc*) content
contexto /kõ'testu/ *m* context
contigo = **com + ti**
continência /kõtʃi'nẽsia/ *f Mil* salute
continen|tal /kõtʃinẽ'taw/ (*pl* **~tais**) *a* continental. **~te** *m* continent
contin|gência /kõtʃĩ'ʒẽsia/ *f* contingency. **~gente** *a* (*eventual*) possible; (*incerto*) contingent ● *m* contingent
continu|ação /kõtʃinua'sãw/ *f* continuation. **~ar** *vt/i* continue; **eles ~am ricos** they are still rich. **~idade** *f*

continuity
contínuo /kõ'tʃinuu/ *a* continuous ● *m* office junior
con|tista /kõ'tʃista/ *m/f* (short) story writer. **~to** *m* (short) story; **~to de fadas** fairy tale; **~to do vigário** confidence trick, swindle
contorcer /kõtor'ser/ *vt* twist. **~se** *vpr* (*de dor*) writhe
contor|nar /kõtor'nar/ *vt* go round; *fig* get round ‹*obstáculo, problema*›; (*cercar*) surround; (*delinear*) outline. **~no** /o/ *m* outline; (*da paisagem*) contour
contra /'kõtra/ *prep* against
contra-atacar /kõtrata'kar/ *vt* counter-attack. **~ataque** *m* counter-attack
contrabaixo /kõtra'baʃu/ *m* double bass
contrabalançar /kõtrabalã'sar/ *vt* counterbalance
contraban|dear /kõtrabãdʒi'ar/ *vt* smuggle. **~dista** *m/f* smuggler. **~do** *m* (*ato*) smuggling; (*artigos*) contraband
contração /kõtra'sãw/ *f* contraction
contracenar /kõtrase'nar/ *vi* **~ com** play up to
contraceptivo /kõtrasep'tʃivu/ *a & m* contraceptive
contracheque /kõtra'ʃeki/ *m* pay slip
contradi|ção /kõtradʒi'sãw/ *f* contradiction. **~tório** *a* contradictory. **~zer** *vt* contradict. **~zer-se** *vpr* ‹*pessoa*› contradict o.s.; ‹*ideias etc*› be contradictory
contragosto /kõtra'gostu/ *m a* **~** reluctantly
contrair /kõtra'ir/ *vt* contract; pick up ‹*hábito, vício*›. **~se** *vpr* contract
contramão /kõtra'mãw/ *f* opposite direction ● *a invar* one way
contramestre /kõtra'mestri/ *m* supervisor; (*em navio*) bosun
contraofensiva /kõtraofẽ'siva/ *f* counter-offensive
contrapartida /kõtrapar'tʃida/ *f fig* compensation; **em ~** on the other hand
contraproducente /kõtraprodu'sẽtʃi/ *a* counterproductive
contrari|ar /kõtrari'ar/ *vt* go against, run counter to; (*aborrecer*) annoy. **~edade** *f* adversity; (*aborrecimento*) annoyance
contrário /kõ'trariu/ *a* opposite; (*desfavorável*) adverse; **~ a** contrary to; ‹*pessoa*› opposed to ● *m* opposite;

pelo ou **ao ~** on the contrary; **ao ~ de** contrary to; **em ~ to** the contrary

contras|tante /kõtras'tãtʃi/ a contrasting. **~tar** vt/i contrast. **~te** m contrast

contratação /kõtrata'sãw/ f (de empregado) recruitment; (de jogador) signing

contra|tante /kõtra'tãtʃi/ m/f contractor. **~tar** vt employ, take on ‹operários›

contra|tempo /kõtra'tẽpu/ m hitch

contra|to /kõ'tratu/ m contract. **~tual** (pl **~tuais**) a contractual

contraven|ção /kõtravẽ'sãw/ f contravention. **~tor** m offender

contribu|ição /kõtribui'sãw/ f contribution. **~inte** m/f contributor; (pagador de impostos) taxpayer. **~ir** vt contribute ● vi contribute; (pagar impostos) pay tax

contrição /kõtri'sãw/ f contrition

contro|lar /kõtro'lar/ vt control; (fiscalizar) check. **~le** /o/, Port **~lo** /o/ m control; (fiscalização) check; **~le de qualidade** quality control

contro|vérsia /kõtro'versia/ f controversy. **~verso** /ɛ/ a controversial

contudo /kõ'tudu/ conj nevertheless

contundir /kõtũ'dʒir/ vt (dar hematoma em) bruise; injure ‹jogador›. **~se** vpr bruise o.s.; ‹jogador› get injured

conturbado /kõtur'badu/ a troubled

contu|são /kõtu'zãw/ f bruise; (de jogador) injury. **~so** a bruised; ‹jogador› injured

convales|cença /kõvale'sẽsa/ f convalescence. **~cer** vi convalesce

convenção /kõvẽ'sãw/ f convention

conven|cer /kõvẽ'ser/ vt convince. **~cido** a (convicto) convinced; (metido) conceited. **~cimento** m (convicção) conviction; (imodéstia) conceitedness

convencio|nal /kõvẽsio'naw/ (pl **~nais**) a conventional

conveni|ência /kõveni'ẽsia/ f convenience. **~ente** a convenient; (cabível) appropriate

convênio /kõ'veniu/ m agreement

convento /kõ'vẽtu/ m convent

convergir /kõver'ʒir/ vi converge

conver|sa /kõ'versa/ f conversation; a **~sa dele** the things he says; **~sa fiada** idle talk. **~sação** f conversation. **~sado** a ‹pessoa› talkative; ‹assunto› talked

about. **~sador** a talkative

conversão /kõver'sãw/ f conversion

conversar /kõver'sar/ vi talk

conver|sível /kõver'sivew/ (pl **~síveis**) a & m convertible. **~ter** vt convert. **~ter-se** vpr be converted. **~tido** m convert

con|vés /kõ'ves/ (pl **~veses**) m deck

convexo /kõ'veksu/ a convex

convic|ção /kõvik'sãw/ f conviction. **~to** a convinced; (ferrenho) confirmed; ‹criminoso› convicted

convi|dado /kõvi'dadu/ m guest. **~dar** vt invite. **~dativo** a inviting

convincente /kõvĩ'sẽtʃi/ a convincing

convir /kõ'vir/ vi (ficar bem) be appropriate; (concordar) agree (**em** on); **~ a** suit, be convenient for; **convém notar que** one should note that

convite /kõ'vitʃi/ m invitation

convi|vência /kõvi'vẽsia/ f coexistence; (relação) close contact. **~ver** vi coexist; (ter relações) associate (**com** with)

convívio /kõ'viviu/ m association (**com** with)

convocar /kõvo'kar/ vt call ‹eleições, greve›; call upon ‹pessoa› (**a** to); (ao serviço militar) call up

convosco = com + vós

convul|são /kõvuw'sãw/ f (do corpo) convulsion; (da sociedade etc) upheaval. **~sionar** vt convulse ‹corpo›; fig churn up. **~sivo** a convulsive

cooper /'kuper/ m jogging; **fazer ~** go jogging

coope|ração /koopera'sãw/ f cooperation. **~rar** vi cooperate. **~rativa** f cooperative. **~rativo** a cooperative

coorde|nação /koordena'sãw/ f coordination. **~nada** f coordinate. **~nar** vt coordinate

copa /'kɔpa/ f (de árvore) top; (aposento) breakfast room; (torneio) cup; pl (naipe) hearts; **a C~ (do Mundo)** the World Cup. **~-cozinha** (pl **~s-cozinhas**) f kitchen-diner

cópia /'kɔpia/ f copy

copiar /kopi'ar/ vt copy

copiloto /kopi'lotu/ m co-pilot

copioso /kopi'ozu/ a ample; ‹refeição› substantial

copo /'kɔpu/ m glass

coque /'kɔki/ m (penteado) bun

coqueiro /ko'keru/ m coconut palm

coqueluche /koke'luʃi/ f (*doença*) whooping cough; (*mania*) fad

coque|tel /koke'tɛw/ (*pl* ~**téis**) *m* cocktail; (*reunião*) cocktail party

cor[1] /kɔr/ *m* **de** ~ by heart

cor[2] /kor/ f colour; **TV a** ~**es** colour TV; **pessoa de** ~ coloured person

coração /kora'sãw/ *m* heart

cora|gem /ko'raʒẽ/ f courage. ~**joso** /o/ *a* courageous

co|ral[1] /ko'raw/ (*pl* ~**rais**) *m* (*animal*) coral

co|ral[2] /ko'raw/ (*pl* ~**rais**) *m* (*de cantores*) choir ● *a* choral

co|rante /ko'rãtʃi/ *a* & *m* colouring. ~**rar** *vt* colour ● *vi* blush

cor|da /'kɔrda/ f rope; *Mus* string; (*para roupa lavada*) clothes line; **dar** ~**da em** (*relógio*) wind; ~**da bamba** tightrope; ~**das vocais** vocal chords. ~**dão** *m* cord; (*de sapatos*) lace; (*policial*) cordon

cordeiro /kor'deru/ *m* lamb

cor|del /kor'dɛw/ (*pl* ~**déis**) *Port m* string; **literatura de** ~**del** trash literature

cor-de-rosa /kordʒi'rɔza/ *a invar* pink

cordi|al /kordʒi'aw/ (*pl* ~**ais**) *a* & *m* cordial. ~**alidade** f cordiality

cordilheira /kordʒi'ʎera/ f chain of mountains

coreano /kori'anu/ *a* & *m* Korean

Coreia /ko'reja/ f Korea

core|ografia /koriogra'fia/ f choreography. ~**ógrafo** *m* choreographer

coreto /ko'retu/ *m* bandstand

coriza /ko'riza/ f runny nose

corja /'kɔrʒa/ f pack; (*de pessoas*) rabble

córner /'kɔrner/ *m* corner

coro /'koru/ *m* chorus

coro|a /ko'roa/ f crown; (*de flores etc*) wreath ● *m/f* 🄳 old man (*f* woman). ~**ação** f coronation. ~**ar** *vt* crown

coro|nel /koro'nɛw/ (*pl* ~**néis**) *m* colonel

coronha /ko'roɲa/ f butt

corpete /kor'petʃi/ *m* bodice

corpo /'kɔrpu/ *m* body; (*físico de mulher*) figure; (*físico de homem*) physique; ~ **a** ~ *m invar* pitched battle. ~ **de bombeiros** fire brigade; ~ **diplomático** diplomatic corps; ~ **docente** teaching staff, *Amer* faculty; ~**ral** (*pl* ~**rais**) *a* physical; (*pena*) corporal

corpu|lência /korpu'lẽsia/ f stoutness. ~**lento** *a* stout

correção /koxe'sãw/ f correction

corre-corre /kɔxi'kɔxi/ *m* (*debandada*) stampede; (*correria*) rush

corre|diço /koxe'dʒisu/ *a* (*porta*) sliding. ~**dor** *m* (*atleta*) runner; (*passagem*) corridor

correia /ko'xeja/ f strap; (*peça de máquina*) belt; (*para cachorro*) lead, *Amer* leash

correio /ko'xeju/ *m* post, mail; (*repartição*) post office; **pôr no** ~ post, *Amer* mail; ~ **aéreo** air mail; ~ **de voz** voicemail; ~ **eletrônico** email

correlação /koxela'sãw/ f correlation

correligionário /koxeliʒio'nariu/ *m* party colleague

corrente /ko'xẽtʃi/ *a* (*água*) running; (*mês, conta*) current; (*estilo*) fluid; (*usual*) common ● f (*de água, eletricidade*) current; (*cadeia*) chain; ~ **de ar** draught. ~**za** /e/ f current; (*de ar*) draught

cor|rer /ko'xer/ *vi* (*à pé*) run; (*de carro*) drive fast, speed; (*fazer rápido*) rush; (*água, sangue*) flow; (*tempo*) elapse; (*boato*) go round ● *vt* draw (*cortina*); run (*risco*). ~**reria** f rush

correspon|dência /koxespõ'dẽsia/ f correspondence. ~**dente** *a* corresponding ● *m/f* correspondent; (*equivalente*) equivalent. ~**der** *vi* ~**der a** correspond to; (*retribuir*) return. ~**der-se** *vpr* correspond (**com** with)

corre|tivo /koxe'tʃivu/ *a* corrective ● *m* punishment. ~**to** /ɛ/ *a* correct

corretor /koxe'tor/ *m* broker; ~ **de imóveis** estate agent, *Amer* realtor

corrida /ko'xida/ f (*prova*) race; (*ação de correr*) run; (*de táxi*) ride

corrigir /koxi'ʒir/ *vt* correct

corrimão /koxi'mãw/ (*pl* ~**s**) *m* handrail; (*de escada*) banister

corriqueiro /koxi'keru/ *a* ordinary, run-of-the-mill

corroborar /koxobo'rar/ *vt* corroborate

corroer /koxo'er/ *vt* corrode (*metal*); *fig* erode. ~**se** *vpr* corrode; *fig* erode

corromper /koxõ'per/ *vt* corrupt. ~**se** *vpr* be corrupted

corro|são /koxo'zãw/ f (*de metal*) corrosion; *fig* erosion. ~**sivo** *a* corrosive

corrup|ção /koxup'sãw/ f corruption. ~**to** *a* corrupt

cor|tada /kor'tada/ f (em tênis) smash; (em pessoa) put-down. **~tante** a cutting. **~tar** vt cut; cut off ‹luz, telefone, perna etc›; cut down ‹árvore›; cut out ‹efeito, vício›; take away ‹prazer›; (com o carro) cut up; (desprezar) cut dead; **~tar o cabelo** (no cabeleireiro) get one's hair cut ● vi cut. **~te**¹ /ɔ/ m cut; (gume) blade; (desenho) cross-section; **sem ~te** ‹faca› blunt; **~te de cabelo** haircut

cor|te² /'kortʃi/ f court. **~tejar** vt court. **~tejo** /e/ m (séquito) retinue; (fúnebre) cortège. **~tês** a (f ~tesa) courteous, polite. **~tesão** (pl ~tesãos) m courtier. **~tesia** f courtesy

corti|ça /kor'tʃisa/ f cork. **~ço** m (casa popular) slum tenement

cortina /kor'tʃina/ f curtain

cortisona /kortʃi'zona/ f cortisone

coruja /ko'ruʒa/ f owl ● a ‹pai, mãe› proud, doting

coruscar /korus'kar/ vi flash

corvo /'korvu/ m crow

cós /kɔs/ m invar waistband

coser /ko'zer/ vt/i sew

cosmético /koz'mɛtʃiku/ a & m cosmetic

cósmico /'kɔzmiku/ a cosmic

cosmo /'kɔzmu/ m cosmos. **~nauta** m/f cosmonaut. **~polita** a cosmopolitan ● m/f globetrotter

costa /'kɔsta/ f coast; pl (dorso) back; **C~ do Marfim** Ivory Coast; **C~ Rica** Costa Rica

costarriquenho /kostaxi'keɲu/ a & m Costa Rican

cos|teiro /kos'teru/ a coastal. **~tela** /ɛ/ f rib. **~teleta** /e/ f chop; pl (suíças) sideburns. **~telinha** f (de porco) spare rib

costu|mar /kostu'mar/ vt **~ma fazer** he usually does; **~mava fazer** he used to do; **~me** m (uso) custom; (traje) costume; **de ~me** usually; **como de ~me** as usual; **ter o ~me de** have a habit of. **~meiro** a customary

costu|ra /kos'tura/ f sewing. **~rar** vt/i sew. **~reira** f (mulher) dressmaker; (caixa) needlework box

co|ta /'kɔta/ f quota. **~tação** f (preço) rate; (apreço) rating. **~tado** a ‹ação› quoted; (conceituado) highly rated. **~tar** vt rate; quote ‹ações›

cote|jar /kote'ʒar/ vt compare. **~jo** /e/ m comparison

cotidiano /kotʃidʒi'anu/ a everyday ● m everyday life

cotonete /koto'nɛtʃi/ m cotton bud

cotove|lada /kotove'lada/ f (para abrir caminho) shove; (para chamar atenção) nudge. **~lo** /e/ m elbow

coura|ça /ko'rasa/ f (armadura) breastplate; (de navio, animal) armour. **~çado** Port m battleship

couro /'koru/ m leather; **~ cabeludo** scalp

couve /'kovi/ f spring greens. **~-de-bruxelas** (pl ~s-de-bruxelas) f Brussels sprout; **~-flor** (pl ~s-flores) f cauliflower

couvert /ku'ver/ (pl ~s) m cover charge

cova /'kɔva/ f (buraco) pit; (sepultura) grave

covar|de /ko'vardʒi/ m/f coward ● a cowardly. **~dia** f cowardice

coveiro /ko'veru/ m gravedigger

covil /ko'viw/ (pl ~vis) m den, lair

covinha /ko'viɲa/ f dimple

co|xa /'koʃa/ f thigh. **~xear** vi hobble

coxia /ko'ʃia/ f aisle

coxo /'koʃu/ a hobbling; **ser ~** hobble

co|zer /ko'zer/ vt/i cook. **~zido** m stew, casserole

cozi|nha /ko'ziɲa/ f (aposento) kitchen; (comida, ação) cooking; (arte) cookery. **~nhar** vt/i cook. **~nheiro** m cook

crachá /kra'ʃa/ m badge, Amer button

crânio /'kraniu/ m skull; (pessoa) genius

crápula /'krapula/ m/f scoundrel

craque /'kraki/ m (de futebol) soccer star; Ⓘ expert

crase /'krazi/ f contraction; **a com ~** a grave (à)

crasso /'krasu/ a crass

cratera /kra'tɛra/ f crater

cravar /kra'var/ vt drive in ‹prego›; dig ‹unha›; stick ‹estaca›; **~ com os olhos** stare at. **~-se** vpr stick

cravejar /krave'ʒar/ vt nail; (com balas) spray, riddle

cravo¹ /'kravu/ m (flor) carnation; (condimento) clove

cravo² /'kravu/ m (na pele) blackhead; (prego) nail

cravo³ /'kravu/ m (instrumento) harpsichord

creche /'krɛʃi/ f crèche

credenci|ais /kredẽsi'ajs/ f pl credentials. **~ar** vt qualify

credi|ário /kredʒi'ariu/ m hire purchase agreement, credit plan. **~bilidade** f credibility. **~tar** vt credit

credifone® /kredʒi'foni/ *m Port* phonecard

crédito /'krɛdʒitu/ *m* credit; **a ~** on credit

cre|do /'krɛdu/ *m* creed ● *int* heavens. **~dor** *m* creditor ● *a* ‹*saldo*› credit

crédulo /'krɛdulu/ *a* gullible

cre|mação /krema'sãw/ *f* cremation. **~mar** *vt* cremate. **~matório** *m* crematorium

cre|me /'krɛmi/ *a invar & m* cream; **~me Chantilly** whipped cream; **~me de leite** (sterilized) cream. **~moso** /o/ *a* creamy

cren|ça /'krẽsa/ *f* belief. **~dice** *f* superstition. **~te** *m* believer; (*protestante*) Protestant ● *a* religious; (*protestante*) Protestant; **estar ~te que** believe that

crepe /'krɛpi/ *m* crepe

crepitar /krepi'tar/ *vi* crackle

crepom /kre'põ/ *m* crepe; **papel ~** tissue paper

crepúsculo /kre'puskulu/ *m* twilight

crer /krer/ *vt/i* believe (**em** in); **creio que** I think (that). **~se** *vpr* believe o.s. to be

cres|cendo /kre'sẽdu/ *m* crescendo. **~cente** *a* growing ● *m* crescent. **~cer** *vi* grow; ‹*bolo*› rise. **~cido** *a* grown. **~cimento** *m* growth

crespo /'krespu/ *a* ‹*cabelo*› frizzy; ‹*mar*› choppy

cretino /kre'tʃinu/ *m* cretin

cria /'kria/ *f* baby; *pl* young

criação /kria'sãw/ *f* creation; (*educação*) upbringing; (*de animais*) raising; (*gado*) livestock

criado /kria'adu/ *m* servant. **~mudo** (*pl* **~s-mudos**) *m* bedside table

criador /kria'dor/ *m* creator; (*de animais*) farmer, breeder

crian|ça /kri'ãsa/ *f* child ● *a* childish. **~çada** *f* kids. **~cice** *f* childishness; (*uma*) childish thing

criar /kri'ar/ *vt* (*fazer*) create; bring up ‹*filhos*›; rear ‹*animais*›; grow ‹*planta*›; pluck up ‹*coragem*›. **~se** *vpr* be brought up, grow up

criati|vidade /kriatʃivi'dadʒi/ *f* creativity. **~vo** *a* creative

criatura /kria'tura/ *f* creature

crime /'krimi/ *m* crime

crimi|nal /krimi'naw/ (*pl* **~nais**) *a* criminal. **~nalidade** *f* crime. **~noso** *m* criminal

crina /'krina/ *f* mane

crioulo /kri'olu/ *a & m* Creole; (*negro*) black

cripta /'kripta/ *f* crypt

crisálida /kri'zalida/ *f* chrysalis

crisântemo /kri'zãtemu/ *m* chrysanthemum

crise /'krizi/ *f* crisis

cris|ma /'krizma/ *f* confirmation. **~mar** *vt* confirm. **~mar-se** *vpr* get confirmed

crista /'krista/ *f* crest

cris|tal /kris'taw/ (*pl* **~tais**) *m* crystal; (*vidro*) glass. **~talino** *a* crystal clear. **~talizar** *vt/i* crystallize

cris|tandade /kristã'dadʒi/ *f* Christendom. **~tão** (*pl* **~tãos**) *a & m* (*f* **~tã**) Christian. **~tianismo** *m* Christianity

Cristo /'kristu/ *m* Christ

> **Cristo Redentor** *Cristo Redentor* ⓘ (Christ the Redeemer) is a statue of Jesus Christ at the peak of the Corcovado mountain in Rio de Janeiro. Inaugurated in 1931, the monument is 38 metres high, and is situated 710 metres above sea level. From the statue, you can see the centre of Rio de Janeiro, the *Pão de Açúcar* (Sugarloaf mountain), the Rodrigo de Freitas Lagoon, and other tourist attractions.

cri|tério /kri'tɛriu/ *m* discretion; (*norma*) criterion. **~terioso** *a* perceptive, discerning

crítica /'kritʃika/ *f* criticism; (*análise*) critique; (*de filme, livro*) review; (*críticos*) critics

criticar /kritʃi'kar/ *vt* criticize; review ‹*filme, livro*›

crítico /'kritʃiku/ *a* critical ● *m* critic

crivar /kri'var/ *vt* (*furar*) riddle

cri|vel /'krivew/ (*pl* **~veis**) *a* credible

crivo /'krivu/ *m* sieve; *fig* scrutiny

crocante /kro'kãtʃi/ *a* crunchy

crochê /kro'ʃe/ *m* crochet

crocodilo /kroko'dʒilu/ *m* crocodile

cromo /'kromu/ *m* chrome; 🅸🅸 (*pessoa*) geek 🅸🅸

cromossomo /kromo'somu/ *m* chromosome

crôni|ca /'kronika/ *f* (*histórica*) chronicle; (*no jornal*) feature; (*conto*) short story. **~co** *a* chronic

cronista /kro'nista/ *m/f* (*de jornal*) feature writer; (*contista*) short story writer; (*historiador*) chronicler

crono|grama /krono'grama/ m schedule. **~logia** f chronology. **~lógico** a chronological. **~metrar** vt time

cronômetro /kro'nometru/ m stopwatch

croquete /kro'ketʃi/ m savoury meatball in breadcrumbs

croqui /kro'ki/ m sketch

crosta /'krosta/ f crust; (em ferida) scab

cru /kru/ a (f ~a) raw; ‹luz, tom, palavra› harsh; ‹linguagem› crude; ‹verdade› unvarnished, plain

cruci|al /krusi'aw/ (pl ~ais) a crucial

crucifi|cação /krusifika'sãw/ f crucifixion. **~car** vt crucify. **~xo** /ks/ m crucifix

cru|el /kru'ɛw/ (pl ~éis) a cruel. **~eldade** f cruelty. **~ento** a bloody

crupe /'krupi/ m croup

crustáceos /krus'tasius/ m pl shellfish

cruz /krus/ f cross

cruza|da /kru'zada/ f crusade. **~do¹** m (soldado) crusader

cru|zado² /kru'zadu/ m (moeda) cruzado. **~zador** m cruiser. **~zamento** m (de ruas) crossroads, junction, Amer intersection; (de raças) cross. **~zar** vt cross ● vi ‹navio› cruise; **~zar com** pass. **~zar-se** vpr cross; ‹pessoas› pass each other. **~zeiro** m (moeda) cruzeiro; (viagem) cruise; (cruz) cross

cu /ku/ m (chulo) arse, Amer ass; **~ de ferro** 🎓 swot 🎓

Cuba /'kuba/ f Cuba

cubano /ku'banu/ a & m Cuban

cúbico /'kubiku/ a cubic

cubículo /ku'bikulu/ m cubicle

cubis|mo /ku'bizmu/ m cubism. **~ta** a & m/f cubist

cubo /'kubu/ m cube; (de roda) hub

cuca /'kuka/ f 🎓 head

cuco /'kuku/ m cuckoo; (relógio) cuckoo clock

cueca /ku'ɛka/ f underpants; pl Port (de mulher) knickers

cueiro /ku'eru/ m baby wrap

cuia /'kuia/ f gourd

cuidado /kui'dadu/ m care; **com ~** carefully; **ter ou tomar ~** be careful. **~so** /o/ a careful

cuidar /kui'dar/ vi **~ de** take care of. **~se** vpr look after o.s.

cujo /'kuʒu/ pron whose

culatra /ku'latra/ f breech; **sair pela ~** fig backfire

culiná|ria /kuli'naria/ f cookery. **~rio** a culinary

culmi|nância /kuwmi'nãsia/ f culmination. **~nante** a culminating. **~nar** vi culminate (**em** in)

cul|pa /'kuwpa/ f guilt; **foi ~pa minha** it was my fault; **ter ~pa de** be to blame for. **~pabilidade** f guilt. **~pado** a guilty ● m culprit. **~par** vt blame (**de** for); (na justiça) find guilty (**de** of). **~par-se** vpr take the blame (**de** for). **~pável** (pl ~páveis) a culpable, guilty

culti|var /kuwtʃi'var/ vt cultivate; grow ‹plantas›. **~vo** m cultivation; (de plantas) growing

cul|to /'kuwtu/ a cultured ● m cult. **~tura** f culture; (de terra) cultivation. **~tural** (pl ~turais) a cultural

cumbuca /kũ'buka/ f bowl

cume /'kumi/ m peak

cúmplice /'kũplisi/ m/f accomplice

cumplicidade /kũplisi'dadʒi/ f complicity

cumprimen|tar /kũprimẽ'tar/ vt/i (saudar) greet; (parabenizar) compliment. **~to** m (saudação) greeting; (elogio) compliment; (de lei, ordem) compliance (**de** with); (de promessa, palavra) fulfilment

cumprir /kũ'prir/ vt keep ‹promessa, palavra›; comply with ‹lei, ordem›; do ‹dever›; carry out ‹obrigações›; serve ‹pena›; **~ com** keep to ● vi **cumpre-nos ir** we should go. **~se** vpr be fulfilled

cúmulo /'kumulu/ m height; **é o ~!** that's the limit!

cunha /'kuɲa/ f wedge; Port (pessoa influente) contact

cunha|da /ku'ɲada/ f sister-in-law. **~do** m brother-in-law

cunhar /ku'ɲar/ vt coin ‹palavra, expressão›; mint ‹moedas›

cunho /'kuɲu/ m hallmark

cupim /ku'pĩ/ m termite

cupom /ku'põ/ m coupon

cúpula /'kupula/ f (abóbada) dome; (de abajur) shade; (chefia) leadership; (reunião de) summit (meeting)

cura /'kura/ f cure ● m curate, priest

curandeiro /kurã'deru/ m (religioso) faith healer; (índio) medicine man; (charlatão) quack

curar /ku'rar/ vt cure; dress ‹ferida›. **~se** vpr be cured

curativo /kura'tʃivu/ m dressing

curá|vel /ku'ravew/ (pl ~veis) a curable

curin|ga /kuˈrĩɡa/ m wild card. **~gão** m joker

curio|sidade /kuriozi'dadʒi/ f curiosity. **~so** /o/ a curious ● m (espectador) onlooker

cur|ral /ku'xaw/ (pl **~rais**) m pen

currículo /ku'xikulu/ m curriculum; (resumo) curriculum vitae, CV

cur|sar /kur'sar/ vt attend ‹escola, aula›; study ‹matéria›. **~so** m course. **~sor** m cursor

curta|-metragem /kurtame'traʒẽ/ (pl **~s-metragens**) m short (film)

cur|tição /kurtʃi'sãw/ f 🄸 enjoyment. **~tir** vt 🄸 enjoy; tan ‹couro›

curto /'kurtu/ a short; ‹conhecimento, inteligência› limited. **~circuito** (pl **~s-circuitos**) m short circuit

cur|va /'kurva/ f curve; (de estrada, rio) bend; **~va fechada** hairpin bend. **~var** vt bend. **~var-se** vpr bend; fig bow (a to). **~vo** a curved; ‹estrada› winding

cus|parada /kuspa'rada/ f spit. **~pe** m spit, spittle. **~pir** vt/i spit

cus|ta /'kusta/ f à **~ta de** at the expense of. **~tar** vt cost ● vi (ser difícil) be hard; **~tar a fazer** (ter dificuldade) find it hard to do; (demorar) take a long time to do. **~tear** vt finance, fund. **~teio** m funding; (relação de despesas) costing. **~to** m cost; a **~to** with difficulty

custódia /kus'tɔdʒia/ f custody

cutelo /ku'telu/ m cleaver

cutícula /ku'tʃikula/ f cuticle

cútis /'kutʃis/ f invar complexion

cutucar /kutu'kar/ vt (com o cotovelo, joelho) nudge; (com o dedo) poke; (com instrumento) prod

czar /zar/ m tsar

....

Dd

....

da = de + a

dádiva /'dadʒiva/ f gift; (donativo) donation

dado /'dadu/ m (de jogar) die, dice; (informação) fact, piece of information; pl data

dador /da'dor/ m Port donor

daí /da'i/ adv (no espaço) from there; (no tempo) then; **~ por diante** from then on; **e ~?** 🄸 so what?

dali /da'li/ adv from over there

dália /'dalia/ f dahlia

dal|tônico /daw'toniku/ a colour-blind. **~tonismo** m colour blindness

dama /'dama/ f lady; (em jogos) queen; pl (jogo) draughts, Amer checkers; **~ de honra** bridesmaid

da|nado /da'nadu/ a damned; (zangado) angry; (travesso) naughty. **~nar-se** vpr get angry; **~ne-se!** 🄸 who cares?

dan|ça /'dãsa/ f dance. **~çar** vt dance ● vi dance; 🄸 ‹pessoa› miss out; ‹coisa› go by the board; ‹criminoso› get caught. **~çarino** m dancer. **~ceteria** f discotheque

da|nificar /danifi'kar/ vt damage. **~ninho** a undesirable. **~no** m (pl) damage. **~noso** /o/ a damaging

dantes /'dãtʃis/ adv formerly

daquela(s), **daquele(s)** = de + aquela(s), aquele(s)

daqui /da'ki/ adv from here; **~ a 2 dias** in 2 days(' time); **~ a pouco** in a minute; **~ em diante** from now on

daquilo = de + aquilo

dar /dar/ vt give; have ‹dormida, lida etc›; do ‹pulo, cambalhota etc›; cause ‹problemas›; produce ‹frutas, leite›; deal ‹cartas›; (lecionar) teach ● vi (ser possível) be possible; (ser suficiente) be enough; **~ com** come across; **~ em** lead to; **ele dá para ator** he'd make a good actor; **~ por** (considerar como) consider to be; (reparar em) notice. **~se** vpr ‹coisa› happen; ‹pessoa› get on

dardo /'dardu/ m dart; (no atletismo) javelin

das = de + as

da|ta /'data/ f date; **de longa ~** long since. **~tar** vt/i date

dati|lografar /datʃilogra'far/ vt/i type. **~lografia** f typing. **~lógrafo** m typist

---

de /dʒi/ ● prep

....► (matéria, conteúdo, qualidade) of; **um jarro ~ água** a jug of water; **uma mesa ~ madeira** a wooden table; **um livro ~ grande interesse** a book of great interest

....► (em descrições) with; **a mulher ~ cabelo castanho** the woman with brown hair; **o rapaz ~ calças azuis** the boy in blue trousers; **uma camiseta ~ manga curta** a short-sleeved shirt

····➤ (*meio de transporte*) by; **~ avião/ trem** by plane/train

····➤ (*com números e expressões de tempo*) **uma nota ~ 10 reais** a 10-real note; **~ dia** during the day

····➤ (*origem, procedência*) from; **eles são ~ São Paulo** they are from São Paulo

····➤ (*posse*) **o cachorro da Ana** Ana's dog; **a chave do carro** the car key; **as pernas da mesa** the table legs

····➤ (*série*) **~ meia em meia hora** every half hour; **~ de dois em dois metros** every two metres

····➤ (*tema, disciplina*) **um livro ~ inglês** an English book; **não entendo nada ~ motores** I don't know a thing about engines

····➤ (*indica autor*) by; **um livro ~ Machado de Assis** a book by Machado de Assis

····➤ (*causa*) **morrer ~ fome** die of hunger; **chorar ~ alegria** cry for joy

debaixo /dʒi'baʃu/ *adv* below; **~ de** under

debalde /dʒi'bawdʒi/ *adv* in vain

debandada /debã'dada/ *f* stampede

deba|te /de'batʃi/ *m* debate; **~te frente a frente** face-to-face debate. **~ter** *vt* debate. **~ter-se** *vpr* grapple

debelar /debe'lar/ *vt* overcome

dé|bil /'dɛbiw/ (*pl* **~beis**) *a* feeble; **~bil mental** retarded (person)

debili|dade /debili'dadʒi/ *f* debility. **~tar** *vt* debilitate. **~tar-se** *vpr* become debilitated

debitar /debi'tar/ *vt* debit

débito /'dɛbitu/ *m* debit

debo|chado /debo'ʃadu/ *a* sardonic. **~char** *vt* mock. **~che** /ɔ/ *m* jibe

debruar /debru'ar/ *vt/i* edge

debruçar-se /debru'sarsi/ *vpr* bend over; **~ sobre** study

debrum /de'brũ/ *m* edging

debulhar /debu'ʎar/ *vt* thresh

debu|tante /debu'tãtʃi/ *f* debutante. **~tar** *vi* debut, make one's debut

década /'dɛkada/ *f* decade; **a ~ dos 60** the sixties

deca|dência /deka'dẽsia/ *f* decadence. **~dente** *a* decadent

decair /deka'ir/ *vi* decline; (*degringolar*) go downhill; ‹*planta*› wilt

decal|car /dekaw'kar/ *vt* trace. **~que** *m* tracing

decapitar /dekapi'tar/ *vt* decapitate

decatlo /de'katlu/ *m* decathlon

de|cência /de'sẽsia/ *f* decency. **~cente** *a* decent

decepar /dese'par/ *vt* cut off

decep|ção /desep'sãw/ *f* disappointment. **~cionar** *vt* disappoint. **~cionar-se** *vpr* be disappointed

decerto /dʒi'sertu/ *adv* certainly

deci|dido /desi'dʒidu/ *a* ‹*pessoa*› determined. **~dir** *vt/i* decide. **~dir-se** *vpr* make up one's mind; **~dir-se por** decide on

decíduo /de'siduu/ *a* deciduous

decifrar /desi'frar/ *vt* decipher

deci|mal /desi'maw/ (*pl* **~mais**) *a & m* decimal

décimo /'dɛsimu/ *a & m* tenth; **~ primeiro** eleventh; **~ segundo** twelfth; **~ terceiro** thirteenth; **~ quarto** fourteenth; **~ quinto** fifteenth; **~ sexto** sixteenth; **~ sétimo** seventeenth; **~ oitavo** eighteenth; **~ nono** nineteenth

deci|são /desi'zãw/ *f* decision. **~sivo** *a* decisive

decla|ração /deklara'sãw/ *f* declaration. **~rado** *a* ‹*inimigo*› sworn; ‹*crente*› avowed; ‹*ladrão*› self-confessed. **~rar** *vt* declare

decli|nação /deklina'sãw/ *f* declension. **~nar** *vt* **~nar (de)** decline ● *vi* decline; ‹*sol*› go down; ‹*chão*› slope down

declínio /de'kliniu/ *m* decline

declive /de'klivi/ *m* (downward) slope, incline

decodificar /dekodʒifi'kar/ *vt* decode

deco|lagem /deko'laʒẽ/ *f* take-off. **~lar** *vi* take off; *fig* get off the ground

decom|por /dekõ'por/ *vt* break down; contort ‹*feições*›. **~por-se** *vpr* break down; ‹*cadáver*› decompose. **~posição** *f* (*de cadáver*) decomposition

deco|ração /dekora'sãw/ *f* decoration; (*aprendizagem*) learning by heart. **~rar** *vt* (*adornar*) decorate; (*aprender*) learn by heart, memorize. **~rativo** *a* decorative. **~reba** /ɛ/ *f* 🄸 rote learning. **~ro** /o/ *m* decorum. **~roso** /o/ *a* decorous

decor|rência /deko'xẽsia/ *f* consequence. **~rente** *a* resulting (**de** from). **~rer** *vi* ‹*tempo*› elapse; ‹*acontecimento*› pass off; (*resultar*) result (**de** from) ● *m* **no ~rer de** in the course of; **com o ~rer do tempo** in time, with the passing of time

deco|tado /deko'tadu/ *a* low-cut. **~te** /ɔ/ *m* neckline

decrépito /de'krɛpitu/ *a* decrepit

decres|cente /dekre'sẽtʃi/ *a* decreasing. **~cer** *vi* decrease

decre|tar /dekre'tar/ *vt* decree; declare ‹*estado de sítio*›. **~to** /ɛ/ *m* decree. **~to-lei** *m* act

decurso /de'kursu/ *m* course

de|dal /de'daw/ (*pl* **~dais**) *m* thimble. **~dão** *m* (*da mão*) thumb; (*do pé*) big toe

dedetizar /dedetʃi'zar/ *vt* spray with insecticide

dedi|cação /dedʒika'sãw/ *f* dedication. **~car** *vt* dedicate; devote ‹*tempo*›. **~car-se** *vpr* dedicate o.s. (a to). **~catória** *f* dedication

dedilhar /dedʒi'ʎar/ *vt* pluck

dedo /'dedu/ *m* finger; (*do pé*) toe; **cheio de ~s** all fingers and thumbs; (*sem graça*) awkward. **~-duro** (*pl* **~s-duros**) *m* sneak; (*político, criminoso*) informer

dedução /dedu'sãw/ *f* deduction

dedurar /dedu'rar/ *vt* sneak on; (*à polícia*) inform on

dedu|tivo /dedu'tʃivu/ *a* deductive. **~zir** *vt* (*descontar*) deduct; (*concluir*) deduce

defa|sado /defa'zadu/ *a* out of step. **~sagem** *f* gap, lag

defecar /defe'kar/ *vi* defecate

defei|to /de'fejtu/ *m* defect; **botar ~to em** find fault with. **~tuoso** /o/ *a* defective

defen|der /defẽ'der/ *vt* defend. **~der-se** *vpr* (*virar-se*) fend for o.s.; (*contra-atacar*) defend o.s. (**de** against). **~siva** *f* **na ~siva** on the defensive. **~sor** *m* defender; (*advogado*) defence counsel

defe|rência /defe'rẽsia/ *f* deference. **~rente** *a* deferential

defesa /de'feza/ *f* defence ● *m* defender

defici|ência /defisi'ẽsia/ *f* deficiency. **~ente** *a* deficient; (*física ou mentalmente*) handicapped ● *m/f* handicapped person

déficit /'dɛfisitʃi/ (*pl* **~s**) *m* deficit

deficitário /defisitʃi'ariu/ *a* in deficit; ‹*empresa*› loss-making

definhar /defi'ɲar/ *vi* waste away; ‹*planta*› wither

defi|nição /defini'sãw/ *f* definition. **~nir** *vt* define. **~nir-se** *vpr* (*descrever-se*) define o.s.; (*decidir-se*) come to a decision; (*explicar-se*) make one's position clear. **~nitivo** *a* definitive. **~nível** (*pl* **~níveis**) *a* definable

defla|ção /defla'sãw/ *f* deflation. **~cionário** *a* deflationary

deflagrar /defla'grar/ *vt* set off ● *vi* break out

defor|mar /defor'mar/ *vt* misshape; deform ‹*corpo*›; distort ‹*imagem*›. **~midade** *f* deformity

defraudar /defraw'dar/ *vt* defraud (**de** of)

defron|tar /defrõ'tar/ *vt* **~tar com** face. **~te** *adv* opposite; **~te de** opposite

defumar /defu'mar/ *vt* smoke

defunto /de'fũtu/ *a & m* deceased

dege|lar /deʒe'lar/ *vt/i* thaw. **~lo** /e/ *m* thaw

degeneração /deʒenera'sãw/ *f* degeneration

degenerar /deʒene'rar/ *vi* degenerate (**em** into)

degolar /dego'lar/ *vt* cut the throat of

degra|dação /degrada'sãw/ *f* degradation. **~dante** *a* degrading. **~dar** *vt* degrade

degrau /de'graw/ *m* step

degringolar /degrĩgo'lar/ *vi* deteriorate, go downhill

degustar /degus'tar/ *vt* taste

dei|tada /dej'tada/ *f* lie-down. **~tado** *a* lying down; (*dormindo*) in bed; Ⓘ (*preguiçoso*) idle. **~tar** *vt* lay down; (*na cama*) put to bed; (*pôr*) put; *Port* (*jogar*) throw ● *vi*, **~tar-se** *vpr* lie down; (*ir para cama*) go to bed

dei|xa /'deʃa/ *f* cue. **~xar** *vt* leave; (*permitir*) let; **~xar de** (*parar*) stop; (*omitir*) fail; **não pôde ~xar de rir** he couldn't help laughing; **~xar alguém nervoso** make sb annoyed; **~xar cair** drop; **~xar a desejar** leave a lot to be desired; **~xa (para lá)** Ⓘ never mind, forget it

dela(s) = **de** + **ela(s)**

delatar /dela'tar/ *vt* report

délavé /dela've/ *a invar* faded

dele(s) = **de** + **ele(s)**

dele|gação /delega'sãw/ *f* delegation; **~gação de autoridade** Com empowerment. **~gacia** *f* police station. **~gado** *m* delegate; **~gado de polícia** police chief. **~gar** *vt* delegate

delei|tar /delej'tar/ *vt* delight. **~tar-se** *vpr* delight (**com** in). **~te** *m* delight. **~toso** /o/ *a* delightful

delgado /dew'gadu/ *a* slender

delibe|ração /delibera'sãw/ f
deliberation. **~rar** vt/i deliberate

delica|deza /delika'deza/ f delicacy;
(cortesia) politeness; **~do** a delicate;
(cortês) polite

delícia /de'lisia/ f delight; **ser uma ~**
‹comida› be delicious; ‹sol etc› be lovely

delici|ar /delisi'ar/ vt delight; **~ar-se**
delight (com in). **~oso** /o/ a delightful,
lovely; ‹comida› delicious

deline|ador /delinia'dor/ m eyeliner.
~ar vt outline

delin|quência /delĩ'kwẽsia/ f
delinquency. **~quente** a & m delinquent

deli|rante /deli'rãtʃi/ a rapturous;
Med delirious. **~rar** vi go into raptures;
‹doente› be delirious

delírio /de'liriu/ m (febre) delirium;
(excitação) raptures

delito /de'litu/ m crime

delonga /de'lõga/ f delay

delta /'dɛwta/ m delta

dema|gogia /demago'ʒia/ f
demagogy. **~gógico** a demagogic.
~gogo /o/ m demagogue

demais /dʒi'majs/ a & adv (muito) very
much; (em demasia) too much; **os ~** the
rest, the others; **é ~!** 🅸 it's great!

deman|da /de'mãda/ f demand; Jurid
action. **~dar** vt sue

demão /de'mãw/ f coat

demar|car /demar'kar/ vt demarcate.
~catório a demarcation

demasia /dema'zia/ f excess; **em ~** too
(much, many)

de|mência /de'mẽsia/ f insanity;
Med dementia. **~mente** a insane; Med
demented

demissão /demi'sãw/ f sacking,
dismissal; **pedir ~** resign

demitir /demi'tʃir/ vt sack, dismiss.
~se vpr resign

demo|cracia /demokra'sia/ f
democracy. **~crata** m/f democrat.
~crático a democratic. **~cratizar**
vt democratize. **~grafia** f demography.
~gráfico a demographic

demo|lição /demoli'sãw/ f
demolition. **~lir** vt demolish

demônio /de'moniu/ m demon

demons|tração /demõstra'sãw/ f
demonstration. **~trar** vt demonstrate.
~trativo a demonstrative

demo|ra /de'mɔra/ f delay. **~rado** a
lengthy. **~rar** vi (levar) take; (tardar a
voltar, terminar etc) be long; (levar muito

tempo) take a long time ● vt delay

dendê /dẽ'de/ m (óleo) palm oil

denegrir /dene'grir/ vt denigrate

dengoso /dẽ'gozu/ a coy

dengue /'dẽgi/ m dengue

denomi|nação /denomina'sãw/ f
denomination. **~nar** vt name

denotar /deno'tar/ vt denote

den|sidade /dẽsi'dadʒi/ f density. **~so**
a dense

den|tado /dẽ'tadu/ a serrated.
~tadura f (set of) teeth; (postiça)
dentures, false teeth. **~tal** (pl **~tais**) a
dental. **~tário** a dental. **~te** m tooth; (de
alho) clove; **~te do siso** wisdom tooth.
~tição f teething; (dentadura) teeth.
~tífrico m toothpaste. **~tista** m/f dentist

dentre =DE + ENTRE

dentro /'dẽtru/ adv inside; **lá ~** in
there; **por ~** on the inside; **~ de** inside;
(tempo) within

dentu|ça /dẽ'tusa/ f buck teeth. **~ço** a
with buck teeth

denúncia /de'nũsia/ f (à polícia etc)
report; (na imprensa etc) disclosure

denunciar /denũsi'ar/ vt (à polícia etc)
report; (na imprensa etc) denounce

deparar /depa'rar/ vi **~ com** come
across

departamento /departa'mẽtu/ m
department

depauperar /depawpe'rar/ vt
impoverish

depenar /depe'nar/ vt pluck ‹aves›;
(roubar) fleece

depen|dência /depẽ'dẽsia/ f
dependence; pl premises. **~dente** a
dependent (de on) ● m/f dependant.
~der vi depend (de on)

depi|lação /depila'sãw/ f depilation.
~lar vt depilate. **~latório** m depilatory
cream

deplo|rar /deplo'rar/ vt deplore.
~rável (pl **~ráveis**) a deplorable

de|poente /depo'ẽtʃi/ m/f witness.
~poimento m (à polícia) statement;
(na justiça) fig testimony

depois /de'pojs/ adv after(wards); **~ de**
after; **~ que** after

depor /de'por/ vi (na polícia) make a
statement; (na justiça) give evidence,
testify ● vt lay down ‹armas›; depose
‹rei, presidente›

depor|tação /deporta'sãw/ f
deportation. **~tar** vt deport

deposi|tante /depozi'tãtʃl/ m/f depositor. **~tar** vt deposit; cast ‹voto›; place ‹confiança›

depósito /de'pozitu/ m deposit; (armazém) warehouse

depra|vação /deprava'sãw/ f depravity. **~vado** a depraved. **~var** vt deprave

depre|ciação /depresia'sãw/ f (perda de valor) depreciation; (menosprezo) deprecation. **~ciar** vt (desvalorizar) devalue; (menosprezar) deprecate. **~ciar-se** vpr ‹bens› depreciate; ‹pessoa› deprecate o.s.. **~ciativo** a deprecatory

depre|dação /depreda'sãw/ f depredation. **~dar** vt wreck

depressa /dʒi'prɛsa/ adv fast, quickly

depres|são /depre'sãw/ f depression. **~sivo** a depressive

depri|mente /depri'mẽtʃi/ a depressing. **~mido** a depressed. **~mir** vt depress. **~mir-se** vpr get depressed

depurar /depu'rar/ vt purify

depu|tação /deputa'sãw/ f deputation. **~tado** m deputy, MP, Amer congressman (f-woman). **~tar** vt delegate

deque /'dɛki/ m (sun)deck

deri|va /de'riva/ f à **~va** adrift; andar à **~va** drift. **~vação** f derivation. **~var** vt derive; (desviar) divert ● vi, **~var-se** vpr derive, be derived (de from); ‹navio› drift

dermatolo|gia /dermatolo'ʒia/ f dermatology. **~gista** m/f dermatologist

derradeiro /dexa'deru/ a last, final

derra|mamento /dexama'mẽtu/ m spill, spillage; **~mamento de sangue** bloodshed. **~mar** vt spill; shed ‹lágrimas›. **~mar-se** vpr spill. **~me** m spill, spillage; **~me cerebral** stroke

derra|pagem /dexa'paʒẽ/ f skidding; (uma) skid. **~par** vi skid

derreter /dexe'ter/ vt melt. **~-se** vpr melt

derro|ta /de'xɔta/ f defeat. **~tar** vt defeat. **~tismo** m defeatism. **~tista** a & m/f defeatist

derrubar /dexu'bar/ vt knock down; bring down ‹governo›

desaba|far /dʒizaba'far/ vi speak one's mind. **~fo** m outburst

desa|bamento /dʒizaba'mẽtu/ m collapse. **~bar** vi collapse; ‹chuva› pour down

desabotoar /dʒizaboto'ar/ vt unbutton

desabri|gado /dʒizabri'gadu/ a homeless. **~gar** vt make homeless

desabrochar /dʒizabro'ʃar/ vi blossom, bloom

desaca|tar /dʒizaka'tar/ vt defy. **~to** m (de pessoa) disrespect; (da lei etc) disregard

desacerto /dʒiza'sertu/ m mistake

desacompanhado /dʒizakõpa'ɲadu/ a unaccompanied

desaconse|lhar /dʒizakõse'ʎar/ vt advise against. **~lhável** (pl **~lháveis**) a inadvisable

desacor|dado /dʒizakor'dadu/ a unconscious. **~do** /o/ m disagreement

desacostu|mado /dʒizakostu'madu/ a unaccustomed. **~mar** vt **~mar alguém de** break sb of the habit of; **~mar-se de** get out of the habit

desacreditar /dʒizakredʒi'tar/ vt discredit

desafeto /dʒiza'fɛtu/ m disaffection

desafi|ador /dʒizafia'dor/ a ‹tarefa› challenging; ‹pessoa› defiant. **~ar** vt challenge; (fazer face a) defy ‹perigo, morte›

desafi|nado /dʒizafi'nadu/ a out of tune. **~nar** vi (cantando) sing out of tune; (tocando) play out of tune ● vt put out of tune

desafio /dʒiza'fiu/ m challenge

desafivelar /dʒizafive'lar/ vt unbuckle

desafo|gar /dʒizafo'gar/ vt vent; (desapertar) relieve. **~gar-se** vpr give vent to one's feelings. **~go** /o/ m (alívio) relief

desafo|rado /dʒizafo'radu/ a cheeky. **~ro** /o/ m cheek; (um) liberty

desafortunado /dʒizafortu'nadu/ a unfortunate

desagra|dar /dʒizagra'dar/ vt displease. **~dável** (pl **~dáveis**) a unpleasant. **~do** m displeasure

desagravo m redress, amends

desagregar /dʒizagre'gar/ vt split up. **~-se** vpr split up

desaguar /dʒiza'gwar/ vt drain ● vi ‹rio› flow (em into)

desajeitado /dʒizaʒej'tadu/ a clumsy

desajuizado /dʒizaʒui'zadu/ a foolish

desajus|tado /dʒizaʒus'tadu/ a Psic maladjusted. **~te** m Psic maladjustment

desalen|tar /dʒizalẽ'tar/ vt dishearten. **~tar-se** vpr get disheartened. **~to** m discouragement

desali|nhado /dʒiali'nadu/ a untidy. **~nho** m untidiness

desalojar /dʒizalo'ʒar/ vt turn out ‹inquilino›; flush out ‹inimigo, ladrões›

desamarrar /dʒizama'xar/ vt untie ● vi cast off

desamarrotar /dʒizamaxo'tar/ vt smooth out

desamassar /dʒizama'sar/ vt smooth out

desambientado /dʒizãbiẽ'tadu/ a unsettled

desampa|rar /dʒizãpa'rar/ vt abandon. **~ro** m abandonment

desandar /dʒizã'dar/ vi ‹molho› separate; **~ a** start to

de|sanimar /dʒizani'mar/ vt discourage ● vi ‹pessoa› lose heart; ‹fato› be discouraging. **~sânimo** m discouragement

desapaixonado /dʒizapaʃo'nadu/ a dispassionate

desaparafusar /dʒizaparafu'zar/ vt unscrew

desapare|cer /dʒizapare'ser/ vi disappear. **~cimento** m disappearance

desapego /dʒiza'pegu/ m detachment; ‹indiferença› indifference

desapercebido /dʒizaperse'bidu/ a unnoticed

desapertar /dʒizaper'tar/ vt loosen

desapon|tamento /dʒizapõta'mẽtu/ m disappointment. **~tar** vt disappoint

desapropriar /dʒizapropri'ar/ vt expropriate

desapro|vação /dʒizaprova'sãw/ f disapproval. **~var** vt disapprove of

desaproveitado /dʒizaprovej-'tadu/ a wasted

desar|mamento /dʒizarma'mẽtu/ m disarmament. **~mar** vt disarm; take down ‹barraca›

desarran|jar /dʒizaxã'ʒar/ vt mess up; upset ‹estômago›. **~jo** m mess; (do estômago) upset

desarregaçar /dʒizaxega'sar/ vt roll down

desarru|mado /dʒizaxu'madu/ a untidy. **~mar** vt untidy; unpack ‹mala›

desarticular /dʒizartʃiku'lar/ vt dislocate

desarvorado /dʒizarvo'radu/ a disoriented, at a loss

desassociar /dʒizasosi'ar/ vt disassociate. **~se** vpr disassociate o.s.

desas|trado /dʒizas'tradu/ a accident-prone. **~tre** m disaster. **~troso** /o/ a disastrous

desatar /dʒiza'tar/ vt untie; **~ a chorar** dissolve in tears

desatarraxar /dʒizataxa'ʃar/ vt unscrew

desaten|cioso /dʒizatẽsi'ozu/ a inattentive. **~to** a oblivious (a to)

desati|nar /dʒizatʃi'nar/ vt bewilder ● vi not think straight. **~no** m mental aberration, bewilderment; (um) folly

desativar /dʒizatʃi'var/ vt deactivate; shut down ‹fábrica›

desatrelar /dʒizatre'lar/ vt unhitch

desatualizado /dʒizatuali'zadu/ a out-of-date

desavença /dʒiza'vẽsa/ f dispute

desavergonhado /dʒizavergo'nadu/ a shameless

desbancar /dʒizbã'kar/ vt outdo

desbaratar /dʒizbara'tar/ vt (desperdiçar) waste

desbocado /dʒizbo'kadu/ a outspoken

desbotar /dʒizbo'tar/ vt/i fade

desbra|vador /dʒizbrava'dor/ m explorer. **~var** vt explore

desbun|dante /dʒizbũ'dãtʃi/ a 🔢 mind-blowing. **~dar** vt 🔢 blow the mind of ● vi 🔢 flip, freak out. **~de** m 🔢 knockout

descabido /dʒiska'bidu/ a inappropriate

descafeinado /dʒiskafej'nadu/ a decaffeinated

descalabro /dʒiska'labru/ m debacle

descalço /dʒis'kawsu/ a barefoot

descambar /dʒiskã'bar/ vi deteriorate, degenerate

descan|sar /dʒiskã'sar/ vt/i rest. **~so** m rest; (de prato, copo) mat

descapotável /dʒiskapu'tavɛł/ a & m Port convertible

desca|rado /dʒiska'radu/ a blatant. **~ramento** m cheek

descarga /dʒis'karga/ f Eletr discharge; (da privada) flush; **dar ~** flush (the toilet)

descarregar /dʒiskaxe'gar/ vt unload ‹mercadorias›; discharge ‹poluentes›; vent ‹raiva› ● vi ‹bateria› go flat; **~ em**

cima de alguém take it out on sb
descarrilhar /dʒiskaxiˈʎar/ vt/i derail
descar|tar /dʒiskarˈtar/ vt discard.
~**tável** (pl ~**táveis**) a disposable
descascar /dʒiskasˈkar/ vt peel ‹frutas, batatas›; shell ‹nozes› ● vi ‹pessoa, pele› peel
descaso /dʒisˈkazu/ m indifference
descen|dência /deseˈdẽsia/ f descent. ~**dente** a descended ● m/f descendant. ~**der** vi descend (**de** from)
descentralizar /dʒisẽtraliˈzar/ vt decentralize
des|cer /deˈser/ vi go down; ‹avião› descend; (do ônibus, trem) get off; (do carro) get out ● vt go down ‹escada, ladeira›; scroll down ‹página›. ~**cida** f descent
desclassificar /dʒisklasifiˈkar/ vt disqualify
desco|berta /dʒiskoˈberta/ f discovery. ~**berto** /ɛ/ a uncovered; ‹conta› overdrawn; **a** ~**berto** overdrawn. ~**bridor** m discoverer. ~**brimento** m discovery. ~**brir** vt discover; (expor) uncover

---

Descobrimentos The term *Descobrimentos* refers to the Age of Discovery in the 15th and 16th centuries, during which the Portuguese engaged in extensive maritime travels in search of new trade routes with the New World. Significant events include the route charted round Africa to India by Vasco da Gama in 1498, and the discovery of Brazil by Pedro Álvares Cabral in 1500.

---

descolar /dʒiskoˈlar/ vt unstick; ▣ (dar) give; (arranjar) get hold of, rustle up; Port ‹avião› take off
descom|por /dʒiskõˈpor/ vt (censurar) scold. ~**se** vpr ‹pessoa› lose one's composure. ~**postura** f (estado) loss of composure; (censura) talking-to
descomprometido /dʒiskõpromeˈtʃidu/ a free
descomu|nal /dʒiskomuˈnaw/ (pl ~**nais**) a extraordinary; (grande) huge
desconcentrar /dʒiskõsẽˈtrar/ vt distract
desconcer|tante /dʒiskõserˈtãtʃi/ a disconcerting. ~**tar** vt disconcert
desconexo /dʒiskoˈneksu/ a incoherent
desconfi|ado /dʒiskõfiˈadu/ a suspicious. ~**ança** f mistrust. ~**ar** vi

suspect
desconfor|tável /dʒiskõforˈtavew/ (pl ~**táveis**) a uncomfortable. ~**to** /o/ m discomfort
descongelar /dʒiskõʒeˈlar/ vt defrost ‹geladeira›; thaw ‹comida›
descongestio|nante /dʒiskõʒestʃioˈnãtʃi/ a & m decongestant. ~**nar** vt decongest
desconhe|cer /dʒiskoɲeˈser/ vt not know. ~**cido** a unknown ● m stranger
desconsiderar /dʒiskõsideˈrar/ vt ignore
desconsolado /dʒiskõsoˈladu/ a disconsolate
descontar /dʒiskõˈtar/ vt deduct; (não levar em conta) discount
desconten|tamento /dʒiskõtẽtaˈmẽtu/ m discontent. ~**te** a discontent
descontinuado /dʒiskõtʃiˈnwadu/ a discontinued
desconto /dʒisˈkõtu/ m discount; **dar um** ~ fig make allowances
descontra|ção /dʒiskõtraˈsãw/ f informality. ~**ído** a informal, casual. ~**ir** vt relax. ~**ir-se** vpr relax
descontro|lar-se /dʒiskõtroˈlarsi/ vpr ‹pessoa› lose control; ‹coisa› go out of control. ~**le** /o/ m lack of control
desconversar /dʒiskõverˈsar/ vi change the subject
descortesia /dʒiskorteˈzia/ f rudeness
descostu|rar /dʒiskostuˈrar/ vt unrip. ~**rar-se** vpr come undone
descrédito /dʒisˈkrɛdʒitu/ m discredit
descren|ça /dʒisˈkrẽsa/ f disbelief. ~**te** a sceptical, disbelieving
des|crever /dʒiskreˈver/ vt describe. ~**crição** f description. ~**critivo** a descriptive
descui|dado /dʒiskuiˈdadu/ a careless. ~**dar** vt neglect. ~**do** m carelessness; (um) oversight
descul|pa /dʒisˈkuwpa/ f excuse; **pedir** ~**pas** apologize. ~**par** vt excuse; ~**pe!** sorry!. ~**par-se** vpr apologize. ~**pável** (pl ~**páveis**) a excusable

---

desde /ˈdezdʒi/ ● prep

····▶ since; **moro aqui** ~ **2008** I have lived here since 2008

····▶ (em expressões) ~ ... **até** ... from ... to ...; ~ **junho até agosto** from June to August; **a loja vende tudo,** ~ **roupas até livros** the shop sells everything, from clothes to books; **~ que** as long as; **~ que você me informe** as long as you let me know

des|dém /dez'dẽj/ m disdain. **~denhar** vt disdain. **~denhoso** /o/ a disdainful

desdentado /dʒizdẽ'tadu/ a toothless

desdita /dʒiz'dʒita/ f unhappiness

desdizer /dʒizdʒi'zer/ vt take back, withdraw ● vi take back what one said

desdo|bramento /dʒizdobra'mẽtu/ m implication. **~brar** vt (abrir) unfold; break down <dados, contas>. **~brar-se** vpr unfold; (empenhar-se) go to a lot of trouble, bend over backwards

dese|jar /deze'ʒar/ vt want; (apaixonadamente) desire; **~jar algo a alguém** wish sb sth. **~jável** (pl **~jáveis**) a desirable. **~jo** /e/ m wish; (forte) desire. **~joso** /o/ a desirous

deselegante /dʒizele'gãtʃi/ a inelegant

desemaranhar /dʒizemara'ɲar/ vt untangle

desembara|çado /dʒizĩbara'sadu/ a <pessoa> confident, nonchalant. **~çar-se** vpr rid o.s. (**de** of). **~ço** m confidence, ease

desembar|car /dʒizĩbar'kar/ vt/i disembark. **~que** m disembarkation; (seção do aeroporto) arrivals

desembocar /dʒizĩbo'kar/ vi flow

desembol|sar /dʒizĩbow'sar/ vt spend, pay out. **~so** /o/ m expenditure

desembrulhar /dʒizĩbru'ʎar/ vt unwrap

desembuchar /dʒizĩbu'ʃar/ vi [I](desabafar) get things off one's chest; (falar logo) spit it out

desempacotar /dʒizĩpako'tar/ vt unpack

desempatar /dʒizĩpa'tar/ vt decide <jogo>

desempe|nhar /dʒizĩpe'ɲar/ vt perform; play <papel>. **~nho** m performance

desempre|gado /dʒizĩpre'gadu/ a unemployed. **~go** /e/ m unemployment

desencadear /dʒizĩkadʒi'ar/ vt set off, trigger

desencaminhar /dʒizĩkami'ɲar/ vt lead astray; embezzle <dinheiro>

desencantar /dʒizĩkã'tar/ vt disenchant

desencon|trar-se /dʒizĩkõ'trarsi/ vpr miss each other, fail to meet. **~tro** m failure to meet

desencorajar /dʒizĩkora'ʒar/ vt discourage

desenferrujar /dʒizĩfexu'ʒar/ vt derust <metal>; stretch <pernas>; brush up <língua>

desenfreado /dʒizĩfri'adu/ a unbridled

desenganar /dʒizĩga'nar/ vt disabuse; declare incurable <doente>

desengonçado /dʒizĩgõ'sadu/ a <pessoa> ungainly

desengre|nado /dʒizĩgre'nadu/ a <carro> in neutral. **~nar** vt put in neutral <carro>; (tecn) disengage

dese|nhar /deze'ɲar/ vt draw. **~nhista** m/f drawer; (industrial) designer. **~nho** /e/ m drawing

desenlace /dʒizĩ'lasi/ m dénouement, outcome

desenrascar-se /dizĩxaʃ'karsi/ vpr Port to get by

desenredar /dʒizĩxe'dar/ vt unravel

desenrolar /dʒizĩxo'lar/ vt unroll <rolo>

desenten|der /dʒizĩtẽ'der/ vt misunderstand. **~der-se** vpr (não se dar bem) not get on. **~dimento** m misunderstanding

desenterrar /dʒizĩte'xar/ vt dig up <cadáver>; unearth <informação>

desentortar /dʒizĩtor'tar/ vt straighten out

desentupir /dʒizĩtu'pir/ vt unblock

desenvol|to /dʒizĩ'vowtu/ a casual, nonchalant. **~tura** f casualness, nonchalance; **com ~tura** nonchalantly. **~ver** vt develop. **~ver-se** vpr develop. **~vimento** m development

desequi|librado /dʒizeki'libradu/ a unbalanced. **~librar** vt unbalance. **~librar-se** vpr become unbalanced. **~líbrio** m imbalance

deser|ção /dezer'sãw/ f desertion. **~tar** vt/i desert. **~to** /e/ a deserted; **ilha ~ta** desert island ● m desert. **~tor** m deserter

desespe|rado /dʒizispe'radu/ a desperate. **~rador** a hopeless. **~rar** vt (desesperançar) make despair ● vi, **~rar-se** vpr despair. **~ro** /e/ m despair

desestabilizar /dʒizistabili'zar/ vt destabilize

desestimular /dʒizistʃimu'lar/ vt discourage

desfal|car /dʒisfaw'kar/ vt embezzle. **~que** m embezzlement

desfa|lecer /dʒisfale'ser/ vt (desmaiar) faint. **~lecimento** m faint

desfavor /dʒisfa'vor/ m disfavour

desfavo|rável /dʒisfavo'ravew/ (pl **~ráveis**) a unfavourable. **~recer** vt be unfavourable to; treat less favourably ‹minorias etc›

desfazer /dʒisfa'zer/ vt undo; unpack ‹mala›; strip ‹cama›; break ‹contrato›; clear up ‹mistério›. **~se** vpr come undone; ‹casamento› break up; ‹sonhos› crumble; **~se em lágrimas** dissolve into tears

desfe|char /dʒisfe'ʃar/ vt throw ‹murro, olhar›. **~cho** /e/ m outcome, dénouement

desfeita /dʒis'fejta/ f slight, insult

desferir /dʒisfe'rir/ vt give ‹pontapé›; launch ‹ataque›; fire ‹flecha›

desfiar /dʒisfi'ar/ vt pick the meat off ‹frango›. **~se** vpr ‹tecido› fray

desfigurar /dʒisfigu'rar/ vt disfigure; fig distort

desfi|ladeiro /dʒisfila'deru/ m pass. **~lar** vi parade. **~le** m parade; **~le de modas** fashion show

desflorestamento /dʒisfloresta'mẽtu/ m deforestation

desforra /dʒis'fɔxa/ f revenge

desfraldar /dʒisfraw'dar/ vt unfurl

desfrutar /dʒisfru'tar/ vt enjoy

desgas|tante /dʒizgas'tãtʃi/ a wearing, stressful. **~tar** vt wear out. **~te** m (de máquina etc) wear and tear; (de pessoa) stress and strain

desgosto /dʒiz'gostu/ m sorrow

desgovernar-se /dʒizgover'narsi/ vpr go out of control

desgraça /dʒiz'grasa/ f misfortune. **~do** a wretched ● m wretch

desgravar /dʒizgra'var/ vt erase

desgrenhado /dʒizgre'ɲadu/ a unkempt

desgrudar /dʒizgru'dar/ vt unstick. **~se** vpr ‹pessoa› tear o.s. away

desidra|tação /dʒizidrata'sãw/ f dehydration. **~tar** vt dehydrate

desig|nação /dezigna'sãw/ f designation. **~nar** vt designate

desi|gual /dʒizi'gwaw/ (pl **~guais**) a unequal; ‹terreno› uneven. **~gualdade** f inequality; (de terreno) unevenness

desilu|dir /dʒizilu'dʒir/ vt disillusion. **~são** f disillusionment

desinfe|tante /dʒizĩfe'tãtʃi/ a & m disinfectant. **~tar** vt disinfect

desinibido /dʒizini'bidu/ a uninhibited

desintegrar-se /dʒizĩte'grarsi/ vpr disintegrate

desinteres|sado /dʒizĩtere'sadu/ a uninterested. **~sante** a uninteresting. **~sar-se** vpr lose interest (de in). **~se** /e/ m disinterest

desintoxicação /dʒizĩtoksika'sãw/ f rehabilitation; **clínica de ~** rehabilitation centre

desis|tência /dezis'tẽsia/ f giving up. **~tir** vt/i **~tir (de)** give up

desle|al /dʒizle'aw/ (pl **~ais**) a disloyal. **~aldade** f disloyalty

deslei|xado /dʒizle'ʃadu/ a sloppy; (no vestir) scruffy. **~xo** m carelessness; (no vestir) scruffiness

desli|gado /dʒizli'gadu/ a ‹luz, TV› off; ‹pessoa› absent-minded. **~gar** vt turn off ‹luz, TV, motor›; hang up, put down ‹telefone› ● vi (ao telefonar) hang up, put the phone down

deslindar /dʒizlĩ'dar/ vt clear up, solve

desli|zante /dʒizli'zãtʃi/ a slippery; ‹inflação› creeping. **~zar** vi slip. **~zar-se** vpr creep. **~ze** m slip; fig (erro) slip-up

deslo|cado /dʒizlo'kadu/ a ‹membro› dislocated; fig out of place. **~calizar** /dʒizlokali'zar/ vt Port ‹fábricas, empresas› relocate. **~car** /dʒizlo'kar/ vt move; Med dislocate ‹fábricas, empresas› relocate. **~car-se** vpr move

deslum|brado /dʒizlũ'bradu/ a fig starry-eyed. **~bramento** m fig wonderment. **~brante** a dazzling. **~brar** vt dazzle. **~brar-se** vpr fig be dazzled

desmai|ado /dʒizmaj'adu/ a unconscious. **~ar** vi faint. **~o** m faint

desman|cha-prazeres /dʒizmãʃapra'zeris/ m/f invar spoilsport. **~char** vt break up; break off ‹noivado›; shatter ‹sonhos›. **~char-se** vpr break up; (no ar, na água, em lágrimas) dissolve

desmantelar /dʒizmãte'lar/ vt dismantle

desmarcar /dʒizmar'kar/ vt cancel ‹encontro›

desmascarar /dʒizmaske'rar/ vt unmask

desma|tamento /dʒizmata'mẽtu/ m deforestation. **~tar** vt clear (of forest)

desmedido /dʒizme'didu/ a excessive

desmemoriado /dʒizmemori'adu/ a forgetful

desmen|tido /dʒizmẽ'tʃidu/ m denial. **~tir** vt deny

desmiolado /dʒizmio'ladu/ a
brainless

desmontar /dʒizmõ'tar/ vt dismantle

desmorali|zante /dʒizmorali'zãtʃi/
a demoralizing. **~zar** vt demoralize

desmoro|namento
/dʒizmorona'mẽtu/ m collapse. **~nar** vt
destroy. **~nar-se** vpr collapse

desnatar /dʒizna'tar/ vi skim ‹leite›

desnecessário /dʒiznese'sariu/ a
unnecessary

desní|vel /dʒiz'nivew/ (pl **~veis**) m
difference in height

desnortear /dʒiznortʃi'ar/ vt
disorientate, Amer disorient

desnutrição /dʒiznutri'sãw/ f
malnutrition

desobe|decer /dʒizobede'ser/
vt/i **~decer (a)** disobey. **~diência** f
disobedience. **~diente** a disobedient

desobrigar /dʒizobri'gar/ vt release
(**de** from)

desobstruir /dʒizobstru'ir/ vt
unblock; empty ‹casa›

desocupado /dʒizoku'padu/ a
unoccupied

desodorante /dʒizodo'rãtʃi/ m, Port
desodorizante /dʒizoduri'zãtʃi/ m
deodorant

deso|lação /dezola'sãw/ f desolation.
~lado a ‹lugar› desolate; ‹pessoa›
desolated. **~lar** vt desolate

desones|tidade /dʒizonestʃi'dadʒi/ f
dishonesty. **~to** /ɛ/ a dishonest

deson|ra /dʒi'zõxa/ f dishonour. **~rar**
vt dishonour. **~roso** /o/ a
dishonourable

desor|deiro /dʒizor'deru/ a
troublemaking ● m troublemaker. **~dem**
f disorder. **~denado** a disorganized;
‹vida› disordered. **~denar** vt disorganize

desorgani|zação
/dʒizorganiza'sãw/ f disorganization.
~zar vt disorganize. **~zar-se** vpr get
disorganized

desorientar /dʒizorie'tar/ vt
disorientate; Amer disorient

desossar /dʒizo'sar/ vt bone

deso|va /dʒi'zɔva/ f roe. **~var** vi spawn

despa|chado /dʒispa'ʃadu/ a efficient.
~chante m/f (de mercadorias) shipping
agent; (de documentos) documentation
agent. **~char** vt deal with; dispatch,
forward ‹mercadorias›. **~cho** m dispatch

desparafusar /dʒisparafu'zar/ vt
unscrew

despedaçar /dʒispeda'sar/ vt (rasgar)
tear to pieces; (quebrar) smash. **~se** vpr
‹vidro, vaso› smash; ‹papel, tecido› tear

despe|dida /dʒispe'dʒida/ f farewell;
~dida de solteiro stag night, Amer
bachelor party. **~dir** vt dismiss; sack
‹empregado›. **~dir-se** vpr say goodbye
(**de** to)

despedimento /diʃpidi'mẽtu/ m Port
dismissal

despei|tado /dʒispej'tadu/ a spiteful.
~to m spite; **a ~to de** despite, in spite of

despe|jar /dʒispe'ʒar/ vt pour out
‹líquido›; empty ‹recipiente›; evict
‹inquilino›. **~jo** /e/ m (de inquilino)
eviction

despencar /dʒispẽ'kar/ vi plummet

despender /dʒispẽ'der/ vt spend
‹dinheiro›

despensa /dʒis'pẽsa/ f pantry, larder

despentear /dʒispẽtʃi'ar/ vt mess up
‹cabelo›; mess up the hair of ‹pessoa›

despercebido /dʒisperse'bidu/ a
unnoticed

desper|diçar /dʒisperdʒi'sar/ vt
waste. **~dício** m waste

desper|tador /dʒisperta'dor/ m alarm
clock. **~tar** vt rouse ‹pessoa›; fig arouse
‹interesse, suspeitas etc› ● vi awake

despesa /dʒis'peza/ f expense

des|pido /des'pidu/ a bare, stripped
(**de** of). **~pir** vt strip (**de** of); strip off
‹roupa›. **~pir-se** vpr strip (off), get
undressed

despo|jar /dʒispo'ʒar/ vt strip (**de** of).
~jar-se vpr divest o.s. (**de** of). **~jo** /o/
m spoils, booty; **~jos mortais** mortal
remains

despontar /dʒispõ'tar/ vi emerge

despor|tista /diʃpur'tiʃta/ Port m/f
sportsman (f -woman). **~tivo** Port a
sporting. **~to** /o/ Port m sport; **carro de
~to** sports car

déspota /'despota/ m/f despot

despótico /des'pɔtʃiku/ a despotic

despovoar /dʒispovo'ar/ vt
depopulate

desprender /dʒisprẽ'der/ vt detach;
(da parede) take down. **~se** vpr come
off; fig detach o.s.

despreocupado /dʒisprioku'padu/
a unconcerned

despreparado /dʒisprepa'radu/ a
unprepared

desprestigiar /dʒisprestʃiʒi'ar/ vt
discredit

despretensioso /dʒispretẽsi'ozu/ a unpretentious

desprevenido /dʒispreve'nidu/ a off one's guard, unprepared; **apanhar ~** catch unawares

despre|zar /dʒispre'zar/ vt despise; (*ignorar*) ignore. **~zível** (pl **~zíveis**) a despicable. **~zo** /e/ m contempt

desproporção /dʒispropor'sãw/ f disproportion

desproporcio|nado /dʒisproporsio'nadu/ a disproportionate. **~nal** (pl **~nais**) a disproportional

despropositado /dʒispropozi'tadu/ a (*absurdo*) preposterous

desprovido /dʒispro'vidu/ a **~ de** without

desqualificar /dʒiskwalifi'kar/ vt disqualify

desqui|tar-se /dʒiski'tarsi/ vpr (legally) separate. **~te** m (legal) separation

desrespei|tar /dʒizxespej'tar/ vt not respect; (*ignorar*) disregard. **~to** m disrespect. **~toso** /o/ a disrespectful

dessa(s), **desse(s)** = de + essa(s), esse(s)

desta = de + esta

desta|camento /dʒistaka'mẽtu/ m detachment. **~car** vt detach; (*ressaltar*) bring out, make stand out. **~car-se** vpr (*desprender-se*) come off; ‹*corredor*› break away; (*sobressair*) stand out (**sobre** against). **~cável** (pl **~cáveis**) a detachable; ‹*caderno*› pull-out

destam|pado /dʒistã'padu/ a (*panela*) uncovered. **~par** vt remove the lid of

destapar /dʒista'par/ vt uncover

destaque /dʒis'taki/ m prominence; (*coisa, pessoa*) highlight; (*do noticiário*) headline

destas, **deste** = de + estas, este

destemido /dʒiste'midu/ a intrepid, courageous

desterrar /dʒiste'xar/ vt (*exilar*) exile

destes = de + estes

destilar /desti'lar/ vt distil. **~ia** f distillery

desti|nado /dʒistʃi'nadu/ a (*fadado*) destined. **~nar** vt intend, mean (**para** for). **~natário** m addressee. **~no** m (*de viagem*) destination; (*sorte*) fate

destituir /dʒistʃitu'ir/ vt remove

desto|ante /dʒisto'ãtʃi/ a ‹*sons*› discordant; ‹*cores*› clashing. **~ar** vi **~ar de** clash with

destrancar /dʒistrã'kar/ vt unlock

destreza /des'treza/ f skill

destrinchar /dʒistrĩ'ʃar/ vt (*expor*) dissect; (*resolver*) sort out

destro /'destru/ a skilful

destro|çar /dʒistro'sar/ vt wreck. **~ços** m pl wreckage

destronar /dʒistro'nar/ vt depose

destroncar /dʒistrõ'kar/ vt rick

destru|ição /dʒistrui'sãw/ f destruction. **~idor** a destructive ● m destroyer. **~ir** vt destroy

desumano /dʒizu'manu/ a inhuman; (*cruel*) inhumane

desunião /dʒizuni'ãw/ f disunity

desu|sado /dʒizu'zadu/ a disused. **~so** m disuse

desvairado /dʒizvaj'radu/ a delirious, raving

desvalori|zação /dʒizvaloriza'sãw/ f devaluation. **~zar** vt devalue

desvanta|gem /dʒizvã'taʒẽ/ f disadvantage. **~joso** /o/ a disadvantageous

desve|lar /dʒizve'lar/ vt unveil; uncover ‹*segredo*›. **~lar-se** vpr go to a lot of trouble. **~lo** /e/ m great care

desvencilhar /dʒizvẽsi'ʎar/ vt extricate, free

desvendar /dʒizvẽ'dar/ vt reveal ‹*segredo*›; solve ‹*mistério*›

desventura /dʒizvẽ'tura/ f misfortune; (*infelicidade*) unhappiness

desviar /dʒizvi'ar/ vt divert ‹*trânsito, rio, atenção, dinheiro*›; avert ‹*golpe, suspeitas, olhos*›. **~se** vpr deviate; ‹*do tema*› digress

desvincular /dʒizvĩku'lar/ vt free

desvio /dʒiz'viu/ m diversion; (*do trânsito*) diversion, Amer detour; (*linha ferroviária*) siding

desvirtuar /dʒizvirtu'ar/ vt misrepresent ‹*verdade*›

deta|lhado /deta'ʎadu/ a detailed. **~lhar** vt detail. **~lhe** m detail

detec|tar /detek'tar/ vt detect. **~tor** m detector

de|tenção /detẽ'sãw/ f (*prisão*) detention. **~tentor** m holder. **~ter** vt (*ter*) hold; (*prender*) detain

detergente /deter'ʒẽtʃi/ m detergent

d

deterio|ração /deteriora'sãw/ f deterioration. **~rar** vt damage. **~rar-se** vpr deteriorate

determi|nação /determina'sãw/ f determination. **~nado** a (certo) certain; (resoluto) determined. **~nar** vt determine

detestar /detes'tar/ vt hate

detetive /dete'tʃivi/ m detective

detido /de'tʃidu/; pp de ▶ **DETER** ● a thorough ● m detainee

detonar /deto'nar/ vt detonate; ⓘ (criticar) pull to pieces ● vi detonate

detrás /de'traʃ/ adv behind ● prep ~ de behind

detrito /de'tritu/ m detritus

deturpar /detur'par/ vt misrepresent, distort

deus /dews/ m (f deusa) god (f goddess). **~dará m ao ~~dará** at the mercy of chance

devagar /dʒiva'gar/ adv slowly

deva|near /devani'ar/ vi daydream. **~neio** m daydream

devas|sar /deva'sar/ vt expose. **~sidão** f debauchery. **~so** a debauched

devastar /devas'tar/ vt devastate

devedor /deve'dor/ a debit ● m debtor

---

dever /de'ver/ ● vt

····▸ (seguido de substantivo) owe; **devo R$5/uma explicação para você** I owe you R$5/an explanation (seguido de infinitivo: obrigação) must; **você deve estudar!** you must study!; **ela já deve estar em casa** she must be at home by now; **não deve ser fácil!** it can't be easy (seguido de infinitivo: conselho, crítica) should; **você não devia sair assim!** you shouldn't go out like that!; **você deveria ter vindo mais cedo** you should have come earlier

● vpr

····▸ **~se a algo** be due to sth; **isso se deve à falta de recursos** that's due to a lack of funds

● m

····▸ duty; **cumprir o ~** do one's duty

····▸ (em expressões) **como deve ser:** **uma carta como deve ser** a proper letter; **coma como deve ser** eat properly

---

de|vido /devi'do/ a due (a to); **~voção** f devotion

de|volução /devolu'sãw/ f return. **~volver** vt return

devorar /devo'rar/ vt devour

devo|tar /devo'tar/ vt devote. **~tar-se** vpr devote o.s. (a to). **~to** /ɔ/ a devout

dez /dɛs/ a & m ten

dezanove /dza'nɔv/ Port a & m nineteen

dezas|seis /dza'sejʃ/ Port a & m sixteen. **~sete** /ɛ/ Port a & m seventeen

dezembro /de'zẽbru/ m December

deze|na /de'zena/ f ten; **uma ~ (de)** about ten. **~nove** /ɔ/ a & m nineteen

dezes|seis /dʒize'sejʃ/ a & m sixteen. **~sete** /ɛ/ a & m seventeen

dezoito /dʒi'zojtu/ a & m eighteen

dia /'dʒia/ m day; **de ~** by day; **(no) ~ 20 de julho** (on) July 20th; **~ de folga** day off; **~ útil** working day. **o ~ a ~** m everyday life

dia|bete /dʒia'betʃi/ f diabetes. **~bético** a & m diabetic

dia|bo /dʒia'bu/ m devil. **~bólico** a diabolical, devilish. **~brete** /e/ m little devil. **~brura** f (de criança) bit of mischief; pl mischief

diadema /dʒia'dema/ m tiara

diafragma /dʒia'fragima/ m diaphragm

diag|nosticar /dʒiagnostʃi'kar/ vt diagnose. **~nóstico** m diagnosis ● a diagnostic

diago|nal /dʒiago'naw/ (pl **~nais**) a & f diagonal

diagra|ma /dʒia'grama/ m diagram. **~mação** f design. **~mador** m designer. **~mar** vt design ‹livro, revista›

dia|lética /dʒia'letʃika/ f dialectics. **~leto** /ɛ/ m dialect

dialogar /dʒialo'gar/ vi talk; Pol hold talks

diálogo /dʒi'alogu/ m dialogue

diamante /dʒia'mãtʃi/ m diamond

diâmetro /dʒi'ametru/ m diameter

dian|te /dʒi'ãtʃi/ adv de ... em **~te** from ... on(wards); **~te de** (enfrentando) faced with; (perante) before. **~teira** f lead. **~teiro** a front

diapasão /dʒiapa'zãw/ m tuning fork

diapositivo /dʒiapozi'tʃivu/ m transparency

diá|ria /dʒi'aria/ f daily rate. **~rio** a daily

diarista /dʒia'rista/ m/f day labourer; (faxineira) daily (help)

diarreia /dʒia'xeja/ f diarrhoea

dica /'dʒika/ f tip, hint

dicção /dʒik'sãw/ f diction

dicionário /dʒisio'nariu/ m dictionary

didáti|ca /dʒi'datʃika/ f teaching methodology. **~co** a teaching; ‹livro› educational; ‹estilo› didactic

die|ta /dʒi'eta/ f diet; **de ~ta** on a diet. **~tista** m/f dietician

difa|mação /dʒifama'sãw/ f defamation. **~mar** vt defame. **~matório** a defamatory

diferen|ça /dʒife'rẽsa/ f difference. **~cial** (pl **~ciais**) a & f differential. **~ciar** vt differentiate. **~ciar-se** vpr differ. **~te** a different

dife|rimento /dʒiferi'mẽtu/ m deferment. **~rir** vt defer ● vi differ

difí|cil /dʒi'fisiw/ (pl **~ceis**) a difficult; (improvável) unlikely

dificilmente /dʒifisiw'mẽtʃi/ adv **~ poderá fazê-lo** he's unlikely to be able to do it

dificul|dade /dʒifikuw'dadʒi/ f difficulty. **~tar** vt make difficult

difteria /dʒifte'ria/ f diphtheria

difun|dir /dʒifũ'dʒir/ vt spread; (pela rádio) broadcast; diffuse ‹luz, calor›. **~dir-se** vpr spread

difu|são /dʒifu'zãw/ f diffusion. **~so** a diffuse

dige|rir /dʒiʒe'rir/ vt digest. **~rível** (pl **~ríveis**) a digestible

diges|tão /dʒiʒes'tãw/ f digestion. **~tivo** a digestive

digi|tal /dʒiʒi'taw/ (pl **~tais**) a digital; **impressão ~tal** fingerprint. **~tar** vt key

dígito /'dʒiʒitu/ m digit

digladiar /dʒigladʒi'ar/ vi do battle

dig|nar-se /dʒig'narsi/ vpr deign (de to). **~nidade** f dignity. **~nificar** vt dignify. **~no** a worthy (de of); (decoroso) dignified

digressão /dʒigrə'sãw/ f Port (de concerto, volta de bicicleta) tour

dilace|rante /dʒilase'rãtʃi/ a ‹dor› excruciating. **~rar** vt tear to pieces

dilapidar /dʒilapi'dar/ vt squander

dilatar /dʒila'tar/ vt expand; Med dilate. **~-se** vpr expand; Med dilate

dilema /dʒi'lema/ m dilemma

diletante /dʒile'tãtʃi/ a & m/f dilettante

dili|gência /dʒili'ʒẽsia/ f diligence; (carruagem) stagecoach. **~gente** a diligent, hard-working

diluir /dʒilu'ir/ vt dilute

dilúvio /dʒi'luviu/ m deluge

dimen|são /dʒimẽ'sãw/ f dimension. **~sionar** vt size up

diminu|ição /dʒiminui'sãw/ f reduction. **~ir** vt reduce ● vi lessen; ‹carro, motorista› slow down. **~tivo** a & m diminutive. **~to** a minute

Dinamarca /dʒina'marka/ f Denmark

dinamar|quês /dʒinamar'kes/ (f **~quesa**) a Danish ● m Dane

dinâmi|ca /dʒi'namika/ f dynamics. **~co** a dynamic

dina|mismo /dʒina'mizmu/ m dynamism. **~mite** f dynamite

dínamo /'dʒinamu/ m dynamo

dinastia /dʒinas'tʃia/ f dynasty

dinda /'dʒida/ f 🔲 godmother

dinheiro /dʒi'ɲeru/ m money

dinossauro /dʒino'sawru/ m dinosaur

diocese /dʒio'sezi/ f diocese

dióxido /dʒi'ɔksidu/ m dioxide; **~ de carbono** carbon dioxide

diplo|ma /dʒi'ploma/ m diploma. **~macia** f diplomacy. **~mar-se** vpr take one's diploma. **~mata** m/f diplomat ● a diplomatic. **~mático** a diplomatic

direção /dʒire'sãw/ f (sentido) direction; (de empresa) management; (condução de carro) driving; (manuseio do volante) steering

direi|ta /dʒi'rejta/ f right. **~tinho** adv exactly right. **~tista** a right-wing ● m/f right-winger, rightist. **~to** a right; (ereto) straight ● adv properly ● m right

dire|tas /dʒi'retas/ f pl direct (presidential) elections. **~to** a direct ● adv directly. **~tor** m director; (de escola) head teacher; (de jornal) editor; **~tor-gerente** managing director. **~toria** f (diretores) board of directors; (sala) boardroom. **~tório** m directory. **~triz** f directive

diri|gente /dʒiri'ʒẽtʃi/ a leading ● m/f leader. **~gir** vt direct; manage ‹empresa›; drive ‹carro›. **~gir-se** vpr (ir) make one's way; **~gir-se a** (falar com) address

dis|cagem /dʒis'kaʒẽ/ f dialling; **~cagem rápida** speed dialling. **~car** vt/i dial

discente /dʒi'sẽtʃi/ a **corpo ~** student body

discer|nimento /dʒiserni'mẽtu/ m discernment. **~nir** vt discern

discipli|na /dʒisi'plina/ f discipline. **~nador** a disciplinary. **~nar** vt discipline

discípulo /dʒi'sipulu/ m disciple

disco-jóquei /dʒisk'ɔkej/ m disc jockey

disco /'dʒisku/ m disc; (de música) record; (no atletismo) discus ● vf 🗓 disco; **~ flexível/rígido** floppy/hard disk; **~ laser** CD, compact disc; **~ voador** flying saucer

discor|dante /dʒiskor'dãtʃi/ a conflicting. **~dar** vi disagree (**de** with)

discote|ca /dʒisko'tɛka/ f discotheque. **~cário** m DJ

discre|pância /dʒiskre'pãsia/ f discrepancy. **~pante** a inconsistent. **~par** vi diverge (**de** from)

dis|creto /dʒis'krɛtu/ a discreet. **~crição** f discretion

discrimi|nação /dʒiskrimina'sãw/ f discrimination; (descrição) description. **~nar** vt discriminate. **~natório** a discriminatory

discur|sar /dʒiskur'sar/ vi speak. **~so** m speech

discussão /dʒisku'sãw/ f discussion; (briga) argument

discu|tir /dʒisku'tʃir/ vt/i discuss; (brigar) argue. **~tível** (pl **~tíveis**) a debatable

disenteria /dʒizẽte'ria/ f dysentery

disfar|çar /dʒisfar'sar/ vt disguise. **~çar-se** vpr disguise o.s. **~ce** m disguise

dis|lético /dʒiz'lɛtʃiku/ a & m dyslexic. **~lexia** f dyslexia. **~léxico** a & m dyslexic

dispa|rada /dʒispa'rada/ f bolt. **~rado** adv o melhor **~rado** the best by a long way. **~rar** vt fire ‹arma› ● vi (com arma) fire; ‹preços, inflação› shoot up; ‹corredor› surge ahead

disparate /dʒispa'ratʃi/ m piece of nonsense; pl nonsense

dis|pêndio /dʒis'pẽdʒiu/ m expenditure. **~pendioso** /o/ a costly

dispen|sa /dʒis'pẽsa/ f exemption. **~sar** vt (distribuir) dispense; (isentar) exempt (**de** from); (prescindir de) dispense with. **~sável** (pl **~sáveis**) a dispensable

dispersar /dʒisper'sar/ vt disperse; waste ‹energias› ● vi, **~se** vpr disperse

disperso /dʒis'pɛrsu/ a scattered

dispo|nibilidade /dʒisponibili'dadʒi/ f availability. **~nível** (pl **~níveis**) a available

dis|por /dʒis'por/ vt arrange ● vi **~por de** have at one's disposal. **~por-se** vpr form up ● m **ao seu ~por** at your disposal. **~posição** f (vontade) willingness; (arranjo) arrangement; (de espírito) frame of mind; (de testamento etc) provision; **à ~posição de alguém** at sb's disposal. **~positivo** m device. **~posto** a prepared, willing (**a** to)

dispu|ta /dʒis'puta/ f dispute. **~tar** vt dispute; (tentar ganhar) compete for

disquete /dʒis'ketʃi/ m diskette, floppy (disk)

dissabores /dʒisa'boris/ m pl troubles

disseminar /dʒisemi'nar/ vt disseminate

dissertação /dʒiserta'sãw/ f dissertation, lecture

dissi|dência /dʒisi'dẽsia/ f dissidence. **~dente** a & m dissident

dissídio /dʒi'sidʒiu/ m dispute

dissimular /dʒisimu'lar/ vt hide ● vi dissimulate

dissipar /dʒisi'par/ vt clear ‹nevoeiro›; dispel ‹dúvidas, suspeitas, ilusões›; dissipate ‹fortuna›. **~se** vpr ‹nevoeiro› clear; ‹dúvidas etc› be dispelled

disso = de + isso

dissolu|ção /dʒisolu'sãw/ f dissolution. **~to** a dissolute

dissolver /dʒisow'ver/ vt dissolve. **~se** vpr dissolve

dissuadir /dʒisua'dʒir/ vt dissuade (**de** from)

distância /dʒis'tãsia/ f distance

distan|ciar /dʒistãsi'ar/ vt distance. **~ciar-se** vpr distance o.s.. **~te** a distant

disten|der /dʒistẽ'der/ vt stretch ‹pernas›; relax ‹músculo›. **~der-se** vpr relax. **~são** f Med pull; **~são muscular** pulled muscle

distin|ção /dʒistʃĩ'sãw/ f distinction. **~guir** vt distinguish (**de** from). **~guir-se** vpr distinguish o.s.. **~tivo** a distinctive ● m badge. **~to** a distinct; ‹senhor› distinguished

disto = de + isto

distor|ção /dʒistor'sãw/ f distortion. **~cer** vt distort

distra|ção /dʒistra'sãw/ f distraction. **~ido** a absent-minded. **~ir** vt distract; (divertir) amuse. **~ir-se** vpr be distracted; (divertir-se) amuse o.s.

distribu|ição /dʒistribui'sãw/ f distribution. **~idor** m distributor. **~idora** f distributor, distribution company. **~ir**

vt distribute

distrito /dʒis'tritu/ m district

distúrbio /dʒis'turbiu/ m trouble

di|tado /dʒi'tadu/ m dictation; (provérbio) saying. **~tador** m dictator. **~tadura** f dictatorship. **~tame** m dictate. **~tar** vt dictate. **~tatorial** (pl **~tatoriais**) a dictatorial

dito /'dʒitu/ a **~ e feito** no sooner said than done ● m remark

ditongo /dʒi'tõgu/ m diphthong

DIU /'dʒiu/ m IUD, coil

diurno /dʒi'urnu/ a day

divã /dʒi'vã/ m couch

divagar /dʒiva'gar/ vi digress

diver|gência /dʒiver'ʒẽsia/ a divergence. **~gente** a divergent. **~gir** vi diverge (**de** from). **~são** f diversion; (divertimento) amusement. **~sidade** f diversity. **~sificar** vt/i diversify. **~so** /ɛ/ a (diferente) diverse; pl (vários) several. **~tido** a (engraçado) funny; (que se curte) enjoyable. **~timento** m enjoyment, fun; (um) amusement. **~tir** vt amuse. **~tir-se** vpr enjoy o.s., have fun

dívida /'dʒivida/ f debt; **~ externa** foreign debt

divi|dendo /dʒivi'dẽdu/ m dividend. **~dido** a (pessoa) torn. **~dir** vt divide; (compartilhar) share. **~dir-se** vpr be divided

divindade /dʒivĩ'dadʒi/ f divinity

divino /dʒi'vinu/ a divine

divi|sa /dʒi'viza/ f (lema) motto; (galão) stripes; (fronteira) border; pl foreign currency. **~são** f division. **~sória** f partition

divorci|ado /dʒivorsi'adu/ a divorced ● m divorcé (f divorcée). **~ar** vt divorce. **~ar-se** vpr get divorced; **~ar-se de** divorce

divórcio /dʒi'vɔrsiu/ m divorce

divul|gado /dʒivuw'gadu/ a widespread. **~gar** vt spread; publish (notícia); divulge (segredo). **~gar-se** vpr be spread

dizer /dʒi'zer/ vt say; **~ a alguém que** tell sb that; **~ para alguém fazer** tell sb to do ● vi **~ com** go with. **~-se** vpr claim to be ● m saying

dizimar /dʒizi'mar/ vt decimate

do ▸ DE + O

dó /dɔ/ m pity; **dar ~** be pitiful; **ter ~ de** feel sorry for

do|ação /doa'sãw/ f donation. **~ador** m donor. **~ar** vt donate

do|bra /'dɔbra/ f fold; (de calça) turn-up, Amer cuff. **~bradiça** f hinge. **~bradiço** a pliable. **~brado** a (duplo) double. **~brar** vt (duplicar) double; (fazer dobra em) fold; (curvar) bend; go round (esquina); ring (sinos); Port dub (filme) ● vi double; (sinos) ring. **~brar-se** vpr bend. **~bro** m double

doca /'dɔka/ f dock

doce /'dosi/ a sweet; (água) fresh ● m sweet; **~ de leite** fudge

docente /do'sẽtʃi/ a teaching; **corpo ~** teaching staff, Amer faculty

dó|cil /'dɔsiw/ (pl **~ceis**) a docile

documen|tação /dokumẽta'sãw/ f documentation. **~tar** vt document. **~tário** a & m documentary. **~to** m document

doçura /do'sura/ f sweetness

dodói /do'dɔj/ 🄝 m ter **~** have a pain ● a poorly, ill

doen|ça /do'ẽsa/ f illness; (infecciosa) fig disease; **~ da vaca louca** mad cow disease. **~te** a ill. **~tio** a (criança, aspecto) sickly; (interesse, curiosidade) morbid

doer /do'er/ vi hurt; (cabeça, músculo) ache

dog|ma /'dɔgima/ m dogma. **~mático** a dogmatic

doido /'dojdu/ a crazy

dois /dojs/ a & m (f **duas**) two

dólar /'dɔlar/ m dollar

dolo|rido /dolo'ridu/ a sore. **~roso** /o/ a painful

dom /dõ/ m gift

do|mador /doma'dor/ m tamer. **~mar** vt tame

doméstica /do'mestʃika/ f housemaid

domesticar /domestʃi'kar/ vt domesticate

doméstico /do'mestʃiku/ a domestic

domi|ciliar /domisili'ar/ a home. **~cílio** m home

domi|nação /domina'sãw/ f domination. **~nador** a domineering. **~nante** a dominant. **~nar** vt dominate; have a command of (língua). **~nar-se** vpr control o.s.

domin|go /do'mĩgu/ m Sunday. **~gueiro** a Sunday

domini|cal /domini'kaw/ (pl **~cais**) a Sunday. **~cano** a & m Dominican

domínio /do'miniu/ m command

dona /'dona/ f owner; **D~** (com nome) Miss. **~ de casa** housewife

d

donativo /dona'tʃivu/ m donation

donde /'dõdʒi/ adv from where; (motivo) from whence

dono /'donu/ m owner

donut /'donut/ m doughnut

donzela /dõ'zela/ f maiden

dopar /do'par/ vt drug

dor /dor/ f pain; (menos aguda) ache; ~ de cabeça headache

dor|mente /dor'mẽtʃi/ a numb ● m sleeper. ~mida f sleep. ~minhoco /o/ m sleepyhead. ~mir vi sleep. ~mitar vi doze. ~mitório m bedroom; (comunitário) dormitory

dorso /'dorsu/ m back; (de livro) spine

dos = de + os

do|sagem /do'zaʒẽ/ f dosage. ~sar vt moderate. ~se /ɔ/ f dose; (de uísque etc) shot, measure

dossiê /dosi'e/ m file

do|tação /dota'sãw/ f endowment. ~tado a gifted; ~tado de endowed with. ~tar vt endow (de with). ~te /ɔ/ m (de noiva) dowry; (dom) endowment

dou|rado /do'radu/ a (de cor) golden; (revestido de ouro) gilded, gilt ● m gilt. ~rar vt gild

dou|to /'dotu/ a learned. ~tor m doctor. ~torado m doctorate, PhD. ~trina f doctrine. ~trinar vt indoctrinate

doutoramento /dotora'mẽtu/ m PhD

doze /'dozi/ a & m twelve

dragão /dra'gãw/ m dragon

dragar /dra'gar/ vt dredge

drágea /'draʒia/ f lozenge

dra|ma /'drama/ m drama. ~malhão m melodrama. ~mático a dramatic. ~matizar vt dramatize. ~maturgo m dramatist, playwright

drapeado /drapi'adu/ a draped

drástico /'drastʃiku/ a drastic

dre|nagem /dre'naʒẽ/ f drainage. ~nar vt drain. ~no /ɛ/ m drain

driblar /dri'blar/ vt (em futebol) dribble round, beat; fig get round

drinque /'drĩki/ m drink

drive /'drajvi/ m disk drive

dro|ga /'drɔga/ f drug; Ⅱ (coisa sem valor) dead loss; (coisa chata) drag ● int damn. ~gado a on drugs ● m drug addict. ~gar vt drug. ~gar-se vpr take drugs. ~garia f dispensing chemist's, pharmacy

duas /'duas/ ▶ **DOIS**

dúbio /'dubiu/ a dubious

dub|lagem /du'blaʒẽ/ f dubbing. ~lar vt dub ‹filme›; mime ‹música›. ~lê m double

ducentésimo /dusẽ'tezimu/ a two-hundredth

ducha /'dusa/ f shower

duche /'duse/ m Port shower

ducto /'duktu/ m duct

duelo /du'ɛlu/ m duel

duende /du'ẽdʒi/ m elf

dueto /du'etu/ m duet

duna /'duna/ f dune

duodécimo /duo'dɛsimu/ a twelfth

duodeno /duo'dɛnu/ m duodenum

dupla /'dupla/ f pair, duo; ‹no tênis› doubles

duplex /du'plɛks/ a invar two-floor ● m invar two-floor apartment, Amer duplex

dupli|car /dupli'kar/ vt/i double. ~cidade f duplicity. ~cata f duplicate

duplo /'duplu/ a double

duque /'duki/ m duke. ~sa /e/ f duchess

du|ração /dura'sãw/ f duration. ~radouro a lasting. ~rante prep during. ~rar vi last. ~rável (pl ~ráveis) a durable

durex® /du'rɛks/ m invar Sellotape®

du|reza /du'reza/ f hardness. ~ro a hard; Ⅱ (sem dinheiro) hard up, broke

dúvida /'duvida/ f doubt; (pergunta) query

duvi|dar /duvi'dar/ vt/i doubt. ~doso /o/ a doubtful

duzentos /du'zẽtus/ a & m two hundred

dúzia /'duzia/ f dozen

DVD /deve'de/ m DVD; gravador de ~ DVD burner; leitor de ~ DVD player

Ee

e /i/ conj and

ébano /'ɛbanu/ m ebony

ébrio /'ɛbriu/ a drunk ● m drunkard

ebulição /ebuli'sãw/ f boiling

eclesiástico /eklezi'astʃiku/ a ecclesiastical

eclético /e'klɛtʃiku/ a eclectic

eclip|sar /eklip'sar/ vt eclipse. **~se** m eclipse

eclodir /eklo'dʒir/ vi emerge; (estourar) break out; ‹flor› open

eco /'ɛku/ m echo; **ter ~** have repercussions. **~ar** vt/i echo

ecografia /ekogra'fia/ f ultrasound (scan)

eco|logia /ekolo'ʒia/ f ecology. **~lógico** /eko'lɔʒiku/ a ecological; **grupo ~lógico** environmental group. **~logista** m/f ecologist

eco|nomia /ekono'mia/ f economy; (ciência) economics; pl (dinheiro poupado) savings. **~nômico** a economic; (rentável, barato) economical. **~nomista** m/f economist. **~nomizar** vt save ● vi economize

ecoponto /ɛkɔ'põtu/ m Port recycling point

ecossistema /ekosis'tema/ m ecosystem

écran /e'krã/ Port m screen

eczema /ek'zɛma/ m eczema

edição /edʒi'sãw/ f edition; (de filmes) editing

edificante /edʒifi'kãtʃi/ a edifying

edifício /edʒi'fisiu/ m building

Edimburgo /edʒi'burgu/ f Edinburgh

edi|tal /edʒi'taw/ (pl ~tais) m announcement. **~tar** vt publish; Comput edit. **~to** m edict. **~tor** m publisher. **~tora** f publishing company. **~torial** (pl ~toriais) a publishing ● m editorial

edredom /edre'dõ/ m, Port **edredão** /edre'dãw/ m quilt

educa|ção /eduka'sãw/ f (ensino) education; (polidez) good manners; **é falta de ~ção** it's rude. **~cional** (pl ~cionais) a education

edu|cado /edu'kadu/ a polite. **~car** vt educate. **~cativo** a educational

EEB /ee'be/ f BSE

efeito /e'fejtu/ m effect; **fazer ~** have an effect; **para todos os ~s** to all intents and purposes; **~ colateral** side effect; **~ estufa** greenhouse effect

efêmero /e'fēmeru/ a ephemeral

efeminado /efemi'nadu/ a effeminate

efervescente /eferve'sētʃi/ a effervescent

efe|tivar /efetʃi'var/ vt bring into effect; (contratar) make a permanent member of staff. **~tivo** a real, effective; ‹cargo, empregado› permanent. **~tuar** vt carry out, effect

efi|cácia /efi'kasia/ f effectiveness. **~caz** a effective

efici|ência /efisi'ēsia/ f efficiency. **~ente** a efficient

efigie /e'fiʒi/ f effigy

Egeu /e'ʒew/ a & m Aegean

égide /'ɛʒidʒi/ f aegis

egipcio /e'ʒipsiu/ a & m Egyptian

Egito /e'ʒitu/ m Egypt

ego /'ɛgu/ m ego. **~cêntrico** a self-centred, egocentric. **~ismo** m selfishness. **~ista** a selfish ● m/f egoist ● m (de rádio etc) earplug

égua /'ɛgwa/ f mare

eis /ejs/ adv (aqui está) here is/are; (isso é) that is

eixo /'ejʃu/ m axle; Mat (entre cidades) axis; **pôr nos ~s** set straight

---

ela /'ɛla/ ● pron

····➤ (pessoa) she; **~ e Catarina são primas** she and Catarina are cousins; (complemento, em comparações) her; **é para ~** it's for her; **você é mais alto do que ~** you're taller than her; (coisa) it; **~ mesma** (she) herself

---

elaborar /elabo'rar/ vt (fazer) make, produce; (desenvolver) work out

elasticidade /elastʃisi'dadʒi/ f (de coisa) elasticity; (de pessoa) suppleness

elástico /e'lastʃiku/ a elastic ● m (de borracha) elastic band; (de calcinha etc) elastic

---

ele /'eli/ ● pron

····➤ (pessoa) he; **~ e José são primos** he and José are cousins; **~ é um rapaz simpático** he's a nice boy; (complemento, em comparações) him; **é para ~** it's for him; **você é mais alto do que ~** you're taller than him; (coisa) it; **~ mesmo** (he) himself

---

elefante /ele'fãtʃi/ m elephant

ele|gância /ele'gãsia/ f elegance. **~gante** a elegant

eleger /ele'ʒer/ vt elect. **~se** vpr get elected

elegia /ele'ʒia/ f elegy

elei|ção /elej'sãw/ f election. **~to** a elected, elect; ‹povo› chosen. **~tor** m voter. **~torado** m electorate. **~toral** (pl ~torais) a electoral

elemen|tar /elemē'tar/ a elementary. **~to** m element

elenco /e'lēku/ m (de filme, peça) cast

e

eles /'elis/, **elas** /'ɛlas/, ● *pron*

····▸ (*sujeito*) they; (*complemento, em comparações*) them; **isto é para eles** this is for them

····▸ (*em expressões*) **agora é que são elas!** now comes the difficult part!; **elas por elas: o plano do governo deu elas por elas** the government's plan made no difference

eletri|cidade /eletrisi'dadʒi/ *f* electricity. **~cista** *m/f* electrician

elétrico /i'lɛktriku/ *Port* tram, *Amer* streetcar ● *a* electric

eletri|ficar /eletrifi'kar/ *vt* electrify. **~zar** *vt* electrify

eletro /e'lɛtru/ *m* ECG. **~cutar** *vt* electrocute. **~do** /o/ *m* electrode. **~domésticos** *m pl* electrical appliances

eletrôni|ca /ele'tronika/ *f* electronics. **~co** *a* electronic

ele|vação /eleva'sãw/ *f* elevation; (*aumento*) rise. **~vado** *a* high; ‹*sentimento, estilo*› elevated. **~vador** *m* lift, *Amer* elevator. **~var** *vt* raise; (*promover*) elevate. **~var-se** *vpr* rise

elimi|nar /elimi'nar/ *vt* eliminate. **~natória** *f* heat. **~natório** *a* eliminatory

elipse /e'lipsi/ *f* ellipse

elíptico /e'liptʃiku/ *a* elliptical

eli|te /e'litʃi/ *f* elite. **~tismo** *m* elitism. **~tista** *a* & *m/f* elitist

elmo /'ɛwmu/ *m* helmet

elo /'ɛlu/ *m* link

elo|giar /eloʒi'ar/ *vt* praise; **~giar alguém por** compliment sb on. **~gio** *m* (*louvor*) praise; (*um*) compliment. **~gioso** /o/ *a* complimentary

elo|quência /elo'kwẽsia/ *f* eloquence. **~quente** *a* eloquent

eluci|dar /elusi'dar/ *vt* elucidate. **~dativo** *a* elucidatory

em /ẽj/ *prep* in; (*sobre*) on; **ela está no Eduardo** she's at Eduardo's (house); **de casa ~ casa** from house to house; **aumentar ~ 10%** increase by 10%

emagre|cer /emagre'ser/ *vi* lose weight, get thinner ● *vt* make thinner. **~cimento** *m* slimming

emanar /ema'nar/ *vi* emanate (**de** from)

emanci|pação /emãsipa'sãw/ *f* emancipation. **~par** *vt* emancipate. **~par-se** *vpr* become emancipated

emara|nhado /emara'ɲadu/ *a* tangled ● *m* tangle. **~nhar** *vt* tangle;

(*envolver*) entangle. **~nhar-se** *vpr* get tangled up; (*envolver-se*) become entangled (**em** in)

embaçar /ĩba'sar/, *Port* **embaciar** /ĩbasi'ar/ *vt* steam up ‹*vidro*› ● *vi* ‹*vidro*› steam up; ‹*olhos*› grow misty

embainhar /ĩbaj'ɲar/ *vt* hem ‹*vestido, calça*›

embaixa|da /ĩba'ʃada/ *f* embassy. **~dor** *m* ambassador. **~triz** *f* ambassador; (*esposa*) ambassador's wife

embaixo /ĩ'baʃu/ *adv* underneath; (*em casa*) downstairs; **~ de** under

emba|lagem /ĩba'laʒẽ/ *f* packaging

emba|lar /ĩba'lar/ *vt* pack; (*move back and forth*) rock ‹*criança*›. **~lo** *m fig* excitement, thrill

embalsamar /ĩbawsa'mar/ *vt* embalm

embara|çar /ĩbara'sar/ *vt* embarrass. **~çar-se** *vpr* get embarrassed (**com** by). **~ço** *m* embarrassment. **~çoso** /o/ *a* embarrassing

embaralhar /ĩbara'ʎar/ *vt* muddle up; shuffle ‹*cartas*›. **~-se** *vpr* get muddled up

embar|cação /ĩbarka'sãw/ *f* vessel. **~cadouro** *m* wharf. **~car** *vt/i* board, embark

embar|gado /ĩbar'gadu/ *a* ‹*voz*› faltering. **~go** *m* embargo

embarque /ĩ'barki/ *m* boarding; (*seção do aeroporto*) departures

embasba|cado /ĩbazba'kadu/ *a* open-mouthed. **~car-se** *vpr* be left open-mouthed

embate /ĩ'batʃi/ *m* (*de carros etc*) crash; *fig* clash

embebedar /ĩbebe'dar/ *vt* make drunk. **~se** *vpr* get drunk

embeber /ĩbe'ber/ *vt* soak; **~se de** soak up; **~se em** get absorbed in

embele|zador /ĩbeleza'dor/ *a* ‹*cirurgia*› cosmetic. **~zar** *vt* embellish; spruce up ‹*casa*›. **~zar-se** *vpr* make o.s. beautiful

embevecer /ĩbeve'ser/ *vt* captivate, engross. **~se** *vpr* get engrossed, be captivated

emblema /ẽ'blema/ *m* emblem

embocadura /ĩboka'dura/ *f* (*de instrumento*) mouthpiece; (*de freio*) bit; (*de rio*) mouth; (*de rua*) entrance

êmbolo /'ẽbulu/ *m* piston

embolsar /ĩbow'sar/ *vt* pocket; (*reembolsar*) reimburse

embora /ĩ'bɔra/ *adv* away ● *conj* although

emborcar /ĩbor'kar/ *vi* overturn; ‹*barco*› capsize

emboscada /ĩbos'kada/ *f* ambush

embrai|agem /ẽbraj'aʒẽ/ *Port f* ▶ EMBREAGEM. ~**ar** *Port vi* ▶ EMBREAR

embre|agem /ẽbri'aʒẽ/ *f* clutch. ~**ar** *vi* let in the clutch

embria|gar /ẽbria'gar/ *vt* intoxicate. ~**gar-se** *vpr* get drunk, become intoxicated. ~**guez** /e/ *f* drunkenness; ~**guez no volante** drunken driving

embri|ão /ẽbri'ãw/ *m* embryo. ~**onário** *a* embryonic

embro|mação /ĩbroma'sãw/ *f* flannel. ~**mar** *vt* flannel, string along; (*enganar*) con ● *vi* stall, drag one's feet

embru|lhada /ĩbru'ʎada/ *f* muddle. ~**lhar** *vt* wrap up ‹*pacote*›; upset ‹*estômago*›; (*confundir*) muddle up. ~**lhar-se** *vpr* ‹*pessoa*› get muddled up. ~**lho** *m* parcel; *fig* mix-up

embur|rado /ĩbu'xadu/ *a* sulky. ~**rar** *vi* sulk

embuste /ĩ'bustʃi/ *m* hoax, put-up job

embu|tido /ĩbu'tʃidu/ *a* built-in, fitted. ~**tir** *vt* build in, fit

emen|da /e'mẽda/ *f* correction, improvement; (*de lei*) amendment. ~**dar** *vt* correct; amend ‹*lei*›. ~**dar-se** *vpr* mend one's ways

ementa /i'mẽta/ *Port f* menu

emer|gência /emer'ʒẽsia/ *f* emergency. ~**gente** *a* emergent. ~**gir** *vi* surface

emi|gração /emigra'sãw/ *f* emigration; (*de aves etc*) migration. ~**grado** *a & m* émigré. ~**grante** *a & m/f* emigrant. ~**grar** *vi* emigrate; ‹*aves, animais*› migrate

emi|nência /emi'nẽsia/ *f* eminence. ~**nente** *a* eminent

emis|são /emi'sãw/ *f* (*de ações etc*) issue; (*na rádio, TV*) transmission, broadcast; (*de som, gases*) emission. ~**sário** *m* emissary. ~**sor** *m* transmitter. ~**sora** *f* (*de rádio*) radio station; (*de TV*) TV station

emitir /emi'tʃir/ *vt* issue ‹*ações, selos etc*›; emit ‹*sons*›; (*pela rádio, TV*) transmit, broadcast

emoção /emo'sãw/ *f* emotion; (*excitação*) excitement

emocio|nal /emosio'naw/ (*pl* ~**nais**) *a* emotional. ~**nante** *a* (*excitante*) exciting; (*comovente*) touching, emotional. ~**nar**

vt (*excitar*) excite; (*comover*) move, touch. ~**nar-se** *vpr* get emotional

emoldurar /emowdu'rar/ *vt* frame

emotivo /emo'tʃivu/ *a* emotional

empacar /ĩpa'kar/ *vi* ‹*cavalo*› baulk; ‹*negociações etc*› grind to a halt; ‹*orador*› dry up

empacotar /ĩpako'tar/ *vt* pack up; (*pôr em pacotes*) packet

empa|da /ẽ'pada/ *f* pie. ~**dão** *m* (large) pie

empalhar /ĩpa'ʎar/ *vt* stuff

empalidecer /ĩpalide'ser/ *vi* turn pale

empanar¹ /ẽpa'nar/ *vt* tarnish, dull

empanar² /ẽpa'nar/ *vt* cook in batter ‹*carne etc*›

empanturrar /ĩpãtu'xar/ *vt* stuff. ~**se** *vpr* stuff o.s. (**de** with)

empapar /ĩpa'par/ *vt* soak

empa|tar /ẽpa'tar/ *vt* draw ‹*jogo*› ● *vi* ‹*times*› draw; ‹*corredores*› tie. ~**te** *m* (*em jogo*) draw; (*em corrida, votação*) tie; (*em xadrez*) *fig* stalemate

empatia /ẽpa'tʃia/ *f* empathy

empecilho /ẽpe'siʎu/ *m* hindrance

empenar /ẽpe'nar/ *vt/i* warp

empe|nhar /ẽpe'nar/ *vt* (*penhorar*) pawn; (*prometer*) pledge. ~**nhar-se** *vpr* do one's utmost (**em** to). ~**nho** /e/ *m* (*compromisso*) pledge; (*diligência*) effort, commitment

emperrar /ĩpe'xar/ *vt* make stick ● *vi* stick

emperti|gado /ĩpertʃi'gadu/ *a* upright. ~**gar-se** *vpr* stand up straight

empilhar /ĩpi'ʎar/ *vt* pile up

empi|nado /ĩpi'nadu/ *a* erect; (*íngreme*) sheer, steep; ‹*nariz*› turned-up; *fig* stuck-up. ~**nar** *vt* stand upright; fly ‹*pipa*›; tip up ‹*copo*›

empírico /ẽ'piriku/ *a* empirical

emplacar /ĩpla'kar/ *vt* notch up ‹*pontos, sucessos, anos*›; license ‹*carro*›

emplastro /ĩ'plastru/ *m* surgical plaster; ~ **de nicotina** nicotine patch

empobre|cer /ĩpobre'ser/ *vt* impoverish. ~**cimento** *m* impoverishment

empoderamento /ẽpodera'mẽtu/ *Port m* empowerment

empoleirar /ĩpole'rar/ *vt* perch. ~**se** *vpr* perch

empol|gação /ĩpowga'sãw/ *f* fascination. ~**gante** *a* fascinating. ~**gar** *vt* fascinate

e

empossar /ĩpoˈsar/ vt swear in

empreen|dedor /ẽpriẽdeˈdor/ a enterprising ● m entrepreneur. **~der** vt undertake. **~dimento** m undertaking

empre|gada /ĩpreˈgada/ f (doméstica) maid. **~gado** m employee. **~gador** m employer. **~gar** vt employ. **~gar-se** vpr get a job. **~gatício** a vínculo **~gatício** contract of employment. **~go** /e/ m (trabalho) job; (uso) use

emprei|tada /ĩprejˈtada/ f commission, contract; (empreendimento) venture. **~teira** f contractor, firm of contractors. **~teiro** m contractor

empre|sa /ĩˈpreza/ f company. **~sa dot.com** dot-com. **~sariado** m business community. **~sarial** (pl **~sariais**) a business. **~sário** m businessman; (de cantor etc) manager

empres|tado /ĩpresˈtadu/ a on loan; **pedir ~tado** (ask to) borrow; **tomar ~tado** borrow. **~tar** vt lend

empréstimo /ĩˈprestʃimu/ m loan

empur|rão /ĩpuˈxãw/ m push. **~rar** vt push

emular /emuˈlar/ vt emulate

enamorado /enamoˈradu/ a (apaixonado) in love

encabeçar /ĩkabeˈsar/ vt head

encabu|lado /ĩkabuˈladu/ a shy. **~lar** vt embarrass. **~lar-se** vpr be shy

encadear /ĩkadeˈar/ vt chain ou link together

encader|nação /ĩkadernaˈsãw/ f binding. **~nado** a bound; (com capa dura) hardback. **~nar** vt bind

encai|xar /ĩkaˈʃar/ vt/i fit. **~xe** m (cavidade) socket; (juntura) joint

encalço /ĩˈkawsu/ m pursuit; **no ~ de** in pursuit of

encalhar /ĩkaˈʎar/ vi (barco) run aground; fig get bogged down; (mercadoria) not sell; ▯ (ficar solteiro) be left on the shelf

encaminhar /ĩkamiˈɲar/ vt (dirigir) steer, direct; (remeter) pass on; set in motion (processo). **~se** vpr set out

encana|dor /ĩkanaˈdor/ m plumber. **~mento** m plumbing

encan|tador /ĩkãtaˈdor/ a enchanting. **~tamento** m enchantment. **~tar** vt enchant. **~to** m charm

encaraco|lado /ĩkarakoˈladu/ a curly. **~lar** vt curl. **~lar-se** vpr curl up

encarar /ĩkaˈrar/ vt confront, face

encarcerar /ĩkarseˈrar/ vt imprison

encardido /ĩkarˈdʒidu/ a grimy

encarecidamente /ĩkaresidaˈmẽtʃi/ adv insistently

encargo /ĩˈkargu/ m task, responsibility

encar|nação /ĩkarnaˈsãw/ f (do espírito) incarnation; (de um personagem) embodiment. **~nar** vt embody; play (papel)

encarre|gado /ĩkaxeˈgadu/ a in charge (de of) ● m person in charge; (de operários) foreman; **~gado de negócios** chargé d'affaires. **~gar** vt **~gar alguém de** put sb in charge of; **~gar-se de** undertake to

encarte /ĩˈkartʃi/ m insert

ence|nação /ĩsenaˈsãw/ f (de peça) production; (fingimento) play-acting. **~nar** vt put on ● vi put it on

ence|radeira /ĩseraˈdera/ f floor polisher. **~rar** vt wax

encer|rado /ĩseˈxadu/ a (assunto) closed. **~ramento** m close. **~rar** vt close. **~rar-se** vpr close

encharcar /ĩʃarˈkar/ vt soak

en|chente /ẽˈʃẽtʃi/ f flood. **~cher** vt fill; ▯ annoy ● vi ▯ be annoying. **~cher-se** vpr fill up; ▯ (fartar-se) get fed up (**de** with)

enciclopédia /ẽsikloˈpedʒia/ f encyclopaedia

enco|berto /ĩkoˈbertu/ a (céu, tempo) overcast. **~brir** vt cover up ● vi (tempo) become overcast

encolher /ĩkoˈʎer/ vt shrug (ombros); pull up (pernas); shrink (roupa) ● vi (roupa) shrink. **~se** vpr (de medo) shrink; (de frio) huddle; (espremer-se) squeeze up

encomen|da /ĩkoˈmẽda/ f order; **de ou sob ~da** to order. **~dar** vt order (a from)

encon|trão /ĩkõˈtrãw/ m bump; (empurrão) shove. **~trar** vt (achar) find; (ver) meet; **~trar com** meet. **~trar-se** vpr (ver-se) meet; (estar) be. **~tro** m meeting; Mil encounter; **ir ao ~tro de** go to meet; fig meet; **ir de ~tro a** run into; fig go against

encorajar /ĩkoraˈʒar/ vt encourage

encor|pado /ĩkorˈpadu/ a stocky; (vinho) full-bodied. **~par** vt/i fill out

encos|ta /ĩˈkɔsta/ f slope. **~tar** vt (apoiar) lean; park (carro); leave on the latch (porta); (pôr de lado) put aside ● vi (carro) pull in. **~tar-se** vpr lean. **~to** /o/ m back

encra|vado /ĩkra'vadu/ a ‹unha, pelo› ingrowing. **~var** vt stick

encren|ca /ĩ'krẽka/ f fix, jam; pl trouble. **~car** vt get into trouble ‹pessoa›; complicate ‹situação› ● vi ‹situação› get complicated; ‹carro› break down. **~car-se** vpr ‹pessoa› get into trouble. **~queiro** m troublemaker

encres|pado /ĩkres'padu/ a ‹mar› choppy. **~par** vt frizz ‹cabelo›. **~par-se** vpr ‹cabelo› go frizzy; ‹mar› get choppy

encruzilhada /ĩkruzi'ʎada/ f crossroads

encurralar /ĩkuxa'lar/ vt hem in

encurtar /ĩkur'tar/ vt shorten

endere|çar /ĩdere'sar/ vt address. **~ço** /e/ m address; Comput **~ço de e-mail** email address

endinheirado /ĩdʒiɲe'radu/ a well-off

endireitar /ĩdʒirej'tar/ vt straighten. **~se** vpr straighten up

endivi|dado /ĩdʒivi'dadu/ a in debt. **~dar** vt put into debt. **~dar-se** vpr get into debt

endoidecer /ĩdojde'ser/ vi get mad

endos|sar /ĩdo'sar/ vt endorse. **~so** /o/ m endorsement

endurecer /ĩdure'ser/ vt/i harden

ener|gético /ener'ʒɛtʃiku/ a energy. **~gia** /ener'ʒia/ f energy; **~gia solar/ nuclear/eólica** solar/nuclear/wind power

enérgico /e'nɛrʒiku/ a vigorous; ‹remédio, discurso› powerful

enevoado /enevu'adu/ a (com névoa) misty; (com nuvens) cloudy

enfarte /ĩ'fartʃi/ m heart attack

ênfase /'ẽfazi/ f emphasis; **dar ~ a** emphasize

enfático /ẽ'fatʃiku/ a emphatic

enfatizar /ẽfatʃi'zar/ vt emphasize

enfei|tar /ĩfej'tar/ vt decorate. **~tar-se** vpr dress up. **~te** m decoration

enfeitiçar /ĩfejtʃi'sar/ vt bewitch

enfer|magem /ĩfer'maʒẽ/ f nursing. **~maria** f ward. **~meira** f nurse. **~meiro** m male nurse. **~midade** f illness. **~mo** a sick ● m patient

enferru|jado /ĩfexu'ʒadu/ a rusty. **~jar** vt/i rust

enfezado /ĩfe'zadu/ a bad-tempered

enfiar /ẽfi'ar/ vt put; slip on ‹roupa›; thread ‹agulha›; string ‹pérolas›

enfileirar /ĩfilej'rar/ vt line up. **~se** vpr line up

enfim /ẽ'fĩ/ adv (finalmente) finally; (resumindo) anyway

enfo|car /ĩfo'kar/ vt tackle. **~que** m approach

enfor|camento /ĩforka'mẽtu/ m hanging. **~car** vt hang. **~car-se** vpr hang o.s.

enfraquecer /ĩfrake'ser/ vt/i weaken

enfrentar /ĩfrẽ'tar/ vt face

enfumaçado /ĩfuma'sadu/ a smoky

enfurecer /ĩfure'ser/ vt infuriate. **~se** vpr get furious

enga|jamento /ĩgaʒa'mẽtu/ m commitment. **~jado** a committed. **~jar-se** vpr get involved (**em** in)

engalfinhar-se /ĩgawfi'ɲarsi/ vpr grapple

enga|nado /ĩga'nadu/ a (errado) mistaken. **~nar** vt deceive; cheat on ‹marido, esposa›; stave off ‹fome›. **~nar-se** vpr be mistaken. **~no** m (erro) mistake; (desonestidade) deception

engarra|famento /ĩgaxafa'mẽtu/ m traffic jam. **~far** vt bottle ‹vinho etc›; block ‹trânsito›

engas|gar /ĩgaz'gar/ vt choke ● vi choke; ‹motor› backfire. **~go** m choking

engastar /ĩgaʃ'tar/ vt set ‹joias›

engatar /ĩga'tar/ vt hitch ‹reboque etc› (**a** to); engage ‹marcha›

engatinhar /ĩgatʃi'ɲar/ vi crawl; fig start out

engave|tamento /ĩgaveta'mẽtu/ m pile-up. **~tar** vt shelve

engelhar /ĩʒe'ʎar/ vi ‹pele› wrinkle

enge|nharia /ĩʒeɲa'ria/ f engineering. **~nheiro** m engineer. **~nho** /e/ m (de pessoa) ingenuity; (de açúcar) sugar mill; (máquina) device. **~nhoca** /ɔ/ f gadget. **~nhoso** a ingenious

engessar /ĩʒe'sar/ vt put in plaster

engodo /ĩ'godu/ m lure

engolir /ĩgo'lir/ vt/i swallow; **~ em seco** gulp

engomar /ĩgo'mar/ vt press; (com goma) starch

engonhar /ẽgo'ɲar/ vi Port faff about ou around

engordar /ĩgor'dar/ vt make fat; fatten ‹animais› ● vi ‹pessoa› put on weight; ‹comida› be fattening

engraçado /ĩgra'sadu/ a funny

engradado /ĩgra'dadu/ m crate

engravidar /ĩgravi'dar/ vt make pregnant ● vi get pregnant

engraxar /ĩgra'ʃar/ vt polish

engre|nado /ĩgre'nadu/ a ‹carro› in gear. **~nagem** f gear; fig mechanism. **~nar** vt put into gear ‹carro›; strike up ‹conversa›. **~nar-se** vpr mesh; fig ‹pessoas› get on

engrossar /ĩgro'sar/ vt thicken; raise ‹voz› ● vi thicken; ‹pessoa› turn nasty

enguia /ẽ'gia/ f eel

engui|çar /ẽgi'sar/ vi break down. **~ço** m breakdown

enig|ma /e'nigima/ m enigma. **~mático** a enigmatic

enjaular /ĩʒaw'lar/ vt cage

enjo|ar /ĩʒo'ar/ vt sicken ● vi, **~ar-se** vpr get sick (**de** of). **~ativo** a ‹comida› sickly; ‹livro etc› boring

enjoo /ĩ'ʒou/ m sickness

enlameado /ĩlami'adu/ a muddy

enlatado /ĩla'tadu/ a tinned, canned. **~s** m pl tinned foods

enle|var /ẽle'var/ vt enthral. **~vo** /e/ m rapture

enlouquecer /ĩloke'ser/ vt drive mad ● vi go mad

enluarado /ĩlua'radu/ a moonlit

enor|me /e'nɔrmi/ a enormous. **~midade** f enormity

enquadrar /ĩkwa'drar/ vt fit ● vi, **~-se** vpr fit in

enquanto /ĩ'kwãtu/ conj while; **~ isso** meanwhile; **por ~** for the time being

enquete /ã'ketʃi/ f survey

enraivecer /ĩxajve'ser/ vt enrage

enredo /ẽ'xedu/ m plot

enrijecer /ĩxiʒe'ser/ vt stiffen. **~se** vpr stiffen

enrique|cer /ĩxike'ser/ vt (dar dinheiro a) make rich; fig enrich ● vi get rich. **~cimento** m enrichment

enro|lado /ĩxo'ladu/ a complicated. **~lar** vt (envolver) roll up; (complicar) complicate; (enganar) cheat. **~lar-se** vpr (envolver-se) roll up; (confundir-se) get mixed up

enroscar /ĩxos'kar/ vt twist

enrouquecer /ĩxoke'ser/ vi go hoarse

enrugar /ĩxu'gar/ vt wrinkle ‹pele, tecido›; furrow ‹testa›

enrustido /ĩxus'tʃidu/ a repressed

ensaboar /ĩsabo'ar/ vt soap

ensai|ar /ĩsaj'ar/ vt (provar) try out; (repetir) rehearse. **~o** m (prova) test; (repetição) rehearsal; (escrito) essay

ensanguentado /ĩsãgwẽ'tadu/ a bloody, bloodstained

enseada /ĩsi'ada/ f inlet

ensebado /ĩse'badu/ a greasy

ensimesmado /ĩsimez'madu/ a lost in thought

ensi|nar /ẽsi'nar/ vt/i teach (**algo a alguém** sb sth); **~nar a nadar** teach sb to swim. **~no** m teaching; (em geral) education

ensolarado /ĩsola'radu/ a sunny

enso|pado /ĩso'padu/ a soaked ● m stew. **~par** vt soak

ensurde|cedor /ĩsurdese'dor/ a deafening. **~cer** vt deafen ● vi go deaf

entabular /ĩtabu'lar/ vt open, start

entalar /ĩta'lar/ vt wedge, jam; (em apertos) get. **~se** vpr get wedged, get jammed; (em apertos) get caught up

entalhar /ĩta'ʎar/ vt carve

entanto /ĩ'tãtu/ m no **~** however

---

então /ĩ'tãw/ ● adv

····▶ (aquela época) **desde ~** since then; **fui no casamento do Pedro e não o vejo desde ~** I went to Pedro's wedding and I haven't seen him since

····▶ (naquele tempo) at that time; **~ era mais magro** I was thinner at that time

····▶ (por isso) so; **eles não vinham, ~ fui embora** they didn't come, so I left

● int

····▶ (para animar) **~, anime-se!** come on, cheer up!

····▶ (para chamar a atenção) **~, o que você pensa que está fazendo?!** hey, what do you think you're doing?!

(em expressões) **e ~?...** (não dar importância) so what?; (para saber informação extra) so, what happened then?

---

entardecer /ĩtarde'ser/ m sunset

ente /'ẽtʃi/ m being

entea|da /ẽtʃi'ada/ f stepdaughter. **~do** m stepson

entedi|ante /ĩtedʒi'ãtʃi/ a boring. **~ar** vt bore. **~ar-se** vpr get bored

enten|der /ĩtẽ'der/ vt understand; **dar a ~der** give to understand; **~der de futebol** know about football. **~der-se** vpr (dar-se bem) get on (**com** with). **~dimento** m understanding

enternecedor /ĩter'nese'dor/ *a*
touching

enter|rar /ĩte'xar/ *vt* bury. **~ro** /e/ *m*
burial; (*cerimônia*) funeral

entidade /ẽtʃi'dadʒi/ *f* entity; (*órgão*)
body

entornar /ĩtor'nar/ *vt* tip over, spill

entorpe|cente /ĩtorpe'sẽtʃi/ *m* drug,
narcotic. **~cer** *vt* numb

entortar /ĩtor'tar/ *vt* make crooked

entrada /ẽ'trada/ *f* entry; (*onde se
entra*) entrance; (*bilhete*) ticket; (*prato*)
starter; (*pagamento*) deposit; *pl* (*no
cabelo*) receding hairline; **dar ~ a** enter;
~ proibida no entry

entranhas /ĩ'traɲas/ *f pl* entrails

entrar /ẽ'trar/ *vi* go/come in; **~ com**
enter ‹*dados*›; put in ‹*dinheiro*›; **~ em
detalhes** go into details; **~ em vigor**
come into force

entravar /ẽtra'var/ *vt* hamper

entre /'ẽtri/ *prep* between; (*em meio a*)
among

entreaberto /ẽtria'bertu/ *a* half-open

entrecortar /ẽtrikor'tar/ *vt*
intersperse; (*cruzar*) intersect

entre|ga /ĩ'trega/ *f* delivery; (*rendição*)
surrender; **~ga a domicílio** home
delivery. **~gar** *vt* hand over; deliver
‹*mercadorias, cartas*›; hand in ‹*caderno,
trabalho escolar*›. **~gar-se** *vpr* give o.s.
up (a to). **~gue** *pp de* ▶ ENTREGAR

entrelaçar /ẽtrela'sar/ *vt* intertwine;
clasp ‹*mãos*›

entrelinhas /ẽtri'liɲas/ *f pl* **ler nas ~**
read between the lines

entremear /ẽtrimi'ar/ *vt* intersperse

entreolhar-se /ẽtrioʎarsi/ *vpr* look at
one another

entretanto /ẽtre'tãtu/ *conj* however

entre|tenimento /ẽtreteni'mẽtu/ *m*
entertainment. **~ter** *vt* entertain

entrever /ẽtre'ver/ *vt* glimpse

entrevis|ta /ẽtre'vista/ *f* interview.
~tador *m* interviewer. **~tar** *vt* interview

entristecer /ĩtriste'ser/ *vt* sadden ● *vi*
be saddened (**com** by)

entroncamento /ĩtrõka'mẽtu/ *m*
junction

entrosar /ĩtro'zar/ *vt/i* integrate

entu|lhar /ĩtu'ʎar/ *vt* cram (**de** with).
~lho *m* rubble

entupir /ĩtu'pir/ *vt* block. **~pir-se** *vpr*
get blocked; (*de comida*) stuff o.s. (**de**
with)

enturmar-se /ĩtur'marsi/ *vpr* mix
in, fit in

entusias|mar /ĩtuziaz'mar/ *vt* fill
with enthusiasm. **~mar-se** *vpr* get
enthusiastic (**com** about). **~mo** *m*
enthusiasm. **~ta** *m/f* enthusiast ● *a*
enthusiastic

entusiástico /ĩtuzi'astʃiku/ *a*
enthusiastic

enumerar /enume'rar/ *vt* enumerate

envelhecer /ĩveʎe'ser/ *vt/i* age

envelope /ẽve'lɔpi/ *m* envelope

envenenar /ĩvene'nar/ *vt* poison;
🚗 soup up ‹*carro*›

envergadura /ĩverga'dura/ *f*
wingspan; *fig* scale

envergo|nhado /ĩvergo'ɲadu/ *a*
ashamed; (*constrangido*) embarrassed.
~nhar *vt* disgrace; (*constranger*)
embarrass. **~nhar-se** *vpr* be ashamed;
(*acanhar-se*) get embarrassed

envernizar /ĩverni'zar/ *vt* varnish

en|viado /ẽvi'adu/ *m* envoy. **~viar** *vt*
send. **~vio** *m* (*ato*) sending; (*remessa*)
consignment

envidraçar /ĩvidra'sar/ *vt* glaze

enviesado /ĩvie'zadu/ *a* (*não vertical*)
slanting; (*torto*) crooked

envol|vente /ĩvow'vẽtʃi/ *a*
compelling, gripping. **~ver** *vt*
(*embrulhar*) wrap; (*enredar*) involve.
~ver-se *vpr* (*enrolar-se*) wrap o.s.;
(*enredar-se*) get involved. **~vimento** *m*
involvement

enxada /ẽ'ʃada/ *f* hoe

enxaguar /ẽʃa'gwar/ *vt* rinse

enxame /ẽ'ʃami/ *m* swarm

enxaqueca /ẽʃa'keka/ *f* migraine

enxergar /ĩʃer'gar/ *vt/i* see

enxer|tar /ĩʃer'tar/ *vt* graft. **~to** /e/
m graft

enxofre /ẽ'ʃofri/ *m* sulphur

enxotar /ĩʃo'tar/ *vt* drive away

enxo|val /ẽʃo'vaw/ (*pl* **~vais**) *m* (*de
noiva*) trousseau; (*de bebê*) layette

enxugar /ĩʃu'gar/ *vt* dry. **~se** *vpr* dry
o.s.

enxurrada /ĩʃu'xada/ *f* torrent; *fig*
flood

enxuto /ĩ'ʃutu/ *a* dry; ‹*corpo*› shapely

enzima /ẽ'zima/ *f* enzyme

epicentro /epi'sẽtru/ *m* epicentre

épico /'ɛpiku/ *a* epic

epidemia /epide'mia/ *f* epidemic

epi|lepsia /epilep'sia/ f epilepsy. **~léptico** a & m epileptic

epílogo /e'pilogu/ m epilogue

episódio /epi'zɔdʒiu/ m episode

epitáfio /epi'tafiu/ m epitaph

época /'ɛpoka/ f time; (da história) age, period; **fazer ~** make history; **móveis da ~** period furniture

epopeia /epo'peja/ f epic

equação /ekwa'sãw/ f equation

equador /ekwa'dor/ m equator; **o E~** Ecuador

equatori|al /ekwatori'aw/ (pl **~ais**) a equatorial. **~ano** a & m Ecuadorian

equilibrar /ekili'brar/ vt balance. **~-se** vpr balance

equilíbrio /eki'libriu/ m balance

equipa /e'kipa/ Port f team

equi|pamento /ekipa'mẽtu/ m equipment. **~par** vt equip

equiparar /ekipa'rar/ vt equate (**com** with). **~-se** vpr compare (**a** with)

equipe /e'kipi/ f team

equitação /ekita'sãw/ f riding

equiva|lência /ekiva'lẽsia/ f equivalence. **~lente** a equivalent. **~ler** vi be equivalent (**a** to)

equivo|cado /ekivo'kadu/ a mistaken. **~car-se** vpr make a mistake

equívoco /e'kivoku/ a equivocal ● m mistake

era /'era/ f era

erário /e'rariu/ m exchequer

ereção /ere'sãw/ f erection

eremita /ere'mita/ m/f hermit

ereto /e'rɛtu/ a erect

erguer /er'ger/ vt raise; erect ‹monumento etc›. **~-se** vpr rise

eri|çado /eri'sadu/ a bristling. **~çar-se** vpr bristle

ermo /'ermu/ a deserted ● m wilderness

erosão /ero'zãw/ f erosion

erótico /e'rɔtʃiku/ a erotic

erotismo /ero'tʃizmu/ m eroticism

er|rado /e'xadu/ a wrong. **~rante** a wandering. **~rar** vt (não fazer certo) get wrong; miss ‹alvo› ● vi (enganar-se) be wrong; (vaguear) wander. **~ro** /e/ m mistake; **fazer um ~ro** make a mistake. **~rôneo** a erroneous

erudi|ção /erudʒi'sãw/ f learning. **~to** a learned; ‹música› classical ● m scholar

erupção /erup'sãw/ f (vulcânica) eruption; (cutânea) rash

erva /'ɛrva/ f herb; **~ daninha** weed. **~-doce** f aniseed

ervilha /er'viʎa/ f pea

esban|jador /izbãʒa'dor/ a extravagant ● m spendthrift. **~jar** vt squander; burst into ‹saúde, imaginação, energia etc›

esbar|rão /izba'xãw/ m bump. **~rar** vi **~rar com** ou **em** bump into ‹pessoa›; come up against ‹problema›

esbelto /iz'bewtu/ a svelte

esbo|çar /izbo'sar/ vt sketch ‹desenho etc›; outline ‹plano etc›; **~çar um sorriso** give a hint of a smile. **~ço** /o/ m (desenho) sketch; (plano) outline; (de um sorriso) hint

esbofetear /izbofetʃi'ar/ vt slap

esborrachar /izboxa'ʃar/ vt squash. **~-se** vpr crash

esbravejar /izbrave'ʒar/ vi rant, rail

esbuga|lhado /izbuga'ʎadu/ a ‹olhos› bulging. **~lhar-se** vpr ‹olhos› pop out

esbura|cado /izbura'kadu/ a full of holes. **~car** vt make holes in

escabroso /iska'brozu/ a fig difficult, tough

escada /is'kada/ f (dentro de casa) stairs; (na rua) steps; (de mão) ladder; **~ de incêndio** fire escape; **~ rolante** escalator. **~ria** f staircase

escafan|drista /iskafã'drista/ m/f diver. **~dro** m diving suit

escala /is'kala/ f scale; (de navio) port of call; (de avião) stopover; **fazer ~** stop over; **sem ~** ‹voo› non-stop

esca|lada /iska'lada/ f fig escalation. **~lão** m echelon, level. **~lar** vt (subir a) scale; (designar) select

escaldar /iskaw'dar/ vt scald; blanch ‹vegetais›

escalfar /iskaw'far/ vt poach

escalonar /iskalo'nar/ vt schedule ‹pagamento›

escama /is'kama/ f scale

escanca|rado /iskãka'radu/ a wide open. **~rar** vt open wide

escandalizar /iskãdali'zar/ vt scandalize. **~-se** vpr be scandalized

escândalo /is'kãdalu/ m (vexame) scandal; (tumulto) fuss, uproar; **fazer um ~** make a scene

escandaloso /iskãda'lozu/ a (chocante) scandalous; (espalhafatoso)

outrageous, loud

Escandinávia /iskãdʒi'navia/ f
Scandinavia

escandinavo /iskãdʒi'navu/ a & m
Scandinavian

escanga|lhado /iskãga'ʎadu/ a
broken. **~lhar** vt break up. **~lhar-se** vpr
fall to pieces; **~lhar-se de rir** split one's
sides laughing

escaninho /iska'niɲu/ m pigeonhole

escanteio /iskã'teju/ m corner

esca|pada /iska'pada/ f (fuga) escape;
(aventura) escapade. **~pamento** m
exhaust. **~par** vi **~par a** ou de (livrar-se)
escape from; (evitar) escape; **~pou-lhe
a palavra** the word slipped out; **o copo
~pou-me das mãos** the glass slipped
out of my hands; **o nome me ~pa** the
name escapes me; **~par de boa** have
a narrow escape. **~patória** f way out;
(desculpa) pretext. **~pe** m escape; (de
carro etc) exhaust. **~pulir** vi escape
(de from)

escaramuça /iskara'musa/ f skirmish

escaravelho /iskara'veʎu/ m beetle

escarcéu /iskar'sɛw/ m uproar, fuss

escarlate /iskar'latʃi/ a scarlet

escarnecer /iskarne'ser/ vt mock

escárnio /is'karniu/ m derision

escarpado /iskar'padu/ a steep

escarrado /iska'xadu/ m **ele é o pai ~**
he's the spitting image of his father

escarro /is'kaxu/ m phlegm

escas|sear /iskasi'ar/ vi run short.
~sez f shortage. **~so** a (raro) scarce;
(ralo) scant

esca|vadeira /iskava'dera/ f digger.
~var vt excavate

esclare|cer /isklare'ser/ vt explain
‹fatos›; enlighten ‹pessoa›. **~cer-se**
vpr ‹fato› be explained; ‹pessoa›
find out. **~cimento** m (de pessoas)
enlightenment; (de fatos) explanation

esclerosado /isklero'zadu/ a senile

escoar /isko'ar/ vt/i drain

esco|cês /isko'ses/ a (f **~cesa**) Scottish
● m (f **~cesa**) Scot

Escócia /is'kɔsia/ f Scotland

esco|la /is'kɔla/ f school; **~la de samba**
samba school. **~lar** a school ● m/f
schoolchild. **~laridade** f schooling

 escola de samba *Escolas de
samba* (samba schools) are local
organizations in which people sing and
dance to samba music, often in
competition with other schools. The
samba schools parade on floats once a
year, during Carnival. The most famous
parades take place in the Rio de Janeiro
Carnival, in the Avenida Marquês de
Sapucaí Sambadrome.

esco|lha /is'koʎa/ f choice. **~lher** vt
choose

escol|ta /is'kɔwta/ f escort. **~tar** vt
escort

escombros /is'kõbrus/ m pl debris

escon|de-esconde /iskõdʒis'kõdʒi/
m hide-and-seek. **~der** vt hide. **~der-se**
vpr hide. **~derijo** m hiding place; (de
bandidos) hideout. **~didas** f pl **às ~didas**
secretly

esco|ra /is'kɔra/ f prop. **~rar** vt prop up.
~rar-se vpr ‹argumento etc› be based
(**em** on)

escore /is'kɔri/ m score

escória /is'kɔria/ f scum, dross

escori|ação /iskoria'sãw/ f graze,
abrasion. **~ar** vt graze

escorpião /iskorpi'ãw/ m scorpion;
E~ Scorpio

escorredor /iskoxe'dor/ m drainer

escorrega /isko'xega/ m slide

escorre|gador /iskoxega'dor/ m
slide. **~gão** m slip. **~gar** vi slip

escor|rer /isko'xer/ vt drain ● vi trickle.
~rido a ‹cabelo› straight

escoteiro /isko'teru/ m boy scout

escotilha /isko'tʃiʎa/ f hatch

esco|va /is'kova/ f brush; **fazer ~va
no cabelo** blow-dry one's hair; **~va
de dentes** toothbrush. **~var** vt brush.
~vinha f **cabelo à ~vinha** crew cut

escra|chado /iskra'ʃadu/ a 🔳
outspoken. **~char** vt 🔳 tell off

escra|vatura /iskrava'tura/ f slavery.
~vidão f slavery. **~vizar** vt enslave. **~vo**
m slave

escre|vente /iskre'vẽtʃi/ m/f clerk.
~ver vt/i write

escri|ta /is'krita/ f writing; **~ta
inteligente** *Telec* predictive text
messaging. **~to** pp de ▶ **ESCREVER** ● a
written; **por ~to** in writing. **~tor** m
writer. **~tório** m office; (numa casa)
study

escritu|ra /iskri'tura/ f (a Bíblia)
scripture; (contrato) deed. **~ração** f
bookkeeping. **~rar** vt keep, write up
‹contas›; draw up ‹documento›

escri|vaninha /iskriva'niɲa/ f bureau, writing desk. **~vão** m (f **~vã**) registrar

escrúpulo /is'krupulu/ m scruple

escrupuloso /iskrupu'lozu/ a scrupulous

escrutínio /iskru'tʃiniu/ m ballot

escu|dar /isku'dar/ vt shield. **~deria** f team. **~do** m shield; (moeda) escudo

escula|chado /iskula'ʃadu/ a 🔲 sloppy. **~char** vt 🔲 mess up <coisa>; tell off <pessoa>. **~cho** m 🔲 (bagunça) mess; (bronca) telling-off

escul|pir /iskuw'pir/ vt sculpt. **~tor** m sculptor. **~tura** f sculpture. **~tural** (pl **~turais**) a statuesque

escuma /is'kuma/ f scum. **~deira** f skimmer

escuna /is'kuna/ f schooner

escu|ras /is'kuras/ f pl **às ~ras** in the dark. **~recer** vt darken ● vi get dark. **~ridão** f darkness. **~ro** a & m dark

escuso /is'kuzu/ a shady

escu|ta /is'kuta/ f listening; **estar à ~ta** be listening; **~ta telefônica** phone tapping. **~tar** vt (perceber) hear; (prestar atenção a) listen to ● vi (poder ouvir) hear; (prestar atenção) listen

esdrúxulo /iz'druʃulu/ a weird

esfacelar /isfase'lar/ vt wreck

esfalfar /isfaw'far/ vt wear out. **~se** vpr get worn out

esfaquear /isfaki'ar/ vt stab

esfarelar /isfare'lar/ vt crumble. **~se** vpr crumble

esfarrapado /isfaxa'padu/ a ragged; <desculpa> lame

es|fera /is'fera/ f sphere. **~férico** a spherical

esferográfi|co /isfero'grafiku/ a caneta **~ca** ballpoint pen

esfiapar /isfia'par/ vt fray. **~se** vpr fray

esfinge /is'fĩʒi/ f sphinx

esfolar /isfo'lar/ vt skin; fig overcharge

esfomeado /isfomi'adu/ a starving, famished

esfor|çar-se /isfor'sarsi/ vpr make an effort. **~ço** /o/ m effort; **fazer ~ço** make an effort

esfre|gaço /isfre'gasu/ m smear. **~gar** vt rub; (para limpar) scrub

esfriar /isfri'ar/ vt cool ● vi cool (down); (sentir frio) get cold

esfumaçado /isfuma'sadu/ a smoky

esfuziante /isfuzi'ãtʃi/ a irrepressible, exuberant

esganar /izga'nar/ vt throttle

esganiçado /izgani'sadu/ a shrill

esgarçar /izgar'sar/ vt/i fray

esgo|tado /izgo'tadu/ a exhausted; <estoque, lotação> sold out. **~tamento** m exhaustion; **~tamento nervoso** nervous breakdown. **~tar** vt exhaust; (gastar) use up. **~tar-se** vpr <pessoa> become exhausted; <estoque, lotação> sell out; <recursos, provisões> run out. **~to** /o/ m drain; (de detritos) sewer

esgri|ma /iz'grima/ f fencing. **~mir** vt brandish ● vi fence. **~mista** m/f fencer

esgrouvinhado /izgrovi'ɲadu/ a tousled, dishevelled

esgueirar-se /izge'rarsi/ vpr slip, sneak

esguelha /iz'geʎa/ f **de ~** askew; <olhar> askance

esgui|char /izgi'ʃar/ vt/i spurt, squirt. **~cho** m jet, spurt

esguio /iz'giu/ a slender

eslavo /iz'lavu/ a Slavic ● m Slav

esmaecer /izmaj'ser/ vi fade

esma|gador /izmaga'dor/ a <vitória, maioria> overwhelming; <provas> incontrovertible. **~gar** vt crush

esmalte /iz'mawtʃi/ m enamel; **~ de unhas** nail varnish

esmeralda /izme'rawda/ f emerald

esme|rar-se /izme'rarsi/ vpr take great care (em over). **~ro** /e/ m great care

esmigalhar /izmiga'ʎar/ vt crumble <pão etc>; shatter <vidro, copo>. **~se** vpr <pão etc> crumble; <vidro, copo> shatter

esmiuçar /izmiu'sar/ vt examine in detail

esmo /'ezmu/ m **a ~** <escolher> at random; <andar> aimlessly; <falar> nonsense

esmola /iz'mɔla/ f donation; pl charity

esmorecer /izmore'ser/ vi flag

esmurrar /izmu'xar/ vt punch

esno|bar /izno'bar/ vt snub ● vi be snobbish. **~be** /iz'nɔbi/ a snobbish ● m/f snob. **~bismo** m snobbishness

esotérico /ezo'teriku/ a esoteric

espa|çar /ispa'sar/ vt space out; make less frequent <visitas, consultas etc>. **~cial** (pl **~ciais**) a space. **~ço** m space; (cultural etc) venue. **~çoso** /o/ a spacious

espada /is'pada/ f sword; pl (naipe) spades. **~chim** m swordsman

espádua /is'padua/ f shoulder blade

espaguete /ispa'getʃi/ m spaghetti

espaire|cer /ispajre'ser/ vt amuse ● vi relax; (dar uma volta) go for a walk. **~cimento** m recreation

espaldar /ispaw'dar/ m back

espalhafato /ispaʎa'fatu/ m (barulho) fuss, uproar; (de roupa etc) extravagance. **~so** /o/ a (barulhento) noisy, rowdy; (ostentoso) extravagant

espalhar /ispa'ʎar/ vt scatter; spread ‹notícia, terror etc›; shed ‹luz›. **~se** vpr spread; ‹pessoas› spread out

espa|nador /ispana'dor/ m feather duster. **~nar** vt dust

espan|camento /ispãka'mẽtu/ m beating. **~car** vt beat up

Espanha /is'paɲa/ f Spain

espa|nhol /ispa'ɲɔw/ (pl **~nhóis**) a (f **~nhola**) Spanish ● m (f **~nhola**) Spaniard; (língua) Spanish; os **~nhóis** the Spanish

espan|talho /ispã'taʎu/ m scarecrow. **~tar** vt (admirar) amaze; (assustar) scare; (afugentar) drive away. **~tar-se** vpr (admirar-se) be amazed; (assustar-se) get scared. **~to** m (susto) fright; (admiração) amazement. **~toso** /o/ a amazing

esparadrapo /ispara'drapu/ m sticking plaster

espargo /is'pargu/ Port m asparagus

esparramar /ispaxa'mar/ vt scatter. **~se** vpr be scattered, spread

espartano /ispar'tanu/ a spartan

espartilho /ispar'tʃiʎu/ m corset

espas|mo /is'pazmu/ m spasm. **~módico** a spasmodic

espatifar /ispatʃi'far/ vt smash. **~se** vpr smash; ‹carro, avião› crash

especi|al /ispesi'aw/ (pl **~ais**) a special. **~alidade** f speciality. **~alista** m/f specialist

especiali|zado /ispesiali'zadu/ a specialized; ‹mão de obra› skilled. **~zar-se** vpr specialize (**em** in)

especiaria /ispesia'ria/ f spice

espécie /is'pɛsi/ f sort, kind; (de animais) species

especifi|cação /ispesifika'sãw/ f specification. **~car** vt specify

específico /ispe'sifiku/ a specific

espécime /is'pesimi/ m specimen

espectador /ispekta'dor/ m (de TV) viewer; (de jogo, espetáculo) spectator; (de acidente etc) onlooker

espectro /is'pɛktru/ m (fantasma) spectre; (de cores) spectrum

especu|lação /ispekula'sãw/ f speculation. **~lador** m speculator. **~lar** vi speculate (**sobre** on). **~lativo** a speculative

espe|lhar /ispe'ʎar/ vt mirror. **~lhar-se** vpr be mirrored. **~lho** /e/ m mirror; **~lho retrovisor** rear-view mirror

espelunca /ispe'lũka/ f 🔢 dive 🔢

espera /is'pɛra/ f wait; **à ~ de** waiting for

esperan|ça /ispe'rãsa/ f hope. **~çoso** /o/ a hopeful

esperar /ispe'rar/ vt (aguardar) wait for; (desejar) hope for; (contar com) expect ● vi wait (**por** for); **fazer alguém ~** keep sb waiting; **espero que ele venha** I hope (that) he comes; **espero que sim/não** I hope so/not

esperma /is'perma/ m sperm

espernear /isperni'ar/ vi kick; fig (reclamar) kick up

esper|talhão /isperta'ʎãw/ m (f **~talhona**) wise guy. **~teza** /e/ f cleverness; (uma) clever move. **~to** /e/ a clever

espes|so /is'pesu/ a thick. **~sura** f thickness

espe|tacular /ispetaku'lar/ a spectacular. **~táculo** m (no teatro etc) show; (cena impressionante) spectacle. **~taculoso** /o/ a spectacular

espe|tar /ispe'tar/ vt (cravar) stick; (furar) skewer. **~tar-se** vpr (cravar-se) stick; (ferir-se) prick o.s.. **~tinho** m skewer; (de carne etc) kebab. **~to** /e/ m spit

espevitado /ispevi'tadu/ a cheeky

espezinhar /ispezi'ɲar/ vt walk all over

espi|a /is'pia/ m/f spy. **~ão** m (f **~ã**) spy. **~ada** f peep. **~ar** vt (observar) spy on; (aguardar) watch for ● vi peer, peep

espicaçar /ispika'sar/ vt goad ‹pessoa›; excite ‹imaginação, curiosidade›

espichar /ispi'ʃar/ vt stretch ● vi shoot up. **~se** vpr stretch out

espiga /is'piga/ f (de trigo etc) ear; (de milho) cob

espina|fração /ispinafra'sãw/ f 🔢 telling-off. **~frar** vt 🔢 tell off. **~fre** m spinach

espingarda /ispĩ'garda/ f rifle, shotgun

espinha /iʃ'piɲa/ f (de peixe) bone; (na pele) spot; ~ **dorsal** spine

espinho /iʃ'piɲu/ m thorn. ~**so** /o/ a thorny; fig difficult, tough

espio|nagem /iʃpio'naʒẽ/ f espionage, spying. ~**nar** vt spy on ● vi spy

espi|ral /iʃpi'raw/ (pl ~**rais**) a & f spiral

espirita /iʃ'pirita/ a & m/f spiritualist

espiritismo /iʃpiri'tʃizmu/ m spiritualism

espírito /iʃ'piritu/ m spirit; (graça) wit

espiritu|al /iʃpiritu'aw/ (pl ~**ais**) a spiritual. ~**oso** /o/ a witty

espir|rar /iʃpi'xar/ vt spurt ● vi ‹pessoa› sneeze; ‹lama, tinta etc› spatter; ‹fogo, lenha, fritura etc› spit. ~**ro** m sneeze

esplêndido /iʃ'plẽdʒidu/ a splendid

esplendor /iʃplẽ'dor/ m splendour

espoleta /iʃpo'leta/ f fuse

espoliar /iʃpoli'ar/ vt plunder, pillage

espólio /iʃ'poliu/ m (herdado) estate; (roubado) spoils

espon|ja /iʃ'põʒa/ f sponge. ~**joso** /o/ a spongy

espon|taneidade /iʃpõtanej'dadʒi/ f spontaneity. ~**tâneo** a spontaneous

espora /iʃ'pora/ f spur

esporádico /iʃpo'radʒiku/ a sporadic

esporear /iʃpori'ar/ vt spur on

espor|te /iʃ'portʃi/ m sport ● a invar ‹roupa› casual; carro ~**te** sports car. ~**tista** m/f sportsman (f-woman). ~**tiva** f sense of humour. ~**tivo** a sporting

espo|sa /iʃ'poza/ f wife. ~**so** m husband

espregui|çadeira /iʃpregisa'dera/ f (tipo cadeira) deckchair; (tipo cama) sun lounger. ~**çar-se** vpr stretch

esprei|ta /iʃ'prejta/ f ficar à ~**ta** lie in wait. ~**tar** vt stalk ‹caça, vítima›; spy on ‹vizinhos, inimigos etc›; look out for ‹ocasião› ● vi peep, spy

espre|medor /iʃpreme'dor/ m squeezer. ~**mer** vt squeeze; wring out ‹roupa›; squash ‹pessoa›. ~**mer-se** vpr squeeze up

espu|ma /iʃ'puma/ f foam; ~**ma de borracha** foam rubber. ~**mante** a ‹vinho› sparkling. ~**mar** vi foam, froth

espúrio /iʃ'puriu/ a spurious

esqua|dra /iʃ'kwadra/ f squad; ~**dra de polícia** Port police station. ~**drão** m squadron. ~**dria** f doors and windows. ~**drinhar** vt explore. ~**dro** m set square

esqualidez /iʃkwali'deʃ/ f squalor

esquálido /iʃ'kwalidu/ a squalid

esquartejar /iʃkwarte'ʒar/ vt chop up

esque|cer /iʃke'ser/ vt/i forget; ~**cer-se de** forget. ~**cido** a forgotten; (com memória fraca) forgetful. ~**cimento** m oblivion; (memória fraca) forgetfulness

esque|lético /iʃke'letʃiku/ a skinny, skeleton-like. ~**leto** /e/ m skeleton

esque|ma /iʃ'kema/ m outline, draft; (operação) scheme; ~**ma de segurança** security operation. ~**mático** a schematic

esquentar /iʃkẽ'tar/ vt warm up; ~ **a cabeça** 🔟 get worked up ● vi warm up; ‹roupa› be warm. ~**se** vpr get annoyed

esquer|da /iʃ'kerda/ f left; à ~**da** (posição) on the left; (direção) to the left. ~**dista** a left-wing ● m/f left-winger. ~**do** /e/ a left

esqui /iʃ'ki/ m ski; (esporte) skiing; ~ **aquático** water skiing. ~**ador** m skier. ~**ar** vi ski

esquilo /iʃ'kilu/ m squirrel

esquina /iʃ'kina/ f corner

esquisi|tice /iʃkizi'tʃisi/ f strangeness; (uma) strange thing. ~**to** a strange

esqui|var-se /iʃki'varsi/ vpr dodge out of the way; ~**var-se de** dodge. ~**vo** a elusive; ‹pessoa› aloof, antisocial

esquizo|frenia /iʃkizofre'nia/ f schizophrenia. ~**frênico** a & m schizophrenic

es|sa /'esa/ pron that (one); ~**sa é boa** that's a good one; ~**sa não** come off it; **por ~sas e outras** for these and other reasons. ~**se** /e/ a that; pl those; 🔟 (este) this; pl these ● pron that one; pl those; 🔟 (este) this one; pl these

essência /e'sẽsia/ f essence

essenci|al /esẽsi'aw/ (pl ~**ais**) a essential; **o** ~**al** what is essential

estabele|cer /iʃtabele'ser/ vt establish. ~**cer-se** vpr establish o.s.. ~**cimento** m establishment

estabili|dade /iʃtabili'dadʒi/ f stability. ~**zar** vt stabilize. ~**zar-se** vpr stabilize

estábulo /iʃ'tabulu/ m cowshed

estaca /iʃ'taka/ f stake; (de barraca) peg; **voltar à ~ zero** go back to square one

estação /iʃta'sãw/ f (do ano) season; (ferroviária etc) station; ~ **balneária** seaside resort

estacar /iʃta'kar/ vi stop short

estacio|namento /istasiona'mētu/ *m* (*ação*) parking; (*lugar*) car park, *Amer* parking lot. **~nar** *vt/i* park

estada /is'tada/ *f*, **estadia** /ista'dʒia/ *f* stay

estádio /is'tadʒiu/ *m* stadium

esta|dista /ista'dʒista/ *m/f* statesman (*f*-woman). **~do** *m* state; **~do civil** marital status; **~do de espírito** state of mind; **Estados Unidos da América** United States of America. **Estado-Maior** *m* Staff. **~dual** (*pl* **~duais**) *a* state

esta|fa /is'tafa/ *f* exhaustion. **~fante** *a* exhausting. **~far** *vt* tire out. **~far-se** *vpr* get tired out

estagi|ar /istaʒi'ar/ *vi* do a traineeship. **~ário** *m* trainee

estágio /is'taʒiu/ *m* traineeship

estag|nado /istagi'nadu/ *a* stagnant. **~nar** *vi* stagnate

estalagem /ista'laʒē/ *f* inn

estalar /ista'lar/ *vt* (*quebrar*) crack; (*fazer barulho com*) click ● *vi* crack

estaleiro /ista'leru/ *m* shipyard

estalo /is'talu/ *m* crack; (*de dedos, língua*) click; **me deu um ~** it clicked (in my mind)

estam|pa /is'tãpa/ *f* print. **~pado** *a* ‹*tecido*› patterned ● *m* (*desenho*) pattern; (*tecido*) print. **~par** *vt* print

estampido /istã'pidu/ *m* bang

estancar /istã'kar/ *vt* staunch. **~se** *vpr* dry up

estância /is'tãsia/ *f* **~ hidromineral** spa

estandarte /istã'dartʃi/ *m* banner

estanho /is'taɲu/ *m* tin

estanque /is'tãki/ *a* watertight

estante /is'tãtʃi/ *f* bookcase

estapafúrdio /istapa'furdʒiu/ *a* weird, odd

estar /is'tar/ ● *vi*

••••➤ (*com lugar*) be; **a Lúcia está em casa** is Lúcia at home?

••••➤ (*achar-se*) **~ doente/cansado** be ill/tired

••••➤ (*aparência*) look; **você está muito bonita!** you look very pretty!

••••➤ **~ em** (*consistir em*) lie in; **o êxito do grupo está na sua originalidade** the group's success lies in their originality

••••➤ **~ a** *Port* (*seguido de infinitivo*) **estavam a jogar** they were playing

● *v aux*

••••➤ (*com gerúndio*) **eles estão brincando** they're playing; **está fazendo 40°C em São Paulo** it's 40°C in São Paulo

••••➤ (*com particípio*) **o arroz está cozido** the rice is cooked; **está aberto** it's open

● *v imp*

••••➤ (*com temperatura*) **está frio/calor** it's cold/hot

••••➤ (*em expressões*) **está bem?** (*de acordo?*) OK?; **você me empresta, está bem?** you'll lend it to me, won't you?; **~ a** *Port* (*com data*) **estamos a dois de junho** it's the second of June; (*com preço*) **a quanto está a banana?** how much are the bananas?; **~ com** (*apoiar*) be rooting for; **força, estou contigo!** go for it! I'm rooting for you; (*doença*) have; **estou com gripe** I've got the flu; **~ de partida** be leaving soon; **estou de partida para Londres** I'm leaving for London soon; **~ em** (*com data*) **estamos em três de abril** it's the third of April; **~ numa** de be into; **ultimamente ela está numa de ouvir rock** she's been into rock music lately; **estar sem** not; **estou sem dinheiro** I haven't got any money; **está sem comer há três dias** she hasn't eaten for three days; **estou!, está lá!** *Port* (*ao telefone*) hello!; **não ~ para** not to be in the mood for; **não estou para brincadeiras** I'm not in the mood for jokes

❗ Quando o verbo **estar** é parte integrante de uma frase como por exemplo **estar acostumado, estar com pressa, estar de acordo, estar de pé,** pesquise pelo adjetivo ou substantivo que o acompanha.

estardalhaço /istarda'ʎasu/ *m* (*barulho*) fuss; (*ostentação*) extravagance

estarre|cedor /istaxese'dor/ *a* horrifying. **~cer** *vt* horrify. **~cer-se** *vpr* be horrified

esta|tal /ista'taw/ (*pl* **~tais**) *a* state-owned ● *f* state company

este|lado /istate'ladu/ *a* sprawling. **~lar** *vt* knock down. **~lar-se** *vpr* go sprawling

estático /is'tatʃiku/ *a* static

estatísti|ca /ista'tʃistʃika/ *f* statistics. **~co** *a* statistical

estati|zação /istatʃiza'sãw/ *f* nationalization. **~zar** *vt* nationalize

estátua /is'tatua/ f statue

estatueta /istatu'eta/ f statuette

estatura /ista'tura/ f stature

estatuto /ista'tutu/ m statute

está|vel /is'tavew/ (pl ~veis) a stable

este[1] /'estʃi/ a invar & m east

este[2] /'estʃi/ a this; pl these ● pron this one; pl these; (mencionado por último) the latter

esteio /is'teju/ m prop; fig mainstay

esteira /is'tera/ f (tapete) mat; (rastro) wake

estelionato /istelio'natu/ m fraud

estender /istē'der/ vt (desdobrar) spread out; (alongar) stretch; (ampliar) extend; hold out <mão>; hang out <roupa>; roll out <massa>; draw out <conversa>. ~se vpr (deitar-se) stretch out; (ir longe) stretch, extend; ~se sobre dwell on

esteno|datilógrafo /istenodatʃi'lɔgrafu/ m shorthand typist. ~grafia f shorthand

estepe /is'tepi/ m spare wheel

esterco /is'terku/ m dung

estéreo /is'teriu/ a invar stereo

estere|otipado /isteriotʃi'padu/ a stereotypical. ~ótipo m stereotype

esté|ril /is'teriw/ (pl ~reis) a sterile

esterili|dade /isterili'dadʒi/ f sterility. ~zar vt sterilize

esterli|no /ister'linu/ a libra ~na pound sterling

esteroide /iste'rɔjdʒi/ m steroid

estética /is'tetʃika/ f aesthetics

esteticista /istetʃi'sista/ m/f beautician

estético /is'tetʃiku/ a aesthetic

estetoscópio /istetos'kɔpiu/ m stethoscope

estiagem /istʃi'aʒẽ/ f dry spell

estibordo /istʃi'bordu/ m starboard

esti|cada /istʃi'kada/ f dar uma ~cada go on. ~car vt stretch ● vi 🄸 go on. ~car-se vpr stretch out

estigma /is'tʃigima/ m stigma. ~tizar vt brand (de as)

estilha|çar /istʃiʎa'sar/ vt shatter. ~çar-se vpr shatter. ~ço m shard, fragment

estilingue /istʃi'lĩgi/ m catapult

estilis|mo /istʃi'lizmu/ m fashion design. ~ta m/f fashion designer

esti|lístico /istʃi'listʃiku/ a stylistic. ~lizar vt stylize. ~lo m style; ~lo de vida lifestyle

esti|ma /es'tʃima/ f esteem. ~mação f estimation; cachorro de ~mação pet dog. ~mado a esteemed; Estimado Senhor Dear Sir. ~mar vt value <bens, joias etc> (em at); estimate <valor, preço etc> (em at); think highly of <pessoa>. ~mativa f estimate

estimu|lante /istʃimu'lãtʃi/ a stimulating ● m stimulant. ~lar vt stimulate; (incentivar) encourage

estímulo /is'tʃimulu/ m stimulus; (incentivo) incentive

estio /is'tʃiu/ m summer

estipu|lação /istʃipula'sãw/ f stipulation. ~lar vt stipulate

estirar /istʃi'rar/ vt stretch. ~se vpr stretch

estirpe /is'tʃirpi/ f stock, line

estivador /istʃiva'dor/ m docker

estocada /isto'kada/ f thrust

estocar /isto'kar/ vt stock ● vi stock up

Estocolmo /isto'kɔwmu/ f Stockholm

esto|far /isto'far/ vt upholster <móveis>. ~fo /o/ m upholstery

estoico /is'tɔjku/ a & m stoic

estojo /is'toʒu/ m case

estômago /is'tomagu/ m stomach

Estônia /is'tonia/ f Estonia

estonte|ante /istõtʃi'ãtʃi/ a stunning, mind-boggling. ~ar vt stun

estopim /isto'pĩ/ m fuse; fig flashpoint

estoque /is'tɔki/ m stock

estore /is'tɔri/ m blind

estória /is'tɔria/ f story

estor|var /istor'var/ vt hinder; obstruct <entrada, trânsito>. ~vo /o/ m hindrance

estou|rado /isto'radu/ a <pessoa> explosive. ~rar vi <bomba, escândalo, pessoa> blow up; <pneu> burst; <guerra> break out; <moda, cantor etc> make it big. ~ro m (de bomba, moda etc) explosion; (de pessoa) outburst; (de pneu) blowout; (de guerra) outbreak

estrábico /is'trabiku/ a <olhos> squinty; <pessoa> squint-eyed

estrabismo /istra'bizmu/ m squint

estraçalhar /istrasa'ʎar/ vt tear to pieces

estrada /is'trada/ f road; ~ de ferro railway, Amer railroad; ~ de rodagem highway; ~ de terra dirt road

estrado /is'tradu/ *m* podium; (*de cama*) base

estragão /istra'gãw/ *m* tarragon

estraga-prazeres /istragapra'zeris/ *m/f invar* spoilsport

estra|gar /istra'gar/ *vt* (*tornar desagradável*) spoil; (*acabar com*) ruin ● *vi* (*quebrar*) break; (*apodrecer*) go off. **~go** *m* damage; *pl* damage; (*de guerra, do tempo*) ravages

estrangeiro /istrã'ʒeru/ *a* foreign ● *m* foreigner; **do ~** from abroad; **para o/no ~** abroad

estrangular /istrãgu'lar/ *vt* strangle

estra|nhar /istra'ɲar/ *vt* (*achar estranho*) find strange; (*não se adaptar a*) find it hard to get used to; (*não se sentir à vontade com*) be shy with; **~nhar que** find it strange that; **estou te ~nhando** that's not like you; **não é de se ~nhar** it's not surprising. **~nheza** /e/ *f* (*esquisitice*) strangeness; (*surpresa*) surprise. **~nho** *a* strange ● *m* stranger

estratagema /istrata'ʒema/ *m* stratagem

estraté|gia /istra'teʒia/ *f* strategy. **~gico** *a* strategic

estrato /is'tratu/ *m* (*camada*) stratum; (*nuvem*) stratus. **~sfera** *f* stratosphere

estre|ante /istri'ãtʃi/ *a* new ● *m/f* newcomer. **~ar** *vt* premiere ‹*peça, filme*›; embark on ‹*carreira*›; wear for the first time ‹*roupa*› ● *vi* ‹*pessoa*› make one's debut; ‹*filme, peça*› open

estrebaria /istreba'ria/ *f* stable

estreia /is'treja/ *f* (*de pessoa*) debut; (*de filme, peça*) premiere

estrei|tar /istrej'tar/ *vt* narrow; take in ‹*vestido*›; make closer ‹*relações, laços*› ● *vi* narrow. **~tar-se** *vpr* ‹*relações*› become closer. **~to** *a* narrow; ‹*relações, laços*› close; ‹*saia*› straight ● *m* strait

estre|la /is'trela/ *f* star. **~lado** *a* ‹*céu*› starry; ‹*ovo*› fried; **~lado por** ‹*filme etc*› starring. **~la-do-mar** (*pl* **~las-do-mar**) *f* starfish. **~lar** *vt* fry ‹*ovo*›; star in ‹*filme, peça*›. **~lato** *m* stardom. **~lismo** *m* star quality

estreme|cer /istreme'ser/ *vt* shake; strain ‹*relações, amizade*› ● *vi* shudder; ‹*relações, amizade*› become strained. **~cimento** *m* shudder; (*de relações, amizade*) strain

estrepar-se /istre'parsi/ *vpr* Ⓘ come a cropper

estrépito /is'trɛpitu/ *m* noise; **com ~** noisily

estrepitoso /istrepi'tozu/ *a* noisy; ‹*sucesso etc*› resounding

estres|sante /istre'sãtʃi/ *a* stressful. **~sar** *vt* stress. **~se** /ɛ/ *m* stress

estria /is'tria/ *f* streak; (*no corpo*) stretch mark

estribeira /istri'bera/ *f* stirrup; **perder as ~s** lose control

estribilho /istri'biʎu/ *m* chorus

estribo /is'tribu/ *m* stirrup

estridente /istri'dẽtʃi/ *a* strident

estripulia /istripu'lia/ *f* antic

estrito /is'tritu/ *a* strict

estrofe /is'trɔfi/ *f* stanza, verse

estrógeno /is'trɔʒenu/ *m* oestrogen

estrogonofe /istrogo'nɔfi/ *m* stroganoff

estron|do /is'trõdu/ *m* crash. **~doso** /o/ *a* loud; ‹*aplausos*› thunderous; ‹*sucesso, fracasso*› resounding

estropiar /istropi'ar/ *vt* cripple ‹*pessoa*›; mangle ‹*palavras*›

estrume /is'trumi/ *m* manure

estrutu|ra /istru'tura/ *f* structure. **~ral** (*pl* **~rais**) *a* structural. **~rar** *vt* structure

estuário /istu'ariu/ *m* estuary

estudan|te /istu'dãtʃi/ *m/f* student. **~til** (*pl* **~tis**) *a* student

estudar /istu'dar/ *vt/i* study

estúdio /is'tudʒiu/ *m* studio

estu|dioso /istudʒi'ozu/ *a* studious ● *m* scholar. **~do** *m* study

estufa /is'tufa/ *f* (*para plantas*) greenhouse; (*de aquecimento*) stove. **~do** *m* stew

estupefato /istupe'fatu/ *a* dumbfounded

estupendo /iste'pẽdu/ *a* stupendous

estupidez /istupi'des/ *f* (*grosseria*) rudeness; (*uma*) rude thing; (*burrice*) stupidity; (*uma*) stupid thing

estúpido /is'tupidu/ *a* (*grosso*) rude, coarse; (*burro*) stupid ● *m* lout

estupor /istu'por/ *m* stupor

estu|prador /istupra'dor/ *m* rapist. **~prar** *vt* rape. **~pro** *m* rape

esturricar /istuxi'kar/ *vt* parch

esvair-se /izva'irsi/ *vpr* fade; **~ em sangue** bleed to death

esvaziar /izvazi'ar/ *vt* empty. **~se** *vpr* empty

esverdeado /izverdʒi'adu/ *a* greenish

e

esvoa|çante /izvoa'sãtʃi/ a ‹cabelo›
flyaway. **~çar** vi flutter

eta /'eta/ int what a

etapa /e'tapa/ f stage; (de corrida, turnê
etc) leg

etário /e'tariu/ a age

éter /'ɛter/ m ether

etéreo /e'tɛriu/ a ethereal

eter|nidade /eterni'dadʒi/ f eternity.
~no /ɛ/ a eternal

éti|ca /'ɛtʃika/ f ethics. **~co** a ethical

etimo|logia /etʃimolo'ʒia/ f
etymology. **~lógico** a etymological

etíope /e'tʃiopi/ a & m/f Ethiopian

Etiópia /etʃi'ɔpia/ f Ethiopia

etique|ta /etʃi'keta/ f (rótulo) label;
(bons modos) etiquette. **~tar** vt label

étnico /'ɛtʃniku/ a ethnic

eu /ew/ pron I ● m self; **mais alto do que
~** taller than me; **sou ~** it's me

EUA m pl USA

eucalipto /ewka'liptu/ m eucalyptus

eufemismo /ewfe'mizmu/ m
euphemism

euforia /ewfo'ria/ f euphoria

euro /'ewru/ m euro

Europa /ew'rɔpa/ f Europe

euro|peu /ewro'pew/ a & m (f **~peia**)
European

eutanásia /ewta'nazia/ f euthanasia

evacu|ação /evakua'sãw/ f
evacuation. **~ar** vt evacuate

evadir /eva'dʒir/ vt evade. **~se** vpr
escape (de from)

evan|gelho /evã'ʒeʎu/ m gospel

evaporar /evapo'rar/ vt evaporate.
~se vpr evaporate

eva|são /eva'zãw/ f escape; (fiscal
etc) evasion; **~ fiscal** tax evasion; **~são
escolar** truancy. **~siva** f excuse. **~sivo**
a evasive

even|to /e'vẽtu/ m event. **~tual**
(pl **~tuais**) a possible. **~tualidade** f
eventuality

evidência /evi'dẽsia/ f evidence

eviden|ciar /evidẽsi'ar/ vt show up.
~ciar-se vpr show up. **~te** a obvious,
evident

evi|tar /evi'tar/ vt avoid; **~tar de beber**
avoid drinking. **~tável** (pl **~táveis**) a
avoidable

evocar /evo'kar/ vt call to mind, evoke
‹passado etc›; call up ‹espíritos etc›

evolu|ção /evolu'sãw/ f evolution. **~ir**
vi evolve

exacerbar /ezaser'bar/ vt exacerbate

exage|rado /ezaʒe'radu/ a over the
top. **~rar** vt (atribuir proporções irreais a)
exaggerate; (fazer em excesso) overdo
● vi (ao falar) exaggerate; (exceder-se)
overdo it. **~ro** /e/ m exaggeration

exa|lação /ezala'sãw/ f fume;
(agradável) scent. **~lar** vt give off
‹perfume etc›

exal|tação /ezawta'sãw/ f (excitação)
agitation; (engrandecimento) exaltation.
~tar vt (excitar) agitate; (enfurecer)
infuriate; (louvar) exalt. **~tar-se** vpr
(excitar-se) get agitated; (enfurecer-se)
get furious

exa|me /e'zami/ m examination; (na
escola) exam(ination). **~me de sangue**
blood test. **~minar** vt examine

exaspe|ração /ezaspera'sãw/ f
exasperation. **~rar** vt exasperate.
~rar-se vpr get exasperated

exa|tidão /ezatʃi'dãw/ f exactness.
~to a exact

exaurir /ezaw'rir/ vt exhaust. **~se** vpr
become exhausted

exaus|tivo /ezaws'tʃivu/ a ‹estudo›
exhaustive; ‹trabalho› exhausting. **~to**
a exhausted

exceção /ese'sãw/ f exception; **abrir ~**
make an exception; **com ~ de** with the
exception of

exce|dente /ese'dẽtʃi/ a & m excess,
surplus. **~der** vt exceed. **~der-se** vpr
overdo it

exce|lência /ese'lẽsia/ f excellence;
(tratamento) excellency. **~lente** a
excellent

excentricidade /esẽtrisi'dadʒi/ f
eccentricity

excêntrico /e'sẽtriku/ a & m eccentric

excep|cional /esepsjo'naw/ (pl
~cionais) a exceptional; (deficiente)
handicapped

exces|sivo /ese'sivu/ a excessive. **~so**
/e/ m excess; **~so de bagagem** excess
baggage; **~so de velocidade** speeding

exce|to /e'sɛtu/ prep except. **~tuar** vt
except

exci|tação /esita'sãw/ f excitement.
~tante a exciting. **~tar** vt excite. **~tar-se**
vpr get excited

excla|mação /isklama'sãw/ f
exclamation. **~mar** vt/i exclaim

exclu|ir /isklu'ir/ vt exclude. **~são**
f exclusion; **com ~são de** with the
exclusion of. **~sividade** f exclusive
rights; **com ~sividade** exclusively. **~sivo**
a exclusive. **~so** a excluded

excomungar /iskomũ'gar/ vt
excommunicate

excremento /iskre'mẽtu/ m
excrement

excur|são /iskur'sãw/ f excursion;
(a pé) hike, walk. **~sionista** m/f day
tripper; (a pé) hiker, walker

execu|ção /ezeku'sãw/ f execution.
~tante m/f performer. **~tar** vt carry out
‹ordem, plano etc›; perform ‹papel,
música›; execute ‹preso, criminoso etc›.
~tivo a & m executive

exem|plar /ezẽ'plar/ a exemplary ● m
(de espécie) example; (de livro, jornal etc)
copy. **~plificar** vt exemplify

exemplo /e'zẽplu/ m example; **a ~
de** following the example of; **por ~** for
example; **dar o ~** set an example

exequí|vel /eze'kwivew/ (pl **~veis**) a
feasible

exer|cer /ezer'ser/ vt exercise;
exert ‹pressão, influência›; carry on
‹profissão›. **~cício** m exercise; Mil drill;
(de profissão) practice; (financeiro)
financial year. **~citar** vt exercise; practise
‹ofício›. **~citar-se** vpr train

exército /e'zɛrsitu/ m army

exibição /ezibi'sãw/ f (de filme,
passaporte etc) showing; (de talento,
força, ostentação) show

exibicionis|mo /ezibisio'nizmu/ m
exhibitionism. **~ta** a & m/f exhibitionist

exi|bido /ezi'bidu/ a ‹pessoa›
pretentious ● m show-off. **~bir** vt
show; (ostentar) show off. **~bir-se** vpr
(ostentar-se) show off

exi|gência /ezi'ʒẽsia/ f demand.
~gente a demanding. **~gir** vt demand

exíguo /e'zigwu/ a (muito pequeno)
tiny; (escasso) minimal

exi|lado /ezi'ladu/ a exiled ● m exile.
~lar vt exile. **~lar-se** vpr go into exile

exílio /e'ziliu/ m exile

exímio /e'zimiu/ a distinguished

eximir /ezi'mir/ vt exempt (de from);
~se de get out of

exis|tência /ezis'tẽsia/ f existence.
~tencial (pl **~tenciais**) a existential.
~tente a existing. **~tir** vi exist

êxito /'ezitu/ m success; (música, filme
etc) hit; **ter ~** succeed

êxodo /'ezodu/ m exodus

exonerar /ezone'rar/ vt (de cargo)
dismiss, sack. **~se** vpr resign

exorbitante /ezorbi'tãtʃi/ a
exorbitant

exor|cismo /ezor'sizmu/ m exorcism.
~cista m/f exorcist. **~cizar** vt exorcize

exótico /e'zɔtʃiku/ a exotic

expan|dir /ispã'dʒir/ vt spread.
~dir-se vpr spread; ‹pessoa› open up;
~dir-se sobre expand upon. **~são** f
expansion. **~sivo** a expansive, open

expatri|ado /ispatri'adu/ a & m
expatriate. **~ar-se** vpr leave one's
country

expectativa /ispekta'tʃiva/ f
expectation; **na ~ de** expecting; **estar
na ~** wait to see what happens; **~ de
vida** life expectancy

expedição /ispedʒi'sãw/ f (de
encomendas, cartas) dispatch;
(de passaporte, diploma etc) issue;
(viagem) expedition

expediente /ispedʒi'ẽtʃi/ a ‹pessoa›
resourceful ● m (horário) working hours;
(meios) expedient; **meio ~** part-time

expe|dir /ispe'dʒir/ vt dispatch
‹encomendas, cartas›; issue ‹passaporte,
diploma›. **~dito** a prompt, quick

expelir /ispe'lir/ vt expel

experi|ência /isperi'ẽsia/ f
experience; (teste, tentativa) experiment.
~ente a experienced

experimen|tação /isperimẽta'sãw/ f
experimentation. **~tado** a experienced.
~tar vt (provar) try out; try on ‹roupa›;
try ‹comida›; (sentir, viver) experience.
~to m experiment

expi|ar /espi'ar/ vt atone for. **~atório** a
bode **~atório** scapegoat

expi|ração /espira'sãw/ f (vencimento)
expiry; (de ar) exhalation. **~rar** vt exhale
● vi (morrer, vencer) expire; (expelir ar)
breath out, exhale

expli|cação /isplika'sãw/ f
explanation. **~car** vt explain. **~car-se**
vpr explain o.s.. **~cável** (pl **~cáveis**) a
explainable

explicitar /isplisi'tar/ vt set out

explícito /is'plisitu/ a explicit

explodir /isplo'dʒir/ vt explode ● vi
explode; ‹ator etc› make it big

explo|ração /isplora'sãw/ f (uso,
abuso) exploitation; (pesquisa)
exploration. **~rar** vt (tirar proveito de)
exploit; (esquadrinhar) explore

e

explo|são /isplo'zãw/ f explosion.
~sivo a & m explosive

expor /es'por/ vt (sujeitar, arriscar)
expose (**a** to); display ‹mercadorias›;
exhibit ‹obras de arte›; (explicar)
expound; **~ a vida** risk one's life. **~se**
vpr expose o.s. (**a** to)

expor|tação /isporta'sãw/ f export.
~tador a exporting ● m exporter.
~tadora f export company. **~tar** vt
export

exposi|ção /ispozi'sãw/ f (de arte etc)
exhibition; (de mercadorias) display; (de
filme fotográfico) exposure; (explicação)
exposition. **~tor** m exhibitor

exposto /is'postu/ a exposed (**a** to);
‹mercadoria, obra de arte› on display

expres|são /ispre'sãw/ f expression.
~sar vt express. **~sar-se** vpr express o.s..
~sivo a expressive; ‹número, quantia›
significant. **~so** /ɛ/ a & m express

exprimir /ispri'mir/ vt express. **~-se**
vpr express o.s.

expropriar /ispropri'ar/ vt expropriate

expul|são /ispuw'sãw/ f expulsion; (de
jogador) sending off. **~sar** vt (de escola,
partido, país etc) expel; (de clube, bar,
festa etc) throw out; (de jogo) send off.
~so pp de ▶ EXPULSAR

expur|gar /ispur'gar/ vt purge;
expurgate ‹livro›. **~go** m purge

êxtase /'estazi/ f ecstasy

extasiado /istazi'adu/ a ecstatic

exten|são /istē'sãw/ f extension;
(tamanho, alcance, duração) extent; (de
terreno) expanse; **~são (de arquivo)**
Comput (file) extension. **~sivo** a
extensive. **~so** a extensive; **por ~so**
in full

extenu|ante /istenu'ãtʃi/ a wearing,
tiring. **~ar** vt tire out. **~ar-se** vpr tire
o.s. out

exterior /isteri'or/ a outside, exterior;
‹aparência› outward; ‹relações, comércio
etc› foreign ● m outside, exterior; (de
pessoa) exterior; **o ~** (outros países)
abroad; **para o/no ~** abroad

exter|minar /istermi'nar/ vt
exterminate. **~mínio** m extermination

exter|nar /ister'nar/ vt show. **~na** /ɛ/ f
location shot. **~no** /ɛ/ a external; ‹dívida
etc› foreign ● m day pupil

extin|ção /istʃĩ'sãw/ f extinction. **~guir**
vt extinguish ‹fogo›; wipe out ‹dívida,
animal, povo›. **~guir-se** vpr ‹fogo, luz›
go out; ‹animal, planta› become extinct.
~to a extinct; ‹organização, pessoa›

defunct. **~tor** m fire extinguisher

extirpar /istʃir'par/ vt remove ‹tumor
etc›; uproot ‹ervas daninhas›; eradicate
‹abusos›

extor|quir /istor'kir/ vt extort. **~são**
f extortion

extra /'estra/ a & m/f extra; **horas ~s**
overtime

extração /istra'sãw/ f extraction;
(da loteria) draw

extraconju|gal /estrakõʒu'gaw/
(pl **~gais**) a extramarital

extracurricular /estrakuxiku'lar/ a
extracurricular

extradi|ção /istradʒi'sãw/ f
extradition. **~tar** vt extradite

extrair /istra'ir/ vt extract; draw
‹números da loteria›

extrajudici|al /estraʒudʒisi'aw/
(pl **~ais**) a out-of-court. **~almente** adv
out of court

extraordinário /istraordʒi'nariu/ a
extraordinary

extrapolar /istrapo'lar/ vt (exceder)
overstep; (calcular) extrapolate ● vi
overstep the mark, go too far

extrasensori|al /estrasẽsori'aw/
(pl **~ais**) a extrasensory

extraterrestre /estrate'xestri/ a & m
extraterrestrial

extrato /is'trato/ m extract; (de conta)
statement

extrava|gância /istrava'gãsia/ f
extravagance. **~gante** a extravagant

extravasar /istrava'zar/ vt release, let
out ‹emoções, sentimentos› ● vi overflow

extra|viado /istravi'adu/ a lost. **~viar**
vt lose, mislay ‹papéis, carta›; lead astray
‹pessoa›; embezzle ‹dinheiro›. **~viar-se**
vpr go astray; ‹carta› get lost. **~vio** m
(perda) misplacement; (de dinheiro)
embezzlement

extre|midade /estremi'dadʒi/ f
end; (do corpo) extremity. **~mismo** m
extremism. **~mista** a & m/f extremist.
~mo /e/ a & m extreme; **o Extremo
Oriente** the Far East. **~moso** /o/ a
doting

extrovertido /istrover'tʃido/ a & m
extrovert

exube|rância /ezube'rãsia/ f
exuberance. **~rante** a exuberant

exultar /ezuw'tar/ vi exult

exumar /ezu'mar/ vt exhume
‹cadáver›; dig up ‹documentos etc›

Ff

fã /fã/ m/f fan

fábrica /'fabrika/ f factory

fabri|cação /fabrika'sãw/ f manufacture. **~cante** m/f manufacturer. **~car** vt manufacture; (*inventar*) fabricate

fábula /'fabula/ f fable; 🛈 (*dinheirão*) fortune

fabuloso /fabu'lozu/ a fabulous

faca /'faka/ f knife. **~da** f knife blow; **dar uma ~da em** fig get some money off

façanha /fa'saɲa/ f feat

facção /fak'sãw/ f faction

face /'fasi/ f face; (*do rosto*) cheek. **~ta** /e/ f facet

fachada /fa'ʃada/ f facade

facho /'faʃu/ m beam

faci|al /fasi'aw/ (pl **~ais**) a facial

fá|cil /'fasiw/ (pl **~ceis**) a easy; ‹*pessoa*› easy-going

facili|dade /fasili'dadʒi/ f ease; (*talento*) facility. **~tar** vt facilitate

facilitismo /facili'tiʒmu/ m o ~ na educação falling education standards

fã-clube /fã'klubi/ m fan club

fac-símile /fak'simili/ m facsimile; (*fax*) fax

fact- Port ▶ **fat-**

facul|dade /fakuw'dadʒi/ f (*mental etc*) faculty; (*escola*) university, *Amer* college; **fazer ~dade** go to university. **~tativo** a optional

fada /'fada/ f fairy. **~do** a destined, doomed. **~madrinha** (pl **~s-madrinhas**) f fairy godmother

fadiga /fa'dʒiga/ f fatigue

fa|dista /fa'dʒista/ m/f fado singer. **~do** m fado

> **fado** *Fado*, literally meaning 🛈 'fate', is a traditional Portuguese style of song dating back to the early 19th century. The songs have a melancholy, plaintive style, and are associated with the Portuguese concept of *saudade* (longing). There are two types of *fado*: Lisbon *fado* is traditionally sung by a woman accompanied by two or three guitarists, whereas Coimbra *fado* is performed by a male soloist.

fagote /fa'gɔtʃi/ m bassoon

fagulha /fa'guʎa/ f spark

fala /'faja/ f beech

faisão /faj'zãw/ m pheasant

faisca /fa'iska/ f spark

fais|cante /fajs'kãtʃi/ a sparkling. **~car** vi spark; (*cintilar*) sparkle

faixa /'faʃa/ f strip; (*cinto*) sash; (*em karatê, judô*) belt; (*da estrada*) lane; (*de ônibus*) bus lane; (*para pedestres*) zebra crossing, *Amer* crosswalk; (*atadura*) bandage; (*de disco*) track; **~ etária** age group

fajuto /fa'ʒutu/ a 🛈 fake

fala /'fala/ f speech

fala-barato /fala'baratu/ m/f invar Port ▶ **TAGARELA**

falácia /fa'lasia/ f fallacy

fa|lado /fa'ladu/ a ‹*língua*› spoken; ‹*caso, pessoa*› talked about. **~lante** a talkative. **~lar** vt/i speak; (*dizer*) say; **~lar com** talk to; **~lar de ou em** talk about; **por ~lar em** speaking of; **sem ~lar em** not to mention; **~loul** 🛈 OK!. **~latório** m (*boatos*) talk; (*som de vozes*) talking

falaz /fa'las/ a fallacious

falcão /faw'kãw/ m falcon

falcatrua /fawka'trua/ f swindle

fale|cer /fale'ser/ vi die, pass away. **~cido** a & m deceased. **~cimento** m death

falência /fa'lẽsia/ f bankruptcy; **ir à ~** go bankrupt

falésia /fa'lezia/ f cliff

fa|lha /'faʎa/ f fault; (*omissão*) failure. **~lhar** vi fail. **~lho** a faulty

fálico /'faliku/ a phallic

fa|lido /fa'lidu/ a & m bankrupt. **~lir** vi go bankrupt. **~lível** (pl **~líveis**) a fallible

falo /'falu/ m phallus

fal|sário /faw'sariu/ m forger. **~sear** vt falsify; **~sete** m falsetto. **~sidade** f falseness; (*mentira*) falsehood

falsifi|cação /fawsifika'sãw/ f forgery. **~cador** m forger. **~car** vt falsify; forge ‹*documentos, notas*›

falso /'fawsu/ a false

fal|ta /'fawta/ f lack; (*em futebol*) foul; **em ~ta** at fault; **por ~ta de** for lack of; **sem ~ta** without fail; **fazer ~ta** be needed; **sentir a ~ta de** miss; **~tar** vi be missing; ‹*aluno*› be absent; **~tam dois dias para** it's two days until; **me ~ta ...** I don't have ...; **~tar a** miss ‹*aula etc*›; break ‹*palavra, promessa*›. **~to** a short (**de** of)

fa|ma /'fama/ f reputation; (*celebridade*) fame. **~migerado** a notorious

família /fa'milia/ f family

famili|ar /famili'ar/ a familiar; (*de família*) family. **~aridade** f familiarity. **~arizar** vt familiarize. **~arizar-se** vpr familiarize o.s.

faminto /fa'mĩtu/ a starving

famoso /fa'mozu/ a famous

fanático /fa'natʃiku/ a fanatical ● m fanatic

fanatismo /fana'tʃizmu/ m fanaticism

fanfarrão /fãfa'xãw/ m braggart

fanhoso /fa'ɲozu/ a nasal; **ser ~** talk through one's nose

fanta|sia /fãta'zia/ f (*faculdade*) imagination; (*devaneio*) fantasy; (*roupa*) fancy dress. **~siar** vt dream up ● vi fantasize. **~siar-se** vpr dress up (**de** as). **~sioso** /o/ a fanciful; ‹*pessoa*› imaginative. **~sista** a imaginative

fantasma /fã'tazma/ m ghost. **~górico** a ghostly

fantástico /fã'tastʃiku/ a fantastic

fantoche /fã'tɔʃi/ m puppet

faqueiro /fa'keru/ m canteen of cutlery

fara|ó /fara'ɔ/ m pharaoh. **~ônico** a fig of epic proportions

farda /'farda/ f uniform. **~do** a uniformed

fardo /'fardu/ m fig burden

fare|jador /fareʒa'dor/ a **cão ~jador** sniffer dog. **~jar** vt sniff out ● vi sniff/smell

farelo /fa'rɛlu/ m bran; (*de pão*) crumb; (*de madeira*) sawdust

farfalhar /farfa'ʎar/ vi rustle

farináceo /fari'nasiu/ a starchy. **~s** m pl starchy foods

farin|ge /fa'rĩʒi/ f pharynx. **~gite** f pharyngitis

farinha /fa'riɲa/ f flour; **~ de rosca** breadcrumbs

far|macêutico /farma'sewtʃiku/ a pharmaceutical ● m (*pessoa*) pharmacist. **~mácia** f (*loja*) chemist's, Amer pharmacy; (*ciência*) pharmacy

faro /'faru/ m sense of smell; fig nose

faroeste /faro'estʃi/ m (*filme*) western; (*região*) wild west

faro|fa /fa'rɔfa/ f fried manioc flour. **~feiro** m day tripper

fa|rol /fa'rɔw/ m (pl **~róis**) m (*de carro*) headlight; (*de trânsito*) traffic light; (*à beira-mar*) lighthouse; **~rol alto** full beam; **~rol baixo** dipped beam. **~roleiro** a boastful ● m big-head.

~rolete /e/ m, Port **~rolim** m sidelight; (*traseiro*) tail light

farpa /'farpa/ f splinter; (*de metal*) fig barb. **~do** a **arame ~do** barbed wire

farra /'faxa/ f partying; **cair na ~** go out and party

farrapo /fa'xapu/ m rag

far|rear /faxi'ar/ vi party. **~rista** m/f raver

far|sa /'farsa/ f (*peça*) farce; (*fingimento*) pretence. **~sante** m/f (*brincalhão*) joker; (*pessoa sem seriedade*) unreliable character

far|tar /far'tar/ vt satiate. **~tar-se** vpr (*saciar-se*) gorge o.s. (**de** with); (*cansar*) tire (**de** of). **~to** a (*abundante*) plentiful; (*cansado*) fed up (**de** with). **~tura** f abundance

fascículo /fa'sikulu/ m instalment

fasci|nação /fasina'sãw/ f fascination. **~nante** a fascinating. **~nar** vt fascinate

fascínio /fa'siniu/ m fascination

fas|cismo /fa'sizmu/ m fascism. **~cista** a & m/f fascist

fase /'fazi/ f phase

fa|tal /fa'taw/ (pl **~tais**) a fatal. **~talismo** m fatalism. **~talista** a fatalistic ● m/f fatalist. **~talmente** adv inevitably

fatia /fa'tʃia/ f slice

fatídico /fa'tʃidʒiku/ a fateful

fati|gante /fatʃi'gãtʃi/ a tiring. **~gar** vt tire, fatigue

Fátima Fátima is a town in central Portugal famous for its Marian shrine, the Basílica of Our Lady of Fátima. The shrine was built to commemorate the reported apparition of the Virgin Mary to three shepherds in 1917, and it attracts millions of Catholic pilgrims every year.

---

fato¹ /'fatu/ m fact; **de ~** as a matter of fact, in fact; **~ consumado** fait accompli

fato² /'fatu/ Port m suit

fator /fa'tor/ m factor

fátuo /'fatuu/ a fatuous

fatu|ra /fa'tura/ f invoice. **~ramento** m turnover. **~rar** vt invoice for ‹*encomenda*›; make ‹*dinheiro*›; fig (*emplacar*) notch up ● vi rake it in

fauna /'fawna/ f fauna

fava /'fava/ f broad bean; **mandar alguém às ~s** tell sb where to get off

favela /fa'vɛla/ f shanty town. **~do** m shanty-dweller

favela *Favela* are Brazilian shanty
towns, characterized by precarious
housing, very little infrastructure
and a lack of official recognition.
The houses in the *favelas* are known as
barracos, and many have no running
water or sanitation. The most famous
shanty towns in Brazil are in Rio de
Janeiro, such as the *Favela da Rocinha*,
which is home to sixty thousand
people.

favo /'favu/ *m* honeycomb

favor /fa'vor/ *m* favour; **a ~ de** in favour
of; **por ~** please; **faça ~** please

favo|rável /favo'ravew/ (*pl* **~ráveis**) *a*
favourable. **~recer** *vt* favour. **~ritismo** *m*
favouritism. **~rito** *a* & *m* favourite

faxi|na /fa'ʃina/ *f* clean-up. **~neiro** *m*
cleaner

fazen|da /fa'zẽda/ *f* (*de café, gado etc*)
farm; (*tecido*) fabric, material; (*pública*)
treasury. **~deiro** *m* farmer

fazer /fa'zer/ ● *vt*

····▸ (*produzir, preparar*) make; **~
uma blusa** make a blouse; **~ muito
ruído** make a lot of noise; **~ um café**
make a coffee; **~ uma pergunta** ask
a question

····▸ (*realizar*) to do; **~ um exame/
lição de casa** do an exam/some
homework

····▸ (*praticar*) do; **~ ginástica/judô**
do gymnastics/judo

····▸ (*favor*) to do; **você me faria um
favor?** can you do me a favour?

····▸ (*comentário, promessa, esforço*)
make; **você precisa ~ um esforço**
you have to make an effort

····▸ (*amor*) make; **faça amor, não
faça guerra** make love not war

····▸ (*anos*) be; **ela faz 20 anos em
março** she'll be 20 in March

····▸ (*profissão*) do; **o que você faz?
Sou piloto** what do you do? I'm a
pilot

····▸ (*obrigar*) make; **~ alguém rir**
make sb laugh; **você me faz vir aqui
todos os dias** you make me come
here everyday

● *vi*

····▸ (*com tempo atmosférico*) **faz
frio/calor** it's cold/hot

····▸ (*em expressões*) **~ bem/mal**
(*ao agir*) be right/wrong; (*à saúde*)
fumar faz mal à saúde smoking is
bad for you; **o exercício faz bem**
exercise is good for you; **~ de conta
que** pretend; **ela fez de conta que
não me viu** she pretended she hadn't
seen me; **não faz mal** (*não importa*) it
doesn't matter

● *vpr*

····▸ **~se de** (*fingir*) pretend; **ele se
fez de burro** he pretended not to
understand

faz-tudo /fas'tudu/ *m/f invar* jack of
all trades

fé /fe/ *f* faith

fe|bre /'febri/ *f* fever; **~bre amarela**
yellow fever; **~bre do feno** hay fever.
~bril (*pl* **~bris**) *a* feverish

fe|chado /fe'ʃadu/ *a* closed; ‹*curva*›
sharp; ‹*sinal*› red; ‹*torneira*› off;
‹*tempo*› overcast; ‹*cara*› stern; ‹*pessoa*›
reserved. **~chadura** *f* lock. **~chamento**
m closure. **~char** *vt* close, shut; turn off
‹*torneira*›; do up ‹*calça, casaco*›; close
‹*negócio*› ● *vi* close, shut; ‹*sinal*› go
red; ‹*tempo*› cloud over; **~char à chave**
lock; **~char a cara** frown. **~cho** /e/ *m*
fastener; **~cho ecler** zip

fécula /'fekula/ *f* starch

fecun|dar /fekũ'dar/ *vt* fertilize. **~do**
a fertile

feder /fe'der/ *vi* stink

fede|ração /federa'sãw/ *f* federation.
~ral (*pl* **~rais**) *a* federal; 🅸 huge.
~rativo *a* federal

fedor /fe'dor/ *m* stink, stench. **~ento**
a stinking

feérico /fee'riku/ *a* magical

feições /fej'sõjs/ *f pl* features

fei|jão /fe'ʒãw/ *m* bean; (*coletivo*) beans.
~joada *f* bean stew. **~joeiro** *m* bean
plant

feijoada *Feijoada* is Brazil's most
typical dish, and is traditionally
made with black beans, pork meat and
pork trimmings, such as the ear, feet,
and tail. It is often served with sautéed
greens, orange and *farofa*, toasted
manioc flour. The dish dates back to
the colonial period when African slaves
had to make use of the parts of the pig
that had been discarded by their
owners. Portugal also has its own
version of *feijoada*, made with pork,
kidney beans, *chouriço* (cured sausage)
and cabbage.

f

feio /'feju/ a ugly; ‹palavra, situação, tempo› nasty; ‹olhar› dirty. **~so** /o/ a plain

fei|ra /'fera/ f market; (industrial) trade fair. **~rante** m/f market trader

feiti|çaria /fejtʃi'sera/ f magic. **~ceira** f witch. **~ceiro** m wizard ● a bewitching. **~ço** m spell

fei|tio /fej'tʃiu/ m (de pessoa) make-up. **~to** pp de ▶ FAZER ● m (ato) deed; (proeza) feat ● conj like; **bem ~to por ele** (it) serves him right. **~tura** f making

feiura /fej'ura/ f ugliness

feixe /'fejʃi/ m bundle

fel /fɛw/ m gall; fig bitterness

felicidade /felisi'dadʒi/ f happiness

felici|tações /felisita'sõjs/ f pl congratulations. **~tar** vt congratulate (**por** on)

felino /fe'linu/ a feline

feliz /fe'lis/ a happy. **~ardo** a lucky. **~mente** adv fortunately

fel|pa /'fewpa/ f (de pano) nap; (penugem) down, fluff. **~pudo** a fluffy

feltro /'fewtru/ m felt

fêmea /'femia/ a & f female

femi|nil /femi'niw/ (pl **~nis**) a feminine. **~nilidade** f femininity. **~nino** a female; ‹palavra› feminine. **~nismo** m feminism. **~nista** a & m/f feminist

fêmur /'femur/ m femur

fen|da /'fẽda/ f crack. **~der** vt/i split, crack

feno /'fenu/ m hay

fenome|nal /fenome'naw/ (pl **~nais**) a phenomenal

fenômeno /fe'nomenu/ m phenomenon

fera /'fɛra/ f wild beast; **ficar uma ~** get really angry; **ser ~ em** 🄑 be brilliant at

féretro /'fɛretru/ m coffin

feriado /feri'adu/ m public holiday

férias /'fɛrias/ f pl holiday(s), Amer vacation; **de ~** on holiday; **tirar ~** take a holiday

feri|da /fe'rida/ f injury; (com arma) wound. **~do** a injured; Mil wounded ● m injured person; **os ~dos** the injured; Mil the wounded. **~r** vt injure; (com arma) wound; (magoar) hurt

fermen|tar /fermẽ'tar/ vt/i ferment. **~to** m yeast; fig ferment; **~to em pó** baking powder

fe|rocidade /ferosi'dadʒi/ f ferocity. **~roz** a ferocious

fer|rado /fe'xadu/ a **estou ~rado** 🄑 I've had it 🄑; **~rado no sono** fast asleep. **~radura** f horseshoe. **~ragem** f ironwork; pl hardware. **~ramenta** f tool; (coletivo) tools. **~rão** m (de abelha) sting. **~rar** vt brand ‹gado›; shoe ‹cavalo›. **~rar-se** vpr 🄑 come a cropper. **~reiro** m blacksmith. **~renho** a ‹partidário etc› staunch; ‹vontade› iron

férreo /'fɛxiu/ a iron

ferro /'fɛxu/ m iron. **~lho** /o/ m bolt. **~velho** (pl **~s-velhos**) m (pessoa) scrap-metal dealer; (lugar) scrap-metal yard. **~via** f railway, Amer railroad. **~viário** a railway ● m railway worker

ferrugem /fe'xuʒẽ/ f rust

fér|til /'fɛrtʃiw/ (pl **~teis**) a fertile

fertili|dade /fertʃili'dadʒi/ f fertility. **~zante** m fertilizer. **~zar** vt fertilize

fer|vente /fer'vẽtʃi/ a boiling. **~ver** vi boil; (de raiva) seethe. **~vilhar** vi bubble; **~vilhar de** swarm with. **~vor** m fervour. **~vura** f boiling

fes|ta /'fɛsta/ f party; (religiosa) festival. **~tejar** vt/i celebrate; (acolher) fete. **~tejo** /e/ m celebration. **~tim** m feast. **~tival** (pl **~tivais**) m festival. **~tividade** f festivity. **~tivo** a festive

festa Every town in Portugal has its own patron saint, and festivals, called festas, are held nationwide during the summer months to celebrate the local saint's day. The festivals consist of colourful processions through the town, coupled with music, street food and much revelry. One of the most famous festivals is the Festa de Santo António in Lisbon during which a mass wedding is held at Lisbon Cathedral in honour of St Anthony, the saint of marriages.

festas juninas Festas juninas are festivals that take place in Brazil over the month of June in honour of various saints: St Anthony on the 13th, St John on the 24th, and St Peter and St Paul on the 29th. During these festivals, various typical dishes are served, such as roasted sweet potato, popcorn, rice pudding, corn bread, and quentão, a hot drink made with wine, sugar, cloves and cinnamon. The festivities often include lighting bonfires, releasing hot-air balloons and dancing to música caipira, Brazilian country music.

feti|che /fe'tʃiʃi/ m fetish. **~chismo** m fetishism. **~chista** m/f fetishist ● a fetishistic

fétido /'fɛtʃidu/ a fetid

feto[1] /'fetu/ m (no útero) foetus

feto[2] /'fetu/ Port m (planta) fern

feu|dal /few'daw/ (pl **~dais**) a feudal. **~dalismo** m feudalism

fevereiro /feve'reru/ m February

fezes /'fezis/ f pl faeces

fiação /fia'sãw/ f Eletr wiring; (fábrica) mill

fia|do /fi'adu/ a ‹conversa› idle ● adv ‹comprar› on credit. **~dor** m guarantor

fiambre /fi'ãbri/ m cooked ham

fiança /fi'ãsa/ f surety; Jurid bail

fiapo /fi'apu/ m thread

fiar /fi'ar/ vt spin ‹lã etc›

fiasco /fi'asku/ m fiasco

fibra /'fibra/ f fibre

---

ficar /fi'kar/ ● vi

••••▶ (estar situado) be; **onde fica a casa deles?** where is their home?

••••▶ (permanecer) stay; **~ em casa** stay at home

••••▶ (restar) be left (over); **~am apenas 3 concorrentes** there were just 3 contestants left

••••▶ (tornar-se) **~ rico/doente/velho/gordo** get rich/ill/old/fat; **~ careca/cego** go bald/blind

••••▶ **~ com** (guardar) **~ com o troco** keep the change

••••▶ **~ de** (prometer) **ele ficou de me ajudar** he promised to help me; (concordar) **ficamos do nos encontrar na terça-feira** we agreed to meet on Tuesday

••••▶ **~ por** (custar) **este vestido ficou por R$30** this dress cost me R$30

••••▶ **~ sem**; (perder) lose; **ela ficou sem o emprego** she lost her job; (esgotar-se) run out of; **fiquei sem açúcar** I ran out of sugar

••••▶ (em expressões) **~ bem/mal**: ‹roupa› **a camisa fica bem em você** the shirt suits you; **~ para trás: ande, não fique para trás** come on, don't get left behind

---

fic|ção /fik'sãw/ f fiction; **~ção científica** science fiction. **~cionista** m/f fiction writer

fi|cha /'fiʃa/ f (de telefone) token; (de jogo) chip; (da caixa) ticket; (de fichário) file card; (na polícia) record; Port (tomada) plug. **~chário** m, Port **~cheiro** m file; (móvel) filing cabinet

fictício /fik'tʃisiu/ a fictitious

fidalgo /fi'dalgu/ m nobleman

fide|digno /fide'dʒignu/ a trustworthy. **~lidade** f fidelity

fiduciário /fidusi'ariu/ a fiduciary ● m trustee

fi|el /fi'ew/ (pl **~éis**) a faithful ● m os **~éis** (na igreja) the congregation

figa /'figa/ f talisman

fígado /'figadu/ f liver

fi|go /'figu/ m fig. **~gueira** f fig tree

figu|ra /fi'gura/ f figure; (carta de jogo) face card; 🅸 (pessoa) character; **fazer (má) ~ra** make a (bad) impression. **~rado** a figurative. **~rante** m/f extra. **~rão** m big shot. **~rar** vi appear, figure. **~rativo** a figurative. **~rinha** f sticker. **~rino** m fashion plate; (de filme, peça) costume design; fig model; **como manda o ~rino** as it should be

fila /'fila/ f line; (de espera) queue, Amer line; (fileira) row; **fazer ~** queue up, Amer stand in line; **~ indiana** single file

filamento /fila'mẽtu/ m filament

filante /fi'lãtʃi/ m/f 🅸 sponger

filan|tropia /filãtro'pia/ f philanthropy. **~trópico** a philanthropic. **~tropo** /o/ m philanthropist

filão /fi'lãw/ m (de ouro) seam; fig money-spinner

filar /fi'lar/ vt 🅸 sponge 🅸, cadge 🅸

filar|mônica /filar'monika/ f philharmonic (orchestra). **~mônico** a philharmonic

filate|lia /filate'lia/ f philately. **~lista** m/f philatelist

filé /fi'lɛ/ m fillet

fileira /fi'lera/ f row

filete /fi'lɛtʃi/ m fillet

fi|lha /'fiʎa/ f daughter. **~lho** m son; **~lho da puta** (vulg) bastard, Amer son of a bitch; **~lho de criação** foster child; **~lho único** only child ● pl (crianças) children. **~lhote** m (de cão) pup; (de lobo etc) cub; pl young

fili|ação /filia'sãw/ f affiliation. **~al** (pl **~ais**) a filial ● f branch

Filipinas /fili'pinas/ f pl Philippines

filipino /fili'pinu/ a & m Filipino

fil|madora /fiwma'dora/ f camcorder. **~magem** f filming. **~mar** vt/i film. **~me** m film

fi|lologia /filolo'ʒia/ f philology. **~lólogo** m philologist

filo|sofar /filozo'far/ vi philosophize. **~sofia** f philosophy. **~sófico** a philosophical

filósofo /fi'lɔzofu/ m philosopher

fil|trar /fiw'trar/ vt filter. **~tro** m filter

fim /fĩ/ m end; **a ~ de** (para) in order to; **estar a ~ de** fancy; **por ~** finally; **sem ~** endless; **ter ~** come to an end; **~ de semana** weekend

fi|nado /fi'nadu/ a & m deceased, departed. **~nal** (pl **~nais**) a final ● m end ● f final. **~nalista** m/f finalist. **~nalizar** vt/i finish

finan|ças /fi'nãsas/ f pl finances. **~ceiro** a financial ● m financier. **~ciamento** m financing; (um) loan. **~ciar** vt finance. **~cista** m/f financier

fincar /fĩ'kar/ vt plant; **~ o pé** fig dig one's heels in

findar /fĩ'dar/ vt/i end

fineza /fi'neza/ f finesse; (favor) kindness

fin|gido /fĩ'ʒidu/ a feigned; ‹pessoa› insincere. **~gimento** m pretence. **~gir** vt pretend; feign ‹doença etc› ● vi pretend; **~gir-se** de pretend to be

fi|ninho /fi'niɲu/ adv **sair de ~ninho** slip away. **~no** a (não grosso) thin; ‹areia, pó etc› fine; (refinado) refined. **~nório** a crafty. **~nura** f thinness; fineness

finito /fi'nitu/ a finite

finlan|dês /fĩlã'des/ a (f **~desa**) Finnish ● m (f **~desa**) Finn; (língua) Finnish

Finlândia /fĩ'lãdʒia/ f Finland

fio /'fiu/ m thread; (elétrico) wire; (de sangue, água) trickle; (de luz, esperança) glimmer; (de navalha etc) edge; **horas a ~** hours on end

fir|ma /'firma/ f firm; (assinatura) signature. **~mamento** m firmament. **~mar** vt fix; (basear) base ● vi settle. **~mar-se** vpr be based (em on). **~me** a firm; ‹tempo› settled ● adv firmly. **~meza** f firmness

fis|cal /fis'kaw/ (pl **~cais**) m inspector. **~calização** f inspection. **~calizar** vt inspect. **~co** m inland revenue, Amer internal revenue service

fis|gada /fiz'gada/ f stabbing pain. **~gar** vt hook

fisi|ca /'fizika/ f physics. **~co** a physical ● m (pessoa) physicist; (corpo) physique

fisio|nomia /fiziono'mia/ f face. **~nomista** m/f ser **~nomista** have a good memory for faces. **~terapeuta** m/f physiotherapist. **~terapia** f physiotherapy

fissura /fi'sura/ f fissure; 🔲 craving. **~do** a **~do em** 🔲 mad about

fita /'fita/ f tape; 🔲 (encenação) play-acting; **fazer ~** 🔲 put on an act; **~ adesiva** Port adhesive tape; **~ métrica** tape measure

fitar /fi'tar/ vt stare at

FIV abr f (= **fertilização in vitro**) IVF

fivela /fi'vɛla/ f buckle

fi|xador /fiksa'dor/ m (de cabelo) setting lotion; (de fotos) fixative. **~xar** vt fix; stick up ‹cartaz›. **~xo** a fixed

flácido /'flasidu/ a flabby

flagelo /fla'ʒɛlu/ m scourge

fla|grante /fla'grãtʃi/ a flagrant; **apanhar em ~grante (delito)** catch in the act. **~grar** vt catch

flame|jante /flame'ʒãtʃi/ a blazing. **~jar** vi blaze

flamengo /fla'mẽgu/ a Flemish ● m Fleming; (língua) Flemish

flamingo /fla'mĩgu/ m flamingo

flâmula /'flamula/ f pennant

flanco /'flãku/ m flank

flanela /fla'nɛla/ f flannel

flanquear /flãki'ar/ vt flank

flash /flɛʃ/ m invar flash

flau|ta /'flawta/ f flute. **~tista** m/f flautist

flecha /'flɛʃa/ f arrow

fler|tar /fler'tar/ vi flirt. **~te** m flirtation

fleuma /'flewma/ f phlegm

flex /flɛks/ m invar ‹carro› flexible-fuel car (car designed to run on petrol and ethanol)

fle|xão /flek'sãw/ f press-up, Amer push-up; Ling inflection. **~xibilidade** f flexibility. **~xionar** vt/i flex ‹perna, braço›; Ling inflect. **~xível** (pl **~xíveis**) a flexible

fliperama /flipe'rama/ m pinball machine

floco /'flɔku/ m flake

flor /flor/ f flower; **a fina ~** the cream; **à ~ da pele** fig on edge

flo|ra /'flɔra/ f flora. **~reado** a full of flowers; fig florid. **~reio** m clever turn of phrase. **~rescer** vi flower. **~resta** /ɛ/ f forest. **~restal** (pl **~restais**) a forest. **~rido** a in flower; fig florid. **~rir** vi flower

flotilha /flo'tʃiʎa/ f flotilla

flu|ência /flu'ẽsia/ f fluency. **~ente** a fluent

flui|dez /flui'des/ f fluidity. **~do** a & m fluid

fluir /flu'ir/ vi flow

fluminense /flumi'nẽsi/ a & m (person) from Rio de Janeiro state

fluorescente /fluore'sẽtʃi/ a fluorescent

flutu|ação /flutua'sãw/ f fluctuation. **~ante** a floating. **~ar** vi float; ‹bandeira› flutter; (hesitar) waver

fluvi|al /fluvi'aw/ (pl **~ais**) a river

fluxo /'fluksu/ m flow. **~grama** m flow chart

fobia /fo'bia/ f phobia

foca /'fɔka/ f seal

focalizar /fokali'zar/ vt focus on

focinho /fo'siɲu/ m snout

foco /'fɔku/ m focus; fig centre

fofo /'fofu/ a soft; ‹pessoa› cuddly

fofo|ca /fo'fɔka/ f piece of gossip; pl gossip. **~car** vi gossip. **~queiro** m gossip ● a gossipy

fo|gão /fo'gãw/ m stove; (de cozinhar) cooker. **~go** /o/ m fire; **tem ~go?** have you got a light?; **ser ~go** 🛈 (ser chato) be a pain in the neck; (ser incrível) be amazing; **~gos de artifício** fireworks. **~goso** /o/ a fiery. **~gueira** f bonfire. **~guete** /e/ m rocket

foice /'fojsi/ f scythe

fol|clore /fow'klɔri/ m folklore. **~clórico** a folk

fole /'fɔli/ m bellows

fôlego /'folegu/ m breath; fig stamina

fol|ga /'fowga/ f rest, break; 🛈 (cara de pau) cheek. **~gado** a ‹roupa› full, loose; ‹vida› leisurely; 🛈 (atrevido) cheeky. **~gar** vt loosen ● vi have time off

fo|lha /'foʎa/ f leaf; (de papel) sheet; **novo em ~lha** brand new; **~lha de pagamento** payroll. **~lhagem** f foliage. **~lhear** vt leaf through. **~lheto** /e/ m pamphlet. **~lhinha** f tear-off calendar. **~lhudo** a leafy

folhado /fo'ʎadu/ m (massa) puff pastry

foli|a /fo'lia/ f revelry. **~ão** m (f **~ona**) reveller

folículo /fo'likulu/ m follicle

fome /'fomi/ f hunger; **estar com ~** be hungry

fomentar /fomẽ'tar/ vt foment

fone /'fɔni/ m (do telefone) receiver; (de rádio etc) headphones

fonema /fo'nema/ m phoneme

fonéti|ca /fo'nɛtʃika/ f phonetics. **~co** a phonetic

fonologia /fonolo'ʒia/ f phonology

fonte /'fõtʃi/ f (de água) spring; fig source

fora /'fɔra/ adv outside; (não em casa) out; (viajando) away ● prep except; **dar um ~** drop a clanger; **dar um ~ em alguém** cut sb dead; chuck ‹namorado›; **por ~** on the outside. **~ de lei** m/f invar outlaw

foragido /fora'ʒidu/ a at large, on the run ● m fugitive

forasteiro /foras'teru/ m outsider

forca /'forka/ f gallows

for|ça /'forsa/ f (vigor) strength; (violência) force; (elétrica) power; **dar uma ~ça a alguém** help sb out; **fazer ~ça** make an effort; **~ças armadas** armed forces. **~çar** vt force. **~ça-tarefa** (pl **~ças-tarefa**) f task force

fórceps /'fɔrseps/ m invar forceps

forçoso /for'sozu/ a forced

for|ja /'fɔrʒa/ f forge. **~jar** vt forge

forma[1] /'fɔrma/ f form; (contorno) shape; (maneira) way; **de qualquer ~** anyway; **manter a ~** keep fit

forma[2] /'fɔrma/ f mould; (de cozinha) baking tin

for|mação /forma'sãw/ f formation; (educação) education; (profissionalizante) training. **~mado** m graduate. **~mal** (pl **~mais**) a formal. **~malidade** f formality. **~malizar** vt formalize. **~mar** vt form; (educar) educate; ‹estudante› graduate. **~mar-se** vpr be formed; ‹estudante› graduate. **~mato** m format. **~matura** f graduation

formatar /forma'tar/ vt Comput format

formidá|vel /formi'davew/ (pl **~veis**) a formidable; (muito bom) tremendous

formi|ga /for'miga/ f ant. **~gamento** m pins and needles. **~gar** vi swarm (de with); ‹perna, mão etc› tingle. **~gueiro** m ants' nest

formosura /formo'zura/ f beauty

fórmula /'fɔrmula/ f formula

formu|lação /formula'sãw/ f
formulation. **~lar** vt formulate. **~lário**
m form

fornalha /for'naʎa/ f furnace

forne|cedor /forne'dor/ m supplier.
~cer vt supply; **~cer algo a alguém**
supply sb with sth. **~cimento** m supply

forno /'fornu/ m oven; (para louça etc)
kiln

foro /'foru/ m forum

forra /'fɔxa/ f **ir à ~** get one's own back

for|ragem /fo'xaʒẽ/ f fodder. **~rar** vt
line ‹roupa, caixa etc›; cover ‹sofá etc›;
carpet ‹assoalho, sala etc›. **~ro** /o/ m
(de roupa, caixa etc) lining; (de sofá etc)
cover; (carpete) (fitted) carpet

forró /fo'xɔ/ m type of Brazilian dance

fortale|cer /fortale'ser/ vt strengthen.
~cimento m strengthening. **~za** /e/ f
fortress

for|te /'fɔrtʃi/ a strong; ‹golpe› hard;
‹chuva› heavy; ‹físico› muscular ● adv
strongly; ‹bater, chover› hard ● m
(militar) fort; (habilidade) strong point,
forte. **~tificação** f fortification. **~tificar**
vt fortify

fortu|ito /for'tuitu/ a chance. **~na** f
fortune

fosco /'fosku/ a dull; ‹vidro› frosted

fosfato /fos'fatu/ m phosphate

fósforo /'fɔsforu/ m match; (elemento
químico) phosphor

fossa /'fɔsa/ f pit; **na ~** fig miserable,
depressed

fós|sil /'fɔsiw/ (pl **~seis**) m fossil

fosso /'fosu/ m ditch; (de castelo) moat

foto /'fɔtu/ f photo. **~cópia** f photocopy.
~copiadora f photocopier. **~copiar**
vt photocopy. **~gênico** a photogenic.
~grafar vt photograph. **~grafia** f
photography. **~gráfico** a photographic

fotógrafo /fo'tɔgrafu/ m
photographer

foz /fɔs/ f mouth

fração /fra'sãw/ f fraction

fracas|sado /fraka'sadu/ a failed ● m
failure. **~sar** vi fail. **~so** m failure

fracionar /frasio'nar/ vt break up

fraco /'fraku/ a weak; ‹luz, som› faint;
‹medíocre› poor ● m weakness, weak
spot

frade /'fradʒi/ m friar

fragata /fra'gata/ f frigate

frá|gil /'fraʒiw/ (pl **~geis**) a fragile;
‹pessoa› frail

fragilidade /fraʒili'dadʒi/ f fragility;
(de pessoa) frailty

fragmen|tar /fragmẽ'tar/ vt
fragment. **~tar-se** vpr fragment. **~to** m
fragment

fra|grância /fra'grãsia/ f fragrance.
~grante a fragrant

fralda /'frawda/ f nappy, Amer diaper

framboesa /frãbo'eza/ f raspberry

França /'frãsa/ f France

fran|cês /frã'ses/ a (f **~cesa**) French ● m
(f **~cesa**) Frenchman (f **~woman**); (língua)
French; **os ~ceses** the French

franco /'frãku/ a (honesto) frank;
(óbvio) clear; (gratuito) free ● m franc.
~atirador (pl **~atiradores**) m sniper; fig
maverick

frangalho /frã'gaʎu/ m tatter

frango /'frãgu/ m chicken

franja /'frãʒa/ f fringe; (do cabelo)
fringe, Amer bangs

fran|quear /frãki'ar/ vt frank ‹carta›.
~queza /e/ f frankness. **~quia** f (de
cartas) franking; Jurid franchise

fran|zino /frã'zinu/ a skinny. **~zir**
vt gather ‹tecido›; wrinkle ‹testa›

fraque /'fraki/ m morning suit

fraqueza /fra'keza/ f weakness; (de luz,
som) faintness

frasco /'frasku/ m bottle

frase /'frazi/ f (oração) sentence;
(locução) phrase. **~ado** m phrasing

frasqueira /fras'kera/ f vanity case

frater|nal /frater'naw/ (pl **~nais**) a
fraternal. **~nidade** f fraternity. **~nizar** vi
fraternize. **~no** a fraternal

fratu|ra /fra'tura/ f fracture. **~rar** vt
fracture. **~rar-se** vpr fracture

frau|dar /fraw'dar/ vt defraud. **~de** f
fraud. **~dulento** a fraudulent

frear /fri'ar/ vt/i brake

freezer /'frizer/ m freezer

fre|guês /fre'ges/ m (f **~guesa**)
customer. **~guesia** f (de loja etc)
clientele; (paróquia) parish

frei /frej/ m brother

freio /'freju/ m brake; (de cavalo) bit

freira /'frera/ f nun

freixo /'frefu/ m ash

fremir /fre'mir/ vi shake

frêmito /'fremitu/ m wave

frenesi /frene'zi/ m frenzy

frenético /fre'netʃiku/ a frantic

frente /ˈfrẽtʃi/ f front; **em ~ a** ou **de** in front of; **para a ~** forward; **pela ~** ahead; **fazer ~ a** face

frequência /freˈkwẽsia/ f frequency; (*assiduidade*) attendance; **com muita ~** often

frequen|tador /frekwẽtaˈdor/ m regular visitor (**de** to). **~tar** vt frequent; (*cursar*) attend. **~te** a frequent

fres|cão /fresˈkãw/ m air-conditioned coach. **~co** /e/ a <comida etc> fresh; <vento, água, quarto> cool; 🅻 (*afetado*) affected; (*exigente*) fussy. **~cobol** m kind of racquetball. **~cor** m freshness. **~cura** f 🅻 (*afetação*) affectation; (*ser exigente*) fussiness; (*coisa sem importância*) trifle

fresta /ˈfresta/ f slit

fre|tar /freˈtar/ vt charter <avião>; hire <caminhão>. **~te** /e/ m freight; (*aluguel de avião*) charter; (*de caminhão*) hire

frevo /ˈfrevu/ m type of Brazilian dance

fria /ˈfria/ f 🅻 difficult situation, spot. **~gem** f chill

fric|ção /frikˈsãw/ f friction. **~cionar** vt rub

fri|eira /friˈera/ f chilblain. **~eza** /e/ f coldness

frigideira /friʒiˈdera/ f frying pan

frígido /ˈfriʒidu/ a frigid

frigorífico /frigoˈrifiku/ m cold store, refrigerator, fridge

frincha /ˈfrĩʃa/ f chink

frio /ˈfriu/ a & m cold; **estar com ~** be cold. **~rento** a sensitive to the cold

frisar /friˈzar/ vt (*enfatizar*) stress; crimp <cabelo>

friso /ˈfrizu/ m frieze

fri|tada /friˈtada/ f fry-up. **~tar** vt fry. **~tas** f pl chips, *Amer* French fries. **~to** a fried; **está ~to** 🅻 he's had it 🅻. **~tura** f fried food

frivolidade /frivoliˈdadʒi/ f frivolity. **frívolo** a frivolous

fronha /ˈfroɲa/ f pillowcase

fronte /ˈfrõtʃi/ f forehead, brow

frontei|ra /frõˈtera/ f border. **~riço** a border

frota /ˈfrɔta/ f fleet

frou|xidão /froʃiˈdãw/ f looseness; (*moral*) laxity. **~xo** a loose; <regulamento> lax; <pessoa> lackadaisical

fru|gal /fruˈgaw/ (*pl* **~gais**) a frugal. **~galidade** f frugality

frus|tração /frustraˈsãw/ f frustration. **~trante** a frustrating. **~trar** vt frustrate

fru|ta /ˈfruta/ f fruit. **~ta-do-conde** (*pl* **~tas-do-conde**) f sweetsop; **~ta-pão** (*pl* **~tas-pão**) f breadfruit. **~teira** f fruit bowl. **~tífero** a fig fruitful. **~to** m fruit

fubá /fuˈba/ m maize flour

fu|çar /fuˈsar/ vi nose around. **~ças** f pl 🅻 face, chops 🅻

fu|ga /ˈfuga/ f escape. **~gaz** a fleeting. **~gida** f escape. **~gir** vi run away; (*soltar-se*) escape; **~gir a** avoid. **~gitivo** a & m fugitive

fulano /fuˈlanu/ m whatever his name is

fuleiro /fuˈleru/ a downmarket, cheap and cheerful

fulgor /fuwˈgor/ m brightness; fig splendour

fuligem /fuˈliʒẽ/ f soot

fulmi|nante /fuwmiˈnãtʃi/ a devastating. **~nar** vt strike down; fig devastate; **~nado por um raio** struck by lightning ● vi (*criticar*) rail

fulo /ˈfulu/ a *Port* furious

fu|maça /fuˈmasa/ f smoke. **~maceira** f cloud of smoke. **~mante**, *Port* **~mador** m smoker. **~mar** vt/i smoke. **~mê** a invar smoked. **~megar** vi smoke. **~mo** /ˈfumu/ m (*tabaco*) tobacco; *Port* (*fumaça*) smoke; (*fumar*) smoking; **~mo passivo** passive smoking

função /fũˈsãw/ f function; **em ~ de** as a result of; **fazer as funções de** function as

funcho /ˈfũʃu/ m fennel

funcio|nal /fũsioˈnaw/ (*pl* **~nais**) a functional. **~nalismo** m civil service. **~namento** m working. **~nar** vi work. **~nário** m employee; **~nário público** civil servant

fun|dação /fũdaˈsãw/ f foundation. **~dador** m founder ● a founding

fundamen|tal /fũdamẽˈtaw/ (*pl* **~tais**) a fundamental. **~tar** vt (*basear*) base; (*justificar*) substantiate. **~to** m foundation

fun|dar /fũˈdar/ vt (*criar*) found; (*basear*) base. **~dar-se** vpr be based (**em** on). **~dear** vi drop anchor, anchor. **~dilho** m seat

fundir /fũˈdʒir/ vt melt <ouro, ferro>; cast <sino, estátua>; (*juntar*) merge. **~se** vpr <ouro, ferro> melt; (*juntar-se*) merge

fundo /ˈfũdu/ a deep ● m (*parte de baixo*) bottom; (*parte de trás*) back;

(de quadro, foto) background; (de dinheiro) fund; **no ~** basically; **~s** m pl (da casa etc) back; (recursos) funds

fúnebre /'funebri/ a funereal

funerário /fune'rariu/ a funeral

funesto /fu'nɛstu/ a fatal

fungar /fũ'gar/ vt/i sniff

fungo /'fũgu/ m fungus

fu|nil /fu'niw/ (pl **~nis**) m funnel. **~nilaria** f panel beating; (oficina) body shop

furacão /fura'kãw/ m hurricane

furado /fu'radu/ a **papo ~** 🄸 hot air

furão /fu'rãw/ m (animal) ferret

furar /fu'rar/ vt pierce ‹orelha etc›; puncture ‹pneu›; make a hole in ‹roupa etc›; jump ‹fila›; break ‹greve› ● vi ‹roupa etc› go into a hole; ‹pneu› puncture; 🄸 ‹programa› fall through

fur|gão /fur'gãw/ m van. **~goneta** /e/ Port f van

fúria /'furia/ f fury

furioso /furi'ozu/ a furious

furo /'furu/ m hole; (de pneu) puncture; (jornalístico) scoop; 🄸 (gafe) blunder, faux pas; **dar um ~** put one's foot in it

furor /fu'ror/ m furore

fur|ta-cor /furta'kor/ a invar iridescent. **~tar** vt steal. **~tivo** a furtive. **~to** m theft

furúnculo /fu'rũkulu/ m boil

fusão /fu'zãw/ f fusion; (de empresas) merger

fusca /'fuska/ f VW beetle

fuselagem /fuze'laʒẽ/ f fuselage

fusí|vel /fu'zivew/ (pl **~veis**) m fuse

fuso /'fuzu/ m spindle; **~ horário** time zone

fustigar /fustʃi'gar/ vt lash; fig (com palavras) lash out at

futebol /futʃi'bɔw/ m football. **~ístico** a football

fú|til /'futʃiw/ (pl **~teis**) a frivolous, inane

futilidade /futʃili'dadʒi/ f frivolity, inanity; (uma) frivolous thing

futu|rismo /futu'rizmu/ m futurism. **~rista** a & m futurist. **~rístico** a futuristic. **~ro** a & m future

fu|zil /fu'ziw/ (pl **~zis**) m rifle. **~zilamento** m shooting. **~zilar** vt shoot ● vi flash. **~zileiro** m rifleman; **~zileiro naval** marine

fuzuê /fuzu'e/ m commotion

Gg

gabarito /gaba'ritu/ m calibre

gabar-se /ga'barsi/ vpr boast (**de** of)

gabinete /gabi'netʃi/ m (em casa) study; (escritório) office; (ministros) cabinet

gado /'gadu/ m livestock; (bovino) cattle

gaélico /ga'ɛliku/ a & m Gaelic

gafanhoto /gafa'ɲotu/ m (pequeno) grasshopper; (grande) locust

gafe /'gafi/ f faux pas, gaffe

gafieira /gafi'era/ f dance; (salão) dance hall

gagá /ga'ga/ a 🄸 senile

ga|go /'gagu/ a stuttering ● m stutterer. **~gueira** f stutter. **~guejar** vi stutter

gaiato /gaj'atu/ a funny

gaiola /gaj'ɔla/ f cage

gaita /'gajta/ f **~ de foles** bagpipes

gaivota /gaj'vɔta/ f seagull

gajo /'gaʒu/ m Port guy, bloke

gala /'gala/ f festa de **~** gala; **roupa de ~** formal dress

galã /ga'lã/ m leading man

galan|tear /galãtʃi'ar/ vt woo. **~teio** m wooing; (um) courtesy

galão /ga'lãw/ m (enfeite) braid; Mil stripe; (medida) gallon; Port (café) white coffee

galáxia /ga'laksia/ f galaxy

galé /ga'lɛ/ f galley

galego /ga'legu/ a & m Galician

galera /ga'lɛra/ f 🄸 crowd

galeria /gale'ria/ f gallery

Gales /'galis/ m **País de G~** Wales

ga|lês /ga'les/ a (f **~lesa**) Welsh ● m (f **~lesa**) Welshman (f-woman); (língua) Welsh

galeto /ga'letu/ m spring chicken

galgar /gaw'gar/ vt (transpor) jump over; climb ‹escada›

galgo /'gawgu/ m greyhound

galheteiro /gaʎe'teru/ m cruet stand

galho /'gaʎu/ m branch; **quebrar um ~** 🄸 help out

galináceos /gali'nasius/ m pl poultry

gali|nha /ga'liɲa/ f chicken. **~nheiro** m chicken coop

galo /'galu/ *m* cock; (*inchação*) bump

galocha /ga'lɔʃa/ *f* Wellington boot

galo|**pante** /galo'pãtʃi/ *a* galloping. **~par** *vi* gallop. **~pe** /ɔ/ *m* gallop

galpão /gaw'pãw/ *m* shed

galvanizar /gawvani'zar/ *vt* galvanize

gama /'gama/ *f* (*musical*) scale; *fig* range

gamado /ga'madu/ *a* besotted (**por** with)

gamão /ga'mãw/ *m* backgammon

gamar /ga'mar/ *vi* fall in love (**por** with)

gana /'gana/ *f* desire

ganância /ga'nãsia/ *f* greed

ganancioso /ganãsi'ozu/ *a* greedy

gancho /'gãʃu/ *m* hook

gangorra /gã'goxa/ *f* see-saw

gangrena /gã'grena/ *f* gangrene

gangue /'gãgi/ *m* gang

ga|**nhador** /gaɲa'dor/ *m* winner ● *a* winning. **~nhar** *vt* win ‹*corrida, prêmio*›; earn ‹*salário*›; get ‹*presente*›; gain ‹*vantagem, tempo, amigo*› ● *vi* win; **~nhar a vida** earn a living. **~nha-pão** *m* livelihood. **~nho** *m* gain; *pl* (*no jogo*) winnings

ga|**nido** *m* squeal; (*de cachorro*) yelp. **~nir** *vi* squeal; ‹*cachorro*› yelp

ganso /'gãsu/ *m* goose

gara|**gem** /ga'raʒẽ/ *f* garage. **~gista** *m/f* garage attendant

garanhão /gara'ɲãw/ *m* stallion

garan|**tia** /garã'tʃia/ *f* guarantee. **~tir** *vt* guarantee

garatujar /garatu'ʒar/ *vt* scribble

gar|**bo** /'garbu/ *m* grace. **~boso** *a* graceful

garça /'garsa/ *f* heron

gar|**çom** /gar'sõ/ *m* waiter. **~çonete** /e/ *f* waitress

gar|**fada** /gar'fada/ *f* forkful. **~fo** *m* fork

gargalhada /garga'ʎada/ *f* gale of laughter; **rir às ~s** roar with laughter

gargalo /gar'galu/ *m* bottleneck; **tomar no ~** drink out of the bottle

garganta /gar'gãta/ *f* throat

gargare|**jar** /gargare'ʒar/ *vi* gargle. **~jo** /e/ *m* gargle

gari /ga'ri/ *m/f* (*lixeiro*) dustman, *Amer* garbage collector; (*varredor de rua*) roadsweeper, *Amer* streetsweeper

garim|**par** /garĩ'par/ *vi* prospect. **~peiro** *m* prospector. **~po** *m* mine

garo|**a** /ga'roa/ *f* drizzle. **~ar** *vi* drizzle

garo|**ta** /ga'rota/ *f* girl. **~to** /o/ *m* boy; *Port* (*café*) coffee with milk

garoupa /ga'ropa/ *f* grouper

garra /'gaxa/ *f* claw; *fig* drive, determination; *pl* (*poder*) clutches

garra|**fa** /ga'xafa/ *f* bottle. **~fada** *f* blow with a bottle. **~fão** *m* flagon

garrancho /ga'xãʃu/ *m* scrawl

garrido /ga'xidu/ *a* (*alegre*) lively

garupa /ga'rupa/ *f* (*de animal*) rump; (*de moto*) pillion seat

gás /gas/ *m* gas; *pl* (*intestinais*) wind, *Amer* gas; **~ lacrimogêneo** tear gas

gasóleo /ga'zɔliu/ *m* diesel oil

gasolina /gazo'lina/ *f* petrol

gaso|**sa** /ga'zɔza/ *f* fizzy lemonade, *Amer* soda. **~so** *a* gaseous; ‹*bebida*› fizzy

gáspea /'gaspia/ *f* upper

gas|**tador** /gasta'dor/ *a* & *m* spendthrift. **~tar** *vt* spend ‹*dinheiro, tempo*›; use up ‹*energia*›; wear out ‹*roupa, sapatos*›. **~to** *m* expense; *pl* spending, expenditure; **dar para o ~to** do

gastrenterite /gastrẽte'ritʃi/ *f* gastroenteritis

gástrico /'gastriku/ *a* gastric

gastrite /gas'tritʃi/ *f* gastritis

gastronomia /gastrono'mia/ *f* gastronomy

ga|**ta** /'gata/ *f* cat; 🔒 sexy woman. **~tão** *m* 🔒 hunk 🔒

gatilho /ga'tʃiʎu/ *m* trigger

ga|**tinha** /ga'tʃiɲa/ *f* 🔒 sexy woman. **~to** *m* cat; 🔒 hunk 🔒; **fazer alguém de ~to-sapato** treat sb like a doormat

gatuno /ga'tunu/ *m* crook ● *a* crooked

gaúcho /ga'uʃu/ *a* & *m* (person) from Rio Grande do Sul

gaveta /ga'veta/ *f* drawer

gavião /gavi'ãw/ *m* hawk

gaze /'gazi/ *f* gauze

gazela /ga'zɛla/ *f* gazelle

gazeta /ga'zeta/ *f* gazette

geada /ʒi'ada/ *f* frost

ge|**ladeira** /ʒela'dera/ *f* fridge. **~lado** *a* frozen; (*muito frio*) freezing ● *m Port* ice cream. **~lar** *vt/i* freeze

gelati|**na** /ʒela'tʃina/ *f* (*sobremesa*) jelly; (*pó*) gelatine. **~noso** /o/ *a* gooey

geleia /ʒe'lɛja/ *f* jam

ge|**leira** /ʒe'lera/ *f* glacier. **~lo** /e/ *m* ice

gema /'ʒema/ f (de ovo) yolk; (pedra) gem; **carioca da ~** carioca born and bred. **~da** f egg yolk whisked with sugar

gêmeo /'ʒemiu/ a & m twin; **Gêmeos** (signo) Gemini

ge|mer /ʒe'mer/ vi moan, groan. **~mido** m moan, groan

gene /'ʒeni/ m gene. **~alogia** f genealogy. **~alógico** a genealogical; **árvore ~alógica** family tree

Genebra /ʒe'nɛbra/ f Geneva

gene|ral /ʒene'raw/ (pl ~rais) m general. **~ralidade** f generality. **~ralização** f generalization. **~ralizar** vt/i generalize. **~ralizar-se** vpr become generalized

genérico /ʒe'nɛriku/ a generic

gênero /'ʒeneru/ m type, kind; (gramatical) gender; (literário) genre; pl goods; **~s alimentícios** foodstuffs; **ela não faz o meu ~** she's not my type

gene|rosidade /ʒenerozi'dadʒi/ f generosity. **~roso** /o/ a generous

genéti|ca /ʒe'nɛtʃika/ f genetics. **~co** a genetic

gengibre /ʒẽ'ʒibri/ m ginger

gengiva /ʒẽ'ʒiva/ f gum

geni|al /ʒeni'aw/ (pl ~ais) a brilliant

gênio /'ʒeniu/ m genius; (temperamento) temperament

genioso /ʒeni'ozu/ a temperamental

geni|tal /ʒeni'taw/ (pl ~tais) a genital

genitivo /ʒeni'tʃivu/ a & m genitive

genocídio /ʒeno'sidʒiu/ m genocide

genro /'ʒẽxu/ m son-in-law

gente /'ʒẽtʃi/ f people; 𝔼 folks; **a ~** (sujeito) we; (objeto) us ● interj 𝔼 gosh

gen|til /ʒẽ'tʃiw/ (pl ~tis) a kind. **~tileza** /e/ f kindness

genuíno /ʒenu'inu/ a genuine

geo|grafia /ʒeogra'fia/ f geography. **~gráfico** a geographical

geógrafo /ʒe'ɔgrafu/ m geographer

geo|logia /ʒeolo'ʒia/ f geology. **~lógico** a geological

geólogo /ʒe'ɔlogu/ m geologist

geo|metria /ʒeome'tria/ f geometry. **~métrico** a geometrical. **~político** a geopolitical

Geórgia /ʒi'ɔrʒia/ f Georgia

georgiano /ʒiorʒi'anu/ a & m Georgian

gera|ção /ʒera'sãw/ f generation. **~dor** m generator

ge|ral /ʒe'raw/ (pl ~rais) a general ● f (limpeza) spring clean; **em ~ral** in general

gerânio /ʒe'raniu/ m geranium

gerar /ʒe'rar/ vt create; generate ‹eletricidade›

gerência /ʒe'rẽsia/ f management

gerenci|ador /ʒerẽsia'dor/ m manager. **~al** (pl ~ais) a management. **~ar** vt manage

gerente /ʒe'rẽtʃi/ m manager ● a managing

gergelim /ʒerʒe'lĩ/ m sesame

geri|atria /ʒeria'tria/ f geriatrics. **~átrico** a geriatric

geringonça /ʒerĩ'gõsa/ f contraption

gerir /ʒe'rir/ vt manage

germânico /ʒer'maniku/ a Germanic

ger|me /'ʒermi/ m germ; **~me de trigo** wheatgerm. **~minar** vi germinate

gerúndio /ʒe'rũdʒiu/ m gerund

gesso /'ʒesu/ m plaster

ges|tação /ʒesta'sãw/ f gestation. **~tante** f pregnant woman

gestão /ʒes'tãw/ f management

ges|ticular /ʒestʃiku'lar/ vi gesticulate. **~to** m gesture

gibi /ʒi'bi/ m 𝔼 comic

Gibraltar /ʒibraw'tar/ f Gibraltar

gigan|te /ʒi'gãtʃi/ a & m giant. **~tesco** /e/ a gigantic

gilete /ʒi'letʃi/ f razor blade ● a & m/f 𝔼 bisexual

gim /ʒĩ/ m gin

ginásio /ʒi'naziu/ m (escola) secondary school; (de ginástica) gymnasium

ginasta /ʒi'nasta/ m/f gymnast

ginásti|ca /ʒi'nastʃika/ f gymnastics; (aeróbica) aerobics. **~co** a gymnastic

ginecolo|gia /ʒinekolo'ʒia/ f gynaecology. **~gista** m/f gynaecologist

gingar /ʒĩ'gar/ vi sway

girafa /ʒi'rafa/ f giraffe

gi|rar /ʒi'rar/ vt/i spin, revolve. **~rassol** (pl ~rassóis) m sunflower. **~ratório** a revolving

gíria /'ʒiria/ f slang; (uma ~) slang expression

giro /'ʒiru/ m spin, turn ● a Port 𝔼 nice, cute

giz /ʒis/ m chalk

gla|cê /gla'se/ m icing. **~cial** (pl **~ciais**) a icy

glamour /gla'mur/ m glamour. **~oso** /o/ a glamorous

glândula /'glãdula/ f gland

glandular /glãdu'lar/ a glandular

glicerina /glise'rina/ f glycerine

glicose /gli'kɔzi/ f glucose

glo|bal /glo'baw/ (pl **~bais**) a (mundial) global; <preço etc> overall. **~bo** /o/ m globe; **~bo ocular** eyeball

globalização /globaliza'sãw/ f globalization

globalizar /globali'zar/ vt globalize

glóbulo /'glɔbulu/ m globule; (do sangue) corpuscle

glória /'glɔria/ f glory

glori|ficar /glorifi'kar/ vt glorify. **~oso** /o/ a glorious

glossário /glo'sariu/ m glossary

glu|tão /glu'tãw/ (f **~tona**) glutton ● a (f **~tona**) greedy

gnomo /gi'nomu/ m gnome

godê /go'de/ a flared

goela /go'ɛla/ f gullet

gogó /go'gɔ/ m Ⓘ Adam's apple

goia|ba /goj'aba/ f guava. **~bada** f guava jelly. **~beira** f guava tree

gol /'gow/ (pl **~s**) m goal

gola /'gɔla/ f collar

gole /'gɔli/ m mouthful

go|lear /goli'ar/ vt thrash. **~leiro** m goalkeeper

golfe /'gowfi/ m golf

golfinho /gow'fiɲu/ m dolphin

golfista /gow'fista/ m/f golfer

golo /'golu/ m Port goal

golpe /'gɔwpi/ m blow; (manobra) trick; **~ (de estado)** coup (d'état); **~ de mestre** masterstroke; **~ de vento** gust of wind; **~ de vista** glance. **~ar** vt hit

goma /'goma/ f gum; (para roupa) starch

gomo /'gomu/ m segment

gôndola /'gõdola/ f rack

gongo /'gõgu/ m gong

gonorrela /gono'xeja/ f gonorrhea

gonzo /'gõzu/ m hinge

googar /gu'gar/ vt google

gorar /go'rar/ vi go wrong, fail

gor|do /'gordu/ a fat. **~ducho** a plump

gordu|ra /gor'dura/ f fat. **~rento** a greasy. **~roso** /u/ a fatty; <pele> greasy, oily

gorgolejar /gorgole'ʒar/ vi gurgle

gorila /go'rila/ m gorilla

gor|jear /gorʒi'ar/ vi twitter. **~jeio** m twittering

gorjeta /gor'ʒeta/ f tip

gorro /'goxu/ m hat

gos|ma /'gɔzma/ f slime. **~mento** a slimy

gos|tar /gos'tar/ vi **~tar de** like. **~to** /o/ m taste; (prazer) pleasure; **para o meu ~to** for my taste; **ter ~to de** taste of. **~toso** a nice; <comida> nice, tasty; Ⓘ <pessoa> gorgeous

go|ta /'gota/ f drop; (que cai) drip; (doença) gout; **foi a ~ta d'água** fig it was the last straw. **~teira** f (buraco) leak; (cano) gutter. **~tejar** vi drip; <telhado> leak ● vt drip

gótico /'gɔtʃiku/ a Gothic

gotícula /go'tʃicula/ f droplet

gourmet /gur'me/ a gourmet; **loja ~** delicatessen

gover|nador /governa'dor/ m governor. **~namental** (pl **~namentais**) a government. **~nanta** f housekeeper. **~nante** a ruling ● m/f ruler. **~nar** vt govern. **~nista** a government ● m/f government supporter. **~no** /e/ m government

go|zação /goza'sãw/ f joking; (uma) send-up. **~zado** a funny. **~zar** vt **~zar (de)** enjoy; Ⓘ (zombar de) make fun of ● vi (ter orgasmo) come. **~zo** m (prazer) enjoyment; (posse) possession; (orgasmo) orgasm; **ser um ~zo** be funny

Grã-Bretanha /grãbre'taɲa/ f Great Britain

graça /'grasa/ f grace; (piada) joke; (humor) humour, funny side; Jurid pardon; **de ~** for nothing; **sem ~** (enfadonho) dull; (não engraçado) unfunny; (envergonhado) embarrassed; **ser uma ~** be lovely; **ter ~** be funny; **não tem ~ sair sozinho** it's no fun to go out alone; **~s a** thanks to

grace|jar /grase'ʒar/ vi joke. **~jo** /e/ m joke

graci|nha /gra'siɲa/ f **ser uma ~nha** be sweet. **~oso** /o/ a gracious

grada|ção /grada'sãw/ f gradation. **~tivo** a gradual

grade /'gradʒi/ f grille, grating; (cerca) railings; **atrás das ~s** behind bars. **~ado** a <janela> barred

grado /'gradu/ m de bom/mau ~ willingly/unwillingly

gradu|ação /gradua'sãw/ f graduation; Mil rank; (variação) gradation. **~ado** a ‹escala› graduated; ‹estudante› graduate; ‹militar› high-ranking; (eminente) respected. **~al** (pl **~ais**) a gradual. **~ar** vt graduate ‹escala›; (ordenar) grade; (regular) regulate. **~ar-se** vpr ‹estudante› graduate

grafia /gra'fia/ f spelling

gráfi|ca /'grafika/ f (arte) graphics; (oficina) print shop. **~co** a graphic ● m (pessoa) printer; (diagrama) graph; pl (de computador) graphics

grã-fino /grã'finu/ 🅸 a posh, upper-class ● m posh person

grafite /gra'fitʃi/ f (mineral) graphite; (de lápis) lead; (pichação) piece of graffiti

grafiteiro /grafi'teru/ m graffitist

grafiti /gra'fiti/ m Port ▶ **grafite**

gra|fologia /grafolo'ʒia/ f graphology. **~fólogo** m graphologist

grama¹ /'grama/ m gramme

grama² /'grama/ f grass. **~do** m lawn; (campo de futebol) field

gramática /gra'matʃika/ f grammar

gramati|cal /gramatʃi'kaw/ (pl **~cais**) a grammatical

gram|peador /grãpia'dor/ m stapler. **~pear** vt staple ‹papéis etc›; tap ‹telefone›. **~po** m (de cabelo) hair clip; (para papéis etc) staple; (ferramenta) clamp

grana /'grana/ f 🅸 cash

granada /gra'nada/ f (projétil) grenade; (pedra) garnet

gran|dalhão /grãda'ʎãw/ a (f **~dalhona**) enormous. **~dão** a (f **~dona**) huge. **~de** a big; fig ‹escritor, amor etc› great. **~deza** /e/ f greatness; (tamanho) magnitude. **~dioso** /o/ a grand

granel /gra'new/ m **a ~** in bulk

granito /gra'nitu/ m granite

granizo /gra'nizu/ m hail

gran|ja /'grãʒa/ f farm. **~jear** vt win, gain

granulado /granu'ladu/ a granulated

grânulo /'granulu/ m granule

grão /grãw/ (pl **~s**) m grain; (de café) bean. **~-de-bico** (pl **~s-de-bico**) m chickpea

grasnar /graz'nar/ vi ‹pato› quack; ‹rã› croak; ‹corvo› caw

grati|dão /gratʃi'dãw/ f gratitude. **~ficação** f (dinheiro a mais) gratuity; (recompensa) gratification. **~ficante** a gratifying. **~ficar** vt (dar dinheiro a) give a gratuity to; (recompensar) gratify

gratinado /gratʃi'nadu/ a & m gratin

grátis /'gratʃis/ adv free

grato /'gratu/ a grateful

gratuito /gra'tuito/ a (de graça) free; (sem motivo) gratuitous

grau /graw/ m degree; **escola de 1°/2° ~** primary/secondary school

graúdo /gra'udu/ a big; (importante) important

gra|vação /grava'sãw/ f (de som) recording; (de desenhos etc) engraving. **~vador** m (pessoa) engraver; (máquina) tape recorder. **~vadora** f record company. **~var** vt record ‹música, disco›; (fixar na memória) memorize; (estampar) engrave

gravata /gra'vata/ f tie; (golpe) stranglehold; **~ borboleta** bow tie

grave /'gravi/ a serious; ‹voz, som› deep; ‹acento› grave

grávida /'gravida/ a pregnant

gravidade /gravi'dadʒi/ f gravity

gravidez /gravi'des/ f pregnancy

gravura /gra'vura/ f engraving; (em livro) illustration

graxa /'graʃa/ f (de sapatos) polish; (de lubrificar) grease

Grécia /'gresia/ f Greece

grego /'gregu/ a & m Greek

grei /grej/ f flock

gre|lha /'greʎa/ f grill. **~lhado** a grilled ● m grill. **~lhar** vt grill

grêmio /'gremiu/ m guild, association

grená /gre'na/ a & m dark red

gre|ta /'greta/ f crack. **~tar** vt/i crack

gre|ve /'grevi/ f strike; **entrar em ~ve** go on strike; **~ve de fome** hunger strike. **~vista** m/f striker

gri|fado /gri'fadu/ a in italics. **~far** vt italicize

griffe /'grifi/ f label, line

gri|lado /gri'ladu/ a 🅸 hung up. **~lar** vt 🅸 bug. **~lar-se** vpr 🅸 get hung up (com about)

grilhão /gri'ʎãw/ m fetter

grilo /'grilu/ m (bicho) cricket; 🅸 (preocupação) hang-up; (problema) hassle; (barulho) squeak

grinalda /gri'nawda/ f garland

gringo /'grĩgu/ 🅸 a foreign ● m foreigner

gri|pado /gri'padu/ *a* **estar/ficar ~pado** have/get the flu. **~par-se** *vpr* get the flu. **~pe** /'gripi/ *f* flu, influenza; **~pe das aves** bird flu; **~pe suína** swine flu

grisalho /gri'zaʎu/ *a* grey

gri|tante /gri'tãtʃi/ *a* ‹erro› glaring, gross; ‹cor› loud, garish. **~tar** *vt/i* shout; ‹de medo› scream. **~taria** *f* shouting. **~to** *m* shout; ‹de medo› scream; **aos ~tos** in a loud voice; **no ~to** 🄸 by force

grogue /'grɔgi/ *a* groggy

grosa /'grɔza/ *f* gross

groselha /gro'zeʎa/ *f* ‹vermelha› redcurrant; ‹espinhosa› gooseberry; **~ negra** blackcurrant

gros|seiro /gro'seru/ *a* rude; ‹tosco, malfeito› rough. **~seria** *f* rudeness; ‹uma› rude thing. **~so** /o/ *a* thick; ‹voz› deep; 🄸 ‹pessoa, atitude› rude. **~sura** *f* thickness; 🄸 ‹grosseria› rudeness

grotesco /gro'tesku/ *a* grotesque

grua /'grua/ *f* crane

gru|dado /gru'dadu/ *a* stuck; *fig* very attached (**em** to). **~dar** *vt/i* stick. **~de** *m* glue. **~dento** *a* sticky

gru|nhido /gru'ɲidu/ *m* grunt. **~nhir** *vi* grunt

grupo /'grupu/ *m* group

gruta /'gruta/ *f* cave

guaraná /gwara'na/ *m* guarana

> **guaraná** *Guaraná* is a common plant native to the Amazon Basin. The term is used to refer to the small fruit of the *guaraná* plant, but also to soft drinks made with guaraná extract, which are very popular in Brazil. *Guaraná* is also used as a stimulant in herbal supplements due to its high caffeine content.

guarani /gwara'ni/ *a* & *m/f* Guarani

guarda /'gwarda/ *f* guard ● *m/f* guard; ‹policial› policeman (*f* -woman); **~ costeira** coastguard. **~chuva** *m* umbrella; **~costas** *m invar* bodyguard; **~florestal** (*pl* **~s-florestais**) *m/f* forest ranger; **~louça** *m* china cupboard; **~noturno** (*pl* **~s-noturnos**) *m* night watchman. **~dor** *m* parking attendant. **~napo** *m* napkin, serviette

guardar /gwar'dar/ *vt* ‹pôr no lugar› put away; ‹conservar› keep; ‹vigiar› guard; ‹não esquecer› remember; **~se de** guard against

guarda|-redes /'gwarda-'xedʃ/ *m invar* Port goalkeeper. **~roupa** *m* wardrobe;

~sol (*pl* **~sóis**) *m* sunshade

guardi|ão /gward3i'ãw/ (*pl* **~ães** ou **~ões**) *m* (*f* **~ã**) guardian

guarita /gwa'rita/ *f* sentry box

guar|necer /gwarne'ser/ *vt* ‹fortificar› garrison; ‹munir› equip; ‹enfeitar› garnish. **~nição** *f* Mil garrison; ‹enfeite› garnish

Guatemala /gwate'mala/ *f* Guatemala

guatemalteco /gwatemaɫ'tɛku/ *a* & *m* Guatemalan

gude /'gudʒi/ *m* **bola de ~** marble

guelra /'gewxa/ *f* gill

guer|ra /'gɛxa/ *f* war. **~reiro** *m* warrior ● *a* warlike. **~rilha** *f* guerrilla war. **~rilheiro** *a* & *m* guerrilla

gueto /'getu/ *m* ghetto

gugar /gu'gar/ *vt* ▶ **googar**

guia /'gia/ *m/f* guide ● *m* guide(book) ● *f* delivery note

Guiana /gi'ana/ *f* Guyana

guianense /gia'nẽsi/ *a* & *m/f* Guyanan

guiar /gi'ar/ *vt* guide; drive ‹veículo› ● *vi* drive. **~se** *vpr* be guided

guichê /gi'ʃe/ *m* window

guidom /gi'dõ/, Port **guidão** /gi'dãw/ *m* handlebars

guilhotina /giʎo'tʃina/ *f* guillotine

guimba /'gĩba/ *f* butt

guinada /gi'nada/ *f* change of direction; **dar uma ~** change direction

guinchar[1] /gĩ'ʃar/ *vi* squeal; ‹freios› screech

guinchar[2] /gĩ'ʃar/ *vt* tow ‹carro›; ‹içar› winch

guincho[1] /'gĩʃu/ *m* squeal; ‹de freios› screech

guincho[2] /'gĩʃu/ *m* ‹máquina› winch; ‹veículo› tow truck

guin|dar /gĩ'dar/ *vt* hoist. **~daste** *m* crane

Guiné /gi'nɛ/ *f* Guinea

gui|sado /gi'zadu/ *m* stew. **~sar** *vt* stew

guitar|ra /gi'taxa/ *f* (electric) guitar. **~rista** *m/f* guitarist

guizo /'gizu/ *m* bell

gu|la /'gula/ *f* greed. **~lodice** *f* greed. **~loseima** *f* delicacy. **~loso** /o/ *a* greedy

gume /'gumi/ *m* cutting edge

guri /gu'ri/ *m* boy. **~a** *f* girl

guru /gu'ru/ *m* guru

gutu|ral /gutu'raw/ (*pl* **~rais**) *a* guttural

g

Hh

há|bil /'abiw/ (*pl* ~**beis**) *a* clever, skilful

habili|dade /abili'dadʒi/ *f* skill; **ter** ~**dade com** be good with. ~**doso** /o/ *a* skilful. ~**tação** *f* qualification. ~**tar** *vt* qualify

habi|tação /abita'sãw/ *f* housing; (*casa*) dwelling. ~**tacional** (*pl* ~**tacionais**) *a* housing. ~**tante** *m/f* inhabitant. ~**tar** *vt* inhabit ● *vi* live. ~**tável** (*pl* ~**táveis**) *a* habitable

hábito /'abitu/ *m* habit

habitu|al /abitu'aw/ (*pl* ~**ais**) *a* habitual. ~**ar** *vt* accustom (**a** to). ~**ar-se** *vpr* get accustomed (**a** to)

hacker /'akεr/ *m/f* BR hacker

hacking *m* BR hacking

hadoque /a'dɔki/ *m* haddock

Haia /'aja/ *f* the Hague

Haiti /aj'tʃi/ *m* Haiti

haitiano /ajtʃi'anu/ *a* & *m* Haitian

hálito /'alitu/ *m* breath

halitose /ali'tɔzi/ *f* halitosis

hall /xɔw/ (*pl* ~**s**) *m* hall; (*de hotel*) foyer

halogênio /alo'ʒenju/ *m* halogen

halte|re /aw'tεri/ *m* dumb-bell. ~**rofilismo** *m* weightlifting. ~**rofilista** *m/f* weightlifter

hambúrguer /ã'burger/ *m* hamburger

hangar /ã'gar/ *m* hangar

haras /'aras/ *m invar* stud farm

hardware /'xarduεr/ *m* hardware

harmo|nia /armo'nia/ *f* harmony. ~**nioso** /o/ *a* harmonious. ~**nizar** *vt* harmonize; (*conciliar*) reconcile. ~**nizar-se** *vpr* (*combinar*) tone in; (*concordar*) coincide

har|pa /'arpa/ *f* harp. ~**pista** *m/f* harpist

haste /'astʃi/ *m* pole; (*de planta*) stem, stalk. ~**ar** *vt* hoist, raise

Havaí /ava'i/ *m* Hawaii

havaiano /avaj'anu/ *a* & *m* Hawaiian

haver /a'ver/ *m* credit; *pl* possessions ● *vt auxiliar* **havia sido** it had been; (*impessoal*) **há** there is/are; **ele trabalha aqui há anos** he's been working here for years; **ela morreu há vinte anos (atrás)** she died twenty years ago

haxixe /a'ʃiʃi/ *m* hashish

he|braico /e'brajku/ *a* & *m* Hebrew. ~**breu** *a* & *m* (*f* ~**breia**) Hebrew

hectare /ek'tari/ *m* hectare

hediondo /edʒi'õdu/ *a* hideous

hein /ẽj/ *int* eh

hélice /'εlisi/ *f* propeller

helicóptero /eli'kɔpteru/ *m* helicopter

hélio /'εliu/ *m* helium

heliporto /eli'portu/ *m* heliport

hem /ẽj/ *int* eh

hematoma /ema'toma/ *m* bruise

hemisfério /emis'feriu/ *m* hemisphere; **Hemisfério Norte/Sul** Northern/Southern Hemisphere

hemo|filia /emofi'lia/ *f* haemophilia. ~**fílico** *a* & *m* haemophiliac. ~**globina** *f* haemoglobin. ~**grama** *m* blood count

hemor|ragia /emoxa'ʒia/ *f* haemorrhage. ~**roidas** *f pl* haemorrhoids

henê /e'ne/ *m* henna

hepatite /epa'tʃitʃi/ *f* hepatitis

hera /'εra/ *f* ivy

heráldi|ca /e'rawdʒika/ *f* heraldry. ~**co** *a* heraldic

herança /e'rãsa/ *f* inheritance; (*de um povo etc*) heritage

her|bicida /erbi'sida/ *m* weedkiller. ~**bívoro** *a* herbivorous ● *m* herbivore

her|dar /er'dar/ *vt* inherit. ~**deiro** *m* heir

hereditário /eredʒi'tariu/ *a* hereditary

here|ge /e'reʒi/ *m/f* heretic. ~**sia** *f* heresy

herético /e'rεtʃiku/ *a* heretical

hermético /er'mεtʃiku/ *a* airtight; *fig* obscure

hérnia /'εrnia/ *f* hernia

her|ói /e'rɔj/ *m* hero. ~**oico** *a* heroic

hero|ína /ero'ina/ *f* (*mulher*) heroine; (*droga*) heroin. ~**ísmo** *m* heroism

herpes /'εrpis/ *m invar* herpes. ~**zoster** *m* shingles

hesi|tação /ezita'sãw/ *f* hesitation. ~**tante** *a* hesitant. ~**tar** *vi* hesitate

hetero|doxo /etero'dɔksu/ *a* unorthodox. ~**gêneo** *a* heterogeneous

heterossexu|al /eteroseksu'aw/ (*pl* ~**ais**) *a* & *m* heterosexual

hexago|nal /eksago'naw/ (*pl* ~**nais**) *a* hexagonal

hexágono /ek'sagonu/ *m* hexagon

hiato /i'atu/ *m* hiatus

hiber|nação /iberna'sãw/ *f* hibernation. ~**nar** *vi* hibernate

híbrido /'ibridu/ *a & m* hybrid; **carro ~** hybrid car

hidrante /i'drãtʃi/ *m* fire hydrant

hidra|tante /idra'tãtʃi/ *a* a moisturising ● *m* moisturizer. **~tar** *vt* moisturize ‹*pele*›. **~to** *m* **~to de carbono** carbohydrate

hidráuli|ca /i'drawlika/ *f* hydraulics. **~co** *a* hydraulic

hidrelétri|ca /idre'lɛtrika/ *f* hydroelectric power station. **~co** *a* hydroelectric

hidro|avião /idroavi'ãw/ *m* seaplane. **~carboneto** /e/ *m* hydrocarbon

hidrófilo /i'drɔfilu/ *a* absorbent; **algodão ~** cotton wool, *Amer* absorbent cotton

hidrofobia /idrofo'bia/ *f* rabies

hidro|gênio /idro'ʒeniu/ *m* hydrogen. **~massagem** *f* **banheira de ~massagem** jacuzzi. **~via** *f* waterway

hiena /i'ena/ *f* hyena

hierarquia /ierar'kia/ *f* hierarchy

hieróglifo /ie'rɔglifu/ *m* hieroglyphic

hífen /'ifẽ/ *m* hyphen

higi|ene /iʒi'eni/ *f* hygiene. **~ênico** *a* hygienic

hilari|ante /ilari'ãtʃi/ *a* a hilarious. **~dade** *f* hilarity

Himalaia /ima'laja/ *m* Himalayas

hin|di /ĩ'dʒi/ *m* Hindi. **~du** *a & m/f* Hindu. **~duísmo** *m* Hinduism. **~duísta** *a & m/f* Hindu

hino /'inu/ *m* hymn; **~ nacional** national anthem

hipermercado /ipermer'kadu/ *m* hypermarket

hipersensí|vel /ipersẽ'sivew/ (*pl* **~veis**) *a* hypersensitive

hipertensão /ipertẽ'sãw/ *f* hypertension

hípico /'ipiku/ *a* horse riding

hipismo /i'pizmu/ *m* horse riding; (*corridas*) horse racing

hip|nose /ipi'nɔzi/ *f* hypnosis. **~nótico** *a* hypnotic. **~notismo** *m* hypnotism. **~notizador** *m* hypnotist. **~notizar** *vt* hypnotize

hipnoterapia /ipnotera'pia/ *f* hypnotherapy

hipocondríaco /ipokõ'driaku/ *a & m* hypochondriac

hipocrisia /ipokri'zia/ *f* hypocrisy

hipócrita /i'pɔkrita/ *m/f* hypocrite ● *a* hypocritical

hipódromo /i'pɔdromu/ *m* race course, *Amer* race track

hipopótamo /ipo'pɔtamu/ *m* hippopotamus

hipote|ca /ipo'teka/ *f* mortgage. **~car** *vt* mortgage. **~cário** *a* mortgage

hipotermia /ipoter'mia/ *f* hypothermia

hipótese /i'pɔtezi/ *f* hypothesis; **na ~ de** in the event of; **na pior das ~s** at worst

hipotético /ipo'tɛtʃiku/ *a* hypothetical

hirto /'irtu/ *a* rigid, stiff

hispânico /is'paniku/ *a* Hispanic

histamina /ista'mina/ *f* histamine

his|terectomia /isterekto'mia/ *f* hysterectomy. **~teria** *f* hysteria. **~térico** *a* hysterical. **~terismo** *m* hysteria

his|tória /is'tɔria/ *f* (*do passado*) history; (*conto*) story; *pl* (*amolação*) trouble. **~toriador** *m* historian. **~tórico** *a* historical; (*marcante*) historic ● *m* history

hoje /'oʒi/ *adv* today; **~ em dia** nowadays; **~ de manhã** this morning; **~ à noite** tonight

Holanda /o'lãda/ *f* Holland

holan|dês /olã'des/ *a* (*f* **~desa**) Dutch ● *m* (*f* **~desa**) Dutchman (*f* -woman); (*língua*) Dutch; **os ~deses** the Dutch

holding /'xɔwdʒĩ/ (*pl* **~s**) *f* holding company

holerite /ole'ritʃi/ *m* pay slip

holo|causto /olo'kawstu/ *m* holocaust. **~fote** /ɔ/ *m* spotlight. **~grama** *m* hologram

homem /'omẽ/ *m* man; **~ de negócios** businessman. **~rã** (*pl* **homens-rã**) *m* frogman

homena|gear /omenaʒi'ar/ *vt* pay tribute to. **~gem** *f* tribute; **em ~gem a** in honour of

homeo|pata /omio'pata/ *m/f* homoeopath. **~patia** *f* homoeopathy. **~pático** *a* homoeopathic

homérico /o'meriku/ *a* (*estrondoso*) booming; (*extraordinário*) phenomenal

homi|cida /omi'sida/ *a* homicidal ● *m/f* murderer. **~cídio** *m* homicide; **~cídio involuntário** manslaughter

homo|geneizado /omoʒenej'zadu/ *a* ‹*leite*› homogenized. **~gêneo** *a* homogeneous

homologar /omolo'gar/ *vt* ratify

homólogo /o'mɔlogu/ *m* opposite number ● *a* equivalent

homônimo /o'monimu/ m (xará) namesake; (vocábulo) homonym

homossexu|al /omoseksu'aw/ (pl ~ais) a & m homosexual. ~alismo m homosexuality

Honduras /õ'duras/ f Honduras

hondurenho /õduˈreɲu/ a & m Honduran

hones|tidade /onestʃiˈdadʒi/ f honesty. ~to /ɛ/ a honest

hono|rário /onoˈrariu/ a honorary. ~rários m pl fees. ~rífico a honorific

hon|ra /'õxa/ f honour. ~radez f honesty, integrity. ~rado a honourable. ~rar vt honour. ~roso /o/ a honourable

hóquei /'ɔkej/ m (field) hockey; ~ sobre gelo ice hockey; ~ sobre patins roller hockey

hora /'ɔra/ f (unidade de tempo) hour; (ocasião) time; que ~s são? what's the time?; a que ~s? at what time?; às três ~s at three o'clock; dizer as ~s tell the time; tem ~s? do you have the time?; em cima da ~ at the last minute; na ~ (naquele momento) at the time; (no ato) on the spot; (a tempo) on time; está na ~ de ir it's time to go; na ~ H (no momento certo) at just the right moment; (no momento crítico) at the crucial moment; meia ~ half an hour; toda ~ all the time; fazer ~ kill time; marcar ~ make an appointment; perder a ~ lose track of time; não tenho ~ my time is my own; não vejo a ~ de ir I can't wait to go; ~s extras overtime; ~s vagas spare time

horário /o'rariu/ a hourly; km ~s km per hour ● m (hora) time; (tabela) timetable; (de trabalho etc) hours; ~ nobre prime time

horda /'ɔrda/ f horde

horista /o'rista/ a paid by the hour ● m/f worker paid by the hour

horizon|tal /orizõ'taw/ (pl ~tais) a & f horizontal. ~te m horizon

hor|monal /ormo'naw/ (pl ~monais) a hormonal. ~mônio m hormone

horóscopo /o'rɔskopu/ m horoscope

horrendo /o'xẽdu/ a horrid

horripi|lante /oxipi'lãtʃi/ a horrifying. ~lar vt horrify

horrí|vel /o'xivew/ (pl ~veis) a horrible, awful

horror /o'xor/ m horror (a of); (coisa horrorosa) horrible thing; ser um ~ be awful; que ~! how awful!

horro|rizar /oxori'zar/ vt/i horrify. ~rizar-se vpr be horrified. ~roso /o/ a horrible

horta /'ɔrta/ f vegetable plot; ~ comercial market garden, Amer truck farm. ~liça f vegetable

hortelã /orte'lã/ f mint; ~pimenta peppermint

horti|cultor /ortʃikuw'tor/ m horticulturalist. ~cultura f horticulture. ~frutigranjeiros m pl fruit and vegetables. ~granjeiros m pl vegetables

horto /'ortu/ m market garden; (viveiro) nursery

hospe|dagem /ospe'daʒẽ/ f accommodation. ~dar vt put up. ~dar-se vpr stay

hóspede /'ɔspidʒi/ m/f guest

hospedei|ra /ospe'dera/ f landlady; ~ra de bordo Port flight attendant. ~ro m landlord

hospício /os'pisiu/ m (de loucos) asylum

hospi|tal /ospi'taw/ (pl ~tais) m hospital. ~talar a hospital. ~taleiro a hospitable. ~talidade f hospitality. ~talizar vt hospitalize

hóstia /'ɔstʃia/ f Host, Communion wafer

hos|til /os'tʃiw/ (pl ~tis) a hostile. ~tilidade f hostility. ~tilizar vt antagonize

ho|tel /o'tɛw/ (pl ~téis) m hotel. ~teleiro a hotel ● m hotelier

huma|nidade /umani'dadʒi/ f humanity. ~nismo m humanism. ~nista a & m/f humanist. ~nitário a & m humanitarian. ~nizar vt humanize. ~no a human; (compassivo) humane. ~nos m pl humans

húmido /'umidu/ a Port humid

humil|dade /umiw'dadʒi/ f humility. ~de a humble

humi|lhação /umiʎa'sãw/ f humiliation. ~lhante a humiliating. ~lhar vt humiliate

humor /u'mor/ m humour; (disposição do espírito) mood; de bom/mau ~ in a good/bad mood

humo|rismo /umo'rizmu/ m humour. ~rista m/f (no palco) comedian; (escritor) humorist. ~rístico a humorous

húngaro /'ũgaru/ a & m Hungarian

Hungria /ũ'gria/ f Hungary

hurra /'uxa/ int hurrah ● m cheer

Ii

ia|te /i'atʃi/ m yacht. **~tismo** m yachting. **~tista** m/f yachtsman (f-woman).

ibérico /i'bɛriku/ a & m Iberian

ibope /i'bɔpi/ m **dar ~** 🔲 be popular

içar /i'sar/ vt hoist

iceberg /ajs'bɛrgi/ (pl **~s**) m iceberg

ícone /'ikoni/ m icon

iconoclasta /ikono'klasta/ m/f iconoclast ● a iconoclastic

icterícia /ikte'risia/ f jaundice

ida /'ida/ f going; **na ~** on the way there; **~ e volta** return, Amer round trip

idade /i'dadʒi/ f age; **meia ~** middle age; **homem de meia ~** middle-aged man; **senhor de ~** elderly man; **Idade Média** Middle Ages

ide|al /ide'aw/ (pl **~ais**) a & m ideal. **~alismo** m idealism. **~alista** m/f idealist ● a idealistic. **~alizar** vt (criar) devise; (sublimar) idealize. **~ar** vt devise. **~ário** m ideas

ideia /i'dɛja/ f idea; **mudar de ~** change one's mind

idem /'idẽ/ adv ditto

idêntico /i'dẽtʃiku/ a identical

identi|dade /idẽtʃi'dadʒi/ f identity. **~ficar** vt identify. **~ficar-se** vpr identify (com with)

ideo|logia /ideolo'ʒia/ f ideology. **~lógico** a ideological

idílico /i'dʒiliku/ a idyllic

idílio /i'dʒiliu/ m idyll

idio|ma /idʒi'oma/ m language. **~mático** a idiomatic

idio|ta /idʒi'ɔta/ m/f idiot ● a idiotic. **~tice** f stupidity; (uma) stupid thing

idola|trar /idola'trar/ vt idolize. **~tria** f idolatry

ídolo /'idulu/ m idol

idôneo /i'doniu/ a suitable

idoso /i'dozu/ a elderly

Iêmen /i'emẽ/ m Yemen

iemenita /ieme'nita/ a & m/f Yemeni

iene /i'eni/ m yen

iglu /i'glu/ m igloo

ignição /igni'sãw/ f ignition

igno|mínia /igno'minia/ f ignominy

igno|rância /igno'rãsia/ f ignorance. **~rante** a ignorant. **~rar** vt

(desconsiderar) ignore; (desconhecer) not know

igreja /i'greʒa/ f church

igu|al /i'gwaw/ (pl **~ais**) a equal; (em aparência) identical; (liso) even ● m/f equal; **por ~al** equally. **~alar** vt equal; level ‹terreno›; **~alar(-se)** a be equal to. **~aldade** f equality. **~alitário** a egalitarian. **~almente** adv equally; (como resposta) the same to you. **~alzinho** a exactly the same (**a** as)

iguaria /igwa'ria/ f delicacy

iídiche /i'idiʃi/ m Yiddish

ile|gal /ile'gaw/ (pl **~gais**) a illegal. **~galidade** f illegality

ilegítimo /ile'ʒitʃimu/ a illegitimate

ilegí|vel /ile'ʒivew/ (pl **~veis**) a illegible

ileso /i'lɛzu/ a unhurt

iletrado /ile'tradu/ a & m illiterate

ilha /'iʎa/ f island

ilharga /i'ʎarga/ f side

ilhéu /i'ʎɛw/ m (f **ilhoa**) islander

ilhós /i'ʎɔs/ m invar eyelet

ilhota /i'ʎɔta/ f small island

ilícito /i'lisitu/ a illicit

ilimitado /ilimi'tadu/ a unlimited

ilógico /i'lɔʒiku/ a illogical

iludir /ilu'dʒir/ vt delude. **~se** vpr delude o.s.

ilumi|nação /ilumina'sãw/ f lighting; (inspiração) enlightenment. **~nar** vt light up, illuminate; (inspirar) enlighten

ilu|são /ilu'zãw/ f illusion; (sonho) delusion. **~sionista** m/f illusionist. **~sório** a illusory

ilus|tração /ilustra'sãw/ f illustration; (erudição) learning. **~trador** m illustrator. **~trar** vt illustrate. **~trativo** a illustrative. **~tre** a illustrious; **~tríssimo senhor** Dear Sir

ímã /'imã/ m magnet

imaculado /imaku'ladu/ a immaculate

imagem /i'maʒẽ/ f image; (da TV) picture

imagi|nação /imaʒina'sãw/ f imagination. **~nar** vt imagine. **~nário** a imaginary. **~nativo** a imaginative. **~nável** (pl **~náveis**) a imaginable. **~noso** /o/ a imaginative

imatu|ridade /imaturi'dadʒi/ f immaturity. **~ro** a immature

imbatível /ĩba'tʃivew/ (pl **~veis**) a unbeatable

imbe|cil /ĩbe'siw/ (pl ~**cis**) a stupid ● m/f imbecile

imberbe /ĩ'berbi/ a (sem barba) beardless

imbricar /ĩbri'kar/ vt overlap. ~**se** vpr overlap

imedia|ções /imedʒia'sõjs/ f pl vicinity. ~**tamente** adv immediately. ~**to** a immediate

imemori|al /imemori'aw/ (pl ~**ais**) a immemorial

imen|sidão /imẽsi'dãw/ f vastness. ~**so** a immense

imergir /imer'ʒir/ vt immerse

imi|gração /imigra'sãw/ f immigration. ~**grante** a & m/f immigrant. ~**grar** vi immigrate

imi|nência /imi'nẽsia/ f imminence. ~**nente** a imminent

imiscuir-se /imisku'irsi/ vpr interfere

imi|tação /imita'sãw/ f imitation. ~**tador** m imitator. ~**tar** vt imitate

imobili|ária /imobili'aria/ f estate agent's, Amer realtor. ~**ário** a property. ~**dade** f immobility. ~**zar** vt immobilize

imo|ral /imo'raw/ (pl ~**rais**) a immoral. ~**ralidade** f immorality

imor|tal /imor'taw/ (pl ~**tais**) a immortal ● m/f member of the Brazilian Academy of Letters. ~**talidade** f immortality. ~**talizar** vt immortalize

imó|vel /i'mɔvew/ (pl ~**veis**) a motionless, immobile ● m building, property; pl property, Amer real estate

impaci|ência /ĩpasi'ẽsia/ f impatience. ~**entar-se** vpr get impatient. ~**ente** a impatient

impacto /ĩ'paktu/, Port **impacte** /ĩ'paktʃi/ m impact

impagá|vel /ĩpa'gavew/ (pl ~**veis**) a priceless

ímpar /'ĩpar/ a unique; ‹número› odd

imparci|al /ĩparsi'aw/ (pl ~**ais**) a impartial. ~**alidade** f impartiality

impasse /ĩ'pasi/ m impasse

impassí|vel /ĩpa'sivew/ (pl ~**veis**) a impassive

impecá|vel /ĩpe'kavew/ (pl ~**veis**) a impeccable

impe|dido /ĩpe'dʒidu/ a ‹rua› blocked; Port (ocupado) engaged, Amer busy; (no futebol) offside. ~**dimento** m prevention; (estorvo) obstruction; (no futebol) offside position. ~**dir** vt stop; (estorvar) hinder; block ‹rua›; ~**dir** alguém de ir ou que alguém vá stop

sb going

impelir /ĩpe'lir/ vt drive

impenetrá|vel /ĩpene'travew/ (pl ~**veis**) a impenetrable

impensá|vel /ĩpẽ'savew/ (pl ~**veis**) a unthinkable

impe|rador /ĩpera'dor/ m emperor. ~**rar** vi reign, rule. ~**rativo** a & m imperative. ~**ratriz** f empress

impercepti|vel /ĩpersep'tʃivew/ (pl ~**veis**) a imperceptible

imperdí|vel /ĩper'dʒivew/ (pl ~**veis**) a unmissable

imperdoá|vel /ĩperdo'avew/ (pl ~**veis**) a unforgivable

imperfei|ção /ĩperfej'sãw/ f imperfection. ~**to** a & m imperfect

imperi|al /ĩperi'aw/ (pl ~**ais**) a imperial ● f Port (de cerveja) glass of draught beer. ~**alismo** m imperialism. ~**alista** a & m/f imperialist

império /ĩ'periu/ m empire

imperioso /ĩperi'ozu/ a imperious; ‹necessidade› pressing

imperme|abilizar /ĩpermiabili'zar/ vt waterproof. ~**ável** (pl ~**áveis**) a waterproof; fig impervious (a to) ● m raincoat

imperti|nência /ĩpertʃi'nẽsia/ f impertinence. ~**nente** a impertinent

impesso|al /ĩpeso'aw/ (pl ~**ais**) a impersonal

ímpeto /'ĩpetu/ m (vontade) urge, impulse; (de emoção) surge; (movimento) start; (na física) impetus

impetuo|sidade /ĩpetuozi'dadʒi/ f impetuosity. ~**so** /o/ a impetuous

impiedoso /ĩpie'dozu/ a merciless

impingir /ĩpĩ'ʒir/ vt foist (a on)

implacá|vel /ĩpla'kavew/ (pl ~**veis**) a implacable

implan|tar /ĩplã'tar/ vt introduce; (no corpo) implant. ~**te** m implant

implemen|tar /ĩplemẽ'tar/ vt implement. ~**to** m implement

impli|cação /ĩplika'sãw/ f implication. ~**cância** f (ato) harassment; (antipatia) grudge; **estar de ~cância com** have it in for. ~**cante** a troublesome ● m/f troublemaker. ~**car** vt (comprometer) implicate; ~**car (em)** (dar a entender) imply; (acarretar, exigir) involve; ~**car com** (provocar) pick on; (antipatizar) not get on with

implícito /ĩ'plisitu/ a implicit

implorar /ĩplo'rar/ *vt* plead for (a from)

imponente /ĩpo'nẽtʃi/ *a* imposing

impopular /ĩpopu'lar/ *a* unpopular

impor /ĩ'por/ *vt* impose (**a** on); command ‹*respeito*›. **~se** *vpr* assert o.s.

impor|tação /ĩporta'sãw/ *f* import. **~tador** *m* importer. **~tadora** *f* import company. **~tados** *m pl* imported goods. **~tância** *f* importance; (*quantia*) amount; **ter ~tância** be important. **~tante** *a* important. **~tar** *vt* import ‹*mercadorias*›; **~tar em** (*montar a*) amount to; (*resultar em*) lead to ● *vi* matter; **~tar-se (com)** mind

importu|nar /ĩportu'nar/ *vt* bother. **~no** *a* annoying

imposição /ĩpozi'sãw/ *f* imposition

impossibili|dade /ĩposibili'dadʒi/ *f* impossibility. **~tar** *vt* make impossible; **~tar alguém de ir, ~tar a alguém ir** prevent sb from going, make it impossible for sb to go

impossí|vel /ĩpo'sivew/ (*pl* **~veis**) *a* impossible

impos|to /ĩ'postu/ *m* tax; **~to de renda** income tax; **~to sobre o valor acrescentado** *Port* VAT. **~tor** *m* impostor. **~tura** *f* deception

impo|tência /ĩpo'tẽsia/ *f* impotence. **~tente** *a* impotent

impreci|são /ĩpresi'zãw/ *f* imprecision. **~so** *a* imprecise

impregnar /ĩpreg'nar/ *vt* impregnate

imprensa /ĩ'prẽsa/ *f* press; **~ marrom** gutter press

imprescindí|vel /ĩpresĩ'dʒivew/ (*pl* **~veis**) *a* essential

impres|são /ĩpre'sãw/ *f* impression; (*no prelo*) printing; **~são digital** fingerprint. **~sionante** *a* (*imponente*) impressive; (*comovente*) striking. **~sionar** *vt* (*causar admiração*) impress; (*comover*) make an impression on. **~sionar-se** *vpr* be impressed (**com** by). **~sionável** (*pl* **~sionáveis**) *a* impressionable. **~sionismo** *m* Impressionism. **~sionista** *a* & *m/f* Impressionist. **~so** *a* printed ● *m* printed sheet; *pl* printed matter. **~sor** *m* printer. **~sora** *f* printer

imprestá|vel /ĩpres'tavew/ (*pl* **~veis**) *a* useless

impre|visível /ĩprevi'zivew/ (*pl* **~visíveis**) *a* unpredictable. **~visto** *a* unforeseen ● *m* unforeseen circumstance

imprimir /ĩpri'mir/ *vt* print

impropério /ĩpro'periu/ *m* term of abuse; *pl* abuse

impróprio /ĩ'propriu/ *a* improper; (*inadequado*) unsuitable (**para** for)

imprová|vel /ĩpro'vavew/ (*pl* **~veis**) *a* unlikely

improvi|sação /ĩproviza'sãw/ *f* improvisation. **~sar** *vt/i* improvise. **~so** *m* **de ~so** on the spur of the moment

impru|dência /ĩpru'dẽsia/ *f* recklessness. **~dente** *a* reckless

impul|sionar /ĩpuwsio'nar/ *vt* drive. **~sivo** *a* impulsive. **~so** *m* impulse

impu|ne /ĩ'puni/ *a* unpunished. **~nidade** *f* impunity

impu|reza /ĩpu'reza/ *f* impurity. **~ro** *a* impure

imun|dície /imũ'dʒisi/ *f* filth. **~do** *a* filthy

imu|ne /i'muni/ *a* immune (**a** to). **~nidade** *f* immunity. **~nizar** *vt* immunize

inabalá|vel /inaba'lavew/ (*pl* **~veis**) *a* unshakeable

iná|bil /i'nabiw/ (*pl* **~beis**) *a* (*desafeitado*) clumsy

inabitado /inabi'tadu/ *a* uninhabited

inacabado /inaka'badu/ *a* unfinished

inaceitá|vel /inasej'tavew/ (*pl* **~veis**) *a* unacceptable

inacessí|vel /inase'sivew/ (*pl* **~veis**) *a* inaccessible

inacreditá|vel /inakredʒi'tavew/ (*pl* **~veis**) *a* unbelievable

inadequado /inade'kwadu/ *a* unsuitable

inadmissí|vel /inadʒimi'sivew/ (*pl* **~veis**) *a* inadmissible

inadvertência /inadʒiver'tẽsia/ *f* oversight

inalar /ina'lar/ *vt* inhale

inalcançá|vel /inawkã'savew/ (*pl* **~veis**) *a* unattainable

inalterá|vel /inawte'ravew/ (*pl* **~veis**) *a* unchangeable

inanição /inani'sãw/ *f* starvation

inanimado /inani'madu/ *a* inanimate

inapto /i'naptu/ *a* (*incapaz*) unfit

inati|vidade /inatʃivi'dadʒi/ *f* inactivity. **~vo** *a* inactive

inato /i'natu/ *a* innate

inaudito /inaw'dʒitu/ *a* unheard of

inaugu|ração /inawgura'sãw/ *f* inauguration. **~ral** (*pl* **~rais**) *a* inaugural. **~rar** *vt* inaugurate

incabí|vel /ĩka'bivew/ (pl ~**veis**) a inappropriate

incalculá|vel /ĩkawku'lavew/ (pl ~**veis**) a incalculable

incandescente /ĩkãde'sẽtʃi/ a red-hot

incansá|vel /ĩkã'savew/ (pl ~**veis**) a tireless

incapaci|tado /ĩkapasi'tadu/ a ‹pessoa› disabled. ~**tar** vt incapacitate

incauto /ĩ'kawtu/ a reckless

incendi|ar /ĩsẽdʒi'ar/ vt set alight. ~**ar-se** vpr catch fire. ~**ário** a incendiary; fig ‹discurso› inflammatory ● m arsonist; fig agitator

incêndio /ĩ'sẽdʒiu/ m fire

incenso /ĩ'sẽsu/ m incense

incenti|var /ĩsẽtʃi'var/ vt encourage. ~**vo** m incentive

incer|teza /ĩser'teza/ f uncertainty. ~**to** /ε/ a uncertain

inces|to /ĩ'sestu/ m incest. ~**tuoso** /o/ a incestuous

in|chação /ĩʃa'sãw/ f swelling. ~**char** vt/i swell

inci|dência /ĩsi'dẽsia/ f incidence. ~**dente** m incident. ~**dir** vi ~**dir em** ‹luz› shine on; ‹imposto› be payable on

incineradora /ĩsinera'dora/ f incinerator

incinerar /ĩsine'rar/ vt incinerate

inci|são /ĩsi'zãw/ f incision. ~**sivo** a incisive

incitar /ĩsi'tar/ vt incite

incli|nação /ĩklina'sãw/ f (do chão) incline; (da cabeça) nod; (propensão) inclination. ~**nado** a ‹chão› sloping; ‹edifício› leaning; (propenso) inclined (a to). ~**nar** vt tilt; nod ‹cabeça› ● vi ‹chão› slope; ‹edifício› lean; (tender) incline (**para** towards). ~**nar-se** vpr lean

inclu|ir /ĩklu'ir/ vt include. ~**são** f inclusion. ~**sive** prep including ● adv inclusive; (até) even. ~**so** a included

incoe|rência /ĩkoe'rẽsia/ f (falta de nexo) incoherence; (inconsequência) inconsistency. ~**rente** a (sem nexo) incoherent; (inconsequente) inconsistent

incógni|ta /ĩ'kɔgnita/ f unknown. ~**to** adv incognito

incolor /ĩko'lor/ a colourless

incólume /ĩ'kɔlumi/ a unscathed

incomodar /ĩkomo'dar/ vt bother ● vi be a nuisance. ~**se** vpr (dar-se ao trabalho) bother (**em** to); ~**se** (**com**) be bothered (by), mind

incômodo /ĩ'komodu/ a (desagradável) tiresome; (sem conforto) uncomfortable ● m nuisance

incompa|rável /ĩkõpa'ravew/ (pl ~**ráveis**) a incomparable. ~**tível** (pl ~**tíveis**) a incompatible

incompe|tência /ĩkõpe'tẽsia/ f incompetence. ~**tente** a incompetent

incompleto /ĩkõ'pletu/ a incomplete

incompreensí|vel /ĩkõpriẽ'sivew/ (pl ~**veis**) a incomprehensible

inconcebí|vel /ĩkõse'bivew/ (pl ~**veis**) a inconceivable

incondicio|nal /ĩkõdʒisio'naw/ (pl ~**nais**) a unconditional; ‹fã, partidário› firm

inconformado /ĩkõfor'madu/ a unreconciled (**com** to)

inconfundí|vel /ĩkõfũ'dʒivew/ (pl ~**veis**) a unmistakeable

inconsciente /ĩkõsi'ẽtʃi/ a & m unconscious

inconsequente /ĩkõse'kwẽtʃi/ a inconsistent

incons|tância /ĩkõs'tãsia/ f changeability. ~**tante** a changeable

inconstitucio|nal /ĩkõstʃitusio'naw/ (pl ~**nais**) a unconstitutional

incontestá|vel /ĩkõtes'tavew/ (pl ~**veis**) a indisputable

incontornável /ĩkõtor'navew/ a unavoidable

inconveniente /ĩkõveni'ẽtʃi/ a (difícil) inconvenient; (desagradável) annoying, tiresome; (indecente) unseemly ● m drawback

incorporar /ĩkorpo'rar/ vt incorporate

incorrer /ĩko'xer/ vi ~**em** ‹multa etc› incur

incorrigí|vel /ĩkoxi'ʒivew/ (pl ~**veis**) a incorrigible

incrédulo /ĩ'kredulu/ a incredulous

incremen|tado /ĩkremẽ'tadu/ a 🆑 stylish. ~**tar** vt build up; 🆑 jazz up. ~**to** m development, growth

incriminar /ĩkrimi'nar/ vt incriminate

incrí|vel /ĩ'krivew/ (pl ~**veis**) a incredible

incu|bação /ĩkuba'sãw/ f incubation. ~**badora** f incubator. ~**bar** vt/i incubate

inculto /ĩ'kuwtu/ a ‹pessoa› uneducated; ‹terreno› uncultivated

incum|bência /ĩkũ'bẽsia/ f task. ~**bir** vt ~**bir alguém de algo/de** assign sb sth/to go ● vi ~**bir a** be up to; ~**bir-se de** take on

incurá|vel /ĩku'ravew/ (pl ~**veis**) a incurable

incursão /ĩkur'sãw/ f incursion

incutir /ĩku'tʃir/ vt instil (**em** in)

indagar /ĩda'gar/ vt inquire (into)

inde|cência /ĩde'sẽsia/ f indecency. ~**cente** a indecent

indecifrá|vel /ĩdesi'fravew/ (pl ~**veis**) a indecipherable

indeciso /ĩde'sizu/ a undecided

indecoroso /ĩdeko'rozu/ a indecorous

indefi|nido /ĩdefi'nidu/ a indefinite. ~**nível** (pl ~**níveis**) a indefinable

indelé|vel /ĩde'lɛvew/ (pl ~**veis**) a indelible

indelica|deza /ĩdelika'deza/ f impoliteness; (uma) impolite thing. ~**do** a impolite

indeni|zação /ĩdeniza'sãw/ f compensation. ~**zar** vt compensate

indepen|dência /ĩdepẽ'dẽsia/ f independence. ~**dente** a independent

indescriti|vel /ĩdiskri'tʃivew/ (pl ~**veis**) a indescribable

indesculpá|vel /ĩdiskuw'pavew/ (pl ~**veis**) a inexcusable

indesejá|vel /ĩdeze'ʒavew/ (pl ~**veis**) a undesirable

indestruti|vel /ĩdistru'tʃivew/ (pl ~**veis**) a indestructible

indeterminado /ĩdetermi'nadu/ a indeterminate

indevido /ĩde'vidu/ a undue

indexar /idek'sar/ vt index; index-link ‹salário, preços›

Índia /'ĩdʒia/ f India

indiano /ĩdʒi'anu/ a & m Indian

indi|cação /ĩdʒika'sãw/ f indication; (do caminho) directions; (nomeação) nomination; (recomendação) recommendation. ~**cador** m indicator; (dedo) index finger ● a indicative (**de** of). ~**car** vt indicate; (para cargo, prêmio) nominate (**para** for); (recomendar) recommend. ~**cativo** a & m indicative

índice /'ĩdʒisi/ m (taxa) rate; (em livro etc) index; ~ **de audiência** ratings

indiciar /ĩdʒisi'ar/ vt charge

indício /ĩ'dʒisiu/ m sign, indication; (de crime) clue

indife|rença /ĩdʒife'rẽsa/ f indifference. ~**rente** a indifferent

indígena /ĩ'dʒiʒena/ a indigenous, native ● m/f native

indiges|tão /ĩdʒiʒes'tãw/ f indigestion. ~**to** a indigestible; fig heavy going

indig|nação /ĩdʒigna'sãw/ f indignation. ~**nado** a indignant. ~**nar** vt make indignant. ~**nar-se** vpr get indignant (**com** about)

indig|nidade /ĩdʒigni'dadʒi/ f indignity. ~**no** a ‹pessoa› unworthy; ‹ato› despicable

índio /'ĩdʒiu/ a & m Indian

indire|ta /ĩdʒi'rɛta/ f hint. ~**to** /ɛ/ a indirect

indis|creto /ĩdʒis'krɛtu/ a indiscreet. ~**crição** f indiscretion

indiscriminado /ĩdʒiskrimi-'nadu/ a indiscriminate

indiscuti|vel /ĩdʒisku'tʃivew/ (pl ~**veis**) a unquestionable

indispensá|vel /ĩdʒispẽ'savew/ (pl ~**veis**) a indispensable

indisponi|vel /ĩdʒispo'nivew/ (pl ~**veis**) a unavailable

indis|por /ĩdʒis'por/ vt upset; ~**por alguém contra** turn sb against. ~**por-se** vpr fall out (**com** with). ~**posição** f indisposition. ~**posto** a (doente) indisposed

indistinto /ĩdʒis'tʃĩtu/ a indistinct

individu|al /ĩdʒividu'aw/ (pl ~**ais**) a individual. ~**alidade** f individuality. ~**alismo** m individualism. ~**alista** a & m/f individualist

indivíduo /ĩdʒi'viduu/ m individual

indizi|vel /ĩdʒi'zivew/ (pl ~**veis**) a unspeakable

índole /'ĩdoli/ f nature

indo|lência /ĩdo'lẽsia/ f indolence. ~**lente** a indolent

indolor /ĩdo'lor/ a painless

Indonésia /ĩdo'nezia/ f Indonesia

indonésio /ĩdo'neziu/ a & m Indonesian

indubitá|vel /ĩdubi'tavew/ (pl ~**veis**) a undoubted

indul|gência /ĩduw'ʒẽsia/ f indulgence. ~**gente** a indulgent

indulto /ĩ'duwtu/ m pardon

indumentária /ĩdumẽ'taria/ f outfit

indústria /ĩ'dustria/ f industry

industri|al /ĩdustri'aw/ (pl ~**ais**) a industrial ● m/f industrialist. ~**alizado** a ‹país› industrialized; ‹mercadoria› manufactured; ‹comida› processed. ~**alizar** vt industrialize ‹país, agricultura *etc*); process ‹*comida, lixo etc*›. **~oso** /o/ *a* industrious

induzir /ĩdu'zir/ *vt* (*persuadir*) induce; (*inferir*) infer (**de** from); **~ em erro** lead astray, mislead sb

inebriante /inebri'ãtʃi/ *a* intoxicating

inédito /i'nɛdʒitu/ *a* unheard-of, unprecedented; (*não publicado*) unpublished

ineficaz /inefi'kas/ *a* ineffective

inefici|ência /inefisi'ẽsia/ *f* inefficiency. **~ente** *a* inefficient

inegá|vel /ine'gavew/ (*pl* **~veis**) *a* undeniable

inépcia /i'nɛpsia/ *f* ineptitude

inepto /i'nɛptu/ *a* inept

inequívoco /ine'kivoku/ *a* unmistakeable

inércia /i'nɛrsia/ *f* inertia

inerente /ine'rẽtʃi/ *a* inherent (**a** in)

inerte /i'nɛrtʃi/ *a* inert

inesgotá|vel /inezgo'tavew/ (*pl* **~veis**) *a* inexhaustible

inesperado /inespe'radu/ *a* unexpected

inesqueci|vel /ineske'sivew/ (*pl* **~veis**) *a* unforgettable

inevitá|vel /inevi'tavew/ (*pl* **~veis**) *a* inevitable

inexato /ine'zatu/ *a* inaccurate

inexis|tência /inezis'tẽsia/ *f* lack. **~tente** *a* non-existent

inexperi|ência /inisperi'ẽsia/ *f* inexperience. **~ente** *a* inexperienced

inexpressivo /inespre'sivu/ *a* expressionless

infalí|vel /ĩfa'livew/ (*pl* **~veis**) *a* infallible

infame /ĩ'fami/ *a* despicable; (*péssimo*) dreadful

infâmia /ĩ'famia/ *f* disgrace

infância /ĩ'fãsia/ *f* childhood

infantaria /ĩfãta'ria/ *f* infantry

infan|til /ĩfã'tʃiw/ *a* ‹*roupa, livro*› children's; (*bobo*) childish. **~tilidade** *f* childishness; (*uma*) childish thing

infarto /ĩ'fartu/ *m* heart attack

infec|ção /ĩfek'sãw/ *f* infection. **~cionar** *vt* infect. **~cioso** *a* infectious

infeliz /ĩfe'lis/ *a* (*não contente*) unhappy; (*inconveniente*) unfortunate; (*desgraçado*) wretched ● *m* (*desgraçado*) wretch. **~mente** *adv* unfortunately

inferi|or /ĩferi'or/ *a* lower; (*em qualidade*) inferior (**a** to). **~oridade** *f* inferiority

inferir /ĩfe'rir/ *vt* infer

infer|nal /ĩfer'naw/ (*pl* **~nais**) *a* infernal. **~nizar** *vt* **~nizar a vida dele** make his life hell. **~no** /ɛ/ *m* hell

infér|til /ĩ'fɛrtʃiw/ (*pl* **~teis**) *a* infertile

infertilidade /ĩfertʃili'dadʒi/ *f* infertility

infestar /ĩfes'tar/ *vt* infest

infetar /ĩfe'tar/ *vt* infect

infidelidade /ĩfideli'dadʒi/ *f* infidelity

infi|el /ĩfi'ɛw/ (*pl* **~éis**) *a* unfaithful

infiltrar /ĩfiw'trar/ *vt* infiltrate; **~se em** infiltrate

ínfimo /'ĩfimu/ *a* lowest; (*muito pequeno*) tiny

infindá|vel /ĩfĩ'davew/ (*pl* **~veis**) *a* unending

infinidade /ĩfini'dadʒi/ *f* infinity; **uma ~ de** an infinite number of

infini|tesimal /ĩfinitezi'maw/ (*pl* **~tesimais**) *a* infinitesimal. **~tivo** *a* & *m* infinitive. **~to** /i/ *a* infinite ● *m* infinity

infla|ção /ĩfla'sãw/ *f* inflation. **~cionar** *vt* inflate. **~cionário** *a* inflationary. **~cionista** *a* & *m/f* inflationist

infla|mação /ĩflama'sãw/ *f* inflammation. **~mar** *vt* inflame. **~mar-se** *vpr* become inflamed. **~matório** *a* inflammatory. **~mável** (*pl* **~máveis**) *a* inflammable

in|flar *vt* inflate. **~flar-se** *vpr* inflate. **~flável** (*pl* **~fláveis**) *a* inflatable

infle|xibilidade /ĩfleksibili'dadʒi/ *f* inflexibility. **~xível** (*pl* **~xíveis**) *a* inflexible

infligir /ĩfli'ʒir/ *vt* inflict (**a** on)

influência /ĩflu'ẽsia/ *f* influence

influen|ciar /ĩfluẽsi'ar/ *vt* **~ciar (em)** influence. **~ciar-se** *vpr* be influenced. **~ciável** (*pl* **~ciáveis**) *a* open to influence. **~te** *a* influential

influir /ĩflu'ir/ *vi* **~ em** ou **sobre** influence

informação /ĩforma'sãw/ *f* information; (*uma*) a piece of information; *Mil* intelligence; *pl* information

infor|mal /ĩfor'maw/ (*pl* **~mais**) *a* informal. **~malidade** *f* informality

infor|mar /ĩfor'mar/ *vt* inform. **~mar-se** *vpr* find out (**de** about). **~mática** /ĩfor'matʃika/ *f* information technology; **especialista em ~mática** IT specialist. **~mativo** *a* informative. **~matizar** *vt* computerize. **~me** *m* *Mil* piece of intelligence

informático /ĩfor'matʃiku/ a computer ● m Port IT specialist

informatização /ĩformatʃiza'sãw/ f computerization

infortúnio /ĩfor'tuniu/ m misfortune

infração /ĩfra'sãw/ f infringement

infraestrutura /ĩfraistru'tura/ f infrastructure

infrator /ĩfra'tor/ m offender

infravermelho /ĩfraver'meʎu/ a infrared

infringir /ĩfrĩ'ʒir/ vt infringe

infrutífero /ĩfru'tʃiferu/ a fruitless

infundado /ĩfũ'dadu/ a unfounded

infundir /ĩfũ'dʒir/ vt (insuflar) infuse; (incutir) instil

infusão /ĩfu'zãw/ f infusion

ingenuidade /ĩʒenui'dadʒi/ f naivety

ingênuo /ĩ'ʒenuu/ a naive

ingerir /ĩʒe'rir/ vt ingest; (engolir) swallow

Inglaterra /ĩgla'texa/ f England

in|glês /ĩ'gles/ a (f ~glesa) English ● m (f ~glesa) Englishman (f-woman); (língua) English; **os ~gleses** the English

ingra|tidão /ĩgratʃi'dãw/ f ingratitude. ~to a ungrateful

ingrediente /ĩgredʒi'ẽtʃi/ m ingredient

íngreme /'ĩgrimi/ a steep

ingres|sar /ĩgre'sar/ vi ~sar em join. ~so m entry; (bilhete) ticket

inhame /i'ɲami/ m yam

ini|bição /inibi'sãw/ f inhibition. ~bir vt inhibit

inici|ado /inisi'adu/ m initiate. ~al (pl ~ais) a & f initial. ~ar vt (começar) begin; (em ciência, seita etc) initiate (em into) ● vi begin. ~ativa f initiative

início /i'nisiu/ m beginning

inigualá|vel /inigwa'lavew/ (pl ~veis) a unparalleled

inimaginá|vel /inimaʒi'navew/ (pl ~veis) a unimaginable

inimi|go /ini'migu/ a & m enemy. ~zade f enmity

ininterrupto /inĩte'xuptu/ a continuous

inje|ção /ĩʒe'sãw/ f injection. ~tado a <olhos> bloodshot. ~tar vt inject. ~tável (pl ~táveis) a <droga> intravenous

injúria /ĩ'ʒuria/ f insult

injuriar /ĩʒuri'ar/ vt insult

injus|tiça /ĩʒus'tʃisa/ f injustice. ~tiçado a wronged. ~to a unfair, unjust

ino|cência /ino'sẽsia/ f innocence. ~centar vt clear (de of). ~cente a innocent

inocular /inoku'lar/ vt inoculate

inócuo /i'nɔkuu/ a harmless

inodoro /ino'dɔru/ a odourless

inofensivo /inofẽ'sivu/ a harmless

inoportuno /inopor'tunu/ a inopportune

inorgânico /inor'ganiku/ a inorganic

inóspito /i'nɔspitu/ a inhospitable

ino|vação /inova'sãw/ f innovation. ~var vt/i innovate

inoxidá|vel /inoksi'davew/ (pl ~veis) a <aço> stainless

inquérito /ĩ'keritu/ m inquiry

inquie|tação /ĩkieta'sãw/ f concern. ~tador, ~tante a worrying. ~tar vt worry. ~tar-se vpr worry. ~to /ɛ/ a uneasy

inquili|nato /ĩkili'natu/ m tenancy. ~no m tenant

inquirir /ĩki'rir/ vt cross-examine <testemunha>

Inquisição /ĩkizi'sãw/ f a ~ the Inquisition

insaciá|vel /ĩsasi'avew/ (pl ~veis) a insatiable

insalubre /ĩsa'lubri/ a unhealthy

insatis|fação /ĩsatʃisfa'sãw/ f dissatisfaction. ~fatório a unsatisfactory. ~feito a dissatisfied

ins|crever /ĩskre'ver/ vt (registrar) register; (gravar) inscribe. ~crever-se vpr register; (em escola etc) enrol. ~crição f (registro) registration; (em clube, escola) enrolment; (em monumento etc) inscription

insegu|rança /ĩsegu'rãsa/ f insecurity. ~ro a insecure

insemi|nação /ĩsemina'sãw/ f insemination. ~nar vt inseminate

insen|satez /ĩsẽsa'tes/ f folly. ~sato a foolish. ~sibilidade f insensitivity. ~sível (pl ~síveis) a insensitive

insepará|vel /ĩsepa'ravew/ (pl ~veis) a inseparable

inserção /ĩser'sãw/ f insertion

inserir /ĩse'rir/ vt insert; enter <dados>

inse|ticida /ĩsetʃi'sida/ m insecticide. ~to /ɛ/ m insect

insígnia /ĩ'signia/ f insignia

insignifi|cância /ĩsignifi'kãsia/ f insignificance. ~cante a insignificant

insincero /ĩsĩ'sɛru/ a insincere

insinu|ante /ĩsinu'ãtʃi/ a suggestive. **~ar** vt/i insinuate

insípido /ĩ'sipidu/ a insipid

insis|tência /ĩsis'tẽsia/ f insistence. **~tente** a insistent. **~tir** vt/i insist (em on)

insolação /ĩsola'sãw/ f sunstroke

inso|lência /ĩso'lẽsia/ f insolence. **~lente** a insolent

insólito /ĩ'sɔlitu/ a unusual

insolú|vel /ĩso'luvew/ (pl **~veis**) a insoluble

insone /ĩ'sɔni/ a ‹noite› sleepless; ‹pessoa› insomniac ● m/f insomniac

insônia /ĩ'sonia/ f insomnia

insosso /ĩ'sosu/ a bland; (sem sabor) tasteless; (sem sal) unsalted

inspe|ção /ĩspe'sãw/ f inspection. **~cionar** vt inspect. **~tor** m inspector

inspi|ração /ĩspira'sãw/ f inspiration. **~rar** vt inspire. **~rar-se** vpr take inspiration (em from)

instabilidade /ĩstabili'dadʒi/ f instability

insta|lação /ĩstala'sãw/ f installation. **~lar** vt install. **~lar-se** vpr install o.s.

instan|tâneo /ĩstã'taniu/ a instant. **~te** m instant

instaurar /ĩstaw'rar/ vt set up

instá|vel /ĩ'stavew/ (pl **~veis**) a unstable; ‹tempo› unsettled

insti|gação /ĩstʃiga'sãw/ f instigation. **~gante** a stimulating. **~gar** vt incite

instin|tivo /ĩstʃĩ'tʃivu/ a instinctive. **~to** m instinct

institu|cional /ĩstʃitusio'naw/ (pl **~cionais**) a institutional. **~ição** f institution. **~ir** vt set up; set ‹prazo›. **~to** m institute

instru|ção /ĩstru'sãw/ f instruction. **~ir** vt instruct; train ‹recrutas›; (informar) advise (**sobre** of)

instrumen|tal /ĩstrumẽ'taw/ (pl **~tais**) a instrumental. **~tista** m/f instrumentalist. **~to** m instrument

instru|tivo /ĩstru'tʃivu/ a instructive. **~tor** m instructor

insubstitui|vel /ĩsubstʃitu'ivew/ (pl **~veis**) a irreplaceable

insucesso /ĩsu'sesu/ m failure

insufici|ência /ĩsufisi'ẽsia/ f insufficiency; (dos órgãos) failure. **~ente** a insufficient

insulina /ĩsu'lina/ f insulin

insul|tar /ĩsuw'tar/ vt insult. **~to** m insult

insuperá|vel /ĩsupe'ravew/ (pl **~veis**) a ‹problema› insurmountable; ‹qualidade› unsurpassed

insuportá|vel /ĩsupor'tavew/ (pl **~veis**) a unbearable

insur|gente /ĩsur'ʒẽtʃi/ a & m/f insurgent. **~gir-se** vpr rise up, revolt. **~reição** f insurrection

intato /ĩ'tatu/ a intact

íntegra /'ĩtegra/ f full text; **na ~** in full

inte|gração /ĩtegra'sãw/ f integration. **~gral** (pl **~grais**) a whole; **arroz/pão ~gral** brown rice/bread. **~grante** a integral ● m/f member. **~grar** vt make up, form; **~grar-se em** become a part of. **~gridade** f integrity

íntegro /'ĩtegru/ a honest

intei|ramente /ĩtera'mẽtʃi/ adv completely. **~rar** vt (informar) fill in, inform (**de** about). **~rar-se** vpr find out (**de** about). **~riço** a in one piece. **~ro** a whole

intelec|to /ĩte'lɛktu/ m intellect. **~tual** (pl **~tuais**) a & m/f intellectual

inteli|gência /ĩteli'ʒẽsia/ f intelligence. **~gente** a clever, intelligent. **~gível** (pl **~gíveis**) a intelligible

intem|périe /ĩtẽ'peri/ f bad weather. **~pestivo** a ill-timed

inten|ção /ĩtẽ'sãw/ f intention; **segundas ~ções** ulterior motives

intencio|nado /ĩtẽsio'nadu/ a **bem ~nado** well-meaning. **~nal** (pl **~nais**) a intentional. **~nar** vt intend

inten|sidade /ĩtẽsi'dadʒi/ f intensity. **~sificar** vt intensify. **~sificar-se** vpr intensify. **~sivo** a intensive. **~so** a intense

intento /ĩ'tẽtu/ m intention

intera|ção /ĩtera'sãw/ f interaction. **~gir** vi interact. **~tivo** a interactive

inter|calar /ĩterka'lar/ vt insert. **~câmbio** m exchange. **~ceptar** vt intercept

intercontinen|tal /ĩterkõtʃinẽ'taw/ (pl **~tais**) a intercontinental

interdepen|dência /ĩterdepẽ'dẽsia/ f interdependence. **~dente** a interdependent

interdi|ção /ĩterdʒi'sãw/ f closure; Jurid injunction. **~tar** vt close ‹rua etc›; (proibir) ban

interes|sante /ĩtere'sãtʃi/ a interesting. **~sar** vt interest ● vi be relevant. **~sar-se** vpr be interested (**em** ou **por** in). **~se** /e/ m interest; (próprio) self-interest. **~seiro** a self-seeking

interestadu|al /ĩteristadu'aw/ (pl **~ais**) a interstate

interface /ĩter'fasi/ f interface

interfe|rência /ĩterfe'rẽsia/ f interference. **~rir** vi interfere

interfone /ĩter'fɔni/ m intercom

interim /'ĩteri/ m interim; **nesse ~** in the interim

interino /ĩte'rinu/ a temporary

interior /ĩteri'or/ a inner; (dentro do país) internal, domestic ● m inside; (do país) country, interior

inter|jeição /ĩterʒej'sãw/ f interjection. **~ligar** vt interconnect. **~locutor** m interlocutor. **~mediário** a & m intermediary

intermédio /ĩter'mɛdʒiu/ m **por ~ de** through

intermi|nável /ĩtermi'navew/ (pl **~veis**) a interminable

internacio|nal /ĩternasio'naw/ (pl **~nais**) a international

inter|nar /ĩter'nar/ vt intern <preso>; admit to hospital <doente>. **~nato** m boarding school

internauta /ĩter'nawta/ m/f Comput netsurfer

Internet /ĩter'nɛt/ f Internet

interno /ĩ'ternu/ a internal

interpelar /ĩterpe'lar/ vt question

interpor /ĩter'por/ vt interpose. **~se** vpr intervene

interpre|tação /ĩterpreta'sãw/ f interpretation. **~tar** vt interpret; perform <papel, música>. **intérprete** m/f (de línguas) interpreter; (de teatro etc) performer

interro|gação /ĩtexoga'sãw/ f interrogation. **~gar** vt interrogate, question. **~gativo** a interrogative. **~gatório** m interrogation

inter|romper /ĩtexõ'per/ vt interrupt. **~rupção** f interruption. **~ruptor** m switch

interurbano /ĩterur'banu/ a long-distance ● m trunk call

intervalo /ĩter'valu/ m interval

inter|venção /ĩtervẽ'sãw/ f intervention. **~vir** vi intervene

intesti|nal /ĩtestʃi'naw/ (pl **~nais**) a intestinal. **~no** m intestine

inti|mação /ĩtʃima'sãw/ f (da justiça) summons. **~mar** vt order; (à justiça) summon

intimidade /ĩtʃimi'dadʒi/ f intimacy; (entre amigos) closeness; (vida íntima) private life; **ter ~ com** be close to

intimidar /ĩtʃimi'dar/ vt intimidate. **~se** vpr be intimidated

íntimo /'ĩtʃimu/ a intimate; <amigo> close; <vida> private ● m close friend

intitular /ĩtʃitu'lar/ vt entitle

intocá|vel /ĩto'kavew/ (pl **~veis**) a untouchable

intole|rância /ĩtole'rãsia/ f intolerance. **~rável** (pl **~ráveis**) a intolerable

intoxi|cação /ĩtoksika'sãw/ f poisoning; **~cação alimentar** food poisoning. **~car** vt poison

intragá|vel /ĩtra'gavew/ (pl **~veis**) a <comida> inedible; <pessoa> unbearable

intransigente /ĩtrãzi'ʒẽtʃi/ a uncompromising

intransi|tável /ĩtrãzi'tavew/ (pl **~táveis**) a impassable. **~tivo** a intransitive

intratá|vel /ĩtra'tavew/ (pl **~veis**) a <pessoa> difficult

intrauterino /ĩtraute'rinu/ a **dispositivo ~** intrauterine device, IUD

intrépido /ĩ'trɛpidu/ a intrepid

intri|ga /ĩ'triga/ f intrigue; (enredo) plot. **~gante** a intriguing. **~gar** vt intrigue

intrincado /ĩtrĩ'kadu/ a intricate

intrínseco /ĩ'trĩsiku/ a intrinsic

introdu|ção /ĩtrodu'sãw/ f introduction. **~tório** a introductory. **~zir** vt introduce

introme|ter-se /ĩtrome'tersi/ vpr interfere. **~tido** a interfering ● m busybody

introspec|ção /ĩtrospek'sãw/ f introspection. **~tivo** a introspective

introvertido /ĩtrover'tʃidu/ a introverted ● m introvert

intruso /ĩ'truzu/ a intrusive ● m intruder

intu|ição /ĩtui'sãw/ f intuition. **~ir** vt intuit. **~itivo** a intuitive. **~ito** m purpose

inumano /inu'manu/ a inhuman

inumerá|vel /inume'ravew/ (pl **~veis**) a innumerable

inúmero /i'numeru/ a countless

inun|dação /inũda'sãw/ f flood. **~dar** vt/i flood

inusitado /inuzi'tadu/ a unusual

inú|til /i'nutʃiw/ (pl ~teis) a useless

inutilizar /inutʃili'zar/ vt render useless; damage ‹aparelho›; thwart ‹esforços›

inutilmente /inutʃiw'mētʃi/ adv in vain

invadir /iva'dʒir/ vt invade

invali|dar /ivali'dar/ vt invalidate; disable ‹pessoa›. ~dez /e/ f disability

inválido /i'validu/ a & m invalid

invariá|vel /ivari'avew/ (pl ~veis) a invariable

inva|são /iva'zãw/ f invasion. ~sor m invader ● a invading

inve|ja /ĩ'veʒa/ f envy. ~jar vt envy. ~jável (pl ~jáveis) a enviable. ~joso /o/ a envious

inven|ção /ivē'sãw/ f invention. ~tar vt invent. ~tário m inventory. ~tivo a inventive. ~tor m inventor

inver|nar /iver'nar/ vi winter, spend the winter. ~no /ɛ/ m winter

inverossí|mil /ivero'simiw/ (pl ~meis) a improbable

inver|são /iver'sãw/ f inversion. ~so a inverse; ‹ordem› reverse ● m reverse. ~ter vt reverse; (colocar de cabeça para baixo) invert

invertebrado /iverte'bradu/ a & m invertebrate

invés /i'ves/ m ao ~ de instead of

investida /ives'tʃida/ f attack

investidura /ivestʃi'dura/ f investiture

investi|gação /ivestʃiga'sãw/ f investigation. ~gar vt investigate

inves|timento /ivestʃi'mētu/ m investment. ~tir vt/i invest; ~tir contra attack

inveterado /ivete'radu/ a inveterate

inviá|vel /ivi'avew/ (pl ~veis) a impracticable

invicto /ĩ'viktu/ a unbeaten

invisí|vel /ivi'zivew/ (pl ~veis) a invisible

invocar /ivo'kar/ vt invoke; 🆒 pester

invólucro /ĩ'volukru/ m covering

involuntário /ivolũ'tariu/ a involuntary

invulnerá|vel /ivuwne'ravew/ (pl ~veis) a invulnerable

iodo /i'odu/ m iodine

ioga /i'ɔga/ f yoga

iogurte /io'gurtʃi/ m yoghurt

ir /ir/ ● vi

····▸ (deslocar-se) go; **vamos para Paris** we are going to Paris; **~ de carro/trem...** go by car/train...; **como vão as coisas em casa?** how are things at home?

····▸ (estar) be; **~ bem vestido** be well dressed

····▸ (começar) **vai fazendo sua lição de casa** start doing your homework

····▸ (em expressões) **~ com** (combinar roupa) go with; **essa camisa não vai com o casaco** that shirt doesn't go with that coat; **~ dar em** (ruas) lead to; **esta rua vai dar no banco** this street leads to the bank; **~ de:** (vestido) **ele foi de palhaço/ de azul** he was dressed as a clown/ in blue; **~ para:** (profissão ou área de estudos) **ele vai para medicina** he is going to study medicine; **~ indo, como vai a sua mãe? Vai indo** how's your mother? Not so bad; **já vou!** coming!; **vamos...?** shall we...?

● v aux

····▸ (seguido de infinitivo) **vamos vender a casa** we are going to sell our house; **você vai gostar** you're going to like it; (em ordens) **vai pôr a mesa!** go and lay the table!; **vá falar com o seu pai!** go and talk to your father!

● vpr

····▸ **~-se** (partir) go; **fui-me embora** I left; (morrer) **ele se foi** he died

ira /'ira/ f wrath

Irã /i'rã/ m Iran

iraniano /irani'anu/ a & m Iranian

Irão /i'rãw/ m Port Iran

Iraque /i'raki/ m Iraq

iraquiano /iraki'anu/ a & m Iraqi

Irlanda /ir'lãda/ f Ireland

irlan|dês /irlã'des/ a (f ~desa) Irish ● m (f ~desa) Irishman (f-woman); (língua) Irish; **os ~deses** the Irish

irmã /ir'mã/ f sister

irmandade /irmã'dadʒi/ f (associação) brotherhood

irmão /ir'mãw/ (pl ~s) m brother

ironia /iro'nia/ f irony

irônico /i'roniku/ a ironic

IRPF abr m (= Imposto de Renda de Pessoa Física) income tax

irracio|nal /ixasio'naw/ (pl ~nais) a irrational

irradiar /ixadʒi'ar/ vt radiate; (*pelo rádio*) broadcast ● vi shine. **~se** vpr spread, radiate

irre|al /ixe'aw/ (*pl* **~ais**) a unreal

irreconheci|vel /ixekoɲe'sivew/ (*pl* **~veis**) a unrecognizable

irrecuperá|vel /ixekupe'ravew/ (*pl* **~veis**) a irretrievable

irrefletido /ixefle'tʃidu/ a rash

irregu|lar /ixegu'lar/ a irregular; (*inconstante*) erratic. **~laridade** f irregularity

irrelevante /ixele'vãtʃi/ a irrelevant

irrepar|vel /ixepa'ravew/ (*pl* **~veis**) a irreparable

irrepreensi|vel /ixepriẽ'sivew/ (*pl* **~veis**) a irreproachable

irrequieto /ixeki'etu/ a restless

irresistí|vel /ixezis'tʃivew/ (*pl* **~veis**) a irresistible

irresoluto /ixezo'lutu/ a ‹*questão*› unresolved; ‹*pessoa*› indecisive

irresponsá|vel /ixespõ'savew/ (*pl* **~veis**) a irresponsible

irreverente /ixeve'rẽtʃi/ a irreverent

irri|gação /ixiga'sãw/ f irrigation. **~gar** vt irrigate

irrisório /ixi'zɔriu/ a derisory

irri|tação /ixita'sãw/ f irritation. **~tadiço** a irritable. **~tante** a irritating. **~tar** vt irritate. **~tar-se** vpr get irritated

irromper /ixõ'per/ vi ~ **em** burst into

IRS /ir'jes/ abr m (*Port* = **Imposto sobre o Rendimento das Pessoas Singulares**) income tax

isca /'iska/ f bait

isen|ção /izẽ'sãw/ f exemption. **~tar** vt exempt. **~to** a exempt

islã /iz'lã/ m Islam

islâmico /iz'lamiku/ a Islamic

isla|mismo /izla'mizmu/ m Islam. **~mita** a & m/f Muslim

islan|dês /izlã'des/ a (*f* **~desa**) Icelandic ● m (*f* **~desa**) Icelander; (*língua*) Icelandic

Islândia /iz'lãdʒia/ f Iceland

iso|lamento /izola'mẽtu/ m isolation; *Eletr* insulation. **~lante** a insulating. **~lar** vt isolate; *Eletr* insulate ● vi (*contra azar*) touch wood, *Amer* knock on wood

isopor /izo'por/ m polystyrene

isqueiro /is'keru/ m lighter

Israel /izxa'ɛw/ m Israel

israe|lense /izraj'lẽsi/ a & m/f Israeli. **~lita** a & m/f Israelite

isso /'isu/ ● pron

·····▶ that; **o que é ~?** what's that?

·····▶ (*em expressões*) **~!** (*aprovação*) Well done!; **nem por ~** not really; **para ~** in order to; **quer passar? Para ~ você terá que estudar** do you want to pass? You'll have to study in order to do that; **por ~** so; **ganhei na loteria, por ~ vou viajar muito** I won the lottery, so I am going to travel a lot

isto /'istu/ pron this; **~ é** that is

Itália /i'talia/ f Italy

italiano /itali'anu/ a & m Italian

itálico /i'taliku/ a & m italic

item /'itẽ/ m item

itine|rante /itʃine'rãtʃi/ a itinerant. **~rário** m itinerary

Iugoslávia /iugoz'lavia/ f Yugoslavia

iugoslavo /iugoz'lavu/ a & m Yugoslavian

IVA /'iva/ abr m VAT

Jj

já /ʒa/ adv already; (*agora*) right away ● conj on the other hand; **desde ~** from now on; **~ não** no longer; **~ que** since; **~, ~** in no time

jabuticaba /ʒabutʃi'kaba/ f jaboticaba

jaca /'ʒaka/ f jack fruit

jacaré /ʒaka're/ m alligator

jacinto /ʒa'sĩtu/ m hyacinth

jactância /ʒak'tãsia/ f boasting

jade /'ʒadʒi/ m jade

jaguar /ʒagu'ar/ m jaguar

jagunço /ʒa'gũsu/ m hired gunman

Jamaica /ʒa'majka/ f Jamaica

jamaicano /ʒamaj'kanu/ a & m Jamaican

jamais /ʒa'majs/ adv never

jamanta /ʒa'mãta/ f juggernaut

janeiro /ʒa'neru/ m January

janela /ʒa'nɛla/ f window; **~ de oportunidade** window of opportunity

jangada /ʒã'gada/ f (fishing) raft

janta /'ʒãta/ f 🔳 dinner

jantar /ʒã'tar/ m dinner ● vi have dinner ● vt have for dinner

Japão /ʒa'pãw/ m Japan

japo|na /ʒaˈpɔna/ f pea jacket ● m/f ① Japanese. **~nês** a & m (f **~nesa**) Japanese

jaqueira /ʒaˈkera/ f jackfruit tree

jaqueta /ʒaˈketa/ f jacket

jarda /ˈʒarda/ f yard

jar|dim /ʒarˈdʒĩ/ m garden. **~dim de infância** (pl **~dins de infância**) f kindergarten

jardim-escola /ʒardʒĩˈskɔla/ m (pl **jardins-escola**) Port nursery school

jardi|nagem /ʒardʒiˈnaʒẽ/ f gardening. **~nar** vi garden. **~neira** f (calça) dungarees; (vestido) pinafore dress, Amer jumper; (ônibus) open-sided bus; (para flores) flower stand. **~neiro** m gardener

jargão /ʒarˈgãw/ m jargon

jar|ra /ˈʒaxa/ f pot. **~ro** m jug

jasmim /ʒazˈmĩ/ m jasmine

jato /ˈʒatu/ m jet

jaula /ˈʒawla/ f cage

ja|zer /ʒaˈzer/ vi lie. **~zida** f deposit. **~zigo** m family grave

jazz /dʒaz/ m jazz. **~ista** m/f jazz artist. **~ístico** a jazzy

jeans /dʒĩːz/ mpl jeans

jeca /ˈʒɛka/ m/f country bumpkin ● a countrified; (cafona) tacky. **~tatu** m/f country bumpkin

jei|tão /ʒejˈtãw/ m ① individual style. **~tinho** m knack. **~to** m way; (de pessoa) manner; (habilidade) skill; **de qualquer ~to** anyway; **de ~to nenhum** no way; **pelo ~to** by the looks of things; **sem ~to** awkward; **dar um ~to** find a way; **dar um ~to em** (arrumar) tidy up; (consertar) fix; (torcer) twist <pé etc>; **ter ~to de** look like; **ter ou levar ~to para** be good at; **tomar ~to** pull one's socks up. **~toso** /o/ a skilful; (de aparência) elegant

je|juar /ʒeʒuˈar/ vi fast. **~jum** m fast

Jeová /ʒioˈva/ m **testemunha de ~** Jehovah's witness

jérsei /ˈʒersej/ m jersey

jesuíta /ʒezuˈita/ a & m/f Jesuit

Jesus /ʒeˈzus/ m Jesus

jibóia /ʒiˈbɔja/ f boa constrictor

jibolar /ʒibojˈar/ vi have a rest to let one's dinner go down

jiló /ʒiˈlɔ/ m okra

jipe /ˈʒipi/ m jeep

jiu-jítsu /ʒiuˈʒitsu/ m jiu-jitsu

joa|lheiro /ʒoaˈʎeru/ m jeweller. **~lheria** f jeweller's (shop)

joaninha /ʒoaˈniɲa/ f ladybird, Amer ladybug; (alfinete) safety pin

joão-ninguém /ʒoãwnĩˈgẽj/ (pl **joões-ninguém**) m nobody

jocoso /ʒoˈkozu/ a jocular

joe|lhada /ʒoeˈʎada/ f blow with the knee. **~lheira** f kneepad. **~lho** /e/ m knee; **de ~lhos** kneeling

jo|gada /ʒoˈgada/ f move. **~gado** a <pessoa> flat out; <papéis, roupa etc> lying around. **~gador** m player; (no cassino etc) gambler. **~gar** vt play; (atirar) throw; (arriscar no jogo) gamble ● vi play; (no cassino etc) gamble; (balançar) toss; **~gar fora** throw away. **~gatina** f gambling

jogging /ˈʒɔgĩ/ m (cooper) jogging; (roupa) track suit

jogo /ˈʒogu/ m (partida) game; (ação de jogar) play; (jogatina) gambling; (conjunto) set; **em ~** at stake; **~ de cintura** fig flexibility, room to manoeuvre; **~ de luz** lighting effects; **~ do bicho** illegal numbers game; **jogos Olímpicos** Olympic Games. **~ da velha** m noughts and crosses

joguete /ʒoˈgetʃi/ m plaything

jóia /ˈʒɔja/ f jewel; (propina) entry fee ● a ① great

joio /ˈʒoju/ m chaff; **separar o ~ do trigo** separate the wheat from the chaff

jóquei /ˈʒɔkej/ m (pessoa) jockey; (lugar) race course

Jordânia /ʒorˈdania/ f Jordan

jordaniano /ʒordaniˈanu/ a & m Jordanian

jor|nada /ʒorˈnada/ f (viagem) journey; **~nada de trabalho** working day. **~nal** (pl **~nais**) m newspaper; (na TV) news

jorna|leco /ʒornaˈlɛku/ m rag, scandal sheet. **~leiro** m (vendedor) newsagent, Amer newsdealer; (entregador) paper boy. **~lismo** m journalism. **~lista** m/f journalist. **~lístico** a journalistic

jor|rar /ʒoˈxar/ vi gush, spurt. **~ro** /ˈʒoxu/ m spurt

jota /ˈʒɔta/ m (letter) J

jovem /ˈʒɔvẽ/ a young; (criado por jovens) youth ● m/f young man (f-woman); pl young people

jovi|al /ʒoviˈaw/ (pl **~ais**) a jovial

juba /ˈʒuba/ f mane

jubileu /ʒubiˈlew/ m jubilee

júbilo /ˈʒubilu/ m joy

ju|daico /ʒuˈdajku/ a Jewish. **~daísmo** m Judaism. **~deu** a (f **~dia**) Jewish ● m (f **~dia**) Jew. **~diação** f ill-treatment; (*uma*) terrible thing. **~diar** *vt* **~diar de** ill-treat

judici|al /ʒudʒisi'aw/ (*pl* **~ais**) *a* judicial. **~ário** *a* judicial ● *m* judiciary. **~oso** /o/ *a* judicious

judô /ʒu'do/ *m* judo

judoca /ʒu'dɔka/ *m/f* judo player

jugo /'ʒugu/ *m* yoke

juiz /ʒu'is/ *m* (f **juíza**) judge; (*em jogos*) referee

juizado /ʒui'zadu/ *m* court

juízo /ʒu'izu/ *m* judgement; (*tino*) sense; (*tribunal*) court; **perder o ~** lose one's head; **ter ~** be sensible; **tomar** ou **criar ~** come to one's senses

jujuba /ʒu'ʒuba/ f (*bala*) fruit jelly

jul|gamento /ʒuwga'mẽtu/ *m* judgement. **~gar** *vt* judge; pass judgement on <*réu*>; (*imaginar*) think. **~gar-se** *vpr* consider o.s.

julho /'ʒuʎu/ *m* July

jumento /ʒu'mẽtu/ *m* donkey

junção /ʒũ'sãw/ f join; (*ação*) joining

junco /'ʒũku/ *m* reed

junho /'ʒuɲu/ *m* June

juni|no /ʒu'ninu/ *a* **festa ~na** St John's Day festival

júnior /'ʒunior/ *a & m* junior

jun|ta /'ʒũta/ f board; *Pol* junta. **~tar** *vt* (*acrescentar*) add; (*uma coisa a outra*) join; (*uma coisa com outra*) combine; save up <*dinheiro*>; gather up <*papéis, lixo etc*> ● *vi* gather. **~tar-se** *vpr* join together; <*multidão*> gather; <*casal*> live together; **~tar-se a** join. **~to** *a* together ● *adv* together; **~to a** next to; **~to com** together with

ju|ra /'ʒura/ f vow. **~rado** *m* juror. **~ramentado** *a* accredited. **~ramento** *m* oath. **~rar** *vt/i* swear. **~ra?** 🔢 really?

júri /'ʒuri/ *m* jury

jurídico /ʒu'ridʒiku/ *a* legal

juris|consulto /ʒuriskõ'suwtu/ *m* legal advisor. **~dição** f jurisdiction. **~prudência** f jurisprudence. **~ta** *m/f* jurist

juros /'ʒurus/ *m pl* interest

jus /ʒus/ *m* **fazer ~ a** live up to

jusante /ʒu'zãtʃi/ f **a ~** downstream

justamente /ʒusta'mẽtʃi/ *adv* exactly; (*com justiça*) fairly

justapor /ʒusta'por/ *vt* juxtapose

justi|ça /ʒus'tʃisa/ f (*perante a lei*) justice; (*para com outros*) fairness;

(*tribunal*) court. **~ceiro** *a* fair-minded ● *m* vigilante

justifi|cação /ʒustʃifika'sãw/ f justification. **~car** *vt* justify. **~cativa** f justification. **~cável** (*pl* **~cáveis**) *a* justifiable

justo /'ʒustu/ *a* fair; (*apertado*) tight ● *adv* just

juve|nil /ʒuve'niw/ (*pl* **~nis**) *a* youthful; (*para jovens*) for young people; <*time, torneio*> junior ● *m* junior championship

juventude /ʒuvẽ'tudʒi/ f youth

Kk

karaokê /karao'ke/ *m* karaoke

karatê /kara'te/ *m* karate

karateca /kara'teka/ *m/f* karate expert

kart /'kartʃi/ (*pl* **~s**) *m* go-kart

ketchup /ke'tʃupi/ *m* ketchup

kickboxing /kikbɔksĩŋ/ *m* kickboxing

kilowatt /kilo'wɔt/ *m* kilowatt

kispo® /'kiʃpu/ *m Port* anorak

kit /'kitʃi/ (*pl* **~s**) *m* kit

kitchenette /kitʃe'netʃi/ f bedsitter

kiwi /ki'vi/ *m* kiwi

Kuwait /ku'wajtʃi/ *m* Kuwait

kuwaitiano /kuwajtʃi'anu/ *a & m* Kuwaiti

Ll

lá /la/ ● *adv*

••••➤ there; **até ~** <*ir*> there; <*esperar etc*> until then; **por ~** (*naquela direção*) that way; (*naquele lugar*) around there; **~ fora** outside; **sei ~** how should I know?

lã /lã/ f wool

labareda /laba'reda/ f flame

lábia /'labia/ f flannel; **ter ~** have the gift of the gab

lábio /'labio/ *m* lip

labirinto /labi'rĩtu/ *m* labyrinth

laboral /labo'raw/ *a Port* labour; **horário ~** working hours

laboratório /labora'tɔriu/ *m*
laboratory

laborioso /labori'ozu/ *a* hard-working

labu|ta /la'buta/ *f* drudgery. **~tar** *vi* slog

laca /'laka/ *f* lacquer

laçada /la'sada/ *f* slip knot

lacaio /la'kaju/ *m* lackey

la|çar /la'sar/ *vt* lasso ‹*boi*›. **~ço** *m* bow; (*de vaqueiro*) lasso; (*vínculo*) tie

lacônico /la'koniku/ *a* laconic

lacraia /la'kraja/ *f* centipede

la|crar /la'krar/ *vt* seal. **~cre** *m* (*substância*) sealing wax; (*fechamento*) seal

lacri|mejar /lakrime'ʒar/ *vi* water. **~mogêneo** *a* ‹*gás*› tear; ‹*filme*› tear-jerking. **~moso** /o/ *a* tearful

lácteo /'laktʃiu/ *a* milk; **Via Láctea** Milky Way

lacticínio /laktʃi'siniu/ *m* ▶ LATICÍNIO

lacuna /la'kuna/ *f* gap

ladainha /lada'iɲa/ *f* litany

la|dear /ladʒi'ar/ *vt* flank; sidestep ‹*dificuldade*›. **~deira** *f* slope

lado /'ladu/ *m* side; **o ~ de cá/lá** this/ that side; **ao ~ de** beside; **~ a ~** side by side; **para este ~** this way; **por outro ~** on the other hand

la|drão /la'drãw/ *m* (*f* **~dra**) thief; (*tubo*) overflow pipe ● *a* thieving

ladrar /la'drar/ *vi* bark

ladri|lhar /ladri'ʎar/ *vt* tile. **~lho** *m* tile

ladroagem /ladro'aʒẽ/ *f* stealing

lagar|ta /la'garta/ *f* caterpillar; (*numa roda*) caterpillar track. **~tear** *vi* bask in the sun. **~tixa** *f* gecko. **~to** *m* lizard

lago /'lagu/ *m* lake

lagoa /la'goa/ *f* lagoon

lagos|ta /la'gosta/ *f* lobster. **~tim** *m* crayfish, *Amer* crawfish

lágrima /'lagrima/ *f* tear

laia /'laja/ *f* kind

laico /'lajku/ *adj* ‹*pessoa*› lay; ‹*ensino*› secular

laivos /'lajvus/ *m pl* traces

laje /'laʒi/ *m* flagstone. **~ar** *vt* pave

lajota /la'ʒɔta/ *f* small paving stone

lama /'lama/ *f* mud. **~çal** (*pl* **~çais**) *m* bog. **~cento** *a* muddy

lamba|da /lã'bada/ *f* lambada. **~teria** *f* lambada club

lam|ber /lã'ber/ *vt* lick. **~bida** *f* lick

lambreta /lã'breta/ *f* moped

lambris /lã'bris/ *m pl* panelling

lambuzar /lãbu'zar/ *vt* smear. **~se** *vpr* get sticky

lamen|tar /lamẽ'tar/ *vt* (*lastimar*) lament; (*sentir*) be sorry; **~tar-se de** lament. **~tável** (*pl* **~táveis**) *a* lamentable. **~to** *m* lament

lâmina /'lamina/ *f* blade; (*de persiana*) slat

laminar /lami'nar/ *vt* laminate

lâmpada /'lãpada/ *f* light bulb; (*abajur*) lamp; **~ compacta** energy-saving lightbulb

lampe|jar /lãpe'ʒar/ *vi* flash. **~jo** /e/ *m* flash

lampião /lãpi'ãw/ *m* lantern

lamúria /la'muria/ *f* moaning

lamuriar-se /lamuri'arsi/ *vpr* moan (*de* about)

lan|ça /'lãsa/ *f* spear. **~çamento** *m* (*de navio, foguete, produto*) launch; (*de filme, disco*) release; (*novo produto*) new line; (*novo filme, disco*) release; (*novo livro*) new title; (*em livro comercial*) entry. **~çar** *vt* (*atirar*) throw; launch ‹*navio, foguete, novo produto, livro*›; release ‹*filme, disco*›; (*em livro comercial*) enter; (*em leilão*) bid; **~çar mão de** make use of. **~ce** *m* (*num filme, jogo*) bit, moment; (*episódio*) episode; (*questão*) matter; (*jogada*) move; (*em leilão*) bid; (*de escada*) flight; (*de casas*) row

lancha /'lãʃa/ *f* launch

lan|char /lã'ʃar/ *vi* have a snack ● *vt* have a snack of. **~che** *m* snack. **~chonete** /ɛ/ *f* snack bar

lancinante /lãsi'nãtʃi/ *a* ‹*dor*› shooting; ‹*grito*› piercing

lânguido /'lãgidu/ *a* languid

lan house *m* internet cafe

lantejoula /lãte'ʒola/ *f* sequin

lanter|na /lã'terna/ *f* lantern; (*de bolso*) torch, *Amer* flashlight. **~nagem** *f* panel beating; (*oficina*) body shop. **~ninha** *m/f* usher; (*f* usherette)

lanugem /la'nuʒẽ/ *f* down

lapela /la'pɛla/ *f* lapel

lapidar /lapi'dar/ *vt* cut ‹*pedra preciosa*›; *fig* polish

lápide /'lapidʒi/ *f* tombstone

lápis /'lapis/ *m invar* pencil

lapiseira /lapi'zera/ *f* propelling pencil; (*caixa*) pencil box

Lapônia /la'ponia/ *f* Lapland

lapso /'lapsu/ *m* lapse

laptop /lap'tɔp/ *m* laptop

la|quê /la'ke/ *m* lacquer. **~quear** *vt* lacquer

lar /lar/ *m* home

laran|ja /la'rãʒa/ *f* orange ● *a invar* orange. **~jada** *f* orangeade. **~jeira** *f* orange tree

lareira /la'rera/ *f* hearth, fireplace

lar|gada /lar'gada/ *f* start; **dar a ~gada** start off. **~gar** *vt* (*soltar*) let go of; give up ‹*estudos, emprego etc*›; **~gar de fumar** give up smoking. **~go** *a* wide; ‹*roupa*› loose ● *m* (*praça*) square; **ao ~go** (*no alto-mar*) out at sea. **~gura** *f* width

larin|ge /la'rĩʒi/ *f* larynx. **~gite** *f* laryngitis

larva /'larva/ *f* larva

lasanha /la'zaɲa/ *f* lasagne

las|ca /'laska/ *f* chip. **~car** *vt/i* chip; **de ~car** ⏹ awful

lástima /'lastʃima/ *f* shame

lastro /'lastru/ *m* ballast

la|ta /'lata/ *f* (*material*) tin; (*recipiente*) tin, *Amer* can; **~ta de lixo** dustbin, *Amer* trash can. **~tão** *m* brass

late|jante /late'ʒãtʃi/ *a* throbbing. **~jar** *vi* throb

latente /la'tẽtʃi/ *a* latent

late|ral /late'raw/ (*pl* **~rais**) *a* side, lateral

laticínio /latʃi'siniu/ *m* dairy product

latido /la'tʃidu/ *m* bark

lati|fundiário /latʃifũdʒi'ariu/ *a* landowning ● *m* landowner. **~fúndio** *m* estate

latim /la'tʃĩ/ *m* Latin

latino /la'tʃinu/ *a & m* Latin. **~americano** *a & m* Latin American

latir /la'tʃir/ *vi* bark

latitude /latʃi'tudʒi/ *f* latitude

lauda /'lawda/ *f* side

laudo /'lawdu/ *m* report, findings

lava /'lava/ *f* lava

lava|bo /la'vabu/ *m* toilet. **~dora** *f* washing machine. **~gem** *f* washing; **~gem a seco** dry cleaning; **~gem cerebral** brainwashing

lavanda /la'vãda/ *f* lavender

lavanderia /lavãde'ria/ *f* laundry

lavar /la'var/ *vt* wash; **~ a seco** dry-clean. **~se** *vpr* wash

lavatório /lava'tɔriu/ *m Port* washbasin

lavoura /la'vora/ *f* (*agricultura*) farming; (*terreno*) field

lav|rador /lavra'dor/ *m* farmhand. **~rar** *vt* work; draw up ‹*documento*›

laxante /la'ʃãtʃi/ *a & m* laxative

lazer /la'zer/ *m* leisure

le|al /le'aw/ (*pl* **~ais**) *a* loyal. **~aldade** *f* loyalty

leão /le'ãw/ *m* lion; **Leão** (*signo*) Leo. **~ de chácara** (*pl* **leões de chácara**) *m* bouncer

lebre /'lɛbri/ *f* hare

lecionar /lesio'nar/ *vt/i* teach

le|gação /lega'sãw/ *f* legation. **~gado** *m* (*pessoa*) legate; (*herança*) legacy

le|gal /le'gaw/ (*pl* **~gais**) *a* legal; ⏹ good; ‹*pessoa*› nice; **tá ~gal** OK. **~galidade** *f* legality. **~galizar** *vt* legalize

legar /le'gar/ *vt* bequeath

legenda /le'ʒẽda/ *f* (*de quadro*) caption; (*de filme*) subtitle; (*inscrição*) inscription

legi|ão /leʒi'ãw/ *f* legion. **~onário** *m* (*romano*) legionary; (*da legião estrangeira*) legionnaire

legis|lação /leʒizla'sãw/ *f* legislation. **~lador** *m* legislator. **~lar** *vi* legislate. **~lativo** *a* legislative ● *m* legislature. **~latura** *f* legislature. **~ta** *m/f* legal expert

legiti|mar /leʒitʃi'mar/ *vt* legitimize. **~midade** *f* legitimacy

legítimo /le'ʒitʃimu/ *a* legitimate

legi|vel /le'ʒivew/ (*pl* **~veis**) *a* legible

légua /'lɛgwa/ *f* league

legume /le'gumi/ *m* vegetable

lei /lej/ *f* law

leigo /'lejgu/ *a* lay ● *m* layman

lei|lão /lej'lãw/ *m* auction. **~loar** *vt* auction. **~loeiro** *m* auctioneer

leitão /lej'tãw/ *m* sucking pig

lei|te /'lejtʃi/ *m* milk; **~te condensado/ desnatado** condensed/skimmed milk. **~teira** *f* (*jarro*) milk jug; (*panela*) milk saucepan. **~teiro** *m* milkman ● *a* ‹*vaca*› dairy

leito /'lejtu/ *m* bed

leitor /lej'tor/ *m* reader

leitoso /lej'tozu/ *a* milky

leitura /lej'tura/ *f* (*ação*) reading; (*material*) reading matter

lema /'lema/ *m* motto

lem|brança /lẽ'brãsa/ *f* memory; (*presente*) souvenir. **~brar** *vt/i* remember; **~brar-se de** remember; **~brar algo a alguém** remind sb of sth. **~brete** /e/ *m* reminder

leme /'lemi/ *m* rudder

len|ço /'lẽsu/ (pl **lenções**) m (para o nariz) handkerchief; (para vestir) scarf. **~ol** /ɔ/ m sheet

len|da /'lẽda/ f legend. **~dário** a legendary

lenha /'leɲa/ f firewood; (uma) log. **~dor** m woodcutter

lente /'lẽtʃi/ f lens; **~ de contato** contact lens

lentidão /lẽtʃi'dãw/ f slowness

lentilha /lẽ'tʃiʎa/ f lentil

lento /'lẽtu/ a slow

leoa /le'oa/ f lioness

leopardo /lio'pardu/ m leopard

le|pra /'lɛpra/ f leprosy. **~proso** /o/ a leprous ● m leper

leque /'lɛki/ m fan; fig array

ler /ler/ vt/i read

LER abr f (= lesão por esforço repetitivo) RSI

ler|deza /ler'deza/ f sluggishness. **~do** /e/ a sluggish

le|são /le'zãw/ f lesion, injury; **~são por esforço repetitivo** repetitive strain injury. **~sar** vt damage

lésbi|ca /'lɛzbika/ f lesbian. **~co** a lesbian

lesionado /lezjo'nadu/ a injured

lesionar /lezjo'nar/ vt injure

lesma /'lɛzma/ f slug

leste /'lɛstʃi/ m east

le|tal /le'taw/ (pl **~tais**) a lethal

le|tão /le'tãw/ a & m (f **~tã**) Latvian

letargia /letar'ʒia/ f lethargy

letivo /le'tʃivu/ a ano **~** academic year

Letônia /le'tonia/ f Latvia

letra /'letra/ f letter; (de música) lyrics, words; (caligrafia) writing; **Letras** Modern Languages; **ao pé da ~** literally; **com todas as ~s** in no uncertain terms; **tirar de ~** take in one's stride; **~ de forma** block letter

letreiro /le'treru/ m sign

leucemia /lewse'mia/ f leukaemia

leva /ɛ/ f batch

levado /le'vadu/ a naughty

levan|tamento /levãta'mẽtu/ m (enquete) survey; (rebelião) uprising; **~tamento de pesos** weightlifting. **~tar** vt raise; lift ‹peso› ● vi get up. **~tar-se** vpr get up; (revoltar-se) rise up

levante /le'vãtʃi/ m east

levar /le'var/ vt take; lead ‹vida›; get ‹tapa, susto etc› ● vi lead (a to)

leve /'lɛvi/ a light; (não grave) slight; **de ~** lightly

levedura /leve'dura/ f yeast

leveza /le'veza/ f lightness

levi|andade /leviã'dadʒi/ f frivolity. **~ano** a frivolous

levitar /levi'tar/ vi levitate

lexi|cal /leksi'kaw/ (pl **~cais**) a lexical

léxico /'lɛksiku/ m lexicon

lexicografia /leksikogra'fia/ f lexicography

lhe /ʎi/ pron (a ele) to him; (a ela) to her; (a você) to you. **~s** pron to them; (a vocês) to you

liba|nês /liba'nes/ a & m (f **~nesa**) Lebanese

Líbano /'libanu/ m Lebanon

libélula /li'bɛlula/ f dragonfly

libe|ração /libera'sãw/ f release. **~ral** (pl **~rais**) a & m liberal. **~ralismo** m liberalism. **~ralizar** vt liberalize. **~rar** vt release

liberdade /liber'dadʒi/ f freedom; **pôr em ~** set free; **~ condicional** probation

líbero /'liberu/ m sweeper

liber|tação /liberta'sãw/ f liberation. **~tar** vt free

Líbia /'libia/ f Libya

libi|dinoso /libidʒi'nozu/ a lecherous. **~do** f libido

líbio /'libiu/ a & m Libyan

li|bra /'libra/ f pound; **Libra** (signo) Libra. **~briano** a & m Libran

lição /li'sãw/ f lesson

licen|ça /li'sẽsa/ f leave; (documento) licence; **com ~ça** excuse me; **de ~ça** on leave; **sob ~ça** under licence. **~ciar** vt (autorizar) license; (dar férias a) give leave to. **~ciar-se** vpr (tirar férias) take leave; (formar-se) graduate. **~ciatura** f degree. **~cioso** /o/ a licentious

licenciado /lisẽsi'adu/ m graduate

liceu /li'sew/ m Port secondary school, Amer high school

licor /li'kor/ m liqueur

lida /'lida/ f slog, grind; (leitura) read

lidar /li'dar/ vt/i **~ com** deal with

lide /'lidʒi/ f (trabalho) work

líder /'lider/ m/f leader

lide|rança /lide'rãsa/ f (de partido etc) leadership; (em corrida, jogo etc) lead. **~rar** vt lead

lido /'lidu/ a well-read

liga /'liga/ f (aliança) league; (tira) garter; (presilha) suspender; (de metais) alloy

li|gação /liga'sãw/ f connection; (telefônica) call; (amorosa) liaison. **~gada** f call, ring. **~gado** a <luz, TV> on; **~gado em** attached to <pessoa>; hooked on <droga>. **~gamento** m ligament. **~gar** vt join, connect; switch on <luz, TV etc>; start up <carro>; bind <amigos> ● vi ring up, call; **~gar para** (telefonar) ring, call; (dar importância) care about; (dar atenção) pay attention to. **~gar-se** vpr join

ligeiro /li'ʒeru/ a light; <ferida, melhora> slight; (ágil) nimble

lilás /li'las/ m lilac ● a invar mauve

lima¹ /'lima/ f (ferramenta) file

lima² /'lima/ f (fruta) lime

limão /li'mãw/ m lime; (amarelo) lemon

limar /li'mar/ vt file

limeira /li'mera/ f lime tree

limiar /limi'ar/ m threshold

limi|tação /limita'sãw/ f limitation. **~tar** vt limit. **~tar-se** vpr limit o.s.; **~tar(-se) com** border on. **~te** m limit; (de terreno) boundary; **passar dos ~tes** go too far; **~te de velocidade** speed limit

limo|eiro /limo'eiru/ m lemon tree. **~nada** f lemonade

lim|pador /lĩpa'dor/ m **~pador de para-brisas** windscreen wiper. **~par** vt clean; wipe <lágrimas, suor>; fig clean up <cidade, organização>. **~peza** /e/ f (ato) cleaning; (qualidade) cleanness; fig clean-up; **~peza pública** sanitation. **~po** a clean; <céu, consciência> clear; <lucro> net, clear; fig pure; **passar a ~po** write up <trabalho>; fig sort out <vida>; **tirar a ~po** get to the bottom of <caso>

limusine /limu'zini/ f limousine

lince /'lĩsi/ f lynx

lindo /'lĩdu/ a beautiful

linear /lini'ar/ a linear

lingote /lĩ'gɔtʃi/ m ingot

língua /'lĩgwa/ f (na boca) tongue; (idioma) language; **~ materna** mother tongue

linguado /lĩ'gwadu/ m sole

lingua|gem /lĩ'gwaʒẽ/ f language. **~jar** m speech, dialect

lingueta /lĩ'gweta/ f bolt

linguiça /lĩ'gwisa/ f pork sausage

lin|guista /lĩ'gwista/ m/f linguist. **~guística** f linguistics. **~guístico** a linguistic

linha /'liɲa/ f line; (fio) thread; **perder a ~** lose one's cool; **~ aérea** airline; **~ de fogo** firing line; **~ de montagem** assembly line. **~gem** f lineage

linho /'liɲu/ m linen; (planta) flax

link /lĩk/ m Comput link, hyperlink

linóleo /li'nɔliu/ m lino(leum)

lipoaspiração /lipoaspira'sãw/ f liposuction

liqui|dação /likida'sãw/ f liquidation; (de loja) clearance sale; (de conta) settlement. **~dar** vt liquidate; settle <conta>; pay off <dívida>; sell off, clear <mercadorias>

liquidificador /likwidʒifika'dor/ m liquidizer

líquido /'likidu/ a liquid; <lucro, salário> net ● m liquid

líri|ca /'lirika/ f Mus lyrics; (poesia) lyric poetry. **~co** a lyrical; <poesia> lyric

lírio /'liriu/ m lily

Lisboa /liz'boa/ f Lisbon

lisboeta /lizbo'eta/ a & m/f (person) from Lisbon

liso /'lizu/ a smooth; (sem desenho) plain; <cabelo> straight; Ⓣ (duro) broke

lison|ja /li'zõʒa/ f flattery. **~jear** vt flatter

lista /'lista/ f list; (listra) stripe; **~ telefônica** telephone directory

listra /'listra/ f stripe. **~do** a striped, stripey

lite|ral /lite'raw/ (pl **~rais**) a literal. **~rário** a literary. **~ratura** f literature

litígio /li'tʃiʒiu/ m dispute; Jurid lawsuit

lito|ral /lito'raw/ (pl **~rais**) m coastline. **~râneo** a coastal

litro /'litru/ m litre

Lituânia /litu'ania/ f Lithuania

lituano /litu'anu/ a & m Lithuanian

living /'livĩ/ (pl **~s**) m living room

livrar /liˈvrar/ vt free; (salvar) save. **~-se** vpr escape; **~-se de** get rid of

livraria /livraˈria/ f bookshop

livre /ˈlivri/ a free; **~ de impostos** tax-free. **~arbítrio** m free will

liv|reiro /liˈvreru/ m bookseller. **~ro** m book; **~ro de consulta** reference book; **~ro de cozinha** cookery book; **~ro de texto** textbook; **~ro eletrônico** e-book

li|xa /ˈliʃa/ f (de unhas) emery board; (para madeira etc) sandpaper. **~xar** vt sand ‹madeira›; file ‹unhas›; **estou me ~xando** 🅸 I couldn't care less

li|xeira /liˈʃeira/ f dustbin, Amer garbage can. **~xeiro** m dustman, Amer garbage collector. **~xo** m rubbish, Amer garbage; (atômico) waste

lobisomem /lobiˈzomẽ/ m werewolf

lobo /ˈlobu/ m wolf. **~-marinho** (pl **~s-marinhos**) m sea lion

lóbulo /ˈlobulu/ m lobe

lo|cação /lokaˈsãw/ f (de imóvel) lease; (de carro) rental. **~cador** m (de casa) landlord. **~cadora** f rental company; (de vídeos) video shop

lo|cal /loˈkaw/ (pl **~cais**) a local ● m site; (de um acidente etc) scene. **~calidade** f locality. **~calização** f location. **~calizar** vt locate. **~calizar-se** vpr (orientar-se) get one's bearings

loção /loˈsãw/ f lotion; **~ após-barba** aftershave lotion

locatário /lokaˈtariu/ m (de imóvel) tenant; (de carro etc) hirer

locomo|tiva /lokomoˈtʃiva/ f locomotive. **~ver-se** vpr get around

locu|ção /lokuˈsãw/ f phrase. **~tor** m announcer

lodo /ˈlodu/ m mud. **~so** /o/ a muddy

logaritmo /logaˈritʃimu/ m logarithm

lógi|ca /ˈlɔʒika/ f logic. **~co** a logical

logo /ˈlɔgu/ adv (em seguida) straightaway; (em breve) soon; (justamente) just; **~ mais** later; **~ antes/depois** just before/straight after; **~ que** as soon as; **até ~** goodbye

logotipo /logoˈtʃipu/ m logo

logradouro /logradoru/ m public place

loiro /ˈlojru/ a ▶ LOURO

lo|ja /ˈlɔʒa/ f shop, Amer store; **~ja de departamentos** department store; **~ja maçônica** Masonic lodge. **~jista** m/f shopkeeper

lom|bada /lõˈbada/ f (de livro) spine; (na rua) speed bump. **~binho** m tenderloin. **~bo** m back; (carne) loin

lona /ˈlona/ f canvas

Londres /ˈlõdris/ f London

londrino /lõˈdrinu/ a London ● m Londoner

longa-metragem /lõgameˈtraʒẽ/ (pl **longas-metragens**) m feature film

longe /ˈlõʒi/ adv far, a long way; **de ~** from a distance; (por muito) by far; **~ disso** far from it

longevidade /lõʒeviˈdadʒi/ f longevity

longínquo /lõˈʒĩkwu/ a distant

longitude /lõʒiˈtudʒi/ f longitude

longo /ˈlõgu/ a long ● m long dress; **ao ~ de** along; (durante) through, over

lontra /ˈlõtra/ f otter

lorde /ˈlɔrdʒi/ m lord

lorota /loˈrɔta/ f 🅸 fib

losango /loˈzãgu/ m diamond

lo|tação /lotaˈsãw/ f capacity; (ônibus) bus; **~tação esgotada** full house. **~tado** a crowded; ‹teatro, ônibus› full. **~tar** vt fill ● vi fill up

lote /ˈlɔtʃi/ m (quinhão) portion; (de terreno) plot, Amer lot; (em leilão) lot; (porção de coisas) batch

loteria /loteˈria/ f lottery

louça /ˈlosa/ f china; (pratos etc) crockery; **lavar a ~** wash up, Amer do the dishes

lou|co /ˈloku/ a mad, crazy ● m madman; **estou ~co para ir** 🅸 I'm dying to go. **~cura** f madness; (uma) crazy thing

louro /ˈloru/ a blond ● m laurel; (condimento) bay leaf

lou|var /loˈvar/ vt praise. **~vável** (pl **~váveis**) a praiseworthy. **~vor** /o/ m praise

lua /ˈlua/ f moon. **~ de mel** f honeymoon

lu|ar /luˈar/ m moonlight. **~arento** a moonlit

lubrifi|cação /lubrifikaˈsãw/ f lubrication. **~cante** a lubricating ● m lubricant. **~car** vt lubricate

lucidez /lusiˈdes/ f lucidity

lúcido /ˈlusidu/ a lucid

lu|crar /luˈkrar/ vi profit (**com** by). **~cratividade** f profitability. **~crativo** a profitable, lucrative. **~cro** m profit

ludibriar /ludʒibriˈar/ vt cheat

lúdico /ˈludʒiku/ a playful

lugar /luˈgar/ m place; (espaço) room; **em ~ de** in place of; **em primeiro ~** in the first place; **em algum ~** somewhere; **em todo ~** everywhere; **dar ~ a** give rise to; **ter ~** take place

lugarejo /luga'reʒu/ m village

lúgubre /'lugubri/ a gloomy, dismal

lula /'lula/ f squid

lume /'lumi/ m fire

luminária /lumi'naria/ f light, lamp; pl illuminations

luminoso /lumi'nozu/ a luminous; ‹ideia› brilliant

lunar /lu'nar/ a lunar ● m mole

lupa /'lupa/ f magnifying glass

lusco-fusco /lusku'fusku/ m twilight

lusitano /luzi'tanu/, **luso** /'luzu/ a & m Portuguese

lus|trar /lus'trar/ vt shine, polish. **~tre** m shine; fig lustre; (luminária) light, lamp. **~troso** /o/ a shiny

lu|ta /'luta/ f fight, struggle; **~ta livre** wrestling. **~tador** m fighter; (de luta livre) wrestler. **~tar** vi fight ● vt do ‹judô etc›

luto /'lutu/ m mourning

luva /'luva/ f glove

luxação /luʃa'sãw/ f dislocation

Luxemburgo /luʃẽ'burgu/ m Luxembourg

luxembur|guês /luʃẽbur'ges/ a (f ~**guesa**) Luxembourg ● m (f ~**guesa**) Luxembourger; (língua) Luxembourgish

luxo /'luʃu/ m luxury; **hotel de ~** luxury hotel; **cheio de ~** 🆇 fussy

luxuoso /luʃu'ozu/ a luxurious

luxúria /lu'ʃuria/ f lust

luxuriante /luʃuri'ãtʃi/ a lush

luz /lus/ f light; **à ~ de** by the light of ‹velas etc›; in the light of ‹fatos etc›; **dar à ~** give birth to

luzidio /luzi'dʒio/ a shiny

luzir /lu'zir/ vi shine

....

Mm

....

maca /'maka/ f stretcher

maçã /ma'sã/ f apple

macabro /ma'kabru/ a macabre

maca|cão /maka'kãw/ m (de trabalho) overalls, Amer coveralls; (tipo de calça) dungarees; (roupa inteiriça) jumpsuit; (para bebê) romper suit. **~co** m monkey;

(aparelho) jack

maçada /ma'sada/ f bore

maçaneta /masa'neta/ f doorknob

maçante /ma'sãtʃi/ a boring

macar|rão /maka'xãw/ m pasta; (espaguete) spaghetti. **~ronada** f pasta with tomato sauce and cheese

macarrônico /maka'xoniku/ a broken

macete /ma'setʃi/ m trick

machado /ma'ʃadu/ m axe

ma|chão /ma'ʃãw/ a tough ● m tough guy. **~chismo** m machismo. **~chista** a chauvinistic ● m male chauvinist. **~cho** a male; ‹homem› macho ● m male

machu|cado /maʃu'kadu/ m injury; (na pele) sore patch. **~car** vt/i hurt. **~car-se** vpr hurt o.s.

maciço /ma'sisu/ a solid; ‹dose etc› massive ● m massif

macieira /masi'era/ f apple tree

maciez /masi'es/ f softness

macilento /masi'lẽtu/ a haggard

macio /ma'siu/ a soft; ‹carne› tender

maço /'masu/ m (de cigarros) packet; (de notas) bundle

ma|çom /ma'sõ/ m freemason. **~çonaria** f freemasonry

maconha /ma'koɲa/ f marijuana

maçônico /ma'soniku/ a Masonic

má-criação /makria'sãw/ f rudeness

macrobiótico /makrobi'ɔtʃiku/ a macrobiotic

macum|ba /ma'kũba/ f Afro-Brazilian cult; (uma) spell. **~beiro** m follower of macumba ● a macumba

madame /ma'dami/ f lady

madeira /ma'dera/ f wood ● m (vinho) Madeira; **~ de lei** hardwood

Madeira /ma'dera/ f Madeira

madeirense /made'rẽsi/ a & m Madeiran

madeixa /ma'deʃa/ f lock

madrasta /ma'drasta/ f stepmother

madrepérola /madre'pɛrola/ f mother of pearl

madressilva /madre'siwva/ f honeysuckle

Madri /ma'dri/ f Madrid

madrinha /ma'driɲa/ f (de batismo) godmother; (de casamento) bridesmaid

madru|gada /madru'gada/ f early morning. **~gador** m early riser. **~gar** vi get up early

maduro /ma'duru/ a ‹fruta› ripe; ‹pessoa› mature

mãe /mãj/ f mother. ~ **de santo** (pl ~**s de santo**) f macumba priestess

maes|tria /majs'tria/ f expertise. ~**tro** m conductor

máfia /'mafia/ f mafia

magazine /maga'zini/ m department store

magia /ma'ʒia/ f magic

mági|ca /'maʒika/ f magic; (uma) magic trick. ~**co** a magic ● m magician

magis|tério /maʒis'teriu/ m teaching; (professores) teachers. ~**trado** m magistrate

magnânimo /mag'nanimu/ a magnanimous

magnata /mag'nata/ m magnate

magnésio /mag'neziu/ m magnesium

mag|nético /mag'netʃiku/ a magnetic. ~**netismo** m magnetism. ~**netizar** vt magnetize; fig mesmerize

mag|nificência /magnifi'sẽsia/ f magnificence. ~**nífico** a magnificent

magnitude /magni'tudʒi/ f magnitude

mago /'magu/ m magician; **os reis** ~**s** the Three Wise Men

mágoa /'magoa/ f sorrow

magoar /mago'ar/ vt/i hurt. ~**se** vpr be hurt

ma|gricela /magri'sɛla/ a skinny. ~**gro** a thin; ‹leite› skimmed; ‹carne› lean; fig meagre

maio /'maju/ m May

maiô /ma'jo/ m swimsuit

maionese /majo'nɛzi/ f mayonnaise

maior /ma'jɔr/ a bigger; ‹escritor, amor etc› greater; **o** ~ **carro** the biggest car; **o** ~ **escritor** the greatest writer; ~ **de idade** of age

Maiorca /ma'jɔrka/ f Majorca

maio|ria /majo'ria/ f majority; **a** ~**ria dos brasileiros** most Brazilians. ~**ridade** f majority, adulthood

mais /majs/ ● adv

····➤ (uso comparativo: com adjetivos) more; ~ **fácil** easier; ~ **inteligente** more intelligent; **é** ~ **alta/elegante que eu** she's taller/slimmer than me

❗ Os adjetivos de uma sílaba formam o comparativo com o acréscimo -er: **mais devagar** slower, **mais rico** richer. Para formar o comparativo da maioria de adjetivos de duas ou mais sílabas, usa-se more + adjetivo: **mais caro** more expensive.

····➤ (uso comparativo: com verbos) **durar** ~ last longer; **trabalhar** ~ work harder; ~ **de** more than; **você viajou** ~ **do que eu** you've travelled more than me; ~ **de 2 semanas** more than 2 weeks; **gosto** ~ **de peixe** I like fish better

····➤ (uso superlativo) most; **a cidade** ~ **bonita do mundo** the most beautiful city in the world; **o** ~ **simpático de todos** the nicest of all; **a loja que vendeu** ~ **livros** the shop that sold most books

❗ Os adjetivos de uma sílaba formam o superlativo com o acréscimo -est: **a cidade mais fria** the coldest city, **a mulher mais rica** the richest woman. Para formar o superlativo da maioria de adjetivos de duas ou mais sílabas, usa-se most + adjetivo: **o mais inteligente** the most intelligent.

····➤ (com pronomes) else; **você tem** ~ **alguma coisa para me dizer?** have you got anything else to tell me?; ~ **alguém?** anyone else?; ~ **nada** nothing else; ~ **ninguém** nobody else

····➤ (em exclamações) **que paisagem** ~ **bonita!** what lovely scenery!

····➤ (em negativas) **não sabemos** ~ **do que disseram no rádio** we only know what it said on the radio; **não foi** ~ **que uma coincidência** it was just a coincidence

● prep

····➤ Mat plus; **5** ~ **5 são 10** 5 plus 5 makes ten

····➤ (em expressões) **a** ~ (para além do necessário) too much, too many; **há 2 cadeiras a** ~ there are 2 chairs too many; (de sobra) spare; **eu tenho uma caneta a** ~ I've got a spare pen; ~ **nada** nothing else; **não tenho** ~ **nada para lhe dizer** I've got nothing else to tell you; ~ **ou menos** more or less; **ela ganha** ~ **ou menos R$200 por dia** she earns around R$200 a day; ~ **dia menos dia** one of these days; **ela vai emigrar,** ~ **dia menos dia** she's going to emigrate one of these days; **além do** ~ what's more

maisena /maj'zena/ f cornflour, Amer cornstarch

maître /mɛtr/ m head waiter

maiúscula /ma'juskula/ f capital letter

majes|tade /maʒes'tadʒi/ f majesty. **~toso** a majestic

major /ma'jɔr/ m major

majoritário /maʒori'tariu/ a majority

mal /maw/ ● adv

····▸ (imperfeitamente) badly; **portar-se ~/falar ~** behave/speak badly; **cheirar ~** smell; **ela ouve muito ~** her hearing is very bad

····▸ (erradamente) wrong; **você escolheu ~** you made the wrong choice

····▸ (quase não) hardly; **eles ~ se falaram** they hardly spoke; (quase nunca) hardly ever; **~ os vemos** we hardly ever see them

····▸ (doente) **estar ~** be quite ill; **sentir-se ~** feel ill

● m

····▸ (dano) harm; **não lhe desejo nenhum ~** I don't wish you any harm

····▸ (maldade) **o bem e o ~** good and evil

····▸ (doença) illness; **tem um ~ incurável** he has an incurable illness

····▸ (problema) **esse foi um ~ menor** that was the least of my troubles

● conj

····▸ (logo que) as soon as; **~ chegaram** as soon as they arrived

····▸ (em expressões) **estar ~ de** (dinheiro) be short of; **não fazer por ~** mean no harm; **ele não faz por ~** he doesn't mean any harm

mala /'mala/ f suitcase; (do carro) boot, Amer trunk; **~ aérea** air courier

malabaris|mo /malaba'rizmu/ m juggling act. **~ta** m/f juggler

mal-agradecido /malagrade'sidu/ a ungrateful

malagueta /mala'geta/ f chilli pepper

malaio /ma'laju/ a & m Malay

Malaísia /mala'izia/ f Malaysia

malaísio /mala'iziu/ a & m Malaysian

malan|dragem /malã'draʒẽ/ f hustling; (uma) clever trick. **~dro** a cunning ● m hustler

malária /ma'laria/ f malaria

mal-assombrado /malasõ'bradu/ a haunted

Malavi /mala'vi/ m Malawi

malcriado /mawkri'adu/ a rude

mal|dade /maw'dadʒi/ f wickedness; (uma) wicked thing; **por ~dade** out of spite. **~dição** f curse. **~dito** a cursed, damned. **~doso** /o/ a wicked

maleá|vel /mali'avew/ (pl **~veis**) a malleable

maledicência /maledi'sẽsia/ f malicious gossip

maléfico /ma'lefiku/ a evil; (prejudicial) harmful

mal-encarado /malĩka'radu/ a shady, dubious ● m shady character

mal-entendido /malĩtẽ'dʒidu/ m misunderstanding

mal-estar /malis'tar/ m (doença) ailment; (constrangimento) discomfort

maleta /ma'leta/ f overnight bag

malévolo /ma'lɛvolu/ a malevolent

malfei|to /maw'fejtu/ a badly done; ‹roupa etc› badly made; fig wrongful. **~tor** m wrongdoer. **~toria** f wrongdoing

ma|lha /'maʎa/ f (ponto) stitch; (tricô) knitting; (tecido) jersey; (casaco) jumper, Amer sweater; (para ginástica) leotard; (de rede) mesh; **fazer ~lha** knit. **~lhado** a ‹animal› dappled; ‹roque› heavy. **~lhar** vt beat; thresh ‹trigo etc› ● vi 🄸 work out

mal-humorado /malumo'radu/ a in a bad mood, grumpy

malícia /ma'lisia/ f (má índole) malice; (astúcia) guile; (humor) innuendo

malicioso /malisi'ozu/ a (mau) malicious; (astuto) crafty; (que põe malícia) dirty-minded

maligno /ma'liginu/ a malignant

malmequer /mawme'ker/ m marigold

malnutrido /mawnu'tridu/ a malnourished

maloca /ma'lɔka/ f Indian village

malo|grar-se /malo'grarsi/ vpr go wrong, fail. **~gro** /o/ m failure

malpassado /mawpa'sadu/ a ‹carne› rare

Malta /'mawta/ f Malta

malte /'mawtʃi/ m malt

maltrapilho /mawtra'piʎu/ a scruffy

maltratar /mawtra'tar/ vt ill-treat, mistreat

malu|co /ma'luku/ a 🄸 mad, crazy 🄸 ● m madman. **~quice** f madness; (uma) crazy thing

malvado /maw'vadu/ a wicked

malver|sação /mawversa'sãw/ f mismanagement; (de fundos)

m

misappropriation. **~sar** vt mismanage; misappropriate ‹dinheiro›

Malvinas /maw'vinas/ f pl Falklands

mamadeira /mama'dera/ f (baby's) bottle

mamãe /ma'mãj/ f mum

mamão /ma'mãw/ m papaya

ma|mar /ma'mar/ vi suckle. **~mata** f 🇮 fiddle

mamífero /ma'miferu/ m mammal

mamilo /ma'milu/ m nipple

mamoeiro /mamo'eru/ m papaya tree

mamografia /mamogra'fia/ f mammography

mamoplastia /mamoplaʃ'tʃia/ f breast surgery, mammoplasty

manada /ma'nada/ f herd

mananci|al /manãsi'aw/ (pl **~ais**) m spring; fig rich source

man|cada /mã'kada/ f blunder. **~car** vi limp. **~car-se** vpr 🇮 take the hint, get the message

man|cha /'mãʃa/ f stain; (na pele) mark. **~char** vt stain

Mancha /'mãʃa/ f **o canal da ~** the English Channel

manchete /mã'ʃetʃi/ f headline

manco /'mãku/ a lame ● m cripple

mandachuva /mãda'ʃuva/ m 🇮 bigwig; (chefe) boss

man|dado /mã'dadu/ m order; **~dado de busca** search warrant; **~dado de prisão** arrest warrant. **~damento** m commandment. **~dante** m/f person in charge. **~dão** a (f **~dona**) bossy. **~dar-se** vpr 🇮 take off. **~dato** m mandate

---

mandar /mã'dar/ ● vt

····▶ (ordenar) tell; **faça o que eu lhe mando** do what I tell you

····▶ (enviar) send; **mande a carta para mim pelo correio** send the letter to me by mail

····▶ (atirar) throw; **mande a bola** throw the ball

····▶ (em expressões) **~ fazer algo** have sth done; **vou ~ consertar o carro** I'm going to have the car repaired; **~ buscar/chamar alguém** send for sb; **mandei buscar o cozinheiro** I sent for the chef; **~ dizer** send word; **~ alguém às favas** tell sb to get lost

---

● vi

····▶ (ser o chefe) be in charge; **quem manda aqui?** who's in charge here?. **~dar-se**

● vpr

····▶ 🇮 take off

---

mandíbula /mã'dʒibula/ f (lower) jaw

mandioca /mãdʒi'ɔka/ f manioc

maneira /ma'nera/ f way; pl (boas) manners; **desta ~** in this way; **de qualquer ~** anyway

mane|jar /mane'ʒar/ vt handle; operate ‹máquina›. **~jável** (pl **~jáveis**) a manageable. **~jo** /e/ m handling

manequim /mane'kĩ/ m (boneco) dummy; (medida) size ● m/f mannequin, model

maneta /ma'neta/ a one-armed ● m/f person with one arm

manga¹ /'mãga/ f (de roupa) sleeve

manga² /'mãga/ f (fruta) mango

manganês /mãga'nes/ m manganese

mangue /'mãgi/ m mangrove swamp

mangueira¹ /mã'gera/ f (tubo) hose

mangueira² /mã'gera/ f (árvore) mango tree

manha /'maɲa/ f tantrum

manhã /ma'ɲã/ f morning; **de ~** in the morning

manhoso /ma'ɲozu/ a wilful

mania /ma'nia/ f (moda) craze; (doença) mania

maníaco /ma'niaku/ a manic ● m maniac. **~depressivo** a & m manic depressive

manicômio /mani'komiu/ m lunatic asylum

manicura /mani'kura/ f manicure; (pessoa) manicurist

manifes|tação /manifesta'sãw/ f manifestation; (passeata) demonstration. **~tante** m/f demonstrator. **~tar** vt manifest, demonstrate. **~tar-se** vpr (revelar-se) manifest o.s.; (exprimir-se) express an opinion. **~to** /ɛ/ a manifest, clear ● m manifesto

manipular /manipu'lar/ vt manipulate

manjedoura /mãʒe'dora/ f manger

manjericão /mãʒeri'kãw/ m basil

mano|bra /ma'nɔbra/ f manoeuvre. **~brar** vt manoeuvre. **~brista** m/f parking valet

m

mansão /mã'sãw/ f mansion

man|sidão /mãsi'dãw/ f gentleness; (do mar) calm. **~sinho** adv de **~sinho** (devagar) slowly; (de leve) gently; (de fininho) stealthily. **~so** a gentle; ‹mar› calm; ‹animal› tame

manta /'mãta/ f blanket; (casaco) cloak

mantel|ga /mã'tejga/ f butter. **~gueira** f butter dish

manter /mã'ter/ vt keep. **~-se** vpr keep; (sustentar-se) keep o.s.

mantimentos /mãtʃi'mẽtus/ m pl provisions

manto /'mãtu/ m mantle

manu|al /manu'aw/ (pl **~ais**) a & m manual. **~fatura** f manufacture; (fábrica) factory. **~faturar** vt manufacture

manuscrito /manus'kritu/ a handwritten ● m manuscript

manu|sear /manuzi'ar/ vt handle. **~seio** m handling

manutenção /manutẽ'sãw/ f maintenance; (de prédio) upkeep

mão /mãw/ (pl **~s**) f hand; (do trânsito) direction; (de tinta) coat; **abrir ~ de** give up; **aguentar a ~** hang on; **dar a ~ a alguém** hold sb's hand; (cumprimentando) shake sb's hand; **deixar alguém na ~** let sb down; **enfiar ou meter a ~ em** hit, slap; **lançar ~ de** make use of; **escrito à ~** written by hand; **ter à ~** have to hand; **de ~s dadas** hand in hand; **em segunda ~** second-hand; **fora de ~** out of the way; **~ única** one way. **~-de-obra** f labour

mapa /'mapa/ m map

maquete /ma'ketʃi/ f model

maqui|agem /maki'aʒẽ/ f make-up. **~ar** vt make up. **~ar-se** vpr put on make-up

maquiavélico /makia'veliku/ a Machiavellian

maqui|lagem, **~lar**, Port **~lhagem**, **~lhar** ▶ MAQUIAGEM

máquina /'makina/ f machine; (ferroviária) engine; **escrever à ~** type; **~ de costura** sewing machine; **~ de escrever** typewriter; **~ de lavar (roupa)** washing machine; **~ de lavar pratos** dishwasher; **~ fotográfica** camera

maqui|nação /makina'sãw/ f machination. **~nal** (pl **~nais**) a mechanical. **~nar** vt/i plot. **~nária** f machinery. **~nista** m/f (ferroviário) engine driver; (de navio) engineer

mar /mar/ m sea

maracu|já /maraku'ʒa/ m passion fruit. **~jazeiro** m passion fruit plant

marasmo /ma'razmu/ f stagnation

marato|na /mara'tona/ f marathon. **~nista** m/f marathon runner

maravi|lha /mara'viʎa/ f marvel; **às mil ~lhas** wonderfully. **~lhar** vt amaze. **~lhar-se** vpr marvel (de at). **~lhoso** /o/ a marvellous

mar|ca /'marka/ f (sinal) mark; (de carro, máquina) make; (de cigarro, sabão etc) brand; **~ca registrada** registered trademark. **~cação** /marka'sãw/ f marking; Port (discagem) dialling; **~ rápida** Port Telec speed dialling. **~cador** m marker; (em livro) bookmark; (placar) scoreboard; (jogador) scorer. **~cante** a outstanding. **~ca-passo** m pacemaker. **~car** vt mark; arrange ‹hora, encontro, jantar etc›; score ‹gol, ponto›; Port (discar) dial ‹relógio, termômetro› show; brand ‹gado›; (observar) keep a close eye on; (impressionar) leave one's mark on; **~car época** make history; **~car hora** make an appointment; **~car o compasso** beat time; **~car os pontos** keep the score ● vi make one's mark

marce|naria /marsena'ria/ f cabinetmaking; (oficina) cabinet maker's workshop. **~neiro** m cabinetmaker

mar|cha /'marʃa/ f march; (de carro) gear; **pôr-se em ~cha** get going; **~cha à ré**, Port **~cha atrás** reverse. **~char** vi march

marci|al /marsi'aw/ (pl **~ais**) a martial. **~ano** a & m Martian

marco¹ /'marku/ m (sinal) landmark

marco² /'marku/ m (moeda) mark

março /'marsu/ m March

maré /ma're/ f tide

mare|chal /mare'ʃaw/ (pl **~chais**) m marshal

maresia /mare'zia/ f smell of the sea

marfim /mar'fĩ/ m ivory

margarida /marga'rida/ f daisy; (para impressora) daisy wheel

margarina /marga'rina/ f margarine

mar|gem /'marʒẽ/ f (de rio) bank; (de lago) shore; (parte em branco) fig margin. **~ginal** (pl **~ginais**) a marginal; (delinquente) delinquent ● m/f delinquent ● f (rua) riverside road. **~ginalidade** f delinquency. **~ginalizar** vt marginalize

marido /ma'ridu/ m husband

marimbondo /marĩ'bõdu/ m hornet

marina /ma'rina/ f marina

mari|nha /ma'riɲa/ f navy; ~**nha mercante** merchant navy. ~**nheiro** m sailor. ~**nho** a marine

marionete /mario'netʃi/ f puppet

mariposa /mari'poza/ f moth

mariscos /ma'riskus/ m seafood

mari|tal /mari'taw/ (pl ~**tais**) a marital

marítimo /ma'ritʃimu/ a sea; ‹cidade› seaside

marmanjo /mar'mãʒu/ m grown-up

marme|lada /marme'lada/ f 🔲 fix. ~**lo** /ɛ/ m quince

marmita /mar'mita/ f (de soldado) mess tin; (de trabalhador) lunch box

mármore /'marmori/ m marble

marmóreo /mar'mɔriu/ a marble

marquise /mar'kizi/ f awning

marreco /ma'xɛku/ m wild duck

Marrocos /ma'xɔkus/ m Morocco

marrom /ma'xõ/ a & m brown

marroquino /maxo'kinu/ a & m Moroccan

Marte /'martʃi/ m.Mars

marte|lada /marte'lada/ f hammer blow. ~**lar** vt/i hammer; ~**lar em** fig go on and on about. ~**lo** /ɛ/ m hammer

mártir /'martʃir/ m/f martyr

mar|tírio /mar'tʃiriu/ m martyrdom; fig torture. ~**tirizar** vt martyr; fig torture

marujo /ma'ruʒu/ m sailor

mar|xismo /mark'sizmu/ m Marxism. ~**xista** a & m/f Marxist

mas /mas/ conj but

mascar /mas'kar/ vt chew

máscara /'maskara/ f mask; (tratamento facial) face pack

mascarar /maska'rar/ vt mask

mascate /mas'katʃi/ m street vendor

mascavo /mas'kavu/ a açúcar ~ brown sugar

mascote /mas'kɔtʃi/ f mascot

masculino /masku'linu/ a male; (para homens) men's; ‹palavra› masculine ● m masculine

másculo /'maskulu/ a masculine

masmorra /maz'moxa/ f dungeon

masoquis|mo /mazo'kizmu/ m masochism. ~**ta** m/f masochist ● a masochistic

massa /'masa/ f mass; (de pão) dough; (de torta, empada) pastry; (macarrão etc) pasta; **cultura de ~** mass culture; **em ~** en masse; **as ~s** the masses

massa|crante /masa'krãtʃi/ a gruelling. ~**crar** vt massacre; fig (maçar) wear out. ~**cre** m massacre

massa|gear /masaʒi'ar/ vt massage. ~**gem** f massage. ~**gista** m/f masseur (f masseuse)

mastigar /mastʃi'gar/ vt chew; (ponderar) chew over

mastro /'mastru/ m mast; (de bandeira) flagpole

mastur|bação /masturba'sãw/ f masturbation. ~**bar-se** vpr masturbate

mata /'mata/ f forest

mata-borrão /matabo'xãw/ m blotting paper

matadouro /mata'doru/ m slaughterhouse

mata|gal /mata'gaw/ (pl ~**gais**) m thicket

mata-moscas /mata'moskas/ m invar fly spray

ma|tança /ma'tãsa/ f slaughter. ~**tar** vt kill; satisfy ‹fome›; quench ‹sede›; guess ‹charada›; (fazer nas coxas) dash off; 🔲 skive off ‹aula, serviço› ● vi kill

mata-ratos /mata'xatus/ m invar rat poison

mate[1] /'matʃi/ m (chá) maté

mate[2] /'matʃi/ a invar matt

matemáti|ca /mate'matʃika/ f mathematics. ~**co** a mathematical ● m mathematician

matéria /ma'tɛria/ f (assunto, disciplina) subject; (no jornal) article; (substância) matter; (usada para fazer algo) material; **em ~ de** in the way of

materi|al /materi'aw/ (pl ~**ais**) m materials ● a material. ~**alismo** m materialism. ~**alista** a materialistic ● m/f materialist. ~**alizar-se** vpr materialize

matéria-prima /materia'prima/ (pl **matérias-primas**) f raw material

mater|nal /mater'naw/ (pl ~**nais**) a maternal. ~**nidade** f maternity; (clínica) maternity hospital. ~**no** /ɛ/ a maternal; **língua ~na** mother tongue

mati|nal /matʃi'naw/ (pl ~**nais**) a morning. ~**nê** f matinee

matiz /ma'tʃis/ m shade; (político) colouring; (pontinha) (de ironia etc) tinge

matizar /matʃi'zar/ vt tinge (**de** with)

mato /'matu/ m scrubland, bush

matraca /ma'traka/ f rattle; (tagarela) chatterbox

matreiro /ma'treru/ a cunning

matriar|ca /matri'arka/ f matriarch. **~cal** (pl **~cais**) a matriarchal

matrícula /ma'trikula/ f enrolment; (taxa) enrolment fee; Port (de carro) number plate, Amer license plate

matricular /matriku'lar/ vt enrol. **~se** vpr enrol

matri|monial /matrimoni'aw/ (pl **~moniais**) a marriage. **~mônio** m marriage

matriz /ma'tris/ f matrix; (útero) womb; (sede) head office

maturidade /maturi'dadʒi/ f maturity

matutino /matu'tʃinu/ a morning ● m morning paper

matuto /ma'tutu/ a countrified ● m country bumpkin

mau /maw/ a (f **má**) bad. **~caráter** m invar bad lot ● a invar no-good; **~olhado** m evil eye

mausoléu /mawzo'lɛw/ m mausoleum

maus-tratos /maws'tratus/ m pl ill-treatment

maxilar /maksi'lar/ m jaw

máxima /'masima/ f maxim

maximizar /masimi'zar/ vt maximize; (exagerar) play up

máximo /'masimu/ a (antes do substantivo) utmost, greatest; (depois do substantivo) maximum ● m maximum; **o ~** 🆇 (o melhor) really something; **ao ~** to the maximum; **no ~** at most

maxixe /ma'ʃiʃi/ m gherkin

me /mi/ pron me; (indireto) (to) me; (reflexivo) myself

meada /mi'ada/ f skein; **perder o fio da ~** lose one's thread

meados /mi'adus/ m pl **~ de maio** mid-May

meandro /mi'ãdru/ f meander; pl fig twists and turns

mecâni|ca /me'kanika/ f mechanics. **~co** a mechanical ● m mechanic

meca|nismo /meka'nizmu/ m mechanism. **~nizar** vt mechanize

mecenas /me'senas/ m invar patron

mecha /'meʃa/ f (de vela) wick; (de bomba) fuse; (porção de cabelos) lock; (cabelo tingido) highlight. **~do** a highlighted

meda|lha /me'daʎa/ f medal. **~lhão** m medallion; (joia) locket

média /'medʒia/ f average; (café) white coffee; **em ~** on average

medi|ação /medʒia'sãw/ f mediation. **~ador** m mediator. **~ante** prep through, by. **~ar** vi mediate

medica|ção /medʒika'sãw/ f medication. **~mento** m medicine

medição /medʒi'sãw/ f measurement

medicar /medʒi'kar/ vt treat ● vi practise medicine. **~se** vpr dose o.s. up

medici|na /medʒi'sina/ f medicine; **~na legal** forensic medicine. **~nal** (pl **~nais**) a medicinal

médico /'medʒiku/ m doctor ● a medical. **~-legal** (pl **~-legais**) a forensic; **~-legista** (pl **~s-legistas**) m/f forensic scientist

medi|da /me'dʒida/ f measure; (dimensão) measurement; **à ~da que** as; **sob ~da** made to measure; **tirar as ~das de alguém** take sb's measurements. **~dor** m meter

medie|val /medʒie'vaw/ (pl **~vais**) a medieval

médio /'medʒiu/ a (típico) average; ‹tamanho, prazo› medium; ‹classe, dedo› middle

mediocre /me'dʒiokri/ a mediocre

mediocridade /medʒiokri'dadʒi/ f mediocrity

medir /me'dʒir/ vt measure; weigh ‹palavras› ● vi measure. **~se** vpr measure o.s.; **quanto você mede?** how tall are you?

medi|tação /medʒita'sãw/ f meditation. **~tar** vi meditate

mediterrâneo /medʒite'xaniu/ a Mediterranean ● m **o Mediterrâneo** the Mediterranean

médium /'medʒiũ/ m/f medium

medo /'medu/ m fear; **ter ~ de** be afraid of; **com ~** afraid. **~nho** /o/ a frightful

medroso /me'drozu/ a fearful, timid

medula /me'dula/ f marrow

megalomania /megaloma'nia/ f megalomania

meia /'meja/ f (comprida) stocking; (curta) sock; (seis) six. **~calça** (pl **~s-calças**) f tights, Amer pantihose; **~idade** f middle age; **~noite** f midnight; **~volta** (pl **~s-voltas**) f about-turn

mei|go /'mejgu/ a sweet. **~guice** f sweetness

meio /'meju/ a half ● adv rather ● m (centro) middle; (ambiente) environment; (recurso) means; **~ litro**

m

half a litre; **dois meses e ~** two and
a half months; **em ~ a** amid; **por
~ de** through; **o ~ ambiente** the
environment; **os ~s de comunicação**
the media; **~s de comunicação social**
Port social media. **~dia** *m* midday; **~fio**
m kerb; **~termo** *m* (*acordo*) compromise

mel /mɛw/ *m* honey

mela|ço /me'lasu/ *m* molasses. **~do** *a*
sticky ● *m* treacle

melancia /melã'sia/ *f* watermelon

melan|colia /melãko'lia/ *f*
melancholy. **~cólico** *a* melancholic

melão /me'lãw/ *m* melon

melar /me'lar/ *vt* make sticky

melhor /me'ʎɔr/ *a* & *adv* better; **o ~**
the best

melho|ra /me'ʎɔra/ *f* improvement;
~ras! get well soon!. **~ramento** *m*
improvement. **~rar** *vt* improve ● *vi*
improve; ‹*doente*› get better

melin|drar /melĩ'drar/ *vt* hurt.
~drar-se *vpr* be hurt. **~droso** /o/ *a*
delicate; ‹*pessoa*› sensitive

melodi|a /melo'dʒia/ *f* melody. **~oso**
/o/ *a* melodious

melodra|ma /melo'drama/ *m*
melodrama. **~mático** *a* melodramatic

meloso /me'lozu/ *a* sickly sweet

melro /'mɛwxu/ *m* blackbird

membrana /mẽ'brana/ *f* membrane

membro /'mẽbru/ *m* member; (*braço,
perna*) limb

memo|rando /memo'rãdu/ *m* memo.
~rável (*pl* **~ráveis**) *a* memorable

memória /me'mɔria/ *f* memory; *pl*
(*autobiografia*) memoirs

men|ção /mẽ'sãw/ *f* mention; **fazer
~ção de** mention. **~cionar** *vt* mention

mendi|cância /mẽdʒi'kãsia/ *f*
begging. **~gar** *vi* beg. **~go** *m* beggar

menina /me'nina/ *f* girl; **a ~ dos olhos
de alguém** the apple of sb's eye

meningite /menĩ'ʒitʃi/ *f* meningitis

meni|nice /meni'nisi/ *f* (*idade*)
childhood. **~no** *m* boy

menopausa /meno'pawza/ *f*
menopause

menor /me'nɔr/ *a* smaller ● *m/f* minor;
o/a ~ the smallest; (*mínimo*) the
slightest, the least

menos /'menos/ *adv* & *pron* less ● *prep*
except; **dois dias a ~** two days less; **a ~
que** unless; **ao ou pelo ~** at least; **o ~
bonito** the least pretty. **~prezar** *vt* look
down upon. **~prezo** /e/ *m* disdain

mensa|geiro /mẽsa'ʒeru/ *m*
messenger. **~gem** /mẽ'saʒẽ ʒ/ *f*
message; **~gem instantânea** *Telec*
instant messaging. **~gem escrita** (*telec*)
text message

men|sal /mẽ'saw/ (*pl* **~sais**) *a* monthly.
~salidade *f* monthly payment.
~salmente *adv* monthly

menstru|ação /mẽstrua'sãw/ *f*
menstruation. **~ada a estar ~ada** be
having one's period. **~al** (*pl* **~ais**) *a*
menstrual. **~ar** *vi* menstruate

menta /'mẽta/ *f* mint

men|tal /mẽ'taw/ (*pl* **~tais**) *a* mental.
~talidade *f* mentality. **~te** *f* mind

men|tir /mẽ'tʃir/ *vi* lie. **~tira** *f* lie.
~tiroso /o/ *a* lying ● *m* liar

mentor /mẽ'tor/ *m* mentor

mercado /mer'kadu/ *m* market. **~ria** *f*
commodity; *pl* goods

mercan|te /mer'kãtʃi/ *a* merchant.
~til (*pl* **~tis**) *a* mercantile

mercê /mer'se/ *f* **à ~ de** at the mercy of

merce|aria /mersia'ria/ *f* grocer's.
~eiro *m* grocer

mercenário /merse'nariu/ *a* & *m*
mercenary

mercúrio /mer'kuriu/ *m* mercury;
Mercúrio Mercury

merda /'mɛrda/ *f* (*vulgar*) shit

mere|cedor /merese'dor/ *a* deserving.
~cer *vt* deserve ● *vi* be deserving.
~cimento *m* merit

merenda /me'rẽda/ *f* packed lunch;
~ escolar school dinner

mere|trício /mere'trisiu/ *m*
prostitution. **~triz** *f* prostitute

mergu|lhador /merguʎa'dor/ *m*
diver. **~lhar** *vt* dip (**em** into) ● *vi* (*na
água*) dive; (*no trabalho*) bury o.s.. **~lho**
m dive; (*esporte*) diving; (*banho de mar*)
dip

meridi|ano /meridʒi'anu/ *m* meridian.
~onal (*pl* **~onais**) *a* southern

mérito /'meritu/ *m* merit

merluza /mer'luza/ *f* hake

mero /'meru/ *a* mere

mês /mes/ (*pl* **meses**) *m* month

mesa /'meza/ *f* table; (*de trabalho*) desk;
~ de centro coffee table; **~ de jantar**
dining table; **~ telefónica** switchboard

mesada /me'zada/ *f* monthly
allowance

mescla /'mɛskla/ *f* mixture, blend

mesmice /mez'misi/ *f* sameness

mesmo /'mezmu/ *a* same ● *adv* (*até*) even; (*justamente*) right; (*de verdade*) really; **você ~** you yourself; **hoje ~** this very day; **~ assim** even so; **~ que** even if; **dá no ~** it comes to the same thing; **fiquei na mesma** I'm none the wiser

mesqui|nharia /meski̯a'ria/ *f* meanness; (*uma*) mean thing. **~nho** *a* mean

mesquita /mes'kita/ *f* mosque

Messias /me'sias/ *m* Messiah

mesti|çagem /mestʃi'saʒẽ/ *f* interbreeding. **~ço** *a* ‹pessoa› of mixed race; ‹animal› cross-bred ● *m* (*pessoa*) person of mixed race; (*animal*) mongrel

mes|trado /mes'tradu/ *m* master's degree. **~tre** /ɛ/ *m* (*f* **~tra**) master; mistress; (*de escola*) teacher ● *a* main; ‹chave› master. **~tre de obras** (*pl* **~tres de obras**) *m* foreman; **~tre-sala** (*pl* **~tres-salas**) *m* master of ceremonies (in carnival procession). **~tria** *f* expertise

meta /'mɛta/ *f* (*de corrida*) finishing post; (*gol*) *fig* goal

meta|bólico /meta'bɔliku/ *a* metabolic. **~bolismo** *m* metabolism

metade /me'tadʒi/ *f* half; **pela ~** halfway

metafísi|ca /meta'fizika/ *f* metaphysics. **~co** *a* metaphysical

metáfora /me'tafora/ *f* metaphor

metafórico /meta'fɔriku/ *a* metaphorical

me|tal /me'taw/ (*pl* **~tais**) *m* metal; *pl* (*numa orquestra*) brass. **~tálico** *a* metallic

meta|lurgia /metalur'ʒia/ *f* metallurgy. **~lúrgica** *f* metal works. **~lúrgico** *a* metallurgical ● *m* metalworker

metamorfose /metamor'fɔzi/ *f* metamorphosis

metano /me'tanu/ *m* methane

meteórico /mete'ɔriku/ *a* meteoric

meteoro /mete'ɔru/ *m* meteor. **~logia** *f* meteorology. **~lógico** *a* meteorological. **~logista** *m/f* (*cientista*) meteorologist; (*na TV*) weather forecaster

meter /me'ter/ *vt* put; **~ medo** be frightening. **~-se** *vpr* (*envolver-se*) get (**em** into); (*intrometer-se*) meddle (**em** in)

meticuloso /metʃiku'lozu/ *a* meticulous

metido /me'tʃidu/ *a* snobbish; **ele é ~ a perito** he thinks he's an expert

metódico /me'tɔdʒiku/ *a* methodical

metodista /meto'dʒista/ *a & m/f* Methodist

método /'mɛtodu/ *m* method

metra|lhadora /metraʎa'dora/ *f* machine gun. **~lhar** *vt* machine-gun

métri|co /'mɛtriku/ *a* metric; **fita ~ca** tape measure

metro[1] /'mɛtru/ *m* metre

metro[2] /'mɛtru/ *m Port* (*metropolitano*) underground, *Amer* subway

metrô /me'tro/ *m* underground, *Amer* subway

metrópole /me'trɔpoli/ *f* metropolis

metropolitano /metropoli'tanu/ *a* metropolitan ● *m Port* underground, *Amer* subway

meu /mew/ *a* (*f* **minha**) my ● *pron* (*f* **minha**) mine; **um amigo ~** a friend of mine; **fico na minha** ⏵ I keep myself to myself

mexer /me'ʃer/ *vt* move; (*com colher etc*) stir ● *vi* move; **~ com** (*comover*) affect, get to; (*brincar com*) tease; (*trabalhar com*) work with; **~ em** touch. **~-se** *vpr* move; (*apressar-se*) get a move on

mexeri|ca /meʃe'rika/ *f* tangerine. **~car** *vi* gossip. **~co** *m* piece of gossip; *pl* gossip. **~queiro** *a* gossiping ● *m* gossip

mexicano /meʃi'kanu/ *a & m* Mexican

México /'mɛʃiku/ *m* Mexico

mexido /me'ʃidu/ *a* **ovos ~s** scrambled eggs

mexilhão /meʃi'ʎãw/ *m* mussel

mi|ado /mi'adu/ *m* miaow. **~ar** *vi* miaow

micreiro /mi'krejru/ *m* PC hacker

micróbio /mi'krɔbiu/ *m* microbe

micro|cosmo /mikro'kɔzmu/ *m* microcosm. **~empresa** /e/ *f* small business. **~empresário** *m* small businessman. **~filme** *m* microfilm. **~fone** *m* microphone. **~onda** *f* microwave. **(forno de) ~ondas** *m* microwave (oven). **~ônibus** *m invar* minibus. **~processador** *m* microprocessor

microrganismo /mikrorga'nizmu/ *m* microorganism

microscó|pico /mikros'kɔpiku/ *a* microscopic. **~pio** *m* microscope

mídia /'midʒia/ *f* media; **~ social** social media

migalha /mi'gaʎa/ *f* crumb

mi|gração /migra'sãw/ f migration.
~grar vi migrate

mijar /mi'ʒar/ vi ① pee. **~jar-se** vpr
wet o.s.. **~jo** m ① pee

mil-/miw/ a & m invar thousand; **estar a
~** be on top form

mila|gre /mi'lagri/ m miracle. **~groso**
/o/ a miraculous

milênio /mi'leniu/ m millennium

milésimo /mi'lezimu/ a thousandth

milha /'miʎa/ f mile

milhão /mi'ʎãw/ m million; **um ~ de
dólares** a million dollars

milhar /mi'ʎar/ m thousand; **~es de
vezes** thousands of times; **aos ~es** in
their thousands

milho /'miʎo/ m maize, Amer corn

milico /mi'liku/ m ① military man; **os
~s** the military

mili|grama /mili'grama/ m milligram.
~litro m millilitre. **milímetro** /e/ m
millimetre

milionário /milio'nariu/ a & m
millionaire

mili|tante /mili'tãtʃi/ a & m militant.
~tar a military ● m soldier

mim /mĩ/ pron me

mimar /mi'mar/ vt spoil

mímica /'mimika/ f mime; (brincadeira)
charades

mi|na /'mina/ f mine. **~nar** vt mine; fig
(prejudicar) undermine

mindinho /mĩ'dʒiɲu/ m little finger,
Amer pinkie

mineiro /mi'neru/ a mining; (de MG)
from Minas Gerais ● m miner; (de MG)
person from Minas Gerais

mine|ração /minera'sãw/ f mining.
~ral (pl **~rais**) a & m mineral. **~rar** vt/i
mine

minério /mi'neriu/ m ore

mingau /mĩ'gaw/ m porridge

míngua /'mĩgwa/ f lack

minguante /mĩ'gwãtʃi/ a **quarto ~**
last quarter

minguar /mĩ'gwar/ vi dwindle

minha /'miɲa/ a & pron ▶ MEU

minhoca /mi'ɲɔka/ f worm

miniatura /minia'tura/ f miniature

mini|malista /minima'lista/ a & a
m/f minimalist. **~mizar** vt minimize;
(subestimar) play down

mínimo /'minimu/ a (muito pequeno)
tiny; (mais baixo) minimum ● m
minimum; **a mínima ideia** the slightest

idea; **no ~** at least

minissaia /mini'saja/ f miniskirt

minis|terial /ministeri'aw/
(pl **~teriais**) a ministerial. **~tério** m
ministry; **Ministério do Interior** Home
Office, Amer Department of the Interior

minis|trar /minis'trar/ vt administer.
~tro m minister; **primeiro ~tro** prime
minister

Minorca /mi'nɔrka/ f Menorca

mino|ritário /minori'tariu/ a
minority. **~ria** f minority

minúcia /mi'nusia/ f detail

minucioso /minusi'ozu/ a thorough

minúscu|la /mi'nuskula/ f small
letter. **~lo** a ‹letra› small; (muito
pequeno) minuscule

minuta /mi'nuta/ f (rascunho) rough
draft

minuto /mi'nutu/ m minute

miolo /mi'olu/ f (de fruta) flesh;
(de pão) crumb; pl brains

míope /'miopi/ a short-sighted

miopia /mio'pia/ f myopia

mira /'mira/ f sight; **ter em ~** have
one's sights on

mirabolante /mirabo'lãtʃi/ a
amazing; ‹ideias, plano› grandiose

mi|ragem /mi'raʒẽ/ f mirage. **~rante**
m lookout. **~rar** vt look at. **~rar-se** vpr
look at o.s.

mirim /mi'rĩ/ a little

miscelânea /mise'lania/ f miscellany

miscigenação /misiʒena'sãw/ f
interbreeding

miserá|vel /mize'ravew/ (pl **~veis**) a
miserable

miséria /mi'zeria/ f misery; (pobreza)
poverty; **uma ~** (pouco dinheiro) a
pittance; **chorar ~** claim poverty

miseri|córdia /mizeri'kɔrdʒia/ f
mercy. **~cordioso** a merciful

misógino /mi'zɔʒinu/ m misogynist
● a misogynistic

miss /'misi/ f beauty queen

missa /'misa/ f mass

missão /mi'sãw/ f mission

mis|sil /'misiw/ (pl **~seis**) m missile;
~sil de longo alcance long-range
missile

missionário /misio'nariu/ m
missionary

missiva /mi'siva/ f missive

mis|tério /mis'teriu/ m mystery.
~terioso /o/ a mysterious. **~ticismo** m

mysticism

místico /'miʃtʃiku/ *m* mystic ● *a* mystical

misto /'miʃtu/ *a* mixed ● *m* mix; **~ quente** toasted ham and cheese sandwich

mistu|ra /mis'tura/ *f* mixture. **~rar** *vt* mix; (*confundir*) mix up. **~rar-se** *vpr* mix (**com** with)

mítico /'mitʃiku/ *a* mythical

mito /'mitu/ *m* myth. **~logia** *f* mythology. **~lógico** *a* mythological

miudezas /miu'dezas/ *f pl* odds and ends

miúdo /mi'udu/ *a* tiny, minute; ‹*chuva*› fine; ‹*despesas*› minor ● *m* (*criança*) child, little one; *pl* (*de galinha*) giblets; **trocar em ~s** go into detail

mixaria /miʃa'ria/ *f* Ⓐ (*soma irrisória*) pittance

mixórdia /mi'ʃɔrdʒia/ *f* muddle

MMS *abr m* (= Serviço de Mensagens Multimédia) MMS

mnemônico /ne'moniku/ *a* mnemonic

mobilar /mobi'lar/ *vt* Port furnish

mobília /mo'bilia/ *f* furniture

mobili|ar /mobili'ar/ *vt* furnish. **~ário** *m* furniture

mobili|dade /mobili'dadʒi/ *f* mobility. **~zar** *vt* mobilize

moça /'mosa/ *f* girl

moçambicano /mosãbi'kanu/ *a & m* Mozambican

Moçambique /mosã'biki/ *m* Mozambique

moção /mo'sãw/ *f* motion

mochila /mo'ʃila/ *f* rucksack

moço /'mosu/ *a* young ● *m* boy, lad

moda /'mɔda/ *f* fashion; **na ~** fashionable

modalidade /modali'dadʒi/ *f* (*esporte*) event

mode|lagem /mode'laʒẽ/ *f* modelling. **~lar** *vt* model (**a** on). **~lar-se** *vpr* model o.s. (**a** on). **~lo** /e/ *a* model ● *m* model

mode|ração /modera'sãw/ *f* moderation. **~rado** *a* moderate. **~rar** *vt* moderate; reduce ‹*velocidade, despesas*›. **~rar-se** *vpr* restrain oneself

moder|nidade /moderni'dadʒi/ *f* modernity. **~nismo** *m* modernism. **~nista** *a & m/f* modernist. **~nizar** *vt* modernize. **~no** /ɛ/ *a* modern

modess™ /'mɔdʒis/ *m invar* ™sanitary towel

modéstia /mo'dɛstʃia/ *f* modesty

modesto /mo'dɛstu/ *a* modest

módico /'mɔdʒiku/ *a* modest

modifi|cação /modʒifika'sãw/ *f* modification. **~car** *vt* modify

mo|dismo /mo'dʒizmu/ *m* idiom. **~dista** *f* dressmaker

modo /'mɔdu/ *m* way; *Ling* mood; *pl* (*maneiras*) manners

modular /modu'lar/ *vt* modulate ● *a* modular

módulo /'mɔdulu/ *m* module

moeda /mo'ɛda/ *f* (*peça de metal*) coin; (*dinheiro*) currency

mo|edor /moe'dor/ *m* **~edor de café** coffee grinder; **~edor de carne** mincer. **~er** *vt* grind ‹*café, trigo*›; squeeze ‹*cana*›; mince ‹*carne*›; (*bater*) beat

mo|fado /mo'fadu/ *a* mouldy. **~far** *vi* moulder. **~fo** /o/ *m* mould

mogno /'mɔgnu/ *m* mahogany

moinho /mo'iɲu/ *m* mill; **~ de vento** windmill

moisés /moj'zɛs/ *m invar* carrycot

moita /'mojta/ *f* bush

mola /'mɔla/ *f* spring

mol|dar /mow'dar/ *vt* mould; cast ‹*metal*›. **~de** /ɔ/ *m* mould; (*para costura etc*) pattern

moldu|ra /mow'dura/ *f* frame. **~rar** *vt* frame

mole /'mɔli/ *a* soft; ‹*pessoa*› listless; Ⓐ (*fácil*) easy ● *adv* easily; **é ~?** Ⓐ can you believe it?

molécula /mo'lekula/ *f* molecule

moleque /mo'lɛki/ *m* (*menino*) lad; (*de rua*) urchin; (*homem*) scoundrel

molestar /moles'tar/ *vt* bother

moléstia /mo'lɛstʃia/ *f* disease

moletom /mole'tõ/ *m* (*tecido*) knitted cotton; (*blusa*) sweatshirt

moleza /mo'leza/ *f* softness; (*de pessoa*) laziness; **viver na ~** lead a cushy life; **ser ~** be easy

mo|lhado /mo'ʎadu/ *a* wet. **~lhar** *vt* wet. **~lhar-se** *vpr* get wet

molho¹ /'mɔʎu/ *m* (*de chaves*) bunch; (*de palha*) sheaf

molho² /'moʎu/ *m* sauce; (*para salada*) dressing; **deixar de ~** leave in soak ‹*roupa*›; **~ inglês** Worcester sauce

molusco /mo'lusku/ *m* mollusc

m

momen|tâneo /momẽ'taniu/ a momentary. **~to** m moment; (força) momentum

Mônaco /'monaku/ m Monaco

monar|ca /mo'narka/ m/f monarch. **~quia** f monarchy. **~quista** a & m/f monarchist

monástico /mo'nastʃiku/ a monastic

monção /mõ'sãw/ f monsoon

mone|tário /mone'tariu/ a monetary. **~tarismo** m monetarism. **~tarista** a & m/f monetarist

monge /'mõʒi/ m monk

monitor /moni'tor/ m monitor; **~ de vídeo** VDU

monitorar /monito'rar/ vt monitor

mono|cromo /mono'krɔmu/ a monochrome. **~gamia** f monogamy

monógamo /mo'nɔgamu/ a monogamous

monograma /mono'grama/ m monogram

monólogo /mo'nɔlogu/ m monologue

mononucleose /mononukli'ɔzi/ f glandular fever

mono|pólio /mono'pɔliu/ m monopoly. **~polizar** vt monopolize

monossílabo /mono'silabu/ a monosyllabic ● m monosyllable

monotonia /monoto'nia/ f monotony

monótono /mo'nɔtonu/ a monotonous

monóxido /mo'nɔksidu/ m **~ de carbono** carbon monoxide

mons|tro /'mõstru/ m monster. **~truosidade** f monstrosity. **~truoso** /o/ a monstrous

monta|dor /mõta'dor/ m (de cinema) editor. **~dora** f assembly company. **~gem** f assembly; (de filme) editing; (de peça teatral) production

monta|nha /mõ'taɲa/ f mountain. **~nha-russa** (pl **~nhas-russas**) f roller coaster. **~nhismo** m mountaineering. **~nhoso** /o/ a mountainous

mon|tante /mõ'tãtʃi/ m amount ● a rising; **a ~tante** upstream. **~tão** m heap. **~tar** vt ride ‹cavalo, bicicleta›; assemble ‹peças, máquina›; put up ‹barraca›; set up ‹empresa, escritório›; mount ‹guarda, diamante›; put on ‹espetáculo, peça›; edit ‹filme›; **~tar a** amount to; **~tar em** (subir em) mount ● vi ride. **~taria** f mount. **~te** m heap; **um ~te de coisas** 🄸 loads of things; **o Monte Branco**

Mont Blanc

Montevidéu /mõtʃivi'dɛw/ f Montevideo

montra /'mõtra/ f Port shop window

monumen|tal /monumẽ'taw/ (pl **~tais**) a monumental. **~to** m monument

mora|da /mo'rada/ f dwelling; Port address. **~dia** f dwelling. **~dor** m resident

mo|ral /mo'raw/ (pl **~rais**) a moral ● f (ética) morals; (de uma história) moral ● m (ânimo) morale; (de pessoa) moral sense. **~ralidade** f morality. **~ralista** a moralistic ● m/f moralist. **~ralizar** vi moralize

morango /mo'rãgu/ m strawberry

morar /mo'rar/ vi live

moratória /mora'tɔria/ f moratorium

mórbido /'mɔrbidu/ a morbid

morcego /mor'segu/ m bat

mor|daça /mor'dasa/ f gag; (para cão) muzzle. **~daz** a scathing. **~der** vt/i bite. **~dida** f bite

mordo|mia /mordo'mia/ f (no emprego) perk; (de casa etc) comfort. **~mo** /o/ m butler

more|na /mo'rena/ f brunette. **~no** a dark; (bronzeado) brown ● m dark person

morfina /mor'fina/ f morphine

moribundo /mori'bũdu/ a dying

moringa /mo'rĩga/ f water jug

morma|cento /morma'sẽtu/ a sultry. **~ço** m sultry weather

morno /'mornu/ a lukewarm

moro|sidade /morozi'dadʒi/ f slowness. **~so** /o/ a slow

morrer /mo'xer/ vi die; ‹luz, dia, ardor, esperança etc› fade; ‹carro› stall

morro /'moxu/ m hill; fig (favela) slum

mortadela /morta'dela/ f mortadella, salami

mor|tal /mor'taw/ (pl **~tais**) a & m mortal. **~talha** f shroud. **~talidade** f mortality. **~tandade** f slaughter. **~te** /ɔ/ f death. **~tífero** a deadly. **~tificar** vt mortify. **~to** /o/ a dead

mosaico /mo'zajku/ m mosaic

mosca /'moska/ f fly

Moscou /mos'ku/, Port **Moscovo** /moʃ'kovu/ f Moscow

mosquito /mos'kitu/ m mosquito

mostarda /mos'tarda/ f mustard

mosteiro /mos'teru/ m monastery

mos|tra /'mɔstra/ f display; **dar ~tras de** show signs of; **pôr à ~tra** show up. **~trador** m face, dial. **~trar** vt show. **~trar-se** vpr (revelar-se) show o.s. to be; (exibir-se) show off. **~truário** m display case

mo|tel /mo'tɛw/ (pl **~téis**) m motel

motim /mo'tʃĩ/ m riot; (na marinha) mutiny

moti|vação /motʃiva'sãw/ f motivation. **~var** vt (incentivar) motivate; (provocar) cause. **~vo** m (razão) reason; (estímulo) motive; (na arte, música) motif; **dar ~vo de** give cause for

moto /'mɔtu/ f motorbike. **~ca** /mo'tɔka/ f 🔟 motorbike

motoci|cleta /motosi'klɛta/ f motorcycle. **~clismo** m motorcycling. **~clista** m/f motorcyclist

motoqueiro /moto'keru/ m 🔟 biker

motor /mo'tor/ m (de carro, avião etc) engine; (elétrico) motor ● a (f **motriz**) ‹força› driving; Anat motor; **~ de arranque** starter motor; **~ de popa** outboard motor

moto|rista /moto'rista/ m/f driver. **~rizado** a motorized. **~rizar** vt motorize

mouse m Comput mouse

mousepad m Comput mousemat

movedi|ço /move'dʒisu/ a unstable, moving; **areia ~ça** quicksand

mó|vel /'mɔvew/ (pl **~veis**) a ‹peça, parte› moving; ‹tropas› mobile; ‹festa› movable ● m piece of furniture; pl furniture

mo|ver /mo'ver/ vt move; (impulsionar) fig drive. **~ver-se** vpr move. **~vido** a driven; **~vido a álcool** alcohol-powered

movimen|tação /movimẽta'sãw/ f bustle. **~tado** a ‹rua, loja› busy; ‹música› upbeat, lively; ‹pessoa, sessão› lively. **~tar** vt liven up. **~tar-se** vpr move. **~to** m movement; Tecn motion; (na rua etc) activity

MP3 m MP3 player

muam|ba /mu'ãba/ f contraband. **~beiro** m smuggler

muco /'muku/ m mucus

muçulmano /musuw'manu/ a & m Muslim

mu|da /'muda/ f (planta) seedling; **~da de roupa** change of clothes. **~dança** f (mudar) move; (de carro) transmission. **~dar** vt/i change; **~dar de assunto** change the subject; **~dar (de casa)** move (house); **~dar de cor** change colour; **~dar de ideia** change one's mind; **~dar de lugar** change places; **~dar de roupa** change (clothes). **~dar-se** vpr move

mu|dez /mu'des/ f silence. **~do** a silent; (deficiente) dumb; ‹telefone› dead ● m mute

mu|gido /mu'ʒidu/ m moo. **~gir** vi moo

muito /'mũitu/ a a lot of; pl many ● pron a lot ● adv (com adjetivo, advérbio) very; (com verbo) a lot; **~ maior** much bigger; **~ tempo** a long time

mula /'mula/ f mule

mulato /mu'latu/ a & m mulatto

muleta /mu'leta/ f crutch

mulher /mu'ʎer/ f woman; (esposa) wife

mulherengo /muʎe'rẽgu/ a womanizing ● m womanizer, ladies' man

mul|ta /'muwta/ f fine. **~tar** vt fine

multicolor /muwtʃiko'lor/ a multicoloured

multidão /muwtʃi'dãw/ f crowd

multinacio|nal /muwtʃinasio'naw/ (pl **~nais**) a & f multinational

multipli|cação /muwtʃiplika'sãw/ f multiplication. **~car** vt multiply. **~car-se** vpr multiply. **~cidade** f multiplicity

múltiplo /'muwtʃiplu/ a & m multiple

multirraci|al /muwtʃixasi'aw/ (pl **~ais**) a multiracial

múmia /'mumia/ f mummy

mun|dano /mũ'danu/ a ‹prazeres etc› worldly; ‹vida, mulher› society. **~dial** (pl **~diais**) a world ● m world championship. **~do** m world; **todo (o) ~do** everybody

munição /muni'sãw/ f ammunition

muni|cipal /munisi'paw/ (pl **~cipais**) a municipal. **~cípio** m (lugar) borough, community; (prédio) town hall; (autoridade) local authority

munir /mu'nir/ vt provide (**de** with). **~se** vpr equip o.s. (**de** with)

mu|ral /mu'raw/ (pl **~rais**) a & m mural. **~ralha** f wall

mur|char /mur'ʃar/ vi ‹planta› wither, wilt; ‹salada› go limp; ‹beleza› fade ● vt wither, wilt ‹planta›. **~cho** a ‹planta› wilting; ‹pessoa› broken

mur|murar /murmu'rar/ vi murmur; (queixar-se) mutter ● vt murmur. **~múrio** m murmur

muro /'muru/ m wall

murro /'muxu/ m punch

musa /'muza/ f muse

muscu|lação /muskula'sãw/ f weight training. **~lar** a muscular. **~latura** f musculature

músculo /'muskulu/ m muscle

musculoso /musku'lozu/ a muscular

museu /mu'zew/ m museum

musgo /'muzgu/ m moss

música /'muzika/ f music; (uma) song; **~ de câmara** chamber music; **~ de fundo** background music; **~ clássica** ou **erudita** classical music

musi|cal /muzi'kaw/ (pl **~cais**) a & m musical. **~car** vt set to music

músico /'muziku/ m musician ● a musical

musse /'musi/ f mousse

mutilar /mutʃi'lar/ vt mutilate; maim <pessoa>

mutirão /mutʃi'rãw/ m joint effort

mútuo /'mutuu/ a mutual

muxoxo /mu'ʃoʃu/ m **fazer ~** tut

....

m Nn
n

....

na = em + a

nabo /'nabu/ m turnip

nação /na'sãw/ f nation

nacio|nal /nasio'naw/ (pl **~nais**) a national; (brasileiro) home-produced. **~nalidade** f nationality. **~nalismo** m nationalism. **~nalista** a & m/f nationalist. **~nalizar** vt nationalize

naco /'naku/ m chunk

nada /'nada/ pron nothing ● adv not at all; **de ~** (não há de quê) don't mention it; **que ~!, ~ disso** no way!

na|dadeira /nada'dera/ f (de peixe) fin; (de mergulhador) flipper. **~dador** m swimmer. **~dar** vi swim

nadador-salvador /nada'dorsawva'dor/ m (pl **nadadores-salvadores**) Port lifeguard

nádegas /'nadegas/ f pl buttocks

nado /'nadu/ m **~ borboleta** butterfly stroke; **~ de costas** backstroke; **~ de peito** breaststroke; **atravessar a ~** swim across

náilon /'najlõ/ m nylon

naipe /'najpi/ m (em jogo de cartas) suit

namo|rada /namo'rada/ f girlfriend. **~rado** m boyfriend. **~rador** a amorous ● m ladies' man. **~rar** vt (ter relação com) go out with; (cobiçar) eye up ● vi <casal> (ter relação) go out together; (beijar-se etc) kiss and cuddle; <homem> have a girlfriend; <mulher> have a boyfriend. **~ro** /o/ m relationship

nanar /na'nar/ vi (col) sleep

nanico /na'niku/ a tiny

nanotecnologia /nãnoteknolo'ʒia/ f nanotechnology

não /nãw/ adv not; (resposta) no ● m no. **~ alinhado** a non-aligned; **~ conformista** a & m/f nonconformist

naquela, naquele, naquilo = em + aquela, aquele, aquilo

narci|sismo /narsi'zizmu/ m narcissism. **~sista** a & m/f narcissist ● a narcissistic. **~so** m narcissus

narcótico /nar'kɔtʃiku/ a & m narcotic

narcotraficante /narkotrafi'kãntʃi/ m/f drug dealer

narcotráfico /narko'trafiku/ m drug trafficking

nari|gudo /nari'gudu/ a with a big nose; **ser ~gudo** have a big nose. **~na** f nostril

nariz /na'ris/ m nose

nar|ração /naxa'sãw/ f narration. **~rador** m narrator. **~rar** vt narrate. **~rativa** f narrative. **~rativo** a narrative

nas = em + as

na|sal /na'zaw/ (pl **~sais**) a nasal. **~salizar** vt nasalize

nas|cença /na'sẽsa/ f birth. **~cente** a nascent ● f source. **~cer** vi be born; <dente, espinha> come through; <planta> sprout; <sol, lua> rise; <dia> dawn; fig <empresa, projeto etc> come into being ● m **o ~cer do sol** sunrise. **~cimento** m birth

nata /'nata/ f cream

natação /nata'sãw/ f swimming

na|tal /na'taw/ (pl **~tais**) a <país, terra> native

Natal /na'taw/ m Christmas

nata|lício /nata'lisiu/ a & m birthday. **~lidade** f **índice de ~lidade** birth rate. **~lino** a Christmas

nati|vidade /natʃivi'dadʒi/ f nativity. **~vo** a & m native

nato /'natu/ a born

natu|ral /natu'raw/ (pl **~rais**) a natural; (oriundo) originating (de from) ● m native (de of)

natura|lidade /naturali'dadʒi/ f naturalness; **com ~lidade** matter-of-factly; **de ~lidade carioca** born in Rio de Janeiro. **~lismo** m naturalism. **~lista** a & m/f naturalist. **~lizar** vt naturalize. **~lizar-se** vpr become naturalized

natureza /natu'reza/ f nature; **~ morta** still life

naturis|mo /natu'rizmu/ m naturism. **~ta** m/f naturist

nau|fragar /nawfra'gar/ vi ‹navio› be wrecked; ‹tripulação› be shipwrecked; fig ‹plano, casamento etc› founder. **~frágio** m shipwreck; fig failure

náufrago /'nawfragu/ m castaway

náusea /'nawzia/ f nausea

nauseabundo /nawzia'bũdu/ a nauseating

náuti|ca /'nawtʃika/ f navigation. **~co** a nautical

na|val /na'vaw/ (pl **~vais**) a naval; **construção ~val** shipbuilding

navalha /na'vaʎa/ f razor. **~da** f cut with a razor

nave /'navi/ f nave; **~ espacial** spaceship

nave|gação /navega'sãw/ f navigation; (tráfego) shipping. **~gador** m navigator; Comput browser. **~gante** m/f seafarer. **~gar** vt navigate; sail ‹mar› ● vi sail; (traçar o rumo) navigate. **~gável** (pl **~gáveis**) a navigable

navio /na'viu/ m ship; **~ cargueiro** cargo ship; **~ de guerra** warship; **~ petroleiro** oil tanker

nazista /na'zista/, Port **nazi** /na'zi/ a & m/f Nazi

neblina /ne'blina/ f mist

nebulo|sa /nebu'lɔza/ f nebula. **~sidade** f cloud. **~so** /o/ a cloudy; fig obscure

neces|saire /nese'ser/ m toilet bag. **~sário** a necessary. **~sidade** f necessity; (que se impõe) need; (pobreza) need. **~sitado** a needy ● m person in need. **~sitar** vt require; (tornar necessário) necessitate; **~sitar de** need

necro|lógio /nekro'lɔʒiu/ m obituary column. **~tério** m mortuary, Amer morgue

nectarina /nekta'rina/ f nectarine

nefasto /ne'fastu/ a fatal

ne|gação /nega'sãw/ f denial; Ling negation; **ser uma ~gação em** be hopeless at; **~gar** vt deny; **~gar-se a** refuse to. **~gativa** f refusal; Ling negative. **~gativo** a & m negative

negli|gência /negli'ʒẽsia/ f negligence. **~genciar** vt neglect. **~gente** a negligent

negoci|ação /negosia'sãw/ f negotiation. **~ador** m negotiator. **~ante** m/f dealer (**de** in). **~ar** vt/i negotiate; **~ar em** deal in. **~ata** f shady deal. **~ável** (pl **~áveis**) a negotiable

negócio /ne'gɔsiu/ m deal; 🔢 (coisa) thing; pl business; **a** ou **de ~s** on business

negocista /nego'sista/ m wheeler-dealer ● a wheeler-dealing

ne|grito /ne'gritu/ m bold. **~gro** /e/ a & m black; (de raça) Negro

nela, **nele** = **em** + **ela**, **ele**

nem /nẽj/ adv not even ● conj ~ ... ~ ... neither ... nor ...; ~ **sempre** not always; ~ **todos** not all; ~ **que** not even if; **que** ~ like; ~ **eu** nor do I

nenê /ne'ne/, **neném** /ne'nẽj/ m baby

nenhum /ne'ɲũ/ a (f **nenhuma**) no ● pron (f **nenhuma**) not one; ~ **dos dois** neither of them; ~ **erro** no mistakes; **erro** ~ no mistakes at all, not a single mistake; ~ **lugar** nowhere

nenúfar /ne'nufar/ m water lily

neoconservador /neokõserva'dor/ a neoconservative

neologismo /neolo'ʒizmu/ m neologism

néon /'neõ/ m neon

neozelan|dês /neozelã'des/ a (f **~desa**) New Zealand ● m (f **~desa**) New Zealander

Nepal /ne'paw/ m Nepal

nervo /'nervu/ m nerve. **~sismo** m (chateação) annoyance; (medo) nervousness. **~so** /o/ a ‹sistema, doença› nervous; (chateado) annoyed; (medroso) nervous; **deixar alguém ~so** get on sb's nerves

nessa(s), **nesse(s)** = **em** + **essa(s)**, **esse(s)**

nesta(s), **neste(s)** = **em** + **esta(s)**, **este(s)**

ne|ta /'neta/ f granddaughter. **~to** /ɛ/ m grandson; pl grandchildren

neuro|logia /newrolo'ʒia/ f neurology. **~lógico** a neurological. **~logista** m/f neurologist

neu|rose /new'rɔzi/ f neurosis. **~rótico** a neurotic

neutrali|dade /newtrali'dadʒi/ f neutrality. **~zar** vt neutralize

neutrão /new'trãw/ m Port ▶ **NÊUTRON**

n

neutro /'newtru/ a neutral

nêutron /'newtrõ/ m neutron

ne|vada /ne'vada/ f snowfall. ~**vado** a snow-covered. ~**var** vi snow. ~**vasca** f snowstorm. ~**ve** /ɛ/ f snow

névoa /'nɛvoa/ f haze

nevoeiro /nevo'eru/ m fog

nexo /'neksu/ m connection; **sem ~** incoherent

Nicarágua /nika'ragwa/ f Nicaragua

nicaraguense /nikara'gwẽsi/ a & m/f Nicaraguan

nicho /'niʃu/ m niche

nicotina /niko'tʃina/ f nicotine

Níger /'niʒer/ m Niger

Nigéria /ni'ʒeria/ f Nigeria

nigeriano /niʒeri'anu/ a & m Nigerian

Nilo /'nilu/ m Nile

ninar /ni'nar/ vt lull to sleep

ninfa /'nĩfa/ f nymph

ninguém /nĩ'gẽj/ pron no one, nobody

ninhada /ni'nada/ f brood

ninharia /nina'ria/ f trifle

ninho /'ninu/ m nest

níquel /'nikew/ m nickel

nisei /ni'sej/ a & m/f Japanese Brazilian

nisso = em + isso

nisto = em + isto

nitidez /nitʃi'des/ f (de imagem etc) sharpness

nítido /'nitʃidu/ a ‹imagem, foto› sharp; ‹diferença, melhora› distinct, clear

nitrogênio /nitro'ʒeniu/ m nitrogen

ni|vel /'nivew/ (pl ~**veis**) m level; a ~**vel de** in terms of

nivelamento /nivela'mẽtu/ m levelling

nivelar /nive'lar/ vt level

no = em + o

nó /nɔ/ m knot; **dar um ~** tie a knot; ~ **dos dedos** knuckle; **um ~ na garganta** a lump in one's throat

nobre /'nɔbri/ a noble; ‹bairro› exclusive ● m/f noble. ~**za** /e/ f nobility

noção /no'sãw/ f notion; pl (rudimentos) elements

nocaute /no'kawtʃi/ m knockout; **pôr alguém ~** knock sb out. ~**ar** vt knock out

nocivo /no'sivu/ a harmful

nódoa /'nɔdoa/ f Port stain

nogueira /no'gera/ f (árvore) walnut tree

noi|tada /noj'tada/ f night. ~**te** f night; (antes de dormir) evening; **à ou de ~te** at night; (antes de dormir) in the evening; **hoje à ~te** tonight; **ontem à ~te** last night; **boa ~te** (ao chegar) good evening; (ao despedir-se) good night; ~**te em branco ou claro** sleepless night

noi|vado /noj'vadu/ m engagement. ~**va** f fiancée; (no casamento) bride. ~**vo** m fiancé; (no casamento) bridegroom; **os ~vos** the engaged couple; (no casamento) the bride and groom; **ficar ~vo** get engaged

no|jento /no'ʒẽtu/ a disgusting. ~**jo** /o/ m disgust

nômade /'nomadʒi/ m/f nomad ● a nomadic

nome /'nomi/ m name; **de ~** by name; **em ~ de** in the name of; ~ **comercial** trade name; ~ **de batismo** Christian name; ~ **de guerra** professional name

nome|ação /nomia'sãw/ f appointment. ~**ar** vt (para cargo) appoint; (chamar pelo nome) name

nomi|nal /nomi'naw/ (pl ~**nais**) a nominal

nonagésimo /nona'ʒezimu/ a ninetieth

nono /'nonu/ a & m ninth

nora /'nɔra/ f daughter-in-law

nordes|te /nor'dɛstʃi/ m north-east. ~**tino** a north-eastern ● m person from the north-east (of Brazil)

nórdico /'nɔrdʒiku/ a Nordic

nor|ma /'nɔrma/ f norm. ~**mal** (pl ~**mais**) a normal

normali|dade /normali'dadʒi/ f normality. ~**zar** vt bring back to normal; normalize ‹relações diplomáticas›. ~**zar-se** vpr return to normal

noroeste /noro'ɛstʃi/ a & m north-west

norte /'nɔrtʃi/ a & m north. ~**africano** a & m North African; ~**americano** a & m North American; ~**coreano** a & m North Korean

nortista /nor'tʃista/ a Northern ● m/f Northerner

Noruega /noru'ɛga/ f Norway

norue|guês /norue'ges/ a & m (f ~**guesa**) Norwegian

nos[1] = em + os

nos[2] /nus/ pron us; (indireto) (to) us; (reflexivo) ourselves

nós /nɔs/ pron we; (depois de preposição) us

nos|sa /'nɔsa/ int gosh. **~so** /ɔ/ a our
● *pron* ours

nos|talgia /nostaw'ʒia/ f nostalgia.
~tálgico a nostalgic

nota /'nɔta/ f note; (*na escola etc*) mark;
(*conta*) bill; **custar uma ~ (preta)** 🔲
cost a bomb; **tomar ~** take note (**de** of);
~ fiscal receipt

no|tação /nota'sãw/ f notation. **~tar**
vt notice, note; **fazer ~tar** point out.
~tável (*pl* **~táveis**) a & m/f notable

notícia /no'tʃisia/ f piece of news; *pl*
news

notici|ar /notʃi'sjar/ vt report. **~ário**
m (*na TV*) news; (*em jornal*) news
section. **~arista** m/f (*na TV*) newsreader;
(*em jornal*) news reporter. **~oso** /o/ a
agência ~osa news agency

notifi|cação /notʃifika'sãw/ f
notification. **~car** vt notify

notívago /no'tʃivagu/ a nocturnal ● m
night person

notório /no'tɔriu/ a well-known

noturno /no'turnu/ a night; (*animal*)
nocturnal

nova /'nɔva/ f piece of news. **~mente**
adv again

novato /no'vatu/ m novice

nove /'nɔvi/ a & m nine. **~centos** a & m
nine hundred

novela /no'vɛla/ f (*na TV*) soap opera;
(*livro*) novella

novembro /no'vẽbru/ m November

noventa /no'vẽta/ a & m ninety

noviço /no'visu/ m novice

novidade /novi'dadʒi/ f novelty;
(*notícia*) piece of news; *pl* (*notícias*) news

novilho /no'viʎu/ m calf

novo /'novu/ a new; (*jovem*) young; **de
~** again; **~ em folha** brand new

noz /nɔs/ f walnut; **~ moscada** nutmeg

nu /nu/ a (f **~a**) (*corpo, pessoa*) naked;
(*braço, parede, quarto*) bare ● m nude;
~ em pelo stark naked; **a verdade ~a e
crua** the plain truth

nuança /nu'ãsa/ f nuance

nu|blado /nu'bladu/ a cloudy. **~blar** vt
cloud. **~blar-se** vpr cloud over

nuca /'nuka/ f nape of the neck

nuclear /nukli'ar/ a nuclear

núcleo /'nukliu/ m nucleus

nu|dez /nu'des/ f nakedness; (*na TV
etc*) nudity; (*da parede etc*) bareness.
~dismo m nudism. **~dista** m/f nudist

nulo /'nulu/ a void

num, numa(s) = em + um, uma(s)

nume|ral /nume'raw/ (*pl* **~rais**) a & m
numeral. **~rar** vt number

numérico /nu'mɛriku/ a numerical

número /'numeru/ m number; (*de
jornal, revista*) issue; (*de sapatos*) size;
(*espetáculo*) act; **fazer ~** make up the
numbers

numeroso /nume'rozu/ a numerous

nunca /'nũka/ adv never; **~ mais** never
again

nuns = em + uns

nupci|al /nupsi'aw/ (*pl* **~ais**) a bridal

núpcias /'nupsias/ f pl marriage

nu|trição /nutri'sãw/ f nutrition. **~trir**
vt nourish; *fig* harbour (*ódio, esperança*).
~tritivo a nourishing; (*valor*) nutritional

nuvem /'nuvẽ/ f cloud

....

Oo

....

o /u/ ● *artigo*

••••➤ the; **~ trem** the train; **~ vizinho
ao lado** the next-door neighbour;
~ João está em casa João is at home

❗ O artigo é omitido em inglês com
nomes próprios, ou com parentes:
o vovô já chegou granddad has
arrived; **onde está o Carlos?** where's
Carlos?

••••➤ (*com partes do corpo, roupa*)
lavei ~ cabelo I washed my hair;
~ sapato está desamarrado your
shoe is undone

❗ Em português, utiliza-se em geral
o artigo para se referir a partes do
corpo, enquanto no inglês usa-se o
pronome possessivo.

••••➤ (*com adjetivo*) **~ interessante...**
what's interesting...; **~ difícil é...** the
difficult thing is...

••••➤ (*com substantivo abstrato*)
~ amor love; **~ sucesso** success;
~ conhecimento knowledge

••••➤ (*com substantivo usado em
sentido geral*) **na prisão** in jail; **no
hospital** in hospital

❗ Observe que o artigo não é
traduzido com substantivos
abstratos ou substantivos usados em
sentido geral: **ele está no hospital**
he's in hospital.

n

o

● *pron*

••••≫ (*ele*) him; **eu ~ vi no sábado à tarde** I saw him on Saturday afternoon

••••≫ (*coisa*) it; **onde é que você ~ guarda** where do you keep it?

••••≫ (*você*) you; **eu ~ avisei?** I told you so!

••••≫ **~ de** (*com características, procedência*) the one with/from; **~ de barba** the one with the beard; **~ do Rio** the one from Rio; **~ que** (*pessoa*) the one; **~ que eu vi era mais alto** the one I saw was taller; (*quem quer que*) whoever; **~ que chegar primeiro faz o café** whoever gets there first has to make the coffee; **~ que** (*como*) what; **nem imagina ~ que foi aquilo** you can't imagine what it was like; **~ que** (*referindo-se a toda a frase anterior*) which; **ele disse que era professor, ~ que não é verdade** he said he was a teacher, which isn't true

ó /ɔ/ *int* 🔢 look

ô /o/ *int* oh

oásis /oˈazis/ *m invar* oasis

oba /ˈoba/ *int* great

obcecar /obiseˈkar/ *vt* obsess

obe|decer /obedeˈser/ *vt* **~decer a** obey. **~diência** *f* obedience. **~diente** *a* obedient

obe|sidade /obeziˈdadʒi/ *f* obesity. **~so** /e/ *a* obese

óbito /ˈɔbitu/ *m* death

obituário /obituˈariu/ *m* obituary

obje|ção /obiʒeˈsãw/ *f* objection. **~tar** *vt/i* object (**a to**)

objeti|va /obiʒeˈtʃiva/ *f* lens. **~vidade** *f* objectivity. **~vo** *a* & *m* objective

objeto /obiˈʒɛtu/ *m* object

objetor /obʒeˈtor/ *m* objector; **~ de consciência** conscientious objector

oblíquo /oˈblikwu/ *a* oblique; ‹*olhar*› sidelong

obliterar /obliteˈrar/ *vt* obliterate

oblongo /oˈblõgu/ *a* oblong

obo|é /oboˈɛ/ *m* oboe. **~ista** *m/f* oboist

obra /ˈɔbra/ *f* work; **em ~s** being renovated; **~ de arte** work of art; **~ de caridade** charity. **~prima** (*pl* **~s-primas**) *f* masterpiece

obri|gação /obrigaˈsãw/ *f* obligation; (*título*) bond. **~gado** *int* thank you; (*não querendo*) no thank you. **~gar** *vt* force,

oblige (**a to**). **~gar-se** *vpr* undertake (**a to**). **~gatório** *a* obligatory, compulsory

obsce|nidade /obiseniˈdadʒi/ *f* obscenity. **~no** /e/ *a* obscene

obscu|ridade /obiskuriˈdadʒi/ *f* obscurity. **~ro** *a* obscure

obséquio /obiˈsekiu/ *m* favour

obsequioso /obisekiˈozu/ *a* obsequious

obser|vação /obiservaˈsãw/ *f* observation. **~vador** *a* observant ● *m* observer. **~vância** *f* observance. **~var** *vt* observe. **~vatório** *m* observatory

obses|são /obiseˈsãw/ *f* obsession. **~sivo** *a* obsessive

obsoleto /obisoˈletu/ *a* obsolete

obstáculo /obisˈtakulu/ *m* obstacle

obstar /obisˈtar/ *vt* stand in the way (**a of**)

obs|tetra /obisˈtɛtra/ *m/f* obstetrician. **~tetrícia** *f* obstetrics. **~tétrico** *a* obstetric

obsti|nação /obistinaˈsãw/ *f* obstinacy. **~nado** *a* obstinate. **~nar-se** *vpr* insist (**em on**)

obstru|ção /obistruˈsãw/ *f* obstruction. **~ir** *vt* obstruct

ob|tenção /obitẽˈsãw/ *f* obtaining. **~ter** *vt* obtain

obtu|ração /obituraˈsãw/ *f* filling. **~rador** *m* shutter. **~rar** *vt* fill ‹*dente*›

obtuso /obiˈtuzu/ *a* obtuse

óbvio /ˈɔbviu/ *a* obvious

ocasi|ão /okaziˈãw/ *f* occasion; (*oportunidade*) opportunity; (*compra*) bargain. **~onal** (*pl* **~onais**) *a* chance. **~onar** *vt* cause

Oceania /osiaˈnia/ *f* Oceania

oce|ânico /osiˈaniku/ *a* ocean. **~ano** *m* ocean

ociden|tal /osidẽˈtaw/ (*pl* **~tais**) *a* western ● *m/f* Westerner. **~te** *m* West

ócio /ˈɔsiu/ *m* (*lazer*) leisure; (*falta de trabalho*) idleness

ocioso /osiˈozu/ *a* idle ● *m* idler

oco /ˈoku/ *a* hollow; ‹*cabeça*› empty

ocor|rência /okoˈxẽsia/ *f* occurrence. **~rer** *vi* occur (**a to**)

ocu|lar /okuˈlar/ *a* **testemunha ~lar** eye witness. **~lista** *m/f* optician

óculos /ˈɔkulus/ *m pl* glasses; **~ de sol** sunglasses

ocul|tar /okuwˈtar/ *vt* conceal. **~to** *a* hidden; (*sobrenatural*) occult

ocu|pação /okupa'sãw/ *f* occupation. **~pado** *a* ‹*pessoa*› busy; ‹*cadeira*› taken; ‹*telefone*› engaged, *Amer* busy. **~par** *vt* occupy; take up ‹*tempo, espaço*›; hold ‹*cargo*›. **~par-se** *vpr* keep busy; **~par-se com** *ou* **de** be involved with ‹*política, literatura etc*›; take care of ‹*cliente, doente, problema*›; occupy one's time with ‹*leitura, palavras cruzadas etc*›

ocupacional /okupasio'naw/ *a* occupational; **terapia ~** occupational therapy

odiar /odʒi'ar/ *vt* hate

ódio /'ɔdʒiu/ *m* hatred, hate; (*raiva*) anger

odioso /odʒi'ozu/ *a* hateful

odontologia /odõtolo'ʒia/ *f* dentistry

odor /o'dor/ *m* odour

oeste /o'ɛstʃi/ *a & m* west

ofe|gante /ofe'gãtʃi/ *a* panting. **~gar** *vi* pant

ofen|der /ofẽ'der/ *vt* offend. **~der-se** *vpr* take offence. **~sa** *f* insult. **~siva** *f* offensive. **~sivo** *a* offensive

ofere|cer /ofere'ser/ *vt* offer. **~cer-se** *vpr* ‹*pessoa*› offer o.s. (**como** as); ‹*ocasião*› arise; **~cer-se para ajudar** offer to help. **~cimento** *m* offer

oferenda /ofe'rẽda/ *f* offering

oferta /o'fɛrta/ *f* offer; **em ~** on offer; **a ~ e a demanda** supply and demand

offline /ɔf'lajni/ *a & adv* Comput offline

ofici|al /ofisi'aw/ (*pl* **~ais**) *a* official ● *m* officer. **~alizar** *vt* make official. **~ar** *vi* officiate

oficina /ofi'sina/ *f* workshop; (*para carros*) garage, *Amer* shop

ofício /o'fisiu/ *m* (*profissão*) trade; (*na igreja*) service

oficioso /ofisi'ozu/ *a* unofficial

ofus|cante /ofus'kãtʃi/ *a* dazzling. **~car** *vt* dazzle ‹*pessoa*›; obscure ‹*sol etc*›; *fig* (*eclipsar*) outshine

OGM /oʒe'em/ *m* Biol GMO

oi /oj/ *int* (*cumprimento*) hi; (*resposta*) yes?

oi|tavo /oi'tavu/ *a & m* eighth. **~tenta** *a & m* eighty. **~to** *a & m* eight. **~tocentos** *a & m* eight hundred

olá /o'la/ *int* hello

olaria /ola'ria/ *f* pottery

óleo /'ɔliu/ *m* oil

oleo|duto /oliu'dutu/ *m* oil pipeline. **~so** /o/ *a* oily

olfato /ow'fatu/ *m* sense of smell

olhada /o'ʎada/ *f* look; **dar uma ~** have a look

olhar /o'ʎar/ *vt* look at; (*assistir*) watch ● *vi* look ● *m* look; **~ para** look at; **~ por** look after; **e olhe lá** 🄸 and that's pushing it

olheiras /o'ʎeras/ *f pl* dark rings under one's eyes

olho /'oʎu/ *m* eye; **a ~ nu** with the naked eye; **custar os ~s da cara** cost a fortune; **ficar de ~** keep an eye out; **ficar de ~ em** keep an eye on; **pôr alguém no ~ da rua** throw sb out; **não pregar o ~** not sleep a wink; **~ gordo** *ou* **grande** envy; **~ mágico** peephole; **~ roxo** black eye

Olimpíada /olĩ'piada/ *f* Olympic Games

olímpico /o'lĩpiku/ *a* ‹*jogos, vila*› Olympic; *fig* blithe

oliveira /oli'vera/ *f* olive tree

olmo /'owmu/ *m* elm

om|breira /õ'brera/ *f* (*para roupa*) shoulder pad; **~bro** *m* shoulder; **dar de ~bros** shrug one's shoulders

omelete /ome'letʃi/, *Port* **omeleta** /ome'leta/ *f* omelette

omis|são /omi'sãw/ *f* omission. **~so** *a* negligent, remiss

omitir /omi'tʃir/ *vt* omit

omni- *Port* ▶ **oni-**

omoplata /omo'plata/ *f* shoulder blade

onça¹ /'õsa/ *f* (*peso*) ounce

onça² /'õsa/ *f* (*animal*) jaguar

onda /'õda/ *f* wave. **pegar ~** 🄸 surf

onde /'õdʒi/ *adv* where; **por ~?** which way?; **~ quer que** wherever

ondu|lação /õdula'sãw/ *f* undulation; (*do cabelo*) wave. **~lado** *a* wavy. **~lante** *a* undulating. **~lar** *vt* wave ‹*cabelo*› ● *vi* undulate

onerar /one'rar/ *vt* burden

ONG /'ɔgi/ *abr f* (= **Organização Não Governamental**) NGO

ônibus /'onibus/ *m invar* bus; **~ espacial** space shuttle

onipotente /onipo'tẽtʃi/ *a* omnipotent

onírico /o'niriku/ *a* dreamlike

onisciente /onisi'ẽtʃi/ *a* omniscient

online /õ'lajni/ *a & adv* Comput online

onomatopeia /onomato'peja/ *f* onomatopoeia

ontem /'õtẽ/ *adv* yesterday

o

onze /'õzi/ a & m eleven

opaco /o'paku/ a opaque

opala /o'pala/ f opal

opção /opi'sãw/ f option

ópera /'ɔpera/ f opera

ope|ração /opera'sãw/ f operation; (bancária etc) transaction. **~rador** m operator. **~rar** vt operate; operate on ‹doente›; work ‹milagre› ● vi operate. **~rar-se** vpr (acontecer) come about; (fazer operação) have an operation. **~rário** a working ● m worker

opereta /ope'reta/ f operetta

opinar /opi'nar/ vt think ● vi express one's opinion

opinião /opini'ãw/ f opinion; **na minha ~** in my opinion; **~ pública** public opinion

ópio /'ɔpiu/ m opium

opor /o'por/ vt put up ‹resistência, argumento›; (pôr em contraste) contrast (a with); **~se** a (não aprovar) oppose; (ser diferente) contrast with

oportu|nidade /oportuni'dadʒi/ f opportunity. **~nista** a & m/f opportunist. **~no** a opportune

oposi|ção /opozi'sãw/ f opposition (a to). **~cionista** a opposition ● m/f opposition politician

oposto /o'postu/ a & m opposite

opres|são /opre'sãw/ f oppression; (no peito) tightness. **~sivo** a oppressive. **~sor** m oppressor

oprimir /opri'mir/ vt oppress; (com trabalho) weigh down ● vi be oppressive

optar /opi'tar/ vi opt (por for); **~ por ir** opt to go

óptica, óptico ▶ ÓTICA, ÓTICO

opu|lência /opu'lẽsia/ f opulence. **~lento** a opulent

ora /'ɔra/ adv & conj now ● int come; **~ essa!** come now! **~ ..., ~ ...** first ..., then...

oração /ora'sãw/ f (prece) prayer; (discurso) oration; (frase) clause

oráculo /o'rakulu/ m oracle

orador /ora'dor/ m orator

oral /o'raw/ a (pl **orais**) a & f oral

orar /o'rar/ vi pray

órbita /'ɔrbita/ f orbit; (do olho) socket

orçamen|tário /orsamẽ'tariu/ a budgetary. **~to** m (plano financeiro) budget; (previsão dos custos) estimate

orçar /or'sar/ vt estimate (**em** at)

ordeiro /or'deru/ a orderly

ordem /'ɔrdẽ/ f order; **por ~ alfabética** in alphabetical order; **~ de pagamento** banker's draft; **~ do dia** agenda

orde|nação /ordena'sãw/ f ordering; (de padre) ordination. **~nado** a ordered ● m wages. **~nar** vt order; put in order ‹papéis, livros etc›; ordain ‹padre›

ordenhar /orde'nar/ vt milk

ordinário /ordʒi'nariu/ a (normal) ordinary; (grosseiro) vulgar; (de má qualidade) inferior; (sem caráter) rough

ore|lha /o'reʎa/ f ear. **~lhão** m phone booth. **~lhudo** a with big ears; **ser ~lhudo** have big ears

orfanato /orfa'natu/ m orphanage

ór|fão /'ɔrfãw/ (pl **~fãos**) a & m (f **~fã**) orphan

orgânico /or'ganiku/ a organic

orga|nismo /orga'nizmu/ m organism; (do Estado etc) institution; **~ geneticamente modificado** GMO. **~nista** m/f organist

organi|zação /organiza'sãw/ f organization. **~zador** a organizing ● m organizer. **~zar** vt organize

órgão /'ɔrgãw/ (pl **~s**) m organ; (do Estado etc) body

orgasmo /or'gazmu/ m orgasm

orgia /or'ʒia/ f orgy

orgu|lhar /orgu'ʎar/ vt make proud. **~lhar-se** vpr be proud (**de** of). **~lho** m pride. **~lhoso** /o/ a proud

orien|tação /oriẽta'sãw/ f orientation; (direção) direction; (vocacional etc) guidance. **~tador** m advisor. **~tal** (pl **~tais**) a eastern; (da Asia) oriental. **~tar** vt direct; (aconselhar) advise; (situar) position. **~tar-se** vpr get one's bearings; **~tar-se por** be guided by. **~te** m east; **Oriente Médio** Middle East; **Extremo Oriente** Far East

orifício /ori'fisiu/ m opening; (no corpo) orifice

origem /o'riʒẽ/ f origin; **dar ~ a** give rise to; **ter ~** originate

origi|nal /oriʒi'naw/ (pl **~nais**) a & m original. **~nalidade** f originality. **~nar** vt give rise to. **~nar-se** vpr originate. **~nário** a ‹planta, animal› native (**de** to); ‹pessoa› originating (**de** from)

oriundo /o'rjũdu/ a originating (**de** from)

orla /'ɔrla/ f border; **~ marítima** seafront

ornamen|tação /ornamẽta'sãw/ f ornamentation. **~tal** (pl **~tais**) a ornamental. **~tar** vt decorate. **~to** m ornament

orques|tra /or'kɛstra/ f orchestra. **~tra sinfônica** symphony orchestra. **~tral** (pl **~trais**) a orchestral. **~trar** vt orchestrate

orquídea /or'kidʒia/ f orchid

ortodoxo /orto'dɔksu/ a orthodox

orto|grafia /ortogra'fia/ f spelling, orthography. **~gráfico** a orthographic

orto|pedia /ortope'dʒia/ f orthopaedics. **~pédico** a orthopaedic. **~pedista** m/f orthopaedic surgeon

orvalho /or'vaʎu/ m dew

---

os /us/, **as** /as/ ● artigo

····▷ the; **os livros que comprei ontem** the books I bought yesterday

● pron

····▷ them; **eu os/as vi no cinema** I saw them at the cinema; **os/as de** (características, procedência) the ones with/from; **os de branco** the ones in white; **as de Salvador** the ones from Salvador; **os da minha avó** my grandmother's ▶ o

---

oscilar /osi'lar/ vi oscillate

ósseo /'ɔsiu/ a bone

os|so /'osu/ m bone. **~sudo** a bony

ostensivo /ostẽ'sivu/ a ostensible

osten|tação /ostẽta'sãw/ f ostentation. **~tar** vt show off. **~toso** a showy, ostentatious

osteopata /ostʃio'pata/ m/f osteopath

ostra /'ostra/ f oyster

ostracismo /ostra'sizmu/ m ostracism

otário /o'tariu/ m 🆇 fool

óti|ca /'ɔtʃika/ f (ciência) optics; (loja) optician's; (ponto de vista) viewpoint. **~co** a optical

otimis|mo /otʃi'mizmu/ m optimism. **~ta** m/f optimist ● a optimistic

otimizar /otʃimi'zar/ vt optimize

ótimo /'ɔtʃimu/ a excellent

otorrino /oto'xinu/ m ear, nose and throat specialist

ou /o/ conj or; **~ ... ~ ...** either ... or ...; **~ seja** in other words

ouriço /o'risu/ m hedgehog. **~-do-mar** (pl **~s-do-mar**) m sea urchin

ouri|ves /o'rivis/ m/f invar jeweller. **~vesaria** f (loja) jeweller's

ouro /'oru/ m gold; pl (naipe) diamonds; **de ~** golden

ou|sadia /oza'dʒia/ f daring; (uma) daring step. **~sado** a daring. **~sar** vt/i dare

outdoor /'awtdor/ (pl **~s**) m billboard

outo|nal /oto'naw/ (pl **~nais**) a autumnal. **~no** /o/ m autumn, Amer fall

outorgar /otor'gar/ vt grant

ou|trem /o'trẽj/ pron (outro) someone else; (outros) others. **~tro** a other ● pron (um) another (one); pl others; **~tra coisa** something else; **~tro dia** the other day; **no ~tro dia** the next day; **~tra vez** again. **~tro copo** another glass. **~trora** adv once upon a time. **~trossim** adv equally

outubro /o'tubru/ m October

ou|vido /o'vidu/ m ear; **de ~vido** by ear; **dar ~vidos a** listen to. **~vinte** m/f listener. **~vir** vt hear; (atentamente) listen to ● vi hear; **~vir dizer que** hear that; **~vir falar de** hear of

ovação /ova'sãw/ f ovation

oval /o'vaw/ (pl **ovais**) a & f oval

ovário /o'variu/ m ovary

ovelha /o'veʎa/ f sheep

overdose /over'dɔzi/ f overdose

óvni /'ɔvni/ m UFO

ovo /'ovu/ m egg; **~ cozido/frito/ mexido/poché** boiled/fried/scrambled/ poached egg

oxi|genar /oksiʒe'nar/ vt bleach ‹cabelo›. **~gênio** m oxygen

ozônio /o'zoniu/ m ozone; **camada de ~** ozone layer

ozono /o'zonu/ m Port ▶ ozônio /o'zonju/

....

Pp

....

pá /pa/ f spade; (de hélice) blade; (de moinho) sail ● m Port 🆇 mate

pacato /pa'katu/ a quiet

pachorra /pa'ʃoxa/ f Port 🆇 patience; **não tenho ~** I can't be bothered

paci|ência /pasi'ẽsia/ f patience. **~ente** a & m/f patient

pacificar /pasifi'kar/ vt pacify

pacífico /pa'sifiku/ a peaceful; **Oceano Pacífico** Pacific Ocean; **ponto ~** undisputed point

pacifis|mo /pasi'fizmu/ m pacifism. **~ta** a & m/f pacifist

o

p

paço /ˈpasu/ m palace

pacote /paˈkɔtʃi/ m (de biscoitos etc) packet; (mandado pelo correio) parcel; (econômico, turístico, software) package

pacto /ˈpaktu/ m pact

pactuar /paktuˈar/ vi ~ com collude with

padaria /padaˈria/ f baker's (shop), bakery

padecer /padeˈser/ vt/i suffer

padeiro /paˈderu/ m baker

padiola /padʒiˈɔla/ f stretcher

padrão /paˈdrãw/ m standard; (desenho) pattern

padrasto /paˈdrastu/ m stepfather

padre /ˈpadri/ m priest

padrinho /paˈdriɲu/ m (de batismo) godfather; (de casamento) best man

padroeiro /padroˈeru/ m patron saint

padronizar /padroniˈzar/ vt standardize

paga /ˈpaga/ f pay. ~mento m payment

pa|gão /paˈgãw/ (pl ~gãos) a & m (f ~gã) pagan

pagar /paˈgar/ vt pay for ‹compra, erro etc›; pay ‹dívida, conta, empregado etc›; pay back ‹empréstimo›; repay ‹gentileza etc› ● vi pay; **eu pago para ver** I'll believe it when I see it

página /ˈpaʒina/ f page; ~ **web** web page

pago /ˈpagu/ a paid ● pp de ▶ PAGAR

pagode /paˈgɔdʒi/ m (torre) pagoda; 𝕀 singalong

pai /paj/ m father; pl (pai e mãe) parents. ~ **de santo** (pl ~s-de-santo) m macumba priest

pai|nel /pajˈnɛw/ (pl ~néis) m panel; (de carro) dashboard

paio /ˈpaju/ m pork sausage

pairar /pajˈrar/ vi hover

país /paˈis/ m country; **P~ de Gales** Wales; **P~es Baixos** Netherlands

paisa|gem /pajˈzaʒẽ/ f landscape. ~**gista** m/f landscape gardener

paisana /pajˈzana/ f à ~ ‹policial› in plain clothes; ‹soldado› in civilian clothes

paixão /pajˈʃãw/ f passion

pala /ˈpala/ f (de boné) peak; (de automóvel) sun visor

palácio /paˈlasiu/ m palace

Palácio do Planalto The Palácio do Planalto is the main working office of the President of Brazil. It 𝑖

is the seat of the government and the President's official residence, and it also houses important government offices, such as the Casa Civil (Chief of Staff) and the Gabinete de Segurança Institucional (Office for Institutional Security).

paladar /palaˈdar/ m palate, taste

palanque /paˈlãki/ m stand

palavra /paˈlavra/ f word; **pedir a ~** ask to speak; **ter ~** be reliable; **tomar a ~** start to speak; **sem ~** ‹pessoa› unreliable; **~ de ordem** watchword; **~s cruzadas** crossword

palavra-chave /palavraˈʃavi/ f (pl **palavras-chave**) password

palavrão /palaˈvrãw/ m swear word

palco /ˈpawku/ m stage

palestino /palesˈtʃinu/ a & m Palestinian

palestra /paˈlɛstra/ f lecture

paleta /paˈleta/ f palette

paletó /paleˈtɔ/ m jacket

palha /ˈpaʎa/ f straw

palha|çada /paʎaˈsada/ f joke. ~**ço** m clown

palhinha /paˈʎiɲa/ f Port (para bebidas) straw

paliativo /paliaˈtʃivu/ a & m palliative

palidez /paliˈdes/ f paleness

pálido /ˈpalidu/ a pale

pali|tar /paliˈtar/ vt pick ● vi pick one's teeth. ~**teiro** m toothpick holder. ~**to** m (para dentes) toothpick; (de fósforo) matchstick; (pessoa magra) beanpole

pal|ma /ˈpawma/ f palm; pl (aplauso) clapping; **bater ~mas** clap. ~**meira** f palm tree. ~**mito** m palm heart. ~**mo** m span; ~**mo a ~mo** inch by inch

palpá|vel /pawˈpavew/ (pl ~**veis**) a palpable

pálpebra /ˈpawpebra/ f eyelid

palpi|tação /pawpitaˈsãw/ f palpitation. ~**tante** a fig thrilling. ~**tar** vi ‹coração› flutter; ‹pessoa› tremble; (dar palpite) stick one's oar in. ~**te** m (pressentimento) hunch; (no jogo etc) tip; **dar ~te** stick one's oar in

panacela /panaˈsela/ f panacea

panaché /panaˈʃɛ/ m Port (bebida) shandy

Panamá /panaˈma/ m Panama

panamenho /panaˈmeɲu/ a & m Panamanian

pan-americano /panameri'kanu/ *a* Pan-American

pança /'pãsa/ *f* paunch

pancada /pã'kada/ *f* blow; **~ d'água** downpour. **~ria** *f* fight, punch-up

pâncreas /'pãkrias/ *m invar* pancreas

pançudo /pã'sudu/ *a* paunchy

panda /'pãda/ *m* panda

pandarecos /pãda'rekus/ *m pl* **aos** ou **em ~** battered

pandeiro /pã'deru/ *m* tambourine

pandemônio /pãde'moniu/ *m* pandemonium

pane /'pani/ *f* breakdown

panela /pa'nɛla/ *f* saucepan; **~ de pressão** pressure cooker

panfleto /pã'fletu/ *m* pamphlet

pânico /'paniku/ *m* panic; **em ~** in a panic; **entrar em ~** panic

panifica|ção /panifika'sãw/ *f* bakery. **~dora** *f* bakery

pano /'panu/ *m* cloth; **~ de fundo** backdrop; **~ de pó** duster; **~ de pratos** tea towel

pano|rama /pano'rama/ *m* panorama. **~râmico** *a* panoramic

panqueca /pã'kɛka/ *f* pancake

panta|nal /pãta'naw/ (*pl* **~nais**) *m* marshland

Pantanal The *Pantanal* is a tropical wetland located within the states of Mato Gross and Mato Grosso do Sul, covering an area of 250 thousand square kilometres. Much of the floodplains are submerged during the rainy season, forming a unique ecosystem which has been designated a UNESCO World Heritage Site, and one of Brazil's most important sites of national heritage. The area is home to hundreds of species of mammals, fish, birds and reptiles, including caimans, capybaras, and piranhas.

pântano /'pãtanu/ *m* marsh

pantanoso /pãta'nozu/ *a* marshy

pantera /pã'tɛra/ *f* panther

pantufa /pã'tufa/ *f* slipper

pão /'pãw/ (*pl* **pães**) *m* bread; **~ de forma** sliced loaf; **~ integral** brown bread. **~ de ló** *m* sponge cake; **~duro** (*pl* **pães-duros**) 𝕀 *a* stingy, tight-fisted ● *m/f* skinflint. **~zinho** *m* bread roll

Pão de Açúcar The *Pão de Açúcar* is a mountain situated at the mouth of Guanabara Bay in Rio de Janeiro. The summit stands at 395 meters above sea level, and is one of the city's most famous landmarks. A cable car (*Bondinho do Pão de Açúcar*) runs tourists up to the top, from which they can view Botafogo Bay, Leme Beach and the vast Atlantic Ocean.

papa /'papa/ *f* (*de nenem*) food; (*arroz etc*) mush

Papa /'papa/ *m* Pope

papagaio /papa'gaju/ *m* parrot

papai /pa'paj/ *m* dad, daddy; **Papai Noel** Father Christmas

papão /pa'pãw/ *m* Port bogeyman

papar /pa'par/ *vt/i* 𝕀 eat

papari|car /papari'kar/ *vt* pamper. **~cos** *m pl* pampering

pa|pel /pa'pew/ (*pl* **~péis**) *m* (*de escrever etc*) paper; (*um*) piece of paper; (*numa peça, filme*) part; *fig* (*função*) role; **de ~pel passado** officially; **~pel de alumínio** aluminium foil; **~pel higiênico** toilet paper. **~pelada** *f* paperwork. **~pelão** *m* cardboard. **~pelaria** *f* stationer's (shop). **~pelzinho** *m* scrap of paper

papo /'papu/ *f* 𝕀 (*conversa*) talk; (*do rosto*) double chin; **bater um ~** 𝕀 have a chat; **~ furado** idle talk

papoula /pa'pola/ *f* poppy

páprica /'paprika/ *f* paprika

paque|ra /pa'kɛra/ *f* 𝕀 pick-up. **~rador** *a* flirtatious ● *m* flirt. **~rar** *vt* flirt with ⟨*pessoa*⟩; eye up ⟨*vestido, carro etc*⟩ ● *vi* flirt

paquista|nês /pakista'nes/ *a & m* (*f*~**nesa**) Pakistani

Paquistão /pakis'tãw/ *m* Pakistan

par /par/ *a* even ● *m* pair; (*parceiro*) partner; **a ~ de** up to date with ⟨*notícias etc*⟩; **sem ~** unequalled

para /'para/ ● *prep*

••••▸ (*uso, finalidade*) for; **é ~ você** it's for you; **muito útil ~ a chuva** very useful for the rain; **muito complicado ~ mim** too complicated for me; **~ que você quer?** what do you want it for?; **detergente ~ máquina** machine detergent

••••▸ (*direção*) **~ sul/norte** towards south/north; **foi ~ a cama** she went to bed; **vai ~ casa!** go home!

····➤ (*com destino a*) ~ **São Paulo** to São Paulo; **o voo** ~ **Salvador** the flight to Salvador

····➤ (*seguido de infinitivo*) **vieram** ~ **ficar** they've come to stay

····➤ (*tempo futuro*) ~ **a próxima semana** for next week; **preciso disto** ~ **segunda** I need it for Monday; **são cinco** ~ **as dez** it's five to ten

····➤ (*lugar impreciso*) **estava (lá)** ~ **Recife** he was somewhere in Recife

····➤ (*em expressões*) ~ **com** to; **foi muito simpático** ~ **com ela** he was very nice to her; **,~ isso: foi** ~ **isso que você me chamou?** you called me here just for that?; ~ **mim** (*opinião*) for me; ~ **mim, ele é o melhor jogador** he is the best player for me; ~ **que** so (that); **ela trabalhou muito** ~ **que ficasse tudo pronto na hora** she worked hard so (that) everything would be ready in time; ~ **si** to yourself; **dizer algo** ~ **si próprio** say sth to o.s.

para|benizar /parabeni'zar/ *vt* congratulate (**por** on). **~béns** *m pl* congratulations

parábola /pa'rabola/ *f* (*conto*) parable; (*curva*) parabola

parabóli|co /para'bɔliku/ *a* **antena ~ca** satellite dish

para|brisa /para'briza/ *m* windscreen, *Amer* windshield. **~choque** *m* bumper

para|da /pa'rada/ *f* stop; (*interrupção*) stoppage; (*militar*) parade; Ⓣ (*coisa difícil*) ordeal, challenge; **~da cardíaca** cardiac arrest. **~deiro** *m* whereabouts

paradisíaco /paradʒi'ziaku/ *a* idyllic

parado /pa'radu/ *a* (*trânsito, carro*) at a standstill, stopped; *fig* (*pessoa*) dull; **ficar** ~ (*pessoa*) stand still; (*trânsito*) stop; (*deixar de trabalhar*) stop work

parado|xal /paradok'saw/ (*pl* **~xais**) *a* paradoxical. **~xo** /ɔ/ *m* paradox

parafina /para'fina/ *f* paraffin

paráfrase /pa'rafrazi/ *f* paraphrase

parafrasear /parafrazi'ar/ *vt* paraphrase

parafuso /para'fuzu/ *m* screw; **entrar em** ~ get into a state

para|gem /pa'raʒẽ/ *f Port* (*parada*) stop; **nestas ~gens** in these parts

parágrafo /pa'ragrafu/ *m* paragraph

Paraguai /para'gwaj/ *m* Paraguay

paraguaio /para'gwaju/ *a & m* Paraguayan

paraíso /para'izu/ *m* paradise

para-lama /para'lama/ *m* (*de carro*) wing, *Amer* fender; (*de bicicleta*) mudguard

parale|la /para'lɛla/ *f* parallel; *pl* (*aparelho*) parallel bars. **~lepípedo** *m* paving stone. **~lo** /ɛ/ *a & m* parallel

para|lisar /parali'zar/ *vt* paralyse; bring to a halt (*fábrica, produção*). **~lisar-se** *vpr* become paralysed; (*fábrica, produção*) grind to a halt. **~lisia** *f* paralysis. **~lítico** *a & m* paralytic. **~médico** *m* paramedic

paranoi|a /para'nɔja/ *f* paranoia. **~co** *a* paranoid

parapeito /para'pejtu/ *m* (*muro*) parapet; (*da janela*) window sill

paraque|das /para'kedas/ *m invar* parachute. **~dista** *m/f* parachutist; (*militar*) paratrooper

parar /pa'rar/ *vt/i* stop; ~ **de fumar** stop smoking; **ir** ~ end up

para-raios /para'xajus/ *m invar* lightning conductor

parasita /para'zita/ *a & m/f* parasite

parceiro /par'seru/ *m* partner

parce|la /par'sela/ *f* (*de terreno*) plot; (*prestação*) instalment. **~lar** *vt* spread (*pagamento*)

parceria /parse'ria/ *f* partnership

parci|al /parsi'aw/ (*pl* **~ais**) *a* partial; (*partidário*) biased. **~alidade** *f* bias

parco /'parku/ *a* frugal; (*recursos*) scant

par|dal /par'daw/ (*pl* **~dais**) *m* sparrow. **~do** *a* (*papel*) brown; (*pessoa*) mulatto

pare|cer /pare'ser/ *vi* (*ter aparência de*) seem; (*ter semelhança com*) be like; **~cer-se com** look like, resemble ● *m* opinion. **~cido** *a* similar (**com** to)

parede /pa'redʒi/ *f* wall

paren|te /pa'rẽtʃi/ *m/f* relative, relation. **~tesco** /e/ *m* relationship

parêntese /pa'rẽtʃizi/ *f* parenthesis; *pl* (*sinais*) brackets, parentheses

paridade /pari'dadʒi/ *f* parity

parir /pa'rir/ *vt* give birth to ● *vi* give birth

parlamen|tar /parlamẽ'tar/ *a* parliamentary ● *m/f* member of parliament. **~tarismo** *m* parliamentary system. **~to** *m* parliament

parmesão /parme'zãw/ *a & m* (**queijo**) ~ Parmesan (cheese)

paródia /pa'rɔdʒia/ *f* parody

parodiar /parodʒi'ar/ *vt* parody

paróquia /pa'rɔkia/ *f* parish

parque /'parki/ *m* park. **~ temático** *m* theme park

parquímetro /par'kimetru/ *m* parking meter

parte /'partʃi/ *f* part; (*quinhão*) share; (*num litígio, contrato*) party; **a maior ~ de** most of; **à ~** (*de lado*) aside; (*separadamente*) separately; **um erro da sua ~** a mistake on your part; **em ~** in part; **em alguma ~** somewhere; **por toda ~** everywhere; **por ~ do pai** on one's father's side; **fazer ~ de** be part of; **tomar ~ em** take part in

parteira /par'tera/ *f* midwife

partici|pação /partʃisipa'sãw/ *f* participation; (*numa empresa, nos lucros*) share. **~pante** *a* participating ● *m/f* participant. **~par** *vi* take part (**de** ou **em** in)

particípio /partʃi'sipiu/ *m* participle

partícula /par'tʃikula/ *f* particle

particu|lar /partʃiku'lar/ *a* private; (*especial*) unusual ● *m* (*pessoa*) private individual; *pl* (*detalhes*) particulars; **em ~lar** (*especialmente*) in particular; (*a sós*) in private. **~laridade** *f* peculiarity

partida /par'tʃida/ *f* (*saída*) departure; (*de corrida*) start; (*de futebol, xadrez etc*) match; **dar ~ em** start up

par|tidário /partʃi'dariu/ *a* partisan ● *m* supporter. **~tido** *a* broken ● *m* (*político*) party; (*casamento, par*) match; **tirar ~tido de** benefit from; **tomar o ~tido de** side with. **~tilha** *f* division. **~tir** *vi* (*sair*) depart; (*corredor*) start; **a ~tir de ...** from ... onwards; **~tir para** Ⅱ resort to; **~tir para outra** do something different, change direction ● *vt* break. **~tir-se** *vpr* break. **~titura** *f* score

partilhar /partʃi'ʎar/ *vt/i* Port share

parto /'partu/ *m* birth

parvo /'parvu/ *a* Port stupid

Páscoa /'paskoa/ *f* Easter

pas|mar /paz'mar/ *vt* amaze. **~mar-se** *vpr* be amazed (**com** at). **~mo** *a* amazed ● *m* amazement

passa /'pasa/ *f* raisin

pas|sada /pa'sada/ *f* **dar uma ~sada em** call in at. **~sadeira** *f* (*mulher*) woman who irons; Port (*faixa*) zebra crossing, Amer crosswalk. **~sado** *a* (*ano, mês, semana*) last; (*tempo, particípio etc*) past; (*fruta, comida*) off; **são duas horas ~sadas** it's gone two o'clock;

bem/mal ~sado well done/rare ● *m* past

passa|geiro /pasa'ʒeru/ *m* passenger ● *a* passing. **~gem** *f* passage; (*bilhete*) ticket; **de ~gem** in passing; **estar de ~gem** be passing through; **~gem de ida e volta** return ticket, Amer round trip ticket

passaporte /pasa'pɔrtʃi/ *m* passport

passar /pa'sar/ *vt* pass; spend (*tempo*); cross (*ponte, rio*); (*a ferro*) iron (*roupa etc*); (*aplicar*) put on (*creme, batom etc*) ● *vi* pass; (*dor, medo, chuva etc*) go; (*ser aceitável*) be passable; **passou a beber muito** he started to drink a lot; **passei dos 30 anos** I'm over thirty; **não passa de um boato** it's nothing more than a rumour; **~ sem** do without; **~ por** go through; go along (*rua*); (*ser considerado*) be taken for; **fazer-se por** pass o.s. off as; **~ por cima de** *fig* overlook ● *m* passing. **~-se** *vpr* happen

passarela /pasa'rela/ *f* (*sobre rua*) footbridge; (*para desfile de moda*) catwalk

pássaro /'pasaru/ *m* bird

passatempo /pasa'tẽpu/ *m* pastime

passe /'pasi/ *m* pass

pas|sear /pasi'ar/ *vi* go out and about; (*viajar*) travel around ● *vt* take for a walk. **~seata** *f* protest march. **~seio** *m* outing; (*volta a pé*) walk; (*volta de carro*) drive; **dar um ~seio** (*a pé*) go for a walk; (*de carro*) go for a drive

passio|nal /pasio'naw/ (*pl* **~nais**) *a* **crime ~nal** crime of passion

passista /pa'sista/ *m/f* dancer

passí|vel /pa'sivew/ (*pl* **~veis**) *a* **~vel de** subject to

passi|vidade /pasivi'dadʒi/ *f* passivity. **~vo** *a* passive ● *m* Com liabilities; Ling passive

passo /'pasu/ *m* step; (*velocidade*) pace; (*barulho*) footstep; **~ a ~** step by step; **a dois ~s de** a stone's throw from; **dar um ~** take a step

pasta /'pasta/ *f* (*matéria*) paste; (*bolsa*) briefcase; (*fichário*) folder; **ministro sem ~** minister without portfolio; **~ de dentes** toothpaste

pas|tagem /pas'taʒẽ/ *f* pasture. **~tar** *vi* graze

pas|tel /pas'tew/ (*pl* **~téis**) *m* (*para comer*) samosa; Port (*doce*) pastry; Port (*pastéis*) pastries; (*para desenhar*) pastel. **~telão** *m* (*comédia*) slapstick. **~telaria** *f* (*loja*) samosa vendor; Port pastry shop

p

pastelaria You can't go very far in Portugal without coming across a *pastelaria*. These are shops or cafes serving a huge variety of cakes and pastries, many of which originated in Portuguese convents. The fillings are often rich in egg yolk, left over after the nuns had used the whites to starch their habits.

pasteurizado /pastewri'zadu/ a pasteurized

pastilha /pas'tʃiʎa/ f pastille

pas|to /'pastu/ m (erva) fodder, feed; (lugar) pasture. **~tor** m (de gado) shepherd; (clérigo) vicar; **~tor alemão** (cachorro) Alsatian. **~toral** (pl **~torais**) a pastoral

pata /'pata/ f paw. **~da** f kick

patamar /pata'mar/ m landing; fig level

patê /pa'te/ m pâté

patente /pa'tẽtʃi/ a obvious ● f Mil rank; (de invenção) patent. **~ar** vt patent ‹produto, invenção›

pater|nal /pater'naw/ (pl **~nais**) a paternal. **~nidade** f paternity. **~no** /ε/ a paternal

pate|ta /pa'teta/ a daft, silly ● m/f fool. **~tice** f stupidity; (uma) silly thing

patético /pa'tɛtʃiku/ a pathetic

patíbulo /pa'tʃibulu/ m gallows

pati|faria /patʃifa'ria/ f roguishness; (uma) dirty trick. **~fe** m scoundrel

patim /pa'tʃĩ/ m skate; **~ de rodas** roller skate

pati|nação /patʃina'sãw/ f skating; (rinque) skating rink. **~nador** m skater. **~nar** vi skate; ‹carro› skid. **~nete** /ε/ m skateboard

pátio /'patʃiu/ m courtyard; (de escola) playground

pato /'patu/ m duck

pato|logia /patolo'ʒia/ f pathology. **~lógico** a pathological. **~logista** m/f pathologist

patrão /pa'trãw/ m boss

pátria /'patria/ f homeland

patriar|ca /patri'arka/ m patriarch. **~cal** (pl **~cais**) a patriarchal

patrimônio /patri'moniu/ m (bens) estate, property; fig (herança) heritage

patri|ota /patri'ɔta/ m/f patriot. **~ótico** a patriotic. **~otismo** m patriotism

patroa /pa'troa/ f boss; **①** (esposa) missus, wife

patro|cinador /patrosina'dor/ m sponsor. **~cinar** vt sponsor. **~cínio** m sponsorship

patru|lha /pa'truʎa/ f patrol. **~lhar** vt/i patrol

pau /paw/ m stick; **①** (cruzeiro) cruzeiro; (chulo) (pênis) prick; pl (naipe) clubs; **a meio ~** at half mast; **rachar ~ ①** (brigar) row, fight like cat and dog. **~lada** f blow with a stick

paulista /paw'lista/ a & m/f (person) from (the state of) São Paulo. **~no** a & m (person) from (the city of) São Paulo

pausa /'pawza/ f pause. **~do** a slow

pauta /'pawta/ f (em papel) lines; (de música) stave; fig (de discussão etc) agenda. **~do** a ‹papel› lined

pavão /pa'vãw/ m peacock

pavilhão /pavi'ʎãw/ m pavilion; (no jardim) summer house

pavimen|tar /pavimẽ'tar/ vt pave. **~to** m floor; (de rua etc) surface

pavio /pa'viu/ m wick

pavor /pa'vor/ m terror; **ter ~ de** be terrified of. **~oso** /o/ a dreadful

paz /pas/ f peace; **fazer as ~es** make up

pé /pɛ/ m foot; (planta) plant; (de móvel) leg; **a ~** on foot; **ao ~ da letra** literally; **estar de ~** ‹festa etc› be on; **ficar de ~** stand up; **em ~** standing (up); **em ~ de igualdade** on an equal footing; **~ de atleta** athlete's foot. **~ de meia** nest egg; **~ de pato** flipper; **~ de vento** gust of wind

peão /pi'ãw/ m Port (pedestre) pedestrian; (no xadrez) pawn

peça /'pesa/ f piece; (de máquina, carro etc) part; (teatral) play; **pregar uma ~ em** play a trick on; **~ de reposição** spare part; **~ de vestuário** item of clothing

pe|cado /pe'kadu/ m sin. **~cador** m sinner. **~caminoso** /o/ a sinful. **~car** vi (contra a religião) sin; fig fall down

pechin|cha /pe'ʃĩʃa/ f bargain. **~char** vi bargain, haggle

peçonhento /peso'ɲẽtu/ a **animais ~s** vermin

pecu|ária /peku'aria/ f livestock farming. **~ário** a livestock. **~arista** m/f livestock farmer

peculi|ar /pekuli'ar/ a peculiar. **~aridade** f peculiarity

peculio /pe'kuliu/ m savings

pedaço /pe'dasu/ m piece; **aos ~s** in pieces; **cair aos ~s** fall to pieces

pedágio /pe'daʒiu/ *m* toll; *(cabine)* tollbooth

peda|gogia /pedago'ʒia/ *f* education. **~gógico** *a* educational. **~gogo** /o/ *m* educationalist

pe|dal /pe'daw/ *(pl* **~dais)** *m* pedal. **~dalar** *vt/i* pedal

pedante /pe'dãtʃi/ *a* pretentious ● *m/f* pseud

pederneira /peder'nera/ *f* flint

pedes|tal /pedes'taw/ *(pl* **~tais)** *m* pedestal

pedestre /pe'dɛstri/ *a & m/f* pedestrian

pedia|tra /pedʒi'atra/ *m/f* paediatrician. **~tria** *f* paediatrics

pedicuro /pedʒi'kuru/ *m* chiropodist, *Amer* podiatrist

pe|dido /pe'dʒidu/ *m* request; *(encomenda)* order; **a ~dido de** at the request of; **~dido de demissão** resignation; **~dido de desculpa** apology. **~dir** *vt* ask for; *(num restaurante etc)* order; **~dir algo a alguém** ask sb for sth; **~dir para algém ir** ask sb to go; **~dir desculpa** apologize; **~dir em casamento** propose to ● *vi* ask; *(num restaurante etc)* order

pedinte /pe'dʒĩtʃi/ *m/f* beggar

pedra /'pɛdra/ stone; **~ de gelo** ice cube; **chuva de ~** hail; **~ pomes** pumice stone

pedregoso /pedre'gozu/ *a* stony

pedreiro /pe'dreru/ *m* builder

pegada /pe'gada/ *f* footprint; *(de goleiro)* save; **~ ecológica** carbon footprint

pegajoso /pega'ʒozu/ *a* sticky

pegar /pe'gar/ *vt* get; catch ‹bola, doença, ladrão, ônibus›; *(segurar)* get hold of; pick up ‹emissora, hábito, mania›; **~ bem/mal** go down well/ badly; **~ fogo** catch fire; **pega essa rua** take that street; **~ em** grab; **~ no sono** get to sleep ● *vi (aderir)* stick; ‹doença› be catching; ‹moda› catch on; ‹carro, motor› start; ‹mentira, desculpa› stick. **~se** *vpr* come to blows

pego /'pɛgu/; *pp de* ▶ **PEGAR**

pei|dar /pej'dar/ *vi (chulo)* fart. **~do** *m (chulo)* fart

pei|to /'pejtu/ *m* chest; *(seio)* breast; *fig (coragem)* guts. **~toril** *(pl* **~toris)** *m* window sill. **~tudo** *a* ‹mulher› busty; *fig (corajoso)* gutsy

pei|xaria /pe'ʃaria/ *f* fishmonger's. **~xe** *m* fish; **Peixes** *(signo)* Pisces. **~xeiro** *m* fishmonger

pela = **por** + **a**

pelado /pe'ladu/ *a (nu)* naked, in the nude

pelan|ca /pe'lãka/ *f* roll of fat; *pl* flab. **~cudo** *a* flabby

pelar /pe'lar/ *vt* peel ‹fruta, batata›; skin ‹animal›; 🅸 *(tomar dinheiro de)* fleece

pelas = **por** + **as**

pele /'pɛli/ *f* skin; *(como roupa)* fur. **~teiro** *m* furrier. **~teria** *f* furrier's

pelica /pe'lika/ *f* **luvas de ~** kid gloves

pelicano /peli'kanu/ *m* pelican

película /pe'likula/ *f* skin

pelo¹ /'pelu/ *m* hair; *(de animal)* coat; **nu em ~** stark naked; **montar em ~** ride bareback

pelo² = **por** + **o**

pelos = **por** + **os**

pelotão /pelo'tãw/ *m* platoon

pelúcia /pe'lusia/ *f* **bicho de ~** soft toy, fluffy animal

peludo /pe'ludu/ *a* hairy

pen /'pɛn/ *f Port* memory stick

pena¹ /'pena/ *f (de ave)* feather; *(de caneta)* nib

pena² /'pena/ *f (castigo)* penalty; *(de amor etc)* pang; **é uma ~ que** it's a pity that; **que ~!** what a pity! **dar ~** be upsetting; **estar com** ou **ter ~ de** feel sorry for; **(não) vale a ~** it's (not) worth it; **vale a ~ tentar** it's worth trying; **~ de morte** death penalty

penada /pe'nada/ *f* stroke of the pen

pe|nal /pe'naw/ *(pl* **~nais)** *a* penal. **~nalidade** *f* penalty. **~nalizar** *vt* penalize

pênalti /'penawtʃi/ *m* penalty

penar /pe'nar/ *vi* suffer

pen|dente /pẽ'dẽtʃi/ *a* hanging; *fig (causa)* pending. **~der** *vi* hang; *(inclinar-se)* slope; *(tender)* be inclined (a to). **~dor** *m* inclination

pen drive *m* memory stick

pêndulo /'pẽdulu/ *m* pendulum

pendu|rado /pẽdu'radu/ *a* hanging; 🅸 *(por fazer, pagar)* outstanding. **~rar** *vt* hang (up); 🅸 put on the slate ‹compra› ● *vi* 🅸 pay later. **~ricalho** *m* pendant

penedo /pe'nedu/ *m* rock

penei|ra /pe'nera/ *f* sieve. **~rar** *vt* sieve, sift ● *vi* drizzle

pene|tra /pe'netra/ *m/f* 🅸 gatecrasher. **~tração** *f* penetration; *fig* perspicacity. **~trante** *a* ‹som, olhar› piercing; ‹dor› sharp; ‹*ferida*› deep; ‹*frio*› biting; ‹*análise, espírito*› incisive, perceptive. **~trar** *vt* penetrate ● *vi* **~trar em** enter ‹*casa*›; *fig* penetrate

penhasco /pe'ɲasku/ *m* cliff

penhoar /peɲo'ar/ *m* dressing gown

penhor /pe'ɲor/ *m* pledge; **casa de ~es** pawnshop

penicilina /penisi'lina/ *f* penicillin

penico /pe'niku/ *m* potty

península /pe'nĩsula/ *f* peninsula

pênis /'penis/ *m invar* penis

penitência /peni'tẽsia/ *f* (*arrependimento*) penitence; (*expiação*) penance

penitenciá|ria /penitẽsi'aria/ *f* prison. **~rio** *a* prison ● *m* prisoner

penoso /pe'nozu/ *a* ‹*experiência, tarefa, assunto*› painful; ‹*trabalho, viagem*› hard, difficult

pensa|dor /pẽsa'dor/ *m* thinker. **~mento** *m* thought

pensão /pẽ'sãw/ *f* (*renda*) pension; (*hotel*) guest house; **~ (alimentícia)** (*paga por ex-marido*) alimony; **~ completa** full board

pen|sar /pẽ'sar/ *vt/i* think (**em** of ou about). **~sativo** *a* thoughtful, pensive

pên|sil /'pẽsiw/ (*pl* **~seis**) *a* **ponte ~sil** suspension bridge

penso /'pẽsu/ *m* (*curativo*) dressing

pentágono /pẽ'tagonu/ *m* pentagon

pentatlo /pẽ'tatlu/ *m* pentathlon

pente /'pẽtʃi/ *m comb*. **~adeira** *f* dressing table. **~ado** *m* hairstyle, hairdo. **~ar** *vt comb*. **~ar-se** *vpr* do one's hair; (*com pente*) comb one's hair

Pentecostes /pẽte'kɔstʃis/ *m* Whitsun

pente-fino /pẽtʃi'finu/ *m* **passar a ~** go over with a fine-tooth comb

pente|lhar /pẽte'ʎar/ *vt* 🆒 bother. **~lho** /e/ *m* pubic hair; 🆒 (*pessoa inconveniente*) pain (in the neck)

penugem /pe'nuʒẽ/ *f* down

penúltimo /pe'nuwtʃimu/ *a* last but one, penultimate

penumbra /pe'nũbra/ *f* half-light

penúria /pe'nuria/ *f* penury, extreme poverty

pepino /pe'pinu/ *m* cucumber

pepita /pe'pita/ *f* nugget

peque|nez /peke'nes/ *f* smallness; *fig* pettiness. **~ninho** *a* tiny. **~no** /e/ *a* small; (*mesquinho*) petty

pequeno-almoço /pikenaw'mosu/ *m* (*pl* **pequenos-almoços**) *Port* breakfast

Pequim /pe'kĩ/ *f* Peking, Beijing

pequinês /peki'nes/ *m* Pekinese

pera /'pera/ *f* pear

perambular /perãbu'lar/ *vi* wander

perante /pe'rãtʃi/ *prep* before

percalço /per'kawsu/ *m* pitfall

perceber /perse'ber/ *vt* realize; *Port* (*entender*) understand; (*psiqu*) perceive

percen|tagem /persẽ'taʒẽ/ *f* percentage. **~tual** (*pl* **~tuais**) *a & m* percentage

percep|ção /persep'sãw/ *f* perception. **~tível** (*pl* **~tíveis**) *a* perceptible

percevejo /perse'veʒu/ *m* (*bicho*) bedbug; (*tachinha*) drawing pin, *Amer* thumbtack

per|correr /perko'xer/ *vt* cross; cover ‹*distância*›; (*viajar por*) travel through. **~curso** *m* journey

percus|são /perku'sãw/ *f* percussion. **~sionista** *m/f* percussionist

percutir /perku'tʃir/ *vt* strike

perda /'perda/ *f* loss; **~ de tempo** waste of time

perdão /per'dãw/ *f* pardon

perder /per'der/ *vt* lose; (*não chegar a ver, pegar*) miss ‹*ônibus, programa na TV etc*›; waste ‹*tempo*›; **~ algo de vista** lose sight of sth ● *vi* lose. **~se** *vpr* get lost; **~se de alguém** lose sb

perdiz /per'dʒis/ *f* partridge

perdoar /perdo'ar/ *vt* forgive (**algo a alguém** sb for sth)

perdulário /perdu'lariu/ *a & m* spendthrift

perdurar /perdu'rar/ *vi* endure; ‹*coisa ruim*› persist

pere|cer /pere'ser/ *vi* perish. **~cível** (*pl* **~cíveis**) *a* perishable

peregri|nação /peregrina'sãw/ *f* peregrination; (*romaria*) pilgrimage. **~nar** *vi* roam; (*por motivos religiosos*) go on a pilgrimage. **~no** *m* pilgrim

pereira /pe'rera/ *f* pear tree

peremptório /perẽp'tɔriu/ *a* peremptory

perene /pe'reni/ *a* perennial

perereca /pere'reka/ *f* tree frog

perfazer /perfa'zer/ *vt* make up

perfeccionis|mo /perfeksio'nizmu/ *m* perfectionism. **~ta** *a & m/f* perfectionist

perfei|ção /perfej'sãw/ f perfection. **~to** a & m perfect

per|fil /per'fiw/ (pl **~fis**) m profile. **~filar** vt line up. **~filar-se** vpr line up

perfu|mado /perfu'madu/ a ‹flor, ar› fragrant; ‹sabonete etc› scented; ‹pessoa› with perfume on. **~mar** vt perfume. **~mar-se** vpr put perfume on. **~maria** f perfumery; 🄸 trimmings, frills. **~me** m perfume

perfu|rador /perfura'dor/ m punch. **~rar** vt punch ‹papel, bilhete›; drill through ‹chão›; perforate ‹úlcera, pulmão etc›. **~ratriz** f drill

pergaminho /perga'miɲu/ m parchment

pergun|ta /per'gũta/ f question; **fazer uma ~ta** ask a question. **~tar** vt/i ask; **~tar algo a alguém** ask sb sth; **~tar por** ask after

perícia /pe'risia/ f (mestria) expertise; (inspeção) investigation; (peritos) experts

perici|al /perisi'aw/ (pl **~ais**) a expert

pericli|tante /perikli'tãtʃi/ a precarious. **~tar** vi be at risk

peri|feria /perife'ria/ f periphery; (da cidade) outskirts. **~férico** a & m peripheral

perigo /pe'rigu/ m danger. **~so** /o/ a dangerous

perímetro /pe'rimetru/ m perimeter

periódico /peri'ɔdʒiku/ a periodic ● m periodical

período /pe'riodu/ m period; **trabalhar meio ~** work part-time

peripécias /peri'pesias/ f pl ups and downs, vicissitudes

periquito /peri'kitu/ m parakeet; (de estimação) budgerigar

periscópio /peris'kɔpiu/ m periscope

perito /pe'ritu/ a & m expert (**em** at)

per|jurar /perʒu'rar/ vi commit perjury. **~júrio** m perjury. **~juro** m perjurer

perma|necer /permane'ser/ vi remain. **~nência** f permanence; (estadia) stay. **~nente** a permanent ● f perm

permeá|vel /permi'avew/ (pl **~veis**) a permeable

permis|são /permi'sãw/ f permission. **~sível** (pl **~síveis**) a permissible. **~sivo** a permissive

permitir /permi'tʃir/ vt allow, permit; **~ a alguém ir** allow sb to go

permutar /permu'tar/ vt exchange

perna /'perna/ f leg

pernicioso /pernisi'ozu/ a pernicious

per|nil /per'niw/ (pl **~nis**) m leg

pernilongo /perni'lõgu/ m (large) mosquito

pernoi|tar /pernoj'tar/ vi spend the night. **~te** m overnight stay

pérola /'perola/ f pearl

perpendicular /perpẽdʒiku'lar/ a perpendicular

perpetrar /perpe'trar/ vt perpetrate

perpetu|ar /perpetu'ar/ vt perpetuate. **~idade** f perpetuity

perpétu|o /per'petuu/ a perpetual; **prisão ~a** life imprisonment

perple|xidade /perpleksi'dadʒi/ f puzzlement. **~xo** /ɛ/ a puzzled

persa /'persa/ a & m/f Persian

perse|guição /persegi'sãw/ f pursuit; (de minorias etc) persecution. **~guidor** m pursuer; (de minorias etc) persecutor. **~guir** vt pursue; persecute ‹minoria, seita etc›

perseve|rança /perseve'rãsa/ f perseverance. **~rante** a persevering. **~rar** vi persevere

persiana /persi'ana/ f blind

pérsico /'persiku/ a **Golfo Pérsico** Persian Gulf

persignar-se /persig'narsi/ vt cross o.s.

persis|tência /persis'tẽsia/ f persistence. **~tente** a persistent. **~tir** vi persist

perso|nagem /perso'naʒẽ/ m/f (pessoa famosa) personality; (em livro, filme etc) character. **~nalidade** f personality. **~nalizar** vt personalize. **~nificar** vt personify

perspectiva /perspek'tʃiva/ f (na arte, ponto de vista) perspective; (possibilidade) prospect

perspi|cácia /perspi'kasia/ f insight, perceptiveness. **~caz** a perceptive

persua|dir /persua'dʒir/ vt persuade (**alguém a s.o. to**). **~são** f persuasion. **~sivo** a persuasive

perten|cente /pertẽ'sẽtʃi/ a belonging (**a to**); (que tem a ver com) pertaining (**a to**). **~cer** vi belong (**a to**); (referir-se) pertain (**a to**). **~ces** m pl belongings

perto /'pertu/ adv near (**de** to); **aqui ~** near here, nearby; **de ~** closely; ‹ver› **close up**

pertur|bação /perturba'sãw/ f disturbance; (do espírito) anxiety. **~bado**

p

a <pessoa> unsettled, troubled. **~bar**
vt disturb. **~bar-se** vpr get upset, be
perturbed

peru /pe'ru/ m turkey

Peru /pe'ru/ m Peru

perua /pe'rua/ f <carro grande> estate
car, Amer station wagon; <caminhonete>
van; <para escolares etc> minibus; ▯
<mulher> brassy woman

peruano /peru'ano/ a & m Peruvian

peruca /pe'ruka/ f wig

perver|são /perver'sãw/ f perversion.
~so a perverse. **~ter** vt pervert

pesadelo /peza'delu/ m nightmare

pesado /pe'zadu/ a heavy; <estilo, livro>
heavy going ● adv heavily

pêsames /'pezamis/ m pl condolences

pesar¹ /pe'zar/ vt weigh; fig <avaliar>
weigh up ● vi weigh; <influir> carry
weight; **~ sobre** <ameaça etc> hang
over. **~se** vpr weigh o.s.

pesar² /pe'zar/ m sorrow. **~oso** /o/ a
sorry, sorrowful

pes|ca /'peska/ f fishing; **ir à ~ca** go
fishing. **~cador** m fisherman. **~car** vt
catch; <retirar da água> fish out ● vi fish;
▯ <entender> understand; <cochilar> nod
off; **~car de** ▯ know all about

pescoço /pes'kosu/ m neck

peseta /pe'zeta/ f peseta

peso /'pezu/ m weight; **de ~** fig
<pessoa> influential; <livro, argumento>
authoritative

pesqueiro /pes'keru/ a fishing

pesqui|sa /pes'kiza/ f research; <uma>
study; pl research; **~sa de mercado**
market research. **~sador** m researcher.
~sar vt/i research

pêssego /'pesigu/ m peach

pessegueiro /pesi'geru/ m peach tree

pessimis|mo /pesi'mizmu/ m
pessimism. **~ta** a pessimistic ● m/f
pessimist

péssimo /'pesimu/ a terrible, awful

pesso|a /pe'soa/ f person; pl people; **em
~a** in person. **~al** (pl **~ais**) a personal
● m staff; ▯ folks

pesta|na /pes'tana/ f eyelash; **tirar
uma ~na** ▯ have a nap. **~nejar** vi blink;
sem ~nejar fig without batting an eyelid

pes|te /'pestʃi/ f <doença> plague;
<criança etc> pest. **~ticida** m pesticide

pétala /'petala/ f petal

peteca /pe'teka/ f kind of shuttlecock;
<jogo> kind of badminton played with

the hand

peteleco /pete'lɛku/ m flick

petição /petʃi'sãw/ f petition

petisco /pe'tʃisku/ m savoury, titbit

petrificar /petrifi'kar/ vt petrify;
<de surpresa> stun. **~se** vpr be petrified;
<de surpresa> be stunned

petroleiro /petro'leru/ a oil ● m oil
tanker

petróleo /pe'trɔliu/ m oil, petroleum;
~ bruto crude oil

petrolífero /petro'liferu/ a oil-
producing

petroquími|ca /petro'kimika/ f
petrochemicals. **~co** a petrochemical

petu|lância /petu'lãsia/ f cheek.
~lante a cheeky

peúga /pi'uga/ f Port sock

pevide /pe'vidʒi/ f Port pip

pia /'pia/ f <do banheiro> washbasin;
<da cozinha> sink; **~ batismal** font

piada /pi'ada/ f joke

pia|nista /pia'nista/ m/f pianist. **~no** m
piano; **~no de cauda** grand piano

piar /pi'ar/ vi <pinto> cheep; <coruja>
hoot

picada /pi'kada/ f <de agulha, alfinete
etc> prick; <de abelha, vespa> sting; <de
mosquito, cobra> bite; <de heroína> shot;
<de avião> nosedive; **o fim da ~** fig the
limit

picadeiro /pika'deru/ m ring

picante /pi'kãtʃi/ a <comida> hot,
spicy; <piada> risqué; <filme, livro>
raunchy

pica-pau /pika'paw/ m woodpecker

picar /pi'kar/ vt <com agulha, alfinete
etc> prick; <abelha, vespa, urtiga> sting;
<mosquito, cobra> bite; <pássaro> peck;
chop <carne, alho etc>; shred <papel> ● vi
<peixe> bite; <lã, cobertor> prickle

picareta /pika'reta/ f pickaxe

pi|chação /piʃa'sãw/ f piece of graffiti;
pl graffiti. **~char** vt spray with graffiti
<muro, prédio>; spray <grafite, desenho>.
~che m pitch

picles /'piklis/ m pl pickles

pico /'piku/ m peak; **20 anos e ~** Port
just over 20

picolé /piko'lɛ/ m ice lolly

pico|tar /piko'tar/ vt perforate. **~te** /ɔ/
m perforations

pie|dade /pie'dadʒi/ f <religiosidade>
piety; <compaixão> pity. **~doso** /o/ a
merciful, compassionate

pie|gas /pi'ɛgas/ a invar ‹filme, livro› sentimental, schmaltzy; ‹pessoa› soppy. **~guice** f sentimentality

piercing m piercing

pifar /pi'far/ vi 🔲 break down, go wrong

pigar|rear /pigaxi'ar/ vi clear one's throat. **~ro** m frog in the throat

pigmento /pig'mẽtu/ m pigment

pig|meu /pig'mew/ a & m (f **~meia**) pygmy

pijama /pi'ʒama/ m pyjamas

pilantra /pi'lãtra/ m/f 🔲 crook

pilão /pi'lãw/ m (na cozinha) pestle; (na construção) ram

pilar /pi'lar/ m pillar

pilastra /pi'lastra/ f pillar

pileque /pi'lɛki/ m drinking session; **tomar um ~** get drunk

pilha /'piʎa/ f (monte) pile; (elétrica) battery

pilhar /pi'ʎar/ vt pillage

pilhéria /pi'ʎɛria/ f joke

pilotar /pilo'tar/ vt fly, pilot ‹avião›; drive ‹carro›

pilotis /pilo'tʃis/ m pl pillars

piloto /pi'lotu/ m pilot; (de carro) driver; (de gás) pilot light ● a invar pilot

pílula /'pilula/ f pill

pimen|ta /pi'mẽta/ f pepper; **~ta-de-Caiena** cayenne pepper. **~ta-do-reino** f black pepper. **~ta-malagueta** (pl **~tas-malagueta**) f chilli pepper. **~tão** m (bell) pepper. **~teira** f pepper pot

PIN /'pin/ m PIN (number)

pinacoteca /pinako'tɛka/ f art gallery

pin|ça /'pĩsa/ f (para tirar pelos) tweezers; (para segurar) tongs; (de siri etc) pincer. **~car** vt pluck ‹sobrancelhas›

pin|cel /pĩ'sɛw/ m (pl **~céis**) m brush. **~celada** f brush stroke. **~celar** vt paint

pin|ga /'pĩga/ f Brazilian rum. **~gado** a ‹café› with a dash of milk. **~gar** vi drip; (começar a chover) spit (with rain) ● vt drip. **~gente** m pendant. **~go** m drop; (no i) dot

pingue-pongue /pĩgi'põgi/ m table tennis

pinguim /pĩ'gwĩ/ m penguin

pi|nha /'piɲa/ f pine cone. **~nheiro** f pine tree. **~nho** m pine

pino /'pinu/ m pin; (para trancar carro) lock; **a ~** upright; **bater ~** ‹carro› knock

pin|ta /'pĩta/ f (sinal) mole; 🔲 (aparência) look. **~tar** vt paint; dye ‹cabelo›; put make-up on ‹rosto, olhos› ● vi paint; 🔲 ‹pessoa› show up; ‹problema, oportunidade› crop up. **~tar-se** vpr put on make-up

pintarroxo /pĩta'xoʃu/ m robin

pinto /'pĩtu/ m chick

pin|tor /pĩ'tor/ m painter. **~tura** f painting

pio¹ /'piu/ m (de pinto) cheep; (de coruja) hoot

pio² /'piu/ a pious

piolho /pi'oʎu/ m louse

pioneiro /pio'neru/ m pioneer ● a pioneering

pior /pi'ɔr/ a & adv worse; **o ~** the worst

pio|ra /pi'ɔra/ f worsening. **~rar** vt make worse, worsen ● vi get worse, worsen

pipa /'pipa/ f (que voa) kite; (de vinho) cask

pipilar /pipi'lar/ vi chirp

pipo|ca /pi'pɔka/ f popcorn. **~car** vi spring up. **~queiro** m popcorn seller

pique /'piki/ m (disposição) energy; **a ~** vertically; **ir a ~** ‹navio› sink

piquenique /piki'niki/ m picnic

pique|te /pi'ketʃi/ m picket. **~teiro** m picket

pirado /pi'radu/ a 🔲 crazy

pirâmide /pi'ramidʒi/ f pyramid

piranha /pi'raɲa/ f piranha; 🔲 (mulher) maneater

pirar /pi'rar/ vi 🔲 flip out 🔲, go mad 🔲

pirata /pi'rata/ a & m/f pirate; **~ informático** Port hacker. **~ria** f piracy; **~ria informática** Port hacking

pírcingue /'pirsinge/ m Port piercing; **~ de corpo** body piercing

pires /'piris/ m invar saucer

pirilampo /piri'lãpu/ m glow-worm

Pirineus /piri'news/ m pl Pyrenees

pirra|ça /pi'xasa/ f spiteful act; **fazer ~ça** be spiteful. **~cento** a spiteful

pirueta /piru'eta/ f pirouette

pirulito /piru'litu/ m lollipop

pi|sada /pi'zada/ f step; (rastro) footprint. **~sar** vt tread on; tread ‹uvas, palco›; (esmagar) trample on ● vi step; **~sar em** step on; (entrar) set foot in

pis|cadela /piska'dɛla/ f wink. **~ca-pisca** m indicator. **~car** vi (com o olho) wink; (pestanejar) blink; ‹estrela, luz› twinkle; ‹motorista› indicate ● m **num ~car de olhos** in a flash

p

piscicultura /pisikuw'tura/ f fish farming; (*lugar*) fish farm

piscina /pi'sina/ f swimming pool

piso /'pizu/ m floor

pisotear /pizotʃi'ar/ vt trample

pista /'pista/ f track; (*da estrada*) carriageway; (*para aviões*) runway; (*de circo*) ring; (*dica*) clue; ~ **de dança** dance floor

pistache /pis'taʃi/ m, **pistacho** /pis'taʃu/ m pistachio (nut)

pisto|la /pis'tɔla/ f pistol; (*para pintar*) spray gun. ~**lão** m influential contact. ~**leiro** m gunman

pitada /pi'tada/ f pinch

piteira /pi'tera/ f cigarette holder

pitoresco /pito'resku/ a picturesque

pitu /pi'tu/ m crayfish

pivete /pi'vetʃi/ m/f child thief

pivô /pi'vo/ m pivot

pixaim /piʃa'ĩ/ a frizzy

pizza /'pitsa/ f pizza. ~**ria** f pizzeria

placa /'plaka/ f plate; (*de carro*) number plate, *Amer* license plate; (*comemorativa*) plaque; (*em computador*) board; ~ **de sinalização** road sign

placar /pla'kar/ m scoreboard; (*escore*) scoreline

plácido /'plasidu/ a placid

plagi|ário /plaʒi'ariu/ m plagiarist. ~**ar** vt plagiarize

plágio /'plaʒiu/ m plagiarism

plaina /'plajna/ f plane

planador /plana'dor/ m glider

planalto /pla'nawtu/ m plateau

planar /pla'nar/ vi glide

planeamento, planear *Port*
▶ PLANEJAMENTO

plane|jamento /planeʒa'mẽtu/ m planning; ~**jamento familiar** family planning. ~**jar** vt plan

planeta /pla'neta/ m planet

planície /pla'nisi/ f plain

planificar /planifi'kar/ vt (*programar*) plan (out)

planilha /pla'niʎa/ f spreadsheet

plano /'planu/ a flat ● m plan; (*superfície, nível*) plane; **primeiro** ~ foreground

planta /'plãta/ f plant; (*do pé*) sole; (*de edifício*) ground plan. ~**ção** f (*ato*) planting; (*terreno*) plantation. ~**do** a **deixar alguém** ~**do** 🆃 keep sb waiting around

plantão /plã'tãw/ m duty; (*noturno*) night duty; **estar de** ~ be on duty

plantar /plã'tar/ vt plant

plas|ma /'plazma/ m plasma. ~**mar** vt mould, shape

plásti|ca /'plastʃika/ f facelift. ~**co** a & m plastic

plataforma /plata'fɔrma/ f platform

plátano /'platanu/ m plane tree

plateia /pla'teja/ f audience; (*parte do teatro*) stalls, *Amer* orchestra

platina /pla'tʃina/ f platinum. ~**dos** m pl points

platônico /pla'toniku/ a platonic

plausí|vel /plaw'zivew/ (pl ~**veis**) a plausible

ple|be /'plɛbi/ f common people. ~**beu** a (f ~**beia**) plebeian ● m (f ~**beia**) commoner. ~**biscito** m plebiscite

plei|tear /plejtʃi'ar/ vt contest. ~**to** m (*litígio*) case; (*eleitoral*) contest

ple|namente /plena'mẽtʃi/ adv fully. ~**nário** a plenary ● m plenary assembly. ~**no** /e/ a full; **em** ~**no verão** in the middle of summer

plissado /pli'sadu/ a pleated

pluma /'pluma/ f feather. ~**gem** f plumage

plu|ral /plu'raw/ (pl ~**rais**) a & m plural

plutônio /plu'toniu/ m plutonium

pluvi|al /pluvi'aw/ (pl ~**ais**) a rain

pneu /pi'new/ m tyre. ~**mático** a pneumatic ● m tyre

pneumonia /pineumo'nia/ f pneumonia

pó /pɔ/ m powder; (*poeira*) dust; **leite em** ~ powdered milk; ~ **de arroz** (face) powder

pobre /'pɔbri/ a poor ● m/f poor man (f woman); **os** ~**s** the poor. ~**za** /e/ f poverty

poça /'posa/ f pool; (*deixada pela chuva*) puddle

poção /po'sãw/ f potion

pocilga /po'siwga/ f pigsty

poço /'posu/ m (*de água, petróleo*) well; (*de mina, elevador*) shaft

podar /po'dar/ vt prune

podcast m podcast

poder /po'der/ ● v aux

····▶ (*capacidade*) can, to be able to; **posso escolher São Paulo ou Porto Alegre** I can choose São Paulo or Porto Alegre; **não podia acreditar**

I couldn't believe it; **desde então, ele não pode andar** he hasn't been able to walk since then

····▶ (*permissão*) can, may; **posso sair?** can ou may I go out?

❚ Há duas traduções possíveis de **poder** quando se pede permissão para fazer algo: *may* e *can*. No entanto, observe que *may* é mais formal do que *can*: **posso entrar?** may I come in?, can I come in? (*probabilidade*) may, could, might; **isso pode ou não ser verdade** that may or may not be true

❚ **could** e **might** exprimem uma probabilidade menor do que **may**

● *m*

····▶ power; **tomar o ~** seize power; **~ de compra** purchasing power; **~ executivo/legislativo** executive/ legislative power; **plenos ~es** full authority

····▶ (*em expressões*) **não ~ com alguém** dislike sb; **não posso com ele!** I can't stand him!; **não ~ mais** be exhausted; **querer é ~** where there's a will, there's a way

pode|rio /pode'riu/ *m* might. **~roso** /o/ *a* powerful

pódio /'pɔdʒiu/ *m* podium

podre /'podri/ *a* rotten; ⬛ (*cansado*) exhausted; (*doente*) grotty; **~ de rico** filthy rich. **~s** *m pl* faults

poei|ra /po'era/ *f* dust. **~rento** *a* dusty

poe|ma /po'ema/ *m* poem; **~sia** *f* (*arte*) poetry; (*poema*) poem. **~ta** *m* poet

poético /po'ɛtʃiku/ *a* poetic

poetisa /poe'tʃiza/ *f* poetess

pois /pojs/ *conj* as, since; **~ é** that's right; **~ não** of course; **~ não?** can I help you?; **~ sim** certainly not

polaco /pu'laku/ *Port a* Polish ● *m* Pole; (*língua*) Polish

polar /po'lar/ *a* polar

polarizar /polari'zar/ *vt* polarize. **~-se** *vpr* polarize

pole|gada /pole'gada/ *f* inch. **~gar** *m* thumb

poleiro /po'leru/ *m* perch

polêmi|ca /po'lemika/ *f* controversy, debate. **~co** *a* controversial

pólen /'pɔlẽ/ *m* pollen

polícia /po'lisia/ *f* police ● *m/f* policeman (f-woman)

polici|al /polisi'aw/ (*pl* **~ais**) *a* ‹carro, inquérito etc› police; ‹romance, filme› detective ● *m/f* policeman (f-woman). **~amento** *m* policing. **~ar** *vt* police

poli|dez /poli'des/ *f* politeness. **~do** *a* polite

poli|gamia /poliga'mia/ *f* polygamy. **~glota** *a* & *m/f* polyglot

Polinésia /poli'nezia/ *f* Polynesia

polinésio /poli'neziu/ *a* & *m* Polynesian

pólio /'pɔliu/ *f* polio

polir /po'lir/ *vt* polish

polissílabo /poli'silabu/ *m* polysyllable

políti|ca /po'litʃika/ *f* politics; (*uma*) policy. **~co** *a* political ● *m* politician

polo[1] /'pɔlu/ *m* pole

polo[2] /'pɔlu/ *m* (*jogo*) polo; **~ aquático** water polo

polo|nês /polo'nes/ *a* (f **~nesa**) Polish ● *m* (f **~nesa**) Pole; (*língua*) Polish

Polônia /po'lonia/ *f* Poland

polpa /'powpa/ *f* pulp

poltrona /pow'trona/ *f* armchair

polu|ente /polu'ẽtʃi/ *a* & *m* pollutant. **~ição** *f* pollution. **~ir** *vt* pollute

polvilhar /powvi'ʎar/ *vt* sprinkle

polvo /'powvu/ *m* octopus

pólvora /'pɔwvora/ *f* gunpowder

polvorosa /powvo'rɔza/ *f* uproar; **em ~** in uproar; ‹pessoa› in a flap

pomada /po'mada/ *f* ointment

pomar /po'mar/ *m* orchard

pom|ba /'põba/ *f* dove. **~bo** *m* pigeon

pomo de Adão /pomudʃia'dãw/ *m* Adam's apple

pom|pa /'põpa/ *f* pomp. **~poso** /o/ *a* pompous

ponche /'põʃi/ *m* punch

ponderar /põde'rar/ *vt/i* ponder

pônei /'ponej/ *m* pony

ponta /'põta/ *f* end; (*de faca, prego*) point; (*de nariz, dedo, língua*) tip; (*de sapato*) toe; *Cine, Teat* (*papel curto*) walk-on part; (*no campo de futebol*) wing; (*jogador*) winger; **na ~ dos pés** on tiptoe; **uma ~ de** a touch of ‹ironia etc›; **aguentar as ~s** ⬛ hold on. **~-cabeça** /e/ *f* **de ~-cabeça** upside down

pontada /põ'tada/ *f* (*dor*) twinge

pontapé /põta'pɛ/ *m* kick; **~ inicial** kick-off

pontaria /põta'ria/ *f* aim; **fazer ~** take aim

p

ponte /'põtʃɪ/ f bridge; ~ **aérea** shuttle; (*em tempo de guerra*) airlift; ~ **de safena** heart bypass; ~ **pênsil** suspension bridge

ponte If a public holiday falls on a Thursday or a Tuesday, it's common for people in Portugal or Brazil to take a day off in between. In Portugal, this practice is called *fazer ponte* (literally "make a bridge") between the holiday and the weekend, and is a very common way of extending holiday celebrations.

ponteiro /põ'teru/ m pointer; (*de relógio*) hand

pontiagudo /põtʃia'gudu/ a sharp

pontilhado /põtʃɪ'ʎadu/ a dotted

ponto /'põtu/ m point; (*de costura, tricô*) stitch; (*no final de uma frase*) full stop, *Amer* period; (*sinalzinho, no i*) dot; (*de ônibus*) stop; (*no teatro*) prompter; **a ~ de** on the point of; **ao ~ ‹carne›** medium; **até certo ~** to a certain extent; **às duas em ~** at exactly two o'clock; **dormir no ~** 🔲 miss the boat; **entregar os ~s** 🔲 give up; **fazer ~** 🔲 hang out; **dois ~s** colon; ~ **de exclamação/interrogação** exclamation/ question mark; ~ **de reciclagem** recycling point; ~ **de táxi** taxi rank, *Amer* taxi stand; ~ **de vista** point of view; ~ **morto** neutral. ~ **e vírgula** m semicolon

pontu|ação /põtua'sãw/ f punctuation. ~**al** (*pl* ~**ais**) a punctual. ~**alidade** f punctuality. ~**ar** vt punctuate

pontudo /põ'tudu/ a pointed

popa /'popa/ f stern

popu|lação /popula'sãw/ f population. ~**lacional** (*pl* ~**lacionais**) a population. ~**lar** a popular. ~**laridade** f popularity. ~**larizar** vt popularize. ~**larizar-se** vpr become popular

pôquer /'poker/ m poker

por /por/ ● prep

••••▸ (*lugar*) **circular pela direita** drive on the right; **passar pelo centro de Brasília** go through the centre of Brasília; **viajar pelo Brasil** travel round Brazil; **você passa ~ uma farmácia?** are you going past a chemist's?; **passo pela sua casa amanhã** I'll drop in tomorrow

••••▸ (*durante*) for; **só ~ uns dias** only for a few days; (*tempo aproximado*) about; ~ **volta de 8 horas** about 8

••••▸ (*causa*) **foi despedido ~ ser preguiçoso** he was sacked for being lazy; ~ **inveja/ciúme/hábito** out of jealousy/envy/habit; **faria qualquer coisa ~ você** I'll do anything for you; **trabalhar ~ dinheiro** work for money

••••▸ (*agente*) by; **assinado/escrito/ pintado ~** signed/written/painted by

••••▸ (*para com*) for; **sentir carinho ~ alguém** to feel affection for sb

••••▸ (*não feito*) ~ **lavar** not yet washed; **tive de deixar o trabalho ~ acabar** I had to leave the work unfinished

••••▸ (*substituição*) **ela irá ~ mim** she'll go instead of me

••••▸ (*preço*) for; **comprei ~ mil euros** I bought it for a thousand euros

••••▸ (*com verbos como agarrar, pegar*) by; **segurei-o pelo braço** I grabbed him by the arm

••••▸ (*em expressões*) ~ **isso** so; ~ **mim** (*no que me diz respeito*) as far as I'm concerned; ~ **mais que** however much

pôr /por/ vt put; put on ‹roupa, chapéu, óculos›; lay ‹mesa, ovos› ● m **o ~ do sol** sunset. ~**se** vpr ‹sol› set; ~**se a** start to; ~**se a caminho** set off

porão /po'rãw/ m (*de prédio*) basement; (*de casa*) cellar; (*de navio*) hold

porca /'pɔrka/ f (*de parafuso*) nut; (*animal*) sow

porção /por'sãw/ f portion; **uma ~ de** (*muitos*) a lot of

porcaria /porka'ria/ f (*sujeira*) filth; (*coisa malfeita*) piece of trash; *pl* trash

porcelana /porse'lana/ f china

porcentagem /porsẽ'taʒẽ/ f percentage

porco /'porku/ a filthy ● m (*animal*) pig; (*carne*) pork. ~**espinho** (*pl* ~**s-espinhos**) m porcupine

porém /po'rẽj/ conj however

pormenor /porme'nɔr/ m detail

por|nô /por'no/ a porn ● m porn film. ~**nografia** f pornography. ~**nográfico** a pornographic

poro /'pɔru/ m pore. ~**so** /o/ a porous

por|quanto /por'kwãtu/ conj since. ~**que** /por'ki/ conj because; *Port* (*por quê?*) why. ~**quê** /por'ke/ adv *Port* why ● m reason why

porquinho|-da-índia /porkiɲuda'idʒia/ (*pl* ~**s-da-índia**) m guinea pig

porrada /poˈxada/ f Ⅱ beating

porre /ˈpɔxi/ m Ⅱ drinking session, booze-up Ⅱ; **de ~** drunk; **tomar um ~** get drunk

porta /ˈpɔrta/ f door

porta-aviões /pɔrtaviˈõjs/ m invar aircraft carrier

porta-bagagens /pɔrtabaˈgaʒãjʃ/ m Port ▶ PORTA-MALAS

porta|-chaves /pɔrtaˈʃavis/ m invar keyholder or key-ring. **~joias** m invar jewellery box; **~lápis** m invar pencil holder; **~luvas** m invar glove compartment; **~malas** m invar boot, Amer trunk; **~níqueis** m invar purse

portador /pɔrtaˈdor/ m bearer

portagem /porˈtaʒẽ/ f Port toll

portanto /porˈtãtu/ conj therefore

portão /porˈtãw/ m gate

portar /porˈtar/ vt carry. **~se** vpr behave

porta|-retrato /pɔrtaxeˈtratu/ m photo frame. **~revistas** m invar magazine rack

portaria /portaˈria/ f (entrada) entrance; (decreto) decree

portá|til (pl **~teis**) a portable

portátil /purˈtatił/ m Port laptop

porta|-toalhas /pɔrtatoˈaʎas/ m invar towel rail. **~voz** m/f spokesman (f-woman)

porte /ˈpɔrtʃi/ m (frete) carriage; (de cartas etc) postage; (de pessoa) bearing; (dimensão) scale; **de grande/pequeno ~** large-/small-scale

porteiro /porˈteru/ m doorman; **~ eletrônico** entryphone

porto /ˈpɔrtu/ m port; **o P~** Oporto. **~ de escala** m port of call; **P~ Rico** m Puerto Rico; **~riquenho** /e/ a & m Puerto Rican; **~ USB** m USB port

portuá|rio /portuˈariu/ a port ● m dock worker, docker

portuense /portuˈẽsi/ a & m/f (person) from Oporto

Portugal /portuˈgaw/ m Portugal

portu|guês /portuˈges/ a & m (f **~guesa**) Portuguese

Português With over 250 million speakers, Portuguese is the sixth most widely spoken language in the world. The **CPLP** (*Comunidade dos Países de Língua Portuguesa*) comprises eight countries that have Portuguese as an official language: Angola, Brazil, Cape Verde, East Timor, Guinea-Bissau, Mozambique, Portugal, and São Tomé and Príncipe. African Portuguese-speaking countries are referred to as the *PALOP* (*Países Africanos de Língua Oficial Portuguesa*).

po|sar /poˈzar/ vi pose. **~se** /o/ f pose; (de filme) exposure

pós-datar /pɔzdaˈtar/ vt post-date

pós-escrito /pɔzisˈkritu/ m postscript

pós-gradua|ção /pɔzgraduaˈsãw/ f postgraduation. **~do** a & m postgraduate

pós-guerra /pɔzˈgexa/ m post-war period; **a Europa do ~** post-war Europe

posi|ção /poziˈsãw/ f position. **~cionar** vt position. **~tivo** a & m positive

posologia /pozoloˈʒia/ f dosage

pos|sante /poˈsãtʃi/ a powerful. **~se** /ɔ/ f (de casa etc) possession, ownership; (do presidente etc) swearing in; pl (pertences) possessions; **tomar ~se** take office; **tomar ~se de** take possession of

posses|são /poseˈsãw/ f possession. **~sivo** a possessive. **~so** /ɛ/ a possessed; (com raiva) furious

possibili|dade /posibiliˈdadʒi/ f possibility. **~tar** vt make possible

possí|vel /poˈsivew/ (pl **~veis**) a possible; **fazer todo o ~vel** do one's best

possuir /posuˈir/ vt possess; (ser dono de) own

posta /ˈpɔsta/ f (de peixe) steak

pos|tal /posˈtaw/ (pl **~tais**) a postal ● m postcard

postar /posˈtar/ vt place. **~se** vpr position o.s.

poste /ˈpɔstʃi/ m post

pôster /ˈposter/ m poster

posteri|dade /posteriˈdadʒi/ f posterity. **~or** a (no tempo) subsequent, later; (no espaço) rear. **~ormente** adv subsequently

postiço /posˈtʃisu/ a false

posto /ˈpostu/ m post; **~ de gasolina**; petrol station, Amer gas station; **~ de saúde** health centre ● pp de ▶ PÔR. **~ que** although

póstumo /ˈpɔstumu/ a posthumous

postura /posˈtura/ f posture

potá|vel /poˈtavew/ (pl **~veis**) a **água ~vel** drinking water

pote /ˈpɔtʃi/ m pot; (de vidro) jar

potência /poˈtẽsia/ f power

P

poten|cial /potẽsi'aw/ (pl ~ciais) a & m potential. ~te a potent

potencializar /potẽsiali'zar/ vt <vendas, crescimento> boost

potenciar /putẽsi'ar/ vt Port ▶ POTENCIALIZAR

potro /'potru/ m foal

pouco /'poku/ a & pron little ● adv not much ● m um ~ a little; ~ a ~ little by little; aos ~s gradually; daqui a ~ shortly; por ~ almost; ~ tempo a short time

pou|pança /po'pãsa/ f saving; (conta) savings account. ~par vt save; spare <vida>

pouquinho /po'kiɲu/ m um ~ (de) a little

pou|sada /po'zada/ f inn. ~sar vi land. ~so m landing

> **pousada** In the 1940s, the Portuguese government decided to create a series of hotels, called *pousadas*, in buildings of historic interest, such as convents, monasteries and castles. Although privately owned now, Portuguese *pousadas* still offer high-quality accommodation in very unique settings. In Brazil, a *pousada* is usually a guest house or a budget hotel.

po|vão /po'vãw/ m common people. ~vo /o/ m people

povo|ação /povoa'sãw/ f settlement. ~ar vt populate

poxa /'poʃa/ int gosh

pra /pra/ prep 1 ▶ PARA

praça /'prasa/ f (largo) square; (mercado) market ● m (soldado) private

prado /'pradu/ m meadow

pra-frente /pra'frẽtʃi/ a invar 1 with it 1, modern

praga /'praga/ f curse; (inseto, doença, pessoa) pest

prag|mático /prag'matʃiku/ a pragmatic. ~matismo m pragmatism

praguejar /prage'ʒar/ vt/i curse

praia /'praja/ f beach

pran|cha /'prãʃa/ f plank; (de surfe) board. ~cheta /e/ f drawing board

pranto /'prãtu/ m weeping

pra|ta /'prata/ f silver. ~taria f (coisas de prata) silverware. ~teado a silver-plated; (cor) silver

prateleira /prate'lera/ f shelf

prática /'pratʃika/ f practice; na ~ in practice

prati|cante /pratʃi'kãtʃi/ a practising ● m/f apprentice; (de esporte etc) player. ~car vt practise; (cometer, executar) carry out ● vi practise. ~cável (pl ~cáveis) a practicable

prático /'pratʃiku/ a practical

prato /'pratu/ m (objeto) plate; (comida) dish; (parte de uma refeição) course; (do toca-discos) turntable; pl (instrumento) cymbals; ~ fundo dish; ~ principal main course

praxe /'praʃi/ f normal practice; de ~ usually

> **praxe** The *código da praxe* refers to a set of rules and traditions to be followed by students at Portuguese universities. Thought to have originated at Portugal's oldest university in Coimbra, the traditions start in freshers' week in which the *caloiros* (freshers) are subjected to various initiation rites and practical jokes, such as being made to walk around town with cans attached to their feet.

prazer /pra'zer/ m pleasure; muito ~ (em conhecê-lo) pleased to meet you. ~oso /o/ a pleasurable

prazo /'prazu/ m term, time; a ~ <compra etc> on credit; a curto/longo ~ in the short/long term; último ~ deadline

preâmbulo /pri'ãbulu/ m preamble

precário /pre'kariu/ a precarious

precaução /prekaw'sãw/ f precaution

preca|ver-se /preka'versi/ vpr take precautions (de against). ~vido a cautious

prece /'presi/ f prayer

prece|dência /prese'dẽsia/ f precedence. ~dente a preceding ● m precedent. ~der vt/i precede

preceito /pre'sejtu/ m precept

precioso /presi'ozu/ a precious

precipício /presi'pisiu/ m precipice

precipi|tação /presipita'sãw/ f haste; (chuva etc) precipitation. ~tado a <fuga> headlong; <decisão, ato> hasty, rash. ~tar vt (lançar) throw; (antecipar) hasten. ~tar-se vpr (lançar-se) throw o.s.; (apressar-se) rush; (agir sem pensar) act rashly

precisamente /presiza'mẽtʃi/ *adv*
precisely

precisão /presi'zãw/ *f* precision,
accuracy

preci|sar /presi'zar/ *vt* (*necessitar*)
need; (*indicar com exatidão*) specify
● *vi* be necessary; **~sar de** need; **~so
ir** I have to go; **~sa-se** wanted. **~so** *a*
(*exato*) precise; (*necessário*) necessary

preço /'presu/ *m* price; **~ de custo** cost
price; **~ fixo** set price

precoce /pre'kɔsi/ *a* (*fruto*) early;
(*velhice, calvície etc*) premature;
(*criança*) precocious

precon|cebido /prekõse'bidu/ *a*
preconceived. **~ceito** *m* prejudice.
~ceituoso *a* prejudiced

preconizar /prekoni'zar/ *vt* advocate

precursor /prekur'sor/ *m* forerunner

preda|dor /preda'dor/ *m* predator.
~tório *a* predatory

predecessor /predese'sor/ *m*
predecessor

predestinar /predestʃi'nar/ *vt*
predestine

predeterminar /predetermi'nar/ *vt*
predetermine

predição /predʒi'sãw/ *f* prediction

predile|ção /predʒile'sãw/ *f*
preference. **~to** /ɛ/ *a* favourite

prédio /'predʒiu/ *m* building

predis|por /predʒis'por/ *vt* prepare
(**para** for); (*tornar parcial*) prejudice
(**contra** against). **~por-se** *vpr* prepare
o.s.. **~posto** *a* predisposed; (*contra*)
prejudiced

predizer /predʒi'zer/ *vt* predict,
foretell

predomi|nância /predomi'nãsia/ *f*
predominance. **~nante** *a* predominant.
~nar *vi* predominate

predomínio /predo'miniu/ *m*
predominance

preencher /priẽ'ʃer/ *vt* fill; fill in, *Amer*
fill out (*formulário*); meet (*requisitos*)

pré|-escola /preis'kɔla/ *f* infant school,
Amer preschool. **~-escolar** *a* preschool;
~-estreia *f* preview; **~-fabricado** *a*
prefabricated

prefácio /pre'fasiu/ *m* preface

prefei|to /pre'fejtu/ *m* mayor. **~tura** *f*
prefecture; (*prédio*) town hall

prefe|rência /prefe'rẽsia/ *f*
preference; (*direito no trânsito*) right of
way; **de ~rência** preferably. **~rencial**

(*pl* **~renciais**) *a* preferential; (*rua*) main.
~rido *a* favourite. **~rir** *vt* prefer (**a** to).
~rível (*pl* **~ríveis**) *a* preferable

prefixo /pre'fiksu/ *m* prefix

prega /'prega/ *f* pleat

pregador[1] /prega'dor/ *m* (*de roupa*)
peg

pre|gador[2] /prega'dor/ *m* (*quem
prega*) preacher. **~gão** *m* (*de vendedor*)
cry; **o ~gão** (*na bolsa de valores*) trading;
(*em leilão*) bidding

pregar[1] /pre'gar/ *vt* fix; (*com prego*)
nail; sew on (*botão*); **não ~ olho** not
sleep a wink; **~ uma peça em** play a
trick on; **~ um susto em alguém** give
sb a fright

pregar[2] /pre'gar/ *vt/i* preach

prego /'pregu/ *m* nail

pregui|ça /pre'gisa/ *f* laziness; (*bicho*)
sloth; **estou com ~ça de ir** I can't be
bothered to go. **~çoso** *a* lazy

pré-histórico /prejs'tɔriku/ *a*
prehistoric

preia-mar /preja'mar/ *f* high tide

prejudi|car /preʒudʒi'kar/ *vt* harm;
damage (*saúde*). **~car-se** *vpr* harm o.s..
~cial (*pl* **~ciais**) *a* harmful, damaging
(**a** to)

prejuízo /preʒu'izu/ *m* damage;
(*financeiro*) loss; **em ~ de** to the
detriment of

prejulgar /preʒuw'gar/ *vt* prejudge

preliminar /prelimi'nar/ *a & m/f*
preliminary

prelo /'prelu/ *m* printing press; **no ~**
being printed

prelúdio /pre'ludʒiu/ *m* prelude

prematuro /prema'turu/ *a* premature

premeditar /premedʒi'tar/ *vt*
premeditate

premente /pre'mẽtʃi/ *a* pressing

premi|ado /premi'adu/ *a* (*romance,
atleta etc*) prizewinning; (*bilhete, número
etc*) winning ● *m* prizewinner. **~ar** *vt*
award a prize to (*romance, atleta etc*);
reward (*honestidade, mérito*)

prêmio /'premiu/ *m* prize; (*de seguro*)
premium; **Grande Prêmio** (*de F1*) Grand
Prix

premir /pre'mir/ *vt Port* press (*tecla*)

premissa /pre'misa/ *f* premiss

premonição /premoni'sãw/ *f*
premonition

pré-na|tal /prena'taw/ (*pl* **~tais**) *a*
antenatal, *Amer* prenatal

p

prenda /ˈprẽda/ f Port present; **~s domésticas** household chores. **~do** a domesticated

pren|dedor /prẽde'dor/ m clip; **~dedor de roupa** clothes peg. **~der** vt (pregar) fix; (capturar) arrest; (atar) tie up ‹cachorro›; tie back ‹cabelo›; (restringir) restrict; (ligar afetivamente) bind; **~der (a atenção de) alguém** grab sb ('s attention)

prenhe /ˈpreɲi/ a pregnant

prenome /pre'nomi/ m first name

pren|sa /ˈprẽsa/ f press. **~sar** vt press

preocu|pação /preokupa'sãw/ f concern. **~pante** a worrying. **~par** vt worry. **~par-se** vpr worry (**com** about)

prepa|ração /prepara'sãw/ f preparation. **~rado** m preparation. **~rar** vt prepare. **~rar-se** vpr prepare, get ready. **~rativos** m pl preparations. **~ro** m preparation; (competência) knowledge; **~ro físico** physical fitness

preponderar /prepõde'rar/ vi prevail (**sobre** over)

preposição /prepozi'sãw/ f preposition

prerrogativa /prexoga'tʃiva/ f prerogative

presa /ˈpreza/ f (de caça) prey; (de cobra) fang; (de elefante) tusk; **~ de guerra** spoils of war

prescin|dir /presĩ'dʒir/ vi **~dir de** dispense with. **~dível** (pl **~díveis**) a dispensable

pres|crever /preskre'ver/ vt prescribe. **~crição** f prescription; (norma) rule

presen|ça /pre'zẽsa/ f presence; **~ça de espírito** presence of mind. **~ciar** vt (estar presente a) be present at; (testemunhar) witness. **~te** a & m present. **~tear** vt **~tear alguém (com algo)** give sb (sth as) a present

presépio /pre'zɛpiu/ m crib

preser|vação /prezerva'sãw/ f preservation. **~var** vt preserve, protect. **~vativo** m (em comida) preservative; (camisinha) condom

presi|dência /prezi'dẽsia/ f presidency; (de uma reunião) chair. **~dencial** (pl **~denciais**) a presidential. **~dencialismo** m presidential system. **~dente** m (f **~denta**) president; (de uma reunião) chairperson

presidiário /prezidʒi'ariu/ m convict

presídio /pre'zidʒiu/ m prison

presidir /prezi'dʒir/ vi preside (**a** over)

presilha /pre'ziʎa/ f fastener; (de cabelo) slide

preso /ˈprezu/ pp de ▶ **PRENDER** ● m prisoner; **ficar ~** get stuck; ‹saia, corda etc› get caught

pressa /ˈprɛsa/ f hurry; **às ~s** in a hurry, hurriedly; **estar com** ou **ter ~** be in a hurry

presságio /pre'saʒiu/ m omen

pressão /pre'sãw/ f pressure; **fazer ~ sobre** put pressure on; **~ arterial** blood pressure

pressen|timento /presẽtʃi'mẽtu/ m premonition, feeling. **~tir** vt sense

pressionar /presio'nar/ vt press ‹botão›; pressure ‹pessoa›

pressupor /presu'por/ vt ‹pessoa› presume; ‹coisa› presuppose

pressurizado /presuri'zadu/ a pressurized

pres|tação /presta'sãw/ f repayment, instalment. **~tar** vt render ‹contas, serviço›; **não ~ta** he/it is no good; **~tar atenção** pay attention; **~tar juramento** take an oath ● vi be of use. **~tativo** a helpful. **~tável** (pl **~táveis**) a serviceable

prestes /ˈprɛstʃis/ a invar **~ a** about to

prestidigita|ção /prestʃidʒiʒita'sãw/ f conjuring. **~dor** m conjurer

pres|tigiar /prestʃiʒi'ar/ vt give prestige to. **~tígio** m prestige. **~tigioso** /o/ a prestigious

préstimo /ˈprɛstʃimu/ m merit

presumir /prezu'mir/ vt presume

presun|ção /prezũ'sãw/ f presumption. **~çoso** /o/ a presumptuous

presunto /pre'zũtu/ m ham

pretendente /pretẽ'dẽtʃi/ m/f (candidato) candidate, applicant

preten|der /pretẽ'der/ vt intend. **~são** f pretension. **~sioso** /o/ a pretentious

preterir /prete'rir/ vt disregard

pretérito /pre'tɛritu/ m preterite

pretexto /pre'testu/ m pretext

preto /ˈpretu/ a & m black. **~ e branco** invar black and white

prevalecer /prevale'ser/ vi prevail

prevenção /prevẽ'sãw/ f (impedimento) prevention; (parcialidade) bias

prevenir /preve'nir/ vt (evitar) prevent; (avisar) warn. **~se** vpr take precautions

preventivo /prevẽ'tʃivu/ a preventive

prever /pre'ver/ vt foresee, predict

previdência /previ'dēsia/ f foresight; ~ **social** social security

prévio /'previu/ a prior

previ|são /previ'zãw/ f prediction, forecast; ~**são do tempo** weather forecast. ~**sível** (pl ~**síveis**) a predictable

pre|zado /pre'zadu/ a esteemed; **Prezado Senhor** Dear Sir. ~**zar** vt think highly of. ~**zar-se** vpr have self-respect

prima /'prima/ f cousin

primário /pri'mariu/ a primary; (fundamental) basic

primata /pri'mata/ m primate

primave|ra /prima'vera/ f spring; (flor) primrose. ~**ril** (pl ~**ris**) a spring

primazia /prima'zia/ f primacy

primei|ra /pri'mera/ f (marcha) first (gear); **de** ~**ra** first-rate; <carne> prime. ~**ra-dama** (pl ~**ras-damas**) f first lady. ~**ranista** m/f first-year (student). ~**ro** a & adv first; **no dia** ~**ro de maio** on the first of May; **em** ~**ro lugar** (para começar) in the first place; (numa corrida, competição) in first place; ~**ro de tudo** first of all; ~**ros socorros** first aid. ~**ro-ministro** (pl ~**ros-ministros**) m (f ~**ra-ministra**) prime-minister

primitivo /primi'tʃivu/ a primitive

primo /'primu/ m cousin ● a **número** ~ prime number. ~**gênito** a & m firstborn

primor /pri'mor/ m perfection

primordi|al /primordʒi'aw/ (pl ~**ais**) a (primitivo) primordial; (fundamental) fundamental

primoroso /primo'rozu/ a exquisite

princesa /prī'seza/ f princess

princi|pado /prīsi'padu/ m principality. ~**pal** (pl ~**pais**) a main ● m principal

príncipe /'prīsipi/ m prince

principiante /prīsipi'ãtʃi/ m/f beginner

princípio /prī'sipiu/ m (início) beginning; (regra) principle; **em** ~ in principle; **por** ~ on principle

priori|dade /priori'dadʒi/ f priority. ~**tário** a priority

prisão /pri'zãw/ f (ato de prender) arrest; (cadeia) prison; (encarceramento) imprisonment; ~ **perpétua** life imprisonment; ~ **de ventre** constipation

prisioneiro /prizio'neru/ m prisoner

prisma /'prizma/ m prism

privação /priva'sãw/ f deprivation

privacidade /privasi'dadʒi/ f privacy

pri|vada /pri'vada/ f toilet. ~**vado** a private; ~**vado de** deprived of. ~**var** vt deprive (**de** of). ~**var-se** vpr deprive o.s. (**de** of)

privati|vo /priva'tʃivu/ a private. ~**zar** vt privatize

privi|legiado /privileʒi'adu/ a privileged; <tratamento> preferential. ~**legiar** vt favour. ~**légio** m privilege

pro [1]= para + o

pró /prɔ/ adv for ● **e** os e os contras the pros and cons

proa /'proa/ f bow, prow

proativo /prɔa'tʃivu/ a proactive

probabilidade /probabili'dadʒi/ f probability

proble|ma /pro'blema/ m problem. ~**mático** a problematic

proce|dência /prose'dēsia/ f origin. ~**dente** a logical; ~**dente de** coming from. ~**der** vi proceed; (comportar-se) behave; (na justiça) take legal action; ~**der de** come from. ~**dimento** m procedure; (comportamento) behaviour; (na justiça) proceedings

proces|sador /prosesa'dor/ m processor; ~**sador de texto** word processor. ~**samento** m processing; (na justiça) prosecution; ~**samento de dados** data processing. ~**sar** vt process; (por crime) prosecute; (por causa civil) sue. ~**so** /ɛ/ m process; (criminal) trial; (civil) lawsuit

procla|mação /proklama'sãw/ f proclamation. ~**mar** vt proclaim

procri|ação /prokria'sãw/ f procreation. ~**ar** vt/i procreate

procu|ra /pro'kura/ f search; (de produto) demand; **à** ~**ra de** in search of. ~**ração** f power of attorney. ~**rado** a sought after, in demand; ~**rado pela polícia** wanted by the police. ~**rador** m (mandatário) proxy; (advogado) public prosecutor. ~**rar** vt look for; (contatar) get in touch with; (ir visitar) look up; ~**rar saber** try to find out

prodígio /pro'dʒiʒiu/ m wonder; (pessoa) prodigy

prodigioso /prodʒiʒi'ozu/ a prodigious

pródigo /'prɔdigu/ a lavish, extravagant

produ|ção /produ'sãw/ f production. ~**tividade** f productivity. ~**tivo** a productive. ~**to** m product; (renda) proceeds; ~**to nacional bruto** gross

P

national product; **~tos agrícolas**
agricultural produce. **~tor** m producer
● **a país ~tor de trigo** wheat-producing
country. **~zido** a 🔢 (*arrumado*) done up.
~zir vt produce

proeminente /proemi'nẽtʃi/ a
prominent

proeza /pro'eza/ f achievement

profa|nar /profa'nar/ vt desecrate.
~no a profane

profecia /profe'sia/ f prophecy

proferir /profe'rir/ vt utter; give
⟨*discurso, palestra*⟩; pass ⟨*sentença*⟩

profes|sar /profe'sar/ vt profess. **~so**
/ɛ/ a professed; ⟨*político etc*⟩ seasoned.
~sor m teacher; **~sor catedrático**
professor

pro|feta /pro'feta/ m prophet. **~fético**
a prophetic. **~fetizar** vt prophesy

profissão /profi'sãw/ f profession

profissio|nal /profisio'naw/ (pl
~nais) a & m/f professional. **~nalismo**
m professionalism. **~nalizante** a
vocational. **~nalizar-se** vpr ⟨*esportista
etc*⟩ turn professional

profun|didade /profũdʒi'dadʒi/ f
depth. **~do** a deep; ⟨*sentimento etc*⟩
profound

profusão /profu'zãw/ f profusion

prog|nosticar /prognostʃi'kar/ vt
forecast. **~nóstico** m forecast; *Med*
prognosis

progra|ma /pro'grama/ m
programme; (*de computador*)
program; (*diversão*) thing to do.
~mação f programming. **~mador** m
programmer. **~mar** vt plan; program
⟨*computador etc*⟩. **~mável** (pl **~máveis**)
a programmable

progredir /progre'dʒir/ vi progress

progres|são /progre'sãw/ f
progression. **~sista** a & m/f progressive.
~sivo a progressive. **~so** /ɛ/ m progress

proi|bição /proibi'sãw/ f ban
(**de** on). **~bido** a forbidden. **~bir** vt
forbid (**alguém de** sb to); ban ⟨*livro,
importações etc*⟩. **~bitivo** a prohibitive

proje|ção /proʒe'sãw/ f projection.
~tar vt plan ⟨*viagem, estrada etc*⟩;
design ⟨*casa, carro etc*⟩; project ⟨*filme,
luz*⟩

projé|til /pro'ʒɛtʃiw/ (pl **~teis**) m
projectile

proje|tista /proʒe'tʃista/ m/f designer.
~to /ɛ/ m project; (*de casa, carro*) design;
~to de lei bill. **~tor** m projector

prol /prɔw/ m **em ~ de** on behalf of

prole /'prɔli/ f offspring. **~tariado** m
proletariat. **~tário** a & m proletarian

prolife|ração /prolifera'sãw/ f
proliferation. **~rar** vi proliferate

prolífico /pro'lifiku/ a prolific

prolixo /pro'liksu/ a verbose, long-
winded

prólogo /'prɔlogu/ m prologue

prolon|gado /prolõ'gadu/ a
prolonged. **~gar** vt prolong. **~gar-se**
vpr go on

promessa /pro'mɛsa/ f promise

prome|tedor /promete'dor/ a
promising. **~ter** vt promise ● vi (*dar
esperança*) show promise; **~ter voltar**
promise to return

promíscuo /pro'miskuu/ a
promiscuous

promis|sor /promi'sor/ a promising.
~sória f promissory note

promoção /promo'sãw/ f promotion

promontório /promõ'tɔriu/ m
promontory

promo|tor /promo'tor/ m promoter;
(*advogado*) prosecutor. **~ver** vt promote

promulgar /promuw'gar/ vt
promulgate

prono|me /pro'nomi/ m pronoun.
~minal (pl **~minais**) a pronominal

pron|tidão /prõtʃi'dãw/ f readiness;
com ~tidão promptly; **estar de ~tidão**
be at the ready. **~tificar** vt get ready.
~tificar-se vpr volunteer (**a** to **para** for).
~to a ready; (*rápido*) prompt ● int that's
that. **~to-socorro** (pl **~tos-socorros**)
m casualty department; *Port* (*reboque*)
tow truck. **~tuário** m (*manual*) manual,
handbook; (*médico*) notes; (*policial*)
record, file

pronto-a-comer /prõtwaku'mer/ m
invar *Port* take-away, *Amer* take-out

pronúncia /pro'nũsia/ f pronunciation

pronunci|ado /pronũsi'adu/
a pronounced. **~amento** m
pronouncement. **~ar** vt pronounce

propagar /propa'gar/ vt propagate
⟨*espécie*⟩; spread ⟨*notícia, ideia, fé*⟩. **~se**
vpr spread; ⟨*espécie*⟩ propagate

propen|são /propẽ'sãw/ f propensity.
~so a inclined (**a** to)

pro|piciar /propisi'ar/ vt provide.
~pício a propitious

propina /pro'pina/ f bribe; *Port*
(*escolar*) fee

propor /pro'por/ *vt* propose. **~se** *vpr* set o.s. ‹*objetivo*›; **~se a estudar** set out to study

proporção /propor'sãw/ *f* proportion

proporcionado /proporsio'nadu/ *a* proportionate (a to); **bem~nado** well proportioned. **~nal** (*pl* **~nais**) *a* proportional. **~nar** *vt* provide

proposição /propozi'sãw/ *f* proposition. **~tado** *a*, **~tal** (*pl* **~tais**) *a* intentional

propósito /pro'pɔzitu/ *m* intention; **a ~** by the way; **a ~ de** on the subject of; **chegar a ~** arrive at the right time; **de ~** on purpose

proposta /pro'pɔsta/ *f* proposal

propriamente /propria'mẽtʃi/ *adv* strictly; **a casa ~ dita** the house proper

propriedade /proprie'dadʒi/ *f* property; (*direito sobre bens*) ownership. **~tário** *m* owner; (*de casa alugada*) landlord

próprio /'prɔpriu/ *a* (*de si*) own; ‹*sentido*› literal; ‹*nome*› proper; **meu ~ carro** my own car; **um carro ~** a car of my own; **o ~ rei** the king himself; **~ a** peculiar to; **~ para** suited to

prorrogação /proxoga'sãw/ *f* extension; (*de dívida*) deferment; (*em futebol etc*) extra time. **~gar** *vt* extend ‹*prazo*›; defer ‹*pagamento*›

prosa /'prɔza/ *f* prose. **~sador** *m* prose writer. **~saico** *a* prosaic

proscrever /proskre'ver/ *vt* proscribe

prospecto /pros'pɛktu/ *m* (*livro*) brochure; (*folheto*) leaflet

prosperar /prospe'rar/ *vi* prosper. **~ridade** *f* prosperity

próspero /'prɔsperu/ *a* prosperous

prosseguimento /prosegi'mẽtu/ *m* continuation. **~guir** *vt* continue ● *vi* proceed, go on

prostituição /prostʃitui'sãw/ *f* prostitution. **~ta** *f* prostitute

prostração /prostra'sãw/ *f* debility. **~trado** *a* prostrate. **~trar** *vt* prostrate; (*enfraquecer*) debilitate. **~trar-se** *vpr* prostrate o.s.

protagonista /protago'nista/ *m/f* protagonist. **~nizar** *vt* be at the centre of ‹*acontecimento*›; feature in ‹*peça, filme*›

proteção /prote'sãw/ *f* protection. **~cionismo** *m* protectionism. **~cionista** *a* & *m/f* protectionist. **~ger** *vt* protect. **~gido** *m* protégé

proteína /prote'ina/ *f* protein

protelar /prote'lar/ *vt* put off

protestante /protes'tãtʃi/ *a* & *m/f* Protestant. **~tar** *vt/i* protest. **~to** /ɛ/ *m* protest

protetor /prote'tor/ *m* protector ● *a* protective

protocolo /proto'kɔlu/ *m* protocol; (*registro*) register

protótipo /pro'tɔtʃipu/ *m* prototype

protuberância /protube'rãsia/ *f* bulge

prova /'prɔva/ *f* (*que comprova*) proof; (*teste*) trial; (*exame*) exam; (*esportiva*) competition; (*de livro etc*) proof; *pl* (*na justiça*) evidence; **à ~va de bala** bulletproof; **pôr à ~va** put to the test. **~vado** *a* proven. **~var** *vt* try ‹*comida*›; try on ‹*roupa*›; try out ‹*carro, novo sistema etc*›; (*comprovar*) prove

provável /pro'vavew/ (*pl* **~veis**) *a* probable

proveito /pro'vejtu/ *m* profit, advantage; **tirar ~ de** (*beneficiar-se*) profit from; (*explorar*) take advantage of. **~so** /o/ *a* useful

proveniência /proveni'ẽsia/ *f* origin. **~ente** *a* originating (*de* from)

proventos /pro'vẽtus/ *m pl* proceeds

prover /pro'ver/ *vt* provide (*de* with)

provérbio /pro'verbiu/ *m* proverb

proveta /pro'veta/ *f* test tube; **bebê de ~** test-tube baby

providência /provi'dẽsia/ *f* (*medida*) measure, step; (*divina*) providence; **tomar ~dências** take steps, take action. **~denciar** *vt* (*prover*) get hold of, provide; (*resolver*) see to, take care of ● *vi* take action

província /pro'vĩsia/ *f* province; (*longe da cidade*) provinces

provincial /provĩsi'aw/ (*pl* **~ais**) *a* provincial. **~ano** *a* & *m* provincial

provir /pro'vir/ *vi* come (*de* from); (*resultar*) be due (*de* to)

provisão /provi'zãw/ *f* provision. **~sório** *a* provisional

provocação /provoka'sãw/ *f* provocation. **~cador, ~cante** *a* provocative. **~car** *vt* provoke; (*ocasionar*) cause

proximidade /prosimi'dadʒi/ *f* closeness; *pl* (*imediações*) vicinity

próximo /'prɔsimo/ *a* (*no tempo*) next; (*perto*) near, close (*de* to); ‹*parente*›

p

close; ‹*futuro*› near ● *m* neighbour, fellow man

pru|dência /pru'dẽsia/ *f* prudence. **~dente** a prudent

prumo /'prumu/ *m* plumb line; **a ~** vertically

prurido /pru'ridu/ *m* itch

pseudônimo /pisew'donimu/ *m* pseudonym

psica|nálise /pisika'nalizi/ *f* psychoanalysis. **~nalista** *m/f* psychoanalyst

psi|cologia /pisikolo'ʒia/ *f* psychology. **~cológico** a psychological. **~cólogo** *m* psychologist

psico|pata /pisiko'pata/ *m/f* psychopath. **~se** /ɔ/ *f* psychosis. **~terapeuta** *m/f* psychotherapist. **~terapia** *f* psychotherapy

psicótico /pisi'kɔtʃiku/ a & *m* psychotic

psique /pi'siki/ *f* psyche

psiqui|atra /pisiki'atra/ *m/f* psychiatrist. **~atria** *f* psychiatry. **~átrico** a psychiatric

psíquico /pi'sikiku/ a psychic

pua /'pua/ *f* bit

puberdade /puber'dadʒi/ *f* puberty

publi|cação /publika'sãw/ *f* publication. **~car** *vt* publish

publici|dade /publisi'dadʒi/ *f* publicity; (*reclame*) advertising. **~tário** a publicity; (*de reclame*) advertising ● *m* advertising executive

público /'publiku/ a public ● *m* public; (*plateia*) audience; **em ~** in public; **o grande ~** the general public

pudera /pu'dɛra/ *int* no wonder!

pudico /pu'dʒiku/ a prudish

pudim /pu'dʒĩ/ *m* pudding

pudor /pu'dor/ *m* modesty, shame

pue|ril /pue'riw/ (*pl* **~ris**) a puerile

pugilis|mo /puʒi'lizmu/ *m* boxing. **~ta** *m* boxer

pu|ído /pu'idu/ a worn through. **~ir** *vt* wear through

pujan|ça /pu'ʒãsa/ *f* power. **~te** a powerful; (*de saúde*) robust

pular /pu'lar/ *vt* jump (over); (*omitir*) skip ● *vi* jump; **~ de contente** jump for joy; **~ carnaval** celebrate Carnival; **~ corda** skip

pulga /'puwga/ *f* flea

pulmão /puw'mãw/ *m* lung

pulo /'pulu/ *m* jump; **dar um ~ em** drop by; **dar ~s** jump up and down

pulôver /pu'lover/ *m* pullover

púlpito /'puwpitu/ *m* pulpit

pul|sar /puw'sar/ *vi* pulsate. **~seira** *f* bracelet. **~so** *m* (*do braço*) wrist; (*batimento arterial*) pulse

pulular /pulu'lar/ *vi* swarm (**de** with)

pulveri|zador /puwveriza'dor/ *m* spray. **~zar** *vt* spray ‹*líquido*›; (*reduzir a pó*) *fig* pulverize

pun|gente /pũ'ʒẽtʃi/ a consuming. **~gir** *vt* afflict

pu|nhado /pu'ɲadu/ *m* handful. **~nhal** (*pl* **~nhais**) *m* dagger. **~nhalada** *f* stab wound. **~nho** *m* fist; (*de camisa etc*) cuff; (*de espada*) hilt

pu|nição /puni'sãw/ *f* punishment. **~nir** *vt* punish. **~nitivo** a punitive

pupila /pu'pila/ *f* pupil

purê /pu're/ *m* purée; **~ de batata** mashed potato

pureza /pu'reza/ *f* purity

pur|gante /pur'gãtʃi/ a & *m* purgative. **~gar** *vt* purge. **~gatório** *m* purgatory

purificar /purifi'kar/ *vt* purify

puritano /puri'tanu/ a & *m* puritan

puro /'puru/ a pure; ‹*aguardente*› neat; **~ e simples** pure and simple. **~sangue** (*pl* **~s-sangues**) a & *m* thoroughbred

púrpura /'purpura/ a purple

purpurina /purpu'rina/ *f* glitter

purulento /puru'lẽtu/ a festering

pus /pus/ *m* pus

pusilânime /puzi'lanimi/ a faint-hearted

pústula /'pustula/ *f* pimple

puta /'puta/ *f* whore ● a *invar* 🄸 **um ~ carro** one hell of a car; **filho da ~** (*vulg*) bastard; **~ que (o) pariu!** (*chulo*) fucking hell!

puto /'putu/ a 🄸 furious

putrefazer /putrefa'zer/ *vi* putrefy

puxa /'puʃa/ *int* gosh

pu|xado /pu'ʃadu/ a 🄸 ‹*exame*› tough; ‹*trabalho*› hard; ‹*aluguel, preço*› steep. **~xador** *m* handle. **~xão** *m* pull, tug. **~xa-puxa** *m* toffee. **~xar** *vt* pull; strike up ‹*conversa*›; bring up ‹*assunto*›; **~xar de uma perna** limp; **~xar para** (*parecer com*) take after; **~xar por** (*exigir muito de*) push (hard). **~xa-saco** *m* 🄸 creep

Qq

QI /ke i/ *m* IQ

quadra /'kwadra/ *f* (*de tênis etc*) court; (*quarteirão*) block. **~do** *a* & *m* square

quadragésimo /kwadra'ʒezimu/ *a* fortieth

qua|dril /kwa'driw/ (*pl* **~dris**) *m* hip

quadrilha /kwa'driʎa/ *f* (*bando*) gang; (*dança*) square dance

quadrinho /kwa'driɲu/ *m* frame; **história em ~s** comic strip

quadro /'kwadru/ *m* picture; (*pintado*) painting; (*tabela*) table; (*pessoal*) staff; (*equipe*) team; (*de uma peça*) scene; **~ interativo** interactive whiteboard. **~negro** (*pl* **~s-negros**) *m* blackboard

quadruplicar /kwadrupli'kar/ *vt/i* quadruple

quádruplo /'kwadruplu/ *a* quadruple. **~s** *m pl* (*crianças*) quads

qual /kwaw/ (*pl* **quais**) *pron* which (one); **o/a ~** (*coisa*) that, which; (*pessoa*) that, who; **~ é o seu nome?** what's your name?; **seja ~ for a decisão** whatever the decision may be

qualidade /kwali'dadʒi/ *f* quality; **na ~ de** in one's capacity as, as

qualifi|cação /kwalifika'sãw/ *f* qualification. **~car** *vt* qualify; (*descrever*) describe (**de** as). **~car-se** *vpr* qualify

qualitativo /kwalita'tʃivu/ *a* qualitative

qualquer /kwaw'kɛr/ ● *a* & *pron*

••••▸ (*não importa qual*) any; **pegue ~ ônibus que vai para o centro** catch any bus that goes downtown; **em ~ caso** in any case; **em ~ momento** at any time; **~ coisa/pessoa** anything/ any one; **~ uma serve** any of them will do; **~ um** (*qualquer pessoa*) **~ um pode se enganar** anyone can make a mistake; **~ um sabe isso** everybody knows that; (*entre dois*) either one; **qual dos dois livros devo levar? ~ um** which of the two books should I take?_either one

••••▸ (*em expressões*) **~ dia** one of these days

quando /'kwãdu/ *adv & conj* when; **~ quer que** whenever; **~ de** at the time of; **~ muito** at most

quantia /kwã'tʃia/ *f* amount

quanti|dade /kwãtʃi'dadʒi/ *f* quantity; **uma ~dade de** a lot of; **em ~dade** in large amounts. **~ficar** *vt* quantify. **~tativo** *a* quantitative

quanto /'kwãtu/ *adv & pron* how much; *pl* how many; **~ tempo?** how long?; **~ mais barato melhor** the cheaper the better; **tão alto ~ eu** as tall as me; **~ ri!** how I laughed!; **~ a** as for; **~ antes** as soon as possible

quaren|ta /kwa'rẽta/ *a* & *m* forty. **~tão** *a* & *m* (*f* **~tona**) forty-year-old. **~tena** /e/ *f* quarantine

quaresma /kwa'rɛzma/ *f* Lent

quarta /'kwarta/ *f* (*dia*) Wednesday; (*marcha*) fourth (gear). **~ de final** (*pl* **~s de final**) *f* quarter final; **~feira** (*pl* **~s-feiras**) *f* Wednesday

quartanista /kwarta'nista/ *m/f* fourth-year (student)

quarteirão /kwarte'rãw/ *m* block

quar|tel /kwar'tɛw/ (*pl* **~téis**) *m* barracks. **~tel-general** (*pl* **~téis-generais**) *m* headquarters

quarteto /kwar'tetu/ *m* quartet; **~ de cordas** string quartet

quarto /'kwartu/ *a* fourth ● *m* (*parte*) quarter; (*aposento*) bedroom; (*guarda*) watch; **são três e/menos um ~** *Port* it's quarter past/to three; **~ de banho** *Port* bathroom; **~ de hora** quarter of an hour; **~ de hóspedes** guest room

quartzo /'kwartzu/ *m* quartz

quase /'kwazi/ *adv* almost, nearly; **~ nada/nunca** hardly anything/ever

quatro /'kwatru/ *a* & *m* four; **de ~** (*no chão*) on all fours; **~ por ~** <*carro*> four-by-four. **~centos** *a* & *m* four hundred

que /ki/ ● *pron rel*

••••▸ (*pessoas, sujeito*) who, that; **o homem ~ esteve aqui ontem** the man who came here yesterday; (*pessoas, complemento*) whom, that; **o rapaz ~ você conheceu** the boy (whom) you met; (*coisas*) that, which; **o carro ~ está estacionado na praça** the car that is parked in the square

❗ quando *que* é complemento, é frequentemente omitido: **a revista que lhe emprestei ontem** *the magazine (that/which) I lent you yesterday*

● *conj*

••••▸ (*integrante*) that; **disse ~ viria esta semana** he said (that) he would come this week; (*em ordens*) **quero**

q

~ **me deixem em paz!** I want to be left alone!; (*em comparações*) than; **o meu irmão é mais alto do** ~ **eu** my brother is taller than me; (*resultado*) that; **estava tão cansada** ~ **adormeci** I was so tired (that) I fell asleep; (*causa*) **não saias** ~ **está a chover muito** don't go out because it's pouring

● *pron*

····▸ (*interrogativo*) what; ~ **horas são?** what time is it?; **em** ~ **andar você mora?** what floor do you live on?; (*com escolha limitada*) which; **com** ~ **carro vamos hoje? o seu ou o meu?** which car shall we take today? yours or mine?; (*exclamação*) what; ~ **casas tão bonitas!** what lovely houses!; ~ **vida!** what a life!; ~ **horror!** how dreadful!; ~ **aborrecimento!** how annoying!

····▸ (*em expressões*) ~ **tal?: que tal foi o filme?** how was the film?; ~ **tal um café?** how about a coffee?

quê /ke/ *pron* what ● *m* **um** ~ something; **não tem de** ~ don't mention it

quebra /'kɛbra/ *f* break; (*de empresa, banco*) crash; (*de força*) cut; **de** ~ in addition. ~**cabeça** *m* jigsaw (puzzle); *fig* puzzle. ~**diço** *a* breakable. ~**do** *a* broken; ‹*carro*› broken down. ~**dos** *m pl* small change. ~**galho** *m* 🄸 stopgap; ~**mar** *m* breakwater; ~**molas** *m invar* speed bump; ~**nozes** *m invar* nutcrackers; ~**pau** *m* 🄸 row; ~**quebra** *m* riot

quebrar /ke'brar/ *vt* break ● *vi* break; ‹*carro etc*› break down; ‹*banco, empresa etc*› crash, go bust. ~**se** *vpr* break

queda /'keda/ *f* fall; **ter uma** ~ **por** have a soft spot for. ~ **de braço** *f* arm wrestling

quei|jeira /ke'ʒera/ *f* cheese dish. ~**jo** *m* cheese; ~**jo prato** Cheddar. ~**jo de minas** *m* Cheshire cheese

queima /'kejma/ *f* burning. ~**da** *f* forest fire. ~**do** *a* burnt; (*bronzeado*) tanned, brown; **cheiro de** ~**do** smell of burning

queimar /kej'mar/ *vt* burn; (*bronzear*) tan ● *vi* burn; ‹*lâmpada*› go; ‹*fusível*› blow. ~**se** *vpr* burn o.s.; (*bronzear-se*) go brown

queima-roupa /kejma'xopa/ *f* à ~ point-blank

quei|xa /'keʃa/ *f* complaint. ~**xar-se** *vpr* complain (**de** about)

queixo /'keʃu/ *m* chin; **bater o** ~ shiver

queixoso /ke'ʃozu/ *a* plaintive ● *m* plaintiff

quem /kẽj/ *pron* who; (*a pessoa que*) anyone who, he who; **de** ~ **é este livro?** whose is this book?; ~ **quer que** whoever; **seja** ~ **for** whoever it is; ~ **falou isso fui eu** it was me who said that; ~ **me dera (que) ...** I wish ..., if only ...

Quênia /'kenia/ *m* Kenya

queniano /keni'anu/ *a* & *m* Kenyan

quen|tão /kẽ'tãw/ *m* mulled wine. ~**te** *a* hot; (*com calor agradável*) warm. ~**tura** *f* heat

quepe /'kɛpi/ *m* cap

quer /kɛr/ *conj* ~ ... ~ ... whether ... or ...

querer /ke'rer/ *vt/i* want; **quero ir** I want to go; **quero que você vá** I want you to go; **eu queria falar com o Sr X** I'd like to speak to Mr X; **vai** ~ **vir amanhã?** do you want to come tomorrow?; **vou** ~ **um cafezinho** I'd like a coffee; **se você quiser** if you want; **queira sentar** do sit down; ~ **dizer** mean; **quer dizer** (*isto é*) that is to say, I mean

querido /ke'ridu/ *a* dear ● *m* darling

quermesse /ker'mɛsi/ *f* fête, fair

querosene /kero'zeni/ *m* kerosene

questão /kes'tãw/ *m* question; (*assunto*) matter; **em** ~ in question; **fazer** ~ **de** really want to; **não faço** ~ **de ir** I don't mind not going

questio|nar /kestʃio'nar/ *vt/i* question. ~**nário** *m* questionnaire. ~**nável** (*pl* ~**náveis**) *a* questionable

quiabo /ki'abu/ *m* okra

quibe /'kibi/ *m* savoury meatball

quicar /ki'kar/ *vt/i* bounce

quiche /'kiʃi/ *f* quiche

quie|to /ki'etu/ *a* (*calado*) quiet; (*imóvel*) still. ~**tude** *f* quiet

quilate /ki'latʃi/ *m* carat; *fig* calibre

quilha /'kiʎa/ *f* keel

quilo /'kilo/ *m* kilo. ~**grama** *m* kilogram. ~**metragem** *f* mileage. ~**métrico** *a* mile-long

quilômetro /ki'lometru/ *m* kilometre

quimbanda /kĩ'bãda/ *m* Afro-Brazilian cult

qui|mera /ki'mera/ *f* fantasy. ~**mérico** *a* fanciful

quími|ca /'kimika/ *f* chemistry. ~**co** *a* chemical ● *m* chemist

quimioterapia /kimiotera'pia/ f chemotherapy

quimono /ki'mɔnu/ m kimono

quina /'kina/ f de ~ edgeways

quindim /kĩ'dʒĩ/ m sweet made of coconut, sugar and egg yolks

quinhão /ki'ɲãw/ m share

quinhentos /ki'ɲẽtus/ a & m five hundred

quinina /ki'nina/ f quinine

quinquagésimo /kwĩkwa'ʒezimu/ a fiftieth

quinquilharias /kĩkiʎa'rias/ f pl knick-knacks

quinta¹ /'kĩta/ f (fazenda) farm

quinta² /'kĩta/ f (dia) Thursday. **~feira** (pl **~s-feiras**) f Thursday

quin|tal /kĩ'taw/ (pl **~tais**) m back yard

quinteiro /kĩ'tajru/ m Port farmer

quinteto /kĩ'tetu/ m quintet

quin|to /'kĩtu/ a & m fifth. **quintuplo** a fivefold. **quintuplos** m pl (crianças) quins

quinze /'kĩzi/ a & m fifteen; **às dez e ~** at quarter past ten; **são ~ para as dez** it's quarter to ten. **~na** /e/ f fortnight. **~nal** (pl **~nais**) a fortnightly. **~nalmente** adv fortnightly

quiosque /ki'ɔski/ m (banca) kiosk; (no jardim) gazebo

quiro|mância /kiro'mãsia/ f palmistry. **~mante** m/f palmist

quisto /'kistu/ m cyst

quitan|da /ki'tãda/ f grocer's (shop). **~deiro** m grocer

qui|tar /ki'tar/ vt pay off ‹dívida›. **~te** a estar **~te** be quits

quociente /kwosi'ẽtʃi/ m quotient

quórum /'kwɔrũ/ m quorum

....

Rr

....

rã /xã/ f frog

rabanete /xaba'netʃi/ m radish

rabear /xabi'ar/ vi ‹caminhão› jack-knife

rabino /xa'binu/ m rabbi

rabis|car /xabis'kar/ vt scribble ● vi (escrever mal) scribble; (fazer desenhos) doodle. **~co** m doodle

rabo /'xabu/ m (de animal) tail; **com o ~ do olho** out of the corner of one's eye. **~ de cavalo** (pl **~s de cavalo**) m pony tail

rabugento /xabu'ʒẽtu/ a grumpy

raça /'xasa/ f (de homens) race; (de animais) breed

ração /xa'sãw/ f (de comida) ration; (para animal) food

racha /'xaʃa/ f crack. **~dura** f crack

rachar /xa'ʃar/ vt (dividir) split; (abrir fendas em) crack; chop ‹lenha›; split ‹despesas› ● vi (dividir-se) split; (apresentar fendas) crack; (ao pagar) split the cost

raci|al /xasi'aw/ (pl **~ais**) a racial

racio|cinar /xasiosi'nar/ vi reason. **~cínio** m reasoning. **~nal** (pl **~nais**) a rational. **~nalizar** vt rationalize

racio|namento /xasiona'mẽtu/ m rationing. **~nar** vt ration

racis|mo /xa'sizmu/ m racism. **~ta** a & m/f racist

radar /xa'dar/ m radar; (na estrada) speed camera

radia|ção /xadʒia'sãw/ f radiation. **~dor** m radiator

radialista /xadʒia'lista/ m/f radio announcer

radiante /xadʒi'ãtʃi/ a (de alegria) overjoyed

radi|cal /xadʒi'kaw/ (pl **~cais**) a & m radical. **~car-se** vpr settle

rádio¹ /'xadʒiu/ m radio ● f radio station

rádio² /'xadʒiu/ m (elemento) radium

radioati|vidade /xadioatʃivi'dadʒi/ f radioactivity. **~vo** a radioactive

radiodifusão /xadʒiodʒifu'zãw/ f broadcasting

radiogra|far /xadʒiogra'far/ vt X-ray ‹pulmões, osso etc›; radio ‹mensagem›. **~fia** f X-ray

radiolo|gia /xadʒiolo'ʒia/ f radiology. **~gista** m/f radiologist

radio|novela /xadʒiono'vɛla/ f radio serial. **~patrulha** f patrol car. **~táxi** m radio taxi. **~terapia** f radiotherapy, ray treatment

raia /'xaja/ f (em corrida) lane; (peixe) ray

rainha /xa'iɲa/ f queen. **~mãe** f queen mother

raio /'xaju/ m (de luz etc) ray; (de círculo) radius; (de roda) spoke; (relâmpago) bolt of lightning; **~ de ação** range

rai|va /'xajva/ f rage; (doença) rabies; **estar com ~va** be furious (**de** with);

q

r

ter ~va de alguém have it in for sb.
~voso a furious; ‹cachorro› rabid

raiz /xa'iz/ f root; ~ quadrada/cúbica
square/cube root

rajada /xa'ʒada/ f (de vento) gust;
(de tiros) burst

ra|lador /xala'dor/ m grater. ~lar vt
grate

ralé /xa'lɛ/ f rabble

ralhar /xa'ʎar/ vi scold

ralo¹ /'xalu/ m (ralador) grater;
(de escoamento) drain

ralo² /'xalu/ a ‹cabelo› thinning; ‹sopa,
tecido› thin; ‹vegetação› sparse; ‹café›
weak

ra|mal /xa'maw/ (pl ~mais) m (telefone)
extension; (de ferrovia) branch line

ramalhete /xama'ʎetʃi/ m posy,
bouquet

ramifi|cação /xamifika'sãw/ f branch.
~car-se vi branch off

ramo /'xamu/ m branch; (profissional
etc) field; (buquê) bunch; Domingo de
Ramos Palm Sunday

rampa /'xãpa/ f ramp

rancor /xã'kor/ m resentment. ~oso
/o/ a resentful

rançoso /xã'sozu/ a rancid

ran|ger /xã'ʒer/ vt grind ‹dentes› ● vi
creak. ~gido m creak

ranhura /xa'ɲura/ f groove; (para
moedas) slot

ranzinza /xã'zĩza/ a cantankerous

rapariga /xapa'riga/ f Port girl

rapaz /xa'pas/ m boy

rapé /xa'pɛ/ m snuff

rapel /ra'pɛw/ m abseiling

rapidez /xapi'des/ f speed

rápido /'xapidu/ a fast ● adv ‹fazer›
quickly; ‹andar› fast

rapina /xa'pina/ f ave de ~ bird of prey

rapo|sa /xa'poza/ f vixen. ~so m fox

rapsódia /xap'sɔdʒia/ f rhapsody

rap|tar /xap'tar/ vt abduct, kidnap
‹criança›. ~to m abduction, kidnapping
(de criança)

raquete /xa'ketʃi/ f, Port raqueta
/xa'keta/ f racquet

raquítico /xa'kitʃiku/ a puny

ra|ramente /xara'mẽtʃi/ adv rarely.
~ridade f rarity. ~ro a rare ● adv rarely

rascunho /xas'kuɲu/ m rough version,
draft

ras|gado /xaz'gadu/ a torn; fig ‹elogios
etc› effusive. ~gão m tear. ~gar vt tear;
(em pedaços) tear up ● vi, ~gar-se vpr
tear. ~go m tear; fig burst

raso /'xazu/ a ‹água› shallow; ‹sapato›
flat; ‹colher etc› level

ras|pão /xas'pãw/ m graze; atingir
de ~pão graze. ~par vt shave ‹cabeça,
pelos›; plane ‹madeira›; (para limpar)
scrape; (tocar de leve) graze; ~par em
scrape

rasteiro /xas'teru/ a ‹planta›
creeping; ‹animal› crawling; ~tejante a
crawling; ‹voz› slurred. ~tejar vi crawl

rasto /'xastu/ m ▶ RASTRO

ras|trear /xastri'ar/ vt track ‹satélite
etc›; scan ‹céu, corpo etc›. ~tro m trail

rasura /xa'zura/ f crossing-out

rasurar /xazu'rar/ vt to cross out

ratear¹ /xatʃi'ar/ vi ‹motor› miss

ra|tear² /xatʃi'ar/ vt share. ~teio m
sharing

ratifi|cação /xatʃifika'sãw/ f
ratification. ~car vt ratify

rato /'xatu/ m rat; (camundongo)
mouse; Port Comput mouse. ~eira f
mousetrap

ravina /xa'vina/ f ravine

razão /xa'zãw/ f reason; (proporção)
ratio ● m ledger; à ~ de at the rate of;
em ~ de on account of; ter ~ be right;
não ter ~ be wrong

razoá|vel /xazo'avew/ (pl ~veis) a
reasonable

ré¹ /xɛ/ f (na justiça) defendant

ré² /xɛ/ f (marcha) reverse; dar ~ reverse

reabastecer /xeabaste'ser/ vt/i refuel

reabilitar /xeabili'tar/ vt rehabilitate

rea|ção /xea'sãw/ f reaction; ~ção em
cadeia chain reaction. ~cionário a & m
reactionary

readmitir /xeadʒimi'tʃir/ vt reinstate
‹funcionário›

reagir /xea'ʒir/ vi react; ‹doente›
respond

reajus|tar /xeaʒus'tar/ vt readjust. ~te
m adjustment

re|al /xe'aw/ (pl ~ais) a ‹verdadeiro› real;
(da realeza) royal

real|çar /xeaw'sar/ vt highlight. ~ce m
prominence

realejo /xea'leʒu/ m barrel organ

realeza /xea'leza/ f royalty

realidade /xeali'dadʒi/ f reality

realimentação /xealimẽta'sãw/ f
feedback

realis|mo /xea'lizmu/ m realism. **~ta** a
realistic ● m/f realist

realização /'xealiza'sãw/ f (de projeto)
implementation; (de sonho, objetivo)
fulfilment; Cine direction

reali|zado /xeali'zadu/ a ‹pessoa›
fulfilled. **~zar** vt (fazer) carry out; (tornar
real) realize ‹sonho, capital›. **~zar-se** vpr
‹sonho› come true; ‹pessoa› fulfil o.s.;
‹casamento, reunião etc› take place

realizador /xializa'dor/ m Port Cine
director

realmente /xeaw'mẽtʃi/ adv really

reaparecer /xeapare'ser/ vi reappear

reativar /xeatʃi'var/ vt reactivate

reaver /xea'ver/ vt get back

reavivar /xeavi'var/ vt revive

rebaixar /xeba'ʃar/ vt lower ‹preço›;
fig demean ● vi ‹preços› drop. **~se** vpr
demean o.s.

rebanho /xe'baɲu/ m herd; (fiéis) flock

reba|ter /xe'batʃi/ m alarm. **~ter**
vt return ‹bola›; refute ‹acusação›;
(ao computador) retype

rebelar-se /xebe'larsi/ vpr rebel

rebel|de /xe'bewdʒi/ a rebellious ● m/f
rebel. **~dia** f rebelliousness

rebelião /xebeli'ãw/ f rebellion

reben|tar /xebẽ'tar/ vt/i
▶ ARREBENTAR. **~to** m (de planta) shoot;
(descendente) offspring

rebite /xe'bitʃi/ m rivet

rebobinar /xebobi'nar/ vt rewind

rebo|cador /xeboka'dor/ m tug. **~car**
vt (tirar) tow; (cobrir com reboco) plaster.
~co /o/ m plaster

rebolar /xebo'lar/ vi swing one's hips

reboque /xe'bɔki/ m towing; (veículo
a ~) trailer; (com guindaste) towtruck;
a ~ on tow

rebote /xe'bɔtʃi/ m (esporte) rebound

rebuçado /xebu'sadu/ m Port sweet,
Amer candy

rebuliço /xebu'lisu/ m commotion

rebuscado /xebus'kadu/ a recherché

recado /xe'kadu/ m message

reca|ída /xeka'ida/ f relapse. **~ir** vi
relapse; ‹acento, culpa› fall

recal|cado /xekaw'kadu/ a repressed.
~car vt repress

recanto /xe'kãtu/ m nook, recess

recapitular /xekapitu'lar/ vt review
● vi recap

recarga /xe'karga/ f (de caneta) refill

recarregar /xekare'gar/ vt recharge
‹bateria›; top up ‹crédito›

reca|tado /xeka'tadu/ a reserved,
withdrawn. **~to** m reserve

recear /xesi'ar/ vt/i fear (por for)

rece|ber /xese'ber/ vt receive; entertain
‹convidados› ● vi (~ber salário) get paid;
(~ber convidados) entertain. **~bimento**
m receipt

receio /xe'seju/ m fear

recei|ta /xe'sejta/ f (de cozinha) recipe;
(médica) prescription; (dinheiro) revenue.
~tar vt prescribe

recém|-casados /xesẽjka'zadus/ m pl
newly-weds. **~chegado** m newcomer;
~nascido a newborn ● m newborn
child, baby

recenseamento /xesẽsja'mẽtu/ m
Port ▶ CENSO

recente /xe'sẽtʃi/ a recent. **~mente**
adv recently

receoso /xese'ozu/ a (apreensivo) afraid

recep|ção /xesep'sãw/ f reception; Port
(de carta) receipt; **~ção de sinal** Telec
reception. **~cionar** vt receive. **~cionista**
m/f receptionist. **~táculo** m receptacle.
~tivo a receptive. **~tor** m receiver

reces|são /xese'sãw/ f recession. **~so**
/ɛ/ m recess

re|chear /xeʃi'ar/ vt stuff ‹frango,
assado›; fill ‹empada›. **~cheio** m (para
frango etc) stuffing; (de empada etc)
filling

rechonchudo /xeʃõ'ʃudu/ a plump

recibo /xe'sibu/ m receipt

reciclagem /xesi'klaʒẽj/ f recycling

reciclar /xesik'lar/ vt recycle

recife /xe'sifi/ m reef

recinto /xe'sĩtu/ m enclosure

recipiente /xesipi'ẽtʃi/ m container

reciprocar /xesipro'kar/ vt reciprocate

recíproco /xe'siproku/ a reciprocal;
‹sentimento› mutual

reci|tal /xesi'taw/ (pl ~tais) m recital.
~tar vt recite

recla|mação /xeklama'sãw/ f
complaint; (no seguro) claim. **~mar**
vt claim ● vi complain (de about);
(no seguro) claim. **~me** m, Port **~mo** m
advertising

reclinar-se /xekli'narsi/ vpr recline

recluso /xe'kluzu/ a reclusive ● m
recluse

r

recobrar /xeko'brar/ vt recover. ~**se** vpr recover

recolher /xeko'ʎer/ vt collect; (retirar) withdraw. ~**se** vpr retire

recomeçar /xekome'sar/ vt/i start again

recomen|dação /xekomẽda'sãw/ f recommendation. ~**dar** vt recommend. ~**dável** (pl ~**dáveis**) a advisable

recompen|sa /xekõ'pẽsa/ f reward. ~**sar** vt reward

reconcili|ação /xekõsilia'sãw/ f reconciliation. ~**ar** vt reconcile. ~**ar-se** vpr be reconciled

reconhe|cer /xekoɲe'ser/ vt recognize; (admitir) acknowledge; Mil reconnoitre; identify ‹corpo›. ~**cimento** m recognition; (gratidão) gratitude; Mil reconnaissance; (de corpo) identification. ~**cível** (pl ~**cíveis**) a recognizable

reconsiderar /xekõside'rar/ vt/i reconsider

reconstituinte /xekõstʃitu'ĩtʃi/ m tonic

reconstituir /xekõstʃitu'ir/ vt reform; reconstruct ‹crime, cena›

reconstruir /xekõstru'ir/ vt rebuild

recor|dação /xekorda'sãw/ f recollection; (objeto) memento. ~**dar** vt recollect; ~**dar-se (de)** recall

recor|de /xe'kɔrdʒi/ a invar & m record. ~**dista** a record-breaking ● m/f record holder

recorrer /xeko'xer/ vi ~ **a** turn to ‹médico, amigo›; resort to ‹violência, tática›; ~ **de** appeal against

recor|tar /xekor'tar/ vt cut out. ~**te** /ɔ/ m cutting, Amer clipping

recostar /xekos'tar/ vt lean back. ~**se** vpr lean back

recreio /xe'kreju/ m recreation; (na escola) break

recriar /xekri'ar/ vt recreate

recriminação /xekrimina'sãw/ f recrimination

recrudescer /xekrude'ser/ vi intensify

recru|ta /xe'kruta/ m/f recruit. ~**tamento** m recruitment. ~**tar** vt recruit

recu|ar /xeku'ar/ vi move back; ‹tropas› retreat; (no tempo) go back; (ceder) back down; (não cumprir) back out (**de** of) ● vt move back. ~**o** m retreat; fig (de intento) climbdown

recupe|ração /xekupera'sãw/ f recovery. ~**rar** vt recover; make up ‹atraso, tempo perdido›. ~**rar-se** vpr

recover (**de** from)

recurso /xe'kursu/ m resort; (coisa útil) resource; (na justiça) appeal; pl resources

recu|sa /xe'kuza/ f refusal. ~**sar** vt refuse; turn down ‹convite, oferta›. ~**sar-se** vpr refuse (**a** to)

reda|ção /xeda'sãw/ f (de livro, contrato) draft; (pessoal) editorial staff; (seção) editorial department; (na escola) composition. ~**tor** m editor

rede /'xedʒi/ f net; (para deitar) hammock; fig (sistema) network; ~ **social** social network. ~ **corporativa** Comput intranet

rédea /'xedʒia/ f rein

redemoinho /xedemo'iɲu/ m ▶ RODAMOINHO

reden|ção /xedẽ'sãw/ f redemption. ~**tor** a redeeming ● m redeemer

redigir /xedʒi'ʒir/ vt draw up ‹contrato›; write ‹artigo›; edit ‹dicionário›

redimir /xedʒi'mir/ vt redeem

redobrar /xedo'brar/ vt redouble

redon|deza /xedõ'deza/ f roundness; pl vicinity. ~**do** a round

redor /xe'dɔr/ m **ao ou em ~ de** around

redução /xedu'sãw/ f reduction

redun|dante /xedũ'dãtʃi/ a redundant. ~**dar** vi ~**dar em** develop into

redu|zido /xedu'zidu/ a limited; (pequeno) small. ~**zir** vt reduce. ~**zir-se** vpr (ficar reduzido) be reduced (**a** to); (resumir-se) come down (**a** to)

reeleger /xeele'ʒer/ vt re-elect

reeleição /xeelej'sãw/ f re-election

reembol|sar /xeẽbow'sar/ vt reimburse ‹pessoa›; refund ‹dinheiro›. ~**so** /o/ m refund; ~**so postal** cash on delivery

reencarnação /xeẽkarna'sãw/ f reincarnation

reentrância /xeẽ'trãsia/ f recess

reescalonar /xeeskalo'nar/ vt reschedule

reescrever /xeeskre'ver/ vt rewrite

refastelar-se /xefaste'larsi/ vpr stretch out

refazer /xefa'zer/ vt redo; rebuild ‹vida›. ~**se** vpr recover (**de** from)

refei|ção /xefej'sãw/ f meal. ~**tório** m dining hall

refém /xe'fẽj/ m hostage

referência /xefeˈrẽsia/ f reference;
com ~ a with reference to

referendum /xefeˈrẽdũ/ m
referendum

refe|rente /xefeˈrẽtʃi/ a **~rente a**
regarding. **~rir** vt report. **~rir-se** vpr
refer (**a** to)

refestelar-se /xefesteˈlarsi/ vpr Port
▶ REFASTELAR-SE

re|fil /xeˈfiw/ (pl **~fis**) m refill

refi|nado /xefiˈnadu/ a refined.
~namento m refinement. **~nar** vt refine.
~naria f refinery

refle|tido /xefleˈtʃidu/ a ‹decisão›
well-thought-out; ‹pessoa› thoughtful.
~tir vt/i reflect. **~tir-se** vpr be reflected.
~xão /ks/ f reflection. **~xivo** /ks/ a
reflexive. **~xo** /eks/ a ‹luz› reflected;
‹ação› reflex ● m (de luz etc) reflection;
(físico) reflex; (no cabelo) streak

refluxo /xeˈfluksu/ m ebb

refo|gado /xefoˈgadu/ m lightly fried
mixture of onions and garlic. **~gar** vt
fry lightly

refor|çar /xeforˈsar/ vt reinforce. **~ço**
/o/ m reinforcement

refor|ma /xeˈfɔrma/ f (da lei etc)
reform; (na casa etc) renovation; (de
militar) discharge; (pensão) pension;
~ma ministerial cabinet reshuffle.
~mado a reformed; Port (aposentado)
retired ● m Port pensioner. **~mar** vt
reform ‹lei, sistema etc›; renovate ‹casa,
prédio›; Port (aposentar) retire. **~mar-se**
vpr Port (aposentar-se) retire; ‹criminoso›
reform. **~matório** m reform school.
~mista a & m/f reformist

refrão /xeˈfrãw/ m chorus

refratário /xefraˈtariu/ a ‹tigela etc›
ovenproof, heatproof

refrear /xefriˈar/ vt rein in ‹cavalo›; fig
curb, keep in check ‹paixões etc›. **~se**
vpr restrain o.s.

refrega /xeˈfrega/ f clash, fight

refres|cante /xefresˈkãtʃi/ a
refreshing. **~car** vt freshen, cool ‹ar›;
refresh ‹pessoa, memória etc› ● vi get
cooler. **~car-se** vpr refresh o.s.. **~co** /e/
m (bebida) soft drink; pl refreshments

refrige|rado /xefriʒeˈradu/ a cooled;
‹casa etc› air-conditioned; (na geladeira)
refrigerated. **~rador** m refrigerator.
~rante m soft drink. **~rar** vt keep cool;
(na geladeira) refrigerate

refugi|ado /xefuʒiˈadu/ m refugee.
~ar-se vpr take refuge

refúgio /xeˈfuʒiu/ m refuge

refugo /xeˈfugu/ m waste, refuse

refutar /xefuˈtar/ vt refute

regaço /xeˈgasu/ m lap

regador /xegaˈdor/ m watering can

regalia /xegaˈlia/ f privilege

regar /xeˈgar/ vt water

regata /xeˈgata/ f regatta

regatear /xegatʃiˈar/ vi bargain, haggle

re|gência /xeˈʒẽsia/ f (de verbo etc)
government. **~gente** m/f (de orquestra)
conductor. **~ger** vt govern ● vi rule

regenerar /xeʒeneˈrar/ vt regenerate

região /xeʒiˈãw/ f region; (de cidade
etc) area

regi|me /xeˈʒimi/ m regime; (dieta)
diet; **fazer ~me** diet. **~mento** m (militar)
regiment; (regulamento) regulations

régio /ˈxeʒiu/ a regal

> **Regiões Autónomas (de Portugal)** *i*
> The autonomous regions of
> Portugal are the archipelagos of
> Madeira and the Azores. Together with
> mainland Portugal, these make up the
> Portuguese Republic. Each autonomous
> region has its own government and
> legislative assembly.

regio|nal /xeʒioˈnaw/ (pl **~nais**) a
regional

registar /xeʒiʃˈtar/ vt Port ▶ **registrar**
/xeʒiʃˈtrar/

registo /xeˈʒiʃtu/ m Port
▶ **registro** /xeˈʒiʃtru/

regis|trador /xeʒistraˈdor/ a **caixa
~tradora** cash register. **~trar** vt register;
(anotar) record. **~tro** m (lista) register;
(de um fato, em banco de dados) record;
(ato de ~trar) registration

rego /ˈxegu/ m (de arado) furrow;
(de roda) rut; (para escoamento) ditch

regozi|jar /xegoziˈʒar/ vt delight.
~jar-se vpr be delighted. **~jo** m delight

regra /ˈxegra/ f rule; pl (menstruações)
periods; **em ~** as a rule

regres|sar /xegreˈsar/ vi return.
~sivo a regressive; **contagem ~siva**
countdown. **~so** /e/ m return

régua /ˈxegwa/ f ruler

regu|lagem /xeguˈlaʒẽ/ f (de carro)
tuning. **~lamento** m regulations. **~lar** a
regular; ‹estatura, qualidade etc› average
● vt regulate; tune ‹carro, motor›; set
‹relógio›; **~lar-se por** go by, be guided
by ● vi work. **~laridade** f regularity.
~larizar vt regularize

r

regurgitar /xegurʒi'tar/ vt bring up

rei /xej/ m king. **~nado** m reign

reincidir /xeĩsi'dʒir/ vi ‹criminoso› reoffend

reino /'xejnu/ m kingdom; fig (da fantasia etc) realm; **Reino Unido** United Kingdom

reiterar /xejte'rar/ vt reiterate

reitor /xej'tor/ m chancellor, Amer president

reivindi|cação /xejvĩdʒika'sãw/ f demand. **~car** vt claim, demand

rejei|ção /xeʒej'sãw/ f rejection. **~tar** vt reject

rejuvenescer /xeʒuvene'ser/ vt rejuvenate ● vi be rejuvenated

relação /xela'sãw/ f relationship; (relatório) account; (lista) list; pl relations; **com** ou **em ~ a** in relation to, regarding

relacio|namento /xelasiona-'mẽtu/ m relationship. **~nar** vt relate (**com** to); (listar) list. **~nar-se** vpr relate (**com** to)

relações-públicas /xelasõjs'publikas/ m/f invar public relations person

relâmpago /xe'lãpagu/ m flash of lightning; pl lightning ● a lightning; **num ~** in a flash

relampejar /xelãpe'ʒar/ vi flash; **relampejou** there was a flash of lightning

relance /xe'lãsi/ m glance; **olhar de ~** glance (at)

rela|tar /xela'tar/ vt relate. **~tivo** a relative. **~to** m account. **~tório** m report

rela|xado /xela'ʃadu/ a relaxed; ‹disciplina› lax; ‹pessoa› lazy, complacent. **~xamento** m (físico) relaxation; (de pessoa) complacency. **~xante** a relaxing ● m tranquillizer. **~xar** vt relax ● vi (descansar) relax; (tornar-se omisso) get complacent. **~xar-se** vpr relax. **~xe** m relaxation

reles /'xelis/ a invar ‹gente› common; ‹ação› despicable

rele|vância /xele'vãsia/ f relevance. **~vante** a relevant. **~var** vt emphasize. **~vo** /e/ m relief; (importância) prominence

religi|ão /xeliʒi'ãw/ f religion. **~oso** /o/ a religious

relin|char /xelĩ'ʃar/ vi neigh. **~cho** m neighing

relíquia /xe'likia/ f relic

relógio /xe'lɔʒiu/ m clock; (de pulso) watch

relu|tância /xelu'tãsia/ f reluctance. **~tante** a reluctant. **~tar** vi be reluctant (**em** to)

reluzente /xelu'zẽtʃi/ a shining, gleaming

relva /'xewva/ f grass. **~do** m lawn

remador /xema'dor/ m rower

remanescente /xemane'sẽtʃi/ a remaining ● m remainder

remar /xe'mar/ vt/i row

rema|tar /xema'tar/ vt finish off. **~te** m finish; (adorno) finishing touch; (de piada) punch line

remediar /xemedʒi'ar/ vt remedy

remédio /xe'mɛdʒiu/ m (contra doença) medicine, drug; (a problema etc) remedy

remelento /xeme'lẽtu/ a bleary

remen|dar /xemẽ'dar/ vt mend; (com pedaço de pano) patch. **~do** m mend; (pedaço de pano) patch

remessa /xe'mesa/ f (de mercadorias) shipment; (de dinheiro) remittance

reme|tente /xeme'tẽtʃi/ m/f sender. **~ter** vt send ‹mercadorias, dinheiro etc›; refer ‹leitor› (**a** to)

remexer /xeme'ʃer/ vt shuffle ‹papéis›; stir up ‹poeira, lama›; wave ‹braços› ● vi rummage. **~se** vpr move around

reminiscência /xemini'sẽsia/ f reminiscence

remir /xe'mir/ vt redeem. **~se** vpr redeem o.s.

remissão /xemi'sãw/ f (de pecados) redemption; (de doença, pena) remission; (num livro) cross reference

remo /'xemu/ m oar; (esporte) rowing

remoção /xemo'sãw/ f removal

remoinho /xemo'iɲu/ m Port ▶ RODAMOINHO

remontar /xemõ'tar/ vi **~ a** ‹coisa› date back to; ‹pessoa› think back to

remorso /xe'mɔrsu/ m remorse

remo|to /xe'mɔtu/ a remote. **~ver** vt remove

remune|ração /xemunera'sãw/ f payment. **~rador** a profitable. **~rar** vt pay

rena /'xena/ f reindeer

re|nal /xe'naw/ (pl **~nais**) a renal, kidney

Renascença /xena'sẽsa/ f Renaissance

renas|cer /xena'ser/ vi be reborn. **~cimento** m rebirth

renda[1] /'xẽda/ f (tecido) lace

ren|da² /'xẽda/ f income; Port (aluguel) rent; **~der** bring in, yield (lucro); earn (juros); fetch (preço); bring (resultado) ● vi (investimento, trabalho, ação) pay off; (comida) go a long way; (produto comprado) give value for money. **~der-se** vpr surrender. **~dição** f surrender. **~dimento** m (renda) income; (de investimento, terreno) yield; (de motor etc) output; (de produto comprado) value for money. **~doso** /o/ a profitable

rene|gado /xene'gadu/ a & m renegade. **~gar** vt renounce

renhido /xe'ɲidu/ a hard-fought

Reno /'xenu/ m Rhine

reno|mado /xeno'madu/ a renowned. **~me** /o/ m renown

reno|vação /xenova'sãw/ f renewal. **~var** vt renew

renque /'xẽki/ m row

ren|tabilidade /xẽtabili'dadʒi/ f profitability. **~tável** (pl **~táveis**) a profitable

rente /'xẽtʃi/ adv ~ a close to ● a (cabelo) cropped

renúncia /xe'nũsia/ f renunciation (a of); (a cargo) resignation (a from)

renunciar /xenũsi'ar/ vi (presidente etc) resign; ~ a give up; waive (direito)

reorganizar /xeorgani'zar/ vt reorganize

repa|ração /xepara'sãw/ f reparation; (conserto) repair. **~rar** vt (consertar) repair; make up for (ofensa, injustiça, erro); make good (danos, prejuízo) ● vi **~rar (em)** notice. **~ro** m (conserto) repair

repar|tição /xepartʃi'sãw/ f division; (seção do governo) department. **~tir** vt divide up

repassar /xepa'sar/ vt revise (matéria, lição)

repatriar /xepatri'ar/ vt repatriate

repe|lente /xepe'lẽtʃi/ a & m repellent. **~lir** vt repel; reject (ideia, proposta etc)

repensar /xepẽ'sar/ vt/i rethink

repen|te /xe'pẽtʃi/ m **de ~te** suddenly; 🄸 (talvez) maybe. **~tino** a sudden

reper|cussão /xeperku'sãw/ f repercussion. **~cutir** vi (som) reverberate; fig (ter efeito) have repercussions

repertório /xeper'tɔriu/ m (músico etc) repertoire; (lista) list

repe|tição /xepetʃi'sãw/ f repetition. **~tido** a repeated; **~tidas vezes**

repeatedly. **~tir** vt repeat ● vi (ao comer) have seconds. **~tir-se** vpr (pessoa) repeat o.s.; (fato, acontecimento) recur. **~titivo** a repetitive

repi|car /xepi'kar/ vt/i ring. **~que** m ring

replay /xe'plej/ (pl **~s**) m action replay

repleto /xe'plɛtu/ a full up

réplica /'xɛplika/ f reply; (cópia) replica

replicar /xepli'kar/ vt answer ● vi reply

repolho /xe'poʎu/ m cabbage

repor /xe'por/ vt (num lugar) put back; (substituir) replace

reportagem /xepor'taʒẽ/ f (uma) report; (ato) reporting

repórter /xe'pɔrter/ m/f reporter

reposição /xepozi'sãw/ f replacement

repou|sar /xepo'sar/ vt/i rest. **~so** m rest

repreen|der /xepriẽ'der/ vt rebuke, reprimand. **~são** f rebuke, reprimand. **~sível** (pl **~síveis**) a reprehensible

represa /xe'preza/ f dam

represália /xe'prezalia/ f reprisal

represen|tação /xeprezẽta'sãw/ f representation; (espetáculo) performance; (ofício de ator) acting. **~tante** m/f representative. **~tar** vt represent; (no teatro) perform (peça); play (papel, personagem) ● vi (ator) act. **~tativo** a representative

repres|são /xepre'sãw/ f repression. **~sivo** a repressive

repri|mido /xepri'midu/ a repressed. **~mir** vt repress

reprise /xe'prizi/ f (na TV) repeat; (de filme) rerun

reprodu|ção /xeprodu'sãw/ f reproduction. **~zir** vt reproduce. **~zir-se** vpr (multiplicar-se) reproduce; (repetir-se) recur

repro|vação /xeprova'sãw/ f disapproval; (em exame) failure. **~var** vt (rejeitar) disapprove of; (em exame) fail; **ser ~vado** (aluno) fail

réptil /'xɛptʃiw/ (pl **~teis**) m reptile

república /xe'publika/ f republic; (de estudantes) hall of residence

republicano /xepubli'kanu/ a & m republican

repudiar /xepudʒi'ar/ vt disown; repudiate (esposa)

repug|nância /xepug'nãsia/ f repugnance. **~nante** a repugnant

repul|sa /xe'puwsa/ f repulsion; (*recusa*) rejection. **~sivo** a repulsive

reputação /xeputa'sãw/ f reputation

requebrar /xeke'brar/ vt swing. **~se** vpr sway

requeijão /xeke'ʒãw/ m cheese spread, cottage cheese

reque|rer /xeke'rer/ vt (*pedir*) apply for; (*exigir*) require. **~rimento** m application

requin|tado /xekĩ'tadu/ a refined. **~tar** vt refine. **~te** m refinement

requisi|ção /xekizi'sãw/ f requisition. **~tar** vt requisition. **~to** m requirement

rês /xes/ (pl **reses**) m head of cattle; pl cattle

rescindir /xesĩ'dʒir/ vt rescind

rés do chão /xezdu'ʃãw/ m invar Port ground floor, Amer first floor

rese|nha /xe'zeɲa/ f review. **~nhar** vt review

reser|va /xe'zɛrva/ f reserve; (*em hotel, avião etc, ressalva*) reservation. **~var** vt reserve. **~vatório** m reservoir. **~vista** m/f reservist

resfri|ado /xesfri'adu/ a estar **~ado** have a cold ● m cold. **~ar** vt cool ● vi get cold; (*tornar-se morno*) cool down. **~ar-se** vpr catch a cold

resga|tar /xezga'tar/ vt (*salvar*) rescue; (*remir*) redeem. **~te** m (*salvamento*) rescue; (*pago por refém*) ransom; (*remissão*) redemption

resguardar /xezgwar'dar/ vt protect. **~se** vpr protect o.s. (**de** from)

residência /xezi'dẽsia/ f residence

residen|cial /xezidẽsi'aw/ (pl **~ciais**) a (*bairro*) residential; (*telefone etc*) home. **~te** a & m/f resident

residir /xezi'dʒir/ vi reside

resíduo /xe'ziduu/ m residue

resig|nação /xezigna'sãw/ f resignation. **~nado** a resigned. **~nar-se** vpr resign o.s. (**com** to)

resiliente /xezili'ẽtʃi/ a resilient

resina /xe'zina/ f resin

resis|tência /xezis'tẽsia/ f resistance; (*de atleta, mental*) endurance; (*de material, objeto*) toughness. **~tente** a strong, tough; (*tecido, roupa*) hard-wearing; (*planta*) hardy; **~tente a** resistant to. **~tir** vi (*opor ~tência*) resist; (*aguentar*) (*pessoa*) hold out; (*objeto*) hold; (*combater*) resist; (*aguentar*) withstand; **~tir ao tempo** stand the test of time

resmun|gar /xezmũ'gar/ vi grumble. **~go** m grumbling

resolu|ção /xezolu'sãw/ f resolution; (*firmeza*) resolve; (*de problema*) solution. **~to** a resolute; **~to a** resolved to

resolver /xezow'ver/ vt (*esclarecer*) sort out; (*problema, enigma*); (*decidir*) decide. **~se** vpr make up one's mind (**a** to)

respaldo /xes'pawdu/ m (*de cadeira*) back; fig (*apoio*) backing

respetivo /xespe'tʃivu/ a respective

respei|tabilidade /xespejtabili'dadʒi/ f respectability. **~tador** a respectful. **~tar** vt respect. **~tável** (pl **~táveis**) a respectable. **~to** m respect (**por** for); **a ~to de** about; **a este ~to** in this respect; **com ~to a** with regard to; **dizer ~to a** a concern. **~toso** /o/ a respectful

respin|gar /xespĩ'gar/ vt/i splash. **~go** m splash

respi|ração /xespira'sãw/ f breathing. **~rador** m respirator. **~rar** vt/i breathe. **~ratório** a respiratory. **~ro** m breath; (*descanso*) break, breather

resplande|cente /xesplãde'sẽtʃi/ a resplendent. **~cer** vi shine

resplendor /xesplẽ'dor/ m brilliance; fig glory

respon|dão /xespõ'dãw/ a (f **~dona**) cheeky. **~der** vt/i answer; (*com insolência*) answer back; **~der a** answer; **~der por** answer for, take responsibility for

responsabili|dade /xespõsabili'dadʒi/ f responsibility. **~zar** vt hold responsible (**por** for). **~zar-se** vpr take responsibility (**por** for)

responsá|vel /xespõ'savew/ (pl **~veis**) a responsible (**por** for)

resposta /xes'pɔsta/ f answer

resquício /xes'kisiu/ m vestige, remnant

ressabiado /xesabi'adu/ a wary, suspicious

ressaca /xe'saka/ f (*depois de beber*) hangover; (*do mar*) undertow

ressaltar /xesaw'tar/ vt emphasize ● vi stand out

ressalva /xe'sawva/ f reservation, proviso; (*proteção*) safeguard

ressarcir /xesar'sir/ vt refund

resse|cado /xese'kadu/ a (*terra*) parched; (*pele*) dry. **~car** vt/i dry up

ressen|tido /xesẽ'tʃidu/ a resentful. **~timento** m resentment. **~tir-se** vpr

~tir-se de (*ofender-se*) resent; (*ser influenciado*) show the effects of

ressequido /xese'kidu/ *a*
▶ RESSECADO

resso|ar /xeso'ar/ *vi* resound. **~nância** *f* resonance. **~nante** *a* resonant. **~nar** *vi* Port snore

ressurgimento /xesurʒi'mētu/ *m* resurgence

ressurreição /xesuxej'sãw/ *f* resurrection

ressuscitar /xesusi'tar/ *vt* revive

restabele|cer /xestabele'ser/ *vt* restore; restore to health ‹*doente*›. **~cer-se** *vpr* recover. **~cimento** *m* restoration; (*de doente*) recovery

res|tante /xes'tãtʃi/ *a* remaining ● *m* remainder. **~tar** *vi* remain; **~ta-me dizer que ...** it remains for me to say that

restau|ração /xestawra'sãw/ *f* restoration. **~rante** *m* restaurant. **~rar** *vt* restore

restitu|ição /xestʃitui'sãw/ *f* return, restitution. **~ir** *vt* (*devolver*) return; restore ‹*forma, força etc*›; reinstate ‹*funcionário*›

resto /'xestu/ *m* rest; *pl* (*de comida*) leftovers; (*de cadáver*) remains; **de ~** besides

restrição /xestri'sãw/ *f* restriction

restringir /xestrĩ'ʒir/ *vt* restrict

restrito /xes'tritu/ *a* restricted

resul|tado /xezuw'tadu/ *m* result. **~tante** *a* resulting (**de** from). **~tar** *vi* result (**de** from **em** in)

resu|mir /xezu'mir/ *vt* (*abreviar*) summarize; (*conter em poucas palavras*) sum up. **~mir-se** *vpr* (*ser expresso em poucas palavras*) be summed up; **~mir-se em** (*ser apenas*) come down to. **~mo** *m* summary; **em ~mo** briefly

resvalar /xezva'lar/ *vi* (*sem querer*) slip; (*deslizar*) slide

reta /'xeta/ *f* (*linha*) straight line; (*de pista etc*) straight; **~ final** home straight

retaguarda /xeta'gwarda/ *f* rearguard

retalho /xe'taʎu/ *m* scrap; **a ~** Port retail

retaliação /xetalia'sãw/ *f* retaliation

retangular /xetãgu'lar/ *a* rectangular

retângulo /xe'tãgulu/ *m* rectangle

retar|dado /xetar'dadu/ *a* retarded ● *m* retard. **~dar** *vt* delay. **~datário** *m* latecomer

retenção /xetẽ'sãw/ *f* retention

reter /xe'ter/ *vt* keep ‹*pessoa*›; hold back ‹*águas, riso, lágrimas*›; (*na memória*) retain. **~se** *vpr* restrain o.s.

rete|sado /xete'zadu/ *a* taut. **~sar** *vt* pull taut

reticência /xetʃi'sẽsia/ *f* reticence

reti|dão /xetʃi'dãw/ *f* rectitude. **~ficar** *vt* rectify

reti|rada /xetʃi'rada/ *f* (*de tropas*) retreat; (*de dinheiro*) withdrawal. **~rado** *a* secluded. **~rar** *vt* withdraw; (*afastar*) move away. **~rar-se** *vpr* ‹*tropas*› retreat; (*afastar-se*) withdraw; (*de uma atividade*) retire. **~ro** *m* retreat

reto /'xetu/ *a* ‹*linha etc*› straight; ‹*pessoa*› honest

retocar /xeto'kar/ *vt* touch up ‹*desenho, maquiagem etc*›; alter ‹*texto*›

reto|mada /xeto'mada/ *f* (*continuação*) resumption; (*reconquista*) retaking. **~mar** *vt* (*continuar com*) resume; (*conquistar de novo*) retake

retoque /xe'tɔki/ *m* finishing touch

retorcer /xetor'ser/ *vt* twist. **~se** *vpr* writhe

retóri|ca /xe'tɔrika/ *f* rhetoric. **~co** *a* rhetorical

retor|nar /xetor'nar/ *vi* return. **~no** *m* return; (*na estrada*) turning place; **dar ~no** do a U-turn

retrair /xetra'ir/ *vt* retract, withdraw. **~se** *vpr* (*recuar*) withdraw; (*encolher-se*) retract

retrasa|do /xetra'zadu/ *a* **a semana ~da** the week before last

retratar¹ /xetra'tar/ *vt* (*desdizer*) retract

retra|tar² /xetra'tar/ *vt* (*em quadro, livro*) portray, depict. **~to** *m* portrait; (*foto*) photo; (*representação*) portrayal; **~to falado** identikit picture

retribuir /xetribu'ir/ *vt* return ‹*favor, visita*›; repay ‹*gentileza*›

retroativo /xetroa'tʃivu/ *a* retroactive; ‹*pagamento*› backdated

retro|ceder /xetrose'der/ *vi* retreat; (*desistir*) back down. **~cesso** /ɛ/ *m* retreat; (*ao passado*) regression

retrógrado /xe'trɔgradu/ *a* retrograde

retrospe|tiva /xetrospe'tʃiva/ *f* retrospective. **~tivo** *a* retrospective. **~to** /ɛ/ *m* look back; **em ~to** in retrospect

retrovisor /xetrovi'zor/ *a & m* (**espelho**) **~** rear-view mirror

retrucar /xetru'kar/ *vt/i* retort

r

retum|bante /xetũˈbãtʃi/ a resounding. **~bar** vi resound

réu /ˈxɛw/ m (f **ré**) defendant

reumatismo /xewmaˈtʃizmu/ m rheumatism

reu|nião /xeuniˈãw/ f meeting; (descontraída) get-together; (de família) reunion; **~nião de cúpula** summit meeting. **~nir** vt bring together ‹pessoas›; combine ‹qualidades›. **~nir-se** vpr meet; ‹amigos, familiares› get together; **~nir-se** a join

revanche /xeˈvãʃi/ f revenge; (jogo) return match

reveillon /xeveˈjõ/ (pl **~s**) m New Year's Eve

reve|lação /xevelaˈsãw/ f revelation; (de fotos) developing; (novo talento) promising newcomer. **~lar** vt reveal; develop ‹filme, fotos›. **~lar-se** vpr (vir a ser) turn out to be

revelia /xeveˈlia/ f **à ~** by default; **à ~ de** without the knowledge of

reven|dedor /xevẽdeˈdor/ m dealer. **~der** vt resell

rever /xeˈver/ vt (ver de novo) see again; (revisar) revise; (examinar) check

reve|rência /xeveˈresia/ f reverence; (movimento do busto) bow; (dobrando os joelhos) curtsey. **~rente** a reverent

reverso /xeˈversu/ m reverse; **o ~ da medalha** the other side of the coin

revés /xeˈvɛs/ m (pl **reveses**) setback

reves|timento /xevestʃiˈmẽtu/ m covering. **~tir** vt cover

reve|zamento /xevezaˈmẽtu/ m alternation. **~zar** vt/i alternate. **~zar-se** vpr alternate

revi|dar /xeviˈdar/ vt return ‹golpe, insulto›; refute ‹crítica›; (retrucar) retort ● vi hit back. **~de** m response

revigorar /xevigoˈrar/ vt strengthen ● vi. **~se** vpr regain one's strength

revi|rar /xeviˈrar/ vt turn out ‹bolsos, gavetas›; turn over ‹terra›; turn inside out ‹roupa›; roll ‹olhos›. **~rar-se** vpr toss and turn. **~ravolta** /ɔ/ f (na política etc) about-face, about-turn; (da situação) turnabout, dramatic change

revi|são /xeviˈzãw/ f (de lições etc) revision; (de máquina, motor) overhaul; (de carro) service; **~são de provas** proofreading. **~sar** vt revise ‹provas, lições›; service ‹carro›. **~sor** m (de bilhetes) ticket inspector; **~sor de provas** proofreader

revis|ta /xeˈvista/ f (para ler) magazine; (teatral) revue; (de tropas etc) review; **passar ~ta** a review. **~tar** vt search

reviver /xeviˈver/ vt relive ● vi revive

revogar /xevoˈgar/ vt revoke ‹lei›; cancel ‹ordem›

revol|ta /xeˈvɔwta/ f (rebelião) revolt; (indignação) disgust. **~tante** a disgusting. **~tar** vt disgust. **~tar-se** vpr (rebelar-se) revolt; (indignar-se) be disgusted. **~to** /o/ a ‹casa, gaveta› upside down; ‹cabelo› dishevelled; ‹mar› rough; ‹mundo, região› troubled; ‹anos› turbulent

revolu|ção /xevoluˈsãw/ f revolution. **~cionar** vt revolutionize. **~cionário** a & m revolutionary

revolver /xevowˈver/ vt turn over ‹terra›; roll ‹olhos›; go through ‹gavetas, arquivos›

revólver /xeˈvɔwver/ m revolver

re|za /ˈxeza/ f prayer. **~zar** vi pray ● vt say ‹missa, oração›; (dizer) state

riacho /xiˈaʃu/ m stream

ribalta /xiˈbawta/ f footlights

ribanceira /xibãˈsera/ f embankment

ribombar /xibõˈbar/ vi rumble

rico /ˈxiku/ a rich ● m rich man; **os ~s** the rich

ricochete /xikoˈʃetʃi/ m ricochet. **~ar** vi ricochet

ricota /xiˈkɔta/ f curd cheese, ricotta

ridicularizar /xidʒikulariˈzar/ vt ridicule

ridículo /xiˈdʒikulu/ a ridiculous

ri|fa /ˈxifa/ f raffle. **~far** vt raffle

rifão /xiˈfãw/ m saying

rifle /ˈxifli/ m rifle

rigidez /xiʒiˈdes/ f rigidity

rígido /ˈxiʒidu/ a rigid

rigor /xiˈgor/ m severity; (meticulosidade) rigour; **vestido a ~** evening dress; **de ~** essential

rigoroso /xigoˈrozu/ a strict; ‹inverno, pena› severe, harsh; ‹lógica, estudo› rigorous

rijo /ˈxiʒu/ a stiff; ‹músculos› firm

rim /xĩ/ m kidney; pl (parte das costas) small of the back

ri|ma /ˈxima/ f rhyme. **~mar** vt/i rhyme

rí|mel /ˈximew/ m (pl **~meis**) m mascara

ringue /ˈxĩgi/ m ring

rinoceronte /xinoseˈrõtʃi/ m rhinoceros

rinque /ˈxĩki/ m rink

rio /'xio/ m river

riqueza /xi'keza/ f wealth; (*qualidade*) richness; pl riches

rir /xir/ vi laugh (**de** at)

risada /xi'zada/ f laugh, laughter; **dar ~** laugh

ris|ca /'xiska/ f stroke; (*listra*) stripe; (*do cabelo*) parting; **à ~ca** to the letter. **~car** vt (*apagar*) cross out ‹erro›; scratch ‹fósforo›; strike ‹mesa, carro etc›; write off ‹amigo›

risco¹ /'xisku/ m (*na parede etc*) scratch; (*no papel*) line; (*esboço*) sketch

risco² m risk

riso /'xizu/ m laugh. **~nho** /o/ a smiling

ríspido /'xispidu/ a harsh

rítmico /'xitʃmiku/ a rhythmic

ritmo /'xitʃimu/ m rhythm

rito /'xitu/ m rite

ritu|al /xitu'aw/ (pl **~ais**) a & m ritual

ri|val /xi'vaw/ (pl **~vais**) a & m/f rival. **~validade** f rivalry. **~valizar** vt rival ● vi vie (**com** with)

rixa /'xiʃa/ f fight

roaming /'xõming/ m Telec roaming

robô /xo'bo/ m robot

robusto /xo'bustu/ a robust

roça /'xɔsa/ f (*campo*) country

rocambole /xokã'bɔli/ m roll

roçar /xo'sar/ vt graze; **~ em** brush against

ro|cha /'xɔʃa/ f rock. **~chedo** /e/ m cliff

roda /'xɔda/ f (*de carro etc*) wheel; (*de amigos etc*) circle; **~ dentada** cog. **~da** f round. **~do a saia ~da** full skirt. **~gigante** (pl **~s-gigantes**) f big wheel, Amer Ferris wheel. **~moinho** m (*de vento*) whirlwind; (*na água*) whirlpool; fig whirl, swirl. **~pé** m skirting board, Amer baseboard

rodar /xo'dar/ vt (*fazer girar*) spin; (*viajar por*) go round; do ‹quilometragem›; shoot ‹filme›; run ‹programa› ● vi (*girar*) spin; (*de carro*) drive round

rodear /xodʒi'ar/ vt (*circundar*) surround; (*andar ao redor de*) go round

rodeio /xo'deju/ m (*ao falar*) circumlocution; (*de gado*) round-up; **falar sem ~s** talk straight

rodela /xo'dela/ f (*de limão etc*) slice; (*peça de metal*) washer

rodízio /xo'dʒiziu/ m rota

rodo /'xodu/ m rake

rodopiar /xodopi'ar/ vi spin round

rodovi|a /xodo'via/ f highway. **~ária** f bus station; **polícia ~ária** traffic police. **~ário** a road

ro|edor /xoe'dor/ m rodent. **~er** vt gnaw; bite ‹unhas›; fig eat away

rogar /xo'gar/ vi request

rojão /xo'ʒãw/ m rocket

rol /xɔw/ (pl **róis**) m roll

rolar /xo'lar/ vt roll ● vi roll; 🄳 (*acontecer*) happen

roldana /xow'dana/ f pulley

roleta /xo'leta/ f (*jogo*) roulette; (*borboleta*) turnstile

rolha /'xoʎa/ f cork

roliço /xo'lisu/ a ‹objeto› cylindrical; ‹pessoa› plump

rolo /'xolu/ m (*de filme, tecido etc*) roll; (*máquina, de cabelo*) roller; **~ compressor** steamroller; **~ de massa** rolling pin

Roma /'xoma/ f Rome

romã /xo'mã/ f pomegranate

roman|ce /xo'mãsi/ m (*livro*) novel; (*caso*) romance. **~cista** m/f novelist

romano /xo'manu/ a & m Roman

romântico /xo'mãtʃiku/ a romantic

romantismo /xomã'tʃizmu/ m (*amor*) romance; (*idealismo*) romanticism

romaria /xoma'ria/ f pilgrimage

rombo /'xõbu/ m hole

Romênia /xo'menia/ f Romania

romeno /xo'menu/ a & m Romanian

rom|per /xõ'per/ vt break; break off ‹relações› ● vi ‹dia› break; ‹sol› rise; **~per com** break up with. **~pimento** m break; (*de relações*) breaking off

ron|car /xõ'kar/ vi (*ao dormir*) snore; ‹estômago› rumble. **~co** m snoring; (*um*) snore; (*de motor*) roar

ron|da /'xõda/ f round, patrol. **~dar** vt (*patrulhar*) patrol; (*espreitar*) prowl around ● vi ‹vigia etc› patrol; ‹animal, ladrão› prowl around

ronronar /xõxo'nar/ vi purr

roque¹ /'xɔki/ m (*em xadrez*) rook

ro|que² /'xɔki/ m (*música*) rock. **~queiro** m rock musician

rosa /'xɔza/ f rose ● a invar pink. **~do** a rosy; ‹vinho› rosé

rosário /xo'zariu/ m rosary

rosbife /xoz'bifi/ m roast beef

rosca /'xoska/ f (*de parafuso*) thread; (*biscoito*) rusk; **farinha de ~** breadcrumbs

r

roseira /xo'zera/ f rose bush

roseta /xo'zeta/ f rosette

rosnar /xoz'nar/ vi ‹cachorro› growl; ‹pessoa› snarl

rosto /'xostu/ m face

rota /'xɔta/ f route

rota|ção /xota'sãw/ f rotation. **~tividade** f turnround. **~tivo** a rotating

rotei|rista /xote'rista/ m/f scriptwriter. **~ro** m (de viagem) itinerary; (de filme, peça) script; (de discussão etc) outline

roti|na /xo'tʃina/ f routine. **~neiro** a routine

rótula /'xɔtula/ f kneecap

rotular /xotu'lar/ vt label (de as)

rótulo /'xɔtulu/ m label

rou|bar /xo'bar/ vt steal ‹dinheiro, carro etc›; rob ‹pessoa, loja etc› ● vi steal; (em jogo) cheat. **~bo** m theft, robbery

rouco /'xoku/ a hoarse; ‹voz› gravelly

rou|pa /'xopa/ f clothes; (uma) outfit; **~pa de baixo** underwear; **~pa de cama** bedclothes. **~pão** m dressing gown

rouquidão /xoki'dãw/ f hoarseness

rouxi|nol /xoʃi'nɔw/ (pl **~nóis**) m nightingale

roxo /'xoʃu/ a purple

rua /'xua/ f street

rubéola /xu'bɛola/ f German measles

rubi /xu'bi/ m ruby

rude /'xudʒi/ a rude

rudimentos /xudʒi'mẽtus/ m pl rudiments, basics

ruela /xu'ɛla/ f backstreet

rufar /xu'far/ vi ‹tambor› roll ● m roll

ruga /'xuga/ f (na pele) wrinkle; (na roupa) crease

ru|gido /xu'ʒidu/ m roar. **~gir** vi roar

ruibarbo /xui'barbu/ m rhubarb

ruído /xu'idu/ m noise

ruidoso /xui'dozu/ a noisy

ruim /xu'ĩ/ a bad

ruína /xu'ina/ f ruin

ruivo /'xuivu/ a ‹cabelo› red; ‹pessoa› red-haired ● m redhead

rulê /xu'le/ a **gola ~** roll-neck

rum /xũ/ m rum

ru|mar /xu'mar/ vi head (para for). **~mo** m course; **~mo a** heading for; **sem ~mo** ‹vida› aimless; ‹andar› aimlessly

rumor /xu'mor/ m (da rua, de vozes) hum; (do trânsito) rumble; (boato) rumour

ru|ral /xu'raw/ (pl **~rais**) a rural

rusga /'xuzga/ f quarrel, disagreement

rush /xaʃ/ m rush hour

Rússia /'xusia/ f Russia

russo /'xusu/ a & m Russian

rústico /'xustʃiku/ a rustic

....

Ss

....

Saara /saa'ra/ m Sahara

sábado /'sabadu/ m Saturday

sabão /sa'bãw/ m soap; **~ em pó** soap powder

sabatina /saba'tʃina/ f test

sabedoria /sabedo'ria/ f wisdom

saber /sa'ber/ vt/i know (de about); (descobrir) find out (de about) ● m knowledge; **eu sei cantar** I know how to sing, I can sing; **sei lá** I've no idea; **que eu saiba** as far as I know

sablá /sabi'a/ m thrush

sabi|chão /sabi'ʃãw/ a & m (f **~chona**) know-it-all

sábio /'sabiu/ a wise ● m wise man

sabone|te /sabo'netʃi/ m bar of soap. **~teira** f soap dish

sabor /sa'bor/ m flavour; **ao ~ de** at the mercy of

sabo|rear /sabori'ar/ vt savour. **~roso** a tasty

sabo|tador /sabota'dor/ m saboteur. **~tagem** f sabotage. **~tar** vt sabotage

saca /'saka/ f sack

sacada /sa'kada/ f balcony

sa|cal /sa'kaw/ (pl **~cais**) a 🔲 boring

saca|na /sa'kana/ 🔲 a (desonesto) devious; (lascivo) dirty-minded, naughty ● m/f rogue. **~nagem** f 🔲 (esperteza) trickery; (sexo) sex; (uma) dirty trick. **~near** vt 🔲 (enganar) do the dirty on; (amolar) take the mickey out of

sacar /sa'kar/ vt/i withdraw ‹dinheiro›; draw ‹arma›; (em tênis, vôlei etc) serve; 🔲 (entender) understand

saçaricar /sasari'kar/ vi play around

sacarina /saka'rina/ f saccharine

saca-rolhas /saka'xoʎas/ m invar corkscrew

sacer|dócio /saser'dɔsiu/ m priesthood. **~dote** /ɔ/ m priest. **~dotisa** f priestess

sachê /sa'ʃe/ *m* sachet

saciar /sasi'ar/ *vt* satisfy

saco /'saku/ *m* bag; **que ~!** 🔲 what a pain! **estar de ~ cheio (de)** 🔲 be fed up (with), be sick (of); **encher o ~ de alguém** 🔲 get on sb's nerves; **puxar o ~ de alguém** 🔲 suck up to sb; **~ de dormir** sleeping bag. **~la** /ɔ/ *f* bag. **~lão** *m* wholesale fruit and vegetable market. **~lejar** *vt* shake

sacramento /sakra'mẽtu/ *m* sacrament

sacri|ficar /sakrifi'kar/ *vt* sacrifice; have put down ‹cachorro etc›. **~fício** *m* sacrifice. **~légio** *m* sacrilege

sacrílego /sa'krilegu/ *a* sacrilegious

sacro /'sakru/ *a* ‹música› religious

sacrossanto /sakro'sãtu/ *a* sacrosanct

sacu|dida /saku'dʒida/ *f* shake. **~dir** *vt* shake

sádico /'sadʒiku/ *a* sadistic ● *m* sadist

sadio /sa'dʒiu/ *a* healthy

sadismo /sa'dʒizmu/ *m* sadism

safa|deza /safa'deza/ *f* (desonestidade) deviousness; (libertinagem) indecency; (uma) dirty trick. **~do** *a* (desonesto) devious; (lascivo) dirty-minded; (esperto) quick; ‹criança› naughty

safena /sa'fena/ *f* **ponte de ~** heart bypass. **~do** *m* bypass patient

safira /sa'fira/ *f* sapphire

safra /'safra/ *f* crop

sagitariano /saʒitari'anu/ *a & m* Sagittarian

Sagitário /saʒi'tariu/ *m* Sagittarius

sagrado /sa'gradu/ *a* sacred

saguão /sa'gwãw/ *m* (de teatro, hotel) foyer, *Amer* lobby; (de estação, aeroporto) concourse

saia /'saja/ *f* skirt. **~-calça** (*pl* **~s-calças**) *f* culottes

saída /sa'ida/ *f* (partida) departure; (porta) *fig* way out; **de ~** at the outset; **estar de ~** be on one's way out

sair /sa'ir/ *vi* (de dentro) go/come out; (partir) leave; (desprender-se) come off; ‹mancha› come out; (resultar) turn out; **~ mais barato** work out cheaper. **~-se** *vpr* fare; **~-se com** (dizer) come out with

sal /saw/ (*pl* **sais**) *m* salt; **~ de frutas** Epsom salts

sala /'sala/ *f* (numa casa) lounge; (num lugar público) hall; (classe) class; **fazer ~ a** entertain; **~ (de aula)** classroom; **~ de embarque** departure lounge; **~ de espera** waiting room; **~ de jantar** dining room; **~ de operação** operating theatre

sala|da /sa'lada/ *f* salad; *fig* jumble, mishmash; **~da de frutas** fruit salad. **~deira** *f* salad bowl

sala e quarto /sali'kwartu/ *m* two-room flat

sala|me /sa'lami/ *m* salami. **~minho** *m* pepperoni

salão /sa'lãw/ *m* hall; (de cabeleireiro) salon; (de carros) show; **~ de beleza** beauty salon

salari|al /salari'aw/ (*pl* **~ais**) *a* wage

salário /sa'lariu/ *m* salary

sal|dar /saw'dar/ *vt* settle. **~do** *m* balance

saleiro /sa'leru/ *m* salt cellar

sal|gadinhos /sawga'dʒinus/ *m pl* snacks. **~gado** *a* salty; ‹preço› exorbitant. **~gar** *vt* salt

salgueiro /saw'geru/ *m* willow; **~ chorão** weeping willow

saliência /sali'ẽsia/ *f* projection

salien|tar /saliẽ'tar/ *vt* (deixar claro) point out; (acentuar) highlight. **~tar-se** *vpr* distinguish o.s.. **~te** *a* prominent

saliva /sa'liva/ *f* saliva

salmão /saw'mãw/ *m* salmon

salmo /'sawmu/ *m* psalm

salmonela /sawmo'nɛla/ *f* salmonella

salmoura /saw'mora/ *f* brine

salpicar /sawpi'kar/ *vt* sprinkle; (sem querer) spatter

salsa /'sawsa/ *f* parsley

salsicha /saw'siʃa/ *f* sausage

saltar /saw'tar/ *vt* (pular) jump; (omitir) skip ● *vi* jump; **~ à vista** be obvious; **~ do ônibus** get off the bus

saltear /sawtʃi'ar/ *vt* sauté ‹batatas etc›

saltitar /sawtʃi'tar/ *vi* hop

salto /'sawtu/ *m* (pulo) jump; (de sapato) heel; **~ com vara** pole vault; **~ em altura** high jump; **~ em distância** long jump. **~-mortal** (*pl* **~s-mortais**) *m* somersault

salu|bre /sa'lubri/ *a* healthy. **~tar** *a* salutary

salva¹ /'sawva/ *f* (de canhões) salvo; (bandeja) salver; **~ de palmas** round of applause

salva² /'sawva/ *f* (erva) sage

salva|ção /sawva'sãw/ *f* salvation. **~dor** *m* saviour

salvaguar|da /sawva'gwarda/ *f* safeguard. **~dar** *vt* safeguard

S

sal|vamento /sawva'mẽtu/ m rescue; (de navio) salvage. **~var** vt save. **~var-se** vpr escape. **~va-vidas** m invar (bóia) lifebelt ● m/f (pessoa) lifeguard ● a barco **~va-vidas** lifeboat. **~vo** a safe ● prep save; **a ~vo** safe

samambaia /samã'baja/ f fern

sam|ba /'sãba/ m samba. **~ba-canção** (pl **~bas-canção**) m slow samba ● a invar **cueca ~ba-canção** boxer shorts; **~ba-enredo** (pl **~bas-enredo**) m samba story. **~bar** vi samba. **~bista** m/f (dançarino) samba dancer; (compositor) composer of sambas. **~bódromo** m Carnival parade ground

samovar /samo'var/ m tea urn

sanar /sa'nar/ vt cure

san|ção /sã'sãw/ f sanction. **~cionar** vt sanction

sandália /sã'dalia/ f sandal

sandes /'sãdiʃ/ f invar Port sandwich

sanduíche /sãdu'iʃi/ m sandwich

sane|amento /sania'mẽtu/ m (esgotos) sanitation; (de finanças) rehabilitation. **~ar** vt set straight ‹finanças›

sanfona /sã'fona/ f (instrumento) accordion; (tricô) ribbing. **~do** a ‹porta› folding; ‹pulôver› ribbed

san|grar /sã'grar/ vt/i bleed. **~grento** a bloody; ‹carne› rare. **~gria** f bloodshed; (de dinheiro) extortion

sangue /'sãgi/ m blood; **~ pisado** bruise. **~-frio** m cool, coolness

sanguessuga /sãgi'suga/ f leech

sanguinário /sãgi'nariu/ a bloodthirsty

sanguíneo /sã'giniu/ a blood

sanidade /sani'dadʒi/ f sanity

sanitário /sani'tariu/ a sanitary. **~s** m pl toilets

san|tidade /sãtʃi'dadʒi/ f sanctity. **~tificar** vt sanctify. **~to** a holy; **todo ~to dia** every single day ● m saint. **~tuário** m sanctuary

são /sãw/ (pl **~s**) a (f **sã**) healthy; (mentalmente) sane; ‹conselho› sound

São /sãw/ a Saint

sapataria /sapata'ria/ f shoe shop

sapate|ado /sapatʃi'adu/ m tap dancing. **~ador** m tap dancer. **~ar** vi tap one's feet; (dançar) tap-dance

sapa|teiro /sapa'teru/ m shoemaker. **~tilha** f pump; **~tilha de balé** ballet shoe

sapato /sa'patu/ m shoe

sapeca /sa'pɛka/ a saucy

sa|pinho /sa'piɲu/ m thrush. **~po** m toad

saque¹ /'saki/ m (do banco) withdrawal; (em tênis, vôlei etc) serve

saque² /'saki/ m (de loja etc) looting. **~ar** vt loot

saraiva /sa'rajva/ f hail. **~da** f hailstorm; **uma ~da de** a hail of

sarampo /sa'rãpu/ m measles

sarar /sa'rar/ vt cure ● vi get better; ‹ferida› heal

sar|casmo /sar'kazmu/ m sarcasm. **~cástico** a sarcastic

sarda /'sarda/ f freckle

Sardenha /sar'deɲa/ f Sardinia

sardento /sar'dẽtu/ a freckled

sardinha /sar'dʒiɲa/ f sardine

sardônico /sar'doniku/ a sardonic

sargento /sar'ʒẽtu/ m sergeant

sarjeta /sar'ʒeta/ f gutter

Satanás /sata'nas/ m Satan

satânico /sa'taniku/ a satanic

satélite /sa'telitʃi/ a & m satellite

sátira /'satʃira/ f satire

satírico /sa'tʃiriku/ a satirical

satirizar /satʃiri'zar/ vt satirize

satisfa|ção /satʃisfa'sãw/ f satisfaction; **dar ~ções a** answer to. **~tório** a satisfactory. **~zer** vt **~zer (a)** satisfy ● vi be satisfactory. **~zer-se** vpr be satisfied

satisfeito /satʃis'fejtu/ a satisfied; (contente) content; (de comida) full

saturar /satu'rar/ vt saturate

Saturno /sa'turnu/ m Saturn

saudação /sawda'sãw/ f greeting

saudade /saw'dadʒi/ f longing; (lembrança) nostalgia; **estar com ~s de** miss; **matar ~s** catch up

saudar /saw'dar/ vt greet

saudá|vel /saw'davew/ (pl **~veis**) a healthy

saúde /sa'udʒi/ f health ● int (ao beber) cheers; (ao espirrar) bless you

saudo|sismo /sawdo'zizmu/ m nostalgia. **~so** /o/ a longing; **estar ~so de** miss; **o nosso ~so amigo** our much-missed friend

sauna /'sawna/ f sauna

saxofo|ne /sakso'foni/ m saxophone. **~nista** m/f saxophonist

sazo|nado /sazo'nadu/ a seasoned. **~nal** (pl **~nais**) a seasonal

se /si/ ● *conj*

····▸ *(causa)* if; **~ chover, não vamos** if it rains, we won't go; **~ fosse rico, comprava uma moto** if I were rich, I'd buy a motorbike

❗ É mais correto dizer if I/he/she/ it **were**, mas coloquialmente usa-se frequentemente **was**. *(dúvida)* whether; **não sei se vou ou se fico** I don't know whether to stay or go

❗ usa-se **whether** e não **if** antes de infinitivo e depois de preposições. *(desejo)* if; **se ao menos você tivesse me dito!** if only you had told me!

● *pron*

····▸ *(reflexo)* (ele) himself, (ela) herself; *(coisa)* itself; *(você)* yourself; *(vocês)* yourselves; *(eles, elas)* themselves; **ela ~ cortou** she's cut herself; **vocês ~ magoaram** you've hurt yourselves; **eles ~ lavaram** they've washed themselves; *(recíproco)* each other, one another; **eles ~ amam** they love each other; **eles ~ telefonam todos os dias** they phone each other every day

····▸ *(passivo)* **registaram-~ três mortos** three deaths were recorded *(sujeito indeterminado)* **fala-~ alemão** German is spoken

····▸ *(em expressões)* **~ bem que** although

sebo /'sebu/ *m (sujeira)* grease; *(livraria)* second-hand bookshop. **~so** /o/ *a* greasy; *‹pessoa›* slimy

seca /'seka/ *f* drought. **~dor** *m* **~dor de cabelo** hairdryer. **~dora** *f* tumble dryer

seção /se'sãw/ *f* section; *(de loja)* department

secar /se'kar/ *vt/i* dry

sec|ção /sek'sãw/ *f* ▶ **SEÇÃO**. **~cionar** *vt* split up

seco /'seku/ *a* dry; *‹resposta, tom›* curt; *‹pessoa, caráter›* cold; *‹barulho, pancada›* dull; **estar ~ por** I'm dying for

secretaria /sekreta'ria/ *f (de empresa)* general office; *(ministério)* department

secretá|ria /sekre'taria/ *f* secretary; **~ria eletrônica** ansaphone. **~rio** *m* secretary

secreto /se'kretu/ *a* secret

secular /seku'lar/ *a (não religioso)* secular; *(antigo)* age-old

século /'sekulu/ *m* century; *pl (muito tempo)* ages

secundário /sekũ'dariu/ *a* secondary

secura /se'kura/ *f* dryness; **estar com uma ~ de** be longing for/to

seda /'seda/ *f* silk

sedativo /seda'tʃivu/ *a & m* sedative

sede[1] /'sedʒi/ *f* headquarters; *(local do governo)* seat

sede[2] /'sedʒi/ *f* thirst **(de** for); **estar com ~** be thirsty

sedentário /sedẽ'tariu/ *a* sedentary

sedento /se'dẽtu/ *a* thirsty **(de** for)

sediar /sedʒi'ar/ *vt* host

sedimen|tar /sedʒimẽ'tar/ *vt* consolidate. **~to** *m* sediment

sedoso /se'dozu/ *a* silky

sedu|ção /sedu'sãw/ *f* seduction. **~tor** *a* seductive. **~zir** *vt* seduce

segmento /seg'mẽtu/ *m* segment

segredo /se'gredu/ *m* secret; *(de cofre etc)* combination

segregar /segre'gar/ *vt* segregate

segui|da /se'gida/ *f* **em ~da** *(imediatamente)* straight away; *(depois)* next; **cinco horas ~das** five hours running. **~do** *a* followed **(de** by). **~dor** *m* follower. **~mento** *m* continuation; **dar ~mento a** go on with

se|guinte /se'gĩtʃi/ *a* following; *‹dia, semana etc›* next. **~guir** *vt/i* follow; *(continuar)* continue; **~guir em frente** *(ir embora)* go; *(indicação na rua)* go straight ahead. **~guir-se** *vpr* follow

segun|da /se'gũda/ *f (dia)* Monday; *(marcha)* second; **de ~da** second-rate; **~das intenções** ulterior motives; **de ~da mão** second-hand. **~da-feira** *(pl ~das-feiras) f* Monday. **~do** *a & m* second ● *adv* secondly ● *prep* according to ● *conj* according to what

segu|rança /segu'rãsa/ *f* security; *(estado de seguro)* safety; *(certeza)* assurance ● *m/f* security guard. **~rar** *vt* hold. **~rar-se** *vpr (controlar-se)* control o.s.; **~rar-se em** hold on to; **fazer ~ro de** insure. **~ro** *a* secure; *(fora de perigo)* safe; *(com certeza)* sure ● *m* insurance; **estar no ~ro** be insured. **~ro-desemprego** *m* unemployment benefit

seio /'seju/ *m* breast, bosom; **no ~ de** within

seis /sejs/ *a & m* six. **~centos** *a & m* six hundred

seita /'sejta/ *f* sect

seixo /'sejʃu/ *m* pebble

sela /'sela/ *f* saddle

S

selar¹ /se'lar/ vt saddle ‹cavalo›

selar² /se'lar/ vt seal; (franquear) stamp

sele|ção /sele'sãw/ f selection; (time) team. **~cionar** vt select. **~to** /ɛ/ a select

selim /se'lĩ/ m saddle

selo /'selu/ m seal; (postal) stamp; (de discos) label

selva /'sɛwva/ f jungle. **~gem** a wild. **~geria** f savagery

sem /sẽj/ prep without; **~ eu saber** without me knowing; **ficar ~ dinheiro** run out of money

semáforo /se'maforu/ m (na rua) traffic lights; (de ferrovia) signal

sema|na /se'mana/ f week. **~nal** (pl **~nais**) a weekly. **~nalmente** adv weekly. **~nário** m weekly

semear /semi'ar/ vt sow

semelhan|ça /seme'ʎãsa/ f similarity. **~te** a similar; (tal) such

sêmen /'semẽ/ m semen

semente /se'mẽtʃi/ f seed; (em fruta) pip

semestre /se'mɛstri/ m six months; (da faculdade etc) term, Amer semester

semi|círculo /semi'sirkulu/ m semicircle. **~final** (pl **~finais**) f semi-final

seminário /semi'nariu/ m (aula) seminar; (colégio religioso) seminary

sem-número /sẽ'numeru/ m **um ~ de** innumerable

sempre /'sẽpri/ adv always; **como ~** as usual; **para ~** for ever; **~ que** whenever

sem-|terra /sẽ'texa/ m/f invar landless labourer. **~teto** a homeless ● m/f homeless person; **~vergonha** a invar brazen ● m/f invar scoundrel

sena|do /se'nadu/ m senate. **~dor** m senator

senão /si'nãw/ conj otherwise; (mas antes) but rather ● m snag

senda /'sẽda/ f path

senha /'seɲa/ f (palavra) password; (número) code; (sinal) signal

senhor /se'ɲor/ m gentleman; (homem idoso) older man; (tratamento) sir ● a (f **~a**) mighty; **Senhor** (com nome) Mr; (Deus) Lord; **o ~** (você) you

senho|ra /se'ɲɔra/ f lady; (mulher idosa) older woman; (tratamento) madam; **Senhora** (com nome) Mrs; **a ~ra** (você) you; **nossa ~ral** ① gosh. **~ria** f **Vossa Senhoria** you. **~rita** f young lady; (tratamento) miss; **Senhorita** (com nome) Miss

se|nil (pl **~nis**) a senile. **~nilidade** f senility

sensação /sẽsa'sãw/ f sensation

sensacio|nal /sẽsasio'naw/ (pl **~nais**) a sensational. **~nalismo** m sensationalism. **~nalista** a sensationalist

sen|sato /sẽ'satu/ a sensible. **~sibilidade** f sensitivity. **~sível** (pl **~síveis**) a sensitive; (que se pode sentir) noticeable. **~so** m sense. **~sual** (pl **~suais**) a sensual

sen|tado /sẽ'tadu/ a sitting. **~tar** vt/i sit. **~tar-se** vpr sit down

sentença /sẽ'tẽsa/ f sentence

sentido /sẽ'tʃidu/ m sense; (direção) direction ● a hurt; **fazer ou ter ~** make sense

sentimen|tal /sẽtʃimẽ'taw/ (pl **~tais**) a sentimental; **vida ~tal** love life. **~to** m feeling

sentinela /sẽtʃi'nɛla/ f sentry

sentir /sẽ'tʃir/ vt feel; (notar) sense; smell ‹cheiro›; taste ‹gosto›; tell ‹diferença›; (ficar magoado por) be hurt by ● vi feel. **~se** vpr feel; **sinto muito** I'm very sorry

sepa|ração /separa'sãw/ f separation. **~rado** a separate; (casal) separated. **~rar** vt separate. **~rar-se** vpr separate

séptico /'sɛptʃiku/ a septic

sepul|tar /sepuw'tar/ vt bury. **~tura** f grave

sequência /se'kwẽsia/ f sequence

sequer /se'kɛr/ adv **nem ~** not even

seques|trador /sekwestra'dor/ m kidnapper; (de avião) hijacker. **~trar** vt kidnap ‹pessoa›; hijack ‹avião›; sequestrate ‹bens›. **~tro** /ɛ/ m (de pessoa) kidnapping; (de avião) hijack; (de bens) sequestration

---

ser /ser/ ● vi

····▸ be; **é alta** she's tall; **sou de Porto Alegre** I'm from Porto Alegre; **2 e 2 são 4** two and two are four; **são três reais** it's three reais; **o banco é na praça** the bank is in the square; (com as horas) **são sete horas** it's seven o'clock; **~ de** (material) be made of; **é de alumínio** it's made of aluminium; (lugar) be from; **ele é do Brasil** he's from Brazil; (grupo esportivo) support; **é do Flamengo** she is a Flamengo supporter

● v aux

····▸ (passiva) to be; **ele será julgado segunda-feira** he will be tried on Monday

● *nm*
····▸ being; **um ~ humano** a human being; **um ~ vivo** a living being

····▸ (*em expressões*) **é que:** (*ênfase*) **é que não me apetece** I just don't feel like it; **seja como for, seja o que for, seja quem for** no matter how/what/who; **sou eu/é você etc** it's me/you etc

sereia /se'reja/ *f* mermaid

serenata /sere'nata/ *f* serenade

sereno /se'renu/ *a* serene; ‹*tempo*› fine

série /'sɛri/ *f* series; (*na escola*) grade; **fora de ~** 🚹 incredible

seriedade /serie'dadʒi/ *f* seriousness

serin|ga /se'rĩga/ *f* syringe. **~gueiro** *m* rubber tapper

sério /'sɛriu/ *a* serious; (*responsável*) responsible; **~?** really?; **falar ~** be serious; **levar a ~** take seriously

sermão /ser'mãw/ *m* sermon

seropositivo /sɛropuzi'tivu/ *a Port* ▶ **soropositivo** /soropozi'tʃivu/

serpen|te /ser'pẽtʃi/ *f* serpent. **~tear** *vi* wind. **~tina** *f* streamer

serra[1] /'sɛxa/ *f* (*montanhas*) mountain range

serra[2] /'sɛxa/ *f* (*de serrar*) saw. **~gem** *f* sawdust. **~lheiro** *m* locksmith

serrano /se'xanu/ *a* mountain

serrar /se'xar/ *vt* saw

ser|tanejo /serta'neʒu/ *a* from the backwoods ● *m* backwoodsman. **~tão** *m* backwoods

servente /ser'vẽtʃi/ *m/f* labourer

Sérvia /'sɛrvia/ *f* Serbia

servi|çal /servi'saw/ (*pl* **~çais**) a helpful ● *m/f* servant. **~ço** *m* service; (*trabalho*) work; (*tarefa*) job; **estar de ~** be on duty. **~dor** *m* servant; *Comput* server. **~dor público** *m* civil servant

ser|vil /ser'viw/ (*pl* **~vis**) *a* servile

sérvio /'sɛrviu/ *a & m* Serbian

servir /ser'vir/ *vt* serve; serve as ● *vi* serve; (*ser adequado*) do; (*ser útil*) be of use; ‹*roupa, sapato etc*› fit; **~ como** ou **de** serve as; **para que serve isso?** what is this (used) for?. **~-se** *vpr* (*ao comer etc*) help o.s. (**de** to); **~-se de** make use of

sessão /se'sãw/ *f* session; (*no cinema*) showing, performance

sessenta /se'sẽta/ *a & m* sixty

seta /'seta/ *f* arrow; (*de carro*) indicator

sete /'sɛtʃi/ *a & m* seven. **~centos** *a & m* seven hundred

setembro /se'tẽbru/ *m* September

setenta /se'tẽta/ *a & m* seventy

sétimo /'sɛtʃimu/ *a* a seventh

setor /se'tor/ *m* sector

setuagésimo /setua'ʒɛzimu/ *a* seventieth

seu /sew/ *a* (*f* **sua**) (*dele*) his; (*dela*) her; (*de coisa*) its; (*deles*) their; (*de você, de vocês*) your ● *pron* (*dele*) his; (*dela*) hers; (*deles*) theirs; (*de você, de vocês*) yours; **~ idiota!** you idiot!; **seu João** Mr John

seve|ridade /severi'dadʒi/ *f* severity. **~ro** /ɛ/ *a* severe

sexagésimo /seksa'ʒɛzimu/ *a* sixtieth

sexo /'sɛksu/ *m* sex; **fazer ~** have sex; **do mesmo ~** ‹*casais, pessoas*› same-sex

sex|ta /'sesta/ *f* Friday. **~ta-feira** (*pl* **~tas-feiras**) *f* Friday; **Sexta-feira Santa** Good Friday. **~to** /e/ *a & m* sixth

sexu|al /seksu'aw/ (*pl* **~ais**) *a* sexual; **vida ~al** sex life

sexy /'sɛksi/ *a invar* sexy

shopping /'ʃɔpĩ/ (*pl* **~s**) *m* shopping centre, *Amer* mall

short /'ʃɔrtʃi/ *m* (*pl* **~s**) shorts; **um ~** a pair of shorts

show /'ʃou/ (*pl* **~s**) *m* show; (*de música*) concert

si /si/ *pron* (*ele*) himself; (*ela*) herself; (*coisa*) itself; (*você*) yourself; (*eles*) themselves; (*vocês*) yourselves; (*qualquer pessoa*) oneself; **em ~** in itself; **fora de ~** beside o.s.; **cheio de ~** full of o.s.; **voltar a ~** come round

sibilar /sibi'lar/ *vi* hiss

SIDA /'sida/ *f Port* ▶ AIDS

side|ral /side'raw/ (*pl* **~rais**) *a* **espaço ~ral** outer space

siderurgia /siderur'ʒia/ *f* iron and steel industry

siderúrgi|ca /side'rurʒika/ *f* steelworks. **~co** *a* iron and steel ● *m* steelworker

sifão /si'fãw/ *m* syphon

sífilis /'sifilis/ *f* syphilis

sigilo /si'ʒilu/ *m* secrecy. **~so** /o/ *a* secret

sigla /'sigla/ *f* acronym

signatário /signa'tariu/ *m* signatory

signifi|cação /signifika'sãw/ *f* significance. **~cado** *m* meaning. **~car** *vt* mean. **~cativo** *a* significant

signo /'signu/ *m* sign

sílaba /'silaba/ *f* syllable

silenciar /silẽsi'ar/ *vt* silence

S

silêncio /si'lẽsiu/ m silence

silencioso /silẽsi'ozu/ a silent ● m silencer, Amer muffler

silhueta /siʎu'eta/ f silhouette

silício /si'lisiu/ m silicon

silicone /sili'kɔni/ m silicone

silo /'silu/ m silo

silvar /siw'var/ vi hiss

sil|vestre /siw'vɛstri/ a wild. **~vicultura** f forestry

sim /sĩ/ adv yes; **acho que ~** I think so

simbólico /sĩ'bɔliku/ a symbolic

simbo|lismo /sĩbo'lizmu/ m symbolism. **~lizar** vt symbolize

símbolo /'sĩbolu/ m symbol

si|metria /sime'tria/ f symmetry. **~métrico** a symmetrical

similar /simi'lar/ a similar

sim|patia /sĩpa'tʃia/ f (qualidade) pleasantness; (afeto) fondness (**por** for); (compreensão, apoio) sympathy; pl sympathies; **ter ~patia por** be fond of. **~pático** a nice

simpati|zante /sĩpatʃi'zãtʃi/ a sympathetic ● m/f sympathizer. **~zar** vi **~zar com** take a liking to ‹pessoa›; sympathize with ‹ideias, partido etc›

simples /'sĩplis/ a invar simple; (único) single ● f (no tênis etc) singles. **~mente** adv simply

simpli|cidade /sĩplisi'dadʒi/ f simplicity. **~ficar** vt simplify

simplório /sĩ'plɔriu/ a simple

simpósio /sĩ'pɔziu/ m symposium

simu|lação /simula'sãw/ f simulation. **~lar** vt simulate

simultâneo /simuw'taniu/ a simultaneous

sina /'sina/ f fate

sinagoga /sina'gɔga/ f synagogue

si|nal /si'naw/ (pl **~nais**) m sign; (aviso, de rádio etc) signal; (de trânsito) traffic light; (no telefone) tone; (dinheiro) deposit; (na pele) mole; **por ~nal** as a matter of fact; **~nal de pontuação** punctuation mark. **~naleira** f traffic lights. **~nalização** f (na rua) road signs. **~nalizar** vt signal; signpost ‹rua, cidade›

since|ridade /sĩseri'dadʒi/ f sincerity. **~ro** /ɛ/ a sincere

sincro|nia /sĩkro'nia/ f synchronization. **~nizar** vt synchronize

sindi|cal /sĩdʒi'kaw/ (pl **~cais**) a trade union. **~calismo** m trade unionism.

~calista m/f trade unionist. **~calizar** vt unionize. **~cato** m trade union

síndico /'sĩdʒiku/ m house manager

síndrome /'sĩdromi/ f syndrome

sinergia /siner'ʒia/ f synergy

sineta /si'neta/ f bell

sin|fonia /sĩfo'nia/ f symphony. **~fônica** f symphony orchestra

Singapura /sĩga'pura/ f Singapore

singe|leza /sĩʒe'leza/ f simplicity. **~lo** /ɛ/ a simple

singu|lar /sĩgu'lar/ a singular; (estranho) peculiar. **~larizar** vt single out

sinis|trado /sinis'tradu/ a damaged. **~tro** a sinister ● m accident

sino /'sinu/ m bell

sinônimo /si'nonimu/ a synonymous ● m synonym

sintaxe /sĩ'taksi/ f syntax

síntese /'sĩtezi/ f synthesis

sin|tético /sĩ'tɛtʃiku/ a (artificial) synthetic; (resumido) concise. **~tetizar** vt summarize

sinto|ma /sĩ'toma/ m symptom. **~mático** a symptomatic

sintoni|zador /sĩtoniza'dor/ m tuner. **~zar** vt tune ‹rádio, TV›; tune in to ‹emissora› ● vi be in tune (**com** with)

sinuca /si'nuka/ f snooker

sinuoso /sinu'ozu/ a winding

sinusite /sinu'zitʃi/ f sinusitis

siri /si'ri/ m crab

Síria /'siria/ f Syria

sírio /'siriu/ a & m Syrian

siso /'sizu/ m good sense

siste|ma /sis'tema/ m system. **~mático** a systematic

sisudo /si'zudu/ a serious

site /sajt/ m Comput website

sítio /'sitʃiu/ m (chácara) farm; Port (local) place; **estado de ~** state of siege

situ|ação /situa'sãw/ f situation; (no governo) party in power. **~ar** vt situate. **~ar-se** vpr be situated; ‹pessoa› position o.s.

smoking /iz'mɔkĩ/ (pl **~s**) m dinner jacket, Amer tuxedo

só /sɔ/ a alone; (sentindo solidão) lonely ● adv only; **um ~ voto** one single vote; **~ um carro** only one car; **a ~s** alone; **imagina ~** just imagine; **~ que** except (that)

soalho /so'aʎu/ m floor

soar /so'ar/ *vt/i* sound

sob /'sobi/ *prep* under

sobera|nia /sobera'nia/ *f* sovereignty. **~no** *a & m* sovereign

soberbo /so'berbu/ *a* ‹pessoa› haughty; (*magnífico*) splendid

sobra /'sɔbra/ *f* surplus; *pl* leftovers; **tempo de ~** (*muito*) plenty of time; **ficar de ~** be left over; **ter algo de ~** (*sobrando*) have sth left over

sobraçar /sobra'sar/ *vt* carry under one's arm

sobrado /so'bradu/ *m* (*casa*) house; (*andar*) upper floor

sobrancelha /sobrã'seʎa/ *f* eyebrow

so|brar /so'brar/ *vi* be left; **~bram-me dois** I have two left

sobre /'sobri/ *prep* (*em cima de*) on; (*por cima de, acima de*) over; (*acerca de*) about

sobreaviso /sobria'vizu/ *m* **estar de ~** be on one's guard

sobrecapa /sobri'kapa/ *f* dust jacket

sobrecarregar /sobrikaxe'gar/ *vt* overload

sobreloja /sobri'lɔʒa/ *f* mezzanine

sobremesa /sobri'meza/ *f* dessert

sobrenatu|ral /sobrinatu'raw/ (*pl* **~rais**) *a* supernatural

sobrenome /sobri'nomi/ *m* surname

sobrepor /sobri'por/ *vt* superimpose

sobrepujar /sobripu'ʒar/ *vt* (*em altura*) tower over; (*em valor, número etc*) surpass; overwhelm ‹adversário›; overcome ‹problemas›

sobrescritar /sobriskri'tar/ *vt* address

sobressair /sobrisa'ir/ *vi* stand out. **~se** *vpr* stand out

sobressalente /sobrisa'lẽtʃi/ *a* spare

sobressal|tar /sobrisaw'tar/ *vt* startle. **~tar-se** *vpr* be startled. **~to** *m* (*movimento*) start; (*susto*) fright

sobretaxa /sobri'taʃa/ *f* surcharge

sobretudo /sobri'tudu/ *adv* above all ● *m* overcoat

sobrevir /sobri'vir/ *vi* happen suddenly; (*seguir*) ensue; **~ a** follow

sobrevi|vência /sobrivi'vẽsia/ *f* survival. **~vente** *a* surviving ● *m/f* survivor. **~ver** *vt/i* **~ver (a)** survive

sobrevoar /sobrivo'ar/ *vt* fly over

sobri|nha /so'briɲa/ *f* niece. **~nho** *m* nephew

sóbrio /'sɔbriu/ *a* sober

socar /so'kar/ *vt* (*esmurrar*) punch; (*amassar*) crush

soci|al /sosi'aw/ (*pl* **~ais**) *a* social; **camisa ~al** dress shirt. **~alismo** *m* socialism. **~alista** *a & m/f* socialist. **~alite** /-a'lajtʃi/ *m/f* socialite. **~ável** (*pl* **~áveis**) *a* sociable

sociedade /sosie'dadʒi/ *f* society; (*parceria*) partnership; **~ anônima** limited company

sócio /'sɔsiu/ *m* (*de empresa*) partner; (*de clube*) member

socioeconômico /sosioeko'nomiku/ *a* socio-economic

soci|ologia /sosiolo'ʒia/ *f* sociology. **~ológico** *a* sociological. **~ólogo** *m* sociologist

soco /'soku/ *m* punch; **dar um ~ em** punch

socor|rer /soko'xer/ *vt* help. **~ro** *m* aid; **primeiros ~ros** first aid ● *int* help

soda /'sɔda/ *f* (*água*) soda water; **~ cáustica** caustic soda

sódio /'sɔdʒiu/ *m* sodium

sofá /so'fa/ *m* sofa. **~-cama** (*pl* **~s-camas**) *m* sofa bed

sofisticado /sofistʃi'kadu/ *a* sophisticated

so|fredor /sofre'dor/ *a* martyred. **~frer** *vt* suffer ‹dor, derrota, danos etc›; have ‹acidente›; undergo ‹operação, mudança etc› ● *vi* suffer; **~frer de** suffer from ‹doença›; have trouble with ‹coração etc›. **~frido** *a* long-suffering. **~frimento** *m* suffering. **~frível** (*pl* **~fríveis**) *a* passable

soft /'softʃi/ (*pl* **~s**) *m* software package. **~ware** *m* software; (*um*) software package

so|gra /'sɔgra/ *f* mother-in-law. **~gro** /o/ *m* father-in-law. **~gros** /ɔ/ *m pl* in-laws

soja /'sɔʒa/ *f* soya, *Amer* soy

sol /sɔw/ (*pl* **sóis**) *m* sun; **faz ~** it's sunny

sola /'sɔla/ *f* sole. **~do** *a* ‹bolo› flat

solapar /sola'par/ *vt* undermine

solar[1] /so'lar/ *a* solar

solar[2] /so'lar/ *vt* sole ‹sapato› ● *vi* ‹bolo› go flat

solavanco /sola'vãku/ *m* jolt; **dar ~s** jolt

soldado /sow'dadu/ *m* soldier

sol|dadura /sowda'dura/ *f* weld. **~dar** *vt* weld

soldo /'sowdu/ *m* pay

soleira /so'lera/ *f* doorstep

S

sole|ne /so'leni/ a solemn. **~nidade** f (cerimônia) ceremony; (qualidade) solemnity

soletrar /sole'trar/ vt spell

solici|tação /solisita'sãw/ f request (de for); (por escrito) application (de for). **~tante** m/f applicant. **~tar** vt request; (por escrito) apply for

solícito /so'lisitu/ a helpful

solidão /soli'dãw/ f loneliness

soli|dariedade /solidarie'dadʒi/ f solidarity. **~dário** a supportive (com of)

soli|dez /soli'des/ f solidity. **~dificar** vt solidify. **~dificar-se** vpr solidify

sólido /'sɔlidu/ a & m solid

solista /so'lista/ m/f soloist

solitá|ria /soli'taria/ f (verme) tapeworm; (cela) solitary confinement. **~rio** a solitary

solo[1] /'sɔlu/ m (terra) soil; (chão) ground

solo[2] /'sɔlu/ m solo

soltar /sow'tar/ vt let go ‹prisioneiros, animal etc›; let loose ‹cães›; (deixar de segurar) let go of; loosen ‹gravata, corda etc›; let down ‹cabelo›; let out ‹grito, suspiro etc›; let off ‹foguetes›; tell ‹piada›; take off ‹freio›. **~se** vpr ‹peça, parafuso› come loose; ‹pessoa› let o.s. go

soltei|ra /sow'tera/ f single woman. **~rão** m bachelor. **~ro** a single ● m single man. **~rona** f spinster

solto /'sowtu/ a (livre) free; ‹cães› loose; ‹cabelo› down; ‹arroz› fluffy; (frouxo) loose; (à vontade) relaxed; (abandonado) abandoned; **correr ~** run wild

solução /solu'sãw/ f solution

soluçar /solu'sar/ vi (ao chorar) sob; (engasgar) hiccup

solucionar /solusio'nar/ vt solve

soluço /so'lusu/ m (ao chorar) sob; (engasgo) hiccup; **estar com ~s** have the hiccups

solú|vel /so'luvew/ (pl **~veis**) a soluble

solvente /sow'vẽtʃi/ a & m solvent

som /sõ/ m sound; (aparelho) stereo; **um ~** 🔲 (música) a bit of music

so|ma /'soma/ f sum. **~mar** vt add up ‹números etc›; (ter como soma) add up to

sombra /'sõbra/ f shadow; (área abrigada do sol) shade; **à ~ de** in the shade of; **sem ~ de dúvida** without a shadow of a doubt

sombre|ado /sõbri'adu/ a shady ● m shading. **~ar** vt shade

sombrinha /sõ'briɲa/ f parasol

sombrio /sõ'briu/ a gloomy

somente /so'mẽtʃi/ adv only

sonâmbulo /so'nãbulu/ m sleepwalker

sonante /so'nãtʃi/ a **moeda ~** hard cash

sonata /so'nata/ f sonata

son|da /'sõda/ f probe. **~dagem** f (no mar) sounding; (de terreno) survey; **~dagem de opinião** opinion poll. **~dar** vt probe; sound ‹profundeza›; fig sound out ‹pessoas, opiniões etc›

soneca /so'nɛka/ f nap; **tirar uma ~** have a nap

sone|gação /sonega'sãw/ f (de impostos) tax evasion. **~gador** m tax dodger. **~gar** vt withhold

soneto /so'netu/ m sonnet

so|nhador /soɲa'dor/ a dreamy ● m dreamer. **~nhar** vt/i dream (com about). **~nho** /'soɲu/ m dream; (doce) doughnut

sono /'sonu/ m sleep; **estar com ~** be sleepy; **pegar no ~** get to sleep. **~lento** a sleepy

sono|plastia /sonoplas'tʃia/ f sound effects. **~ridade** f sound quality. **~ro** /ɔ/ a sound; ‹voz› sonorous; ‹consoante› voiced

sonso /'sõsu/ a devious

sopa /'sopa/ f soup

sopapo /so'papu/ m slap; **dar um ~ em** slap

sopé /so'pɛ/ m foot

sopeira /so'pera/ f soup tureen

soprano /so'pranu/ m/f soprano

so|prar /so'prar/ vt blow ‹folhas etc›; blow up ‹balão›; blow out ‹vela› ● vi blow. **~pro** m blow; (de vento) puff; **instrumento de ~pro** wind instrument

soquete[1] /so'ketʃi/ f ankle sock

soquete[2] /so'ketʃi/ m socket

sordidez /sordʒi'des/ f sordidness; (imundície) squalor

sórdido /'sɔrdʒidu/ a (reles) sordid; (imundo) squalid

soro /'soru/ m (remédio) serum; (de leite) whey

soropositivo /soropozi'tʃivu/ a HIV-positive

sorrateiro /soxa'teru/ a crafty

sor|ridente /soxiˈdẽtʃi/ a smiling. **~rir** vi smile. **~riso** m smile

sorte /ˈsɔxtʃi/ f luck; (destino) fate; **pessoa de ~** lucky person; **por ~** luckily; **ter** ou **dar ~** be lucky; **tive a ~ de conhecê-lo** I was lucky enough to meet him; **tirar a ~** draw lots; **trazer ~** bring good luck

sor|tear /soxtʃiˈar/ vt draw for <prêmio>; select in a draw <pessoa>. **~teio** m draw

sorti|do /soxˈtʃidu/ a assorted. **~mento** m assortment

sorumbático /sorũˈbatʃiku/ a sombre, gloomy

sorver /soxˈver/ vt sip <bebida>

sósia /ˈsɔzia/ m/f double

soslaio /sozˈlaju/ m **de ~** sideways; <olhar> askance

sosse|gado /soseˈgadu/ a <vida> quiet; **ficar ~gado** <pessoa> rest assured. **~gar** vt reassure ● vi rest. **~go** /e/ m peace

sótão /ˈsɔtãw/ (pl **~s**) m attic, loft

sotaque /soˈtaki/ m accent

soterrar /soteˈxar/ vt bury

soutien /sutiˈã/ (pl **~s**) m Port bra

sova|co /soˈvaku/ m armpit. **~queira** f BO, body odour

soviético /soviˈetʃiku/ a & m Soviet

sovi|na /soˈvina/ a stingy, mean, Amer cheap ● m/f cheapskate. **~nice** f stinginess, meanness, Amer cheapness

sozinho /soˈziɲu/ a (sem ninguém) alone, on one's own; (por si próprio) by o.s.; **falar ~** talk to o.s.

spam m (em correio eletrônico) spam

spray /isˈprej/ (pl **~s**) m spray

squash /isˈkwɛʃ/ m squash

stand /isˈtãdʒi/ (pl **~s**) m stand

status /isˈtatus/ m status

stripper /isˈtriper/ (pl **~s**) m/f stripper

striptease /istripiˈtʃizi/ m striptease

sua /ˈsua/ a & pron ▶ SEU

su|ado /suˈadu/ a <pessoa, roupa> sweaty; fig hard-earned. **~ar** vt/i sweat; **~ar por/para** fig work hard for/to; **~ar frio** come out in a cold sweat

sua|ve /suˈavi/ a <toque, subida> gentle; <gosto, cheiro, dor, inverno> mild; <música, voz> soft; <vinho> smooth; <trabalho> light; <prestações> easy. **~vidade** f gentleness; mildness; softness; smoothness; ▶ SUAVE. **~vizar** vt soften; soothe <dor, pessoa>

subalterno /subawˈtεrnu/ a & m subordinate

subconsciente /subikõsiˈẽtʃi/ a & m subconscious

subdesenvolvido /subidʒizĩvowˈvidu/ a underdeveloped

súbdito /ˈsubditu/ m Port ▶ SÚDITO

subdividir /subidʒiviˈdʒir/ vt subdivide

subemprego /subĩˈpregu/ m menial job

subemprei|tar /subĩprejˈtar/ vt subcontract. **~teiro** m subcontractor

subenten|der /subĩtẽˈder/ vt infer. **~dido** a implied ● m insinuation

subestimar /subestʃiˈmar/ vt underestimate

su|bida /suˈbida/ f (ação) ascent; (ladeira) incline; (de preços etc) fig rise. **~bir** vi go up; <rio, águas> rise ● vt go up, climb; **~bir em** climb <árvore>; get up onto <mesa>; get on <ônibus>

súbito /ˈsubitu/ a sudden; **(de) ~** suddenly

subjacente /subiʒaˈsẽtʃi/ a underlying

subjeti|vidade /subiʒetʃiviˈdadʒi/ f subjectivity. **~vo** a subjective

subjugar /subiʒuˈgar/ vt subjugate

subjuntivo /subiʒũˈtʃivu/ a & m subjunctive

sublevar-se /subleˈvarsi/ vpr rise up

sublime /suˈblimi/ a sublime

subli|nhado /subliˈɲadu/ m underlining. **~nhar** vt underline

sublocar /subloˈkar/ vt/i sublet

submarino /subimaˈrinu/ a underwater ● m submarine

submer|gir /subimerˈʒir/ vt submerge. **~gir-se** vpr submerge. **~so** a submerged

submeter /subimeˈter/ vt subject (a to); put down, subdue <povo, rebeldes etc>; submit <projeto>. **~se** vpr (render-se) submit; **~se a** (sofrer) undergo

submis|são /subimiˈsãw/ f submission. **~so** a submissive

submundo /subiˈmũdu/ m underworld

subnutrição /subinutriˈsãw/ f malnutrition

subordi|nado /subordʒiˈnadu/ a & m subordinate. **~nar** vt subordinate (a to)

subor|nar /suborˈnar/ vt bribe. **~no** /o/ m bribe

S

subproduto /subipro'dutu/ *m* by-product

subs|crever /subiskre'ver/ *vt* sign ‹carta etc›; subscribe to ‹opinião›; subscribe ‹dinheiro› (**para** to). **~crever-se** *vpr* sign one's name. **~crição** *f* subscription. **~crito** *pp de* ▶ SUBSCREVER

subsequente /subise'kwẽtʃi/ *a* subsequent

subserviente /subiservi'ẽtʃi/ *a* subservient

subsidiar /subisidʒi'ar/ *vt* subsidize

subsidiá|ria /subisidʒi'aria/ *f* subsidiary. **~rio** *a* subsidiary

subsídio /subi'sidʒiu/ *m* subsidy

subsistência /subisis'tẽsia/ *f* subsistence

subsolo /subi'sɔlu/ *m* (porão) basement

substância /subis'tãsia/ *f* substance

substan|cial /subistãsi'aw/ (*pl* **~ciais**) *a* substantial. **~tivo** *m* noun

substitu|ição /subistʃitui'sãw/ *f* replacement; substitution. **~ir** *vt* (pôr B no lugar de A) replace (**A por B** A with B); (usar B em vez de A) substitute (**A por B** B for A). **~to** *a & m* substitute

subterfúgio /subiter'fuʒiu/ *m* subterfuge

subterrâneo /subite'xaniu/ *a* underground

sub|til /sub'til/ (*pl* **~tis**) *a* Port ▶ SUTIL

subtra|ção /subitra'sãw/ *f* subtraction. **~ir** *vt* subtract ‹números›; (roubar) steal

suburbano /subur'banu/ *a* suburban

subúrbio /su'burbiu/ *m* suburbs

subven|ção /subivẽ'sãw/ *f* grant, subsidy. **~cionar** *vt* subsidize

subver|são /subiver'sãw/ *f* subversion. **~sivo** *a & m* subversive

suca|ta /su'kata/ *f* scrap metal. **~tear** *vt* scrap

sucção /suk'sãw/ *f* suction

suce|der /suse'der/ *vi* (acontecer) happen ● *vt* **~der a** succeed ‹rei etc›; (vir depois) follow. **~der-se** *vpr* follow on from one another. **~dido** *a* **bem~dido** successful

suces|são /suse'sãw/ *f* succession. **~sivo** *a* successive. **~so** /ɛ/ *m* success; (música) hit; **fazer** ou **ter ~so** be successful. **~sor** *m* successor

sucinto /su'sĩtu/ *a* succinct

suco /'suku/ *m* juice

suculento /suku'lẽtu/ *a* juicy

sucumbir /sukũ'bir/ *vi* succumb (**a** to)

sucur|sal /sukur'saw/ (*pl* **~sais**) *f* branch

Sudão /su'dãw/ *m* Sudan

sudário /su'dariu/ *m* shroud

sudeste /su'dɛstʃi/ *a & m* south-east; **o Sudeste Asiático** South East Asia

súdito /'sudʒitu/ *m* subject

sudoeste /sudo'estʃi/ *a & m* southwest

Suécia /su'esia/ *f* Sweden

sueco /su'eku/ *a & m* Swedish

suéter /su'eter/ *m/f* sweater

sufici|ência /sufisi'ẽsia/ *f* sufficiency. **~ente** *a* enough, sufficient; **o ~ente** enough

sufixo /su'fiksu/ *m* suffix

suflê /su'fle/ *m* soufflé

sufo|cante /sufo'kãtʃi/ *a* stifling. **~car** *vt* (asfixiar) suffocate; fig stifle ● *vi* suffocate. **~co** /o/ *m* hassle; **estar num ~co** be having a tough time

sufrágio /su'fraʒiu/ *m* suffrage

sugar /su'gar/ *vt* suck

sugerir /suʒe'rir/ *vt* suggest

suges|tão /suʒes'tãw/ *f* suggestion; **dar uma ~tão** make a suggestion. **~tivo** *a* suggestive

Suíça /su'isa/ *f* Switzerland

suíças /su'isas/ *f pl* sideburns

sui|cida /sui'sida/ *a* suicidal; **ataque ~** suicide bombing; **bombardeador ~** suicide bomber ● *m/f* suicide (victim). **~cidar-se** *vpr* commit suicide. **~cídio** *m* suicide

suíço /su'isu/ *a & m* Swiss

suíno /su'inu/ *a & m* pig

suíte /su'itʃi/ *f* suite

su|jar /su'ʒar/ *vt* dirty; fig sully ‹reputação etc› ● *vi*, **~se** *vpr* get dirty; **~jar-se com alguém** queer one's pitch with sb. **~jeira** *f* dirt; (uma) dirty trick

suje|tar /suʒej'tar/ *vt* subject (**a** to). **~tar-se** *vpr* subject o.s. (**a** to). **~to a** *a* subject (**a** to) ● *m* (de oração) subject; (pessoa) person

su|jidade /suʒi'dadʒi/ *f Port* dirt. **~jo** *a* dirty

sul /suw/ *a invar & m* south. **~africano** *a & m* South African; **~americano** *a & m* South American; **~coreano** *a & m* South Korean

sul|car /suw'kar/ *vt* furrow ‹testa›. **~co** *m* furrow

sulfúrico /suw'furiku/ a sulphuric

sulista /su'lista/ a southern ● m/f southerner

sultão /suw'tãw/ m sultan

sumário /su'mariu/ a <justiça> summary; <roupa> skimpy, brief

su|miço /su'misu/ m disappearance; **dar ~miço em** spirit away; **tomar chá de ~miço** disappear. **~mido** a <cor, voz> faint. **~mir** vi disappear; **ele anda ~mido** he's disappeared

sumo /'sumu/ m Port juice

sumptuoso /sũtu'ozu/ a Port ▶ SUNTUOSO

sunga /'sũga/ f swimming trunks

suntuoso /sũtu'ozu/ a sumptuous

suor /su'or/ m sweat

superar /supe'rar/ vt overcome <dificuldade etc>; surpass <expetativa, pessoa>

superá|vel /supe'ravew/ (pl ~veis) a surmountable. **~vit** (pl ~vits) m surplus

superestimar /superestʃi'mar/ vt overestimate

superestrutura /superistru'tura/ f superstructure

superfici|al /superfisi'aw/ (pl ~ais) a superficial

superfície /super'fisi/ f surface; (medida) area

supérfluo /su'perfluu/ a superfluous

superintendência /superĩtẽ-'dẽsia/ f bureau

superi|or /superi'or/ a (de cima) upper; <ensino> higher; <número, temperatura etc> greater (**a** than); (melhor) superior (**a** to) ● m superior. **~oridade** f superiority

superlativo /superla'tʃivu/ a & m superlative

superlota|ção /superlota'sãw/ f overcrowding. **~do** a overcrowded

supermercado /supermer'kadu/ m supermarket

superpotência /superpo'tẽsia/ f superpower

superpovoado /superpovo'adu/ a overpopulated

supersecreto /superse'kretu/ a top secret

supersensí|vel /supersẽ'sivew/ (pl ~veis) a oversensitive

supersônico /super'soniku/ a supersonic

supersti|ção /superstʃi'sãw/ f superstition. **~cioso** /o/ a superstitious

supervi|são /supervi'zãw/ f supervision. **~sionar** vt supervise. **~sor** m supervisor

supetão /supe'tãw/ m **de ~** all of a sudden

suplantar /suplã'tar/ vt supplant

suplemen|tar /suplemẽ'tar/ a supplementary ● vt supplement. **~to** m supplement

suplente /su'plẽtʃi/ a & m/f substitute

supletivo /suple'tʃivu/ a supplementary; **ensino ~** adult education

súplica /'suplika/ f plea; **tom de ~** pleading tone

suplicar /supli'kar/ vt plead for; (em juízo) petition for

suplício /su'plisiu/ m torture; fig (aflição) torment

supor /su'por/ vt suppose

supor|tar /supor'tar/ vt (sustentar) support; (tolerar) stand, bear. **~tável** (pl ~táveis) a bearable. **~te** /ɔ/ m support

suposição /supozi'sãw/ f supposition

supositório /supozi'tɔriu/ m suppository

supos|tamente /suposta'mẽtʃi/ adv supposedly. **~to** /o/ a supposed; **~to que** supposing that

supre|macia /suprema'sia/ f supremacy. **~mo** /e/ a supreme

supressão /supre'sãw/ f (de lei, cargo, privilégio) abolition; (de jornal, informação, nomes) suppression; (de palavras, cláusula) deletion

suprimento /supri'mẽtu/ m supply

suprimir /supri'mir/ vt abolish <lei, cargo, privilégio>; suppress <jornal, informação, nomes>; delete <palavras, cláusula>

suprir /su'prir/ vt provide for <família, necessidades>; make up for <falta>; make up <quantia>; supply <o que falta>; (substituir) take the place of; **~ alguém de** provide sb with; **~ A por B** substitute B for A

supurar /supu'rar/ vi turn septic

sur|dez /sur'des/ f deafness. **~do** a deaf; <consoante> voiceless ● m deaf person; **os ~dos** the deaf. **~do-mudo** (pl ~dos-mudos) a deaf and dumb ● m deaf mute

sur|fe /'surfi/ m surfing. **~fista** m/f surfer

S

sur|gimento /surʒi'mẽtu/ m
appearance. **~gir** vi arise; **~gir à mente**
spring to mind

Suriname /suri'nami/ m Surinam

surpreen|dente /surprië'dẽtʃi/
a surprising. **~der** vt surprise ● vi be
surprising. **~der-se** vpr be surprised
(**de** at)

surpre|sa /sur'preza/ f surprise; **de
~sa** by surprise. **~so** /e/ a surprised

sur|ra /'suxa/ f thrashing. **~rado**
a ‹roupa› worn-out. **~rar** vt thrash
‹pessoa›; wear out ‹roupa›

surrealis|mo /suxea'lizmu/ m
surrealism. **~ta** a & m/f surrealist

surtir /sur'tʃir/ vt produce; **~ efeito** be
effective

surto /'surtu/ m outbreak

susce|tibilidade /susetʃibili-'dadʒi/ f
(de pessoa) sensitivity. **~tível** (pl **~tíveis**)
a ‹pessoa› touchy, sensitive; **~tível a**
open to

suscitar /susi'tar/ vt cause; raise
‹dúvida, suspeita›

suspei|ta /sus'pejta/ f suspicion. **~tar**
vt/i **~tar** (**de**) suspect. **~to** a suspicious;
(duvidoso) suspect ● m suspect. **~toso**
/o/ a suspicious

suspen|der /suspẽ'der/ vt suspend.
~são f suspension. **~se** m suspense. **~so**
a suspended. **~sórios** m pl braces, Amer
suspenders

suspi|rar /suspi'rar/ vi sigh; **~rar por**
long for. **~ro** m sigh; (doce) meringue

sussur|rar /susu'xar/ vt/i whisper. **~ro**
m whisper

sustar /sus'tar/ vt/i stop

sustenido /suste'nidu/ a Mús sharp;
tecla ~ hash key

sustentabilidade /sustẽtabili'dadʒi/
f sustainability

susten|táculo /sustẽ'takulu/ m
mainstay. **~tar** vt support; (afirmar)
maintain. **~to** m support; (ganha-pão)
livelihood

sustentável /sustẽ'tavew/ a
sustainable

susto /'sustu/ m fright

sutiã /sutʃi'ã/ m bra

su|til /su'tʃiw/ (pl **~tis**) a subtle. **~tileza**
/e/ f subtlety

sutu|ra /su'tura/ f suture. **~rar** vt suture

SUV m (carro) SUV

sweatshirt /swet'ʃarte/ f Port
sweatshirt

Tt

tá /ta/ int 🔢 OK; ▶ ESTAR

taba|caria /tabaka'ria/ f tobacconist's.
~co m tobacco

tabefe /ta'bɛfi/ m slap

tabe|la /ta'bɛla/ f table. **~lar** vt tabulate

tablado /ta'bladu/ m platform

tabu /ta'bu/ a & m taboo

tábua /'tabua/ f board; **~ de passar
roupa** ironing board

tabuleiro /tabu'leru/ m (de xadrez etc)
board

tabuleta /tabu'leta/ f (letreiro) sign

taça /'tasa/ f (prêmio) cup; (de
champanhe etc) glass

ta|cada /ta'kada/ f shot; **de uma ~cada**
in one go. **~car** vt hit ‹bola›; 🔢 throw

tacha /'taʃa/ f tack

tachar /ta'ʃar/ vt brand (**de** as)

tachinha /ta'ʃĩna/ f drawing pin, Amer
thumbtack

tácito /'tasitu/ a tacit

taciturno /tasi'turnu/ a taciturn

taco /'taku/ m (de golfe) club; (de bilhar)
cue; (de hóquei) stick

tagare|la /taga'rɛla/ a chatty, talkative
● m/f chatterbox. **~lar** vi chatter

tailan|dês /tajlã'des/ a & m (f **~desa**)
Thai

Tailândia /taj'lãdʒia/ f Thailand

tailleur /ta'jer/ (pl **~s**) m suit

Taiti /taj'tʃi/ m Tahiti

tal /taw/ (pl **tais**) a such; **que ~?** what
do you think?; Port how are you?; **que
~ uma cerveja?** how about a beer?; **~
como** such as; **~ qual** just like; **um ~
de João** someone called John; **e ~** and
so on

tala /'tala/ f splint

talão /ta'lãw/ m stub; **~ de cheques**
chequebook

talco /'tawku/ m talc

talen|to /ta'lẽtu/ m talent. **~toso** /o/
a talented

talhar /ta'ʎar/ vt slice ‹dedo, carne›;
carve ‹pedra, imagem›

talharim /taʎa'rĩ/ m tagliatelle

talher /ta'ʎer/ m set of cutlery; pl
cutlery

talho /'taʎu/ m Port butcher's

talismã /taliz'mã/ *m* charm, talisman

talo /'talu/ *m* stalk

talvez /taw'ves/ *adv* perhaps; ~ **ele venha amanhã** he may come tomorrow

tamanco /ta'mãku/ *m* clog

tamanho /ta'maɲu/ *m* size ● *adj* such

tâmara /'tamara/ *f* date

tamarindo /tama'rĩdu/ *m* tamarind

também /tã'bẽj/ *adv* also; ~ **não** not ... either, neither

tam|bor /tã'bor/ *m* drum. ~**borilar** *vi* ‹*dedos*› drum; ‹*chuva*› patter. ~**borim** *m* tambourine

Tâmisa /'tamiza/ *m* Thames

tam|pa /'tãpa/ *f* lid. ~**pão** *m* (*vaginal*) tampon. ~**par** *vt* put the lid on ‹*recipiente*›; (*tapar*) cover. ~**pinha** *f* top ● *m/f* 🇮 shorthouse

tampouco /tã'poku/ *adv* nor, neither

tanga /'tãga/ *f* G-string; (*avental*) loincloth

tangente /tã'ʒẽtʃi/ *f* tangent; **pela ~** *fig* narrowly

tangerina /tãʒe'rina/ *f* tangerine

tango /'tãgu/ *m* tango

tanque /'tãki/ *m* tank; (*para lavar roupa*) sink

tanto /'tãtu/ *a & pron* so much; *pl* so many ● *adv* so much; ~ ... **como** ... both ... and ...; ~ **(...) quanto** as much (...) as; ~ **melhor** so much the better; ~ **tempo** so long; **vinte e ~s anos** twenty odd years; **nem ~** not as much; **um ~ difícil** somewhat difficult; ~ **que** to the extent that

Tanzânia /tã'zania/ *f* Tanzania

tão /tãw/ *adv* so; ~ **grande quanto** as big as. ~ **somente** *adv* solely

tapa /'tapa/ *m ou f* slap; **dar um ~ em** slap

tapar /ta'par/ *vt* (*cobrir*) cover; block ‹*luz, vista*›; cork ‹*garrafa*›

tapeçaria /tapesa'ria/ *f* (*pano*) tapestry; (*loja*) carpet shop

tape|tar /tape'tar/ *vt* carpet. ~**te** /e/ *m* carpet; ~**te de rato** *Port* (*comput*) mousemat

tapioca /tapi'ɔka/ *f* tapioca

tapume /ta'pumi/ *m* fence

taquicardia /takikar'dʒia/ *f* palpitations

taquigra|far /takigra'far/ *vt/i* write in shorthand. ~**fia** *f* shorthand

tara /'tara/ *f* fetish. ~**do** a sex-crazed; **ser ~do por** be crazy about ● *m* sex

maniac

tar|dar /tar'dar/ *vi* (*atrasar*) be late; (*demorar muito*) be long ● *vt* delay; ~**dar a responder** take a long time to answer, be a long time answering; **o mais ~dar** at the latest; **sem mais ~dar** without further delay. ~**de** *adv* late; ~**de da noite** late at night ● *f* afternoon; **hoje à ~de** this afternoon. ~**dinha** *f* late afternoon. ~**dio** a late

tarefa /ta'refa/ *f* task, job

tarifa /ta'rifa/ *f* tariff; ~ **de embarque** airport tax

tarimbado /tarĩ'badu/ a experienced

tarja /'tarʒa/ *f* strip

ta|rô /ta'ro/ *m* tarot. ~**rólogo** *m* tarot reader

tartamu|dear /tartamudʒi'ar/ *vi* stammer. ~**do** a stammering ● *m* stammerer

tártaro /'tartaru/ *m* tartar

tartaruga /tarta'ruga/ *f* (*bicho*) turtle; (*material*) tortoiseshell

tatear /tatʃi'ar/ *vt* feel ● *vi* feel one's way

táti|ca /'tatʃika/ *f* tactics. ~**co** a tactical

tá|til /'tatʃiw/ (*pl* ~**teis**) a tactile

tato /'tatu/ *m* (*sentido*) touch; (*diplomacia*) tact

tatu /ta'tu/ *m* armadillo

tatu|ador /tatua'dor/ *m* tattooist. ~**agem** *f* tattoo. ~**ar** *vt* tattoo

tauromaquia /tawroma'kia/ *f* bullfighting

taxa /'taʃa/ *f* (*a pagar*) charge; (*índice*) rate; ~ **de câmbio** exchange rate; ~ **de juros** interest rate; ~ **rodoviária** road tax

taxar /ta'ʃar/ *vt* tax

taxativo /taʃa'tʃivu/ a firm, categorical

táxi /'taksi/ *m* taxi

taxiar /taksi'ar/ *vi* taxi

taxímetro /tak'simetru/ *m* taxi meter

taxista /tak'sista/ *m/f* taxi driver

tchã /tʃã/ *m* 🇮 special something

tchau /tʃaw/ *int* goodbye, bye

tcheco /'tʃeku/ a & *m* Czech

Tchecoslováquia /tʃekoslo'vakia/ *f* Czechoslovakia

te /tʃi/ *pron* you; (*a ti*) to you

tear /tʃi'ar/ *m* loom

tea|tral /tʃia'traw/ (*pl* ~**trais**) a theatrical; ‹*grupo*› theatre. ~**tro** *m* theatre. ~**trólogo** *m* playwright

t

tece|lagem /tese'laʒẽ/ f (*trabalho*) weaving; (*fábrica*) textile factory. **~lão** m (f **~lã**) weaver

te|cer /te'ser/ vt/i weave. **~cido** m cloth; (*no corpo*) tissue

te|cla /'tɛkla/ f key. **~cladista** m/f (*músico*) keyboard player; (*de computador*) keyboard operator. **~clado** m keyboard. **~clar** vt key (in)

técni|ca /'tɛknika/ f technique. **~co** a technical ● m specialist; (*de time*) manager; (*que mexe com máquinas*) technician

tecno|crata /tekno'krata/ m/f technocrat. **~logia** f technology. **~lógico** a technological

teco-teco /tɛku'tɛku/ m light aircraft

tédio /'tɛdʒiu/ m boredom

tedioso /tedʒi'ozu/ a boring, tedious

Teerã /tee'rã/ f Teheran

tela /'teja/ f web

tei|ma /'tejma/ f persistence. **~mar** vi insist; **~mar em ir** insist on going. **~mosia** f stubbornness. **~moso** /o/ a stubborn; ‹*ruído*› insistent

teixo /'tejʃu/ m yew

Tejo /'teʒu/ m Tagus

tela /'tɛla/ f (*de cinema, TV etc*) screen; (*tecido, pintura*) canvas. **~ plana** f flat screen

telecoman|dado /telekomã'dadu/ a remote-controlled. **~do** m remote control

telecomunicação /telekomunika'sãw/ f telecommunication

teleférico /tele'fɛriku/ m cable car

telefo|nar /telefo'nar/ vi telephone; **~nar para alguém** phone sb. **~ne** /o/ m telephone; (*número*) phone number; **~ne celular** cell phone; **~ne sem fio** cordless phone. **~nema** /e/ m phone call. **~nia** f telephone technology

telefôni|co /tele'foniku/ a telephone; **cabine ~ca** phone box, Amer phone booth; **mesa ~ca** switchboard

telefonista /telefo'nista/ m/f (*da companhia telefônica*) operator; (*dentro de empresa etc*) telephonist

tele|grafar /telegra'far/ vt/i telegraph. **~gráfico** a telegraphic

telégrafo /te'lɛgrafu/ m telegraph

tele|grama /tele'grama/ m telegram. **~guiado** a remote-controlled

telejor|nal /teleʒor'naw/ (*pl* **~nais**) m television news

telemóvel /tele'mɔvew/ m Port mobile phone, Amer cell phone

tele|novela /teleno'vɛla/ f TV soap opera. **~objetiva** f telephoto lens

tele|patia /telepa'tʃia/ f telepathy. **~pático** a telepathic

telescó|pico /teles'kɔpiku/ a telescopic. **~pio** m telescope

telespectador /telespekta'dor/ m television viewer ● a viewing

teletrabalho /teletra'baʎu/ m teleworking

televi|são /televi'zãw/ f television; **~são a cabo** cable television; **~são digital** digital television. **~sionar** vt televise. **~sivo** a television. **~sor** m television set

telex /te'lɛks/ m invar telex

telha /'teʎa/ f tile. **~do** m roof

te|ma /'tema/ m theme. **~mático** a thematic

temer /te'mer/ vt fear ● vi be afraid; **~ por** fear for

teme|rário /teme'rariu/ a reckless. **~ridade** f recklessness. **~roso** /o/ a fearful

te|mido /te'midu/ a feared. **~mível** (*pl* **~míveis**) a fearsome. **~mor** m fear

tempão /tẽ'pãw/ m **um ~** a long time

temperado /tẽpe'radu/ a ‹*clima*› temperate ● pp de ▶ **TEMPERAR**

temperamen|tal /tẽperamẽ'taw/ (*pl* **~tais**) a temperamental. **~to** m temperament

temperar /tẽpe'rar/ vt season ‹*comida*›; temper ‹*aço*›

temperatura /tẽpera'tura/ f temperature

tempero /tẽ'peru/ m seasoning

tempestade /tẽpes'tadʒi/ f storm

templo /'tẽplu/ m temple

tempo /'tẽpu/ m (*período*) time; (*atmosférico*) weather; (*do verbo*) tense; (*de jogo*) half; **ao mesmo ~** at the same time; **nesse meio ~** in the meantime; **o ~ todo** all the time; **de todos os ~s** of all time; **quanto ~** how long; **multo/ pouco ~** a long/short time; **~ integral** full time

tempo|rada /tẽpo'rada/ f (*sazão*) season; (*tempo*) while. **~ral** (*pl* **~rais**) a temporal ● m storm. **~rário** a temporary

te|nacidade /tenasi'dadʒi/ f tenacity. **~naz** a tenacious ● f tongs

tenção /tẽ'sãw/ f intention

tencionar /tēsio'nar/ *vt* intend

tenda /'tēda/ *f* tent

tendão /tē'dãw/ *m* tendon; **~ de Aquiles** Achilles tendon

tendência /tē'dēsia/ *f* (*moda*) trend; (*propensão*) tendency

tendencioso /tēdēsi'ozu/ *a* tendentious

ten|der /tē'der/ *vi* tend (**para** towards); **~de a engordar** he tends to get fat; **o tempo ~de a ficar bom** the weather is improving

tenebroso /tene'brozu/ *a* dark; *fig* (*terrível*) dreadful

tenente /te'nētʃi/ *m/f* lieutenant

tênis /'tenis/ *m invar* (*jogo*) tennis; (*sapato*) trainer; **um ~** (*par*) a pair of trainers; **~ de mesa** table tennis

tenista /te'nista/ *m/f* tennis player

tenor /te'nor/ *m* tenor

tenro /'tēxu/ *a* tender

ten|são /tē'sãw/ *f* tension; **~são (arterial)** blood pressure. **~so** *a* tense

tentação /tēta'sãw/ *f* temptation

tentáculo /tē'takulu/ *m* tentacle

ten|tador /tēta'dor/ *a* tempting. **~tar** *vt* try; (*seduzir*) tempt ● *vi* try. **~tativa** *f* attempt. **~tativo** *a* tentative

tênue /'tenui/ *a* faint

teo|logia /teolo'ʒia/ *f* theology. **~lógico** *a* theological

teólogo /te'ɔlogu/ *m* theologian

teor /te'or/ *m* (*de gordura etc*) content; (*de carta, discurso*) drift

teo|rema /teo'rema/ *m* theorem. **~ria** *f* theory

teórico /te'ɔriku/ *a* theoretical

teorizar /teori'zar/ *vt* theorize

tépido /'tepidu/ *a* tepid

---

ter /ter/ ● *vt*

••••➤ (*posse*) have got, have; **você tem irmãos?** have you got any brothers or sisters?, do you have any brothers or sisters?; **ele não tem dinheiro nenhum** he doesn't have any money

❗ **ter** pode ser traduzido como *have* ou *have got*, mas observe que *have got* é muito mais comum em inglês britânico.

••••➤ (*idade, tamanho*) be; **a minha filha tem 10 anos** my daughter is ten; **tem três metros de comprimento** it's three metres long

---

••••➤ (*doença, dor*) have; **~ dor de dente/pneumonia/febre** to have toothache/pneumonia/a temperature

••••➤ (*sentir*) **~ medo** be scared; **~ frio** be cold; **~ ciúmes** be jealous

❗ Observe que **ter + substantivo** em geral é traduzido como *to be* + **adjetivo** quando significa 'sentir': **tenho medo** *I'm scared*.

••••➤ (*dar à luz*) **~ um bebê** have a baby

● *v aux*

••••➤ (*estar obrigado a*) **~ que** *ou* **de fazer algo** have to do sth; **tiveram que ir embora imediatamente** they had to leave straight away; **você tem de dizer a ele** you must tell him

••••➤ (*seguido de particípio*) **tenho dito muitas vezes...** I have often said...

••••➤ (*em expressões*) **ir ~ com** (*encontrar-se*) meet up with; **fiquei de ir ~ com ele logo** I arranged to meet up with him later

---

tera|peuta /tera'pewta/ *m/f* therapist. **~pêutico** *a* therapeutic. **~pia** *f* therapy

terça /'tersa/ *f* Tuesday. **~-feira** (*pl* **~s-feiras**) *f* Tuesday; **Terça-Feira Gorda** Shrove Tuesday

tercei|ra /ter'sera/ *f* (*marcha*) third. **~ranista** *m/f* third-year. **~ro** *a* third ● *m* third party

terço /'tersu/ *m* third

ter|çol (*pl* **~çóis**) *m* stye

tergal /ter'gaw/ *m* Terylene

térmi|co /'termiku/ *a* thermal; **garrafa ~ca** Thermos® flask

termi|nal /termi'naw/ (*pl* **~nais**) *a* & *m* terminal; **~nal de vídeo** VDU. **~nante** *a* definite. **~nar** *vt* finish ● *vi* ⟨*pessoa, coisa*⟩ finish; ⟨*coisa*⟩ end; **~nar com alguém** (*cortar relação*) break up with sb

ter|minologia /terminolo'ʒia/ *f* terminology. **~mo**¹ /'termu/ *m* term; **pôr ~mo a** put an end to; **meio ~mo** compromise

termo² /'termu/ *m Port* Thermos® (flask)

ter|mômetro /ter'mometru/ *m* thermometer. **~mostato** *m* thermostat

terno¹ /'ternu/ *m* suit

ter|no² /'tɛrnu/ *a* tender. **~nura** *f* tenderness

terra /'texa/ *f* land; (*solo, elétrico*) earth; (*chão*) ground; **a Terra** Earth; **por ~** on the ground; **~ natal** homeland

t

terraço /te'xasu/ m terrace

terra|cota /texa'kɔta/ f terracotta.
~moto /texa'mɔtu/ m Port earthquake.
~plenagem f earth moving

terreiro /te'xeru/ m meeting place for
Afro-Brazilian cults

terremoto /texe'mɔtu/ m earthquake

terreno /te'xenu/ a earthly ● m
ground; Geog terrain; (um) piece of land;
~ baldio piece of waste ground

térreo /'texiu/ a ground-floor; **(andar)
~** ground-floor, Amer first-floor

terrestre /te'xestri/ a ‹animal, batalha,
forças› land; (da Terra) of the Earth, the
Earth's; ‹alegrias etc› earthly

terrificante /texifi'kãtʃi/ a terrifying

terrina /te'xina/ f tureen

territori|al /texitori'aw/ (pl ~ais) a
territorial

território /texi'tɔriu/ m territory

terrí|vel /te'xivew/ (pl ~veis) a terrible

terror /te'xor/ m terror; **filme de ~**
horror film

terroris|mo /texo'rizmu/ m terrorism.
~ta a & m/f terrorist

tese /'tezi/ f theory; (escrita) thesis

teso /'tezu/ a (apertado) taut; (rígido)
stiff

tesoura /te'zora/ f scissors; **uma ~** a
pair of scissors

tesou|reiro /tezo'reru/ m treasurer.
~ro m treasure; (do Estado) treasury

testa /'tɛsta/ f forehead. **~ de ferro**
(pl ~s-de-ferro) m frontman

testamento /testa'mẽtu/ m will;
(na Bíblia) testament

tes|tar /tes'tar/ vt test. **~te** /ɛ/ m test

testemu|nha /teste'muɲa/ f witness;
~nha ocular eye witness. **~nhar** vt bear
witness to ● vi testify. **~nho** m evidence,
testimony

testículo /tes'tʃikulu/ m testicle

teta /'teta/ f teat

tétano /'tetanu/ m tetanus

teto /'tetu/ m ceiling; **~ solar** sun roof

tétrico /'tetriku/ a (triste) dismal;
(medonho) horrible

teu /tew/ a (f **tua**) a your ● pron yours

têx|til /'testʃiw/ (pl ~teis) m textile

tex|to /'testu/ m text. **~tura** f texture

texugo /te'ʃugu/ m badger

tez /tes/ f complexion

ti /tʃi/ pron you

tia /'tʃia/ f aunt. **~avó** (pl ~s-avós) f
great aunt

tiara /tʃi'ara/ f tiara

tíbia /'tʃibia/ f shin bone

ticar /tʃi'kar/ vt tick

tico /'tʃiku/ m **um ~ de** a little bit of

tiete /tʃi'etʃi/ m/f fan

tifo /'tʃifu/ m typhoid

tigela /tʃi'ʒela/ f bowl; **de meia ~**
small-time

tigre /'tʃigri/ m tiger. **~sa** /e/ f tigress

tijolo /tʃi'ʒolu/ m brick

til /tʃiw/ (pl **tis**) m tilde

tilintar /tʃili'tar/ vi jingle ● m jingling

timão /tʃi'mãw/ m tiller

timbre /'tʃibri/ m (insígnia) crest; (em
papel) heading; (de som) tone; (de vogal)
quality

time /'tʃimi/ m team

timidez /tʃimi'des/ f shyness

tímido /'tʃimidu/ a shy

tímpano /'tʃipanu/ m (tambor)
kettledrum; (no ouvido) eardrum

tina /'tʃina/ f vat

tingir /tʃi'ʒir/ vt dye ‹tecido, cabelo›;
fig tinge

ti|nido /tʃi'nidu/ m tinkling. **~nir** vi
tinkle; ‹ouvidos› ring; (tremer) tremble;
estar ~nindo fig be in peak condition

tino /'tʃinu/ m sense, judgement; **ter ~
para** have a flair for

tin|ta /'tʃita/ f (para pintar) paint; (para
escrever) ink; (para tingir) dye. **~teiro**
m inkwell

tintim /tʃi'tʃi/ m **contar ~ por ~** give a
blow-by-blow account of

tin|to /'tʃitu/ a dyed; ‹vinho› red. **~tura**
f dye; fig tinge. **~turaria** f dry cleaner's

tio /'tʃiu/ m uncle; pl (e tia) uncle and
aunt. **~avô** (pl ~s-avôs) m great uncle

típico /'tʃipiku/ a typical

tipo /'tʃipu/ m type

tipoia /tʃi'pɔja/ f sling

tique /'tʃiki/ m (sinal) tick; (do rosto etc)
twitch

tíquete /'tʃiketʃi/ m ticket

tiquinho /tʃi'kiɲu/ m **um ~ de** a tiny
bit of

tira /'tʃira/ f strip ● m/f 🄸 copper, Amer
cop

tiracolo /tʃira'kɔlu/ m **a ~** ‹bolsa› over
one's shoulder; ‹pessoa› in tow

tiragem /tʃi'raʒẽ/ f (de jornal)
circulation

tira|-gosto /tʃira'gostu/ *m* snack.
~manchas *m invar* stain remover

ti|rania /tʃira'nia/ *f* tyranny. **~rânico** *a* tyrannical. **~rano** *m* tyrant

tirar /tʃi'rar/ *vt* (*afastar*) take away; (*de dentro*) take out; take off ‹*roupa, sapato, tampa*›; take ‹*foto, cópia, férias*›; clear ‹*mesa*›; get ‹*nota, diploma, salário*›; get out ‹*mancha*›

tiritar /tʃiri'tar/ *vi* shiver

tiro /'tʃiru/ *m* shot; **~ ao alvo** shooting; **é ~ e queda** 🅸 it can't fail. **~teio** *m* shoot-out

titânio /tʃi'taniu/ *m* titanium

titere /'tʃiteri/ *m* puppet

ti|tia /tʃi'tʃia/ *f* auntie. **~tio** *m* uncle

tititi /tʃitʃi'tʃi/ *m* 🅸 talk

titubear /tʃitubi'ar/ *vi* stagger, totter; *fig* (*hesitar*) waver

titular /tʃitu'lar/ *m/f* title holder; (*de time*) captain ● *vt* title

título /'tʃitulu/ *m* title; (*obrigação*) bond; **a ~ de** on the basis of; **a ~ pessoal** on a personal basis; **~ eleitoral** electoral register

toa /'toa/ *f* **à ~** (*sem rumo*) aimlessly; (*ao acaso*) at random; (*sem motivo*) without reason; (*em vão*) for nothing; (*desocupado*) at a loose end; (*de repente*) out of the blue

toada /to'ada/ *f* melody

toalete /toa'letʃi/ *m* toilet

toalha /to'aʎa/ *f* towel; **~ de mesa** tablecloth

tobogã /tobo'gã/ *m* (*rampa*) slide; (*trenó*) toboggan

toca /'tɔka/ *f* burrow

toca|-discos /tɔka'dʒiskus/ *m invar* record player. **~fitas** *m invar* tape player

tocaia /to'kaja/ *f* ambush

tocante /to'kãtʃi/ *a* (*enternecedor*) moving

tocar /to'kar/ *vt* touch; play ‹*piano, música, disco etc*›; ring ‹*campainha*› ● *vi* touch; ‹*pianista, música, disco etc*› play; **~ a** (*dizer respeito*) concern; **~ em** touch; touch on ‹*assunto*›; ‹*campainha, telefone, sino*› ring. **~-se** *vpr* touch; (*mancar-se*) take the hint

tocha /'tɔʃa/ *f* torch

toco /'toku/ *m* (*de árvore*) stump; (*de cigarro*) butt

toda /'toda/ *f* **a ~** at full speed

todavia /toda'via/ *conj* however

todo /'todu/ *a* all; (*cada*) every; *pl* all; **~ o dinheiro** all the money; **~ dia, ~s os dias** every day; **~s os alunos** all the pupils; **o dia ~** all day; **em ~ lugar** everywhere; **~ mundo, ~s** everyone; **~s nós** all of us; **ao ~** in all. **~-poderoso** *a* almighty

todo-o-terreno /todute'xenu/ *a & m* Port Auto four-by-four

tofe /'tɔfi/ *m* toffee

toga /'tɔga/ *f* gown; (*de romano*) toga

toicinho /toj'siɲu/ *m* bacon

toldo /'towdu/ *m* awning

tole|rância /tole'rãsia/ *f* tolerance. **~rante** *a* tolerant. **~rar** *vt* tolerate. **~rável** (*pl* **~ráveis**) *a* tolerable

to|lice /to'lisi/ *f* foolishness; (*uma*) foolish thing. **~lo** /o/ *a* foolish ● *m* fool

tom /tõ/ *m* tone; **~ de toque** *Telec* ringtone

to|mada /to'mada/ *f* (*conquista*) capture; (*elétrica*) plughole; (*de filme*) shot. **~mar** *vt* take; (*beber*) drink; **~mar café** have breakfast

tomara /to'mara/ *int* I hope so; **~ que** let's hope that. **~que caia** *a invar* ‹*vestido*› strapless

tomate /to'matʃi/ *m* tomato

tom|bar /tõ'bar/ *vt* (*derrubar*) knock down; list ‹*edifício*› ● *vi* fall over, fall; **levar um ~bo** have a fall. **~bo** *m* fall; **levar um ~bo** have a fall

tomilho /to'miʎu/ *m* thyme

tomo /'tomu/ *m* volume

tona /'tona/ *f* **trazer à ~** bring up; **vir à ~** emerge

tonalidade /tonali'dadʒi/ *f* (*de música*) key; (*de cor*) shade

to|nel /to'nɛw/ (*pl* **~néis**) *m* cask. **~nelada** *f* tonne

tôni|ca /'tonika/ *f* tonic; *fig* (*assunto*) keynote. **~co** *a & m* tonic

tonificar /tonifi'kar/ *vt* tone up

ton|tear /tõtʃi'ar/ *vt* **~tear alguém** make sb's head spin. **~teira** *f* dizziness. **~to** *a* (*zonzo*) dizzy; (*bobo*) stupid; (*atrapalhado*) flustered. **~tura** *f* dizziness

to|pada /to'pada/ *f* trip; **dar uma ~pada em** stub one's toe on. **~par** *vt* agree to, accept; **~par com** bump into ‹*pessoa*›; come across ‹*coisa*›

topázio /to'paziu/ *m* topaz

topete /to'petʃi/ *m* quiff

tópico /'tɔpiku/ *a* topical ● *m* topic

topless /topi'les/ *a invar & adv* topless

topo /'topu/ *m* top

t

topografia /topograˈfia/ f topography

topônimo /toˈponimu/ m place name

toque /ˈtɔki/ m touch; (da campainha, do telefone) ring; (de instrumento) playing; **dar um ~ em** 🄸 have a word with

Tóquio /ˈtɔkiu/ f Tokyo

tora /ˈtɔrà/ f log

toranja /toˈrãʒa/ f grapefruit

tórax /ˈtɔraks/ m invar thorax

tor|ção /torˈsãw/ f (do braço etc) sprain. **~cedor** m supporter. **~cer** vt twist; (machucar) sprain; (espremer) wring ‹roupa›; (centrifugar) spin ‹roupa› ● vi (gritar) cheer (por for); (desejar sucesso) keep one's fingers crossed (**por** for **para que** that). **~cer-se** vpr twist about. **~cicolo** /ɔ/ m stiff neck. **~cida** f (torção) twist; (torcedores) supporters; (gritaria) cheering

tormen|ta /torˈmẽta/ f storm. **~to** m torment. **~toso** /o/ a stormy

tornado /torˈnadu/ m tornado

tornar /torˈnar/ vt make. **~-se** vpr become

torne|ado /torniˈadu/ a **bem ~ado** shapely. **~ar** vt turn

torneio /torˈneju/ m tournament

torneira /torˈnera/ f tap, Amer faucet

torniquete /torniˈketʃi/ m (para ferido) tourniquet; Port (de entrada) turnstile

torno /ˈtornu/ m lathe; (de ceramista) wheel; **em ~ de** around

tornozelo /tornoˈzelu/ m ankle

toró /toˈrɔ/ m downpour

torpe /ˈtɔrpi/ a dirty

torpe|dear /torpedʒiˈar/ vt torpedo. **~do** /e/ m torpedo

torpor /torˈpor/ m torpor

torra|da /toˈxada/ f piece of toast; pl toast. **~deira** f toaster

torrão /toˈxãw/ m (de terra) turf; (de açúcar) lump

torrar /toˈxar/ vt toast ‹pão›; roast ‹café›; blow ‹dinheiro›; sell off ‹mercadorias›

torre /ˈtoxi/ f tower; (em xadrez) rook; **~ de controle** control tower. **~ão** m turret

torrefação /toxefaˈsãw/ f (ação) roasting; (fábrica) coffee-roasting plant

torren|cial /toxẽsiˈaw/ (pl **~ciais**) a torrential. **~te** f torrent

torresmo /toˈxezmu/ m crackling

tórrido /ˈtɔxidu/ a torrid

torrone /toˈxoni/ m nougat

torso /ˈtorsu/ m torso

torta /ˈtɔrta/ f pie, tart

tor|to /ˈtortu/ a crooked; **a ~ e a direito** left, right and centre. **~tuoso** a winding

tortu|ra /torˈtura/ f torture. **~rador** m torturer. **~rar** vt torture

to|sa /ˈtɔza/ f (de cachorro) clipping; (de ovelhas) shearing. **~são** m fleece. **~sar** vt clip ‹cachorro›; shear ‹ovelhas›; crop ‹cabelo›

tosco /ˈtosku/ a rough, coarse

tosquiar /toskiˈar/ vt shear ‹ovelha›

tos|se /ˈtɔsi/ f cough; **~se de cachorro** whooping cough. **~sir** vi cough

tostão /tosˈtãw/ m penny

tostar /tosˈtar/ vt brown ‹carne›; tan ‹pele, pessoa›. **~-se** vpr (ao sol) go brown

to|tal /toˈtaw/ (pl **~tais**) a & m total

totali|dade /totaliˈdadʒi/ f entirety. **~tário** a totalitarian. **~zar** vt total

touca /ˈtoka/ f bonnet; (de freira) wimple; **~ de banho** bathing cap. **~dor** m dressing table

toupeira /toˈpera/ f mole

tou|rada /toˈrada/ f bullfight. **~reiro** m bullfighter. **~ro** m bull; **Touro** (signo) Taurus

tóxico /ˈtɔksiku/ a toxic ● m toxic substance

toxicômano /toksiˈkomanu/ m drug addict

toxina /tokˈsina/ f toxin

traba|lhador /trabaʎaˈdor/ a ‹pessoa› hard-working; ‹classe› working ● m worker. **~lhar** vt work ● vi work; (numa peça, filme) act. **~lheira** f big job. **~lhista** a labour. **~lho** m work; (um) job; (na escola) assignment; **dar-se o ~lho de** go to the trouble of; **~lho de parto** labour; **~lhos forçados** hard labour. **~lhoso** a laborious

traça /ˈtrasa/ f moth

tração /traˈsãw/ f traction

tra|çar /traˈsar/ vt draw; draw up ‹plano›; set out ‹ordens›. **~ço** m stroke; (entre frases) dash; (vestígio) trace; (característica) trait; pl (do rosto) features

tradi|ção /tradʒiˈsãw/ f tradition. **~cional** (pl **~cionais**) a traditional

tradu|ção /traduˈsãw/ f translation. **~tor** m translator. **~zir** vt/i translate (de from para into)

trafe|gar /trafe'gar/ vi run. **~gável** (pl **~gáveis**) a open to traffic

tráfego /'trafegu/ m traffic

trafi|cância /trafi'kãsia/ f trafficking. **~cante** /trafi'kãtʃi/ m/f trafficker; **~cante de droga** drug dealer; **~cante sexual** sex trafficker. **~car** vt/i traffic (com i)

tráfico /'trafiku/ m traffic

tra|gada /tra'gada/ f (de bebida) swallow; (de cigarro) drag. **~gar** vt swallow; inhale ‹fumaça›

tragédia /tra'ʒedʒia/ f tragedy

trágico /'traʒiku/ a tragic

trago /'tragu/ m (de bebida) swallow; (de cigarro) drag; **de um ~** in one go

trai|ção /traj'sãw/ f (ato) betrayal; (deslealdade) treachery; (da pátria) treason. **~coeiro** a treacherous. **~dor** a treacherous ● m traitor

trailer /'trejler/ (pl **~s**) m (de filme etc) trailer; (casa móvel) caravan, Amer trailer

traineira /traj'nera/ f trawler

training /'trejnĩ/ (pl **~s**) m track suit

trair /tra'ir/ vt betray; be unfaithful to ‹marido, mulher›. **~se** vpr give o.s. away

tra|jar /tra'ʒar/ vt wear. **~jar-se** vpr dress (**de** in). **~je** m outfit; **~je a rigor** evening dress; **~je espacial** space suit

traje|to /tra'ʒetu/ m (percurso) journey; (caminho) route. **~tória** f trajectory; fig course

tralha /'traʎa/ f (trastes) junk

tra|ma /'trama/ f plot. **~mar** vt/i plot

trambi|que /trã'biki/ m con. **~queiro** m con artist

tramitar /trami'tar/ vi be processed

trâmites /'tramitʃis/ m pl channels

tramoia /tra'mɔja/ f scheme

trampolim /trãpo'lĩ/ m (de ginástica) trampoline; (de piscina) fig springboard

tranca /'trãka/ f bolt; (em carro) lock

trança /'trãsa/ f (de cabelo) plait

tran|cafiar /trãkafi'ar/ vt lock up. **~car** vt lock; cancel ‹matrícula›

trançar /trã'sar/ vt plait ‹cabelo›; weave ‹palha etc›

tranco /'trãku/ m jolt; **aos ~s e barrancos** in fits and starts

tranqueira /trã'kera/ f junk

tranqui|lidade /trãkwili'dadʒi/ f tranquillity. **~lizador** a reassuring. **~lizante** m tranquillizer ● a reassuring. **~lizar** vt reassure. **~lizar-se** vpr be

reassured. **~lo** a ‹bairro, sono› peaceful; ‹pessoa, voz, mar› calm; ‹consciência› clear; ‹sucesso, lucro› sure-fire ● adv with no trouble

transa /'trãza/ f 🔢 (negócio) deal; (caso) affair. **~ção** f transaction. **~do** a 🔢 ‹roupa, pessoa, casa› stylish; ‹relação› healthy

Transamazônica /trãzama'zonika/ f trans-Amazonian highway

transar /trã'zar/ 🔢 vt set up; do ‹drogas› ● vi (negociar) deal; (fazer sexo) have sex

transatlântico /trãzat'lãtʃiku/ a transatlantic ● m liner

transbordar /trãzbor'dar/ vi overflow

transcen|dental /trãsẽdẽ'taw/ (pl **~dentais**) a transcendental. **~der** vt/i **~der (a)** transcend

trans|crever /trãskre'ver/ vt transcribe. **~crição** f transcription. **~crito** a transcribed ● m transcript

transe /'trãzi/ m trance

transeunte /trãzi'ũtʃi/ m/f passer-by

transfe|rência /trãsfe'rẽsia/ f transfer. **~ridor** m protractor. **~rir** vt transfer. **~rir-se** vpr transfer

transfor|mação /trãsforma'sãw/ f transformation. **~mador** m transformer. **~mar** vt transform. **~mar-se** vpr be transformed

trânsfuga /'trãsfuga/ m/f deserter; (de um país) defector

transfusão /trãsfu'zãw/ f transfusion

trans|gredir /trãzgre'dʒir/ vt infringe. **~gressão** f infringement

transi|ção /trãzi'sãw/ f transition. **~cional** (pl **~cionais**) a transitional

transi|gente /trãzi'ʒẽtʃi/ a open to compromise. **~gir** vi compromise

transis|tor /trãzis'tor/ m transistor. **~torizado** a transistorized

transi|tar /trãzi'tar/ vi pass. **~tável** (pl **~táveis**) a passable. **~tivo** a transitive

trânsito /'trãzitu/ m traffic; **em ~** in transit

transitório /trãzi'tɔriu/ a transitory

translúcido /trãz'lusidu/ a translucent

transmis|são /trãzmi'sãw/ f transmission. **~sor** m transmitter

transmitir /trãzmi'tʃir/ vt transmit ‹programa, calor, doença›; convey ‹notícia, ordens›; transfer ‹herança, direito›. **~se** vpr ‹doença› be transmitted

t

transpa|recer /trãspare'ser/ vi be
visible; fig ‹emoção, verdade› come
out. **~rência** f transparency. **~rente** a
transparent

transpi|ração /trãspira'sãw/ f
perspiration. **~rar** vt exude ● vi (suar)
perspire; ‹notícia› trickle through;
‹verdade› come out

transplan|tar /trãsplã'tar/ vt
transplant. **~te** m transplant

transpor /trãs'por/ vt cross ‹rio,
fronteira›; get over ‹obstáculo,
dificuldade›; transpose ‹letras, música›

transpor|tadora /trãsporta'dora/ f
transport company. **~tar** vt transport;
(em contas) carry forward. **~te** m
transport; **~te coletivo** public transport

transposto /trãs'postu/ pp de
▶ TRANSPOR

transtor|nar /trãstor'nar/ vt mess
up ‹papéis, casa›; disrupt ‹rotina,
ambiente›; disturb, upset ‹pessoa›.
~nar-se vpr ‹pessoa› be rattled. **~no** /o/
m (de casa, rotina) disruption; (de pessoa)
disturbance; (contratempo) upset; **~no
obsessivo compulsivo** Psic obsessive-
compulsive disorder

transver|sal /trãzver'saw/ (pl ~sais)
a (rua) **~sal** cross street. **~so** /ɛ/ a
transverse

transvi|ado /trãzvi'adu/ a wayward.
~ar vt lead astray

trapa|ça /tra'pasa/ f swindle. **~cear** vi
cheat. **~ceiro** a crooked ● m cheat

trapa|lhada /trapa'ʎada/ f bungle.
~lhão a (f **~lhona**) f bungling ● m
(f **~lhona**) bungler

trapézio /tra'peziu/ m trapeze

trapezista /trape'zista/ m/f trapeze
artist

trapo /'trapu/ m rag

traqueia /tra'keja/ f windpipe, trachea

traquejo /tra'keʒu/ m knack

traquinas /tra'kinas/ a invar
mischievous

trás /tras/ adv de ~ from behind; **a roda
de ~** the back wheel; **de ~ para frente**
back to front; **para ~** backwards; **deixar
para ~** leave behind; **por ~ de** behind

traseiro /tra'zeru/ a rear, back ● m
bottom

trasladar /trazla'dar/ vt transport

traspas|sado /traspa'sadu/ a ‹paletó›
double-breasted. **~sar** vt pierce

traste /'trastʃi/ m (pessoa) pain; (coisa)
piece of junk

tra|tado /tra'tadu/ m (pacto) treaty;
(estudo) treatise. **~tamento** m
treatment; (título) title. **~tar** vt treat;
negotiate ‹preço, venda› ● vi (manter
relações) have dealings (**com** with);
(combinar) negotiate (**com** with);
~tar de deal with; **~tar alguém de**
ou **por** address sb. as; **~tar de voltar**
(tentar) seek to return; (resolver) decide
to return; **~tar-se de** be a matter of.
~tável (pl **~táveis**) a ‹doença› treatable;
‹pessoa› accommodating. **~tos** m pl
maus~tos ill-treatment

trator /tra'tor/ m tractor

trauma /'trawma/ m trauma. **~tizante**
a traumatic. **~tizar** vt traumatize

tra|vão /tra'vãw/ m Port brake. **~var**
vt lock ‹rodas, músculos›; stop ‹carro›;
block ‹passagem›; strike up ‹amizade,
conversa›; wage ‹luta, combate› ● vi
Port brake

trave /'travi/ f beam, joist; (do gol)
crossbar

traves|sa /tra'vesa/ f (trave) crossbar;
(rua) side street; (prato) dish; (pente)
slide. **~são** m dash. **~seiro** m pillow. **~sia**
f crossing. **~so** /e/ a ‹criança› naughty.
~sura f prank; pl mischief

travesti /traves'tʃi/ m transvestite;
(artista) drag artist. **~do** a in drag

trazer /tra'zer/ vt bring; bear ‹nome,
ferida›; wear ‹barba, chapéu, cabelo
curto›

trecho /'treʃu/ m (de livro etc) passage;
(de rua etc) stretch

treco /'treku/ m 🗊 (coisa) thing;
(ataque) turn

trégua /'tregwa/ f truce; fig respite

trei|nador /trejna'dor/ m trainer.
~namento m training. **~nar** vt train
‹atleta, animal›; practise ‹língua etc›
● vi ‹atleta› train; ‹pianista, principiante›
practise. **~no** m training; (um) training
session

trejeito /tre'ʒejtu/ m grimace

trela /'trela/ f lead, Amer leash

treliça /tre'lisa/ f trellis

trem /trẽj/ m train; **~ de aterrissagem**
undercarriage; **~ de carga** goods train,
Amer freight train

trema /'trema/ m dieresis

treme|deira /treme'dera/ f shiver.
~licar vi tremble. **~luzir** vi glimmer,
flicker

tremendo /tre'mẽdu/ a tremendous

tre|mer /tre'mer/ vi tremble; ‹terra›
shake. **~mor** m tremor; (tremedeira)

shiver. **~mular** *vi* ‹*bandeira*› flutter; ‹*luz, estrela*› glimmer, flicker

trêmulo /'tremulu/ *a* trembling; ‹*luz*› flickering

trena /'trena/ *f* tape measure

trenó /tre'nɔ/ *m* sledge, *Amer* sled; (*puxado a cavalos etc*) sleigh

tre|padeira /trepa'dera/ *f* climbing plant. **~par** *vt* climb ● *vi* climb; (*chulo*) fuck

três /tres/ *a* & *m* three

tresloucado /trezlo'kadu/ *a* deranged

trevas /'trevas/ *f pl* darkness

trevo /'trevu/ *m* (*planta*) clover; (*rodoviário*) interchange

treze /'trezi/ *a* & *m* thirteen

trezentos /tre'zẽtus/ *a* & *m* three hundred

triagem /tri'aʒẽ/ *f* (*escolha*) selection; (*separação*) sorting; **fazer uma ~ de** sort

tri|angular /triãgu'lar/ *a* triangular. **~ângulo** *m* triangle

tri|bal /tri'baw/ (*pl* **~bais**) *a* tribal. **~bo** *f* tribe

tribu|na /tri'buna/ *f* rostrum. **~nal** (*pl* **~nais**) *m* court

tribu|tação /tributa'sãw/ *f* taxation. **~tar** *vt* tax. **~tário** *a* tax ● *m* tributary. **~to** *m* tribute

tri|cô /tri'ko/ *m* knitting; **artigos de ~cô** knitwear. **~cotar** *vt/i* knit

tridimensio|nal /tridʒimẽsio'naw/ (*pl* **~nais**) *a* three-dimensional

trigêmeo /tri'ʒemiu/ *m* triplet

trigésimo /tri'ʒezimu/ *a* thirtieth

tri|go /'trigu/ *m* wheat. **~gueiro** *a* dark

trilha /'triʎa/ *f* path; (*pista, de disco*) track; **~ sonora** soundtrack

trilhão /tri'ʎãw/ *m* billion, *Amer* trillion

trilho /'triʎu/ *m* track

trilogia /trilo'ʒia/ *f* trilogy

trimes|tral /trimes'traw/ (*pl* **~trais**) *a* quarterly. **~tre** /ɛ/ *m* quarter; (*do ano letivo*) term

trincar /trĩ'kar/ *vt/i* crack

trincheira /trĩ'ʃera/ *f* trench

trinco /'trĩku/ *m* latch

trindade /trĩ'dadʒi/ *f* trinity

trinta /'trĩta/ *a* & *m* thirty

trio /'triu/ *m* trio; **~ elétrico** music float

tripa /'tripa/ *f* gut

tripé /tri'pɛ/ *m* tripod

tripli|car /tripli'kar/ *vt/i*, **~-se** *vpr* treble. **~cata** *f* triplicate

triplo /'triplu/ *a* & *m* triple

tripu|lação /tripula'sãw/ *f* crew. **~lante** *m/f* crew member. **~lar** *vt* man

triste /'tristʃi/ *a* sad. **~za** /e/ *f* sadness; **é uma ~za** 🔢 it's pathetic

tritu|rador /tritura'dor/ *m* (*de papel*) shredder; **~rador de lixo** waste disposal unit. **~rar** *vt* shred ‹*legumes, papel*›; grind up ‹*lixo*›

triun|fal /triũ'faw/ (*pl* **~fais**) *a* triumphal. **~fante** *a* triumphant. **~far** *vi* triumph. **~fo** *m* triumph

trivi|al /trivi'aw/ (*pl* **~ais**) *a* trivial. **~alidade** *f* triviality; *pl* trivia

triz /tris/ *m* **por um ~** narrowly, by a hair's breadth; **não foi atropelado por um ~** he narrowly missed being knocked down

tro|ca /'trɔka/ *f* exchange; **em ~ca de** in exchange for. **~cadilho** *m* pun. **~cado** *m* change. **~cador** *m* conductor. **~car** *vt* (*dar e receber*) exchange (**por** for); change ‹*dinheiro, lençóis, lâmpada, lugares etc*›; (*transpor*) change round; (*confundir*) mix up; **~car de roupa/trem/lugar** change clothes/trains/places. **~car-se** *vpr* change. **~ca-troca** *m* swap. **~co** /o/ *m* change; **a ~co de quê?** what for?; **dar o ~co em alguém** pay sb back

troço /'trɔsu/ *m* 🔢 (*coisa*) thing; (*ataque*) turn; **me deu um ~** I had a funny turn

troféu /tro'fɛw/ *m* trophy

trólebus /'trɔlebus/ *m invar* trolley bus

trom|ba /'trõba/ *f* (*de elefante*) trunk; (*cara amarrada*) long face. **~bada** *f* crash. **~ba-d'água** (*pl* **~bas-d'água**) *f* downpour. **~badinha** *m* bag snatcher. **~bar** *vi* **~bar com** crash into ‹*poste, carro*›; bump into ‹*pessoa*›

trombo|ne /trõ'boni/ *m* trombone. **~nista** *m/f* trombonist

trompa /'trõpa/ *f* French horn; **~ de Falópio** fallopian tube

trompe|te /trõ'petʃi/ *m* trumpet. **~tista** *m/f* trumpeter

tron|co /'trõku/ *m* trunk. **~cudo** *a* stocky

trono /'tronu/ *m* throne

tropa /'trɔpa/ *f* troop; (*exército*) army; *pl* troops; **~ de choque** riot police

trope|ção /trope'sãw/ *m* trip; (*erro*) slip-up. **~çar** *vi* trip; (*errar*) slip up. **~ço** /e/ *m* stumbling block

trôpego /'tropegu/ *a* unsteady

t

tropi|cal /tropi'kaw/ (*pl* **~cais**) *a*
tropical

trópico /'trɔpiku/ *m* tropic

tro|tar /tro'tar/ *vi* trot. **~te** /ɔ/ *m* (*de cavalo*) trot; (*de estudantes*) practical joke; (*mentira*) hoax

trouxa /'troʃa/ *f* (*de roupa etc*) bundle ● *m/f* 🔢 sucker 🔢 ● *a* 🔢 gullible

tro|vão /tro'vãw/ *m* clap of thunder; *pl* thunder. **~vejar** *vi* thunder. **~voada** *f* thunderstorm. **~voar** *vi* thunder

trucidar /trusi'dar/ *vt* slaughter

trucu|lência /truku'lẽsia/ *f* barbarity. **~lento** *a* (*cruel*) barbaric; (*brigão*) belligerent

trufa /'trufa/ *f* truffle

trunfo /'trũfu/ *m* trump; *fig* trump card

truque /'truki/ *m* trick

truta /'truta/ *f* trout

tu /tu/ *pron* you

tua /'tua/ ▶ TEU

tuba /'tuba/ *f* tuba

tubarão /tuba'rãw/ *m* shark

tubá|rio /tu'bariu/ *a* **gravidez ~ria** ectopic pregnancy

tuberculose /tubercu'lɔzi/ *f* tuberculosis

tubo /'tubu/ *m* tube; (*no corpo*) duct

tubulação /tubula'sãw/ *f* ducting

tucano /tu'kanu/ *m* toucan

---

tudo /'tudu/ ● *pron*

····➤ all; **é ~ por hoje** that's all for today; (*todas as coisas*) everything; **~ tinha ido** everything had gone

····➤ (*em expressões*) **dar/fazer ~ por ~** give one's all; **no fim de ~** after all; **por ~ e por nada** over the slightest thing; **dar ~ por ou para algo** (*desejar muito*) give one's all for sth

---

t **tufão** /tu'fãw/ *m* typhoon

tulipa /tu'lipa/ *f* tulip

u **tumba** /'tũba/ *f* tomb

tumor /tu'mor/ *m* tumour; **~ cerebral** brain tumour

túmulo /'tumulu/ *m* grave

tumul|to /tu'muwtu/ *m* commotion; (*motim*) riot. **~tuado** *a* disorderly, rowdy. **~tuar** *vt* disrupt ● *vi* cause a commotion. **~tuoso** *a* tumultuous

tú|nel /'tunew/ (*pl* **~neis**) *m* tunnel

túnica /'tunika/ *f* tunic

Tunísia /tu'nizia/ *f* Tunisia

tupiniquim /tupini'kĩ/ *a* Brazilian

turbante /tur'bãtʃi/ *m* turban

turbilhão /turbi'ʎãw/ *m* whirlwind

turbina /tur'bina/ *f* turbine

turbu|lência /turbu'lẽsia/ *f* turbulence. **~lento** *a* turbulent

turco /'turku/ *a & m* Turkish

turfa /'turfa/ *f* peat

turfe /'turfe/ *m* horse racing

turis|mo /tu'rizmu/ *m* tourism; **fazer ~mo** go sightseeing. **~ta** *m/f* tourist

turístico /tu'ristʃiku/ *a* ‹ponto, indústria› tourist; ‹viagem› sightseeing

turma /'turma/ *f* group; (*na escola*) class

turnê /tur'ne/ *f* tour

turno /'turnu/ *m* (*de trabalho*) shift; (*de competição, eleição*) round

turquesa /tur'keza/ *m/f & a invar* turquoise

Turquia /tur'kia/ *f* Turkey

turra /'tuxa/ *f* **às ~s com** at loggerheads with

tur|var /tur'var/ *vt* cloud. **~vo** *a* cloudy

tutano /tu'tanu/ *m* marrow

tutela /tu'tela/ *f* guardianship

tutor /tu'tor/ *m* guardian

tutu /tu'tu/ *m* (*vestido*) tutu; (*prato*) beans with bacon and manioc flour

TV /te've/ *f* TV

············

Uu

············

ubíquo /u'bikwu/ *a* ubiquitous

Ucrânia /u'krania/ *f* Ukraine

ucraniano /ukrani'anu/ *a & m* Ukrainian

ué /u'ɛ/ *int* hang on

ufa /'ufa/ *int* phew

ufanis|mo /ufa'nizmu/ *m* chauvinism. **~ta** *a & m/f* chauvinist

Uganda /u'gãda/ *m* Uganda

ui /ui/ *int* (*de dor*) ouch; (*de nojo*) ugh; (*de espanto*) oh

uísque /u'iski/ *m* whisky

ui|var /ui'var/ *vi* howl. **~vo** *m* howl

úlcera /'uwsera/ *f* ulcer

ulterior /uwteri'or/ *a* further

ulti|mamente /uwtʃima'mẽtʃi/ *adv* recently. **~mar** *vt* finalize. **~mato** *m* ultimatum

último /'uwtʃimu/ a last; ‹moda, notícia etc› latest; **em ~ caso** as a last resort; **nos ~s anos** in recent years; **por ~** last

ultra|jante /uwtra'ʒɐ̃tʃi/ a offensive. **~jar** vt offend. **~je** m outrage

ultraleve /uwtra'lɛvi/ m microlite

ultra|mar /uwtra'mar/ m overseas. **~marino** a overseas

ultrapas|sado /uwtrapa'sadu/ a outdated. **~sagem** f overtaking, Amer passing. **~sar** vt (de carro) overtake, Amer pass; (ser superior a) surpass; (exceder) exceed; (extrapolar) go beyond ● vi overtake, Amer pass

ultrassonografia /uwtrasonogra'fia/ f ultrasound scan

ultravioleta /uwtravio'leta/ a ultraviolet

ulu|lante /ulu'lɐ̃tʃi/ a fig blatant. **~lar** vi wail

um /ũ/ (f **uma**, pl **uns**, f pl **umas**)
● artigo

••••► a, an (antes de som vocálico); **~ carro** a car; **uma maçã** an apple

❗ a forma an emprega-se antes de uma vogal ou som vocálico; **uma árvore** a tree; **um braço** an arm. **uns, umas** some; **preciso de uns sapatos novos** I need some new shoes; **já que você vai lá, compre umas bananas** get some bananas while you're there

● a

••••► (numeral) one; **disse ~ quilo, não dois** I said one kilo, not two; (aproximadamente) about; **uns quinze dias** about a fortnight

● pron

••••► one; (plural) some; **como não tinha gravata, emprestei-lhe uma** he didn't have a tie so I lent him one; **uns gostam, outros não** some like it, some don't

••••► (em expressões) **~ ao outro, uma à outra** etc each other; **ajudaram-se uns aos outros** they helped each other; **~ a ~, ~ por ~** one by one; **verifiquei os itens da lista ~ a ~** I went through the things on the list one by one

umbanda /ũ'bɐ̃da/ m Afro-Brazilian cult

umbigo /ũ'bigu/ m navel

umbili|cal /ũbili'kaw/ (pl **~cais**) a umbilical

umedecer /umede'ser/ vt moisten. **~se** vpr moisten

umidade /umi'dadʒi/ f moisture; (desagradável) damp; (do ar) humidity

úmido /'umidu/ a moist; ‹parede, roupa etc› damp; ‹ar, clima› humid

unânime /u'nɐnimi/ a unanimous

unanimidade /unanimi'dadʒi/ f unanimity

undécimo /ũ'dɛsimu/ a eleventh

unguento /ũ'gwẽtu/ m ointment

unha /'uɲa/ f nail; (de animal, utensílio) claw

união /uni'ɐ̃w/ f union; (concórdia) unity; (ato de unir) joining; **~ civil** (entre pessoas do mesmo sexo) civil partnership; **União Européia** European Union, EU

unicamente /unika'mẽtʃi/ adv only

único /'uniku/ a only; (ímpar) unique

uni|dade /uni'dadʒi/ f unit. **~do** a united; ‹família› close

unifi|cação /unifika'sɐ̃w/ f unification. **~car** vt unify

unifor|me /uni'fɔrmi/ a uniform; ‹superfície› even ● m uniform. **~midade** f uniformity. **~mizado** a ‹policial etc› uniformed; (padronizado) standardized. **~zar** vt (padronizar) standardize

unilate|ral /unilate'raw/ (pl **~rais**) a unilateral

unir /u'nir/ vt unite ‹povo, nações, família etc›; (ligar, casar) join; (combinar) combine (a ou com with). **~se** vpr (aliar-se) unite (a with); (juntar-se) join together; (combinar-se) combine (a ou com with)

unissex /uni'sɛks/ a invar unisex

uníssono /u'nisonu/ m **em ~** in unison

univer|sal /univer'saw/ (pl **~sais**) a universal

universi|dade /universi'dadʒi/ f university. **~tário** a university ● m university student

universo /uni'vɛrsu/ m universe

untar /ũ'tar/ vt grease ‹fôrma›; spread ‹pão›; smear ‹corpo›

upa /'upa/ int (incentivando) ups-a-daisy; (ao cair algo etc) whoops

urânio /u'raniu/ m uranium

Urano /u'ranu/ m Uranus

urbanis|mo /urba'nizmu/ m town planning. **~ta** m/f town planner

urbani|zado /urbani'zadu/ a built-up. **~zar** vt urbanize

urbano /ur'banu/ a (da cidade) urban; (refinado) urbane

U

urdir /ur'dʒir/ vt weave; (maquinar) hatch

urdu /ur'du/ m Urdu

ur|gência /ur'ʒesia/ f urgency. **~gente** a urgent. **~gir** vi be urgent; ‹tempo› press; **~ge irmos** we must go urgently

uri|na /u'rina/ f urine. **~nar** vt pass ● vi urinate. **~nol** (pl **~nóis**) m (penico) chamber pot; (em banheiro) urinal

urna /'urna/ f (para cinzas) urn; (para votos) ballot box; pl fig polls

ur|rar /u'xar/ vt/i roar. **~ro** m roar

urso /'ursu/ m bear. **~branco** (pl **~s-brancos**) m polar bear

urti|cária /urtʃi'karia/ f nettle rash. **~ga** f nettle

urubu /uru'bu/ m black vulture

Uruguai /uru'gwaj/ m Uruguay

uruguaio /uru'gwaju/ a & m Uruguayan

urze /'urzi/ f heather

usado /u'zadu/ a used; ‹roupa› worn; ‹palavra› common

usar /u'zar/ vt wear ‹roupa, óculos, barba etc›; **~ (de)** (utilizar) use

USB a & m USB; **porta ~** USB port

usina /u'zina/ f plant; **~ termonuclear** nuclear power station

uso /'uzu/ m use; (de palavras, linguagem) usage; (praxe) practice

usu|al /uzu'aw/ (pl **~ais**) a common. **~ário** m user. **~fruir** vt enjoy ‹coisas boas›; have the use of ‹prédio, jardim etc›. **~fruto** m use

usuário /uzu'arju/ m Comput user; **nome do ~** username

usurário /uzu'rariu/ a money-grubbing ● m moneylender

usurpar /uzur'par/ vt usurp

uten|sílio /ute'siliu/ m utensil. **~te** m/f Port user

útero /'uteru/ m uterus, womb

UTI /ute'i/ f intensive care unit

u **útil** /'utʃiw/ (pl **úteis**) a useful; **dia ~** workday

v **utili|dade** /utʃili'dadʒi/ f usefulness; (uma) utility. **~tário** a utilitarian. **~zar** vt (empregar) use; (tornar útil) utilize. **~zável** (pl **~záveis**) a usable

utilizador /utʃiliza'dor/ m Port ▶ USUÁRIO

utopia /uto'pia/ f Utopia

utópico /u'tɔpiku/ a Utopian

uva /'uva/ f grape

úvula /'uvula/ f uvula

Vv

vaca /'vaka/ f cow

vaci|lante /vasi'lãtʃi/ a wavering; ‹luz› flickering. **~lar** vi waver; ‹luz› flicker; Ⓣ (bobear) slip up

vaci|na /va'sina/ f vaccine. **~nação** f vaccination. **~nar** vt vaccinate

vácuo /'vakuu/ m vacuum

va|diar /vadʒi'ar/ vi (viver ocioso) laze around; (fazer cera) mess about. **~dio** a idle ● m idler

vaga /'vaga/ f (posto) vacancy; (para estacionar) parking place

vagabun|dear /vagabũdʒi'ar/ vi (perambular) roam; (vadiar) laze around. **~do** a ‹pessoa, vida› idle; ‹produto, objeto› shoddy ● m tramp; (pessoa vadia) bum

vaga-lume /vaga'lumi/ m glow-worm

va|gão /va'gãw/ m (de passageiros) carriage, Amer car; (de carga) wagon. **~gão-leito** (pl **~gões-leitos**) m sleeping car; **~gão-restaurante** (pl **~gões-restaurantes**) m dining car

vagar[1] /va'gar/ vi ‹pessoa› wander about; ‹barco› drift

vagar[2] /va'gar/ vi ‹cargo, apartamento› become vacant

vagaroso /vaga'rozu/ a slow

vagem /'vaʒẽ/ f green bean

vagi|na /va'ʒina/ f vagina. **~nal** (pl **~nais**) a vaginal

vago[1] /'vagu/ a (indefinido) vague

vago[2] /'vagu/ a (desocupado) vacant; ‹tempo› spare

vaguear /vagi'ar/ vi roam

vai|a /'vaja/ f boo. **~ar** vi boo

vai|dade /vaj'dadʒi/ f vanity. **~doso** a vain

vaivém /vaj'vẽj/ m comings and goings, toing and froing

vala /'vala/ f ditch; **~ comum** mass grave

vale[1] /'vali/ m (de rio etc) valley

vale[2] /'vali/ m (ficha) voucher; **~ postal** postal order

valen|tão /valẽ'tãw/ a (f **~tona**) tough ● m tough guy. **~te** a brave. **~tia** f bravery; (uma) feat

valer /va'ler/ vt be worth ● vi be valid; **~ algo a alguém** earn sb sth; **~se de**

avail o.s. of; **~ a pena** be worth it; **vale a pena tentar** it's worth trying; **mais vale desistir** it's better to give up; **vale tudo** anything goes; **fazer ~** enforce ‹*lei*›; stand up for ‹*direitos*›; **para ~** (*a sério*) for real; (*muito*) really

vale|-refeição /vali'refeȷˈsãw/ (*pl* **~s-refeição**) *m* luncheon voucher

valeta /va'leta/ *f* gutter

valete /va'letʃi/ *m* jack

valia /va'lia/ *f* value

validar /vali'dar/ *vt* validate

válido /'validu/ *a* valid

valioso /vali'ozu/ *a* valuable

valise /va'lizi/ *f* travelling bag

valor /va'lor/ *m* value; (*valentia*) valour; *pl* (*títulos*) securities; **no ~ de** to the value of; **sem ~** worthless; **objetos de ~** valuables; **~ nominal** face value

valori|zação /valoriza'sãw/ *f* (*apreciação*) valuing; (*aumento no valor*) increase in value. **~zado** a highly valued. **~zar** *vt* (*apreciar*) value; (*aumentar o valor de*) increase the value of. **~zar-se** *vt* ‹*coisa*› increase in value; ‹*pessoa*› value o.s.

val|sa /'vawsa/ *f* waltz. **~sar** *vi* waltz

válvula /'vawvula/ *f* valve

vampiro /vã'piru/ *m* vampire

vandalismo /vãda'lizmu/ *m* vandalism

vândalo /'vãdalu/ *m* vandal

vangloriar-se /vãglori'arsi/ *vpr* brag (*de about*)

vanguarda /vã'gwarda/ *f* vanguard; (*de arte*) avant-garde

vanta|gem /vã'taʒẽ/ *f* advantage; **contar ~gem** boast; **levar ~gem** have the advantage (**a** over); **tirar ~gem de** take advantage of. **~joso** /o/ *a* advantageous

vão /vãw/ (*pl* **~s**) *a* (*f* **vã**) vain; **em ~** in vain ● *m* gap

vapor /va'por/ *m* (*fumaça*) steam; (*gás*) vapour; (*barco*) steamer; **máquina a ~** steam engine; **a todo ~** at full blast

vaporizar /vapori'zar/ *vt* vaporize; (*com spray*) spray

vaqueiro /va'keru/ *m* cowboy

vaquinha /va'kiɲa/ *f* collection, whip-round

vara /'vara/ *f* rod; **~ civil** civil district; **~ mágica** ou **de condão** magic wand

va|ral /va'raw/ (*pl* **~rais**) *m* washing line

varanda /va'rãda/ *f* veranda

varão /va'rãw/ *m* male

varar /va'rar/ *vt* (*furar*) pierce; (*passar por*) sweep through

varejão /vare'ʒãw/ *m* wholesale store

varejeira /vare'ʒera/ *f* bluebottle

vare|jista /vare'ʒista/ *a* retail ● *m/f* retailer. **~jo** /e/ *m* retail trade; **vender a ~jo** sell retail

vari|ação /varia'sãw/ *f* variation. **~ado** a varied. **~ante** *a* & *f* variant. **~ar** *vt/i* vary; **para ~ar** for a change. **~ável** (*pl* **~áveis**) *a* variable; ‹*tempo*› changeable

varicela /vari'sɛla/ *f* chickenpox

variedade /varie'dadʒi/ *f* variety

varinha /va'riɲa/ *f* **~ de condão** magic wand; **~ mágica** Port (*utensílio culinário*) hand mixer

varíola /va'riola/ *f* smallpox

vários /'varius/ *a pl* several

variz /va'ris/ *f* varicose vein

varo|nil /varo'niw/ (*pl* **~nis**) *a* manly

var|rer /va'xer/ *vt* sweep; *fig* sweep away. **~rido** a **um doido ~rido** a raving lunatic

Varsóvia /var'sɔvia/ *f* Warsaw

vasculhar /vasku'ʎar/ *vt* search through

vasectomia /vazekto'mia/ *f* vasectomy

vaselina /vaze'lina/ *f* vaseline

vasilha /va'ziʎa/ *f* jug

vaso /'vazu/ *m* pot; (*para flores*) vase; **~ sanguíneo** blood vessel

vassoura /va'sora/ *f* broom

vas|tidão /vastʃi'dãw/ *f* vastness. **~to** a vast

vatapá /vata'pa/ *m* spicy North-Eastern dish

Vaticano /vatʃi'kanu/ *m* Vatican

vati|cinar /vatʃisi'nar/ *vt* prophesy. **~cínio** *m* prophecy

va|zamento /vaza'mẽtu/ *m* leak. **~zante** *f* ebb tide. **~zão** *m* outflow; **dar ~zão a** *fig* give vent to. **~zar** *vt/i* leak

vazio /va'ziu/ *a* empty ● *m* emptiness; (*um*) void

veado /vi'adu/ *m* deer

ve|dação /veda'sãw/ *f* (*de casa, janela*) insulation; (*em motor etc*) gasket. **~dar** *vt* seal ‹*recipiente, abertura*›; stanch ‹*sangue*›; seal off ‹*saída, área*›; **~dar algo (a alguém)** prohibit sth (for s.o.)

vedete /ve'dɛte/ *f* star

vee|mência /vee'mẽsia/ *f* vehemence. **~mente** *a* vehement

V

vege|tação /veʒeta'sãw/ f vegetation. **~tal** (pl **~tais**) a & m vegetable. **~tar** vi vegetate. **~tariano** a & m vegetarian

vela /'veja/ f vein

veicular /veiku'lar/ vt convey; place ‹anúncios›

veículo /ve'ikulu/ m vehicle; **~ utilitário desportivo** sports utility vehicle, SUV; (de comunicação etc) medium

vela[1] /'vɛla/ f (de barco) sail; (esporte) sailing

vela[2] /'vɛla/ f candle; (em motor) spark plug; **segurar a ~** 🎲 play gooseberry

velar[1] /ve'lar/ vt (cobrir) veil

velar[2] /ve'lar/ vt watch over ● vi keep vigil

veleidade /velej'dadʒi/ f whim

ve|leiro /ve'leru/ m sailing boat. **~lejar** vi sail

velhaco /ve'ʎaku/ a crooked ● m crook

ve|lharia /veʎa'ria/ f old thing. **~lhice** f old age. **~lho** /ɛ/ a old ● m old man. **~lhote** /ɔ/ m old man

velocidade /velosi'dadʒi/ f speed; Port (marcha) gear; **a toda** ~ at full speed; **~ máxima** speed limit

velocímetro /velo'simetru/ m speedometer

velocista /velo'sista/ m/f sprinter

velório /ve'lɔriu/ m wake

veloz /ve'los/ a fast

veludo /ve'ludu/ m velvet; **~ cotelê** corduroy

ven|cedor /vẽse'dor/ a winning ● m winner. **~cer** vt win over ‹adversário etc›; win ‹partida, corrida, batalha› ● vi (triunfar) win; ‹prestação, aluguel, dívida› fall due; ‹contrato, passaporte, prazo› expire; ‹apólice› mature. **~cido** a dar-se por **~cido** give in. **~cimento** m (de dívida, aluguel) due date; (de contrato, prazo) expiry date; (de alimento, remédio etc) best before date; (salário) payment; pl, earnings

venda[1] /'vẽda/ f sale; (loja) general store; **à ~** on sale; **pôr à ~** put up for sale

ven|da[2] /'vẽda/ f blindfold. **~dar** vt blindfold

venda|val /vẽda'vaw/ (pl **~vais**) m gale, storm

ven|dável /vẽ'davew/ (pl **~dáveis**) a saleable. **~dedor** m (de loja) shop assistant; (em geral) seller. **~der** vt/i sell; **estar ~dendo saúde** be bursting with health

vendeta /vẽ'deta/ f vendetta

veneno /ve'nenu/ m poison; (de cobra etc, malignidade) venom. **~so** /o/ a poisonous; (maldoso) venomous

vene|ração /venera'sãw/ f reverence; (de Deus etc) worship. **~rar** vt revere; worship ‹Deus etc›

vené|reo /ve'neriu/ a doença **~rea** venereal disease

Veneza /ve'neza/ f Venice

veneziana /venezi'ana/ f shutter

Venezuela /venezu'ɛla/ f Venezuela

venezuelano /venezue'lanu/ a & m Venezuelan

venta /'vẽta/ f nostril

ven|tania /vẽta'nia/ f gale. **~tar** vi be windy. **~tarola** /ɔ/ f fan

venti|lação /vẽtʃila'sãw/ f ventilation. **~lador** m fan. **~lar** vt ventilate; air ‹sala, roupa›

ven|to /'vẽtu/ m wind; **de ~to em popa** smoothly. **~toinha** f (cata-vento) weather vane; Port (ventilador) fan. **~tosa** /ɔ/ f sucker. **~toso** /o/ a windy

ven|tre /'vẽtri/ m belly. **~tríloquo** m ventriloquist

Vênus /'venus/ f Venus

ver /ver/ vt see; watch ‹televisão›; (resolver) see to ● vi see; **ter a ~ com** have to do with; **vai ~ que ela não sabe** 🎲 I bet she doesn't know; **vê se você não volta tarde** see you don't get back late; **viu?** 🎲 right? ● **a meu ~** in my view. **~-se** vpr (no espelho etc) see o.s.; (em estado, condição) find o.s.; (um ao outro) see each other

veracidade /verasi'dadʒi/ f truthfulness

vera|near /verani'ar/ vi spend the summer. **~neio** m summer holiday, Amer summer vacation. **~nista** m/f holidaymaker, Amer vacationer

verão /ve'rãw/ m summer

veraz /ve'ras/ a truthful

ver|bal /ver'baw/ (pl **~bais**) a verbal. **~bete** /e/ m entry. **~bo** m verb. **~borragia** f waffle. **~boso** /o/ a verbose

verbas /'verbas/ f pl funds

verda|de /ver'dadʒi/ f truth; **de ~de** ‹coisa› real; ‹fazer› really; **na ~de** actually; **para falar a ~de** to tell the truth. **~deiro** a ‹declaração, pessoa› truthful; (real) true

verde /'verdʒi/ a & m green; **jogar ~ para colher maduro** fish for information. **~abacate** *a invar* avocado; **~amarelo** *a* yellow and green; (*brasileiro*) Brazilian; (*nacionalista*) nationalistic; **~esmeralda** *a invar* emerald green. **~jar** *vi* turn green

verdu|ra /ver'dura/ *f* (*para comer*) greens; (*da natureza*) greenery. **~reiro** *m* greengrocer, *Amer* produce dealer

vereador /veria'dor/ *m* councillor

vereda /ve'reda/ *f* path

veredito /vere'dʒitu/ *m* verdict

vergar /ver'gar/ *vt/i* bend

vergo|nha /ver'goɲa/ *f* (*pudor*) shame; (*constrangimento*) embarrassment; (*timidez*) shyness; (*uma*) disgrace; **ter ~nha** be ashamed; be embarrassed; be shy; **cria ou tome ~nha na cara!** you should be ashamed of yourself!. **~nhoso** *a* shameful

verídico /ve'ridʒiku/ *a* true

verificar /verifi'kar/ *vt* check, verify <*fatos, dados etc*>; **~ que** ascertain that; **~ se** check that. **~se** *vpr* <*previsão etc*> come true; <*acidente etc*> happen

verme /'vermi/ *m* worm

verme|lhidão /vermeʎi'dãw/ *f* redness. **~lho** /e/ *a & m* red; **no ~lho** (*endividado*) in the red

vernáculo /ver'nakulu/ *a & m* vernacular

verniz /ver'nis/ *f* varnish; (*couro*) patent leather

veros|símil /vero'simiw/ (*pl* **~simeis**) *a* plausible. **~similhança** *f* plausibility

verruga /ve'xuga/ *f* wart

ver|sado /ver'sadu/ *a* well-versed (**em** in). **~são** *f* version. **~sar** *vi* **~sar sobre** concern. **~sátil** (*pl* **~sáteis**) *a* versatile. **~satilidade** *f* versatility. **~sículo** *m* (*da Bíblia*) verse. **~so**[1] /e/ *m* verse

verso[2] /e/ *m* (*de página*) reverse, other side; **vide ~** see over

vértebra /'vertebra/ *f* vertebra

verte|brado /verte'bradu/ *a & m* vertebrate. **~bral** (*pl* **~brais**) *a* spinal

ver|tente /ver'tẽtʃi/ *f* slope. **~ter** *vt* (*derramar*) pour; shed <*lágrimas, sangue*>; (*traduzir*) render (**para** into)

verti|cal /vertʃi'kaw/ (*pl* **~cais**) *a & f* vertical. **~gem** *f* dizziness. **~ginoso** /o/ *a* dizzy

vesgo /'vezgu/ *a* cross-eyed

vesícula /ve'zikula/ *f* gall bladder

vespa /'vespa/ *f* wasp

véspera /'vespera/ *f a* **~** the day before; **a ~ de** the eve of; **a ~ de Natal**

Christmas Eve; **nas ~s de** on the eve of

vespertino /vesper'tʃinu/ *a* evening

ves|te /'vestʃi/ *f* robe. **~tiário** *m* (*para se trocar*) changing room; (*para guardar roupa*) cloakroom

vestibular /vestʃibu'lar/ *m* university entrance exam

> **vestibular** The *vestibular* is a   *i*
> highly competitive exam that is
> taken by any student wishing to apply
> to university in Brazil. Candidates are
> tested on various subjects, such as
> Portuguese Language, History,
> Geography, Maths, etc. The most
> popular courses, such as Medicine,
> Dentistry, and Engineering, have as
> many as 70 applicants per place, and
> students are selected for admission
> based on their overall *vestibular* grade.

---

vestíbulo /ves'tʃibulu/ *m* hall(way); (*do teatro*) foyer

vestido /ves'tʃidu/ *m* dress ● *a* dressed (**de** in)

vestígio /ves'tʃiʒiu/ *m* trace

vesti|menta /vestʃi'mẽta/ *f* (*de sacerdote*) vestments. **~tir** *vt* (*pôr*) put on; (*usar*) wear; (*pôr roupa em*) dress; (*dar roupa a*) clothe. **~tir-se** *vpr* dress; **~tir-se de branco/de padre** dress in white/as a priest. **~tuário** *m* clothing

vetar /ve'tar/ *vt* veto

veterano /vete'ranu/ *a & m* veteran

veterinário /veteri'nariu/ *a* veterinary ● *m* vet

veto /'vetu/ *m* veto

véu /vɛw/ *m* veil

vexa|me /ve'ʃami/ *m* disgrace; **dar um ~me** make a fool of o.s.. **~minoso** /o/ *a* disgraceful

vexar /ve'ʃar/ *vt* shame. **~se** *vpr* be ashamed (**de** of)

vez /ves/ *f* (*ocasião*) time; (*turno*) turn; **às ~es** sometimes; **cada ~ mais** more and more; **de ~** for good; **desta ~** this time; **de ~ em quando** now and again, from time to time; **de uma ~** (*ao mesmo tempo*) at once; (*de um golpe*) in one go; **de uma ~ por todas** once and for all; **duas ~es** twice; **em ~ de** instead of; **fazer as ~es de** take the place of; **mais uma ~, outra ~** again; **muitas ~es** (*com muita frequência*) often; (*repetidamente*) many times; **raras ~es** seldom; **repetidas ~es** repeatedly; **uma ~** once; **uma ~ que** since

via /'via/ f (*estrada*) road; (*rumo, meio*) way; (*exemplar*) copy; pl (*trâmites*) channels ● *prep* via; **em ~s de** on the point of; **por ~ aérea/marítima** by air/ sea; **por ~ das dúvidas** just in case; **por ~ de regra** as a rule; **Via Láctea** Milky Way

viabili|dade /viabili'dadʒi/ f feasibility. **~zar** *vt* make feasible

viação /via'sãw/ f (*transporte*) road transport; (*estradas*) road network; (*companhia*) bus company

viaduto /via'dutu/ m viaduct; (*rodoviário*) flyover, *Amer* overpass

via|gem /vi'aʒẽ/ f (*uma*) trip, journey; (*em geral*) travelling; pl (*de uma pessoa*) travels; (*em geral*) travels; **boa ~gem!** have a good trip! **~gem de negócios** business trip. **~jado** a well-travelled. **~jante** a travelling ● *m/f* traveller. **~jar** *vi* travel; **estar ~jando** 🇧🇷 (*com o pensamento longe*) be miles away

viário /vi'ariu/ a road; **anel ~** ring road

viatura /via'tura/ f vehicle

viá|vel /vi'avew/ (*pl* **~veis**) a feasible

víbora /'vibora/ f viper

vi|bração /vibra'sãw/ f vibration; *fig* thrill. **~brante** a vibrant. **~brar** *vt* shake ● *vi* vibrate; *fig* be thrilled (**com** by)

vice /'visi/ m/f deputy

vice-cam|peão /visikãpi'ãw/ m (*f~peã*) runner-up

vicejar /vise'ʒar/ *vi* flourish

vice-presiden|te /visiprezi'dẽtʃi/ m (*f~ta*) vice-president

vice-rei /visi'xej/ m viceroy

vice-versa /visi'vɛrsa/ *adv* vice versa

vici|ado /visi'adu/ a addicted (**em** to) ● m addict; **um ~ado em drogas** a drug addict. **~ar** *vt* (*falsificar*) tamper with; (*estragar*) ruin *vi* ‹*droga*› be addictive. **~ar-se** *vpr* get addicted (**em** to)

vício /'visiu/ m vice

vicioso /visi'ozu/ a **círculo ~** vicious circle

vicissitudes /visisi'tudʒis/ f pl ups and downs

viço /'visu/ m (*de plantas*) exuberance; (*de pessoa, pele*) freshness. **~so** /o/ a ‹*planta*› lush; ‹*pele, pessoa*› fresh

vida /'vida/ f life; **sem ~** lifeless; **dar ~** a liven up

videira /vi'dera/ f vine

vidente /vi'dẽtʃi/ m/f clairvoyant

vídeo /'vidʒiu/ m video; (*tela*) screen

vídeo|cassete /vidʒiuka'setʃi/ m (*fita*) video tape; (*aparelho*) video, *Amer* VCR. **~clipe** m video. **~clube** m video club. **~game** m video game. **~teipe** m video tape

vidra|ça /vi'drasa/ f window pane. **~çaria** f (*fábrica*) glassworks; (*vidraças*) glazing. **~ceiro** m glazier

vi|drado /vi'dradu/ a glazed; **estar ~drado em** ou **por** 🇧🇷 love. **~drar** *vt* glaze ● *vi* 🇧🇷 fall in love (**em** ou **por** with). **~dro** m (*material*) glass; (*pote*) jar; (*janela*) window; **~dro fumê** tinted glass

viela /vi'ɛla/ f alley

Viena /vi'ena/ f Vienna

Vietnã /vietʃi'nã/ m, *Port* **Vietname** /viet'nam/ m Vietnam

vietnamita /vietna'mita/ a & m/f Vietnamese

viga /'viga/ f joist

vigarice /viga'risi/ f swindle

vigário /vi'gariu/ m vicar

vigarista /viga'rista/ m/f swindler, con artist

vi|gência /vi'ʒẽsia/ f (*qualidade*) force; (*tempo*) period in force. **~gente** a in force

vigésimo /vi'ʒɛzimu/ a twentieth

vigi|a /vi'ʒia/ f (*guarda*) watch; (*em navio*) porthole ● m night watchman. **~ar** *vt* (*observar*) watch; (*cuidar de*) watch over; (*como sentinela*) guard ● *vi* keep watch

vigi|lância /viʒi'lãsia/ f vigilance. **~lante** a vigilant

vigília /vi'ʒilia/ f vigil

vigor /vi'gor/ m vigour; **em ~** in force

vigo|rar /vigo'rar/ *vi* be in force. **~roso** a vigorous

VIH /veia'ga/ *abr* m (= **Vírus da Imunodeficiência Humana**) HIV

vil /viw/ (*pl* **vis**) a base, despicable

vila /'vila/ f (*cidadezinha*) small town; (*casa elegante*) villa; (*conjunto de casas*) housing estate; **~ olímpica** Olympic village

vi|lania /vila'nia/ f villainy. **~lão** m (*f~lã*) villain

vilarejo /vila'reʒu/ m village

vilipendiar /vilipẽdʒi'ar/ *vt* disparage

vime /'vimi/ m wicker

vina|gre /vi'nagri/ m vinegar. **~grete** /ɛ/ m vinaigrette

vin|car /vĩ'kar/ vt crease; line ‹rosto›. **~co** m crease; (no rosto) line

vincular /vĩku'lar/ vt bond, tie

vínculo /'vĩkulu/ m link, bond; **~ empregatício** contract of employment

vinda /'vĩda/ f coming; **dar as boas ~s a** welcome

vindicar /vĩdʒi'kar/ vt vindicate

vindima /vĩ'dʒima/ f vintage

vin|do /'vĩdu/ pp e pres de **vir**. **~douro** a coming

vin|gança /vĩ'gãsa/ f vengeance, revenge. **~gar** vt avenge ● vi ‹flores› thrive; ‹criança› survive; ‹plano, empreendimento› be successful. **~gar-se** vpr take one's revenge (**de** for **em** on). **~gativo** a vindictive

vinha /'viɲa/ f vineyard

vinhedo /vi'ɲedu/ m vineyard

vinheta /vi'ɲeta/ f (na TV etc) sequence

vinho /'viɲu/ m wine ● a invar maroon; **~ do Porto** port

> **vinho verde** *Vinho verde* (literally 'green wine') is a light, slightly sparkling Portuguese wine originating from the Minho area in the north of the country. The 'green' in its name refers to its young age rather than to its colour, and it is available in white, red and rosé varieties.

vinícola /vi'nikola/ a wine-growing

vinicul|tor /vinikuw'tor/ m wine grower. **~tura** f wine growing

vinil /vi'niw/ m vinyl

vinte /'vĩtʃi/ a & m twenty. **~na** /e/ f score

viola /vi'ɔla/ f viola

violação /viola'sãw/ f violation

violão /vio'lãw/ m guitar

violar /vio'lar/ vt violate

vio|lência /vio'lẽsia/ f violence; (uma) act of violence. **~lentar** vt rape ‹mulher›. **~lento** a violent

violeta /vio'leta/ f violet ● a invar violet

violi|nista /violi'nista/ m/f violinist. **~no** m violin

violonce|lista /violõse'lista/ m/f cellist. **~lo** /ɛ/ m cello

vir /vir/ vi come; **o ano que vem** next year; **venho lendo os jornais** I have been reading the papers; **vem cá** come here; ⟨!⟩ listen; **isso não vem ao caso** that's irrelevant; **~ a ser** turn out to be; **~ com** give ‹argumento etc›

virabrequim /virabre'kĩ/ m crankshaft

viração /vira'sãw/ f breeze

vira-casaca /viraka'zaka/ m/f turncoat

vira|da /vi'rada/ f turn. **~do** a ‹roupa› inside out; (de cabeça para baixo) upside down; **~do para** facing

vira-lata /vira'lata/ m mongrel

virar /vi'rar/ vt turn; turn over ‹disco, barco etc›; turn inside out ‹roupa›; turn out ‹bolsos›; tip ‹balde, água etc› ● vi turn; ‹barco› turn over; (tornar-se) become; **vira e mexe** every so often. **~se** vpr turn round; (na vida) get by, cope; **~se para** turn to

viravolta /vira'vɔwta/ f about-turn

virgem /'virʒẽ/ a ‹fita› blank; ‹floresta, noiva etc› virgin ● f virgin; **Virgem** (signo) Virgo

virgindade /virʒĩ'dadʒi/ f virginity

vírgula /'virgula/ f comma; (decimal) point

vi|ril /vi'riw/ (pl **~ris**) a virile

virilha /vi'riʎa/ f groin

virilidade /virili'dadʒi/ f virility

virtu|al /virtu'aw/ (pl **~ais**) a virtual

virtude /vir'tudʒi/ f virtue

virtuo|sismo /virtuo'zizmu/ m virtuosity. **~so** /o/ a virtuous ● m virtuoso

virulento /viru'lẽtu/ a virulent

vírus /'virus/ m invar virus

visão /vi'zãw/ f vision; (aspeto, ponto de vista) view

visar /vi'zar/ vt aim at ‹caça, alvo›; **~ (a)** aim for ‹objetivo›; ‹medida, ação› be aimed at

vísceras /'viseras/ f pl innards

viscon|de /vis'kõdʒi/ m viscount. **~dessa** /e/ f viscountess

viscoso /vis'kozu/ a viscous

viseira /vi'zera/ f visor

visibilidade /vizibili'dadʒi/ f visibility

visionário /vizio'nariu/ a & m visionary

visi|ta /vi'zita/ f visit; (visitante) visitor; **fazer uma ~ta a alguém** pay s.o. a visit. **~tante** a visiting ● m/f visitor. **~tar** vt visit

visí|vel /vi'zivew/ (pl **~veis**) a visible

vislum|brar /vizlũ'brar/ vt (entrever) glimpse; (imaginar) envisage. **~bre** m glimpse

visom /vi'zõ/ m mink

visor /vi'zor/ m viewfinder

V

vis|ta /'vista/ f sight; (*dos olhos*) eyesight; (*panorama*) view; **à ~ta** (*visível*) in view; (*em dinheiro*) in cash; **à primeira ~ta** at first sight; **pôr à ~ta** put on show; **de ~ta** ‹*conhecer*› by sight; **em ~ta de** in view of; **ter em ~ta** have in view; **dar na ~ta** attract attention; **fazer ~ta** look nice; **fazer ~ta grossa** turn a blind eye (**a** to); **perder de ~ta** lose sight of; **a perder de ~ta** as far as the eye can see; **uma ~ta de olhos** a quick look. **~to** a seen ● *m* visa; **pelo ~to** by the looks of things; **~to que** seeing that

visto|ria /visto'ria/ f inspection. **~riar** *vt* inspect

vistoso /vis'tozu/ a eye-catching

visu|al /vizu'aw/ (*pl* ~**ais**) a visual ● *m* look. **~alizar** *vt* visualize

vi|tal /vi'taw/ (*pl* ~**tais**) a vital. **~talício** a for life. **~talidade** f vitality

vita|mina /vita'mina/ f vitamin; (*bebida*) liquidized fruit drink. **~minado** a with added vitamins. **~mínico** a vitamin

vitela /vi'tɛla/ f (*carne*) veal

viticultura /vitʃikuw'tura/ f viticulture

vítima /'vitʃima/ f victim

viti|mar /vitʃi'mar/ *vt* (*matar*) claim the life of; **ser ~mado por** fall victim to

vitória /vi'tɔria/ f victory

vitorioso /vitori'ozu/ a victorious

vi|tral /vi'traw/ (*pl* ~**trais**) *m* stained glass window

vitrine /vi'trini/ f shop window

vitrola /vi'trɔla/ f jukebox

viú|va /vi'uva/ f widow. **~vo** a widowed ● *m* widower

viva /'viva/ f cheer ● *int* hurray; **~ a rainha** long live the queen

vivacidade /vivasi'dadʒi/ f vivacity

vivalma /vi'vawma/ f **não há ~ lá fora** there's not a soul outside

vivar /vi'var/ *vt/i* cheer

vivaz /vi'vas/ a lively, vivacious; ‹*planta*› hardy

viveiro /vi'veru/ *m* (*de plantas*) nursery; (*de peixes*) fishpond; (*de aves*) aviary; *fig* breeding ground

vivência /vi'vẽsia/ f experience

vivenda /vi'vẽda/ f *Port* detached house

viver /vi'ver/ *vt/i* live (**de** on); **ele vive reclamando** he's always complaining ● *m* life

víveres /'viveris/ *m pl* provisions

vívido /'vividu/ a vivid

vivissecção /vivisek'sãw/ f vivisection

vivo /'vivu/ a (*que vive*) living; (*animado*) lively; ‹*cor*› bright ● *m* **os ~s** the living; **ao ~** live; **estar ~** be alive; **dinheiro ~** cash

vizi|nhança /vizi'nãsa/ f neighbourhood. **~nho** a neighbouring ● *m* neighbour

vo|ador /voa'dor/ a flying. **~ar** *vi* fly; (*explodir*) blow up; **sair ~ando** rush off

vocabulário /vokabu'lariu/ *m* vocabulary

vocábulo /vo'kabulu/ *m* word

voca|ção /voka'sãw/ f vocation. **~cional** (*pl* ~**cionais**) a vocational; **orientação ~cional** careers guidance

vo|cal /vo'kaw/ (*pl* ~**cais**) a vocal

você /vo'se/ *pron* you. **~s** *pron* you

vociferar /vosife'rar/ *vi* shout abuse

vodca /'vɔdʒka/ f vodka

voga /'vɔga/ f (*moda*) vogue

vo|gal /vo'gaw/ (*pl* ~**gais**) f vowel

volante /vo'lãtʃi/ *m* (*de carro*) steering wheel

volá|til /vo'latʃiw/ (*pl* ~**teis**) a volatile

vôlei /'volej/ *m*, **voleibol** /volej'bɔl/ *m* volleyball

volt /'vɔwtʃi/ (*pl* ~**s**) *m* volt

volta /'vɔwta/ f (*retorno*) return; (*da pista*) lap; (*resposta*) response; **às ~s com** tied up with; **de ~** back; **em ~ de** around; **na ~** on the way back; **na ~ do correio** by return of post; **por ~ de** around; **dar a ~ ao mundo** go round the world; **dar a ~ por cima** make a comeback; **dar meia ~** turn round; **dar uma ~** (*a pé*) go for a walk; (*de carro*) go for a drive; **dar uma ~ em** turn round; **dar ~s** spin round; **ter ~** get a response; **~ e meia** every so often. **~do a ~do para** geared towards

voltagem /vow'taʒẽ/ f voltage

voltar /vow'tar/ *vi* go/come back, return; **~ a si** come to; **~ a fazer** do again; **~ atrás** backtrack ● *vt* rewind ‹*fita*›. **~se** *vpr* turn round; **~se para/contra** turn to/against

volu|me /vo'lumi/ *m* volume. **~moso** a sizeable; ‹*som*› loud

voluntário /volũ'tariu/ a & *m* volunteer

volúpia /vo'lupia/ f sensuality, lust

voluptuoso /voluptu'ozu/ a sensual; ‹*mulher*› voluptuous

volú|vel /vo'luvew/ (pl **~veis**) a fickle

vomitar /vomi'tar/ vt/i vomit

vômito /'vomitu/ m vomit; pl vomiting

vontade /võ'tadʒi/ f will; **à ~** (bem) at ease; (quanto quiser) as much as one likes; **fique à ~** make yourself at home; **tem comida à ~** there's plenty of food; **estar com ~ de** feel like; **isso me dá ~ de chorar** it makes me feel like crying; **fazer a ~ de alguém** do what sb wants

voo /'vou/ m flight; **levantar ~** take off; **~ livre** hang-gliding

voraz /vo'ras/ a voracious

vos /vus/ pron you; (a vocês) to you

vós /vɔs/ pron you

vosso /'vɔsu/ a your ● pron yours

vo|tação /vota'sãw/ f vote. **~tante** m/f voter. **~tar** vt vote on ‹lei etc›; (dedicar) devote; (prometer) vow ● vi vote (**em** for)

voto /'vɔtu/ m (em votação) vote; (promessa) vow; pl (desejos) wishes

vo|vó /vo'vɔ/ f grandma. **~vô** m grandpa

voz /vɔs/ f voice; **dar ~ de prisão a alguém** place s.o. under arrest

vozerio /voze'riu/ m shouting

vul|cânico /vuw'kaniku/ a volcanic. **~cão** m volcano

vul|gar /vuw'gar/ a ordinary; (baixo) vulgar. **~garizar** vt popularize; (tornar baixo) vulgarize. **~go** adv commonly known as

vulne|rabilidade /vuwnerabili'dadʒi/ f vulnerability. **~rável** (pl **~ráveis**) a vulnerable

vul|to /'vuwtu/ m (figura) figure; (tamanho) bulk; (importância) importance; **de ~to** important. **~toso** /o/ a bulky

Xx

xadrez /ʃa'dres/ m (jogo) chess; (desenho) check; Ⓣ (prisão) prison ● a invar check

xaile /'ʃajle/ m ▶ **xale**

xale /'ʃali/ m shawl

xampu /ʃã'pu/ m shampoo

xará /ʃa'ra/ m/f namesake

xarope /ʃa'rɔpi/ m syrup

xaxim /ʃa'ʃĩ/ m plant fibre

xenofobia /ʃenofo'bia/ f xenophobia

xenófobo /ʃe'nɔfobu/ a xenophobic ● m xenophobe

xepa /'ʃepa/ f scraps

xeque¹ /'ʃɛki/ m (árabe) sheikh

xeque² /'ʃɛki/ m (no xadrez) check. **~~mate** m checkmate

xere|ta /ʃe'reta/ Ⓣ a nosy ● m/f nosy parker. **~tar** vi Ⓣ nose around

xerez /ʃe'res/ m sherry

xerife /ʃe'rifi/ m sheriff

xerocar /ʃero'kar/ vt photocopy

xerox /ʃe'rɔks/ m invar photocopy

xexelento /ʃeʃe'lẽtu/ Ⓣ a scruffy ● m scruff

xícara /'ʃikara/ f cup

xiita /ʃi'ita/ a & m/f Shiite

xilofone /ʃilo'foni/ m xylophone

xingar /ʃĩ'gar/ vt swear at ● vi swear

xis /ʃis/ m invar letter X; **o ~ do problema** the crux of the problem

xixi /ʃi'ʃi/ m Ⓣ wee; **fazer ~** do a wee Ⓣ

xô /ʃo/ int shoo

xucro /'ʃukru/ a ignorant

Ww

walkie-talkie /uɔki'tɔki/ (pl **~s**) m walkie-talkie

Walkman® /uɔk'mɛn/ m invar Walkman®

WAP /uap/ a (telec) WAP

watt /u'ɔtʃi/ (pl **~s**) m watt

web /uɛb/ m web, WWW

windsur|fe /uĩ'surfi/ m windsurfing. **~fista** m/f windsurfer

Zz

zagueiro /za'geru/ m full back

Zaire /'zajri/ m Zaire

Zâmbia /'zãbia/ f Zambia

zan|gado /zã'gadu/ a cross, annoyed. **~gar** vt annoy. **~gar-se** vpr get cross, get annoyed (**com** with)

zanzar /zã'zar/ vi wander

zarpar /zar'par/ vi set off; (de navio) set sail

zebra /'zebra/ f zebra; (*pessoa*) fool; (*resultado*) upset

ze|lador /zela'dor/ m caretaker, *Amer* janitor. ~**lar** *vt* ~**lar (por)** take care of. ~**lo** /e/ m zeal; ~**lo por** devotion to. ~**loso** /o/ a zealous

zé-ninguém /zenĩ'gẽ/ m **ser um** ~ to be a nobody

zero /'zɛru/ m zero; (*em escores*) nil. ~~**quilômetro** a *invar* brand new

ziguezague /zigi'zagi/ m zigzag. ~**ar** *vi* zigzag

Zimbábue /zĩ'babui/ m Zimbabwe

zinco /'zĩku/ m zinc

ziper /'ziper/ m zip, zipper

zodíaco /zo'dʒiaku/ m zodiac

zoeira /zo'era/ f din

zom|bador /zõba'dor/ a mocking. ~**bar** *vi* ~**bar (de)** mock. ~**baria** f mockery

zona /'zona/ f (*área*) zone; (*de cidade*) district; (*desordem*) mess; (*tumulto*) commotion; (*bairro do meretrício*) red-light district

zonzo /'zõzu/ a dizzy

zoo /'zou/ m zoo

zoo|logia /zoolo'ʒia/ f zoology. ~**lógico** a zoological

zoólogo /zo'ɔlogu/ m zoologist

zulu /zu'lu/ a & m/f Zulu

zum /zũ/ m zoom lens

zumbi /zũ'bi/ m zombie

zum|bido /zũ'bidu/ m buzz; (*no ouvido*) ringing. ~**bir** *vi* buzz

zu|nido /zu'nidu/ m (*de vento, bala*) whistle; (*de inseto*) buzz. ~**nir** *vi* ‹*vento, bala*› whistle; ‹*inseto*› buzz

zunzum /zũ'zũ/ m rumour

Zurique /zu'riki/ f Zurich

zurrar /zu'xar/ *vi* bray

a /ə/ *emphatic* /eɪ/

❗ before vowel or mute h **an** /ən/ *emphatic* /æn/ ● *indefinite article*

····▸ um(a); **~ pencil** um lápis; **~ pen** uma caneta

❗ When talking about what people do, **a** is not translated into Portuguese **she's a doctor** *ela é médica*

❗ **a** is not translated into Portuguese in the numbers **a hundred** and a **thousand a hundred** years ago *há cem anos*; **there were a thousand people there** *havia mil pessoas lá*

····▸ per; **two pounds ~ metre** duas libras o metro; **sixty miles ~n hour** sessenta milhas por hora, (P) à hora; **once ~ year** uma vez por ano; **twice ~ year** duas vezes por ano

aback /ə'bæk/ *adv* **taken ~** desconcertado, (P) surpreendido

abandon /ə'bændən/ *vt* abandonar ● *n* abandono *m*. **~ed** *a* abandonado; ‹*behaviour*› livre, dissoluto

abate /ə'beɪt/ *vt/i* abater, abrandar, diminuir

abattoir /'æbətwɑː(r)/ *n* matadouro *m*

abbey /'æbɪ/ *n* abadia *f*, mosteiro *m*

abbreviat|e /ə'briːvɪeɪt/ *vt* abreviar. **~ion** /-'eɪʃn/ *n* abreviação *f*; (*short form*) abreviatura *f*

abdicat|e /'æbdɪkeɪt/ *vt/i* abdicar. **~ion** /-'keɪʃn/ *n* abdicação *f*

abdom|en /'æbdəmən/ *n* abdômen *m*, (P) abdómen *m*. **~inal** /-'dɒmɪnl/ *a* abdominal

abduct /æb'dʌkt/ *vt* raptar. **~ion** /-ʃn/ *n* rapto *m*

aberration /æbə'reɪʃn/ *n* aberração *f*

abeyance /ə'beɪəns/ *n* **in ~** ‹*matter*› em suspenso; ‹*custom*› em desuso

abhor /əb'hɔː(r)/ *vt* (*pt* abhorred) abominar, ter horror a. **~rence** /-'hɒrəns/ *n* horror *m*. **~rent** /-'hɒrənt/ *a* abominável, execrável

abide /ə'baɪd/ *vt* (*pt* abided) suportar, tolerar; **~ by** ‹*promise*› manter; ‹*rules*› acatar

ability /ə'bɪlətɪ/ *n* capacidade *f* (**to do** para or de fazer); (*cleverness*) habilidade

f, esperteza *f*

abject /'æbdʒekt/ *a* abjeto, (P) abjecto

ablaze /ə'bleɪz/ *a* em chamas; *fig* aceso, (P) excitado

abl|e /'eɪbl/ *a* (**er, est**) capaz (**to** de); **be ~ to** (*have power, opportunity*) ser capaz de, poder; (*know how to*) ser capaz de, saber. **~y** *adv* habilmente

abnormal /æb'nɔːml/ *a* anormal. **~ity** /-'mælətɪ/ *n* anormalidade *f*. **~ly** *adv* (*unusually*) excepcionalmente

aboard /ə'bɔːd/ *adv* a bordo ● *prep* a bordo de

aboli|sh /ə'bɒlɪʃ/ *vt* abolir, extinguir. **~tion** /æbə'lɪʃn/ *n* abolição *f*, extinção *f*

abominable /ə'bɒmɪnəbl/ *a* abominável, detestável

abort /ə'bɔːt/ *vt/i* (fazer) abortar. **~ive** *a* ‹*attempt etc*› abortado, malogrado

abortion /ə'bɔːʃn/ *n* aborto *m*; **have an ~** fazer um aborto, ter um aborto

abound /ə'baʊnd/ *vi* abundar (**in** em)

about /ə'baʊt/ *adv* (*approximately*) aproximadamente, cerca de; (*here and there*) aqui e ali; (*all round*) por todos os lados, em roda, em volta; (*in existence*) por aí; **~ here** por aqui; **be ~ to** estar prestes a; **he was ~ to eat** ia comer; **how or what ~ leaving?** e se nós fôssemos embora?; **know/talk ~** saber/ falar sobre ● *prep* acerca de, sobre; (*round*) em torno de; (*somewhere in*) em, por. **~-face**, **~-turn** *ns* reviravolta *f*

above /ə'bʌv/ *adv* acima, por cima ● *prep* sobre; **he's not ~ lying** ele não é de mentir; **~ all** sobretudo. **~ board** a franco, honesto ● *adv* com lisura; **~-mentioned** *a* acima, supracitado

abrasive /ə'breɪsɪv/ *a* abrasivo; *fig* agressivo ● *n* abrasivo *m*

abreast /ə'brest/ *adv* lado a lado; **keep ~ of** manter-se a par de

abridge /ə'brɪdʒ/ *vt* abreviar

abroad /ə'brɔːd/ *adv* no estrangeiro; (*far and wide*) por todo o lado; **go ~** ir para o estrangeiro

abrupt /ə'brʌpt/ *a* (*sudden, curt*) brusco; (*steep*) abrupto

abscess /'æbsɪs/ *n* abscesso *m*, (P) abcesso *m*

a

abscond /əb'skɒnd/ *vi* evadir-se, andar fugido

absen|t¹ /'æbsənt/ *a* ausente; ‹look etc› distraído. **~ce** *n* ausência *f*; (lack) falta *f*. **~t-minded** *a* distraído; **~t-mindedness** *n* distracção *f*, (P) distracção *f*

absent² /əb'sent/ *v refl* **~ o.s.** ausentar-se

absentee /æbsen'tiː/ *n* ausente *mf*, (P) absentista *m*

absolute /'æbsəluːt/ *a* absoluto; 🔟 ‹coward etc› autêntico, (P) verdadeiro. **~ly** *adv* absolutamente

absor|b /əb'sɔːb/ *vt* absorver. **~ption** *n* absorção *f*

absorbent /əb'sɔːbənt/ *a* absorvente; **~ cotton** *Amer* algodão hidrófilo *m*

abst|ain /əb'stein/ *vi* abster-se (**from** de). **~ention** /-'stenʃn/ *n* abstenção *f*

abstemious /əb'stiːmiəs/ *a* abstêmio, (P) abstémio, sóbrio

abstract¹ /'æbstrækt/ *a* abstrato

abstract² /əb'strækt/ *vt* (take out) extrair; (separate) abstrair

absurd /əb'sɜːd/ *a* absurdo. **~ity** *n* absurdo *m*

abundan|t /ə'bʌndənt/ *a* abundante. **~ce** *n* abundância *f*

abuse¹ /ə'bjuːz/ *vt* (misuse) abusar de; (ill-treat) maltratar; (insult) injuriar, insultar

abus|e² /ə'bjuːs/ *n* (wrong use) abuso *m* (**of** de); (insults) insultos *mpl*. **~ive** *a* injurioso, ofensivo

abysmal /ə'bizməl/ *a* abismal; 🔟 (bad) abissal

abyss /ə'bis/ *n* abismo *m*

academic /ækə'demik/ *a* acadêmico, (P) académico, universitário; (scholarly) intelectual; *pej* académico; (P) teórico ● *n* universitário

academy /ə'kædəmi/ *n* academia *f*

accelerat|e /ək'seləreit/ *vt* acelerar ● *vi* acelerar-se; *Auto* acelerar. **~ion** /-'reiʃn/ *n* aceleração *f*

accelerator /ək'seləreitə(r)/ *n Auto* acelerador *m*

accent¹ /'æksənt/ *n* acento *m*; (local pronunciation) sotaque *m*

accent² /æk'sent/ *vt* acentuar

accept /ək'sept/ *vt* aceitar. **~able** *a* aceitável. **~ance** *n* aceitação *f*; (approval) aprovação *f*

access /'ækses/ *n* acesso *m* (**to** a). **~ible** /ək'sesəbl/ *a* acessível

accessory /ək'sesəri/ *a* acessório ● *n* acessório *m*; *Jur* (person) cúmplice *m*

accident /'æksidənt/ *n* acidente *m*, desastre *m*; (chance) acaso *m*. **~al** /-'dentl/ *a* acidental, fortuito. **~ally** /-'dentəli/ *adv* acidentalmente, por acaso

acclaim /ə'kleim/ *vt* aclamar ● *n* aplauso *m*, aclamações *fpl*

acclimatiz|e /ə'klaimətaiz/ *vt/i* aclimatar(-se)

accommodat|e /ə'kɒmədeit/ *vt* acomodar; (lodge) alojar; (adapt) adaptar; (supply) fornecer; (oblige) fazer a vontade de. **~ing** *a* obsequioso, amigo de fazer vontades. **~ion** /-'deiʃn/ *n* acomodação *f*; (rooms) alojamento *m*, quarto *m*

accompan|y /ə'kʌmpəni/ *vt* acompanhar. **~iment** *n* acompanhamento *m*

accomplice /ə'kʌmplis/ *n* cúmplice *mf*

accomplish /ə'kʌmpliʃ/ *vt* (perform) executar, realizar; (achieve) realizar, conseguir fazer. **~ed** *a* acabado. **~ment** *n* realização *f*; (ability) talento *m*, dote *m*

accord /ə'kɔːd/ *vi* concordar ● *vt* conceder ● *n* acordo *m*; **of one's own ~** por vontade própria, espontaneamente. **~ance** *n* **in ~ance with** em conformidade com, de acordo com

according /ə'kɔːdiŋ/ *adv* **~ to** conforme. **~ly** *adv* (therefore) por conseguinte, por consequência; (appropriately) conformemente

accordion /ə'kɔːdiən/ *n* acordeão *m*

accost /ə'kɒst/ *vt* abordar, abeirar-se de

account /ə'kaunt/ *n Comm* conta *f*; (description) relato *m*; (importance) importância *f* ● *vt* considerar; **~ for** dar contas de, explicar; **on ~ of** por causa de; **on no ~** em caso algum; **take into ~** ter ou levar em conta. **~ number** *n* número *f* da conta, (P) número *m* de conta . **~able** /-əbl/ *a* responsável (**for** por)

accountant /ə'kauntənt/ *n* contador(a) *m/f*, (P) contabilista *mf*

accumulat|e /ə'kjuːmjʊleit/ *vt/i* acumular(-se). **~ion** /-'leiʃn/ *n* acumulação *f*, acréscimo *m*

accura|te /'ækjərət/ *a* exato, preciso. **~cy** *n* exatidão *f*, precisão *f*

accus|e /ə'kjuːz/ *vt* acusar; **the ~ed** o acusado. **~ation** /ækjuː'zeiʃn/ *n* acusação f

accustom /əˈkʌstəm/ vt acostumar, habituar; **get ~ed to** acostumar-se a, habituar-se a. **~ed** a acostumado, habituado

ace /eɪs/ n ás m

ache /eɪk/ n dor f ● vi doer; **my leg ~s** dói-me a perna, tenho dores na perna

achieve /əˈtʃiːv/ vt realizar, efetuar; <success> alcançar. **~ment** n realização f; <feat> feito m, façanha f, sucesso m

acid /ˈæsɪd/ a ácido; <wine> azedo; <words> áspero ● n ácido m. **~ity** /əˈsɪdətɪ/ n acidez f

acknowledge /əkˈnɒlɪdʒ/ vt reconhecer; ~ **(receipt of)** acusar a recepção de. **~ment** n reconhecimento m; (letter etc) acusação f de recebimento, (P) aviso m de recepção

acne /ˈæknɪ/ n acne mf

acorn /ˈeɪkɔːn/ n bolota f, glande f

acoustic /əˈkuːstɪk/ a acústico. **~s** npl acústica f

acquaint /əˈkweɪnt/ vt ~ **sb with sth** pôr alguém a par de algo; **be ~ed with** <person, fact> conhecer. **~ance** n (knowledge, person) conhecimento m; (person) conhecido m

acqui|re /əˈkwaɪə(r)/ vt adquirir. **~sition** /ækwɪˈzɪʃn/ n aquisição f

acquit /əˈkwɪt/ vt (pt acquitted) absolver; ~ **o.s. well** sair-se bem. **~tal** n absolvição f

acrid /ˈækrɪd/ a acre

acrimon|ious /ækrɪˈməʊnɪəs/ a acrimonioso

acrobat /ˈækrəbæt/ n acrobata mf. **~ic** /-ˈbætɪk/ a acrobático. **~ics** /-ˈbætɪks/ npl acrobacia f

acronym /ˈækrənɪm/ n sigla f

across /əˈkrɒs/ adv & prep (side to side) de lado a lado (de), de um lado para o outro (de); (on the other side) do outro lado (de); (crosswise) através (de), de través; **go** or **walk ~** atravessar; **swim ~** atravessar a nado

act /ækt/ n (deed) Theatr ato m; (in variety show) número m; (decree) lei f ● vi agir, atuar; Theatr representar; (function) funcionar; (pretend) fingir ● vt <part, role> desempenhar; ~ **as** servir de. **~ing** a interino ● n Theatr desempenho m

action /ˈækʃn/ n ação f; Mil combate m; **out of ~** fora de combate; Techn avariado; **take ~** agir, atuar

activ|e /ˈæktɪv/ a ativo; <interest> vivo; <volcano> em atividade. **~ity** /-ˈtɪvətɪ/ n

atividade f

ac|tor /ˈæktə(r)/ n ator m. **~tress** n atriz f

actual /ˈæktʃʊəl/ a real, verdadeiro; <example> concreto; **the ~ pen which** a própria caneta que. **~ly** adv (in fact) na realidade

acupunctur|e /ˈækjʊpʌŋktʃə(r)/ n acupuntura f, (P) acupunctura f. **~ist** n acupunturador m, (P) acupuncturista mf

acute /əˈkjuːt/ a agudo; <mind> perspicaz; <emotion> intenso, vivo; <shortage> grande. **~ly** adv vivamente

ad /æd/ n 🅸 anúncio m

AD abbr dC

adamant /ˈædəmənt/ a inflexível

adapt /əˈdæpt/ vt/i adaptar(-se). **~ation** /ædæpˈteɪʃn/ n adaptação f

adaptab|le /əˈdæptəbl/ a adaptável

add /æd/ vt/i acrescentar; ~ **(up)** somar; ~ **up to** (total) elevar-se a

adder /ˈædə(r)/ n víbora f

addict /ˈædɪkt/ n viciado m; **drug ~** viciado em droga, viciado da droga, (P) toxicodependente

addict|ed /əˈdɪktɪd/ a **be ~ed to** <drink, drugs> also fig ter o vício de. **~ion** /-ʃn/ n Med dependência f; fig vício m. **~ive** a que produz dependência

addition /əˈdɪʃn/ n adição f; **in ~** além disso; **in ~ to** além de. **~al** /-ʃənl/ a adicional, suplementar

address /əˈdres/ n endereço m; (speech) discurso m ● vt endereçar; (speak to) dirigir-se a

adequa|te /ˈædɪkwət/ a adequado; (satisfactory) satisfatório

adhere /ədˈhɪə(r)/ vi aderir (to a)

adhesive /ədˈhiːsɪv/ a & n adesivo m; ~ **plaster** esparadrapo m, (P) adesivo m

adjacent /əˈdʒeɪsnt/ a adjacente; contíguo (to a)

adjective /ˈædʒektɪv/ n adjetivo m

adjoin /əˈdʒɔɪn/ vt confinar com, ficar contíguo a

adjourn /əˈdʒɜːn/ vt adiar ● vi suspender a sessão; ~ **to** (go) passar a, ir para

adjudicate /əˈdʒuːdɪkeɪt/ vt/i julgar; (award) adjudicar

adjust /əˈdʒʌst/ vt/i (alter) ajustar, regular; (arrange) arranjar; ~ **(o.s.) to** adaptar-se a. **~able** a regulável. **~ment** n Techn regulação f, afinação f; (of person) adaptação f

ad lib /ædˈlɪb/ vi (pt ad libbed) 🅸 improvisar ● adv à vontade

a **administer** /ədˈmɪnɪstə(r)/ vt
administrar

administrat|e /ədˈmɪnɪstreɪt/ vt
administrar, gerir. **~ion** /-ˈstreɪʃn/ n
administração f. **~or** n administrador m

admirable /ˈædmərəbl/ a admirável

admiral /ˈædmərəl/ n almirante m

admir|e /ədˈmaɪə(r)/ vt admirar.
~ation /-mɪˈreɪʃn/ n admiração f. **~er**
/-ˈmaɪərə(r)/ n admirador m

admission /ədˈmɪʃn/ n admissão f;
(to museum, theatre, etc) ingresso m, (P)
entrada f; (confession) confissão f

admit /ədˈmɪt/ vt (pt admitted)
(let in) admitir, permitir a entrada a;
(acknowledge) reconhecer, admitir; **~ to**
confessar. **~tance** n admissão f

admoni|sh /ədˈmɒnɪʃ/ vt admoestar

adolescen|t /ædəˈlesnt/ a & n
adolescente mf. **~ce** n adolescência f

adopt /əˈdɒpt/ vt adotar; **~ed child**
filho adotivo. **~ion** /-ʃn/ n adoção f

ador|e /əˈdɔː(r)/ vt adorar. **~able**
a adorável. **~ation** /ædəˈreɪʃn/ n
adoração f

adorn /əˈdɔːn/ vt adornar, enfeitar

adrenalin /əˈdrenəlɪn/ n adrenalina f

adrift /əˈdrɪft/ a & adv à deriva

adult /ˈædʌlt/ a & n adulto m. **~hood** n
idade f adulta, (P) maioridade f

adulterat|e /əˈdʌltəreɪt/ vt adulterar

adulter|y /əˈdʌltərɪ/ n adultério m.
~er, ~ess ns adúlter/o, -a mf. **~ous** a
adúltero

advance /ədˈvɑːns/ vt/i avançar ● n
avanço m; (payment) adiantamento m ●
‹payment, booking› adiantado; **in ~** com
antecedência. **~d** a avançado. **~ment** n
promoção f, ascensão f

advantage /ədˈvɑːntɪdʒ/ n vantagem
f; **take ~ of** aproveitar-se de, tirar
partido de; (person) explorar. **~ous**
/ædvənˈteɪdʒəs/ a vantajoso

adventur|e /ədˈventʃə(r)/ n aventura f.
~er n aventureiro m, explorador m. **~ous**
a aventuroso

adverb /ˈædvɜːb/ n advérbio m

adversary /ˈædvəsərɪ/ n adversário m,
antagonista mf

advers|e /ˈædvɜːs/ a (contrary) adverso;
(unfavourable) desfavorável. **~ity**
/ədˈvɜːsətɪ/ n adversidade f

advert /ˈædvɜːt/ n 🄸 anúncio m

advertise /ˈædvətaɪz/ vt/i anunciar,
fazer publicidade (de); (sell) pôr um
anúncio (para); **~ for** procurar. **~r** /-ə(r)/

n anunciante mf

advertisement /ədˈvɜːtɪsmənt/ n
anúncio m; (advertising) publicidade f

advice /ədˈvaɪs/ n conselho(s) mpl;
Comm aviso m

advis|e /ədˈvaɪz/ vt aconselhar;
(inform) avisar, informar; **~e against**
desaconselhar. **~able** a aconselhável.
~er n conselheiro m; (in business)
consultor m. **~ory** a consultivo

advocate[1] /ˈædvəkət/ n Jur advogado
m; (supporter) defensor(a) mf

advocate[2] /ˈædvəkeɪt/ vt advogar,
defender

aerial /ˈeərɪəl/ a aéreo ● n antena f

aerobics /eəˈrəʊbɪks/ n ginástica f
aeróbica

aeroplane /ˈeərəpleɪn/ n avião m

aerosol /ˈeərəsɒl/ n aerossol m

aesthetic /iːsˈθetɪk/ a estético

affair /əˈfeə(r)/ n (business) negócio m;
(romance) ligação f, aventura f; (matter)
assunto m; **love ~** paixão f

affect /əˈfekt/ vt afetar. **~ation**
/æfekˈteɪʃn/ n afetação f. **~ed** a afetado,
pretencioso

affection /əˈfekʃn/ n afeição f, afeto m

affectionate /əˈfekʃənət/ a afetuoso,
carinhoso

affiliat|e /əˈfɪlɪeɪt/ vt afiliar; **~ed
company** filial f. **~ion** /-ˈeɪʃn/ n afiliação f

affirm /əˈfɜːm/ vt afirmar. **~ation**
/æfəˈmeɪʃn/ n afirmação f

affirmative /əˈfɜːmətɪv/ a afirmativo
● n afirmativa f

afflict /əˈflɪkt/ vt afligir. **~ion** /-ʃn/ n
aflição f

affluen|t /ˈæfluənt/ a rico, afluente.
~ce n riqueza f, afluência f

afford /əˈfɔːd/ vt (have money for)
permitir-se, ter meios (para); **can you ~
the time?** você teria tempo?; **I can't ~ a
car** eu não posso comprar um carro; **we
can't ~ to lose** não podemos perder

affront /əˈfrʌnt/ n afronta f ● vt insultar

afloat /əˈfləʊt/ adv & a à tona, a flutuar;
(at sea) no mar; ‹business› lançado, (P)
sem dívidas

afraid /əˈfreɪd/ a **be ~** ter medo (**of,
to** de **that** que); (be sorry) lamentar,
ter muita pena; **I'm ~ (that)** (regret to
say) lamento or tenho muita pena de
dizer que

Africa /ˈæfrɪkə/ n África f. **~n** a & n
africano m

after /ˈɑːftə(r)/ adv depois ● prep depois de ● conj depois que; ~ **all** afinal de contas; ~ **doing** depois de fazer; **be** ~ (seek) querer, pretender. ~**effect** n sequela f, efeito m retardado; (of drug) efeito m secundário

aftermath /ˈɑːftəmæθ/ n consequências fpl

afternoon /ɑːftəˈnuːn/ n tarde f

aftershave /ˈɑːftəʃeɪv/ n loção f pós-barba, (P) loção f para a barba

afterthought /ˈɑːftəθɔːt/ n reflexão f posterior; **as an** ~ pensando melhor

afterwards /ˈɑːftəwədz/ adv depois, mais tarde

again /əˈgen/ adv de novo, outra vez; (on the other hand) por outro lado; **then** ~ além disso

against /əˈgenst/ prep contra

age /eɪdʒ/ n idade f; (period) época f, idade f; ~**s** 🆑 (very long time) há séculos mpl; **of** ~ /ur maior; **ten years of** ~ com/ de dez anos; **under** ~ menor ● vt/i (pres p **ageing**) envelhecer. ~ **group** n faixa etária f. ~**less** a sempre jovem

aged[1] /eɪdʒd/ a ~ **six** de seis anos de idade

aged[2] /ˈeɪdʒɪd/ a idoso, velho

agen|cy /ˈeɪdʒənsɪ/ n agência f; (means) intermédio m. ~**t** n agente mf

agenda /əˈdʒendə/ n ordem f do dia

aggravat|e /ˈægrəveɪt/ vt agravar; 🆑 (annoy) irritar. ~**ion** /-ˈveɪʃn/ n (worsening) agravamento m; (exasperation) irritação f; 🆑 (trouble) aborrecimentos mpl

aggregate /ˈægrɪgeɪt/ vt/i agregar(-se) ● /ˈægrɪgət/ a total, global ● n (total, mass, materials) agregado m; **in the** ~ no todo

aggress|ive /əˈgresɪv/ a agressivo; (weapons) ofensivo. ~**ion** /-ʃn/ n agressão f. ~**or** n agressor m

agil|e /ˈædʒaɪl/ a ágil. ~**ity** /əˈdʒɪlətɪ/ n agilidade f

agitat|e /ˈædʒɪteɪt/ vt agitar. ~**ion** /-ˈteɪʃn/ n agitação f

agnostic /ægˈnɒstɪk/ a & n agnóstico m

ago /əˈgəʊ/ adv há; **a month** ~ há um mês; **long** ~ há muito tempo

agon|y /ˈægənɪ/ n agonia f; (mental) angústia f. ~**ize** vi atormentar-se, torturar-se

agree /əˈgriː/ vt/i concordar; (of figures) acertar; ~ **that** reconhecer que; ~ **to do** concordar em or aceitar fazer; ~ **to sth** concordar com alguma coisa; **seafood doesn't** ~ **with me** não me dou bem com mariscos. ~**d** a ‹time, place› combinado; **be** ~**d** estar de acordo

agreeable /əˈgriːəbl/ a agradável; **be** ~ **to** estar de acordo com

agreement /əˈgriːmənt/ n acordo m; Gramm concordância f; (contract) contrato m; **in** ~ de acordo

agricultur|e /ˈægrɪkʌltʃə(r)/ n agricultura f. ~**al** /-ˈkʌltʃərəl/ a agrícola

aground /əˈgraʊnd/ adv **run** ~ (of ship) encalhar

ahead /əˈhed/ adv à frente, adiante; (in advance) adiantado; ~ **of sb** diante de alguém, à frente de alguém; ~ **of time** antes da hora, adiantado; **straight** ~ sempre em frente

aid /eɪd/ vt ajudar; ~ **and abet** ser cúmplice de ● n ajuda f; **in** ~ **of** em auxílio de, a favor de

AIDS /eɪdz/ n Med AIDS f, (P) sida m. ~ **awareness** n conscientização f sobre a AIDS, (P) consciencialização f sobre a SIDA; ~ **virus** n vírus m da AIDS, (P) vírus m da SIDA

aim /eɪm/ vt ‹gun› apontar; ‹efforts› dirigir; (send) atirar (**at** para) ● vi visar ● n alvo m; ~ **at** visar; ~ **to** aspirar a, tencionar; **take** ~ fazer pontaria. ~**less** a, ~**lessly** adv sem objetivo

air /eə(r)/ n ar m; **in the** ~ ‹rumour› espalhado; ‹plans› no ar; **on the** ~ Radio no ar ● vt arejar; ‹views› expor ‹base etc› aéreo; ~ **force** Força f Aérea; ~ **hostess** aeromoça f, (P) hospedeira f de bordo; ~ **raid** ataque m aéreo. ~**conditioned** a com ar condicionado; ~ **conditioning** n condicionamento m do ar, (P) ar m condicionado; ~ **strike** n ataque m aéreo

aircraft /ˈeəkrɑːft/ n (pl invar) avião m. ~ **carrier** n porta-aviões m

airfield /ˈeəfiːld/ n campo m de aviação

airgun /ˈeəgʌn/ n espingarda f de pressão

airlift /ˈeəlɪft/ n ponte f aérea ● vt transportar em ponte aérea

airline /ˈeəlaɪn/ n linha f aérea

airmail /ˈeəmeɪl/ n correio m aéreo; **by** ~ por avião

airport /ˈeəpɔːt/ n aeroporto m

airtight /ˈeətaɪt/ a hermético

airy /ˈeərɪ/ a (-ier, -iest) arejado; ‹manner› desenvolto

aisle /aɪl/ n (of church) nave f lateral; (gangway) coxia f

ajar /əˈdʒɑː(r)/ *adv & a* entreaberto

à la carte /ɑːlɑːˈkɑːt/ *adv & a* à la carte, (P) à lista

alarm /əˈlɑːm/ *n* alarme *m*; (*clock*) campainha *f* ● *vt* alarmar. **~ clock** *n* despertador *m*. **~ing** *a* alarmante

alas /əˈlæs/ *int* ai! ai de mim!

album /ˈælbəm/ *n* álbum *m*

alcohol /ˈælkəhɒl/ *n* álcool *m*. **~ic** /-ˈhɒlɪk/ *a* ‹person, drink› alcoólico ● *n* alcoólico *m*. **~ism** *n* alcoolismo *m*

alcove /ˈælkəʊv/ *n* recesso *m*, alcova *f*

ale /eɪl/ *n* cerveja *f* inglesa

alert /əˈlɜːt/ *a* (*lively*) vivo; (*watchful*) vigilante ● *n* alerta *m*; **be on the ~** estar alerta ● *vt* alertar

algebra /ˈældʒɪbrə/ *n* álgebra *f*

Algeria /ælˈdʒɪərɪə/ *n* Argélia *f*

alias /ˈeɪlɪəs/ *n* (*pl* **-ases**) outro nome *m*, nome falso *m*, (P) pseudónimo *m* ● *adv* aliás

alibi /ˈælɪbaɪ/ *n* (*pl* **-is**) álibi *m*, (P) alibi *m*

alien /ˈeɪlɪən/ *n & a* estrangeiro *m*; **~ to** (*contrary*) contrário *a*; (*differing*) alheio *a*, estranho *a*

alienat|e /ˈeɪlɪəneɪt/ *vt* alienar

alight[1] /əˈlaɪt/ *vi* descer; (*bird*) pousar

alight[2] /əˈlaɪt/ *a* (*on fire*) em chamas; (*lit up*) aceso

align /əˈlaɪn/ *vt* alinhar. **~ment** *n* alinhamento *m*

alike /əˈlaɪk/ *a* semelhante, parecido ● *adv* da mesma maneira; **look** or **be ~** parecer-se

alimony /ˈælɪmənɪ/ *n* pensão *f* alimentar, (P) de alimentos

alive /əˈlaɪv/ *a* vivo; **~ to** sensível *a*; **~ with** fervilhando de, (P) a fervilhar de

alkali /ˈælkəlaɪ/ *n* (*pl* **-is**) álcali *m*, (P) alcali *m*

---

all /ɔːl/ ● *a*

····▸ (*with singular noun*) todo, toda; **~ the wine** o vinho todo; **~ my money** todo o meu dinheiro

····▸ (*with plural noun*) todos, todas; **~ the men** todos os homens; **~ the women** todas as mulheres

● *pron*

····▸ (*plural*) todos, todas; **~ are here** todos estão aqui; **are we ~ going?** vamos todos?

····▸ (*everything*) tudo; **~ she said was...** tudo o que ela disse foi...; **I ate ~ of it** Eu comi tudo

---

····▸ (*in phrases*) **~ in** de modo geral; **in ~** (*in total*) no total; **not at ~** (*in no way*) de modo algum; **it was not at ~ expensive** não foi nem um pouco caro; (*answer to 'thank you'*) de nada

● *adv*

····▸ (*completely*) completamente; **~ by myself** completamente só; **~ in white** todo de branco; (*in scores*) **two ~** dois a dois

····▸ (*in phrases*) **~ along** todo o tempo; **~ but** quase, todos menos; **~ in** (*exhausted*) esgotado; **~ over** (*in all parts of*) por todo; **I ache ~ over** dói-me o corpo inteiro; **~ the better/less/more/worse** *etc* tanto melhor/menos/mais/pior *etc*; **~ right** bem; (*as a response*) está bem.

~-in *a* tudo incluído; **~-out** *a* ‹effort› máximo; **~-round** *a* completo

allegation /ælɪˈɡeɪʃn/ *n* alegação *f*

allege /əˈledʒ/ *vt* alegar

allegiance /əˈliːdʒəns/ *n* fidelidade *f*, lealdade *f*

allerg|y /ˈælədʒɪ/ *n* alergia *f*. **~ic** /əˈlɜːdʒɪk/ *a* alérgico

alleviate /əˈliːvɪeɪt/ *vt* aliviar

alley /ˈælɪ/ *n* (*pl* **-eys**) (*street*) viela *f*; (*for bowling*) pista *f*

alliance /əˈlaɪəns/ *n* aliança *f*

allied /ˈælaɪd/ *a* aliado

alligator /ˈælɪɡeɪtə(r)/ *n* jacaré *m*

allocat|e /ˈæləkeɪt/ *vt* (*share out*) distribuir; (*assign*) destinar. **~ion** /-ˈkeɪʃn/ *n* atribuição *f*

allot /əˈlɒt/ *vt* (*pt* **allotted**) atribuir. **~ment** *n* atribuição *f*; (*share*) distribuição *f*; (*land*) horta *f* alugada

allow /əˈlaʊ/ *vt* permitir; (*grant*) conceder, dar; (*reckon on*) contar com; (*agree*) admitir, reconhecer; **~ sb to** permitir a alguém (+ *inf*) ou que (+ *subj*); **~ for** levar em conta

allowance /əˈlaʊəns/ *n* (*for employees*) ajudas *fpl* de custo; (*monthly, for wife, child*) benefício *m*; (*tax*) desconto *m*; **make ~ for** (*person*) levar em consideração, ser indulgente para com; (*take into account*) atender a, levar em consideração

alloy /əˈlɔɪ/ *n* liga *f*

allude /əˈluːd/ *vi* **~ to** aludir a

allure /əˈlʊə(r)/ *vt* seduzir, atrair

allusion /əˈluːʒn/ *n* alusão *f*

ally[1] /ˈælaɪ/ *n* (*pl* **-lies**) aliado *m*

ally² /əˈlaɪ/ vt aliar; ~ oneself with/to aliar-se com/a

almighty /ɔːlˈmaɪtɪ/ a todo-poderoso; **I** grande; formidável

almond /ˈɑːmənd/ n amêndoa f; ~ **paste** maçapão m

almost /ˈɔːlməʊst/ adv quase

alone /əˈləʊn/ a & adv só; **leave** ~ (abstain from interfering with) deixar em paz; **let** ~ (without considering) sem or para não falar de

along /əˈlɒŋ/ prep ao longo de ● adv (onward) para diante; **all** ~ durante todo o tempo; ~ **with** com; **move** ~, **please** ande, por favor

alongside /əlɒŋˈsaɪd/ adv Naut atracado; **come** ~ acostar ● prep ao lado de

aloof /əˈluːf/ adv à parte ● a distante

aloud /əˈlaʊd/ adv em voz alta

alphabet /ˈælfəbet/ n alfabeto m. ~**ical** /-ˈbetɪkl/ a alfabético

alpine /ˈælpaɪn/ a alpino, alpestre

Alps /ælps/ npl **the** ~ os Alpes mpl

Al-Qaeda /ˌælkæˈiːdə/ pr n Al-Qaeda f, (P) Alcaida f

already /ɔːlˈredɪ/ adv já

also /ˈɔːlsəʊ/ adv também

altar /ˈɔːltə(r)/ n altar m

alter /ˈɔːltə(r)/ vt/i alterar(-se), modificar(-se). ~**ation** /-ˈreɪʃn/ n alteração f; (to garment) modificação f

alternate¹ /ɔːlˈtɜːnət/ a alternado

alternat|e² /ˈɔːltəneɪt/ vt/i alternar(-se); ~**ing current** Electr corrente f alterna

alternative /ɔːlˈtɜːnətɪv/ a alternativo ● n alternativa f. ~**ly** adv em alternativa; or ~**ly** ou então

although /ɔːlˈðəʊ/ conj embora, conquanto

altitude /ˈæltɪtjuːd/ n altitude f

altogether /ɔːltəˈɡeðə(r)/ adv (completely) completamente; (in total) ao todo; (on the whole) de modo geral

aluminium /æljʊˈmɪnɪəm/ Amer **aluminum** /əˈluːmɪnəm/ n alumínio m

always /ˈɔːlweɪz/ adv sempre

am /æm/ ▶ BE

a.m. /eɪˈem/ adv da manhã

amass /əˈmæs/ vt amontoar, juntar

amateur /ˈæmətə(r)/ n & a amador m. ~**ish** a pej de amador, (P) amadorístico

amaz|e /əˈmeɪz/ vt assombrar, espantar. ~**ed** a assombrado. ~**ement** n assombro m

Amazon /ˈæməzən/ n **the** ~ o Amazonas

ambassador /æmˈbæsədə(r)/ n embaixador m

amber /ˈæmbə(r)/ n âmbar m; (traffic light) luz f amarela

ambigu|ous /æmˈbɪɡjʊəs/ a ambíguo. ~**ity** /-ˈɡjuːətɪ/ n ambiguidade f

ambiti|on /æmˈbɪʃn/ n ambição f. ~**ous** a ambicioso

ambivalen|t /æmˈbɪvələnt/ a ambivalente

amble /ˈæmbl/ vi caminhar sem pressa

ambulance /ˈæmbjʊləns/ n ambulância f

ambush /ˈæmbʊʃ/ n emboscada f ● vt fazer uma emboscada para, (P) fazer uma emboscada a

amend /əˈmend/ vt emendar, corrigir. ~**ment** n (to rule) emenda f. ~**s** n **make** ~**s for** reparar, compensar

amenities /əˈmiːnətɪz/ npl (pleasant features) atrativos mpl; (facilities) confortos mpl, comodidades fpl

America /əˈmerɪkə/ n América f. ~**n** a & n americano m. ~**nism** /-nɪzəm/ n americanismo m

> **American dream** O conceito de "sonho americano" baseia-se na ideia de que qualquer pessoa que vive nos Estados Unidos pode alcançar o sucesso se trabalhar arduamente. Para os imigrantes e para as minorias, o conceito inclui também liberdade e igualdade de direitos.

amiable /ˈeɪmɪəbl/ a amável

amicable /ˈæmɪkəbl/ a amigável, amigo

amid(st) /əˈmɪd(st)/ prep entre, no meio de

amiss /əˈmɪs/ a & adv mal; **sth** ~ qq coisa que não está bem; **take sth** ~ levar qq coisa a mal

ammonia /əˈməʊnɪə/ n amoníaco m

ammunition /æmjʊˈnɪʃn/ n munições fpl

amnesia /æmˈniːzɪə/ n amnésia f

amnesty /ˈæmnəstɪ/ n anistia f, (P) amnistia f

among(st) /əˈmʌŋ(st)/ prep entre, no meio de; ~ **ourselves** (aqui) entre nós

amoral /eɪˈmɒrəl/ a amoral

amorous /ˈæmərəs/ a amoroso

a

amount /əˈmaʊnt/ n quantidade f; (*total*) montante m; (*sum of money*) quantia f ● vi ~ **to** elevar-se a; fig equivaler a

amp /æmp/ n 🄸 ampere m

amphibi|an /æmˈfɪbɪən/ n anfíbio m. **~ous** a anfíbio

ampl|e /ˈæmpl/ a (**-er, -est**) (*large, roomy*) amplo; (*enough*) suficiente, bastante

amplif|y /ˈæmplɪfaɪ/ vt ampliar, amplificar. **~ier** n amplificador m

amputat|e /ˈæmpjʊteɪt/ vt amputar. **~ion** /-ˈteɪʃn/ n amputação f

amus|e /əˈmjuːz/ vt divertir. **~ement** n divertimento m. **~ing** a divertido

an /ən, æn/ ▶ A

anaem|ia /əˈniːmɪə/ n anemia f. **~ic** a anêmico, (P) anémico

anaesthetic /ænɪsˈθetɪk/ n anestético m, (P) anestésico m; **give an ~ to** anestesiar

anaesthetist /əˈniːsθətɪst/ n anestesista mf

anagram /ˈænəgræm/ n anagrama m

analog(ue) /ˈænəlɒg/ a análogo

analogy /əˈnælədʒɪ/ n analogia f

analys|e /ˈænəlaɪz/ vt analisar. **~t** /-ɪst/ n analista mf

analysis /əˈnæləsɪs/ n (pl **-yses** /-əsiːz/) análise f

analytic(al) /ænəˈlɪtɪk(l)/ a analítico

anarch|y /ˈænəkɪ/ n anarquia f. **~ist** n anarquista mf

anatomy /əˈnætəmɪ/ n anatomia f. **~ical** /ænəˈtɒmɪkl/ a anatômico, (P) anatómico

ancest|or /ˈænsestə(r)/ n antepassado m

ancestry /ˈænsestrɪ/ n ascendência f, estirpe f

anchor /ˈæŋkə(r)/ n âncora f ● vt/i ancorar

ancient /ˈeɪnʃənt/ a antigo

and /ənd emphatic ænd/ conj e; **go ~ see** vá ver; **better ~ better/less ~ less** etc cada vez melhor/menos etc

anecdote /ˈænɪkdəʊt/ n anedota f

angel /ˈeɪndʒl/ n anjo m. **~ic** /ænˈdʒelɪk/ a angélico, angelical

anger /ˈæŋgə(r)/ n cólera f, zanga f ● vt irritar

angle[1] /ˈæŋgl/ n ângulo m

angle[2] /ˈæŋgl/ vi (*fish*) pescar (à linha); **~ for** fig <*compliments, information*> andar

à procura de. **~r** /-ə(r)/ n pescador m

Anglo-Saxon /ˈæŋgləʊˈsæksn/ a & n anglo-saxão m

angr|y /ˈæŋgrɪ/ a (**-ier, -iest**) zangado; **get ~y** zangar-se (**with** com)

anguish /ˈæŋgwɪʃ/ n angústia f

angular /ˈæŋgjʊlə(r)/ a angular; <*features*> anguloso

animal /ˈænɪml/ a & n animal m

animate[1] /ˈænɪmət/ a animado

animat|e[2] /ˈænɪmeɪt/ vt animar; **~ed cartoon** filme m de bonecos animados or (P) de desenhos animados. **~ion** /-ˈmeɪʃn/ n animação f

animosity /ænɪˈmɒsətɪ/ n animosidade f

aniseed /ˈænɪsiːd/ n semente f de anis

ankle /ˈæŋkl/ n tornozelo m; **~ sock** mela f soquete

annex /əˈneks/ vt anexar

annexe /ˈæneks/ n anexo m

annihilate /əˈnaɪəleɪt/ vt aniquilar

anniversary /ænɪˈvɜːsərɪ/ n aniversário m

announce /əˈnaʊns/ vt anunciar. **~ment** n anúncio m. **~r** /-ə(r)/ n Radio, TV locutor m

annoy /əˈnɔɪ/ vt irritar, aborrecer. **~ance** n aborrecimento m. **~ed** a aborrecido (**with** com); **get ~ed** aborrecer-se. **~ing** a irritante

annual /ˈænjʊəl/ a anual ● n Bot planta f anual; (*book*) anuário m

annul /əˈnʌl/ vt (pt **annulled**) anular

anomal|y /əˈnɒməlɪ/ n anomalia f

anonym|ous /əˈnɒnɪməs/ a anônimo, (P) anónimo

anorak /ˈænəræk/ n anoraque m, anorak m

another /əˈnʌðə(r)/ a & pron (um) outro; **~ ten minutes** mais dez minutos; **to one ~** um ao outro, uns aos outros

answer /ˈɑːnsə(r)/ n resposta f; (*solution*) solução f ● vt responder a; <*prayer*> atender a ● vi responder; **~ the door** atender à porta; **~ back** retrucar, (P) responder torto; **~ for** responder por. **~ing machine** n secretária f eletrônica, (P) atendedor m de chamadas

ant /ænt/ n formiga f

antagonis|m /ænˈtægənɪzəm/ n antagonismo m. **~tic** /-ˈnɪstɪk/ a antagónico, (P) antagónico, hostil

antagonize /ænˈtægənaɪz/ vt antagonizar, hostilizar

Antarctic /æn'tɑːktɪk/ n Antártico, (P) Antárctico m ● a antártico, (P) antárctico

antelope /'æntɪləʊp/ n antílope m

antenatal /ˌæntɪ'neɪtl/ a pré-natal

antenna /æn'tenə/ n (pl -ae /-iː/) antena f

anthem /'ænθəm/ n cântico m; national ~ hino m nacional

anthology /æn'θɒlədʒɪ/ n antologia f

anthropolog|y /ˌænθrə'pɒlədʒɪ/ n antropologia f. ~**ist** n antropólogo m

anti- /'ænti/ pref anti-

antibiotic /ˌæntɪbaɪ'ɒtɪk/ n antibiótico m

antibody /'æntɪbɒdɪ/ n anticorpo m

anticipat|e /æn'tɪsɪpeɪt/ vt (foresee, expect) prever; (forestall) antecipar-se a. ~**ion** /-'peɪʃn/ n antecipação f; (expectation) expectativa f; in ~**ion of** na previsão or antecipação de

anticlimax /ˌæntɪ'klaɪmæks/ n anticlímax m; (let-down) decepção f; it was an ~ não correspondeu à expectativa

anticlockwise /ˌæntɪ'klɒkwaɪz/ adv & a no sentido contrário ao dos ponteiros do relógio

antics /'æntɪks/ npl (of clown) palhaçadas fpl; (behaviour) comportamento m bizarro

antidote /'æntɪdəʊt/ n antídoto m

antifreeze /'æntɪfriːz/ n anticongelante m

antipathy /æn'tɪpəθɪ/ n antipatia f

antiquated /'æntɪkweɪtɪd/ a antiquado

antique /æn'tiːk/ a antigo ● n antiguidade f; ~ **dealer** antiquário m; ~ **shop** loja f de antiguidades, (P) antiquário m

antiquity /æn'tɪkwətɪ/ n antiguidade f

antiseptic /ˌæntɪ'septɪk/ a & n antisséptico m

antisocial /ˌæntɪ'səʊʃl/ a antissocial; (unsociable) insociável

antlers /'æntləz/ npl chifres mpl, esgalhos mpl

antonym /'æntənɪm/ n antônimo m, (P) antónimo m

anus /'eɪnəs/ n ânus m

anvil /'ænvɪl/ n bigorna f

anxiety /æŋ'zaɪətɪ/ n ansiedade f; (eagerness) ânsia f

anxious /'æŋkʃəs/ a (worried, eager) ansioso (to de, por)

any /'enɪ/ a & pron qualquer, quaisquer; (in neg and interr sentences) algum, alguns; (in neg sentences) nenhum, nenhuns; (every) todo; at ~ **moment** a qualquer momento; at ~ **rate** de qualquer modo, em todo o caso; in ~ **case** em todo o caso; have you ~ **money/friends**? você tem (algum) dinheiro/(alguns) amigos?; I don't have ~ **time** não tenho nenhum tempo or tempo nenhum or tempo algum; has she ~? ela tem algum?; she doesn't have ~ ela não tem nenhum ● adv (at all) de modo algum or nenhum; (a little) um pouco; ~ **the less/the worse** etc menos/pior etc

anybody /'enɪbɒdɪ/ pron qualquer pessoa; (somebody) alguém; (after negative) ninguém; he didn't see ~ ele não viu ninguém

anyhow /'enɪhaʊ/ adv (no matter how) de qualquer modo; (badly) de qualquer maneira, ao acaso; (in any case) em todo o caso; you can try, ~ em todo o caso, você pode tentar

anyone /'enɪwʌn/ pron = ANYBODY

anything /'enɪθɪŋ/ pron (something) alguma coisa; (no matter what) qualquer coisa; (after negative) nada; ~ **you do** tudo o que você fizer; he didn't say ~ não disse nada; it is ~ **but cheap** é tudo menos barato

anyway /'enɪweɪ/ adv de qualquer modo; (in any case) em todo o caso

anywhere /'enɪweə(r)/ adv (somewhere) em qualquer parte; (after negative) em parte alguma/nenhuma; ~ **else** em qualquer outro lado; ~ **you go** onde quer que você vá; he doesn't go ~ ele não vai a lado nenhum

apart /ə'pɑːt/ adv à parte; (separated) separado; (into pieces) aos bocados; ~ **from** à parte, além de; ten metres ~ a dez metros de distância entre si; come ~ desfazer-se; keep ~ manter separado; take ~ desmontar

apartment /ə'pɑːtmənt/ n Amer apartamento m; ~**s** aposentos mpl

apath|y /'æpəθɪ/ n apatia f

ape /eɪp/ n macaco m ● vt macaquear

aperitif /ə'perətɪf/ n aperitivo m

apex /'eɪpeks/ n ápice m, cume m

apologetic /əˌpɒlə'dʒetɪk/ a ‹tone etc› apologético, de desculpas; be ~ desculpar-se

apologize /ə'pɒlədʒaɪz/ vi desculpar-se (for de, por to junto de, perante) pedir desculpa (for por)

a

apology /ə'pɒlədʒɪ/ n desculpa f; (*defence of belief*) apologia f

apostle /ə'pɒsl/ n apóstolo m

apostrophe /ə'pɒstrəfɪ/ n apóstrofe f

appal /ə'pɔːl/ vt (pt **-led**) estarrecer. **~ling** a estarrecedor

apparatus /æpə'reɪtəs/ n aparelho m

apparent /ə'pærənt/ a aparente. **~ly** adv aparentemente

apparition /æpə'rɪʃn/ n aparição f

appeal /ə'piːl/ vi Jur apelar (**to** para); (*attract*) atrair (**to** a); (*for funds*) angariar ● n apelo m; (*attractiveness*) atrativo m; (*for funds*) angariação f; **~ to sb for sth** pedir algo a alguém. **~ing** a (*attractive*) atraente

appear /ə'pɪə(r)/ vi aparecer; (*seem*) parecer; (*in court, theatre*) apresentar-se. **~ance** n aparição f; (*aspect*) aparência f; (*in court*) comparecimento m, (P) comparência f

appease /ə'piːz/ vt apaziguar

appendicitis /əpendɪ'saɪtɪs/ n apendicite f

appendix /ə'pendɪks/ n (pl **-ices** /-siːz/) (*of book*) apêndice m; (pl **-ixes** /-ksɪz/) Anat apêndice m

appetite /'æpɪtaɪt/ n apetite m

appetizer /'æpɪtaɪzə(r)/ n (*snack*) tira-gosto m, (P) aperitivo m; (*drink*) aperitivo m

appetizing /'æpɪtaɪzɪŋ/ a apetitoso

applau|d /ə'plɔːd/ vt/i aplaudir. **~se** n aplauso(s) m(pl)

apple /'æpl/ n maçã f; **~ tree** macieira f

appliance /ə'plaɪəns/ n aparelho m, instrumento m, utensílio m; **household ~s** utensílios mpl domésticos

applicable /'æplɪkəbl/ a aplicável

applicant /'æplɪkənt/ n candidato m (**for** a)

application /æplɪ'keɪʃn/ n aplicação f; (*request*) pedido m; (*form*) formulário m; (*for job*) candidatura f

apply /ə'plaɪ/ vt aplicar ● vi **~y to** (*refer*) aplicar-se a; (*ask*) dirigir-se a; **~y for** ‹*job, grant*› candidatar-se a; **~y o.s. to** aplicar-se a. **~ied** a aplicado

appoint /ə'pɔɪnt/ vt (*to post*) nomear; ‹*time, date*› marcar. **well-~ed** a bem equipado, bem provido. **~ment** n nomeação f; (*meeting*) entrevista f; (*with friends*) encontro m; (*with doctor etc*) consulta f, (P) marcação f; (*job*) posto m

apprais|e /ə'preɪz/ vt avaliar. **~al** n avaliação f

appreciable /ə'priːʃəbl/ a apreciável

appreciat|e /ə'priːʃɪeɪt/ vt (*value*) apreciar; (*understand*) compreender; (*be grateful for*) estar/ficar grato por ● vi encarecer. **~ion** /-'eɪʃn/ n apreciação f; (*rise in value*) encarecimento m; (*gratitude*) reconhecimento m. **~ive** /ə'priːʃɪətɪv/ a apreciador; (*grateful*) reconhecido

apprehen|d /æprɪ'hend/ vt (*seize, understand*) apreender; (*dread*) recear. **~sion** n apreensão f

apprehensive /æprɪ'hensɪv/ a apreensivo

apprentice /ə'prentɪs/ n aprendiz, -a mf ● vt pôr como aprendiz (**to** de). **~ship** n aprendizagem f

approach /ə'prəʊtʃ/ vt aproximar; (*with request or offer*) abordar ● vi aproximar-se ● n aproximação f; **~ to** ‹*problem*› abordagem f de; ‹*place*› acesso m a; ‹*person*› diligência junto de. **~able** a acessível

appropriate¹ /ə'prəʊprɪət/ a apropriado, próprio

appropriate² /ə'prəʊprɪeɪt/ vt apropriar-se de

approval /ə'pruːvl/ n aprovação f; **on ~** Comm sob condição, à aprovação

approv|e /ə'pruːv/ vt/i aprovar; **~e of** aprovar

approximate¹ /ə'prɒksɪmət/ a aproximado. **~ly** adv aproximadamente

approximat|e² /ə'prɒksɪmeɪt/ vt/i aproximar(-se) de. **~ion** /-'meɪʃn/ n aproximação f

apricot /'eɪprɪkɒt/ n damasco m

April /'eɪprəl/ n Abril m; **~ Fool's Day** o primeiro de Abril, o dia das mentiras; **make an ~ fool of** pregar uma mentira em, (P) pregar uma mentira a

apron /'eɪprən/ n avental m

apt /æpt/ a apto; ‹*pupil*› dotado; **be ~ to** ser propenso a

aptitude /'æptɪtjuːd/ n aptidão f, (P) aptitude f

aqualung /'ækwəlʌŋ/ n escafandro autônomo, (P) autónomo m

aquarium /ə'kweərɪəm/ n (pl **-ums**) aquário m

Aquarius /ə'kweərɪəs/ n Astr Aquário m

aquatic /ə'kwætɪk/ a aquático; ‹*sport*› náutico, aquático

Arab /'ærəb/ a & n árabe mf. **~ic** a & n Lang árabe m, arábico m; **~ic numerals** algarismos mpl árabes or arábicos

Arabian /ə'reɪbɪən/ a árabe

arable /'ærəbl/ a arável

arbitrary /'ɑːbɪtrərɪ/ a arbitrário

arbitrat|e /'ɑːbɪtreɪt/ vi arbitrar. ~**ion**
/-'treɪʃn/ n arbitragem f

arc /ɑːk/ n arco m; ~ **lamp** lâmpada f de
arco; ~ **welding** soldadura f a arco

arcade /ɑː'keɪd/ n (shop) arcada f;
amusement ~ fliperama m

arch /ɑːtʃ/ n arco m; (vault) abóbada f
● vt/i arquear(-se)

arch- /ɑːtʃ/ pref arqui-

archaeolog|y /ɑːkɪ'ɒlədʒɪ/ n
arqueologia f. ~**ical** /-ə'lɒdʒɪkl/ a
arqueológico. ~**ist** n arqueólogo m

archaic /ɑː'keɪɪk/ a arcaico

archbishop /ɑːtʃ'bɪʃəp/ n arcebispo m

archer /'ɑːtʃə(r)/ n arqueiro m. ~**y** n tiro
m ao arco

archetype /'ɑːkɪtaɪp/ n arquétipo m

architect /'ɑːkɪtekt/ n arquiteto m

architectur|e /'ɑːkɪtektʃə(r)/
n arquitetura f. ~**al** /-'tektʃərəl/ a
arquitetônico, (P) arquitetónico

archiv|es /'ɑːkaɪvz/ npl arquivo m

archway /'ɑːtʃweɪ/ n arcada f

Arctic /'ɑːktɪk/ n ártico m ● a ártico;
~ **weather** tempo m glacial

ardent /'ɑːdnt/ a ardente

ardour /'ɑːdə(r)/ n ardor m

arduous /'ɑːdjʊəs/ a árduo

are /ɑː(r)/ emphatic ɑː(r)/ ▶ BE

area /'eərɪə/ n área f

arena /ə'riːnə/ n arena f

Argentin|a /ɑːdʒən'tiːnə/ n Argentina
f. ~**ian** /-'tɪnɪən/ a & n argentino m

argu|e /'ɑːgjuː/ vi discutir; (reason)
argumentar, arguir ● vt (debate) discutir;
~**e that** alegar que

argument /'ɑːgjʊmənt/ n (dispute)
disputa f; (reasoning) argumento m.
~**ative** /-'mentətɪv/ a que gosta de
discutir, argumentativo

arid /'ærɪd/ a árido

Aries /'eəriːz/ n Astr áries m, Carneiro m

arise /ə'raɪz/ vi (pt arose, pp arisen)
surgir; ~ **from** resultar de

aristocracy /ærɪ'stɒkrəsɪ/ n
aristocracia f

aristocrat /'ærɪstəkræt/ n aristocrata
mf. ~**ic** /-'krætɪk/ a aristocrático

arithmetic /ə'rɪθmətɪk/ n aritmética f

arm[1] /ɑːm/ n braço m; ~ **in** ~ de braço
dado

arm[2] /ɑːm/ vt armar; ~**ed robbery**
assalto à mão armada m ● n Mil arma f

armament /'ɑːməmənt/ n
armamento m

armchair /'ɑːmtʃeə(r)/ n cadeira f de
braços, poltrona f

armour /'ɑːmə(r)/ n armadura f; (on
tanks etc) blindagem f. ~**ed** a blindado

armpit /'ɑːmpɪt/ n axila f, sovaco m

arms /ɑːmz/ npl armas fpl; **coat of** ~
brasão m

army /'ɑːmɪ/ n exército m

aroma /ə'rəʊmə/ n aroma m. ~**tic**
/ærə'mætɪk/ a aromático

arose /ə'rəʊz/ ▶ ARISE

around /ə'raʊnd/ adv em redor, em
volta; (here and there) por aí ● prep em
redor de, em torno de, em volta de;
(approximately) aproximadamente;
~ **here** por aqui

arouse /ə'raʊz/ vt despertar; (excite)
excitar

arrange /ə'reɪndʒ/ vt arranjar;
‹time, date› combinar; ~ **to do sth**
combinar fazer algo. ~**ment** n arranjo
m; (agreement) acordo m; **make** ~**ments**
(for) (plans) tomar disposições (para);
(preparations) fazer preparativos (para)

arrears /ə'rɪəz/ npl dívidas fpl em atraso,
atrasos mpl; **in** ~ em atraso

arrest /ə'rest/ vt (by law) deter, prender;
‹process, movement› deter ● n captura f;
under ~ sob prisão

arrival /ə'raɪvl/ n chegada f; **new** ~
recém-chegado m

arrive /ə'raɪv/ vi chegar

arrogan|t /'ærəgənt/ a arrogante. ~**ce**
n arrogância f

arrow /'ærəʊ/ n flecha f, seta f

arson /'ɑːsn/ n fogo m posto. ~**ist** n
incendiário m

art[1] /ɑːt/ n arte f; **the** ~**s** Univ letras fpl;
fine ~**s** belas-artes fpl; ~ **gallery** museu
m (de arte); (private) galeria f de arte

artery /'ɑːtərɪ/ n artéria f

arthritis /ɑː'θraɪtɪs/ n artrite f

artichoke /'ɑːtɪtʃəʊk/ n alcachofra f;
Jerusalem ~ topinambo m

article /'ɑːtɪkl/ n artigo m

articulate[1] /ɑː'tɪkjʊlət/ a que se
exprime com clareza; ‹speech› bem
articulado

articulat|e[2] /ɑː'tɪkjʊleɪt/ vt/i articular;
~**ed lorry** camião m articulado

artificial /ɑːtɪ'fɪʃl/ a artificial

a

artillery /ɑːˈtɪləɪ/ n artilharia f

artisan /ɑːˈtɪˈzæn/ n artífice mf, artesão m, artesã f

artist /ˈɑːtɪst/ n artista mf. **~ic** /-ˈtɪstɪk/ a artístico

artiste /ɑːˈtiːst/ n artista mf

as /əz emphatic æz/ adv & conj como; (while) enquanto; (when) quando; ~ **a gift** de presente; ~ **tall** ~ tão alto quanto, (P) tão alto como; ~ **if** como se; ~ **much** tanto, tantos; ~ **many** quanto, quantos; ~ **soon** logo que; ~ **well** (also) também; ~ **well** ~ (in addition to) assim como; ~ **for**, ~ **to** quanto a; ~ **from** a partir de ● pron que; **I ate the same** ~ **him** comi o mesmo que ele

asbestos /æzˈbestəs/ n asbesto m, amianto m

ASBO, **Asbo** /ˈæzbəʊ/ abbr (pl ASBOs, Asbos) Ordem f de Comportamento Antissocial

ascend /əˈsend/ vt/i subir; ~ **the throne** ascender ou subir ao trono

ascent /əˈsent/ n ascensão f; (slope) subida f, rampa f

ascertain /æsəˈteɪn/ vt certificar-se de; ~ **that** certificar-se de que

ash¹ /æʃ/ n ~(-tree) freixo m

ash² /æʃ/ n cinza f; **A~ Wednesday** Quarta-feira f de Cinzas

ashamed /əˈʃeɪmd/ a **be** ~ ter vergonha, ficar envergonhado (of de, por)

ashore /əˈʃɔː(r)/ adv em terra; **go** ~ desembarcar

ashtray /ˈæʃtreɪ/ n cinzeiro m

Asia /ˈeɪʃə/ n Ásia f. **~n** a & n asiático m

aside /əˈsaɪd/ adv de lado, de parte ● n Theat aparte m; ~ **from** Amer à parte

ask /ɑːsk/ vt/i pedir; ‹a question› perguntar; (invite) convidar; ~ **sb sth** pedir algo a alguém; ~ **about** informar-se de; ~ **after sb** pedir notícias de alguém, perguntar por alguém; ~ **for** pedir; ~ **sb in** mandar entrar alguém; ~ **sb to do sth** pedir a alguém para fazer algo

askew /əˈskjuː/ adv & a de través, de esguelha

asleep /əˈsliːp/ adv & a adormecido; (numb) dormente; **fall** ~ adormecer

asparagus /əˈspærəgəs/ n (plant) espargo m, (P) espargo m; Culin aspargos mpl, (P) espargo m

aspect /ˈæspekt/ n aspecto m; (direction) exposição f

asphalt /ˈæsfælt/ n asfalto m ● vt asfaltar

asphyxiat|e /əsˈfɪksɪeɪt/ vt/i asfixiar. **~ion** /-ˈeɪʃn/ n asfixia f

aspir|e /əsˈpaɪə(r)/ vi ~**e to** aspirar a. **~ation** /əspəˈreɪʃn/ n aspiração f

aspirin /ˈæsprɪn/ n aspirina f

ass /æs/ n burro m; **make an** ~ **of o.s.** fazer papel de palhaço, (P) fazer figura de parvo

assail /əˈseɪl/ vt assaltar, agredir. **~ant** n assaltante mf, agressor m

assassin /əˈsæsɪn/ n assassino m

assassinat|e /əˈsæsɪneɪt/ vt assassinar. **~ion** /-ˈeɪʃn/ n assassinato m

assault /əˈsɔːlt/ n assalto m ● vt assaltar, atacar

assemble /əˈsembl/ vt ‹people› reunir; (fit together) montar ● vi reunir-se

assembly /əˈsemblɪ/ n assembleia f; ~ **line** linha f de montagem

assent /əˈsent/ n assentimento m ● vi ~ **to** consentir em

assert /əˈsɜːt/ vt afirmar; ‹one's rights› reivindicar; ~ **o.s.** impor-se. **~ion** /-ʃn/ n asserção f. **~ive** a dogmático, peremptório

assess /əˈses/ vt avaliar; ‹payment› estabelecer o montante de. **~ment** n avaliação f

asset /ˈæset/ n (advantage) vantagem f; **~s** Comm ativo m; (possessions) bens mpl

assign /əˈsaɪn/ vt atribuir, destinar; Jur transmitir; ~ **sb to** designar alguém para

assignment /əˈsaɪnmənt/ n tarefa f, missão f; Jur transmissão f

assimilat|e /əˈsɪmɪleɪt/ vt/i assimilar(-se)

assist /əˈsɪst/ vt/i ajudar. **~ance** n ajuda f, assistência f

assistant /əˈsɪstənt/ n (helper) assistente mf, auxiliar mf; (in shop) ajudante mf, empregado m ● a adjunto

associat|e¹ /əˈsəʊʃɪeɪt/ vt associar ● vi ~**e with** conviver com. **~ion** /-ˈeɪʃn/ n associação f

associate² /əˈsəʊʃɪət/ a & n associado m

assort|ed /əˈsɔːtɪd/ a variados; ‹foods› sortidos. **~ment** n sortimento m, (P) sortido m

assume /əˈsjuːm/ vt assumir; (presume) supor, presumir

assumption /əˈsʌmpʃn/ n suposição f

assurance /əˈʃʊərəns/ n certeza f, garantia f; (insurance) seguro m; (self-

confidence) segurança *f*, confiança *f*

assure /ə'ʃʊə(r)/ *vt* assegurar. **~d** *a* certo, garantido; **rest ~d that** ficar certo que

asterisk /'æstərɪsk/ *n* asterisco *m*

asthma /'æsmə/ *n* asma *f*

astonish /ə'stɒnɪʃ/ *vt* espantar. **~ment** *n* espanto *m*

astound /ə'staʊnd/ *vt* assombrar

astray /ə'streɪ/ *adv* & *a* **go ~** perder-se, extraviar-se; **lead ~** desencaminhar

astride /ə'straɪd/ *adv* & *prep* escarranchado (em)

astrolog|y /ə'strɒlədʒɪ/ *n* astrologia *f*. **~er** *n* astrólogo *m*

astronaut /'æstrənɔːt/ *n* astronauta *mf*

astronom|y /ə'strɒnəmɪ/ *n* astronomia *f*. **~er** *n* astrônomo *m*, (P) astrónomo *m*. **~ical** /æstrə'nɒmɪkl/ *a* astronômico, (P) astronómico

astute /ə'stjuːt/ *a* astuto, astucioso

asylum /ə'saɪləm/ *n* asilo *m*

---

at /ət *emphatic* æt/ ● *prep*

·····➤ (*position*) em; (*at home*) em casa; (*at school*) na escola; (*at sea*) no mar; (*at the door*) à porta

❗ The preposition *em* often contracts with definite and indefinite articles *o*, *a* and *um*, *uma* to form *no*, *na* and *num*, *numa*

·····➤ (*at someone's house*) na casa de; **~ Peter's** na casa do Pedro; (*at someone's business*) em; **~ the doctor's** no médico

·····➤ (*time*) **~ two o'clock** às duas horas; **~ three years of age** aos três anos ; **~ night** à noite; **~ Christmas/ Easter** no Natal/na Páscoa

·····➤ (*price*) a; **~ £2.20 each** a duas libras e vinte cada

·····➤ (*speed*) **~ 50 mph** a cinquenta milhas por hora

·····➤ (*in email addresses*=@) arroba

·····➤ (*in phrases*) **~ once** imediatamente; **~ the same time** ao mesmo tempo; **~ times** às vezes; **be good/bad ~ sth** ser bom/ruim em aco; **two ~ a time** dois de cada vez; **be angry/surprised ~ sb** estar brabo/ surpreendido com alguém

---

ate /et/ ▶ **EAT**

atheis|t /'eɪθɪɪst/ *n* ateu *m*. **~m** /-zəm/ *n* ateísmo *m*

athlet|e /'æθliːt/ *n* atleta *mf*. **~ic** /-'letɪk/ *a* atlético. **~ics** /-'letɪks/ *n(pl)* atletismo *m*

Atlantic /ət'læntɪk/ *a* atlântico ● *n* **~ (Ocean)** Atlântico *m*

atlas /'ætləs/ *n* atlas *m*

atmospher|e /'ætməsfɪə(r)/ *n* atmosfera *f*

atom /'ætəm/ *n* átomo *m*. **~ic** /ə'tɒmɪk/ *a* atômico, (P) atómico; **~(ic) bomb** bomba *f* atômica, (P) atómica

atone /ə'təʊn/ *vi* **~ for** expiar

atrocious /ə'trəʊʃəs/ *a* atroz

atrocity /ə'trɒsətɪ/ *n* atrocidade *f*

attach /ə'tætʃ/ *vt/i* (*affix*) ligar(-se), prender(-se); (*join*) juntar(-se). **~ed** *a* <document> junto, anexo; be **~ed** to (*like*) estar apegado a. **~ment** *n* ligação *f*; (*affection*) apego *m*; (*accessory*) acessório *m*; (*in email*) anexo *m*

attack /ə'tæk/ *n* ataque *m* ● *vt/i* atacar. **~er** *n* atacante *mf*

attain /ə'teɪn/ *vt* atingir. **~able** *a* atingível

attempt /ə'tempt/ *vt* tentar ● *n* tentativa *f*

attend /ə'tend/ *vt/i* atender (**to** a); (*escort*) acompanhar; (*look after*) tratar; <meeting> comparecer a; <school> frequentar. **~ance** *n* comparecimento *m*; (*times present*) frequência *f*; (*people*) assistência *f*

attendant /ə'tendənt/ *a* concomitante, que acompanha ● *n* empregado *m*; (*servant*) servidor *m*

attention /ə'tenʃn/ *n* atenção *f*; **~!** Mil sentido! **pay ~** prestar atenção (**to** a)

attentive /ə'tentɪv/ *a* atento; (*considerate*) atencioso

attic /'ætɪk/ *n* sótão *m*, água-furtada *f*

attitude /'ætɪtjuːd/ *n* atitude *f*

attorney /ə'tɜːnɪ/ *n* (*pl* **-eys**) procurador *m*; *Amer* advogado *m*

attract /ə'trækt/ *vt* atrair. **~ion** /-ʃn/ *n* atração *f*; (*charm*) atrativo *m*

attractive /ə'træktɪv/ *a* atraente

attribute[1] /ə'trɪbjuːt/ *vt* **~ to** atribuir a

attribute[2] /'ætrɪbjuːt/ *n* atributo *m*

aubergine /'əʊbəʒiːn/ *n* berinjela *f*

auburn /'ɔːbən/ *a* cor de acaju, castanho-avermelhado

auction /'ɔːkʃn/ *n* leilão *m* ● *vt* leiloar. **~eer** /-ə'nɪə(r)/ *n* leiloeiro *m*, (P) pregoeiro *m*

audaci|ous /ɔːˈdeɪʃəs/ a audacioso, audaz. **~ty** /-ˈæsəti/ n audácia f
audible /ˈɔːdəbl/ a audível
audience /ˈɔːdɪəns/ n auditório m; Theat, Radio (interview) audiência f
audiovisual /ˌɔːdɪəʊˈvɪʒʊəl/ a audiovisual
audit /ˈɔːdɪt/ n auditoria f ● vt fazer uma auditoria
audition /ɔːˈdɪʃn/ n audição f ● vt dar/ fazer uma audição
auditor /ˈɔːdɪtə(r)/ n perito-contador m, (P) perito-contabilista m
auditorium /ɔːdɪˈtɔːrɪəm/ n auditório m
augment /ɔːgˈment/ vt/i aumentar(-se)
August /ˈɔːgəst/ n agosto m
aunt /ɑːnt/ n tia f
au pair /əʊˈpeə(r)/ n au pair f
aura /ˈɔːrə/ n aura f, emanação f
auspicious /ɔːˈspɪʃəs/ a auspicioso
auster|e /ɔːˈstɪə(r)/ a austero. **~ity** /-erəti/ n austeridade f
Australia /ɒˈstreɪlɪə/ n Austrália f. **~n** a & n australiano m
Austria /ˈɒstrɪə/ n Áustria f. **~n** a & n austríaco m
authentic /ɔːˈθentɪk/ a autêntico. **~ity** /-ənˈtɪsəti/ n autenticidade f
authenticate /ɔːˈθentɪkeɪt/ vt autenticar
author /ˈɔːθə(r)/ n autor m, autora f
authoritarian /ɔːθɒrɪˈteərɪən/ a autoritário
authorit|y /ɔːˈθɒrəti/ n autoridade f; (permission) autorização f. **~ative** /-ɪtətɪv/ a (trusted) autorizado; (manner) autoritário
authoriz|e /ˈɔːθəraɪz/ vt autorizar. **~ation** /-ˈzeɪʃn/ n autorização f
autistic /ɔːˈtɪstɪk/ a autista, autístico
autobiography /ɔːtəˈbaɪɒɡrəfɪ/ n autobiografia f
autograph /ˈɔːtəɡrɑːf/ n autógrafo m ● vt autografar
automat|e /ˈɔːtəmeɪt/ vt automatizar. **~ion** /ɔːtəˈmeɪʃn/ n automação f
automatic /ɔːtəˈmætɪk/ a automático ● n (car) automático m. **~ally** /-klɪ/ adv automaticamente
automobile /ˈɔːtəməbiːl/ n Amer automóvel m
autonom|y /ɔːˈtɒnəmɪ/ n autonomia f. **~ous** a autônomo, (P) autónomo
autopsy /ˈɔːtɒpsɪ/ n autópsia f

autumn /ˈɔːtəm/ n outono m. **~al** /-ˈtʌmnəl/ a outonal
auxiliary /ɔːgˈzɪlɪərɪ/ a & n auxiliar mf; **~ verb** verbo m auxiliar
avail /əˈveɪl/ vt **~ o.s. of** servir-se de ● vi (be of use) valer ● n **of no ~** inútil; **to no ~** sem resultado, em vão
availab|le /əˈveɪləbl/ a disponível. **~ility** /-ˈbɪləti/ n disponibilidade f
avalanche /ˈævəlɑːnʃ/ n avalanche f
avaric|e /ˈævərɪs/ n avareza f
avatar /ˈævətɑː(r)/ n avatar m
avenge /əˈvendʒ/ vt vingar
avenue /ˈævənjuː/ n avenida f; fig (line of approach) via f
average /ˈævərɪdʒ/ n média f ● a médio ● vt tirar a média de; (produce, do) fazer em média ● vi **~ out at** dar de média, dar uma média de; **on ~** em média
avers|e /əˈvɜːs/ a **be ~e to** ser avesso a. **~ion** /-ʃn/ n aversão f, repugnância f
avert /əˈvɜːt/ vt (turn away) desviar; (ward off) evitar
aviary /ˈeɪvɪərɪ/ n aviário m
aviation /eɪvɪˈeɪʃn/ n aviação f
avid /ˈævɪd/ a ávido
avocado /ævəˈkɑːdəʊ/ n (pl -s) abacate m
avoid /əˈvɔɪd/ vt evitar. **~able** a que se pode evitar, evitável. **~ance** n evitação f
await /əˈweɪt/ vt aguardar
awake /əˈweɪk/ vt/i (pt awoke, pp awoken) acordar ● a **be ~** estar acordado
awaken /əˈweɪkən/ vt/i despertar. **~ing** n despertar m
award /əˈwɔːd/ vt atribuir, conferir; Jur adjudicar ● n recompensa f, prêmio m, (P) prémio m; <scholarship> bolsa f
aware /əˈweə(r)/ a ciente, cônscio; **be ~ of** estar consciente de or ter consciência de; **become ~ of** tomar consciência de; **make sb ~ of** sensibilizar alguém para. **~ness** n consciência f
away /əˈweɪ/ adv (at a distance) longe; (to a distance) para longe; (absent) fora; (persistently) sem parar; (entirely) completamente; **eight miles ~** a oito milhas (de distância); **four days ~** daí a quatro dias ● a & n **~ (match)** jogo m fora de casa
awe /ɔː/ n assombro m, admiração f reverente, terror m respeitoso. **~some** a assombroso

awful /'ɔːfl/ a terrível. **~ly** adv muito, terrivelmente

awkward /'ɔːkwəd/ a difícil; (clumsy, difficult to use) desajeitado, maljeitoso; (inconvenient) inconveniente; (embarrassing) embaraçoso; (embarrassed) embaraçado; **an ~ customer** ⚏ um freguês perigoso or intratável

awning /'ɔːnɪŋ/ n toldo m

awoke, awoken /ə'wəʊk, ə'wəʊkən/ ▶ AWAKE

awry /ə'raɪ/ adv torto; **go ~** dar errado; **be ~** estar torto

axe /æks/ n machado m ● vt (pres p **axing**) (reduce) cortar; (dismiss) despedir

axis /'æksɪs/ n (pl **axes** /-iːz/) eixo m

axle /'æksl/ n eixo (de roda) m

Azores /ə'zɔːz/ n Açores mpl

....

Bb

....

BA abbr (= Bachelor of Arts) ▶ BACHELOR

baboon /bə'buːn/ n babuíno m

baby /'beɪbɪ/ n bebê m, (P) bebé m; **~ carriage** Amer carrinho m de bebê, (P) bebé. **~sit** vi tomar conta de crianças; **~sitter** n baby-sitter mf, babá f

babyish /'beɪbɪʃ/ a infantil

bachelor /'bætʃələ(r)/ n solteiro m; **B~ of Arts/Science** Bacharel m em Letras/Ciências

back /bæk/ n (of person, hand, chair) costas fpl; (of animal) dorso m; (of car, train) parte f traseira; (of house, room) fundo m; (of coin) reverso m; (of page) verso m; Football beque m; zagueiro m, (P) defesa m; **at the ~ of beyond** em casa do diabo, no fim do mundo ● a traseiro, posterior; ‹taxes› em atraso; **~ number** número m atrasado ● adv atrás, para trás; (returned) de volta ● vt (support) apoiar; ‹horse› apostar em; ‹car› (fazer) recuar ● vi recuar; **~ down** desistir (**from** de); **~ out** (of an undertaking etc) fugir (ao combinado etc); **~ up** Auto fazer marcha à ré, (P) atrás; Comput tirar um back-up de. **~up** n apoio m; Comput back-up m; Amer (traffic jam) engarrafamento m ● a de reserva; Comput backup

backache /'bækeɪk/ n dor f nas costas

backbiting /'bækbaɪtɪŋ/ n maledicência f

backbone /'bækbəʊn/ n espinha f dorsal

backdate /bæk'deɪt/ vt antedatar

backer /'bækə(r)/ n (of horse) apostador m; (of cause) partidário m, apoiante mf; Comm patrocinador m, financiador m

backfire /bæk'faɪə(r)/ vi Auto dar explosões no tubo de escape; fig sair o tiro pela culatra

background /'bækgraʊnd/ n (of picture) fundo m, segundo-plano m; (context) contexto m; (environment) meio m; (experience) formação f

backhand /'bækhænd/ n Tennis esquerda f. **~ed** a com as costas da mão; **~ed compliment** cumprimento m ambíguo

backing /'bækɪŋ/ n apoio m; Comm patrocínio m

backlash /'bæklæʃ/ n fig reação f violenta; repercussões fpl

backlog /'bæklɒg/ n acumulação m (de trabalho etc)

backside /'bæksaɪd/ n ⚏ (buttocks) traseiro m

backstage /bæk'steɪdʒ/ a & adv por detrás dos bastidores

backstroke /'bækstrəʊk/ n nado m de costas

backtrack /'bæktræk/ vi fig voltar atrás

backward /'bækwəd/ a retrógrado; (retarded) atrasado; ‹step, look, etc› para trás

backwards /'bækwədz/ adv para trás; (walk) para trás; (fall) de costas, para trás; (in reverse order) de trás para diante, às avessas; **go ~ and forwards** ir e vir, andar para trás e para a frente; **know sth ~** saber algo de trás para a frente

backwater /'bækwɔːtə(r)/ n pej (place) lugar m atrasado

bacon /'beɪkən/ n toucinho m defumado; (in rashers) bacon m

bacteria /bæk'tɪərɪə/ npl bactérias fpl

bad /bæd/ a (worse, worst) mau; ‹accident› grave; ‹food› estragado; (ill) doente; **feel ~** sentir-se mal; **~ language** palavrões mpl. **~mannered** a mal-educado; **~tempered** a mal-humorado. **~ly** adv mal; (seriously) gravemente; **want ~ly** (desire) desejar imensamente, ter grande vontade de; (need) precisar muito de

badge /bædʒ/ n emblema m; (policeman's) crachá m, (P) distintivo m

b

badger /'bædʒə(r)/ n texugo m ● vt atormentar; (pester) importunar

badminton /'bædmɪntən/ n badminton m

baffle /'bæfl/ vt atrapalhar, desconcertar

bag /bæg/ n saco m; (handbag) bolsa f, carteira f; ~s (luggage) malas fpl ● vt (pt bagged) ensacar; Ⅱ (take) embolsar

baggage /'bægɪdʒ/ n bagagem f

baggy /'bægɪ/ a <clothes> muito largo, bufante

bagpipes /'bægpaɪps/ npl gaita f de foles

Bahamas /bə'hɑːməz/ npl the ~ as Bahamas fpl

bail¹ /beɪl/ n fiança f ● vt pôr em liberdade sob fiança; **be out on ~** estar solto sob fiança

bail² /beɪl/ vt ~ (out) Naut esgotar, tirar água de

bailiff /'beɪlɪf/ n (officer) oficial m de diligências; (of estate) feitor m

bait /beɪt/ n isca f ● vt pôr isca; fig atormentar (com insultos); atazanar

bak|e /beɪk/ vt/i cozer (no forno); <bread, cakes, etc> assar; (in the sun) torrar. ~er n padeiro m; (of cakes) doceiro m. ~ing n cozedura f; (batch) fornada f; ~ing tin forma f. ~ing powder n fermento m em pó

bakery /'beɪkərɪ/ n padaria f; (cakes) confeitaria f

balance /'bæləns/ n equilíbrio m; (scales) balança f; (sum) saldo m; Comm balanço m; ~ **of power** equilíbrio m político; ~ **of trade** balança f comercial ● vt equilibrar; (weigh up) pesar; <budget> equilibrar ● vi equilibrar-se. ~ **sheet** n balanço m. ~d a equilibrado

balcony /'bælkənɪ/ n balcão m; (in a house) varanda f

bald /bɔːld/ a (-er, -est) calvo, careca; <tyre> careca. ~ing a be ~ing ficar calvo. ~ly adv a nu e cru, (P) secamente. ~ness n calvície f

bale¹ /beɪl/ n (of straw) fardo m; (of cotton) balote m ● vt enfardar

bale² /beɪl/ vi ~ **out** saltar de paraquedas

balk /bɔːk/ vt frustrar, contrariar ● vi ~ **at** assustar-se com, recuar perante

ball¹ /bɔːl/ n bola f

ball² /bɔːl/ n (dance) baile m

ballad /'bæləd/ n balada f

ballerina /bælə'riːnə/ n bailarina f

ballet /'bæleɪ/ n balé m, (P) ballet m, bailado m

balloon /bə'luːn/ n balão m

ballot /'bælət/ n escrutínio m ● vt (members) consultar por voto secreto ● vi Pol votar. ~ **(paper)** n cédula f eleitoral, (P) boletim m de voto; ~ **box** n urna f

ballroom /'bɔːlruːm/ n salão m de baile

balm /bɑːm/ n bálsamo m. ~y a balsâmico; (mild) suave

bamboo /bæm'buː/ n bambu m

ban /bæn/ vt (pt banned) banir; ~ **from** proibir de ● n proibição f

banal /bə'nɑːl/ a banal. ~ity /-ælətɪ/ n banalidade f

banana /bə'nɑːnə/ n banana f

band /bænd/ n (for fastening) cinta f, faixa f; (strip) tira f, banda f; Mus, Mil banda f; Mus (dance, jazz) conjunto m; (group) bando m ● vi ~ **together** juntar-se

bandage /'bændɪdʒ/ n atadura f, (P) ligadura f ● vt ligar

bandit /'bændɪt/ n bandido m

bandstand /'bændstænd/ n coreto m

bandwagon /'bændwægən/ n **climb on the ~** fig apanhar o trem, (P) o comboio

bang /bæŋ/ n (blow) pancada f; (loud noise) estouro m, estrondo m; (of gun) detonação f ● vt/i (hit, shut) bater ● vi explodir ● int pum; ~ **in the middle** jogar no meio; **shut the door with a ~** bater (com) a porta

banger /'bæŋə(r)/ n (firework) bomba f; Ⅹ (sausage) salsicha f; (old) ~ Ⅹ (car) calhambeque m Ⅱ

bangle /'bæŋgl/ n pulseira f, bracelete m

banish /'bænɪʃ/ vt banir, desterrar

banisters /'bænɪstəz/ npl corrimão m

banjo /'bændʒəʊ/ n (pl -os) banjo m

bank¹ /bæŋk/ n (of river) margem f; (of earth) talude m; (of sand) banco m ● vt amontoar ● vi Aviat inclinar-se numa curva

bank² /bæŋk/ n Comm banco m; ~ **account** conta f bancária; ~ **holiday** feriado m nacional; ~ **rate** taxa f bancária ● vt depositar no banco; ~ **on** contar com; ~ **with** ter conta em

bank|er /'bæŋkə(r)/ n banqueiro m. ~ing /-ɪŋ/ n operações fpl bancárias; (career) carreira f bancária, banca f

banknote /'bæŋknəʊt/ n nota f de banco

bankrupt /'bæŋkrʌpt/ a & n falido m; **go ~** falir ● vt levar à falência. **~cy** n falência f, bancarrota f

banner /'bænə(r)/ n bandeira f, estandarte m

banquet /'bæŋkwɪt/ n banquete m

banter /'bæntə(r)/ n gracejo m, brincadeira f ● vi gracejar, brincar

baptism /'bæptɪzəm/ n batismo m

Baptist /'bæptɪst/ n batista mf

baptize /bæp'taɪz/ vt batizar

bar /bɑː(r)/ n (of chocolate) tablette f, barra f; (of metal, soap, sand etc) barra f; (of door, window) tranca f; (in pub) bar m; (counter) balcão m, bar m; Mus barra f de compasso; fig (obstacle) barreira f; (in law court) teia f; **the B~** a advocacia f; **~ code** código m de barra; **behind ~s** na cadeia ● vt (pt **barred**) (obstruct) barrar; (prohibit) proibir (**from** de); (exclude) excluir; ‹door, window› trancar ● prep salvo, exceto; **~ none** sem exceção

Barbados /bɑː'beɪdɒs/ n Barbados mpl

barbarian /bɑː'beərɪən/ n bárbaro m

barbari|c /bɑː'bærɪk/ a bárbaro. **~ty** /-ətɪ/ n barbaridade f

barbarous /'bɑːbərəs/ a bárbaro

barbecue /'bɑːbɪkjuː/ n (grill) churrasqueira f; (occasion, food) churrasco m ● vt assar

barbed /bɑːbd/ a **~ wire** arame m farpado

barber /'bɑːbə(r)/ n barbeiro m

bare /beə(r)/ a (-er, -est) nu; ‹room› vazio; (mere) mero ● vt pôr à mostra, pôr a nu, descobrir

bareback /'beəbæk/ adv em pelo

barefaced /'beəfeɪst/ a descarado

barefoot /'beə(r)fʊt/ adv descalço

barely /'beəlɪ/ adv apenas, mal

bargain /'bɑːgɪn/ n (deal) negócio m; (good buy) pechincha f ● vi negociar; (haggle) regatear; **~ for** esperar

barge /bɑːdʒ/ n barcaça f ● vi **~ in** interromper (despropositadamente); (into room) irromper

bark[1] /bɑːk/ n (of tree) casca f

bark[2] /bɑːk/ n (of dog) latido m ● vi latir; **his ~ is worse than his bite** cão que ladra não morde

barley /'bɑːlɪ/ n cevada f

barmaid /'bɑːmeɪd/ n empregada f de bar

barman /'bɑːmən/ n (pl **-men**) barman m, empregado m de bar

barmy /'bɑːmɪ/ a ▣ maluco ▣

barn /bɑːn/ n celeiro m

barometer /bə'rɒmɪtə(r)/ n barômetro m, (P) barómetro m

baron /'bærən/ n barão m. **~ess** n baronesa f

barracks /'bærəks/ n quartel m, caserna f

barrage /'bærɑːʒ/ n barragem f; fig enxurrada f; Mil fogo m de barragem

barrel /'bærəl/ n (of oil, wine) barril m; (of gun) cano m

barren /'bærən/ a estéril; ‹soil› árido, estéril

barricade /bærɪ'keɪd/ n barricada f ● vt barricar

barrier /'bærɪə(r)/ n barreira f; (hindrance) entrave m, barreira f

barrister /'bærɪstə(r)/ n advogado m

barrow /'bærəʊ/ n carrinho m de mão

barter /'bɑːtə(r)/ n troca f ● vt trocar

base /beɪs/ n base f ● vt basear (**on** em) ● a baixo, ignóbil. **~less** a infundado

baseball /'beɪsbɔːl/ n beisebol m

basement /'beɪsmənt/ n porão m, (P) cave f

bash /bæʃ/ vt bater com violência ● n pancada f forte; **have a ~ at** experimentar

bashful /'bæʃfl/ a tímido

basic /'beɪsɪk/ a básico, elementar, fundamental. **~ally** adv basicamente, no fundo

basin /'beɪsn/ n bacia f; (for food) tigela f; Naut ante-doca f; (for washing) pia f

basis /'beɪsɪs/ n (pl **bases** /-siːz/) base f

bask /bɑːsk/ vi **~ in the sun** apanhar sol

basket /'bɑːskɪt/ n cesto m

basketball /'bɑːskɪtbɔːl/ n basquete(bol) m

Basque /bɑːsk/ a & n basco m

bass[1] /bæs/ n (pl **bass**) (fish) perca f

bass[2] /beɪs/ a Mus grave ● n (pl **basses**) Mus baixo m

bassoon /bə'suːn/ n fagote m

bastard /'bɑːstəd/ n (illegitimate child) bastardo m; ▣ pej safado m ▣; ▣ not pej cara m ▣

bat[1] /bæt/ n Cricket pá f; Baseball bastão m; Table Tennis rafuete f ● vt/i (pt **batted**) bater (em); **without ~ting an eyelid** sem pestanejar

b

bat² /bæt/ n Zool morcego m

batch /bætʃ/ n (loaves) fornada f; (people) monte m; (goods) remessa f; (papers, letters etc) batelada f, monte m

bath /bɑːθ/ n (pl -s /bɑːðz/) banho m; (tub) banheira f; ~s (washing) banho m público; (swimming) piscina f ● vt dar banho a ● vi tomar banho

bathe /beɪð/ vt dar banho em; <wound> limpar ● vi tomar banho (de mar) ● n banho m (de mar). ~r /-ə(r)/ n banhista mf

bathing /'beɪðɪŋ/ n banho m de mar. ~ costume/suit n traje m de banho, (P) fato m de banho

bathrobe /'bɑːθrəʊb/ n Amer roupão m

bathroom /'bɑːθruːm/ n banheiro m, (P) casa f de banho

battalion /bə'tælɪən/ n batalhão m

batter /'bætə(r)/ vt bater, espancar, maltratar ● n Culin (for cakes) massa f de bolos; Culin (for frying) massa f de empanar. ~ed a <car, pan> amassado; <child, wife> maltratado, espancado

battery /'bætərɪ/ n Mil, Auto bateria f; Electr pilha f

battle /'bætl/ n batalha f; fig luta f ● vi combater, batalhar, lutar

battlefield /'bætlfiːld/ n campo m de batalha

battleship /'bætlʃɪp/ n couraçado m

baulk /bɔːlk/ vt/i = BALK

bawl /bɔːl/ vt/i berrar

bay¹ /beɪ/ n Bot loureiro m

bay² /beɪ/ n Geog baía f; ~ window janela f saliente

bay³ /beɪ/ n (bark) latido m ● vi latir; at ~ (animal; also fig) cercado, (P) em apuros; keep at ~ manter à distância

bayonet /'beɪənɪt/ n baioneta f

bazaar /bə'zɑː(r)/ n bazar m

BC abbr (= before Christ) a C

bcc abbr (= blind carbon copy) Cco Com cópia oculta

be /biː/ ● vi (pres am, are, is, pt was, were, pp been);

❗ Portuguese has two verbs meaning be: ser and estar. As a general rule, ser is used to describe a permanent state or inherent characteristic, e.g. I'm Brazilian sou brasileiro, whereas estar is used to describe temporary states, e.g. I'm tired estou cansado.

····▶ (identity or characteristic) ser; I'm Portuguese sou português; it's yellow é amarelo

····▶ (temporary state) estar; I'm angry/bored estou brabo/entediado

····▶ (situation) ficar; where's the town centre? onde é que fica o centro?; it's 10 minutes away fica a 10 minutos

····▶ (cost) ser; how much is it? quanto é?; it's £15 são 15 libras

····▶ (feelings) estar com; I'm hungry/thirsty/sleepy estou com fome/sede/sono; I'm cold estou com frio

····▶ (health) estar; how are you? como está?; he's ill ele está doente

····▶ (age) ter; he's twenty ele tem vinte anos

····▶ (weather) estar; it's hot/cold está calor/frio; it's 30 degrees today hoje estão 30 graus

····▶ (become) ficar; he was disappointed ficou desapontado

● v aux

····▶ (in continuous tense) I am working estou trabalhando, (P) estou a trabalhar; She is leaving next week ela vai embora na próxima semana

····▶ (in passives) he was killed ele foi morto; the window has been fixed a janela foi consertada

····▶ (in tag questions) their house is lovely, isn't it? a casa deles é linda, não é?

····▶ (in short answers) are you a doctor? yes, I am é médico? sim, sou.

····▶ (with infinitive) she is to go immediately ela tem que ir imediatamente; they are to be married in August eles vão casar em agosto

beach /biːtʃ/ n praia f

beacon /'biːkən/ n farol m; (marker) baliza f

bead /biːd/ n conta f; ~ of sweat gota f de suor

beak /biːk/ n bico m

beam /biːm/ n (of wood) trave f, viga f; (of light) raio m; (of torch) feixe m de luz ● vt/i (radiate) irradiar; fig sorrir radiante. ~ing a radiante

bean /biːn/ n feijão m; broad ~ fava f; coffee ~s café m em grão; runner ~ feijão m verde

bear¹ /beə(r)/ n urso m

bear² /beə(r)/ vt/i (pt bore, pp borne) sustentar, suportar; (endure) aguentar, suportar; <*child*> dar à luz; **~ in mind** ter em mente, lembrar; **~ left** virar à esquerda; **~ on** relacionar-se com, ter a ver com; **~ out** confirmar; **~ up!** coragem!. **~able** a tolerável, suportável. **~er** n portador m

beard /bɪəd/ n barba f. **~ed** a barbado, com barba

bearing /'beərɪŋ/ n (*manner*) porte m; (*relevance*) relação f; *Naut* marcação f; **get one's ~s** orientar-se

beast /biːst/ n (*animal, person*) besta f, animal m; (*in fables*) fera f; **~ of burden** besta f de carga

beat /biːt/ vt/i (*pt* beat, *pp* beaten) bater; **~ about the bush** estar com rodeios; **~ a retreat** bater em retirada; **~ it** ▣ (*go away*) pôr-se a andar; **it ~s me** ▣ não consigo entender; **~ up** espancar ● n *Med* batimento m; *Mus* compasso m, ritmo m; (*of drum*) toque m; (*of policeman*) ronda f, (*P*) giro m. **~ing** n sova f

beautician /bjuːˈtɪʃn/ n esteticista mf

beautiful /'bjuːtɪfl/ a belo, lindo

beautify /'bjuːtɪfaɪ/ vt embelezar

beauty /'bjuːtɪ/ n beleza f; **~ parlour** instituto m de beleza; **~ spot** sinal m no rosto, mosca f; (*place*) local m pitoresco

beaver /'biːvə(r)/ n castor m

became /bɪˈkeɪm/ ▶ BECOME

because /bɪˈkɒz/ conj porque ● adv **~ of** por causa de

beckon /'bekən/ vt/i **~ (to)** fazer sinal (para)

become /bɪˈkʌm/ vt/i (*pt* became, *pp* become) tornar-se; (*befit*) ficar bem a; **what has ~ of her?** que é feito dela?

becoming /bɪˈkʌmɪŋ/ a que fica bem, apropriado

bed /bed/ n cama f; (*layer*) camada f; (*of sea*) fundo m; (*of river*) leito m; (*of flowers*) canteiro m; **~ and breakfast (b & b)** quarto m com café da manhã, (*P*) com pequeno-almoço ● vt/i (*pt* bedded) **~ down** ir deitar-se; **~ in** plantar. **~sit(ter)** n ▣ misto m de quarto e sala; **go to ~** ir para cama; **in ~** na cama. **~ding** n roupa f de cama

---

ⓘ **bed and breakfast** Os *bed and breakfast*, ou *B&B*, são casas particulares ou pequenos hotéis que oferecem alojamento e café da manhã aos hóspedes a preços normalmente baixos.

---

bedclothes /'bedkləʊðz/ n roupa f de cama

bedroom /'bedruːm/ n quarto m de dormir

bedside /'bedsaɪd/ n cabeceira f; **~ manner** (*doctor's*) modos mpl que inspiram confiança

bedspread /'bedspred/ n colcha f

bedtime /'bedtaɪm/ n hora f de deitar, hora f de ir para a cama

bee /biː/ n abelha f; **make a ~line for** ir direto a

beech /biːtʃ/ n faia f

beef /biːf/ n carne f de vaca

beefburger /'biːfbɜːgə(r)/ n hambúrguer m

beehive /'biːhaɪv/ n colmeia f

been /biːn/ ▶ BE

beer /bɪə(r)/ n cerveja f

beet /biːt/ n beterraba f

beetle /'biːtl/ n escaravelho m

beetroot /'biːtruːt/ n (raiz de) beterraba f

before /bɪˈfɔː(r)/ prep (*time*) antes de; (*place*) em frente de ● adv antes; (*already*) já ● conj antes que; **~ leaving** antes de partir; **~ he leaves** antes que ele parta, antes de ele partir

beforehand /bɪˈfɔːhænd/ adv de antemão, antecipadamente

befriend /bɪˈfrend/ vt tornar-se amigo de; (*be helpful to*) auxiliar

beg /beg/ vt/i (*pt* begged) mendigar; (*entreat*) suplicar; **~ sb's pardon** pedir desculpa a alguém; **~ the question** fazer uma petição de princípio; **it's going ~ging** está sobrando, (*P*) a sobrar

began /bɪˈgæn/ ▶ BEGIN

beggar /'begə(r)/ n mendigo m, pedinte mf; ▣ (*person*) cara m ▣

begin /bɪˈgɪn/ vt/i (*pt* began, *pp* begun, *pres p* beginning) começar, principiar. **~ner** n principiante mf. **~ning** n começo m, princípio m

begrudge /bɪˈgrʌdʒ/ vt ter inveja de; (*give*) dar de má vontade; **~ doing** fazer de má vontade or a contragosto

beguile /bɪˈgaɪl/ vt enganar

begun /bɪˈgʌn/ ▶ BEGIN

behalf /bɪˈhɑːf/ n **on ~ of** em nome de; (*in the interest of*) em favor de

behave /bɪˈheɪv/ vi portar-se; **~ (o.s.)** portar-se bem

behaviour /bɪˈheɪvjə(r)/ n conduta f, comportamento m

behead /bɪ'hed/ vt decapitar

behind /bɪ'haɪnd/ prep atrás de ● adv atrás; (late) com atraso ● n ⬛ (buttocks) traseiro m ⬛; ~ **the times** antiquado, retrógrado; **leave ~** deixar para trás

beige /beɪʒ/ a & n bege m, (P) beige m

being /'biːɪŋ/ n ser m; **bring into ~** criar; **come into ~** nascer, originar-se

belated /bɪ'leɪtɪd/ a tardio, atrasado

belch /beltʃ/ vi arrotar ● vt ~ **out** ‹smoke› vomitar, lançar ● n arroto m

belfry /'belfrɪ/ n campanário m

Belgi|um /'beldʒəm/ n Bélgica f. **~an** a & n belga mf

belief /bɪ'liːf/ n crença f; (trust) confiança f; (opinion) convicção f

believ|e /bɪ'liːv/ vt/i acreditar; **~e in** acreditar em. **~able** a crível. **~er** /-ə(r)/ n crente mf

belittle /bɪ'lɪtl/ vt depreciar

bell /bel/ n sino m; (small) sineta f; (on door, of phone) campainha f; (on cat, toy) guizo m

bellow /'beləʊ/ vt/i berrar, bramir; ~ **out** rugir

belly /'belɪ/ n barriga f, ventre m

belong /bɪ'lɒŋ/ vi ~ (**to**) pertencer (a); ‹club› ser sócio (de)

belongings /bɪ'lɒŋɪŋz/ npl pertences mpl; **personal ~** objetos mpl de uso pessoal

beloved /bɪ'lʌvɪd/ a & n amado m

below /bɪ'ləʊ/ prep abaixo de, debaixo de ● adv abaixo, em baixo; (on page) abaixo

belt /belt/ n cinto m; Techn correia f; fig zona f ● vt ⬛ (hit) zurzir ● vi ⬛ (rush) safar-se

bemused /bɪ'mjuːzd/ a estonteado, confuso; (thoughtful) pensativo

bench /bentʃ/ n banco m; (seat, working-table) bancada f; **the ~** Jur os magistrados (no tribunal)

bend /bend/ vt/i (pt, pp bent) curvar(-se); ‹arm, leg› dobrar; (road, river) fazer uma curva, virar ● n curva f; ~ **over** debruçar-se or inclinar-se sobre

beneath /bɪ'niːθ/ prep abaixo de, debaixo de; fig abaixo de ● adv debaixo, em baixo

benefactor /'benɪfæktə(r)/ n benfeitor m

beneficial /benɪ'fɪʃl/ a benéfico, proveitoso

beneficiary /benɪ'fɪʃərɪ/ n beneficiário m

benefit /'benɪfɪt/ n (advantage, performance) benefício m; (profit) proveito m; (allowance) subsídio m ● vt/i (pt benefited, pres p benefiting) (be useful to) beneficiar (by de); (do good to) beneficiar, fazer bem a; (receive benefit) lucrar; ganhar (by, from com)

benevolen|t /bɪ'nevələnt/ a benevolente. **~ce** n benevolência f

bent /bent/ ▶ BEND n (skill) aptidão f; jeito m (for para); (liking) queda f (for para) ● a curvado; (twisted) torcido; ⬛ (dishonest) desonesto; ~ **on** decidido a

bequeath /bɪ'kwiːð/ vt legar

bereave|d /bɪ'riːvd/ a **the ~d wife**/etc a esposa/etc do falecido; **the ~d family** a família enlutada. **~ment** n luto m

beret /'bereɪ/ n boina f

Bermuda /bə'mjuːdə/ n Bermudas fpl

berry /'berɪ/ n baga f

berth /bɜːθ/ n (in ship) beliche m; (in train) couchette f; (anchorage) ancoradouro m ● vi atracar; **give a wide ~ to** passar ao largo, (P) de largo

beside /bɪ'saɪd/ prep ao lado de, junto de; ~ **o.s.** fora de si; **be ~ the point** não ter nada a ver com o assunto, não vir ao caso

besides /bɪ'saɪdz/ prep além de; (except) fora, salvo ● adv além disso

besiege /bɪ'siːdʒ/ vt sitiar, cercar; ~ **with** assediar

best /best/ a & n (**the**) ~ (o/a) melhor mf ● adv melhor; ~ **man** padrinho m de casamento; **at (the) ~** na melhor das hipóteses; **do one's ~** fazer o (melhor) que se pode; **make the ~ of** tirar o melhor partido de; **the ~ part of** a maior parte de; **to the ~ of my knowledge** que eu saiba

bestseller /best'selə(r)/ n best-seller m

bet /bet/ n aposta f ● vt/i (pt bet or betted) apostar (on em)

betray /bɪ'treɪ/ vt trair. **~al** n traição f

better /'betə(r)/ a & adv melhor; **all the ~** tanto melhor; ~ **off** (richer) mais rico; **he's ~ off at home** é melhor para ele ficar em casa; **I'd ~ go** é melhor ir-me embora; **get ~** melhorar ● vt melhorar ● n **our ~s** os nossos superiores mpl; **the ~ part of it** a maior parte disso; **get the ~ of sb** levar a melhor em relação a alguém

between /bɪ'twiːn/ prep entre ● adv **in ~** no meio, no intervalo; ~ **you and me** aqui entre nós

beverage /'bevərɪdʒ/ n bebida f

beware /bɪ'weə(r)/ vi acautelar-se (of com) tomar cuidado (of com)

bewilder /bɪ'wɪldə(r)/ vt desorientar. **~ment** n desorientação f, confusão f

bewitch /bɪ'wɪtʃ/ vt encantar, cativar

beyond /bɪ'jɒnd/ prep além de; (doubt, reach) fora de ● adv além; **it's ~ me** isso ultrapassa-me; **he lives ~ his means** ele vive acima dos seus meios

bias /'baɪəs/ n parcialidade f; pej (prejudice) preconceito m; Sewing viés m ● vt (pt biased) influenciar; **~ed against** de prevenção contra, (P) de pé atrás contra. **~ed** a parcial

bib /bɪb/ n babeiro m, babette m

Bible /'baɪbl/ n Bíblia f

biblical /'bɪblɪkl/ a bíblico

bibliography /bɪblɪ'ɒɡrəfɪ/ n bibliografia f

biceps /'baɪseps/ n bíceps m

bicker /'bɪkə(r)/ vi questionar, discutir

bicycle /'baɪsɪkl/ n bicicleta f ● vi andar de bicicleta

bid /bɪd/ n oferta f, lance m; (attempt) tentativa f ● vt/i (pt bid, pres p bidding) fazer uma oferta, lançar, oferecer como lance. **~der** n licitante mf; **the highest ~der** quem dá or oferece mais

bide /baɪd/ vt **~ one's time** esperar pelo bom momento

big /bɪɡ/ a (bigger, biggest) grande; 🔲 (generous) generoso; **~ shot** 🔲 mandachuva m ● adv 🔲 em grande; **talk ~** gabar-se 🔲; **think ~** 🔲 ter grandes planos. **~-headed** a pretensioso, convencido

bigamy /'bɪɡəmɪ/ n bigamia f. **~ist** n bígamo m. **~ous** a bígamo

bigot /'bɪɡət/ n fanático m, intolerante mf. **~ed** a fanático, intolerante. **~ry** n fanatismo m, intolerância f

bigwig /'bɪɡwɪɡ/ n 🔲 mandachuva m

bike /baɪk/ n 🔲 bicicleta f

bikini /bɪ'ki:nɪ/ n (pl -is) biquíni m

bile /baɪl/ n bílis f

bilingual /baɪ'lɪŋɡwəl/ a bilíngue

bilious /'bɪlɪəs/ a bilioso

bill[1] /bɪl/ n (invoice) fatura f; (in restaurant) conta f; Pol projeto m de lei; Amer (banknote) nota f de banco; (poster) cartaz m; **~ of exchange** letra f de câmbio ● vt faturar; Theatr anunciar, pôr no programa; **~ sb for** apresentar a alguém a conta de

bill[2] /bɪl/ n (of bird) bico m

billiards /'bɪlɪədz/ n bilhar m

billion /'bɪlɪən/ n (10^9) mil milhões; (10^{12}) um milhão de milhões

bin /bɪn/ n (for storage) caixa f, lata f; (for rubbish) lata f do lixo, (P) caixote m

bind /baɪnd/ vt (pt bound) (tie) atar; <book> encadernar; Jur obrigar; (cover the edge of) debruar ● n 🔲 (bore) chatice f 🔲; **be ~ing on** ser obrigatório para

binding /'baɪndɪŋ/ n encadernação f; (braid) debrum m

binge /bɪndʒ/ n 🔲 **go on a ~** cair na farra; (overeat) empanturrar-se. **~ drinking** n: consumo excessivo de álcool em pouco tempo

bingo /'bɪŋɡəʊ/ n bingo m ● int acerte!

binoculars /bɪ'nɒkjʊləz/ npl binóculo m

biochemistry /baɪəʊ'kemɪstrɪ/ n bioquímica f

biodegradable /baɪəʊdɪ'ɡreɪdəbl/ a biodegradável

biodiesel /'baɪəʊdi:zl/ n biodiesel m

biography /baɪ'ɒɡrəfɪ/ n biografia f. **~er** n biógrafo m

biology /baɪ'ɒlədʒɪ/ n biologia f. **~ical** /-ə'lɒdʒɪkl/ a biológico. **~ist** n biólogo m

birch /bɜ:tʃ/ n (tree) bétula f

bird /bɜ:d/ n ave f, pássaro m; 🔲 (girl) garota f 🔲; **~ sanctuary** refúgio m ornitológico. **~ flu** n gripe f aviária, (P) gripe f das aves; **~watcher** n ornitófilo m

Biro® /'baɪərəʊ/ n (pl -os) (caneta) esferográfica f, Bic® f

birth /bɜ:θ/ n nascimento m; **~ certificate** certidão f de nascimento; **~ control/rate** controle m /índice m de natalidade; **give ~ to** dar à luz. **~place** n lugar m de nascimento

birthday /'bɜ:θdeɪ/ n aniversário m, (P) dia m de anos; **his ~ is on 9 July** ele faz anos no dia 9 de julho

birthmark /'bɜ:θmɑ:k/ n sinal m

biscuit /'bɪskɪt/ n biscoito m, bolacha f

bishop /'bɪʃəp/ n bispo m

bit[1] /bɪt/ n (small piece, short time) pedaço m, bocado m; (of bridle) freio m; (of tool) broca f; **a ~** um pouco

bit[2] /bɪt/ ▶ BITE

bitch /bɪtʃ/ n cadela f; 🔲 (woman) peste f; fig cadela f 🔲 ● vt/i 🔲 (criticize) malhar, (P) cortar (em) 🔲; 🔲 (grumble) resmungar. **~y** a 🔲 maldoso

bite /baɪt/ vt/i (pt bit, pp bitten) morder; (insect) picar ● n mordida f; (sting) picada f; **have a ~ (to eat)** comer qualquer coisa

biting /'baɪtɪŋ/ a cortante

bitter /'bɪtə(r)/ a amargo; (*weather*) glacial. **~ly** adv amargamente; **it's ~ly cold** está um frio de rachar. **~ness** n amargura f; (*resentment*) ressentimento

bizarre /bɪ'zɑː(r)/ a bizarro

black /blæk/ a (**-er, -est**) negro, preto; **~ and blue** coberto de nódoas negras; **~ coffee** café m (sem leite); **~ eye** olho m negro; **~ ice** gelo m negro sobre o asfalto; **~ market** mercado m negro ● n negro m, preto m; **a ~** (*person*) um preto, um negro ● vt enegrecer; (*goods*) boicotar

blackberry /'blækbəri/ n amora f silvestre

blackbird /'blækbɜːd/ n melro m

blackboard /'blækbɔːd/ n quadro m preto

blackcurrant /'blækkʌrənt/ n groselha f negra

blacken /'blækən/ vt/i escurecer; **~ sb's name** difamar, denegrir

blacklist /'blæklɪst/ n lista f negra ● vt pôr na lista negra

blackmail /'blækmeɪl/ n chantagem f ● vt fazer chantagem. **~er** n chantagista mf

blackout /'blækaʊt/ n (*wartime*) blecaute m, (P) blackout m; *Med* desmaio m; *Electr* falta f de corrente; *Theatr* apagar m de luzes

bladder /'blædə(r)/ n bexiga f

blade /bleɪd/ n lâmina f; (*of oar, propeller*) pá f; (*of grass*) ervinha f, folhinha f de erva

blame /bleɪm/ vt culpar ● n culpa f; **be to ~** ser o culpado. **~less** a irrepreensível; (*innocent*) inocente

bland /blænd/ a (**-er, -est**) (*of manner*) suave; (*mild*) brando; (*insipid*) insípido

blank /blæŋk/ a (*space, cheque*) em branco; (*look*) vago; (*wall*) nu ● n espaço m em branco; (*cartridge*) cartucho m sem bala

blanket /'blæŋkɪt/ n cobertor m; *fig* manto m ● vt (*pt* **blanketed**) cobrir com cobertor; (*cover thickly*) encobrir, recobrir; **wet ~** desmancha-prazeres mf

blare /bleə(r)/ vt/i ressoar, atroar ● n clangor m; (*of horn*) buzinar m

blasé /'blɑːzeɪ/ a blasé

blasphem|y /'blæsfəmɪ/ n blasfémia f, (P) blasfémia f

blast /blɑːst/ n (*gust*) rajada f; (*sound*) som m; (*explosion*) explosão f ● vt dinamitar; **~!** drogal, (P) raiosl. **~ed** a maldito.

blatant /'bleɪtnt/ a flagrante; (*shameless*) descarado

blaze /bleɪz/ n chamas fpl; (*light*) clarão m; (*outburst*) explosão f ● vi arder; (*shine*) resplandecer, brilhar; **~ a trail** abrir o caminho, ser pioneiro

blazer /'bleɪzə(r)/ n blazer m

bleach /bliːtʃ/ n descolorante, descorante m; (*household*) água f sanitária, (P) lixívia f ● vt/i branquear; (*hair*) oxigenar

bleak /bliːk/ a (**-er, -est**) (*place*) desolado; (*chilly*) frio; *fig* desanimador

bleary-eyed /'blɪəriaɪd/ a com olhos injetados

bleat /bliːt/ n balido m ● vi balir

bleed /bliːd/ vt/i (*pt* **bled**) sangrar

bleep /bliːp/ n bip m. **~er** n bip m

blemish /'blemɪʃ/ n defeito m; (*on reputation*) mancha f ● vt manchar

blend /blend/ vt/i misturar(-se); (*go well together*) combinar-se ● n mistura f. **~er** n *Culin* liquidificador m

bless /bles/ vt abençoar; **be ~ed with** ter a felicidade de ter. **~ing** n benção f; (*thing one is glad of*) felicidade f; **it's a ~ing in disguise** há males que vêm para bem

blessed /'blesɪd/ a bem-aventurado; 🄸 (*cursed*) maldito

blew /bluː/ ▶ BLOW¹

blight /blaɪt/ n doença f de plantas; *fig* influência f maligna ● vt arruinar, frustrar

blind /blaɪnd/ a cego; **~ alley** (*also fig*) beco m sem saída; **~ man/woman** cego m /cega f ● vt cegar ● n (*on window*) persiana f; (*deception*) ardil m; **be ~ to** não ver; **turn a ~ eye to** fingir não ver, fechar os olhos a. **~ly** adv às cegas. **~ness** n cegueira f

blindfold /'blaɪndfəʊld/ a & adv de olhos vendados ● n venda f ● vt vendar os olhos a

bling /blɪŋ/, **bling bling** /'blɪŋ blɪŋ/ ns 🄸 bling-bling m, estilo adotado principalmente por rappers, que se caracteriza pelo uso de muitas joias

blink /blɪŋk/ vi piscar

bliss /blɪs/ n felicidade f, beatitude f. **~ful** a felicíssimo

blister /'blɪstə(r)/ n bolha f, empola f ● vi empolar

blizzard /'blɪzəd/ n tempestade f de neve, nevasca f

bloated /'bləʊtɪd/ a inchado

blob /blɒb/ n pingo m grosso; (stain) mancha f

block /blɒk/ n bloco m; (buildings) quarteirão m; (in pipe) entupimento m; ~ **(of flats)** prédio (de andares) m; ~ **letters** maiúsculas fpl ● vt bloquear, obstruir; <pipe> entupir. **~age** n obstrução f

blockade /blɒ'keɪd/ n bloqueio m ● vt bloquear

blog /blɒg/ n blogue m, (P) blog m ● vi blogar

blogger /'blɒgə(r)/ n blogueiro m, (P) bloguista m

bloke /bləʊk/ n 🔢 sujeito m 🔢; cara m 🔢

blond /blɒnd/ a & n louro m

blonde /blɒnd/ a & n loura f

blood /blʌd/ n sangue m ● a <bank, donor, transfusion, etc> de sangue; <poisoning> do sangue; <group, vessel> sanguíneo; ~ **pressure** tensão f arterial; ~ **test** exame m de sangue. **~curdling** a horrendo

bloodhound /'blʌdhaʊnd/ n sabujo m

bloodshed /'blʌdʃed/ n derramamento m de sangue, carnificina f

bloodshot /'blʌdʃɒt/ a injetado de sangue

bloodstream /'blʌdstriːm/ n sangue m, fluxo m sanguíneo

bloodthirsty /'blʌdθɜːstɪ/ a sanguinário

bloody /'blʌdɪ/ a (-ier, -iest) ensanguentado; (with much bloodshed) sangrento; 🔢 grande; maldito ● adv 🔢 pra burro. **~minded** a 🔢 do contra 🔢; chato 🔢

bloom /bluːm/ n flor f, (beauty) frescura f, viço m; **in ~** em flor ● vi florir; fig vicejar

blossom /'blɒsəm/ n flor f, **in ~** em flor ● vi (flower) florir, desabrochar; (develop, flourish) florescer, desabrochar

blot /blɒt/ n mancha f ● vt (pt blotted) manchar; (dry) secar; ~ **out** apagar; (hide) tapar, toldar

blotch /blɒtʃ/ n mancha f. **~y** a manchado

blouse /blaʊz/ n blusa f, (in uniform) blusão m

blow¹ /bləʊ/ vt/i (pt blew, pp blown) soprar; (fuse) fundir-se, queimar; 🔢 (squander) esbanjar; <trumpet etc> tocar; ~ **a whistle** apitar; ~ **one's nose** assoar o nariz; ~ **out** <candle> apagar, soprar; ~ **over** passar □ ~ **away**, ~ **off** vt levar, soprar ● vi voar, ir pelos ares (fora) □ ~ **up** vt (explode) explodir; <tyre> encher; <photograph> ampliar ● vi (explode) explodir. **~dry** vt <hair> fazer um brushing ● n brushing m

blow² /bləʊ/ n pancada f; (slap) bofetada f; (punch) murro m; fig golpe m

blowlamp /'bləʊlæmp/ n maçarico m

blown /bləʊn/ ▶ BLOW¹

blue /bluː/ a (-er, -est) azul; (indecent) indecente ● n azul m; **come out of the ~** ser inesperado. **~s** n Mus blues; **have the ~s** 🔢 estar deprimido

bluebell /'bluːbel/ n jacinto m dos bosques

bluebottle /'bluːbɒtl/ n mosca f varejeira

blueprint /'bluːprɪnt/ n cópia f fotográfica de planta; fig projeto m

bluff /blʌf/ vi blefar, (P) fazer bluff ● vt enganar (fingindo), blefar ● n blefe m, (P) bluff m

blunder /'blʌndə(r)/ vi cometer um erro crasso; (move) avançar às cegas or tateando ● n erro m crasso, (P) bronca f

blunt /blʌnt/ a (-er, -est) embotado; <person> direto ● vt embotar. **~ly** adv sem rodeios

blur /blɜː(r)/ n mancha f ● vt (pt blurred) (smear) manchar; (make indistinct) toldar

blurb /blɜːb/ n contracapa f, sinopse f de um livro

blurt /blɜːt/ vt ~ **out** deixar escapar

blush /blʌʃ/ vi corar ● n rubor m, vermelhidão f

bluster /'blʌstə(r)/ vi (wind) soprar em rajadas; (swagger) andar com ar fanfarrão. **~y** a borrascoso

boar /bɔː(r)/ n varrão m; **wild ~** javali m

board /bɔːd/ n tábua f; (for notices) quadro m, (P) placard m; (food) pensão f; Admin conselho m ● vt/i cobrir com tábuas; <aircraft, ship, train> embarcar (em); <bus, train> subir (em); **full ~** pensão f completa; **half ~** meia-pensão f; **on ~** a bordo; ~ **up** entaipar; ~ **with** ser pensionista em casa de. **~er** n pensionista mf; (at school) interno m. **~ing card** n cartão m de embarque; **~ing school** n internato m

boast /bəʊst/ vi gabar-se ● vt orgulhar-se de ● n gabarolice f. **~ful** a vaidoso

boat /bəʊt/ n barco m; **in the same ~** nas mesmas circunstâncias

bob /bɒb/ vt/i (pt bobbed) (curtsy) inclinar-se; (hair) cortar pelos ombros, (P) cortar à joãozinho; **~ (up and down)** andar para cima e para baixo

bobsleigh /'bɒbsleɪ/ n trenó m

bodily /'bɒdɪlɪ/ a corporal, físico ● adv (in person) fisicamente, em pessoa; (lift) em peso

body /'bɒdɪ/ n corpo m; (organization) organismo m; **in a ~** em massa; **the main ~ of** o grosso de. **~(work)** n (of car) carroçaria f; **~building** n body building m; **~ piercing** n piercing m no corpo, (P) pírcingue m de corpo

bodyguard /'bɒdɪgɑːd/ n guarda-costas m; (escort) escolta f

bog /bɒg/ n pântano m ● vt **get ~ged down** atolar-se; fig ficar emperrado

bogus /'bəʊgəs/ a falso

boil[1] /bɔɪl/ n Med furúnculo m

boil[2] /bɔɪl/ vt/i ferver; **come to the ~** ferver; **~ down to** resumir-se a; **~ over** transbordar, (P) a ferver **~ing hot** fervendo; **~ing point** ponto m de ebulição

boiler /'bɔɪlə(r)/ n caldeira f; **~ suit** macacão m, (P) fato m de macaco

boisterous /'bɔɪstərəs/ a turbulento; (noisy and cheerful) animado

bold /bəʊld/ a (-er, -est) ousado; (of colours) vivo. **~ness** n ousadia f

Bolivia /bə'lɪvɪə/ n Bolívia f. **~n** a & n boliviano m

bolster /'bəʊlstə(r)/ n travesseiro m ● vt sustentar; ajudar; **~ one's spirits** levantar o moral

bolt /bəʊlt/ n (on door etc) ferrolho m; (for nut) parafuso m; (lightning) relâmpago m; **~ upright** reto or (P) direito como um fuso ● vt aferrolhar; (food) engolir ● vi fugir, disparar

bomb /bɒm/ n bomba f ● vt bombardear. **~er** n (aircraft) bombardeiro m; (person) bombista mf

bombard /bɒm'bɑːd/ vt bombardear

bombastic /bɒm'bæstɪk/ a bombástico

bombshell /'bɒmʃel/ n granada f; fig bomba f

bond /bɒnd/ n (agreement) compromisso m; (link) laço m, vínculo m; Comm obrigação f; **in ~** em depósito na alfândega

bondage /'bɒndɪdʒ/ n escravidão f, servidão f

bone /bəʊn/ n osso m; (of fish) espinha f; **~ idle** preguiçoso ● vt desossar. **~ dry** a completamente seco, ressecado

bonfire /'bɒnfaɪə(r)/ n fogueira f

bonnet /'bɒnɪt/ n chapéu m; Auto capô m do motor, (P) capot m

bonus /'bəʊnəs/ n bónus m, (P) bónus m

bony /'bəʊnɪ/ a (-ier, -iest) ossudo; ‹meat, fish› cheio de ossos/de espinhas

boo /buː/ int fora ● vt/i vaiar ● n vaia f

boob /buːb/ n 🔲 (mistake) asneira f; disparate m ● vi 🔲 fazer asneira(s)

booby /'buːbɪ/ n **~ prize** prêmio or (P) prémio m de consolação; **~ trap** bomba f armadilhada

book /bʊk/ n livro m; **~s** Comm contas fpl, escrita f; **~ of matches** carteira f de fósforos; **~ of tickets** (bus, tube) caderneta f de módulos; **~ing office** bilheteria f, (P) bilheteira f ● vt (enter) averbar, registrar; Comm escriturar; (reserve) marcar, reservar; **be fully ~ed** ter a lotação esgotada

bookcase /'bʊkkeɪs/ n estante f

bookkeep|er /'bʊkkiːpə(r)/ n guarda-livros m. **~ing** n contabilidade f, escrituração f

booklet /'bʊklɪt/ n brochura f

bookmaker /'bʊkmeɪkə(r)/ n book (maker) m

bookmark /'bʊkmɑːk/ n marca f de livro, marcador m de página

bookseller /'bʊkselə(r)/ n livreiro m

bookshop /'bʊkʃɒp/ n livraria f

bookstall /'bʊkstɔːl/ n quiosque m

boom /buːm/ vi ribombar; (of trade) prosperar ● n (sound) ribombo m; Comm boom m, prosperidade f

boon /buːn/ n bênção f, vantagem f

boost /buːst/ vt desenvolver, promover; ‹morale› levantar; ‹price› aumentar ● n força f 🔲. **~er** n Med dose suplementar f; (vaccine) revacinação f, (P) reforço m

boot /buːt/ n bota f; Auto portamala f, bagageira f ● vt **~ (up)** Comput dar carga em; **to ~** (in addition) ainda por cima

booth /buːð/ n barraca f; (telephone, voting) cabine f

booty /'buːtɪ/ n saque m, pilhagem f

booze /buːz/ vi 🔲 embebedar-se 🔲; encharcar-se 🔲 ● n 🔲 pinga f 🔲

border /'bɔːdə(r)/ n borda f, margem f; (frontier) fronteira f; (garden bed) canteiro m ● vi **~ on** confinar com;

(*be almost the same as*) atingir as raias de

borderline /'bɔːdəlaɪn/ n linha f divisória; ~ **case** caso m limite

bore[1] /bɔː(r)/ ▸ BEAR[2]

bore[2] /bɔː(r)/ vt/i Techn furar, perfurar ● n (*of gun barrel*) calibre m

bore[3] /bɔː(r)/ vt aborrecer, entediar ● n maçante m; (*thing*) chatice f; **be ~d** aborrecer-se, maçar-se. **~dom** n tédio m. **boring** a tedioso, maçante

born /bɔːn/ a nascido; **be ~** nascer

borne /bɔːn/ ▸ BEAR[2]

borough /'bʌrə/ n município m

borrow /'bɒrəʊ/ vt pedir emprestado (**from** a)

bosom /'bʊzəm/ n peito m; (*woman's; also fig*) (*midst*) seio m; ~ **friend** amigo íntimo m

boss /bɒs/ n 🄸 patrão m; patroa f; mandachuva m 🄸 ● vt mandar; ~ **sb about** 🄸 mandar em alguém

bossy /'bɒsɪ/ a mandão, autoritário

botan|y /'bɒtənɪ/ n botânica f. **~ical** /bə'tænɪkl/ a botânico. **~ist** /-ɪst/ n botânico m

botch /bɒtʃ/ vt atamancar; (*spoil*) estragar, escangalhar

both /bəʊθ/ a & pron ambos, os dois; ~ **of us** nós dois; ~ **the books** ambos os livros ● adv ~ ... **and** não só ... mas também, tanto ... como

bother /'bɒðə(r)/ vt/i incomodar(-se) ● n (*inconvenience*) incómodo m, (P) incómodo m; trabalho m; (*effort*) custo m, trabalho m; (*worry*) preocupação f; **don't** ~ não se incomode; **I can't be ~ed** não posso me dar o trabalho

bottle /'bɒtl/ n garrafa f; (*small*) frasco m; (*for baby*) mamadeira f, (P) biberão m ● vt engarrafar; ~ **up** reprimir. ~ **opener** n saca-rolhas m

bottleneck /'bɒtlnek/ n (*obstruction*) entrave m; (*traffic jam*) engarrafamento m

bottom /'bɒtəm/ n fundo m; (*of hill*) sopé m; (*buttocks*) traseiro m ● a inferior; (*last*) último m; **from top to ~** de alto a baixo

bough /baʊ/ n ramo m

bought /bɔːt/ ▸ BUY

boulder /'bəʊldə(r)/ n pedregulho m

bounce /baʊns/ vi saltar; (*of person*) pular, dar pulos; 🄴 (*of cheque*) ser devolvido ● vt fazer saltar ● n (*of ball*) salto m, (P) ressalto m

bound[1] /baʊnd/ vi pular; (*move by jumping*) ir aos pulos ● n pulo m

bound[2] /baʊnd/ ▸ BIND ● a **be ~ for** ir com destino a, ir para; **be ~ to** (*obliged*) ser obrigado a; (*certain*) haver de; **she's ~ to like it** ela há de gostar disso

boundary /'baʊndrɪ/ n limite m

bound|s /baʊndz/ npl limites mpl; **out of ~s** interdito; **~ed by** limitado por. **~less** a sem limites

bouquet /bʊ'keɪ/ n ramo m de flores; (*wine*) aroma m

bout /baʊt/ n período m; Med ataque m; Boxing combate m

boutique /buː'tiːk/ n boutique f

bow[1] /bəʊ/ n (*weapon*) Mus arco m; (*knot*) laço m. ~ **tie** n gravata borboleta f, (P) laço m

bow[2] /baʊ/ n vénia f, (P) vénia f ● vt/i inclinar(-se), curvar-se

bow[3] /baʊ/ n Naut proa f

bowels /'baʊəlz/ npl intestinos mpl; fig entranhas fpl

bowl[1] /bəʊl/ n (*basin*) bacia f; (*for food*) tigela f; (*of pipe*) fornilho m

bowl[2] /bəʊl/ n (*ball*) boliche m, (P) bola f de madeira ● vt Cricket lançar; ~ **over** siderar, varar. **~ing** n boliche m, (P) bowling m. **~s** npl boliche m, (P) jogo m com bolas de madeira. **~ing alley** n pista f

bowler[1] /'bəʊlə(r)/ n Cricket lançador m

bowler[2] /'bəʊlə(r)/ n ~ **(hat)** (chapéu de) coco m

box[1] /bɒks/ n caixa f; Theatr camarote m; **B~ing Day** feriado m no primeiro dia útil depois do Natal ● vt pôr dentro duma caixa; ~ **in** fechar. ~ **office** n bilheteria f, (P) bilheteira f

box[2] /bɒks/ vt/i Sport lutar boxe; ~ **the ears of** esbofetear. **~er** n pugilista m, boxeur m. **~ing** n boxe m, pugilismo m

boy /bɔɪ/ n rapaz m. **~friend** n namorado m. **~ish** a de menino

boycott /'bɔɪkɒt/ vt boicotar ● n boicote m

bra /brɑː/ n soutien m

brace /breɪs/ n braçadeira f; (*dental*) aparelho m; (*tool*) berbequim m; (*of birds*) par m ● vt apoiar, firmar; ~ **o.s.** concentrar as energias, fazer força; (*for blow*) preparar-se. **~s** npl (*for trousers*) suspensórios mpl

bracelet /'breɪslɪt/ n bracelete m, pulseira f

bracing /'breɪsɪŋ/ a tonificante, estimulante

bracket /'brækɪt/ n suporte m; (group) grupo m; **age/income** ~ faixa f etária/ salarial; **round** ~s parênteses mpl; **square** ~s parênteses mpl, colchetes mpl ● vt (pt **bracketed**) pôr entre parênteses; (put together) pôr em pé de igualdade, agrupar

brag /bræg/ vi (pt **bragged**) gabar-se (about de)

braid /breɪd/ n galão m; (of hair) trança f

Braille /breɪl/ n braile m

brain /breɪn/ n cérebro m; miolos mpl 🔟; fig inteligência f; ~s Culin miolos mpl. ~**less** a estúpido

brainwash /'breɪnwɒʃ/ vt fazer uma lavagem cerebral

brainwave /'breɪnweɪv/ n ideia f genial

brainy /'breɪnɪ/ a (**-ier, -iest**) inteligente, esperto

braise /breɪz/ vt Culin estufar

brake /breɪk/ n travão m ● vt/i travar; ~ **light** farol m do freio, (P) luz f de travagem

branch /brɑːntʃ/ n ramo m; (of road) ramificação f; (of railway line) ramal m; Comm sucursal f; (of bank) balcão m ● vi ~ (**off**) bifurcar-se, ramificar-se

brand /brænd/ n marca f; ~ **name** marca f de fábrica ● vt marcar; ~ **sb as** tachar alguém de, (P) rotular alguém de. ~**new** a novo em folha

brandish /'brændɪʃ/ vt brandir

brandy /'brændɪ/ n aguardente f, conhaque m

brass /brɑːs/ n latão m; **the** ~ Mus os metais mpl; **top** ~ 🔟 os chefões 🔟 ● a de cobre, de latão; **get down to** ~ **tacks** tratar das coisas sérias

brassiere /'bræsɪə(r)/ n soutien m

brat /bræt/ n pej fedelho m

bravado /brə'vɑːdəʊ/ n bravata f

brave /breɪv/ a (**-er, -est**) bravo, valente ● vt arrostar. ~**ry** /-ərɪ/ n bravura f

brawl /brɔːl/ n briga f, rixa f, desordem f ● vi brigar

brawn /brɔːn/ n força f muscular, músculo m. ~**y** a musculoso

bray /breɪ/ n zurro m ● vi zurrar

brazen /'breɪzn/ a descarado

Brazil /brə'zɪl/ n Brasil m; ~ **nut** castanha f do Pará. ~**ian** a & n brasileiro m

breach /briːtʃ/ n quebra f; (gap) brecha f ● vt abrir uma brecha em; ~ **of contract** quebra f de contrato; ~ **of the peace** perturbação f da ordem pública;

~ **of trust** abuso m de confiança

bread /bred/ n pão m. ~**winner** n ganha-pão m

breadcrumbs /'bredkrʌmz/ npl migalhas fpl; Culin farinha f de rosca

breadth /bredθ/ n largura f; (of mind, view) abertura f

break /breɪk/ vt (pt **broke**, pp **broken**) partir, quebrar; ‹vow, silence, etc› quebrar; ‹law› transgredir; ‹journey› interromper; ‹news› dar; ‹a record› bater; ~ **one's arm/leg** quebrar or (P) partir o braço/a perna ● vi partir-se, quebrar-se; ‹voice, weather› mudar; ~ **in** forçar uma entrada; ~ **out** rebentar ● n quebra f, ruptura f; (interval) intervalo m; 🔟 (opportunity) oportunidade f; chance f □ ~ **down** vt analisar ● vi (of person) ir-se abaixo; (of machine) avariar-se. ~ **off** vt quebrar ● vi desligar-se. ~ **up** vt/i terminar ● vi (of schools) entrar em férias. ~**able** a quebrável. ~**age** n quebra f

breakdown /'breɪkdaʊn/ n Techn avaria f, pane f; Med esgotamento m nervoso; (of figures) análise f ● a Auto de pronto-socorro; ~ **van** pronto-socorro m

breaker /'breɪkə(r)/ n vaga f de rebentação

breakfast /'brekfəst/ n café m da manhã, (P) pequeno-almoço

breakthrough /'breɪkθruː/ n descoberta f decisiva, avanço m

breakwater /'breɪkwɔːtə(r)/ n quebra-mar m

breast /brest/ n peito m. ~**feed** vt amamentar; ~**stroke** n estilo m bruços

breath /breθ/ n respiração f; **bad** ~ mau hálito m; **out of** ~ sem fôlego; **under one's** ~ num murmúrio, baixo. ~**less** a ofegante

breath|e /briːð/ vt/i respirar; ~**e in** inspirar; ~**e out** expirar. ~**ing** n respiração f. ~**ing space** n pausa f

breather /'briːðə(r)/ n pausa f de descanso, momento m para respirar

breathtaking /'breθteɪkɪŋ/ a assombroso, arrebatador

bred /bred/ ▶ **BREED**

breed /briːd/ vt (pt **bred**) criar ● vi reproduzir-se ● n raça f. ~**er** n criador m. ~**ing** n criação f; fig educação f

breez|e /briːz/ n brisa f. ~**y** a fresco

brevity /'brevətɪ/ n brevidade f

brew /bruː/ vt ‹beer› fabricar; ‹tea› fazer; fig armar; tramar ● vi fermentar; ‹tea› preparar; fig armar-se; preparar-se

● n decocção f; (tea) infusão f. **~er** n cervejeiro m. **~ery** n cervejaria f

bribe /braɪb/ n suborno m ● vt subornar. **~ry** /-ərɪ/ n suborno m, corrupção f

brick /brɪk/ n tijolo m

bricklayer /'brɪkleɪə(r)/ n pedreiro m

bridal /'braɪdl/ a nupcial

bride /braɪd/ n noiva f

bridegroom /'braɪdɡrʊm/ n noivo m

bridesmaid /'braɪdzmeɪd/ n dama f de honra, (P) de honor

bridge¹ /brɪdʒ/ n ponte f; (of nose) cana f ● vt **~ a gap** preencher uma lacuna

bridge² /brɪdʒ/ n Cards bridge m

bridle /'braɪdl/ n cabeçada f, freio m ● vt refrear

brief¹ /briːf/ a (-er, -est) breve. **~s** npl (men's) cueca f, (P) slip m; (women's) calcinhas fpl, (P) cuecas fpl. **~ly** adv brevemente

brief² /briːf/ n Jur sumário m; (case) causa f; (instructions) instruções fpl ● vt dar instruções a

briefcase /'briːfkeɪs/ n pasta f

brigad|e /brɪ'ɡeɪd/ n brigada f

bright /braɪt/ a (-er, -est) brilhante; (of colour) vivo; (of light) forte; ‹room› claro; (cheerful) alegre; (clever) inteligente. **~ness** n (sheen) brilho m; (clarity) claridade f; (intelligence) inteligência f

brighten /'braɪtn/ vt alegrar ● vi (of weather) clarear; (of face) animar-se, iluminar-se

brillian|t /'brɪljənt/ a brilhante. **~ce** n brilho m

brim /brɪm/ n borda f; (of hat) aba f ● vi (pt brimmed) **~ over** transbordar, cair por fora

bring /brɪŋ/ vt (pt brought) trazer; **~ about** causar; **~ back** trazer (de volta); (call to mind) relembrar; **~ down** trazer para baixo; ‹bird, plane› abater; (prices) baixar; **~ forward** adiantar, apresentar; **~ it off** ser bem sucedido (em alguma coisa); **~ out** (take out) tirar; (show) revelar; ‹book› publicar; **~ round** or **to** reanimar, fazer voltar a si; **~ to bear** ‹pressure etc› exercer; **~ up** educar; Med vomitar; ‹question› levantar

brink /brɪŋk/ n beira f, borda f

brisk /brɪsk/ a (-er, -est) ‹pace, movement› vivo, rápido; ‹business, demand› grande

bristl|e /'brɪsl/ n pelo m

Britain /'brɪtən/ n Grã-Bretanha f

British /'brɪtɪʃ/ a britânico; **the ~** o povo m britânico, os britânicos mpl

brittle /'brɪtl/ a frágil

broach /brəʊtʃ/ vt abordar, entabular, encetar

broad /brɔːd/ a (-er, -est) largo; (daylight) pleno; **~band** banda f larga; **~ bean** fava f. **~minded** a tolerante, liberal. **~ly** adv de modo geral

broadband /'brɔːdbænd/ n banda larga f

broadcast /'brɔːdkɑːst/ vt/i (pt broadcast) transmitir, fazer uma transmissão; ‹person› cantar, falar etc na rádio or na TV ● n emissão f. **~ing** a & n (de) rádiodifusão f

broaden /'brɔːdn/ vt/i alargar(-se)

broccoli /'brɒkəlɪ/ n inv brócolis mpl, (P) brócolos mpl

brochure /'brəʊʃə(r)/ n brochura f

broke /brəʊk/ ▶ BREAK a 🅰 depenado 🅰 liso, (P) 🅰 teso 🅰

broken /'brəʊkən/ a **~ English** inglês m estropeado. **~hearted** a com o coração despedaçado

broker /'brəʊkə(r)/ n corretor m, broker m

bronchitis /brɒŋ'kaɪtɪs/ n bronquite f

bronze /brɒnz/ n bronze m

brooch /brəʊtʃ/ n broche m

brood /bruːd/ n ninhada f ● vi chocar; fig cismar. **~y** a (hen) choca; fig sorumbático

brook /brʊk/ n regato m, ribeiro m

broom /bruːm/ n vassoura f; Bot giesta f

broth /brɒθ/ n caldo m

brothel /'brɒθl/ n bordel m

brother /'brʌðə(r)/ n irmão m. **~in-law** n (pl **~s-in-law**) cunhado m. **~hood** n irmandade f; fraternidade f. **~ly** a fraternal

brought /brɔːt/ ▶ BRING

brow /braʊ/ n (forehead) testa f; (of hill) cume m; (eyebrow) sobrancelha f

brown /braʊn/ a (-er, -est) castanho ● n castanho m ● vt/i acastanhar; (in the sun) bronzear, tostar; ‹meat› alourar

browse /braʊz/ vi (through book) folhear; (of animal) pastar; (in a shop) olhar sem comprar. **~r** n Comput navegador m

bruise /bruːz/ n hematoma m, contusão f ● vt causar um hematoma. **~d** a coberto de hematomas, contuso; ‹fruit› machucado, (P) pisado

b

brunette /bruːˈnet/ n morena f

brunt /brʌnt/ n **the ~ of** o maior peso de, o pior de

brush /brʌʃ/ n escova f; (painter's) pincel m; (skirmish) escaramuça f; **~ against** roçar; **~ aside** não fazer caso de; **~ off** ⚀ (reject) mandar passear ⚀; **~ up (on)** aperfeiçoar

brusque /bruːsk/ a brusco

Brussels /ˈbrʌslz/ n Bruxelas f; **~ sprouts** couve-de-Bruxelas f

brutal /ˈbruːtl/ a brutal. **~ity** /-ˈtælətɪ/ n brutalidade f

brute /bruːt/ n & a (animal, person) bruto m; **by ~ force** por força bruta

BSc abbr (= Bachelor of Science) ▶ BACHELOR

BSE /ˈbiːesˈiː/ n EEB, encefalopatia espongiforme bovina

btw abbr (= by the way) a propósito; Thursday, ~, is also the day that our new kitchen gets delivered a propósito, quinta-feira é também o dia em que nos entregam a nova cozinha

bubb|le /ˈbʌbl/ n bolha f; (of soap) bola f de sabão ● vi borbulhar; **~le over** transbordar. **~le gum** n chiclete m, (P) pastilha f elástica. **~ly** a efervescente

buck¹ /bʌk/ n macho m ● vi dar galões, (P) corcovear ☐ **~ up** vt/i animar(-se); ⚀ (rush) apressar-se; despachar-se

buck² /bʌk/ n Amer ⚀ dólar m

buck³ /bʌk/ n **pass the ~**⚀ fazer o jogo do empurra ⚀

bucket /ˈbʌkɪt/ n balde m

buckle /ˈbʌkl/ n fivela f ● vt/i afivelar(-se); (bend) torcer(-se), vergar; **~ down to** empenhar-se

bud /bʌd/ n botão m, rebento m ● vi (pt budded) rebentar; **in ~** em botão

Buddhis|t /ˈbʊdɪst/ a & n budista mf. **~m** /-zəm/ n budismo m

budding /ˈbʌdɪŋ/ a nascente, em botão, incipiente

budge /bʌdʒ/ vt/i mexer(-se)

budget /ˈbʌdʒɪt/ n orçamento m ● vi (pt budgeted) **~ for** prever no orçamento m

buff /bʌf/ n (colour) cor f de camurça; ⚀ fanático m; entusiasta mf ● vt polir

buffalo /ˈbʌfələʊ/ n (pl -oes) búfalo m; Amer bisão m

buffer /ˈbʌfə(r)/ n para-choque m

buffet¹ /ˈbʊfeɪ/ n (meal, counter) bufê m, (P) bufete m

buffet² /ˈbʌfɪt/ vt (pt buffeted) esbofetear

bug /bʌg/ n (insect) bicho m; (bedbug) percevejo m; ⚀ (germ) vírus m; ⚀ (device) microfone m de escuta; ⚀ (defect) defeito m ● vt (pt bugged) grampear; Amer ⚀ (annoy) chatear ⚀

buggy /ˈbʌgɪ/ n (for baby) carrinho m

bugle /ˈbjuːgl/ n clarim m

build /bɪld/ vt/i (pt built) construir, edificar ● n físico m, compleição f ☐ **~ up** vt/i criar; (increase) aumentar; (accumulate) acumular(-se). **~up** n acumulação f; fig publicidade f. **~er** n construtor m, empreiteiro m; (workman) operário m

building /ˈbɪldɪŋ/ n edifício m, prédio m; **~ site** canteiro m de obras; **~ society** sociedade f de investimentos imobiliários

built /bɪlt/ ▶ BUILD. **~-in** a incorporado; **~-in wardrobe** armário m embutido na parede; **~-up** a urbanizado

bulb /bʌlb/ n bolbo m; Electr lâmpada f. **~ous** a bolboso

Bulgaria /bʌlˈgeərɪə/ n Bulgária f

bulg|e /bʌldʒ/ n bojo m, saliência f ● vi inchar; (jut out) fazer uma saliência. **~ing** a inchado; <pocket etc> cheio

bulk /bʌlk/ n quantidade f, volume m; **in ~** por grosso; (loose) a granel; **the ~ of** a maior parte de. **~y** a volumoso

bull /bʊl/ n touro m. **~seye** n (of target) centro m do alvo, mosca f

bulldog /ˈbʊldɒg/ n buldogue m

bulldoze /ˈbʊldəʊz/ vt terraplanar. **~r** /-ə(r)/ n bulldozer m

bullet /ˈbʊlɪt/ n bala f. **~proof** a à prova de balas; <vehicle> blindado

bulletin /ˈbʊlətɪn/ n boletim m

bullfight /ˈbʊlfaɪt/ n tourada f, corrida f de touros. **~er** n toureiro m. **~ing** n tauromaquia f

bullring /ˈbʊlrɪŋ/ n arena f, (P) praça f de touros

bully /ˈbʊlɪ/ n mandão m, pessoa f prepotente; Schol terror m, o mau ● vt intimidar; (treat badly) atormentar; (coerce) forçar (**into** a)

bum¹ /bʌm/ n ⚀ (buttocks) traseiro m; bunda f⚀

bum² /bʌm/ n Amer ⚀ vagabundo m

bump /bʌmp/ n choque m, embate m; (swelling) inchaço m; (on head) galo m ● vt/i bater, chocar; **~ into** bater em, chocar com; (meet) esbarrar com, encontrar. **~y** a <surface> irregular; <ride> aos solavancos

bumper /'bʌmpə(r)/ n para-choques m inv ● a excepcional

bun /bʌn/ n pãozinho m doce com passas; (hair) coque m

bunch /bʌntʃ/ n (of flowers) ramo m; (of keys) molho m; (of people) grupo m; (of grapes) cacho m

bundle /'bʌndl/ n molho m ● vt atar num molho; (push) despachar

bung /bʌŋ/ n batoque m, rolha f ● vt rolhar; 🅸 (throw) atirar; deitar; ~ up entupir

bungalow /'bʌŋgələʊ/ n chalé m; (outside Europe) bungalô m, (P) bungalow m

bungle /'bʌŋgl/ vt fazer malfeito, estragar

bunion /'bʌnjən/ n Med joanete m

bunk /bʌŋk/ n (in train) couchette f; (in ship) beliche m. ~ beds npl beliches mpl

bunker /'bʌŋkə(r)/ n Mil abrigo m, casamata f, bunker m; Golf obstáculo m em cova de areia

buoy /bɔɪ/ n boia f ● vt ~ up animar

buoyan|t /'bɔɪənt/ a flutuante; fig alegre. ~cy n fig alegria f; exuberância f

burden /'bɜːdn/ n fardo m ● vt carregar, sobrecarregar

bureau /'bjʊərəʊ/ n (pl -eaux /-əʊz/) (desk) secretária f; (office) seção f, (P) secção f

bureaucracy /bjʊə'rɒkrəsɪ/ n burocracia f

bureaucrat /'bjʊərəkræt/ n burocrata mf. ~ic /-'krætɪk/ a burocrático

burger /'bɜːgə(r)/ n hambúrguer m

burglar /'bɜːglə(r)/ n ladrão m, assaltante mf. ~ alarm n alarme m contra ladrões. ~ize vt Amer assaltar. ~y n assalto m

burgle /'bɜːgl/ vt assaltar

burial /'berɪəl/ n enterro m

burka, burkha /'bɜːkə, 'bʊrkɑ/ n burca f

burly /'bɜːlɪ/ a (-ier, -iest) robusto e corpulento, forte

Burm|a /'bɜːmə/ n Birmânia f. ~ese /-'miːz/ a & n birmanês m

burn /bɜːn/ vt (pt burned or burnt) queimar ● vi queimar(-se), arder ● n queimadura f; ~ down reduzir a cinzas. ~er n (of stove) bico m de gás

burnt /bɜːnt/ ▶ BURN

burp /bɜːp/ n 🅸 arroto m ● vi 🅸 arrotar

burrow /'bʌrəʊ/ n toca f ● vi cavar, fazer uma toca

burst /bɜːst/ vt/i (pt burst) arrebentar; ~ into ‹flames, room etc› irromper em; ~ into tears desatar num choro, desfazer-se em lágrimas; ~ out laughing desatar a rir ● n estouro m, rebentar m; (of anger, laughter) explosão f; (of firing) rajada f; (of energy) acesso m

bury /'berɪ/ vt sepultar, enterrar; (hide) esconder; (engross, thrust) mergulhar

bus /bʌs/ n (pl buses) ônibus m, (P) autocarro m; ~ lane faixa f de ônibus, (P) de autocarro. ~ stop n paragem f

bush /bʊʃ/ n arbusto m; (land) mato m. ~y a espesso

business /'bɪznɪs/ n (trade, shop, affair) negócio m; (task) função f; (occupation) ocupação f; have no ~ to não ter o direito de; it's no ~ of yours não é da sua conta; mind your own ~ cuide da sua vida; that's my ~ isso é meu problema. ~like a eficiente, sistemático. ~man n homem m de negócios, comerciante m

busker /'bʌskə(r)/ n músico m ambulante

bust¹ /bʌst/ n busto m

bust² /bʌst/ vt/i (pt busted or bust) 🅸 ▶ BURST, ▶ BREAK ● a falido; go ~ falir. ~up n 🅸 discussão f, (P) bulha f

bustl|e /'bʌsl/ vi andar numa azáfama; (hurry) apressar-se ● n azáfama f. ~ing a animado, movimentado

bus|y /'bɪzɪ/ a (-ier, -iest) ocupado; ‹street› movimentado; ‹day› atarefado ● vt ~y o.s. with ocupar-se com. ~ily adv ativamente, atarefadamente

busybody /'bɪzɪbɒdɪ/ n intrometido m, pessoa f abelhuda

but /bʌt/ conj mas ● prep exceto, (P) excepto, senão ● adv apenas, só; all ~ todos menos; (nearly) quase, por pouco não; ~ for sem, se não fosse; last ~ one/two penúltimo/antepenúltimo; nobody ~ ninguém a não ser

butcher /'bʊtʃə(r)/ n açougueiro m, (P) homem m do talho; fig carrasco m; the ~'s açougue m, (P) talho m ● vt chacinar

butler /'bʌtlə(r)/ n mordomo m

butt /bʌt/ n (of gun) coronha f; (of cigarette) ponta f; (target) alvo m de troça, de ridículo etc; (cask) barril m ● vt/i dar cabeçada em; ~ in interromper

butter /'bʌtə(r)/ n manteiga f ● vt pôr manteiga em

b

buttercup /'bʌtəkʌp/ n botão-de-ouro m

butterfly /'bʌtəflaɪ/ n borboleta f

buttock /'bʌtək/ n nádega f

button /'bʌtn/ n botão m ● vt/i abotoar(-se)

buttonhole /'bʌtnhəʊl/ n casa f de botão; (in lapel) botoeira f ● vt fig obrigar a ouvir

buttress /'bʌtrɪs/ n contraforte m; fig esteio m ● vt sustentar

buy /baɪ/ vt (pt bought) comprar (from a); 🅧 (believe) engolir 🆃 ● n compra f. ~er n comprador m

buzz /bʌz/ n zumbido m ● vi zumbir; ~ off pôr-se a andar. ~er n campainha f

by /baɪ/ prep (near) junto de, perto de; (along, past, means) por; (according to) conforme; (before) antes de; ~ accident/ mistake sem querer; ~ bike/car etc de bicicleta/carro etc; ~ day/night de dia/noite; ~ the kilo por quilo; ~ land/ sea/air por terra/mar/ar; ~ now a esta hora; ~ oneself sozinho ● adv (near) perto; ~ and ~ muito em breve; ~ and large no conjunto. ~election n eleição f suplementar; ~product n derivado m

bye(-bye) /baɪ(baɪ)/ int 🆃 adeus; adeusinho

bypass /'baɪpɑːs/ n (estrada) secundária f, desvio m; Med by-pass m, ponte f de safena ● vt fazer um desvio; fig contornar

bystander /'baɪstændə(r)/ n circunstante mf, espectador m

byte /baɪt/ n byte m

Cc

cab /kæb/ n táxi m; (of lorry, train) cabina f, cabine f

cabaret /'kæbəreɪ/ n variedades fpl, cabaré m

cabbage /'kæbɪdʒ/ n couve f, repolho m

cabin /'kæbɪn/ n cabana f; (in plane) cabina f; (in ship) camarote m

cabinet /'kæbɪnɪt/ n armário m; C~ Pol gabinete m

cable /'keɪbl/ n cabo m ● n funicular m, teleférico m; ~ railway funicular m; ~ television televisão f a cabo. ~ channel n canal de tevê a cabo f, (P) canal de televisão por cabo m

cache /kæʃ/ n (esconderijo m de) tesouro m, armas fpl, provisões fpl

cackle /'kækl/ n cacarejo m ● vi cacarejar

cactus /'kæktəs/ n (pl es or cacti /-taɪ/) cacto m

caddie /'kædɪ/ n Golf caddie m

caddy /'kædɪ/ n lata f para o chá

cadet /kə'det/ n cadete m

cadge /kædʒ/ vt/i filar, (P) cravar

Caesarean /sɪ'zeərɪən/ a ~ (section) cesariana f

cafe /'kæfeɪ/ n café m

cafeteria /kæfɪ'tɪərɪə/ n cafeteria f, restaurante m self-service

cafetière /kæfə'tjeə(r)/ n cafeteira de pistão f

caffeine /'kæfiːn/ n cafeína f

cage /keɪdʒ/ n gaiola f

cagey /'keɪdʒɪ/ a 🆃 (secretive) misterioso; reservado

cake /keɪk/ n bolo m; a piece of ~ 🆃 canja f 🆃. ~d a empastado; his shoes were ~d with mud tinha os sapatos cobertos de lama

calamity /kə'læmətɪ/ n calamidade f

calcium /'kælsɪəm/ n cálcio m

calculat|e /'kælkjʊleɪt/ vt/i calcular; Amer (suppose) supor. ~ed a ‹action› deliberado, calculado. ~ing a calculista. ~ion /-'leɪʃn/ n cálculo m. ~or n calculador m, (P) máquina f de calcular

calendar /'kælɪndə(r)/ n calendário m

calf[1] /kɑːf/ n (pl calves) (young cow or bull) vitelo m, bezerro m; (of other animals) cria f

calf[2] /kɑːf/ n (pl calves) (of leg) barriga f da perna

calibre /'kælɪbə(r)/ n calibre m

call /kɔːl/ vt/i chamar; (summon) convocar; (phone) telefonar; ~ (in or round) (visit) passar por casa de; be ~ed (named) chamar-se; ~ back (phone) tornar a telefonar; (visit) voltar; ~ for (demand) pedir, requerer; (fetch) ir buscar; ~ off cancelar; ~ on (visit) visitar, fazer uma visita a; ~ out (to) chamar; ~ up Mil mobilizar, recrutar; (phone) telefonar ● n chamada f; (bird's cry) canto m; (shout) brado m, grito m; be on ~ estar de serviço. ~ centre n central f telefônica, (P) telefónica. ~er n visitante f, visita f; (phone) chamador m, (P) pessoa f que faz a chamada. ~ing n vocação f

callous /'kæləs/ a insensível

calm /kɑːm/ a (-er, -est) calmo ● n calma f ● vt/i ~ **(down)** acalmar(-se). ~**ness** n calma f

calorie /ˈkælərɪ/ n caloria f

camcorder /ˈkæmkɔːdə(r)/ n câmera f or (P) câmara f de filmar

came /keɪm/ ▶ COME

camel /ˈkæml/ n camelo m

camera /ˈkæmərə/ n máquina f fotográfica; Cine, TV câmera f, (P) câmara. ~**man** n (pl -**men**) operador m; ~**phone** n celular com câmera m, (P) telemóvel com câmara m

camouflage /ˈkæməflɑːʒ/ n camuflagem f ● vt camuflar

camp¹ /kæmp/ n acampamento m ● vi acampar. ~ **bed** n cama f de campanha. ~**er** n campista mf; (car) autocaravana f. ~**ing** n campismo m

camp² /kæmp/ a afetado, efeminado

campaign /kæmˈpeɪn/ n campanha f ● vi fazer campanha

campsite /ˈkæmpsaɪt/ n área f de camping, (P) parque m de campismo

campus /ˈkæmpəs/ n (pl -**puses** /-pəsɪz/) campus m, (P) cidade f universitária

can¹ /kæn/ n vasilha f de lata; (for food) lata f (de conserva) ● vt (pt **canned**) enlatar; ~**ned music** música f em fita para locais públicos. ~ **opener** n abridor m de latas, (P) abrelatas m

can² /kæn unstressed kən /(pres **can**, pt **could**) ● v aux

····▶ (be able to) poder, conseguir; **I ~'t do it** não consigo fazer isso; **I could if I had time** poderia se tivesse tempo; **she ~ help you** ela pode ajudá-lo

····▶ (know how to) saber; **I ~ speak English** sei falar inglês; **he ~ drive** ele sabe dirigir

····▶ (be allowed to) poder, ser permitido; **you ~'t park here** não é permitido estacionar aqui; **nobody ~ take pictures** ninguém pode tirar fotografias

····▶ (in requests) poder; ~ **I have a glass of water, please?** podia me dar um copo de água, por favor?; **could you ring me tomorrow?** podia me telefonar amanhã?

····▶ (with verbs of perception); **I ~ hear you** eu consigo ouvir você; ~ **they see us?** eles conseguem nos ver?

····▶ could (possibility); **we could have won** podíamos ter ganhado; **I could phone her now, if you want** poderia telefonar para ela agora, se você quiser

Canad|a /ˈkænədə/ n Canadá m. ~**ian** /kəˈneɪdɪən/ a & n canadense mf, (P) canadiano m

canal /kəˈnæl/ n canal m

canary /kəˈneərɪ/ n canário m. **C~ Islands** npl as (Ilhas) Canárias

cancel /ˈkænsl/ vt (pt **cancelled**) cancelar; (cross out) riscar; ‹stamps› inutilizar ◻ ~ **out** vi fig neutralizar-se mutuamente. ~**lation** /-ˈleɪʃn/ n cancelamento m

cancer /ˈkænsə(r)/ n câncer m, cancro m; **C~** Astrol Caranguejo m, Câncer m. ~**ous** a canceroso

candid /ˈkændɪd/ a franco

candida|te /ˈkændɪdeɪt/ n candidato m

candle /ˈkændl/ n vela f; (in church) vela f, círio m

candlestick /ˈkændlstɪk/ n castiçal m

candy /ˈkændɪ/ n bala f, (P) açúcar cândi; Amer (sweet, sweets) doce(s) m. ~ **floss** n algodão-doce m

cane /keɪn/ n cana f; (walking stick) bengala f; (for baskets) verga f; Schol (for punishment) vergasta f ● vt vergastar

canine /ˈkeɪnaɪn/ a & n canino m

cannabis /ˈkænəbɪs/ n cânhamo m, maconha f

cannibal /ˈkænɪbl/ n canibal mf. ~**ism** /-zəm/ n canibalismo m

cannon /ˈkænən/ n inv canhão m

cannot /ˈkænət/ (= can not) ▶ CAN²

canny /ˈkænɪ/ a (-ier, -iest) astuto, manhoso

canoe /kəˈnuː/ n canoa f ● vi andar de canoa

canon /ˈkænən/ n cônego m, (P) cónego m; (rule) cânone m

can't /kɑːnt/ (= can not) ▶ CAN²

canteen /kænˈtiːn/ n cantina f; (flask) cantil m; (for cutlery) estojo m

canter /ˈkæntə(r)/ n meio galope m, cânter m ● vi andar a meio galope

canvas /ˈkænvəs/ n lona f; (for painting or tapestry) tela f

canvass /ˈkænvəs/ vt/i angariar votos or fregueses

canyon /ˈkænjən/ n canhão m, (P) desfiladeiro m

cap /kæp/ n (with peak) boné m; (without peak) barrete m; (of nurse) touca f; (of bottle, pen, tube, etc) tampa f; Mech tampa f, tampão m ● vt (pt capped) ‹bottle, pen, tube, etc› tapar, tampar; (rates) impôr um limite a; (outdo) suplantar; Sport selecionar, (P) seleccionar; ~ped with encimado de, coroado de

capab|le /'keɪpəbl/ a ‹person› capaz (of de); ‹things, situations› suscetível (of de). ~ility /-'bɪləti/ n capacidade f

capacity /kə'pæsəti/ n capacidade f; in one's ~ as na (sua) qualidade de

cape¹ /keɪp/ n (cloak) capa f

cape² /keɪp/ n Geog cabo m

caper¹ /'keɪpə(r)/ vi andar aos pinotes

caper² /'keɪpə(r)/ n Culin alcaparra f

capital /'kæpɪtl/ a capital; ~ (letter) maiúscula f ● n (town) capital f; (money) capital m; ~ punishment pena f de morte

capitalis|t /'kæpɪtəlɪst/ a & n capitalista mf. ~m /-zəm/ n capitalismo m

> **Capitol** O Capitólio, como é conhecida a sede do Congresso (Congress) dos Estados Unidos, é situado em Washington DC. Como está situado em Capitol Hill, a imprensa utiliza com frequência este termo para se referir ao Congresso dos Estados Unidos.

Capricorn /'kæprɪkɔ:n/ n Astrol Capricórnio m

capsicum /'kæpsɪkəm/ n pimento m

capsize /kæp'saɪz/ vt/i virar(-se)

capsule /'kæpsju:l/ n cápsula f

captain /'kæptɪn/ n capitão m; Navy capitão-de-mar-e-guerra m ● vt capitanear, comandar

caption /'kæpʃn/ n legenda f; (heading) título m

captivate /'kæptɪveɪt/ vt cativar

captiv|e /'kæptɪv/ a & n cativo m, prisioneiro m. ~ity /-'tɪvəti/ n cativeiro m

captor /'kæptə(r)/ n captor m

capture /'kæptʃə(r)/ vt capturar; ‹attention› prender ● n captura f

car /kɑ:(r)/ n carro m; ~ ferry barca f para carros; ~ phone telefone m de carro. ~ park n (parque m de) estacionamento m; ~ wash n estação f de lavagem

carafe /kə'ræf/ n garrafa f para água ou vinho

caramel /'kærəmel/ n caramelo m

carat /'kærət/ n quilate m

caravan /'kærəvæn/ n caravana f, reboque m

carbohydrate /kɑ:bəʊ'haɪdreɪt/ n hidrato m de carbono

carbon /'kɑ:bən/ n carbono m; ~ copy cópia f em papel carbono, (P) químico; ~ monoxide óxido m de carbono; ~ paper papel m carbono, (P) químico. ~ footprint n pegada f de carbono, (P) pegada f ecológica ; ~ neutral a carbono m neutro ; ~ offsetting n compensação f de carbono

carburettor /kɑ:bju'retə(r)/ n carburador m

carcass /'kɑ:kəs/ n carcaça f

card /kɑ:d/ n cartão m; (postcard) postal m; (playing card) carta f. ~ game(s) n(pl) jogo(s) m(pl) de cartas; ~ index n fichário m, (P) ficheiro m

cardboard /'kɑ:dbɔ:d/ n cartão m, papelão m

cardigan /'kɑ:dɪgən/ n casaco m de lã

cardinal /'kɑ:dɪnl/ a cardeal, principal; ~ number numeral m cardinal ● n Relig cardeal m

care /keə(r)/ n cuidado m; (concern) interesse m ● vi ~ about (be interested) estar interessado por; (be worried) estar preocupado com; ~ for (like) gostar de; (look after) tomar conta de; take ~ tomar cuidado; take ~ of cuidar de; (deal with) tratar de; he couldn't ~ less ele está pouco ligando, ele não dá a menor ⓘ

career /kə'rɪə(r)/ n carreira f ● vi ir a toda a velocidade, ir numa carreira

carefree /'keəfri:/ a despreocupado

careful /'keəfl/ a cuidadoso; (cautious) cauteloso; ~! cuidado!

careless /'keəlɪs/ a descuidado (about com). ~ness n descuido m, negligência f

caress /kə'res/ n carícia f ● vt acariciar

caretaker /'keəteɪkə(r)/ n zelador m duma casa vazia; (janitor) zelador m, (P) porteiro m

cargo /'kɑ:gəʊ/ n (pl -oes) carregamento m, carga f

Caribbean /kærɪ'bi:ən/ a caraíba; the ~ as Caraíbas fpl

caricature /'kærɪkətjʊə(r)/ n caricatura f ● vt caricaturar

caring /'keərɪŋ/ a carinhoso, afetuoso

carnage /'kɑ:nɪdʒ/ n carnificina f

carnation /kɑ:'neɪʃn/ n cravo m

carnival /'kɑːnɪvl/ n carnaval m

carol /'kærəl/ n cântico or canto m de Natal m

carp[1] /kɑːp/ n inv carpa f

carp[2] /kɑːp/ vi ~ **(at)** criticar

carpent|er /'kɑːpɪntə(r)/ n carpinteiro m. ~**ry** n carpintaria f

carpet /'kɑːpɪt/ n tapete m; **with fitted ~s** (estar) atapetado; **be on the ~** 🆒 ser chamado à ordem ● vt (pt **carpeted**) atapetar

carriage /'kærɪdʒ/ n carruagem f; (of goods) frete m, transporte m; (cost, bearing) porte m

carrier /'kærɪə(r)/ n transportador m; (company) transportadora f; Med portador m; ~ **(bag)** saco m de plástico

carrot /'kærət/ n cenoura f

carry /'kærɪ/ vt/i levar; <goods> transportar; (involve) acarretar; (have for sale) ter à venda; **be carried away** entusiasmar-se, deixar-se levar; ~ **off** levar à força; <prize> incluir; ~ **it off** sair-se bem (de); ~ **on** continuar, 🆒 (flirt) flertar; 🆒 (behave) portar-se (mal); ~ **out** executar; <duty> cumprir; ~ **through** levar a cabo

cart /kɑːt/ n carroça f; carro m ● vt acarretar; 🆒 carregar com

carton /'kɑːtn/ n embalagem f de cartão or de plástico; (of yogurt) embalagem f, pote m; (of milk) pacote m

cartoon /kɑːˈtuːn/ n desenho m humorístico, caricatura f; (strip) estória f em quadrinhos, (P) banda f desenhada; (film) desenhos mpl animados. ~**ist** n caricaturista mf; (of strip, film) desenhador m

cartridge /'kɑːtrɪdʒ/ n cartucho m

carv|e /kɑːv/ vt esculpir, talhar; <meat> trinchar; ~**ing knife** faca f de trinchar, trinchante m. ~**ing** n obra f de talha; (on tree trunk) incisão f

case[1] /keɪs/ n caso m; Jur causa f, processo m; Phil argumentos mpl; **in any ~** em todo caso; **in ~ (of)** no caso (de); **in that ~** nesse caso

case[2] /keɪs/ n caixa f; (crate) caixa f, caixote m; (for camera, jewels, spectacles, etc) estojo m; (suitcase) mala f; (for cigarettes) cigarreira f

cash /kæʃ/ n dinheiro m, numerário m, cash m; **be short of ~** ter pouco dinheiro; **in ~** em dinheiro; **pay ~** pagar em dinheiro; ~ **desk** caixa f; ~ **dispenser** caixa f electrônica, (P) multibanco m; ~ **register** caixa f registradora, (P) registadora f ● vt (obtain money for) cobrar, receber; (give money for) pagar; ~ **a cheque** (receive/ give) cobrar/descontar um cheque; ~ **in** receber; ~ **in (on)** aproveitar-se de. ~ **flow** n cash-flow m

cashback /'kæʃbæk/ n cashback m possibilidade que o cliente tem de pagar acima do valor da compra com cartão de crédito e receber 'troco'

cashew /kæˈʃuː/ n caju m

cashier /kæˈʃɪə(r)/ n caixa mf

cashmere /kæʃˈmɪə(r)/ n caxemira f

casino /kəˈsiːnəʊ/ n (pl -os) casino m

casserole /'kæsərəʊl/ n caçarola f; (stew) estufado m

cassette /kəˈset/ n cassette f; ~ **player** gravador m. ~ **recorder** n gravador m

cast /kɑːst/ vt (pt cast) lançar, arremessar; (shed) despojar-se de; (vote) dar; <metal> fundir; <shadow> projetar ● n Theatr elenco m; (mould) molde m; Med aparelho m de gesso. ~**-iron** a de ferro fundido; fig muito forte; ~**-offs** npl roupa f velha

castanets /kæstəˈnets/ npl castanholas fpl

castaway /'kɑːstəweɪ/ n náufrago m

caste /kɑːst/ n casta f

castigate /'kæstɪɡeɪt/ vt castigar

castle /'kɑːsl/ n castelo m; Chess torre f

castor /'kɑːstə(r)/ n roda f de pé de móvel; ~ **sugar** açúcar m em pó

casual /'kæʒʊəl/ a (chance) <meeting> casual; (careless, unmethodical) descuidado; (informal) informal; ~ **clothes** roupa f prática or de lazer; ~ **work** trabalho m ocasional

casualty /'kæʒʊəltɪ/ n (dead) morto m; (death) morte f; (injured) ferido m; (victim) vítima f; Mil baixa f

cat /kæt/ n gato m. ~**seyes**® npl reflectores mpl

catalogue /'kætəlɒɡ/ n catálogo m ● vt catalogar

Catalonia /kætəˈləʊnɪə/ n Catalunha f

catalyst /'kætəlɪst/ n catalisador m

catapult /'kætəpʌlt/ n (child's) atiradeira f, (P) fisga f ● vt catapultar

cataract /'kætərækt/ f (waterfall & Med) catarata f

catarrh /kəˈtɑː(r)/ n catarro m

catastroph|e /kəˈtæstrəfɪ/ n catástrofe f. ~**ic** /kætəsˈtrɒfɪk/ a catastrófico

catch /kætʃ/ vt (pt **caught**) apanhar; (grasp) agarrar; (hear) perceber; ~ **sb's eye** atrair a atenção de alguém; ~ **sight of** avistar ● vi prender-se (**in** em); (get stuck) ficar preso; ~ **fire** pegar fogo, (P) incendiar-se; ~ **on** 𝕀 pegar, tornar-se popular; ~ **up (with)** pôr-se a par (com); ‹work› pôr em dia ● n apanha f; (of fish) pesca f; (trick) ratoeira f; (snag) problema m; (on door) trinco m; (fastener) fecho m. **~phrase** n clichê m

catching /'kætʃɪŋ/ a contagioso, infeccioso

catchy /'kætʃɪ/ a que pega fácil

categorical /kætɪ'gɒrɪkl/ a categórico

category /'kætɪgərɪ/ n categoria f

cater /'keɪtə(r)/ vi fornecer comida (para clubes, casamentos, etc); ~ **for** (pander to) satisfazer; ‹consumers› dirigir-se a. **~er** n fornecedor m. **~ing** n catering m

caterpillar /'kætəpɪlə(r)/ n lagarta f

cathedral /kə'θiːdrəl/ n catedral f

catholic /'kæθəlɪk/ a universal; (eclectic) eclético. **C~** a & n católico m. **~ism** /kə'θɒlɪsɪzəm/ n catolicismo m

cattle /'kætl/ npl gado m

catty /'kætɪ/ a (dissimuladamente) maldoso, com perfídia

caught /kɔːt/ ▶ CATCH

cauliflower /'kɒlɪflaʊə(r)/ n couve-flor f

cause /kɔːz/ n causa f ● vt causar; ~ **sth to grow/move** etc fazer algo crescer/mexer etc

cauti|on /'kɔːʃn/ n cautela f; (warning) aviso m ● vt avisar. **~ous** /'kɔːʃəs/ a cauteloso

cavalry /'kævəlrɪ/ n cavalaria f

cave /keɪv/ n caverna f, gruta f ● vi ~ **in** desabar, dar de si

caveman /'keɪvmæn/ n (pl **-men**) troglodita m, homem m das cavernas; fig (tipo) primário m

cavern /'kævən/ n caverna f

caviare /'kævɪɑː(r)/ n caviar m

cavity /'kævətɪ/ n cavidade f

cc abbr (= **carbon copy**) cópia f com papel carbono, (P) cópia f carbono

CD /siː'diː/ ▶ COMPACT DISC

cease /siːs/ vt/i cessar. **~fire** n cessar-fogo m. **~less** a incessante

cedar /'siːdə(r)/ n cedro m

cedilla /sɪ'dɪlə/ n cedilha f

ceiling /'siːlɪŋ/ n lit & fig teto m

celebrat|e /'selɪbreɪt/ vt/i celebrar, festejar. **~ion** /-'breɪʃn/ n celebração f, festejo m

celebrated /'selɪbreɪtɪd/ a célebre

celebrity /sɪ'lebrətɪ/ n celebridade f

celery /'selərɪ/ n aipo m

celiba|te /'selɪbət/ a celibatário. **~cy** n celibato m

cell /sel/ n (of prison, convent) cela f; Biol, Pol, Electr célula f; ~ **phone** celular m, (P) telemóvel

cellar /'selə(r)/ n porão m, cave f; (for wine) adega f, cave f

cell|o /'tʃeləʊ/ n (pl **-os**) violoncelo m. **~ist** n violoncelista mf

cellphone /'selfəʊn/ n celular m, (P) telemóvel m

cellular /'seljʊlə(r)/ a celular

Celt /kelt/ n celta mf. **~ic** a celta, céltico

cement /sɪ'ment/ n cimento m ● vt cimentar

cemetery /'semətrɪ/ n cemitério m

censor /'sensə(r)/ n censor m ● vt censurar. **~ship** n censura f

censure /'senʃə(r)/ n censura f, crítica f ● vt censurar, criticar

census /'sensəs/ n recenseamento m, censo m

cent /sent/ n cêntimo m

centenary /sen'tiːnərɪ/ n centenário m

centigrade /'sentɪgreɪd/ a centígrado

centimetre /'sentɪmiːtə(r)/ n centímetro m

central /'sentrəl/ a central; ~ **heating** aquecimento m central. **~ize** vt centralizar

centre /'sentə(r)/ n centro m ● vt (pt **centred**) centrar ● vi ~ **on** concentrar-se em, fixar-se em

century /'sentʃərɪ/ n século m

ceramic /sɪ'ræmɪk/ a ‹object› em cerâmica. **~s** n cerâmica f

cereal /'sɪərɪəl/ n cereal m

ceremonial /serɪ'məʊnɪəl/ a de cerimônia ● n cerimonial m

ceremon|y /'serɪmənɪ/ n cerimônia f, (P) cerimónia f. **~ious** /-'məʊnɪəs/ a cerimonioso

certain /'sɜːtn/ a certo; **be ~** ter a certeza; **for ~** com certeza, ao certo; **make ~** confirmar, verificar. **~ly** adv com certeza, certamente. **~ty** n certeza f

certificate /sə'tɪfɪkət/ n certificado m; (birth, marriage) certidão f; (health) atestado m

certif|y /'sɜːtɪfaɪ/ *vt/i* certificar

chafe /tʃeɪf/ *vt/i* esfregar; (*make/become sore*) esfolar/ficar esfolado; *fig* irritar(-se)

chaffinch /'tʃæfɪntʃ/ *n* tentilhão *m*

chain /tʃeɪn/ *n* corrente *f*, cadeia *f*; (*series*) cadeia *f*; ~ **store** loja *f* pertencente a uma cadeia ● *vt* acorrentar; ~ **reaction** reação *f* em cadeia. ~**smoke** *vi* fumar cigarros um atrás do outro

chair /tʃeə(r)/ *n* cadeira *f*; (*position of chairman*) presidência *f*; *Univ* cátedra *f* ● *vt* presidir

chairman /'tʃeəmən/ *n* (*pl* -men) presidente *mf*

chalet /'ʃæleɪ/ *n* chalé *m*

chalk /tʃɔːk/ *n* greda *f*, cal *f*; (*for writing*) giz *m* ● *vt* traçar com giz

challeng|e /'tʃælɪndʒ/ *n* desafio *m*; (*by sentry*) interpelação *f* ● *vt* desafiar; (*question the truth of*) contestar. ~**er** *n* *Sport* pretendente (ao título) *mf*. ~**ing** *a* estimulante, que constitui um desafio

chamber /'tʃeɪmbə(r)/ *n old use* aposento *m*; ~ **music** música *f* de câmara; **C~ of Commerce** Câmara *f* de Comércio. ~**maid** *n* arrumadeira *f*, (*P*) criada *f*

chamois /'ʃæmɪ/ *n* ~**(-leather)** camurça *f*

champagne /ʃæm'peɪn/ *n* champanhe *m*

champion /'tʃæmpɪən/ *n* campeão *m*, campeã *f* ● *vt* defender. ~**ship** *n* campeonato *m*

chance /tʃɑːns/ *n* acaso *m*; (*luck*) sorte *f*; (*opportunity*) oportunidade *f*, chance *f*; (*likelihood*) hipótese *f*, probabilidade *f*; (*risk*) risco *m* ● *a* casual, fortuito ● *vi* calhar ● *vt* arriscar; **by** ~ por acaso

chancellor /'tʃɑːnsələ(r)/ *n* chanceler *m*; **C~ of the Exchequer** Ministro *m* das Finanças

chancy /'tʃɑːnsɪ/ *a* arriscado

chandelier /ʃændə'lɪə(r)/ *n* lustre *m*

change /tʃeɪndʒ/ *vt* mudar; (*exchange*) trocar *‹clothes, house, trains, etc›* mudar de; ~ **hands** (*ownership*) mudar de dono; ~ **one's mind** mudar de ideia(s) ● *vi* mudar; (~ *clothes*) mudar-se, mudar de roupa; ~ **into** *‹a butterfly etc›* transformar-se em; *‹evening dress etc›* pôr; ~ **over** passar, mudar (**to** para) ● *n* mudança *f*; (*money*) troco *m*; **a** ~ **of clothes** uma muda de roupa. ~**able** *a* variável

channel /'tʃænl/ *n* canal *m* ● *vt* (*pt* **channelled**) canalizar; **the C~ Islands** as Ilhas do Canal da Mancha; **the (English) C~** o Canal da Mancha

chant /tʃɑːnt/ *n* cântico *m* ● *vt/i* cantar, entoar

chao|s /'keɪɒs/ *n* caos *m*. ~**tic** /-'ɒtɪk/ *a* caótico

chap /tʃæp/ *n* 🔲 sujeito *m*; cara *m* 🔲, (*P*) tipo *m*

chapel /'tʃæpl/ *n* capela *f*

chaplain /'tʃæplɪn/ *n* capelão *m*

chapter /'tʃæptə(r)/ *n* capítulo *m*

character /'kærəktə(r)/ *n* caráter *m*, (*P*) carácter *m*; (*in novel, play*) personagem *m*; (*reputation*) fama *f*; (*eccentric person*) excêntrico *m*; (*letter*) caractere *m*, (*P*) carácter *m*. ~**ize** *vt* caracterizar

characteristic /kærəktə'rɪstɪk/ *a* característico ● *n* característica *f*

charade /ʃə'rɑːd/ *n* charada *f*

charcoal /'tʃɑːkəʊl/ *n* carvão *m* de lenha

charge /tʃɑːdʒ/ *n* preço *m*; *Electr, Mil* carga *f*; *Jur* acusação *f*; (*task, custody*) cargo *m* ● *vt/i* *‹price›* cobrar; *‹enemy›* atacar; *Jur* incriminar; **be in** ~ **of** ter a cargo; **take** ~ **of** encarregar-se de

chariot /'tʃærɪət/ *n* carro *m* de guerra or triunfal

charisma /kə'rɪzmə/ *n* carisma *m*. ~**tic** /kærɪz'mætɪk/ *a* carismático

charit|y /'tʃærətɪ/ *n* caridade *f*; (*society*) instituição *f* de caridade. ~**able** *a* caridoso

charm /tʃɑːm/ *n* encanto *m*, charme *m*; (*spell*) feitiço *m*; (*talisman*) amuleto *m* ● *vt* encantar. ~**ing** *a* encantador

chart /tʃɑːt/ *n* *Naut* carta *f*; (*table*) mapa *m*, gráfico *m*, tabela *f* ● *vt* fazer o mapa de

charter /'tʃɑːtə(r)/ *n* carta *f*; ~ **(flight)** (voo) charter *m* ● *vt* fretar

chase /tʃeɪs/ *vt* perseguir ● *vi* 🔲 correr (**after** atrás de) ● *n* caça *f*, perseguição *f*; ~ **away** or **off** afugentar, expulsar

chasm /'kæzm/ *n* abismo *m*

chassis /'ʃæsɪ/ *n* chassi *m*

chaste /tʃeɪst/ *a* casto

chastise /tʃæs'taɪz/ *vt* castigar

chastity /'tʃæstətɪ/ *n* castidade *f*

chat /tʃæt/ *n* conversa *f*; **have a** ~ bater um papo, (*P*) dar dois dedos de conversa ● *vi* (*pt* **chatted**) conversar, cavaquear. ~**room** *n* sala *f* de chat. ~**ty** *a* conversador

chatter /'tʃætə(r)/ vi tagarelar; **his teeth are ~ing** seus dentes estão tiritando ● n tagarelice f

chauffeur /'ʃəʊfə(r)/ n motorista m, chofer (particular) m, chauffeur m

chauvinis|t /'ʃəʊvɪnɪst/ n chauvinista mf; **male ~t** pej machista m. **~m** /-zəm/ n chauvinismo m

cheap /tʃiːp/ a (**-er, -est**) barato; ‹fare, rate› reduzido

cheapen /'tʃiːpən/ vt depreciar

cheat /tʃiːt/ vt enganar, trapacear ● vi (at games) roubar, (P) fazer batota; (in exams) copiar ● n intrujão m; (at games) trapaceiro m, (P) batoteiro m

check¹ /tʃek/ vt/i (examine) verificar; ‹tickets› revisar; (restrain) controlar, refrear; **~ in** assinar o registro or (P) registo; (at airport) fazer o check-in; **~ out** pagar a conta ● n verificação f; (tickets) controle m; (curb) freio m; Chess xeque m; Amer (bill) conta f; Amer (cheque) cheque m. **~in** n check-in m; **~out** n caixa f; **~up** n exame m médico, check-up m

check² /tʃek/ n (pattern) xadrez m. **~ed** a de xadrez

cheek /tʃiːk/ n face f; fig descaramento m. **~y** a descarado

cheer /tʃɪə(r)/ n alegria f; (shout) viva m ● vt/i aclamar, aplaudir; **~s!** à sua!, (P) vossa (saúde)!; (thank you) obrigado; **~ (up)** animar(-se). **~ful** a bem disposto; alegre

cheerio /tʃɪərɪ'əʊ/ int 🄸 até logo, (P) adeusinho 🄸

cheese /tʃiːz/ n queijo m

cheetah /'tʃiːtə/ n chita f, lobo-tigre m

chef /ʃef/ n cozinheiro-chefe m

chemical /'kemɪkl/ a químico ● n produto m químico

chemist /'kemɪst/ n farmacêutico m; (scientist) químico m. **~'s (shop)** n farmácia f. **~ry** n química f

cheque /tʃek/ n cheque m. **~book** n talão m de cheques, (P) livro m de cheques; **~ card** n cartão m de banco

cherish /'tʃerɪʃ/ vt estimar, querer; ‹hope› acalentar

cherry /'tʃerɪ/ n cereja f

chess /tʃes/ n jogo m de xadrez. **~board** n tabuleiro m de xadrez

chest /tʃest/ n peito m; (for money, jewels) cofre m; **~ of drawers** cômoda f, (P) cómoda f

chestnut /'tʃesnʌt/ n castanha f

chew /tʃuː/ vt mastigar. **~ing gum** n chiclete m, (P) pastilha f elástica

chic /ʃiːk/ a chique

chick /tʃɪk/ n pinto m

chicken /'tʃɪkɪn/ n galinha f ● vi **~ out** 🅇 acovardar-se. **~pox** n catapora f, (P) varicela f

chief /tʃiːf/ n chefe m ● a principal. **~ly** adv principalmente

child /tʃaɪld/ n (pl **children** /'tʃɪldrən/) criança f; (son) filho m; (daughter) filha f. **~hood** n infância f, meninice f. **~ish** a infantil; (immature) acriançado, pueril. **~less** a sem filhos. **~like** a infantil. **~minder** n babá f que cuida de crianças em sua própria casa, (P) ama

childbirth /'tʃaɪldbɜːθ/ n parto m

Chile /'tʃɪlɪ/ n Chile m. **~an** a & n chileno m

chill /tʃɪl/ n frio m; Med resfriado m, (P) constipação f ● vt/i arrefecer; Culin refrigerar. **~y** a frio; **be** or **feel ~y** ter frio

chilli /'tʃɪlɪ/ n (pl **-ies**) malagueta f

chime /tʃaɪm/ n carrilhão m; (sound) música m de carrilhão ● vt/i tocar

chimney /'tʃɪmnɪ/ n (pl **-eys**) chaminé f

chimpanzee /tʃɪmpæn'ziː/ n chimpanzé m

chin /tʃɪn/ n queixo m

china /'tʃaɪnə/ n porcelana f; (crockery) louça f

Chin|a /'tʃaɪnə/ n China f. **~ese** /-'niːz/ a & n chinês m

chink¹ /tʃɪŋk/ n (crack) fenda f, fresta f

chink² /tʃɪŋk/ n tinir m ● vt/i (fazer) tinir

chip /tʃɪp/ n (broken piece) bocado m; Culin batata f frita em palitos; (gambling) ficha f; (electronic) chip m, circuito m integrado ● vt/i (pt **chipped**) lascar(-se)

chiropodist /kɪ'rɒpədɪst/ n calista mf

chirp /tʃɜːp/ n pipilar m; (of cricket) cricri m ● vi pipilar; ‹cricket› cantar, fazer cricri

chivalr|y /'ʃɪvlrɪ/ n cavalheirismo m. **~ous** a cavalheiresco

chive /tʃaɪv/ n cebolinho m

chlorine /'klɔːriːn/ n cloro m

chocolate /'tʃɒklɪt/ n chocolate m

choice /tʃɔɪs/ n escolha f ● a escolhido, seleto, (P) selecionado

choir /'kwaɪə(r)/ n coro m

choirboy /'kwaɪəbɔɪ/ n menino m de coro, corista m, (P) coralista m

choke /tʃəʊk/ vt/i sufocar; (on food) engasgar(-se) ● n Auto afogador m, (P) botão m do ar 🄸

cholesterol /kə'lestərɒl/ n colesterol m

choose /tʃuːz/ vt/i (pt chose, pp chosen) escolher; (prefer) preferir; ~ **to do** decidir fazer

choosy /'tʃuːzɪ/ a 🔢 exigente; difícil de contentar

chop /tʃɒp/ vt/i (pt chopped) cortar ● n ‹wood› machadada f; Culin costeleta f; ~ **down** abater. ~per n cutelo m; ✖ (helicopter) helicóptero m

choppy /'tʃɒpɪ/ a ‹sea› picado

chopstick /'tʃɒpstɪk/ n fachis m, pauzinho m

choral /'kɔːrəl/ a coral

chord /kɔːd/ n Mus acorde m

chore /tʃɔː(r)/ n trabalho m; (unpleasant task) tarefa f maçante; **household ~s** afazeres mpl domésticos

choreograph|er /kɒrɪ'ɒɡrəfə(r)/ n coreógrafo m. ~y n coreografia f

chorus /'kɔːrəs/ n coro m; (of song) refrão m, estribilho m

chose, chosen /tʃəʊz, 'tʃəʊzn/ ▶ CHOOSE

Christ /kraɪst/ n Cristo m

christen /'krɪsn/ vt batizar. ~ing n batismo m

Christian /'krɪstʃən/ a & n cristão m; ~ **name** nome m de batismo. ~ity /-strænətɪ/ n cristandade f

Christmas /'krɪsməs/ n Natal m ● a do Natal; ~ **card** cartão m de Boas Festas; ~ **Day/Eve** dia m /véspera f de Natal; ~ **tree** árvore f de Natal

chrome /krəʊm/ n cromo m

chromosome /'krəʊməsəʊm/ n cromossoma m

chronic /'krɒnɪk/ a crônico, (P) crónico

chronicle /'krɒnɪkl/ n crônica f, (P) crónica f

chronological /krɒnə'lɒdʒɪkl/ a cronológico

chrysanthemum /krɪ'sænθəməm/ n crisântemo m

chubby /'tʃʌbɪ/ a (-ier, -iest) gorducho, rechonchudo

chuck /tʃʌk/ vt 🔢 deitar; atirar; ~ **out** ‹person› expulsar; ‹thing› jogar fora, (P) deitar fora

chuckle /'tʃʌkl/ n riso m abafado ● vi rir sozinho

chum /tʃʌm/ n 🔢 amigo m íntimo, camarada mf. ~my a amigável

chunk /tʃʌŋk/ n (grande) bocado m, naco m

church /tʃɜːtʃ/ n igreja f

churchyard /'tʃɜːtʃjɑːd/ n cemitério m

churlish /'tʃɜːlɪʃ/ a grosseiro, indelicado

churn /tʃɜːn/ n batedeira f; (milk can) vasilha f de leite ● vt bater; ~ **out** produzir em série

chutney /'tʃʌtnɪ/ n (pl -eys) chutney m

cider /'saɪdə(r)/ n sidra f, (P) cidra f

cigar /sɪ'ɡɑː(r)/ n charuto m

cigarette /sɪɡə'ret/ n cigarro m

cinema /'sɪnəmə/ n cinema m

cinnamon /'sɪnəmən/ n canela f

circle /'sɜːkl/ n círculo m; Theat balcão m ● vt dar a volta a ● vi descrever círculos, voltear

circuit /'sɜːkɪt/ n circuito m

circuitous /sɜː'kjuːɪtəs/ a indireto, tortuoso

circular /'sɜːkjʊlə(r)/ a circular

circulat|e /'sɜːkjʊleɪt/ vt/i (fazer) circular. ~ion /-'leɪʃn/ n circulação f; (sales of newspaper) tiragem f

circumcis|e /'sɜːkəmsaɪz/ vt circuncidar. ~ion /-'sɪʒn/ n circuncisão f

circumference /sə'kʌmfərəns/ n circunferência f

circumflex /'sɜːkəmfleks/ n circunflexo m

circumstance /'sɜːkəmstəns/ n circunstância f; ~**s** (means) situação f econômica, (P) económica

circus /'sɜːkəs/ n circo m

cistern /'sɪstən/ n reservatório m; (of WC) autoclismo m

cit|e /saɪt/ vt citar. ~ation /-'teɪʃn/ n citação f

citizen /'sɪtɪzn/ n cidadão m, cidadã f; (of town) habitante mf. ~ship n cidadania f

citrus /'sɪtrəs/ n ~ **fruit** citrino m

city /'sɪtɪ/ n cidade f

The City Área situada dentro dos limites da antiga cidade de Londres. Atualmente é o centro financeiro da capital, na qual muitas instituições financeiras têm as suas sedes centrais. Muitas vezes, quando se fala de *The City*, está se referindo a essas sedes e não à área da cidade propriamente dita.   *i*

---

civic /'sɪvɪk/ a cívico

civil /'sɪvl/ a civil; ‹rights› cívico; (polite) delicado; ~ **servant** funcionário m público; **C~ Service** Administração f Pública; ~ **war** guerra f civil.

~ partnership n união m civil entre homossexuais, (P) união f de facto entre pessoas do mesmo sexo. **~ity** /-'vɪlətɪ/ n civilidade f, cortesia f

civilian /sɪ'vɪlɪən/ a & n civil mf, paisano m

civiliz|e /'sɪvəlaɪz/ vt civilizar. **~ation** /-'zeɪʃn/ n civilização f

claim /kleɪm/ vt reclamar; (assert) pretender ● vi (from insurance) reclamar ● n reivindicação f; (assertion) afirmação f; (right) direito m; (from insurance) reclamação f

clairvoyant /kleə'vɔɪənt/ n vidente mf ● a clarividente

clam /klæm/ n molusco m

clamber /'klæmbə(r)/ vi trepar

clammy /'klæmɪ/ a (-ier, -iest) úmido, (P) húmido e pegajoso

clamour /'klæmə(r)/ n clamor m, vociferação f ● vi **~ for** exigir aos gritos

clamp /klæmp/ n grampo m; (for car) bloqueador m ● vt prender com grampo; ⟨a car⟩ bloquear; **~ down on** apertar, suprimir; 🈂 cair em cima de 🈂

clan /klæn/ n clã m

clang /klæŋ/ n tinir m

clap /klæp/ vt/i (pt clapped) aplaudir; (put) meter ● n aplauso m; (of thunder) ribombo m; **~ one's hands** bater palmas

claret /'klærət/ n clarete m

clarif|y /'klærɪfaɪ/ vt esclarecer. **~ication** /-ɪ'keɪʃn/ n esclarecimento m

clarinet /klærɪ'net/ n clarinete m

clarity /'klærətɪ/ n claridade f

clash /klæʃ/ n choque m; (sound) estridor m; fig conflito m ● vt/i entrechocar(-se); (of colours) destoar

clasp /klɑːsp/ n (fastener) fecho m; (hold, grip) aperto m de mão ● vt apertar, serrar

class /klɑːs/ n classe f ● vt classificar

classic /'klæsɪk/ a & n clássico m. **~s** npl letras fpl clássicas, (P) estudos mpl clássicos. **~al** a clássico

classif|y /'klæsɪfaɪ/ vt classificar; **~ied advertisement** anúncio m classificado. **~ication** /-ɪ'keɪʃn/ n classificação f

classroom /'klɑːsruːm/ n sala f de aulas

clatter /'klætə(r)/ n estardalhaço m ● vi fazer barulho

clause /klɔːz/ n cláusula f; Gram oração f

claustrophob|ia /klɔːstrə'fəʊbɪə/ n claustrofobia f. **~ic** a claustrofóbico

claw /klɔː/ n garra f; (of lobster) tenaz f, pinça f ● vt (seize) agarrar; (scratch) arranhar; (tear) rasgar

clay /kleɪ/ n argila f, barro m

clean /kliːn/ a (-er, -est) limpo ● adv completamente ● vt limpar ● vi **~ up** fazer a limpeza. **~er** n faxineira f, (P) mulher f da limpeza; (of clothes) empregado m da tinturaria

cleans|e /klenz/ vt limpar; fig purificar; **~ing cream** creme m de limpeza

clear /klɪə(r)/ a (-er, -est) claro; ⟨glass⟩ transparente; (without obstacles) livre; ⟨profit⟩ líquido; ⟨sky⟩ limpo; **~ of** (away from) afastado de ● adv claramente ● vt ⟨snow, one's name, etc⟩ limpar; ⟨the table⟩ tirar; ⟨jump⟩ transpor; ⟨debt⟩ saldar; Jur absolver; (through customs) despachar; **~ out** (clean) fazer a limpeza; **~ up** (tidy) arrumar; ⟨mystery⟩ desvendar ● vi ⟨fog⟩ dissipar-se; ⟨sky⟩ limpar; **~ off** or **out** 🈂 sair andando, zarpar; **~ up** (of weather) clarear, limpar

clearance /'klɪərəns/ n autorização f; (for ship) despacho m; (space) espaço m livre; **~ sale** liquidação f, saldos mpl

clearing /'klɪərɪŋ/ n clareira f

cleaver /'kliːvə(r)/ n cutelo m

clench /klentʃ/ vt ⟨teeth, fists⟩ cerrar; (grasp) agarrar

clergy /'klɜːdʒɪ/ n clero m. **~man** (pl -men) n clérigo m, sacerdote m

cleric /'klerɪk/ n clérigo m. **~al** a Relig clerical; (of clerks) de escritório

clerk /klɑːk/ n auxiliar m de escritório

clever /'klevə(r)/ a (-er, -est) esperto, inteligente; (skilful) hábil, habilidoso

cliché /'kliːʃeɪ/ n chavão m, lugar-comum m, clichê m

click /klɪk/ n estalido m, clique m ● vi dar um estalido; Comput clicar

client /'klaɪənt/ n cliente mf

cliff /klɪf/ n penhasco m. **~s** npl falésia f

climat|e /'klaɪmɪt/ n clima m. **~ change** n alterações fpl climáticas

climax /'klaɪmæks/ n clímax m, ponto m culminante

climb /klaɪm/ vt ⟨stairs⟩ subir; ⟨tree, wall⟩ subir em, trepar em, (P) subir, trepar; ⟨mountain⟩ escalar ● vi subir, trepar ● n subida f; (mountain) escalada f; **~ down** descer; fig dar a mão à palmatória fig. **~er** n Sport alpinista mf; (plant) trepadeira f

cling /klɪŋ/ vi (pt clung) **~ (to)** agarrar-se (a); (stick) colar-se (a)

clinic /'klɪnɪk/ n clínica f

clinical /'klɪnɪkl/ a clínico

clink /klɪŋk/ n tinido m ● vt/i (fazer) tilintar

clip[1] /klɪp/ n (for paper) clipe m; (for hair) grampo m, (P) gancho m; (for tube) braçadeira f ● vt (pt clipped) prender

clip[2] /klɪp/ vt (pt clipped) cortar; (trim) aparar ● n tosquia f; ▣ (blow) murro m. **~ping** n recorte m

cloak /kləʊk/ n capa f, manto m

cloakroom /'kləʊkruːm/ n vestiário m; (toilet) toalete m, (P) lavabo m

clock /klɒk/ n relógio m ● vi **~ in/out** marcar o ponto (à entrada/à saída); **~ up** ▣ ‹miles etc› fazer

clockwise /'klɒkwaɪz/ a & adv no sentido dos ponteiros do relógio

clockwork /'klɒkwɜːk/ n mecanismo m; **go like ~** ir às mil maravilhas

clog /klɒg/ n tamanco m, soco m ● vt/i (pt clogged) entupir(-se)

cloister /'klɔɪstə(r)/ n claustro m

close[1] /kləʊs/ a (-er, -est) próximo (to de); ‹link, collaboration› estreito; ‹friend› íntimo; ‹weather› abafado; **have a ~ shave** fig escapar por um triz ● adv perto; **~ at hand, ~ by** muito perto; **~ together** (crowded) espremido. **~-up** n grande plano m. **~ly** adv de perto

close[2] /kləʊz/ vt/i fechar(-se); (end) terminar; (of shop etc) fechar ● n fim m; **~d shop** organização f que só admite trabalhadores sindicalizados

closet /'klɒzɪt/ n armário m

closure /'kləʊʒə(r)/ n encerramento m

clot /klɒt/ n coágulo m ● vi (pt clotted) coagular

cloth /klɒθ/ n pano m; (tablecloth) toalha f de mesa

cloth|e /kləʊð/ vt vestir. **~ing** n vestuário m, roupa f

clothes /kləʊðz/ npl roupa f, vestuário m. **~ line** n varal m para roupa

cloud /klaʊd/ n nuvem f ● vt/i toldar(-se). **~ computing** n computação f na nuvem. **~y** a nublado, toldado; ‹liquid› turvo

clout /klaʊt/ n cascudo m, (P) carolo m; ▣ (power) poder m efectivo ● vt ▣ bater

clove /kləʊv/ n cravo m; **~ of garlic** dente m de alho

clover /'kləʊvə(r)/ n trevo m

clown /klaʊn/ n palhaço m ● vi fazer palhaçadas

club /klʌb/ n clube m; (weapon) cacete m; **~s** Cards paus mpl ● vt/i (pt clubbed) dar bordoadas or cacetadas (em); **~ together** (share costs) cotizar-se

clue /kluː/ n indício m, pista f; (in crossword) definição f; **not have a ~** não fazer a menor ideia

clump /klʌmp/ n maciço m, tufo m

clumsy /'klʌmzɪ/ a (-ier, -iest) desajeitado

clung /klʌŋ/ ▸ CLING

cluster /'klʌstə(r)/ n (pequeno) grupo m; Bot cacho m ● vt/i agrupar(-se)

clutch /klʌtʃ/ vt agarrar (em), apertar ● vi agarrar-se (at a) ● n Auto embreagem f, (P) embraiagem f. **~es** npl garras fpl

clutter /'klʌtə(r)/ n barafunda f, desordem f ● vt atravancar

coach /kəʊtʃ/ n ônibus m, (P) autocarro m, camioneta f; (of train) carruagem f; Sport treinador m ● vt (tutor) dar aulas a; Sport treinar

coal /kəʊl/ n carvão m

coalition /kəʊə'lɪʃn/ n coligação f

coarse /kɔːs/ a (-er, -est) grosseiro

coast /kəʊst/ n costa f ● vi costear; (cycle) descer em roda-livre; (car) ir em ponto morto

coastguard /'kəʊstgɑːd/ n polícia f marítima

coastline /'kəʊstlaɪn/ n litoral m

coat /kəʊt/ n casaco m; (of animal) pelo m; (of paint) camada f, demão f; **~ of arms** brasão m ● vt cobrir. **~ing** n camada f

coax /kəʊks/ vt levar com afagos ou lisonjas, convencer

cobble /'kɒbl/ n **~(-stone)** pedra f de calçada

cobweb /'kɒbweb/ n teia f de aranha

cocaine /kəʊ'keɪn/ n cocaína f

cock /kɒk/ n (male bird) macho m; (rooster) galo m ● vt ‹gun› engatilhar; ‹ears› fitar

cockerel /'kɒkərəl/ n frango m, galo m novo

cockney /'kɒknɪ/ n (pl -eys) (person) londrino m; (dialect) dialeto m do leste de Londres

cockpit /'kɒkpɪt/ n cabine f

cockroach /'kɒkrəʊtʃ/ n barata f

cocktail /'kɒkteɪl/ n cocktail m, coquetel m; **fruit ~** salada f de fruta

cocky /'kɒkɪ/ a (-ier, -iest) convencido ▣

cocoa /'kəʊkəʊ/ n cacau m

coconut /'kəʊkənʌt/ n coco m

cod /kɒd/ n (pl invar) bacalhau m; **~liver oil** óleo m de fígado de bacalhau

code /kəʊd/ n código m ● vt codificar

coerc|e /kəʊ'ɜːs/ vt coagir. **~ion** /-ʃn/ n coação f

coexist /kəʊɪg'zɪst/ vi coexistir. **~ence** n coexistência f

coffee /'kɒfɪ/ n café m; **~bar** café m. **~ table** n mesa f baixa

coffin /'kɒfɪn/ n caixão m

cogent /'kəʊdʒənt/ a convincente; (relevant) pertinente

cognac /'kɒnjæk/ n conhaque m

cohabit /kəʊ'hæbɪt/ vi coabitar

coherent /kə'hɪərənt/ a coerente

coil /kɔɪl/ vt/i enrolar(-se) ● n rolo m; Electr bobina f; (one ring) espiral f; (contraceptive) dispositivo m intrauterino, DIU

coin /kɔɪn/ n moeda f ● vt cunhar

coincide /kəʊɪn'saɪd/ vi coincidir

coinciden|ce /kəʊ'ɪnsɪdəns/ n coincidência f. **~tal** /-'dentl/ a que acontece por coincidência

colander /'kʌləndə(r)/ n peneira f, (P) coador m

cold /kəʊld/ a (-er, -est) frio; **be or feel ~** estar com frio; **it's ~** está frio; **~ cream** creme m para a pele ● n frio m; Med resfriado m, constipação f. **~blooded** a (person) insensível; (deed) a sangue frio. **~ness** n frio m; (of feeling) frieza f

coleslaw /'kəʊlslɔː/ n salada f de repolho cru

colic /'kɒlɪk/ n cólica f(pl)

collaborat|e /kə'læbəreɪt/ vi colaborar. **~ion** /-'reɪʃn/ n colaboração f. **~or** n colaborador m

collapse /kə'læps/ vi desabar; Med ter um colapso ● n colapso m

collapsible /kə'læpsəbl/ a desmontável, dobrável

collar /'kɒlə(r)/ n gola f; (of shirt) colarinho m; (of dog) coleira f ● vt 🔢 pôr a mão a. **~bone** n clavícula f

colleague /'kɒliːg/ n colega mf

collect /kə'lekt/ vt (gather) juntar; (fetch) ir/vir buscar; (money, rent) cobrar; (as hobby) colecionar ● vi juntar-se; **call ~** Amer chamar a cobrar. **~ion** /-ʃn/ n coleção f, (in church) coleta f, (of mail) tiragem f; coleta f, (P) abertura f. **~or** n (as hobby) colecionador m

college /'kɒlɪdʒ/ n colégio m

collide /kə'laɪd/ vi colidir

colliery /'kɒlɪərɪ/ n mina f de carvão

collision /kə'lɪʒn/ n colisão f, choque m; fig conflito m

colloquial /kə'ləʊkwɪəl/ a coloquial

colon /'kəʊlən/ n Gram dois pontos mpl; Anat cólon m

colonel /'kɜːnl/ n coronel m

colonize /'kɒlənaɪz/ vt colonizar

colon|y /'kɒlənɪ/ n colônia f, (P) colónia f. **~ial** /kə'ləʊnɪəl/ a & n colonial mf

colossal /kə'lɒsl/ a colossal

colour /'kʌlə(r)/ n cor f ● a (photo, TV, etc) a cores; (film) colorido ● vt colorir, dar cor a ● vi (blush) corar. **~blind** a daltônico, (P) daltónico. **~ful** a colorido. **~ing** n (of skin) cor f; (in food) corante m. **~less** a descolorido

coloured /'kʌləd/ a (pencil, person) de cor ● n pessoa f de cor

column /'kɒləm/ n coluna f

columnist /'kɒləmnɪst/ n colunista mf

coma /'kəʊmə/ n coma m

comb /kəʊm/ n pente m ● vt pentear; (search) vasculhar; **~ one's hair** pentear-se

combat /'kɒmbæt/ n combate m ● vt (pt combated) combater

combination /kɒmbɪ'neɪʃn/ n combinação f

combine /kəm'baɪn/ vt/i combinar(-se), juntar(-se), reunir(-se)

combustion /kəm'bʌstʃən/ n combustão f

come /kʌm/ vi (pt came, pp come) vir; (arrive) chegar; (occur) suceder; **~ about** acontecer; **~ across** encontrar, dar com; **~ away** or **off** soltar-se; **~ back** voltar; **~ by** obter; **~ down** descer; (price) baixar; **~ from** vir de; **~ in** entrar; **~ into** (money) herdar; **~ off** (succeed) ter êxito; (fare) sair-se; **~ on!** vamos!; **~ out** sair; **~ round** (after fainting) voltar a si; (be converted) deixar-se convencer; **~ to** (amount to) montar a; **~ up** subir; (seeds) despontar; fig surgir; **~ up with** (idea) ter, vir com, propor. **~back** n regresso m; (retort) réplica f; **~down** n humilhação f

comedian /kə'miːdɪən/ n comediante mf

comedy /'kɒmədɪ/ n comédia f

comet /'kɒmɪt/ n cometa m

comfort /'kʌmfət/ n conforto m ● vt confortar, consolar. ~ **food** n comida f de conforto; ~ **zone** n zona f de conforto; **to be in/out of one's** ~ **zone** estar dentro/fora da sua zona de conforto. ~**able** a confortável

comic /'kɒmɪk/ a cómico, (P) cómico ● n cómico m, (P) cómico m; (periodical) estórias fpl em quadrinhos, (P) revista f de banda desenhada; ~ **strip** estória f em quadrinhos, (P) banda f desenhada

coming /'kʌmɪŋ/ n vinda f; ~**s and goings** idas e vindas fpl ● a próximo

comma /'kɒmə/ n vírgula f

command /kə'mɑːnd/ n Mil comando m; (order) ordem f; (mastery) domínio m ● vt comandar; ‹respect› inspirar, impor. ~**er** n comandante m

commemorat|e /kə'meməreɪt/ vt comemorar. ~**ion** /-'reɪʃn/ n comemoração f. ~**ive** a comemorativo

commence /kə'mens/ vt/i começar

commend /kə'mend/ vt louvar; (entrust) confiar. ~**able** a louvável. ~**ation** /kɒmen'deɪʃn/ n louvor m

comment /'kɒment/ n comentário m ● vi comentar; ~ **on** comentar, fazer comentários

commentary /'kɒməntrɪ/ n comentário m; Radio, TV relato m

commentat|e /'kɒmənteɪt/ vi fazer um relato. ~**or** n Radio, TV comentarista mf, (P) comentador m

commerce /'kɒmɜːs/ n comércio m

commercial /kə'mɜːʃl/ a comercial ● n publicidade (comercial) f. ~**ize** vt comercializar

commiserat|e /kə'mɪzəreɪt/ vi ~ **with** compadecer-se de. ~**ion** /-'reɪʃn/ n comiseração f, pesar m

commission /kə'mɪʃn/ n comissão f; (order for work) encomenda f ● vt encomendar; Mil nomear; ~ **to do** encarregar de fazer; **out of** ~ fora de serviço ativo. ~**er** n comissário m; Police chefe m

commit /kə'mɪt/ vt (pt committed) cometer; (entrust) confiar; ~ **o.s.** comprometer-se, empenhar-se; ~ **suicide** suicidar-se; ~ **to memory** decorar. ~**ment** n compromisso m

committee /kə'mɪtɪ/ n comissão f, comitê m, (P) comité m

commodity /kə'mɒdətɪ/ n artigo m, mercadoria f

common /'kɒmən/ a (-er, -est) comum; (usual) usual, corrente; pej (ill-bred) ordinário; ~ **law** direito m consuetudinário; **C~ Market** Mercado m Comum; ~ **sense** bom senso m, senso m comum ● n prado m público, (P) baldio m; **House of C~s** Câmara f dos Comuns; **in** ~ em comum. ~**room** n sala f comum. ~**ly** adv mais comum

commoner /'kɒmənə(r)/ n plebeu m

commonplace /'kɒmənpleɪs/ a banal ● n lugar-comum m

Commonwealth A associação das antigas colónias e territórios que formavam o Império Britânico. De dois em dois anos, celebra-se um encontro de cúpula dos respectivos chefes de governo. Entre os países-membros existem inúmeros vínculos culturais, educativos e desportivos. Nos Estados Unidos, o termo *Commonwealth* emprega-se oficialmente quando se refere ao conjunto de quatro estados: Kentucky, Massachusetts, Pensilvânia e Virgínia.

commotion /kə'məʊʃn/ n agitação f, confusão f, barulheira f

communal /'kɒmjʊnl/ a (of a commune) comunal; (shared) comum

commune /'kɒmjuːn/ n comuna f

communicat|e /kə'mjuːnɪkeɪt/ vt/i comunicar. ~**ion** /-'keɪʃn/ n comunicação f; ~**ion cord** sinal m de alarme. ~**ive** /-ətɪv/ a comunicativo

communion /kə'mjuːnɪən/ n comunhão f

communis|t /'kɒmjʊnɪst/ n comunista mf ● a comunista. ~**m** /-zəm/ n comunismo m

community /kə'mjuːnətɪ/ n comunidade f; ~ **centre** centro m comunitário

commute /kə'mjuːt/ vi viajar diariamente para o trabalho. ~**r** /-ə(r)/ n pessoa f que viaja diariamente para o trabalho

compact¹ /kəm'pækt/ a compacto. ~ **disc** n cd m

compact² /'kɒmpækt/ n estojo m de pó-de-arroz, (P) caixa f

companion /kəm'pænɪən/ n companheiro m. ~**ship** n companhia f, convívio m

company /'kʌmpənɪ/ n companhia f; (guests) visitas fpl; **keep sb** ~ fazer companhia a alguém

comparable /'kɒmpərəbl/ a comparável

compar|e /kəm'peə(r)/ vt/i
comparar(-se) (**to, with** com). **~ative**
/-'pærətɪv/ a comparativo; ‹comfort etc›
relativo

comparison /kəm'pærɪsn/ n
comparação f

compartment /kəm'pɑːtmənt/ n
compartimento m

compass /'kʌmpəs/ n bússola f; **~es**
compasso m

compassion /kəm'pæʃn/ n compaixão
f. **~ate** a compassivo

compatib|le /kəm'pætəbl/
a compatível. **~ility** /-'bɪləti/ n
compatibilidade f

compel /kəm'pel/ vt (pt **compelled**)
compelir, forçar. **~ling** a irresistível,
convincente

compensat|e /'kɒmpənseit/
vt/i compensar. **~ion** /-'seɪʃn/ n
compensação f; (financial) indenização f,
(P) indemnização f

compete /kəm'piːt/ vi competir;
~ with rivalizar com

competen|t /'kɒmpɪtənt/ a
competente. **~ce** n competência f

competition /kɒmpə'tɪʃn/ n
competição f; Comm concorrência f

competitive /kəm'petɪtɪv/ a ‹sport,
prices› competitivo; **~ examination**
concurso m

competitor /kəm'petɪtə(r)/ n
competidor m, concorrente mf

compile /kəm'paɪl/ vt compilar, coligir.
~r /-ə(r)/ n compilador m

complacen|t /kəm'pleɪsnt/
a satisfeito consigo mesmo, (P)
complacente. **~cy** n (auto-)satisfação f,
(P) complacência f

complain /kəm'pleɪn/ vi queixar-se
(**about** de)

complaint /kəm'pleɪnt/ n queixa f;
(in shop) reclamação f; Med doença f,
achaque m

complement /'kɒmplɪmənt/
n complemento m ● vt completar,
complementar. **~ary** /-'mentrɪ/ a
complementar

complet|e /kəm'pliːt/ a completo;
(finished) acabado; (downright) perfeito
● vt completar; ‹a form› preencher.
~ely adv completamente. **~ion** /-ʃn/ n
conclusão f, feitura f, realização f

complex /'kɒmpleks/ a complexo
● n complexo m. **~ity** /kəm'pleksəti/ n
complexidade f

complexion /kəm'plekʃn/ n cor f da
tez, tez f; fig caráter m, (P) carácter m,
aspecto m

compliance /kəm'plaɪəns/ n
docilidade f; (agreement) conformidade
f; **in ~ with** em conformidade com

complicat|e /'kɒmplɪkeɪt/ vt
complicar. **~ed** a complicado. **~ion**
/-'keɪʃn/ n complicação f

compliment /'kɒmplɪmənt/
n cumprimento m, elogio m ● vt
/'kɒmplɪment/ cumprimentar, elogiar

complimentary /kɒmplɪ'mentrɪ/
a amável, elogioso; **~ copy** oferta f;
~ ticket bilhete m grátis

comply /kəm'plaɪ/ vi **~ with** agir em
conformidade com

component /kəm'pəʊnənt/ n
componente m; (of machine) peça f ● a
componente, constituinte

compose /kəm'pəʊz/ vt compor; **~
o.s.** acalmar-se, dominar-se. **~d** a calmo,
senhor de si. **~r** /-ə(r)/ n compositor m

composition /kɒmpə'zɪʃn/ n
composição f.

compost /'kɒmpɒst/ n húmus m,
adubo m

composure /kəm'pəʊʒə(r)/ n calma f,
domínio m de si mesmo

compound /'kɒmpaʊnd/ n composto
m; (enclosure) cercado m, recinto m ● a
composto; **~ fracture** fratura f exposta

comprehen|d /kɒmprɪ'hend/ vt
compreender. **~sion** n compreensão f

comprehensive /kɒmprɪ'hensɪv/ a
compreensivo, vasto; (insurance) contra
todos os riscos; **~ school** escola f de
ensino secundário técnico e acadêmico
or (P) académico

compress /kəm'pres/ vt comprimir.
~ion /-ʃn/ n compressão f

comprise /kəm'praɪz/ vt compreender,
abranger

compromise /'kɒmprəmaɪz/ n
compromisso m ● vt comprometer ● vi
chegar a um meio-termo

compulsion /kəm'pʌlʃn/ n
(constraint) coação f; Psych desejo m
irresistível, compulsão f

compulsive /kəm'pʌlsɪv/ a Psych
compulsivo; ‹liar, smoker etc› inveterado

compulsory /kəm'pʌlsərɪ/ a
obrigatório, compulsório

computer /kəm'pjuːtə(r)/ n
computador m; **~ science** informática f.
~ize vt computerizar

comrade /'kɒmreɪd/ n camarada mf

con[1] /kɒn/ vt (pt **conned**) 🅰 enganar ● n 🅰 intrujice f; vigarice f; burla f; **~ man** 🅰 intrujão m, vigarista m, burlão m

con[2] /kɒn/ ▶ **PRO**[1]

concave /'kɒŋkeɪv/ a côncavo

conceal /kən'siːl/ vt ocultar, esconder

concede /kən'siːd/ vt conceder, admitir; (in a game etc) ceder, dar-se por vencido

conceit /kən'siːt/ n presunção f. **~ed** a presunçoso, presumido, cheio de si

conceivabl|e /kən'siːvəbl/ a concebível

conceive /kən'siːv/ vt/i conceber

concentrat|e /'kɒnsntreɪt/ vt/i concentrar(-se). **~ion** /-'treɪʃn/ n concentração f

concept /'kɒnsept/ n conceito m

conception /kən'sepʃn/ n concepção f

concern /kən'sɜːn/ n (worry) preocupação f; (business) negócio m ● vt dizer respeito a, respeitar; **~ o.s. with, be ~ed with** interessar-se por, ocupar-se de; (regard) dizer respeito a; **it's no ~ of mine** não me diz respeito. **~ing** prep sobre, respeitante a

concerned /kən'sɜːnd/ a inquieto; preocupado (**about** com)

concert /'kɒnsət/ n concerto m

concession /kən'seʃn/ n concessão f

conclu|de /kən'kluːd/ vt concluir ● vi terminar. **~sion** n conclusão f

conclusive /kən'kluːsɪv/ a conclusivo

concoct /kən'kɒkt/ vt preparar por mistura; fig (invent) fabricar. **~ion** /-ʃn/ n mistura f; fig invenção f; mentira f

concrete /'kɒnkriːt/ n concreto m, (P) cimento m ● a concreto ● vt concretar, (P) cimentar

concur /kən'kɜː(r)/ vi (pt **concurred**) concordar; (of circumstances) concorrer

concussion /kən'kʌʃn/ n comoção f cerebral

condemn /kən'dem/ vt condenar. **~ation** /kɒndem'neɪʃn/ n condenação f

condens|e /kən'dens/ vt/i condensar(-se). **~ation** /kɒnden'seɪʃn/ n condensação f

condescend /kɒndɪ'send/ vi condescender; (lower o.s.) rebaixar-se

condition /kən'dɪʃn/ n condição f; **on ~ that** com a condição de que ● vt condicionar. **~al** a condicional. **~er** n (for hair) condicionador m, creme m rinse

condolences /kən'dəʊlənsɪz/ npl condolências fpl, pêsames mpl, sentimentos mpl

condom /'kɒndəm/ n preservativo m

condone /kən'dəʊn/ vt desculpar, fechar os olhos a

conducive /kən'djuːsɪv/ a **be ~ to** contribuir para, ser propício a

conduct[1] /kən'dʌkt/ vt conduzir, dirigir; ⟨orchestra⟩ reger

conduct[2] /'kɒndʌkt/ n conduta f

conductor /kən'dʌktə(r)/ n maestro m; Electr (of bus) condutor m

cone /kəʊn/ n cone m; Bot pinha f; (for ice cream) casquinha f, (P) cone m

confectioner /kən'fekʃnə(r)/ n confeiteiro m, (P) pasteleiro m. **~y** n confeitaria f, (P) pastelaria f

conference /'kɒnfərəns/ n conferência f; **in ~** em reunião f

confess /kən'fes/ vt/i confessar; Relig confessar(-se). **~ion** /-ʃn/ n confissão f

confetti /kən'fetɪ/ n confetes mpl, (P) confeti mpl

confide /kən'faɪd/ vt confiar ● vi **~ in** confiar em

confiden|t /'kɒnfɪdənt/ a confiante, confiado. **~ce** n confiança f; (boldness) confiança f em si; (secret) confidência f, **~ce trick** vigarice f; **in ~ce** em confidência

confidential /kɒnfɪ'denʃl/ a confidencial

confine /kən'faɪn/ vt fechar; (limit) limitar (**to** a). **~ment** n detenção f; Med parto m

confirm /kən'fɜːm/ vt confirmar. **~ation** /kɒnfə'meɪʃn/ n confirmação f. **~ed** a (bachelor) inveterado

confiscat|e /'kɒnfɪskeɪt/ vt confiscar. **~ion** /-'keɪʃn/ n confiscação f

conflict[1] /'kɒnflɪkt/ n conflito m

conflict[2] /kən'flɪkt/ vi estar em contradição. **~ing** a contraditório

conform /kən'fɔːm/ vt/i conformar(-se)

confront /kən'frʌnt/ vt confrontar, defrontar, enfrentar; **~ with** confrontar-se com. **~ation** /kɒnfrʌn'teɪʃn/ n confrontação f

confus|e /kən'fjuːz/ vt confundir. **~ed** a confuso. **~ing** a que faz confusão. **~ion** /-ʒn/ n confusão f

congeal /kən'dʒiːl/ vt/i congelar, solidificar

congenial /kən'dʒiːnɪəl/ a (agreeable) simpático

congest|ed /kən'dʒestɪd/ a
congestionado. **~ion** /-tʃn/ n (traffic)
congestionamento m; Med congestão f

congratulat|e /kən'grætjʊleɪt/ vt
felicitar; dar os parabéns (**on** por). **~ions**
/-'leɪʃnz/ npl felicitações fpl, parabéns mpl

congregat|e /'kɒŋɡrɪgeɪt/ vi reunir-se.
~ion /-'geɪʃn/ n (in church) congregação
f, fiéis mpl

congress /'kɒŋɡres/ n congresso m;
C~ Amer Congresso m

> **Congress** O Congresso é o órgão
> legislativo dos Estados Unidos.
> Reúne-se no Capitólio (*Capitol*) e é
> composto por duas câmaras: o Senado
> e a Câmara de Representantes. O
> Congresso é renovado de dois em dois
> anos, e a sua função é elaborar leis que
> devem ser aprovadas, primeiro pelas
> duas câmaras e posteriormente pelo
> Presidente.

conjecture /kən'dʒektʃə(r)/ n
conjectura f, (P) conjetura f ● vt/i
conjecturar, (P) conjeturar

conjugat|e /'kɒndʒʊgeɪt/ vt conjugar.
~ion /-'geɪʃn/ n conjugação f

conjunction /kən'dʒʌŋkʃn/ n
conjunção f

conjur|e /'kʌndʒə(r)/ vi fazer truques
mágicos ● vt **~e up** fazer aparecer. **~or**
n mágico m, prestidigitador m

connect /kə'nekt/ vt/i ligar(-se); (of
train) fazer ligação. **~ed** a ligado; **be
~ed with** estar relacionado com

connection /kə'nekʃn/ n relação f; Rail
(phone call) ligação f; Electr contacto m

connectivity /kɒnek'tɪvəti/ n
conectividade f

connoisseur /kɒnə'sɜː(r)/ n
conhecedor m, apreciador m

conquer /'kɒŋkə(r)/ vt vencer;
‹country› conquistar. **~or** n
conquistador m

conquest /'kɒŋkwest/ n conquista f

conscience /'kɒnʃəns/ n consciência f

conscientious /kɒnʃi'enʃəs/ a
consciencioso

conscious /'kɒnʃəs/ a consciente.
~ness n consciência f

conscript¹ /kən'skrɪpt/ vt recrutar.
~ion /-ʃn/ n serviço m militar obrigatório

conscript² /'kɒnskrɪpt/ n recruta m

consecrate /'kɒnsɪkreɪt/ vt consagrar

consecutive /kən'sekjʊtɪv/ a
consecutivo, seguido

consensus /kən'sensəs/ n consenso m

consent /kən'sent/ vi consentir (**to** em)
● n consentimento m

consequence /'kɒnsɪkwəns/ n
consequência f

consequent /'kɒnsɪkwənt/ a
resultante (**on, upon** de). **~ly** adv por
consequência, por conseguinte

conservation /kɒnsə'veɪʃn/ n
conservação f

conservative /kən'sɜːvətɪv/ a
conservador; (estimate) moderado.
● **C~** a & n conservador m

conservatory /kən'sɜːvətrɪ/ n
(greenhouse) estufa f; (house extension)
jardim m de inverno

conserve /kən'sɜːv/ vt conservar

consider /kən'sɪdə(r)/ vt considerar;
(allow for) levar em consideração.
~ation /-'reɪʃn/ n consideração f. **~ing**
prep em vista de, tendo em conta

considerabl|e /kən'sɪdərəbl/ a
considerável; (much) muito

considerate /kən'sɪdərət/ a
atencioso, delicado

consign /kən'saɪn/ vt consignar.
~ment n consignação f

consist /kən'sɪst/ vi consistir (**of**, em)

consisten|t /kən'sɪstənt/ a
(unchanging) constante; (not
contradictory) coerente; **~t with**
conforme com. **~cy** n consistência f; fig
coerência f. **~tly** adv regularmente

consol|e /kən'səʊl/ vt consolar. **~ation**
/kɒnsə'leɪʃn/ n consolação f; **~ation
prize** prêmio m or (P) prémio m de
consolação

consolidat|e /kən'sɒlɪdeɪt/ vt/i
consolidar(-se). **~ion** /-'deɪʃn/ n
consolidação f

consonant /'kɒnsənənt/ n consoante f

conspicuous /kən'spɪkjʊəs/ a
conspícuo, visível; (striking) notável;
make o.s. ~ fazer-se notar, chamar a
atenção

conspira|cy /kən'spɪrəsɪ/ n
conspiração f. **~cy theory** n teoria f da
conspiração

conspire /kən'spaɪə(r)/ vi conspirar

constable /'kʌnstəbl/ n polícia m

constant /'kɒnstənt/ a constante. **~ly**
adv constantemente

constellation /kɒnstə'leɪʃn/ n
constelação f

constipation /kɒnstɪ'peɪʃn/ n prisão
f de ventre

constituency /kən'stɪtjʊənsɪ/ n (pl -cies) círculo m eleitoral

constituent /kən'stɪtjʊənt/ a & n constituinte m

constitut|e /'kɒnstɪtjuːt/ vt constituir. ~ion /-'tjuːʃn/ n constituição f. ~ional /-'tjuːʃənl/ a constitucional

constrain /kən'streɪn/ vt constranger

constraint /kən'streɪnt/ n constrangimento m

constrict /kən'strɪkt/ vt constringir, apertar

construct /kən'strʌkt/ vt construir. ~ion /-ʃn/ n construção f; under ~ion em construção

constructive /kən'strʌktɪv/ a construtivo

consul /'kɒnsl/ n cônsul m

consulate /'kɒnsjʊlət/ n consulado m

consult /kən'sʌlt/ vt consultar. ~ation /kɒnsl'teɪʃn/ n consulta f

consultant /kən'sʌltənt/ n consultor m; Med especialista mf

consume /kən'sjuːm/ vt consumir. ~r /-ə(r)/ n consumidor m

consumption /kən'sʌmpʃn/ n consumo m

contact /'kɒntækt/ n contato m, (P) contacto m; ‹person› relação f; ~ lenses lentes fpl de contato or (P) contacto ● vt contactar

contagious /kən'teɪdʒəs/ a contagioso

contain /kən'teɪn/ vt conter; ~ o.s. conter-se. ~er n recipiente m; (for transport) contentor m

contaminat|e /kən'tæmɪneɪt/ vt contaminar. ~ion /-'neɪʃn/ n contaminação f

contemplat|e /'kɒntempleɪt/ vt contemplar; (intend) ter em vista; (consider) esperar, pensar em. ~ion /-'pleɪʃn/ n contemplação f

contemporary /kən'temprərɪ/ a & n contemporâneo m

contempt /kən'tempt/ n desprezo m. ~ible a desprezível. ~uous /-tʃʊəs/ a desdenhoso

contend /kən'tend/ vt afirmar, sustentar ● vi ~ with lutar contra. ~er n adversário m, contendor m

content[1] /kən'tent/ a satisfeito, contente ● vt contentar. ~ed a satisfeito, contente. ~ment n contentamento m, satisfação f

content[2] /'kɒntent/ n conteúdo m; (table of) ~s índice m

contention /kən'tenʃn/ n disputa f, contenda f; (assertion) argumento m

contest[1] /'kɒntest/ n competição f; (struggle) luta f

contest[2] /kən'test/ vt contestar; (compete for) disputar. ~ant n concorrente mf

context /'kɒntekst/ n contexto m

continent /'kɒntɪnənt/ n continente m; the C~ a Europa (continental) f. ~al /-'nentl/ a continental; (of mainland Europe) europeu; ~al breakfast café m da manhã europeu, (P) pequeno-almoço m europeu; ~al quilt edredom m, (P) edredão m

contingen|t /kən'tɪndʒənt/ a & n contingente m. ~cy n contingência f; ~cy plan plano m de emergência

continual /kən'tɪnjʊəl/ a contínuo. ~ly adv continuamente

continu|e /kən'tɪnjuː/ vt/i continuar. ~ation /-tɪnju'eɪʃn/ n continuação f

continuity /kɒntɪ'njuːətɪ/ n continuidade f

continuous /kən'tɪnjʊəs/ a contínuo. ~ly adv continuamente

contort /kən'tɔːt/ vt contorcer; fig distorcer. ~ion /-ʃn/ n contorção f

contour /'kɒntʊə(r)/ n contorno m

contraband /'kɒntrəbænd/ n contrabando m

contraception /kɒntrə'sepʃn/ n contracepção f

contraceptive /kɒntrə'septɪv/ a & n contraceptivo m

contract[1] /'kɒntrækt/ n contrato m

contract[2] /kən'trækt/ vt/i contrair(-se); (make a contract) contratar. ~ion /-ʃn/ n contração f

contractor /kən'træktə(r)/ n empreiteiro m; (firm) firma f empreiteira de serviços, (P) recrutadora f de mão-de-obra temporária

contradict /kɒntrə'dɪkt/ vt contradizer. ~ion /-ʃn/ n contradição f. ~ory a contraditório

contrary[1] /'kɒntrərɪ/ a & n (opposite) contrário m ● adv ~ to contrariamente a; on the ~ ao or pelo contrário

contrary[2] /kən'treərɪ/ a (perverse) do contra, embirrento

contrast[1] /'kɒntrɑːst/ n contraste m

contrast[2] /kən'trɑːst/ vt/i contrastar. ~ing a contrastante

contraven|e /kɒntrə'viːn/ vt infringir. **~tion** /-'venʃn/ n contravenção f

contribut|e /kən'trɪbjuːt/ vt/i contribuir (**to** para); (to newspaper etc) colaborar (**to** em). **~ion** /kɒntrɪ'bjuːʃn/ n contribuição f. **~or** /-'trɪbjuːtə(r)/ n contribuinte mf; (to newspaper) colaborador m

contrivance /kən'traɪvəns/ n (invention) engenho m; (device) engenhoca f; (trick) maquinação f

control /kən'trəʊl/ vt (pt controlled) (check, restrain) controlar; ‹firm etc› dirigir ● n controle m; (management) direção f; **~s** (of car, plane) comandos mpl; (knobs) botões mpl; **be in ~ of** dirigir; **under ~** sob controle

controversial /kɒntrə'vɜːʃl/ a controverso, discutível

controversy /'kɒntrəvɜːsɪ/ n controvérsia f

convalesce /kɒnvə'les/ vi convalescer. **~nce** n convalescença f

convene /kən'viːn/ vt convocar ● vi reunir-se

convenience /kən'viːnɪəns/ n conveniência f; **~s** (appliances) comodidades fpl; (lavatory) privada f, (P) casa f de banho; **at your ~** quando (e como) lhe convier; **~ foods** alimentos mpl semiprontos

convenient /kən'viːnɪənt/ a conveniente; **be ~ for** convir a. **~ly** adv sem inconveniente; (situated) bem; (arrive) a propósito

convent /'kɒnvənt/ n convento m; **~ school** colégio m de freiras

convention /kən'venʃn/ n convenção f; (custom) uso m, costume m. **~al** a convencional

converge /kən'vɜːdʒ/ vi convergir

conversation /kɒnvə'seɪʃn/ n conversa f. **~al** a de conversa, coloquial

converse[1] /kən'vɜːs/ vi conversar

converse[2] /'kɒnvɜːs/ a & n inverso m. **~ly** /kən'vɜːslɪ/ adv ao invés, inversamente

conver|t[1] /kən'vɜːt/ vt converter; (house) transformar. **~sion** /-ʃn/ n conversão f; ‹house› transformação f. **~tible** a convertível, conversível ● n Auto conversível m

convert[2] /'kɒnvɜːt/ n convertido m, converso m

convex /'kɒnveks/ a convexo

convey /kən'veɪ/ vt transmitir; ‹goods› transportar; ‹idea, feeling› comunicar;

~or belt tapete m rolante, correia f transportadora

convict[1] /kən'vɪkt/ vt declarar culpado. **~ion** /-ʃn/ n condenação f; (opinion) convicção f

convict[2] /'kɒnvɪkt/ n condenado m

convinc|e /kən'vɪns/ vt convencer. **~ing** a convincente

convoy /'kɒnvɔɪ/ n escolta f

convuls|e /kən'vʌls/ vt convulsionar; fig abalar; **be ~ed with laughter** torcer-se de riso

coo /kuː/ vi (pt cooed) arrulhar ● n arrulho m

cook /kʊk/ vt/i cozinhar; **~ up** 🅣 cozinhar fig, fabricar ● n cozinheira f, cozinheiro m

cooker /'kʊkə(r)/ n fogão m

cookery /'kʊkərɪ/ n cozinha f; **~ book** livro m de culinária

cookie /'kʊkɪ/ n Amer biscoito m

cool /kuːl/ a (-er, -est) fresco; (calm) calmo; (unfriendly) frio ● n frescura f; 🆇 (composure) sangue-frio m ● vt/i arrefecer. **~ box** n geladeira f portátil. **in the ~** no fresco. **~ly** /'kuːllɪ/ adv calmamente; fig friamente. **~ness** n frescura f; fig frieza f

coop /kuːp/ n galinheiro m ● vt **~ up** engaiolar, fechar

co-operat|e /kəʊ'ɒpəreɪt/ vi cooperar. **~ion** /-'reɪʃn/ n cooperação f

cooperative /kəʊ'ɒpərətɪv/ a cooperativo ● n cooperativa f

coordinat|e /kəʊ'ɔːdɪneɪt/ vt coordenar. **~ion** /-'neɪʃn/ n coordenação f

cop /kɒp/ n 🆇 porco m 🆇, (P) chui m 🆇

cope /kəʊp/ vi aguentar-se, arranjar-se; **~ with** poder com, dar conta de

copious /'kəʊpɪəs/ a copioso

copper[1] /'kɒpə(r)/ n cobre m ● a de cobre

copper[2] /'kɒpə(r)/ n 🆇 porco m 🆇, (P) chui m 🆇

coppice /'kɒpɪs/, **copse** /kɒps/ ns mata f de corte

copulat|e /'kɒpjʊleɪt/ vi copular

copy /'kɒpɪ/ n cópia f; (of book) exemplar m; (of newspaper) número m ● vt/i copiar

copyright /'kɒpɪraɪt/ n direitos mpl autorais, (P) direitos npl de autor

coral /'kɒrəl/ n coral m

cord /kɔːd/ n cordão m; Electr fio m

cordial /'kɔːdɹəl/ a & n cordial m

cordon /'kɔːdn/ n cordão m ● vt ~ **off** fechar (com um cordão de isolamento)

corduroy /'kɔːdərɔɪ/ n veludo m cotelé

core /kɔː(r)/ n âmago m; (of apple, pear) coração m

cork /kɔːk/ n cortiça f; (for bottle) rolha f ● vt rolhar

corkscrew /'kɔːkskruː/ n saca-rolhas m

corn[1] /kɔːn/ n trigo m; Amer (maize) milho m; (seed) grão m; ~ **on the cob** espiga f de milho, cozinhada inteira

corn[2] /kɔːn/ n (hard skin) calo m

corner /'kɔːnə(r)/ n canto m; (of street) esquina f; (bend in road) curva f ● vt encurralar; (market) monopolizar ● vi dar uma curva, virar

cornet /'kɔːnɪt/ n Mus cornetim m; (for ice cream) casquinha f, (P) cone m

cornflakes /'kɔːnfleɪks/ npl cornflakes mpl, cereais mpl

cornflour /'kɔːnflaʊə(r)/ n fécula f de milho, maisena f

corny /'kɔːnɪ/ a 🄵 batido, (P) estafado

coronation /kɒrə'neɪʃn/ n coroação f

coroner /'kɒrənə(r)/ n magistrado m que investiga os casos de morte suspeita

corporal[1] /'kɔːpərəl/ n Mil cabo m

corporal[2] /'kɔːpərəl/ a ~ **punishment** castigo m corporal

corporate /'kɔːpərət/ a coletivo; (body) corporativo

corporation /kɔːpə'reɪʃn/ n corporação f; (of town) municipalidade f

corps /kɔː(r)/ n (pl corps /kɔːz/) corpo m

corpse /kɔːps/ n cadáver m

correct /kə'rekt/ a correto; **the ~ time** a hora certa; **you are ~** você tem razão ● vt corrigir. **~ion** /-ʃn/ n correção f, emenda f

correlat|e /'kɒrəleɪt/ vt/i correlacionar(-se). **~ion** /-'leɪʃn/ n correlação f

correspond /kɒrɪ'spɒnd/ vi corresponder (**to, with** a). **~ence** n correspondência f. **~ent** n correspondente mf. **~ing** a correspondente

corridor /'kɒrɪdɔː(r)/ n corredor m

corro|de /kə'rəʊd/ vt/i corroer(-se). **~sion** n corrosão f

corrugated /'kɒrəgeɪtɪd/ a corrugado; ~ **cardboard** cartão m canelado; ~ **iron** chapa f ondulada

corrupt /kə'rʌpt/ a corrupto ● vt corromper. **~ion** /-ʃn/ n corrupção f

corset /'kɔːsɪt/ n espartilho m; (elasticated) cinta f elástica

Corsica /'kɔːsɪkə/ n Córsega f

cosmetic /kɒz'metɪk/ n cosmético m ● a cosmético; fig superficial

cosmonaut /'kɒzmənɔːt/ n cosmonauta mf

cosmopolitan /kɒzmə'pɒlɪtən/ a & n cosmopolita mf

cosset /'kɒsɪt/ vt (pt cosseted) proteger

cost /kɒst/ vt (pt cost) custar; (pt costed) fixar o preço de ● n custo m; **~s** jur custos mpl; **at all ~s** custe o que custar; **to one's** ~ à sua custa; ~ **of living** custo m de vida

costly /'kɒstlɪ/ a (**-ier, -iest**) caro ● a caro; (valuable) precioso

costume /'kɒstjuːm/ n traje m

cos|y /'kəʊzɪ/ a (**-ier, -iest**) confortável, íntimo ● n abafador m (do bule do chá)

cot /kɒt/ n cama f de bêbê, (P) de bebé, berço m

cottage /'kɒtɪdʒ/ n pequena casa f de campo; ~ **cheese** requeijão m, ricota f; ~ **industry** artesanato m; ~ **pie** empada f de carne picada

cotton /'kɒtn/ n algodão m; (thread) fio m, linha f; ~ **wool** algodão m hidrófilo

couch /kaʊtʃ/ n divã m

couchette /kuː'ʃet/ n couchette f

cough /kɒf/ vi tossir ● n tosse f

could /kʊd, kəd/ pt of ▶ CAN[2]

council /'kaʊnsl/ n conselho m; ~ **house** casa f de bairro popular

councillor /'kaʊnsələ(r)/ n vereador m

counsel /'ka.ʊnsl/ n conselho m; (pl invar) Jur advogado m. **~lor** n conselheiro m

count[1] /kaʊnt/ vt/i contar; ~ **on** contar com ● n conta f. **~down** n (rocket) contagem f regressiva or (P) decrescente

count[2] /kaʊnt/ n (nobleman) conde m

counter[1] /'kaʊntə(r)/ n (in shop) balcão m; (in game) ficha f, (P) tento m

counter[2] /'kaʊntə(r)/ adv ~ **to** contrário a; ~ **to** (in the opposite direction) em sentido contrário a ● a oposto ● vt opor; ‹blow› aparar ● vi ripostar

counter- /'kaʊntə(r)/ pref contra-

counteract /kaʊntər'ækt/ vt neutralizar, frustrar

C

counter-attack /ˈkaʊntərətæk/ n contra-ataque m ● vt/i contra-atacar

counterbalance /ˈkaʊntəbæləns/ n contrapeso m ● vt contrabalançar

counterfeit /ˈkaʊntəfɪt/ a falsificado, falso ● n falsificação f ● vt falsificar

counterfoil /ˈkaʊntəfɔɪl/ n talão m, canhoto m

counterpart /ˈkaʊntəpɑːt/ n equivalente m; (person) homólogo m

counterproductive /ˈkaʊntəprədʌktɪv/ a contraproducente

countersign /ˈkaʊntəsaɪn/ vt subscrever documento já assinado; ‹cheque› contrassinar

countess /ˈkaʊntɪs/ n condessa f

countless /ˈkaʊntlɪs/ a sem conta, incontável, inúmero

country /ˈkʌntrɪ/ n país m; (homeland) pátria f; (countryside) campo m

countryside /ˈkʌntrɪsaɪd/ n campo m

county /ˈkaʊntɪ/ n condado m

coup /kuː/ n ~ (d'état) golpe m (de estado)

couple /ˈkʌpl/ n par m, casal m; a ~ of um par de ● vt/i unir(-se), ligar(-se); Techn acoplar

coupon /ˈkuːpɒn/ n cupão m

courage /ˈkʌrɪdʒ/ n coragem f. ~ous /kəˈreɪdʒəs/ a corajoso

courgette /kʊəˈʒet/ n abobrinha f

courier /ˈkʊrɪə(r)/ n correio m; (for tourists) guia mf; (for parcels, mail) estafeta f

course /kɔːs/ n curso m; (series) série f; Culin prato m; (for golf) campo m; fig caminho m; in due ~ na altura devida, oportunamente; in the ~ of durante; of ~ está claro, com certeza

court /kɔːt/ n (of monarch) corte f; (courtyard) pátio m; Tennis court m; quadra f, (P) campo m; Jur tribunal m ● vt cortejar; (danger) provocar; ~ martial (pl courts martial) conselho m de guerra

courteous /ˈkɜːtɪəs/ a cortês, delicado

courtesy /ˈkɜːtəsɪ/ n cortesia f

courtyard /ˈkɔːtjɑːd/ n pátio m

cousin /ˈkʌzn/ n primo m; first/second ~ primo m em primeiro/segundo grau

cove /kəʊv/ n angra f, enseada f

cover /ˈkʌvə(r)/ vt/i cobrir; ~ up tapar; fig encobrir ● n cobertura f; (for bed) colcha f; (for book, furniture) capa f; (lid) tampa f; (shelter) abrigo m; ~ charge serviço m; take ~ abrigar-se; under separate ~ em separado. ~ing n cobertura f; ~ing letter carta (que acompanha um documento) f. ~-up n fig encobrimento m

coverage /ˈkʌvərɪdʒ/ n (of events) reportagem f, cobertura f

covet /ˈkʌvɪt/ vt cobiçar

cow /kaʊ/ n vaca f

coward /ˈkaʊəd/ n covarde mf. ~ly a covarde

cowardice /ˈkaʊədɪs/ n covardia f

cowboy /ˈkaʊbɔɪ/ n cowboy m, vaqueiro m

cower /ˈkaʊə(r)/ vi encolher-se (de medo)

cowshed /ˈkaʊʃed/ n estábulo m

coy /kɔɪ/ a (-er, -est) (falsamente) tímido

crab /kræb/ n caranguejo m

crack /kræk/ n fenda f; (in glass) rachadura f; (noise) estalo m; 🅰 (joke) piada f; (drug) crack m ● a 🅵 de elite ● vt/i estalar; ‹nut› quebrar, (P) partir; ‹joke› contar; ‹problem› resolver; ‹voice› mudar; ~ down on 🅵 cair em cima de, arrochar; get ~ing 🅵 pôr mãos à obra

cracker /ˈkrækə(r)/ n busca-pé m, bomba f de estalo; Culin bolacha f de água e sal

crackers /ˈkrækəz/ a 🅰 desmiolado; maluco 🅵

crackle /ˈkrækl/ vi crepitar ● n crepitação f

cradle /ˈkreɪdl/ n berço m ● vt embalar

craft[1] /krɑːft/ n ofício m; (technique) arte f; (cunning) manha f, astúcia f

craft[2] /krɑːft/ n (invar) (boat) embarcação f

craftsman /ˈkrɑːftsmən/ n (pl -men) artífice mf. ~ship n arte f

crafty /ˈkrɑːftɪ/ a (-ier, -iest) manhoso, astucioso

crag /kræg/ n penhasco m. ~gy a escarpado, íngreme

cram /kræm/ vt (pt crammed) ~ (for an exam) decorar, (P) empinar; ~ into/ with entulhar com

cramp /kræmp/ n cãibra f ● vt restringir, tolher. ~ed a apertado

crane /kreɪn/ n grua f; (bird) grou m ● vt ‹neck› esticar

crank[1] /kræŋk/ n Techn manivela f. ~-shaft n Techn cambota f

crank[2] /kræŋk/ n excêntrico m. ~y a excêntrico

crash /kræʃ/ n acidente m; (noise)
estrondo m; Comm falência f; (financial)
colapso m, crash m ● vt/i (fall/strike) cair/
bater com estrondo; ‹two cars› chocar,
bater; Comm abrir falência; ‹plane›
cair; ~ **out** 🇮 (go to sleep) apagar,
(P) apagar-se; (be out of competition,
race) ser eliminado, (P) cair de sono
● a ‹course, programme› intensivo.
~ **helmet** n capacete m; ~**land** vi fazer
uma aterrissagem forçada, (P) uma
aterragem forçada

crate /kreɪt/ n engradado m

crater /'kreɪtə(r)/ n cratera f

crav|e /kreɪv/ vt/i ~**e (for)** ansiar por.
~**ing** n desejo m irresistível, ânsia f

crawl /krɔːl/ vi rastejar; (of baby)
engatinhar, (P) andar de gatas; (of
car) mover-se lentamente ● n rastejo
m; (swimming) crawl m; **be ~ing with**
fervilhar de, estar cheio de

crayfish /'kreɪfɪʃ/ n (pl invar) lagostim m

crayon /'kreɪən/ n crayon m, lápis m
de pastel

craze /kreɪz/ n moda f, febre f

craz|y /'kreɪzɪ/ a (-ier, -iest) doido;
louco (about por). ~**iness** n loucura f

creak /kriːk/ n rangido m ● vi ranger

cream /kriːm/ n (milk fat; also fig) nata
f; (cosmetic) Culin creme m ● a creme
invar ● vt desnatar; ~ **cheese** queijo-
creme m. ~**y** a cremoso

crease /kriːs/ n vinco m ● vt/i
amarrotar(-se)

creat|e /kriː'eɪt/ vt criar. ~**ion** /-ʃn/ n
criação f. ~**ive** a criador, criativo. ~**or** n
criador m

creature /'kriːtʃə(r)/ n criatura f

crèche /kreɪʃ/ n creche f

credentials /krɪ'denʃlz/ npl
credenciais fpl; (of competence etc)
referências fpl

credib|le /'kredəbl/ a crível, verossímil.
~**ility** /-'bɪlətɪ/ n credibilidade f

credit /'kredɪt/ n crédito m; (honour)
honra f; ~**s** (cinema) créditos mpl; ~ **card**
cartão m de crédito ● vt (pt **credited**)
acreditar em; Comm creditar; ~ **sb with**
atribuir a alguém. ~**or** n credor m

creditable /'kredɪtəbl/ a louvável,
honroso

creed /kriːd/ n credo m

creek /kriːk/ n enseada f estreita; **be up
the ~** 🇽 estar frito 🇽

creep /kriːp/ vi (pt **crept**) rastejar; (move
stealthily) mover-se furtivamente ● n 🇽

cara m nojento, (P) tipo m nojento; **give
sb the ~s** dar arrepios a alguém. ~**er** n
(planta f) trepadeira f. ~**y** a arrepiante

cremat|e /krɪ'meɪt/ vt cremar. ~**ion**
/-ʃn/ n cremação f

crematorium /kremə'tɔːrɪəm/ n
(pl **-ia**) crematório m

crêpe /kreɪp/ n crepe m; ~ **paper** papel
m crepom, (P) plissado

crept /krept/ ▶ CREEP

crescent /'kresnt/ n crescente m;
(street) rua f em semicírculo

cress /kres/ n agrião m

crest /krest/ n (of bird, hill) crista f; (on
coat of arms) timbre m

crevasse /krɪ'væs/ n fenda(em geleira) f

crevice /'krevɪs/ n racha f, fenda f

crew[1] /kruː/ ▶ CROW

crew[2] /kruː/ n tripulação f; (gang)
bando m. ~ **cut** n corte m à escovinha;
~ **neck** n gola f redonda e um pouco
subida, meia gola

crib[1] /krɪb/ n berço m; (Christmas)
presépio m

crib[2] /krɪb/ vt/i (pt **cribbed**) 🇮 colar,
(P) 🇽 cabular 🇽 ● n cópia f, plágio m;
(translation) burro m 🇽

cricket[1] /'krɪkɪt/ n críquete m. ~**er** n
jogador m de críquete

cricket[2] /'krɪkɪt/ n (insect) grilo m

crime /kraɪm/ n crime m; (minor) delito
m; (collectively) criminalidade f

criminal /'krɪmɪnl/ a & n criminoso m

crimson /'krɪmzn/ a & n carmesim m

cring|e /krɪndʒ/ vi encolher-se

crinkle /'krɪŋkl/ vt/i enrugar(-se) ● n
vinco m, ruga f

cripple /'krɪpl/ n aleijado m, coxo m ● vt
estropiar; fig paralisar

crisis /'kraɪsɪs/ n (pl **crises** /-siːz/) crise f

crisp /krɪsp/ a (-er, -est) Culin crocante;
‹air› fresco; ‹manners, reply› decidido.
~**s** npl batatas fpl fritas redondas

criterion /kraɪ'tɪərɪən/ n (pl **-ia**)
critério m

critic /'krɪtɪk/ n crítico m. ~**al** a
crítico. ~**ally** adv de forma crítica; (ill)
gravemente

criticism /'krɪtɪsɪzəm/ n crítica f

criticize /'krɪtɪsaɪz/ vt/i criticar

croak /krəʊk/ n (frog) coaxar m; (raven)
crocitar m, crocito m ● vi (frog) coaxar;
(raven) crocitar

crochet /'krəʊʃeɪ/ n crochê m ● vt fazer
em crochê

crockery /'krɒkərɪ/ n louça f

crocodile /'krɒkədaɪl/ n crocodilo m

crocus /'krəʊkəs/ n (pl **-uses** /-sɪz/) croco m

crony /'krəʊnɪ/ n camarada mf, amigão m, parceiro m

crook /krʊk/ n 🄸 (criminal) vigarista mf; (stick) cajado m

crooked /'krʊkɪd/ a torcido; (winding) tortuoso; (askew) torto; 🄸 (dishonest) desonesto

crop /krɒp/ n colheita f, fig quantidade f; (haircut) corte m rente ● vt (pt **cropped**) cortar ● vi ~ **up** aparecer, surgir

croquet /'krəʊkeɪ/ n croquet m, croqué m

cross /krɒs/ n cruz f ● vt/i cruzar; <cheque> cruzar, (P) barrar; (oppose) contrariar; (of paths) cruzar-se ● a zangado; ~ **off** or **out** riscar; ~ **o.s.** benzer-se; ~ **sb's mind** passar pela cabeça or pelo espírito de alguém, ocorrer a alguém; **talk at ~ purposes** falar sem se entender. ~**country** a & adv à corta-mato; ~**examine** vt fazer o contrainterrogatório (de testemunhas); ~**eyed** a vesgo, estrábico; ~**fire** n fogo m cruzado; ~**section** n corte m transversal; fig grupo or sector m representativo m

crossbar /'krɒsbɑː(r)/ n barra f transversal f; (of bicycle) travessão m

crossing /'krɒsɪŋ/ n cruzamento m; (by boat) travessia f; (on road) passagem f

crossroads /'krɒsrəʊdz/ n encruzilhada f, cruzamento m

crossword /'krɒswɜːd/ n palavras fpl cruzadas

crotch /krɒtʃ/ n entrepernas fpl

crouch /kraʊtʃ/ vi agachar-se

crow /krəʊ/ n corvo m; **as the ~ flies** em linha reta ● vi (cock) cantar; cantar; fig rejubilar-se (**over** com)

crowbar /'krəʊbɑː(r)/ n alavanca f, pé-de-cabra m

crowd /kraʊd/ n multidão f ● vi afluir ● vt encher; ~ **into** apinhar-se em. ~**ed** a cheio, apinhado

crown /kraʊn/ n coroa f; (of hill) topo m, cume m ● vt coroar; <tooth> pôr uma coroa em

crucial /'kruːʃl/ a crucial

crucifix /'kruːsɪfɪks/ n crucifixo m

crucify /'kruːsɪfaɪ/ vt crucificar. ~**ixion** /-'fɪkʃn/ n crucificação f

crude /kruːd/ a (**-er**, **-est**) (raw) bruto; (rough, vulgar) grosseiro; ~ **oil** petróleo m bruto

cruel /krʊəl/ a (**crueller**, **cruellest**) cruel. ~**ty** n crueldade f

cruise /kruːz/ n cruzeiro m ● vi cruzar; (of tourists) fazer um cruzeiro; (of car) ir a velocidade de cruzeiro; ~**ing speed** velocidade f de cruzeiro. ~**er** n cruzador m

crumb /krʌm/ n migalha f, farelo m

crumble /'krʌmbl/ vt/i desfazer(-se); <bread> esmigalhar(-se); (collapse) desmoronar-se

crumple /'krʌmpl/ vt/i amarrotar(-se)

crunch /krʌntʃ/ vt trincar; (under one's feet) fazer ranger

crusade /kruː'seɪd/ n cruzada f. ~**r** /-ə(r)/ n cruzado m; fig militante mf

crush /krʌʃ/ vt esmagar; <clothes, papers> amassar, amarrotar ● n aperto m; **a ~ on** 🄸 uma paixonite or (P) paixoneta por

crust /krʌst/ n côdea f, crosta f. ~**y** a crocante

crutch /krʌtʃ/ n muleta f; (crotch) entrepernas fpl

crux /krʌks/ n (pl **cruxes**) o ponto crucial

cry /kraɪ/ n grito m; **a far ~ from** muito diferente de ● vi (weep) chorar; (call out) gritar

crypt /krɪpt/ n cripta f

cryptic /'krɪptɪk/ a críptico, enigmático

crystal /'krɪstl/ n cristal m. ~**lize** vt/i cristalizar(-se)

cub /kʌb/ n cria f, filhote m; **C~** (Scout) lobito m

Cuba /'kjuːbə/ n Cuba f

cubbyhole /'kʌbɪhəʊl/ n cochicho m; (snug place) cantinho m

cube /kjuːb/ n cubo m. ~**ic** a cúbico

cubicle /'kjuːbɪkl/ n cubículo m, compartimento m; (at swimming pool) cabine f

cuckoo /'kʊkuː/ n cuco m

cucumber /'kjuːkʌmbə(r)/ n pepino m

cuddle /'kʌdl/ vt/i abraçar com carinho; (nestle) aninhar(-se) ● n abracinho m, festinha f. ~**y** a fofo, aconchegante

cue¹ /kjuː/ n Theat deixa f; (hint) sugestão f, sinal m

cue² /kjuː/ n (billiards) taco m

cuff /kʌf/ n punho m; (blow) sopapo m; **off the ~** de improviso ● vt dar um sopapo. **~link** n botão m de punho

cul-de-sac /'kʌldəsæk/ n (pl **culs-de-sac**) beco m sem saída

culinary /'kʌlɪnərɪ/ a culinário

cull /kʌl/ vt (select) escolher; (kill) abater seletivamente ● n abate m

culminat|e /'kʌlmɪneɪt/ vi ~**e in** acabar em. **~ion** /-'neɪʃn/ n auge m, ponto m culminante

culprit /'kʌlprɪt/ n culpado m

cult /kʌlt/ n culto m

cultivat|e /'kʌltɪveɪt/ vt cultivar. **~ion** /-'veɪʃn/ n cultivo m, cultivação f

cultural /'kʌltʃərəl/ a cultural

culture /'kʌltʃə(r)/ n cultura f. **~d** a culto

cumbersome /'kʌmbəsəm/ a (unwieldy) pesado; incómodo, (P) incómodo

cumulative /'kjuːmjʊlətɪv/ a cumulativo

cunning /'kʌnɪŋ/ a astuto, manhoso ● n astúcia f, manha f

cup /kʌp/ n xícara f, (P) chávena f; (prize) taça f; **C~ Final** Final de Campeonato f

cupboard /'kʌbəd/ n armário m

curable /'kjʊərəbl/ a curável

curator /kjʊə'reɪtə(r)/ n (museum) conservador m; Jur curador m

curb /kɜːb/ n freio m ● vt refrear; (price increase etc) sustar

curdle /'kɜːdl/ vt/i coalhar

cure /kjʊə(r)/ vt curar ● n cura f

curfew /'kɜːfjuː/ n toque m de recolher, recolher m obrigatório

curio /'kjʊərɪəʊ/ n (pl **-os**) curiosidade f

curi|ous /'kjʊərɪəs/ a curioso. **~osity** /-'ɒsətɪ/ n curiosidade f

curl /kɜːl/ vt/i encaracolar(-se) ● n caracol m; **~ up** enroscar(-se)

curler /'kɜːlə(r)/ n rolo m

curly /'kɜːlɪ/ a (**-ier, -iest**) encaracolado, crespo

currant /'kʌrənt/ n passa f de Corinto

currency /'kʌrənsɪ/ n moeda f corrente; (general use) circulação f; **foreign ~** moeda f estrangeira

current /'kʌrənt/ a (common) corrente; ‹event, price, etc› atual; **~ account** conta f corrente; **~ affairs** atualidades fpl ● n corrente f. **~ly** adv atualmente

curriculum /kə'rɪkjʊləm/ n (pl **-la**) currículo m, programa m de estudos. **~ vitae** n curriculum vitae m

curry[1] /'kʌrɪ/ n caril m

curry[2] /'kʌrɪ/ vt **~ favour with** procurar agradar a

curse /kɜːs/ n maldição f, praga f; (bad language) palavrão m ● vt amaldiçoar, praguejar contra ● vi praguejar; (swear) dizer palavrões

cursor /'kɜːsə(r)/ n cursor m

cursory /'kɜːsərɪ/ a apressado, superficial; **a ~ look** uma olhada superficial

curt /kɜːt/ a brusco

curtail /kɜː'teɪl/ vt abreviar; ‹expenses etc› reduzir

curtain /'kɜːtn/ n cortina f; Theat pano m

curtsy /'kɜːtsɪ/ n reverência f ● vi fazer uma reverência

curve /kɜːv/ n curva f ● vt/i curvar(-se); (of road) fazer uma curva

cushion /'kʊʃn/ n almofada f ● vt ‹a blow› amortecer; fig proteger

cushy /'kʊʃɪ/ a (**-ier, -iest**) ▯ fácil; agradável; **~ job** sinecura f, tacho m fig

custard /'kʌstəd/ n creme m

custodian /kʌ'stəʊdɪən/ n guarda m

custod|y /'kʌstədɪ/ n (safe keeping) custódia f; Jur detenção f; (of child) tutela f

custom /'kʌstəm/ n costume m; Comm freguesia f, clientela f. **~ary** a habitual

customer /'kʌstəmə(r)/ n freguês m, cliente mf

customs /'kʌstəmz/ npl alfândega f ● a alfandegário; **~ clearance** desembaraço m alfandegário; **~ officer** funcionário m da alfândega

cut /kʌt/ vt/i (pt cut, pres p **cutting**) cortar; ‹prices etc› reduzir; **~ back** or **down (on)** reduzir; **~ in** intrometer-se; Auto cortar; **~ off** cortar; fig isolar; **~ out** recortar; (leave out) suprimir; **~ short** encurtar, (P) atalhar ● n corte m, golpe m; (of clothes, hair) corte m; (piece) pedaço m; (prices etc) redução f, corte m; 🅰 (share) comissão f, (P) talhada f 🅰. **~back** n corte m; **~out** n figura f para recortar; **~price** a a preço(s) reduzido(s)

cute /kjuːt/ a (**-er, -est**) ▯ (clever) esperto; (attractive) bonito, (P) giro ▯

cutlery /'kʌtlərɪ/ n talheres mpl

cutlet /'kʌtlɪt/ n costeleta f

cutting /'kʌtɪŋ/ a cortante ● n (from newspaper) recorte m; (plant) estaca f; **~ edge** gume m

CV abbr ▶ CURRICULUM VITAE

cybercafe /'saɪbəkæfeɪ/ n lan house f, (P) cibercafé m

cyberspace /'saɪbəspeɪs/ n ciberespaço m

cybersquatter /'saɪbəskwɒtə(r)/ n: pessoa que compra nome de domínio de marca famosa para vendê-lo depois com lucro; (P) ciberespeculador/a mf

cyberterrorism /'saɪbətərɪzəm/ n terrorismo m cibernético, (P) ciberterrorismo m

cycl|e /'saɪkl/ n ciclo m; (bicycle) bicicleta f ● vi andar de bicicleta; ~ **lane** ciclovia f. ~**ing** n ciclismo m. ~**ist** n ciclista mf

cyclone /'saɪkləʊn/ n ciclone m

cylind|er /'sɪlɪndə(r)/ n cilindro m. ~**rical** a cilíndrico

cymbals /'sɪmblz/ npl Mus pratos mpl

cynic /'sɪnɪk/ n cínico m. ~**al** a cínico. ~**ism** /-sɪzəm/ n cinismo m

Cypr|us /'saɪprəs/ n Chipre m. ~**iot** /'sɪprɪət/ a & n cipriota mf

cyst /sɪst/ n quisto m

Czech /tʃek/ a & n tcheco m, (P) checo m

Dd

dab /dæb/ vt (pt dabbed) aplicar levemente ● n a ~ **of** uma aplicaçãozinha de; ~ **sth on** aplicar qq coisa em gestos leves

dabble /'dæbl/ vi ~ **in** interessar-se por, fazer um pouco de (como amador)

dad /dæd/ n 🄸 paizinho m 🄸. ~**dy** n (children's use) papai m, (P) papá m. ~**dy-long-legs** n pernilongo m

daffodil /'dæfədɪl/ n narciso m

daft /dɑːft/ a (-er, -est) doido, maluco

dagger /'dægə(r)/ n punhal m; at ~s **drawn** prestes a lutar (**with** com)

Dáil Éireann *i* É o nome da câmara baixa do Parlamento da República da Irlanda. Pronuncia-se /'ɛːr(ə)n, 'eɪrʲən/ e é formada por 166 representantes ou deputados, normalmente conhecidos por *TDs*, que representam 41 circunscrições. São eleitos através do sistema de representação proporcional. De acordo com a Constituição, deve haver um deputado por cada 20.000 ou 30.000 pessoas.

daily /'deɪlɪ/ a diário, cotidiano, quotidiano ● adv diariamente, todos os dias ● n (newspaper) diário m; 🄸 (charwoman) faxineira f, (P) mulher f a dias

dainty /'deɪntɪ/ a (-ier, -iest) delicado; (pretty, neat) gracioso

dairy /'deərɪ/ n leiteria f, (P) leitaria; ~ **products** laticínios mpl

daisy /'deɪzɪ/ n margarida f

dam /dæm/ n barragem f, represa f ● vt (pt dammed) represar

damag|e /'dæmɪdʒ/ n estrago(s) mpl; ~**es** Jur perdas fpl e danos mpl ● vt estragar, danificar

dame /deɪm/ n old use dama f; Amer 🔳 mulher f

damn /dæm/ vt Relig condenar ao inferno; (swear at) amaldiçoar, maldizer; fig (condemn) condenar; **I'll be ~ed if** que um raio me atinja se ● int raios!, bolas! ● n **not care a** ~ 🄸 estar pouco ligando 🄸, (P) estar-se marimbando 🄸 ● a 🄸 do diabo 🄸, danado ● adv 🄸 muitíssimo. ~**ation** /-'neɪʃn/ n danação f, condenação f

damp /dæmp/ n umidade f, (P) humidade f ● a (-er, -est) úmido, (P) húmido ● vt umedecer, (P) humedecer. ~**en** vt = DAMP. ~**ness** n umidade f, (P) humidade f

dance /dɑːns/ vt/i dançar ● n dança f; ~ **hall** sala f de baile. ~**r** /-ə(r)/ n dançarino m; (professional) bailarino m

dandelion /'dændɪlaɪən/ n dente-de-leão m

dandruff /'dændrʌf/ n caspa f

Dane /deɪn/ n dinamarquês m

danger /'deɪndʒə(r)/ n perigo m; **be in** ~ **of** correr o risco de. ~**ous** a perigoso

dangle /'dæŋgl/ vi oscilar, pender ● vt ter or trazer dependurado; (hold) balançar; fig ‹hopes, etc› acenar com

Danish /'deɪnɪʃ/ a dinamarquês ● n Lang dinamarquês m

dare /deə(r)/ vt ~ **to do** ousar fazer; ~ **sb to do** desafiar alguém a fazer; **I** ~ **say** creio ● n desafio m

daredevil /'deədevl/ n louco m, temerário m

daring /'deərɪŋ/ a audacioso ● n audácia f

dark /dɑːk/ a (-er, -est) escuro, sombrio; (gloomy) sombrio; (of colour) escuro; (of skin) moreno; ~ **horse** concorrente mf que é uma incógnita ● n escuridão f, escuro m; (nightfall) anoitecer *m*, cair *m* da noite; **be in the ~ about** *fig* ignorar. **~room** *n* câmara *f* escura. **~ness** *n* escuridão *f*

darken /'dɑːkən/ *vt/i* escurecer

darling /'dɑːlɪŋ/ *a* & *n* querido *m*

darn /dɑːn/ *vt* serzir, remendar

dart /dɑːt/ *n* dardo *m*, flecha *f*; **~s** (*game*) jogo *m* de dardos ● *vi* lançar-se

dartboard /'dɑːtbɔːd/ *n* alvo *m*

dash /dæʃ/ *vi* precipitar-se; **~ off** partir a toda a velocidade; (*letter*) escrever à pressa ● *vt* arremessar; (*hopes*) destruir ● *n* corrida *f*; (*stroke*) travessão *m*; (*Morse*) traço *m*; **a ~ of** um pouco de

dashboard /'dæʃbɔːd/ *n* painel *m* de instrumentos, quadro *m* de bordo

data /'deɪtə/ *npl* dados *mpl*; **~ capture** aquisição *f* de informações, recolha *f* de dados; **~ processing** processamento *m* or tratamento *m* de dados. **~base** *n* base *f* de dados

date¹ /deɪt/ *n* data *f*; 🔢 encontro *m* marcado ● *vt/i* datar; 🔢 andar com; **out of ~** desatualizado; **to ~** até à data; **up to ~** (*style*) moderno; (*information etc*) em dia. **~d** *a* antiquado

date² /deɪt/ *n* (*fruit*) tâmara *f*

daub /dɔːb/ *vt* borrar, pintar toscamente

daughter /'dɔːtə(r)/ *n* filha *f*. **~-in-law** *n* (*pl* **~s-in-law**) nora *f*

daunt /dɔːnt/ *vt* assustar, intimidar, desencorajar

dawdle /'dɔːdl/ *vi* perder tempo

dawn /dɔːn/ *n* madrugada *f* ● *vi* madrugar, amanhecer; **~ on** *fig* fazer-se luz no espírito de, começar a perceber

day /deɪ/ *n* dia *m*; (*period*) época *f*, tempo *m*; **the ~ before** véspera. **~dream** *n* devaneio *m* ● *vi* devanear

daybreak /'deɪbreɪk/ *n* romper *m* do dia, aurora *f*, amanhecer *m*

daylight /'deɪlaɪt/ *n* luz *f* do dia; **~ robbery** roubar descaradamente

daytime /'deɪtaɪm/ *n* dia *m*, dia *m* claro

daze /deɪz/ *vt* aturdir ● *n* **in a ~** aturdido

dazzle /'dæzl/ *vt* deslumbrar; (*with headlights*) ofuscar

dead /ded/ *a* morto; (*numb*) dormente; **~ end** beco *m* sem saída; **in the ~ centre** bem no meio ● *adv* completamente, de todo; **stop ~** estacar ● *n* **the ~** os mortos; **in the ~ of the night** a horas mortas, na calada da noite. **~pan** *a* inexpressivo

deaden /'dedn/ *vt* (*sound, blow*) amortecer; (*pain*) aliviar

deadline /'dedlaɪn/ *n* prazo *m* final

deadlock /'dedlɒk/ *n* impasse *m*

deadly /'dedlɪ/ *a* (**-ier, -iest**) mortal; (*weapon*) mortífero

deaf /def/ *a* (**-er, -est**) surdo; **turn a ~ ear** fingir que não ouve; **~ mute** surdo-mudo *m*. **~ness** *n* surdez *f*

deafen /'defn/ *vt* ensurdecer. **~ing** *a* ensurdecedor

deal /diːl/ *vt* (*pt* **dealt**) distribuir; (*a blow, cards*) dar ● *vi* negociar ● *n* negócio *m*; *Cards* vez de dar *f*; **a great ~** muito (**of** de); **~ in** negociar em; **~ with** (*person*) tratar (com); (*affair*) tratar de. **~er** *n* comerciante *m*; (*agent*) concessionário *m*; representante *m*

dealt /delt/ ▶ **DEAL**

dean /diːn/ *n* decano *m*

dear /dɪə(r)/ *a* (**-er, -est**) (*cherished*) caro, querido; (*expensive*) caro ● *n* amor *m* ● *adv* caro ● *int* oh **~!** meu Deus!. **~ly** *adv* (*very much*) muito; (*pay*) caro

dearth /dɜːθ/ *n* escassez *f*

death /deθ/ *n* morte *f*; **~ certificate** certidão *f* de óbito; **~ penalty** pena *f* de morte; **~ rate** taxa *f* de mortalidade. **~ trap** *n* lugar *m* perigoso, ratoeira *f*. **~ly** *a* de morte, mortal

debase /dɪ'beɪs/ *vt* degradar

debat|e /dɪ'beɪt/ *n* debate *m* ● *vt* debater. **~able** *a* discutível

debauchery /dɪ'bɔːtʃərɪ/ *n* deboche *m*, devassidão *f*

debit /'debɪt/ *n* débito *m* ● *vt* (*pt* **debited**) debitar

debris /'deɪbriː/ *n* destroços *mpl*

debt /det/ *n* dívida *f*; **in ~** endividado. **~or** *n* devedor *m*

debut /'deɪbjuː/ *n* (*of actor, play etc*) estreia *f*

decade /'dekeɪd/ *n* década *f*

decaden|t /'dekədənt/ *a* decadente. **~ce** *n* decadência *f*

decaffeinated /diː'kæfiːneɪtɪd/ *a* sem cafeína

decapitate /dɪ'kæpɪteɪt/ *vt* decapitar

decay /dɪ'keɪ/ *vi* apodrecer, estragar-se; (*food*) *fig* deteriorar-se; (*building*) degradar-se ● *n* apodrecimento *m*; (*of tooth*) cárie *f*; *fig* declínio *m*; decadência *f*

deceased /dɪ'siːst/ *a* & *n* falecido *m*, defunto *m*

deceit /dɪ'siːt/ *n* engano *m*. **~ful** *a* enganador

d

deceive /dɪ'siːv/ vt enganar, iludir

December /dɪ'sembə(r)/ n dezembro m

decen|t /'diːsnt/ a decente; Ⅱ (good) (bastante) bom; Ⅱ (likeable) simpático. ~cy n decência f

decentralize /diː'sentrəlaɪz/ vt descentralizar

decept|ive /dɪ'septɪv/ a enganador, ilusório. ~ion /-ʃn/ n engano m

decide /dɪ'saɪd/ vt/i decidir; ~ on decidir-se por; ~ to do decidir fazer. ~d /-ɪd/ a decidido; (clear) definido, nítido. ~dly /-ɪdlɪ/ adv decididamente

decimal /'desɪml/ a decimal ● n (fração f,) decimal m; ~ point vírgula f decimal

decipher /dɪ'saɪfə(r)/ vt decifrar

decision /dɪ'sɪʒn/ n decisão f

decisive /dɪ'saɪsɪv/ a decisivo; (manner) decidido

deck /dek/ n convés m; (of cards) baralho m. ~chair n espreguiçadeira f

declar|e /dɪ'kleə(r)/ vt declarar. ~ation /deklə'reɪʃn/ n declaração f

decline /dɪ'klaɪn/ vt (refuse) declinar, recusar delicadamente; Gram declinar ● vi (deteriorate) declinar; (fall) baixar ● n declínio m; (fall) abaixamento m

decode /diː'kəʊd/ vt descodificar

decompos|e /diːkəm'pəʊz/ vt/i decompor(-se). ~ition /-ɒmpə'zɪʃn/ n decomposição f

décor /'deɪkɔː(r)/ n decoração f

decorat|e /'dekəreɪt/ vt decorar, enfeitar; (paint) pintar; (paper) pôr papel em. ~ion /-'reɪʃn/ n decoração f; (medal etc) condecoração f. ~ive /-ətɪv/ a decorativo

decoy[1] /'diːkɔɪ/ n chamariz m, engodo m; (trap) armadilha f

decoy[2] /dɪ'kɔɪ/ vt atrair, apanhar

decrease[1] /diː'kriːs/ vt/i diminuir

decrease[2] /'diːkriːs/ n diminuição f

decrepit /dɪ'krepɪt/ a decrépito

dedicat|e /'dedɪkeɪt/ vt dedicar. ~ed a dedicado. ~ion /-'keɪʃn/ n dedicação f; (in book) dedicatória f

deduce /dɪ'djuːs/ vt deduzir

deduct /dɪ'dʌkt/ vt deduzir; (from pay) descontar

deduction /dɪ'dʌkʃn/ n dedução f; (from pay) desconto m

deed /diːd/ n ato m; Jur contrato m

deep /diːp/ a (-er, -est) profundo; take a ~ breath respirar fundo ● adv

profundamente. ~ freeze n congelador m ● ~freeze vt congelar

deepen /'diːpən/ vt/i aprofundar(-se); (mystery, night) adensar-se

deer /dɪə(r)/ n (pl invar) veado m

deface /dɪ'feɪs/ vt danificar, degradar

default /dɪ'fɔːlt/ vi faltar ● n by ~ à revelia; win by ~ Sport ganhar por não comparecimento, (P) comparência ● n Comput default m

defeat /dɪ'fiːt/ vt derrotar; (thwart) malograr ● n derrota f; (of plan, etc) malogro m

defect[1] /'diːfekt/ n defeito m. ~ive /dɪ'fektɪv/ a defeituoso

defect[2] /dɪ'fekt/ vi desertar. ~ion n defecção m. ~or n trânsfuga mf, dissidente mf; (political) asilado m político

defence /dɪ'fens/ n defesa f. ~less a indefeso

defend /dɪ'fend/ vt defender. ~ant n Jur réu m, acusado m. ~er n advogado m de defesa, defensor m

defensive /dɪ'fensɪv/ a defensivo ● n on the ~ na defensiva f; (person, sport) na retranca f Ⅱ

defer /dɪ'fɜː(r)/ vt (pt deferred) adiar, diferir ● vi ~ to ceder, deferir

deferen|ce /'defərəns/ n deferência f. ~tial /-'renʃl/ a deferente

defian|ce /dɪ'faɪəns/ n desafio m; in ~ of sem respeito por. ~t a de desafio

deficien|t /dɪ'fɪʃnt/ a deficiente; be ~t in ter falta de. ~cy n deficiência f

deficit /'defɪsɪt/ n déficit m

define /dɪ'faɪn/ vt definir

definite /'defɪnɪt/ a definido; (clear) categórico, claro; (certain) certo; ~ly decididamente; (clearly) claramente

definition /defɪ'nɪʃn/ n definição f

definitive /dɪ'fɪnətɪv/ a definitivo

deflat|e /dɪ'fleɪt/ vt esvaziar; (person) desemproar, desinchar. ~ion /-ʃn/ n esvaziamento m; Econ deflação f

deflect /dɪ'flekt/ vt/i desviar(-se)

deform /dɪ'fɔːm/ vt deformar. ~ed a deformado, disforme. ~ity n deformidade f

defraud /dɪ'frɔːd/ vt defraudar

defrost /diː'frɒst/ vt descongelar

deft /deft/ a (-er, -est) hábil

defuse /diː'fjuːz/ vt (a bomb) desativar; (a situation) acalmar

defy /dɪ'faɪ/ vt desafiar; (attempts) resistir a; (the law) desobedecer a;

(*public opinion*) opor-se a

degrad|e /dɪˈɡreɪd/ *vt* degradar

degree /dɪˈɡriː/ *n* grau *m*; *Univ* diploma *m*; **to a ~** ao mais alto grau, muito

dehydrate /diːˈhaɪdreɪt/ *vt/i* desidratar(-se)

de-ice /diːˈaɪs/ *vt* descongelar, degelar; (*windscreen*) tirar o gelo de

deign /deɪn/ *vt* **~ to do** dignar-se (a) fazer

deity /ˈdiːɪtɪ/ *n* divindade *f*

dejected /dɪˈdʒektɪd/ *a* abatido

delay /dɪˈleɪ/ *vt* atrasar; (*postpone*) retardar ● *vi* atrasar-se ● *n* atraso *m*, demora *f*

delegate¹ /ˈdelɪɡət/ *n* delegado *m*

delegat|e² /ˈdelɪɡeɪt/ *vt* delegar. **~ion** /-ˈɡeɪʃn/ *n* delegação *f*

delet|e /dɪˈliːt/ *vt* riscar. **~ion** /-ʃn/ *n* rasura *f*

deliberate¹ /dɪˈlɪbərət/ *a* deliberado; (*steps etc*) compassado

deliberat|e² /dɪˈlɪbəreɪt/ *vt/i* deliberar

delica|te /ˈdelɪkət/ *a* delicado. **~cy** *n* delicadeza *f*; ‹*food*› gulodice *f*; iguaria *f*, (*P*) acepipe *m*

delicatessen /delɪkəˈtesn/ *n* (*shop*) mercearias *fpl* finas

delicious /dɪˈlɪʃəs/ *a* delicioso

delight /dɪˈlaɪt/ *n* grande prazer *m*, delícia *f*; (*thing*) delícia *f*, encanto *m* ● *vt* deliciar ● *vi* **~ in** deliciar-se com. **~ed** *a* deliciado, encantado. **~ful** *a* delicioso, encantador

delinquen|t /dɪˈlɪŋkwənt/ *a & n* delinquente *mf*

deliri|ous /dɪˈlɪrɪəs/ *a* delirante; **be ~ous** delirar. **~um** /-əm/ *n* delírio *m*

deliver /dɪˈlɪvə(r)/ *vt* entregar; ‹*letters*› distribuir; (*free*) libertar; *Med* fazer o parto. **~y** *n* entrega *f*; (*letters*) distribuição *f*; *Med* parto *m*

delu|de /dɪˈluːd/ *vt* enganar; **~de o.s.** ter ilusões. **~sion** /-ʒn/ *n* ilusão *f*

deluge /ˈdeljuːdʒ/ *n* dilúvio *m* ● *vt* inundar

de luxe /dɪˈlʌks/ *a* de luxo

delve /delv/ *vi* **~ into** pesquisar, rebuscar

demand /dɪˈmɑːnd/ *vt* exigir; (*ask to be told*) perguntar ● *n* exigência *f*; *Comm* procura *f*; (*claim*) reivindicação *f*; **in ~** procurado. **~ing** *a* exigente; ‹*work*› puxado, custoso

demeanour /dɪˈmiːnə(r)/ *n* comportamento *m*, conduta *f*

demented /dɪˈmentɪd/ *a* louco, demente; **become ~** enlouquecer

demo /ˈdeməʊ/ *n* (*pl* **-os**) 🆒 manifestação *f*, (*P*) manif *f*

democracy /dɪˈmɒkrəsɪ/ *n* democracia *f*

democrat /ˈdeməkræt/ *n* democrata *mf*. **~ic** /-ˈkrætɪk/ *a* democrático

demoli|sh /dɪˈmɒlɪʃ/ *vt* demolir. **~tion** /deməˈlɪʃn/ *n* demolição *f*

demon /ˈdiːmən/ *n* demônio *m*, (*P*) demónio *m*

demonstrat|e /ˈdemənstreɪt/ *vt* demonstrar ● *vi Pol* fazer uma manifestação, manifestar-se. **~ion** /-ˈstreɪʃn/ *n* demonstração *f*; *Pol* manifestação *f*. **~or** *n Pol* manifestante *mf*

demonstrative /dɪˈmɒnstrətɪv/ *a* demonstrativo

demoralize /dɪˈmɒrəlaɪz/ *vt* desmoralizar

demote /dɪˈməʊt/ *vt* fazer baixar de posto, despromover, rebaixar

demure /dɪˈmjʊə(r)/ *a* recatado, modesto

den /den/ *n* antro *m*, covil *m*; (*room*) cantinho *m*, recanto *m*

denial /dɪˈnaɪəl/ *n* negação *f*; (*refusal*) recusa *f*; (*statement*) desmentido *m*

denim /ˈdenɪm/ *n* brim *m*; **~s** (*jeans*) jeans *mpl*, (*P*) calças *f* de ganga

Denmark /ˈdenmɑːk/ *n* Dinamarca *f*

denomination /dɪnɒmɪˈneɪʃn/ *n* denominação *f*; *Relig* confissão *f*, seita *f*; (*money*) valor *m*

denote /dɪˈnəʊt/ *vt* denotar

denounce /dɪˈnaʊns/ *vt* denunciar

dens|e /dens/ *a* (**-er, -est**) denso; 🆒 ‹*person*› obtuso. **~ity** *n* densidade *f*

dent /dent/ *n* mossa *f*, depressão *f* ● *vt* dentear

dental /ˈdentl/ *a* dentário, dental

dentist /ˈdentɪst/ *n* dentista *mf*. **~ry** *n* odontologia *f*

denture /ˈdentʃə(r)/ *n* dentadura (postiça) *f*

deny /dɪˈnaɪ/ *vt* negar; ‹*rumour*› desmentir; (*disown*) renegar; (*refuse*) recusar

deodorant /diːˈəʊdərənt/ *n & a* desodorante *m*, (*P*) desodorizante *m*

depart /dɪˈpɑːt/ vi partir; ~ **from** (deviate) afastar-se de, desviar-se de

department /dɪˈpɑːtmənt/ n departamento m; (in shop, office) seção f, (P) secção f; (government) repartição f; ~ **store** loja f de departamentos, (P) grande armazém m

departure /dɪˈpɑːtʃə(r)/ n partida f; a ~ **from** ‹custom, diet etc› uma mudança de; a new ~ uma nova orientação

depend /dɪˈpend/ vi ~ **on** depender de; (trust) contar com. ~**able** a de confiança. ~**ence** n dependência f. ~**ent (on)** a dependente (de)

dependant /dɪˈpendənt/ n dependente mf

depict /dɪˈpɪkt/ vt descrever; (in pictures) representar

deplor|e /dɪˈplɔː(r)/ vt deplorar. ~**able** a deplorável

deport /dɪˈpɔːt/ vt deportar. ~**ation** /diːpɔːˈteɪʃn/ n deportação f

depose /dɪˈpəʊz/ vt depor

deposit /dɪˈpɒzɪt/ vt (pt deposited) depositar ● n depósito m; ~ **account** conta f de depósito a prazo

depot /ˈdepəʊ/ n Mil depósito m; (buses) garagem f; Amer (station) rodoviária f; estação f de trem, (P) de comboio

deprav|e /dɪˈpreɪv/ vt depravar

depreciat|e /dɪˈpriːʃɪeɪt/ vt/i depreciar(-se). ~**ion** /-ˈeɪʃn/ n depreciação f

depress /dɪˈpres/ vt deprimir; (press down) carregar em. ~**ion** /-ʃn/ n depressão f

deprivation /deprɪˈveɪʃn/ n privação f

deprive /dɪˈpraɪv/ vt ~ **of** privar de. ~**d** a privado; (underprivileged) deserdado (da sorte), destituído; ‹child› carente

depth /depθ/ n profundidade f; be out of one's ~ perder pé, (P) não ter pé; fig ficar desnorteado, estar perdido; in the ~(s) of no mais fundo de, nas profundezas de

deputy /ˈdepjʊtɪ/ n (pl -ies) delegado m ● a adjunto; ~ **chairman** vice-presidente m

derail /dɪˈreɪl/ vt descarrilhar; be ~**ed** descarrilhar. ~**ment** n descarrilhamento m

deranged /dɪˈreɪndʒd/ a ‹mind› transtornado, louco

derelict /ˈderəlɪkt/ a abandonado

derivative /dɪˈrɪvətɪv/ a derivado; ‹work› pouco original ● n derivado m

deriv|e /dɪˈraɪv/ vt ~**e from** tirar de ● vi ~**e from** derivar de. ~**ation** /derɪˈveɪʃn/ n derivação f

derogatory /dɪˈrɒgətrɪ/ a pejorativo; ‹remark› depreciativo

derv /dɜːv/ n gasóleo m

descend /dɪˈsend/ vt/i descer, descender; be ~**ed from** descender de. ~**ant** n descendente mf

descent /dɪˈsent/ n descida f; (lineage) descendência f, origem f

descri|be /dɪsˈkraɪb/ vt descrever. ~**ption** /-ˈkrɪpʃn/ n descrição f. ~**ptive** /-ˈkrɪptɪv/ a descritivo

desecrate /ˈdesɪkreɪt/ vt profanar

desert[1] /ˈdezət/ a & n deserto m; ~ **island** ilha f deserta

desert[2] /dɪˈzɜːt/ vt/i desertar. ~**ed** a abandonado. ~**er** n desertor m. ~**ion** /-ʃn/ n deserção f

deserv|e /dɪˈzɜːv/ vt merecer. ~**edly** /dɪˈzɜːvɪdlɪ/ adv merecidamente, a justo título. ~**ing** a ‹person› merecedor; ‹action› meritório

design /dɪˈzaɪn/ n desenho m; (artistic) design m; (style of dress) modelo m; (pattern) padrão m, motivo m ● vt desenhar; (devise) conceber. ~**er** n desenhador m; (of dresses) costureiro m; (of machine) inventor m

designat|e /ˈdezɪgneɪt/ vt designar. ~**ion** /-ˈneɪʃn/ n designação f

desir|e /dɪˈzaɪə(r)/ n desejo m ● vt desejar. ~**able** a desejável, atraente

desk /desk/ n secretária f; (of pupil) carteira f; (in hotel) recepção f; (in bank) caixa f

desolat|e /ˈdesələt/ a desolado. ~**ion** /-ˈleɪʃn/ n desolação f

despair /dɪˈspeə(r)/ n desespero m ● vi desesperar (of de)

desperate /ˈdespərət/ a desesperado; (criminal) capaz de tudo; be ~ **for** ter uma vontade doida de

desperation /despəˈreɪʃn/ n desespero m

despicable /dɪˈspɪkəbl/ a desprezível

despise /dɪˈspaɪz/ vt desprezar

despite /dɪˈspaɪt/ prep apesar de, a despeito de, mau grado

desponden|t /dɪˈspɒndənt/ a desanimado

dessert /dɪˈzɜːt/ n sobremesa f. ~ **spoon** n colher f de sobremesa

destination /destɪˈneɪʃn/ n destino m, destinação f

destiny /'destɪnɪ/ n destino m

destitute /'destɪtjuːt/ a destituído, indigente

destroy /dɪ'strɔɪ/ vt destruir. **~uction** /-'strʌkʃn/ n destruição f. **~uctive** a destrutivo, destruidor

detach /dɪ'tætʃ/ vt separar, arrancar. **~able** a separável; ‹lining etc› solto. **~ed** a separado; (impartial) imparcial; (unemotional) desprendido; **~ed house** casa f sem parede-meia com outra

detachment /dɪ'tætʃmənt/ n separação f; (indifference) desprendimento m; Mil destacamento m; (impartiality) imparcialidade f

detail /'diːteɪl/ n pormenor m, detalhe m ● vt detalhar; ‹troops› destacar. **~ed** a detalhado

detain /dɪ'teɪn/ vt reter; (in prison) deter. **~ee** /diːteɪ'niː/ n detido m

detect /dɪ'tekt/ vt detectar. **~ion** /-ʃn/ n detecção f

detective /dɪ'tektɪv/ n detetive m; **~ story** romance m policial

detention /dɪ'tenʃn/ n detenção f; **be given a ~** (school) ficar de castigo na escola

deter /dɪ'tɜː(r)/ vt (pt deterred) dissuadir; (hinder) impedir

detergent /dɪ'tɜːdʒənt/ a & n detergente m

deteriorate /dɪ'tɪərɪəreɪt/ vi deteriorar(-se). **~ion** /-'reɪʃn/ n deterioração f

determine /dɪ'tɜːmɪn/ vt determinar; **~e to do** decidir fazer. **~ation** /-'neɪʃn/ n determinação f. **~ed** a determinado; **~ed to do** decidido a fazer

deterrent /dɪ'terənt/ n dissuasivo m

detest /dɪ'test/ vt detestar. **~able** a detestável

detonate /'detəneɪt/ vt/i detonar. **~or** n espoleta f, detonador m

detour /'diːtʊə(r)/ n desvio m

detract /dɪ'trækt/ vi **~ from** depreciar, menosprezar

detriment /'detrɪmənt/ n detrimento m. **~al** /-'mentl/ a prejudicial

devalue /diː'væljuː/ vt desvalorizar. **~ation** /-'eɪʃn/ n desvalorização f

devastate /'devəsteɪt/ vi devastar; fig (overwhelm) arrasar. **~ing** a devastador; (criticism) de arrasar

develop /dɪ'veləp/ vt/i (pt developed) desenvolver(-se); (get) contrair; (build on) urbanizar; (film) revelar; **~ into**

tornar-se; **~ing country** país m em vias de desenvolvimento. **~ment** n desenvolvimento m; (film) revelação f; (of land) urbanização f

deviate /'diːvɪeɪt/ vi desviar-se. **~ion** /-'eɪʃn/ n desvio m

device /dɪ'vaɪs/ n dispositivo m; (scheme) processo m; **left to one's own ~s** entregue a si mesmo

devil /'devl/ n diabo m

devious /'diːvɪəs/ a tortuoso; fig ‹means› escuso; fig ‹person› pouco franco

devise /dɪ'vaɪz/ vt imaginar, inventar

devoid /dɪ'vɔɪd/ a **~ of** desprovido de, destituído de

devote /dɪ'vəʊt/ vt dedicar, devotar. **~ed** a dedicado, devotado. **~ion** /-ʃn/ n devoção f

devotee /devə'tiː/ n **~ of** adepto m de, entusiasta mf de

devour /dɪ'vaʊə(r)/ vt devorar

devout /dɪ'vaʊt/ a devota; ‹prayer› fervoroso

dew /djuː/ n orvalho m

dexterity /dek'sterətɪ/ n destreza f, jeito m. **~rous** /'dekstrəs/ a destro, hábil

diabetes /daɪə'biːtiːz/ n diabetes f. **~ic** /-'betɪk/ a diabético

diabolical /daɪə'bɒlɪkl/ a diabólico

diagnose /'daɪəgnəʊz/ vt diagnosticar

diagnosis /daɪəg'nəʊsɪs/ n (pl -oses /-siːz/) diagnóstico m

diagonal /daɪ'ægənl/ a & n diagonal f

diagram /'daɪəgræm/ n diagrama m, esquema m

dial /'daɪəl/ n mostrador m ● vt (pt dialled) ‹number› marcar, discar; **~ling code** código m de discagem; **~ling tone** sinal m de discar

dialect /'daɪəlekt/ n dialeto m

dialogue /'daɪəlɒg/ n diálogo m

diameter /daɪ'æmɪtə(r)/ n diâmetro m

diamond /'daɪəmənd/ n diamante m, brilhante m; (shape) losango m; **~s** Cards ouros mpl

diaper /'daɪəpə(r)/ n Amer fralda f

diarrhoea /daɪə'rɪə/ n diarreia f

diary /'daɪərɪ/ n agenda f; (record) diário m

dice /daɪs/ n (pl invar) dado m

dictate /dɪk'teɪt/ vt/i ditar. **~ion** /-ʃn/ n ditado m

dictator /dɪk'teɪtə(r)/ n ditador m. **~ship** n ditadura f

dictionary /'dɪkʃənrɪ/ n dicionário m

did /dɪd/ ▶ DO

diddle /'dɪdl/ vt 🗓 trapacear; enganar

didn't /'dɪdnt/ (= did not) ▶ DO

die /daɪ/ vi (pres p dying) morrer; **be dying to** estar doido para; ~ **down** diminuir, baixar; ~ **out** desaparecer, extinguir-se

diesel /'diːzl/ n diesel m; ~ **engine** motor m a diesel

diet /'daɪət/ n dieta f ● vi fazer dieta, estar de dieta

differ /'dɪfə(r)/ vi diferir; (disagree) discordar

differen|t /'dɪfrənt/ a diferente. ~**ce** n diferença f; (disagreement) desacordo m. ~**ly** adv diferentemente

differentiate /dɪfə'renʃɪeɪt/ vt/i diferençar(-se), diferenciar(-se)

difficult /'dɪfɪkəlt/ a difícil. ~**y** n dificuldade f

diffiden|t /'dɪfɪdənt/ a acanhado, inseguro. ~**ce** n acanhamento m, insegurança f

diffuse¹ /dɪ'fjuːs/ a difuso

diffus|e² /dɪ'fjuːz/ vt difundir

dig /dɪg/ vt/i (pt dug, pres p digging) cavar; (thrust) espetar ● n (with elbow) cotovelada f; (with finger) cutucada f, (P) espetadela f; (remark) ferroada f; Archaeol escavação f; ~**s** 🗓 quarto m alugado; ~ **up** desenterrar

digest /dɪ'dʒest/ vt/i digerir. ~**ible** a digerível, digestível. ~**ion** /-ʃn/ n digestão f

digit /'dɪdʒɪt/ n dígito m

digital /'dɪdʒɪtl/ a digital; ~ **clock** relógio m digital. ~ **camera** n câmera f digital, (P) câmara f digital; ~ **television** n televisão f ou TV digital

dignif|y /'dɪgnɪfaɪ/ vt dignificar. ~**ied** a digno

dignitary /'dɪgnɪtərɪ/ n dignitário m

dignity /'dɪgnətɪ/ n dignidade f

digress /daɪ'gres/ vi digressar, divagar; ~ **from** desviar-se de. ~**ion** /-ʃn/ n digressão f

dilapidated /dɪ'læpɪdeɪtɪd/ a <house> arruinado, degradado; <car> estragado

dilat|e /daɪ'leɪt/ vt/i dilatar(-se)

dilemma /dɪ'lemə/ n dilema m

diligen|t /'dɪlɪdʒənt/ a diligente, aplicado. ~**ce** n diligência f, aplicação f

dilute /daɪ'ljuːt/ vt diluir ● a diluído

dim /dɪm/ a (**dimmer, dimmest**) (weak) fraco; (dark) sombrio; (indistinct) vago; 🗓 (stupid) burro 🗓 ● vt/i (pt dimmed) <light> baixar. ~**ly** adv (shine) fracamente; (remember) vagamente

dime /daɪm/ n Amer moeda f de dez centavos

dimension /daɪ'menʃn/ n dimensão f

diminish /dɪ'mɪnɪʃ/ vt/i diminuir

diminutive /dɪ'mɪnjʊtɪv/ a diminuto ● n diminutivo m

dimple /'dɪmpl/ n covinha f

din /dɪn/ n barulheira f, (P) chinfrim m

dine /daɪn/ vi jantar. ~**r** /-ə(r)/ n (person) comensal m; Rail vagão-restaurante m; Amer (restaurant) lanchonete f

dinghy /'dɪŋgɪ/ n (pl -ghies) bote m; (inflatable) bote m de borracha, (P) barco m de borracha

dingy /'dɪndʒɪ/ a (-ier, -iest) com ar sujo, esquálido

dining room /'daɪnɪŋruːm/ n sala f de jantar

dinner /'dɪnə(r)/ n jantar m; (lunch) almoço m. ~ **jacket** n smoking m

dinosaur /'daɪnəsɔː(r)/ n dinossauro m

dip /dɪp/ vt/i (pt dipped) mergulhar; (lower) baixar ● n mergulho m; (bathe) banho m rápido, mergulho m; (slope) descida f; Culin molho m; ~ **into** <book> folhear; ~ **one's headlights** baixar para médios

diploma /dɪ'pləʊmə/ n diploma m

diplomacy /dɪ'pləʊməsɪ/ n diplomacia f

diplomat /'dɪpləmæt/ n diplomata mf. ~**ic** /-'mætɪk/ a diplomático

dire /daɪə(r)/ a (-er, -est) terrível; <need, poverty> extremo

direct /dɪ'rekt/ a direto ● adv diretamente ● vt dirigir; ~ **sb to** indicar a alguém o caminho para

direction /dɪ'rekʃn/ n direção f, sentido m; ~**s** instruções fpl; ~**s for use** modo m de emprego

directly /dɪ'rektlɪ/ adv diretamente; (at once) imediatamente, logo

director /dɪ'rektə(r)/ n diretor m

directory /dɪ'rektərɪ/ n (telephone) ~ lista f telefônica or (P) telefónica

dirt /dɜːt/ n sujeira, sujidade f; ~ **cheap** 🗓 baratíssimo

dirty /'dɜːtɪ/ a (-ier, -iest) sujo; <word> obsceno ● vt/i sujar(-se); ~ **trick** golpe m baixo, (P) boa partida f

disability /dɪsə'bɪlətɪ/ n deficiência f

disable /dɪsˈeɪbl/ vt incapacitar. ~d a inválido, deficiente

disadvantage /dɪsədˈvɑːntɪdʒ/ n desvantagem f

disagree /dɪsəˈɡriː/ vi discordar (**with** de); ~ with ‹food, climate› não fazer bem. ~ment n desacordo m; (quarrel) desentendimento m

disagreeable /dɪsəˈɡriːəbl/ a desagradável

disappear /dɪsəˈpɪə(r)/ vi desaparecer. ~ance n desaparecimento m

disappoint /dɪsəˈpɔɪnt/ vt desapontar, decepcionar. ~ment n desapontamento m, decepção f

disapprov|e /dɪsəˈpruːv/ vi ~e (of) desaprovar. ~al n desaprovação f

disarm /dɪˈsɑːm/ vt/i desarmar. ~ament n desarmamento m

disast|er /dɪˈzɑːstə(r)/ n desastre m. ~rous a desastroso

disband /dɪsˈbænd/ vt/i debandar; ‹troops› dispersar

disbelief /dɪsbɪˈliːf/ n incredulidade f

disc /dɪsk/ n disco m; ~ jockey disc(o) jockey m

discard /dɪsˈkɑːd/ vt pôr de lado, descartar(-se) de; ‹old clothes etc› desfazer-se de

discern /dɪˈsɜːn/ vt discernir. ~ible a perceptível. ~ing a perspicaz. ~ment n discernimento m, perspicácia f

discharge[1] /dɪsˈtʃɑːdʒ/ vt descarregar; (dismiss) despedir, mandar embora; ‹duty› cumprir; ‹liquid› vazar, (P) deitar; ‹patient› dar alta a; ‹prisoner› absolver, pôr em liberdade; ‹pus› purgar, (P) deitar

discharge[2] /ˈdɪstʃɑːdʒ/ n descarga f; (dismissal) despedimento m; (of patient) alta f; (of prisoner) absolvição f; Med secreção f

disciple /dɪˈsaɪpl/ n discípulo m

disciplin|e /ˈdɪsɪplɪn/ n disciplina f ● vt disciplinar; (punish) castigar. ~ary a disciplinar

disclaim /dɪsˈkleɪm/ vt Jur repudiar; (deny) negar. ~er n desmentido m

disclos|e /dɪsˈkləʊz/ vt revelar. ~ure /-ʒə(r)/ n revelação f

disco /ˈdɪskəʊ/ n (pl -os) 🄳 discoteca f

discolour /dɪsˈkʌlə(r)/ vt/i descolorir(-se); (in sunlight) desbotar(-se)

discomfort /dɪsˈkʌmfət/ n mal-estar m; (lack of comfort) desconforto m

disconcert /dɪskənˈsɜːt/ vt desconcertar. ~ing a desconcertante

disconnect /dɪskəˈnekt/ vt desligar

discontent /dɪskənˈtent/ n descontentamento m. ~ed a descontente

discontinue /dɪskənˈtɪnjuː/ vt descontinuar, suspender

discord /ˈdɪskɔːd/ n discórdia f

discount[1] /ˈdɪskaʊnt/ n desconto m

discount[2] /dɪsˈkaʊnt/ vt descontar; (disregard) dar o desconto a

discourage /dɪsˈkʌrɪdʒ/ vt desencorajar

discourte|ous /dɪsˈkɜːtɪəs/ a indelicado

discover /dɪsˈkʌvə(r)/ vt descobrir. ~y n descoberta f; (of island etc) descobrimento m

discredit /dɪsˈkredɪt/ vt (pt discredited) desacreditar ● n descrédito m

discreet /dɪˈskriːt/ a discreto

discrepancy /dɪˈskrepənsɪ/ n discrepância f

discretion /dɪˈskreʃn/ n discrição f; (prudence) prudência f

discriminat|e /dɪˈskrɪmɪneɪt/ vt/i discriminar; ~e against tomar partido contra, fazer discriminação contra. ~ing a discriminador; (having good taste) com discernimento. ~ion /-ˈneɪʃn/ n discernimento m; (bias) discriminação f

discus /ˈdɪskəs/ n disco m

discuss /dɪˈskʌs/ vt discutir. ~ion /-ʃn/ n discussão f

disdain /dɪsˈdeɪn/ n desdém m ● vt desdenhar. ~ful a desdenhoso

disease /dɪˈziːz/ n doença f. ~d a ‹plant› atacado por doença; ‹person, animal› doente

disembark /dɪsɪmˈbɑːk/ vt/i desembarcar

disenchant /dɪsɪnˈtʃɑːnt/ vt desencantar. ~ment n desencantamento m

disengage /dɪsɪnˈɡeɪdʒ/ vt desprender, soltar; Mech desengatar

disentangle /dɪsɪnˈtæŋɡl/ vt desembaraçar, desenredar

disfigure /dɪsˈfɪɡə(r)/ vt desfigurar

disgrace /dɪsˈɡreɪs/ n vergonha f; (disfavour) desgraça f ● vt desonrar. ~ful a vergonhoso

disgruntled /dɪsˈɡrʌntld/ a descontente

d

disguise /dɪsˈgaɪz/ vt disfarçar • n disfarce m; **in ~** disfarçado

disgust /dɪsˈgʌst/ n repugnância f • vt repugnar. **~ing** a repugnante

dish /dɪʃ/ n prato m • vt **~ out** [I] distribuir; **~ up** servir; **the ~es** (crockery) a louça f

dishcloth /ˈdɪʃklɒθ/ n pano m de prato

dishearten /dɪsˈhɑːtn/ vt desencorajar, desalentar

dishonest /dɪsˈɒnɪst/ a desonesto. **~y** n desonestidade f

dishonour /dɪsˈɒnə(r)/ n desonra f • vt desonrar. **~able** a desonroso

dishwasher /ˈdɪʃwɒʃə(r)/ n lavadora f de pratos, (P) máquina f de lavar a louça

disillusion /dɪsɪˈluːʒn/ vt desiludir. **~ment** n desilusão f

disinfect /dɪsɪnˈfekt/ vt desinfetar, (P) desinfectar. **~ant** n desinfetante m, (P) desinfectante m

disinherit /dɪsɪnˈherɪt/ vt deserdar

disintegrate /dɪsˈɪntɪgreɪt/ vt/i desintegrar(-se)

disinterested /dɪsˈɪntrəstɪd/ a desinteressado

disjointed /dɪsˈdʒɔɪntɪd/ a ‹talk› descosido, desconexo

disk /dɪsk/ n Comput disco m Amer ▶ **DISC**; **~ drive** unidade f de disco

dislike /dɪsˈlaɪk/ n aversão f, antipatia f • vt não gostar de, antipatizar com

dislocat|e /ˈdɪsləkeɪt/ vt ‹limb› deslocar

dislodge /dɪsˈlɒdʒ/ vt desalojar

disloyal /dɪsˈlɔɪəl/ a desleal. **~ty** n deslealdade f

dismal /ˈdɪzməl/ a tristonho

dismantle /dɪsˈmæntl/ vt desmantelar

dismay /dɪsˈmeɪ/ n consternação f • vt consternar

dismiss /dɪsˈmɪs/ vt despedir; (from mind) afastar, pôr de lado. **~al** n despedimento m

dismount /dɪsˈmaʊnt/ vi desmontar

disobedien|t /dɪsəˈbiːdɪənt/ a desobediente. **~ce** n desobediência f

disobey /dɪsəˈbeɪ/ vt/i desobedecer (a)

disorder /dɪsˈɔːdə(r)/ n desordem f; Med perturbações fpl, disfunção f. **~ly** a desordenado; (riotous) desordeiro

disown /dɪsˈəʊn/ vt repudiar

disparaging /dɪsˈpærɪdʒɪŋ/ a depreciativo

dispatch /dɪsˈpætʃ/ vt despachar • n despacho m

dispel /dɪsˈpel/ vt (pt dispelled) dissipar

dispensary /dɪsˈpensərɪ/ n dispensário m, farmácia f

dispense /dɪsˈpens/ vt dispensar • vi **~ with** dispensar, passar sem. **~r** /-ə(r)/ n (container) distribuidor m

dispers|e /dɪsˈpɜːs/ vt/i dispersar(-se)

dispirited /dɪsˈpɪrɪtɪd/ a desanimado

display /dɪsˈpleɪ/ vt exibir, mostrar; ‹feeling› manifestar, dar mostras de • n exposição f; (of computer) apresentação f visual; Comm objetos mpl expostos

displeas|e /dɪsˈpliːz/ vt desagradar a; **~ed with** descontente com. **~ure** /-ˈpleʒə(r)/ n desagrado m

disposable /dɪsˈpəʊzəbl/ a descartável

dispos|e /dɪsˈpəʊz/ vt dispor • vi **~e of** desfazer-se de; **well ~ed towards** bem disposto para com. **~al** n (of waste) eliminação f; **at sb's ~al** à disposição de alguém

disposition /dɪspəˈzɪʃn/ n disposição f; (character) índole f

disproportionate /dɪsprəˈpɔːʃənət/ a desproporcionado

disprove /dɪsˈpruːv/ vt refutar

dispute /dɪsˈpjuːt/ vt contestar; (fight for, quarrel) disputar • n disputa f; (industrial) Pol conflito m; **in ~** em questão

disqualif|y /dɪsˈkwɒlɪfaɪ/ vt tornar inapto; Sport desqualificar; **~y from driving** apreender a carteira de motorista, (P) a carta de condução. **~ication** /-ɪˈkeɪʃn/ n desqualificação f

disregard /dɪsrɪˈgɑːd/ vt não fazer caso de • n indiferença f (for por)

disrepair /dɪsrɪˈpeə(r)/ n mau estado m, abandono m, degradação f

disreputable /dɪsˈrepjʊtəbl/ a pouco recomendável; (in appearance) com mau aspecto; (in reputation) vergonhoso, de má fama

disrepute /dɪsrɪˈpjuːt/ n descrédito m

disrespect /dɪsrɪˈspekt/ n falta f de respeito. **~ful** a desrespeitoso, irreverente

disrupt /dɪsˈrʌpt/ vt perturbar; ‹plans› transtornar; (break up) dividir. **~ion** /-ʃn/ n perturbação f. **~ive** a perturbador

dissatisf|ied /dɪˈsætɪsfaɪd/ a descontente. **~action** /dɪsætɪsˈfækʃn/ n descontentamento m

dissect /dɪ'sekt/ vt dissecar. **~ion** /-ʃn/ n dissecação f

dissent /dɪ'sent/ vi dissentir, discordar ● n dissensão f, desacordo m

dissertation /dɪsə'teɪʃn/ n dissertação f

disservice /dɪs'sɜːvɪs/ n **do sb a ~** prejudicar alguém

dissident /'dɪsɪdənt/ a & n dissidente mf

dissimilar /dɪ'sɪmɪlə(r)/ a diferente

dissociate /dɪ'səʊʃɪeɪt/ vt dissociar, desassociar

dissolve /dɪ'zɒlv/ vt/i dissolver(-se)

dissuade /dɪ'sweɪd/ vt dissuadir

distance /'dɪstəns/ n distância f; **from a ~** de longe; **in the ~** ao longe, à distância

distant /'dɪstənt/ a distante; ‹relative› afastado

distil /dɪ'stɪl/ vt (pt distilled) destilar

distillery /dɪ'stɪlərɪ/ n destilaria f

distinct /dɪ'stɪŋkt/ a distinto; (marked) claro, nítido. **~ion** /-ʃn/ n distinção f. **~ive** a distintivo, característico. **~ly** adv distintamente; (markedly) claramente

distinguish /dɪ'stɪŋgwɪʃ/ vt/i distinguir. **~ed** a distinto

distort /dɪ'stɔːt/ vt distorcer; (misrepresent) deturpar. **~ion** /-ʃn/ n distorção f; (misrepresentation) deturpação f

distract /dɪ'strækt/ vt distrair. **~ed** a (distraught) desesperado, fora de si. **~ing** a enlouquecedor. **~ion** /-ʃn/ n distração f

distraught /dɪ'strɔːt/ a desesperado, fora de si

distress /dɪ'stres/ n (physical) dor f; (anguish) aflição f; (poverty) miséria f; (danger) perigo m ● vt afligir. **~ing** a aflitivo, doloroso

distribut|e /dɪ'strɪbjuːt/ vt distribuir. **~ion** /-'bjuːʃn/ n distribuição f. **~or** n distribuidor m

district /'dɪstrɪkt/ n região f; (of town) zona f

distrust /dɪs'trʌst/ n desconfiança f ● vt desconfiar de

disturb /dɪ'stɜːb/ vt perturbar; (move) desarrumar; (bother) incomodar. **~ance** n (noise, disorder) distúrbio m. **~ed** a perturbado. **~ing** a perturbador

disused /dɪs'juːzd/ a fora de uso, desusado, em desuso

ditch /dɪtʃ/ n fosso m ● vt 🅰 (abandon) abandonar; largar

dither /'dɪðə(r)/ vi hesitar

ditto /'dɪtəʊ/ adv idem

div|e /daɪv/ vi mergulhar; (rush) precipitar-se ● n mergulho m; (of plane) picada f; 🅰 (place) espelunca f. **~er** n mergulhador m. **~ing board** n prancha f de saltos

diverge /daɪ'vɜːdʒ/ vi divergir

diverse /daɪ'vɜːs/ a diverso

diversify /daɪ'vɜːsɪfaɪ/ vt diversificar

diversity /daɪ'vɜːsətɪ/ n diversidade f

diver|t /daɪ'vɜːt/ vt desviar; (entertain) divertir. **~sion** /-ʃn/ n diversão f; (traffic) desvio m

divide /dɪ'vaɪd/ vt/i dividir(-se); **~ in two** (branch, river, road) bifurcar-se

dividend /'dɪvɪdend/ n dividendo m

divine /dɪ'vaɪn/ a divino

divinity /dɪ'vɪnətɪ/ n divindade f; Theology teologia f

division /dɪ'vɪʒn/ n divisão f

divorce /dɪ'vɔːs/ n divórcio m ● vt/i divorciar(-se) de. **~d** a divorciado

divorcee /dɪvɔː'siː/ n divorciado m

divulge /daɪ'vʌldʒ/ vt divulgar

DIY abbr ▶ DO-IT-YOURSELF

dizz|y /'dɪzɪ/ a (-ier, -iest) tonto; **be** or **feel ~y** ter tonturas, sentir-se tonto. **~iness** n tontura f, vertigem f

---

do /duː/ unstressed də/ (pres **do**, 3rd person sing. **does**, pt **did**, pp **done**) ● vt

••••▸ (carry out) fazer; **she's ~ing her homework** ela está fazendo os deveres; **what are you ~ing?** o que você está fazendo?; **~ something!** faça alguma coisa!; **~ the washing-up** lavar a louça; **~ the cleaning** fazer a faxina

••••▸ (as job) **what does she ~?** o que ela faz?

••••▸ (arrange) **~ one's hair** pentear-se; **~ one's make-up** maquiar-se

••••▸ (cheat) enganar; **this isn't a genuine antique, you've been done** esta antiguidade é falsa, você foi enganado

● vi

••••▸ (get on) ir; **how are they ~ing at school?** como eles vão na escola?; **how are you ~ing?** como vai?

••••▸ (with as or adverb) fazer; **~ as they ~** faça como eles; **he can ~ as**

he likes ele pode fazer do jeito que gosta; **you did well** você fez bem

····▸ (*be suitable*) servir; **this will ~** isso serve

····▸ (*be sufficient*) bastar; **one bottle of water will ~** uma garrafa de água basta; **will £20 ~?** £20 chegam?

····▸ (*in phrases*) **that does it!** chegal; **well done!** muito bem!

● *v aux*

····▸ (*in questions and negatives*) **~ you see?** vê?; **I ~ not smoke** não fumo; **Mary didn't phone** a Mary não telefonou; **Don't ~ that!** não faça isso!

····▸ (*in tag questions*) **you like chocolate, don't you?** você gosta de chocolate, não gosta?; **he lives in London, doesn't he?** ele mora em Londres, não mora?

····▸ (*as verb substitute*) **you speak Portuguese better than I ~** você fala português melhor do que eu

····▸ (*in short answers*) **does he work there?** yes, he does/no, he doesn't ele trabalha ali? sim, trabalha/não, não trabalha

····▸ (*for emphasis*) **I ~ like her** gosto mesmo dela

● *n* (*pl* dos, *or* do's)

····▸ festa *f*; *npl* **dos and don'ts** regras a seguir

□ **~ away with** ● *vt* eliminar. **~ in** ● *vt* (*kill* ▪) matar, liquidar. **~ up** ● *vt* (*fasten*) ‹shoelaces› amarrar; ‹buttons, coat, zip› fechar; ‹house› renovar. **~ without** ● *vt* passar sem. **~ with:** ● *vt* (*need*) **I could ~ with a cup of tea** me cairia bem uma xícara de chá; **it could ~ with a wash** precisa de uma lavagem; (*connected with*) **it's to ~ with** tem a ver com; **it's nothing to ~ with** não tem nada a ver com

docile /ˈdəʊsaɪl/ *a* dócil

dock¹ /dɒk/ *n* doca *f* ● *vt* levar à doca ● *vi* entrar na doca. **~er** *n* estivador *m*

dock² /dɒk/ *n Jur* banco *m* dos réus

dockyard /ˈdɒkjɑːd/ *n* estaleiro *m*

doctor /ˈdɒktə(r)/ *n* médico *m*, doutor *m*; *Univ* doutor *m* ● *vt* (*cat*) capar; *fig* adulterar; falsificar

doctorate /ˈdɒktərət/ *n* doutorado *m*, (P) doutoramento *m*

doctrine /ˈdɒktrɪn/ *n* doutrina *f*

document /ˈdɒkjʊmənt/ *n* documento *m* ● *vt* documentar. **~ary** /-ˈmentrɪ/ *a* documental ● *n* documentário *m*

dodge /dɒdʒ/ *vt/i* esquivar(-se), furtar(-se) a ● *n* ▯ truque *m*

dodgy /ˈdɒdʒɪ/ *a* (**-ier, -iest**) ▯ delicado; difícil; embaraçoso; arriscado

does /dʌz/ ▸ DO

doesn't /ˈdʌznt/ (= does not) ▸ DO

dog /dɒg/ *n* cão *m* ● *vt* (*pt* **dogged**) ir no encalço de, perseguir. **~-eared** *a* com os cantos dobrados

dogged /ˈdɒgɪd/ *a* obstinado, persistente

dogma /ˈdɒgmə/ *n* dogma *m*. **~tic** /-ˈmætɪk/ *a* dogmático

dogsbody /ˈdɒgzbɒdɪ/ *n* ▯ pau-para-toda-obra *m* ▯; factótum *m*

do-it-yourself *a* faça-você-mesmo

doldrums /ˈdɒldrəmz/ *npl* **be in the ~** estar com a neura; ‹business› estar parado

dole /dəʊl/ *vt* **~ out** distribuir ● *n* ▯ auxílio *m* de desemprego; **on the ~** ▯ desempregado (titular de auxílio)

doll /dɒl/ *n* boneca *f* ● *vt/i* **~ up** ▯ embonecar(-se)

dollar /ˈdɒlə(r)/ *n* dólar *m*

dolphin /ˈdɒlfɪn/ *n* golfinho *m*

domain /dəʊˈmeɪn/ *n* domínio *m*

dome /dəʊm/ *n* cúpula *f*; (*vault*) abóbada *f*

domestic /dəˈmestɪk/ *a* (*of home, animal, flights*) doméstico; ‹trade› interno; ‹news› nacional. **~ated** /-keɪtɪd/ ‹animal› domesticado; ‹person› que gosta de trabalhos caseiros

dominant /ˈdɒmɪnənt/ *a* dominante

dominat|e /ˈdɒmɪneɪt/ *vt/i* dominar. **~ion** /-ˈneɪʃn/ *n* dominação *f*, domínio *m*

domineer /dɒmɪˈnɪə(r)/ *vi* **~ over** mandar (em), ser autocrático (para com). **~ing** *a* mandão, autocrático

domino /ˈdɒmɪnəʊ/ *n* (*pl* **-oes**) dominó *m*

donat|e /dəʊˈneɪt/ *vt* fazer doação de, doar, dar. **~ion** /-ʃn/ *n* donativo *m*

done /dʌn/ ▸ DO

donkey /ˈdɒŋkɪ/ *n* burro *m*

donor /ˈdəʊnə(r)/ *n* (*of blood*) doador *m*, (P) dador *m*

don't /dəʊnt/ (= do not) ▸ DO

doodle /ˈduːdl/ *vi* rabiscar

doom /duːm/ n ruína f; (*fate*) destino m; **be ~ed to** ser/estar condenado a; **~ed (to failure)** condenado ao fracasso

door /dɔː(r)/ n porta f

doorman /'dɔːmən/ n (pl **-men**) porteiro m

doormat /'dɔːmæt/ n capacho m

doorstep /'dɔːstep/ n degrau m da porta

doorway /'dɔːweɪ/ n vão m da porta, (P) entrada f

dope /dəʊp/ n ① droga f; ② (*idiot*) imbecil mf ● vt dopar, drogar

dormant /'dɔːmənt/ a dormente; (*inactive*) inativo; (*latent*) latente

dormitory /'dɔːmɪtrɪ/ n dormitório m; *Amer Univ* residência f

dos|e /dəʊs/ n dose f ● vt medicar. **~age** n dosagem f; (*on label*) posologia f

dot /dɒt/ n ponto m; **on the ~** no momento preciso ● vt **be ~ted with** estar pejado de; **~ted line** linha f pontilhada

dot-com /dɒt'kɒm/ n empresa f dot. com

dote /dəʊt/ vi **~ on** ser louco por

double /'dʌbl/ a duplo; ‹room, bed› de casal; **~ chin** papada f; **~ Dutch** algaraviada f, fala f incompreensível; **~ glazing** (janela f de) vidro m duplo ● adv duas vezes mais ● n dobro m; **~s** *Tennis* dupla f, (P) pares mpl; **at the ~** a passo acelerado ● vt/i dobrar, duplicar; (*fold*) dobrar em dois. **~ bass** n contrabaixo m; **~-cross** vt enganar; **~-decker** n ônibus m, (P) autocarro m de dois andares. **doubly** adv duplamente

doubt /daʊt/ n dúvida f ● vt duvidar de; **~ if** or **that** duvidar que. **~ful** a duvidoso; (*hesitant*) que tem dúvidas. **~less** adv sem dúvida, indubitavelmente

dough /dəʊ/ n massa f

doughnut /'dəʊnʌt/ n sonho m, (P) bola f de Berlim

dove /dʌv/ n pomba f

dowdy /'daʊdɪ/ a (**-ier, -iest**) sem graça, sem gosto

down[1] /daʊn/ n (*feathers, hair*) penugem f

down[2] /daʊn/ adv (*to lower place*) abaixo, para baixo; (*in lower place*) em baixo; **be ~** ‹level, price› descer; ‹sun› estar posto; **come** or **go ~** descer; **~ under** na Austrália; **~ with** abaixo ● prep por (+n) (n+) abaixo; **~ the hill/street** etc pelo monte/pela rua etc abaixo ● vt ① (*knock down*) jogar or (P) atirar abaixo; ① (*drink*) esvaziar. **~-and-out** n marginal m; **~hearted** a desencorajado, desanimado; **~-to-earth** a terra-a-terra invar

downcast /'daʊnkɑːst/ a abatido, deprimido, desmoralizado

downfall /'daʊnfɔːl/ n queda f, ruína f

downhill /daʊn'hɪl/ adv **go ~** descer; fig ir abaixo ● a /'daʊnhɪl/ a descer, descendente

download /daʊn'ləʊd/ vt *Comput* baixar

downpour /'daʊnpɔː(r)/ n aguaceiro m forte, (P) chuvada f

downright /'daʊnraɪt/ a franco; (*utter*) autêntico, verdadeiro ● adv positivamente

downstairs /daʊn'steəz/ adv (at/to) em/para baixo, no/para o andar de baixo ● /'daʊnsteəz/ a ‹flat etc› de baixo, do andar de baixo

downstream /'daʊnstriːm/ adv rio abaixo

downtown /'daʊntaʊn/ a & adv (de, em, para) o centro da cidade; **~ Boston** o centro de Boston

downtrodden /'daʊntrɒdn/ a espezinhado, oprimido

downward /'daʊnwəd/ a descendente. **~(s)** adv para baixo

dowry /'daʊərɪ/ n dote m

doze /dəʊz/ vi dormitar; **~ off** cochilar ● n soneca f, cochilo m

dozen /'dʌzn/ n dúzia f; **~s of** ① dezenas de, dúzias de

Dr abbr (= **Doctor**) Dr

drab /dræb/ a insípido; (*of colour*) morto, apagado

draft[1] /drɑːft/ n rascunho m; *Comm* ordem f de pagamento ● vt fazer o rascunho de; (*draw up*) redigir; **the ~** *Amer Mil* recrutamento m

draft[2] /drɑːft/ n *Amer* = **DRAUGHT**

d

drag /dræg/ *vt/i* (*pt* **dragged**) arrastar(-se); ‹*river*› dragar; (*pull away*) arrancar ● *n* ⓘ (*task*) chatice *f* ⓧ; ⓘ (*person*) estorvo *m*; ⓧ (*clothes*) travesti *m*

dragon /'drægən/ *n* dragão *m*

dragonfly /'drægənflaɪ/ *n* libélula *f*

drain /dreɪn/ *vt* drenar; ‹*vegetables*› escorrer; ‹*glass, tank*› esvaziar; (*use up*) esgotar ● *vi* ~ (**off**) escoar-se ● *n* cano *m*; ~(**pipe**) cano *m* de esgoto. ~**s** *npl* (*sewers*) esgotos *mpl*. ~**age** *n* drenagem *f*. ~**ing board** *n* escorredouro *m*

drama /'drɑːmə/ *n* arte *f* dramática; (*play, event*) drama *m*. ~**tic** /drə'mætɪk/ *a* dramático. ~**tist** /'dræmətɪst/ *n* dramaturgo *m*. ~**tize** /'dræmətaɪz/ *vt* dramatizar

drank /dræŋk/ ▶ **DRINK**

drape /dreɪp/ *vt* ~ **round/over** dispor (tecido) em pregas à volta de or sobre. ~**s** *npl Amer* cortinas *fpl*

drastic /'dræstɪk/ *a* drástico, violento

draught /drɑːft/ *n* corrente *f* de ar; *Naut* calado *m*; ~**s** (*game*) (jogo *m* das) damas *fpl*; ~ **beer** chope *m*, (*P*) cerveja à caneca, imperial *f* ⓘ. ~**y** *a* com correntes de ar, ventoso

draw /drɔː/ *vt* (*pt* **drew**, *pp* **drawn**) puxar; (*attract*) atrair; ‹*picture*› desenhar; (*in lottery*) tirar à sorte; ‹*line*› traçar; (*open curtains*) abrir; (*close curtains*) fechar ● *vi* desenhar; *Sport* empatar; (*come*) vir ● *n Sport* empate *m*; (*lottery*) sorteio *m*; ~ **back** recuar; ~ **in** (*of days*) diminuir; ~ **near** aproximar-se; ~ **out** ‹*money*› levantar; ~ **up** deter-se, parar; ‹*document*› redigir; ‹*chair*› aproximar, chegar

drawback /'drɔːbæk/ *n* inconveniente *m*, desvantagem *f*

drawer /drɔː(r)/ *n* gaveta *f*

drawing /'drɔːɪŋ/ *n* desenho *m*. ~ **board** *n* prancheta *f*; ~ **pin** *n* percevejo *m*

drawl /drɔːl/ *n* fala *f* arrastada

drawn /drɔːn/ ▶ **DRAW**

dread /dred/ *n* terror *m* ● *vt* temer

dreadful /'dredfl/ *a* medonho, terrível

dream /driːm/ *n* sonho *m* ● *vt/i* (*pt* **dreamed**, *or* **dreamt**) sonhar (*of* com) ● *a* (*ideal*) dos seus sonhos; ~ **up** imaginar. ~**er** *n* sonhador *m*. ~**y** *a* sonhador; ‹*music*› romântico

dreary /'drɪərɪ/ *a* (**-ier, -iest**) tristonho; (*boring*) aborrecido

dredge /dredʒ/ *n* draga *f* ● *vt/i* dragar. ~**r** /-ə(r)/ *n* draga *f*; (*for sugar*) polvilhador *m*

dregs /dregz/ *npl* depósito *m*, sedimento *m*; *fig* escória *f*

drench /drentʃ/ *vt* encharcar

dress /dres/ *n* vestido *m*; (*clothing*) roupa *f* ● *vt/i* vestir(-se); ‹*food*› temperar; ‹*wound*› fazer curativo, (*P*) pensar, (*P*) tratar; ‹*rehearsal*› ensaio *m* geral; ~ **up as** fantasiar-se de; **get** ~**ed** vestir-se

dresser /'dresə(r)/ *n* (*furniture*) guarda-louça *m*

dressing /'dresɪŋ/ *n* (*sauce*) tempero *m*; (*bandage*) curativo *m*, (*P*) penso *m*. ~ **gown** *n* roupão *m*; ~ **room** *n Sport* vestiário *m*; *Theat* camarim *m*; ~**table** *n* toucador *m*

dressmak|er /'dresmeɪkə(r)/ *n* costureira *f*, modista *f*. ~**ing** *n* costura *f*

dressy /'dresɪ/ *a* (**-ier, -iest**) elegante, chique *invar*

drew /druː/ ▶ **DRAW**

dribble /'drɪbl/ *vi* pingar; ‹*person*› babar-se; ‹*football*› driblar

dried /draɪd/ *a* ‹*fruit etc*› seco

drier /'draɪə(r)/ *n* secador *m*

drift /drɪft/ *vi* ir à deriva; (*pile up*) amontoar-se ● *n* força *f* da corrente; (*pile*) monte *m*; (*of events*) rumo *m*; (*meaning*) sentido *m*. ~**er** *n* pessoa *f* sem rumo

drill /drɪl/ *n* (*tool*) broca *f*; (*training*) exercício *m*, treino *m*; (*routine procedure*) exercícios *mpl* ● *vt* furar, perfurar; (*train*) treinar; ‹*tooth*› abrir ● *vi* treinar-se

drink /drɪŋk/ *vt/i* (*pt* **drank**, *pp* **drunk**) beber ● *n* bebida *f*; **a** ~ **of water** um copo de água; ~**ing water** água *f* potável. ~**able** *a* potável; (*palatable*) bebível. ~**er** *n* bebedor *m*

drip /drɪp/ *vi* (*pt* **dripped**) pingar ● *n* pingar *m*; ⓧ (*person*) banana *mf* ⓘ. ~**-dry** *vt* deixar escorrer ● *a* que não precisa passar

drive /draɪv/ *vt* (*pt* **drove**, *pp* **driven** /'drɪvn/) empurrar, impelir, levar; ‹*car, animal*› dirigir, conduzir, (*P*) guiar; ‹*machine*› acionar; ~ **at** chegar a; ~ **in** (*force in*) enterrar; ~ **mad** (*fazer*) enlouquecer, pôr fora de si ● *vi* dirigir, conduzir, (*P*) guiar; ~ **away** ‹*car*› partir ● *n* passeio *m* de carro; (*private road*) entrada *f* para veículos; *fig* energia *f*; *Psych* drive *m*, compulsão *f*, impulso *m*; (*campaign*) campanha *f*. ~**-in** *n* ‹*bank, cinema etc*› banco *m*, cinema *etc* em que se é atendido no carro, drive-in *m*

drivel /ˈdrɪvl/ n baboseira f, bobagem f

driver /ˈdraɪvə(r)/ n condutor m; (of taxi, bus) chofer m, motorista mf

driving /ˈdraɪvɪŋ/ n condução f. ~ **licence** n carteira f de motorista, (P) carta f de condução; ~ **school** n auto-escola f, (P) escola f de condução; ~ **test** n exame m de motorista or (P) de condução

drizzle /ˈdrɪzl/ n chuvisco m ● vi chuviscar

drone /drəʊn/ n zumbido m; (male bee) zangão m ● vi zumbir; fig falar monotonamente

drool /druːl/ vi babar(-se)

droop /druːp/ vi pender, curvar-se

drop /drɒp/ n gota f; (fall) queda f; (distance) altura f de queda ● vt/i (pt dropped) (deixar) cair; (fall, lower) baixar; ~ **(off)** (person from car) deixar, largar; ~ **a line** escrever duas linhas (to a); ~ **in** passar por (on em casa de); ~ **off** (doze) adormecer; ~ **out** (withdraw) retirar-se; (of student) abandonar. **~out** n marginal mf, marginalizado m

droppings /ˈdrɒpɪŋz/ npl excrementos mpl de animal; (of birds) cocô, (P) cocó m 🔲; porcaria f 🔲

drought /draʊt/ n seca f

drove /drəʊv/ ▶ DRIVE

drown /draʊn/ vt/i afogar(-se)

drowsy /ˈdraʊzɪ/ a sonolento; **be** or **feel ~** ter vontade de dormir

drudge /drʌdʒ/ n mouro m de trabalho. **~ry** /-ərɪ/ n trabalho m penoso e monótono, estafa f

drug /drʌɡ/ n droga f; Med medicamento m, remédio m ● vt (pt drugged) drogar; ~ **addict** drogado m, tóxico-dependente m

drugstore /ˈdrʌɡstɔː(r)/ n Amer farmácia f que vende também sorvetes etc, (P) drogaria f

drum /drʌm/ n Mus tambor m; (for oil) barril m, tambor m; **~s** Mus bateria f ● vi (pt drummed) tocar tambor; (with one's fingers) tamborilar ● vt ~ **into sb** fazer entrar na cabeça de alguém; ~ **up** ⟨support⟩ conseguir obter; ⟨business⟩ criar. **~mer** n tambor m; (in pop group etc) baterista m, (P) bateria m

drunk /drʌŋk/ ▶ DRINK a embriagado, bêbedo; **get ~** embebedar-se, embriagar-se ● n bêbedo m. **~ard** n alcoólico m, bêbedo m. **~en** a embriagado, bêbedo; (habitually) bêbedo

dry /draɪ/ a (**drier, driest**) seco; ⟨day⟩ sem chuva; **be** or **feel ~** ter sede ● vt/i secar; ~ **up** ⟨dishes⟩ secar a louça; (of supplies) esgotar-se. **~-clean** vt limpar a seco; **~-cleaner's** n (loja de) lavagem f a seco, lavanderia f. **~ness** n secura f

dual /ˈdjuːəl/ a duplo; ~ **carriageway** estrada f dividida por faixa central

dub /dʌb/ vt (pt dubbed) ⟨film⟩ dobrar; ⟨nickname⟩ apelidar de

dubious /ˈdjuːbɪəs/ a duvidoso; ⟨character, compliment⟩ dúbio; **feel ~ about** ter dúvidas quanto a

duchess /ˈdʌtʃɪs/ n duquesa f

duck /dʌk/ n pato m ● vi abaixar-se rapidamente ● vt ⟨head⟩ baixar; ⟨person⟩ batizar, pregar uma amona em. **~ling** n patinho m

duct /dʌkt/ n canal m, tubo m

dud /dʌd/ a 🔲 (thing) que não presta ou não funciona; 🔲 (coin) falso; 🔲 (cheque) sem fundos, (P) careca 🔲

due /djuː/ a devido; (expected) esperado; ~ **to** devido a, por causa de; **in ~ course** no tempo devido ● adv ~ **east** /etc exatamente, /etc a ● n devido m; **~s** direitos mpl; (of club) cota f

duel /ˈdjuːəl/ n duelo m

duet /djuːˈet/ n dueto m

dug /dʌɡ/ ▶ DIG

duke /djuːk/ n duque m

dull /dʌl/ a (-er, -est) (boring) enfadonho; ⟨colour⟩ morto; ⟨mirror⟩ embaçado; ⟨weather⟩ encoberto; ⟨sound⟩ surdo; (stupid) burro

duly /ˈdjuːlɪ/ adv devidamente; (in due time) no tempo devido

dumb /dʌm/ a (-er, -est) mudo; 🔲 (stupid) bronco 🔲; burro 🔲

dumbfound /dʌmˈfaʊnd/ vt pasmar

dummy /ˈdʌmɪ/ n imitação f, coisa f simulada; (of tailor) manequim m; (of baby) chupeta f

dump /dʌmp/ vt ⟨rubbish⟩ jogar fora; (put down) deixar cair; 🔲 (abandon) largar ● n monte m de lixo; (tip) lixeira f; Mil depósito m; 🔲 buraco m

dunce /dʌns/ n burro m; **~'s cap** orelhas fpl de burro

dune /djuːn/ n duna f

dung /dʌŋ/ n esterco m; (manure) estrume m

dungarees /dʌŋɡəˈriːz/ npl macacão m, (P) fato m de macaco

dungeon /ˈdʌndʒən/ n calabouço m, masmorra f

dupe /djuːp/ vt enganar ● n trouxa m

duplicate¹ /ˈdjuːplɪkət/ n duplicado m
● a idêntico

duplicate² /ˈdjuːplɪkeɪt/ vt duplicar,
fazer em duplicado; (on machine)
fotocopiar

duplicity /djuːˈplɪsɪtɪ/ n duplicidade f

durable /ˈdjʊərəbl/ a resistente;
(enduring) duradouro, durável

duration /djuˈreɪʃn/ n duração f

duress /djuˈres/ n under ~ sob coação f

during /ˈdjʊərɪŋ/ prep durante

dusk /dʌsk/ n crepúsculo m, anoitecer m

dust /dʌst/ n pó m, poeira f ● vt limpar o
pó de; (sprinkle) polvilhar

dustbin /ˈdʌstbɪn/ n lata f do lixo, (P)
caixote m

duster /ˈdʌstə(r)/ n pano m do pó

dustman /ˈdʌstmən/ n (pl -men) lixeiro
m, (P) homem m do lixo

dusty /ˈdʌstɪ/ a (-ier, -iest) poeirento,
empoeirado

Dutch /dʌtʃ/ a holandês; **go ~** pagar
cada um a sua despesa ● n Lang
holandês m. **~man** n holandês m

dutiful /ˈdjuːtɪfl/ a cumpridor; (showing
respect) respeitador

dut|y /ˈdjuːtɪ/ n dever m; (tax) impostos
mpl; **~ies** (of official etc) funções fpl; **off
~y** de folga; **on ~y** de serviço. **~y-free**
a isento de impostos; **~y-free shop** free
shop m

duvet /ˈdjuːveɪ/ n edredom m, (P)
edredão m de penas

DVD abbr (= Digital Versatile Disc)
DVD m. **~ burner** n gravador m de DVD;
~ player n leitor m de DVD

dwarf /dwɔːf/ n (pl -fs) anão m

dwell /dwel/ vi (pt dwelt) morar; **~ on**
alongar-se sobre. **~ing** n habitação f

dwindle /ˈdwɪndl/ vi diminuir,
reduzir-se

dye /daɪ/ vt (pres p dyeing) tingir ● n
tinta f

dying /ˈdaɪɪŋ/ ▶ DIE

dynamic /daɪˈnæmɪk/ a dinâmico

dynamite /ˈdaɪnəmaɪt/ n dinamite f
● vt dinamitar

dynamo /ˈdaɪnəməʊ/ n (pl -os)
dínamo m

dysentery /ˈdɪsəntrɪ/ n disenteria f

dyslex|ia /dɪsˈleksɪə/ n dislexia f. **~ic**
a disléxico

Ee

each /iːtʃ/ a & pron cada; **~ one** cada
um; **~ other** um ao outro, uns aos
outros; **they like ~ other** gostam um do
outro/uns dos outros; **know/love/** etc
~ other conhecer-se/amar-se/ etc

eager /ˈiːɡə(r)/ a ansioso (**to** por)
desejoso (**for** de); ‹supporter›
entusiástico; **be ~ to** ter vontade de.
~ly adv com impaciência, ansiosamente;
(keenly) com entusiasmo. **~ness**
n ansiedade f, desejo m; (keenness)
entusiasmo m

eagle /ˈiːɡl/ n águia f

ear /ɪə(r)/ n ouvido m; (external part)
orelha f. **~drum** n tímpano m; **~ring** n
brinco m

earache /ˈɪəreɪk/ n dor f de ouvidos

earl /ɜːl/ n conde m

early /ˈɜːlɪ/ (-ier, -iest) adv cedo ● a
primeiro; ‹hour› matinal; ‹fruit›
temporão; ‹retirement› antecipado;
have an ~ dinner jantar cedo; **in ~
summer** no princípio do verão

earmark /ˈɪəmɑːk/ vt destinar; reservar
(**for** para)

earn /ɜːn/ vt ganhar; (deserve) merecer

earnest /ˈɜːnɪst/ a sério; **in ~** a sério

earnings /ˈɜːnɪŋz/ npl salário m;
(profits) ganhos mpl, lucros mpl

earshot /ˈɪəʃɒt/ n within ~ ao alcance
da voz

earth /ɜːθ/ n terra f ● vt Electr ligar
à terra; **why on ~?** por que diabo?,
porque cargas d'água?. **~ly** a terrestre,
terreno

earthenware /ˈɜːθənweə(r)/ n louça f
de barro, falança f

earthquake /ˈɜːθkweɪk/ n tremor m
de terra, terremoto m, (P) terramoto m

earthy /ˈɜːθɪ/ a terroso, térreo; (coarse)
grosseiro

ease /iːz/ n facilidade f; (comfort) bem-
estar m; **at ~** à vontade; Mil descansar;
ill at ~ pouco à vontade; **with ~**
facilmente ● vt/i (from pain, anxiety)
acalmar(-se); (slow down) afrouxar;
(slide) deslizar; **~ in/out** fazer entrar/sair
com cuidado

easel /ˈiːzl/ n cavalete m

east /iːst/ n este m, leste m, oriente m;
the E~ o Oriente ● a este, (de) leste,
oriental ● adv a/para leste; **~ of** para

o leste de. **~erly** a oriental, leste, a/de leste. **~ward** a, **~ward(s)** adv para leste

Easter /'iːstə(r)/ n Páscoa f; **~ egg** ovo m de Páscoa

eastern /'iːstən/ a oriental, leste

easy /'iːzɪ/ a (**-ier, -iest**) fácil; (relaxed) natural, descontraído; **take it ~** levar as coisas com calma; **~ chair** poltrona f. **~going** a bonacheirão. **easily** adv facilmente

eat /iːt/ vt/i (pt **ate**, pp **eaten**) comer; **~ into** corroer. **~able** a comestível

eaves /iːvz/ npl beiral m

eavesdrop /'iːvzdrɒp/ vi (pt **-dropped**) escutar por detrás da porta

ebb /eb/ n vazante f, baixa-mar m ● vi vazar; fig declinar

e-book /'iːbʊk/ n livro m eletrônico, (P) eletrónico

EC /iːˈsiː/ abbr (= European Commission) CE f

eccentric /ɪkˈsentrɪk/ a & n excêntrico m. **~ity** /eksenˈtrɪsətɪ/ n excentricidade f

ecclesiastical /ɪkliːzɪˈæstɪkl/ a eclesiástico

echo /'ekəʊ/ n (pl **-oes**) eco m ● vt/i (pt **echoed**, pres p **echoing**) ecoar; fig repetir

eclipse /ɪˈklɪps/ n eclipse m ● vt eclipsar

ecolog|y /iːˈkɒlədʒɪ/ n ecologia f. **~ical** /iːkəˈlɒdʒɪkl/ a ecológico

e-commerce /'iːkɒmɜːs/ n comércio m eletrônico or (P) eletrónico

economic /iːkəˈnɒmɪk/ a econômico, (P) económico; (profitable) rentável. **~al** a econômico, (P) económico. **~s** n economia f política

economist /ɪˈkɒnəmɪst/ n economista mf

econom|y /ɪˈkɒnəmɪ/ n economia f. **~ize** vt/i economizar

ecstasy /'ekstəsɪ/ n êxtase m

ecstatic /ɪkˈstætɪk/ a extático

eczema /'eksɪmə/ n eczema m

edge /edʒ/ n borda f, beira f; (of town) periferia f, limite m; (of knife) fio m ● vt debruar ● vi (move) avançar pouco a pouco

edgy /'edʒɪ/ a irritadiço, nervoso

edible /'edɪbl/ a comestível

edifice /'edɪfɪs/ n edifício m

Edinburgh Festival É o evento cultural mais importante da Grã-Bretanha, que se celebra em agosto, na capital da Escócia desde 1947. O festival atrai um grande número de visitantes e um aspecto muito relevante do evento são os espetáculos que não formam parte do programa oficial, e aos quais se dá o nome de the Fringe.

edit /'edɪt/ vt (pt **edited**) ‹newspaper› dirigir; ‹text› editar

edition /ɪˈdɪʃn/ n edição f

editor /'edɪtə(r)/ n (of newspaper) diretor m; (P) diretor m; editor m responsável; (of text) organizador m de texto; **the ~ (in chief)** redator-chefe m. **~ial** /edɪˈtɔːrɪəl/ a & n editorial m

educat|e /'edʒʊkeɪt/ vt instruir; ‹mind, public› educar. **~ed** a instruído; educado. **~ion** /-ˈkeɪʃn/ n educação f; (schooling) ensino m. **~ional** /-ˈkeɪʃənl/ a educativo, pedagógico

eel /iːl/ n enguia f

eerie /'ɪərɪ/ a (**-ier, -iest**) arrepiante, misterioso

effect /ɪˈfekt/ n efeito m ● vt efetuar; **come into ~** entrar em vigor; **in ~** na realidade; **take ~** ter efeito

effective /ɪˈfektɪv/ a eficaz, eficiente; (striking) sensacional; (actual) efetivo. **~ly** adv (efficiently) eficazmente; (strikingly) de forma sensacional; (actually) efetivamente. **~ness** n eficácia f

effeminate /ɪˈfemɪnət/ a efeminado, afeminado

effervescent /efəˈvesnt/ a efervescente

efficien|t /ɪˈfɪʃnt/ a eficiente, eficaz. **~cy** n eficiência f. **~tly** adv eficientemente

effort /'efət/ n esforço m. **~less** a fácil, sem esforço

e.g. /iːˈdʒiː/ abbr por ex

egg[1] /eg/ n ovo m. **~plant** n beringela f

egg[2] /eg/ vt **~ on** 🅟 incitar

eggshell /'egʃel/ n casca f de ovo

ego /'egəʊ/ n (pl **-os**) ego m, eu m. **~ism** n egoísmo m. **~ist** n egoísta mf. **~tism** n egotismo m. **~tist** n egotista mf

Egypt /'iːdʒɪpt/ n Egito m. **~ian** /ɪˈdʒɪpʃn/ a & n egípcio m

eh /eɪ/ int 🅟 hã?

eiderdown /'aɪdədaʊn/ n edredão m, edredom m

eight /eɪt/ a & n oito m. **~h** a & n oitavo m

eighteen /eɪˈtiːn/ a & n dezoito m. **~th** a & n décimo oitavo m

eight|y /'eɪtɪ/ a & n oitenta m. **~ieth** a & n octogésimo m

either /'aɪðə(r)/ a & pron um e outro; (with negative) nem um nem outro; (each) cada ● adv também não ● conj ~ ... or ou ... ou; (with negative) nem ... nem

ejaculate /ɪ'dʒækjʊleɪt/ vt/i ejacular; (exclaim) exclamar

eject /ɪ'dʒekt/ vt expelir; (expel) expulsar, despejar, ejetar

elaborate[1] /ɪ'læbərət/ a elaborado, rebuscado, minucioso

elaborate[2] /ɪ'læbəreɪt/ vt elaborar ● vi entrar em pormenores; ~ on estender-se sobre

elapse /ɪ'læps/ vi decorrer

elastic /ɪ'læstɪk/ a & n elástico m; ~ band elástico m

elat|ed /ɪ'leɪtɪd/ a radiante, exultante. **~ion** n exultação f

elbow /'elbəʊ/ n cotovelo m

elder[1] /'eldə(r)/ a mais velho. **~s** npl pessoas fpl mais velhas

elder[2] /'eldə(r)/ n (tree) sabugueiro m

elderly /'eldəlɪ/ a idoso; **the ~** as pessoas de idade

eldest /'eldɪst/ a & n o mais velho m

elect /ɪ'lekt/ vt eleger ● a eleito. **~ion** /-kʃn/ n eleição f

electric /ɪ'lektrɪk/ a elétrico

electrician /ɪlek'trɪʃn/ n eletricista m

electricity /ɪlek'trɪsətɪ/ n eletricidade f

electrify /ɪ'lektrɪfaɪ/ vt eletrificar; fig (excite) eletrizar

electrocute /ɪ'lektrəkjuːt/ vt eletrocutar

electronic /ɪlek'trɒnɪk/ a eletrônico, (P) electrónico. **~s** n eletrônica f, (P) eletrónica f

elegan|t /'elɪgənt/ a elegante. **~ce** n elegância f

element /'elɪmənt/ n elemento m; (of heater etc) resistência f. **~ary** /-'mentrɪ/ a elementar; (school) primário

elephant /'elɪfənt/ n elefante m

elevat|e /'elɪveɪt/ vt elevar. **~ion** /-'veɪʃn/ n elevação f

elevator /'elɪveɪtə(r)/ n Amer (lift) elevador m; ascensor m

eleven /ɪ'levn/ a & n onze m. **~th** a & n décimo primeiro m; **at the ~th hour** à última hora

eligible /'elɪdʒəbl/ a (for office) idóneo, (P) idóneo (for para); (desirable) aceitável; **be ~ for** (entitled to) ter direito a

eliminat|e /ɪ'lɪmɪneɪt/ vt eliminar

elite /eɪ'liːt/ n elite f

elm /elm/ n olmo m, ulmeiro m

elocution /elə'kjuːʃn/ n elocução f

elope /ɪ'ləʊp/ vi fugir

eloquen|t /'eləkwənt/ a eloquente. **~ce** n eloquência f

else /els/ adv mais; **everybody ~** todos os outros; **nobody ~** mais ninguém; **nothing ~** nada mais; **or ~** ou então, senão; **somewhere ~** noutro lado qualquer. **~where** adv noutro lado

elusive /ɪ'luːsɪv/ a (person) esquivo, difícil de apanhar; (answer) evasivo

emaciated /ɪ'meɪʃɪeɪtɪd/ a emaciado, macilento

email /'iːmeɪl/ n correio m eletrônico, (P) eletrónico, e-mail m; ~ **address** endereço m de e-mail

embankment /ɪm'bæŋkmənt/ n (of river) dique m; (of railway) terrapleno m; talude m, (P) aterro m

embargo /ɪm'bɑːgəʊ/ n (pl -oes) embargo m

embark /ɪm'bɑːk/ vt/i embarcar; ~ **on** (business etc) embarcar em, meter-se em [1]; (journey) começar

embarrass /ɪm'bærəs/ vt embaraçar, confundir. **~ment** n embaraço m, atrapalhação f

embassy /'embəsɪ/ n embaixada f

embellish /ɪm'belɪʃ/ vt embelezar, enfeitar

embezzle /ɪm'bezl/ vt desviar (fundos). **~ment** n desfalque m

emblem /'embləm/ n emblema m

embod|y /ɪm'bɒdɪ/ vt encarnar; (include) incorporar, incluir. **~iment** n personificação f

embrace /ɪm'breɪs/ vt/i abraçar(-se); (offer, opportunity) acolher ● n abraço m

embroider /ɪm'brɔɪdə(r)/ vt bordar. **~y** n bordado m

embryo /'embrɪəʊ/ n (pl -os) embrião m

emerald /'emərəld/ n esmeralda f

emerge /ɪ'mɜːdʒ/ vi emergir, surgir

emergency /ɪ'mɜːdʒənsɪ/ n emergência f; (urgent case) urgência f; ~ **exit** saída f de emergência; **in an ~** em caso de urgência

emigrant /'emɪgrənt/ n emigrante mf

emigrat|e /'emɪgreɪt/ vi emigrar. **~ion** /-'greɪʃn/ n emigração f

eminent /'emɪnənt/ a eminente

emi|t /ɪˈmɪt/ vt (pt **emitted**) emitir. **~ssion** /-ʃn/ n emissão f

emotion /ɪˈməʊʃn/ n emoção f. **~al** a ‹person, shock› emotivo; ‹speech, scene› emocionante

emperor /ˈempərə(r)/ n imperador m

emphasis /ˈemfəsɪs/ n ênfase f; **lay ~ on** pôr em relevo

emphasize /ˈemfəsaɪz/ vt enfatizar, sublinhar; ‹syllable, word› acentuar

emphatic /ɪmˈfætɪk/ a enfático; ‹manner› enérgico

empire /ˈempaɪə(r)/ n império m

employ /ɪmˈplɔɪ/ vt empregar. **~ee** /emplɔɪˈiː/ n empregado m. **~er** n patrão m. **~ment** n emprego m; **~ment agency** agência f de emprego

empower /ɪmˈpaʊə(r)/ vt autorizar (**to do** a fazer)

empress /ˈemprɪs/ n imperatriz f

empt|y /ˈempti/ a vazio; ‹promise› falso; **on an ~y stomach** com o estômago vazio, em jejum ● vt/i esvaziar(-se). **~iness** n vazio m

emulsion /ɪˈmʌlʃn/ n emulsão f

enable /ɪˈneɪbl/ vt **~ sb to do** permitir a alguém fazer

enact /ɪˈnækt/ vt Jur decretar; Theat representar

enamel /ɪˈnæml/ n esmalte m ● vt (pt **enamelled**) esmaltar

enchant /ɪnˈtʃɑːnt/ vt encantar. **~ing** a encantador. **~ment** n encantamento m

encircle /ɪnˈsɜːkl/ vt cercar, rodear

enclose /ɪnˈkləʊz/ vt ‹land› cercar; (with letter) enviar incluso/junto. **~d** a ‹space› fechado; (with letter) anexo, incluso, junto

enclosure /ɪnˈkləʊʒə(r)/ n cercado m, recinto m; (with letter) documento m anexo

encore /ɒŋˈkɔː(r)/ int & n bis m

encounter /ɪnˈkaʊntə(r)/ vt encontrar, deparar com ● n encontro m

encourage /ɪnˈkʌrɪdʒ/ vt encorajar. **~ment** n encorajamento m

encroach /ɪnˈkrəʊtʃ/ vi **~ on** ‹land› invadir; ‹time› abusar de

encycloped|ia /ɪnsaɪkləˈpiːdɪə/ n enciclopédia f. **~ic** a enciclopédico

end /end/ n fim m; (farthest part) extremo m, ponta f; **in the ~** por fim; **no ~ of** 🔢 muito, enorme, imenso; **on ~** (upright) em pé; (consecutive) a fio, de seguida ● vt/i acabar, terminar; **~ up** (arrive finally) ir parar (**in** a/em); **~ up**

doing acabar por fazer

endanger /ɪnˈdeɪndʒə(r)/ vt pôr em perigo

endeavour /ɪnˈdevə(r)/ n esforço m ● vi esforçar-se (**to** por)

ending /ˈendɪŋ/ n fim m; (of word) terminação f

endless /ˈendlɪs/ a interminável; ‹times› sem conta; ‹patience› infinito

endorse /ɪnˈdɔːs/ vt ‹document› endossar; ‹action› aprovar. **~ment** n Auto averbamento m

endow /ɪnˈdaʊ/ vt doar. **~ment** n doação f

endur|e /ɪnˈdjʊə(r)/ vt suportar ● vi durar. **~ance** n resistência f

enemy /ˈenəmi/ n & a inimigo m

energetic /enəˈdʒetɪk/ a enérgico

energy /ˈenədʒi/ n energia f

enforce /ɪnˈfɔːs/ vt aplicar

engage /ɪnˈɡeɪdʒ/ vt ‹staff› contratar; Mech engrenar ● vi **~ in** envolver-se em, lançar-se em. **~d** a noivo; (busy) ocupado. **~ment** n noivado m; (undertaking, appointment) compromisso m; Mil combate m

engine /ˈendʒɪn/ n motor m; (of train) locomotiva f

engineer /endʒɪˈnɪə(r)/ n engenheiro m ● vt engenhar. **~ing** n engenharia f

England /ˈɪŋɡlənd/ n Inglaterra f

English /ˈɪŋɡlɪʃ/ a inglês ● n Lang inglês m; **the ~** os ingleses mpl. **~man** n inglês m. **~woman** n inglesa f

engrav|e /ɪnˈɡreɪv/ vt gravar. **~ing** n gravura f

engrossed /ɪnˈɡrəʊst/ a absorto (**in** em)

engulf /ɪnˈɡʌlf/ vt engolfar, tragar

enhance /ɪnˈhɑːns/ vt aumentar; (heighten) realçar

enigma /ɪˈnɪɡmə/ n enigma m. **~tic** /enɪɡˈmætɪk/ a enigmático

enjoy /ɪnˈdʒɔɪ/ vt gostar de; (benefit from) gozar de; **~ o.s.** divertir-se. **~able** a agradável. **~ment** n prazer m

enlarge /ɪnˈlɑːdʒ/ vt aumentar; **~ upon** alargar-se sobre. **~ment** n ampliação f

enlighten /ɪnˈlaɪtn/ vt esclarecer. **~ment** n esclarecimento m, elucidação f

enlist /ɪnˈlɪst/ vt recrutar; fig aliciar; granjear ● vi alistar-se

enliven /ɪnˈlaɪvn/ vt animar

enmity /ˈenməti/ n inimizade f

enormous /ɪˈnɔːməs/ a enorme

enough /ɪˈnʌf/ a bastante m, suficiente m ● adv & n bastante m, suficiente m ● int basta!, chega!

enquir|e /ɪnˈkwaɪə(r)/ vt/i perguntar, indagar; ~e about informar-se de, pedir informações sobre. ~y n pedido m de informações

enrage /ɪnˈreɪdʒ/ vt enfurecer, enraivecer

enrich /ɪnˈrɪtʃ/ vt enriquecer

enrol /ɪnˈrəʊl/ vt/i (pt enrolled) inscrever(-se); Schol matricular(-se). ~ment n inscrição f; Schol matrícula f

ensemble /ɒnˈsɒmbl/ n conjunto m

ensu|e /ɪnˈsjuː/ vi seguir-se. ~ing a decorrente

ensure /ɪnˈʃʊə(r)/ vt assegurar; ~ that assegurar-se de que

entail /ɪnˈteɪl/ vt acarretar

entangle /ɪnˈtæŋgl/ vt emaranhar, enredar

enter /ˈentə(r)/ vt ‹room, club etc› entrar em; (register) registar; ‹data› entrar com ● vi entrar (into em); ~ for inscrever-se em

enterprise /ˈentəpraɪz/ n empresa f, empreendimento m; fig iniciativa f

enterprising /ˈentəpraɪzɪŋ/ a empreendedor

entertain /entəˈteɪn/ vt entreter; ‹guests› receber; ‹ideas› alimentar, nutrir. ~er n artista mf. ~ment n entretenimento m; (performance) espetáculo m

enthral /ɪnˈθrɔːl/ vt (pt enthralled) fascinar

enthuse /ɪnˈθjuːz/ vi ~ over entusiasmar-se por

enthusias|m /ɪnˈθjuːzɪæzm/ n entusiasmo m. ~t n entusiasta mf. ~tic /-ˈæstɪk/ a entusiástico

entice /ɪnˈtaɪs/ vt atrair; ~ to do induzir a fazer. ~ment n tentação f, engodo m

entire /ɪnˈtaɪə(r)/ a inteiro. ~ly adv inteiramente

entirety /ɪnˈtaɪərətɪ/ n in its ~ por inteiro, na (sua) totalidade

entitle /ɪnˈtaɪtl/ vt dar direito; ~d a ‹book› intitulado; be ~d to sth ter direito a algo. ~ment n direito m

entrance /ˈentrəns/ n entrada f (to para); (right to enter) admissão f

entrant /ˈentrənt/ n Sport concorrente mf; (in exam) candidato m

entreat /ɪnˈtriːt/ vt rogar, suplicar. ~y n rogo m, súplica f

entrust /ɪnˈtrʌst/ vt confiar

entry /ˈentrɪ/ n entrada f; (on list) item m; (in dictionary) verbete m; ~ form ficha f de inscrição, (P) boletim m de inscrição; no ~ entrada proibida

envelop /ɪnˈveləp/ vt (pt enveloped) envolver

envelope /ˈenvələʊp/ n envelope m, sobrescrito m

enviable /ˈenvɪəbl/ a invejável

envious /ˈenvɪəs/ a invejoso; be ~ of ter inveja de

environment /ɪnˈvaɪərənmənt/ n meio m; (ecological) meio ambiente m. ~al /-ˈmentl/ a do meio; (ecological) do ambiente

envisage /ɪnˈvɪzɪdʒ/ vt encarar; (foresee) prever

envoy /ˈenvɔɪ/ n enviado m

envy /ˈenvɪ/ n inveja f ● vt invejar, ter inveja de

epic /ˈepɪk/ n epopeia f ● a épico

epidemic /epɪˈdemɪk/ n epidemia f

epilep|sy /ˈepɪlepsɪ/ n epilepsia f. ~tic /-ˈleptɪk/ a & n epiléptico m, (P) epilético m

episode /ˈepɪsəʊd/ n episódio m

epitom|e /ɪˈpɪtəmɪ/ n (summary) epítome m; (embodiment) modelo m. ~ize vt fig representar; encarnar; (summarize) resumir

epoch /ˈiːpɒk/ n época f. ~-making a que marca uma época

equal /ˈiːkwəl/ a & n igual m; ~ to (task) à altura de ● vt (pt equalled) igualar, ser igual a. ~ity /iːˈkwɒlətɪ/ n igualdade f. ~ly adv igualmente; (similarly) de igual modo

equalize /ˈiːkwəlaɪz/ vt/i igualar; Sport empatar

equate /ɪˈkweɪt/ vt equacionar (with com); (treat as equal) equiparar (with a)

equation /ɪˈkweɪʒn/ n equação f

equator /ɪˈkweɪtə(r)/ n equador m

equilibrium /iːkwɪˈlɪbrɪəm/ n equilíbrio m

equip /ɪˈkwɪp/ vt (pt equipped) equipar (with com); munir (with de). ~ment n equipamento m

equitable /ˈekwɪtəbl/ a equitativo

equity /ˈekwətɪ/ n equidade f

equivalent /ɪˈkwɪvələnt/ a & n equivalente m

era /ˈɪərə/ n era f, época f

eradicate /ɪˈrædɪkeɪt/ vt erradicar, suprimir

erase /ɪˈreɪz/ vt apagar. ~r /-ə(r)/ n borracha (de apagar) f

erect /ɪˈrekt/ a ereto ● vt erigir. ~ion /-ʃn/ n ereção f; (building) construção f, edifício m

ero|de /ɪˈrəʊd/ vt corroer. ~sion /ɪˈrəʊʒn/ n erosão f

erotic /ɪˈrɒtɪk/ a erótico

err /ɜː(r)/ vi (pt **erred**) errar

errand /ˈerənd/ n recado m

erratic /ɪˈrætɪk/ a errático, irregular; ‹person› variável, imprevisível

erroneous /ɪˈrəʊnɪəs/ a errôneo, (P) erróneo, errado

error /ˈerə(r)/ n erro m

erupt /ɪˈrʌpt/ vi ‹war, fire› irromper; ‹volcano› entrar em erupção. ~ion /-ʃn/ n erupção f

escalat|e /ˈeskəleɪt/ vt/i intensificar(-se); (of prices) subir em espiral

escalator /ˈeskəleɪtə(r)/ n escada f rolante

escape /ɪˈskeɪp/ vi escapar-se ● vt escapar a ● n fuga f; (of prisoner) evasão f, fuga f; ~ **from sb** escapar de alguém; ~ **to** fugir para; **have a lucky** or **narrow** ~ escapar por um triz

escapism /ɪˈskeɪpɪzəm/ n escapismo m

escort[1] /ˈeskɔːt/ n escolta f; (of woman) cavalheiro m, acompanhante m

escort[2] /ɪˈskɔːt/ vt escoltar; (accompany) acompanhar

Eskimo /ˈeskɪməʊ/ n (pl **-os**) esquimó mf

especial /ɪˈspeʃl/ a especial. ~**ly** adv especialmente

espionage /ˈespɪɒnɑːʒ/ n espionagem f

espresso /eˈspresəʊ/ n (pl **-os**) (coffee) expresso m, (P) bica f

essay /ˈeseɪ/ n ensaio m; Schol redação f

essence /ˈesns/ n essência f

essential /ɪˈsenʃl/ a essencial ● n the ~**s** o essencial m. ~**ly** adv essencialmente

establish /ɪˈstæblɪʃ/ vt estabelecer; ‹business, state› fundar; (prove) provar, apurar. ~**ment** n estabelecimento m; (institution) instituição f; **the E~ment** o Establishment m, a classe f dirigente

estate /ɪˈsteɪt/ n propriedade f; (possessions) bens mpl; (inheritance) herança f; ~ **agent** agente m imobiliário; (housing) ~ conjunto m habitacional;

~ **car** perua f, (P) carrinha f

esteem /ɪˈstiːm/ vt estimar ● n estima f

estimate[1] /ˈestɪmət/ n cálculo m, avaliação f; Comm orçamento m, estimativa f

estimat|e[2] /ˈestɪmeɪt/ vt calcular, estimar. ~**ion** /-ˈmeɪʃn/ n opinião f

estuary /ˈestʃʊərɪ/ n estuário m

etc abbr (= et cetera) etc

eternal /ɪˈtɜːnl/ a eterno

eternity /ɪˈtɜːnətɪ/ n eternidade f

ethic /ˈeθɪk/ n ética f; ~**s** ética f. ~**al** a ético

ethnic /ˈeθnɪk/ a étnico

etiquette /ˈetɪket/ n etiqueta f

eulogy /ˈjuːlədʒɪ/ n elogio m (fúnebre)

euphemism /ˈjuːfəmɪzəm/ n eufemismo m

euro /ˈjʊərəʊ/ n euro m

Europe /ˈjʊərəp/ n Europa f. **E~an** /-ˈpɪən/ a & n europeu m; **E~an Union** União Europeia

evacuat|e /ɪˈvækjʊeɪt/ vt evacuar. ~**ion** /-ˈeɪʃn/ n evacuação f

evade /ɪˈveɪd/ vt evadir

evaluate /ɪˈvæljʊeɪt/ vt avaliar

evangelical /iːvænˈdʒelɪkl/ a evangélico

evaporat|e /ɪˈvæpəreɪt/ vt/i evaporar(-se); ~**ed milk** leite m evaporado. ~**ion** /-ˈreɪʃn/ n evaporação f

evasion /ɪˈveɪʒn/ n evasão f

evasive /ɪˈveɪsɪv/ a evasivo

eve /iːv/ n véspera f

even /ˈiːvn/ a regular; ‹surface› liso, plano; ‹amounts› igual; ‹number› par; **get** ~ **with** ajustar contas com ● vt/i ~ **up** igualar(-se), acertar ● adv mesmo; ~ **better** ainda melhor. ~**ly** adv uniformemente

evening /ˈiːvnɪŋ/ n entardecer m, anoitecer m; (whole evening) serão m; ~ **class** aula f à noite (para adultos); ~ **dress** traje m de cerimônia or (P) cerimónia or de rigor; (woman's) vestido m de noite

event /ɪˈvent/ n acontecimento m; **in the** ~ **of** no caso de. ~**ful** a movimentado, memorável

eventual /ɪˈventʃʊəl/ a final. ~**ly** adv por fim; (in future) eventualmente

ever /ˈevə(r)/ adv jamais; (at all times) sempre; **do you** ~ **go?** você já foi alguma vez?, costumas ir?; **the best I** ~ **saw** o melhor que já vi; ~ **so** [1]

muitíssimo, tão; **hardly ~** quase nunca.
~ since adv desde então ● prep desde
● conj desde que

evergreen /'evəgri:n/ n sempre-verde
f, planta f de folhas persistentes ● a
persistente

everlasting /'evəlɑːstɪŋ/ a eterno

every /'evrɪ/ a cada; **~ now and then**
de vez em quando, volta e meia; **~ one**
cada um; **~ other day** dia sim dia não,
de dois em dois dias; **~ three days** de
três em três dias

everybody /'evrɪbɒdɪ/ pron todo o
mundo, todos

everyday /'evrɪdeɪ/ a cotidiano, (P)
quotidiano, diário; (common) do dia a
dia, vulgar

everyone /'evrɪwʌn/ pron todo o
mundo, todos

everything /'evrɪθɪŋ/ pron tudo

everywhere /'evrɪweə(r)/ adv
(position) em todo lugar, em toda parte;
(direction) a todo lugar, a toda parte

evict /ɪ'vɪkt/ vt expulsar, despejar. **~ion**
/-ʃn/ n despejo m

evidence /'evɪdəns/ n evidência f;
(proof) prova f; (testimony) testemunho
m, depoimento m; **~ of** sinal de; **give ~**
testemunhar; **in ~** em evidência

evident /'evɪdənt/ a evidente. **~ly** adv
evidentemente

evil /'iːvl/ a mau ● n mal m

evo|ke /ɪ'vəʊk/ vt evocar. **~cative**
/ɪ'vɒkətɪv/ a evocativo

evolution /iːvə'luːʃn/ n evolução f

evolve /ɪ'vɒlv/ vi evolucionar, evoluir
● vt desenvolver, produzir

ex- /eks/ pref ex-

exact /ɪg'zækt/ a exato ● vt exigir (**from**
de). **~ing** a exigente; (task) difícil. **~ly**
adv exatamente

exaggerat|e /ɪg'zædʒəreɪt/ vt/i
exagerar. **~ion** /-'reɪʃn/ n exagero m

exam /ɪg'zæm/ n 🏛 exame m

examination /ɪgzæmɪ'neɪʃn/ n
exame m; Jur interrogatório m

examine /ɪg'zæmɪn/ vt examinar;
(witness etc) interrogar. **~r** /-ə(r)/ n
examinador m

example /ɪg'zɑːmpl/ n exemplo m; **for
~** por exemplo; **make an ~ of** castigar
para servir de exemplo

exasperat|e /ɪg'zæspəreɪt/ vt
exasperar. **~ion** /-'reɪʃn/ n exaspero m

excavat|e /'ekskəveɪt/ vt escavar;
(uncover) desenterrar. **~ion** /-'veɪʃn/ n

escavação f

exceed /ɪk'siːd/ vt exceder; (speed
limit) ultrapassar, exceder

excel /ɪk'sel/ vi (pt **excelled**)
distinguir-se ● vt superar, ultrapassar

excellen|t /'eksələnt/ a excelente. **~ce**
n excelência f

except /ɪk'sept/ prep exceto, fora; **~ for**
a não ser, menos, salvo ● vt excetuar.
~ion /-ʃn/ n exceção f; **take ~ion to**
(object to) achar inaceitável; (be offended
by) achar ofensivo

exceptional /ɪk'sepʃənl/ a
excepcional, (P) excecional

excerpt /'eksɜːpt/ n trecho m, excerto m

excess¹ /ɪk'ses/ n excesso m

excess² /'ekses/ a excedente, em
excesso; **~ fare** excesso m, suplemento
m; **~ luggage** excesso m de peso

excessive /ɪk'sesɪv/ a excessivo

exchange /ɪks'tʃeɪndʒ/ vt trocar
● n troca f; (of currency) câmbio m;
(telephone) **~** central f telefônica, (P)
telefónica; **~ rate** taxa f de câmbio

excit|e /ɪk'saɪt/ vt excitar; (rouse)
despertar; (enthuse) entusiasmar.
~able a excitável. **~ed** a excitado;
get ~ed excitar-se, entusiasmar-se.
~ement n excitação f. **~ing** a excitante,
emocionante

exclaim /ɪk'skleɪm/ vi exclamar

exclamation /eksklə'meɪʃn/ n
exclamação f; **~ mark** ponto m de
exclamação

exclu|de /ɪk'skluːd/ vt excluir. **~ding**
prep excluído. **~sion** /ɪk'skluːʒn/ n
exclusão f

exclusive /ɪk'skluːsɪv/ a (rights etc)
exclusivo; (club etc) seleto; (news item)
(em) exclusivo; **~ of** sem incluir. **~ly** adv
exclusivamente

excruciating /ɪk'skruːʃɪeɪtɪŋ/ a
excruciante, atroz

excursion /ɪk'skɜːʃn/ n excursão f

excus|e¹ /ɪk'skjuːz/ vt desculpar;
~e me! desculpe!, com licença! **~e
from** (exempt) dispensar de. **~able** a
desculpável

excuse² /ɪk'skjuːs/ n desculpa f

ex-directory /eksdɪ'rektərɪ/ a que
não vem no anuário or (P) na lista

execute /'eksɪkjuːt/ vt executar

execution /eksɪ'kjuːʃn/ n execução f

executive /ɪg'zekjʊtɪv/ a & n
executivo m

exemplary /ɪg'zemplərɪ/ a exemplar

exemplify /ɪgˈzemplɪfaɪ/ vt exemplificar, ilustrar

exempt /ɪgˈzempt/ a isento (**from** de) ● vt dispensar, eximir. **~ion** /-ʃn/ isenção f

exercise /ˈeksəsaɪz/ n exercício m ● vt ‹powers, restraint etc› exercer; ‹dog› levar para passear ● vi fazer exercício; **~ book** caderno m (de exercícios)

exert /ɪgˈzɜːt/ vt empregar, exercer; **~ o.s.** esforçar-se, fazer um esforço. **~ion** /-ʃn/ n esforço m

exhaust /ɪgˈzɔːst/ vt esgotar ● n Auto (tubo de) escape m. **~ed** a esgotado, exausto. **~ion** /-stʃən/ n esgotamento m, exaustão f

exhaustive /ɪgˈzɔːstɪv/ a exaustivo, completo

exhibit /ɪgˈzɪbɪt/ vt exibir, mostrar; ‹thing, collection› expor ● n objeto m, exposto

exhibition /eksɪˈbɪʃn/ n exposição f; (act of showing) demonstração f

exhilarat|e /ɪgˈzɪləreɪt/ vt regozijar; (invigorate) animar, estimular. **~ion** /-ˈreɪʃn/ n animação f, alegria f

exile /ˈeksaɪl/ n exílio m; (person) exilado m ● vt exilar, desterrar

exist /ɪgˈzɪst/ vi existir. **~ence** n existência f; **be in ~ence** existir

exit /ˈeksɪt/ n saída f

exorbitant /ɪgˈzɔːbɪtənt/ a exorbitante

exotic /ɪgˈzɒtɪk/ a exótico

expand /ɪkˈspænd/ vt/i expandir(-se); (extend) estender(-se), alargar(-se); ‹gas, liquid, metal› dilatar(-se). **~sion** n expansão f; (extension) alargamento m; (of gas etc) dilatação f

expanse /ɪkˈspæns/ n extensão f

expatriate /eksˈpætrɪət/ a & n expatriado m

expect /ɪkˈspekt/ vt esperar; (suppose) crer, supor; (require) contar com, esperar; ‹baby› esperar; **~ to do** contar fazer. **~ation** /ekspekˈteɪʃn/ n expectativa f

expectan|t /ɪkˈspektənt/ a **~t mother** gestante f. **~cy** n expectativa f

expedient /ɪkˈspiːdɪənt/ a oportuno ● n expediente m

expedition /ekspɪˈdɪʃn/ n expedição f

expel /ɪkˈspel/ vt (pt **expelled**) expulsar; ‹gas, poison etc› expelir

expend /ɪkˈspend/ vt despender

expenditure /ɪkˈspendɪtʃə(r)/ n despesa f, gasto m

expense /ɪkˈspens/ n despesa f; (cost) custo m; **at sb's ~** à custa de alguém; **at the ~ of** fig à custa de

expensive /ɪkˈspensɪv/ a caro, dispendioso; ‹tastes, habits› de luxo

experience /ɪkˈspɪərɪəns/ n experiência f ● vt experimentar; (feel) sentir. **~d** a experiente

experiment /ɪkˈsperɪmənt/ n experiência f ● vi (fazer) fazer uma experiência. **~al** /-ˈmentl/ a experimental

expert /ˈekspɜːt/ a & n perito m

expertise /ekspɜːˈtiːz/ n perícia f, competência f

expir|e /ɪkˈspaɪə(r)/ vi expirar. **~y** n fim m de prazo, expiração f

expl|ain /ɪkˈspleɪn/ vt explicar. **~anation** /ekspləˈneɪʃn/ n explicação f. **~anatory** /ɪkˈsplæ-nətrɪ/ a explicativo

explicit /ɪkˈsplɪsɪt/ a explícito

explo|de /ɪkˈspləʊd/ vt/i (fazer) explodir. **~sion** /ɪkˈspləʊʒn/ n explosão f. **~sive** a & n explosivo m

exploit[1] /ˈeksplɔɪt/ n façanha f

exploit[2] /ɪkˈsplɔɪt/ vt explorar. **~ation** /eksplɔɪˈteɪʃn/ n exploração f

explor|e /ɪkˈsplɔː(r)/ vt explorar; fig examinar. **~ation** /ekspləˈreɪʃn/ n exploração f. **~er** n explorador m

export[1] /ɪkˈspɔːt/ vt exportar. **~er** n exportador m

export[2] /ˈekspɔːt/ n exportação f

expos|e /ɪkˈspəʊz/ vt expor; (disclose) revelar; (unmask) desmascarar. **~ure** /-ʒə(r)/ n exposição f; (cold) frio m

express[1] /ɪkˈspres/ a expresso, categórico ● adv (por) expresso ● n (train) rápido m, expresso m. **~ly** adv expressamente

express[2] /ɪkˈspres/ vt exprimir. **~ion** /-ʃn/ n expressão f. **~ive** a expressivo

expulsion /ɪkˈspʌlʃn/ n expulsão f

exquisite /ˈekskwɪzɪt/ a requintado

exten|d /ɪkˈstend/ vt (stretch) estender; (enlarge) aumentar, ampliar; (prolong) prolongar; (grant) oferecer ● vi (stretch) estender-se; (in time) prolongar-se. **~sion** /ɪkˈstenʃn/ n (incl phone) extensão f; (of deadline) prorrogação f; (building) anexo m

extensive /ɪkˈstensɪv/ a extenso; ‹damage, study› vasto. **~ly** adv muito

extent /ɪk'stent/ n extensão f; (degree) medida f; **to some ~** até certo ponto, em certa medida; **to such an ~ that** a tal ponto que

exterior /ɪk'stɪərɪə(r)/ a & n exterior m

exterminat|e /ɪk'stɜ:mɪneɪt/ vt exterminar. **~ion** /-'neɪʃn/ n exterminação f, extermínio m

external /ɪk'stɜ:nl/ a externo. **~ly** adv exteriormente

extinct /ɪk'stɪŋkt/ a extinto. **~ion** /-ʃn/ n extinção f

extinguish /ɪk'stɪŋgwɪʃ/ vt extinguir, apagar. **~er** n extintor m

extort /ɪk'stɔ:t/ vt extorquir (**from** a). **~ion** /-ʃn/ n extorsão f

extortionate /ɪk'stɔ:ʃənət/ a exorbitante

extra /'ekstrə/ a extra, adicional; **~ strong** extra-forte; **~ time** Football prorrogação f, (P) prolongamento m ● adv extra, excepcionalmente, (P) excecionalmente ● n extra m; Cine, Theat extra mf, figurante mf

extra- /'ekstrə/ pref extra-

extract¹ /ɪk'strækt/ vt extrair; ‹promise, tooth› arrancar; fig obter. **~ion** /-ʃn/ n extração f; (descent) origem f

extract² /'ekstrækt/ n extrato m

extraordinary /ɪk'strɔ:dnrɪ/ a extraordinário

extravagan|t /ɪk'strævəgənt/ a extravagante; (wasteful) esbanjador. **~ce** n extravagância f; (wastefulness) esbanjamento m

extrem|e /ɪk'stri:m/ a & n extremo m. **~ely** adv extremamente. **~ist** n extremista mf

extricate /'ekstrɪkeɪt/ vt desembaraçar, livrar

extrovert /'ekstrəvɜ:t/ n extrovertido m

exuberan|t /ɪg'zju:bərənt/ a exuberante

exude /ɪg'zju:d/ vt ‹charm etc› destilar; ressumar, (P) transpirar

exult /ɪg'zʌlt/ vi exultar

eye /aɪ/ n olho m ● vt (pt **eyed**, pres p **eyeing**) olhar; **keep an ~ on** vigiar; **see ~ to ~** concordar inteiramente. **~-opener** n revelação f; **~shadow** n sombra f

eyeball /'aɪbɔ:l/ n globo m ocular

eyebrow /'aɪbraʊ/ n sobrancelha f

eyelash /'aɪlæʃ/ n pestana f

eyelid /'aɪlɪd/ n pálpebra f

eyesight /'aɪsaɪt/ n vista f

eyesore /'aɪsɔ:(r)/ n monstruosidade f, horror m

eyewitness /'aɪwɪtnɪs/ n testemunha f ocular

....

Ff

....

fable /'feɪbl/ n fábula f

fabric /'fæbrɪk/ n tecido m; (structure) edifício m

fabricat|e /'fæbrɪkeɪt/ vt fabricar; (invent) urdir, inventar. **~ion** /-'keɪʃn/ n fabrico m; (invention) invenção f

fabulous /'fæbjʊləs/ a fabuloso

face /feɪs/ n face f, cara f, rosto m; (expression) face f; (grimace) careta f; (of clock) mostrador m; **~ to ~** cara a cara, frente a frente; **in the ~ of** em vista de; **on the ~ of it** a julgar pelas aparências; **pull ~s** fazer caretas ● vt (look towards) encarar; (confront) enfrentar ● vi (be opposite) estar de frente para; **~ up to** enfrentar. **~cloth** n toalha f de rosto; **~lift** n cirurgia f plástica do rosto; **~ pack** n máscara de beleza f

faceless /'feɪslɪs/ a fig anônimo, (P) anónimo

facet /'fæsɪt/ n faceta f

facetious /fə'si:ʃəs/ a faceto; pej 🔟 engraçadinho 🔟 pej

facial /'feɪʃl/ a facial

facile /'fæsaɪl/ a fácil; (superficial) superficial

facilitate /fə'sɪlɪteɪt/ vt facilitar

facilit|y /fə'sɪlətɪ/ n facilidade f; **~ies** (means) facilidades fpl; (installations) instalações fpl

facsimile /fæk'sɪmǝlɪ/ n facsímile m

fact /fækt/ n fato m, (P) facto m; **in ~, as a matter of ~** na realidade

faction /'fækʃn/ n facção f, (P) fação f

factor /'fæktə(r)/ n fator m

factory /'fæktərɪ/ n fábrica f

factual /'fæktʃʊəl/ a concreto, real

faculty /'fækltɪ/ n faculdade f

fad /fæd/ n capricho m, mania f; (craze) moda f

fade /feɪd/ vt/i ‹colours› desbotar; ‹sound› diminuir; (disappear) apagar(-se)

faff /fæf/ vi enrolar 'ele ficou enrolando o dia todo', (P) engonhar 'esteve aí só a engonhar todo o dia'

fag /fæg/ n ⊞ (chore) estafa f; ⊠ (cigarette) cigarro m

fail /feɪl/ vt/i falhar; (in an examination) reprovar; (omit, neglect) deixar de; Comm falir ● n without ~ sem falta

failing /'feɪlɪŋ/ n deficiência f ● prep na falta de, à falta de

failure /'feɪljə(r)/ n fracasso m, (P) falhanço m; (of engine) falha f; (of electricity) falta f; (person) fracassado m

faint /feɪnt/ a (-er, -est) (indistinct) apagado; (weak) fraco; (giddy) tonto ● vi desmaiar ● n desmaio m. ~**ness** n debilidade f; (indistinctness) apagado m

fair[1] /feə(r)/ n feira f. ~**ground** n parque m de diversões, (P) largo m de feira

fair[2] /feə(r)/ a (-er, -est) <hair> louro; <weather> bom; (of moderate quality) razoável; (just) justo; ~ **play** jogo m limpo, fair play m. ~**ly** adv razoavelmente. ~**ness** n justiça f. ~ **trade** n comércio m justo

fairy /'feərɪ/ n fada f; ~ **story**, ~ **tale** conto m de fadas

faith /feɪθ/ n fé f; (religion) religião f; (loyalty) lealdade f; **in good** ~ de boa fé

faithful /'feɪθfl/ a fiel ● adv fielmente; **yours** ~**ly** atenciosamente. ~**ness** n fidelidade f

fake /feɪk/ n <thing> imitação f; <person> impostor m ● a falsificado ● vt falsificar; (pretend) simular, fingir

falcon /'fɔlkən/ n falcão m

fall /fɔːl/ vi (pt fell, pp fallen) cair; ~ **back** bater em retirada; ~ **back on** recorrer a; ~ **behind** atrasar-se (**with** em); ~ **down** or **off** cair; ~ **flat** falhar, não resultar; ~ **flat on one's face** estatelar-se; ~ **for** <a trick> cair em, deixar-se levar por; ⊞ <a person> apaixonar-se por, ficar caído por ⊞; ~ **in** <roof> ruir; Mil alinhar-se, pôr-se em forma; ~ **out** brigar, (P) zangar-se (**with** com); ~ **through** (of plans) falhar ● n quedas f; Amer (autumn) outono m. ~**s** npl (waterfall) queda-d'água f, cataratas fpl. ~**out** n poeira f radioativa

fallac|y /'fæləsɪ/ n falácia f, engano m

fallen /'fɔːlən/ ▶ FALL

fallible /'fæləbl/ a falível

false /fɔːls/ a falso; ~ **teeth** dentadura f. ~**ly** adv falsamente

falsehood /'fɔːlshʊd/ n falsidade f, mentira f

falsify /'fɔːlsɪfaɪ/ vt (pt -**fied**) falsificar; <a story> deturpar

falter /'fɔːltə(r)/ vi vacilar; (of the voice) hesitar

fame /feɪm/ n fama f

familiar /fə'mɪlɪə(r)/ a familiar; (intimate) íntimo; **be** ~ **with** estar familiarizado com

familiarity /fəmɪlɪ'ærɪtɪ/ n familiaridade f

familiarize /fə'mɪlɪəraɪz/ vt familiarizar (**with/to** com); (make well known) tornar conhecido

family /'fæməlɪ/ n família f; ~ **doctor** médico m da família; ~ **tree** árvore f genealógica

famine /'fæmɪn/ n fome f

famished /'fæmɪʃt/ a esfomeado, faminto; **be** ~ ⊞ estar morrendo de fome, (P) estar a morrer de fome

famous /'feɪməs/ a famoso

fan[1] /fæn/ n (in the hand) leque m; (mechanical) ventilador m, (P) ventoinha f ● vt (pt fanned) abanar; <a fire> also fig atiçar ● vi ~ **out** abrir-se em leque; ~ **belt** correia f da ventoinha

fan[2] /fæn/ n ⊞ fã mf; ~ **mail** correio m de fãs

fanatic /fə'nætɪk/ n fanático m. ~**al** a fanático. ~**ism** /-sɪzəm/ n fanatismo m

fanciful /'fænsɪfl/ a fantasioso, fantasista

fancy /'fænsɪ/ n fantasia f; (liking) gosto m; **it took my** ~ gostei disso, (P) deu-me no gosto; **a passing** ~ um entusiasmo passageiro; ~ **dress** traje m fantasia ● a extravagante, fantástico; (of buttons etc) de fantasia; (of prices) exorbitante ● vt imaginar; ⊞ (like) gostar de; ⊞ (want) apetecer

fanfare /'fænfeə(r)/ n fanfarra f

fang /fæŋ/ n presa f, dente m canino

fantastic /fæn'tæstɪk/ a fantástico

fantas|y /'fæntəsɪ/ n fantasia f. ~**ize** vt fantasiar, imaginar

far /fɑː(r)/ adv longe; (much, very) muito ● a distante, longínquo; (end, side) outro; ~ **away**, ~ **off** ao longe; **as** ~ **as** (up to) até; **as** ~ **as I know** tanto quanto saiba; **the F~ East** o Extremo-Oriente m. ~**-fetched** a forçado; (unconvincing) pouco plausível; ~**-reaching** a de grande alcance

farc|e /fɑːs/ n farsa f. ~**ical** a de farsa; ridículo

fare /feə(r)/ n preço m da passagem; (in taxi) tarifa f, preço m da corrida; (passenger) passageiro m; (food) comida f ● vi (get on) dar-se

farewell /feə'wel/ *int & n* adeus *m*

farm /fɑːm/ *n* quinta *f*, fazenda *f* ● *vt* cultivar ● *vi* ser fazendeiro, (P) lavrador; **~ out** (*of work*) delegar a tarefeiros. **~er** *n* fazendeiro *m*, (P) lavrador *m*. **~ing** *n* agricultura *f*, lavoura *f*

farmhouse /'fɑːmhaʊs/ *n* casa *f* da fazenda, (P) quinta

farmyard /'fɑːmjɑːd/ *n* quintal de fazenda *m*, (P) pátio *m* de quinta

farth|er /'fɑːðə(r)/ *adv* mais longe ● *a* mais distante. **~est** *adv* mais longe ● *a* o mais distante

fascinat|e /'fæsɪneɪt/ *vt* fascinar. **~ion** /-'neɪʃn/ *n* fascínio *m*, fascinação *f*

fascis|t /'fæʃɪst/ *n* fascista *mf*. **~m** /-zəm/ *n* fascismo *m*

fashion /'fæʃn/ *n* moda *f*; (*manner*) maneira *f* ● *vt* amoldar, (P) moldar. **~able** *a* na moda

fast¹ /fɑːst/ *a* (**-er, -est**) rápido; (*colour*) fixo, que não desbota ● *adv* depressa; (*firmly*) firmemente; **be ~** (*of clock*) adiantar-se, estar adiantado; **~ asleep** profundamente adormecido, ferrado no sono. **~ food** *n* fast-food *f*

fast² /fɑːst/ *vi* jejuar ● *n* jejum *m*

fasten /'fɑːsn/ *vt/i* prender; ‹door, window› fechar(-se); ‹seat-belt› apertar. **~er ~ing** *ns* fecho *m*

fastidious /fə'stɪdɪəs/ *a* exigente

fat /fæt/ *n* gordura *f* ● *a* (**fatter, fattest**) gordo

fatal /'feɪtl/ *a* fatal; **~ injuries** ferimentos *mpl* mortais. **~ity** /fə'tæləti/ *n* fatalidade *f*. **~ly** *adv* fatalmente, mortalmente

fate /feɪt/ *n* (*destiny*) destino *m*; (*one's lot*) destino *m*, sorte *f*. **~ful** *a* fatídico

father /'fɑːðə(r)/ *n* pai *m* ● *vt* gerar. **~-in-law** *n* (*pl* **~s-in-law**) sogro *m*. **~ly** *a* paternal

fathom /'fæðəm/ *n* braça *f* ● *vt* **~ (out)** (*comprehend*) compreender

fatigue /fə'tiːg/ *n* fadiga *f* ● *vt* fatigar

fatten /'fætn/ *vt/i* engordar. **~ing** *a* que engorda

fatty /'fæti/ *a* (**-ier, -iest**) gorduroso; ‹tissue› adiposo

fault /fɔːlt/ *n* defeito *m*, falha *f*; (*blame*) falta *f*, culpa *f*; *Geol* falha *f*; **at ~** culpado; **it's your ~** é culpa sua. **~less** *a* impecável. **~y** *a* defeituoso

favour /'feɪvə(r)/ *n* favor *m* ● *vt* favorecer; (*prefer*) preferir; **do sb a ~** fazer um favor a alguém. **~able** *a* favorável

favourit|e /'feɪvərɪt/ *a & n* favorito *m*. **~ism** /-ɪzəm/ *n* favoritismo *m*

fawn¹ /fɔːn/ *n* cervo *m* novo ● *a* (*colour*) castanho claro

fawn² /fɔːn/ *vi* **~ on** adular, bajular

fax /fæks/ *n* fax *m*, fac-símile *m*; **~ machine** fax *m* ● *vt* mandar um fax

fear /fɪə(r)/ *n* medo *m*, receio *m*, temor *m*; (*likelihood*) perigo *m* ● *vt* recear, ter medo de. **for ~ of/that** com medo de/ que. **~ful** *a* (*terrible*) medonho; (*timid*) medroso, receoso. **~less** *a* destemido, intrépido

feasib|le /'fiːzəbl/ *a* factível, praticável; (*likely*) plausível. **~ility** /-'bɪləti/ *n* possibilidade *f*; (*plausibility*) plausibilidade *f*

feast /fiːst/ *n* festim *m*; *Relig also fig* festa *f* ● *vt/i* festejar; (*eat and drink*) banquetear-se; **~ on** regalar-se com

feat /fiːt/ *n* feito *m*, façanha *f*

feather /'feðə(r)/ *n* pena *f*, pluma *f*

feature /'fiːtʃə(r)/ *n* feição *f*, traço *m*; (*quality*) característica *f*; (*film*) longa-metragem *f*; (*article*) artigo *m* em destaque ● *vt* representar; ‹film› ter como protagonista ● *vi* figurar

February /'febrʊəri/ *n* fevereiro *m*

fed /fed/ ► FEED ● *a* **be ~ up** estar farto 🔲(**with de**)

federa|l /'fedərəl/ *a* federal. **~tion** /-'reɪʃn/ *n* federação *f*

fee /fiː/ *n* preço *m*; **~(s)** (*of doctor, lawyer etc*) honorários *mpl*; (*member's subscription*) quota *f*; (P) *Univ* propinas *fpl*; (*enrolment/registration*) matrícula *f*; **school ~s** mensalidades *fpl* escolares

feeble /'fiːbl/ *a* (**-er, -est**) débil, fraco

feed /fiːd/ *vt* (*pt* **fed**) alimentar, dar de comer a; (*suckle*) alimentar, (*supply*) alimentar, abastecer ● *vi* alimentar-se ● *n* comida *f*; (*breastfeeding*) amamentação *f*; *Mech* alimentação *f*

feedback /'fiːdbæk/ *n* reação *f*; *Electr* regeneração *f*, (P) feedback *m*

feel /fiːl/ *vt* (*pt* **felt**) sentir; (*touch*) apalpar, tatear ● *vi* (*tired, lonely etc*) sentir-se; **~ hot/thirsty** ter calor/sede; **~ as if** ter a impressão (de) que; **~ like** ter vontade de

feeling /'fiːlɪŋ/ *n* sentimento *m*; (*physical*) sensação *f*

feet /fiːt/ ► FOOT

feign /feɪn/ *vt* fingir

feline /'fiːlaɪn/ *a* felino

fell[1] /fel/ vt abater, derrubar

fell[2] /fel/ ▶ **FALL**

fellow /'feləʊ/ n companheiro m, camarada m; (of society, college) membro m; ☐ cara m, (P) tipo m ☐

felt[1] /felt/ n feltro m

felt[2] /felt/ ▶ **FEEL**

female /'fi:meɪl/ a <animal etc> fêmea f, <voice, sex etc> feminino ● n mulher f; (animal) fêmea f

feminin|e /'femənɪn/ a & n feminino m. ~ity /-'nɪnəti/ n feminilidade f

feminist /'femɪnɪst/ n feminista mf

fenc|e /fens/ n tapume m, cerca f ● vt cercar ● vi esgrimir. ~er n esgrimista mf. ~ing n esgrima f; (fences) tapume m

fend /fend/ vi ~ **for o.s.** defender-se, virar-se ☐, governar-se ● vt ~ **off** defender-se de

fender /'fendə(r)/ n guarda-fogo m; Amer (mudguard) para-lama m, (P) guarda-lamas m

fennel /'fenl/ n (herb) funcho m, erva-doce f

ferment[1] /fə'ment/ vt/i fermentar; (excite) excitar

ferment[2] /'fɜ:ment/ n fermento m; fig efervescência f

fern /fɜ:n/ n feto m

feroc|ious /fə'rəʊʃəs/ a feroz. ~ity /-'rɒsəti/ n ferocidade f

ferry /'feri/ n barco m de travessia, ferry(-boat) m ● vt transportar

fertil|e /'fɜ:taɪl/ a fértil, fecundo. ~ity /fə'tɪləti/ n fertilidade f, fecundidade f. ~ize /-əlaɪz/ vt fertilizar, fecundar

fertilizer /'fɜ:təlaɪzə(r)/ n adubo m, fertilizante m

fervent /'fɜ:vənt/ a fervoroso

fervour /'fɜ:və(r)/ n fervor m, ardor m

fester /'festə(r)/ vt/i infectar; fig envenenar

festival /'festɪvl/ n festival m; Relig festa f

festiv|e /'festɪv/ a festivo; ~**e season** período m das festas. ~ity /fes'tɪvəti/ n festividade f, regozijo m; ~**ities** festas fpl, festividades fpl

festoon /fe'stu:n/ vt engrinaldar (**with** de or com)

fetch /fetʃ/ vt (go for) ir buscar; (bring) trazer; (be sold for) vender-se por, render

fetching /'fetʃɪŋ/ a atraente

fête /feɪt/ n festa or feira f de caridade ao ar livre f ● vt festejar

fetish /'fetɪʃ/ n fetiche m, ídolo m; (obsession) mania f

feud /fju:d/ n discórdia f, inimizade f. ~al a feudal

fever /'fi:və(r)/ n febre f. ~ish a febril

few /fju:/ a & n poucos mpl; ~ **books** poucos livros; **they are** ~ são poucos. **a** ~ a & n alguns mpl; **a good** ~, **quite a** ~ bastantes

fiancé /fɪ'ɒnseɪ/ n noivo m. ~e n noiva f

fiasco /fɪ'æskəʊ/ n (pl -os) fiasco m

fib /fɪb/ n lorota f, cascata f, peta f, mentira f ● vi (pt fibbed) mentir

fibre /'faɪbə(r)/ n fibra f

fibreglass /'faɪbəglɑ:s/ n fibra f de vidro

fickle /'fɪkl/ a leviano, inconstante

fiction /'fɪkʃn/ n ficção f; (works of) ~ romances mpl, obras fpl de ficção. ~al a de ficção, fictício

fictitious /fɪk'tɪʃəs/ a fictício

fiddle /'fɪdl/ n ☐ violino m; ☒ (swindle) trapaça f, (P) aldrabice f ● vi ☒ trapacear ☒, (P) aldrabar ● vt ☒ (falsify) falsificar, cozinhar ☒; ~ **with** ☐ brincar com, remexer em, (P) estar a brincar com, estar a (re)mexer em

fidelity /fɪ'deləti/ n fidelidade f

fidget /'fɪdʒɪt/ vi (pt fidgeted) estar irrequieto, remexer-se; ~ **with** remexer em. ~**y** a irrequieto; (impatient) impaciente

field /fi:ld/ n campo m; **F~ Marshal** marechal de campo m ● vt/i Cricket (estar pronto para) apanhar ou interceptar or (P) intercetar a bola

fieldwork /'fi:ldwɜ:k/ n trabalho m de campo; Mil fortificação f de campanha

fiend /fi:nd/ n diabo m, demônio m, (P) demónio m. ~**ish** a diabólico

fierce /fɪəs/ a (-er, -est) feroz; <storm, attack> violento; <heat> intenso, abrasador. ~**ness** n ferocidade f; (of storm, attack) violência f; (of heat) intensidade f

fiery /'faɪəri/ a (-ier, -iest) ardente; <temper, speech> inflamado

fifteen /fɪf'ti:n/ a & n quinze m. ~**th** a & n décimo quinto m

fifth /fɪfθ/ a & n quinto m

fift|y /'fɪfti/ a & n cinquenta m. ~**y-~y** a meias. ~**ieth** a & n quinquagésimo m

fig /fɪg/ n figo m

fight /faɪt/ vi (pt fought) lutar, combater; ~ **over sth** lutar por algo; ~ **shy of** esquivar-se de, fugir de ● vt lutar contra, combater ● *n* luta *f*; (*quarrel, brawl*) briga *f*. **~er** *n* lutador *m*; *Mil* combatente *mf*; (*plane*) caça *m*. **~ing** *n* combate *m*

figurative /'fɪɡərətɪv/ *a* figurado

figure /'fɪɡə(r)/ *n* (*number*) algarismo *m*; (*diagram, body*) figura *f*; **~ of speech** figura *f* de retórica ● *vt* imaginar, supor; **~ out** compreender ● *vi* (*appear*) figurar (**in** em). **~head** *n* figura *f* de proa; *pej* (*person*) testa de ferro *m*; chefe *m* nominal

file[1] /faɪl/ *n* (*tool*) lixa *f*, lima *f* ● *vt* lixar, limar

file[2] /faɪl/ *n* fichário *m*, (P) dossier *m*; (*box, drawer*) fichário *m*, (P) ficheiro *m*; *Comput* arquivo *m*; (*line*) fila *f*; **(in) single ~e** (em) fila indiana ● *vt* arquivar ● *vi* **~e (past)** desfilar, marchar em fila; **~e in/out** entrar/sair em fila; **~ing cabinet** fichário *m*, (P) ficheiro *m*. **~ extension** *n Comput* extensão *f* de arquivo justo

fill /fɪl/ *vt/i* encher(-se); <*vacancy*> preencher ● *n* **eat one's ~** comer o que quiser; **have one's ~** estar farto; **~ in** <*form*> preencher; **~ out** (*get fat*) engordar; **~ up** encher até cima; *Auto* encher o tanque, (P) atestar o depósito

fillet /'fɪlɪt/ *n* (*meat, fish*) filé *m*, (P) filete *m* ● *vt* (*pt* filleted) <*meat, fish*> cortar em filés, (P) filetes

filling /'fɪlɪŋ/ *n* recheio *m*; (*of tooth*) obturação *f*, (P) chumbo *m*; **~ station** posto *m* de gasolina

film /fɪlm/ *n* filme *m*; **~ star** estrela or vedete *f* de cinema, astro *m* ● *vt/i* filmar

filter /'fɪltə(r)/ *n* filtro *m*; **~ coffee** café *m* de filtro ● *vt/i* filtrar(-se)

filth /fɪlθ/ *n* imundície *f*; *fig* obscenidade *f*. **~y** a imundo; *fig* obsceno

fin /fɪn/ *n* barbatana *f*

final /'faɪnl/ *a* final; (*conclusive*) decisivo ● *n Sport* final *f*. **~s** *npl* (*exams*) finais *fpl*. **~ist** *n* finalista *mf*. **~ly** *adv* finalmente, por fim; (*once and for all*) definitivamente

finale /fɪ'nɑːlɪ/ *n* final *m*

finalize /'faɪnəlaɪz/ *vt* finalizar

financ|e /'faɪnæns/ *n* finança(s) *f* ● *a* financeiro ● *vt* financiar

financial /faɪ'nænʃl/ *a* financeiro

find /faɪnd/ *vt* (*pt* found) <*sth lost*> achar, encontrar; (*think*) achar; (*discover*) descobrir; *Jur* declarar ● *n* achado *m* □ **~ out** *vt* apurar, descobrir ● *vi* informar-se (**about** sobre)

fine[1] /faɪn/ *n* multa *f* ● *vt* multar

fine[2] /faɪn/ *a* (-er, -est) fino; (*splendid*) belo, lindo; **~ arts** belas artes *fpl*; **~ weather** bom tempo ● *adv* (muito) bem; (*small*) fino, fininho

finesse /fɪ'nes/ *n* finura *f*, sutileza *f*, (P) subtileza *f*

finger /'fɪŋɡə(r)/ *n* dedo *m* ● *vt* apalpar. **~nail** *n* unha *f*

fingerprint /'fɪŋɡəprɪnt/ *n* impressão *f* digital

fingertip /'fɪŋɡətɪp/ *n* ponta *f* do dedo

finicky /'fɪnɪkɪ/ *a* meticuloso, miudinho

finish /'fɪnɪʃ/ *vt/i* acabar, terminar ● *n* fim *m*; (*of race*) chegada *f*; (*on wood, clothes*) acabamento *m*; **~ doing** acabar de fazer; **~ up doing** acabar por fazer; **~ up in** ir parar a, acabar em

finite /'faɪnaɪt/ *a* finito

Fin|land /'fɪnlənd/ *n* Finlândia *f*. **~n** *n* finlandês *m*. **~nish** *a* & *n Lang* finlandês *m*

fir /fɜː(r)/ *n* abeto *m*

fire /'faɪə(r)/ *n* fogo *m*; (*conflagration*) incêndio *m*; (*heater*) aquecedor *m*; **on ~** em chamas; **set ~ to** pôr fogo a/em; **~ brigade** bombeiros *mpl*; **~ station** quartel *m* dos bombeiros; **~ alarm** *n* alarme *m* de incêndio; **~ engine** *n* carro *m* de bombeiro; **~ escape** *n* saída *f* de incêndio; **~ extinguisher** *n* extintor *m* de incêndio ● *vt* <*bullet, gun, etc*> disparar; (*dismiss*) despedir; *fig* (*stimulate*) inflamar ● *vi* atirar; fazer fogo (**at** sobre)

firearm /'faɪərɑːm/ *n* arma *f* de fogo

fireman /'faɪəmən/ *n* (*pl* -men) bombeiro *m*

fireplace /'faɪəpleɪs/ *n* chaminé *f*, lareira *f*

firewood /'faɪəwʊd/ *n* lenha *f*

firework /'faɪəwɜːk/ *n* fogo *m* de artifício

firing squad /'faɪərɪŋskwɒd/ *n* pelotão *m* de execução

firm[1] /fɜːm/ *n* firma *f* comercial

firm[2] /fɜːm/ *a* (-er, -est) firme; (*belief*) firme, inabalável

first /fɜːst/ *a* & *n* primeiro *m*; *Auto* primeira *f*; **~ name** nome *m* próprio; **for the ~ time** pela primeira vez; **~ aid** primeiros socorros *mpl* ● *adv* primeiro, em primeiro lugar; **at ~** a princípio, no início; **~ of all** antes de mais nada. **~-class** *a* de primeira classe; **~-rate** *a* excelente. **~ly** *adv* primeiramente, em primeiro lugar

fish /fɪʃ/ *n* (*pl* usually invar) peixe *m* ● *vt/i* pescar; **~ out** 𝕀 tirar. **~ing** *n* pesca *f*; **go ~ing** ir pescar, (P) ir à pesca. **~y** *a* de peixe; *fig* (*dubious*) suspeito

fisherman /'fɪʃəmən/ *n* (*pl* **-men**) pescador *m*

fishmonger /'fɪʃmʌŋgə(r)/ *n* dono *m* /empregado *m* de peixaria; **~'s (shop)** peixaria *f*

fission /'fɪʃn/ *n* fissão *f*, cisão *f*

fist /fɪst/ *n* punho *m*, mão *f* fechada, (P) punho *m*

fit[1] /fɪt/ *n* acesso *m*, ataque *m*; (*of generosity*) rasgo *m*

fit[2] /fɪt/ *a* (**fitter, fittest**) de boa saúde, em forma; (*proper*) próprio; (*good enough*) em condições; (*able*) capaz ● *vt/i* (*pt* **fitted**) assentar, ficar bem (a); (*into space*) caber; (*match*) ajustar-se (a); (*install*) instalar; **~ out** equipar; **~ted carpet** carpete *m*, (P) alcatifa *f* ● *n* **be a good ~** assentar bem; **be a tight ~** estar justo. **~ness** *n* saúde *f*, (P) condição *f* física

fitting /'fɪtɪŋ/ *a* apropriado ● *n* (*clothes*) prova *f*; **~s** (*fixtures*) instalações *fpl*; (*fitments*) mobiliário *m*; **~ room** cabine *f* (de provas)

five /faɪv/ *a* & *n* cinco *m*

fix /fɪks/ *vt* fixar; (*mend, prepare*) arranjar ● *n* **in a ~** em apuros, (P) numa alhada; **~ sb up with sth** conseguir algo para alguém. **~ed** *a* fixo

fixation /fɪk'seɪʃn/ *n* fixação *f*; (*obsession*) obsessão *f*

fixture /'fɪkstʃə(r)/ *n* equipamento *m*, instalação *f*; *Sport* (data *f* marcada para) competição *f*

fizz /fɪz/ *vi* efervescer, borbulhar ● *n* efervescência *f*. **~y** *a* gasoso

fizzle /'fɪzl/ *vi* **~ out** ⟨*plan etc*⟩ acabar em nada or (P) em águas de bacalhau 🔢

flab /flæb/ *n* 🔢 gordura *f*; banha *f* 🔢. **~by** *a* flácido

flabbergasted /'flæbəgɑːstɪd/ *a* 🔢 espantado; pasmado 🔢

flag[1] /flæg/ *n* bandeira *f* ● *vt* (*pt* **flagged**) fazer sinal; **~ down** fazer sinal para parar. **~pole** *n* mastro *m* (de bandeira)

flag[2] /flæg/ *vi* (*pt* **flagged**) (*droop*) cair, pender, tombar; (*of person*) esmorecer

flagrant /'fleɪgrənt/ *a* flagrante

flagstone /'flægstəʊn/ *n* laje *f*

flair /fleə(r)/ *n* jeito *m*, habilidade *f*

flak|e /fleɪk/ *n* floco *m*; (*paint*) lasca *f* ● *vi* descamar-se, lascar-se. **~y** *a* ⟨*paint*⟩ descamado, lascado

flamboyant /flæm'bɔɪənt/ *a* flamejante; (*showy*) flamante, vistoso; (*of manner*) extravagante

flame /fleɪm/ *n* chama *f*, labareda *f* ● *vi* flamejar; **burst into ~s** incendiar-se

flamingo /flə'mɪŋgəʊ/ *n* (*pl* **-os**) flamingo *m*

flammable /'flæməbl/ *a* inflamável

flan /flæn/ *n* torta *f*, (P) tarte *f*

flank /flæŋk/ *n* flanco *m* ● *vt* flanquear

flannel /'flænl/ *n* flanela *f*; (*for face*) toalha *f* de rosto

flap /flæp/ *vi* (*pt* **flapped**) bater ● *vt* **~ its wings** bater as asas ● *n* (*of table, pocket*) aba *f*; 🔢 (*panic*) pânico *m*

flare /fleə(r)/ *vi* **~ up** irromper em chamas; (*of war*) rebentar; *fig* (*of person*) enfurecer-se ● *n* chamejar *m*; (*dazzling light*) clarão *m*; (*signal*) foguete *m* de sinalização. **~d** *a* ⟨*skirt*⟩ evasê

flash /flæʃ/ *vi* brilhar subitamente; (*on and off*) piscar; *Auto* fazer sinal com o pisca-pisca; **~ past** passar como uma bala, (P) passar como um bólide ● *vt* fazer brilhar; (*send*) lançar, dardejar; (*flaunt*) fazer alarde de, ostentar ● *n* clarão *m*, lampejo *m*; *Photo* flash *m*

flashback /'flæʃbæk/ *n* cena *f* retrospectiva *or* (P) retrospetiva, flashback *m*

flashlight /'flæʃlaɪt/ *n* lanterna *f* elétrica

flashy /'flæʃi/ *a* espalhafatoso, que dá nas vistas

flask /flɑːsk/ *n* frasco *m*; (*vacuum flask*) garrafa *f* térmica, (P) termo *m*

flat /flæt/ *a* (**flatter, flattest**) plano, chato; ⟨*tyre*⟩ arriado, vazio, furado; (*battery*) fraco; ⟨*refusal*⟩ categórico; ⟨*fare, rate*⟩ fixo; (*monotonous*) monótono; *Mus* bemol; (*out of tune*) desafinado; **~ out** (*drive*) em alta velocidade; (*work*) a dar tudo por tudo ● *n* apartamento *m*; 🔢 (*tyre*) furo *m* no pneu; *Mus* bemol *m*. **~ly** *adv* categoricamente

flatter /'flætə(r)/ *vt* lisonjear, adular. **~ing** *a* lisonjeiro, adulador. **~y** *n* lisonja *f*

flaunt /flɔːnt/ *vt/i* pavonear(-se), ostentar

flavour /'fleɪvə(r)/ *n* sabor *m* (**of** a) ● *vt* dar sabor a, temperar. **~ing** *n* aroma *m* sintético; (*seasoning*) tempero *m*

flaw /flɔː/ *n* falha *f*, imperfeição *f*. **~less** *a* perfeito

flea /fliː/ *n* pulga *f*

fled /fled/ ▶ **FLEE**

flee /fliː/ *vi* (*pt* **fled**) fugir ● *vt* fugir de

fleece /fliːs/ n lã f de carneiro, velo m
● vt fig esfolar; roubar

fleet /fliːt/ n (of warships) esquadra f;
(of merchant ships, vehicles) frota f

fleeting /ˈfliːtɪŋ/ a curto, fugaz

Flemish /ˈflemɪʃ/ a & n Lang flamengo m

flesh /fleʃ/ n carne f; (of fruit) polpa f

flew /fluː/ ▶ FLY²

flex[1] /fleks/ vt flexionar

flex[2] /fleks/ n Electr fio f flexível

flexib|le /ˈfleksəbl/ a flexível. ~ility
/-ˈbɪləti/ n flexibilidade f

flick /flɪk/ n (light blow) safanão m; (with
fingertip) piparote m ● vt dar um safanão
em; (with fingertip) dar um piparote a;
~ through folhear

flicker /ˈflɪkə(r)/ vi vacilar, oscilar,
tremular ● n oscilação f, tremular m;
(light) luz f trémula

flier /ˈflaɪə(r)/ n = FLYER

flight[1] /flaɪt/ n (flying) voo m; ~ of
stairs lance m de escada

flight[2] /flaɪt/ n (fleeing) fuga f; put to ~
pôr em fuga; take ~ pôr-se em fuga

flimsy /ˈflɪmzɪ/ a (-ier, -iest) ‹material›
fino; ‹object› frágil; ‹excuse etc› fraco,
esfarrapado

flinch /flɪntʃ/ vi (wince) retrair-se; (draw
back) recuar; (hesitate) hesitar

fling /flɪŋ/ vt/i (pt flung) atirar(-se),
arremessar(-se); (rush) precipitar-se

flint /flɪnt/ n sílex m; (for lighter) pedra f

flip /flɪp/ vt (pt flipped) fazer girar com
o dedo e o polegar ● n pancadinha f;
~ through folhear

flippant /ˈflɪpənt/ a irreverente,
petulante

flirt /flɜːt/ vt namoriscar, flertar, (P)
flartar ● n namorador m, namoradeira
f. ~ation /-ˈteɪʃn/ n namorico m, flerte
m, (P) flirt m. ~atious a namorador m,
namoradeira f

flit /flɪt/ vi (pt flitted) esvoaçar

float /fləʊt/ vt/i (fazer) flutuar;
(company) lançar ● n boia f; (low cart)
carro m alegórico

flock /flɒk/ n (of sheep; congregation)
rebanho m; (of birds) bando m; (crowd)
multidão f ● vi afluir, juntar-se

flog /flɒg/ vt (pt flogged) açoitar;
▣ (sell) vender

flood /flʌd/ n inundação f, cheia f; (of
tears) dilúvio m, rio m ● vt inundar, alagar
● vi estar inundado; ‹river› transbordar;
fig ‹people› afluir

floodlight /ˈflʌdlaɪt/ n projetor m,
holofote m ● vt (pt floodlit) iluminar

floor /flɔː(r)/ n o chão m, soalho m;
(for dancing) pista f; (storey) andar m
● vt assoalhar; (baffle) desconcertar,
embatucar

flop /flɒp/ vi (pt flopped) (drop)
(deixar-se) cair; (move helplessly)
debater-se; ▣ (fail) ser um fiasco ● n
▣ fiasco m. ~py a mole, tombado; ~py
(disk) disquete m

floral /ˈflɔːrəl/ a floral

florid /ˈflɒrɪd/ a florido

florist /ˈflɒrɪst/ n florista mf

flounder /ˈflaʊndə(r)/ vi esbracejar,
debater-se; fig meter os pés pelas mãos

flour /ˈflaʊə(r)/ n farinha f

flourish /ˈflʌrɪʃ/ vi florescer, prosperar
● vt brandir ● n floreado m; (movement)
gesto m elegante

flout /flaʊt/ vt escarnecer (de)

flow /fləʊ/ vi correr, fluir; (traffic)
mover-se; (hang loosely) flutuar; (gush)
jorrar ● n corrente f; (of tide; also fig)
enchente f; ~ into (of river) desaguar
em; ~ chart organograma m

flower /ˈflaʊə(r)/ n flor f ● vi florir,
florescer. ~ bed n canteiro m. ~y a
florido

flown /fləʊn/ ▶ FLY²

flu /fluː/ n ▣ gripe f

fluctuat|e /ˈflʌktʃʊeɪt/ vi flutuar,
oscilar. ~ion /-ˈeɪʃn/ n flutuação f,
oscilação f

fluen|t /ˈfluːənt/ a fluente; be ~t
(in a language) falar correntemente
(uma língua). ~cy n fluência f. ~tly adv
fluentemente

fluff /flʌf/ n cotão m; (down) penugem
f ● vt ▣ (bungle) estender-se em ▣;
executar mal. ~y a penugento, fofo

fluid /ˈfluːɪd/ a & n fluido m

fluke /fluːk/ n bambúrrio m ▣; golpe
m de sorte

flung /flʌŋ/ ▶ FLING

flunk /flʌŋk/ vt/i Amer ▣ levar pau ▣,
(P) chumbar ▣

fluorescent /flʊəˈresnt/ a fluorescente

fluoride /ˈflʊəraɪd/ n flúor m

flush[1] /flʌʃ/ vi corar, ruborizar-se
● vt lavar com água, (P) lavar a jorros
de água; ~ the toilet dar descarga,
(P) puxar o autoclismo ● n rubor m,
vermelhidão f; fig excitação f; (of water)
jorro m ● a ~ with ao nível de, rente a

flush[2] /flʌʃ/ vt ~ out desalojar

fluster /ˈflʌstə(r)/ vt atarantar, perturbar, enervar

flute /fluːt/ n flauta f

flutter /ˈflʌtə(r)/ vi esvoaçar; ‹wings› bater; ‹heart› palpitar ● vt bater; ~ **one's eyelashes** pestanejar ● n (of wings) batimento m; fig agitação f

flux /flʌks/ n **in a state of** ~ em mudança f contínua

fly[1] /flaɪ/ n mosca f

fly[2] /flaɪ/ vi (pt **flew**, pp **flown**) voar; ‹passengers› ir de/viajar de avião; (rush) correr ● vt pilotar; ‹passengers, goods› transportar por avião; ‹flag› hastear, (P) arvorar ● n (of trousers) braguilha f

flyer /ˈflaɪə(r)/ n aviador m; Amer (circular) prospecto m, (P) prospeto m

flying /ˈflaɪɪŋ/ a voador; **with** ~ **colours** com grande êxito, esplendidamente; ~ **saucer** disco m voador; ~ **start** bom arranque m; ~ **visit** visita f de médico

flyover /ˈflaɪəʊvə(r)/ n viaduto m

foal /fəʊl/ n potro m

foam /fəʊm/ n espuma f ● vi espumar

fob /fɒb/ vt (pt **fobbed**) ~ **off** iludir, entreter com artifícios; ~ **off on** impingir a

focus /ˈfəʊkəs/ n (pl **-cuses** or **-ci**) /-saɪ/ foco m; **in** ~ focado, em foco; **out of** ~ desfocado ● vt/i (pt **focused**) focar

fodder /ˈfɒdə(r)/ n forragem f

foetus /ˈfiːtəs/ n (pl **-tuses**) feto m

fog /fɒg/ n nevoeiro m ● vt/i (pt **fogged**) enevoar(-se). ~**horn** n sereia f de nevoeiro. ~**gy** a enevoado, brumoso; **it is** ~**gy** está nevoento or (P) de nevoeiro

foible /ˈfɔɪbl/ n fraqueza f, ponto m fraco

foil[1] /fɔɪl/ n papel m de alumínio; fig contraste m

foil[2] /fɔɪl/ vt frustrar

fold /fəʊld/ vt/i dobrar(-se); ‹arms› cruzar; ⒤ (fail) falir ● n dobra f. ~**er** n pasta f; (leaflet) prospecto m or (P) prospeto m (desdobrável) m. ~**ing** a dobrável, dobradiço

foliage /ˈfəʊlɪɪdʒ/ n folhagem f

folk /fəʊk/ n povo m; ~**s** (family, people) gente f ⒤, pessoal m ⒤ ● a folclórico, popular. ~**lore** n folclore m

follow /ˈfɒləʊ/ vt/i seguir; **it** ~**s that** quer dizer que; ~ **suit** ‹cards› servir o naipe jogado; fig seguir o exemplo, fazer o mesmo; ~ **up** (letter etc) dar seguimento a. ~**er** n partidário m,

seguidor m. ~**ing** n partidários mpl ● a seguinte ● prep em seguimento a

folly /ˈfɒlɪ/ n loucura f

fond /fɒnd/ a **-er -est** carinhoso; ‹hope› caro; **be** ~ **of** gostar de, ser amigo de. ~**ness** n (for people) afeição f; (for thing) gosto m

fondle /ˈfɒndl/ vt acariciar

font /fɒnt/ n pia f batismal

food /fuːd/ n alimentação f, comida f; (nutrient) alimento m ● a alimentar; ~ **poisoning** envenenamento m alimentar

fool /fuːl/ n idiota mf, parvo m ● vt enganar ● vi ~ **around** andar sem fazer nada

foolhardy /ˈfuːlhɑːdɪ/ a imprudente, atrevido

foolish /ˈfuːlɪʃ/ a idiota, parvo. ~**ness** n idiotice f, parvoíce f

foolproof /ˈfuːlpruːf/ a infalível

foot /fʊt/ n (pl **feet**) (of person, bed, stairs) pé m; (of animal) pata f; (measure) pé m (= 30,48 cm); **on** ~ a pé; **on** or **to one's feet** de pé; **put one's** ~ **in it** cometer uma gafe; **to be under sb's feet** atrapalhar alguém ● vt ~ **the bill** pagar a conta. ~**bridge** n passarela f

football /ˈfʊtbɔːl/ n bola f de futebol; (game) futebol m; ~ **pools** loteria f esportiva, (P) totobola m. ~**er** n futebolista mf, jogador m de futebol

foothills /ˈfʊthɪlz/ npl contrafortes mpl

foothold /ˈfʊthəʊld/ n ponto m de apoio

footing /ˈfʊtɪŋ/ n **firm** ~ apoio m seguro; **on an equal** ~ em pé de igualdade

footlights /ˈfʊtlaɪts/ npl ribalta f

footnote /ˈfʊtnəʊt/ n nota f de rodapé

footpath /ˈfʊtpɑːθ/ n (pavement) calçada f, (P) passeio m; (in open country) atalho m, caminho m

footprint /ˈfʊtprɪnt/ n pegada f

footstep /ˈfʊtstep/ n passo m

footwear /ˈfʊtweə(r)/ n calçado m

---

for unstressed /fə(r)/ emphatic fɔː(r)/ ● prep

····▸ (expressing purpose) para; ~ **me** para mim; **music** ~ **dancing** música para dançar; **what is it** ~? para que serve isto?; **what have you got** ~ **a cold?** o que tem para gripe?

····▸ (on behalf of, in place of) por; **I did it** ~ **you** fiz isso por si; **I took her classes** ~ **her** fiquei com as turmas dela; **I'm speaking ~ everyone in this department** falo por todos neste departamento

····➤ (expressing worth) no valor de; **a check/bill ~ ten euros** um cheque/ uma conta no valor de dez euros

····➤ (expressing reason) por; **famous ~ its wine** famoso pelo seu vinho; **he was sentenced to death ~ murder** ele foi condenado à morte por homicídio; **~ fear/love of** por medo/ amor de

❗ the preposition *por* often contracts with the definite articles *o* and *a* to form *pelo*, *pela*

····➤ (expressing direction) para; **the train ~ Oxford** o trem para Oxford

····➤ (with a time period that is still continuing) há; **I've been waiting ~ two hours** estou esperando há duas horas; **I haven't seen him ~ ten years** há dez anos que não o vejo; (with a time period that has ended) durante; **I waited ~ two hours** esperei durante duas horas; (with a future time period) durante; **I'm going to Paris ~ six weeks** vou para Paris por seis semanas; **he'll be away ~ a few weeks** ele vai ficar fora durante algumas semanas

····➤ (with distances) durante; **I drove ~ 50 kilometres** dirigi durante 50 quilômetros

● conj

····➤ porque, visto que; **he's not coming, ~ he has no money** ele não vem, porque não tem dinheiro

forbade /fəˈbæd/ ▶ FORBID

forbid /fəˈbɪd/ vt (pt **forbade**, pp **forbidden**) proibir; **you are ~den to smoke** você está proibido de fumar, (P) estás proibido de fumar. **~ding** a severo, intimidante

force /fɔːs/ n força f; **come into ~** entrar em vigor; **the ~s** as Forças Armadas ● vt forçar; **~ into** fazer entrar à força; **~ on** impor a. **~d** a forçado. **~ful** a enérgico

force-feed /ˈfɔːsfiːd/ vt (pt **-fed**) alimentar à força

forceps /ˈfɔːseps/ n ; pl invar fórceps m

forcibl|e /ˈfɔːsəbl/ a convincente; (done by force) à força. **~y** adv à força

ford /fɔːd/ n vau m ● vt passar a vau, vadear

fore /fɔː(r)/ a dianteiro ● n **to the ~** em evidência

forearm /ˈfɔːrɑːm/ n antebraço m

forecast /ˈfɔːkɑːst/ vt (pt **forecast**) prever ● n previsão f; **weather ~** boletim m meteorológico, previsão f do tempo

forefinger /ˈfɔːfɪŋɡə(r)/ n (dedo) indicador m

foregone /ˈfɔːɡɒn/ a **~ conclusion** resultado m previsto

foreground /ˈfɔːɡraʊnd/ n primeiro plano m

forehead /ˈfɒrɪd/ n testa f

foreign /ˈfɒrən/ a estrangeiro; ‹trade› externo; ‹travel› ao/no estrangeiro; **F~ Office** Ministério m dos Negócios Estrangeiros. **~er** n estrangeiro m

foreman /ˈfɔːmən/ n (pl **foremen**) contramestre m; (of jury) primeiro jurado m

foremost /ˈfɔːməʊst/ a principal, primeiro ● adv **first and ~** antes de mais nada, em primeiro lugar

forename /ˈfɔːneɪm/ n prenome m

forerunner /ˈfɔːrʌnə(r)/ n precursor m

foresee /fɔːˈsiː/ vt (pt **-saw**, pp **-seen**) prever. **~able** a previsível

foresight /ˈfɔːsaɪt/ n previsão f, previdência f

forest /ˈfɒrɪst/ n floresta f

forestry /ˈfɒrɪstrɪ/ n silvicultura f

forever /fəˈrevə(r)/ adv (endlessly) constantemente, para sempre

foreword /ˈfɔːwɜːd/ n prefácio m

forfeit /ˈfɔːfɪt/ n penalidade f, preço m; (in game) prenda f ● vt perder

forgave /fəˈɡeɪv/ ▶ FORGIVE

forge[1] /fɔːdʒ/ vi **~ ahead** tomar a dianteira, avançar

forge[2] /fɔːdʒ/ n forja f ● vt ‹metal, friendship› forjar; (counterfeit) falsificar, forjar. **~r** /-ə(r)/ n falsificador m, forjador m. **~ry** /-ərɪ/ n falsificação f

forget /fəˈɡet/ vt/i (pt **forgot**, pp **forgotten**) esquecer; **~ o.s.** portar-se com menos dignidade, esquecer-se de quem é. **~-me-not** n miosótis m. **~ful** a esquecido. **~fulness** n esquecimento m

forgive /fəˈɡɪv/ vt (pt **forgave**, pp **forgiven**) perdoar (sb for sth algo a alguém). **~ness** n perdão m

forgo /fɔːˈɡəʊ/ vt (pt **forwent**, pp **forgone**) renunciar a

fork /fɔːk/ n garfo m; (for digging etc) forquilha f; (in road) bifurcação f ● vi bifurcar; **~ out** 🔘 desembolsar. **~-lift truck** n empilhadeira f

forlorn /fə'lɔːn/ a abandonado, desolado

form /fɔːm/ n forma f; (document) impresso m, formulário m; Schol classe f ● vt/i formar(-se)

formal /'fɔːml/ a formal; ‹dress› de cerimónia or (P) cerimónia. **~ity** /-'mælətɪ/ n formalidade f

format /'fɔːmæt/ n formato m ● vt (pl **formatted**) ‹disk› formatar

formation /fɔː'meɪʃn/ n formação f

former /'fɔːmə(r)/ a antigo; (first of two) primeiro; **the ~** aquele. **~ly** adv antigamente

formidable /'fɔːmɪdəbl/ a formidável, tremendo

formula /'fɔːmjʊlə/ n (pl **-ae** /-iː/; or **-as**) fórmula f

formulate /'fɔːmjʊleɪt/ vt formular

forsake /fə'seɪk/ vt (pt **forsook**, pp **forsaken**) abandonar

fort /fɔːt/ n Mil forte m

forth /fɔːθ/ adv adiante, para a frente; **and so ~** e assim por diante, etcetera; **go back and ~** andar de trás para diante

forthcoming /fɔːθ'kʌmɪŋ/ a que está para vir, próximo; (communicative) comunicativo, receptivo, (P) recetivo; ‹book› no prelo

forthright /'fɔːθraɪt/ a franco, direto

fortify /'fɔːtɪfaɪ/ vt fortificar. **~ication** /-ɪ'keɪʃn/ n fortificação f

fortitude /'fɔːtɪtjuːd/ n fortitude f, fortaleza f

fortnight /'fɔːtnaɪt/ n quinze dias mpl, (P) quinzena f. **~ly** a quinzenal ● adv de quinze em quinze dias

fortress /'fɔːtrɪs/ n fortaleza f

fortunate /'fɔːtʃənət/ a feliz, afortunado; **be ~** ter sorte. **~ly** adv felizmente

fortune /'fɔːtʃən/ n sorte f; (wealth) fortuna f; **have the good ~ to** ter a sorte de. **~ teller** n cartomante mf

forty /'fɔːtɪ/ a & n quarenta m. **~ieth** a & n quadragésimo m

forum /'fɔːrəm/ n fórum m, foro m

forward /'fɔːwəd/ a (in front) dianteiro; (towards the front) para a frente; (advanced) adiantado; (pert) atrevido ● n Sport atacante m, (P) avançado m ● adv **~(s)** para a frente, para diante; **come ~** apresentar-se; **go ~** avançar ● vt ‹letter› remeter; ‹goods› expedir; fig (help) favorecer

fossil /'fɒsl/ a & n fóssil m

foster /'fɒstə(r)/ vt fomentar; ‹child› criar. **~child** n filho m adotivo; **~mother** n mãe f adotiva

fought /fɔːt/ ▶ FIGHT

foul /faʊl/ a (-er, -est) infecto; ‹language› obsceno; ‹weather› mau; **~ play** jogo m desleal; (crime) crime m ● n Football falta f ● vt sujar, emporcalhar. **~mouthed** a de linguagem obscena

found[1] /faʊnd/ ▶ FEEL

found[2] /faʊnd/ vt fundar. **~ation** /-'deɪʃn/ n fundação f; (basis) fundamento m. **~ations** npl (of building) alicerces mpl

founder[1] /'faʊndə(r)/ n fundador m

founder[2] /'faʊndə(r)/ vi afundar-se

foundry /'faʊndrɪ/ n fundição f

fountain /'faʊntɪn/ n fonte f. **~ pen** n caneta-tinteiro f, (P) caneta f de tinta permanente

four /fɔː(r)/ a & n quatro m. **~th** a & n quarto m

fourteen /fɔː'tiːn/ a & n catorze m. **~th** a & n décimo quarto m

fowl /faʊl/ n ave f de capoeira

fox /fɒks/ n raposa f ● vt 🇬🇧 deixar perplexo; enganar; **be ~ed** ficar perplexo

foyer /'fɔɪeɪ/ n foyer m

fraction /'frækʃn/ n fração f; (small bit) bocadinho m, partícula f

fracture /'fræktʃə(r)/ n fratura f ● vt/i fraturar(-se)

fragile /'frædʒaɪl/ a frágil

fragment /'frægmənt/ n fragmento m

fragran|t /'freɪgrənt/ a fragrante, perfumado. **~ce** n fragrância f, perfume m

frail /freɪl/ a (-er, -est) frágil

frame /freɪm/ n Techn (of spectacles) armação f; (of picture) moldura f; (of window) caixilho m; (body) corpo m, (P) estrutura f ● vt colocar a armação em; ‹picture› emoldurar; fig formular; 🇬🇧 incriminar falsamente; tramar; **~ of mind** estado m de espírito

framework /'freɪmwɜːk/ n estrutura f; (context) quadro m, esquema m

France /frɑːns/ n França f

franchise /'fræntʃaɪz/ n Pol direito m de voto; Comm concessão f, franchise f

frank[1] /fræŋk/ a franco

frank[2] /fræŋk/ vt franquear

frantic /'fræntɪk/ a frenético

fraternal /frə'tɜːnl/ a fraternal

fraud /frɔːd/ n fraude f; (person) impostor m. ~ulent /'frɔːdjʊlənt/ a fraudulento

fraught /frɔːt/ a ~ with cheio de

fray[1] /freɪ/ n rixa f

fray[2] /freɪ/ vt/i desfiar(-se), puir, esgarçar(-se)

freak /friːk/ n aberração f, anomalia f ● a anormal; ~ of nature aborto m da natureza. ~ish a anormal

freckle /'frekl/ n sarda f

free /friː/ a (freer, freest) livre; (gratis) grátis; (lavish) liberal ● vt (pt freed) libertar (from de); (rid) livrar (of de); ~ of charge grátis, de graça; a ~ hand carta f branca. ~lance a independente, free-lance; ~-range a ‹egg› de galinha criada ao ar livre. ~ly adv livremente

freedom /'friːdəm/ n liberdade f

freez|e /friːz/ vt/i (pt froze, pp frozen) gelar; Culin, Finance congelar(-se) ● n gelo m; Culin, Finance congelamento m. ~er n congelador m. ~ing a gélido, glacial; below ~ing abaixo de zero

freight /freɪt/ n frete m

French /frentʃ/ a francês; ~ window porta f envidraçada ● n Lang francês m; the ~ os franceses. ~man n francês m; ~woman n francesa f

frenz|y /'frenzɪ/ n frenesi m

frequen|t[1] /'friːkwənt/ a frequente. ~cy n frequência f. ~tly adv frequentemente

frequent[2] /frɪ'kwent/ vt frequentar

fresh /freʃ/ a (-er, -est) fresco; (different, additional) novo; 🇺🇸 (cheeky) descarado; atrevido. ~ness n frescura f

fret /fret/ vt/i (pt fretted) ralar(-se). ~ful a rabugento

friction /'frɪkʃn/ n fricção f

Friday /'fraɪdɪ/ n sexta-feira f; Good ~ Sexta-Feira f Santa

fridge /frɪdʒ/ n 🇺🇸 geladeira f, (P) frigorífico m

fried /fraɪd/ ▶ FRY ● a frito

friend /frend/ n amigo m. ~ship n amizade f

friendl|y /'frendlɪ/ a (-ier, -iest) amigável, amigo, simpático. ~iness n simpatia f, gentileza f

fright /fraɪt/ n medo m, susto m; give sb a ~ pregar um susto em alguém. ~ful a medonho, assustador

frighten /'fraɪtn/ vt assustar; ~ off afugentar. ~ed a assustado; be ~ed (of) ter medo (de)

frigid /'frɪdʒɪd/ a frígido. ~ity /-'dʒɪdətɪ/ n frigidez f, frieza f; Psych frigidez f

frill /frɪl/ n babado m, (P) folho m

fringe /frɪndʒ/ n franja f; (of area) borda f; (of society) margem f; ~ benefits (work) regalias fpl extras; ~ theatre teatro m alternativo, teatro m de vanguarda

frisk /frɪsk/ vi pular, brincar ● vt revistar

fritter[1] /'frɪtə(r)/ n bolinho m frito, (P) frito m

fritter[2] /'frɪtə(r)/ vt ~ away desperdiçar

frivol|ous /'frɪvələs/ a frívolo. ~ity /-'vɒlətɪ/ n frivolidade f

fro /frəʊ/ (= to and fro) ▶ TO

frock /frɒk/ n vestido m

frog /frɒg/ n rã f

frolic /'frɒlɪk/ vi (pt frolicked) brincar, fazer travessuras ● n brincadeira f, travessura f

from /frəm emphatic frɒm/ prep de; (with time, prices etc) de, a partir de; (according to) por, a julgar por

front /frʌnt/ n Meteo, Mil, Pol (of car, train) frente f; (of shirt) peitilho m; (of building; also fig) fachada f; (promenade) calçada f à beira-mar f ● a da frente; (first) primeiro; in ~ (of) em frente (de); ~ door porta f da rua; ~-wheel drive tração f dianteira

frontier /'frʌntɪə(r)/ n fronteira f

frost /frɒst/ n gelo m, temperatura f abaixo de zero; (on ground, plants etc) geada f ● vt/i cobrir(-se) de geada. ~bite n queimadura f de frio; ~bitten a queimado pelo frio. ~ed a ‹glass› fosco. ~y a glacial

froth /frɒθ/ n espuma f ● vi espumar, fazer espuma. ~y a espumoso

frown /fraʊn/ vi franzir as sobrancelhas ● n franzir m de sobrancelhas; ~ on desaprovar

froze, frozen /frəʊz, 'frəʊzn/ ▶ FREEZE

froze, frozen /frəʊz, 'frəʊzn/ ▶ FREEZE

frugal /'fruːgl/ a poupado; ‹meal› frugal

fruit /fruːt/ n fruto m; (collectively) fruta f; ~ machine caça-níqueis mpl, (P) máquina f de jogo; ~ salad salada f de frutas. ~y a que tem gosto ou cheiro de fruta

fruit|ful /'fruːtfl/ a frutífero, produtivo. ~less a infrutífero

fruition /fruː'ɪʃn/ n come to ~ realizar-se

frustrat|e /frʌ'streɪt/ vt frustrar. **~ion** /-ʃn/ n frustração f

fry /fraɪ/ vt/i (pt **fried**) fritar. **~ing pan** n frigideira f

fudge /fʌdʒ/ n Culin doce m de leite, (P) doce m acaramelado ● vt/i ~ **(the issue)** lançar a confusão

fuel /'fjuːəl/ n combustível m; (for car) carburante m ● vt (pt **fuelled**) abastecer de combustível; fig atear

fugitive /'fjuːdʒətɪv/ a & n fugitivo m

fulfil /fʊl'fɪl/ vt (pt **fulfilled**) cumprir, realizar; <condition> satisfazer; ~ **o.s.** realizar-se. **~ment** n realização f; (of condition) satisfação f

full /fʊl/ a (-er, -est) cheio; <meal> completo; <price> total, por inteiro; <skirt> rodado; ~ **moon** lua f cheia; ~ **stop** ponto m final; **at ~ speed** a toda velocidade; **to the ~** ao máximo; **be ~ up** 🔟 (after eating) estar cheio 🔟 ● adv **in** ~ integralmente. **~scale** a em grande; **~size** a em tamanho natural; **~time** a & adv a tempo integral, full-time. **~y** adv completamente

fumble /'fʌmbl/ vi tatear; (in the dark) andar tateando; ~ **with** estar atrapalhado com, andar às voltas com

fume /fjuːm/ vi defumar, (P) deitar fumo, fumegar; (with anger) ferver. **~s** npl gases mpl

fun /fʌn/ n divertimento m; **for ~** de brincadeira; **make ~ of** zombar de, fazer troça de. **~fair** n parque m de diversões, (P) feira f de diversões, (P) feira f popular

function /'fʌŋkʃn/ n função f ● vi funcionar. **~al** a funcional

fund /fʌnd/ n fundos mpl ● vt financiar

fundamental /fʌndə'mentl/ a fundamental

funeral /'fjuːnərəl/ n enterro m, funeral m ● a fúnebre

fungus /'fʌŋgəs/ n (pl **-gi** /-gaɪ/) fungo m

funnel /'fʌnl/ n funil m; (of ship) chaminé f

funn|y /'fʌnɪ/ a (-ier, -iest) engraçado, divertido; (odd) esquisito. **~ily** adv comicamente; (oddly) estranhamente; **~ily enough** por incrível que pareça

fur /fɜː(r)/ n pelo m; (for clothing) pele f; (in kettle) depósito m, crosta f; ~ **coat** casaco m de pele

furious /'fjʊərɪəs/ a furioso

furnace /'fɜːnɪs/ n fornalha f

furnish /'fɜːnɪʃ/ vt mobiliar, (P) mobilar; (supply) prover (with de). **~ings** npl

mobiliário m e equipamento m

furniture /'fɜːnɪtʃə(r)/ n mobília f

furry /'fɜːrɪ/ a (-ier, -iest) peludo; <toy> de pelúcia, (P) de peluche

furth|er /'fɜːðə(r)/ a mais distante; (additional) adicional, suplementar ● adv mais longe; (more) mais ● vt promover; **~er education** ensino m supletivo, cursos mpl livres, (P) educação f superior. **~est** a o mais distante ● adv mais longe

furthermore /fɜːðə'mɔː(r)/ adv além disso

fury /'fjʊərɪ/ n fúria f, furor m

fuse[1] /fjuːz/ vt/i fundir(-se); fig amalgamar ● n fusível m; **the lights ~d** os fusíveis queimaram

fuse[2] /fjuːz/ n (of bomb) espoleta f

fuselage /'fjuːzəlɑːʒ/ n fuselagem f

fuss /fʌs/ n história(s) f(pl), escarcéu m ● vi preocupar-se com ninharias; **make a ~ of** ligar demasiado para or (P) a, criar caso com, fazer um espalhafato com. **~y** a exigente, complicado

futile /'fjuːtaɪl/ a fútil

future /'fjuːtʃə(r)/ a & n futuro m; **in ~** no futuro, de agora em diante

futuristic /fjuːtʃə'rɪstɪk/ a futurista, futurístico

fuzz /fʌz/ n penugem f; (hair) cabelo m frisado

fuzzy /'fʌzɪ/ a <hair> frisado; <photo> pouco nítido, desfocado

f

g

Gg

gabble /'gæbl/ vt/i tagarelar, falar, ler muito depressa ● n tagarelice f, algaravia f

gable /'geɪbl/ n empena f, oitão m

gadget /'gædʒɪt/ n pequeno utensílio m; (fitting) dispositivo m; (device) engenhoca f 🔟

Gaelic /'geɪlɪk/ n galês m

gag /gæg/ n mordaça f; (joke) gag m, piada f ● vt (pt **gagged**) amordaçar

gaiety /'geɪətɪ/ n alegria f

gaily /'geɪlɪ/ adv alegremente

gain /geɪn/ vt ganhar ● vi (of clock) adiantar-se; ~ **weight** aumentar de peso; ~ **on** (get closer to) aproximar-se de ● n ganho m; (increase) aumento m

gait /geɪt/ n (modo de) andar m

gala /'gɑːlə/ n gala m; *Sport* festival m

galaxy /'gæləksɪ/ n galáxia f

gale /geɪl/ n vento m forte

gallant /'gælənt/ a galhardo, valente; (*chivalrous*) galante, cortês. **~ry** n galhardia f, valentia f; (*chivalry*) galanteria f, cortesia f

gallery /'gælərɪ/ n galeria f

galley /'gælɪ/ n (pl -eys) galera f; (*ship's kitchen*) cozinha f

gallon /'gælən/ n galão m = 4,546 litros, Amer = 3.785 litros

gallop /'gæləp/ n galope m ● vi (pt galloped) galopar

gallows /'gæləʊz/ npl forca f

galore /gə'lɔː(r)/ adv à beça, em abundância

gambl|e /'gæmbl/ vt/i jogar ● n jogo (de azar) m; *fig* risco m; **~e on** apostar em. **~er** n jogador m

game /geɪm/ n jogo m; *Football* desafio m; (*animals*) caça f ● a bravo; **~ for** pronto para

gamekeeper /'geɪmkiːpə(r)/ n guarda-florestal m

gammon /'gæmən/ n presunto m defumado

gang /gæŋ/ n bando m, gang m; (*of workmen*) turma f, (P) grupo m ● vi **~ up** ligar-se (**on** contra)

gangling /'gæŋglɪŋ/ a desengonçado

gangrene /'gæŋgriːn/ n gangrena f

gangster /'gæŋstə(r)/ n gângster m, bandido m

gangway /'gæŋweɪ/ n passagem f; (*aisle*) coxia f; (*on ship*) portaló m; (*from ship to shore*) passadiço m

gaol /dʒeɪl/ n & vt = JAIL

gap /gæp/ n abertura f, brecha f; (*in time*) intervalo m; (*deficiency*) lacuna f

gap|e /geɪp/ vi ficar boquiaberto or embasbacado. **~ing** a escancarado

gap year Na Grã-Bretanha, é o período de tempo entre o final dos estudos no ensino secundário e a entrada na universidade. Muitos estudantes dedicam este período a obter experiência laboral relacionada com as suas futuras carreiras profissionais. Outros realizam atividades não-relacionadas com os estudos, e para alguns é uma oportunidade para poupar dinheiro ou viajar.

garage /'gærɑːʒ/ n garagem f; (*service station*) posto m de gasolina, (P) estação f de serviço ● vt pôr na garagem

garbage /'gɑːbɪdʒ/ n lixo m; **~ can** Amer lata f do lixo, (P) caixote m do lixo

garden /'gɑːdn/ n jardim m ● vi jardinar. **~er** n jardineiro m. **~ing** n jardinagem f

gargle /'gɑːgl/ vi gargarejar ● n gargarejo m

garish /'geərɪʃ/ a berrante, espalhafatoso

garland /'gɑːlənd/ n grinalda f

garlic /'gɑːlɪk/ n alho m

garment /'gɑːmənt/ n peça f de vestuário, roupa f

garnish /'gɑːnɪʃ/ vt enfeitar, guarnecer ● n guarnição f

garrison /'gærɪsn/ n guarnição f ● vt guarnecer

garrulous /'gærələs/ a tagarela

garter /'gɑːtə(r)/ n liga f

gas /gæs/ n (pl gases) gás m; *Med* anestésico m; Amer 🔲 (*petrol*) gasolina f ● vt (pt gassed) asfixiar; *Mil* gasear ● vi 🔲 fazer conversa fiada; **~ fire** aquecedor m a gás; **~ mask** máscara f antigás; **~ meter** medidor m or (P) contador m do gás

gash /gæʃ/ n corte m, lanho m ● vt cortar

gasket /'gæskɪt/ n junta f

gasoline /'gæsəliːn/ n Amer gasolina f

gasp /gɑːsp/ vi arfar, arquejar; *fig* (*with rage, surprise*) ficar sem ar ● n arquejo m

gastric /'gæstrɪk/ a gástrico

gastronomy /gæ'strɒnəmɪ/ n gastronomia f

gate /geɪt/ n portão m; (*of wood*) cancela f; (*barrier*) barreira f; (*airport*) porta f

gatecrash /'geɪtkræʃ/ vt/i entrar (numa festa) sem convite

gateway /'geɪtweɪ/ n (porta de) entrada f

gather /'gæðə(r)/ vt reunir, juntar; (*pick up, collect*) apanhar; (*amass, pile up*) acumular, juntar; (*conclude*) deduzir; ‹cloth› franzir ● vi reunir-se; (*pile up*) acumular-se; **~ speed** ganhar velocidade. **~ing** n reunião f

gaudy /'gɔːdɪ/ a (-ier, -iest) (*bright*) berrante; (*showy*) espalhafatoso

gauge /geɪdʒ/ n medida f padrão; (*device*) indicador m; (*railway*) bitola f ● vt medir, avaliar

gaunt /gɔːnt/ a emagrecido, macilento; (grim) lúgubre, desolado

gauze /gɔːz/ n gaze f

gave /geɪv/ ▶ GIVE

gawky /'gɔːkɪ/ a (-ier, -iest) desajeitado

gay /geɪ/ a (-er, -est) alegre; ▣ (homosexual) homossexual; gay

gaze /geɪz/ vi ~ (at) olhar fixamente (para) ● n contemplação f

GB abbr ▶ GREAT BRITAIN

gear /gɪə(r)/ n equipamento m; Techn engrenagem f; Auto velocidade f; in ~ engrenado; out of ~ em ponto morto ● vt equipar; (adapt) adaptar

gearbox /'gɪəbɒks/ n caixa f de mudança, caixa f de transmissão, (P) caixa f de velocidades

geese /giːs/ ▶ GOOSE

gel /dʒel/ n geleia f

gelatine /'dʒelətiːn/ n gelatina f

gem /dʒem/ n gema f, pedra f preciosa

Gemini /'dʒemɪnaɪ/ n Astr Gêmeos mpl, (P) Gémeos mpl

gender /'dʒendə(r)/ n gênero m, (P) género m

gene /dʒiːn/ n gene m

genealogy /dʒiːnɪ'ælədʒɪ/ n genealogia f

general /'dʒenrəl/ a geral; ~ election eleições fpl legislativas; in ~ em geral ● n general m. ~ practitioner n clínico-geral m, (P) médico m de família. ~ly adv geralmente

generalize /'dʒenrəlaɪz/ vt/i generalizar. ~ation /-'zeɪʃn/ n generalização f

generate /'dʒenəreɪt/ vt gerar, produzir

generation /dʒenə'reɪʃn/ n geração f

generator /'dʒenəreɪtə(r)/ n gerador m

generous /'dʒenərəs/ a generoso; (plentiful) abundante. ~osity /-'rɒsətɪ/ n generosidade f

genetic /dʒɪ'netɪk/ a genético. ~s n genética f

genial /'dʒiːnɪəl/ a agradável

genius /'dʒiːnɪəs/ n (pl -uses) gênio m, (P) génio m

genocide /'dʒenəsaɪd/ n genocídio m

gent /dʒent/ n the G~s ▣ banheiros mpl de homens, (P) lavabos mpl para homens

genteel /dʒen'tiːl/ a elegante, fino, refinado

gentle /'dʒentl/ a (er, est) brando, suave. ~eness n brandura f, suavidade f. ~y adv brandamente, suavemente

gentleman /'dʒentlmən/ n (pl -men) senhor m; (well-bred) cavalheiro m

genuine /'dʒenjuɪn/ a genuíno, verdadeiro; (belief) sincero

geography /dʒɪ'ɒgrəfɪ/ n geografia f. ~ical /dʒɪə'græfɪkl/ a geográfico

geology /dʒɪ'ɒlədʒɪ/ n geologia f. ~ical /dʒɪə'lɒdʒɪkl/ a geológico. ~ist n geólogo m

geometry /dʒɪ'ɒmətrɪ/ n geometria f. ~ic(al) /dʒɪə'metrɪk(l)/ a geométrico

geranium /dʒə'reɪnɪəm/ n gerânio m

geriatric /dʒerɪ'ætrɪk/ a geriátrico

germ /dʒɜːm/ n germe m, micróbio m

German /'dʒɜːmən/ a & n alemão m, alemã f; Lang alemão m; G~ measles rubéola f. G~ic /dʒə'mænɪk/ a germânico. G~y n Alemanha f

germinate /'dʒɜːmɪneɪt/ vi germinar

gesticulate /dʒe'stɪkjʊleɪt/ vi gesticular

gesture /'dʒestʃə(r)/ n gesto m

---

get /get/ ● vt (pt got, pp got, gotten US pres p getting)

····▶ (receive) receber; **we got a letter** recebemos uma carta

····▶ (obtain, achieve) conseguir, obter; **I got a job in São Paulo** consegui um emprego em São Paulo; **he ~s good grades** ele tem boas notas

····▶ (buy) comprar; **~ sb a present** comprar um presente para alguém

····▶ (fetch) ir buscar; **go and ~ a chair** vá buscar uma cadeira

····▶ (travel by) apanhar; **we can ~ the bus** podemos pegar o ônibus

····▶ (understand) perceber; **I don't ~ it** não percebo

····▶ (experience) ter; **~ a surprise** ter uma surpresa; **~ a shock** ter um choque

····▶ ‹illness› pegar, apanhar; **~ the flu/a cold** pegar uma gripe

····▶ (cause to be done) **~ the TV repaired** mandar arrumar a televisão; **~ one's hair cut** (ir) cortar o cabelo

····▶ (ask or persuade) **~ sb to do sth** fazer com que alguém faça algo; **he got his sister to help him with the homework** ele convenceu a irmã a ajudá-lo no trabalho de casa

g

● *vi*

····▶ (*become*) tornar-se, ficar; **he is getting old** está ficando velho; **he got rich** ficou rico

····▶ (*into state/condition*) ~ **married** casar-se; ~ **hurt** ficar ferido; ~ **better/ worse** melhorar/piorar

····▶ (*arrive*) chegar; ~ **to the airport** chegar ao aeroporto

□ ~ **about** ● *vi* (*person*) deslocar-se. ~ **along** ● *vi* (*progress*) **how is she getting along?** como ela está progredindo?. ~ **along with** ● *vi* dar-se bem com. ~ **at** ● *vt* (*have access to*) alcançar; (*criticize*) criticar; (*mean*) querer dizer, insinuar; **what are you getting at?** o que você está insinuando?. ~ **away** ● *vi* escapar. ~ **back** ● *vi* voltar ● *vt* recuperar. ~ **by** ● *vi* safar-se. ~ **down** ● *vt/i* descer. ~ **in** ● *vi* (*enter*) entrar; ‹*bus, train*› chegar. ~ **into** ● *vt* (*dress*) vestir. ~ **off** ● *vi* (*from bus, train, horse*) descer ● *vt* (*remove*) remover; ‹*bus, train, horse*› descer de. ~ **on** ● *vi* ‹*bus*› subir; (*be on good terms*) ~ **on well with sb** dar-se bem com alguém; (*make progress*) **how are you getting on?** como você está indo?. ~ **out** ● *vi* sair. ~ **over** ● *vt* ‹*illness*› recuperar. ~ **round** ● *vt* ‹*rule*› contornar; ‹*person*› convencer. ~ **through** ● *vi* (*on the phone*) estabelecer contato. ~ **up** ● *vi* levantar-se

getaway /'getəweɪ/ *n* fuga *f*

get-up *n* 🄳 apresentação *f*

ghastly /'gɑːstlɪ/ *a* (**-ier, -iest**) horrível; (*pale*) lívido

gherkin /'gɜːkɪn/ *n* pepino *m* pequeno para conservas, cornichão *m*

ghetto /'getəʊ/ *n* (*pl* **-os**) gueto *m*, ghetto *m*

ghost /gəʊst/ *n* fantasma *m*, espectro *m*. ~**ly** *a* fantasmagórico, espectral

giant /'dʒaɪənt/ *a & n* gigante *m*

gibberish /'dʒɪbərɪʃ/ *n* algaravia *f*, linguagem *f* incompreensível

giblets /'dʒɪblɪts/ *npl* miúdos *mpl*, miudezas *fpl*

giddy /'gɪdɪ/ *a* (**-ier, -iest**) estonteante, vertiginoso; **be or feel** ~ ter tonturas or vertigens

gift /gɪft/ *n* presente *m*, dádiva *f*; (*ability*) dom *m*, dote *m*. ~~**-wrap** *vt* (*pt* **-wrapped**) fazer um embrulho de presente

gifted /'gɪftɪd/ *a* dotado

gig /gɪg/ *n* 🄸 show *m*; sessão *f* de jazz etc

gigantic /dʒaɪ'gæntɪk/ *a* gigantesco

giggle /'gɪgl/ *vi* dar risadinhas nervosas ● *n* risinho *m* nervoso

gild /gɪld/ *vt* dourar

gilt /gɪlt/ *a & n* dourado *m*. ~~**-edged** *a* de toda a confiança

gimmick /'gɪmɪk/ *n* truque *m*, artifício *m*

gin /dʒɪn/ *n* gin *m*, genebra *f*

ginger /'dʒɪndʒə(r)/ *n* gengibre *m* ● *a* louro-avermelhado, ruivo; ~ **ale,** ~ **beer** cerveja *f* de gengibre, (*P*) ginger ale *m*

gingerbread /'dʒɪndʒəbred/ *n* pão *m* de gengibre

gingerly /'dʒɪndʒəlɪ/ *adv* cautelosamente

gipsy /'dʒɪpsɪ/ *n* = GYPSY

giraffe /dʒɪ'rɑːf/ *n* girafa *f*

girder /'gɜːdə(r)/ *n* trave *f*, viga *f*

girl /gɜːl/ *n* (*child*) menina *f*; (*young woman*) moça *f*, (*P*) rapariga *f*. ~**friend** *n* amiga *f*; (*of boy*) namorada *f*

gist /dʒɪst/ *n* essencial *m*

give /gɪv/ *vt/i* (*pt* **gave**, *pp* **given**) dar; (*bend, yield*) ceder; ~ **away** dar; ‹*secret*› revelar, trair; ~ **back** devolver; ~ **in** dar-se por vencido, render-se; ~ **off** emitir; ~ **way** ceder; ‹*traffic*› dar prioridade; (*collapse*) dar de si □ ~ **out** *vt* anunciar ● *vi* esgotar-se. ~ **up** *vt/i* desistir (de), renunciar (a); ~ **o.s. up** entregar-se

given /'gɪvn/ ▶ GIVE *a* dado; ~ **name** nome *m* de batismo

glacier /'glæsɪə(r)/ *n* glaciar *m*, geleira *f*

glad /glæd/ *a* contente. ~**ly** *adv* com (todo o) prazer

glam|our /'glæmə(r)/ *n* fascinação *f*, encanto *m*, (*P*) glamour *m*. ~**orize** *vt* tornar fascinante. ~**orous** *a* fascinante, sedutor, glamoroso

glance /glɑːns/ *n* relance *m*, olhar *m*; **at first** ~ à primeira vista ● *vi* ~ **at** dar uma olhada a

gland /glænd/ *n* glândula *f*

glar|e /gleə(r)/ *vi* brilhar intensamente, faiscar ● *n* luz *f* crua; *fig* olhar *m* feroz; ~**e at** olhar ferozmente para. ~**ing** *a* brilhante; (*obvious*) flagrante

glass /glɑːs/ *n* vidro *m*; (*vessel, its contents*) copo *m*; (*mirror*) espelho *m*; ~**es** óculos *mpl*. ~**y** *a* vítreo

glaze /gleɪz/ *vt* ‹*door etc*› envidraçar; ‹*pottery*› vidrar ● *n* vidrado *m*

gleam /gliːm/ n raio m de luz frouxa; fig vislumbre m ● vi luzir, brilhar

glee /gliː/ n alegria f

glib /glɪb/ a que tem a palavra fácil, verboso

glide /glaɪd/ vi deslizar; ‹bird, plane› planar. **~r** /-ə(r)/ n planador m

glimmer /'glɪmə(r)/ n luz f trêmula or (P) trémula, ténue ● vi tremular

glimpse /glɪmps/ n vislumbre m; **catch a ~ of** entrever, ver de relance

glint /glɪnt/ n brilho m, reflexo m ● vi brilhar, cintilar

glisten /'glɪsn/ vi reluzir

glitter /'glɪtə(r)/ vi luzir, resplandecer ● n esplendor m, cintilação f

gloat /gləʊt/ vi **~ over** ter um prazer maligno em, exultar com

global /'gləʊbl/ a global

globalization /ˌgləʊbəlaɪ'zeɪʃən, Amer -lɪ'z-/ n globalização f

globe /gləʊb/ n globo m

gloom /gluːm/ n obscuridade f; fig tristeza f. **~y** a sombrio; (sad) triste; (pessimistic) pessimista

glorif|y /'glɔːrɪfaɪ/ vt glorificar; **a ~ied waitress**/etc pouco mais que uma garçonete/etc, (P) empregada-de-mesa/etc

glorious /'glɔːrɪəs/ a glorioso

glory /'glɔːrɪ/ n glória f; (beauty) esplendor m ● vi **~ in** orgulhar-se de

gloss /glɒs/ n brilho m ● a brilhante ● vt **~ over** minimizar, encobrir. **~y** a brilhante

glossary /'glɒsərɪ/ n (pl **-ries**) glossário m

glove /glʌv/ n luva f; **~ compartment** porta-luvas m

glow /gləʊ/ vi arder; ‹person› resplandecer ● n brasa f. **~ing** a fig entusiástico

glucose /'gluːkəʊs/ n glucose f

glue /gluː/ n cola f ● vt (pres p **gluing**) colar

glum /glʌm/ a (**glummer**, **glummest**) sorumbático; (dejected) abatido

glut /glʌt/ n superabundância f

glutton /'glʌtn/ n glutão m. **~ous** a glutão. **~y** n gula f

GMO /dʒiːɛm'əʊ/ n OGM m, organismo m geneticamente modificado

gnash /næʃ/ vt **~ one's teeth** ranger os dentes

gnat /næt/ n mosquito m

gnaw /nɔː/ vt/i roer

go /gəʊ/ ● vi (3rd person sing pres. tense **goes**, pt **went**, pp **gone**)

⋯▸ ir; **~ to school/town/the cinema** ir à escola/à cidade/ao cinema; **~ shopping/swimming/riding** ir às compras/nadar/andar a cavalo; **~ for a walk** sair para um passeio; **~ for a nap** tirar uma soneca

⋯▸ (leave) ir; **I must be ~ing** tenho de ir

⋯▸ (vanish) ir-se, desaparecer; **the money's gone** o dinheiro acabou; **my bike's gone** a minha bicicleta desapareceu; **my headache is gone** a minha dor de cabeça desapareceu

⋯▸ (work, function) funcionar; **is the car ~ing?** o carro funciona?

⋯▸ (become) ficar; **~ blind** ficar cego; **~ pale/red** ficar pálido/corado

⋯▸ (turn out, progress) ir correr; **how's it ~ing?** como vai tudo?; **how did the exam ~?** como correu o exame?

⋯▸ (match) combinar; **the two colours don't ~ [together]** as duas cores não combinam

⋯▸ (in future tenses) **be ~ing to** ir (+ inf); **it's ~ing to rain** vai chover; **I'm not ~ing to do it** não vou fazer isso

● n (pl **goes**)

⋯▸ (turn) vez f; **it's your ~** é a sua vez

⋯▸ (try) tentativa f; **have a ~ at doing sth** fazer uma tentativa de aco

⋯▸ (energy) dinamismo m; **Mary's always got plenty of ~** a Mary sempre foi muito dinâmica

⋯▸ (in phrases) **on the ~** em grande atividade; **make a ~ of sth** tornar aco um sucesso.

~ahead n luz f verde ● a dinâmico; **~between** n intermediário

□ **~ across** ● vi ir para diante. **~ away** ● vi ir embora. **~ back** ● vi voltar. **~ back on** ● vi voltar atrás com; (return) voltar. **~ by** ● vi (pass) passar. **~ down** ● vi descer; ‹sun› pôr-se; ‹ship› afundar. **~ for** ● vt ir buscar; (like) gostar de; (attack) atacar. **~ in** ● vi entrar. **~ in for** ● vt ‹exam› apresentar-se a. **~ off** ● vi ir embora; (explode) arrebentar; (sound) soar; (decay) estragar. **~ on** ● vi continuar; (happen) acontecer. **~ out** ● vi sair; ‹light› apagar. **~ over** ● vt

(*check*) verificar, examinar. ~ **round**
● *vi* (*be enough*) chegar. ~ **through**
● *vt* (*check*) verificar, examinar.
~ **under** ● *vi* ir abaixo. ~ **up** ● *vi* subir.
~ **without** ● *vt* passar sem

goal /gəʊl/ *n* meta *f*; (*area*) baliza *f*;
(*score*) gol *m*, (P) golo *m*. ~**post** *n* trave *f*

goalkeeper /'gəʊlkiːpə(r)/ *n* goleiro
m, (P) guarda-redes *m*

goat /gəʊt/ *n* cabra *f*

gobble /'gɒbl/ *vt* comer com
sofreguidão, devorar

god /gɒd/ *n* deus *m*. ~**daughter** *n*
afilhada *f*. ~**dess** *n* deusa *f*. ~**father** *n*
padrinho *m*. ~**ly** *a* devoto. ~**mother**
n madrinha *f*; ~**son** *n* afilhado *m*

God /gɒd/ *n* Deus *m*

godsend /'gɒdsend/ *n* achado *m*,
dádiva *f* do céu

goggles /'gɒglz/ *npl* óculos *mpl* de
proteção

going /'gəʊɪŋ/ *n* **it is slow/hard**
~ é demorado/difícil ● *a* ‹*price,
rate*› corrente; atual. ~**s-on** *npl*
acontecimentos *mpl* estranhos

gold /gəʊld/ *n* ouro *m* ● *a* de/em ouro.
~ **mine** *n* mina *f* de ouro

golden /'gəʊldən/ *a* de ouro; (*like
gold*) dourado; (*opportunity*) único;
~ **wedding** bodas *fpl* de ouro

goldfish /'gəʊldfɪʃ/ *n* peixe *m* dourado/
vermelho

goldsmith /'gəʊldsmɪθ/ *n* ourives
m inv

golf /gɒlf/ *n* golfe *m*; ~ **club** clube *m* de
golfe, associação *f* de golfe; (*stick*) taco
m. ~ **course** *n* campo *m* de golfe. ~**er** *n*
jogador *m* de golfe

gone /gɒn/ ▶ **go** *a* ido, passado; ~ **six
o'clock** depois das seis

gong /gɒŋ/ *n* gongo *m*

good /gʊd/ *a* (**better, best**) bom; **as** ~
as praticamente; G~ **Friday** Sexta-feira
f Santa; ~ **name** bom nome *m* ● *n* bem
m; **for** ~ para sempre; **it is no** ~ não
adianta; **it is no** ~ **shouting**/*etc* não
adianta gritar/*etc*. ~ **afternoon** *int* boa(s)
tarde(s); ~ **evening/night** *int* boa(s)
noite(s); ~**looking** *a* bonito; ~ **morning**
int bom dia

goodbye /gʊd'baɪ/ *int & n* adeus *m*

goodness /'gʊdnɪs/ *n* bondade *f*; **my**
~**l** meu Deus!

goods /gʊdz/ *npl* Comm mercadorias
fpl; ~ **train** trem *m* de carga, (P) comboio
m de mercadorias

goodwill /gʊd'wɪl/ *n* boa vontade *f*

goose /guːs/ *n* (*pl* **geese**) ganso *m*.
~**flesh**, ~**pimples** *ns* pele *f* de galinha

gooseberry /'guzbərɪ/ *n* (*fruit*)
groselha *f*; (*bush*) groselheira *f*

gore[2] /gɔː(r)/ *vt* perfurar

gorge /gɔːdʒ/ *n* desfiladeiro *m*,
garganta *f* ● *vt* ~ **o.s.** empanturrar-se

gorgeous /'gɔːdʒəs/ *a* magnífico,
maravilhoso

gorilla /gə'rɪlə/ *n* gorila *m*

gormless /'gɔːmlɪs/ *a* 🅧 estúpido

gorse /gɔːs/ *n* giesta *f*, tojo *m*, urze *f*

gory /'gɔːrɪ/ *a* (-**ier**, -**iest**) sangrento

gosh /gɒʃ/ *int* puxa!, (P) caramba!

gospel /'gɒspl/ *n* evangelho *m*

gossip /'gɒsɪp/ *n* bisbilhotice *f*, fofoca
f; (*person*) bisbilhoteiro *m*, fofoqueiro *m*
● *vi* (*pt* **gossiped**) bisbilhotar

got /gɒt/ ▶ **get**; **have** ~ ter; **have** ~ **to
do** ter que fazer, (P) ter de fazer

Gothic /'gɒθɪk/ *a* gótico

gourmet /'gʊəmeɪ/ *n* gastrônomo *m*,
(P) gastrónomo *m*, gourmet *m*

govern /'gʌvn/ *vt/i* governar. ~**ess**
n preceptora *f*. ~**or** *n* governador *m*;
(*of school, hospital etc*) diretor *m*

government /'gʌvənmənt/ *n*
governo *m*

gown /gaʊn/ *n* vestido *m*; (*of judge,
teacher*) toga *f*

GP *abbr* ▶ **GENERAL PRACTITIONER**

grab /græb/ *vt* (*pt* **grabbed**) agarrar,
apanhar

grace /greɪs/ *n* graça *f* ● *vt* honrar;
(*adorn*) ornar; **say** ~ dar graças. ~**ful** *a*
gracioso

gracious /'greɪʃəs/ *a* gracioso; (*kind*)
amável, afável

grade /greɪd/ *n* categoria *f*; (*of goods*)
classe *f*, qualidade *f*; (*on scale*) grau *m*;
(*school mark*) nota *f* ● *vt* classificar

gradient /'greɪdɪənt/ *n* gradiente *m*,
declive *m*

gradual /'grædʒʊəl/ *a* gradual,
progressivo. ~**ly** *adv* gradualmente

graduate[1] /'grædʒʊət/ *n* diplomado *m*,
graduado *m*, licenciado *m*

graduat|e[2] /'grædʒʊeɪt/ *vt/i*
formar(-se). ~**ion** /-'eɪʃn/ *n* colação *f* de
grau, (P) formatura *f*

graffiti /grə'fiːtiː/ *npl* graffiti *mpl*

graft /grɑːft/ *n* Med, Bot enxerto *m*;
(*work*) batalha *f* ● *vt* enxertar; (*work*)
batalhar

grain /greɪn/ n grão m; (collectively) cereais mpl; (in wood) veio m; **against the ~** fig contra a maneira de ser

gram /græm/ n grama m

gramm|ar /'græmə(r)/ n gramática f. **~atical** /grə'mætɪkl/ a gramatical

grand /grænd/ a (-er, -est) grandioso, magnífico; ‹duke, master› grão; **~ piano** piano m de cauda

grand|child /'grændtʃaɪld/ n (pl -children) neto m. **~daughter** n neta f. **~father** n avô m. **~mother** n avó f. **~parents** npl avós mpl. **~son** n neto m

grandeur /'grændʒə(r)/ n grandeza f

grandiose /'grændɪəʊs/ a grandioso

grandstand /'grændstænd/ n tribuna f principal

granite /'grænɪt/ n granito m

grant /grɑːnt/ vt conceder; ‹a request› ceder a; (admit) admitir (that que) ● n subsídio m; Univ bolsa f; **take for ~ed** dar por garantido, contar com

grape /greɪp/ n uva f

grapefruit /'greɪpfruːt/ n inv grapefruit m, toranja f

graph /grɑːf/ n gráfico m

graphic /'græfɪk/ a gráfico; fig vívido. **~s** npl Comput gráficos mpl

grapple /'græpl/ vi **~ with** estar engalfinhado com; fig estar às voltas com

grasp /grɑːsp/ vt agarrar; (understand) compreender ● n domínio m; (reach) alcance m; fig (understanding) compreensão f

grasping /'grɑːspɪŋ/ a ganancioso

grass /grɑːs/ n erva f; (lawn) grama f, (P) relva f; (pasture) pastagem f; 🅴 (informer) delator m ● vt cobrir com grama, (P) relva; 🅴 (betray) delatar; **~ roots** Pol bases fpl. **~y** a coberto de erva

grasshopper /'grɑːshɒpə(r)/ n gafanhoto m

grate¹ /greɪt/ n (fireplace) lareira f; (frame) grelha f

grate² /greɪt/ vt ralar ● vi ranger; **~ one's teeth** ranger os dentes. **~r** /-ə(r)/ n ralador m

grateful /'greɪtfl/ a grato, agradecido

gratify /'grætɪfaɪ/ vt (pt -fied) contentar, satisfazer. **~ing** a gratificante

gratis /'greɪtɪs/ a & adv grátis (invar), de graça

gratitude /'grætɪtjuːd/ n gratidão f, reconhecimento m

gratuitous /grə'tjuːɪtəs/ a gratuito; (uncalled-for) sem motivo

gratuity /grə'tjuːɪtɪ/ n gratificação f, gorjeta f

grave¹ /greɪv/ n cova f, sepultura f, túmulo m

grave² /greɪv/ a (-er, -est) grave, sério

grave³ /grɑːv/ a **~ accent** acento m grave

gravel /'grævl/ n cascalho m miúdo, saibro m

gravestone /'greɪvstəʊn/ n lápide f, campa f

graveyard /'greɪvjɑːd/ n cemitério m

gravity /'grævətɪ/ n gravidade f

gravy /'greɪvɪ/ n molho (de carne) m

graze¹ /greɪz/ vt/i pastar

graze² /greɪz/ vt roçar; (scrape) esfolar ● n esfoladura f, (P) esfoladela f

greas|e /griːs/ n gordura f ● vt engordurar; Culin untar; Mech lubrificar; **~e-proof paper** papel m vegetal. **~y** a gorduroso

great /greɪt/ a (-er, -est) grande; 🅸 (splendid) esplêndido. **~grandfather** n bisavô m; **~grandmother** n bisavó f. **~ly** adv grandemente, muito. **~ness** n grandeza f

Great Britain /greɪt'brɪtən/ n Grã-Bretanha f

Greece /griːs/ n Grécia f

greed /griːd/ n cobiça f, ganância f; (for food) gula f. **~y** a cobiçoso, ganancioso; (for food) guloso

Greek /griːk/ a & n grego m

green /griːn/ a (-er, -est) verde ● n verde m; (grass) gramado m, (P) relvado m; **~s** hortaliças fpl; **~ belt** zona f verde, paisagem f protegida; **~ light** luz f verde. **~ery** n verdura f

> **green card** Nos Estados Unidos, é o documento oficial que qualquer pessoa que não seja cidadão norte-americano deve obter para morar e trabalhar neste país. No Reino Unido, é o documento que se deve obter da companhia de seguros para que a cobertura de uma apólice continue em vigor quando se conduz um veículo no estrangeiro.

greengrocer /'griːngrəʊsə(r)/ n quitandeiro m, (P) vendedor m de hortaliças

greenhouse /'griːnhaʊs/ n estufa f; **~ effect** efeito estufa, (P) efeito de estufa

g

Greenland /'gri:nlənd/ n Groenlândia f, (P) Gronelândia f

greet /gri:t/ vt acolher. **~ing** n saudação f; (welcome) acolhimento m. **~ings** npl cumprimentos mpl; (Christmas etc) votos mpl, desejos mpl

grenade /grɪ'neɪd/ n granada f

grew /gru:/ ▶ GROW

grey /greɪ/ a (-er, -est) cinzento; ‹hair› grisalho ● n cinzento m

greyhound /'greɪhaʊnd/ n galgo m

grid /grɪd/ n (grating) gradeamento m, grade f; Electr rede f

g **grief** /gri:f/ n dor f; **come to ~** acabar mal

grievance /'gri:vns/ n razão f de queixa

grieve /gri:v/ vt sofrer, afligir ● vi sofrer; **~ for** chorar por

grill /grɪl/ n grelha f; (food) grelhado m; (place) grill m ● vt grelhar; (question) submeter a interrogatório cerrado, apertar com perguntas ● vi grelhar

grille /grɪl/ n grade f; (of car) grelha f

grim /grɪm/ a (**grimmer, grimmest**) sinistro; (without mercy) implacável

grimace /grɪ'meɪs/ n careta f ● vi fazer careta(s)

grim|e /graɪm/ n sujeira f. **~y** a encardido, sujo

grin /grɪn/ vi (pt **grinned**) sorrir abertamente, dar um sorriso largo ● n sorriso m aberto

grind /graɪnd/ vt (pt **ground**) triturar; ‹coffee› moer; (sharpen) amolar, afiar; **~ one's teeth** ranger os dentes; **~ to a halt** parar freando, (P) travar lentamente

grip /grɪp/ vt (pt **gripped**) agarrar; (interest) prender ● n (of hands) aperto m; (control) controle m, domínio m; **come to ~s with** fazer face a. **~ping** a apaixonante

grisly /'grɪzlɪ/ a (-ier, -iest) macabro, horrível

gristle /'grɪsl/ n cartilagem f

grit /grɪt/ n areia f, grão m de areia; fig (pluck) coragem f; fortaleza f ● vt (pt **gritted**) ‹road› jogar or (P) deitar areia em; ‹teeth› cerrar

groan /grəʊn/ vi gemer ● n gemido m

grocer /'grəʊsə(r)/ n dono/a m/f de mercearia. **~ies** npl artigos mpl de mercearia. **~y** n (shop) mercearia f

groggy /'grɒgɪ/ a (-ier, -iest) grogue, fraco das pernas

groin /grɔɪn/ n virilha f

groom /gru:m/ n noivo m; (for horses) moço m de estrebaria ● vt ‹horse› tratar de; fig preparar

groove /gru:v/ n ranhura f; (for door, window) calha f; (in record) estria f; fig rotina f

grope /grəʊp/ vi tatear; **~ for** procurar às cegas

gross /grəʊs/ a (-er, -est) (vulgar) grosseiro; (flagrant) flagrante; (of error) crasso; (of weight, figure etc) bruto ● n (pl invar) grosa f. **~ly** adv grosseiramente; (very) extremamente

grotesque /grəʊ'tesk/ a grotesco

grotty /'grɒtɪ/ a 🅇 sórdido

grouch /graʊtʃ/ vi 🅘 ralhar. **~y** a 🅘 rabugento

ground[1] /graʊnd/ n chão m, solo m; (area) terreno m; (reason) razão f, motivo m; **~s** jardins mpl; (of coffee) borra(s) f (pl); **~ floor** térreo m, (P) rés do chão m ● vt/i Naut encalhar; ‹plane› reter em terra. **~less** a infundado, sem fundamento

ground[2] /graʊnd/ ▶ GRIND

grounding /'graʊndɪŋ/ n bases fpl, conhecimentos mpl básicos

groundsheet /'graʊndʃi:t/ n impermeável m para o chão

groundwork /'graʊndwɜ:k/ n trabalhos mpl de base or preliminares

group /gru:p/ n grupo m ● vt/i agrupar(-se)

grouse[1] /graʊs/ n (pl invar) galo m silvestre

grouse[2] /graʊs/ vi 🅘 (grumble) resmungar; 🅘 (complain) queixar-se

grovel /'grɒvl/ vi (pt **grovelled**) humilhar-se; fig rebaixar-se

grow /grəʊ/ vi (pt **grew**, pp **grown**) crescer; (become) tornar-se; **~ old** envelhecer; **~ up** crescer, tornar-se adulto ● vt cultivar

growl /graʊl/ vi rosnar ● n rosnadela f

grown /grəʊn/ a **~ man** homem feito. **~-up** a adulto ● n pessoa f adulta

growth /grəʊθ/ n crescimento m; (increase) aumento m; Med tumor m

grub /grʌb/ n larva f; 🅇 (food) boia f; rango m, (P) comida f

grubby /'grʌbɪ/ a (-ier, -iest) sujo, porco

grudge /grʌdʒ/ vt dar/reconhecer de má vontade; **~ doing** fazer de má vontade; **~ sb sth** dar algo a alguém de má vontade ● n má vontade f; **have**

a ~ **against** ter ressentimento contra. **grudgingly** adv relutantemente

gruelling /ˈgruːəlɪŋ/ a estafante, extenuante

gruesome /ˈgruːsəm/ a macabro

gruff /grʌf/ a (-er, -est) carrancudo, rude

grumble /ˈgrʌmbl/ vi resmungar (**at** contra, por)

grumpy /ˈgrʌmpɪ/ a (-ier, -iest) mal-humorado, rabugento

grunt /grʌnt/ vi grunhir ● n grunhido m

guarantee /gærənˈtiː/ n garantia f ● vt garantir

guard /gɑːd/ vt guardar, proteger ● vi ~ **against** precaver-se contra ● n guarda f; (person) guarda m; (on train) condutor m. ~**ian** n guardião m, defensor m; (of orphan) tutor m

guarded /ˈgɑːdɪd/ a cauteloso, circunspeto, (P) circunspecto

guerrilla /gəˈrɪlə/ n guerrilheiro m; ~ **warfare** guerrilha f, guerra f de guerrilhas

guess /ges/ vt/i adivinhar; (suppose) supor ● n suposição f, conjetura f

guesswork /ˈgeswɜːk/ n suposição f, conjetura(s) f(pl)

guest /gest/ n convidado m; (in hotel) hóspede mf. ~ **house** n pensão f

guidance /ˈgaɪdns/ n orientação f, direção f, (P) direcção f

guide /gaɪd/ n guia mf ● vt guiar; ~**d missile** míssil m guiado; (remote-control) míssil m teleguiado. ~ **dog** n cão m de cego, cão-guia m; ~**lines** npl diretrizes fpl

Guide /gaɪd/ n Guia f

guidebook /ˈgaɪdbʊk/ n guia m (turístico)

guilt /gɪlt/ n culpa f. ~**y** a culpado

guinea pig /ˈgɪnɪpɪg/ n cobaia f, porquinho-da-índia m

guitar /gɪˈtɑː(r)/ n guitarra f, violão m, (P) viola f. ~**ist** n guitarrista mf, tocador m de violão, (P) viola f

gulf /gʌlf/ n golfo m; (hollow) abismo m

gull /gʌl/ n gaivota f

gullible /ˈgʌləbl/ a crédulo

gully /ˈgʌlɪ/ n barranco m; (drain) sarjeta f

gulp /gʌlp/ vt engolir, devorar ● vi engolir em seco ● n trago m

gum¹ /gʌm/ n Anat gengiva f

gum² /gʌm/ n goma f; (chewing gum) chiclete m; goma f elástica, (P) pastilha f elástica ● vt (pt **gummed**) colar

gun /gʌn/ n (pistol) pistola f; (rifle) espingarda f; (cannon) canhão m ● vt (pt **gunned**) ~ **down** abater a tiro

gunfire /ˈgʌnfaɪə(r)/ n tiroteio m

gunman /ˈgʌnmən/ n (pl -men) bandido m armado, atirador m

gunpowder /ˈgʌnpaʊdə(r)/ n pólvora f

gunshot /ˈgʌnʃɒt/ n tiro m

gurgle /ˈgɜːgl/ n gorgolejo m ● vi gorgolejar

gush /gʌʃ/ vi jorrar ● n jorro m. ~**ing** a efusivo, derretido

gust /gʌst/ n (of wind) rajada f; (of smoke) nuvem f. ~**y** a ventoso

gusto /ˈgʌstəʊ/ n gosto m, entusiasmo m

gut /gʌt/ n tripa f; ~**s** (belly) barriga f; 🆃 (courage) coragem f ● vt (pt **gutted**) estripar; ‹fish› limpar; ‹fire› destruir o interior de

gutter /ˈgʌtə(r)/ n calha f, canaleta f; (in street) sarjeta f, valeta f

guy /gaɪ/ n 🆃 (man) cara m, (P) tipo m 🆃

guzzle /ˈgʌzl/ vt/i comer/beber com sofreguidão, encher-se (de)

gym /dʒɪm/ n 🆃 (gymnasium) ginásio m; 🆃 (gymnastics) ginástica f

gym|nasium /dʒɪmˈneɪzɪəm/ n ginásio m. ~**nast** /ˈdʒɪmnæst/ n ginasta mf. ~**nastics** /-ˈnæstɪks/ npl ginástica f

gynaecolog|y /gaɪnɪˈkɒlədʒɪ/ n ginecologia f. ~**ist** n ginecologista mf

gypsy /ˈdʒɪpsɪ/ n cigano m

Hh

haberdashery /ˈhæbədæʃərɪ/ n armarinho m, (P) retrosaria f

habit /ˈhæbɪt/ n hábito m, costume m; (costume) hábito m; **be in/get into the ~ of** ter/apanhar o hábito de

habit|able /ˈhæbɪtəbl/ a habitável. ~**ation** /-ˈteɪʃn/ n habitação f

habitat /ˈhæbɪtæt/ n habitat m

habitual /həˈbɪtʃʊəl/ a habitual, costumeiro; ‹smoker, liar› inveterado. ~**ly** adv habitualmente

hack¹ /hæk/ n (horse) cavalo m de aluguel or (P) aluguer; (writer) escrevinhador m pej. ~**er** n Comput micreiro *m*, hacker *m*, (*P*) pirata *m* informático

hack² /hæk/ *vt* cortar, despedaçar; **~ to pieces** cortar em pedaços

hackneyed /'hæknɪd/ *a* banal, batido

had /hæd/ ▶ HAVE

haddock /'hædək/ *n* (*invar*) hadoque *m*, eglefim *m*; **smoked ~** hadoque *m* fumado

haemorrhage /'hemərɪdʒ/ *n* hemorragia *f*

haemorrhoids /'hemərɔɪdz/ *npl* hemorroidas *fpl*

haggard /'hægəd/ *a* desfigurado, com o rosto desfeito, magro e macilento

haggle /'hægl/ *vi* **~ (over)** regatear

hail¹ /heɪl/ *vt* saudar; ‹*taxi*› fazer sinal para, chamar ● *vi* **~ from** vir de

hail² /heɪl/ *n* granizo *m*, (*P*) saraiva *f*, (*P*) chuva de pedra *f* ● *vi* chover granizo, (*P*) saraivar

hailstone /'heɪlstəun/ *n* pedra *f* de granizo

hair /heə(r)/ *n* (*on head*) cabelo(s) *m*(*pl*); (*on body*) pêlos *mpl*; (*single strand*) cabelo *m*; (*of animal*) pêlo *m*. **~do** *n* 🔢 penteado *m*; **~dryer** *n* secador *m* de cabelo; **~raising** *a* horripilante, de pôr os cabelos em pé; **~style** *n* estilo *m* de penteado

hairbrush /'heəbrʌʃ/ *n* escova *f* para o cabelo

haircut /'heəkʌt/ *n* corte *m* de cabelo

hairdresser /'heədresə(r)/ *n* cabeleireiro *m*, cabeleireira *f*

hairpin /'heəpɪn/ *n* grampo *m*, (*P*) gancho *m* para o cabelo; **~ bend** curva *f* fechada, quase em V

hairy /'heərɪ/ *a* (**-ier, -iest**) peludo, cabeludo; 🔣 (*terrifying*) de pôr os cabelos em pé; horripilante

hake /heɪk/ *n* (*pl invar*) abrótea *f*

half /hɑːf/ *n* (*pl* **halves** /hɑːvz/) metade *f*, meio *m*; **go halves** dividir as despesas ● *a* meio; **~ a dozen** meia dúzia; **~ an hour** meia hora ● *adv* ao meio. **~caste** *n* mestiço *m*; **~hearted** *a* sem grande entusiasmo; **~term** *n* férias *fpl* no meio do trimestre; **~time** *n* meio-tempo *m*; **~way** *a* & *adv* a meio caminho; **~wit** *n* idiota *mf*

halibut /'hælɪbət/ *n* (*pl invar*) halibute *m*

hall /hɔːl/ *n* sala *f*; (*entrance*) vestíbulo *m*, entrada *f*; (*mansion*) solar *m*; **~ of residence** residência *f* de estudantes

hallmark /'hɔːlmɑːk/ *n* (*on gold etc*) marca *f* de contraste; *fig* cunho *m*; selo *m*

hallo /hə'ləu/ *int* & *n* (*greeting, surprise*) olá; (*on phone*) está

Halloween /hæləu'iːn/ *n* véspera *f* do Dia de Todos os Santos *or* (*P*) Dia das Bruxas

hallucination /həluːsɪ'neɪʃn/ *n* alucinação *f*

halo /'heɪləu/ *n* (*pl* **-oes**) halo *m*, auréola *f*

halt /hɔːlt/ *n* parada *f*, (*P*) paragem *f* ● *vt* deter, fazer parar ● *vi* fazer alto, parar

halve /hɑːv/ *vt* dividir ao meio; ‹*time etc*› reduzir à metade

ham /hæm/ *n* presunto *m*

hamburger /'hæmbɜːgə(r)/ *n* hambúrguer *m*

hammer /'hæmə(r)/ *n* martelo *m* ● *vt/i* martelar; *fig* bater com força

hammock /'hæmək/ *n* rede (de dormir) *f*

hamper¹ /'hæmpə(r)/ *n* cesto *m*, (*P*) cabaz *m*

hamper² /'hæmpə(r)/ *vt* dificultar, atrapalhar

hamster /'hæmstə(r)/ *n* hamster *m*

hand /hænd/ *n* mão *f*; (*of clock*) ponteiro *m*; (*writing*) letra *f*; (*worker*) trabalhador *m*; *Cards* mão *f*; (*measure*) palmo *m*; (**helping**) **~** ajuda *f*, mão *f*; **at ~** à mão; **on the one ~... on the other ~** por um lado ... por outro; **out of ~** incontrolável; **to ~** à mão ● *vt* dar, entregar; **~ in** or **over** entregar; **~ out** distribuir. **~baggage** *n* bagagem *f* de mão; **~out** *n* impresso *m*, folheto *m*; (*money*) esmola *f*, donativo *m*

handbag /'hændbæg/ *n* carteira *f*, bolsa de mão *f*, mala de mão *f*

handbook /'hændbuk/ *n* manual *m*

handbrake /'hændbreɪk/ *n* freio *m* de mão, (*P*) travão *m* de mão

handcuffs /'hændkʌfs/ *npl* algemas *fpl*

handful /'hændful/ *n* mão-cheia *f*, punhado *m*; (*a few*) punhado *m*; (*difficult task*) mão de obra *f*; **she's a ~** 🔢 ela é danada

handicap /'hændɪkæp/ *n* (*in competition*) handicap *m*; (*disadvantage*) desvantagem *f* ● *vt* (*pt* **handicapped**) prejudicar. **~ped** *a* deficiente; **mentally ~ped** deficiente mental

handicraft /'hændɪkrɑːft/ *n* artesanato *m*, trabalho *m* manual

handiwork /'hændɪwɜːk/ *n* obra *f*, trabalho *m*

handkerchief /'hæŋkətʃɪf/ n lenço m

handle /'hændl/ n (of door etc) maçaneta f, puxador m; (of cup etc) asa f; (of implement) cabo m; (of pan etc) alça f, (P) pega ● vt (touch) manusear, tocar; (operate with hands) manejar; (deal in) negociar em; (deal with) tratar de; ‹person› lidar com; **fly off the ~** 🗲 perder as estribeiras

handlebar /'hændlbɑː(r)/ n guidão m, (P) guiador m

handmade /'hændmeɪd/ a feito à mão

handshake /'hændʃeɪk/ n aperto m de mão

handsome /'hænsəm/ a bonito; fig generoso

handwriting /'hændraɪtɪŋ/ n letra f, caligrafia f

handy /'hændɪ/ a (-ier, -iest) (convenient, useful) útil, prático; ‹person› jeitoso; (near) à mão

handyman /'hændɪmæn/ n (pl -men) faz-tudo m

hang /hæŋ/ vt (pt hung) pendurar, suspender; ‹head› baixar (pt hanged) ‹criminal› enforcar; **~ on to** (hold tightly) agarrar-se a; **~ up** ‹phone› desligar ● vi estar dependurado, pender; ‹criminal› ser enforcado; **~ about** andar por aí; **~ back** hesitar; **~ on** (wait) aguardar; **~ out** 🗲 (live) morar ● n **get the ~ of** 🗲 pegar o jeito de, (P) apanhar. **~gliding** n asa-delta f; **~up** n 🗲 complexo m

hangar /'hæŋə(r)/ n hangar m

hanger /'hæŋə(r)/ n (for clothes) cabide m. **~-on** n parasita mf

hangover /'hæŋəʊvə(r)/ n (from drinking) ressaca f

hanker /'hæŋkə(r)/ vi **~ after** ansiar por, suspirar por

happen /'hæpən/ vi acontecer, suceder; **he ~s to be out** por acaso ele não está. **~ing** n acontecimento m

happ|y /'hæpɪ/ a (-ier, -iest) feliz; **be ~y with** estar contente com. **~y-go-lucky** a despreocupado. **~ily** adv com satisfação; **she smiled ~ily** ela sorriu feliz; (fortunately) felizmente. **~iness** n felicidade f

harass /'hærəs/ vt amofinar, atormentar, perseguir. **~ment** n amofinação f, perseguição f; **sexual ~ment** assédio m sexual

harbour /'hɑːbə(r)/ n porto m; (shelter) abrigo m ● vt abrigar, dar asilo a; fig (in the mind) ocultar; obrigar

hard /hɑːd/ a (-er, -est) duro; (difficult) difícil; **~-boiled egg** ovo m cozido; **~ disk** disco m rígido, (P) duro; **~ of hearing** meio surdo; **~ shoulder** acostamento m, (P) berma f alcatroada; **~ water** água f dura ● adv muito, intensamente; (look) fixamente; (pull) com força; (think) a fundo, a sério; **~ by** muito perto; **~ up** 🗲 sem dinheiro, teso 🗲, liso 🗲. **~back** n livro m encadernado.

hardboard /'hɑːdbɔːd/ n madeira f compensada, madeira f prensada

harden /'hɑːdn/ vt/i endurecer. **~ed** a (callous) calejado; (robust) enrijado

hardly /'hɑːdlɪ/ adv mal, dificilmente, a custo; **~ ever** quase nunca

hardship /'hɑːdʃɪp/ n provação f, adversidade f; (suffering) sofrimento m; (financial) privação f

hardware /'hɑːdweə(r)/ n ferragens fpl; Comput hardware m

hardy /'hɑːdɪ/ a (-ier, -iest) resistente

hare /heə(r)/ n lebre f

harm /hɑːm/ n mal m; **out of ~'s way** a salvo; **there's no ~ in** não há mal em ● vt prejudicar, fazer mal a. **~ful** a prejudicial, nocivo. **~less** a inofensivo

harmonica /hɑː'mɒnɪkə/ n gaita f de boca, (P) beiços

harmon|y /'hɑːmənɪ/ n harmonia f. **~ious** /-'məʊnɪəs/ a harmonioso. **~ize** vt/i harmonizar(-se)

harness /'hɑːnɪs/ n arreios mpl ● vt arrear; fig (use) aproveitar; utilizar

harp /hɑːp/ n harpa f ● vi **~ on (about)** repisar

harpsichord /'hɑːpsɪkɔːd/ n cravo m

harrowing /'hærəʊɪŋ/ a dilacerante, lancinante

harsh /hɑːʃ/ a (-er, -est) duro, severo; ‹texture, voice› áspero; ‹light› cru; ‹colour› gritante; ‹climate› rigoroso. **~ness** n dureza f

harvest /'hɑːvɪst/ n colheita f, ceifa f ● vt colher, ceifar

has /hæz/ ▶ HAVE

hash /hæʃ/ n picadinho m, carne f cozida; fig (jumble) bagunça f; **make a ~ of** fazer uma bagunça de. **~ key** n tecla f sustenido, (P) tecla f cardinal

hashish /'hæʃɪʃ/ n haxixe m

hassle /'hæsl/ n 🗲 (quarrel) discussão f; 🗲 (struggle) dificuldade f ● vt 🗲 aborrecer

haste /heɪst/ n pressa f; **make ~** apressar-se

hasten /'heɪsn/ vt/i apressar(-se)

hast|y /'heɪstɪ/ a (**-ier, -iest**) apressado; (too quick) precipitado

hat /hæt/ n chapéu m

hatch[1] /hætʃ/ n (for food) postigo m; Naut escotilha f

hatch[2] /hætʃ/ vt/i chocar; <a plot etc> tramar, urdir

hatchback /'hætʃbæk/ n carro m de três ou cinco portas

hate /heɪt/ n ódio m ● vt odiar, detestar. **~ful** a odioso, detestável

hatred /'heɪtrɪd/ n ódio m

haughty /'hɔːtɪ/ a (**-ier, -iest**) altivo, soberbo, arrogante

haul /hɔːl/ vt arrastar, puxar; <goods> transportar em camião ● n (booty) presa f; (fish caught) apanha f; (distance) percurso m. **~age** n transporte m de cargas

haunt /hɔːnt/ vt rondar, frequentar; <ghost> assombrar; <thought> obcecar ● n lugar m favorito; **~ed house** casa f mal-assombrada

have /hæv unstressed həv, əv/ ● vt (3 sing pres **has**, pt and pp **had**)

····➤ (possess) ter; **I ~ (got) a car** tenho um carro; **they ~ (got) problems** eles têm problemas

····➤ (do sth) (have a try) tentar; **~ a bath** tomar banho; **~ a meal** comer uma refeição; **~ a walk** dar um passeio

····➤ (take, esp. in restaurant, shop) **I'll ~ the soup** vou querer a sopa; **I'll ~ the red dress** vou levar o vestido vermelho

····➤ (receive) receber; **I had a letter from her** recebi uma carta dela

····➤ (have sth done) mandar fazer; **we had the house painted** mandamos pintar a casa; **~ one's hair cut** cortar o cabelo

● v aux

····➤ (in perfect tenses) ter; **~ done** ter feito; **I ~ seen him** eu o vi

····➤ (in tag questions) **you've seen her, ~n't you?** você a viu, não viu?; **you ~n't seen her, have you?** você não a viu, viu?

····➤ (in short answers) **'you've never met him'** -'**yes, I ~'** 'você nunca o conheceu'- 'sim, conheci'

····➤ (must) **~ to** ter de; **I ~ to go** tenho de ir; **you don't ~ to do it** você não tem que fazer isso

□ **have on** ● vt (be wearing) ter vestido; **~ sb on** gozar com alguém. **have out** ● vt <tooth, tonsils> extrair; **~ it out with sb** pôr a coisa em pratos limpos com alguém

havoc /'hævək/ n estragos mpl; **play ~ with** causar estragos em

hawk[1] /hɔːk/ n falcão m

hawk[2] /hɔːk/ vt vender de porta em porta. **~er** n vendedor m ambulante

hawthorn /'hɔːθɔːn/ n pilriteiro m, estripeiro m

hay /heɪ/ n feno m; **~ fever** febre f do feno

haystack /'heɪstæk/ n palheiro m

hazard /'hæzəd/ n risco m; **~ warning lights** pisca-alerta m ● vt arriscar. **~ous** a arriscado

haze /heɪz/ n bruma f, neblina f, cerração f

hazel /'heɪzl/ n aveleira f. **~nut** n avelã f

hazy /'heɪzɪ/ a (**-ier, -iest**) brumoso, encoberto; fig (vague) vago

he /hiː/ pron ele ● n macho m

head /hed/ n cabeça f; (chief) chefe m; (of beer) espuma f; **~ first** de cabeça; **~s or tails** cara ou coroa?; **~ waiter** chefe m de garçons, (P) empregados de mesa ● a principal ● vt encabeçar, estar à frente de ● vi **~ for** dirigir-se para. **~dress** n toucador m; **~on** a frontal ● adv de frente. **~er** n Football cabeçada f

headache /'hedeɪk/ n dor f de cabeça

heading /'hedɪŋ/ n cabeçalho m, título m; (subject category) rubrica f

headlamp /'hedlæmp/ n farol m

headland /'hedlənd/ n promontório m

headlight /'hedlaɪt/ n farol m

headline /'hedlaɪn/ n título m, cabeçalho m

headlong /'hedlɒŋ/ a de cabeça; (rash) precipitado ● adv de cabeça; (rashly) precipitadamente

head|master /hed'mɑːstə(r)/ n diretor m. **~mistress** n diretora f

headphone /'hedfəʊn/ n fone m de cabeça, (P) auscultador m

headquarters /hed'kwɔːtəz/ npl sede f; Mil quartel m general

headrest /'hedrest/ n apoio m para a cabeça

headroom /'hedru:m/ n Auto espaço m para a cabeça; (bridge) limite m de altura, altura f máxima

headstrong /'hedstrɒŋ/ a teimoso

headway /'hedweɪ/ n progresso m; **make ~** fazer progressos

heady /'hedɪ/ a (-ier, -iest) empolgante

heal /hi:l/ vt/i curar(-se), sarar; ‹wound› cicatrizar

health /helθ/ n saúde f; **~ centre** posto m de saúde, (P) centro m de saúde; **~ foods** alimentos mpl naturais. **~y** a saudável, sadio

heap /hi:p/ n monte m, pilha f ● vt amontoar, empilhar; **~s of money** 🗉 dinheiro aos montes 🗉

hear /hɪə(r)/ vt/i (pt heard /hɜ:d/) ouvir; **~, hear!** apoiado! **~ from** ter notícias de; **~ of** or **about** ouvir falar de; **I won't ~ of it** nem quero ouvir falar nisso. **~ing** n ouvido m, audição f; Jur audiência f. **~ing-aid** n aparelho m de audição, (P) aparelho m auditivo

hearsay /'hɪəseɪ/ n boato m; **it's only ~** é só por ouvir dizer

hearse /hɜ:s/ n carro m funerário

heart /hɑ:t/ n coração m; **~s** Cards copas fpl; **at ~** no fundo; **by ~** de cor; **~ attack** ataque m de coração; **lose ~** perder a coragem, desanimar. **~beat** n pulsação f, batida f; **~breaking** a de partir o coração; **~broken** a com o coração partido, desfeito; **~to-heart** a com o coração nas mãos

heartburn /'hɑ:tbɜ:n/ n azia f

hearten /'hɑ:tn/ vt animar, encorajar

heartfelt /'hɑ:tfelt/ a sincero, sentido

hearth /hɑ:θ/ n lareira f

heartless /'hɑ:tlɪs/ a insensível, desalmado, cruel

heart|y /'hɑ:tɪ/ a (-ier, -iest) caloroso; ‹meal› abundante. **~ily** adv calorosamente; ‹eat, laugh› com vontade

heat /hi:t/ n calor m; fig ardor m; (contest) eliminatória f ● vt/i aquecer. **~stroke** n insolação f. **~wave** n onda f de calor. **~er** n aquecedor m. **~ing** n aquecimento m

heated /'hi:tɪd/ a fig acalorado; aceso

heathen /'hi:ðn/ n pagão m, pagã f

heather /'heðə(r)/ n urze f

heave /hi:v/ vt/i (lift) içar; ‹a sigh› soltar; (retch) ter náuseas; 🗉 (throw) atirar

heaven /'hevn/ n céu m. **~ly** a celestial; 🗉 divino

heav|y /'hevɪ/ a (-ier, -iest) pesado; ‹blow, rain› forte; ‹cold, drinker› grande; ‹traffic› intenso. **~ily** adv pesadamente; ‹drink, smoke etc› desalmadamente

heavyweight /'hevɪweɪt/ n Boxing peso-pesado m

Hebrew /'hi:bru:/ a hebreu, hebraico ● n Lang hebreu m

heckle /'hekl/ vt interromper, interpelar

hectic /'hektɪk/ a muito agitado, febril

hedge /hedʒ/ n sebe f ● vt cercar ● vi (in answering) usar de evasivas; **~ one's bets** fig resguardar-se

hedgehog /'hedʒhɒg/ n ouriço-cacheiro m

heed /hi:d/ vt prestar atenção a, escutar ● n pay **~ to** prestar atenção a, dar ouvidos a

heel /hi:l/ n calcanhar m; (of shoe) salto m; 🗷 canalha m

hefty /'heftɪ/ a (-ier, -iest) robusto e corpulento

height /haɪt/ n altura f; (of mountain, plane) altitude f; fig auge m; cúmulo m

heighten /'haɪtn/ vt/i aumentar, elevar(-se)

heir /eə(r)/ n herdeiro m. **~ess** n herdeira f

heirloom /'eəlu:m/ n peça f de família, (P) relíquia f de família

held /held/ ▶ HOLD¹

helicopter /'helɪkɒptə(r)/ n helicóptero m

hell /hel/ n inferno m; **for the ~ of it** só por gozo. **~ish** a infernal

hello /hə'ləʊ/ int & n = HALLO

helm /helm/ n leme m

helmet /'helmɪt/ n capacete m

help /help/ vt/i ajudar ● n ajuda f; **home ~** empregada f, faxineira f, (P) mulher f a dias; **~ o.s.** to servir-se de; **he cannot ~ laughing** ele não pode conter o riso; **it can't be ~ed** não há remédio. **~er** n ajudante mf. **~ful** a útil; (serviceable) de grande ajuda. **~less** a impotente

helping /'helpɪŋ/ n porção f, dose f

hem /hem/ n bainha f ● vt (pt hemmed) fazer a bainha; **~ in** cercar, encurralar

hemisphere /'hemɪsfɪə(r)/ n hemisfério m

hemp /hemp/ n cânhamo m

hen /hen/ n galinha f

h

hence /hens/ adv (from now) a partir desta altura; (for this reason) daí, por isso; **a week ~** daqui a uma semana. **~forth** adv de agora em diante, doravante

henpecked /'henpekt/ a mandado, (P) dominado pela mulher

her /hɜː(r)/ pron a (a ela); (after prep) ela; **(to) ~** lhe; **I know ~** conheço-a ● a seu(s), sua(s), dela

herald /'herəld/ vt anunciar

heraldry /'herəldrı/ n heráldica f

herb /hɜːb/ n erva f culinária or medicinal

herd /hɜːd/ n manada f; (of pigs) vara f ● vi **~ together** juntar-se em rebanho

here /hɪə(r)/ adv aqui ● int tome; aqui está; **to/from ~** para aqui/daqui

hereafter /hɪər'ɑːftə(r)/ adv de/para o futuro, daqui em diante ● n **the ~** a vida de além-túmulo, (P) a vida f para além da morte

hereby /hɪə'baɪ/ adv Jur pelo presente ato ou decreto, etc

hereditary /hɪ'redɪtrɪ/ a hereditário

here|sy /'herəsɪ/ n heresia f. **~tic** n herege mf. **~tical** /hɪ'retɪkl/ a herético

heritage /'herɪtɪdʒ/ n herança f, patrimônio m, (P) património m

hermit /'hɜːmɪt/ n eremita m

hernia /'hɜːnɪə/ n hérnia f

hero /'hɪərəʊ/ n (pl -oes) herói m

heroic /hɪ'rəʊɪk/ a heroico

heroin /'herəʊɪn/ n heroína f

heroine /'herəʊɪn/ n heroína f

heroism /'herəʊɪzəm/ n heroísmo m

heron /'herən/ n garça f

herring /'herɪŋ/ n arenque m

hers /hɜːz/ poss pron o(s) seu(s), a(s) sua(s), o(s) dela, a(s) dela; **it is ~** é (o) dela or o seu

herself /hɜː'self/ pron ela mesma/ própria; (reflexive) se; **by ~** sozinha; **for ~** para si mesma/própria; **to ~** a/para si mesma/própria; **Mary ~ said so** foi a própria Maria que o disse

hesitant /'hezɪtənt/ a hesitante

hesitat|e /'hezɪteɪt/ vt hesitar. **~ion** /-'teɪʃn/ n hesitação f

heterosexual /hetərəʊ'seksjʊəl/ a & n heterossexual mf

hexagon /'heksəgən/ n hexágono m. **~al** /-'ægənl/ a hexagonal

hey /heɪ/ int eh, olá

heyday /'heɪdeɪ/ n auge m, apogeu m

hi /haɪ/ int olá, viva

hibernat|e /'haɪbəneɪt/ vi hibernar. **~ion** /-'neɪʃn/ n hibernação f

hiccup /'hɪkʌp/ n soluço m ● vi soluçar, estar com soluços

hide[1] /haɪd/ vt/i (pt **hid**, pp **hidden**) esconder(-se) **(from** de). **~-and-seek** (game) esconde-esconde m, (P) jogo m das escondidas; **~out** n 🄣 esconderijo m

hide[2] /haɪd/ n pele f, couro m

hideous /'hɪdɪəs/ a horrendo, medonho

hiding /'haɪdɪŋ/ n 🄣 (thrashing) sova f; surra f; **go into ~** esconder-se

hierarchy /'haɪərɑːkɪ/ n hierarquia f

hi-fi /haɪ'faɪ/ a & n (de) alta fidelidade f

high /haɪ/ a (-er, -est) alto; <price, number> elevado; <voice, pitch> agudo; **~ chair** cadeira f alta para crianças; **~ jump** salto m em altura; **~-rise building** edifício m alto, (P) torre f; **~ school** escola f secundária; **in the ~ season** em plena estação; **~ spot** ponto m culminante; **~ street** rua f principal; **~ tide** maré f alta; **~er education** ensino m superior ● n alta f ● adv alto; **two metres ~** com dois metros de altura. **~-handed** a autoritário, prepotente; **~-speed** a ultrarápido

highbrow /'haɪbraʊ/ a & n 🄣 intelectual m

highlight /'haɪlaɪt/ n fig ponto m alto ● vt salientar, pôr em relevo, realçar

highly /'haɪlɪ/ adv altamente, extremamente; **speak ~ of** falar bem de. **~-strung** a muito sensível, nervoso, tenso

Highness /'haɪnɪs/ n Alteza f

> **high school** Nos Estados Unidos, é o último ciclo de ensino secundário, geralmente frequentado por alunos de idades entre os 14 e os 18 anos. Na Grã-Bretanha, alguns colégios de ensino secundário também se chamam *high schools*. ⓘ

highway /'haɪweɪ/ n estrada f, rodovia f; **H~ Code** Código m Nacional de Trânsito

hijab /hɪ'dʒɑːb/ n hijab m

hijack /'haɪdʒæk/ vt sequestrar ● n sequestro m. **~er** n (of plane) pirata (do ar) m

hike /haɪk/ n caminhada no campo f ● vi fazer uma caminhada. **~r** /-ə(r)/ n excursionista mf, caminhante mf

hilarious /hɪ'leərɪəs/ a divertido, desopilante

hill /hɪl/ n colina f, monte m; (slope) ladeira f, subida f. **~y** a acidentado

hillside /'hɪlsaɪd/ n encosta f, vertente f

him /hɪm/ pron o (a ele); (after prep) ele; (to) ~ lhe; **I know** ~ conheço-o

himself /hɪm'self/ pron ele mesmo/ próprio; (reflexive) se; **by** ~ sozinho; **for** ~ para si mesmo/próprio; **to** ~ a/para si mesmo/próprio; **Peter** ~ **saw it** foi o próprio Pedro que o viu

hind /haɪnd/ a traseiro, posterior

hind|er /'hɪndə(r)/ vt empatar, estorvar; (prevent) impedir. **~rance** n estorvo m

hindsight /'haɪndsaɪt/ n **with** ~ em retrospecto, (P) em retrospetiva

Hindu /hɪn'duː/ n & a hindu mf. **~ism** /-ɪzəm/ n hinduísmo m

hinge /hɪndʒ/ n dobradiça f ● vi ~ **on** depender de

hint /hɪnt/ n insinuação f, indireta f; (advice) sugestão f; dica f 🄸 ● vt dar a entender, insinuar ● vi ~ **at** fazer alusão a

hip /hɪp/ n quadril m, anca f

hippie /'hɪpɪ/ n hippie mf

hippopotamus /hɪpə'pɒtəməs/ n (pl -muses) hipopótamo m

hire /'haɪə(r)/ vt alugar; ‹person› contratar ● n aluguel m, (P) aluguer m

his /hɪz/ a seu(s), sua(s), dele ● poss pron o(s) seu(s), a(s) sua(s), o(s) dele, a(s) dele; **it is** ~ é (o) dele or o seu

Hispanic /hɪs'pænɪk/ a hispânico

hiss /hɪs/ n silvo m; (for disapproval) assobio m, vaia f ● vt/i sibilar; (for disapproval) assobiar, vaiar

historian /hɪ'stɔːrɪən/ n historiador m

histor|y /'hɪstərɪ/ n história f. **~ic(al)** /hɪ'stɒrɪk(l)/ a histórico

hit /hɪt/ vt (pt hit, pres p hitting) atingir, bater em; (knock against, collide with) chocar com, ir de encontro a; (strike a target) acertar em; (find) descobrir; (affect) atingir; ~ **it off** dar-se bem (with com) ● vi ~ **on** dar com ● n pancada f; fig (success) sucesso m. **~-and-run** a (driver) que foge depois do desastre; **~-or-miss** a ao acaso

hitch /hɪtʃ/ vt atar, prender; (to a hook) enganchar; ~ **up** puxar para cima; ~ **a lift, ~-hike** viajar de carona or (P) boleia ● n sacão m; (snag) problema m. **~-hiker** n o que viaja de carona, boleia

HIV abbr (= human immunodeficiency virus) HIV m, (P) VIH m; **~-positive** soropositivo, (P) seropositivo; **to be ~-positive/negative** ser soropositivo/ soronegativo, (P) ser seropositivo/ seronegativo, ter um resultado positivo/ negativo no teste de VIH

hive /haɪv/ n colmeia f ● vt ~ **off** separar e tornar independente

hoard /hɔːd/ vt juntar, açambarcar ● n provisão f; (of valuables) tesouro m

hoarding /'hɔːdɪŋ/ n tapume m, outdoor m

hoarse /hɔːs/ a (-er, -est) rouco. **~ness** n rouquidão f

hoax /həʊks/ n (malicious) logro m, embuste m; (humorous) trote m ● vt (malicious) enganar, lograr; passar um trote, pregar uma peça em

hob /hɒb/ n placa f de aquecimento (do fogão)

hobble /'hɒbl/ vi coxear ● vt pear

hobby /'hɒbɪ/ n passatempo m favorito. ~ **horse** n fig tópico m favorito

hockey /'hɒkɪ/ n hóquei m

hoe /həʊ/ n enxada f ● vt trabalhar com enxada

hog /hɒg/ n porco m; (greedy person) glutão m ● vt (pt hogged) 🄸 açambarcar

hoist /hɔɪst/ vt içar ● n guindaste m, (P) monta-cargas m

hold¹ /həʊld/ vt (pt held) segurar; (contain) levar; (possess) ter, possuir; (occupy) ocupar; (keep, maintain) conservar, manter; (affirm) manter; ~ **on to** guardar; (cling to) agarrar-se a; ~ **one's breath** suster a respiração; ~ **one's tongue** calar-se; ~ **the line** não desligar; ~ **up** (support) sustentar; (delay) demorar; (rob) assaltar ● vi (of rope etc) aguentar(-se); ~ **back** reter; ~ **on** 🄸 esperar; ~ **out** resistir; ~ **with** aguentar ● n (influence) domínio m; **get** ~ **of** pôr as mãos em; fig apanhar. **~-up** n atraso m; Auto engarrafamento m; (robbery) assalto m. **~er** n detentor m; (of post, title etc) titular mf; (for object) suporte m

hold² /həʊld/ n (of ship, plane) porão m

holdall /'həʊldɔːl/ n saco m de viagem

holding /'həʊldɪŋ/ n (land) propriedade f; Comm ações fpl, valores mpl, holding m

hole /həʊl/ n buraco m ● vt abrir buraco(s) em, esburacar

holiday /'hɒlədeɪ/ n férias fpl; (day off; public) feriado m ● vi passar férias.

~maker n pessoa f em férias; (in summer) veranista mf, (P) veraneante mf

holiness /'həʊlɪnɪs/ n santidade f

Holland /'hɒlənd/ n Holanda f

hollow /'hɒləʊ/ a oco, vazio; fig falso; <cheeks> fundo; <sound> surdo ● n (in the ground) cavidade f; (in the hand) cova f

holly /'hɒlɪ/ n azevinho m

holster /'həʊlstə(r)/ n coldre m

holy /'həʊlɪ/ a (-ier, -iest) santo, sagrado; <water> benta; **H~ Ghost, H~ Spirit** Espírito m Santo

homage /'hɒmɪdʒ/ n homenagem f; **pay ~ to** prestar homenagem a

home /həʊm/ n casa f, lar m; (institution) lar m, asilo m; (country) país m natal ● a caseiro, doméstico; (of family) de família; Pol nacional, interno; <football match> em casa; **H~ Office** Ministério m do Interior; **~ town** cidade f or terra f natal; **~ truth** dura verdade f, verdade(s) f(pl) amarga(s) ● adv (at) **~** em casa; **come/go ~** vir/ir para casa; **make oneself at ~** não fazer cerimónia or (P) cerimónia. **~-made** a caseiro. **~less** a sem casa, desabrigado

homeland /'həʊmlænd/ n pátria f

homely /'həʊmlɪ/ a (-ier, -iest) (simple) simples; Amer (ugly) sem graça

homesick /'həʊmsɪk/ a **be ~** ter saudades (de casa)

homework /'həʊmwɜːk/ n trabalho m de casa, dever m de casa

homicide /'hɒmɪsaɪd/ n homicídio m; (person) homicida mf

homoeopath|y /həʊmɪˈɒpəθɪ/ n homeopatia f. **~ic** a homeopático

homosexual /hɒmə'sekʃʊəl/ a & n homossexual mf

honest /'ɒnɪst/ a honesto; (frank) franco. **~y** n honestidade f

honey /'hʌnɪ/ n mel m; 🔲 (darling) querido m; querida f; meu bem m

honeycomb /'hʌnɪkəʊm/ n favo m de mel

honeymoon /'hʌnɪmuːn/ n lua f de mel

honorary /'ɒnərərɪ/ a honorário

honour /'ɒnə(r)/ n honra f ● vt honrar. **~able** a honrado, honroso

hood /hʊd/ n capuz m; (car roof) capota f, (P) tejadilho m; Amer (bonnet) capô m, (P) capot m

hoodie /'hʊdɪ/ n moletom m com capuz, (P) sweatshirt f com capuz

hoodwink /'hʊdwɪŋk/ vt enganar

hoof /huːf/ n (pl -fs) casco m

hook /hʊk/ n gancho m; (on garment) colchete m; (for fishing) anzol m ● vt enganchar; <fish> apanhar, pescar; **off the ~** livre de dificuldades; <phone> desligado

hooked /hʊkt/ a **be ~ on** 🔲 ter o vício de, estar viciado em

hookey /'hʊkɪ/ n **play ~** Amer 🔲 fazer gazeta

hooligan /'huːlɪgən/ n desordeiro m

hoop /huːp/ n arco m; (of cask) cinta f

hooray /huːˈreɪ/ int & n = **HURRAH**

hoot /huːt/ n (of owl) pio m de mocho; (of horn) buzinada f; (jeer) apupo m ● vi (of owl) piar; (of horn) buzinar; (jeer) apupar. **~er** n buzina f; (of factory) sirene f

Hoover® /'huːvə(r)/ n aspirador de pó m, (P) aspirador m ● vt passar o aspirador

hop¹ /hɒp/ vi (pt hopped) saltar num pé só, (P) ao pé coxinho; **~ in** 🔲 subir, saltar 🔲; **~ it** 🔲 pôr-se a andar 🔲; **~ out** 🔲 descer, saltar 🔲 ● n salto m

hop² /hɒp/ n (plant) lúpulo m; **~s** espigas fpl de lúpulo

hope /həʊp/ n esperança f ● vt/i esperar; **~ for** esperar (ter). **~ful** a esperançoso; (promising) promissor; **be ~ful (that)** ter esperança (que), confiar (em que). **~fully** adv esperançosamente; (it is hoped that) é de esperar que. **~less** a desesperado, sem esperança; (incompetent) incapaz

horde /hɔːd/ n horda f

horizon /həˈraɪzn/ n horizonte m

horizontal /hɒrɪ'zɒntl/ a horizontal

hormone /'hɔːməʊn/ n hormônio m, (P) hormona f

horn /hɔːn/ n chifre m, corno m; (of car) buzina f; Mus trompa f. **~y** a caloso, calejado

hornet /'hɔːnɪt/ n vespão m

horoscope /'hɒrəskəʊp/ n horóscopo m

horrible /'hɒrəbl/ a horrível, horroroso

horrid /'hɒrɪd/ a horrível, horripilante

horrific /həˈrɪfɪk/ a horrífico

horr|or /'hɒrə(r)/ n horror m ● a (film etc) de terror. **~ify** vt horrorizar, horripilar

horse /hɔːs/ n cavalo m. **~ chestnut** n castanha-da-Índia f; **~ racing** n corrida f de cavalos, hipismo m; **~radish** n rábano m

horseback /'hɔːsbæk/ n **on ~** a cavalo

horseplay /'hɔːspleɪ/ n brincadeira f grosseira, abrutalhada f

horsepower /'hɔːspaʊə(r)/ n cavalo-vapor m

horseshoe /'hɔːsʃuː/ n ferradura f

horticultur|e /'hɔːtɪkʌltʃə(r)/ n horticultura f

hose /həʊz/ n **~(-pipe)** mangueira f ● vt regar com a mangueira

hospice /'hɒspɪs/ n hospício m; (for travellers) hospedaria f

hospit|able /hə'spɪtəbl/ a hospitaleiro. **~ality** /-'tæləti/ n hospitalidade f

hospital /'hɒspɪtl/ n hospital m

host[1] /həʊst/ n anfitrião m, dono m da casa. **~ess** n anfitriã f, dona f da casa

host[2] /həʊst/ n **a ~ of** uma multidão de, um grande número de

host[3] /həʊst/ n Relig hóstia f

hostage /'hɒstɪdʒ/ n refém m

hostel /'hɒstl/ n residência f de estudantes etc, pousada f

hostil|e /'hɒstaɪl/ a hostil. **~ity** /hɒ'stɪləti/ n hostilidade f

hot /hɒt/ a (hotter, hottest) quente; Culin picante; **be or feel ~** estar com or ter calor; **it is ~** está or faz calor; **~ dog** cachorro-quente m; **~ line** linha direta f esp entre chefes de estado; **~-water bottle** saco m de água quente ● vt/i (pt hotted) **~ up** 🄸 aquecer

hotbed /'hɒtbed/ n fig foco m

hotel /həʊ'tel/ n hotel m

hound /haʊnd/ n cão m de caça e de corrida, sabujo m ● vt acossar, perseguir

hour /'aʊə(r)/ n hora f. **~ly** adv de hora em hora ● a de hora em hora; **~ly pay** retribuição f horária; **paid ~ly** pago por hora

house[1] /haʊs/ n (pl **~s** /'haʊzɪz/) casa f; Pol câmara f; **on the ~** por conta da casa. **~-warming** n inauguração f da casa

house[2] /haʊz/ vt alojar; (store) arrecadar, guardar

houseboat /'haʊsbəʊt/ n casa f flutuante

household /'haʊshəʊld/ n família f, agregado m familiar. **~er** n ocupante mf; (owner) proprietário m

housekeep|er /'haʊskiːpə(r)/ n governanta f. **~ing** n (work) tarefas fpl domésticas

housewife /'haʊswaɪf/ n (pl **-wives**) dona f de casa

housework /'haʊswɜːk/ n tarefas fpl domésticas

housing /'haʊzɪŋ/ n alojamento m; **~ estate** zona f residencial

hovel /'hɒvl/ n casebre m, tugúrio m

hover /'hɒvə(r)/ vi pairar; (linger) deixar-se ficar, demorar-se

hovercraft /'hɒvəkrɑːft/ n (invar) aerobarco m, hovercraft m

how /haʊ/ adv como; **~ long/old is…?** que comprimento/idade tem…?; **~ far?** a que distância?; **~ many?** quantos?; **~ much?** quanto?; **~ often?** com que frequência; **~ pretty it is** como é lindo; **~ about a walk?** e se fôssemos dar uma volta?; **~ are you?** como vai?; **~ do you do?** muito prazer!; **and ~!** oh se é!

however /haʊ'evə(r)/ adv de qualquer maneira; (though) contudo, no entanto, todavia; **~ small it may be** por menor que seja

howl /haʊl/ n uivo m ● vi uivar

hub /hʌb/ n cubo m da roda; fig centro m. **~cap** n calota f, (P) tampão m da roda

hubbub /'hʌbʌb/ n chinfrim m

huddle /'hʌdl/ vt/i apinhar(-se); **~ together** aconchegar-se

huff /hʌf/ n **in a ~** com raiva, zangado

hug /hʌg/ vt (pt hugged) abraçar, apertar nos braços; (keep close to) chegar-se a ● n abraço m

huge /hjuːdʒ/ a enorme

hull /hʌl/ n (of ship) casco m

hullo /hə'ləʊ/ int & n = HALLO

hum /hʌm/ vt/i (pt hummed) cantar com a boca fechada; (of insect, engine) zumbir ● n zumbido m

human /'hjuːmən/ a humano ● n **~ (being)** ser m humano

humane /hjuː'meɪn/ a humano, compassivo

humanitarian /hjuːmænɪ'teəriən/ a humanitário

humanity /hjuː'mænəti/ n humanidade f

humbl|e /'hʌmbl/ a (-er, -est) humilde ● vt humilhar

humdrum /'hʌmdrʌm/ a monótono, rotineiro

humid /'hjuːmɪd/ a úmido, (P) húmido. **~ity** /-'mɪdəti/ n umidade f, (P) humidade f

humiliat|e /hjuː'mɪlieɪt/ vt humilhar. **~ion** /-'eɪʃn/ n humilhação f

h

humility /hjuːˈmɪlətɪ/ n humildade f

hum|our /ˈhjuːmə(r)/ n humor m ● vt fazer a vontade de. **~orous** a humorístico; ‹person› divertido, espirituoso

hump /hʌmp/ n corcova f; (of the back) corcunda f ● vt corcovar, arquear; **the ~** 🈁 a neura 🇮

hunch¹ /hʌntʃ/ vt curvar; **~ed up** curvado

hunch² /hʌntʃ/ n 🇮 palpite m

hunchback /ˈhʌntʃbæk/ n corcunda mf

hundred /ˈhʌndrəd/ a cem ● n centena f, cento m; **~s of** centenas de. **~th** a & n centésimo m

hundredweight /ˈhʌndrədweɪt/ n quintal m (= 50,8 kg, Amer = 45,36 kg)

hung /hʌŋ/ ▶ HANG

Hungar|y /ˈhʌŋgərɪ/ n Hungria f. **~ian** /-ˈgeərɪən/ a & n húngaro m

hunger /ˈhʌŋgə(r)/ n fome f ● vi **~ for** ter fome de; fig desejar vivamente, ansiar por

hungr|y /ˈhʌŋgrɪ/ a (**-ier**, **-iest**) esfomeado, faminto; **be ~y** ter fome, estar com fome

hunk /hʌŋk/ n grande naco m

hunt /hʌnt/ vt/i caçar ● n caça f; **~ for** andar à caça de, andar à procura de. **~er** n caçador m. **~ing** n caça f, caçada f

hurdle /ˈhɜːdl/ n obstáculo m

hurl /hɜːl/ vt arremessar, lançar com força

hurrah, hurray /hʊˈrɑː, hʊˈreɪ/ int & n hurra m, viva m

hurricane /ˈhʌrɪkən/ n furacão m

hurried /ˈhʌrɪd/ a apressado. **~ly** adv apressadamente, às pressas

hurry /ˈhʌrɪ/ vt/i apressar(-se), despachar(-se) ● n pressa f; **be in a ~** estar com ou ter pressa; **do sth in a ~** fazer algo à pressa; **~ up!** ande logo, (P) despache-se

hurt /hɜːt/ vt (pt hurt) fazer mal a; (injure, offend) magoar, ferir ● vi doer ● a magoado, ferido ● n mal m; ‹feelings› mágoa f. **~ful** a prejudicial; ‹remark etc› que magoa

hurtle /ˈhɜːtl/ vi despenhar-se; (move rapidly) precipitar-se ● vt arremessar

husband /ˈhʌzbənd/ n marido m, esposo m

hush /hʌʃ/ vt (fazer) calar; **~ up** abafar, encobrir ● vi calar-se; **~!** silêncio! ● n silêncio m. **~-hush** a 🇮 muito em segredo

husky /ˈhʌskɪ/ a (**-ier**, **-iest**) (hoarse) rouco, enrouquecido; (burly) corpulento ● n cão m esquimó

hustle /ˈhʌsl/ vt empurrar, dar encontrões a ● n empurrão m; **~ and bustle** grande movimento m, azáfama f

hut /hʌt/ n cabana f, barraca f de madeira

hutch /hʌtʃ/ n coelheira f

hybrid /ˈhaɪbrɪd/ a & n híbrido m. **~ car** n carro m híbrido

hydraulic /haɪˈdrɔːlɪk/ a hidráulico

hydroelectric /haɪdrəʊˈlektrɪk/ a hidrelétrico, (P) hidroeléctrico

hydrogen /ˈhaɪdrədʒən/ n hidrogênio m, (P) hidrogénio m

hygiene /ˈhaɪdʒiːn/ n higiene f

hygienic /haɪˈdʒiːnɪk/ a higiênico, (P) higiénico

hymn /hɪm/ n hino m, cântico m

hyper- /ˈhaɪpə(r)/ pref hiper-

hypermarket /ˈhaɪpəmɑːkɪt/ n hipermercado m

hyphen /ˈhaɪfn/ n hífen m, traço de união m. **~ate** vt hifenizar

hypno|sis /hɪpˈnəʊsɪs/ n hipnose f. **~tic** /-ˈnɒtɪk/ a hipnótico

hypnot|ize /ˈhɪpnətaɪz/ vt hipnotizar. **~ism** /-ɪzəm/ n hipnotismo m

hypochondriac /haɪpəˈkɒndrɪæk/ n hipocondríaco m

hypocrisy /hɪˈpɒkrəsɪ/ n hipocrisia f

hypocrit|e /ˈhɪpəkrɪt/ n hipócrita mf. **~ical** /-ˈkrɪtɪkl/ a hipócrita

hypodermic /haɪpəˈdɜːmɪk/ a hipodérmico ● n seringa f

hypothe|sis /haɪˈpɒθəsɪs/ n (pl **-theses** /-siːz/) hipótese f. **~tical** /-əˈθetɪkl/ a hipotético

hyster|ia /hɪˈstɪərɪə/ n histeria f. **~ical** /hɪˈsterɪkl/ a histérico

I i

I /aɪ/ pron eu

Iberian /aɪˈbɪːrɪən/ a ibérico ● n ibero m

ice /aɪs/ n gelo m; **~ hockey** hóquei m sobre o gelo; **~ lolly** picolé m ● vt/i gelar; ‹cake› cobrir com glacé or (P) glace ● vi **~ up** gelar. **~box** n Amer geladeira f, (P) frigorífico m; **~ (cream)** n sorvete m, (P) gelado m; **~ cube** n cubo m or pedra f de gelo; **~ pack** n saco m de gelo; **~ rink** n rinque m de patinagem, (P) patinagem f no gelo; **~ skating** n patinação f, (P) patinagem f no gelo

iceberg /'aɪsbɜːɡ/ n iceberg m; fig pedaço m de gelo

Iceland /'aɪslənd/ n Islândia f

icicle /'aɪsɪkl/ n pingente m de gelo

icing /'aɪsɪŋ/ n Culin cobertura f de açúcar, glacê m, (P) glace m

icy /'aɪsɪ/ a (-ier, -iest) gelado, gélido, glacial; <road> com gelo

idea /aɪ'dɪə/ n ideia f

ideal /aɪ'dɪəl/ a & n ideal m. **~ize** vt idealizar. **~ly** adv idealmente

idealis|t /aɪ'dɪəlɪst/ n idealista mf. **~m** /-zəm/ n idealismo m. **~tic** /-'lɪstɪk/ a idealista

identical /aɪ'dentɪkl/ a idêntico

identif|y /aɪ'dentɪfaɪ/ vt identificar ● vi **~y with** identificar-se com. **~ication** /-ɪ'keɪʃn/ n identificação f

identity /aɪ'dentətɪ/ n identidade f; **~ card** carteira f de identidade, (P) bilhete m de identidade

ideolog|y /aɪdɪ'ɒlədʒɪ/ n ideologia f. **~ical** /-ɪə'lɒdʒɪkl/ ideológico

idiom /'ɪdɪəm/ n idioma m; (phrase) expressão f idiomática. **~atic** /-'mætɪk/ a idiomático

idiosyncrasy /ɪdɪə'sɪŋkrəsɪ/ n idiossincrasia f, peculiaridade f

idiot /'ɪdɪət/ n idiota mf. **~ic** /-'ɒtɪk/ a idiota

idl|e /'aɪdl/ a (-er, -est) (not active; lazy) ocioso; (unemployed) sem trabalho; (of machines) parado; fig (useless) inútil ● vt/i (of engine) estar em ponto morto. **~eness** n ociosidade f

idol /'aɪdl/ n ídolo m. **~ize** vt idolatrar

idyllic /ɪ'dɪlɪk/ a idílico

i.e. abbr isto é, quer dizer

if /ɪf/ conj se

igloo /'ɪɡluː/ n iglu m

ignite /ɪɡ'naɪt/ vt/i inflamar(-se), acender; (catch fire) pegar fogo; (set fire to) atear fogo a

ignition /ɪɡ'nɪʃn/ n Auto ignição f; **~ (key)** chave f de ignição

ignoran|t /'ɪɡnərənt/ a ignorante; **be ~t** of ignorar. **~ce** n ignorância f

ignore /ɪɡ'nɔː(r)/ vt não fazer caso de, passar por cima de; <person in the street etc> fingir não ver

ill /ɪl/ a (sick) doente; **~ at ease** pouco à vontade; **~ will** má vontade f, animosidade f ● adv mal ● n mal m. **~-advised** a pouco aconselhável; **~-bred** a mal-educado; **~-fated** a malfadado; **~-treat** vt maltratar

illegal /ɪ'liːɡl/ a ilegal

illegible /ɪ'ledʒəbl/ a ilegível

illegitima|te /ɪlɪ'dʒɪtɪmət/ a ilegítimo. **~cy** n ilegitimidade f

illitera|te /ɪ'lɪtərət/ a analfabeto; (uneducated) iletrado. **~cy** n analfabetismo m

illness /'ɪlnɪs/ n doença f

illogical /ɪ'lɒdʒɪkl/ a ilógico

illuminat|e /ɪ'luːmɪneɪt/ vt iluminar; (explain) esclarecer. **~ion** /-'neɪʃn/ n iluminação f. **~ions** npl luminárias fpl

illusion /ɪ'luːʒn/ n ilusão f

illusory /ɪ'luːsərɪ/ a ilusório

illustrat|e /'ɪləstreɪt/ vt ilustrar. **~ion** /-'streɪʃn/ n ilustração f

illustrious /ɪ'lʌstrɪəs/ a ilustre

image /'ɪmɪdʒ/ n imagem f; **(public) ~** imagem f pública

imaginary /ɪ'mædʒɪnərɪ/ a imaginário

imaginat|ion /ɪmædʒɪ'neɪʃn/ n imaginação f. **~ive** /ɪ'mædʒɪnətɪv/ a imaginativo

imagin|e /ɪ'mædʒɪn/ vt imaginar. **~able** a imaginável

imbalance /ɪm'bæləns/ n desequilíbrio m

imbecile /'ɪmbəsiːl/ a & n imbecil mf

imitat|e /'ɪmɪteɪt/ vt imitar. **~ion** /-'teɪʃn/ n imitação f

immaculate /ɪ'mækjʊlət/ a imaculado; (impeccable) impecável

immaterial /ɪmə'tɪərɪəl/ a (of no importance) irrelevante; **that's ~ to me** para mim tanto faz

immature /ɪmə'tjʊə(r)/ a imaturo

immediate /ɪ'miːdɪət/ a imediato. **~ly** adv imediatamente ● conj logo que, assim que

immens|e /ɪ'mens/ a imenso

immers|e /ɪ'mɜːs/ vt mergulhar, imergir; **be ~ed in** fig estar imerso em. **~ion** /-ʃn/ n imersão f; **~ion heater** aquecedor m de água elétrico

immigr|ate /'ɪmɪɡreɪt/ vi imigrar. **~ant** n & a imigrante mf, imigrado m. **~ation** /-'ɡreɪʃn/ n imigração f

imminen|t /'ɪmɪnənt/ a iminente

i

immobil|e /ɪˈməʊbaɪl/ a imóvel. **~ize** /-əlaɪz/ vt imobilizar

immoral /ɪˈmɒrəl/ a imoral. **~ity** /ɪməˈrælətɪ/ n imoralidade f

immortal /ɪˈmɔːtl/ a imortal. **~ity** /-ˈtælətɪ/ n imortalidade f. **~ize** vt imortalizar

immun|e /ɪˈmjuːn/ a imune; imunizado (**from** contra). **~ity** n imunidade f

imp /ɪmp/ n diabrete m

impact /ˈɪmpækt/ n impacto m

impair /ɪmˈpeə(r)/ vt deteriorar; (damage) prejudicar

impart /ɪmˈpɑːt/ vt comunicar; transmitir (**to** a)

impartial /ɪmˈpɑːʃl/ a imparcial. **~ity** /-ʃɪˈælətɪ/ n imparcialidade f

impassable /ɪmˈpɑːsəbl/ a ‹road, river› impraticável, intransitável; ‹barrier etc› intransponível

impatien|t /ɪmˈpeɪʃənt/ a impaciente. **~ce** n impaciência f

impeccable /ɪmˈpekəbl/ a impecável

impede /ɪmˈpiːd/ vt impedir, estorvar

impediment /ɪmˈpedɪmənt/ n impedimento m, obstáculo m; (speech) ~ defeito (na fala) m

impel /ɪmˈpel/ vt (pt impelled) impelir; forçar (**to do** a fazer)

impending /ɪmˈpendɪŋ/ a iminente

impenetrable /ɪmˈpenɪtrəbl/ a impenetrável

imperative /ɪmˈperətɪv/ a imperativo; ‹need etc› imperioso ● n imperativo m

imperceptible /ɪmpəˈseptəbl/ a imperceptível, (P) imperceptível

imperfect /ɪmˈpɜːfɪkt/ a imperfeito. **~ion** /-əˈfekʃn/ n imperfeição f

imperial /ɪmˈpɪərɪəl/ a imperial; (of measures) legal na GB. **~ism** /-lɪzəm/ n imperialismo m

impersonal /ɪmˈpɜːsənl/ a impessoal

impersonat|e /ɪmˈpɜːsəneɪt/ vt fazer-se passar por; Theat fazer or representar (o papel) de. **~ion** /-ˈneɪʃn/ n imitação f

impetuous /ɪmˈpetʃʊəs/ a impetuoso

impetus /ˈɪmpɪtəs/ n ímpeto m

impinge /ɪmˈpɪndʒ/ vi ~ **on** afetar; (encroach) infringir

implacable /ɪmˈplækəbl/ a implacável

implant /ɪmˈplɑːnt/ vt implantar

implement¹ /ˈɪmplɪmənt/ n instrumento m, utensílio m

implement² /ˈɪmplɪment/ vt implementar, executar

implicit /ɪmˈplɪsɪt/ a implícito; (unquestioning) absoluto, incondicional

implore /ɪmˈplɔː(r)/ vt implorar, suplicar, rogar

imply /ɪmˈplaɪ/ vt implicar; (hint) sugerir, dar a entender, insinuar

impolite /ɪmpəˈlaɪt/ a indelicado, incorreto

import¹ /ɪmˈpɔːt/ vt importar. **~er** n importador m

import² /ˈɪmpɔːt/ n importação f; (meaning) significado m; (importance) importância f

importan|t /ɪmˈpɔːtnt/ a importante. **~ce** n importância f

impos|e /ɪmˈpəʊz/ vt impôr; (inflict) infligir ● vi ~**e on** abusar de. **~ition** /-əˈzɪʃn/ n imposição f; (unfair burden) abuso m

imposing /ɪmˈpəʊzɪŋ/ a imponente

impossib|le /ɪmˈpɒsəbl/ a impossível. **~ility** /-ˈbɪlətɪ/ n impossibilidade f

impostor /ɪmˈpɒstə(r)/ n impostor m

impoten|t /ˈɪmpətənt/ a impotente. **~ce** n impotência f

impoverish /ɪmˈpɒvərɪʃ/ vt empobrecer

impracticable /ɪmˈpræktɪkəbl/ a impraticável

impractical /ɪmˈpræktɪkl/ a pouco prático

imprecise /ɪmprɪˈsaɪs/ a impreciso

impregnate /ˈɪmpregneɪt/ vt impregnar (**with** de)

impresario /ɪmprɪˈsɑːrɪəʊ/ n (pl -os) empresário m

impress /ɪmˈpres/ vt impressionar, causar impressão a; (imprint) imprimir; ~ **sth on sb** inculcar algo em alguém

impression /ɪmˈpreʃn/ n impressão f. **~able** a impressionável. **~ist** n impressionista mf

impressive /ɪmˈpresɪv/ a impressionante, imponente

imprint¹ /ˈɪmprɪnt/ n impressão f, marca f

imprint² /ɪmˈprɪnt/ vt imprimir

imprison /ɪmˈprɪzn/ vt prender, aprisionar. **~ment** n aprisionamento m, prisão f

improbab|le /ɪmˈprɒbəbl/ a improvável

impromptu /ɪmˈprɒmptjuː/ a & adv
de improviso ● n impromptu m

improper /ɪmˈprɒpə(r)/ a impróprio;
(indecent) indecente, pouco decente;
(wrong) incorreto

improve /ɪmˈpruːv/ vt/i melhorar; ~ on
aperfeiçoar. ~ment n melhoria f; (in
house etc) melhoramento m; (in health)
melhoras fpl

improvis|e /ˈɪmprəvaɪz/ vt/i
improvisar. ~ation /-ˈzeɪʃn/ n
improvisação f

imprudent /ɪmˈpruːdnt/ a
imprudente

impuden|t /ˈɪmpjʊdənt/ a descarado,
insolente. ~ce n descaramento m,
insolência f

impulse /ˈɪmpʌls/ n impulso m

impulsive /ɪmˈpʌlsɪv/ a impulsivo

impur|e /ɪmˈpjʊə(r)/ a impuro. ~ity n
impureza f

in /ɪn/ prep em, dentro de; ~ Lisbon/
English em Lisboa/inglês; ~ winter no
inverno; ~ an hour (at end of, within)
numa hora; ~ the rain na/à chuva;
~ doing ao fazer; ~ the evening à
tardinha; the best ~ o melhor em ● adv
dentro; (at home) em casa; (in fashion)
na moda; we are ~ for vamos ter ● n
the ~s and outs meandros mpl. ~-laws
npl 🆃 sogros mpl; ~-patient n doente m
internado

inability /ɪnəˈbɪlətɪ/ n incapacidade f
(to do para fazer)

inaccessible /ɪnækˈsesəbl/ a
inacessível

inaccura|te /ɪnˈækjərət/ a inexato.
~cy n inexatidão f, falta f de rigor

inaction /ɪnˈækʃn/ n inação f

inactiv|e /ɪnˈæktɪv/ a inativo. ~ity
/-ˈtɪvətɪ/ n inação f

inadequa|te /ɪnˈædɪkwət/ a
inadequado, impróprio; (insufficient)
insuficiente. ~cy n inadequação f;
(insufficiency) insuficiência f

inadvertently /ɪnədˈvɜːtəntlɪ/ adv
inadvertidamente; (unintentionally) sem
querer, sem ser por mal

inadvisable /ɪnədˈvaɪzəbl/ a
desaconselhável, não aconselhável

inane /ɪˈneɪn/ a tolo, oco

inanimate /ɪnˈænɪmət/ a inanimado

inappropriate /ɪnəˈprəʊprɪət/ a
impróprio, inadequado

inarticulate /ɪnɑːˈtɪkjʊlət/ a
inarticulado; (of person) incapaz de se

exprimir claramente

inattentive /ɪnəˈtentɪv/ a desatento

inaugural /ɪˈnɔːgjʊrəl/ a inaugural

inaugurat|e /ɪˈnɔːgjʊreɪt/ vt
inaugurar. ~ion /-ˈreɪʃn/ n inauguração f

inauspicious /ɪnɔːˈspɪʃəs/ a pouco
auspicioso

inborn /ɪnˈbɔːn/ a inato

inbox /ˈɪnbɒks/ n caixa f de entrada

inbred /ɪnˈbred/ a inato, congênito, (P)
congénito

incalculable /ɪnˈkælkjʊləbl/ a
incalculável

incapable /ɪnˈkeɪpəbl/ a incapaz

incendiary /ɪnˈsendɪərɪ/ a incendiário
● n bomba f incendiária

incense[1] /ˈɪnsens/ n incenso m

incense[2] /ɪnˈsens/ vt exasperar,
enfurecer

incentive /ɪnˈsentɪv/ n incentivo,
estímulo

incessant /ɪnˈsesənt/ a incessante. ~ly
adv incessantemente, sem cessar

incest /ˈɪnsest/ n incesto m. ~uous
/ɪnˈsestjʊəs/ a incestuoso

inch /ɪntʃ/ n polegada f (= 2,54 cm)
● vt/i avançar palmo a palmo or pouco a
pouco; within an ~ of a um passo de

incidence /ˈɪnsɪdəns/ n incidência f;
(rate) percentagem f

incident /ˈɪnsɪdənt/ n incidente m

incidental /ɪnsɪˈdentl/ a incidental,
acessório; (casual) acidental; ⟨expenses⟩
eventuais; ⟨music⟩ de cena, incidental.
~ly adv incidentalmente; (by the way) a
propósito

incinerat|e /ɪnˈsɪnəreɪt/ vt incinerar.
~or n incinerador m

incision /ɪnˈsɪʒn/ n incisão f

incisive /ɪnˈsaɪsɪv/ a incisivo

incite /ɪnˈsaɪt/ vt incitar, instigar.
~ment n incitamento m

inclination /ɪnklɪˈneɪʃn/ n inclinação
f, tendência f

incline[1] /ɪnˈklaɪn/ vt/i inclinar(-se); be
~d to inclinar-se para; (have tendency)
ter tendência para

incline[2] /ˈɪnklaɪn/ n inclinação f,
declive m

inclu|de /ɪnˈkluːd/ vt incluir; (in letter)
enviar junto or em anexo. ~ding prep
inclusive. ~sion n inclusão f

inclusive /ɪnˈkluːsɪv/ a & adv inclusive;
be ~ of incluir

incognito /ɪnkɒgˈniːtəʊ/ a & adv incógnito

incoherent /ɪnkəˈhɪərənt/ a incoerente

income /ˈɪŋkʌm/ n rendimento m; ~ **tax** imposto sobre a renda, (P) imposto sobre o rendimento

incoming /ˈɪnkʌmɪŋ/ a ‹tide› enchente; ‹tenant etc› novo

incomparable /ɪnˈkɒmpərəbl/ a incomparável

incompatible /ɪnkəmˈpætəbl/ a incompatível

incompeten|t /ɪnˈkɒmpɪtənt/ a incompetente. ~**ce** n incompetência f

incomplete /ɪnkəmˈpliːt/ a incompleto

incomprehensible /ɪnkɒmprɪˈhensəbl/ a incompreensível

inconceivable /ɪnkənˈsiːvəbl/ a inconcebível

inconclusive /ɪnkənˈkluːsɪv/ a inconcludente

incongruous /ɪnˈkɒŋgrʊəs/ a incongruente; (absurd) absurdo

inconsiderate /ɪnkənˈsɪdərət/ a impensado, inconsiderado; (lacking in regard) pouco atencioso, sem consideração (pelos sentimentos etc de outrem)

inconsisten|t /ɪnkənˈsɪstənt/ a incoerente; (at variance) contraditório; ~**t with** incompatível com. ~**cy** n incoerência f

inconspicuous /ɪnkənˈspɪkjʊəs/ a que não dá nas vistas, que não chama a atenção

incontinen|t /ɪnˈkɒntɪnənt/ a incontinente. ~**ce** n incontinência f

inconvenien|t /ɪnkənˈviːnɪənt/ a inconveniente, incômodo, (P) incómodo. ~**ce** n inconveniência f; (drawback) inconveniente m ● vt incomodar

incorporate /ɪnˈkɔːpəreɪt/ vt incorporar; (include) incluir

incorrect /ɪnkəˈrekt/ a incorreto

incorrigible /ɪnˈkɒrɪdʒəbl/ a incorrigível

increas|e[1] /ɪnˈkriːs/ vt/i aumentar. ~**ing** a crescente. ~**ingly** adv cada vez mais

increase[2] /ˈɪnkriːs/ n aumento m; on the ~ aumentando, crescendo, (P) em crescimento, em alta

incredible /ɪnˈkredəbl/ a incrível

incredulous /ɪnˈkredjʊləs/ a incrédulo

incriminat|e /ɪnˈkrɪmɪneɪt/ vt incriminar

incubat|e /ˈɪnkjʊbeɪt/ vt incubar. ~**ion** /-ˈbeɪʃn/ n incubação f. ~**or** n incubadora f

incur /ɪnˈkɜːr/ vt (pt incurred) ‹displeasure, expense etc› incorrer em; ‹debts› contrair

incurable /ɪnˈkjʊərəbl/ a incurável, que não tem cura

indebted /ɪnˈdetɪd/ a ~ **to sb** em dívida (para) com alguém (for por)

indecen|t /ɪnˈdiːsnt/ a indecente. ~**t assault** n atentado m contra o pudor. ~**cy** n indecência f

indecision /ɪndɪˈsɪʒn/ n indecisão f

indecisive /ɪndɪˈsaɪsɪv/ a inconcludente, não decisivo; (hesitating) indeciso

indeed /ɪnˈdiːd/ adv realmente, deveras, mesmo; (in fact) de fato, (P) facto; **very much** ~ muitíssimo

indefinite /ɪnˈdefɪnət/ a indefinido; (time) indeterminado. ~**ly** adv indefinidamente

indent /ɪnˈdent/ vt ‹notch› recortar; Typ entrar. ~**ation** /-ˈteɪʃn/ n recorte m; Typ entrada f

independen|t /ɪndɪˈpendənt/ a independente. ~**ce** n independência f

indescribable /ɪndɪˈskraɪbəbl/ a indescritível

indestructible /ɪndɪˈstrʌktəbl/ a indestrutível

indeterminate /ɪndɪˈtɜːmɪnət/ a indeterminado

index /ˈɪndeks/ n (pl indexes) (in book) índice m; (in library) catálogo m ● vt indexar; ~ **card** ficha (de fichário), (P) ficheiro f; ~ **finger** index m, (dedo) indicador m. ~**-linked** a ligado ao índice de inflação

India /ˈɪndɪə/ n Índia f. ~**n** a & n (of India) indiano (m); (American) índio (m)

indicat|e /ˈɪndɪkeɪt/ vt indicar. ~**ion** /-ˈkeɪʃn/ n indicação f. ~**or** n indicador m; Auto pisca-pisca m; (board) quadro m

indicative /ɪnˈdɪkətɪv/ a & n indicativo m

indict /ɪnˈdaɪt/ vt acusar. ~**ment** n acusação f

indifferen|t /ɪnˈdɪfrənt/ a indiferente; (not good) medíocre. ~**ce** n indiferença f

indigenous /ɪnˈdɪdʒɪnəs/ a indígena; natural (**to** de)

indigest|ion /ɪndɪˈdʒestʃən/ n
indigestão f. **~ible** /-ˈtəbl/ a indigesto

indign|ant /ɪnˈdɪgnənt/ a indignado.
~ation /-ˈneɪʃn/ n indignação f

indirect /ɪndɪˈrekt/ a indireto. **~ly** adv
indiretamente

indiscr|eet /ɪndɪˈskriːt/ a indiscreto;
(not wary) imprudente. **~etion** /-ˈeʃn/
n indiscrição f; (action, remark etc)
deslize m

indiscriminate /ɪndɪˈskrɪmɪnət/
a que tem falta de discernimento;
(random) indiscriminado. **~ly** adv
sem discernimento; (at random)
indiscriminadamente, ao acaso

indispensable /ɪndɪˈspensəbl/
a indispensável

indispos|ed /ɪndɪˈspəʊzd/
a indisposto

indisputable /ɪndɪˈspjuːtəbl/
a indisputável, incontestável

indistinct /ɪndɪˈstɪŋkt/ a indistinto

indistinguishable /ɪndɪˈstɪŋgwɪʃ-
əbl/ a indistinguível, imperceptível;
(identical) indiferenciável

individual /ɪndɪˈvɪdʒʊəl/ a
individual ● n indivíduo m. **~ity**
/-ˈælətɪ/ n individualidade f. **~ly** adv
individualmente

indivisible /ɪndɪˈvɪzəbl/ a indivisível

indoctrinat|e /ɪnˈdɒktrɪneɪt/ vt (en)
doutrinar

indolen|t /ˈɪndələnt/ a indolente. **~ce**
n indolência f

indoor /ˈɪndɔː(r)/ a (de) interior,
interno; (under cover) coberto; ‹games›
de salão. **~s** /ɪnˈdɔːz/ adv dentro de
casa, no interior

induce /ɪnˈdjuːs/ vt induzir, levar;
(cause) causar, provocar

indulge /ɪnˈdʌldʒ/ vt satisfazer;
(spoil) fazer a(s) vontade(s) de ● vi **~ in**
entregar-se a

indulgen|t /ɪnˈdʌldʒənt/ a indulgente.
~ce n (leniency) indulgência f; (desire)
satisfação f

industrial /ɪnˈdʌstrɪəl/ a industrial;
‹unrest etc› trabalhista; ‹action›
reivindicativo; **~ estate** zona f
industrial. **~ist** n industrial m. **~ized** a
industrializado

industrious /ɪnˈdʌstrɪəs/ a
trabalhador, aplicado

industry /ˈɪndəstrɪ/ n indústria f; (zeal)
aplicação f, diligência f, zelo m

inebriated /ɪˈniːbrɪeɪtɪd/ a
embriagado, ébrio

inedible /ɪˈnedɪbl/ a não comestível

ineffective /ɪnɪˈfektɪv/ a ineficaz;
‹person› ineficiente, incapaz

ineffectual /ɪnɪˈfektʃʊəl/ a ineficaz,
improfícuo

inefficien|t /ɪnɪˈfɪʃnt/ a ineficiente.
~cy n ineficiência f

ineligible /ɪnˈelɪdʒəbl/ a inelegível;
(undesirable) indesejável; **be ~ for** não
ter direito a

inept /ɪˈnept/ a inepto

inequality /ɪnɪˈkwɒlətɪ/ n
desigualdade f

inevitable /ɪnˈevɪtəbl/ a inevitável,
fatal

inexcusable /ɪnɪkˈskjuːzəbl/
a indesculpável, imperdoável

inexhaustible /ɪnɪgˈzɔːstəbl/
a inesgotável, inexaurível

inexpensive /ɪnɪkˈspensɪv/ a barato,
em conta

inexperience /ɪnɪkˈspɪərɪəns/ n
inexperiência f, falta f de experiência.
~d a inexperiente

inexplicable /ɪnˈeksplɪkəbl/
a inexplicável

infallib|le /ɪnˈfæləbl/ a infalível

infam|ous /ˈɪnfəməs/ a infame. **~y** n
infâmia f

infan|t /ˈɪnfənt/ n bebé m, (P) bebé
m; (child) criança f. **~cy** n infância f;
(babyhood) primeira infância f

infantile /ˈɪnfəntaɪl/ a infantil

infantry /ˈɪnfəntrɪ/ n infantaria f

infatuat|ed /ɪnˈfætʃʊeɪtɪd/ a **~ed
with** cego or perdido por. **~ion** /-ˈeɪʃn/ n
cegueira f, paixão f

infect /ɪnˈfekt/ vt infetar, (P) infectar;
~ sb with contagiar ou contaminar
alguém com. **~ion** /-ʃn/ n infecção f,
(P) infeção f, contágio m. **~ious** /-ʃəs/ a
infeccioso, contagioso

infer /ɪnˈfɜː(r)/ vt (pt inferred) inferir,
deduzir. **~ence** /ˈɪnfərəns/ n inferência f

inferior /ɪnˈfɪərɪə(r)/ a inferior; ‹work
etc› de qualidade inferior ● n inferior mf;
(in rank) subalterno m. **~ity** /-ˈɒrətɪ/ n
inferioridade f

infernal /ɪnˈfɜːnl/ a infernal

infertil|e /ɪnˈfɜːtaɪl/ a infértil,
estéril. **~ity** /-əˈtɪlətɪ/ n infertilidade f,
esterilidade f

infest /ɪnˈfest/ vt infestar (**with** de).
~ation n infestação f

i

infidelity /ɪnfɪˈdelətɪ/ n infidelidade f

infiltrat|e /ˈɪnfɪltreɪt/ vt/i infiltrar(-se). **~ion** /-ˈtreɪʃn/ n infiltração f

infinite /ˈɪnfɪnət/ a & n infinito m. **~ly** adv infinitamente

infinitive /ɪnˈfɪnətɪv/ n infinitivo m

infinity /ɪnˈfɪnətɪ/ n infinidade f, infinito m

infirm /ɪnˈfɜːm/ a débil, fraco

inflam|e /ɪnˈfleɪm/ vt inflamar. **~mable** /-æməbl/ a inflamável. **~mation** /-əˈmeɪʃn/ n inflamação f

inflate /ɪnˈfleɪt/ vt ‹balloon etc› encher de ar; ‹prices› causar inflação de

inflation /ɪnˈfleɪʃn/ n inflação f. **~ary** a inflacionário

inflection /ɪnˈflekʃn/ n inflexão f; Gram flexão f, desinência f

inflexible /ɪnˈfleksəbl/ a inflexível

inflict /ɪnˈflɪkt/ vt infligir; impor (**on** a)

influence /ˈɪnflʊəns/ n influência f ● vt influenciar, influir sobre

influential /ɪnflʊˈenʃl/ a influente

influenza /ɪnflʊˈenzə/ n gripe f

influx /ˈɪnflʌks/ n afluência f, influxo m

inform /ɪnˈfɔːm/ vt informar; **~ against** or **on** denunciar; **keep ~ed** manter ao corrente or a par. **~ant** n informante mf. **~er** n delator m, denunciante mf

informal /ɪnˈfɔːml/ a informal; (simple) simples; sem cerimônia; (P) cerimónia; (unofficial) oficioso; (colloquial) familiar; ‹dress› de passeio, à vontade; ‹dinner, gathering› íntimo. **~ity** /-ˈmælətɪ/ n informalidade f; (simplicity) simplicidade f; (intimacy) intimidade f. **~ly** adv informalmente, sem cerimônia, (P) cerimónia, à vontade

information /ɪnfəˈmeɪʃn/ n informação f; (facts, data) informações fpl; **~ technology** tecnologia f de informação

informative /ɪnˈfɔːmətɪv/ a informativo

infrared /ɪnfrəˈred/ a infravermelho

infrequent /ɪnˈfriːkwənt/ a pouco frequente. **~ly** adv raramente

infringe /ɪnˈfrɪndʒ/ vt infringir; **~ on** transgredir; ‹rights› violar. **~ment** n infração f; (rights) violação f

infuriat|e /ɪnˈfjʊərieɪt/ vt enfurecer, enraivecer. **~ing** a enfurecedor, de enfurecer, de dar raiva

infus|e /ɪnˈfjuːz/ vt infundir, incutir; ‹herbs, tea› pôr de infusão. **~ion** /-ʒn/ n infusão f

ingen|ious /ɪnˈdʒiːnɪəs/ a engenhoso, bem pensado. **~uity** /-ɪˈnjuːətɪ/ n engenho m, habilidade f, imaginação f

ingenuous /ɪnˈdʒenjʊəs/ a cândido, ingênuo, (P) ingénuo

ingrained /ɪnˈɡreɪnd/ a arraigado, enraizado; ‹dirt› entranhado

ingratiate /ɪnˈɡreɪʃɪeɪt/ vt **~ o.s. with** insinuar-se junto de, cair nas or ganhar as boas graças de

ingratitude /ɪnˈɡrætɪtjuːd/ n ingratidão f

ingredient /ɪnˈɡriːdɪənt/ n ingrediente m

inhabit /ɪnˈhæbɪt/ vt habitar. **~able** a habitável. **~ant** n habitante mf

inhale /ɪnˈheɪl/ vt inalar, aspirar. **~r** /-ə(r)/ n inalador m

inherent /ɪnˈhɪərənt/ a inerente. **~ly** adv inerentemente, em si

inherit /ɪnˈherɪt/ vt herdar (**from** de). **~ance** n herança f

inhibit /ɪnˈhɪbɪt/ vt inibir; (prevent) impedir; **be ~ed** ser (um) inibido. **~ion** /-ˈbɪʃn/ n inibição f

inhospitable /ɪnˈhɒspɪtəbl/ a inóspito; (of person) inospitaleiro, pouco/nada hospitaleiro

inhuman /ɪnˈhjuːmən/ a desumano

inhumane /ɪnhjuːˈmeɪn/ a inumano, cruel

inimitable /ɪˈnɪmɪtəbl/ a inimitável

initial /ɪˈnɪʃl/ a & n inicial f ● vt (pt initialled) assinar com as iniciais, rubricar. **~ly** adv inicialmente

initiat|e /ɪˈnɪʃɪeɪt/ vt iniciar (**into** em); ‹scheme› lançar. **~ion** /-ˈeɪʃn/ n iniciação f; (start) início m

initiative /ɪˈnɪʃətɪv/ n iniciativa f

inject /ɪnˈdʒekt/ vt injetar; fig insuflar. **~ion** /-ʃn/ n injeção f

injure /ˈɪndʒə(r)/ vt (harm) fazer mal a, prejudicar, lesar; (hurt) ferir

injury /ˈɪndʒərɪ/ n ferimento m, lesão f; (wrong) mal m

injustice /ɪnˈdʒʌstɪs/ n injustiça f

ink /ɪŋk/ n tinta f

inkling /ˈɪŋklɪŋ/ n ideia f, suspeita f

inlaid /ɪnˈleɪd/ ▶ HIRE

inland /ˈɪnlənd/ a interior ● /ɪnˈlænd/ adv no interior, para o interior; **the I~ Revenue** o Fisco, a Receita Federal

inlay[1] /ɪnˈleɪ/ vt (pt inlaid) embutir, incrustar

inlay² /'ɪnleɪ/ n incrustação f, obturação f

inlet /'ɪnlet/ n braço m de mar, enseada f; Techn admissão f

inmate /'ɪnmeɪt/ n residente mf; (in hospital) internado m; (in prison) presidiário m

inn /ɪn/ n estalagem f

innate /ɪ'neɪt/ a inato

inner /'ɪnə(r)/ a interior, interno; fig íntimo; ~ **city** centro m da cidade. ~**most** a mais profundo, mais íntimo. ~ **tube** n câmara f de ar

innings /'ɪnɪŋz/ n Cricket vez f de bater; Pol período m no poder

innocen|t /'ɪnəsnt/ a & n inocente mf. ~**ce** n inocência f

innocuous /ɪ'nɒkjʊəs/ a inócuo, inofensivo

innovat|e /'ɪnəveɪt/ vi inovar. ~**ion** /-'veɪʃn/ n inovação f. ~**or** n inovador m

innuendo /ɪnjuː'endəʊ/ n (pl -oes) insinuação f, indireta f

innumerable /ɪ'njuːmərəbl/ a inumerável

inoculat|e /ɪ'nɒkjʊleɪt/ vt inocular. ~**ion** /-'leɪʃn/ n inoculação f, vacina f

inoffensive /ɪnə'fensɪv/ a inofensivo

inopportune /ɪn'ɒpətjuːn/ a inoportuno

inordinate /ɪ'nɔːdɪnət/ a excessivo, desmedido. ~**ly** adv excessivamente, desmedidamente

input /'ɪnpʊt/ n (data) dados mpl; Electr (power) energia f; (computer process) entrada f, dados mpl

inquest /'ɪnkwest/ n inquérito m

inquir|e /ɪn'kwaɪə(r)/ vi informar-se ● vt perguntar, indagar, inquirir; ~**e about** procurar informações sobre, indagar; ~**e into** inquirir, indagar. ~**ing** a ‹look› interrogativo; ‹mind› inquisitivo. ~**y** n (question) pergunta f; Jur inquérito m; (investigation) investigação f

inquisition /ɪnkwɪ'zɪʃn/ n inquisição f

inquisitive /ɪn'kwɪzətɪv/ a curioso, inquisitivo; (prying) intrometido, bisbilhoteiro

insan|e /ɪn'seɪn/ a louco, doido. ~**ity** /ɪn'sænətɪ/ n loucura f, demência f

insanitary /ɪn'sænɪtrɪ/ a insalubre, anti-higiénico, (P) anti-higiénico

insatiable /ɪn'seɪʃəbl/ a insaciável

inscri|be /ɪn'skraɪb/ vt inscrever; ‹book› dedicar. ~**ption** /-ɪpʃn/ n inscrição f; (in book) dedicatória f

inscrutable /ɪn'skruːtəbl/ a impenetrável, misterioso

insect /'ɪnsekt/ n inseto m

insecur|e /ɪnsɪ'kjʊə(r)/ a (not firm) inseguro, mal seguro; (unsafe) Psych inseguro. ~**ity** n insegurança f, falta f de segurança

insensitive /ɪn'sensɪtɪv/ a insensível

inseparable /ɪn'seprəbl/ a inseparável

insert¹ /ɪn'sɜːt/ vt inserir; ‹key› meter, colocar; (add) pôr, inserir. ~**ion** /-ʃn/ n inserção f

insert² /'ɪnsɜːt/ n coisa f inserida, enxerto m

inside /ɪn'saɪd/ n interior m; ~**s** 🄸 tripas fpl 🄸; ~ **out** de dentro para fora, do avesso; (thoroughly) por dentro e por fora, a fundo ● a interior, interno ● adv no interior, dentro, por dentro ● prep dentro de; (of time) em menos de

insight /'ɪnsaɪt/ n penetração f, perspicácia f; (glimpse) vislumbre m

insignificant /ɪnsɪg'nɪfɪkənt/ a insignificante

insincer|e /ɪnsɪn'sɪə(r)/ a insincero. ~**ity** /-'serətɪ/ n insinceridade f, falta f de sinceridade

insinuat|e /ɪn'sɪnjʊeɪt/ vt insinuar. ~**ion** /-'eɪʃn/ n (act) insinuação f; (hint) indireta f, insinuação f

insipid /ɪn'sɪpɪd/ a insípido, sem sabor

insist /ɪn'sɪst/ vt/i ~ **(on/that)** insistir (em/em que)

insisten|t /ɪn'sɪstənt/ a insistente. ~**ce** n insistência f

insolen|t /'ɪnsələnt/ a insolente. ~**ce** n insolência f

insoluble /ɪn'sɒljʊbl/ a insolúvel

insolvent /ɪn'sɒlvənt/ a insolvente

insomnia /ɪn'sɒmnɪə/ n insônia f, (P) insónia f

inspect /ɪn'spekt/ vt inspecionar, examinar; ‹tickets› fiscalizar; ‹passport› controlar; ‹troops› passar revista a. ~**ion** /-ʃn/ n inspeção f, exame m; ‹ticket› fiscalização f; ‹troops› revista f. ~**or** n inspetor m; (on train) fiscal m

inspir|e /ɪn'spaɪə(r)/ vt inspirar. ~**ation** /-ə'reɪʃn/ n inspiração f

instability /ɪnstə'bɪlətɪ/ n instabilidade f

install /ɪn'stɔːl/ vt instalar; ‹heater etc› montar, instalar. ~**ation** /-ə'leɪʃn/ n instalação f

instalment /ɪn'stɔːlmənt/ n prestação f; (of serial) episódio m

instance /'ɪnstəns/ n exemplo m, caso m; **for** ~ por exemplo; **in the first** ~ em primeiro lugar

instant /'ɪnstənt/ a imediato; ‹food› instantâneo ● n instante m. ~ **messaging** n mensagem f instantânea. ~**ly** adv imediatamente, logo

instantaneous /ɪnstən'teɪnɪəs/ a instantâneo

instead /ɪn'sted/ adv em vez disso, em lugar disso; ~ **of** em vez de, em lugar de

instigat|e /'ɪnstɪgeɪt/ vt instigar, incitar. ~**ion** /-'geɪʃn/ n instigação f. ~**or** n instigador m

instil /ɪn'stɪl/ vt (pt **instilled**) instilar, insuflar

instinct /'ɪnstɪŋkt/ n instinto m. ~**ive** /ɪn'stɪŋktɪv/ a instintivo

institut|e /'ɪnstɪtjuːt/ n instituto m ● vt instituir; ‹legal proceedings› intentar; ‹inquiry› ordenar. ~**ion** /-'tjuːʃn/ n instituição f; (school) estabelecimento m de ensino; (hospital) estabelecimento m hospitalar

instruct /ɪn'strʌkt/ vt instruir; (order) mandar, ordenar; ‹a solicitor etc› dar instruções a; ~ **sb in sth** ensinar algo a alguém. ~**ion** /-ʃn/ n instrução f. ~**ions** /-ʃnz/ npl instruções fpl, modo m de emprego; (orders) ordens fpl. ~**ive** a instrutivo. ~**or** n instrutor m

instrument /'ɪnstrʊmənt/ n instrumento m; ~ **panel** painel m de instrumentos

instrumental /ɪnstrʊ'mentl/ a instrumental; **be** ~ **in** ter um papel decisivo em. ~**ist** n instrumentalista mf

insubordinat|e /ɪnsə'bɔːdɪnət/ a insubordinado. ~**ion** /-'neɪʃn/ n insubordinação f

insufferable /ɪn'sʌfrəbl/ a intolerável, insuportável

insufficient /ɪnsə'fɪʃnt/ a insuficiente

insular /'ɪnsjʊlə(r)/ a insular; fig (narrow-minded) bitolado, limitado, (P) tacanho

insulat|e /'ɪnsjʊleɪt/ vt isolar; ~**ing tape** fita f isolante. ~**ion** /-'leɪʃn/ n isolamento m

insulin /'ɪnsjʊlɪn/ n insulina f

insult[1] /ɪn'sʌlt/ vt insultar, injuriar. ~**ing** a insultante, injurioso

insult[2] /'ɪnsʌlt/ n insulto m, injúria f

insur|e /ɪn'ʃʊə(r)/ vt segurar, pôr no seguro; Amer ▶ ENSURE. ~**ance** n seguro m; ~**ance policy** apólice f de seguro

insurmountable /ɪnsə'maʊntəbl/ a insuperável

intact /ɪn'tækt/ a intato, (P) intacto

intake /'ɪnteɪk/ n admissão f; Techn admissão f, entrada f; (of food) ingestão f

intangible /ɪn'tændʒəbl/ a intangível

integral /'ɪntɪgrəl/ a integral; **be an** ~ **part of** ser parte integrante de

integrat|e /'ɪntɪgreɪt/ vt/i integrar(-se); ~**ed circuit** circuito m integrado. ~**ion** /-'greɪʃn/ n integração f

integrity /ɪn'tegrətɪ/ n integridade f

intellect /'ɪntəlekt/ n intelecto m, inteligência f. ~**ual** /-'lektʃʊəl/ a & n intelectual m

intelligen|t /ɪn'telɪdʒənt/ a inteligente. ~**ce** n inteligência f; Mil informações fpl

intelligible /ɪn'telɪdʒəbl/ a inteligível

intend /ɪn'tend/ vt tencionar; (destine) reservar, destinar. ~**ed** a intencional, proposital

intens|e /ɪn'tens/ a intenso; ‹person› emotivo. ~**ely** adv intensamente; (very) extremamente. ~**ity** n intensidade f

intensif|y /ɪn'tensɪfaɪ/ vt intensificar. ~**ication** /-ɪ'keɪʃn/ n intensificação f

intensive /ɪn'tensɪv/ a intensivo; ~ **care** tratamento m intensivo

intent /ɪn'tent/ n intento m, desígnio m, propósito m ● a atento, concentrado; ~ **on** absorto em; (intending to) decidido a. ~**ly** adv atentamente

intention /ɪn'tenʃn/ n intenção f. ~**al** a intencional. ~**ally** adv de propósito

inter /ɪn'tɜː(r)/ vt (pt **interred**) enterrar

inter- /'ɪntə(r)/ pref inter-

interact /ɪntə'rækt/ vi agir uns sobre os outros. ~**ion** /-ʃn/ n interação f

intercede /ɪntə'siːd/ vi interceder

intercept /ɪntə'sept/ vt interceptar, (P) intercetar

interchange[1] /ɪntə'tʃeɪndʒ/ vt permutar, trocar. ~**able** a permutável

interchange[2] /'ɪntətʃeɪndʒ/ n permuta f, intercâmbio m; (road junction) trevo m de trânsito, (P) nó m

intercom /'ɪntəkɒm/ n interfone m, (P) intercomunicador m

interconnected /ɪntəkə'nektɪd/ a ‹facts, events etc› ligado

intercourse /'ɪntəkɔːs/ n (sexual) relações fpl sexuais

interest /'ɪntrəst/ n interesse m; (legal share) título m; (in finance) juro(s) *m(pl)*; **rate of ~** taxa *f* de juros ● *vt* interessar. **~ed** *a* interessado; **be ~ed in** interessar-se por. **~ing** *a* interessante

interface /'ɪntəfeɪs/ *n* interface *f*

interfer|e /ɪntə'fɪə(r)/ *vi* interferir; intrometer-se (**in** em); (*meddle, hinder*) interferir (**with** com); (*tamper*) mexer indevidamente (**with** em). **~ence** *n* interferência *f*

interim /'ɪntərɪm/ *n* **in the ~** nesse/ neste ínterim *m*, (P) interim *m* ● *a* interino, provisório

interior /ɪn'tɪərɪə(r)/ *a & n* interior *m*

interjection /ɪntə'dʒekʃn/ *n* interjeição *f*

interlock /ɪntə'lɒk/ *vt/i* entrelaçar; ‹*pieces of puzzle etc*› encaixar(-se); Mech ‹*wheels*› engrenar, engatar

intermarr|iage /ɪntə'mærɪdʒ/ *n* casamento *m* entre membros de diferentes famílias, raças etc; (*between near relations*) casamento *m* consanguíneo. **~y** *vi* ligar-se por casamento

intermediary /ɪntə'miːdɪərɪ/ *a & n* intermediário *m*

intermediate /ɪntə'miːdɪət/ *a* intermédio, intermediário

interminable /ɪn'tɜːmɪnəbl/ *a* interminável, infindável

intermission /ɪntə'mɪʃn/ *n* intervalo *m*

intermittent /ɪntə'mɪtnt/ *a* intermitente. **~ly** *adv* intermitentemente

intern /ɪn'tɜːn/ *vt* internar. **~ment** *n* internamento *m*

internal /ɪn'tɜːnl/ *a* interno, interior; *Amer* **the ~ Revenue** a Receita Federal, (P) o Fisco. **~ly** *adv* internamente, interiormente

international /ɪntə'næʃnəl/ *a & n* internacional *mf*

Internet /'ɪntənet/ *n* Internet *f*. **~ cafe** *n* lan house *f*, (P) cibercafé *m*

interpret /ɪn'tɜːprɪt/ *vt/i* interpretar. **~ation** /-'teɪʃn/ *n* interpretação *f*. **~er** *n* intérprete *mf*

interrogat|e /ɪn'terəgeɪt/ *vt* interrogar. **~ion** /-'geɪʃn/ *n* interrogação *f*; (*by police etc*) interrogatório *m*

interrogative /ɪntə'rɒgətɪv/ *a* interrogativo ● *n* (*pronoun*) pronome *m* interrogativo

interrupt /ɪntə'rʌpt/ *vt* interromper. **~ion** /-ʃn/ *n* interrupção *f*

intersect /ɪntə'sekt/ *vt/i* intersetar(-se), (P) intersectar(-se); ‹*roads*› cruzar-se.

~ion /-ʃn/ *n* intersecção *f*, (P) interseção *f*; (*crossroads*) cruzamento *m*

intersperse /ɪntə'spɜːs/ *vt* entremear, intercalar; (*scatter*) espalhar

interval /'ɪntəvl/ *n* intervalo *m*; **at ~s** a intervalos

interven|e /ɪntə'viːn/ *vi* (*interfere*) intervir; (*of time*) decorrer; (*occur*) sobrevir, intervir. **~tion** /-'venʃn/ *n* intervenção *f*

interview /'ɪntəvjuː/ *n* entrevista *f* ● *vt* entrevistar. **~ee** *n* entrevistado *m*. **~er** *n* entrevistador *m*

intestin|e /ɪn'testɪn/ *n* intestino *m*. **~al** *a* intestinal

intima|te¹ /'ɪntɪmət/ *a* íntimo; (*detailed*) profundo. **~cy** *n* intimidade *f*. **~tely** *adv* intimamente

intimate² /'ɪntɪmeɪt/ *vt* (*announce*) dar a conhecer, fazer saber; (*imply*) dar a entender

intimidat|e /ɪn'tɪmɪdeɪt/ *vt* intimidar. **~ion** /-'deɪʃn/ *n* intimidação *f*

into /'ɪntə emphatic 'ɪntʊ/ *prep* para dentro de; **divide ~ three** dividir em três; **~ pieces** aos/em bocados; **translate ~** traduzir para

intolerable /ɪn'tɒlərəbl/ *a* intolerável, insuportável

intoleran|t /ɪn'tɒlərənt/ *a* intolerante. **~ce** *n* intolerância *f*

intonation /ɪntə'neɪʃn/ *n* entoação *f*, entoação *f*, inflexão *f*

intoxicat|ed /ɪn'tɒksɪkeɪtɪd/ *a* embriagado, etilizado. **~ion** /-'keɪʃn/ *n* embriaguez *f*

intranet /'ɪntrənet/ *n* rede *f* corporativa

intransigent /ɪn'trænsɪdʒənt/ *a* intransigente

intransitive /ɪn'trænsətɪv/ *a* ‹*verb*› intransitivo

intravenous /ɪntrə'viːnəs/ *a* intravenoso

intrepid /ɪn'trepɪd/ *a* intrépido, arrojado

intrica|te /'ɪntrɪkət/ *a* intrincado, complexo. **~cy** *n* complexidade *f*

intrigu|e /ɪn'triːg/ *vt/i* intrigar ● *n* intriga *f*. **~ing** *a* intrigante, curioso

intrinsic /ɪn'trɪnsɪk/ *a* intrínseco. **~ally** /-klɪ/ *adv* intrinsecamente

introduce /ɪntrə'djuːs/ *vt* ‹*programme, question*› apresentar; (*bring in, insert*) introduzir; (*initiate*) iniciar; **~ sb to sb** ‹*person*› apresentar alguém a alguém

introduct|ion /ɪntrə'dʌkʃn/ n
introdução f; (of/to person) apresentação
f. ~ory /-tərɪ/ a introdutório, de
introdução; ‹letter, words› de
apresentação

introspective /ɪntrə'spektɪv/
a introspectivo, (P) introspetivo

introvert /'ɪntrəvɜːt/ n & a
introvertido m

intru|de /ɪn'truːd/ vi intrometer-se,
ser a mais. ~der n intruso m. ~sion n
intrusão f. ~sive a intruso

intuit|ion /ɪntjuː'ɪʃn/ n intuição f. ~ive
/ɪn'tjuːɪtɪv/ a intuitivo

inundate /'ɪnʌndeɪt/ vt inundar
(with de)

invade /ɪn'veɪd/ vt invadir. ~r /-ə(r)/ n
invasor m

invalid[1] /'ɪnvəlɪd/ n inválido m

invalid[2] /ɪn'vælɪd/ a inválido. ~ate vt
invalidar

invaluable /ɪn'væljʊəbl/ a inestimável

invariabl|e /ɪn'veərɪəbl/ a invariável.
~y adv invariavelmente

invasion /ɪn'veɪʒn/ n invasão f

invent /ɪn'vent/ vt inventar. ~ion
n invenção f. ~ive a inventivo. ~or n
inventor m

inventory /'ɪnvəntrɪ/ n inventário m

inver|t /ɪn'vɜːt/ vt inverter. ~ted
commas npl aspas fpl. ~sion n inversão f

invest /ɪn'vest/ vt investir; ‹time, effort›
dedicar ● vi fazer um investimento; ~
in ⏰ (buy) gastar dinheiro em. ~ment
n investimento m. ~or n investidor m,
financiador m

investigat|e /ɪn'vestɪgeɪt/ vt
investigar. ~ion /-'geɪʃn/ n investigação
f; under ~ion em estudo. ~or n
investigador m

invidious /ɪn'vɪdɪəs/ a antipático,
odioso

invigorate /ɪn'vɪgəreɪt/ vt revigorar;
(encourage) estimular

invincible /ɪn'vɪnsəbl/ a invencível

invisible /ɪn'vɪzəbl/ a invisível

invit|e /ɪn'vaɪt/ vt convidar; (bring on)
pedir, provocar. ~ation /ɪnvɪ'teɪʃn/ n
convite m. ~ing a (tempting) tentador;
(pleasant) acolhedor, convidativo

invoice /'ɪnvɔɪs/ n fatura f ● vt faturar

involuntary /ɪn'vɒləntrɪ/ a
involuntário

involve /ɪn'vɒlv/ vt implicar, envolver;
~d in implicado em. ~d a (complex)
complicado; (at stake) em jogo;

(emotionally) envolvido. ~ment n
envolvimento m, participação f

invulnerable /ɪn'vʌlnərəbl/ a
invulnerável

inward /'ɪnwəd/ a interior; ‹thought
etc› íntimo. ~(s) adv para dentro,
para o interior. ~ly adv interiormente,
intimamente

iodine /'aɪədiːn/ n iodo m; (antiseptic)
tintura f de iodo

IOU /aɪəʊ'juː/ n, abbr vale m

IQ /aɪ'kjuː/ abbr (= intelligence
quotient) QI m, (quociente m de
inteligência)

Iran /ɪ'rɑːn/ n Irã m, (P) Irão m

Iraq /ɪ'rɑːk/ n Iraque m

irascible /ɪ'ræsəbl/ a irascível

irate /aɪ'reɪt/ a irado, enraivecido

Ireland /'aɪələnd/ n Irlanda f

iris /'aɪərɪs/ n Anat, Bot íris f

Irish /'aɪərɪʃ/ a & n (language) irlandês
m. ~man n irlandês m. ~woman n
irlandesa f

iron /'aɪən/ n ferro m; (appliance) ferro
m de engomar ● a de ferro ● vt passar
a ferro; ~ out fazer desaparecer; fig
aplanar, resolver. ~ing n do the ~ing
passar a roupa. ~ing board n tábua f de
passar roupa, (P) tábua f de engomar

ironic(al) /aɪ'rɒnɪk(l)/ a irônico, (P)
irónico

ironmonger /'aɪənmʌŋgə(r)/ n
ferreiro m, (P) ferrageiro m. ~'s n (shop)
loja f de ferragens

irony /'aɪərənɪ/ n ironia f

irrational /ɪ'ræʃənl/ a irracional;
‹person› ilógico, que não raciocina

irreconcilable /ɪrekən'saɪləbl/ a
irreconciliável

irrefutable /ɪrɪ'fjuːtəbl/ a irrefutável

irregular /ɪ'regjʊlə(r)/ a irregular. ~ity
/-'lærətɪ/ n irregularidade f

irrelevant /ɪ'reləvənt/ a irrelevante,
que não é pertinente

irreparable /ɪ'repərəbl/ a irreparável,
irremediável

irreplaceable /ɪrɪ'pleɪsəbl/ a
insubstituível

irresistible /ɪrɪ'zɪstəbl/ a irresistível

irresolute /ɪ'rezəluːt/ a irresoluto

irrespective /ɪrɪ'spektɪv/ a ~ of sem
levar em conta, independente de

irresponsible /ɪrɪ'spɒnsəbl/ a
irresponsável

irreverent /ɪ'revərənt/ a irreverente

irreversible /ɪrɪˈvɜːsəbl/ a irreversível; ‹decision› irrevogável

irrigat|e /ˈɪrɪɡeɪt/ vt irrigar. **~ion** /-ˈɡeɪʃn/ n irrigação f

irritable /ˈɪrɪtəbl/ a irritável, irascível

irritat|e /ˈɪrɪteɪt/ vt irritar. **~ion** /-ˈteɪʃn/ n irritação f

is /ɪz/ ► BE

Islam /ˈɪzlɑːm/ n Islã m, (P) Islão. **~ic** /ɪzˈlæmɪk/ a islâmico

island /ˈaɪlənd/ n ilha f; **traffic ~** abrigo m de pedestres, (P) placa f de refúgio

isolat|e /ˈaɪsəleɪt/ vt isolar. **~ion** /-ˈleɪʃn/ n isolamento m

Israel /ˈɪzreɪl/ n Israel m. **~i** /ɪzˈreɪlɪ/ a & n israelense mf, (P) israelita mf

issue /ˈɪʃuː/ n questão f, (outcome) resultado m; (of magazine etc) número m; (of stamps, money etc) emissão f; **at ~** em questão; **take ~ with** entrar em discussão com, discutir com ● vt distribuir, dar; ‹stamps, money etc› emitir; ‹orders› dar ● vi **~ from** sair de

---

it /ɪt/ ● pron

····➤ (subject) ele, ela; **'Where's the book/chair?' – '~'s in the kitchen'** 'onde está o livro/a cadeira?' – '(ele/ela) está na cozinha'

····➤ (object) o, a; **~'s my book and I want it** o livro é meu e eu quero; **that's my pen, give ~ to me** essa caneta é minha, me dê(!)

····➤ (with preposition) **we talked a lot about ~** falamos muito sobre isso; **Elliott went to ~** o Elliott foi lá

····➤ (non-specific) isto, isso, aquilo; **that's ~** é isso; **take ~** leve isso

····➤ (impersonal) **~ is cold** está frio; **~ is raining** está chovendo; **~ will snow** vai nevar; **~ is the 6th of May today** hoje é seis de maio; **who is ~?** quem é?

---

italic /ɪˈtælɪk/ a itálico. **~s** npl itálico m

Ital|y /ˈɪtəlɪ/ n Itália f. **~ian** /ɪˈtælɪən/ a & n (person) Lang italiano m

itch /ɪtʃ/ n coceira f, (P) comichão f; fig (desire) desejo m ardente ● vi coçar, sentir comichão, comichar; **my arm ~es** estou com coceira or (P) comichão no braço; **I am ~ing to** estou morto por 🄸. **~y** a que dá coceira or (P) comichão

item /ˈaɪtəm/ n item m, artigo m; (on programme) número m; (on agenda) ponto m; **news ~** notícia f. **~ize** /-aɪz/ vt discriminar, especificar

itinerant /aɪˈtɪnərənt/ a itinerante; ‹musician, actor› ambulante

itinerary /aɪˈtɪnərərɪ/ n itinerário m

its /ɪts/ a seu, sua, seus, suas

it's /ɪts/ (= **it is**, **it has**) ► BE, ► HAVE

itself /ɪtˈself/ pron ele mesmo, ele próprio, ela mesma, ela própria; (reflexive) se; (after prep) si mesmo, si próprio, si mesma, si própria; **by ~** sozinho, por si

IVF abbr (= **in vitro fertilization**) FIV f

ivory /ˈaɪvərɪ/ n marfim m

ivy /ˈaɪvɪ/ n hera f

The Ivy League O grupo de universidades mais antigas e conceituadas dos Estados Unidos. Situadas no nordeste do país, compõem a Ivy League as universidades de Harvard, Yale, Columbia, Cornell, Dartmouth College, Brown, Princeton e Pennsylvania. O termo provém da hera que cresce nos edifícios antigos destas universidades.

Jj

jab /dʒæb/ vt (pt **jabbed**) espetar ● n espetadela f; 🄸 (injection) picada f, (P) injeção f

jabber /ˈdʒæbə(r)/ vi tagarelar; (indistinctly) falar confusamente ● n tagarelice f; (indistinct speech) algaravia f; (indistinct voices) algaraviada f

jack /dʒæk/ n Techn macaco m; Cards valete m; **the Union J~** a bandeira f inglesa ● vt **~ up** levantar com macaco

jacket /ˈdʒækɪt/ n casaco (curto) m; (of book) sobrecapa f, (of potato) casca f

jackpot /ˈdʒækpɒt/ n sorte f grande; **hit the ~** ganhar a sorte grande

jacuzzi® /dʒəˈkuːzɪ/ n jacuzzi m, banheira f de hidromassagem

jade /dʒeɪd/ n (stone) jade m

jaded /ˈdʒeɪdɪd/ a (tired) estafado; (bored) enfastiado

jagged /ˈdʒæɡɪd/ a recortado, denteado; (sharp) pontiagudo

jail /dʒeɪl/ n prisão f ● vt prender, colocar na cadeia. **~er** n carcereiro m, (P) guarda mf prisional

jam¹ /dʒæm/ n geleia f, compota f, (P) geleia

jam² /dʒæm/ vt/i (pt **jammed**) (wedge) entalar; (become wedged) entalar-se; (crowd) apinhar(-se); Mech bloquear; Radio provocar interferências em; ~ **one's brakes on** Ⓘ pôr o pé no freio, (P) no travão subitamente, apertar o freio subitamente ● n (crush) aperto m; (traffic) engarrafamento m; Ⓘ (difficulty) apuro m; aperto m. **~packed** a Ⓘ abarrotado (**with** de)

Jamaica /dʒəˈmeɪkə/ n Jamaica f

jangle /ˈdʒæŋgl/ n som m estridente ● vi retinir

janitor /ˈdʒænɪtə(r)/ n porteiro m; (caretaker) zelador m

January /ˈdʒænjʊərɪ/ n janeiro m

Japan /dʒəˈpæn/ n Japão m. **~ese** /dʒæpəˈniːz/ a & n japonês m

jar¹ /dʒɑː(r)/ n pote m. **jam~** n frasco m de geleia

jar² /dʒɑː(r)/ vt/i (pt **jarred**) ressoar; bater ruidosamente (**against** contra); (of colours) destoar; (disagree) discordar (**with** de) ● n (shock) choque m. **~ring** a dissonante

jargon /ˈdʒɑːgən/ n jargão m, gíria f profissional

jaundice /ˈdʒɔːndɪs/ n icterícia f

jaunt /dʒɔːnt/ n (trip) passeata f

jaunty /ˈdʒɔːntɪ/ a (**-ier, -iest**) (cheerful) alegre, jovial; (sprightly) desenvolto

javelin /ˈdʒævlɪn/ n dardo m

jaw /dʒɔː/ n maxilar m, mandíbula f

jazz /dʒæz/ n jazz m ● vt ~ **up** animar. **~y** a Ⓘ espalhafatoso

jealous /ˈdʒeləs/ a ciumento; (envious) invejoso. **~y** n ciúme m; (envy) inveja f

jeans /dʒiːnz/ npl (blue-)jeans mpl, calça f de zuarte, (P) calças fpl de ganga

jeep /dʒiːp/ n jipe m

jeer /dʒɪə(r)/ vt/i ~ **at** (laugh) fazer troça de; (scorn) escarnecer de; (boo) vaiar ● n (mockery) troça f; (booing) vaia f

jelly /ˈdʒelɪ/ n gelatina f

jellyfish /ˈdʒelɪfɪʃ/ n água-viva f

jeopard|y /ˈdʒepədɪ/ n perigo m. **~ize** vt comprometer, pôr em perigo

jerk /dʒɜːk/ n solavanco m, (P) safanão m; ⓧ (fool) idiota mf ● vt/i sacudir; (move jerkily) mover (-se) aos solavancos, (P) mover (-se) aos sacões. **~y** a sacudido

jersey /ˈdʒɜːzɪ/ n (pl **-eys**) camisola f, pulôver m, suéter m; (fabric) jérsei m, (P) malha f

jest /dʒest/ n gracejo m, graça f ● vi gracejar, brincar

Jesus /ˈdʒiːzəs/ n Jesus m

jet¹ /dʒet/ n azeviche m. **~-black** a negro de azeviche

jet² /dʒet/ n jato m; (plane) (avião a) jato m; ~ **lag** cansaço m provocado pela diferença de fuso horário. **~-propelled** a de propulsão a jato

jetty /ˈdʒetɪ/ n (breakwater) quebra-mar m; (landing stage) desembarcadouro m, cais m

Jew /dʒuː/ n judeu m

jewel /ˈdʒuːəl/ n joia f. **~ler** n joalheiro m; **~ler's (shop)** joalheria f, (P) joalharia f. **~lery** n joias fpl

Jewish /ˈdʒuːɪʃ/ a judeu

jib /dʒɪb/ vi (pt **jibbed**) recusar-se a avançar; (of a horse) empacar; ~ **at** opor-se a, ter relutância em ● n (sail) bujarrona f

jig /dʒɪg/ n jiga f

jiggle /ˈdʒɪgl/ vt (rock) balançar; (jerk) sacolejar, (P) sacudir

jigsaw /ˈdʒɪgsɔː/ n ~**(-puzzle)** puzzle m, quebra-cabeça m, (P) quebra-cabeças m

jilt /dʒɪlt/ vt deixar; abandonar; dar um fora em Ⓘ; (P) mandar passear Ⓘ

jingle /ˈdʒɪŋgl/ vt/i tilintar, tinir ● n tilintar m, tinido m; (advertising etc) música f de anúncio

jinx /dʒɪŋks/ n Ⓘ pessoa or coisa f azarenta f; fig (spell) azar m

jitter|s /ˈdʒɪtəz/ npl **the ~s** Ⓘ nervos mpl. **~y** /-ərɪ/ a **be ~y** Ⓘ estar nervoso, ter os nervos à flor da pele Ⓘ

job /dʒɒb/ n trabalho m; (post) emprego m; **have a ~ doing** ter dificuldade em fazer; **it is a good ~ that** felizmente que. **~less** a desempregado

jobcentre /ˈdʒɒbsentə(r)/ n posto m de desemprego, (P) centro m de emprego

jockey /ˈdʒɒkɪ/ n (pl **-eys**) jóquei m

jocular /ˈdʒɒkjʊlə(r)/ a jocoso, galhofeiro, brincalhão

jog /dʒɒg/ vt (pt **jogged**) dar um leve empurrão em, tocar em; (memory) refrescar ● vi Sport fazer jogging. **~ging** n jogging m

join /dʒɔɪn/ vt juntar, unir; (become member) fazer-se sócio de, entrar para; ~ **sb** juntar-se a alguém ● vi (of roads) juntar-se, entroncar-se; (of rivers) confluir; ~ **up** alistar-se ● n junção f, junta f □ ~ **in** vt/i participar (em)

joiner /ˈdʒɔɪnə(r)/ n marceneiro m

joint /dʒɔɪnt/ a comum, conjunto; (*effort*) conjunto; ~ **author** coautor m ● n junta f, junção f; *Anat* articulação f; *Culin* quarto m; (*roast meat*) carne f assada; 🅇 (*place*) espelunca f. ~**ly** adv conjuntamente

jok|e /dʒəʊk/ n piada f, gracejo m ● vi gracejar. ~**er** n brincalhão m; *Cards* curinga f de baralho, (P) diabo m. ~**ingly** adv na brincadeira

joll|y /'dʒɒlɪ/ a (-ier, -iest) alegre, bem-disposto ● adv 🅸 muito

jolt /dʒəʊlt/ vt sacudir, sacolejar ● vi ir aos solavancos ● n solavanco m; (*shock*) choque m, sobressalto m

jostle /'dʒɒsl/ vt dar um encontrão or encontrões em, empurrar ● vi empurrar, acotovelar-se

jot /dʒɒt/ n (**not a**) ~ nada ● vt (pt **jotted**) ~ (**down**) apontar, tomar nota de. ~**ter** n (*pad*) bloco m de notas

journal /'dʒɜːnl/ n diário m; (*newspaper*) jornal m; (*periodical*) periódico m, revista f. ~**ism** n jornalismo m. ~**ist** n jornalista mf

journey /'dʒɜːnɪ/ n (pl **-eys**) viagem f; (*distance*) trajeto m ● vi viajar

jovial /'dʒəʊvɪəl/ a jovial

joy /dʒɔɪ/ n alegria f. ~**ride** n passeio m em carro roubado. ~**ful**, ~**ous** adjs alegre

jubil|ant /'dʒuːbɪlənt/ a cheio de alegria, jubiloso. ~**ation** /-'leɪʃn/ n júbilo m, regozijo m

jubilee /'dʒuːbɪliː/ n jubileu m

Judaism /'dʒuːdeɪɪzəm/ n Judaísmo m

judder /'dʒʌdə(r)/ vi trepidar, vibrar ● n trepidação f, vibração f

judge /dʒʌdʒ/ n juiz m ● vt julgar. ~**ment** n (*judging*) julgamento m, juízo m; (*opinion*) juízo m; (*decision*) julgamento m

judic|iary /dʒuː'dɪʃərɪ/ n magistratura f, (*system*) judiciário m. ~**ial** a judiciário

judicious /dʒuː'dɪʃəs/ a judicioso

judo /'dʒuːdəʊ/ n judô m, (P) judo m

jug /dʒʌɡ/ n (*tall*) jarro m; (*round*) botija f. **milk-**~ n leiteira f

juggle /'dʒʌɡl/ vt/i fazer malabarismos (**with** com). ~**r** /-ə(r)/ n malabarista mf

juic|e /dʒuːs/ n suco m, (P) sumo m. ~**y** a suculento; 🅸 <*story etc*> picante

jukebox /'dʒuːkbɒks/ n juke-box m, (P) máquina f de música

July /dʒuː'laɪ/ n julho m

jumble /'dʒʌmbl/ vt misturar ● n mistura f; ~ **sale** venda f de caridade de objetos usados

jumbo /'dʒʌmbəʊ/ a ~ **jet** (avião) jumbo m

jump /dʒʌmp/ vt/i saltar; (*start*) sobressaltar(-se); (*of prices etc*) subir repentinamente; ~ **at** aceitar imediatamente; ~ **the gun** agir prematuramente; ~ **the queue** furar a fila; ~ **to conclusions** tirar conclusões apressadas ● n salto m; (*start*) sobressalto m; (*of prices*) alta f

jumper /'dʒʌmpə(r)/ n pulôver m, suéter m, (P) camisola f de lã

jumpy /'dʒʌmpɪ/ a nervoso

junction /'dʒʌŋkʃn/ n junção f; (*of roads etc*) entroncamento m

June /dʒuːn/ n junho m

jungle /'dʒʌŋɡl/ n selva f, floresta f

junior /'dʒuːnɪə(r)/ a júnior; (*in age*) mais novo (**to** que); (*in rank*) subalterno; <*school*> primária; ~ **to** (*in rank*) abaixo de ● n o mais novo m; *Sport* júnior mf

junk /dʒʌŋk/ n ferro-velho m, velharias fpl; (*rubbish*) lixo m; ~ **food** comida f sem valor nutritivo, comida f de plástico; ~ **mail** material m impresso, enviado por correio, sem ter sido solicitado; ~ **shop** loja f de ferro-velho, bricabraque m

junkie /'dʒʌŋkɪ/ n 🅇 drogado m

jurisdiction /dʒʊərɪs'dɪkʃn/ n jurisdição f

juror /'dʒʊərə(r)/ n jurado m

jury /'dʒʊərɪ/ n júri m

just /dʒʌst/ a justo ● adv justamente, exatamente; (*only*) só; ~ **listen!** escuta sól; ~ **as** assim como; (*with time*) assim que; **he has** ~ **left** ele acabou de sair; ~ **as tall as** exatamente tão alto quanto; ~ **as well that** ainda bem que; ~ **before** um momento antes (de). ~**ly** adv com justiça, justamente

justice /'dʒʌstɪs/ n justiça f; **J**~ **of the Peace** juiz m de paz

justifiabl|e /'dʒʌstɪfaɪəbl/ a justificável. ~**y** adv com razão, justificadamente

justif|y /'dʒʌstɪfaɪ/ vt justificar. ~**ication** /-ɪ'keɪʃn/ n justificação f

jut /dʒʌt/ vi (pt **jutted**) ~ **out** fazer saliência, sobressair

juvenile /'dʒuːvənaɪl/ a (*youthful*) juvenil; (*childish*) pueril, infantil; (*delinquent*) jovem; (*court*) de menores ● n jovem mf

Kk

kaleidoscope /kə'laɪdəskəʊp/ n caleidoscópio m

kangaroo /kæŋgə'ruː/ n canguru m

karate /kə'rɑːtɪ/ n karatê m, karaté m

kebab /kə'bæb/ n churrasquinho m, espetinho m

keel /kiːl/ n quilha f ● vi ~ **over** virar-se

keen /kiːn/ a (-er, -est) (sharp) agudo; (eager) entusiástico; (of appetite) devorador; (of intelligence) vivo; (of wind) cortante. ~**ly** adv vivamente; (eagerly) com entusiasmo. ~**ness** n vivacidade f; (enthusiasm) entusiasmo m

keep /kiːp/ (pt kept) vt guardar; ‹family› sustentar; ‹animals› ter, criar; (celebrate) festejar; (conceal) esconder; (delay) demorar; (prevent) impedir (from de); ‹promise› cumprir; ‹shop› ter; ~ **in/ out** impedir de entrar/de sair; ~ **up** conservar; ~ **up (with)** acompanhar ● vi manter-se, conservar-se; (remain) ficar; ~ **(on)** continuar ‹doing fazendo or (P) a fazer› ● n sustento m; (of castle) torre f de menagem □ ~ **back** vt (withhold) reter ● vi manter-se afastado. ~**er** n guarda mf

keeping /'kiːpɪŋ/ n guarda f, cuidado m; **in ~ with** em harmonia com, (P) de harmonia com

keepsake /'kiːpseɪk/ n (thing) lembrança f, recordação f

keg /keg/ n barril m pequeno

kennel /'kenl/ n casota (de cão) f. ~**s** npl canil m

kept /kept/ ▶ KEEP

kerb /kɜːb/ n meio fio m, (P) borda f do passeio

kernel /'kɜːnl/ n (of nut) miolo m

kerosene /'kerəsiːn/ n (paraffin) querosene m, (P) petróleo m; (aviation fuel) gasolina f

ketchup /'ketʃəp/ n molho m de tomate, ketchup m

kettle /'ketl/ n chaleira f

key /kiː/ n chave f; (of piano etc) tecla f; Mus clave f ● a chave ● vt ~ **in** digitar, bater; ~**ed up** tenso. ~**ring** n chaveiro m, porta-chaves m invar

keyboard /'kiːbɔːd/ n teclado m

keyhole /'kiːhəʊl/ n buraco m da fechadura

khaki /'kɑːkɪ/ a & n cáqui invar m, (P) caqui invar m

kick /kɪk/ vt/i dar um pontapé or pontapés (a em); ‹ball› chutar (em); (of horse) dar um coice or coices, escoicear; ~ **out** 🄸 pôr na rua; ~ **up** ‹fuss, racket› fazer ● n pontapé m; (of gun, horse) coice m; 🄸 (thrill) excitação f; prazer m. ~**off** n chute m inicial, kick-off m

kid /kɪd/ n (goat) cabrito m; 🅇 (child) garoto m; (leather) pelica f ● vt/i (pt kidded) 🄸 brincar (com)

kidnap /'kɪdnæp/ vt (pt kidnapped) raptar. ~**ping** n rapto m

kidney /'kɪdnɪ/ n rim m

kill /kɪl/ vt matar; fig (put an end to) acabar com ● n matança f. ~**er** n assassino m. ~**ing** n matança f, massacre m; (of game) caçada f ● a 🄸 (funny) de morrer de rir; 🄸 (exhausting) de morte

killjoy /'kɪldʒɔɪ/ n desmancha-prazeres mf

kilo /'kiːləʊ/ n (pl -os) quilo m

kilogram /'kɪləgræm/ n quilograma m

kilometre /'kɪləmiːtə(r)/ n quilômetro m, (P) quilómetro m

kilowatt /'kɪləwɒt/ n quilowatt m

kilt /kɪlt/ n kilt m, saiote m escocês, (P) saia f escocesa

kin /kɪn/ n família f, parentes mpl; **next of ~** os parentes mais próximos

kind[1] /kaɪnd/ n espécie f, gênero m, (P) género m, natureza f; **in ~** em gêneros or (P) géneros; fig (in the same form) na mesma moeda; ~ **of** 🄸 (somewhat) de certo modo, um pouco

kind[2] /kaɪnd/ a (-er, -est) (good) bom; (friendly) gentil, amável. ~-**hearted** a bom, bondoso. ~**ness** n bondade f

kindergarten /'kɪndəgɑːtn/ n jardim de infância m, (P) infantário m

kindly /'kaɪndlɪ/ a (-ier, -iest) benévolo, bondoso ● adv bondosamente, gentilmente, com simpatia; ~ **wait** tenha a bondade de esperar

king /kɪŋ/ n rei m. ~-**size(d)** a de tamanho grande

kingdom /'kɪŋdəm/ n reino m

kingfisher /'kɪŋfɪʃə(r)/ n pica-peixe m, martim-pescador m

kink /kɪŋk/ n (in rope) volta f, nó m; fig perversão f. ~**y** a 🄸 excêntrico; pervertido; (of hair) encarapinhado

kiosk /'kiːɒsk/ n quiosque m; **telephone ~** cabine telefônica, (P) telefónica

kip /kɪp/ n 🔲 sono m ● vi (pt **kipped**) 🔲 dormir

kipper /'kɪpə(r)/ n arenque m defumado

kiss /kɪs/ n beijo m ● vt/i beijar(-se)

kit /kɪt/ n equipamento m; (set of tools) ferramenta f; (for assembly) kit m ● vt (pt **kitted**) ~ **out** equipar

kitchen /'kɪtʃɪn/ n cozinha f; ~ **garden** horta f; ~ **sink** pia f, (P) lava-louças m

kite /kaɪt/ n (toy) pipa f, (P) papagaio m de papel

kitten /'kɪtn/ n gatinho m

kitty /'kɪtɪ/ n (fund) fundo m comum, vaquinha f; Cards bolo m

knack /næk/ n jeito m

knapsack /'næpsæk/ n mochila f

knead /niːd/ vt amassar

knee /niː/ n joelho m

kneecap /'niːkæp/ n rótula f

kneel /niːl/ vi (pt **knelt**) ~ **(down)** ajoelhar(-se)

knelt /nelt/ ▶ KNEEL

knew /njuː/ ▶ KNOW

knickers /'nɪkəz/ npl calcinhas (de senhora) fpl

knife /naɪf/ n (pl **knives**) faca f ● vt esfaquear, apunhalar

knight /naɪt/ n cavaleiro m; Chess cavalo m. ~**hood** n grau m de cavaleiro

knit /nɪt/ vt (pt **knitted**, or **knit**) tricotar ● vi tricotar, fazer tricô; fig (unite) unir-se; (of bones) soldar-se; ~ **one's brow** franzir as sobrancelhas. ~**ting** n malha f, tricô m

knitwear /'nɪtweə(r)/ n roupa f de malha, malhas fpl

knob /nɒb/ n (of door) maçaneta f; (of drawer) puxador m; (of radio, TV etc) botão m; (of butter) noz f. ~**bly** a nodoso

knock /nɒk/ vt/i bater (em); 🔲 (criticize) desancar (em); ~ **down** ‹chair, pedestrian› deitar no chão, derrubar; (demolish) jogar or (P) deitar abaixo; 🔲 (reduce) baixar, reduzir; (at auction) adjudicar (**to** a); ~ **out** pôr fora de combate, eliminar; (stun) assombrar; ~ **over** entornar; ~ **up** ‹meal etc› arranjar às pressas □ ~ **about** vt tratar mal ● vi (wander) andar a esmo; ~ **off** vt 🔲 (complete quickly) despachar; 🔲 (steal) roubar ● vi 🔲 parar de trabalhar; fechar a loja 🔲. ~**down** a ‹price› muito baixo; ~**kneed** a de pernas de tesoura; ~**out** n Boxing nocaute m, KO m. ~**er** n aldrava f

knot /nɒt/ n nó m ● vt (pt **knotted**) atar com nó, dar nó or nós em

knotty /'nɒtɪ/ a (**-ier, -iest**) nodoso, cheio de nós; (difficult) complicado, espinhoso

know /nəʊ/ vt/i (pt **knew**, pp **known**) saber (**that** que); (person, place) conhecer; ~ **about** ‹cars etc› saber sobre, saber de; ~ **of** ter conhecimento de, ter ouvido falar de ● n **in the** ~ 🔲 por dentro. ~**all** n sabe-tudo m 🔲; ~**how** n know-how m, conhecimentos mpl técnicos, culturais etc. ~**ingly** adv com ar conhecedor; (consciously) conscientemente

knowledge /'nɒlɪdʒ/ n conhecimento m; (learning) saber m. ~**able** a conhecedor, entendido, versado

known /nəʊn/ ▶ KNOW a conhecido

knuckle /'nʌkl/ n nó m dos dedos ● vi ~ **under** ceder, submeter-se

Koran /kə'rɑːn/ n Alcorão m, Corão m

Korea /kə'rɪə/ n Coreia f

kosher /'kəʊʃə(r)/ a aprovado pela lei judaica; 🔲 como deve ser

kowtow /kaʊ'taʊ/ vi prostrar-se (**to** diante de); (act obsequiously) bajular

k

l

Ll

lab /læb/ n 🔲 laboratório m

label /'leɪbl/ n (on bottle etc) rótulo m; (on clothes, luggage) etiqueta f ● vt (pt **labelled**) rotular; etiquetar, pôr etiqueta em

laboratory /lə'bɒrətrɪ/ n laboratório m

laborious /lə'bɔːrɪəs/ a laborioso, trabalhoso

labour /'leɪbə(r)/ n trabalho m, labuta f; (workers) mão de obra f; **in** ~ em trabalho de parto ● vi trabalhar; (try hard) esforçar-se ● vt alongar-se sobre, insistir em. ~**ed** a ‹writing› laborioso, sem espontaneidade; ‹breathing, movement› difícil. ~**saving** a que poupa trabalho

Labour /'leɪbə(r)/ n (party) Partido m Trabalhista, os trabalhistas ● a trabalhista

labourer /'leɪbərə(r)/ n trabalhador m; (on farm) trabalhador m rural

labyrinth /'læbərɪnθ/ n labirinto m

lace /leɪs/ n renda f; (of shoe) cordão m de sapato, (P) atacador m ● vt atar; ‹drink› juntar um pouco (de aguardente, rum etc)

lack /læk/ n falta f ● vt faltar (a), não ter; **be ~ing** faltar; **be ~ing in** carecer de

laconic /lə'kɒnɪk/ a lacônico, (P) lacónico

lacquer /'lækə(r)/ n laca f

lad /læd/ n rapaz m, moço m

ladder /'lædə(r)/ n escada f de mão, (P) escadote m; (in stocking) fio m corrido, (P) malha f (caída) ● vi deixar correr um fio, (P) deixar cair uma malha ● vt fazer malhas em

laden /'leɪdn/ a carregado (**with** de)

ladle /'leɪdl/ n concha (de sopa) f

lady /'leɪdɪ/ n senhora f; (title) Lady f; **young ~** jovem f. **~-in-waiting** n dama f de companhia, (P) dama f de honor; **~like** a senhoril, elegante. **Ladies** n (toilets) toalete m das Senhoras, (P) lavabos m para Senhoras

ladybird /'leɪdɪbɜːd/ n joaninha f

lag[1] /læg/ vi (pt lagged) atrasar-se, ficar para trás ● n atraso m

lag[2] /læg/ vt (pt lagged) ‹pipes etc› revestir com isolante térmico

lager /'lɑːgə(r)/ n cerveja f leve e clara; "loura" f ▣

lagoon /lə'guːn/ n lagoa f

laid /leɪd/ ▶ LAY[2]

lain /leɪn/ ▶ LIE[2]

lair /leə(r)/ n toca f, covil m

lake /leɪk/ n lago m

lamb /læm/ n cordeiro m, carneiro m; (meat) carneiro m, borrego m

lambswool /'læmzwʊl/ n lã f

lame /leɪm/ a (-er, -est) coxo; fig (unconvincing) fraco

lament /lə'ment/ n lamento m, lamentação f ● vt/i lamentar(-se) (de/por)

laminated /'læmɪneɪtɪd/ a laminado

lamp /læmp/ n lâmpada f

lamp post /'læmppəʊst/ n poste (do candeeiro) (de iluminação pública) m

lampshade /'læmpʃeɪd/ n abajur m, quebra-luz m

lance /lɑːns/ n lança f ● vt lancetar

land /lænd/ n terra f; (country) país m; (plot) terreno m; (property) terras fpl ● a de terra, terrestre; ‹policy etc› agrário ● vt/i desembarcar; Aviat aterrissar, (P) aterrar; (fall) ir parar (**on** em/a); ▣ (obtain) arranjar; ‹a blow› aplicar, mandar. **~locked** a rodeado de terra

landing /'lændɪŋ/ n desembarque m; Aviat aterrissagem f, (P) aterragem f; (top of stairs) patamar m

land|lady /'lændleɪdɪ/ n (of rented house) senhoria f, proprietária f; (who lets rooms) dona f da casa; (of boarding house) dona f da pensão; (of inn etc) proprietária f, estalajadeira f. **~lord** n (of rented house) senhorio m, proprietário m; (of inn etc) proprietário m, estalajadeiro m

landmark /'lændmɑːk/ n (conspicuous feature) ponto m de referência; fig marco m

landscape /'lændskeɪp/ n paisagem f ● vt projetar paisagisticamente

landslide /'lændslaɪd/ n desabamento or desmoronamento m de terras m; fig Pol vitória f esmagadora

lane /leɪn/ n senda f, caminho m; (in country) estrada f pequena; (in town) viela f, ruela f; (of road) faixa f, pista f; (of traffic) fila f; Aviat corredor m; Naut rota f

language /'læŋgwɪdʒ/ n língua f; (speech, style) linguagem f; **bad ~** linguagem f grosseira; **~ lab** laboratório m de línguas

languid /'læŋgwɪd/ a lânguido

languish /'læŋgwɪʃ/ vi elanguescer

lank /læŋk/ a (of hair) escorrido, liso

lanky /'læŋkɪ/ a (-ier, -iest) desengonçado, escanifrado

lantern /'læntən/ n lanterna f

lap[1] /læp/ n colo m; Sport volta f completa. **~dog** n cãozinho m de estimação, cão m de colo

lap[2] /læp/ vt **~ up** beber lambendo ● vi marulhar

lapel /lə'pel/ n lapela f

lapse /læps/ vi decair, degenerar-se; (expire) caducar ● n lapso m; Jur prescrição f; **~ into** ‹thought› mergulhar em; ‹bad habit› adquirir

lard /lɑːd/ n banha f de porco

larder /'lɑːdə(r)/ n despensa f

large /lɑːdʒ/ a (-er, -est) grande; **at ~** à solta, em liberdade; **by and ~** em geral. **~ly** adv largamente, em grande parte. **~ness** n grandeza f

lark[1] /lɑːk/ n (bird) cotovia f

lark[2] /lɑːk/ n ▣ pândega f; brincadeira f ● vi **~ about** ▣ fazer travessuras, brincar

larva /'lɑːvə/ n (pl -vae /-viː/) larva f

laryngitis /lærɪn'dʒaɪtɪs/ n laringite f

larynx /'lærɪŋks/ n laringe f

laser /'leɪzə(r)/ n laser m; **~ printer** impressora f a laser

lash /læʃ/ vt chicotear, açoitar; ‹rain› fustigar ● n chicote m; (stroke) chicotada f; (eyelash) pestana f, cílio m; **~ out** atacar, atirar-se a; **①** (spend) esbanjar dinheiro em algo

lasso /læ'suː/ n (pl -os) laço m ● vt laçar

last[1] /lɑːst/ a último; **~ night** ontem à noite, a noite passada; **the ~ straw** a gota d'água ● adv no fim, em último lugar; (most recently) a última vez ● n último m; **at (long) ~** por fim, finalmente; **to the ~** até ao fim. **~-minute** a de última hora. **~ly** adv finalmente, em último lugar

last[2] /lɑːst/ vt/i durar, continuar. **~ing** a duradouro, durável

latch /lætʃ/ n trinco m

late /leɪt/ a (-er, -est) atrasado; (recent) recente; (former) antigo, ex-, anterior; ‹hour, fruit etc› tardio; (deceased) falecido ● adv tarde; **in ~ July** no fim de julho; **of ~** ultimamente; **at the ~st** o mais tardar. **~ness** n atraso m

lately /'leɪtlɪ/ adv nos últimos tempos, ultimamente

latent /'leɪtnt/ a latente

lateral /'lætərəl/ a lateral

lather /'lɑːðə(r)/ n espuma f de sabão ● vt ensaboar ● vi fazer espuma

Latin /'lætɪn/ n Lang latim m ● a latino. **~ America** n América f Latina; **~ American** a & n latino-americano m

latitude /'lætɪtjuːd/ n latitude f

latter /'lætə(r)/ a último, mais recente ● n **the ~** este, esta. **~ly** adv recentemente

laudable /'lɔːdəbl/ a louvável

laugh /lɑːf/ vi rir (at de); **~ off** disfarçar com uma piada ● n riso m. **~able** a irrisório, ridículo. **~ing stock** n objeto m de troça

laughter /'lɑːftə(r)/ n riso m, risada f

launch[1] /lɔːntʃ/ vt lançar ● n lançamento m; **~ into** lançar-se or meter-se em; **~ing pad** plataforma f de lançamento

launch[2] /lɔːntʃ/ n (boat) lancha f

launder /'lɔːndə(r)/ vt lavar e passar

launderette /lɔːn'dret/ n lavandaria or (P) lavandaria f automática

laundry /'lɔːndrɪ/ n lavandaria f; (clothes) roupa f, (P) lavandaria f; **do the ~** lavar a roupa

laurel /'lɒrəl/ n loureiro m, louro m

lava /'lɑːvə/ n lava f

lavatory /'lævətrɪ/ n privada f, (P) casa de banho f; (room) toalete m, (P) lavabo m

lavender /'lævəndə(r)/ n alfazema f, lavanda f

lavish /'lævɪʃ/ a pródigo; (plentiful) copioso, generoso; (lush) suntuoso, (P) sumptuoso ● vt ser pródigo em, encher de

law /lɔː/ n lei f; (profession, study) direito m; **~ and order** ordem f pública. **~-abiding** a cumpridor da lei, respeitador da lei. **~ful** a legal, legítimo. **~fully** adv legalmente, legitimamente. **~less** a sem lei; (act) ilegal; (person) rebelde

law court /'lɔːkɔːt/ n tribunal m

lawn /lɔːn/ n gramado m, (P) relvado m. **~ mower** n cortador m de grama, (P) máquina f de cortar a relva

lawsuit /'lɔːsuːt/ n processo m, ação f judicial

lawyer /'lɔːjə(r)/ n advogado m

lax /læks/ a negligente; (discipline) frouxo; (morals) relaxado. **~ity** n negligência f; (of discipline) frouxidão f; (of morals) relaxamento m

laxative /'læksətɪv/ n laxante m, laxativo m

lay[1] /leɪ/ a leigo; **~ opinion** opinião f de um leigo

lay[2] /leɪ/ vt (pt laid) pôr, colocar; ‹trap› preparar, pôr; ‹eggs, table, siege› pôr; ‹plan› fazer; **~ on** ‹gas, water etc› instalar, ligar; ‹entertainment etc› organizar, providenciar; ‹food› servir; **~ out** ‹design› traçar, planejar; (spread out) estender, espalhar; ‹money› gastar ● vi pôr (ovos); **~ aside** pôr de lado; **~ down** pousar; ‹condition, law, rule› impor; ‹arms› depor; ‹one's life› oferecer; ‹policy› ditar; **~ hold of** agarrar(-se a) □ **~ off** vt ‹worker› suspender do trabalho ● vi **①** parar; desistir. **~ up** vt (store) juntar; ‹ship, car› pôr fora de serviço

lay[3] /leɪ/ ▶ LIE[2]

layabout /'leɪəbaʊt/ n **①** vadio m

lay-by /'leɪbaɪ/ n acostamento m, (P) berma f

layer /'leɪə(r)/ n camada f

layman /'leɪmən/ n (pl -men) leigo m

layout /'leɪaʊt/ n disposição f; Typ composição f

laze /leɪz/ vi descansar, vadiar

laz|y /'leɪzɪ/ a (-ier, -iest) preguiçoso. **~iness** n preguiça f. **~ybones** n 🔲 vadio m; vagabundo m

lead¹ /li:d/ vt/i (pt led) conduzir, guiar, levar; ‹team etc› chefiar, liderar; ‹life› levar; ‹choir, band etc› dirigir; ~ away levar; ~ on fig encorajar; ~ the way ir na frente; ~ up to conduzir a ● n (distance) avanço m; (first place) dianteira f; (clue) indício m, pista f; (leash) coleira f; Electr cabo m; Theatr papel m principal; (example) exemplo m; in the ~ na frente

lead² /led/ n chumbo m; (of pencil) grafite f

leader /'li:də(r)/ n chefe m, líder m; (of country, club, union etc) dirigente mf; Pol líder; (of orchestra) regente mf, maestro m; (in newspaper) editorial m. **~ship** n direção f, liderança f

leading /'li:dɪŋ/ a principal; ~ article artigo m de fundo, editorial m

leaf /li:f/ n (pl leaves) folha f; (flap of table) aba f ● vi ~ through folhear. **~y** a frondoso

leaflet /'li:flɪt/ n prospecto m, folheto m informativo

league /li:g/ n liga f; Sport campeonato m da Liga; in ~ with de coligação com, em conluio com

leak /li:k/ n (escape) fuga f; (hole) buraco m ● vt/i ‹roof, container› pingar; Electr, Gas ter um escapamento, (P) ter uma fuga; Naut fazer água; ~ (out) fig (divulge) divulgar; fig (become known) transpirar, divulgar-se. **~y** a que tem um vazamento, (P) que tem uma fuga

lean¹ /li:n/ a (-er, -est) magro

lean² /li:n/ vt/i (pt leaned, or leant /lent/) encostar(-se); apoiar-se (on em); (be slanting) inclinar(-se); ~ back/forward or over inclinar-se para trás/para a frente; ~ on 🔲 pressionar

leaning /'li:nɪŋ/ a inclinado ● n inclinação f

leap /li:p/ vt (pt leaped or leapt /lept/) galgar, saltar por cima de; ~ year ano m bissexto ● vi saltar ● n salto m, pulo m. **~frog** n eixo-badeixo m, (P) jogo m do eixo

learn /lɜ:n/ vt/i (pt learned or learnt) aprender; (be told) vir a saber, ouvir dizer. **~er** n principiante mf, aprendiz m

learn|ed /'lɜ:nɪd/ a erudito. **~ing** n saber m, erudição f

lease /li:s/ n arrendamento m, aluguel m, (P) aluguer m ● vt arrendar, (P) alugar

leash /li:ʃ/ n coleira f

least /li:st/ a o menor ● n o mínimo m, o menos m ● adv o menos; at ~ pelo menos; not in the ~ de maneira alguma

leather /'leðə(r)/ n couro m, cabedal m

leave /li:v/ vt/i (pt left) deixar; (depart from) sair/partir (de), ir-se (de); be left (over) restar, sobrar; ~ alone deixar em paz, não tocar; ~ out omitir ● n licença f, permissão f; ~ of absence licença f; on ~ Mil de licença; take one's ~ despedir-se (of de)

Leban|on /'lebənən/ n Líbano m

lecherous /'letʃərəs/ a lascivo

lecture /'lektʃə(r)/ n conferência f; Univ aula f teórica; fig sermão m ● vi dar uma conferência; Univ dar aula(s) ● vt pregar um sermão a alguém 🔲. **~r** /-ə(r)/ n conferente mf, conferencista mf; Univ professor m

led /led/ ▶ LEAD¹

ledge /ledʒ/ n rebordo m, saliência f; (of window) peitoril m

ledger /'ledʒə(r)/ n livro-mestre m, razão m

leech /li:tʃ/ n sanguessuga f

leek /li:k/ n alho-poró m, (P) alho-porro m

leer /lɪə(r)/ vi ~ (at) olhar de modo malicioso or manhoso (para) ● n olhar m malicioso or manhoso

leeway /'li:weɪ/ n Naut deriva f; fig liberdade f de ação, margem f 🔲

left¹ /left/ ▶ LEAVE; ~ luggage (office) depósito m de bagagens. **~overs** npl restos mpl, sobras fpl

left² /left/ a esquerdo; Pol de esquerda ● n esquerda f ● adv à/para a esquerda. **~-hand** a da esquerda; (position) à esquerda; **~-handed** a canhoto; **~-wing** a Pol de esquerda

leg /leg/ n perna f; (of table) pé m, perna f; (of journey) etapa f; pull sb's ~ brincar or mexer com alguém; stretch one's **~s** esticar as pernas. **~room** n espaço m para as pernas

legacy /'legəsɪ/ n legado m

legal /'li:gl/ a legal; ‹affairs etc› jurídico; ~ adviser advogado m. **~ity** /li:'gælətɪ/ n legalidade f. **~ly** adv legalmente

legalize /'li:gəlaɪz/ vt legalizar

legend /'ledʒənd/ n lenda f. **~ary** /'ledʒəndrɪ/ a lendário

leggings /'legɪŋz/ npl perneiras fpl; (women's) legging m, (P) leggings m

legib|le /'ledʒəbl/ a legível

legion /'li:dʒən/ n legião f

legislat|e /'ledʒɪsleɪt/ vt legislar. **~ion** /-'leɪʃn/ n legislação f

legislat|ive /'ledʒɪslətɪv/ a legislativo

legitima|te /lɪ'dʒɪtɪmət/ a legítimo. **~cy** n legitimidade f

leisure /'leʒə(r)/ n lazer m, tempo m livre; **at one's ~** ao bel prazer, (P) a seu belo prazer; **~ centre** centro m de lazer. **~ly** a pausado, compassado ● adv sem pressa, devagar

lemon /'lemən/ n limão m

lemonade /lemə'neɪd/ n limonada f

lend /lend/ vt (pt lent) emprestar; (contribute) dar; **~ a hand to** (help) ajudar; **~ itself to** prestar-se a. **~er** n pessoa f que empresta. **~ing** n empréstimo m

length /leŋθ/ n comprimento m; (in time) período m; (of cloth) corte m; **at ~** extensamente; (at last) por fim, finalmente. **~y** a longo, demorado

lengthen /'leŋθən/ vt/i alongar(-se)

lengthways /'leŋθweɪz/ adv ao comprido, em comprimento, longitudinalmente

lenien|t /'liːnɪənt/ a indulgente, clemente. **~cy** n indulgência f, clemência f

lens /lenz/ n (of spectacles) lente f; Photo objetiva f

lent /lent/ ▸ LEND

Lent /lent/ n Quaresma f

lentil /'lentl/ n lentilha f

Leo /'liːəʊ/ n Astr Leão m

leopard /'lepəd/ n leopardo m

leotard /'liːəʊtɑːd/ n collant(s) m(pl), (P) maillot m de ginástica ou dança

leper /'lepə(r)/ n leproso m

leprosy /'leprəsɪ/ n lepra f

lesbian /'lezbɪən/ a lésbico ● n lésbica f

less /les/ a (in number) menor (than que) ● n, adv & prep menos; **~ and ~** cada vez menos

lessen /'lesn/ vt/i diminuir

lesser /'lesə(r)/ a menor; **to a ~ degree** em menor grau

lesson /'lesn/ n lição f

let /let/ vt (pt let, pres p letting) deixar, permitir; (lease) alugar, arrendar; **~ alone** deixar em paz; (not to mention) sem falar em, para não o falar em; **~ down** baixar; (deflate) esvaziar; (disappoint) desapontar; (fail to help) deixar na mão; **~ in** deixar entrar; **~ o.s. in for** <task, trouble> meter-se em; **~ off** <gun> disparar; <firework>

soltar, (P) deitar; (excuse) desculpar; **~ out** deixar sair; **~ through** deixar passar; **~ up** 🄸 abrandar, diminuir ● v aux **~'s go** vamos; **~ him do it** que o faça ele; **~ me know** diga-me, avise-me ● n aluguel m, (P) aluguer m ● vt/i **~ go** soltar □ **~ on** 🄸 vt revelar (**that** que) ● vi descoser-se 🄸, (P) descair-se 🄸. **~-down** n desapontamento m; **~-up** n 🄸 pausa f; trégua f

lethal /'liːθl/ a fatal, mortal

letharg|y /'leθədʒɪ/ n letargia f, apatia f. **~ic** /lɪ'θɑːdʒɪk/ a letárgico, apático

letter /'letə(r)/ n (symbol) letra f; (message) carta f. **~ bomb** n carta-bomba f; **~ box** n caixa f do correio. **~ing** n letras fpl

lettuce /'letɪs/ n alface f

leukaemia /luː'kiːmɪə/ n leucemia f

level /'levl/ a plano; (on surface) horizontal; (in height) no mesmo nível (**with** que) ● n nível m; **on the ~** 🄸 franco, sincero ● vt (pt levelled) nivelar; <gun, missile> apontar; <accusation> dirigir; **~ crossing** passagem f de nível. **~-headed** a equilibrado, sensato

lever /'liːvə(r)/ n alavanca f ● vt **~ up** levantar com alavanca

leverage /'liːvərɪdʒ/ n influência f

levy /'levɪ/ vt <tax> cobrar ● n imposto m

lewd /luːd/ a (-er, -est) libidinoso, obsceno

liabilit|y /laɪə'bɪlətɪ/ n responsabilidade f; 🄸 (handicap) desvantagem f; **~ies** dívidas fpl

liable /'laɪəbl/ a **~ to do** suscetível de fazer; **~ to** <illness etc> suscetível a; <fine> sujeito a; **~ for** responsável por

liaise /lɪ'eɪz/ vi 🄸 servir de intermediário (**between** entre); fazer a ligação (**with** com)

liaison /lɪ'eɪzn/ n ligação f

liar /'laɪə(r)/ n mentiroso m

libel /'laɪbl/ n difamação f ● vt (pt libelled) difamar

liberal /'lɪbərəl/ a liberal. **~ly** adv liberalmente

Liberal /'lɪbərəl/ a & n liberal mf

liberat|e /'lɪbəreɪt/ vt libertar. **~ion** /-'reɪʃn/ n libertação f; (of women) emancipação f

libert|y /'lɪbətɪ/ n liberdade f; **at ~y to** livre de; **take ~ies** tomar liberdades

libido /lɪ'biːdəʊ/ n (pl -os) libido m

Libra /'liːbrə/ n Astr Balança f, Libra f

librar|y /'laɪbrərɪ/ n biblioteca f. **~ian** /-'brɛərɪən/ n bibliotecário m

Libya /'lɪbɪə/ n Líbia f. **~n** a & n líbio m

lice /laɪs/ n ▶ LOUSE

licence /'laɪsns/ n licença f; (*for TV*) taxa f; (*for driving*) carteira f, (P) carta f; (*behaviour*) libertinagem f

license /'laɪsns/ vt dar licença para, autorizar ● n *Amer* ▶ LICENCE; **~ plate** placa f do carro, (P) placa f de matrícula, matrícula f

lick /lɪk/ vt lamber; ☒ (*defeat*) bater ☒; **dar uma surra em** ☒ ● n lambidela f; **a ~ of paint** uma mão de pintura

lid /lɪd/ n tampa f

lie[1] /laɪ/ n mentira f ● vi (*pt* lied, *pres p* lying) mentir; **give the ~ to** desmentir

lie[2] /laɪ/ vi (*pt* lay, *pp* lain, *pres p* lying) estar deitado; (*remain*) ficar; (*be situated*) estar, encontrar-se; (*in grave*) (*on ground*) jazer; **~ down** descansar; **~ in, have a ~in** dormir até tarde; **~ low** ☒ (*hide*) andar escondido

lieu /luː/ n **in ~ of** em vez de

lieutenant /leftˈnənt/ n *Army* tenente m; *Navy* 1.° tenente m

life /laɪf/ n (*pl* lives) vida f; **~ cycle** ciclo m vital; **~ expectancy** probabilidade f de vida, (P) esperança f média de vida; **~ insurance** seguro m de vida. **~guard** n salva-vidas m; **~ jacket** n colete m salva-vidas; **~size(d)** a (de) tamanho natural *invar*

lifebelt /'laɪfbelt/ n cinto m salva-vidas, (P) boia f de salvação

lifeboat /'laɪfbəʊt/ n barco m salva-vidas

lifeless /'laɪflɪs/ a sem vida

lifelike /'laɪflaɪk/ a natural, real; (*of portrait*) muito parecido

lifelong /'laɪflɒŋ/ a de toda a vida, perpétuo

lifestyle /'laɪfstaɪl/ n estilo m de vida

lifetime /'laɪftaɪm/ n vida f; **the chance of a ~** uma oportunidade única

lift /lɪft/ vt/i levantar(-se), erguer(-se); ☒ (*steal*) roubar; surripiar ☒; (*of fog*) levantar, dispersar-se ● n ascensor m, elevador m; **give a ~ to** dar carona, (P) boleia a ☒. **~-off** n decolagem f, (P) descolagem f

ligament /'lɪɡəmənt/ n ligamento m

light[1] /laɪt/ n luz f; (*lamp*) lâmpada f; (*on vehicle*) farol m; (*spark*) lume m ● a claro ● vt (*pt* lit, *or* lighted) (*ignite*) acender; (*illuminate*) iluminar; **bring to ~** trazer à luz, revelar; **come to ~** vir à luz; **~ up** iluminar(-se), acender(-se)

light[2] /laɪt/ a & adv (*-er*, *-est*) leve. **~-headed** a (*dizzy*) estonteado, tonto; (*frivolous*) leviano; **~-hearted** a alegre, despreocupado. **~ly** adv de leve, levemente, ligeiramente. **~ness** n leveza f

lighten[1] /'laɪtn/ vt/i iluminar(-se); (*make brighter*) clarear

lighten[2] /'laɪtn/ vt/i ‹*load etc*› aligeirar(-se), tornar mais leve

lighter /'laɪtə(r)/ n isqueiro m

lighthouse /'laɪthaʊs/ n farol m

lighting /'laɪtɪŋ/ n iluminação f

lightning /'laɪtnɪŋ/ n relâmpago m; (*thunderbolt*) raio m ● a muito rápido; **like ~** como um relâmpago

lightweight /'laɪtweɪt/ a leve

like[1] /laɪk/ a semelhante (a), parecido (com) ● prep como ● conj ☒ como ● n igual m, coisa f parecida; **the ~s of you** gente como você(s). **~-minded** a da mesma opinião

like[2] /laɪk/ vt gostar (de); **I would ~** gostaria (de), queria; **if you ~** se quiser; **would you ~?** gostaria?, queria?. **~able** a simpático

like|ly /'laɪklɪ/ a (*-ier*, *-iest*) provável ● adv provavelmente; **he is ~ly to come** é provável que ele venha; **not ~ly!** ☒ nem morto ☒, nem por sonhos. **~lihood** n probabilidade f

liken /'laɪkn/ vt comparar (**to** com)

likeness /'laɪknɪs/ n semelhança f

likewise /'laɪkwaɪz/ adv também; (*in the same way*) da mesma maneira

liking /'laɪkɪŋ/ n gosto m, inclinação f; (*for person*) afeição f; **take a ~ to** (*thing*) tomar gosto por; (*person*) simpatizar com

lilac /'laɪlək/ n lilás m ● a lilás *invar*

lily /'lɪlɪ/ n lírio m, lis m; **~ of the valley** lírio-do-vale m

limb /lɪm/ n membro m

lime[1] /laɪm/ n cal f

lime[2] /laɪm/ n (*fruit*) limão m, (P) lima f

lime[3] /laɪm/ n **~(-tree)** tília f

limelight /'laɪmlaɪt/ n **be in the ~** estar em evidência

limit /'lɪmɪt/ n limite m ● vt limitar. **~ation** /-'teɪʃn/ n limitação f. **~ed company** n sociedade f anónima, (P) anónima de responsabilidade limitada

limousine /'lɪməziːn/ n limusine f

limp[1] /lɪmp/ vi mancar, coxear ● n **have a ~** coxear

limp[2] /lɪmp/ a (**-er, -est**) mole, frouxo

line[1] /laɪn/ n linha f; (string) fio m; (rope) corda f; (row) fila f; (of poem) verso m; (wrinkle) ruga f; (of business) ramo m; (of goods) linha f; Amer (queue) fila f, (P) fila f; **in ~ with** de acordo com ● vt marcar com linhas; <streets etc> ladear, enfileirar-se ao longo de; **~d paper** papel m pautado; **~ up** alinhar(-se), enfileirar(-se); (in queue) pôr(-se) em fila, (P) fila. **~up** n (players) formação f

line[2] /laɪn/ vt (garment) forrar (**with** de)

linear /'lɪnɪə(r)/ a linear

linen /'lɪnɪn/ n <sheets etc> roupa f (branca) de cama; (material) linho m

liner /'laɪnə(r)/ n navio m de linha regular, (P) paquete m

linesman /'laɪnzmən/ n Football, Tennis juiz m de linha

linger /'lɪŋgə(r)/ vi demorar-se, deixar-se ficar; (of smells etc) persistir

lingerie /'lænʒərɪ/ n roupa f de baixo/ interior (de senhora), lingerie f

linguist /'lɪŋgwɪst/ n linguista mf

linguistic /lɪŋ'gwɪstɪk/ a linguístico. **~s** n linguística f

lining /'laɪnɪŋ/ n forro m

link /lɪŋk/ n laço m; (of chain; also fig) elo m; (on web page) link m ● vt unir, ligar; (relate) ligar; <arm> enfiar; **~ up** (of roads) juntar-se (**with** a)

lint /lɪnt/ n Med curativo m de fibra de algodão; (fluff) cotão m

lion /'laɪən/ n leão m. **~ess** n leoa f

lip /lɪp/ n lábio m, beiço m; (edge) borda f; (of jug etc) bico m; **pay ~service to** fingir pena, admiração etc. **~read** vt/i entender pelos movimentos dos lábios, ler lábios

lipstick /'lɪpstɪk/ n batom m, (P) bâton m

liqueur /lɪ'kjʊə(r)/ n licor m

liquid /'lɪkwɪd/ n & a líquido m. **~ize** vt liquidificar. **~izer** n liquidificador m

liquor /'lɪkə(r)/ n bebida f alcoólica

liquorice /'lɪkərɪs/ n alcaçuz m

Lisbon /'lɪzbən/ n Lisboa f

lisp /lɪsp/ n ceceio m ● vi cecear

list[1] /lɪst/ n lista f ● vt fazer uma lista de; (enter) pôr na lista

list[2] /lɪst/ vi (of ship) adernar ● n adernamento m

listen /'lɪsn/ vi escutar, prestar atenção; **~ to, ~ in (to)** escutar, pôr-se à escuta. **~er** n ouvinte mf

listless /'lɪstlɪs/ a sem energia, apático

lit /lɪt/ ► LIGHT[1]

literal /'lɪtərəl/ a literal. **~ly** adv literalmente

litera|te /'lɪtərət/ a alfabetizado. **~cy** n alfabetização f, instrução f

literature /'lɪtrətʃə(r)/ n literatura f; 🄸 (leaflets etc) folhetos mpl

lithe /laɪð/ a ágil, flexível

litigation /lɪtɪ'geɪʃn/ n litígio m

litre /'liːtə(r)/ n litro m

litter /'lɪtə(r)/ n lixo m; (animals) ninhada f ● vt cobrir de lixo; **~ed with** coberto de. **~ bin** n lata f, (P) caixote m do lixo

little /'lɪtl/ a pequeno; (not much) pouco ● n pouco m ● adv pouco, mal, nem; **a ~** um pouco (de); **he ~ knows** ele mal/nem sabe; **~ by ~** pouco a pouco

live[1] /laɪv/ a vivo; <wire> eletrizado; <broadcast> em direto, ao vivo

live[2] /lɪv/ vt/i viver; (reside) habitar, morar, viver; **~ down** fazer esquecer; **~ it up** cair na farra; **~ on** viver de; (continue) continuar a viver; **~ up to** mostrar-se à altura de; (fulfil) cumprir

livelihood /'laɪvlɪhʊd/ n modo m de vida

lively /'laɪvlɪ/ a (**-ier, -iest**) vivo, animado. **~iness** n vivacidade f, animação f

liven /'laɪvn/ vt/i **~ up** animar(-se)

liver /'lɪvə(r)/ n fígado m

livestock /'laɪvstɒk/ n gado m

livid /'lɪvɪd/ a lívido; 🄸 (furious) furioso

living /'lɪvɪŋ/ a vivo ● n vida f; (livelihood) modo m de vida, sustento m; **earn or make a ~** ganhar a vida; **standard of ~** nível m de vida. **~ room** n sala f de estar

lizard /'lɪzəd/ n lagarto m

load /ləʊd/ n carga f; (of lorry, ship) carga f, carregamento m; (weight, strain) peso m; **~s of** 🄸 ● vt carregar. **~ed** a <dice> viciado; 🆇 (rich) cheio da nota, (P) podre de rico

loaf[1] /ləʊf/ n (pl loaves) pão m

loaf[2] /ləʊf/ vi vadiar. **~er** n preguiçoso m, vagabundo m

loan /ləʊn/ n empréstimo m ● vt emprestar; **on ~** emprestado

loath /ləʊθ/ a sem vontade de, pouco disposto a, relutante em

loath|e /ləʊð/ vt detestar. **~ing** n repugnância f, aversão f

lobby /ˈlɒbɪ/ n entrada f, vestíbulo m; Pol lobby m, grupo m de pressão ● vt fazer pressão sobre

lobster /ˈlɒbstə(r)/ n lagosta f

local /ˈləʊkl/ a local; ‹shops etc› do bairro ● n pessoa f do lugar; 🍺 (pub) taberna f/pub m do bairro; **~ government** administração f municipal. **~ly** adv localmente

locality /ləʊˈkælətɪ/ n localidade f; (position) lugar m

localization /ləʊkəˈlaɪzeɪʃn/ n localização f

locat|e /ləʊˈkeɪt/ vt localizar; (situate) situar. **~ion** /-ʃn/ n localização f. **on ~ion** (cinema) em external, (P) no exterior

lock[1] /lɒk/ n (hair) mecha f de cabelo

lock[2] /lɒk/ n (on door etc) fecho m, fechadura f; (on canal) comporta f; **under ~ and key** a sete chaves ● vt/i fechar à chave; Auto ‹wheels› imobilizar(-se); **~ in** fechar à chave, encerrar; **~ out** fechar a porta para deixar na rua, ficar trancado do lado de fora; **~ up** fechar a casa. **~out** n lockout m

locker /ˈlɒkə(r)/ n compartimento m com chave

locket /ˈlɒkɪt/ n medalhão m

locksmith /ˈlɒksmɪθ/ n serralheiro m, chaveiro m

locomotion /ləʊkəˈməʊʃn/ n locomoção f

locomotive /ˈləʊkəməʊtɪv/ n locomotiva f

locum /ˈləʊkəm/ n Med substituto m

locust /ˈləʊkəst/ n gafanhoto m

lodge /lɒdʒ/ n casa f do guarda numa propriedade; (of porter) portaria f ● vt alojar; ‹money› depositar; **~ a complaint** apresentar uma queixa ● vi estar alojado (**with** em casa de); (become fixed) alojar-se. **~r** /-ə(r)/ n hóspede mf

lodgings /ˈlɒdʒɪŋz/ n quarto m mobiliado; (flat) apartamento m

loft /lɒft/ n sótão m

lofty /ˈlɒftɪ/ a (**-ier, -iest**) elevado; (haughty) altivo

log /lɒg/ n tronco m, toro m; **sleep like a ~** dormir como uma pedra ● vt (pt **logged**) Naut/Aviat lançar no diário de bordo; **~ off** acabar de usar, terminar a sessão (de utilizador); **~ on** iniciar a sessão

loggerheads /ˈlɒgəhedz/ npl **at ~** às turras (**with** com)

logic /ˈlɒdʒɪk/ a lógico. **~al** a lógico. **~ally** adv logicamente

logistics /ləˈdʒɪstɪks/ n logística f

logo /ˈləʊgəʊ/ n (pl **-os**) 🏷 emblema m; logotipo m, (P) logótipo m

loiter /ˈlɔɪtə(r)/ vi andar vagarosamente; (stand about) rondar

loll /lɒl/ vi refestelar-se

loll|ipop /ˈlɒlɪpɒp/ n pirulito m, (P) chupa-chupa m. **~y** n 🍭 pirulito m; (P) chupa-chupa m; 💰 (money) grana f, pasta f

London /ˈlʌndən/ n Londres

lone /ləʊn/ a solitário. **~r** /-ə(r)/ n solitário m. **~some** a solitário

lonely /ˈləʊnlɪ/ a (**-ier, -iest**) solitário; ‹person› só, solitário

long[1] /lɒŋ/ a (**-er, -est**) longo, comprido; **~ face** cara f triste; **~ jump** salto m em distância, (P) em comprimento; **~playing record** LP m; **~ wave** ondas fpl longas; **so ~!** 🤙 até logo! ● adv muito tempo, longamente; **how ~ is...?** (in size) qual é o comprimento de...?; **how ~?** (in time) quanto tempo?; **he will not be ~** ele não vai demorar; **a ~ time** muito tempo; **a ~ way** longe; **as or so ~ as** contanto que, desde que; **~ ago** há muito tempo; **before ~** (future) daqui a pouco, dentro em pouco; (past) pouco (tempo) depois; **in the ~ run** no fim de contas; **~ before** muito (tempo) antes. **~-distance** a ‹flight› de longa distância; ‹phone call› interurbano; **~-range** a de longo alcance; ‹forecast› a longo prazo; **~-sighted** a que enxerga mal a distância, (P) hipermetrope; **~-standing** a de longa data; **~-suffering** a com paciência exemplar/de santo; **~-term** a a longo prazo; **~-winded** a prolixo

long[2] /lɒŋ/ vi **~ for** ansiar por, ter grande desejo de; **~ to** desejar. **~ing** n desejo m ardente

longevity /lɒnˈdʒevətɪ/ n longevidade f, vida f longa

longhand /ˈlɒŋhænd/ n escrita f à mão

longitude /'lɒndʒɪtjuːd/ n longitude f

loo /luː/ n 🔢 banheiro m, (P) casa f de banho

look /lʊk/ vt/i olhar; (seem) parecer; **~ after** tomar conta de, olhar por; **~ at** olhar para; **~ down on** desprezar; **~ for** procurar; **~ forward to** aguardar com impaciência; **~ in on** visitar; **~ into** examinar, investigar; **~ like** parecer-se com, ter ar de; **~ on** (as spectator) ver, assistir; (regard as) considerar; **~ out** ter cautela; **~ out for** procurar; (watch) estar à espreita de; **~ round** olhar em redor; **~ up** <word> procurar; (visit) ir ver; **~ up to** respeitar ● n olhar m; (appearance) ar m, aspecto m; (good) **~s** beleza f. **~out** n Mil posto m de observação; (watcher) vigia m

loom[1] /luːm/ n tear m

loom[2] /luːm/ vi surgir indistintamente; fig ameaçar

loony /'luːnɪ/ n & a 🔢 maluco m 🔢; doido m

loop /luːp/ n laçada f; (curve) volta f, arco m; Aviat loop m ● vt dar uma laçada

loophole /'luːphəʊl/ n (in rule) saída f, furo m

loose /luːs/ a (-er, -est) <knot etc> frouxo; <page etc> solto; <clothes> folgado; (not packed) a granel; (inexact) vago; <morals> dissoluto, imoral; **at a ~ end** sem saber o que fazer, sem ocupação definida; **break ~** soltar-se. **~ly** adv sem apertar; (roughly) vagamente

loosen /'luːsn/ vt (slacken) soltar, desapertar; (untie) desfazer, desatar

loot /luːt/ n saque m ● vt pilhar, saquear. **~er** n assaltante mf, salteador m. **~ing** n pilhagem f, saque m

lop /lɒp/ vt (pt lopped) **~ off** cortar, podar

lopsided /lɒp'saɪdɪd/ a torto, inclinado para um lado

lord /lɔːd/ n senhor m; (title) lord m; **the ~** o Senhor; **the L~'s Prayer** o Pai-Nosso; (good) **L~!** meu Deus!

lorry /'lɒrɪ/ n caminhão m, camião m

lose /luːz/ vt/i (pt lost) perder; **get lost** perder-se; **get lost** 🔢 vai passear! 🔢. **~r** /-ə(r)/ n perdedor m

loss /lɒs/ n perda f; **be at a ~** estar perplexo; **at a ~ for words** sem saber o que dizer

lost /lɒst/ ▶ LOSE ● a perdido; **~ property** objetos mpl perdidos (e achados)

lot[1] /lɒt/ n sorte f; (at auction, land) lote m; **draw ~s** tirar à sorte

lot[2] /lɒt/ n **the ~** tudo; (people) todos mpl; **a ~ (of)**, **~s (of)** 🔢 uma porção (de), (P) um monte (de) 🔢; **quite a ~ (of)** 🔢 uma boa porção (de), (P) montes (de) 🔢

lotion /'ləʊʃn/ n loção f

lottery /'lɒtərɪ/ n loteria f, (P) lotaria f

loud /laʊd/ a (-er, -est) alto, barulhento, ruidoso; (of colours) berrante ● adv alto; **out ~** em voz alta

loudspeaker /laʊd'spiːkə(r)/ n alto-falante m, (P) altifalante m

lounge /laʊndʒ/ vi recostar-se preguiçosamente ● n sala f, salão m

louse /laʊs/ n (pl lice) piolho m

lousy /'laʊzɪ/ a (-ier, -iest) piolhento; 🔢 (very bad) péssimo

lout /laʊt/ n pessoa f grosseira, arruaceiro m

lovable /'lʌvəbl/ a amoroso, adorável

love /lʌv/ n amor m; Tennis zero m, nada m ● vt amar, estar apaixonado por; (like greatly) gostar muito de; **in ~** apaixonado (**with** por); **~ affair** aventura f amorosa; **she sends you her ~** ela lhe manda lembranças, (P) ela manda-lhe cumprimentos

lovely /'lʌvlɪ/ a (-ier, -iest) lindo; 🔢 (delightful) encantador; delicioso

lover /'lʌvə(r)/ n namorado m, apaixonado m; (illicit) amante m; (devotee) admirador m, apreciador m

lovesick /'lʌvsɪk/ a perdido de amor

loving /'lʌvɪŋ/ a amoroso, terno, extremoso

low /ləʊ/ a (-er, -est) baixo ● adv baixo ● n baixa f; (low pressure) área de baixa pressão f. **~cut** a decotado; **~down** a baixo, reles ● n 🔢 a verdade autêntica, (P) a verdade nua e crua; **~fat** a de baixo teor de gordura; **~key** a fig moderado; discreto

lower /'ləʊə(r)/ a & adv ▶ LOW ● vt baixar; **~ o.s.** (re)baixar-se (**to** a)

lowlands /'ləʊləndz/ npl planície(s) f(pl)

lowly /'ləʊlɪ/ a (-ier, -iest) humilde, modesto

loyal /'lɔɪəl/ a leal. **~ly** adv lealmente

lozenge /'lɒzɪndʒ/ n (shape) losango m; (tablet) pastilha f

lubric|ate /'luːbrɪkeɪt/ vt lubrificar. **~ant** n lubrificante m. **~ation** /-'keɪʃn/ n lubrificação f

lucid /'lu:sɪd/ a lúcido. **~ity** /lu:-'sɪdətɪ/ n lucidez f

luck /lʌk/ n sorte f; **bad ~** pouca sorte f; **for ~** para dar sorte; **good ~!** boa sorte

luck|y /'lʌkɪ/ a (**-ier, -iest**) sortudo, com sorte; ‹*event etc*› feliz; ‹*number etc*› que dá sorte. **~ily** adv felizmente

lucrative /'lu:krətɪv/ a lucrativo, rentável

ludicrous /'lu:dɪkrəs/ a ridículo, absurdo

lug /lʌg/ vt (pt lugged) arrastar

luggage /'lʌgɪdʒ/ n bagagem f. **~ rack** n porta-bagagem m

lukewarm /'lu:kwɔ:m/ a morno; fig sem entusiasmo; indiferente

lull /lʌl/ vt (send to sleep) embalar; ‹*suspicions*› acalmar ● n calmaria f, (P) acalmia f

lullaby /'lʌləbaɪ/ n canção f de embalar

lumbago /lʌm'beɪgəʊ/ n lumbago m

lumber /'lʌmbə(r)/ n trastes mpl velhos; (wood) madeira f cortada ● vt **~ sb with** sobrecarregar alguém com

luminous /'lu:mɪnəs/ a luminoso

lump /lʌmp/ n bocado m; (swelling) caroço m; (in the throat) nó m; (in liquid) grumo m; (of sugar) torrão m ● vt **~ together** amontoar, juntar indiscriminadamente; **~ sum** quantia f total; (payment) pagamento m feito de uma vez. **~y** a grumoso, encaroçado

lunacy /'lu:nəsɪ/ n loucura f

lunar /'lu:nə(r)/ a lunar

lunatic /'lu:nətɪk/ n lunático m; **~ asylum** manicômio m, (P) manicómio m

lunch /lʌntʃ/ n almoço m ● vi almoçar. **~time** n hora f do almoço

luncheon /'lʌntʃən/ n (formal) almoço m; **~ meat** carne f enlatada, (P) carnes frias fpl; **~ voucher** senha f de almoço

lung /lʌŋ/ n pulmão m

lunge /lʌndʒ/ n mergulho m, movimento m súbito para a frente; (thrust) arremetida f ● vi mergulhar; arremessar-se (**at** para cima de, contra)

lurch[1] /lɜ:tʃ/ n **leave sb in the ~** deixar alguém em apuros

lurch[2] /lɜ:tʃ/ vi ir aos ziguezagues, dar guinadas; (stagger) cambalear

lure /lʊə(r)/ vt atrair, tentar ● n chamariz m, engodo m; **the ~ of the sea** a atração do mar

lurid /'lʊərɪd/ a berrante; fig (sensational) sensacional; fig (shocking) horrífico

lurk /lɜ:k/ vi esconder-se à espreita; (prowl) rondar; (be latent) estar latente

luscious /'lʌʃəs/ a apetitoso; (voluptuous) desejável

lush /lʌʃ/ a viçoso, luxuriante

Lusitanian /lusɪ'teɪnɪən/ a & n lusitano m

lust /lʌst/ n luxúria f, sensualidade f; fig cobiça f; desejo m ardente ● vi **~ after** cobiçar, desejar ardentemente. **~ful** a sensual

lustre /'lʌstə(r)/ n lustre m; fig prestígio m

lusty /'lʌstɪ/ a (**-ier, -iest**) robusto

lute /lu:t/ n alaúde m

Luxemburg /'lʌksəmbɜ:g/ n Luxemburgo m

luxuriant /lʌg'ʒʊərɪənt/ a luxuriante

luxurious /lʌg'ʒʊərɪəs/ a luxuoso

luxury /'lʌkʃərɪ/ n luxo m ● a de luxo

lying /'laɪɪŋ/ ▶ LIE[1], LIE[2]

lynch /lɪntʃ/ vt linchar

lyric /'lɪrɪk/ a lírico. **~s** npl Mus letra f. **~al** a lírico

Mm

MA abbr (= Master of Arts) ▶ MASTER

mac /mæk/ n 🔢 impermeável m; gabardine f

macabre /mə'kɑ:brə/ a macabro

macaroni /mækə'rəʊnɪ/ n macarrão m

macaroon /mækə'ru:n/ n bolinho m seco de amêndoa ralada

machine /mə'ʃi:n/ n máquina f, legível à máquina f, (P) legível por máquina f ● vt fazer à máquina; (sewing) coser à máquina. **~ gun** n metralhadora f; **~-readable** a em linguagem de máquina, legível à máquina, (P) legível por máquina

machinery /mə'ʃi:nərɪ/ n maquinaria f; (working parts; also fig) mecanismo m

machinist /mə'ʃi:nɪst/ n maquinista m

macho /'mætʃəʊ/ a machista

mackerel /'mækrəl/ n (pl invar) cavala f

mackintosh /'mækɪntɒʃ/ n impermeável m, gabardine f

mad /mæd/ a (**madder, maddest**) doido, louco; ‹*dog*› raivoso; 🔢 (angry) furioso 🔢; **~ cow disease** doença f da vaca louca or (P) das vacas loucas; **be ~**

about ser doido por; **like** ~ como (um) doido. **~ly** adv loucamente; (frantically) enlouquecidamente. **~ness** n loucura f

Madagascar /mædə'gæskə(r)/ n Madagáscar m

madam /'mædəm/ n senhora f; **no, ~** não senhora

madden /'mædn/ vt endoidecer, enlouquecer; **it's ~ing** é de enlouquecer

made /meɪd/ ▶ MAKE; **~ to measure** feito sob medida, (P) à medida

Madeira /mə'dɪərə/ n Madeira f; (wine) Madeira m

madman /'mædmən/ n (pl -men) doido m

Mafia /'mæfɪə/ n Máfia f

magazine /mægə'ziːn/ n revista f, magazine m; (of gun) carregador m

maggot /'mægət/ n larva f

magic /'mædʒɪk/ n magia f ● a mágico. **~al** a mágico

magician /mə'dʒɪʃn/ n (conjuror) mágico m, prestidigitador m; (wizard) feiticeiro m

magistrate /'mædʒɪstreɪt/ n magistrado m

magnanim|ous /mæg'nænɪməs/ a magnânimo. **~ity** n /-ə'nɪməti/ n magnanimidade f

magnet /'mægnɪt/ n ímã m, (P) íman m. **~ic** /-'netɪk/ a magnético. **~ism** /-ɪzəm/ n magnetismo f

magnificen|t /mæg'nɪfɪsnt/ a magnífico. **~ce** n magnificência f

magnif|y /'mægnɪfaɪ/ vt aumentar; (sound) ampliar, amplificar; **~ying glass** lupa f. **~ication** /-ɪ'keɪʃn/ n aumento m, ampliação f

magnitude /'mægnɪtjuːd/ n magnitude f

magpie /'mægpaɪ/ n pega f

mahogany /mə'hɒgənɪ/ n mogno m

maid /meɪd/ n criada f, empregada f; **old ~** solteirona f

maiden /'meɪdn/ n old use donzela f ● a (aunt) solteira; (speech, voyage) inaugural; **~ name** nome m de solteira

mail[1] /meɪl/ n correio m; (letters) correio m, correspondência f ● a postal ● vt postar, pôr no correio; (send by mail) mandar pelo correio. **~bag** n mala f postal; **~box** n Amer caixa f do correio; **~ing list** n lista f de endereços; **~ order** n encomenda f por correspondência, (P) por correio

mail[2] /meɪl/ n (armour) cota f de malha

mailman /'meɪlmæn/ n (pl -men) Amer carteiro m

maim /meɪm/ vt mutilar, aleijar

main[1] /meɪn/ a principal ● n **in the ~** em geral, essencialmente; **~ road** estrada f principal. **~ly** adv principalmente, sobretudo

main[2] /meɪn/ n (water/gas) ~ cano m de água/gás; **the ~s** Electr a rede f elétrica

mainland /'meɪnlənd/ n continente m

mainstay /'meɪnsteɪ/ n fig esteio m

mainstream /'meɪnstriːm/ n tendência f dominante, linha f principal

maintain /meɪn'teɪn/ vt manter, sustentar; (rights) defender, manter

maintenance /'meɪntənəns/ n (care, continuation) manutenção f; (allowance) pensão f

maisonette /meɪzə'net/ n dúplex m

maize /meɪz/ n milho m

majestic /mə'dʒestɪk/ a majestoso

majesty /'mædʒəstɪ/ n majestade f

major /'meɪdʒə(r)/ a maior; (very important) de vulto; **~ road** estrada f principal ● n major m ● vi ~ **in** Amer Univ especializar-se em

majority /mə'dʒɒrətɪ/ n maioria f; (age) maioridade f ● a majoritário, (P) maioritário; **the ~ of people** a maioria or a maior parte das pessoas

make /meɪk/ vt/i (pt made) fazer; (decision) tomar; (destination) chegar a; (cause to) fazer (+ inf) or (com) que (+ subj); **you ~ me angry** você me aborrece, (P) tu aborreces-me; **be made of** ser feito de; **~ o.s. at home** estar à vontade/como em sua casa; **~ it** chegar; (succeed) triunfar; **I ~ it two o'clock** são duas pelo meu relógio; **~ as if to** fazer or fingir que; **~ believe** fingir; **~ do with** arranjar-se com, contentar-se com; **~ for** dirigir-se para; (contribute to) ajudar a; **~ off** fugir (with com); **~ out** avistar, distinguir; (understand) entender; (claim) pretender; (a cheque) passar, emitir; **~ over** ceder, transferir (to a brand) marca f; **on the ~** 🅱 oportunista ◻ **~ up** vt fazer, compor; (story) inventar; (deficit) suprir; **~ up one's mind** decidir-se; **~ up (one's face)** maquilhar-se, (P) maquilhar-se ● vi fazer as pazes; **~ up for** compensar. **~-believe** a fingido ● n fantasia f; **~-up** n maquilagem f, (P) maquilhagem f; (of object) composição f; Psych maneira f de ser, natureza f

maker /ˈmeɪkə(r)/ n fabricante mf
makeshift /ˈmeɪkʃɪft/ n solução f temporária ● a provisório
making /ˈmeɪkɪŋ/ n be the ~ of fazer, ser a causa do sucesso de; **in the** ~ em formação; **he has the ~s of** ele tem as qualidades essenciais de
maladjusted /mælə'dʒʌstɪd/ a desajustado, inadaptado
malaise /mæ'leɪz/ n mal-estar m
malaria /mə'leərɪə/ n malária f
Malay /mə'leɪ/ a & n malaio m. ~sia /-ʒə/ n Malásia f
male /meɪl/ a ‹voice, sex› masculino; Biol, Techn macho ● n (human) homem m, indivíduo m do sexo masculino; (arrival) macho m
malevolen|t /mə'levələnt/ a malévolo
malfunction /mæl'fʌŋkʃn/ n mau funcionamento m ● vi funcionar mal
malice /ˈmælɪs/ n maldade f, malícia f; **bear sb** ~ guardar rancor a alguém
malicious /mə'lɪʃəs/ a maldoso, malicioso
malign /mə'laɪn/ vt caluniar, difamar
malignan|t /mə'lɪɡnənt/ a ‹tumour› maligno; (malevolent) malévolo
mallet /ˈmælɪt/ n maço m
malnutrition /mælnjuː'trɪʃn/ n desnutrição f, subalimentação f, subnutrição f
malpractice /mæl'præktɪs/ n abuso m; (incompetence) incompetência f profissional, negligência f
malt /mɔːlt/ n malte m
Malt|a /ˈmɔːltə/ n Malta f
maltreat /mæl'triːt/ vt maltratar. ~ment n mau(s) trato(s) m(pl)
mammal /ˈmæml/ n mamífero m
mammoth /ˈmæməθ/ n mamute m ● a gigantesco, colossal
man /mæn/ n (pl men) homem m; (in sports team) jogador m; Chess peça f; ~ **in the street** o homem m da rua, (P) o cidadão m comum; ~ **to man** de homem para homem ● vt (pt manned) prover de pessoal; Mil guarnecer; Naut guarnecer, equipar, tripular; (be on duty at) estar de serviço em. ~hour n hora f de trabalho per capita, homem-hora m; ~hunt n caça f ao homem; ~made a artificial
manage /ˈmænɪdʒ/ vt ‹household› governar; ‹tool› manejar; ‹boat, affair, crowd› manobrar; ‹shop› dirigir, gerir; **I could** ~ **another drink** até que tomaria mais um drinque 🆃, (P) até

tomava mais outra bebida 🆃; ~ **to do** conseguir fazer; **managing director** diretor m geral ● vi arranjar-se. ~able a manejável; (easily controlled) controlável. ~ment n gerência f, direção f
manager /ˈmænɪdʒə(r)/ n diretor m; (of bank, shop) gerente m; (of actor) empresário m, representante m; Sport treinador m. ~ess /-'res/ n diretora f; gerente f. ~ial /-'dʒɪərɪəl/ a diretivo, administrativo; ~ial staff gestores mpl
mandate /ˈmændeɪt/ n mandato m
mandatory /ˈmændətrɪ/ a obrigatório
mane /meɪn/ n crina f; (of lion) juba f
mango /ˈmæŋɡəʊ/ n (pl -oes) manga f
manhandle /ˈmænhændl/ vt mover à força de braço; (treat roughly) tratar com brutalidade
manhole /ˈmænhəʊl/ n poço m de inspeção
manhood /ˈmænhʊd/ n idade f adulta; (quality) virilidade f
mania /ˈmeɪnɪə/ n mania f. ~c /-ɪæk/ n maníaco m
manicur|e /ˈmænɪkjʊə(r)/ n manicure f ● vt fazer, arranjar
manifest /ˈmænɪfest/ a manifesto ● vt manifestar. ~ation /-'steɪʃn/ n manifestação f
manifesto /mænɪ'festəʊ/ n (pl -os) manifesto m
manipulat|e /mə'nɪpjʊleɪt/ vt manipular. ~ion /-'leɪʃn/ n manipulação f
mankind /mæn'kaɪnd/ n humanidade f, gênero m, (P) género m humano, raça f humana
manly /ˈmænlɪ/ a viril, másculo
manner /ˈmænə(r)/ n maneira f, modo m; (attitude) modo m(pl); (kind) espécie f; ~s maneiras fpl; **bad** ~s má-criação f, falta f de educação; **good** ~s (boa) educação f
mannerism /ˈmænərɪzəm/ n maneirismo m, afetação f
manoeuvre /mə'nuːvə(r)/ n manobra f ● vt/i manobrar
manor /ˈmænə(r)/ n solar m
manpower /ˈmænpaʊə(r)/ n mão de obra f
mansion /ˈmænʃn/ n mansão f
manslaughter /ˈmænslɔːtə(r)/ n homicídio m involuntário
mantelpiece /ˈmæntlpiːs/ n (shelf) consolo m da lareira, (P) prateleira f da chaminé

manual /ˈmænjʊəl/ a manual ● n manual m

manufacture /mænjʊˈfæktʃə(r)/ vt fabricar ● n fabrico m, fabricação f. **~r** /-ə(r)/ n fabricante mf

manure /məˈnjʊə(r)/ n estrume m

manuscript /ˈmænjʊskrɪpt/ n manuscrito m

many /ˈmenɪ/ a (**more, most**) muitos; **~ a man/tear**/etc muitos homens/ muitas lágrimas/etc; **~ of us/them/ you** muitos de nós/deles/de vocês; **you may take as ~ as you want** você pode levar quantos quiser; **how ~?** quantos?; **one too ~** um a mais ● n muitos; (many people) muita gente f; **a great ~** muitíssimos

map /mæp/ n mapa m ● vt (pt mapped) fazer um mapa de, mapear; **~ out** planear em pormenor; ‹route› traçar

maple /ˈmeɪpl/ n bordo m

mar /mɑː(r)/ vt (pt marred) estragar; ‹beauty› desfigurar

marathon /ˈmærəθən/ n maratona f

marble /ˈmɑːbl/ n mármore m; (for game) bola f de gude, (P) berlinde f

march /mɑːtʃ/ vi marchar ● vt **~ off** fazer marchar, conduzir à força; **he was ~ed off to prison** levaram-no à força para a prisão ● n marcha f

March /mɑːtʃ/ n março m

mare /meə(r)/ n égua f

margarine /mɑːdʒəˈriːn/ n margarina f

margin /ˈmɑːdʒɪn/ n margem f. **~al** a marginal; **~al seat** Pol lugar m ganho com pequena maioria. **~ally** adv por uma pequena margem, muito pouco

marigold /ˈmærɪɡəʊld/ n cravo-de-defunto m, (P) malmequer m

marijuana /mærɪˈwɑːnə/ n maconha f, marijuana f

marina /məˈriːnə/ n marina f

marinade /mærɪˈneɪd/ n marinada f, vinha d'alho, escabeche m ● vt pôr em marinada, pôr em vinha d'alho

marine /məˈriːn/ a marinho; (of ship, trade etc) marítimo ● n ‹shipping› marinha f; ‹sailor› fuzileiro m naval

marital /ˈmærɪtl/ a marital, conjugal, matrimonial; **~ status** estado m civil

maritime /ˈmærɪtaɪm/ a marítimo

mark[1] /mɑːk/ n (currency) marco m

mark[2] /mɑːk/ n marca f; (trace) marca f, sinal m; (stain) mancha f; Schol nota f; (target) alvo m; **make one's ~** ganhar

nome ● vt marcar; ‹exam etc› marcar, classificar; **~ out** marcar; **~ out for** escolher para, designar para; **~ time** marcar passo. **~er** n marcador m. **~ing** n marcas fpl, marcação f

marked /mɑːkt/ a marcado. **~ly** /-ɪdlɪ/ adv manifestamente, visivelmente

market /ˈmɑːkɪt/ n mercado m; **on the ~** à venda; **~ garden** horta f de legumes para venda; **~ research** pesquisa f de mercado ● vt vender; (launch) comercializar, lançar. **~place** n mercado m. **~ing** n marketing m

marksman /ˈmɑːksmən/ n (pl -**men**) atirador m especial

marmalade /ˈmɑːməleɪd/ n compota f de laranja, (P) geleia

maroon /məˈruːn/ a & n bordô m, (P) bordeaux m

marooned /məˈruːnd/ a abandonado em ilha, costa deserta etc; fig (stranded) encalhado fig

marquee /mɑːˈkiː/ n barraca or tenda f grande f; Amer (awning) toldo m

marriage /ˈmærɪdʒ/ n casamento m, matrimônio m, (P) matrimónio m; **~ certificate** certidão f de casamento. **~able** a casadouro

marrow /ˈmærəʊ/ n (of bone) tutano m, medula f; (vegetable) abóbora f; **chilled to the ~** gelado até aos ossos

marr|y /ˈmærɪ/ vt casar(-se) com; (give or unite in marriage) casar; **get ~ied** casar-se ● vi casar-se. **~ied** a casado; ‹life› de casado, conjugal

Mars /mɑːz/ n Marte m

marsh /mɑːʃ/ n pântano m. **~y** a pantanoso

marshal /ˈmɑːʃl/ n Mil marechal m; (steward) mestre m de cerimónias, (P) cerimónias ● vt (pt marshalled) dispor em ordem, ordenar; (usher) conduzir, escoltar

marshmallow /mɑːʃˈmæləʊ/ n marshmallow m

martial /ˈmɑːʃl/ a marcial; **~ law** lei f marcial

martyr /ˈmɑːtə(r)/ n mártir mf ● vt martirizar. **~dom** n martírio m

marvel /ˈmɑːvl/ n maravilha f, prodígio m ● vi (pt marvelled) (feel wonder) maravilhar-se (at com); (be astonished) pasmar (at com)

marvellous /ˈmɑːvələs/ a maravilhoso

Marxis|t /ˈmɑːksɪst/ a & n marxista mf. **~m** /-zəm/ n marxismo m

marzipan /ˈmɑːzɪpæn/ n maçapão m

m

mascara /mæˈskɑːrə/ n rímel m

mascot /ˈmæskət/ n mascote f

masculin|e /ˈmæskjʊlɪn/ a masculino ● n masculino m. **~ity** /-ˈlɪnəti/ n masculinidade f

mash /mæʃ/ n (pulp) papa f ● vt esmagar; **~ed potatoes** purê m or (P) puré m de batata(s)

mask /mɑːsk/ n máscara f ● vt mascarar

masochis|t /ˈmæsəkɪst/ n masoquista mf. **~m** /-zəm/ n masoquismo m

mason /ˈmeɪsn/ n maçom m; (building) pedreiro m. **~ry** n maçonaria f, mação m; (building) alvenaria f

mass[1] /mæs/ n Relig missa f

mass[2] /mæs/ n massa f; (heap) montão m; **the ~es** as massas, a grande massa ● vt/i aglomerar(-se), reunir(-se) em massa. **~-produce** vt produzir em série/ massa

massacre /ˈmæsəkə(r)/ n massacre m ● vt massacrar

massage /ˈmæsɑːʒ/ n massagem f ● vt massagear, fazer massagens em, (P) dar massagens a

masseu|r /mæˈsɜː(r)/ n massagista m. **~se** /mæˈsɜːz/ n massagista f

massive /ˈmæsɪv/ a (heavy) maciço; (huge) enorme

mast /mɑːst/ n mastro m; (for radio etc) antena f

master /ˈmɑːstə(r)/ n (in school) professor m, mestre m; (expert) mestre m; (boss) patrão m; (owner) dono m; **~** (boy) menino m; **M~ of Arts**/etc Licenciado m em Letras/etc ● vt dominar. **~ key** n chave-mestra f; **~mind** n (of scheme etc) cérebro m ● vt planejar, dirigir; **~ stroke** n golpe m de mestre. **~y** n domínio m (over sobre); (knowledge) conhecimento m; (skill) perícia f

masterly /ˈmɑːstəli/ a magistral

masterpiece /ˈmɑːstəpiːs/ n obra-prima f

masturbat|e /ˈmæstəbeɪt/ vi masturbar-se. **~ion** /-ˈbeɪʃn/ n masturbação f

mat /mæt/ n tapete m pequeno; (at door) capacho m; **(table) ~** n (of cloth) paninho m de mesa; (for hot dishes) descanso m para pratos

match[1] /mætʃ/ n fósforo m

match[2] /mætʃ/ n (contest) competição f, torneio m; (game) partida f; (equal) par m, parceiro m, igual mf; fig (marriage) casamento m; (marriage partner) partido m ● vt/i (set against) contrapôr (against a); (equal) igualar; (go with) condizer; (be alike) ir com, emparceirar com; **her shoes ~ed her bag** os sapatos dela combinavam com a bolsa. **~ing** a condizente, a condizer

matchbox /ˈmætʃbɒks/ n caixa f de fósforos

mat|e[1] /meɪt/ n companheiro m, camarada mf; (of birds, animals) macho m, fêmea f; (assistant) ajudante mf ● vt/i acasalar(-se) (with com)

mate[2] /meɪt/ n Chess mate m, xeque-mate m

material /məˈtɪərɪəl/ n material m; (fabric) tecido m; (equipment) apetrechos mpl ● a material; (significant) importante

materialis|m /məˈtɪərɪəlɪzəm/ n materialismo m. **~tic** /-ˈlɪstɪk/ a materialista

materialize /məˈtɪərɪəlaɪz/ vi realizar-se, concretizar-se; (appear) aparecer

maternal /məˈtɜːnəl/ a maternal

maternity /məˈtɜːnəti/ n maternidade f ● a ‹clothes› de grávida; **~ hospital** maternidade f; **~ leave** licença f de maternidade

mathematic|s /mæθəˈmætɪks/ n matemática f. **~al** a matemático. **~ian** /-əˈtɪʃn/ n matemático m

maths /mæθs/ n 🇬🇧 matemática f

matinee /ˈmætɪneɪ/ n matinê f, (P) matinée f

matrimon|y /ˈmætrɪməni/ n matrimônio m, (P) matrimónio m

matron /ˈmeɪtrən/ n matrona f; (in school) inspetora f; (former use) (senior nursing officer) enfermeira-chefe f

matt /mæt/ a fosco, sem brilho, mate

matted /ˈmætɪd/ a emaranhado

matter /ˈmætə(r)/ n (substance) matéria f; (affair) assunto m, caso m, questão f; (pus) pus m; **as a ~ of fact** na verdade; **no ~ what happens** não importa o que acontecer; **what is the ~?** o que é que há?, (P) o que é que se passa?; **what is the ~ with you?** o que é que você tem? ● vi importar; **it does not ~** não importa. **~-of-fact** a prosaico, terra a terra

mattress /ˈmætrɪs/ n colchão m

matur|e /məˈtjʊə(r)/ a maduro, amadurecido ● vt/i amadurecer; Comm vencer-se. **~ity** n madureza f, maturidade f; Comm vencimento m

maul /mɔːl/ vt maltratar, atacar

Mauritius /məˈrɪʃəs/ n Ilha f Maurícia

mausoleum /mɔːsəˈliəm/ n mausoléu m

mauve /məʊv/ ● a & n lilás m

maxim /ˈmæksɪm/ n máxima f

maxim|um /ˈmæksɪməm/ a & n (pl **-ima**) máximo m. **~ize** vt aumentar ao máximo, maximizar

---

may /meɪ/ ● v aux (pt **might**)

····▶ (possibility) poder; he **~** come talvez ele venha; he **~** have missed his train ele pode ter perdido o trem; it **~** rain talvez chova

····▶ (permission) you **~** leave pode ir; **~** I smoke? posso fumar?

····▶ (wish) **~** he be happy que ele seja feliz; **~** the best man win! que ganhe o melhor!

····▶ (in phrases) I **~** as well go bem que eu podia ir embora; we **~** as well give up bem que podíamos desistir

---

May /meɪ/ n maio. **M~ Day** n o primeiro de maio

maybe /ˈmeɪbɪ/ adv talvez

mayhem /ˈmeɪhem/ n (disorder) distúrbios mpl violentos; (havoc) estragos mpl

mayonnaise /meɪəˈneɪz/ n maionese f

mayor /meə(r)/ n prefeito m. **~ess** n prefeita f; (mayor's wife) mulher f do prefeito

maze /meɪz/ n labirinto m

me /miː/ pron me; (after prep) mim; with **~** comigo; he knows **~** ele me conhece; it's **~** sou eu

meadow /ˈmedəʊ/ n prado m, campina f

meagre /ˈmiːgə(r)/ a (thin) magro; (scanty) escasso

meal[1] /miːl/ n refeição f

meal[2] /miːl/ n (grain) farinha f grossa

mean[1] /miːn/ a (-er, -est) mesquinho; (unkind) mau

mean[2] /miːn/ a médio; **Greenwich ~ time** tempo m médio de Greenwich ● n média f

mean[3] /miːn/ vt (pt **meant**) (intend) tencionar or ter (a) intenção (**to** de); (signify) querer dizer, significar; (entail) dar em resultado, resultar provavelmente em; (refer to) referir-se a; **be meant for** destinar-se a; I didn't **~** it desculpe, foi sem querer; he **~s what**

he says ele está falando sério, (P) ele está a falar a sério

meaning /ˈmiːnɪŋ/ n sentido m, significado m. **~ful** a significativo. **~less** a sem sentido

means /miːnz/ n meio(s) m(pl) ● npl meios mpl pecuniários, recursos mpl; **by ~ of** por meio de, através de; **by all ~** com certeza; **by no ~** de modo nenhum

meant /ment/ ▶ MEAN[3]

mean|time /ˈmiːntaɪm/ adv (**in the**) **~time** entretanto. **~while** /-waɪl/ adv entretanto

measles /ˈmiːzlz/ n sarampo m; **German ~** rubéola f

measly /ˈmiːzlɪ/ a 🆇 miserável; ínfimo

measure /ˈmeʒə(r)/ n medida f ● vt/i medir; **made to ~** feito sob medida; **~ up to** mostrar-se à altura de, (P) à medida. **~d** a medido, calculado. **~ment** n medida f

meat /miːt/ n carne f. **~y** a carnudo; fig (substantial) substancial

mechanic /mɪˈkænɪk/ n mecânico m

mechanic|al /mɪˈkænɪkl/ a mecânico. **~s** n mecânica f ● npl mecanismo m

mechan|ism /ˈmekənɪzəm/ n mecanismo m. **~ize** vt mecanizar

medal /ˈmedl/ n medalha f. **~list** n condecorado m; **be a gold ~list** ser medalha de ouro

medallion /mɪˈdæliən/ n medalhão m

meddle /ˈmedl/ vi (interfere) imiscuir-se; intrometer-se (**in** em); (tinker) mexer (**with** em). **~some** a intrometido, abelhudo

media /ˈmiːdɪə/ ▶ MEDIUM npl; **the ~** a mídia, (P) os media mpl, os meios de comunicação social or de massa

mediat|e /ˈmiːdɪeɪt/ vi servir de intermediário, mediar. **~ion** /-ˈeɪʃn/ n mediação f. **~or** n mediador m, intermediário m

medical /ˈmedɪkl/ a médico ● n 🆇 (examination) exame m médico

medicat|ed /ˈmedɪkeɪtɪd/ a medicinal. **~ion** /-ˈkeɪʃn/ n medicamentação f, medicação f

medicinal /mɪˈdɪsɪnl/ a medicinal

medicine /ˈmedsn/ n medicina f; (substance) remédio m, medicamento m

medieval /medɪˈiːvl/ a medieval

mediocr|e /miːdɪˈəʊkə(r)/ a medíocre. **~ity** /-ˈɒkrətɪ/ n mediocridade f

meditat|e /ˈmedɪteɪt/ vt/i meditar. **~ion** /-ˈteɪʃn/ n meditação f

Mediterranean /medɪtə'reɪnɪən/ a mediterrâneo ● n the M~ o Mediterrâneo

medium /'miːdɪəm/ n (pl media) meio m (pl mediums) (person) médium mf ● a médio; ~ wave Radio onda f média; the happy ~ o meio-termo

medley /'medlɪ/ n (pl -eys) miscelânea f

meek /miːk/ a (-er, -est) manso, submisso, sofrido

meet /miːt/ vt (pt met) encontrar; (intentionally) encontrar-se com, ir ter com; (at station etc) ir esperar, ir buscar; (make the acquaintance of) conhecer; (conform with) ir ao encontro de, satisfazer; ‹opponent, obligation etc› fazer face a; ‹bill, expenses› pagar ● vi encontrar-se; (get acquainted) familiarizar-se; (in session) reunir-se; ~ with encontrar; ‹accident, misfortune› sofrer, ter

meeting /'miːtɪŋ/ n reunião f, encontro m; (between two people) encontro m. ~ place n ponto m de encontro

megalomania /megəlǝʊ'meɪnɪə/ n megalomania f, mania f de grandeza, (P) das grandezas

megaphone /'megəfəʊn/ n megafone m, porta-voz m

melancholy /'melənkɒlɪ/ n melancolia f ● a melancólico

mellow /'meləʊ/ a (-er, -est) ‹fruit, person› amadurecido, maduro; ‹sound, colour› quente, suave ● vt/i amadurecer; (soften) suavizar

melodious /mɪ'ləʊdɪəs/ a melodioso

melodrama /'melədrɑːmə/ n melodrama m. ~tic /-ǝ'mætɪk/ a melodramático

melod|y /'melədɪ/ n melodia f. ~ic /mɪ'lɒdɪk/ a melódico

melon /'melən/ n melão m

melt /melt/ vt/i ‹metals› fundir(-se); ‹butter, snow etc› derreter(-se); (fade away) desvanecer(-se). ~ing pot n cadinho m

member /'membə(r)/ n membro m; (of club etc) sócio m; M~ of Parliament deputado m. ~ship n qualidade f de sócio; (members) número m de sócios; (fee) cota f; ~ship card carteira f, (P) cartão m de sócio

memento /mɪ'mentəʊ/ n (pl -oes) lembrança f, recordação f

memo /'meməʊ/ n (pl -os) ⛶ nota f; apontamento m; lembrete m

memoir /'memwɑː(r)/ n (record, essay) memória f, memorial m. ~s npl memórias fpl

memorable /'memərəbl/ a memorável

memorandum /memə'rændəm/ n (pl -da, or -dums) nota f, lembrete m; (diplomatic) memorando m

memorial /mɪ'mɔːrɪəl/ n monumento m comemorativo ● a comemorativo

memorize /'meməraɪz/ vt decorar, memorizar, aprender de cor

memory /'memərɪ/ n memória f; from ~ de memória, de cor; in ~ of em memória de. ~ stick n pente m de memória, (P) dispositivo m de memória externa or pen f

men /men/ ▶ MAN

menac|e /'menəs/ n ameaça f; (nuisance) praga f, chaga f ● vt ameaçar

mend /mend/ vt consertar, reparar; (darn) remendar; ~ one's ways corrigir-se, emendar-se ● n conserto m; (darn) remendo m; on the ~ melhorando

menial /'miːnɪəl/ a humilde

meningitis /menɪn'dʒaɪtɪs/ n meningite f

menopause /'menəpɔːz/ n menopausa f

menstruation /menstrʊ'eɪʃn/ n menstruação f

mental /'mentl/ a mental; ‹hospital› de doentes mentais, psiquiátrico

mentality /men'tælətɪ/ n mentalidade f

mention /'menʃn/ vt mencionar; don't ~ it! não tem de quê, de nada ● n menção f

menu /'menjuː/ n (pl -us) menu m, (P) ementa f

merchandise /'mɜːtʃəndaɪz/ n mercadorias fpl ● vt/i negociar

merchant /'mɜːtʃənt/ n mercador m ● a ‹ship, navy› mercante; ~ bank banco m comercial

merciful /'mɜːsɪfl/ a misericordioso

merciless /'mɜːsɪlɪs/ a impiedoso, sem dó

mercury /'mɜːkjʊrɪ/ n mercúrio m

mercy /'mɜːsɪ/ n piedade f, misericórdia f; at the ~ of à mercê de

mere /mɪə(r)/ a mero, simples. ~ly adv meramente, simplesmente, apenas

merge /mɜːdʒ/ vt/i fundir(-se), amalgamar(-se); Comm ‹companies› fundir(-se). **~r** /-ə(r)/ n fusão f

meringue /mə'ræŋ/ n merengue m, suspiro m

merit /'merɪt/ n mérito m ● vt (pt **merited**) merecer

mermaid /'mɜːmeɪd/ n sereia f

merriment /'merɪmənt/ n divertimento m, alegria f, folguedo m

merry /'merɪ/ a (**-ier**, **-iest**) alegre, divertido; **~ Christmas** Feliz Natal. **~-go-round** n carrossel m; **~making** n festa f, divertimento m

mesh /meʃ/ n malha f

mess /mes/ n (disorder) desordem f, trapalhada f; (trouble) embrulhada f, trapalhada f; (dirt) porcaria f; Mil (place) cantina f, messe f; Mil (food) rancho m; **make a ~ of** estragar ● vt **~ up** (make untidy) desarrumar; (make dirty) sujar; (confuse) atrapalhar, estragar ● vi **~ about** perder tempo; (behave foolishly) fazer asneiras; **~ about with** (tinker with) entreter-se com, andar às voltas com

message /'mesɪdʒ/ n mensagem f; (informal) recado m

messenger /'mesɪndʒə(r)/ n mensageiro m

Messiah /mɪ'saɪə/ n Messias m

messy /'mesɪ/ a (**-ier**, **-iest**) desarrumado, bagunçado; (dirty) sujo, porco

met /met/ ▶ MEET

metabolism /mɪ'tæbəlɪzm/ n metabolismo m

metal /'metl/ n metal m ● a de metal. **~lic** /mɪ'tælɪk/ a metálico; ‹paint, colour› metalizado

metaphor /'metəfə(r)/ n metáfora f. **~ical** /-'fɒrɪkl/ a metafórico, (P) metafórico

meteor /'miːtɪə(r)/ n meteoro m

meteorolog|y /miːtɪə'rɒlədʒɪ/ n meteorologia f. **~ical** /-ə'lɒdʒɪkl/ a meteorológico

meter[1] /'miːtə(r)/ n contador m

meter[2] /'miːtə(r)/ n Amer ▶ METRE

method /'meθəd/ n método m

methodical /mɪ'θɒdɪkl/ a metódico

Methodist /'meθədɪst/ n metodista mf

methylated /'meθɪleɪtɪd/ a **~ spirit** álcool m metílico

meticulous /mɪ'tɪkjʊləs/ a meticuloso

metre /'miːtə(r)/ n metro m

metric /'metrɪk/ a métrico

metropol|is /mə'trɒpəlɪs/ n metrópole f. **~itan** /metrə'pɒlɪtən/ a metropolitano

mettle /'metl/ n têmpera f, caráter m; (spirit) brio m

mew /mjuː/ n miado m ● vi miar

Mexic|o /'meksɪkəʊ/ n México m. **~an** a & n mexicano m

miaow /miː'aʊ/ n & vi = MEW

mice /maɪs/ ▶ MOUSE

mickey /'mɪkɪ/ n **take the ~ out of** 🖾 fazer troça de, gozar 🄸

micro- /'maɪkrəʊ/ pref micro-

microchip /'maɪkrəʊtʃɪp/ n microchip m

microfilm /'maɪkrəʊfɪlm/ n microfilme m

microlight /'maɪkrəʊlaɪt/ n Aviat ultraleve m

microphone /'maɪkrəfəʊn/ n microfone m

microscop|e /'maɪkrəskəʊp/ n microscópio m. **~ic** /-'skɒpɪk/ a microscópico

microwave /'maɪkrəweɪv/ n microonda f; **~ oven** forno m de micro-ondas, (P) micro-ondas m

mid /mɪd/ a meio; **in ~-air** no ar, em pleno voo; **in ~-March** em meados de março

midday /mɪd'deɪ/ n meio-dia m

middle /'mɪdl/ a médio, meio; (quality) médio, mediano; **M~ Ages** Idade f Média; **~ class** classe f média; **M~ East** Médio Oriente m; **~ name** segundo nome m ● n meio m; **in the ~ of** no meio de. **~-aged** a de meia idade; **~-class** a burguês

middleman /'mɪdlmæn/ n (pl **-men**) intermediário m

midge /mɪdʒ/ n mosquito m

midget /'mɪdʒɪt/ n anão m ● a minúsculo

Midlands /'mɪdləndz/ npl região f do centro da Inglaterra

midnight /'mɪdnaɪt/ n meia-noite f

midriff /'mɪdrɪf/ n diafragma m; (abdomen) ventre m

midst /mɪdst/ n **in the ~ of** no meio de

midsummer /mɪd'sʌmə(r)/ n pleno verão m; (solstice) solstício m do verão

midway /mɪd'weɪ/ adv a meio caminho

midwife /'mɪdwaɪf/ n (pl **-wives**) parteira f

m

might[1] /maɪt/ n potência f; (strength) força f. **~y** a poderoso; fig (great) imenso ● adv 🄸 muito

might[2] /maɪt/ ▶ MAY

migraine /'mi:greɪn/ n enxaqueca f

migrant /'maɪgrənt/ a migratório ● n (person) migrante mf, emigrante mf

migrat|e /maɪ'greɪt/ vi migrar. **~ion** /-ʃn/ n migração f

mike /maɪk/ n 🄸 microfone m

mild /maɪld/ a (-er, -est) brando, manso; ‹illness, taste› leve; ‹climate› temperado; ‹weather› ameno. **~ly** adv brandamente, mansamente; **to put it ~ly** para não dizer coisa pior. **~ness** n brandura f

mildew /'mɪldju:/ n bolor m, mofo m; (in plants) míldio m

mile /maɪl/ n milha f (=1,6 km); **~s too big/etc** 🄸 grande demais, (P) demasiado grande. **~age** n (loosely) quilometragem f

milestone /'maɪlstəʊn/ n marco m miliário; fig data f or acontecimento m importante, marco m

militant /'mɪlɪtənt/ a & n militante mf

military /'mɪlɪtrɪ/ a militar

milk /mɪlk/ n leite m ● a (product) lácteo ● vt ordenhar; fig (exploit) explorar. **~shake** n milk-shake m, batido m. **~y** a (like milk) leitoso; ‹tea etc› com muito leite; **M~y Way** Via f Láctea

milkman /'mɪlkmən/ n (pl **-men**) leiteiro m

mill /mɪl/ n moinho m; (factory) fábrica f ● vt moer ● vi ~ **around** aglomerar-se; ‹crowd› apinhar-se. **pepper~** n moedor m de pimenta

millennium /mɪ'lenɪəm/ n (pl **-iums**, or **-ia**) milénio m, (P) milénio m

millet /'mɪlɪt/ n painço m, milhete m

milligram /'mɪlɪgræm/ n miligrama m

millilitre /'mɪlɪli:tə(r)/ n mililitro m

millimetre /'mɪlɪmi:tə(r)/ n milímetro m

million /'mɪlɪən/ n milhão m; **a ~ pounds** um milhão de libras. **~aire** /-'neə(r)/ n milionário m

mime /maɪm/ n mímica f; (actor) mímico m ● vt/i exprimir por mímica, mimar

mimic /'mɪmɪk/ vt (pt **mimicked**) imitar ● n imitador m, parodiante mf

mince /mɪns/ vt picar ● n carne f moída, (P) carne f picada. **~ pie** n pastel m recheado com massa de passas, amêndoas, especiarias etc. **~r** n máquina f de moer

mincemeat /'mɪnsmi:t/ n massa f de passas, amêndoas, especiarias etc usada para recheio; **make ~ of** 🄸 arrasar, aniquilar

mind n espírito m, mente f; (intellect) intelecto m; (sanity) razão f; **to be out of one's ~** estar fora de si; **have a good ~ to** estar disposto a; **make up one's ~** decidir-se; **presence of ~** presença f de espírito; **to my ~** a meu ver ● vt (look after) tomar conta de, tratar de; (heed) prestar atenção a; (object to) importar-se com, incomodar-se com; **do you ~ if I smoke?** não se incomoda or (P) importa-se que eu fume?; **do you ~ helping me?** quer fazer o favor de me ajudar?; **never ~** não se importe, não tem importância; **~ful of** atento a, consciente de. **~less** a insensato

minder /'maɪndə(r)/ n pessoa f que toma conta de crianças mf; (bodyguard) guarda-costas mf

mine[1] /maɪn/ poss pron o(s) meu(s), a(s) minha(s); **it is ~** é (o) meu or (a) minha

min|e[2] /maɪn/ n mina f ● vt escavar, explorar; (extract) extrair; Mil minar. **~er** n mineiro m. **~ing** n exploração f mineira ● a mineiro

minefield /'maɪnfi:ld/ n campo m minado

mineral /'mɪnərəl/ n mineral m; (soft drink) bebida f gasosa; **~ water** água f mineral

minesweeper /'maɪnswi:pə(r)/ n caça-minas m

mingle /'mɪŋgl/ vt/i misturar(-se) (with com)

miniature /'mɪnɪtʃə(r)/ n miniatura f ● a miniatural

minibus /'mɪnɪbʌs/ n (public) micro-ônibus m, (P) autocarro m pequeno, miniautocarro m

minim|um /'mɪnɪməm/ a & n (pl **-ma**) mínimo m. **~al** a mínimo. **~ize** vt minimizar, dar pouca importância a

miniskirt /'mɪnɪskɜ:t/ n minissaia f

minist|er /'mɪnɪstə(r)/ n ministro m; Relig pastor m. **~erial** /-'stɪərɪəl/ a ministerial. **~ry** n ministério m

mink /mɪŋk/ n (fur) marta f, visão m

minor /'maɪnə(r)/ a & n menor mf

minority /maɪ'nɒrətɪ/ n minoria f ● a minoritário

mint[1] /mɪnt/ n the **M~** a Casa da Moeda; **a ~** uma fortuna; **in ~**

condition em perfeito estado, como novo, impecável ● *vt* cunhar

mint² /mɪnt/ *n* (*plant*) hortelã *f*; (*sweet*) pastilha *f* de hortelã

minus /ˈmaɪnəs/ *prep* menos; ⊟ (*without*) sem ● *n* menos *m*

minute¹ /ˈmɪnɪt/ *n* minuto *m*; **~s** (*of meeting*) ata *f*

minute² /maɪˈnjuːt/ *a* diminuto, minúsculo; (*detailed*) minucioso

mirac‖le /ˈmɪrəkl/ *n* milagre *m*. **~ulous** /mɪˈrækjʊləs/ *a* milagroso, miraculoso

mirage /ˈmɪrɑːʒ/ *n* miragem *f*

mire /maɪə(r)/ *n* lodo *m*, lama *f*

mirror /ˈmɪrə(r)/ *n* espelho *m*; (*in car*) retrovisor *m* ● *vt* refletir, espelhar

mirth /mɜːθ/ *n* alegria *f*, hilaridade *f*

misadventure /mɪsədˈventʃə(r)/ *n* desgraça *f*; **death by ~** morte *f* acidental

misanthropist /mɪsˈænθrəpɪst/ *n* misantropo *m*

misapprehension /mɪsæprɪˈhenʃn/ *n* mal-entendido *m*

misbehav‖e /mɪsbɪˈheɪv/ *vi* portar-se mal, proceder mal. **~iour** /-ˈheɪvɪə(r)/ *n* mau comportamento *m*, má conduta *f*

miscalculat‖e /mɪsˈkælkjʊleɪt/ *vt/i* calcular mal, enganar-se. **~ion** /-ˈleɪʃn/ *n* erro *m* de cálculo

miscarr‖y /mɪsˈkærɪ/ *vi* abortar (espontaneamente), ter um aborto (espontâneo); (*fail*) falhar, malograr-se. **~iage** /-ɪdʒ/ *n* aborto (espontâneo) *m*; **~iage of justice** erro *m* judiciário

miscellaneous /mɪsəˈleɪnɪəs/ *a* variado, diverso

mischief /ˈmɪstʃɪf/ *n* (*of children*) diabrura *f*, travessura *f*; (*harm*) mal *m*, dano *m*; **get into ~** fazer disparates; **make ~** criar ou semear discórdias

mischievous /ˈmɪstʃɪvəs/ *a* endiabrado, travesso

misconception /mɪskənˈsepʃn/ *n* ideia *f* errada, (*P*) ideia *f*, falso conceito *m*

misconduct /mɪsˈkɒndʌkt/ *n* conduta *f* imprópria

misconstrue /mɪskənˈstruː/ *vt* interpretar mal

misdemeanour /mɪsdɪˈmiːnə(r)/ *n* delito *m*

miser /ˈmaɪzə(r)/ *n* avarento *m*, sovina *mf*. **~ly** *a* avarento, sovina

miserable /ˈmɪzrəbl/ *a* infeliz; (*wretched*, *mean*) desgraçado, miserável

misery /ˈmɪzərɪ/ *n* infelicidade *f*

misfire /mɪsˈfaɪə(r)/ *vi* ‹*plan, gun, engine*› falhar

misfit /ˈmɪsfɪt/ *n* inadaptado *m*

misfortune /mɪsˈfɔːtʃən/ *n* desgraça *f*, infelicidade *f*, pouca sorte *f*

misgiving(s) /mɪsˈgɪvɪŋ(z)/ *n(pl)* dúvida(s) *f(pl)*, receio(s) *m(pl)*

misguided /mɪsˈgaɪdɪd/ *a* (*mistaken*) desencaminhado; (*misled*) mal aconselhado, enganado

mishap /ˈmɪshæp/ *n* contratempo *m*, desastre *m*

misinform /mɪsɪnˈfɔːm/ *vt* informar mal

misinterpret /mɪsɪnˈtɜːprɪt/ *vt* interpretar mal

misjudge /mɪsˈdʒʌdʒ/ *vt* julgar mal

mislay /mɪsˈleɪ/ *vt* (*pt* **mislaid**) perder, extraviar

mislead /mɪsˈliːd/ *vt* (*pt* **misled**) induzir em erro, enganar. **~ing** *a* enganador

mismanage /mɪsˈmænɪdʒ/ *vt* dirigir mal. **~ment** *n* má gestão *f*, desgoverno *m*

misnomer /mɪsˈnəʊmə(r)/ *n* termo *m* impróprio

misogynist /mɪˈsɒdʒɪnɪst/ *n* misógino *m*

misprint /ˈmɪsprɪnt/ *n* erro *m* tipográfico

mispronounce /mɪsprəˈnaʊns/ *vt* pronunciar mal

misquote /mɪsˈkwəʊt/ *vt* citar incorretamente

misread /mɪsˈriːd/ *vt* (*pt* **misread** /-ˈred/) ler ou interpretar mal

misrepresent /mɪsreprɪˈzent/ *vt* deturpar, desvirtuar

miss /mɪs/ *vt/i* ‹*chance, bus etc*› perder; ‹*target*› errar, falhar; (*notice the loss of*) dar pela falta de; (*regret the absence of*) sentir a falta de, ter saudades de; **he ~es her/Portugal** ele sente a falta ou tem saudades dela/de Portugal/*etc*; **~ out** omitir; **~ the point** não compreender ● *n* falha *f*; **it was a near ~** foi ou escapou por um triz

Miss /mɪs/ *n* (*pl* **Misses**) Senhorita *f*, (*P*) Menina *f*

missile /ˈmɪsaɪl/ *n* míssil *m*; (*object thrown*) projétil *m*

missing /ˈmɪsɪŋ/ *a* que falta; (*lost*) perdido; ‹*person*› desaparecido; **a book with a page ~** um livro com uma página a menos

mission /ˈmɪʃn/ *n* missão *f*

m

missionary /'mɪʃənrɪ/ *n* missionário *m*

misspell /mɪs'spel/ *vt* (*pt* **misspelt** or **misspelled**) escrever mal

mist /mɪst/ *n* neblina *f*, névoa *f*, bruma *f*; *fig* névoa *f* ● *vt/i* enevoar(-se); ‹*window*› embaçar(-se)

mistake /mɪ'steɪk/ *n* engano *m*, erro *m* ● *vt* (*pt* **mistook**, *pp* **mistaken**) compreender mal; (*choose wrongly*) enganar-se em; ~ **for** confundir com, tomar por. ~**n** /-ən/ *a* errado; **be ~n** enganar-se. ~**nly** /-ənlɪ/ *adv* por engano

mistletoe /'mɪsltəʊ/ *n* visco *m*

mistreat /mɪs'triːt/ *vt* maltratar

mistress /'mɪstrɪs/ *n* senhora *f*, dona *f*; (*teacher*) professora *f*; (*lover*) amante *f*

mistrust /mɪs'trʌst/ *vt* desconfiar de, duvidar de ● *n* desconfiança *f*

misty /'mɪstɪ/ *a* (**-ier, -iest**) enevoado, brumoso; ‹*window*› embaçado; (*indistinct*) indistinto

misunderstand /mɪsʌndə'stænd/ *vt* (*pt* **-stood**) compreender mal. ~**ing** *n* mal-entendido *m*

misuse[1] /mɪs'juːz/ *vt* empregar mal; ‹*power etc*› abusar de

misuse[2] /mɪs'juːs/ *n* mau uso *m*; (*abuse*) abuso *m*; (*of funds*) desvio *m*

mitten /'mɪtn/ *n* luva *f* com uma única divisão entre o polegar e os dedos, mitene *f*

mix /mɪks/ *vt/i* misturar(-se); ~ **with** associar-se com; ~ **up** misturar bem; *fig* (*confuse*) confundir ● *n* mistura *f*. ~**up** *n* trapalhada *f*, confusão *f*. ~**er** *n* Culin batedeira *f*

mixed /mɪkst/ *a* ‹*school etc*› misto; (*assorted*) sortido; **be ~ up** 🄸 estar confuso

mixed-race *a* ‹*couple, marriage*› mestiço

mixture /'mɪkstʃə(r)/ *n* mistura *f*; **cough ~** xarope *m* para a tosse

MMS *abbr* (= **Multimedia Messaging Service**) MMS *m*

moan /məʊn/ *n* gemido *m* ● *vi* gemer; (*complain*) queixar-se; lastimar-se (**about** de)

moat /məʊt/ *n* fosso *m*

mob /mɒb/ *n* multidão *f*; (*tumultuous*) turba *f*; 🄴 (*gang*) bando *m* ● *vt* (*pt* **mobbed**) cercar, assediar

mobil|e /'məʊbaɪl/ *a* móvel; ~**e home** caravana *f*, trailer *m*; ~**e phone** celular *m* ● *n* celular *m*, (*P*) telemóvel *m*; **don't forget to switch your ~ off** não se

esquece de desligar o celular, (*P*) não te esqueças de desligar o telemóvel. ~**ity** /-'bɪlətɪ/ *n* mobilidade *f*

mobiliz|e /'məʊbɪlaɪz/ *vt/i* mobilizar

mock /mɒk/ *vt/i* zombar de, gozar ● *a* falso. ~**up** *n* maqueta *f*

mockery /'mɒkərɪ/ *n* troça *f*, gozação *f*, (*P*) gozo *m*, (*P*) um gozo *m*; **a ~ of** uma gozação de

mode /məʊd/ *n* modo *m*; (*fashion*) moda *f*

model /'mɒdl/ *n* modelo *m* ● *a* modelo; (*exemplary*) exemplar; (*toy*) em miniatura ● *vt* (*pt* **modelled**) modelar; ‹*clothes*› apresentar ● *vi* ser or trabalhar como modelo

modem /'məʊdem/ *n* modem *m*

moderate[1] /'mɒdərət/ *a* & *n* moderado *m*. ~**ly** *adv* moderadamente; ~**ly good** sofrível

moderat|e[2] /'mɒdəreɪt/ *vt/i* moderar(-se). ~**ion** /-'reɪʃn/ *n* moderação *f*; **in ~ion** com moderação

modern /'mɒdn/ *a* moderno; ~ **languages** línguas *fpl* vivas or modernas. ~**ize** *vt* modernizar

modest /'mɒdɪst/ *a* modesto. ~**y** *n* modéstia *f*

modif|y /'mɒdɪfaɪ/ *vt* modificar. ~**ication** /-ɪ'keɪʃn/ *n* modificação *f*

module /'mɒdjuːl/ *n* módulo *m*

moist /mɔɪst/ *a* (**-er, -est**) úmido, (*P*) húmido. ~**ure** /'mɔɪstʃə(r)/ *n* umidade *f*, (*P*) humidade *f*. ~**urizer** /-tʃəraɪzə(r)/ *n* creme *m* hidratante

moisten /'mɔɪsn/ *vt/i* umedecer, (*P*) humedecer

mole[1] /məʊl/ *n* (*on skin*) sinal *m* na pele

mole[2] /məʊl/ *n* (*animal*) toupeira *f*

molecule /'mɒlɪkjuːl/ *n* molécula *f*

molest /mə'lest/ *vt* meter-se com, molestar

mollycoddle /'mɒlɪkɒdl/ *vt* mimar

molten /'məʊltən/ *a* fundido

moment /'məʊmənt/ *n* momento *m*

momentar|y /'məʊməntrɪ/ *a* momentâneo. ~**ily** /'məʊməntrəlɪ/ *adv* momentaneamente

momentous /mə'mentəs/ *a* grave, importante

momentum /mə'mentəm/ *n* ímpeto *m*, velocidade *f* adquirida

Monaco /'mɒnəkəʊ/ *n* Mônaco *m*, (*P*) Mónaco *m*

monarch /'mɒnək/ n monarca mf. **~y** n monarquia f

monast|ery /'mɒnəstrɪ/ n mosteiro m, convento m. **~ic** /mə-'næstɪk/ a monástico

Monday /'mʌndɪ/ n segunda-feira f

monetary /'mʌnɪtrɪ/ a monetário

money /'mʌnɪ/ n dinheiro m; **~ order** vale m postal. **~ box** n cofre m; **~lender** n agiota mf, usurário

mongrel /'mʌŋgrəl/ n (cão) vira-lata m, (P) rafeiro m

monitor /'mɒnɪtə(r)/ n chefe m de turma; Techn monitor m ● vt controlar; ‹a broadcast› monitorar or monitorizar (a transmissão)

monk /mʌŋk/ n monge m, frade m

monkey /'mʌŋkɪ/ n (pl **-eys**) macaco m. **~ nut** n amendoim m

mono /'mɒnəʊ/ n (pl **-os**) gravação f mono ● a mono invar

monogram /'mɒnəgræm/ n monograma m

monologue /'mɒnəlɒg/ n monólogo m

monopol|y /mə'nɒpəlɪ/ n monopólio m. **~ize** vt monopolizar

monosyllab|le /'mɒnəsɪləbl/ n monossílabo m. **~ic** /-'læbɪk/ a monossilábico

monotone /'mɒnətəʊn/ n tom m uniforme

monoton|ous /mə'nɒtənəs/ a monótono. **~y** n monotonia f

monsoon /mɒn'suːn/ n monção f

monst|er /'mɒnstə(r)/ n monstro m. **~rous** a monstruoso

monstrosity /mɒn'strɒsətɪ/ n monstruosidade f

month /mʌnθ/ n mês m

monthly /'mʌnθlɪ/ a mensal ● adv mensalmente ● n (periodical) revista f mensal

monument /'mɒnjʊmənt/ n monumento m. **~al** /-'mentl/ a monumental

moo /muː/ n mugido m ● vi mugir

mood /muːd/ n humor m, disposição f; **in a good/bad ~** de bom/mau humor. **~y** a de humor instável; (sullen) carrancudo

moon /muːn/ n lua f

moon|light /'muːnlaɪt/ n luar m. **~lit** a iluminado pela lua, enluarado

moonlighting /'muːnlaɪtɪŋ/ n 🄵 segundo emprego m; esp à noite

moor[1] /mʊə(r)/ n charneca f

moor[2] /mʊə(r)/ vt amarrar, atracar

moose /muːs/ n (pl invar) n alce m

moot /muːt/ a discutível ● vt levantar

mop /mɒp/ n esfregão m ● vt (pt **mopped**) **~ (up)** limpar; **~ of hair** trunfa f

mope /məʊp/ vi estar or andar abatido e triste

moped /'məʊped/ n moto f pequena, (P) motorizada f

moral /'mɒrəl/ a moral ● n moral f; **~s** moral f, bons costumes mpl

morale /mə'rɑːl/ n moral m

morality /mə'rælətɪ/ n moralidade f

morbid /'mɔːbɪd/ a mórbido

more /mɔː(r)/ a & adv mais (**than** (do) que) ● n mais m; **some ~ tea/pens/ etc** mais chá/canetas/etc; **there is no ~ bread** não há mais pão; **~ or less** mais ou menos

moreover /mɔː'rəʊvə(r)/ adv além disso, de mais a mais

morgue /mɔːg/ n morgue f, necrotério m

morning /'mɔːnɪŋ/ n manhã f; **in the ~** de manhã

Morocc|o /mə'rɒkəʊ/ n Marrocos m

moron /'mɔːrɒn/ n idiota mf

morose /mə'rəʊs/ a taciturno e insociável, carrancudo

morphine /'mɔːfiːn/ n morfina f

morsel /'mɔːsl/ n bocado (esp de comida) m

mortal /'mɔːtl/ a & n mortal mf. **~ity** /mɔː'tælətɪ/ n mortalidade f

mortar /'mɔːtə(r)/ n argamassa f; (bowl) almofariz m; Mil morteiro m

mortgage /'mɔːgɪdʒ/ n hipoteca f ● vt hipotecar

mortify /'mɔːtɪfaɪ/ vt mortificar

mortuary /'mɔːtʃərɪ/ n casa f mortuária

mosaic /məʊ'zeɪɪk/ n mosaico m

Moscow /'mɒskəʊ/ n Moscou m, (P) Moscovo m

mosque /mɒsk/ n mesquita f

mosquito /mə'skiːtəʊ/ n (pl **-oes**) mosquito m

moss /mɒs/ n musgo m. **~y** a musgoso

most /məʊst/ a o mais, o maior; (majority) a maioria de, a maior parte de; **for the ~ part** na maior parte, na grande maioria ● *n* mais *m*; (*majority*) maioria, a maior parte, o máximo ● *adv* o mais; (*very*) muito; **at ~** no máximo; **make the ~ of** aproveitar ao máximo, tirar o melhor partido de. **~ly** *adv* sobretudo

motel /məʊˈtel/ *n* motel *m*

moth /mɒθ/ *n* mariposa *f*, (*P*) borboleta *f* noturna. (**clothes-**)**~** *n* traça *f*. **~ball** *n* bola *f* de naftalina

mother /ˈmʌðə(r)/ *n* mãe *f*; **M~'s Day** o Dia da(s) Mãe(s) ● *vt* tratar como a um filho. **~hood** *n* maternidade *f*. **~-in-law** *n* (*pl* **~s-in-law**) sogra *f*; **~-of-pearl** *n* madrepérola *f*; **~-to-be** *n* futura mãe *f*. **~ly** *a* maternal

motif /məʊˈtiːf/ *n* tema *m*

motion /ˈməʊʃn/ *n* movimento *m*; (*proposal*) moção *f* ● *vt/i* **~ (to) sb to** fazer sinal a alguém para. **~less** *a* imóvel

motivat|e /ˈməʊtɪveɪt/ *vt* motivar. **~ion** /-ˈveɪʃn/ *n* motivação *f*

motive /ˈməʊtɪv/ *n* motivo *m*

motor /ˈməʊtə(r)/ *n* motor *m*; (*car*) automóvel *m* ● *a* Anat motor; ‹*boat*› a motor ● *vi* ir de automóvel; **~ bike** ⓘ moto *f* ⓘ; **~ car** carro *m*; **~ cycle** motocicleta *f*; **~ cyclist** motociclista *mf*; **~ vehicle** veículo *m* automóvel. **~ing** *n* automobilismo *m*. **~ized** *a* motorizado

motorist /ˈməʊtərɪst/ *n* motorista *mf*, automobilista *mf*

motorway /ˈməʊtəweɪ/ *n* rodovia *f*, (*P*) autoestrada *f*

mottled /ˈmɒtld/ *a* sarapintado, pintalgado

motto /ˈmɒtəʊ/ *n* (*pl* **-oes**) divisa *f*, lema *m*

mould[1] /məʊld/ *n* (*container*) forma *f*, molde *m*; Culin forma *f* ● *vt* moldar. **~ing** *n* Archit moldura *f*

mould[2] /məʊld/ *n* (*fungi*) bolor *m*, mofo *m*. **~y** *a* bolorento

moult /məʊlt/ *vi* estar na muda

mound /maʊnd/ *n* monte *m* de terra or de pedras; (*small hill*) montículo *m*

mount /maʊnt/ *vt/i* montar ● *n* (*support*) suporte *m*; (*for gem etc*) engaste *m*; **~ up** aumentar, subir

mountain /ˈmaʊntɪn/ *n* montanha *f*; **~ bike** mountain bike *f*, bicicleta *f* de montanha. **~ous** *a* montanhoso

mountaineer /maʊntɪˈnɪə(r)/ *n* alpinista *mf*. **~ing** *n* alpinismo *m*

mourn /mɔːn/ *vt/i* **~ (for)** chorar (a morte de); **~ (over)** sofrer (por). **~er** *n*

pessoa *f* que acompanha o enterro. **~ing** *n* luto *m*; **in ~ing** de luto

mournful /ˈmɔːnfl/ *a* triste; (*sorrowful*) pesaroso

mouse /maʊs/ *n* (*pl* **mice**) camundongo *m*, (*P*) rato *m*. **~mat** *n* mousepad *m*, (*P*) tapete de rato *m*

mousetrap /ˈmaʊstræp/ *n* ratoeira *f*

mousse /muːs/ *n* mousse *f*

moustache /məˈstɑːʃ/ *n* bigode *m*

mouth[1] /maʊθ/ *n* boca *f*

mouth[2] /maʊð/ *vt/i* declamar; (*silently*) articular sem som

mouthful /ˈmaʊθfʊl/ *n* bocado *m*

mouthpiece /ˈmaʊθpiːs/ *n* Mus bocal *m*, boquilha *f*; *fig* (*person*) porta-voz *mf*

mouthwash /ˈmaʊθwɒʃ/ *n* líquido *m* para bochecho

movable /ˈmuːvəbl/ *a* móvel

move /muːv/ *vt/i* mover(-se), mexer(-se), deslocar(-se); (*emotionally*) comover; (*incite*) convencer, levar a; (*act*) agir; (*propose*) propor; (*depart*) ir, partir; (*go forward*) avançar; **~ (out)** mudar-se, sair; **~ back** recuar; **~ forward** avançar; **~ in** mudar-se para; **~ on!** circulem!; **~ over, please** chegue-se para lá, por favor ● *n* movimento *m*; (*in game*) jogada *f*; (*player's turn*) vez *f*; (*house change*) mudança *f*; **on the ~** em marcha

movement /ˈmuːvmənt/ *n* movimento *m*

movie /ˈmuːvɪ/ *n* Amer filme *m*; **the ~s** o cinema

moving /ˈmuːvɪŋ/ *a* (*touching*) comovente; (*movable*) móvil; (*in motion*) em movimento

mow /məʊ/ *vt* (*pp* **mowed**, *or* **mown**) ceifar; ‹*lawn*› cortar a grama, (*P*) relva; **~ down** ceifar. **~er** *n* (*for lawn*) máquina *f* de cortar a grama, (*P*) relva

MP *abbr* (= Member of Parliament) ▶ **MEMBER**

MP3 player *n* MP3 *m*

Mr /ˈmɪstə(r)/ *n* (*pl* **Messrs**) Senhor *m*; **~ Smith** o Sr Smith

Mrs /ˈmɪsɪz/ *n* Senhora *f*; **~ Smith** a Sra Smith; **Mr and ~ Smith** o Sr Smith e a mulher

Ms /mɪz/ *n* Senhora D. *f*

much /mʌtʃ/ (**more, most**) *a*, *adv* & *n* muito *m*; **very ~** muito, muitíssimo; **you may have as ~ as you need** você pode levar o que precisar; **~ of it** muito or grande parte dele; **so ~ the better/worse** tanto melhor/pior; **how ~?**

quanto?; **not ~** não muito; **too ~** demasiado, demais; **he's not ~ of a gardener** não é lá grande jardineiro

muck /mʌk/ n estrume m; ⓘ (dirt) porcaria f ● vi ~ **about** 🄴 entreter-se, perder tempo; ~ **in** 🄴 ajudar, dar uma mão ● vt ~ **up** 🄴 estragar. **~y** a sujo

mucus /'mjuːkəs/ n muco m

mud /mʌd/ n lama f. **~dy** a lamacento, enlameado

muddle /'mʌdl/ vt baralhar, atrapalhar, confundir ● vi ~ **through** sair-se bem, desenrascar-se 🄴 ● n desordem f; (mix-up) confusão f, trapalhada f

mudguard /'mʌdgɑːd/ n para-lama m, (P) para-lamas m

muffle /'mʌfl/ vt abafar; ~ **(up)** agasalhar(-se); **~d sounds** sons mpl abafados. **~r** /-ə(r)/ n cachecol m

mug /mʌg/ n caneca f; 🄴 (face) cara f; 🄴 (fool) trouxa mf ⓘ ● vt (pt mugged) assaltar, agredir. **~ger** n assaltante mf. **~ging** n assalto m

muggy /'mʌgɪ/ a abafado

mule /mjuːl/ n mulo m; (female) mula f

mull /mʌl/ vt ~ **over** ruminar; fig matutar em

multi- /'mʌltɪ/ pref mult(i)-

multicoloured /'mʌltɪkʌləd/ a multicolor

multinational /mʌltɪ'næʃnəl/ a & n multinacional f

multiple /'mʌltɪpl/ a & n múltiplo m

multipl|y /'mʌltɪplaɪ/ vt/i multiplicar(-se). **~ication** /-ɪ'keɪʃn/ n multiplicação f

multistorey /mʌltɪ'stɔːrɪ/ a (car park) em vários níveis, de vários andares

multitude /'mʌltɪtjuːd/ n multidão f

mum[1] /mʌm/ a **keep ~** ⓘ ficar calado

mum[2] /mʌm/ n ⓘ mamãe f ⓘ, (P) mamã f ⓘ

mumble /'mʌmbl/ vt/i resmungar, resmonear

mummy[1] /'mʌmɪ/ n (body) múmia f

mummy[2] /'mʌmɪ/ n (esp child's lang) mamãe f, (P) mamã f, mãezinha f ⓘ

mumps /mʌmps/ n caxumba f, parotidite f, papeira f

munch /mʌntʃ/ vt mastigar

mundane /mʌn'deɪn/ a banal; (worldly) mundano

municipal /mjuː'nɪsɪpl/ a municipal. **~ity** /-'pælətɪ/ n municipalidade f

munitions /mjuː'nɪʃnz/ npl munições fpl

mural /'mjʊərəl/ a & n mural m

murder /'mɜːdə(r)/ n assassínio m, assassinato m ● vt assassinar. **~er** n assassino m, assassina f. **~ous** a assassino, sanguinário; (of weapon) mortífero

murky /'mɜːkɪ/ a (-ier, -iest) escuro, sombrio

murmur /'mɜːmə(r)/ n murmúrio m ● vt/i murmurar

muscle /'mʌsl/ n músculo m ● vi ~ **in** ⓘ impor-se, intrometer-se

muscular /'mʌskjʊlə(r)/ a muscular; (brawny) musculoso

muse /mjuːz/ vi meditar, cismar

museum /mjuː'zɪəm/ n museu m

mush /mʌʃ/ n papa f de farinha de milho. **~y** a mole; (sentimental) piegas inv

mushroom /'mʌʃrʊm/ n cogumelo m ● vi pulular, multiplicar-se com rapidez

music /'mjuːzɪk/ n música f. **~al** a musical ● n (show) comédia f musical, musical m. **~al box** n caixa f de música; **~ stand** n estante f de música

musician /mjuː'zɪʃn/ n músico m

musk /mʌsk/ n almíscar m

Muslim /'mʊzlɪm/ a & n muçulmano m

mussel /'mʌsl/ n mexilhão m

must /mʌst/ v aux dever; **you ~ go** é necessário que você parta; **he ~ be old** ele deve ser velho; **I ~ have done it** eu devo tê-lo feito ● n **be a ~** ⓘ ser imprescindível

mustard /'mʌstəd/ n mostarda f

muster /'mʌstə(r)/ vt/i juntar(-se), reunir(-se); **pass ~** ser aceitável

musty /'mʌstɪ/ a (-ier, -iest) mofado, bolorento

mutation /mjuː'teɪʃn/ n mutação f

mute /mjuːt/ a & n mudo m

muted /'mjuːtɪd/ a (sound) em surdina; (colour) suave

mutilat|e /'mjuːtɪleɪt/ vt mutilar. **~ion** /-'leɪʃn/ n mutilação f

mutin|y /'mjuːtɪnɪ/ n motim f ● vi amotinar-se. **~ous** a amotinado

mutter /'mʌtə(r)/ vt/i resmungar

mutton /'mʌtn/ n (carne de) carneiro m

mutual /'mjuːtʃʊəl/ a mútuo; ⓘ (common) comum. **~ly** adv mutuamente

muzzle /'mʌzl/ n focinho m; (device) focinheira f, (P) açaime m; (of gun) boca f

m

● *vt* amordaçar; ‹*dog*› pôr focinheira(P) açaime em

my /maɪ/ *a* meu(s), minha(s)

myself /maɪ'self/ *pron* eu mesmo, eu próprio; (*reflexive*) me; (*after prep*) mim (próprio, mesmo); **by ~** sozinho

mysterious /mɪ'stɪərɪəs/ *a* misterioso

mystery /'mɪstərɪ/ *n* mistério *m*

mystic /'mɪstɪk/ *a* & *n* místico *m*. **~al** *a* místico. **~ism** /-sɪzəm/ *n* misticismo *m*

mystify /'mɪstɪfaɪ/ *vt* deixar perplexo

mystique /mɪ'stiːk/ *n* mística *f*

myth /mɪθ/ *n* mito *m*. **~ical** *a* mítico

mytholog|y /mɪ'θɒlədʒɪ/ *n* mitologia *f*. **~ical** /mɪθə'lɒdʒɪkl/ *a* mitológico

Nn

nab /næb/ *vt* (*pt* **nabbed**) 🅰 apanhar em flagrante; apanhar com a boca na botija 🅿; pilhar

nag /næg/ *vt/i* (*pt* **nagged**) implicar (com), criticar constantemente; (*pester*) apoquentar

nail /neɪl/ *n* prego *m*; (*of finger, toe*) unha *f*; **~ polish** esmalte *m*, (P) verniz *m* para as unhas; **hit the ~ on the head** acertar em cheio; **on the ~** sem demora ● *vt* pregar. **~ file** *n* lixa *f* de unhas

naïve /naɪ'iːv/ *a* ingênuo, (P) ingénuo

naked /'neɪkɪd/ *a* nu; **to the ~ eye** a olho nu, à vista desarmada. **~ness** *n* nudez *f*

name /neɪm/ *n* nome *m*; *fig* reputação *f*; fama ● *vt* (*mention; appoint*) nomear; (*give a name to*) chamar, dar o nome de; ‹*a date*› marcar; **be ~d after** ter o nome de. **~less** *a* sem nome, anônimo, (P) anónimo

namely /'neɪmlɪ/ *adv* a saber

namesake /'neɪmseɪk/ *n* homônimo *m*, (P) homónimo *m*

nanny /'nænɪ/ *n* ama *f*, babá *f*

nap[1] /næp/ *n* soneca *f* ● *vi* (*pt* **napped**) dormitar, tirar um cochilo, fazer uma sesta; **catch ~ping** apanhar desprevenido

nap[2] /næp/ *n* (*of material*) felpa *f*

napkin /'næpkɪn/ *n* guardanapo *m*; (*for baby*) fralda *f*

nappy /'næpɪ/ *n* fralda *f*. **~ rash** *n* assadura *f*

narcotic /nɑː'kɒtɪk/ *a* & *n* narcótico *m*

narrat|e /nə'reɪt/ *vt* narrar. **~ion** /-ʃn/ *n* narrativa *f*. **~or** *n* narrador *m*

narrative /'nærətɪv/ *n* narrativa *f* ● *a* narrativo

narrow /'nærəʊ/ *a* (-er, -est) estreito; *fig* restrito ● *vt/i* estreitar(-se); (*limit*) limitar(-se). **~ly** *adv* (*only just*) por pouco; (*closely, carefully*) de perto, com cuidado. **~-minded** *a* a bitolado, de visão limitada

nasal /'neɪzl/ *a* nasal

nast|y /'nɑːstɪ/ *a* (-ier, -iest) (*malicious, of weather*) mau; (*unpleasant*) desagradável, intragável; (*rude*) grosseiro

nation /'neɪʃn/ *n* nação *f*. **~wide** *a* em todo o país, em escala ou a nível nacional

national /'næʃnəl/ *a* nacional ● *n* natural *mf*; **~ anthem** hino *m* nacional. **~ism** *n* nacionalismo *m*. **~ize** *vt* nacionalizar

nationality /næʃə'nælətɪ/ *n* nacionalidade *f*

National Trust Fundação britânica 🅸 cujo objetivo é a conservação de lugares de interesse histórico ou de beleza natural. É financiada por doações e subvenções privadas. É a maior proprietária de terras da Grã-Bretanha. Na Escócia, é um organismo independente chamado *National Trust for Scotland*.

---

native /'neɪtɪv/ *n* natural *mf*, nativo *m* ● *a* nativo; (*country*) natal; (*inborn*) inato; **be a ~ of** ser natural de; **~ language** língua *f* materna; **~ speaker of Portuguese** falante *m* nativo de Português

Nativity /nə'tɪvətɪ/ *n* **the ~** a Natividade *f*

natter /'nætə(r)/ *vi* fazer conversa fiada, falar à toa, tagarelar

natural /'nætʃrəl/ *a* natural; **~ history** história *f* natural. **~ist** *n* naturalista *mf*. **~ly** *adv* naturalmente; (*by nature*) por natureza

naturaliz|e /'nætʃrəlaɪz/ *vt/i* naturalizar(-se); ‹*animal, plant*› aclimatar(-se). **~ation** /-'zeɪʃn/ *n* naturalização *f*

nature /'neɪtʃə(r)/ *n* natureza *f*; (*kind*) gênero *m*, (P) género *m*; (*of person*) índole *f*

naughty /'nɔːtɪ/ *a* (-ier, -iest) ‹*child*› levado; (*indecent*) picante

nause|a /'nɔːsɪə/ n náusea f. **~ating, ~ous** a nauseabundo, repugnante

nautical /'nɔːtɪkl/ a náutico; **~ mile** milha f marítima

naval /'neɪvl/ a naval; ‹officer› de marinha

nave /neɪv/ n nave f

navel /'neɪvl/ n umbigo m

navigable /'nævɪgəbl/ a navegável

navigat|e /'nævɪgeɪt/ vt ‹sea etc› navegar; ‹ship› pilotar ● vi navegar. **~ion** /-'geɪʃn/ n navegação f. **~or** n navegador m

navy /'neɪvɪ/ n marinha f de guerra; **~ (blue)** azul-marinho m invar

near /nɪə(r)/ adv perto, quase; **~ to** perto de; **draw ~** aproximar(-se) (**to** de) ● prep perto de ● a próximo; **N~ East** Oriente m Próximo, (P) Próximo Oriente m ● vt aproximar-se de, chegar-se a. **~ by** adv perto, próximo. **~ness** n proximidade f

nearby /'nɪəbaɪ/ a & adv próximo, perto

nearly /'nɪəlɪ/ adv quase, por pouco; **not ~ as pretty/etc** as longe de ser tão bonita/etc como

neat /niːt/ a (-er, -est) (bem) cuidado; ‹room› bem arrumado; ‹spirits› puro, sem gelo. **~ly** adv (with care) com cuidado; (cleverly) habilmente. **~ness** n aspecto m cuidado

necessar|y /'nesəsərɪ/ a necessário. **~ily** adv necessariamente

necessitate /nɪ'sesɪteɪt/ vt exigir, obrigar a, tornar necessário

necessity /nɪ'sesətɪ/ n necessidade f; (thing) coisa f indispensável, artigo m de primeira necessidade

neck /nek/ n pescoço m; (of dress) gola f; **~ and neck** emparelhados

necklace /'neklɪs/ n colar m

neckline /'neklaɪn/ n decote m

nectarine /'nektərɪn/ n pêssego m

née /neɪ/ a em solteira; **Ann Jones ~ Drewe** Ann Jones cujo nome de solteira era Drewe

need /niːd/ n necessidade f ● vt precisar de, necessitar de; **you ~ not come** não tem de or não precisa (de) vir. **~less** a inútil, desnecessário. **~lessly** adv inutilmente, sem necessidade

needle /'niːdl/ n agulha f ● vt 🔟 (provoke) provocar

needlework /'niːdlwɜːk/ n costura f; (embroidery) bordado m

needy /'niːdɪ/ a (-ier, -iest) necessitado, carenciado, carente

negation /nɪ'geɪʃn/ n negação f

negative /'negətɪv/ a negativo ● n negativa f, negação f; Photo negativo m; **in the ~** ‹answer› na negativa; Gram na forma negativa. **~ly** adv negativamente

neglect /nɪ'glekt/ vt descuidar; ‹opportunity› desprezar; ‹family› não cuidar de; ‹duty› não cumprir; **~ to** (omit to) esquecer-se de ● n falta f de cuidado(s), descuido m; **(state of) ~** abandono m. **~ful** a negligente

negligen|t /'neglɪdʒənt/ a negligente. **~ce** n negligência f, desleixo m

negligible /'neglɪdʒəbl/ a insignificante, ínfimo

negotiable /nɪ'gəʊʃəbl/ a negociável

negotiat|e /nɪ'gəʊʃɪeɪt/ vt/i negociar; ‹obstacle› transpor; ‹difficulty› vencer. **~ion** /-sɪ'eɪʃn/ n negociação f. **~or** n negociador m

Negro /'niːgrəʊ/ a & n (pl **oes**) negro m, preto m

neigh /neɪ/ n relincho m ● vi relinchar

neighbour /'neɪbə(r)/ n vizinho m. **~hood** n vizinhança f. **~ing** a vizinho. **~ly** a de boa vizinhança

neither /'naɪðə(r)/ a & pron nenhum(a) (de dois or duas), nem um nem outro, nem uma nem outra ● adv tampouco, também não ● conj nem; **~ big nor small** nem grande nem pequeno; **~ am I** nem eu

neocon /'niːəʊkɒn/ a & n neoconservador mf

neon /'niːɒn/ n néon m

nephew /'nevjuː/ n sobrinho m

nerve /nɜːv/ n nervo m; fig (courage) coragem f; 🔟 (impudence) descaramento m, (P) lata f 🔟; **get on sb's nerves** irritar, dar nos nervos de alguém. **~-racking** a de arrasar os nervos, enervante

nervous /'nɜːvəs/ a nervoso; **be or feel ~** (afraid) ter receio/um certo medo; **~ breakdown** esgotamento m nervoso. **~ly** adv nervosamente. **~ness** n nervosismo m; (fear) receio m

nest /nest/ n ninho m ● vi aninhar-se, fazer or ter ninho. **~ egg** n pé-de-meia m

nestle /'nesl/ vi aninhar-se

net¹ /net/ n rede f ● vt (pt **netted**) apanhar na rede. **~ting** n rede f; **wire ~ting** rede f de arame

net² /net/ a ‹weight etc› líquido

Netherlands /'neðələndz/ npl the ~ os Países Baixos

nettle /'netl/ n urtiga f

network /'netwз:k/ n rede f, cadeia f

neuro|sis /njʊə'rəʊsɪs/ n (pl -oses /-siːz/) neurose f. ~**tic** /-'rɒtɪk/ a & n neurótico m

neuter /'njuːtə(r)/ a & n neutro m ● vt castrar, capar

neutral /'njuːtrəl/ a neutro; ~ (**gear**) ponto m morto. ~**ity** /-'træləti/ n neutralidade f

never /'nevə(r)/ adv nunca; ▣ (not) não; **he** ~ **refuses** ele nunca recusa; **I** ~ **saw him** ▣ nunca o vi; ~ **mind** não faz mal, deixe para lá. ~~**ending** a interminável

nevertheless /nevəðə'les/ adv & conj contudo, no entanto

new /njuː/ a (-er, -est) novo; ~ **moon** lua f nova; ~ **year** ano m novo; **N~ Year's Day** dia m de Ano Novo; **N~ Year's Eve** véspera f de Ano Novo; **N~ Zealand** Nova Zelândia f; **N~ Zealander** neozelandês m. ~**born** a recém-nascido. ~**ness** n novidade f

New Age n Nova Era f, o Movimento Nova Era f

newcomer /'njuːkʌmə(r)/ n recém-chegado m

newfangled /njuː'fæŋgld/ a pej moderno

newly /'njuːlɪ/ adv há pouco, recentemente. ~~**weds** npl recém-casados mpl

news /njuːz/ n notícia(s) f(pl); Radio noticiário m, notícia(s) fpl; TV telejornal m. ~**caster**, ~**reader** n locutor m; ~**flash** n notícia f de última hora

newsagent /'njuːzeɪdʒənt/ n jornaleiro m

newsletter /'njuːzletə(r)/ n boletim m informativo

newspaper /'njuːzpeɪpə(r)/ n jornal m

newsreel /'njuːzriːl/ n atualidades fpl

newt /njuːt/ n tritão m

next /nekst/ a próximo; (adjoining) pegado, ao lado, contíguo; (following) seguinte ● adv a seguir; ~ **to** ao lado de; ~ **to nothing** quase nada ● n seguinte mf; ~ **of kin** parente m mais próximo. ~**door** a do lado

nib /nɪb/ n bico m, (P) aparo m

nibble /'nɪbl/ vt mordiscar, dar dentadinhas em

nice /naɪs/ a (-er, -est) agradável, bom; (kind) simpático, gentil; (pretty) bonito; (respectable) bem-educado; correto; (subtle) fino, subtil. ~**ly** adv agradavelmente; (well) bem

nicety /'naɪsətɪ/ n sutileza f, (P) subtileza f

niche /nɪtʃ/ n nicho m; fig bom lugar m

nick /nɪk/ n corte m, chanfradura f; ▣ (prison) cadeia f ● vt dar um corte em; ▣ (steal) roubar, limpar ▣; ▣ (arrest) apanhar; pôr a mão em ▣; **in good** ~ ▣ em boa forma, em bom estado; **in the** ~ **of time** mesmo a tempo

nickel /'nɪkl/ n níquel m; Amer moeda f de cinco cêntimos

nickname /'nɪkneɪm/ n apelido m, (P) alcunha f; (short form) diminutivo m ● vt apelidar de

nicotine /'nɪkətiːn/ n nicotina f

niece /niːs/ n sobrinha f

Nigeria /naɪ'dʒɪərɪə/ n Nigéria f. ~**n** a & n nigeriano m

night /naɪt/ n noite f; **at** ~ à/de noite; **by** ~ de noite ● a de noite, noturno. ~**cap** n (drink) bebida f tomada na hora de deitar; ~**club** n boate f, (P) boîte f; ~**dress**, ~**gown** ns camisola f de dormir, (P) camisa f de noite; ~**life** n vida f noturna; ~ **school** n escola f noturna; ~**time** n noite f

nightfall /'naɪtfɔːl/ n anoitecer m

nightingale /'naɪtɪŋgeɪl/ n rouxinol m

nightly /'naɪtlɪ/ a noturno ● adv de noite, à noite, todas as noites

nightmare /'naɪtmeə(r)/ n pesadelo m

nil /nɪl/ n nada m; Sport zero m ● a nulo

nimble /'nɪmbl/ a (-er, -est) ágil, ligeiro

nin|e /naɪn/ a & n nove m. ~**th** a & n nono m

nineteen /naɪn'tiːn/ a & n dezenove m, (P) dezanove m. ~**th** a & n décimo nono m

ninet|y /'naɪntɪ/ a & n noventa m. ~**ieth** a & n nonagésimo m

nip /nɪp/ vt/i (pt nipped) apertar, beliscar; ▣ (rush) ir correndo; ir num pulo ▣; ~ **in the bud** cortar pela raiz ● n aperto m, beliscão m; (drink) gole m, trago m; **a** ~ **in the air** um frio cortante

nipple /'nɪpl/ n mamilo m

nippy /'nɪpɪ/ a (-ier, -iest) ▣ (quick) rápido; ▣ (chilly) cortante

nitrogen /'naɪtrədʒən/ n azoto m, nitrogênio m, (P) nitrogénio m

nitwit /'nɪtwɪt/ n 🔲 imbecil m

no /nəʊ/ a nenhum; ~ **entry** entrada f proibida; ~ **money/time/**etc nenhum dinheiro/tempo/etc; ~ **man's land** terra f de ninguém; ~ **one** ▶ NOBODY ● adv não; ~ **smoking** é proibido fumar; ~ **way!** 🔲 de modo nenhum! ● n (pl **noes**) não m

nob|le /'nəʊbl/ a (**-er, -est**) nobre. **~ility** /-'bɪlətɪ/ n nobreza f

nobleman /'nəʊblmən/ n (pl **-men**) nobre m, fidalgo m

nobody /'nəʊbɒdɪ/ pron ninguém ● n nulidade f; **he knows** ~ ele não conhece ninguém; ~ **is there** não tem ninguém lá, (P) não está lá ninguém

no-brainer /nəʊ'breɪnə(r)/ n trivialidade f

nocturnal /nɒk'tɜːnl/ a noturno

nod /nɒd/ vt/i (pt **nodded**) ~ (**one's head**) acenar (com) a cabeça; ~ (**off**) cabecear ● n aceno m com a cabeça (para dizer que sim or para cumprimentar)

noise /nɔɪz/ n ruído m, barulho m. **~less** a silencioso

nois|y /'nɔɪzɪ/ a (**-ier, -iest**) ruidoso, barulhento

nomad /'nəʊmæd/ n nômada mf, (P) nómada mf. **~ic** /-'mædɪk/ a nômada, (P) nómada

nominal /'nɒmɪnl/ a nominal; ⟨fee, sum⟩ simbólico

nominat|e /'nɒmɪneɪt/ vt (appoint) nomear; (put forward) propor. **~ion** /-'neɪʃn/ n nomeação f

non- /nɒn/ pref não, sem, in-, a-, anti-, des-. **~stick** a não-aderente

nonchalant /'nɒnʃələnt/ a indiferente, desinteressado

non-commissioned /nɒnkə-'mɪʃnd/ a ~ **officer** sargento m, cabo m

non-committal /nɒnkə'mɪtl/ a evasivo

nondescript /'nɒndɪskrɪpt/ a insignificante, medíocre, indefinível

none /nʌn/ pron (person) nenhum, ninguém; (thing) nenhum, nada; ~ **of us** nenhum de nós; **I have** ~ não tenho nenhum; ~ **of that!** nada disso! ● adv ~ **too** não muito; **he is** ~ **the happier** nem por isso ele é mais feliz; ~ **the less** contudo, no entanto, apesar disso

nonentity /nɒ'nentətɪ/ n nulidade f, zero à m esquerda, João Ninguém m

non-existent /nɒnɪg'zɪstənt/ a inexistente

nonplussed /nɒn'plʌst/ a perplexo, pasmado

nonsens|e /'nɒnsns/ n absurdo m, disparate m. **~ical** /-'sensɪkl/ a absurdo, disparatado

non-smoker /nɒn'sməʊkə(r)/ n nãofumante m, (P) nãofumador m

non-stop /nɒn'stɒp/ a ininterrupto, contínuo; ⟨train⟩ direto; ⟨flight⟩ sem escala ● adv sem parar

noodles /'nuːdlz/ npl talharim m, (P) macaronete m

nook /nʊk/ n (re)canto m

noon /nuːn/ n meio-dia m

noose /nuːs/ n laço m corrediço

nor /nɔː(r)/ conj & adv nem, também não; ~ **do I** nem eu

norm /nɔːm/ n norma f

normal /'nɔːml/ a & n normal m; **above/below** ~ acima/abaixo do normal. **~ity** /nɔː'mælətɪ/ n normalidade f. **~ly** adv normalmente

north /nɔːθ/ n norte m ● a norte, do norte; (of country, people etc) setentrional ● adv a, ao/para o norte; **N~ America** América f do Norte. **~erly** /'nɔːðəlɪ/ a do norte. **~ward(s)** adv para o norte. **N~ American** a & n norteamericano m; **~east** n nordeste m; **~west** n noroeste m

northern /'nɔːðən/ a do norte

Norw|ay /'nɔːweɪ/ n Noruega f. **~egian** /nɔː'wiːdʒən/ a & n norueguês m

nose /nəʊz/ n nariz m; (of animal) focinho m ● vi ~ **about** farejar; **pay through the** ~ pagar um preço exorbitante

nosebleed /'nəʊzbliːd/ n hemorragia f nasal or pelo nariz

nosedive /'nəʊzdaɪv/ n voo m picado

nostalg|ia /nɒ'stældʒə/ n nostalgia f. **~ic** a nostálgico

nostril /'nɒstrəl/ n narina f; (of horse) venta f (usually pl)

nosy /'nəʊzɪ/ a (**-ier, -iest**) 🔲 bisbilhoteiro

---

not /nɒt/ ● adv

····▶ não; ~ **at all** nada, de modo nenhum; (reply to thanks) de nada; **he is** ~ **at all bored** ele não está nem um pouco entediado; ~ **yet** ainda não; **I suppose** ~ creio que não

---

notable /'nəʊtəbl/ a notável ● n notabilidade f

notably /ˈnəʊtəblɪ/ adv notavelmente; (particularly) especialmente

notch /nɒtʃ/ n corte m em V ● vt marcar com cortes; ~ **up** ‹score etc› marcar

note /nəʊt/ n nota f; (banknote) nota (de banco) f; (short letter) bilhete m ● vt notar

notebook /ˈnəʊtbʊk/ n livrinho m de notas, (P) bloco m de notas

noted /ˈnəʊtɪd/ a conhecido, famoso

notepaper /ˈnəʊtpeɪpə(r)/ n papel m de carta

noteworthy /ˈnəʊtwɜːðɪ/ a notável

nothing /ˈnʌθɪŋ/ n nada m; (person) nulidade f, zero m; **he eats** ~ ele não come nada; ~ **big**/etc nada (de) grande/ etc; ~ **else** nada mais; ~ **much** pouca coisa; **for** ~ (free) de graça; (in vain) em vão ● adv nada, de modo algum or nenhum, de maneira alguma or nenhuma

notice /ˈnəʊtɪs/ n anúncio m, notícia f; (in street, on wall) letreiro m; (warning) aviso m; (attention) atenção f; **(advance)** ~ pré-aviso m; **at short** ~ num prazo curto; **a week's** ~ o prazo de uma semana; **hand in one's** ~ pedir demissão; **take** ~ reparar (**of** em); **take no** ~ não fazer caso (**of** de) ● vt notar, reparar. ~**board** n quadro m para afixar anúncios etc

noticeabl|e /ˈnəʊtɪsəbl/ a visível. ~**y** adv visivelmente

notif|y /ˈnəʊtɪfaɪ/ vt participar, notificar. ~**ication** /-ɪˈkeɪʃn/ n participação f, notificação f

notion /ˈnəʊʃn/ n noção f

notor|ious /nəʊˈtɔːrɪəs/ a notório. ~**iety** /-əˈraɪətɪ/ n fama f

notwithstanding /nɒtwɪθˈstændɪŋ/ prep apesar de, não obstante ● adv mesmo assim, ainda assim ● conj embora, conquanto, apesar de (que)

nougat /ˈnuːgɑː/ n nugá m, torrone m, (P) nogado m

nought /nɔːt/ n zero m

noun /naʊn/ n substantivo m, nome m

nourish /ˈnʌrɪʃ/ vt alimentar, nutrir. ~**ing** a alimentício, nutritivo. ~**ment** n alimento m, sustento m

novel /ˈnɒvl/ n romance m ● a novo, original. ~**ist** n romancista mf. ~**ty** n novidade f

November /nəʊˈvembə(r)/ n novembro m

novice /ˈnɒvɪs/ n (beginner) noviço m, novato m; Relig noviço m

now /naʊ/ adv agora; **by** ~ a estas horas, por esta altura; **from** ~ **on** de agora em diante; ~ **and again,** ~ **and then** de vez em quando; **right** ~ já ● conj ~ **(that)** agora que

nowadays /ˈnaʊədeɪz/ adv hoje em dia, presentemente, atualmente

nowhere /ˈnəʊweə(r)/ adv (position) em lugar nenhum, em lado nenhum; (direction) a lado nenhum, a parte alguma or nenhuma

nozzle /ˈnɒzl/ n bico m, bocal m; (of hose) agulheta f

nuance /ˈnjuːɑːns/ n nuance f, matiz m

nuclear /ˈnjuːklɪə(r)/ a nuclear

nucleus /ˈnjuːklɪəs/ n (pl -lei /-lɪaɪ/) núcleo m

nud|e /njuːd/ a & n nu m; **in the** ~**e** nu. ~**ity** n nudez f

nudge /nʌdʒ/ vt tocar com o cotovelo, cutucar ● n ligeira cotovelada f, cutucada f

nudis|t /ˈnjuːdɪst/ n nudista mf

nuisance /ˈnjuːsns/ n aborrecimento m; chatice f 🔠; (person) chato m 🔠

null /nʌl/ a nulo; ~ **and void** Jur írrito e nulo

numb /nʌm/ a entorpecido, dormente ● vt entorpecer, adormecer

number /ˈnʌmbə(r)/ n número m; (numeral) algarismo m ● vt numerar; (amount to) ser em número de; (count) contar, incluir. ~ **plate** n chapa (do carro) f, (P) matrícula f (do carro)

numeral /ˈnjuːmərəl/ n número m, algarismo m

numerate /ˈnjuːmərət/ a que tem conhecimentos básicos de matemática

numerical /njuːˈmerɪkl/ a numérico

numerous /ˈnjuːmərəs/ a numeroso

nun /nʌn/ n freira f, religiosa f

nurs|e /nɜːs/ n enfermeira f, enfermeiro m; (nanny) ama(-seca) f, babá f ● vt cuidar de, tratar de; ‹hopes etc› alimentar, acalentar. ~**ing** n enfermagem f; ~**ing home** clínica f de repouso, (P) lar m de idosos

nursery /ˈnɜːsərɪ/ n quarto m de crianças; (for plants) viveiro m; **(day)** ~ creche f; ~ **rhyme** poema or canção f infantil m; ~ **school** jardim m de infância

nurture /ˈnɜːtʃə(r)/ vt educar

nut /nʌt/ n Bot noz f; Techn porca f de parafuso

nutcrackers /ˈnʌtkrækəz/ npl quebra-nozes m invar

nutmeg /'nʌtmeg/ n noz-moscada f

nutrient /'njuːtrɪənt/ n substância f nutritiva, nutriente m

nutrit|ion /njuːˈtrɪʃn/ n nutrição f. **~ious** a nutritivo

nutshell /'nʌtʃel/ n casca f de noz; **in a ~** em poucas palavras, em suma

nuzzle /'nʌzl/ vt esfregar com o focinho

nylon /'naɪlɒn/ n nylon m; **~s** meias fpl de nylon

Oo

oak /əʊk/ n carvalho m

OAP abbr (= old-age pensioner) ▸ OLD

oar /ɔː(r)/ n remo m

oasis /əʊˈeɪsɪs/ n (pl oases /-siːz/) oásis m

oath /əʊθ/ n juramento m; (swear word) praga f

oatmeal /'əʊtmiːl/ n farinha f de aveia; (porridge) papa f de aveia

oats /əʊts/ npl aveia f

obedien|t /əˈbiːdɪənt/ a obediente. **~ce** n obediência f

obes|e /əʊˈbiːs/ a obeso. **~ity** n obesidade f

obey /əˈbeɪ/ vt/i obedecer (a)

obituary /əˈbɪtʃʊərɪ/ n necrológio m, (P) necrologia f

object[1] /'ɒbdʒɪkt/ n objeto m; (aim) objetivo m; Gram complemento m

object[2] /əbˈdʒekt/ vt/i objetar (que); **~ to** opor-se a, discordar de. **~ion** /-ʃn/ n objeção f

objectionable /əbˈdʒekʃnəbl/ a censurável; (unpleasant) desagradável

objectiv|e /əbˈdʒektɪv/ a objetivo. **~ity** /-ˈtɪvətɪ/ n objetividade f

obligation /ɒblɪˈɡeɪʃn/ n obrigação f; **be under an ~ to sb** dever favores a alguém

obligatory /əˈblɪɡətrɪ/ a obrigatório

oblig|e /əˈblaɪdʒ/ vt obrigar; (do a favour) fazer um favor a, obsequiar. **~ed** a obrigado (to a); **~ed to sb** em dívida (para) com alguém. **~ing** a prestável, amável

oblique /əˈbliːk/ a oblíquo

obliterat|e /əˈblɪtəreɪt/ vt obliterar. **~ion** /-ˈreɪʃn/ n obliteração f

oblivion /əˈblɪvɪən/ n esquecimento m

oblivious /əˈblɪvɪəs/ a esquecido; sem consciência (of/to de)

oblong /'ɒblɒŋ/ a oblongo, alongado ● n retângulo m

obnoxious /əbˈnɒkʃəs/ a ofensivo, detestável

oboe /'əʊbəʊ/ n oboé m

obscen|e /əbˈsiːn/ a obsceno. **~ity** /-ˈenətɪ/ n obscenidade f

obscur|e /əbˈskjʊə(r)/ a obscuro ● vt obscurecer; (conceal) encobrir. **~ity** n obscuridade f

obsequious /əbˈsiːkwɪəs/ a demasiado obsequioso, subserviente

observan|t /əbˈzɜːvənt/ a observador. **~ce** n observância f, cumprimento m

observatory /əbˈzɜːvətrɪ/ n observatório m

observ|e /əbˈzɜːv/ vt observar. **~ation** /ɒbzəˈveɪʃn/ n observação f; **keep under ~ation** vigiar. **~er** n observador m

obsess /əbˈses/ vt obcecar. **~ion** /-ʃn/ n obsessão f. **~ive** a obsessivo

obsessive-compulsive disorder n transtorno obsessivo-compulsivo m

obsolete /'ɒbsəliːt/ a obsoleto, antiquado

obstacle /'ɒbstəkl/ n obstáculo m

obstetric|s /əbˈstetrɪks/ n obstetrícia f. **~ian** /ɒbstɪˈtrɪʃn/ n obstetra mf

obstina|te /'ɒbstɪnət/ a obstinado. **~cy** n obstinação f

obstruct /əbˈstrʌkt/ vt obstruir, bloquear; (hinder) estorvar, obstruir. **~ion** /-ʃn/ n obstrução f; (thing) obstáculo m

obtain /əbˈteɪn/ vt obter ● vi prevalecer, estar em vigor. **~able** a que se pode obter

obtrusive /əbˈtruːsɪv/ a importuno; ‹thing› demasiado em evidência; que dá muito na(s) vista(s) 🄸

obvious /'ɒbvɪəs/ a óbvio, evidente. **~ly** adv obviamente

occasion /əˈkeɪʒn/ n ocasião f; (event) acontecimento m ● vt ocasionar; **on ~** de vez em quando, ocasionalmente

occasional /əˈkeɪʒənl/ a ocasional. **~ly** adv de vez em quando, ocasionalmente

occult /ɒˈkʌlt/ a oculto

occupation /ɒkjʊˈpeɪʃn/ n ocupação f. **~al** a profissional; ‹therapy› ocupacional

occup|y /'ɒkjʊpaɪ/ vt ocupar. **~ant ~ier** ns ocupante mf

n
o

occur /əˈkɜː(r)/ vi (pt **occurred**) ocorrer, acontecer, dar-se; (arise) apresentar-se, aparecer; **~ to sb** ocorrer a alguém

occurrence /əˈkʌrəns/ n acontecimento m, ocorrência f

ocean /ˈəʊʃn/ n oceano m

o'clock /əˈklɒk/ adv **it is one ~** é uma hora; **it is six ~** são seis horas

octagon /ˈɒktəgən/ n octógono m. **~al** /-ˈtægənl/ a octogonal

October /ɒkˈtəʊbə(r)/ n outubro m

octopus /ˈɒktəpəs/ n (pl **-puses**) polvo m

odd /ɒd/ a (**-er, -est**) estranho, singular; ‹number› ímpar; (left over) de sobra; (not of set) desemparelhado; (occasional) ocasional; **~ jobs** (paid) biscates mpl; (in garden etc) trabalhos mpl diversos; **twenty ~** vinte e tantos. **~ity** n singularidade f; (thing) curiosidade f. **~ly** adv de modo estranho

oddment /ˈɒdmənt/ n resto m, artigo m avulso

odds /ɒdz/ npl probabilidades fpl; (in betting) ganhos mpl líquidos; **at ~** em desacordo; (quarrelling) de mal, brigado; **it makes no ~** não faz diferença; **~ and ends** artigos mpl avulsos, coisas fpl pequenas

odious /ˈəʊdɪəs/ a odioso

odour /ˈəʊdə(r)/ n odor m. **~less** a inodoro

o

of /əv emphatic ɒv/ ● prep

····▶ de; **a friend ~ mine** um amigo meu; **the mother ~ the twins** a mãe dos gêmeos; **the fifth ~ June** (dia) cinco de junho; **take six ~ them** leve seis deles; **the works ~ Shakespeare** as obras de Shakespeare; **made ~ gold** (feito) de ouro

❗ the preposition *de* often contracts with: definite articles *o* and *a* to form *do, da*; demonstrative pronouns *este, esse, aquele, isto, isso, aquilo* to form *deste, desse, daquele, disto, disso, daquilo*; personal pronouns *ele, ela* to form *dele, dela*.

····▶ (on the part of) da parte de; **it was nice ~ him/John** foi simpático da parte dele/da parte do John →For translations of expressions such as **of course** and **consist of** see entries **course** and **consist**

off /ɒf/ adv embora, fora; (switched off) apagado, desligado; (taken off) tirado, tirado; (cancelled) cancelado;

‹food› estragado; **be well ~** ser abastado ● prep (fora) de; (distant from) a alguma distância de; **be ~** (depart) ir-se embora, partir; **be better/worse ~** estar em melhor/pior situação; **a day ~** um dia de folga; **20% ~** redução de 20%; **on the ~ chance that** no caso de; **~ colour** indisposto, adoentado. **~ licence** n loja f de bebidas alcoólicas; **~load** vt descarregar; **~putting** a desconcertante; **~stage** adv fora de cena; **~white** a branco-sujo

offal /ˈɒfl/ n miudezas fpl, fressura f

offence /əˈfens/ n (feeling) ofensa f; (crime) delito m, transgressão f; **give ~ to** ofender; **take ~** ofender-se (**at** com)

offend /əˈfend/ vt ofender; **be ~ed** ofender-se (**at** com). **~er** n delinquente mf

offensive /əˈfensɪv/ a ofensivo; (disgusting) repugnante ● n ofensiva f

offer /ˈɒfə(r)/ vt (pt **offered**) oferecer ● n oferta f; **on ~** em promoção. **~ing** n oferenda f

offhand /ɒfˈhænd/ a espontâneo; (curt) seco ● adv de improviso, sem pensar

office /ˈɒfɪs/ n escritório m; (post) cargo m; (branch) filial f; **~ hours** horas fpl de expediente; **in ~** no poder; **take ~** assumir o cargo

officer /ˈɒfɪsə(r)/ n oficial m; (policeman) agente m

official /əˈfɪʃl/ a oficial ● n funcionário m. **~ly** adv oficialmente

officiate /əˈfɪʃɪeɪt/ vi Relig oficiar; **~ as** presidir, exercer as funções de

officious /əˈfɪʃəs/ a intrometido

offing /ˈɒfɪŋ/ n **in the ~** fig em perspectiva

> **off-licence** No Reino Unido, toda e qualquer loja que tenha uma licença para vender bebidas alcoólicas que devem ser consumidas fora do local. Abrem quando os *pubs* estão fechados e também costumam vender bebidas não alcoólicas, tabaco, guloseimas, etc. Muitas vezes alugam copos para festas, etc.

offset /ˈɒfset/ vt (pt **-set**, pres p **-setting**) compensar, contrabalançar

offshoot /ˈɒfʃuːt/ n rebento m; fig efeito m secundário

offshore /ˈɒfʃɔː(r)/ a ao largo da costa

offside /ɒfˈsaɪd/ a & adv offside, em impedimento, (P) fora de jogo

offspring /ˈɒfsprɪŋ/ n (pl invar) descendência f, prole f

often /ˈɒfn/ adv muitas vezes, frequentemente; **every so ~** de vez em quando; **how ~?** quantas vezes?

oh /əʊ/ int oh, ah

oil /ɔɪl/ n óleo m; (petroleum) petróleo m; **~ rig** plataforma f de poço de petróleo; **~ well** poço m de petróleo ● vt lubrificar. **~ painting** n pintura f a óleo. **~y** a oleoso; ‹food› gorduroso

oilfield /ˈɔɪlfiːld/ n campo m petrolífero

ointment /ˈɔɪntmənt/ n pomada f

OK /əʊˈkeɪ/ a & adv 🄸 (está) bem; (está) certo; (está) legal

old /əʊld/ a (-er, -est) velho; ‹person› velho, idoso; (former) antigo; **how ~ is he?** que idade tem ele?; **of ~** (d)antes, antigamente; **~ age** velhice f; **~-age pensioner** reformado m, aposentado m, pessoa f de terceira idade; **~ boy** antigo aluno m; **~ girl** antiga aluna f; **~ maid** solteirona f; **~ man** homem m idoso, velho m; **~ woman** mulher f idosa, velha f. **~-fashioned** a fora de moda

olive /ˈɒlɪv/ n azeitona f ● a de azeitona; **~ oil** azeite m

Olympic /əˈlɪmpɪk/ a olímpico; **~ Games** Jogos mpl Olímpicos. **~s** npl Olimpíadas fpl

omelette /ˈɒmlɪt/ n omelete f

omen /ˈəʊmən/ n agouro m

ominous /ˈɒmɪnəs/ a agourento

omi|t /əˈmɪt/ vt (pt omitted) omitir. **~ssion** /-ʃn/ n omissão f

on /ɒn/ prep sobre, em cima de, de, em; **~ arrival** na chegada, ao chegar; **~ foot** a pé etc; **~ doing** ao fazer; **~ time** na hora, dentro do horário; **~ Tuesday** na terça-feira; **~ Tuesdays** às terças-feiras ● adv para diante, para a frente; (switched on) aceso, ligado; (tap) aberto; (machine) em funcionamento; (put on) posto; (happening) em curso; **walk/etc ~** continuar a andar/etc; **be ~ at** Film, TV estar levando ou passando, (P) estar a dar; **~ and off** de vez em quando; **~ and ~** sem parar

once /wʌns/ adv uma vez; (formerly) noutro(s) tempo(s) ● conj uma vez que, desde que; **all at ~** de repente; (simultaneously) todos ao mesmo tempo; **just this ~** só esta vez; **~ (and) for all** duma vez para sempre; **~ upon a time** era uma vez. **~-over** n 🄸 vista f de olhos

oncoming /ˈɒnkʌmɪŋ/ a que se aproxima, próximo; **the ~ traffic** o trânsito que vem do sentido oposto, (P) no sentido contrário

one /wʌn/ a um(a); (sole) único ● n um(a) mf ● pron um(a) mf; (impersonal) se; **~ by** um a um; **a big/red/etc~** um grande/vermelho/etc; **this/that~** este/esse; **~ another** um ao outro, uns aos outros. **~-sided** a parcial; **~-way** a ‹street› mão única, (P) via f de sentido único; ‹ticket› simples

oneself /wʌnˈself/ pron si, si mesmo/próprio; (reflexive) se; **by ~** sozinho

onion /ˈʌnɪən/ n cebola f

online /ɒnˈlaɪn/ a conectado or (P) ligado (à Internet), online

onlooker /ˈɒnlʊkə(r)/ n espectador m, circunstante mf

only /ˈəʊnlɪ/ a único; **an ~ child** um filho único ● adv apenas, só, somente; **he ~ has six** ele só tem seis; **not ~ ... but also** não só ... mas também; **~ too** muito, mais que ● conj só que

onset /ˈɒnset/ n começo m; (attack) ataque m

onslaught /ˈɒnslɔːt/ n ataque m violento, assalto m

onward(s) /ˈɒnwəd(z)/ adv para a frente/diante

ooze /uːz/ vt/i escorrer, verter

opal /ˈəʊpl/ n opala f

opaque /əʊˈpeɪk/ a opaco, tosco

open /ˈəʊpən/ a aberto; ‹view› aberto, amplo; (free to all) aberto ao público; (attempt) franco; **in the ~ air** ao ar livre; **keep an ~ house** receber muito, abrir a porta para todos; **~ secret** segredo m de polichinelo; **~ sea** mar m alto ● vt/i abrir(-se); (of shop, play) abrir; **~ on to** dar para; **~ out** or **up** abrir(-se). **~-heart** a (of surgery) de coração aberto; **~-minded** a que tem uma mente aberta; **~-plan** a sem divisórias. **~ness** n abertura f; (frankness) franqueza f

opener /ˈəʊpənə(r)/ n (tins) abridor m de latas, (P) abre-latas m invar; (bottles) saca-rolhas m invar

opening /ˈəʊpənɪŋ/ n abertura f; (beginning) começo m; (opportunity) oportunidade f; (job) vaga f

openly /ˈəʊpənlɪ/ adv abertamente

Open University A universidade à distância na Grã-Bretanha, fundada em 1969. As aulas são lecionadas por correspondência, através de material impresso, material enviado pela Internet e de programas de televisão emitidos pela BBC. Também há cursos de verão aos quais os alunos devem assistir presencialmente. Não se exige nenhuma qualificação acadêmica para entrar na *Open University*.

opera /'ɒprə/ n ópera f. **~ glasses** npl binóculo (de teatro) m, (P) binóculos mpl. **~tic** /ɒpə'rætɪk/ a de ópera, operático

operat|e /'ɒpəreɪt/ vt/i operar; Techn (pôr a) funcionar; **~e on** Med operar. **~ing theatre** n Med anfiteatro m, sala f de operações. **~ion** /-'reɪʃn/ n operação f; **in ~ion** em vigor; Techn em funcionamento. **~ional** /-'reɪʃnl/ a operacional. **~or** n operador m; (telephonist) telefonista mf

operative /'ɒpərətɪv/ a (surgical) operatório; ‹law etc› em vigor

opinion /ə'pɪnɪən/ n opinião f, parecer m; **in my ~** a meu ver. **~ poll** n sondagem (de opinião) f. **~ated** /-eɪtɪd/ a dogmático, opinioso

opium /'əʊpɪəm/ n ópio m

Oporto /ə'pɔːtəʊ/ n Porto m

opponent /ə'pəʊnənt/ n adversário m, antagonista mf, oponente mf

opportune /'ɒpətjuːn/ a oportuno

opportunity /ɒpə'tjuːnətɪ/ n oportunidade f

oppos|e /ə'pəʊz/ vt opor-se a; **~ed to** oposto a. **~ing** a oposto

opposite /'ɒpəzɪt/ a & n oposto m, contrário m ● adv em frente ● prep **~ (to)** em frente de/a

opposition /ɒpə'zɪʃn/ n oposição f

oppress /ə'pres/ vt oprimir. **~ion** /-ʃn/ n opressão f. **~ive** a opressivo

opt /ɒpt/ vi **~ for** optar por; **~ out** recusar-se a participar (of de); **~ to do** escolher fazer

optical /'ɒptɪkl/ a óptico; **~ illusion** ilusão óptica f

optician /ɒp'tɪʃn/ n oculista mf

optimis|t /'ɒptɪmɪst/ n otimista mf. **~m** /-zəm/ n otimismo m. **~tic** /-'mɪstɪk/ a otimista

optimum /'ɒptɪməm/ a & n (pl **-ima**) ótimo m, (P) óptimo m

option /'ɒpʃn/ n escolha f, opção f; **have no ~ (but)** não ter outro remédio (senão)

optional /'ɒpʃənl/ a opcional, facultativo

opulen|t /'ɒpjʊlənt/ a opulento. **~ce** n opulência f

or /ɔː(r)/ conj ou; (with negative) nem; **~ else** senão

oracle /'ɒrəkl/ n oráculo m

oral /'ɔːrəl/ a oral

orange /'ɒrɪndʒ/ n laranja f; (colour) laranja m, cor f de laranja ● a de laranja; (colour) alaranjado, cor de laranja

orator /'ɒrətə(r)/ n orador m. **~y** n oratória f

orbit /'ɔːbɪt/ n órbita f ● vt (pt **orbited**) gravitar em torno de

orchard /'ɔːtʃəd/ n pomar m

orchestra /'ɔːkɪstrə/ n orquestra f. **~l** /-'kestrəl/ a orquestral

orchestrate /'ɔːkɪstreɪt/ vt orquestrar

orchid /'ɔːkɪd/ n orquídea f

ordain /ɔː'deɪn/ vt decretar; Relig ordenar

ordeal /ɔː'diːl/ n prova f, provação f

order /'ɔːdə(r)/ n ordem f; Comm encomenda f; pedido m ● vt ordenar; ‹goods etc› encomendar; **in ~ that** para que; **in ~ to** para

orderly /'ɔːdəlɪ/ a ordenado, em ordem; (not unruly) ordeiro ● n Mil ordenança f; Med servente m de hospital

ordinary /'ɔːdɪnrɪ/ a normal, ordinário, vulgar; **out of the ~** fora do comum

ordination /ɔːdɪ'neɪʃn/ n Relig ordenação f

ore /ɔː(r)/ n minério m

organ /'ɔːgən/ n órgão m. **~ist** n organista mf

organic /ɔː'gænɪk/ a orgânico

organism /'ɔːgənɪzəm/ n organismo m

organiz|e /'ɔːgənaɪz/ vt organizar. **~ation** /-'zeɪʃn/ n organização f. **~er** n organizador m

orgasm /'ɔːgæzəm/ n orgasmo m

orgy /'ɔːdʒɪ/ n orgia f

Orient /'ɔːrɪənt/ n **the ~** o Oriente m

orientat|e /'ɔːrɪənteɪt/ vt orientar. **~ion** /-'teɪʃn/ n orientação f

origin /'ɒrɪdʒɪn/ n origem f

original /ə'rɪdʒənl/ a original; (not copied) original. **~ity** /-'nælətɪ/ n originalidade f. **~ly** adv originalmente; (in the beginning) originariamente

originat|e /ə'rɪdʒəneɪt/ vt/i originar(-se). **~e from** provir de

ornament /'ɔːnəmənt/ n ornamento m; (object) peça f decorativa. **~al**

/-'mentl/ a ornamental

ornate /ɔː'neɪt/ a florido, floreado

ornitholog|y /ɔːnɪ'θɒlədʒɪ/ n ornitologia f

orphan /'ɔːfn/ n órfã(o) f(m) ● vt deixar órfão. **~age** n orfanato m

orthodox /'ɔːθədɒks/ a ortodoxo

orthopaedic /ɔːθə'piːdɪk/ a ortopédico

oscillate /'ɒsɪleɪt/ vi oscilar, vacilar

ostensibl|e /ɒs'tensəbl/ a aparente, pretenso. **~y** adv aparentemente, pretensamente

ostentati|on /ɒsten'teɪʃn/ n ostentação f. **~ous** /-'teɪʃəs/ a ostentoso, ostensivo

osteopath /'ɒstɪəpæθ/ n osteopata mf

ostracize /'ɒstrəsaɪz/ vt pôr de lado, marginalizar

ostrich /'ɒstrɪtʃ/ n avestruz mf

other /'ʌðə(r)/ a, n & pron outro m; (some) **~s** outros; **the ~ day** no outro dia; **the ~ one** o outro ● adv **~ than** diferente de, senão

otherwise /'ʌðəwaɪz/ adv de outro modo ● conj senão, caso contrário

otter /'ɒtə(r)/ n lontra f

ouch /aʊtʃ/ int ai!, uil

ought /ɔːt/ v aux (pt ought) dever; **you ~ to stay** você devia ficar; **he ~ to succeed** ele deve vencer; **I ~ to have done it** eu devia tê-lo feito

ounce /aʊns/ n onça f (= 28,35 g)

our /'aʊə(r)/ a nosso(s), nossa(s)

ours /'aʊəz/ poss pron o(s) nosso(s), a(s) nossa(s)

ourselves /aʊə'selvz/ pron nós mesmos/próprios; (reflexive) nos; **by ~** sozinhos

oust /aʊst/ vt expulsar, obrigar a sair

out /aʊt/ adv fora; (of light, fire) apagado; (in blossom) aberto, desabrochado, em flor; (of tide) baixo; **be ~** não estar em casa, estar fora (de casa); (wrong) enganar-se; **be ~ to** estar resolvido a; **run/etc ~** sair correndo or (P) a correr/etc; **~ of** fora de; (without) sem; **~ of pity/etc** por pena/etc; **made ~ of** feito de or em; **take ~** tirar de; **5 ~ of 6** 5 (de) entre 6; **~ of date** fora de moda; (not valid) fora do prazo; **~ of doors** ao ar livre; **~ of one's mind** doido; **~ of order** quebrado, (P) avariado; **~ of place** deslocado; **~ of the way** afastado. **~-and-** a completo,

rematado; **~patient** n doente mf de consulta externa

outboard /'aʊtbɔːd/ a **~ motor** motor m de popa

outbox /'aʊtbɒks/ n caixa f de saída

outbreak /'aʊtbreɪk/ n (of flu etc) surto m, epidemia f; (of war) deflagração f

outburst /'aʊtbɜːst/ n explosão f

outcast /'aʊtkɑːst/ n pária m

outcome /'aʊtkʌm/ n resultado m

outcry /'aʊtkraɪ/ n clamor m; (protest) protesto m

outdated /aʊt'deɪtɪd/ a fora da moda, ultrapassado

outdo /aʊt'duː/ vt (pt -did, pp -done) ultrapassar, superar

outdoor /'aʊtdɔː(r)/ a ao ar livre. **~s** /-'dɔːz/ adv fora de casa, ao ar livre

outer /'aʊtə(r)/ a exterior; **~ space** espaço (cósmico) m

outfit /'aʊtfɪt/ n equipamento m; (clothes) roupa f

outgoing /'aʊtgəʊɪŋ/ a que vai sair; (of minister etc) demissionário; fig sociável. **~s** npl despesas fpl

outgrow /aʊt'grəʊ/ vt (pt -grew, pp -grown) crescer mais do que; ‹clothes› já não caber em

outing /'aʊtɪŋ/ n saída f, passeio m

outlandish /aʊt'lændɪʃ/ a exótico, estranho

outlaw /'aʊtlɔː/ n fora da lei mf, bandido m ● vt banir, proscrever

outlay /'aʊtleɪ/ n despesa(s) f(pl)

outlet /'aʊtlet/ n saída f, escoadouro m; (for goods) mercado m, saída f; (for feelings) escape m, vazão m; Electr tomada f

outline /'aʊtlaɪn/ n contorno m; (summary) plano m geral, esquema m, esboço m ● vt contornar; (summarize) descrever em linhas gerais

outlive /aʊt'lɪv/ vt sobreviver a

outlook /'aʊtlʊk/ n (view) vista f; (mental attitude) visão f; (future prospects) perspectiva(s) f(pl), (P) perspetiva(s) f(pl)

outlying /'aʊtlaɪɪŋ/ a afastado, remoto

outnumber /aʊt'nʌmbə(r)/ vt ultrapassar em número

outpost /'aʊtpəʊst/ n posto m avançado

output /'aʊtpʊt/ n rendimento m; (of computer) saída f, output m

o

outrage /'aʊtreɪdʒ/ n atrocidade f, crime m; (scandal) escândalo m • vt ultrajar

outrageous /aʊt'reɪdʒəs/ a (shocking) escandaloso; (very cruel) atroz

outright /'aʊtraɪt/ adv completamente; (at once) imediatamente; (frankly) abertamente • a completo; (refusal) claro

outset /'aʊtset/ n início m, começo m, princípio m

outside[1] /aʊt'saɪd/ n exterior m • adv (lá) (por) fora • prep (para) fora de, além de; (in front of) diante de; **at the ~** no máximo

outside[2] /'aʊtsaɪd/ a exterior

outsider /aʊt'saɪdə(r)/ n estranho m; (in race) cavalo m com poucas probabilidades de vencer, azarão m

outsize /'aʊtsaɪz/ a tamanho extra invar

outskirts /'aʊtskɜːts/ npl arredores mpl, subúrbios mpl, arrabaldes mpl

outspoken /aʊt'spəʊkn/ a franco

outstanding /aʊt'stændɪŋ/ a saliente, proeminente; (debt) por saldar; (very good) notável, destacado

outstretched /aʊt'stretʃt/ a (arm) estendido, esticado

outward /'aʊtwəd/ a para o exterior; (sign etc) exterior; (journey) de ida. **~ly** adv exteriormente. **~s** adv para o exterior

outwit /aʊt'wɪt/ vt (pt -witted) ser mais esperto que, enganar

oval /'əʊvl/ n & a oval m

Oval Office O Salão Oval é o escritório oficial do Presidente dos Estados Unidos, situado na ala oeste da Casa Branca. A forma oval foi exigida por George Washington para ter contato visual com todos os presentes durante as reuniões. A princípio, o presidente queria que todas as divisões da Casa Branca fossem ovais, mas logo percebeu que este desenho era pouco prático.

ovary /'əʊvərɪ/ n ovário m

ovation /əʊ'veɪʃn/ n ovação f

oven /'ʌvn/ n forno m

over /'əʊvə(r)/ prep sobre, acima de, por cima de; (across) de para o/do outro lado de; (during) durante, em; (more than) mais de • adv por cima; (too) demais, demasiadamente; (ended) acabado; **the film is ~** o filme já acabou;

jump/etc**~** saltar/etc por cima; **he has some ~** ele tem uns de sobra; **all ~ the country** em/por todo o país; **all ~ the table** por toda a mesa; **~ and above** (besides, in addition to) (para) além de; **~ and ~** repetidas vezes; **~ there** ali, lá, acolá

over- /'əʊvə(r)/ pref sobre-, super-; (excessively) demais, demasiado

overall[1] /'əʊvərɔːl/ n bata f; **~s** macacão m, (P) fato-macaco m

overall[2] /'əʊvərɔːl/ a global; (length etc) total • adv globalmente

overbalance /əʊvə'bæləns/ vt/i (fazer) perder o equilíbrio

overbearing /əʊvə'beərɪŋ/ a autoritário, despótico; (arrogant) arrogante

overboard /'əʊvəbɔːd/ adv (pela) borda fora

overcast /əʊvə'kɑːst/ a encoberto, nublado

overcharge /əʊvə'tʃɑːdʒ/ vt **~ sb (for)** cobrar demais a alguém (por)

overcoat /'əʊvəkəʊt/ n casacão m; (for men) sobretudo m

overcome /əʊvə'kʌm/ vt (pt -came, pp -come) superar, vencer; **~ by** sucumbindo a, dominado or vencido por

overcrowded /əʊvə'kraʊdɪd/ a apinhado, superlotado; (country) superpovoado

overdo /əʊvə'duː/ vt (pt -did, pp -done) exagerar, levar longe demais; **~ne** Culin cozinhado demais

overdose /'əʊvədəʊs/ n dose f excessiva, (P) overdose f

overdraft /'əʊvədrɑːft/ n saldo m negativo

overdraw /əʊvə'drɔː/ vt (pt -drew, pp -drawn) sacar a descoberto, (P) ter a conta a descoberto

overdue /əʊvə'djuː/ a em atraso, atrasado; (belated) tardio

overestimate /əʊvər'estɪmeɪt/ vt sobrestimar, atribuir valor excessivo a

overexpose /əʊvərɪk'spəʊz/ vt expor demais

overflow[1] /əʊvə'fləʊ/ vt/i extravasar; transbordar (**with** de)

overflow[2] /'əʊvəfləʊ/ n (outlet) descarga f; (excess) excesso m

overgrown /əʊvə'grəʊn/ a que cresceu demais; (garden etc) invadido pela vegetação

overhang /əʊvə'hæŋ/ vt (pt **-hung**) estar sobranceiro a, pairar sobre ● vi projetar-se ● n saliência f

overhaul[1] /əʊvə'hɔːl/ vt fazer uma revisão em

overhaul[2] /'əʊvəhɔːl/ n revisão f

overhead[1] /əʊvə'hed/ adv em or por cima, ao or no alto

overhead[2] /'əʊvəhed/ a aéreo. **~s** npl despesas fpl gerais

overhear /əʊvə'hɪə(r)/ vt (pt **-heard**) (eavesdrop) ouvir sem conhecimento do falante; (hear by chance) ouvir por acaso

overjoyed /əʊvə'dʒɔɪd/ a radiante, felicíssimo

overlap /əʊvə'læp/ vt/i (pt **-lapped**) sobrepor(-se) parcialmente; fig coincidir

overleaf /əʊvə'liːf/ adv no verso

overload /əʊvə'ləʊd/ vt sobrecarregar

overlook /əʊvə'lʊk/ vt deixar passar; (of window) dar para; (of building) dominar

overnight /əʊvə'naɪt/ adv durante a noite; fig dum dia para o outro ● a <train> da noite; <stay, journey, etc> de noite, noturno; fig súbito

overpass /əʊvə'pɑːs/ n passagem f superior

overpay /əʊvə'peɪ/ vt (pt **-paid**) pagar em excesso

overpower /əʊvə'paʊə(r)/ vt dominar, subjugar; fig esmagar. **~ing** a esmagador; <heat> sufocante, insuportável

overpriced /əʊvə'praɪst/ a muito caro

overrid|e /əʊvə'raɪd/ vt (pt **-rode**, pp **-ridden**) prevalecer sobre, passar por cima de. **~ing** a primordial, preponderante; (importance) maior

overripe /'əʊvəraɪp/ a demasiado maduro

overrule /əʊvə'ruːl/ vt anular, rejeitar; <claim> indeferir

overrun /əʊvə'rʌn/ vt (pt **-ran**, pp **-run**, pres p **-running**) invadir; <a limit> exceder, ultrapassar

overseas /əʊvə'siːz/ a ultramarino; (abroad) estrangeiro ● adv no ultramar, no estrangeiro

oversee /əʊvə'siː/ vt (pt **-saw**, pp **-seen**) supervisionar. **~r** /'əʊvəsiːə(r)/ n capataz m

overshadow /əʊvə'ʃædəʊ/ vt fig eclipsar; ofuscar

oversight /'əʊvəsaɪt/ n lapso m

oversleep /əʊvə'sliːp/ vi (pt **-slept**) acordar tarde, dormir demais

overt /'əʊvɜːt/ a manifesto, claro, patente

overtake /əʊvə'teɪk/ vt/i (pt **-took**, pp **-taken**) ultrapassar

overthrow /əʊvə'θrəʊ/ vt (pt **-threw**, pp **-thrown**) derrubar, depor ● n /'əʊvəθrəʊ/ Pol derrubada f, (P) deposição

overtime /'əʊvətaɪm/ n horas fpl extras

overtones /'əʊvətəʊnz/ npl fig tom m; implicação f

overture /'əʊvətjʊə(r)/ n Mus abertura f; fig proposta f; abordagem f

overturn /əʊvə'tɜːn/ vt/i virar(-se); <car, plane> capotar, virar-se

overweight /əʊvə'weɪt/ a be **~** ter excesso de peso

overwhelm /əʊvə'welm/ vt oprimir; (defeat) esmagar; (amaze) assoberbar. **~ing** a esmagador; <urge> irresistível

overwork /əʊvə'wɜːk/ vt/i sobrecarregar(-se) com trabalho ● n excesso m de trabalho

overwrought /əʊvə'rɔːt/ a muito agitado, superexcitado

ow|e /əʊ/ vt dever. **~ing** a devido; **~ing to** devido a

owl /aʊl/ n coruja f

own[1] /əʊn/ a próprio; **a house/etc of one's ~** uma casa/etc própria; **get one's ~ back** 🔲 ir à forra, (P) desforrar-se; **hold one's ~** aguentar-se; **on one's ~** sozinho

own[2] /əʊn/ vt possuir; **~ up (to)** 🔲 confessar. **~er** n proprietário m, dono m. **~ership** n posse f, propriedade f

ox /ɒks/ n (pl **oxen**) boi m

Oxbridge Termo usado para se referir simultaneamente às universidades mais antigas e prestigiadas do Reino Unido, Oxford e Cambridge, especialmente quando se quer destacar o meio privilegiado com que estão relacionadas. Ultimamente, foram feitos grandes esforços para atrair alunos de todos os meios sociais.

oxygen /'ɒksɪdʒən/ n oxigénio m, (P) oxigénio m

oyster /'ɔɪstə(r)/ n ostra f

ozone /'əʊzəʊn/ n ozônio m, (P) ozono m; **~ layer** camada f de ozônio, (P) ozono m

Pp

pace /peɪs/ n passo m; fig ritmo m; **keep ~ with** acompanhar, manter-se a par de ● vt percorrer passo a passo ● vi ~ **up and down** andar de um lado para o outro

pacemaker /'peɪsmeɪkə(r)/ n Med marca-passo m, (P) pacemaker m

Pacific /pə'sɪfɪk/ a pacífico ● n ~ **(Ocean)** (Oceano) Pacífico m

pacifist /'pæsɪfɪst/ n pacifista mf

pacify /'pæsɪfaɪ/ vt pacificar, apaziguar

pack /pæk/ n pacote m; Mil mochila f; (of hounds) matilha f; (of lies) porção f, (of cards) baralho m ● vt empacotar; ‹suitcase› fazer; ‹box, room› encher; (press down) atulhar, encher até não caber mais ● vi fazer as malas; ~ **into** (cram) apinhar em, comprimir em; **send ~ing** pôr a andar, mandar passear. **~ed** a apinhado; **~ed lunch** merenda f

package /'pækɪdʒ/ n pacote m, embrulho m ● vt embalar; ~ **deal** pacote m de propostas; ~ **holiday** pacote m turístico

packet /'pækɪt/ n pacote m; (of cigarettes) maço m

pact /pækt/ n pacto m

pad /pæd/ n (in clothing) chumaço m; (for writing) bloco m de papel/de notas; (for ink) almofada (de carimbo) f; **(launching)** ~ rampa f de lançamento ● vt (pt **padded**) enchumaçar, acolchoar; fig ‹essay etc› encher linguiça, (P) pôr palha em Ⓔ. **~ding** n chumaço m; fig linguiça f, (P) palha f Ⓔ

paddle[1] /'pædl/ n remo m de canoa

paddle[2] /'pædl/ vi chapinhar, molhar os pés; **~ing pool** piscina f de plástico para crianças

paddock /'pædək/ n cercado m; (at racecourse) paddock m

padlock /'pædlɒk/ n cadeado m ● vt fechar com cadeado

paediatrician /piːdɪə'trɪʃn/ n pediatra mf

pagan /'peɪgən/ a & n pagão m, pagã f

page[1] /peɪdʒ/ n (of book etc) página f

page[2] /peɪdʒ/ vt mandar chamar

pageant /'pædʒənt/ n espetáculo m (histórico); (procession) cortejo m. **~ry** n pompa f

paid /peɪd/ ▸ PAY ● a put ~ **to** Ⓔ (end) pôr fim a

pail /peɪl/ n balde m

pain /peɪn/ n dor f; **~s** esforços mpl; **be in ~** sofrer, ter dores; **take ~s to** esforçar-se por ● vt magoar. **~killer** n analgésico m. **~ful** a doloroso; (grievous) (laborious) penoso. **~less** a sem dor, indolor

painstaking /'peɪnzteɪkɪŋ/ a cuidadoso, esmerado, meticuloso

paint /peɪnt/ n tinta f; **~s** (in box) tintas fpl ● vt/i pintar. **~er** n pintor m. **~ing** n pintura f

paintbrush /'peɪntbrʌʃ/ n pincel m

pair /peə(r)/ n par m; **a ~ of scissors** uma tesoura; **a ~ of trousers** um par de calças; **in ~s** aos pares ● vi ~ **off** formar pares

Pakistan /pɑːkɪ'stɑːn/ n Paquistão m. **~i** a & n paquistanês m

pal /pæl/ n Ⓔ colega mf; amigo m

palace /'pælɪs/ n palácio m

palat|e /'pælət/ n palato m. **~able** a saboroso, gostoso; fig agradável

palatial /pə'leɪʃl/ a suntuoso, (P) sumptuoso

pale /peɪl/ a (-er, -est) pálido; ‹colour› claro ● vi empalidecer. **~ness** n palidez f

Palestin|e /'pælɪstaɪn/ n Palestina f. **~ian** /-'stɪnɪən/ a & n palestino m, (P) palestiniano

palette /'pælɪt/ n paleta f

palm /pɑːm/ n (of hand) palma f; (tree) palmeira f ● vt ~ **off** impingir (on a); P~ **Sunday** Domingo m de Ramos

palpable /'pælpəbl/ a palpável

palpitat|e /'pælpɪteɪt/ vi palpitar. **~ion** /-'teɪʃn/ n palpitação f

paltry /'pɔːltrɪ/ a (-ier, -iest) irrisório

pamper /'pæmpə(r)/ vt mimar, paparicar or apaparicar

pamphlet /'pæmflɪt/ n panfleto m, folheto m

pan /pæn/ n panela f; (for frying) frigideira f ● vt (pt **panned**) Ⓔ criticar severamente

panacea /pænə'sɪə/ n panaceia f

panache /pə'næʃ/ n brio m, estilo m, panache m

pancake /'pænkeɪk/ n crepe m, panqueca f

panda /'pændə/ n panda m

pandemonium /pændɪ'məʊnɪəm/ n pandemônio m, (P) pandemónio m, caos m

pander /'pændə(r)/ vi ~ to prestar-se a servir, ir ao encontro de, fazer concessões a

pane /peɪn/ n vidraça f

panel /'pænl/ n painel m; (jury) júri m; (speakers) convidados mpl; (instrument) ~ painel m de instrumentos, (P) de bordo. **~ling** n apainelamento m. **~list** n convidado m de painel

pang /pæŋ/ n pontada f, dor f aguda e súbita; **~s** (of hunger) ataques mpl de fome; **~s of conscience** remorsos mpl

panic /'pænɪk/ n pânico m ● vt/i (pt **panicked**) desorientar(-se), (fazer) entrar em pânico. **~stricken** a tomado de pânico

panoram|a /pænə'rɑːmə/ n panorama m. **~ic** /-'ræmɪk/ a panorâmico

pansy /'pænzɪ/ n amor-perfeito m

pant /pænt/ vi ofegar, arquejar

panther /'pænθə(r)/ n pantera f

panties /'pæntɪz/ npl ⬚ calcinhas fpl, (P) cuecas fpl

pantomime /'pæntəmaɪm/ n pantomima f

pantry /'pæntrɪ/ n despensa f

pants /pænts/ npl ⬚ (underwear) cuecas fpl, ⬚ (trousers) calças fpl

paper /'peɪpə(r)/ n papel m; (newspaper) jornal m; (exam) prova f escrita; (essay) comunicação f; **on** ~ por escrito ● vt forrar com papel. **~s** npl (for identification) documentos mpl. ~ **clip** n clipe m

paperback /'peɪpəbæk/ a & n ~ **(book)** livro m de capa mole

paperweight /'peɪpəweɪt/ n pesa-papéis m invar, (P) pisa-papéis m invar

paperwork /'peɪpəwɜːk/ n trabalho m de secretária; pej papelada f

paprika /'pæprɪkə/ n páprica f, (P) paprica f

par /pɑː(r)/ n **be below** ~ estar abaixo do padrão desejado; **on a** ~ **with** em igualdade com

parable /'pærəbl/ n parábola f

parachut|e /'pærəʃuːt/ n pára-quedas m invar ● vi descer de paraquedas. **~ist** n paraquedista mf

parade /pə'reɪd/ n Mil parada f militar; (procession) procissão f ● vi desfilar ● vt alardear

paradise /'pærədaɪs/ n paraíso m

paradox /'pærədɒks/ n paradoxo m. **~ical** /-'dɒksɪkl/ a paradoxal

paraffin /'pærəfɪn/ n querosene m, (P) petróleo m

paragon /'pærəgən/ n modelo m de perfeição

paragraph /'pærəgrɑːf/ n parágrafo m

parallel /'pærəlel/ a & n paralelo m ● vt (pt **parelleled**) comparar(-se)

paralyse /'pærəlaɪz/ vt paralisar

paraly|sis /pə'ræləsɪs/ n paralisia f. **~tic** /-'lɪtɪk/ a & n paralítico m

paramedic /pærə'medɪk/ n paramédico

parameter /pə'ræmɪtə(r)/ n parâmetro m

paramount /'pærəmaʊnt/ a supremo, primordial

parapet /'pærəpɪt/ n parapeito m

paraphernalia /pærəfə'neɪlɪə/ n equipamento m, parafernália f; tralha f ⬚

paraphrase /'pærəfreɪz/ n paráfrase f ● vt parafrasear

paraplegic /pærə'pliːdʒɪk/ n paraplégico m

parasite /'pærəsaɪt/ n parasita mf

parasol /'pærəsɒl/ n sombrinha f; (on table) parasol m, guarda-sol m

parcel /'pɑːsl/ n embrulho m; (for post) encomenda f

parch /pɑːtʃ/ vt ressecar; **be ~ed** estar com muita sede

parchment /'pɑːtʃmənt/ n pergaminho m

pardon /'pɑːdn/ n perdão m; Jur perdão m, indulto m; **I beg your** ~ perdão, desculpe; **(I beg your)** ~? como? ● vt (pt **pardoned**) perdoar

parent /'peərənt/ n pai m, mãe f. **~s** npl pais mpl. **~al** /pə'rentl/ a dos pais, paterno, materno

parenthesis /pə'renθəsɪs/ n (pl **-theses** /-siːz/) parêntese m, parêntesis m

parish /'pærɪʃ/ n paróquia f; (municipal) freguesia f. **~ioner** /pə'rɪʃənə(r)/ n paroquiano m

park /pɑːk/ n parque m ● vt estacionar. **~ing** n estacionamento m; **no ~ing** estacionamento proibido. **~ing meter** n parquímetro m

parliament /'pɑːləmənt/ n parlamento m, assembleia f. **~ary** /-'mentrɪ/ a parlamentar

p

dos Comuns. A primeira tem de mais de 750 membros, a maioria deles nomeados, com um número de cargos hereditários, algo que está sendo reformado no momento. A Câmara dos Comuns tem de 650 membros eleitos. Ver *Dáil Éireann, Scottish Parliament, Welsh Assembly.*

parochial /pəˈrəʊkɪəl/ *a* paroquial; *fig* provinciano; tacanho

parody /ˈpærədɪ/ *n* paródia *f* ● *vt* parodiar.

parole /pəˈrəʊl/ *n* **on ~** em liberdade condicional ● *vt* pôr em liberdade condicional

parquet /ˈpɑːkeɪ/ *n* parquê *m*, parquete *m*

parrot /ˈpærət/ *n* papagaio *m*

parsley /ˈpɑːslɪ/ *n* salsa *f*

parsnip /ˈpɑːsnɪp/ *n* cherovia *f*, pastinaga *f*

parson /ˈpɑːsn/ *n* pároco *m*, pastor *m*

part /pɑːt/ *n* parte *f*; (*of serial*) episódio *m*; (*of machine*) peça *f*; *Theat* papel *m*; (*side in dispute*) partido *m*; **in ~** em parte; **on the ~ of** da parte de; **~ of speech** categoria *f* gramatical; **take ~ in** tomar parte em; **these ~s** estas partes ● *a* parcial ● *adv* em parte ● *vt/i* separar(-se) (**from** de). **~time** *a* & *adv* tempo parcial, em part-time

partial /ˈpɑːʃl/ *a* (*incomplete, biased*) parcial; **be ~ to** gostar de. **~ity** /-ɪˈælɪtɪ/ *n* parcialidade *f*; (*liking*) predileção *f* (**for** por). **~ly** *adv* parcialmente

particip|ate /pɑːˈtɪsɪpeɪt/ *vi* participar (**in** em). **~ant** *n* /-ənt/ participante *mf*. **~ation** /-ˈpeɪʃn/ *n* participação *f*

particle /ˈpɑːtɪkl/ *n* partícula *f*; (*of dust*) grão *m*; *fig* mínimo *m*

particular /pəˈtɪkjʊlə(r)/ *a* especial, particular; (*fussy*) exigente; (*careful*) escrupuloso. **~s** *npl* pormenores *mpl*. **in ~** *adv* em especial, particularmente. **~ly** *adv* particularmente

parting /ˈpɑːtɪŋ/ *n* separação *f*; (*in hair*) risca *f* ● *a* de despedida

partisan /pɑːtɪˈzæn/ *n* partidário *m*; *Mil* guerrilheiro *m*

partition /pɑːˈtɪʃn/ *n* (*of room*) tabique *m*, divisória *f*; *Pol* (*division*) partilha *f*, divisão *f* ● *vt* dividir, repartir; **~ off** dividir por meio de tabique

partly /ˈpɑːtlɪ/ *adv* em parte

partner /ˈpɑːtnə(r)/ *n* sócio *m*; *Cards, Sport* parceiro *m*; *Dancing* par *m*.

~ship *n* associação *f*, parceria *f*; *Comm* sociedade *f*

partridge /ˈpɑːtrɪdʒ/ *n* perdiz *f*

party /ˈpɑːtɪ/ *n* festa *f*, reunião *f*; (*group*) grupo *m*; *Pol* partido *m*; *Jur* parte *f*; **~ line** (*telephone*) linha *f* coletiva

pass /pɑːs/ *vt/i* (*pt* **passed**) passar; (*overtake*) ultrapassar; ‹*exam*› passar; (*approve*) passar; ‹*law*› aprovar; **~ (by)** passar por; **~ away** falecer; **~ out** or **round** distribuir; **~ out** Ⅰ (*faint*) perder os sentidos, desmaiar; **~ over** (*disregard, overlook*) passar por cima de; **~ up** Ⅰ (*forgo*) deixar perder ● *n* (*permit*) *Sport* passe *m*; *Geog* desfiladeiro *m*, garganta *f*; (*in exam*) aprovação *f*; **make a ~ at** Ⅰ atirar-se para (*P*) ● atirar-se a Ⅰ

passable /ˈpɑːsəbl/ *a* passável; ‹*road*› transitável

passage /ˈpæsɪdʒ/ *n* passagem *f*; (*voyage*) travessia *f*; (*corridor*) corredor *m*, passagem *f*

passenger /ˈpæsɪndʒə(r)/ *n* passageiro *m*

passer-by /pɑːsəˈbaɪ/ *n* (*pl* **passers-by**) transeunte *mf*

passion /ˈpæʃn/ *n* paixão *f*. **~ate** *a* apaixonado, exaltado

passive /ˈpæsɪv/ *a* passivo. **~ smoking** *n* fumo *m* passivo

passport /ˈpɑːspɔːt/ *n* passaporte *m*

password /ˈpɑːswɜːd/ *n* senha *f*

past /pɑːst/ *a* passado; (*former*) antigo; **these ~ months** estes últimos meses ● *n* passado *m* ● *prep* para além de; (*in time*) mais de; (*in front of*) diante de ● *adv* em frente; **be ~ it** já não ser capaz; **it's five ~ eleven** são onze e cinco

pasta /ˈpæstə/ *n* prato *m* de massa(s)

paste /peɪst/ *n* cola *f*; *Culin* massa(s) *f(pl)*; (*dough*) massa *f*; (*jewellery*) strass *m*, (*P*) vidro *m* ● *vt* colar

pastel /ˈpæstl/ *n* pastel *m* ● *a* pastel *invar*

pasteurize /ˈpæstʃəraɪz/ *vt* pasteurizar

pastime /ˈpɑːstaɪm/ *n* passatempo *m*

pastry /ˈpeɪstrɪ/ *n* massa *f* (de pastelaria); (*tart*) pastel *m*

pasture /ˈpɑːstʃə(r)/ *n* pastagem *f*

pasty¹ /ˈpæstɪ/ *n* empadinha *f*

pasty² /ˈpeɪstɪ/ *a* pastoso

pat /pæt/ *vt* (*pt* **patted**) (*hit gently*) dar pancadinhas em; (*caress*) fazer festinhas a ● *n* pancadinha *f*, (*caress*) festinha *f* ● *adv* a propósito; (*readily*) prontamente ● *a* preparado, pronto

patch /pætʃ/ n remendo m; (*over eye*) tapa-olho m; (*spot*) mancha f; (*small area*) pedaço m; (*of vegetables*) canteiro m, (P) leira f; **bad ~** mau bocado m; **not be a ~ on** não chegar aos pés de ● vt ~ **up** remendar; **~ up a quarrel** fazer as pazes. **~work** n obra f de retalhos. **~y** a desigual

pâté /'pæteɪ/ n patê m

patent /'peɪtnt/ a & n patente f; **~ leather** verniz m, polimento m ● vt patentear

paternal /pə'tɜ:nl/ a paternal; (*relative*) paterno

paternity /pə'tɜ:nətɪ/ n paternidade f

path /pɑ:θ/ n (pl -s /pɑ:ðz/) caminho m, trilha f; (*in park*) aleia f, (P) alameda f; (*of rocket*) trajetória f

pathetic /pə'θetɪk/ a patético; [T] (*contemptible*) desgraçado [T], desprezível

patholog|y /pə'θɒlədʒɪ/ n patologia f. **~ist** n patologista mf

patience /'peɪʃns/ n paciência f

patio /'pætɪəʊ/ n (pl -os) pátio m

patriot /'pætrɪət/ n patriota mf. **~ic** /-'ɒtɪk/ a patriótico. **~ism** /-ɪzəm/ n patriotismo m

patrol /pə'trəʊl/ n patrulha f ● vt/i patrulhar. **~ car** n carro m de patrulha

patron /'peɪtrən/ n (*of the arts etc*) patrocinador m, mecenas mf; protetor m; (*of charity*) benfeitor m; (*customer*) freguês m, cliente mf; **~ saint** padroeiro m, patrono m

patron|age /'pætrənɪdʒ/ n freguesia f, clientela f; (*support*) patrocínio m. **~ize** vt ser cliente de; (*support*) patrocinar; (*condescend*) tratar com ares de superioridade

patter[1] /'pætə(r)/ n (*of rain*) tamborilar m, chuviscar m; **~ of steps** som m leve de passos miúdos, corridinha f leve

patter[2] /'pætə(r)/ n (*of class, profession*) gíria f, jargão m; (*chatter*) conversa f fiada

pattern /'pætn/ n padrão m; (*for sewing*) molde m; (*example*) modelo m

paunch /pɔ:ntʃ/ n pança f

pause /pɔ:z/ n pausa f ● vi pausar, fazer (uma) pausa

pav|e /peɪv/ vt pavimentar; **~e the way** preparar o caminho (**for** para). **~ing stone** n paralelepípedo m, laje f

pavement /'peɪvmənt/ n passeio m

pavilion /pə'vɪlɪən/ n pavilhão m

paw /pɔ:/ n pata f ● vt dar patadas em; (*horse*) escarvar; [T] (*person*) pôr as patas em cima de

pawn[1] /pɔ:n/ n Chess peão m; fig joguete m

pawn[2] /pɔ:n/ vt empenhar; **~shop** casa f de penhores, prego m [T]

pawnbroker /'pɔ:nbrəʊkə(r)/ n penhorista mf, dono m de casa de penhores, agiota mf

pay /peɪ/ vt/i (pt **paid**) pagar; (*interest*) render; (*visit, compliment*) fazer; **~ attention** prestar atenção; **~ back** restituir; **~ for** pagar; **~ homage** prestar homenagem; **~ in** depositar ● n pagamento m; (*wages*) vencimento m, ordenado m, salário m; **in the ~ of** em pagamento de. **~slip** n contracheque m, (P) folha f de pagamento

payable /'peɪəbl/ a pagável

pay as you go n pagamento m de acordo com o uso, (P) pré-pagamento m

payment /'peɪmənt/ n pagamento m; fig (*reward*) recompensa f

payroll /'peɪrəʊl/ n folha f de pagamentos; **be on the ~** fazer parte da folha de pagamentos de uma firma

pea /pi:/ n ervilha f

peace /pi:s/ n paz f; **disturb the ~** perturbar a ordem pública

peaceful /'pi:sfl/ a pacífico; (*calm*) calmo, sereno

peacemaker /'pi:smeɪkə(r)/ n mediador m, pacificador m

peach /pi:tʃ/ n pêssego m

peacock /'pi:kɒk/ n pavão m

peak /pi:k/ n pico m, cume m, cimo m; (*of cap*) pala f; (*maximum*) máximo m; **~ hours** horas fpl de ponta; Electr horas fpl de carga máxima; **~ed cap** boné m de pala

peal /pi:l/ n (*of bells*) repique m; (*of laughter*) gargalhada f, risada f

peanut /'pi:nʌt/ n amendoim m; **~s** [x] (*small sum*) uma bagatela f

pear /peə(r)/ n pera f

pearl /pɜ:l/ n pérola f

peasant /'peznt/ n camponês m, aldeão m

peat /pi:t/ n turfa f

pebble /'pebl/ n seixo m, calhau m

peck /pek/ vt/i bicar; (*attack*) dar bicadas (em) ● n bicada f; [T] (*kiss*) beijo m seco or (P) repenicado, beijoca f; **~ing order** hierarquia f, ordem f de importância

p

peckish /'pekɪʃ/ a be ~ 🔲 ter vontade de comer

peculiar /pɪ'kjuːlɪə(r)/ a bizarro, singular; (special) peculiar (to a) característico (to de). ~ity /-'ærətɪ/ n singularidade f; (feature) peculiaridade f

pedal /'pedl/ n pedal m ● vi (pt pedalled) pedalar

pedantic /pɪ'dæntɪk/ a pedante

peddle /'pedl/ vt vender de porta em porta; <drugs> fazer tráfico de

pedestal /'pedɪstl/ n pedestal m

pedestrian /pɪ'destrɪən/ n pedestre mf, (P) peão m ● a pedestre; fig prosaico; ~ crossing faixa f para pedestres, (P) passadeira f

pedigree /'pedɪgriː/ n estirpe f, linhagem f; (of animal) raça f ● a de raça

pedlar /'pedlə(r)/ n vendedor m ambulante

peek /piːk/ vi espreitar ● n espreitadela f

peel /piːl/ n casca f ● vt descascar ● vi <skin> pelar; <paint> escamar-se, descascar; <wallpaper> descolar-se

peep /piːp/ vi espreitar ● n espreitadela f. ~hole n vigia f; (in door) olho m mágico

peer[1] /pɪə(r)/ vi ~ at/into (searchingly) perscrutar; (with difficulty) esforçar-se por ver

peer[2] /pɪə(r)/ n (equal, noble) par m

peeved /piːvd/ a 🔲 irritado; chateado 🔲

peevish /'piːvɪʃ/ a irritável

peg /peg/ n cavilha f; (for washing) pregador m de roupa, (P) mola f; (for coats etc) cabide m; (for tent) estaca f ● vt (pt pegged) prender com estacas; off the ~ prêt-à-porter, (P) pronto-a-vestir m inv

pejorative /pɪ'dʒɒrətɪv/ a pejorativo

pelican /'pelɪkən/ n pelicano m; ~ crossing passagem f com sinais manobrados pelos pedestres, (P) peões

pellet /'pelɪt/ n bolinha f; (for gun) grão m de chumbo

pelt[1] /pelt/ n pele f

pelt[2] /pelt/ vt bombardear (with com) ● vi chover a cântaros; (run fast) correr em disparada ou disparado

pelvis /'pelvɪs/ n Anat pélvis m, bacia f

pen[1] /pen/ n (enclosure) cercado m ● vt encurralar. play~ n cercado m, (P) parque m

pen[2] /pen/ n caneta f ● vt (pt penned) escrever. ~friend n correspondente mf

penal /'piːnl/ a penal. ~ize vt impôr uma penalidade a; Sport penalizar

penalty /'penltɪ/ n pena f; (fine) multa f; Sport penalidade f; ~ kick pênalti m, (P) pénálti f

penance /'penəns/ n penitência f

pence /pens/ ▶ PENNY

pencil /'pensl/ n lápis m ● vt (pt pencilled) escrever or desenhar a lápis. ~ sharpener n apontador m, (P) apara-lápis m invar or afia-lápis m inv

pendant /'pendənt/ n berloque m

pending /'pendɪŋ/ a pendente ● prep (during) durante; (until) até

pendulum /'pendjʊləm/ n pêndulo m

penetrat|e /'penɪtreɪt/ vt/i penetrar (em). ~ing a penetrante. ~ion /-'treɪʃn/ n penetração f

penguin /'peŋgwɪn/ n pinguim m

penicillin /penɪ'sɪlɪn/ n penicilina f

peninsula /pə'nɪnsjʊlə/ n península f

penis /'piːnɪs/ n pênis m, (P) pénis m

penitentiary /penɪ'tenʃərɪ/ n Amer penitenciária f, cadeia f

penknife /'pennaɪf/ n (pl -knives) canivete m

penniless /'penɪlɪs/ a sem vintém, sem um tostão

penny /'penɪ/ n (pl pennies, or pence) pêni m, (P) péni m; fig centavo m; vintém m

pension /'penʃn/ n pensão f; (in retirement) aposentadoria f, (P) reforma f ● vt ~ off reformar, aposentar. ~er n (old-age) ~er reformado m

pensive /'pensɪv/ a pensativo

penthouse /'penthaʊs/ n cobertura f, (P) apartamento de luxo (no último andar)

pent-up /'pentʌp/ a reprimido

penultimate /pen'ʌltɪmət/ a penúltimo

people /'piːpl/ npl pessoas fpl ● n gente f, povo m ● vt povoar; the Portuguese ~ os portugueses mpl; ~ say dizem, diz-se

pep /pep/ n vigor m ● vt ~ up animar; ~ talk discurso m de encorajamento

pepper /'pepə(r)/ n pimenta f; (vegetable) pimentão m, (P) pimento m ● vt apimentar. ~y a apimentado, picante

peppermint /'pepəmɪnt/ n hortelã-pimenta f; (sweet) bala f, (P) pastilha f de hortelã-pimenta

per /pɜː(r)/ *prep* por; ~ **annum** por ano; ~ **cent** por cento; ~ **kilo**/*etc* o quilo/*etc*

perceive /pə'siːv/ *vt* perceber; (*notice*) aperceber-se de

percentage /pə'sentɪdʒ/ *n* percentagem *f*

perceptible /pə'septəbl/ *a* perceptível, (*P*) percetível

percept|ion /pə'sepʃn/ *n* percepção *f*, (*P*) perceção *f*. ~**ive** /-tɪv/ *a* perceptivo, (*P*) percetivo, penetrante, perspicaz

perch[1] /pɜːtʃ/ *n* poleiro *m* ● *vi* empoleirar-se, pousar

perch[2] /pɜːtʃ/ *n* (*fish*) perca *f*

percolat|e /'pɜːkəleɪt/ *vt/i* filtrar(-se), passar. ~**or** *n* máquina *f* de café com filtro, cafeteira *f*

percussion /pə'kʌʃn/ *n* percussão *f*

perennial /pə'renɪəl/ *a* perene; (*plant*) perene

perfect[1] /'pɜːfɪkt/ *a* perfeito. ~**ly** *adv* perfeitamente

perfect[2] /pə'fekt/ *vt* aperfeiçoar. ~**ion** /-ʃn/ *n* perfeição *f*. ~**ionist** *n* perfeccionista *mf*, (*P*) perfecionista *mf*

perform /pə'fɔːm/ *vt* ‹*a task*› *Mus* executar; ‹*a function*› *Theat* desempenhar ● *vi* representar; ‹*function*› funcionar. ~**ance** *n* (*of task*) *Mus* execução *f*; (*of function*) *Theat* desempenho *m*; (*of car*) performance *f*, comportamento *m*, rendimento *m*; [1] (*fuss*) drama *m*; cena *f*. ~**er** *n* artista *mf*

perfume /'pɜːfjuːm/ *n* perfume *m*

perhaps /pə'hæps/ *adv* talvez

peril /'perəl/ *n* perigo *m*. ~**ous** *a* perigoso

perimeter /pə'rɪmɪtə(r)/ *n* perímetro *m*

period /'pɪərɪəd/ *n* período *m*, época *f*; (*era*) época *f*; (*lesson*) hora *f* de aula; período *m* letivo; *Med* período *m*; (*full stop*) ponto (final) *m* ● *a* (*of novel*) de costumes; (*of furniture*) de estilo. ~**ic** /-'ɒdɪk/ *a* periódico. ~**ical** /-'ɒdɪkl/ *n* periódico *m*. ~**ically** /-'ɒdɪklɪ/ *adv* periodicamente

peripher|y /pə'rɪfərɪ/ *n* periferia *f*. ~**al** *a* periférico; *fig* marginal; à margem

perish /'perɪʃ/ *vi* morrer, perecer; (*rot*) estragar-se, deteriorar-se. ~**able** *a* (*of goods*) deteriorável

perjur|e /'pɜːdʒə(r)/ *vpr* ~**e o.s.** jurar falso, perjurar. ~**y** *n* perjúrio *m*

perk[1] /pɜːk/ *vt/i* ~ **up** [1] arrebitar(-se). ~**y** *a* [1] vivo; animado

perk[2] /pɜːk/ *n* [1] regalia *f*; extra *m*

perm /pɜːm/ *n* permanente *f* ● *vt* **have one's hair ~ed** fazer uma permanente

permanen|t /'pɜːmənənt/ *a* permanente. ~**ce** *n* permanência *f*. ~**tly** *adv* permanentemente, a título permanente

permissible /pə'mɪsəbl/ *a* permissível, admissível

permission /pə'mɪʃn/ *n* permissão *f*, licença *f*

permissive /pə'mɪsɪv/ *a* permissivo; ~ **society** sociedade *f* permissiva. ~**ness** *n* permissividade *f*

permit[1] /pə'mɪt/ *vt* (*pt* **permitted**) permitir; consentir (**sb to** a alguém que)

permit[2] /'pɜːmɪt/ *n* licença *f*; (*pass*) passe *m*

permutation /pɜːmjuː'teɪʃn/ *n* permutação *f*, permuta *f*

perpendicular /pɜːpən'dɪkjʊlə(r)/ *a & n* perpendicular *f*

perpetrat|e /'pɜːpɪtreɪt/ *vt* perpetrar. ~**or** *n* autor *m*

perpetual /pə'petʃʊəl/ *a* perpétuo

perpetuate /pə'petʃʊeɪt/ *vt* perpetuar

perplex /pə'pleks/ *vt* deixar perplexo. ~**ed** *a* perplexo

persecut|e /'pɜːsɪkjuːt/ *vt* perseguir. ~**ion** /-'kjuːʃn/ *n* perseguição *f*

persever|e /pɜːsɪ'vɪə(r)/ *vi* perseverar. ~**ance** *n* perseverança *f*

Persian /'pɜːʃn/ *a & n Lang* persa *m*

persist /pə'sɪst/ *vi* persistir (**in doing** em fazer). ~**ence** *n* persistência *f*. ~**ent** *a* persistente; (*obstinate*) teimoso; (*continual*) contínuo, constante. ~**ently** *adv* persistentemente

person /'pɜːsn/ *n* pessoa *f*; **in ~** em pessoa

personal /'pɜːsənl/ *a* pessoal; ‹*secretary*› particular; ~ **stereo** estéreo *m* pessoal, walkman *m*. ~**ly** *adv* pessoalmente

personality /pɜːsə'nælətɪ/ *n* personalidade *f*; (*on TV*) vedete *f*, (*P*) vedeta *f*

personify /pə'sɒnɪfaɪ/ *vt* personificar

personnel /pɜːsə'nel/ *n* pessoal *m*

perspective /pə'spektɪv/ *n* perspectiva *f*, (*P*) perspetiva *f*

perspir|e /pə'spaɪə(r)/ *vi* transpirar. ~**ation** /-ə'reɪʃn/ *n* transpiração *f*

persua|de /pə'sweɪd/ *vt* persuadir (**to** a). ~**sion** /-'sweɪʒn/ *n* persuasão *f*; (*belief*) crença *f*, convicção *f*. ~**sive** /-'sweɪsɪv/ *a* persuasivo

p

pert /pɜːt/ a (*saucy*) atrevido, descarado; (*lively*) vivo

pertinent /'pɜːtɪnənt/ a pertinente

perturb /pə'tɜːb/ vt perturbar, transtornar

Peru /pə'ruː/ n Peru m. **~vian** a & n peruano m

peruse /pə'ruːz/ vt ler com atenção

perva|de /pə'veɪd/ vt espalhar-se por, invadir. **~sive** a penetrante

pervers|e /pə'vɜːs/ a que insiste no erro; (*wicked*) perverso; (*wayward*) caprichoso. **~ity** n obstinação f; (*wickedness*) perversidade f; (*waywardness*) capricho m, birra f

perver|t¹ /pə'vɜːt/ vt perverter. **~sion** n perversão f

pervert² /'pɜːvɜːt/ n pervertido m, tarado m

pessimis|t /'pesɪmɪst/ n pessimista mf. **~m** /-zəm/ n pessimismo m. **~tic** /-'mɪstɪk/ a pessimista

pest /pest/ n praga f, inseto m novico; (*animal*) animal m daninho; (*person*) peste f

pester /'pestə(r)/ vt incomodar ▯

pesticide /'pestɪsaɪd/ n pesticida m

pet /pet/ n animal m de estimação; (*favourite*) preferido m, querido m ● a ‹rabbit etc› de estimação ● vt (pt petted) acariciar; **~ name** nome m usado em família

petal /'petl/ n pétala f

peter /'piːtə(r)/ vi **~ out** extinguir-se, acabar pouco a pouco, morrer fig

petition /pɪ'tɪʃn/ n petição f ● vt requerer

petrify /'petrɪfaɪ/ vt petrificar

petrol /'petrəl/ n gasolina f; **~ pump** bomba f de gasolina; **~ station** posto m de gasolina; **~ tank** tanque m de gasolina

petroleum /pɪ'trəʊlɪəm/ n petróleo m

petticoat /'petɪkəʊt/ n combinação f, anágua f

petty /'petɪ/ a (-ier, -iest) pequeno, insignificante; (*mean*) mesquinho; **~ cash** fundo m para pequenas despesas, caixa f pequena

petulan|t /'petjʊlənt/ a petulante, irritável. **~ce** n irritabilidade f

pew /pjuː/ n banco (de igreja) m

phantom /'fæntəm/ n fantasma m

pharmaceutical /fɑːmə'sjuːtɪkl/ a farmacêutico

pharmac|y /'fɑːməsɪ/ n farmácia f. **~ist** n farmacêutico m

phase /feɪz/ n fase f ● vt **~ in/out** introduzir/retirar progressivamente

PhD abbr of **Doctor of Philosophy** n doutorado m, (P) doutoramento m

pheasant /'feznt/ n faisão m

phenomen|on /fɪ'nɒmɪnən/ n (pl -ena) fenômeno m, (P) fenómeno m. **~al** a fenomenal

philanthrop|ist /fɪ'lænθrəpɪst/ n filantropo m. **~ic** /-ən'θrɒpɪk/ a filantrópico

Philippines /'fɪlɪpiːnz/ npl **the ~** as Filipinas fpl

philistine /'fɪlɪstaɪn/ n filisteu m

philosoph|y /fɪ'lɒsəfɪ/ n filosofia f. **~er** n filósofo m. **~ical** /-ə'sɒfɪkl/ a filosófico

phlegm /flem/ n Med catarro m, fleuma f

phobia /'fəʊbɪə/ n fobia f

phone /fəʊn/ n ▯ telefone m; **on the ~** no or (P) ao telefone; **~ book** lista f telefônica, (P) telefónica; **~ box** cabine f telefônica or (P) telefónica; **~ call** chamada f, telefonema m ● vt/i ▯ telefonar (para); **~ back** voltar a telefonar, ligar de volta. **~-in** n programa m de rádio ou tv com participação dos ouvintes

phonecard /'fəʊnkɑːd/ n cartão m para uso em telefone público

phonetic /fə'netɪk/ a fonético. **~s** n fonética f

phoney /'fəʊnɪ/ a (-ier, -iest) ▯ falso; fingido ● n ▯ (*person*) fingido m; ▯ (*thing*) falso m, (P) falsificação f

photo /'fəʊtəʊ/ n (pl -os) ▯ retrato m; foto f

photocop|y /'fəʊtəʊkɒpɪ/ n fotocópia f ● vt fotocopiar. **~ier** n fotocopiadora f

photogenic /fəʊtəʊ'dʒenɪk/ a fotogênico, (P) fotogénico

photograph /'fəʊtəɡrɑːf/ n fotografia f ● vt fotografar. **~er** /fə-'tɒɡrəfə(r)/ n fotógrafo m. **~ic** /-'ɡræfɪk/ a fotográfico. **~y** /fə-'tɒɡrəfɪ/ n fotografia f

phrase /freɪz/ n expressão f, frase f; Gram locução f, frase f elíptica ● vt exprimir. **~ book** n livro m de expressões idiomáticas

physical /'fɪzɪkl/ a físico

physician /fɪ'zɪʃn/ n médico m

physicist /'fɪzɪsɪst/ n físico m

physics /'fɪzɪks/ n física f

physiology /fɪzɪ'ɒlədʒɪ/ n fisiologia f

physiotherap|y /fɪzɪəʊ'θerəpɪ/ *n* fisioterapia *f*. **~ist** *n* fisioterapeuta *mf*

physique /fɪ'ziːk/ *n* físico *m*

pian|o /pɪ'ænəʊ/ *n* (*pl* **-os**) piano *m*. **~ist** /'pɪənɪst/ *n* pianista *mf*

pick[1] /pɪk/ *n* (*tool*) picareta *f*

pick[2] /pɪk/ *vt* escolher; ‹*flowers, fruit etc*› colher; ‹*lock*› forçar; ‹*teeth*› palitar; **~ a quarrel with** puxar *or* (*P*) pedir uma briga com; **~ holes in an argument** descobrir os pontos fracos dum argumento; **~ sb's pocket** bater *or* (*P*) roubar a carteira de alguém; **~ off** tirar, arrancar; **~ on** implicar com; **~ out** escolher; (*identify*) identificar, reconhecer ● *n* escolha *f*; (*best*) o/a melhor; **take one's ~** escolher livremente ◻ **~ up** *vt* apanhar; ‹*speed*› ganhar

pickaxe /'pɪkæks/ *n* picareta *f*

picket /'pɪkɪt/ *n* piquete *m*; (*single striker*) grevista *mf* de piquete ● *vt* (*pt* **picketed**) colocar um piquete em ● *vi* fazer piquete

pickings /'pɪkɪŋz/ *npl* restos *mpl*

pickle /'pɪkl/ *n* vinagre *m*; **~s** picles *mpl*, (*P*) pickles *mpl*; **in a ~** ◻ numa encrenca ◻ ● *vt* conservar em vinagre

pickpocket /'pɪkpɒkɪt/ *n* batedor *m* de carteiras, (*P*) carteirista *m*

picnic /'pɪknɪk/ *n* piquenique *m* ● *vi* (*pt* **picnicked**) piquenicar, (*P*) fazer um piquenique

picture /'pɪktʃə(r)/ *n* imagem *f*; (*illustration*) estampa *f*, ilustração *f*; (*painting*) quadro *m*, pintura *f*; (*photo*) fotografia *f*, retrato *m*; (*drawing*) desenho *m*; *fig* descrição *f*; quadro *m*; **the ~s** o cinema ● *vt* imaginar; (*describe*) pintar, descrever

picturesque /pɪktʃə'resk/ *a* pitoresco

pie /paɪ/ *n* torta *f*, (*P*) tarte *f*; (*of meat*) empada *f*

piece /piːs/ *n* pedaço *m*, bocado *m*; (*of machine, in game*) peça *f*; (*of currency*) moeda *f*; **a ~ of advice/furniture/***etc* um conselho/um móvel/*etc*; **take to ~s** desmontar ● *vt* **~ together** juntar, montar

piecemeal /'piːsmiːl/ *a* aos poucos, pouco a pouco

pier /pɪə(r)/ *n* molhe *m*

pierc|e /pɪəs/ *vt* furar, penetrar. **~ing** *a* penetrante; (*of scream, pain*) lancinante

piety /'paɪətɪ/ *n* piedade *f*, devoção *f*

pig /pɪg/ *n* porco *m*. **~-headed** *a* cabeçudo, teimoso

pigeon /'pɪdʒɪn/ *n* pombo *m*. **~hole** *n* escaninho *m*

piggy /'pɪgɪ/ *a* como um porco; **~ bank** cofre *m* de criança. **~back** *adv* nas costas, (*P*) porquinho-mealheiro *m*

pigment /'pɪgmənt/ *n* pigmento *m*. **~ation** /-'teɪʃn/ *n* pigmentação *f*

pigsty /'pɪgstaɪ/ *n* pocilga *f*, chiqueiro *m*

pigtail /'pɪgteɪl/ *n* trança *f*

pilchard /'pɪltʃəd/ *n* peixe *m* pequeno da família do arenque, sardinha *f* europeia

pile /paɪl/ *n* pilha *f*; (*of carpet*) pelo *m* ● *vt/i* amontoar(-se); empilhar(-se) (**into** em); **a ~ of** ◻ um monte de ◻; **~ up** acumular(-se). **~-up** *n* choque *m* em cadeia

piles /paɪlz/ *npl* hemorroidas *fpl*

pilfer /'pɪlfə(r)/ *vt* furtar

pilgrim /'pɪlgrɪm/ *n* peregrino *m*, romeiro *m*. **~age** *n* peregrinação *f*, romaria *f*

pill /pɪl/ *n* pílula *f*, comprimido *m*

pillar /'pɪlə(r)/ *n* pilar *m*. **~ box** *n* marco *m* do correio

pillow /'pɪləʊ/ *n* travesseiro *m*

pillowcase /'pɪləʊkeɪs/ *n* fronha *f*

pilot /'paɪlət/ *n* piloto *m* ● *vt* (*pt* **piloted**) pilotar. **~ light** *n* piloto *m*; *Electr* lâmpada *f* testemunho; (*gas*) piloto *m*

pimple /'pɪmpl/ *n* borbulha *f*, espinha *f*

pin /pɪn/ *n* alfinete *m*; *Techn* cavilha *f*; **have ~s and needles** estar com uma cãibra ● *vt* (*pt* **pinned**) pregar *or* prender com alfinete(s); (*hold down*) prender, segurar; **~ sb down** *fig* obrigar alguém a definir-se, apertar (com) alguém *fig*; **~ up** pregar. **~point** *vt* localizar com precisão; **~stripe** *a* de listras finas; **~up** *n* ◻ pin-up *f*

PIN /pɪn/ *abbr* (= **personal identification number**) PIN *m*, (*P*) código *m* PIN

pinafore /'pɪnəfɔː(r)/ *n* avental *m*; **~ dress** veste *f*

pincers /'pɪnsəz/ *npl* (*tool*) torquês *f*, (*P*) alicate *m*; *Med* pinça *f*; *Zool* pinça(s) *f(pl)*, tenaz(es) *f(pl)*

pinch /pɪntʃ/ *vt* apertar; ⊠ (*steal*) surripiar ◻ ● *n* aperto *m*; (*tweak*) beliscão *m*; (*small amount*) pitada *f*; **at a ~** em caso de necessidade

pine[1] /paɪn/ *n* (*tree*) pinheiro *m*; (*wood*) pinho *m*

pine[2] /paɪn/ *vi* **~ away** definhar, consumir-se; **~ for** suspirar por

p

pineapple /'paɪnæpl/ n abacaxi m, (P) ananás m

ping-pong /'pɪŋpɒŋ/ n pingue-pongue m

pink /pɪŋk/ a & n rosa m

pinnacle /'pɪnəkl/ n pináculo m

pint /paɪnt/ n quartilho m (= 0,57 l, Amer = 0,47 l)

pioneer /paɪə'nɪə(r)/ n pioneiro m ● vt ser o pioneiro em, preparar o caminho para

pious /'paɪəs/ a piedoso, devoto

pip /pɪp/ n (seed) pevide f

pipe /paɪp/ n cano m, tubo m; (of smoker) cachimbo m ● vt encanar, canalizar; ~ **down** calar a boca

pipeline /'paɪplaɪn/ n (for oil) oleoduto m; (for gas) gaseoduto m, (P) gasoduto m; **in the** ~ fig encaminhado

piping /'paɪpɪŋ/ n tubagem f; ~ **hot** muito quente

pira|te /'paɪərət/ n pirata m. ~**cy** n pirataria f

Pisces /'paɪsiːz/ n Astr Peixe m

pistol /'pɪstl/ n pistola f

piston /'pɪstən/ n êmbolo m, pistão m

pit /pɪt/ n (hole) cova f, fosso m, (mine) poço m; (quarry) pedreira f ● vt (pt pitted) picar, esburacar; fig opor; ~ **o.s. against** (struggle) medir-se com

pitch¹ /pɪtʃ/ n breu m. ~-**black** a escuro como breu

pitch² /pɪtʃ/ vt (throw) lançar; ‹tent› armar ● vi cair ● n (slope) declive m; (of sound) som m; (of voice) altura f; Sport campo m

pitfall /'pɪtfɔːl/ n fig cilada f; perigo m inesperado

pith /pɪθ/ n (of orange) parte f branca da casca, mesocarpo m; fig (essential part) cerne m; âmago m

pithy /'pɪθɪ/ a (-ier, -iest) preciso, conciso

piti|ful /'pɪtɪfl/ a lastimoso; (contemptible) miserável. ~**less** a impiedoso

pittance /'pɪtns/ n salário m miserável, miséria f

pity /'pɪtɪ/ n dó m, pena f, piedade f; **it's a** ~ é uma pena; **take** ~ **on** ter pena de; **what a** ~! que pena! ● vt compadecer-se de

pivot /'pɪvət/ n eixo m ● vt (pt pivoted) girar em torno de

placard /'plækɑːd/ n (poster) cartaz m

placate /plə'keɪt/ vt apaziguar, aplacar

place /pleɪs/ n lugar m, sítio m; (house) casa f; (seat, rank etc) lugar m ● vt colocar, pôr; ~ **an order** fazer uma encomenda; **at/to my** ~ em or na/a minha casa. ~ **mat** n pano m de mesa individual

placid /'plæsɪd/ a plácido

plagiar|ize /'pleɪdʒəraɪz/ vt plagiar. ~**ism** n plágio m

plague /pleɪg/ n peste f; (of insects) praga f ● vt atormentar, atazanar

plaice /pleɪs/ n (pl invar) solha f

plain /pleɪn/ a (-er, -est) claro; (candid) franco; (simple) simples; (not pretty) sem beleza; (not patterned) liso; **in** ~ **clothes** à paisana ● adv com franqueza ● n planície f. ~**ly** adv claramente; (candidly) francamente

plaintiff /'pleɪntɪf/ n queixoso m

plait /plæt/ vt entrançar ● n trança f

plan /plæn/ n plano m, projeto m; (of a house, city etc) plano m, planta f ● vt (pt planned) planear, planejar ● vi fazer planos; ~ **to do** ter a intenção de fazer

plane¹ /pleɪn/ n (level) plano m; (aeroplane) avião m ● a plano

plane² /pleɪn/ n (tool) plaina f ● vt aplainar

planet /'plænɪt/ n planeta m

plank /plæŋk/ n prancha f

planning /'plænɪŋ/ n planeamento m, planejamento m; ~ **permission** permissão f para construir

plant /plɑːnt/ n planta f; Techn aparelhagem f; (factory) fábrica f ● vt plantar; ~ **a bomb** colocar uma bomba. ~**ation** /-'teɪʃn/ n plantação f

plaque /plɑːk/ n placa f; (on teeth) tártaro m, pedra f

plaster /'plɑːstə(r)/ n reboco m; (adhesive) esparadrapo m, band-aid m, (P) gesso m; **in** ~ engessado; ~ **of Paris** gesso m ● vt rebocar; (cover) cobrir (**with** com, de)

plastic /'plæstɪk/ a plástico ● n plástica f; ~ **surgery** cirurgia f plástica

plate /pleɪt/ n prato m; (in book) gravura f ● vt revestir de metal

plateau /'plætəʊ/ n (pl -eaux /-əʊz/) planalto m, platô m

platform /'plætfɔːm/ n estrado m; (for speaking) tribuna f; Rail plataforma f, cais m; fig programa m de partido político; ~ **ticket** bilhete m de gare

platinum /'plætɪnəm/ n platina f

platitude /'plætɪtjuːd/ n banalidade f, lugar-comum m

platonic /plə'tɒnɪk/ a platônico, (P) platónico

plausible /'plɔːzəbl/ a plausível; ‹person› convincente

play /pleɪ/ vt/i (for amusement) brincar; ‹instrument› tocar; ‹cards, game› jogar; ‹opponent› jogar contra; ‹match› disputar; ~ **down** minimizar; ~ **on** (take advantage of) aproveitar-se de; ~ **safe** jogar pelo seguro; ~ **up** 🄸 dar problemas (a) ● n jogo m; Theat peça f; (movement) folga f, margem f. ~**group** n jardim m de infância

playboy /'pleɪbɔɪ/ n playboy m

player /'pleɪə(r)/ n jogador m; Theat artista mf; Mus artista mf, executante mf, instrumentista mf

playful /'pleɪfl/ a brincalhão m

playground /'pleɪɡraʊnd/ n pátio m de recreio

playing /'pleɪɪŋ/ n atuação f. ~ **card** n carta f de jogar; ~ **field** n campo m de jogos

playwright /'pleɪraɪt/ n dramaturgo m

plc abbr of (= **public limited company**) SARL

plea /pliː/ n súplica f; (reason) pretexto m, desculpa f; Jur alegação f da defesa

plead /pliːd/ vt/i pleitear; (as excuse) alegar; ~ **guilty** confessar-se culpado; ~ **with** implorar a

pleasant /'pleznt/ a agradável

please /pliːz/ vt/i agradar (a), dar prazer (a); **they ~e themselves, they do as they ~e** eles fazem como bem entendem ● adv por favor, (P) se faz favor. ~**ed** a contente; satisfeito (**with** com). ~**ing** a agradável

pleasur|e /'pleʒə(r)/ n prazer m. ~**able** a agradável

pleat /pliːt/ n prega f ● vt preguear

pledge /pledʒ/ n penhor m, garantia f; fig promessa f ● vt prometer; (pawn) empenhar

plentiful /'plentɪfl/ a abundante

plenty /'plentɪ/ n abundância f, fartura f; ~ **(of)** muito (de); (enough) bastante (de)

pliable /'plaɪəbl/ a flexível

pliers /'plaɪəz/ npl alicate m

plight /plaɪt/ n triste f situação

plinth /plɪnθ/ n plinto m

plod /plɒd/ vi (pt **plodded**) caminhar lentamente; ‹work› trabalhar; marrar 🄳

plonk /plɒŋk/ n 🄳 vinho m ordinário, (P) carrascão m

plot /plɒt/ n complô m, conspiração f; (of novel etc) trama f; (of land) lote m ● vt/i (pt **plotted**) conspirar; (mark out) traçar

plough /plaʊ/ n arado m ● vt/i arar; ~ **back** reinvestir; ~ **into** colidir; ~ **through** abrir caminho por

ploy /plɔɪ/ n 🄸 estratagema m

pluck /plʌk/ vt apanhar; ‹bird› depenar; ‹eyebrows› depilar; Mus tanger; ~ **up courage** ganhar coragem ● n coragem f. ~**y** a corajoso

plug /plʌɡ/ n tampão m; Electr tomada f, (P) ficha f ● vt (pt **plugged**) tapar com tampão; 🄸 (publicize) fazer grande propaganda de ● vi ~ **away** 🄸 trabalhar com afinco; ~ **in** Electr ligar

plum /plʌm/ n ameixa f

plumb /plʌm/ adv exatamente ● vt sondar

plumb|er /'plʌmə(r)/ n bombeiro m, encanador m, (P) canalizador m. ~**ing** n encanamento m, (P) canalização f

plummet /'plʌmɪt/ vi (pt **plummeted**) despencar

plump /plʌmp/ a (-er, -est) rechonchudo, roliço ● vi ~ **for** optar por

plunder /'plʌndə(r)/ vt pilhar, saquear ● n pilhagem f, saque m; (goods) despojo m

plunge /plʌndʒ/ vt/i mergulhar, atirar(-se), afundar(-se) ● n mergulho m; **take the** ~ fig decidir-se, dar o salto fig

plural /'plʊərəl/ a plural; ‹noun› no plural ● n plural m

plus /plʌs/ prep mais ● a positivo ● n sinal +; fig qualidade f positiva

plush /plʌʃ/ n pelúcia f, peluche m ● a de pelúcia, de peluche; 🄸 de luxo

ply /plaɪ/ vt (tool) manejar; (trade) exercer; ~ **sb with drink** encher alguém de bebidas ● vi ‹ship, bus› fazer carreira entre dois lugares

plywood /'plaɪwʊd/ n madeira f compensada, (P) contraplacado m

p.m. /piː'em/ adv da tarde, da noite

pneumatic /njuː'mætɪk/ a pneumático; ~ **drill** broca f pneumática

pneumonia /njuː'məʊnɪə/ n pneumonia f

poach /pəʊtʃ/ vt/i (steal) caçar/pescar em propriedade alheia ou ilegalmente; Culin fazer pochê, (P) escalfar; ~**ed eggs** ovos mpl pochês, (P) ovos mpl escalfados

p

pocket /'pɒkɪt/ n bolso m, algibeira f ● a de algibeira ● vt meter no bolso. **~book** n (notebook) livro m de apontamentos; Amer (handbag) carteira f; **~ money** n (monthly) mesada f; (weekly) semanada f, dinheiro m para pequenas despesas

pod /pɒd/ n vagem f

podcast /'pɒdkɑːst/ n podcast m

poem /'pəʊɪm/ n poema m

poet /'pəʊɪt/ n poeta m, poetisa f. **~ic** /-'etɪk/ a poético

poetry /'pəʊɪtrɪ/ n poesia f

poignant /'pɔɪnjənt/ a pungente, doloroso

point /pɔɪnt/ n ponto m; (tip) ponta f; (decimal point) vírgula f; (meaning) sentido m, razão m; Electr tomada f; **~s** Rail agulhas fpl; **on the ~ of** prestes a, quase a; **~ of view** ponto m de vista; **that is a good ~** (remark) é uma boa observação; **to the ~** a propósito; **what is the ~?** de que adianta? ● vt/i (aim) apontar (at para); (show) apontar; indicar (at/to para); **~ out** apontar, fazer ver. **~-blank** a & adv à queima-roupa; fig categórico

pointed /'pɔɪntɪd/ a pontiagudo; (of remark) intencional, contundente

pointer /'pɔɪntə(r)/ n ponteiro m; 🔢 (hint) sugestão f

pointless /'pɔɪntlɪs/ a inútil, sem sentido

poise /pɔɪz/ n equilíbrio m; (carriage) porte m; fig (self-possession) presença f; segurança f. **~d** a equilibrado; ‹person› seguro de si

poison /'pɔɪzn/ n veneno m, peçonha f ● vt envenenar. **blood-~ing** n envenenamento m do sangue. **food-~ing** n intoxicação f alimentar. **~ous** a venenoso

poke /pəʊk/ vt/i espetar; (with elbow) acotovelar; ‹fire› atiçar ● n espetadela f; (with elbow) cotovelada f; **~ about** esgaravatar, remexer, procurar; **~ fun at** fazer troça/pouco de; **~ out** ‹head› enfiar

poker[1] /'pəʊkə(r)/ n atiçador m

poker[2] /'pəʊkə(r)/ n Cards pôquer m, (P) póquer m

poky /'pəʊkɪ/ a (-ier, -iest) acanhado, apertado

Poland /'pəʊlənd/ n Polónia f, (P) Polónia f

polar /'pəʊlə(r)/ a polar; **~ bear** urso m branco

pole[1] /pəʊl/ n vara f; (for flag) mastro m; (post) poste m

pole[2] /pəʊl/ n Geog polo m

Pole /pəʊl/ n polaco m

police /pə'liːs/ n polícia f; **~ state** estado m policial; **~ station** distrito m, delegacia f, (P) esquadra f de polícia ● vt policiar

police|man /pə'liːsmən/ n (pl -men) policial m, (P) polícia m, guarda m, agente m de polícia. **~woman** n (pl -women) polícia f feminina, (P) mulher-polícia f

policy[1] /'pɒlɪsɪ/ n (plan of action) política f

policy[2] /'pɒlɪsɪ/ n (insurance) apólice f de seguro

polio /'pəʊlɪəʊ/ n polio f

polish /'pɒlɪʃ/ vt polir, dar lustro em; ‹shoes› engraxar; ‹floor› encerar ● n (for shoes) graxa f; (for floor) cera f; (for nails) esmalte m, (P) verniz m; (shine) polimento m; fig requinte m; **~ off** acabar (rapidamente); **~ up** ‹language› aperfeiçoar. **~ed** a requintado, elegante

Polish /'pəʊlɪʃ/ a & n polonês m, (P) polaco m

polite /pə'laɪt/ a polido, educado, delicado. **~ness** n delicadeza f, cortesia f

political /pə'lɪtɪkl/ a político

politician /pɒlɪ'tɪʃn/ n político m

politics /'pɒlətɪks/ n política f

poll /pəʊl/ n votação f; (survey) sondagem f, pesquisa f; **go to the ~s** votar, ir às urnas ● vt ‹votes› obter. **~ing booth** n cabine f de voto

pollen /'pɒlən/ n pólen m

pollut|e /pə'luːt/ vt poluir. **~ion** /-ʃn/ n poluição f

polo /'pəʊləʊ/ n polo m; **~ neck** gola f rolê

polyester /pɒlɪ'estə/ n poliéster m

polythene /'pɒlɪθiːn/ n politeno m. **~ bag** n saco m de plástico

pomegranate /'pɒmɪɡrænɪt/ n romã f

pomp /pɒmp/ n pompa f

pomp|ous /'pɒmpəs/ a pomposo. **~osity** /-'pɒsətɪ/ n imponência f

pond /pɒnd/ n lagoa f, lago m; (artificial) tanque m, lago m

ponder /'pɒndə(r)/ vt/i ponderar; meditar (over sobre)

pony /'pəʊnɪ/ n pônei m, (P) pónei m. **~tail** n rabo m de cavalo

poodle /'puːdl/ n caniche m

pool¹ /puːl/ n (*puddle*) charco m, poça f; (*for swimming*) piscina f

pool² /puːl/ n (*fund*) fundo m comum; *Econ, Comm* pool m; (*game*) forma f de bilhar; **~s** loteca f, (P) totobola m ● vt pôr num fundo comum

poor /pʊə(r)/ a (**-er, -est**) pobre; (*not good*) medíocre. **~ly** adv mal ● a doente

pop¹ /pɒp/ n estalido m, ruído m seco ● vt/i (*pt* **popped**) dar um estalido, estalar; (*of cork*) saltar; **~ in/out/off** entrar/sair/ir-se embora; **~ up** aparecer de repente, saltar

pop² /pɒp/ n música f pop ● a pop *invar*

popcorn /'pɒpkɔːn/ n pipoca f

pope /pəʊp/ n papa m

poplar /'pɒplə(r)/ n choupo m, álamo m

poppy /'pɒpɪ/ n papoula f

popular /'pɒpjʊlə(r)/ a popular; (*in fashion*) em voga, na moda; **be ~ with** ser popular entre. **~ity** /-'lærətɪ/ n popularidade f. **~ize** vt popularizar, vulgarizar

populat|e /'pɒpjʊleɪt/ vt povoar. **~ion** /-'leɪʃn/ n população f

populous /'pɒpjʊləs/ a populoso

porcelain /'pɔːslɪn/ n porcelana f

porch /pɔːtʃ/ n alpendre m; *Amer* varanda f

porcupine /'pɔːkjʊpaɪn/ n porco-espinho m

pore¹ /pɔː(r)/ n poro m

pore² /pɔː(r)/ vi **~ over** examinar, estudar

pork /pɔːk/ n carne f de porco

pornograph|y /pɔː'nɒgrəfɪ/ n pornografia f. **~ic** /-ə'græfɪk/ a pornográfico

porridge /'pɒrɪdʒ/ n (papa f de) flocos mpl de aveia

port¹ /pɔːt/ n (*harbour*) porto m

port² /pɔːt/ n (*wine*) (vinho do) Porto m

portable /'pɔːtəbl/ a portátil

porter¹ /'pɔːtə(r)/ n (*carrier*) carregador m

porter² /'pɔːtə(r)/ n (*doorkeeper*) porteiro m

portfolio /pɔːt'fəʊlɪəʊ/ n (*pl* **-os**) portfólio m; (*case, post*) pasta f; (*securities*) carteira f de investimentos

porthole /'pɔːthəʊl/ n vigia f

portion /'pɔːʃn/ n (*share, helping*) porção f; (*part*) parte f

portrait /'pɔːtrɪt/ n retrato m

portray /pɔː'treɪ/ vt retratar, pintar; *fig* descrever. **~al** n retrato m

Portug|al /'pɔːtjʊgl/ n Portugal m. **~uese** /-'giːz/ a & n *invar* português m

pose /pəʊz/ vt/i (fazer) posar; <*question*> fazer, colocar ● n pose f, postura f; **~ as** fazer-se passar por

poser /'pəʊzə(r)/ n quebra-cabeças m

posh /pɒʃ/ a 🆇 chique *invar*

position /pə'zɪʃn/ n posição f; (*job*) lugar m, colocação f; (*state*) situação f ● vt colocar

positive /'pɒzətɪv/ a positivo; (*definite*) categórico, definitivo; 🆄 (*downright*) autêntico; **she's ~ that** ela tem certeza que. **~ly** adv positivamente; (*absolutely*) completamente

possess /pə'zes/ vt possuir. **~ion** /-ʃn/ n posse f; (*thing possessed*) possessão f

possessive /pə'zesɪv/ a possessivo

possib|le /'pɒsəbl/ a possível. **~ility** /-'bɪlətɪ/ n possibilidade f

possibly /'pɒsəblɪ/ adv possivelmente, talvez; **if I ~ can** se me for possível; **i cannot ~ leave** estou impossibilitado de partir

post¹ /pəʊst/ n (*pole*) poste m ● vt <*notice*> afixar, pregar

post² /pəʊst/ n (*station, job*) posto m ● vt colocar; (*appoint*) colocar

post³ /pəʊst/ n (*mail*) correio m; **P~ Office** agência f dos correios, (P) estação f dos correios; (*corporation*) Departamento m dos Correios e Telégrafos, (P) Correios, Telégrafos e Telefones mpl (CTT) ● a postal ● vt mandar pelo correio; **keep ~ed** manter informado. **~ code** n código m postal

post- /pəʊst/ pref pós-

postage /'pəʊstɪdʒ/ n porte m

postal /'pəʊstl/ a postal; **~ order** vale m postal

postcard /'pəʊstkɑːd/ n cartão-postal m, (P) bilhete m postal

poster /'pəʊstə(r)/ n cartaz m

posterity /pɒ'sterətɪ/ n posteridade f

postgraduate /pəʊst'grædʒʊet/ n pós-graduado m

posthumous /'pɒstjʊməs/ a póstumo. **~ly** adv a título póstumo

postman /'pəʊstmən/ n (*pl* **-men**) carteiro m

postmark /'pəʊstmɑːk/ n carimbo m do correio

post-mortem /pəʊst'mɔːtəm/ n autópsia f

postpone /pə'spəʊn/ vt adiar. **~ment** n adiamento m

postscript /'pəʊsskrɪpt/ n postscriptum m

posture /'pɒstʃə(r)/ n postura f, posição f ● vi posar

post-war /'pəʊstwɔː(r)/ a de aprósguerra, (P) do pós-guerra

pot /pɒt/ n pote m; (for cooking) panela f; (for plants) vaso m; 🅇 (marijuana) maconha f, (P) marijuana f; **go to ~** 🅇 ‹business› arruinar, degringolar 🅸;🅇 ‹person› estar arruinado or liquidado; **take ~ luck** aceitar o que houver; **take a ~shot** dar um tiro de perto (**at** em); (at random) dar um tiro a esmo (**at** em) ● vt (pt **potted**) **~ (up)** plantar em vaso. **~ belly** n pança f, barriga f

potato /pə'teɪtəʊ/ n (pl **-oes**) batata f

poten|t /pə'təʊtnt/ a potente, poderoso; ‹drink› forte. **~cy** n potência f

potential /pə'tenʃl/ a & n potencial m. **~ly** adv potencialmente

pothol|e /'pɒthəʊl/ n caverna f, caldeirão m; (in road) buraco m

potion /'pəʊʃn/ n poção f

potted /'pɒtɪd/ a (of plant) de vaso; (preserved) de conserva

potter[1] /'pɒtə(r)/ n oleiro m, ceramista mf. **~y** n olaria f, cerâmica f

potter[2] /'pɒtə(r)/ vi entreter-se com isto ou aquilo

potty[1] /'pɒtɪ/ a (**-ier**, **-iest**) 🅇 doido, pirado 🅇, (P) chanfrado 🅸

potty[2] /'pɒtɪ/ n **-ties** 🅸 penico m de criança

pouch /paʊtʃ/ n bolsa f; (for tobacco) tabaqueira f

poultry /'pəʊltrɪ/ n aves fpl domésticas, carne f de aves domésticas

pounce /paʊns/ vi atirar-se (**on** sobre, para cima de)● n salto m

pound[1] /paʊnd/ n (weight) libra f (= 453 g); (money) libra f

pound[2] /paʊnd/ n (for dogs) canil m municipal; (for cars) parque m de viaturas rebocadas

pound[3] /paʊnd/ vt/i (crush) esmagar, pisar; (of heart) bater com força; (bombard) bombardear; (on piano etc) martelar

pour /pɔː(r)/ vt deitar, derramar ● vi correr; ‹rain› chover torrencialmente; **~ in/out** (of people) afluir/sair em massa; **~ off** or **out** esvaziar, vazar; **~ing rain** chuva f torrencial

pout /paʊt/ vt/i **~ (one's lips)** (sulk) fazer beicinho; (in annoyance) ficar de trombas ● n beicinho m

poverty /'pɒvətɪ/ n pobreza f, miséria f. **~stricken** a pobre

powder /'paʊdə(r)/ n pó m; (for face) pó de arroz m ● vt polvilhar; ‹face› empoar. **~ room** n toalete m, toucador m. **~y** a como pó

power /'paʊə(r)/ n poder m; Maths, Mech potência f; (energy) energia f; Electr corrente f; **~ cut** corte m de energia, blecaute m, (P) blackout m; **~ station** central f elétrica; **~ed by** movido a; ‹jet etc› de propulsão. **~ful** a poderoso; Mech potente. **~less** a impotente

practicable /'præktɪkəbl/ a viável

practical /'præktɪkl/ a prático; **~ joke** brincadeira f de mau gosto

practically /'præktɪklɪ/ adv praticamente

practice /'præktɪs/ n prática f; (of law etc) exercício m; Sport treino m; (clients) clientela f; **in ~** (in fact) na prática; (well-trained) em forma; **out of ~** destreinado, sem prática; **put into ~** pôr em prática

practis|e /'præktɪs/ vt/i ‹skill, sport› praticar, exercitar-se em; ‹profession› exercer; (put into practice) pôr em prática. **~ed** a experimentado, experiente. **~ing** a ‹Catholic etc› praticante

practitioner /præk'tɪʃənə(r)/ n praticante mf; **general ~** médico m de clínica geral or de família

pragmatic /præg'mætɪk/ a pragmático

praise /preɪz/ vt louvar, elogiar ● n elogio(s) m(pl), louvor(es) m(pl)

praiseworthy /'preɪzwɜːðɪ/ a louvável, digno de louvor

pram /præm/ n carrinho m de bebê, (P) bebé

prance /prɑːns/ vi (of horse) curvetear, empinar-se; (of person) pavonear-se

prank /præŋk/ n brincadeira f de mau gosto

prawn /prɔːn/ n camarão m grande, (P) gamba f

pray /preɪ/ vi rezar, orar

prayer /preə(r)/ n oração f; **the Lord's P~** o Padre-Nosso. **~ book** n missal m

pre- /priː/ pref pré-

preach /priːtʃ/ vt/i pregar (**at** a). **~er** n pregador m

prearrange /priːəˈreɪndʒ/ vt combinar or arranjar de antemão

precarious /prɪˈkeərɪəs/ a precário; (of position) instável, inseguro

precaution /prɪˈkɔːʃn/ n precaução f. **~ary** a de precaução

preced|e /prɪˈsiːd/ vt preceder. **~ing** a precedente

precedent /ˈpresɪdənt/ n precedente m

precinct /ˈpriːsɪŋkt/ n precinto m; Amer (district) circunscrição f; (pedestrian) ~ área f de pedestres, (P) zona f para peões

precious /ˈpreʃəs/ a precioso

precipice /ˈpresɪpɪs/ n precipício m

precipitat|e /prɪˈsɪpɪteɪt/ vt precipitar ● a /-ɪtət/ precipitado. **~ion** /-ˈteɪʃn/ n precipitação f

precis|e /prɪˈsaɪs/ a preciso; (careful) meticuloso. **~ely** adv precisamente. **~ion** /-ˈsɪʒn/ n precisão f

preclude /prɪˈkluːd/ vt evitar, excluir, impedir

precocious /prɪˈkəʊʃəs/ a precoce

preconc|eived /priːkənˈsiːvd/ a preconcebido. **~eption** /priːkənˈsepʃn/ n ideia f preconcebida

precursor /priːˈkɜːsə(r)/ n precursor m

predator /ˈpredətə(r)/ n animal m de rapina, predador m. **~y** a predatório

predecessor /ˈpriːdɪsesə(r)/ n predecessor m, antecessor m

predicament /prɪˈdɪkəmənt/ n situação f difícil

predict /prɪˈdɪkt/ vt predizer, prognosticar. **~able** a previsível. **~ion** /-ʃn/ n predição f, (P) previsão f, prognóstico m

predictive text messaging n previsão f de texto, (P) escrita f inteligente

predominant /prɪˈdɒmɪnənt/ a predominante, preponderante. **~ly** adv predominantemente, preponderantemente

predominate /prɪˈdɒmɪneɪt/ vi predominar

pre-eminent /priːˈemɪnənt/ a preeminente, superior

pre-empt /priːˈempt/ vt adquirir por preempção. **~ive** a antecipado; Mil preventivo

preen /priːn/ vt alisar; ~ o.s. enfeitar-se

prefab /ˈpriːfæb/ n 🔢 casa f pré-fabricada. **~ricated** /-ˈfæbrɪkeɪtɪd/ a pré-fabricado

preface /ˈprefɪs/ n prefácio m

prefect /ˈpriːfekt/ n aluno m autorizado a disciplinar outros; (official) prefeito m

prefer /prɪˈfɜː(r)/ vt (pt preferred) preferir. **~able** /ˈprefrəbl/ a preferível

preferen|ce /ˈprefrəns/ n preferência f. **~tial** /-əˈrenʃl/ a preferencial, privilegiado

prefix /ˈpriːfɪks/ n (pl -ixes) prefixo m

pregnan|t /ˈpregnənt/ a ‹woman› grávida; ‹animal› prenhe. **~cy** n gravidez f

prehistoric /priːhɪˈstɒrɪk/ a pré-histórico

prejudice /ˈpredʒʊdɪs/ n preconceito m, ideia f preconcebida, prejuízo m; (harm) prejuízo m ● vt influenciar. **~d** a com preconceitos

preliminar|y /prɪˈlɪmɪnərɪ/ a preliminar. **~ies** npl preliminares mpl, preâmbulos mpl

prelude /ˈpreljuːd/ n prelúdio m

premarital /priːˈmærɪtl/ a antes do casamento, pré-marital

premature /ˈpremətjʊə(r)/ a prematuro

premeditated /priːˈmedɪteɪtɪd/ a premeditado

premier /ˈpremɪə(r)/ a primeiro ● n Pol primeiro-ministro m

premises /ˈpremɪsɪz/ npl local m, edifício m; on the ~ neste estabelecimento, no local

premium /ˈpriːmɪəm/ n prêmio m, (P) prémio m; at a ~ a peso de ouro

premonition /priːməˈnɪʃn/ n pressentimento m

preoccup|ation /priːɒkjʊˈpeɪʃn/ n preocupação f. **~ied** /-ˈɒkjʊpaɪd/ a preocupado

preparation /prepəˈreɪʃn/ n preparação f; **~s** preparativos mpl

preparatory /prɪˈpærətrɪ/ a preparatório; ~ school escola f primária particular

prepare /prɪˈpeə(r)/ vt/i preparar(-se) (for para); **~d** to pronto a, preparado para

preposition /prepəˈzɪʃn/ n preposição f

preposterous /prɪˈpɒstərəs/ a absurdo, disparatado, ridículo

prerequisite /priːˈrekwɪzɪt/ n condição f prévia

prerogative /prɪˈrɒɡətɪv/ n prerrogativa f

p

Presbyterian /prezbɪˈtɪərɪən/ a & n presbiteriano m

prescri|be /prɪˈskraɪb/ vt prescrever; Med receitar, prescrever. **~ption** /-ɪpʃn/ n prescrição f; Med receita f

presence /ˈprezns/ n presença f; **~ of mind** presença f de espírito

present[1] /ˈpreznt/ a & n presente mf; **at ~** no momento, presentemente

present[2] /ˈpreznt/ n (gift) presente m, prenda f

present[3] /prɪˈzent/ vt apresentar; ‹film etc› dar; **~ sb with** oferecer a alguém. **~able** a apresentável. **~ation** /preznˈteɪʃn/ n apresentação f. **~er** n apresentador m

presently /ˈprezntlɪ/ adv dentro em pouco, daqui a pouco; Amer (now) neste momento

preservative /prɪˈzɜːvətɪv/ n preservativo m, conservante m

preserv|e /prɪˈzɜːv/ vt preservar; (maintain) Culin conservar ● n reserva f; fig área f; terreno m; (jam) compota f. **~ation** /prezəˈveɪʃn/ n conservação f

preside /prɪˈzaɪd/ vi presidir (**over** a)

presiden|t /ˈprezɪdənt/ n presidente mf. **~cy** n presidência f. **~tial** /-ˈdenʃl/ a presidencial

press /pres/ vt/i carregar (**on** em); (squeeze) espremer; (urge) pressionar; (iron) passar a ferro; **be ~ed for** estar apertado com falta de; **~ on (with)** continuar (com), prosseguir (com) ● n imprensa f; Mech prensa f; (for wine) lagar m; **~ conference** entrevista f coletiva, (P) conferência f de imprensa

pressing /ˈpresɪŋ/ a premente, urgente

pressure /ˈpreʃə(r)/ n pressão f; **~ group** grupo m de pressão ● vt fazer pressão sobre. **~ cooker** n panela f de pressão

pressurize /ˈpreʃəraɪz/ vt pressionar, fazer pressão sobre

prestige /preˈstiːʒ/ n prestígio m

prestigious /preˈstɪdʒəs/ a prestigioso

presumably /prɪˈzjuːməblɪ/ adv provavelmente, presumivelmente

presum|e /prɪˈzjuːm/ vt presumir; **~e to** tomar a liberdade de, atrever-se a. **~ption** /-ˈzʌmpʃn/ n presunção f

presumptuous /prɪˈzʌmptʃuəs/ a presunçoso

pretence /prɪˈtens/ n fingimento m; (claim) pretensão f; (pretext) desculpa f, pretexto m

pretend /prɪˈtend/ vt/i fingir (**to do** fazer); **~ to** (lay claim to) ter pretensões a, ser pretendente a; (profess to have) pretender ter

pretentious /prɪˈtenʃəs/ a pretencioso

pretext /ˈpriːtekst/ n pretexto m

pretty /ˈprɪtɪ/ a (-ier, -iest) bonito, lindo ● adv bastante

prevail /prɪˈveɪl/ vi prevalecer; **~ on sb to** convencer alguém a. **~ing** a dominante

prevalen|t /ˈprevələnt/ a geral, dominante. **~ce** n frequência f

prevent /prɪˈvent/ vt impedir (**from doing** de fazer); (avoid) evitar. **~able** a que se pode evitar, evitável. **~ion** /-ʃn/ n prevenção f. **~ive** a preventivo

preview /ˈpriːvjuː/ n pré-estréia f, (P) anteestreia f

previous /ˈpriːvɪəs/ a precedente, anterior; **~ to** antes de. **~ly** adv antes, anteriormente

pre-war /priːˈwɔː(r)/ a do pré-guerra, (P) de antes da guerra

prey /preɪ/ n presa f ● vi **~ on** dar caça a; (worry) preocupar, atormentar; **bird of ~** ave f de rapina, predador m

price /praɪs/ n preço m ● vt marcar o preço de. **~less** a inestimável; 🄳 (amusing) impagável

prick /prɪk/ vt picar, furar ● n picada f; **~ up one's ears** arrebitar a(s) orelha(s)

prickl|e /ˈprɪkl/ n pico m, espinho m; (sensation) picada f. **~y** a espinhoso, que pica; ‹person› irritável

pride /praɪd/ n orgulho m ● vpr **~ o.s. on** orgulhar-se de

priest /priːst/ n padre m, sacerdote m. **~hood** n sacerdócio m; (clergy) clero m

prim /prɪm/ a (**primmer, primmest**) formal, cheio de nove-horas 🄳; (prudish) pudico

primary /ˈpraɪmərɪ/ a primário; (chief, first) primeiro; **~ school** escola f primária

prime[1] /praɪm/ a primeiro, principal; (first-rate) de primeira qualidade; **P~ Minister** Primeiro-Ministro m; **~ number** número m primo

prime[2] /praɪm/ vt aprontar, aprestar; (with facts) preparar; ‹surface› preparar, aparelhar

primeval /praɪˈmiːvl/ a primitivo

primitive /ˈprɪmɪtɪv/ a primitivo

primrose /ˈprɪmrəʊz/ n primavera f, prímula f

prince /prɪns/ n príncipe m

princess /prɪn'ses/ n princesa f

principal /'prɪnsəpl/ a principal ● n Schol diretor m. **~ly** adv principalmente

principle /'prɪnsəpl/ n princípio m; **in/ on ~** em/por princípio

print /prɪnt/ vt imprimir; (write) escrever em letra de imprensa; **~ed matter** impressos mpl ● n marca f, impressão f; (letters) letra f de imprensa; (photo) prova (fotográfica) f; (engraving) gravura f; **out of ~** esgotado. **~out** n cópia f impressa

print|er /'prɪntə(r)/ n tipógrafo m; Comput impressora f. **~ing** n impressão f, tipografia f

prior /'praɪə(r)/ a anterior, precedente; **~ to** antes de

priority /praɪ'ɒrətɪ/ n prioridade f

prise /praɪz/ vt forçar (com alavanca); **~ open** arrombar

prison /'prɪzn/ n prisão f. **~er** n prisioneiro m

pristine /'prɪstiːn/ a primitivo; ‹condition› perfeito, como novo

privacy /'prɪvəsɪ/ n privacidade f, intimidade f; (solitude) isolamento m

private /'praɪvət/ a privado; (confidential) confidencial; ‹lesson, life, house etc› particular; ‹ceremony› íntimo ● n soldado m raso; **in ~** em particular; (of ceremony) na intimidade. **~ly** adv particularmente; (inwardly) no fundo, interiormente

privilege /'prɪvəlɪdʒ/ n privilégio m. **~d** a privilegiado; **be ~d to** ter o privilégio de

prize /praɪz/ n prêmio m, (P) prémio m ● a premiado; ‹fool etc› perfeito ● vt ter em grande apreço, apreciar muito. **~giving** n distribuição f de prêmios, (P) prémios, **~winner** n premiado, vencedor m

pro /prəʊ/ n **the ~s and cons** os prós e os contras

pro- /prəʊ/ pref (acting for) pro-; (favouring) pró-

probab|le /'prɒbəbl/ a provável. **~ility** /-'bɪlətɪ/ n probabilidade f. **~ly** adv provavelmente

probation /prə'beɪʃn/ n (testing) estágio m, tirocínio m; Jur liberdade f condicional

probe /prəʊb/ n Med sonda f; fig (investigation) inquérito m ● vt/i **~ (into)** sondar, investigar

problem /'prɒbləm/ n problema m ● a difícil. **~atic** /-'mætɪk/ a problemático

procedure /prə'siːdʒə(r)/ n procedimento m, processo m, norma f

proceed /prə'siːd/ vi prosseguir, ir para diante, avançar; **~ to do** passar a fazer; **~ with sth** continuar ou avançar com alguma coisa. **~ing** n procedimento m

proceedings /prə'siːdɪŋz/ npl Jur processo m; (report) ata f

proceeds /'prəʊsiːdz/ npl produto m, lucro m, proventos mpl

process /'prəʊses/ n processo m; **in ~** em curso; **in the ~ of doing** sendo feito ● vt tratar; Photo revelar

procession /prə'seʃn/ n procissão f, cortejo m

procl|aim /prə'kleɪm/ vt proclamar. **~amation** /prɒklə'meɪʃn/ n proclamação f

procure /prə'kjʊə(r)/ vt obter

prod /prɒd/ vt/i (pt prodded) (push) empurrar; (poke) espetar; fig (urge) incitar ● n espetadela f; fig incitamento m

prodigy /'prɒdɪdʒɪ/ n prodígio m

produc|e¹ /prə'djuːs/ vt/i produzir; (bring out) tirar, extrair; (show) apresentar, mostrar; (cause) causar, provocar; Theat pôr em cena. **~er** n produtor m. **~tion** /-'dʌkʃn/ n produção f; Theat encenação f

produce² /'prɒdjuːs/ n produtos (agrícolas) mpl

product /'prɒdʌkt/ n produto m

productiv|e /prə'dʌktɪv/ a produtivo. **~ity** /prɒdʌk'tɪvətɪ/ n produtividade f

profess /prə'fes/ vt professar; **~ to do** alegar fazer

profession /prə'feʃn/ n profissão f. **~al** a profissional; (well done) de profissional; ‹person› que exerce uma profissão liberal ● n profissional mf

professor /prə'fesə(r)/ n professor (universitário) m

proficien|t /prə'fɪʃnt/ a proficiente, competente. **~cy** n proficiência f, competência f

profile /'prəʊfaɪl/ n perfil m

profit /'prɒfɪt/ n proveito m; (money) lucro m ● vi (pt profited) **~ by** aproveitar-se de; **~ from** tirar proveito de. **~able** a proveitoso; (of business) lucrativo, rentável

profound /prə'faʊnd/ a profundo

profus|e /prə'fjuːs/ a profuso. **~ion** /-ʒn/ n profusão f

p

program /'prəʊgræm/ n **(computer)**
~ programa m ● vt (pt **programmed**)
programar. **~mer** n programador m

programme /'prəʊgræm/ n
programa m

progress[1] /'prəʊgres/ n progresso m;
in ~ em curso, em andamento

progress[2] /prə'gres/ vi progredir. **~ion**
/-ʃn/ n progressão f

progressive /prə'gresɪv/ a
progressivo; (reforming) progressista.
~ly adv progressivamente

prohibit /prə'hɪbɪt/ vt proibir (**sb from
doing** alguém de fazer)

project[1] /prə'dʒekt/ vt projetar
● vi ressaltar, sobressair. **~ion** /-ʃn/
n projeção f; (protruding) saliência f,
ressalto m

project[2] /'prɒdʒekt/ n projeto m

projectile /prə'dʒektaɪl/ n projétil m

projector /prə'dʒektə(r)/ n projetor m

prolific /prə'lɪfɪk/ a prolífico

prologue /'prəʊlɒg/ n prólogo m

prolong /prə'lɒŋ/ vt prolongar

> **prom** Nos Estados Unidos, um *i*
> *prom* é o baile de formatura que
> se celebra para os estudantes que
> terminam o *High School*. Em Londres,
> *the Proms* são uma série de concertos
> de música clássica aos quais uma
> grande parte do público assiste de pé.
> Ocorre no *Royal Albert Hall* no verão,
> durante oito semanas. Oficialmente,
> são conhecidos como os *Henry Wood
> Promenade Concerts*, em memória ao
> seu fundador.

promenade /prɒmə'nɑːd/ n passeio
m ● vt/i passear

prominen|t /'prɒmɪnənt/ a
(projecting; important) proeminente;
(conspicuous) bem à vista, conspícuo.
~ce n proeminência f. **~tly** adv bem à
vista

promiscu|ous /prə'mɪskjʊəs/ a
promíscuo, de costumes livres. **~ity**
/prɒmɪs'kjuːətɪ/ n promiscuidade f,
liberdade f de costumes

promis|e /'prɒmɪs/ n promessa f
● vt/i prometer. **~ing** a prometedor,
promissor

promot|e /prə'məʊt/ vt promover.
~ion /-'məʊʃn/ n promoção f

prompt /prɒmpt/ a pronto, rápido,
imediato; (punctual) pontual ● adv em

ponto ● vt levar; *Theat* soprar, servir
de ponto para. **~er** n ponto m. **~ly** adv
prontamente; pontualmente

prone /prəʊn/ a deitado (de bruços);
~ **to** propenso a

pronoun /'prəʊnaʊn/ n pronome m

pron|ounce /prə'naʊns/ vt
pronunciar; (declare) declarar. **~ounced**
a pronunciado. **~ouncement** n
declaração f. **~unciation** /-ʌnsɪ'eɪʃn/ n
pronúncia f

proof /pruːf/ n prova f; (of liquor) teor
m alcoólico, graduação f ● a **~ against**
à prova de

prop[1] /prɒp/ n suporte m; lit & fig apoio
m; esteio m ● vt (pt **propped**) sustentar,
suportar, apoiar; ~ **against** apoiar
contra

prop[2] /prɒp/ n I *Theat* acessório m, (P)
adereço m

propaganda /prɒpə'gændə/ n
propaganda f

propel /prə'pel/ vt (pt **propelled**)
propulsionar, impelir

propeller /prə'pelə(r)/ n hélice f

proper /'prɒpə(r)/ a correto; (seemly)
conveniente; (real) propriamente dito;
I (thorough) belo; ~ **noun** substantivo
m próprio. **~ly** adv corretamente;
(rightly) com razão, acertadamente;
(accurately) propriamente

property /'prɒpətɪ/ n (house)
imóvel m; (land, quality) propriedade f;
(possessions) bens mpl

prophecy /'prɒfəsɪ/ n profecia f

prophesy /'prɒfɪsaɪ/ vt/i profetizar;
~ **that** predizer que

prophet /'prɒfɪt/ n profeta m. **~ic**
/prə'fetɪk/ a profético

proportion /prə'pɔːʃn/ n proporção f.
~al, **~ate** adjs proporcional

proposal /prə'pəʊzl/ n proposta f;
(of marriage) pedido m de casamento

propos|e /prə'pəʊz/ vt propor
● vi pedir em casamento; **~e to do**
propor-se fazer. **~ition** /prɒpə-'zɪʃn/
n proposição f; I (matter) caso m;
questão f

proprietor /prə'praɪətə(r)/ n
proprietário m

propriety /prə'praɪətɪ/ n propriedade
f, correção f

prose /prəʊz/ n prosa f

prosecut|e /'prɒsɪkjuːt/ vt *Jur* processar.
~ion /-'kjuːʃn/ n *Jur* acusação f

p

prospect[1] /'prɒspekt/ n perspectiva f

prospect[2] /prə'spekt/ vt/i pesquisar, prospectar, (P) prospetar

prospective /prə'spektɪv/ a futuro; (possible) provável

prosper /'prɒspə(r)/ vi prosperar

prosper|ous /'prɒspərəs/ a próspero. ~ity /-'sperətɪ/ n prosperidade f

prostitut|e /'prɒstɪtjuːt/ n prostituta f. ~ion /-'tjuːʃn/ n prostituição f

prostrate /'prɒstreɪt/ a prostrado

protect /prə'tekt/ vt proteger. ~ion /-ʃn/ n proteção f. ~ive a protetor. ~or n protetor m

protégé /'prɒtɪʒeɪ/ n protegido m. ~e n protegida f

protein /'prəʊtiːn/ n proteína f

protest[1] /'prəʊtest/ n protesto m

protest[2] /prə'test/ vt/i protestar. ~er n Pol manifestante mf

Protestant /'prɒtɪstənt/ a & n protestante mf

protocol /'prəʊtəkɒl/ n protocolo m

prototype /'prəʊtətaɪp/ n protótipo m

protract /prə'trækt/ vt prolongar, arrastar

protrud|e /prə'truːd/ vi sobressair, sair do alinhamento

proud /praʊd/ a (er, -est) orgulhoso

prove /pruːv/ vt provar, demonstrar ● vi ~ (to be) easy/ etc verificar-se ser fácil/etc; ~ o.s. dar provas de si. ~n /-n/ a provado

proverb /'prɒvɜːb/ n provérbio m. ~ial /prə'vɜːbɪəl/ a proverbial

provid|e /prə'vaɪd/ vt prover; munir (sb with sth alg de alguma coisa) ● vi ~ for providenciar para; <person> prover de, cuidar de; (allow for) levar em conta; ~ed, ~ing (that) desde que, contanto que

providence /'prɒvɪdəns/ n providência f

province /'prɒvɪns/ n província f; fig competência f

provincial /prə'vɪnʃl/ a provincial; (rustic) provinciano

provision /prə'vɪʒn/ n provisão f; (stipulation) disposição f; ~s (food) provisões fpl

provisional /prə'vɪʒənl/ a provisório. ~ly adv provisoriamente

proviso /prə'vaɪzəʊ/ n (pl -os) condição f

provo|ke /prə'vəʊk/ vt provocar. ~cation /prɒvə'keɪʃn/ n provocação f. ~cative /-'vɒkətɪv/ a provocante

prowess /'praʊɪs/ n proeza f, façanha f

prowl /praʊl/ vi rondar ● n be on the ~ andar à espreita

proximity /prɒk'sɪmətɪ/ n proximidade f

proxy /'prɒksɪ/ n by ~ por procuração

prude /pruːd/ n puritano m, pudico m

pruden|t /'pruːdnt/ a prudente. ~ce n prudência f

prune[1] /pruːn/ n ameixa f seca

prune[2] /pruːn/ vt podar

pry /praɪ/ vi bisbilhotar; ~ into meter o nariz em, intrometer-se em

psalm /sɑːm/ n salmo m

pseudo- /'sjuːdəʊ/ pref pseudo-

pseudonym /'sjuːdənɪm/ n pseudônimo m, (P) pseudónimo m

psychiatr|y /saɪ'kaɪətrɪ/ n psiquiatria f. ~ic /-'rætrɪk/ a psiquiátrico. ~ist n psiquiatra mf

psychic /'saɪkɪk/ a psíquico; <person> com capacidade de telepatia

psychoanalys|e /saɪkəʊ'ænəlaɪz/ vt psicanalisar. ~t /-ɪst/ n psicanalista mf

psychoanalysis /saɪkəʊə'næləsɪs/ n psicanálise f

psycholog|y /saɪ'kɒlədʒɪ/ n psicologia f. ~ical /-ə'lɒdʒɪkl/ a psicológico. ~ist n psicólogo m

psychopath /'saɪkəʊpæθ/ n psicopata mf

pub /pʌb/ n pub m

---

pub Na Grã-Bretanha, é o estabelecimento onde se vende cerveja e outras bebidas (alcoólicas e não alcoólicas) para consumo no local. *Pub* é a forma abreviada de *public house*. Os pubs costumam oferecer comida e uma série de jogos, sobretudo dardos, bilhar, etc. O horário de abertura depende da licença, sendo o horário normal das 11 às 23 horas.

---

puberty /'pjuːbətɪ/ n puberdade f

public /'pʌblɪk/ a público; <holiday> feriado; in ~ em público; ~ house pub m; ~ relations relações fpl públicas; ~ school escola f particular; Amer escola f oficial. ~-spirited a de espírito cívico, patriótico. ~ly adv publicamente

p

publication /pʌblɪˈkeɪʃn/ n publicação f

publicity /pʌˈblɪsətɪ/ n publicidade f

publicize /ˈpʌblɪsaɪz/ vt fazer publicidade de/a

public school Em Inglaterra e no País de Gales, é um colégio privado para alunos entre os 13 e os 18 anos. A maioria desses colégios são internatos só para rapazes ou só para raparigas. Nos Estados Unidos e na Escócia, o termo refere-se a uma escola pública.

publish /ˈpʌblɪʃ/ vt publicar. ~**er** n editor m. ~**ing** n publicação f; ~**ing house** editora f

pudding /ˈpʊdɪŋ/ n pudim m; (dessert) doce m

puddle /ˈpʌdl/ n poça f de água, charco m

puff /pʌf/ n baforada f ● vt/i lançar baforadas; (breathe hard) arquejar, ofegar; ~ **at** ‹cigar etc› dar baforadas em; ~ **out** (swell) inchar(-se). ~ **pastry** n massa f folhada

puffy /ˈpʌfɪ/ a inchado

pull /pʊl/ vt/i puxar; ‹muscle› distender; ~ **a face** fazer uma careta; ~ **one's weight** fig fazer a sua quota-parte; ~ **sb's leg** brincar com alguém, meter-se com alguém; ~ **away** or **out** Auto arrancar; ~ **down** puxar para baixo; ‹building› demolir; ~ **in** Auto encostar(-se); ~ **off** tirar; fig sair-se bem em, conseguir alcançar; ~ **o.s. together** recompor-se, refazer-se; ~ **out** partir; (extract) arrancar, tirar; ~ **through** sair-se bem; ~ **up** puxar para cima; (uproot) arrancar; Auto parar ● n puxão m; fig (influence) influência f; empenho m; **give a ~** dar um puxão

pullover /ˈpʊləʊvə(r)/ n pulôver m

pulp /pʌlp/ n polpa f; (for paper) pasta f de papel

pulpit /ˈpʊlpɪt/ n púlpito m

pulsate /pʌlˈseɪt/ vi pulsar, bater, palpitar. ~**ion** /-ˈseɪʃn/ n pulsação f

pulse /pʌls/ n pulso m; **feel sb's ~** tirar o pulso de alguém

pummel /ˈpʌml/ vt (pt pummelled) esmurrar

pump[1] /pʌmp/ n bomba f ● vt/i bombear; ‹person› arrancar or extrair informações de; ~ **up** encher com bomba

pump[2] /pʌmp/ n (shoe) sapato m

pumpkin /ˈpʌmpkɪn/ n abóbora f

pun /pʌn/ n trocadilho m, jogo m de palavras

punch[1] /pʌntʃ/ vt esmurrar, dar um murro or soco; (perforate) furar, perfurar; ‹a hole› fazer ● n murro m, soco m; (device) furador m. ~**line** n remate m; ~**up** n □ pancadaria f

punch[2] /pʌntʃ/ n (drink) ponche m

punctual /ˈpʌŋktʃʊəl/ a pontual. ~**ity** /-ˈælətɪ/ n pontualidade f

punctuat|**e** /ˈpʌŋktʃʊeɪt/ vt pontuar. ~**ion** /-ˈeɪʃn/ n pontuação f

puncture /ˈpʌŋktʃə(r)/ n (in tyre) furo m ● vt/i furar

pungent /ˈpʌndʒənt/ a acre, pungente

punish /ˈpʌnɪʃ/ vt punir, castigar. ~**able** a punível. ~**ment** n punição f, castigo m

punt /pʌnt/ n (boat) chalana f

punter /ˈpʌntə(r)/ n (gambler) jogador m; □ (customer) freguês m, cliente m

puny /ˈpjuːnɪ/ a (-ier, -iest) fraco, débil

pup(py) /ˈpʌpɪ/ n cachorro m, cachorrinho m

pupil /ˈpjuːpl/ n aluno m; (of eye) pupila f

puppet /ˈpʌpɪt/ n lit & fig fantoche m; marionete f

purchase /ˈpɜːtʃəs/ vt comprar (**from sb** de alguém) ● n compra f. ~**r** /-ə(r)/ n comprador m

pur|**e** /ˈpjʊə(r)/ a (-er, -est) puro. ~**ely** adv puramente. ~**ity** n pureza f

purge /pɜːdʒ/ vt purgar; Pol sanear ● n Med purgante m; Pol saneamento m

purif|**y** /ˈpjʊərɪfaɪ/ vt purificar. ~**ication** /-ɪˈkeɪʃn/ n purificação f

puritan /ˈpjʊərɪtən/ n puritano m. ~**ical** /-ˈtænɪkl/ a puritano

purple /ˈpɜːpl/ a roxo, purpúreo ● n roxo m, púrpura f

purpose /ˈpɜːpəs/ n propósito m; (determination) firmeza f; **on ~** de propósito; **to no ~** em vão. ~**built** a construído especialmente

purposely /ˈpɜːpəslɪ/ adv de propósito, propositadamente

purr /pɜː/ n ronrom m ● vi ronronar

purse /pɜːs/ n carteira f; Amer bolsa f ● vt franzir

pursue /pəˈsjuː/ vt perseguir; (go on with) prosseguir; (engage in)

entregar-se a, dedicar-se a. **~r** /-ə(r)/ n
perseguidor m

pursuit /pəˈsjuːt/ n perseguição f; fig
atividade f

pus /pʌs/ n pus m

push /pʊʃ/ vt/i empurrar; ‹button›
apertar, premir, carregar; (thrust) enfiar;
🔟 (recommend) insistir; **be ~ed for**
‹time etc› estar com pouco; **be ~ing
thirty**/etc 🔟 estar beirando os or (P) à
beira dos trinta/etc; **give the ~ to** 🔟
dar o fora em alguém; **~ sb around**
fazer alguém de bobo or (P) de parvo;
~ back repelir; **~ off** 🔟 dar o fora, (P)
mandar embora; **~ on** continuar; **~ up**
(lift) levantar; ‹prices› forçar o aumento
de ● n empurrão m; (effort) esforço m;
(drive) energia f. **~chair** n carrinho m (de
criança); **~over** n canja f 🔟, coisa f fácil;
~up n Amer flexão f. **~er** n fornecedor m
(de droga). **~y** a 🔟 agressivo, furão

put /pʊt/ vt/i (pt put, pres p putting)
colocar, pôr; ‹question› fazer, colocar;
~ the damage at a million estimar
os danos em um milhão; **I'd ~ it at a
thousand** eu diria mil; **~ sth tactfully**
dizer alguma coisa com tato; **~ across**
comunicar; **~ away** guardar; **~ back**
repor; (delay) retardar, atrasar; **~ by** pôr
de lado; **~ down** pôr em lugar baixo;
(write) anotar; (pay) pagar; (suppress)
sufocar, reprimir; **~ forward** ‹plan›
submeter; **~ in** (insert) introduzir; (fix)
instalar; submeter; **~ in for** fazer um
pedido, candidatar-se; **~ off** (postpone)
adiar; (disconcert) desanimar; (displease)
desagradar; **~ sb off sth** tirar o gosto
de alguém por algo; **~ on** ‹clothes›
pôr, vestir; ‹radio› ligar; ‹light›
acender; ‹speed, weight› ganhar;
‹accent› adotar; **~ out** pôr para fora;
(stretch) esticar; (extinguish) extinguir,
apagar; (disconcert) desconcertar;
(inconvenience) incomodar; **~ up**
levantar; ‹building› erguer, construir;
colocar; aumentar; hospedar; oferecer;
~up job embuste m; **~ up with**
suportar, aturar

putty /ˈpʌti/ n massa de vidraceiro f,
betume m

puzzl|e /ˈpʌzl/ n puzzle m, quebra-
cabeça(s) m ● vt deixar perplexo, intrigar
● vi quebrar a cabeça, ser intrigante.
~ing a intrigante

pyjamas /pəˈdʒɑːməz/ npl pijama m

pylon /ˈpaɪlɒn/ n poste m

pyramid /ˈpɪrəmɪd/ n pirâmide f

python /ˈpaɪθn/ n píton m

Qq

quack[1] /kwæk/ n (of duck) grasnido m
● vi grasnar

quack[2] /kwæk/ n charlatão m

quadrangle /ˈkwɒdræŋgl/ n
quadrângulo m; (of college) pátio m
quadrangular

quadruped /ˈkwɒdrʊped/ n
quadrúpede m

quadruple /ˈkwɒdrʊpl/ a & n
quádruplo m ● /kwɒˈdrʊpl/ vt/i
quadruplicar. **~ts** /-plɪts/ npl
quadrigêmeos mpl, (P) quadrigémeos mpl

quaint /kweɪnt/ a (-er, -est) pitoresco;
(whimsical) estranho, bizarro

quake /kweɪk/ vi tremer ● n 🔟 tremor
m de terra

qualification /kwɒlɪfɪˈkeɪʃn/
n qualificação f; (accomplishment)
habilitação f; (diploma) diploma m, título
m; (condition) requisito m, condição f; fig
restrição f; reserva f

qualif|y /ˈkwɒlɪfaɪ/ vt qualificar; fig
(moderate) atenuar, moderar; fig (limit)
pôr ressalvas or restrições a ● vi fig (be
entitled to) ter os requisitos (for para);
Sport classificar-se; **he ~ied as a vet**
ele formou-se em veterinária. **~ied** a
formado; (able) qualificado, habilitado;
(moderated) atenuado; (limited) limitado

quality /ˈkwɒlətɪ/ n qualidade f

qualm /kwɑːm/ n escrúpulo m

quandary /ˈkwɒndərɪ/ n dilema m

quantity /ˈkwɒntətɪ/ n quantidade f

quarantine /ˈkwɒrəntiːn/ n
quarentena f

quarrel /ˈkwɒrəl/ n zanga f, questão
f, discussão f ● vi (pt quarrelled)
zangar-se, questionar, discutir. **~some** a
conflituoso, brigão

quarry[1] /ˈkwɒrɪ/ n (prey) presa f, caça f

quarry[2] /ˈkwɒrɪ/ n (excavation)
pedreira f

quarter /ˈkwɔːtə(r)/ n quarto m; (of
year) trimestre m; Amer (coin) quarto
m de dólar; 25 cêntimos mpl; (district)
bairro m, quarteirão m; **~s** (lodgings)
alojamento m, residência f; Mil quartel
m; **from all ~s** de todos os lados; **~ of
an hour** quarto de hora; **(a) ~ past
six** seis e quinze; **(a) ~ to seven** quinze
para as sete ● vt dividir em quarto;

p

q

Mil aquartelar. **~final** *n Sport* quarta *f or* (*P*) quartos *mpl* de final. **~ly** *a* trimestral ● *adv* trimestralmente

quartet /kwɔː'tet/ *n* quarteto *m*

quartz /kwɔːts/ *n* quartzo *m* ● *a* ‹*watch etc*› de quartzo

quash /kwɒʃ/ *vt* reprimir; *Jur* revogar

quaver /'kweɪvə(r)/ *vi* tremer, tremular ● *n Mus* colcheia *f*

quay /kiː/ *n* cais *m*

queasy /'kwiːzɪ/ *a* delicado; **feel ~** estar enjoado

queen /kwiːn/ *n* rainha *f*; *Cards* dama *f*

queer /kwɪə(r)/ *a* (**-er, -est**) estranho; (*slightly ill*) indisposto; ▣ (*homosexual*) bicha; maricas ▣; (*dubious*) suspeito ● *n* ▣ bicha *m*; maricas *m* ▣

quell /kwel/ *vt* reprimir, abafar, sufocar

quench /kwentʃ/ *vt* ‹*fire, flame*› apagar; ‹*thirst*› matar, saciar

query /'kwɪərɪ/ *n* questão *f* ● *vt* questionar

quest /kwest/ *n* busca *f*, procura *f*; **in ~ of** em demanda de

question /'kwestʃən/ *n* pergunta *f*, interrogação *f*; (*problem, affair*) questão *f*; **in ~** em questão or em causa; **out of the ~** fora de toda a questão, (*P*) fora de questão; **there's no ~ of** nem pensar em; **without ~** sem dúvida; **~ mark** ponto *m* de interrogação ● *vt* perguntar, interrogar; (*doubt*) pôr em dúvida or em causa. **~able** *a* discutível

questionnaire /kwestʃə'neə(r)/ *n* questionário *m*

q queue /kjuː/ *n* fila *f* ● *vi* (*pres p* queuing) fazer fila

r quibble /'kwɪbl/ *vi* tergiversar, usar de evasivas; (*raise petty objections*) discutir por coisas insignificantes

quick /kwɪk/ *a* (**-er, -est**) rápido; **be ~** despachar-se; **have a ~ temper** exaltar-se facilmente ● *adv* depressa. **~ly** *adv* rapidamente, depressa. **~ness** *n* rapidez *f*

quicken /'kwɪkən/ *vt/i* apressar(-se)

quicksand /'kwɪksænd/ *n* areia *f* movediça

quid /kwɪd/ *n invar* ▣ libra *f*

quiet /'kwaɪət/ *a* (**-er, -est**) quieto, sossegado, tranquilo ● *n* quietude *f*, sossego *m*, tranquilidade *f*; **keep ~** calar-se; **on the ~** às escondidas, na calada. **~ly** *adv* sossegadamente, silenciosamente. **~ness** *n* sossego *m*, tranquilidade *f*, calma *f*

quieten /'kwaɪətn/ *vt/i* sossegar, acalmar(-se)

quilt /kwɪlt/ *n* coberta *f* acolchoada; (**continental**) **~** edredão *m* de penas ● *vt* acolchoar

quintet /kwɪn'tet/ *n* quinteto *m*

quirk /kwɜːk/ *n* mania *f*, singularidade *f*

quit /kwɪt/ *vt* (*pt* quitted) deixar ● *vi* ir-se embora; (*resign*) demitir-se, desistir; **~ doing** *Amer* parar or deixar de fazer

quite /kwaɪt/ *adv* completamente, absolutamente; (*rather*) bastante; **~ (so)!** isso mesmo!, exatamente! **~ a few** bastante, alguns/algumas; **~ a lot** bastante

quiver /'kwɪvə(r)/ *vi* tremer, estremecer ● *n* tremor *m*, estremecimento *m*

quiz /kwɪz/ *n* (*pl* quizzes) teste *m*; (*game*) concurso *m* ● *vt* (*pt* quizzed) interrogar

quizzical /'kwɪzɪkl/ *a* zombeteiro, (*P*) gozão *m* Ⓘ

quota /'kwəʊtə/ *n* cota *f*, quota *f*

quotation /kwəʊ'teɪʃn/ *n* citação *f*; (*estimate*) orçamento *m*; **~ marks** aspas *fpl*

quote /kwəʊt/ *vt* citar; (*estimate*) fazer um orçamento ● *n* Ⓘ (*passage*) citação *f*; Ⓘ (*estimate*) orçamento *m*

Rr

rabbi /'ræbaɪ/ *n* rabino *m*

rabbit /'ræbɪt/ *n* coelho *m*

rabid /'ræbɪd/ *a fig* fanático; ferrenho; ‹*dog*› raivoso

rabies /'reɪbiːz/ *n* raiva *f*

race[1] /reɪs/ *n* corrida *f* ● *vt* ‹*horse*› fazer correr ● *vi* correr, dar or fazer uma corrida; (*rush*) ir em grande or a toda (a) velocidade. **~track** *n* pista *f*

race[2] /reɪs/ *n* (*group*) raça *f* ● *a* racial

racecourse /'reɪskɔːs/ *n* hipódromo *m*

racehorse /'reɪshɔːs/ *n* cavalo *m* de corrida

racial /'reɪʃl/ *a* racial

racing /'reɪsɪŋ/ *n* corridas *fpl*; **~ car** carro *m* de corridas

racis|t /'reɪsɪst/ *a &* n racista *mf*. **~m** /-zəm/ *n* racismo *m*

rack[1] /ræk/ *n* (*for luggage*) porta-bagagem *m*, bagageiro *m*; (*for plates*) escorredor m de prato ● vt ~ **one's brains** dar tratos à imaginação, (P) dar voltas à cabeça

rack² /ræk/ n **go to ~ and ruin** arruinar-se; (of buildings etc) cair em ruínas

racket¹ /'rækɪt/ n Sport raquete f, (P) raqueta f

racket² /'rækɪt/ n (din) barulheira f; (swindle) roubalheira f; ⊠ (business) negociata f ⊞

racy /'reɪsɪ/ a (-ier, -iest) vivo, vigoroso

radar /'reɪdɑː(r)/ n radar m ● a de radar

radian|t /'reɪdɪənt/ a radiante. ~**ce** n brilho m

radiator /'reɪdɪeɪtə(r)/ n radiador m

radical /'rædɪkl/ a & n radical m

radio /'reɪdɪəʊ/ n (pl -os) rádio f; (set) (aparelho de) rádio m; ~ **station** estação f de rádio, emissora f ● vt transmitir pela rádio

radioactiv|e /reɪdɪəʊ'æktɪv/ a radioativo. ~**ity** /-'tɪvətɪ/ n radioatividade f

radish /'rædɪʃ/ n rabanete m

radius /'reɪdɪəs/ n (pl -dii /-dɪaɪ/) raio m

raffle /'ræfl/ n rifa f ● vt rifar

raft /rɑːft/ n jangada f

rafter /'rɑːftə(r)/ n trave f, viga f

rag¹ /ræg/ n farrapo m; (for wiping) trapo m; pej (newspaper) jornaleco m. ~**s** npl farrapos mpl, andrajos mpl; **in ~s** maltrapilho.

rag² /ræg/ vt (pt ragged) zombar de

rage /reɪdʒ/ n raiva f, fúria f ● vi estar furioso; (of storm) rugir; (of battle) estar acesa; **be all the ~** ⊞ fazer furor, estar na moda ⊞

ragged /'rægɪd/ a <clothes, person> esfarrapado, roto; <edge> esfiapado, esgarçado

raid /reɪd/ n Mil ataque m; (by police) batida f; (by criminals) assalto m ● vt fazer um ataque or uma batida or um assalto. ~**er** n atacante m, assaltante m

rail /reɪl/ n (of stairs) corrimão m; (of ship) amurada f; (on balcony) parapeito m; (for train) trilho m, (P) carril m; (for curtain) varão m; **by ~** por estrada, (P) caminho de ferro

railings /'reɪlɪŋz/ npl grade f

railroad /'reɪlrəʊd/ n Amer ▶ RAILWAY

railway /'reɪlweɪ/ n estrada f, (P) caminho m de ferro; ~ **line** linha f do trem or (P) do comboio; ~ **station** estação f ferroviária, (P) estação f de

caminho de ferro

rain /reɪn/ n chuva f; ~ **forest** floresta f tropical ● vi chover. ~**storm** n tempestade f com chuva; ~**water** n água f da chuva

rainbow /'reɪnbəʊ/ n arco-íris m

raincoat /'reɪnkəʊt/ n impermeável m

raindrop /'reɪndrɒp/ n pingo m de chuva

rainfall /'reɪnfɔːl/ n precipitação f, pluviosidade f

rainy /'reɪnɪ/ a (-ier, -iest) chuvoso

raise /reɪz/ vt levantar, erguer; (breed) criar; (voice) levantar; (question) fazer, levantar; (price etc) aumentar, subir; (funds) angariar; (loan) obter ● n Amer aumento m

raisin /'reɪzn/ n passa f

rake /reɪk/ n ancinho m ● vt juntar, alisar com ancinho; (search) revolver, remexer; ~ **in** (money) ganhar a rodos; ~ **up** desenterrar, ressuscitar

rally /'rælɪ/ vt/i reunir(-se); (reassemble) reagrupar(-se), reorganizar(-se); (health) restabelecer(-se); (strength) recuperar as forças ● n (recovery) recuperação f; (meeting) comício m, assembleia f; Auto rally m, rali m

ram /ræm/ n (sheep) carneiro m ● vt (pt rammed) (beat down) calcar; (push) meter à força; (crash into) bater contra

rambl|e /'ræmbl/ n caminhada f, perambulação f ● vi perambular, vaguear; ~ **on** divagar. ~**er** n caminhante mf; (plant) trepadeira f. ~**ing** a <speech> desconexo

ramp /ræmp/ n rampa f

rampage /ræm'peɪdʒ/ vi causar distúrbios violentos

rampant /'ræmpənt/ a **be ~** vicejar, florescer; <diseases etc> grassar

ramshackle /'ræmʃækl/ a <car> desconjuntado; <house> caindo aos pedaços

ran /ræn/ ▶ RUN

ranch /rɑːntʃ/ n rancho m, estância f

rancid /'rænsɪd/ a rançoso

random /'rændəm/ a feito, tirado etc ao acaso ● n **at ~** ao acaso, a esmo, aleatoriamente

randy /'rændɪ/ a (-ier, -iest) lascivo, sensual

rang /ræŋ/ ▶ RING²

range /reɪndʒ/ n (distance) alcance m; (scope) âmbito m; (variety) gama f, variedade f; (stove) fogão m; (of voice) registro m, (P) registo m; (of temperature) variação f; **~ of mountains** cordilheira f, serra f ● vt dispor, ordenar ● vi estender-se; (vary) variar. **~r** n guarda-florestal m

rank[1] /ræŋk/ n fila f, fileira f; Mil posto m; (social position) classe f, categoria f; **the ~ and file** a massa f, gente f comum ● vt/i **~ among** contar(-se) entre

rank[2] /ræŋk/ a (-er, -est) ‹plants› luxuriante; ‹smell› fétido; (out-and-out) total

ransack /'rænsæk/ vt (search) espionar, (P) espiar, revistar, remexer; (pillage) pilhar, saquear

ransom /'rænsəm/ n resgate m ● vt resgatar; **hold to ~** prender como refém

rant /rænt/ vi usar linguagem bombástica

rap /ræp/ n pancadinha f seca ● vt/i (pt rapped) bater, dar uma pancada seca em

rape /reɪp/ vt violar, estuprar ● n violação f, estupro m

rapid /'ræpɪd/ a rápido. **~ity** /rə'pɪdətɪ/ n rapidez f

rapids /'ræpɪdz/ npl rápidos mpl

rapist /'reɪpɪst/ n violador m, estuprador m

rapport /ræ'pɔː(r)/ n bom m relacionamento

raptur|e /'ræptʃə(r)/ n êxtase m. **~ous** a extático; ‹welcome etc› entusiástico

rar|e[1] /reə(r)/ a (-er, -est) raro. **~ely** adv raramente, raras vezes. **~ity** n raridade f

rare[2] /reə(r)/ a (-er, -est) Culin malpassado

rarefied /'reərɪfaɪd/ a rarefeito; (refined) requintado

rascal /'rɑːskl/ n (dishonest) patife m; (mischievous) maroto m

rash[1] /ræʃ/ n erupção f cutânea; irritação f na pele 🆄

rash[2] /ræʃ/ a (-er, -est) imprudente, precipitado. **~ly** adv imprudentemente, precipitadamente

rasher /'ræʃə(r)/ n fatia f (de presunto ou de bacon)

raspberry /'rɑːzbrɪ/ n framboesa f

rat /ræt/ n rato m, (P) ratazana f; **~ race** fig luta f renhida para vencer na vida, arrivismo m

rate /reɪt/ n (ratio) razão f; (speed) velocidade f; (price) tarifa f; (of exchange) (taxa f de) câmbio m; (of interest) taxa f; **~s** (taxes) impostos mpl municipais, taxas fpl; **at this ~** desse jeito, desse modo; **at any ~** de qualquer modo, pelo menos; **at the ~ of** à razão de ● vt avaliar; fig (consider) considerar

rather /'rɑːðə(r)/ adv (by preference) antes; (fairly) muito, bastante; (a little) um pouco; **I would ~ go** preferia ir

rating /'reɪtɪŋ/ n Comm rating m, (P) valor m; (sailor) praça f, marinheiro m; Radio, TV índice m de audiência

ratio /'reɪʃɪəʊ/ n (pl -os) proporção f

ration /'ræʃn/ n ração f ● vt racionar

rational /'ræʃnəl/ a racional; ‹person› sensato, razoável. **~ize** vt racionalizar

rattle /'rætl/ vt/i matraquear; (of door, window) bater; (of bottles) chocalhar; 🆃 agitar; mexer com os nervos de ● n (baby's toy) guizo m, chocalho m; (of football fan) matraca f; (sound) matraquear m, chocalhar m; **~ off** despejar 🆃

rattlesnake /'rætlsneɪk/ n cobra f cascavel

raucous /'rɔːkəs/ a áspero, rouco

ravage /'rævɪdʒ/ vt devastar, causar estragos a. **~s** npl devastação f, estragos mpl

rave /reɪv/ vi delirar; (in anger) urrar; **~ about** delirar (de entusiasmo) com

raven /'reɪvn/ n corvo m

ravenous /'rævənəs/ a esfomeado; (greedy) voraz

ravine /rə'viːn/ n ravina f, barranco m

raving /'reɪvɪŋ/ a **~ lunatic** doido m varrido ● adv **~ mad** loucamente

ravish /'rævɪʃ/ vt (rape) violar; (enrapture) arrebatar, encantar. **~ing** a arrebatador, encantador

raw /rɔː/ a (-er, -est) cru; (not processed) bruto; (wound) em carne viva; (weather) frio e úmido, (P) húmido; (immature) inexperiente, verde; **~ deal** tratamento m injusto; **~ material** matéria-prima f

ray /reɪ/ n raio m

razor /'reɪzə(r)/ n navalha f de barba. **~ blade** n lâmina f de barbear

re /riː/ prep a respeito de, em referência a, relativo a

re- /riː/ pref re-

reach /riːtʃ/ vt chegar a atingir; (contact) contatar; (pass) passar; **~ for** estender a mão para agarrar ● vi estender-se, chegar ● n alcance m; **out of ~** fora de alcance; **within ~ of** ao alcance de; (close to) próximo de

react /rɪ'ækt/ vi reagir

reaction /rɪˈækʃn/ n reação f. **~ary** a & n reacionário m

reactor /rɪˈæktə(r)/ n reator m

read /riːd/ vt/i (pt **read** /red/) ler; fig (interpret) interpretar; (study) estudar; (of instrument) marcar, indicar ● n Ⅰ leitura f; **~ about** ler um artigo sobre; **~ out** ler em voz alta. **~able** a agradável or fácil de ler; (legible) legível. **~er** n leitor m; (book) livro m de leitura. **~ing** n leitura f; (of instrument) registro m, (P) registo m

readily /ˈredɪlɪ/ adv de boa vontade, prontamente; (easily) facilmente

readjust /riːəˈdʒʌst/ vt reajustar, readaptar ● vi readaptar-se, reajustar-se

ready /ˈredɪ/ a (**-ier, -iest**) pronto; **~ money** dinheiro m vivo, (P) pagamento m à vista ● n **at the ~** pronto para disparar. **~-made** a pronto; **~-to-wear** a prêt-à-porter, (P) pronto-a-vestir

real /rɪəl/ a real, verdadeiro; (genuine) autêntico; **~ estate** Amer bens mpl imobiliários ● adv Amer Ⅰ realmente

realis|t /ˈrɪəlɪst/ n realista mf. **~m** /-zəm/ n realismo m. **~tic** /-ˈlɪstɪk/ a realista. **~tically** /-ˈlɪstɪkəlɪ/ adv realisticamente

reality /rɪˈælətɪ/ n realidade f. **~ TV** n reality show m, (P) reality TV f; televisão f de reality shows

realiz|e /ˈrɪəlaɪz/ vt dar-se conta de, aperceber-se de, perceber; (fulfil; turn into cash) realizar. **~ation** /-ˈzeɪʃn/ n consciência f, noção f; (fulfilment) realização f

really /ˈrɪəlɪ/ adv realmente, na verdade

realm /relm/ n reino m; fig domínio m; esfera f

reap /riːp/ vt (cut) ceifar; (gather) fig colher

reappear /riːəˈpɪə(r)/ vi reaparecer

rear¹ /rɪə(r)/ n traseira f, retaguarda f; **bring up the ~** ir na retaguarda, fechar a marcha ● a traseiro, de trás, posterior. **~-view mirror** n espelho m retrovisor

rear² /rɪə(r)/ vt levantar, erguer; ‹children, cattle› criar; **~ one's head** levantar a cabeça ● vi (of horse etc) empinar-se

rearrange /riːəˈreɪndʒ/ vt arranjar doutro modo, reorganizar

reason /ˈriːzn/ n razão f; **within ~** razoável ● vt/i raciocinar, argumentar; **~ with sb** procurar convencer alguém. **~ing** n raciocínio m

reasonable /ˈriːznəbl/ a razoável

reassur|e /riːəˈʃʊə(r)/ vt tranquilizar, sossegar. **~ance** n garantia f. **~ing** a animador, reconfortante

rebate /ˈriːbeɪt/ n (refund) reimbolso m; (discount) desconto m, abatimento m

rebel¹ /ˈrebl/ n rebelde mf

rebel² /rɪˈbel/ vi (pt **rebelled**) rebelar-se, revoltar-se, sublevar-se. **~lion** n rebelião f, revolta f. **~lious** a rebelde

rebound¹ /rɪˈbaʊnd/ vi repercutir, ressoar; fig (backfire) recair (**on** sobre)

rebound² /ˈriːbaʊnd/ n ricochete m

rebuff /rɪˈbʌf/ vt receber mal; repelir Ⅰ ● n rejeição f

rebuild /riːˈbɪld/ vt (pt **rebuilt**) reconstruir

rebuke /rɪˈbjuːk/ vt repreender ● n reprimenda f

recall /rɪˈkɔːl/ vt chamar, mandar regressar; (remember) lembrar-se de ● n (summons) ordem f de regresso

recant /rɪˈkænt/ vi retratar-se

recap /ˈriːkæp/ vt/i (pt **recapped**) Ⅰ recapitular ● n recapitulação f

recapitulat|e /riːkəˈpɪtʃʊleɪt/ vt/i recapitular

reced|e /rɪˈsiːd/ vi recuar, retroceder. **his hair is ~ing** ele está ficando or (P) a ficar com entradas. **~ing** a ‹forehead, chin› recuado, voltado para dentro

receipt /rɪˈsiːt/ n recibo m; (receiving) recepção f, (P) receção; **~s** Comm receitas fpl

receive /rɪˈsiːv/ vt receber. **~r** /-ə(r)/ n (of stolen goods) receptador m, (P) recetador m; (of phone) fone m, (P) auscultador m; Radio, TV receptor m, (P) recetor m; (**official**) **~** síndico m de massa falida

recent /ˈriːsnt/ a recente. **~ly** adv recentemente

receptacle /rɪˈseptəkl/ n recipiente m, receptáculo m, (P) recetáculo m

reception /rɪˈsepʃn/ n recepção f, (P) receção; (welcome) acolhimento m; (signal) recepção f, (P) receção f (de sinal). **~ist** n recepcionista mf, (P) rececionista mf

receptive /rɪˈseptɪv/ a receptivo, (P) recetivo

recess /rɪˈses/ n recesso m; (of legislature) recesso m; Amer Schol recreio m

recession /rɪˈseʃn/ n recessão f, depressão f (económica)

recharge /riːˈtʃɑːdʒ/ vt tornar a carregar, recarregar

r

recipe /ˈresəpɪ/ n Culin receita f

recipient /rɪˈsɪpɪənt/ n recipiente mf; (of letter) destinatário m

reciprocate /rɪˈsɪprəkeɪt/ vt/i reciprocar(-se), retribuir, fazer o mesmo

recital /rɪˈsaɪtl/ n (music etc) recital m

recite /rɪˈsaɪt/ vt recitar; (list) enumerar

reckless /ˈreklɪs/ a inconsciente, imprudente, estouvado

reckon /ˈrekən/ vt/i calcular; (judge) considerar; (think) supor, pensar; ~ on contar com, depender de; ~ with contar com, levar em conta

reclaim /rɪˈkleɪm/ vt (demand) reclamar; ‹land› recuperar

reclin|e /rɪˈklaɪn/ vt/i reclinar(-se)

recluse /rɪˈkluːs/ n solitário m, recluso m

recognition /rekəgˈnɪʃn/ n reconhecimento m; **beyond ~** irreconhecível; **gain ~** ganhar nome, ser reconhecido

recogniz|e /ˈrekəgnaɪz/ vt reconhecer. ~able /ˈrekəgnaɪzəbl/ a reconhecível

recoil /rɪˈkɔɪl/ vi recuar; ‹gun› dar coice ● n recuo m; (gun) coice m; ~ from doing recusar-se a fazer

recollect /rekəˈlekt/ vt recordar-se de. ~ion /-ʃn/ n recordação f, memória f

recommend /rekəˈmend/ vt recomendar. ~ation /-ˈdeɪʃn/ n recomendação f

recompense /ˈrekəmpens/ vt recompensar ● n recompensa f

reconcil|e /ˈrekənsaɪl/ vt ‹people› reconciliar; ‹facts› conciliar; ~e o.s. to resignar-se a, conformar-se com. ~iation /-sɪlɪˈeɪʃn/ n reconciliação f

reconnaissance /rɪˈkɒnɪsns/ n reconhecimento m

reconnoitre /rekəˈnɔɪtə(r)/ vt/i (pres p -tring) Mil reconhecer, fazer um reconhecimento (de)

reconsider /riːkənˈsɪdə(r)/ vt reconsiderar

reconstruct /riːkənˈstrʌkt/ vt reconstruir. ~ion /-ʃn/ n reconstrução f

record[1] /rɪˈkɔːd/ vt registar; ‹disc, tape etc› gravar; ~ that referir/relatar que. ~ing n (disc, tape etc) gravação f

record[2] /ˈrekɔːd/ n (register) registro m, (P) registo m; (mention) menção f, nota f; (file) arquivo m; Mus disco m; Sport record(e) m; **have a (criminal) ~** ter cadastro; **off the ~** (unofficial) oficioso; (secret) confidencial ● a record(e) invar.

~ **player** n toca-discos m invar, (P) gira-discos m invar

recorder /rɪˈkɔːdə(r)/ n Mus flauta f de ponta; Techn instrumento m registrador, (P) de registo

recount[1] /rɪˈkaʊnt/ vt narrar em pormenor, relatar

recount[2] /ˈriːkaʊnt/ n Pol nova contagem f

recoup /rɪˈkuːp/ vt compensar; (recover) recuperar

recover /rɪˈkʌvə(r)/ vt recuperar ● vi restabelecer-se. ~y n recuperação f; ‹health› recuperação f, restabelecimento m

recreation /rekrɪˈeɪʃn/ n recreação f, recreio m; (pastime) passatempo m. ~al a recreativo

recruit /rɪˈkruːt/ n recruta m ● vt recrutar. ~ment n recrutamento m

rectang|le /ˈrektæŋgl/ n retângulo m. ~ular /-ˈtæŋgjʊlə(r)/ a retangular

rectify /ˈrektɪfaɪ/ vt retificar

recuperate /rɪˈkjuːpəreɪt/ vt/i recuperar(-se)

recur /rɪˈkɜː(r)/ vi (pt recurred) repetir-se; (come back) voltar (to a)

recurren|t /rɪˈkʌrənt/ a frequente, (P) frequente, repetido, periódico. ~ce n repetição f

recycle /riːˈsaɪkl/ vt reciclar

red /red/ a (redder, reddest) encarnado, vermelho; ‹hair› ruivo; ~ **carpet** fig recepção f or (P) receção f solene, tratamento m especial; **R~ Cross** Cruz f Vermelha; ~ **herring** fig pista f falsa; ~ **light** luz f vermelha; ~ **tape** fig papelada f, burocracia f; ~ **wine** vinho m tinto ● n encarnado m, vermelho m; **in the ~** em déficit. ~**-handed** a em flagrante (delito); com a boca na botija 🗓; ~**-hot** a escaldante, incandescente

redden /ˈredn/ vt/i avermelhar(-se); (blush) corar, ruborizar-se

redecorate /riːˈdekəreɪt/ vt decorar; pintar de novo

red|eem /rɪˈdiːm/ vt ‹sins etc› redimir; ‹sth pawned› tirar do prego 🗓; ‹voucher etc› resgatar. ~**emption** /rɪˈdempʃn/ n resgate m; (of honour) salvação f

redirect /riːdaɪˈrekt/ vt ‹letter› reendereçar

redness /ˈrednɪs/ n vermelhidão f, cor f vermelha

redo /riːˈduː/ vt (pt -did, pp -done) refazer

redress /rɪ'dres/ vt reparar; (set right) remediar, emendar; **~ the balance** restabelecer o equilíbrio ● n reparação f

reduc|e /rɪ'djuːs/ vt reduzir; ‹temperature etc› baixar. **~tion** /rɪ'dʌkʃən/ n redução f

redundan|t /rɪ'dʌndənt/ a redundante, supérfluo; ‹worker› desempregado; **be made ~t** ficar desempregado. **~cy** n demissão f por excesso de pessoal

reed /riːd/ n cara f, junco m; Mus palheta f

reef /riːf/ n recife m

reek /riːk/ n mau cheiro m ● vi cheirar mal, tresandar; **he ~s of wine** ele está com cheiro de or tresanda a vinho

reel /riːl/ n carretel m; (spool) bobina f ● vi cambalear, vacilar ● vt **~ off** recitar 🅘

refectory /rɪ'fektərɪ/ n refeitório m

refer /rɪ'fɜː(r)/ vt/i (pt referred) **~ to** referir-se a; (concern) aplicar-se a, dizer respeito a; (consult) consultar; (direct) remeter a/para

referee /refə'riː/ n árbitro m; (for job) pessoa f que dá referências ● vt (pt refereed) arbitrar

reference /'refrəns/ n referência f; (testimonial) referências fpl; **in or with ~ to** com referência a; **~ book** livro m de consulta, obra f de referência

referendum /refə'rendəm/ n (pl -dums, or -da) referendo m, plebiscito m

refill[1] /riː'fɪl/ vt encher de novo; ‹pen etc› pôr carga nova em

refill[2] /'riːfɪl/ n ‹pen etc› carga f nova, (P) recarga f

refine /rɪ'faɪn/ vt refinar. **~d** a refinado; ‹taste, manners etc› requintado. **~ment** n ‹taste, manners etc› refinamento m, requinte m; Tech refinação f. **~ry** /-ərɪ/ n refinaria f

reflect /rɪ'flekt/ vt/i refletir (on/upon em). **~ion** /-ʃn/ n reflexão f; (image) reflexo m. **~or** n refletor m

reflective /rɪ'flektɪv/ a refletor; (thoughtful) refletido, ponderado

reflex /'riːfleks/ a & n reflexo m

reflexive /rɪ'fleksɪv/ a Gram reflexivo, (P) reflexo

reform /rɪ'fɔːm/ vt/i reformar(-se) ● n reforma f. **~er** n reformador m

refrain[1] /rɪ'freɪn/ n refrão m, estribilho m

refrain[2] /rɪ'freɪn/ vi abster-se (from de)

refresh /rɪ'freʃ/ vt refrescar; (of rest etc) restaurar; **~ one's memory** avivar or refrescar a memória. **~ing** a refrescante; (of rest etc) reparador. **~ments** npl refeição f leve; (drinks) refrescos mpl

refresher /rɪ'freʃə(r)/ n **~ course** curso m de reciclagem

refrigerat|e /rɪ'frɪdʒəreɪt/ vt refrigerar. **~or** n frigorífico m, refrigerador m, geladeira f

refuel /riː'fjuːəl/ vt/i (pt refuelled) reabastecer(-se) (de combustível)

refuge /'refjuːdʒ/ n refúgio m, asilo m; **take ~** refugiar-se

refugee /refjʊ'dʒiː/ n refugiado m

refund[1] /rɪ'fʌnd/ vt reembolsar

refund[2] /'riːfʌnd/ n reembolso m

refus|e[1] /rɪ'fjuːz/ vt/i recusar(-se). **~al** n recusa f; **first ~al** preferência f, primeira opção f

refuse[2] /'refjuːs/ n refugo m, lixo m. **~ collector** n lixeiro m, (P) homem m do lixo

refute /rɪ'fjuːt/ vt refutar

regain /rɪ'geɪn/ vt recobrar, recuperar

regal /'riːɡl/ a real, régio

regard /rɪ'ɡɑːd/ vt considerar; (gaze) olhar ● n consideração f, estima f; (gaze) olhar m; **~s** cumprimentos mpl; (less formally) lembranças fpl, saudades fpl. **as ~s ~ing** prep no que diz respeito a, quanto a. **~less** adv apesar de tudo; **~less of** apesar de

regatta /rɪ'ɡætə/ n regata f

regenerate /rɪ'dʒenəreɪt/ vt regenerar

regime /reɪ'ʒiːm/ n regime m

regiment /'redʒɪmənt/ n regimento m. **~al** /-'mentl/ a de regimento, regimental

region /'riːdʒən/ n região f; **in the ~ of** por volta de. **~al** a regional

regist|er /'redʒɪstə(r)/ n registro m, (P) registo m ● vt (record) anotar; (notice) fixar, registar, prestar atenção a; ‹birth, letter› registrar, (P) registar; ‹vehicle› matricular; ‹emotions etc› exprimir ● vi inscrever-se. **~er office** n registro m, (P) registo m. **~ration** /-'streɪʃn/ n registro m, (P) registo m; (for course) inscrição f, matrícula f; **~ration (number)** número m de placa or de matrícula

registrar /redʒɪ'strɑː(r)/ n oficial m do registro, (P) registo m civil; Univ secretário m

regret /rɪ'ɡret/ n pena f, pesar m; (repentance) remorso m; **I have no**

~s não estou arrependido ● vt (pt **regretted**) lamentar; sentir (**to do** fazer); (feel repentance) arrepender-se de, lamentar. **~fully** adv com pena, pesarosamente. **~table** a lamentável. **~tably** adv infelizmente

regular /'regjʊlə(r)/ a regular; (usual) normal; ☐ (thorough) perfeito; verdadeiro; autêntico ● n ☐ ‹client› cliente mf habitual. **~ity** /-'lærətɪ/ n regularidade f. **~ly** adv regularmente

regulat|e /'regjʊleɪt/ vt regular. **~ion** /-'leɪʃn/ n regulação f; (rule) regulamento m, regra f

rehabilitat|e /ri:ə'bɪlɪteɪt/ vt reabilitar. **~ion** /-'teɪʃn/ n reabilitação f

rehears|e /rɪ'hɜːs/ vt ensaiar. **~al** n ensaio m; **dress ~al** ensaio m geral

reign /reɪn/ n reinado m ● vi reinar (over em)

reimburse /ri:ɪm'bɜːs/ vt reembolsar. **~ment** n reembolso m

rein /reɪn/ n rédea f

reincarnation /ri:ɪnkɑː'neɪʃn/ n reencarnação f

reindeer /'reɪndɪə(r)/ n invar rena f

reinforce /ri:ɪn'fɔːs/ vt reforçar; **~d concrete** concreto m armado, (P) cimento m or betão m armado. **~ment** n reforço m; **~ments** reforços mpl

reinstate /ri:ɪn'steɪt/ vt reintegrar, reintroduzir

reiterate /ri:'ɪtəreɪt/ vt reiterar

reject¹ /rɪ'dʒekt/ vt rejeitar. **~ion** /-ʃn/ n rejeição f

reject² /'ri:dʒekt/ n (artigo de) refugo m

rejoic|e /rɪ'dʒɔɪs/ vi regozijar-se (**at/ over** com). **~ing** n regozijo m

rejuvenate /ri:'dʒu:vəneɪt/ vt rejuvenescer

relapse /rɪ'læps/ n recaída f ● vi recair

relate /rɪ'leɪt/ vt relatar; (associate) relacionar ● vi **~ to** ter relação com; (get on with) entender-se com. **~d** a aparentado; ‹ideas etc› afim, relacionado

relation /rɪ'leɪʃn/ n relação f; (person) parente mf. **~ship** n parentesco m; (link) relação f; (affair) ligação f

relative /'relətɪv/ n parente mf ● a relativo. **~ly** adv relativamente

relax /rɪ'læks/ vt/i relaxar(-se); fig descontrair(-se). **~ation** /ri:læk'seɪʃn/ n relaxamento m; fig descontração f; (recreation) distração f. **~ing** a relaxante

relay¹ /'ri:leɪ/ n turma f, (P) turno m; **~ race** corrida f de revezamento, (P) estafetas

relay² /rɪ'leɪ/ vt (message) retransmitir

release /rɪ'li:s/ vt libertar, soltar; Mech desengatar, soltar; ‹bomb, film, record› lançar; ‹news› dar, publicar; ‹gas, smoke› soltar, libertar, emitir ● n libertação f; Mech desengate m; (bomb, film, record) lançamento m; (news) publicação f; (gas, smoke) emissão f; **new ~** estreia f

relegate /'relɪgeɪt/ vt relegar

relent /rɪ'lent/ vi ceder. **~less** a implacável, inexorável, inflexível

relevan|t /'reləvənt/ a relevante, pertinente, a propósito; **be ~ to** ter a ver com, dizer respeito a. **~ce** n pertinência f, relevância f

reliab|le /rɪ'laɪəbl/ a de confiança, com que se pode contar; ‹source etc› fidedigno; ‹machine etc› seguro, confiável. **~ility** /-'bɪlətɪ/ n confiabilidade f

reliance /rɪ'laɪəns/ n (dependence) segurança f; (trust) confiança f; fé f (on em)

relic /'relɪk/ n relíquia f; **~s** vestígios mpl, ruínas fpl

relief /rɪ'li:f/ n alívio m; (assistance) auxílio m, assistência f; (outline, design) relevo m; **~ road** estrada f alternativa

relieve /rɪ'li:v/ vt aliviar; (help) socorrer; (take over from) revezar, substituir; Mil render

religion /rɪ'lɪdʒən/ n religião f

religious /rɪ'lɪdʒəs/ a religioso

relinquish /rɪ'lɪŋkwɪʃ/ vt abandonar, renunciar a

relish /'relɪʃ/ n prazer m, gosto m; Culin molho m condimentado ● vt saborear, apreciar, gostar de

relocate /ri:ləʊ'keɪt/ vt/i transferir(-se), mudar(-se)

reluctan|t /rɪ'lʌktənt/ a relutante (**to** em); pouco inclinado (**to** a). **~ce** n relutância f. **~tly** adv a contragosto, relutantemente

rely /rɪ'laɪ/ vi **~ on** contar com; (depend) depender de

remain /rɪ'meɪn/ vi ficar, permanecer. **~s** npl restos mpl; (ruins) ruínas fpl. **~ing** a restante

remainder /rɪ'meɪndə(r)/ n restante m, remanescente m

remand /rɪ'mɑːnd/ vt reconduzir à prisão para detenção provisória ● n on

~ sob prisão preventiva

remark /rɪˈmɑːk/ n observação f, comentário m ● vt observar, comentar ● vi ~ **on** fazer observações or comentários sobre. ~**able** a notável

remarr|y /riːˈmæri/ vt/i tornar a casar(-se) (com)

remed|y /ˈremədi/ n remédio m ● vt remediar. ~**ial** /rɪˈmiːdɪəl/ a Med corretivo

rememb|er /rɪˈmembə(r)/ vt lembrar-se de, recordar-se de. ~**rance** n lembrança f, recordação f

remind /rɪˈmaɪnd/ vt (fazer) lembrar (**sb of sth** algo a alguém); ~ **sb to do** lembrar a alguém que faça. ~**er** n o que serve para fazer lembrar; (note) lembrete m

reminisce /remɪˈnɪs/ vi (re) lembrar (coisas passadas). ~**nces** npl reminiscências fpl

reminiscent /remɪˈnɪsnt/ a ~ **of** que faz lembrar, evocativo de

remit /rɪˈmɪt/ vt (pt **remitted**) (money) remeter. ~**tance** n remessa (de dinheiro) f

remnant /ˈremnənt/ n resto m; (trace) vestígio m; (of cloth) retalho m

remorse /rɪˈmɔːs/ n remorsos m. ~**ful** a arrependido, com remorsos. ~**less** a implacável

remote /rɪˈməʊt/ a remoto, distante; ‹person› distante; (slight) vago, leve; ~ **control** comando m à distância, telecomando m. ~**ly** adv de longe; vagamente

remov|e /rɪˈmuːv/ vt tirar, remover; (lead away) levar; (dismiss) demitir; (get rid of) eliminar. ~**al** n remoção f; (dismissal) demissão f; (from house) mudança f

remunerat|e /rɪˈmjuːnəreɪt/ vt remunerar. ~**ion** /-ˈreɪʃn/ n remuneração f

rename /riːˈneɪm/ vt rebatizar

render /ˈrendə(r)/ vt retribuir; ‹services› prestar; Mus interpretar; (translate) traduzir

renegade /ˈrenɪɡeɪd/ n renegado m

renew /rɪˈnjuː/ vt renovar; (resume) retomar. ~**able** a renovável. ~**al** n renovação f; (resumption) reatamento m

renounce /rɪˈnaʊns/ vt renunciar a; (disown) renegar, repudiar

renovat|e /ˈrenəveɪt/ vt renovar. ~**ion** /-ˈveɪʃn/ n renovação f

renown /rɪˈnaʊn/ n renome m. ~**ed** a conceituado, célebre, de renome

rent /rent/ n aluguel m, (P) aluguer m, renda f ● vt alugar, arrendar. ~**al** n (charge) aluguel m, (P) aluguer m; renda f; (act of renting) aluguel m, (P) aluguer m

renunciation /rɪnʌnsɪˈeɪʃn/ n renúncia f

reopen /riːˈəʊpən/ vt/i reabrir(-se)

reorganize /riːˈɔːɡənaɪz/ vt/i reorganizar(-se)

rep /rep/ n 🄸 vendedor m; caixeiro-viajante m

repair /rɪˈpeə(r)/ vt reparar, consertar ● n reparo m, conserto m; **in good** ~ em bom estado (de conservação)

repatriat|e /riːˈpætrɪeɪt/ vt repatriar. ~**ion** /-ˈeɪʃn/ n repatriamento m

repay /riːˈpeɪ/ vt (pt **repaid**) pagar, devolver, reembolsar; (reward) recompensar. ~**ment** n pagamento m, reembolso m

repeal /rɪˈpiːl/ vt revogar ● n revogação f

repeat /rɪˈpiːt/ vt/i repetir(-se) ● n repetição f; (broadcast) retransmissão f. ~**edly** adv repetidas vezes, repetidamente

repel /rɪˈpel/ vt (pt **repelled**) repelir. ~**lent** a & n repelente m

repent /rɪˈpent/ vi arrepender-se (**of** de). ~**ance** n arrependimento m. ~**ant** a arrependido

repercussion /riːpəˈkʌʃn/ n repercussão f

repertoire /ˈrepətwɑː(r)/ n repertório m

repertory /ˈrepətri/ n repertório m

repetit|ion /repɪˈtɪʃn/ n repetição f. ~**ious** ~**ive** /rɪˈpetətɪv/ a repetitivo

repetitive strain injury n lesão f por esforço repetitivo

replace /rɪˈpleɪs/ vt colocar no mesmo lugar, repor; (take the place of) substituir. ~**ment** n reposição f; (substitution) substituição f; (person) substituto m

replenish /rɪˈplenɪʃ/ vt voltar a encher, reabastecer; (renew) renovar

replica /ˈreplɪkə/ n réplica f, cópia f, reprodução f

reply /rɪˈplaɪ/ vt/i responder, replicar ● n resposta f, réplica f

report /rɪˈpɔːt/ vt relatar; (notify) informar; (denounce) denunciar, apresentar queixa de ● vi fazer um relatório; ~ **(on)** ‹news item› fazer

r

uma reportagem (sobre); **~ to** (go) apresentar-se a ● n (in newspapers) reportagem f; (of company, doctor) relatório m; Schol boletim m escolar; (sound) detonação f; (rumour) rumores mpl. **~edly** adv segundo consta. **~er** n repórter m

repossess /riːpə'zes/ vt reapossar-se de, retomar

represent /reprɪ'zent/ vt representar. **~ation** /-'teɪʃn/ n representação f

representative /reprɪ'zentətɪv/ a representativo ● n representante mf

repress /rɪ'pres/ vt reprimir. **~ion** /-ʃn/ n repressão f. **~ive** a repressor, repressivo

reprieve /rɪ'priːv/ n suspensão f temporária; (temporary relief) tréguas fpl ● vt suspender temporariamente; fig dar tréguas a

reprimand /'reprɪmɑːnd/ vt repreender ● n repreensão f, reprimenda f

reprint /'riːprɪnt/ n reimpressão f, reedição f ● vt reimprimir

reproach /rɪ'prəʊtʃ/ vt censurar; repreender (**sb for sth** alguém por algo, algo a alguém) ● n censura f; **above ~** irrepreensível. **~ful** a repreensivo, reprovador

reproduce /riːprə'djuːs/ vt/i reproduzir(-se). **~tion** /-'dʌkʃn/ n reprodução f. **~tive** /-'dʌktɪv/ a reprodutivo, reprodutor

reptile /'reptaɪl/ n réptil m

republic /rɪ'pʌblɪk/ n república f. **~an** a & n republicano m

repugnant /rɪ'pʌgnənt/ a repugnante. **~ce** n repugnância f

repulse /rɪ'pʌls/ vt repelir, repulsar. **~ion** /-ʃn/ n repulsa f. **~ive** a repulsivo, repelente, repugnante

reputable /'repjʊtəbl/ a respeitado, honrado; ‹firm, make etc› de renome, conceituado

reputation /repjʊ'teɪʃn/ n reputação f

repute /rɪ'pjuːt/ n reputação f. **~d** /-ɪd/ a suposto, putativo; **~d to be** tido como, tido na conta de. **~dly** /-ɪdlɪ/ adv segundo consta, com fama de

request /rɪ'kwest/ n pedido m ● vt pedir; solicitar (**of, from** a)

require /rɪ'kwaɪə(r)/ vt requerer. **~d** a requerido; (needed) necessário, preciso. **~ment** n fig requisito m; (need) necessidade f; (demand) exigência f

resale /'riːseɪl/ n revenda f

rescue /'reskjuː/ vt salvar; socorrer (**from** de) ● n salvamento m; (help) socorro m, ajuda f. **~r** /-ə(r)/ n salvador m

research /rɪ'sɜːtʃ/ n pesquisa f, investigação f ● vt/i pesquisar; fazer investigação (**into** sobre). **~er** n investigador m

resemble /rɪ'zembl/ vt assemelhar-se a, parecer-se com. **~ance** n semelhança f; similaridade f (**to** com)

resent /rɪ'zent/ vt ressentir(-se de), ficar ressentido com. **~ful** a ressentido. **~ment** n ressentimento m

reservation /rezə'veɪʃn/ n (booking) reserva f; Amer reserva (de índios) f

reserve /rɪ'zɜːv/ vt reservar ● n reserva f; Sport suplente mf; **in ~** de reserva. **~d** a reservado

reservoir /'rezəvwɑː(r)/ n (lake, supply etc) reservatório m; (container) depósito m

reshuffle /riː'ʃʌfl/ vt Pol remodelar ● n Pol reforma (do Ministério) f, remodelação f (ministerial)

reside /rɪ'zaɪd/ vi residir

resident /'rezɪdənt/ a residente ● n morador m, habitante mf; (foreigner) residente mf; (in hotel) hóspede mf. **~ce** n residência f; (of students) residência f, lar m; **~ce permit** visto m de residência

residential /rezɪ'denʃl/ a residencial

residue /'rezɪdjuː/ n resíduo m

resign /rɪ'zaɪn/ vt (post) demitir-se; **~ o.s. to** resignar-se a ● vi demitir-se, apresentar a demissão. **~ation** /rezɪg'neɪʃn/ n resignação f; (from job) demissão f. **~ed** a resignado

resilient /rɪ'zɪlɪənt/ a (springy) elástico; (person) resistente. **~ce** n elasticidade f; (of person) resistência f

resin /'rezɪn/ n resina f

resist /rɪ'zɪst/ vt/i resistir (a). **~ance** n resistência f. **~ant** a resistente

resolute /'rezəluːt/ a resoluto. **~ion** /-'luːʃn/ n resolução f

resolve /rɪ'zɒlv/ vt resolver; **~ to do** resolver fazer ● n resolução f. **~d** a (resolute) resoluto; (decided) resolvido (**to** a)

resonant /'rezənənt/ a ressonante. **~ce** n ressonância f

resort /rɪ'zɔːt/ vi **~ to** recorrer a, valer-se de ● n recurso m; (place) estância f, local m turístico; **as a last ~** em último recurso; **seaside ~** praia f, balneário m, (P) estância f balnear

resound /rɪ'zaʊnd/ vi reboar; ressoar (**with** com). **~ing** a ressoante; fig retumbante

resource /rɪˈsɔːs/ n recurso m; ~s recursos mpl, riquezas fpl. ~ful a expedito, engenhoso, desembaraçado. ~fulness n expediente m, engenho m

respect /rɪˈspekt/ n respeito m ● vt respeitar; **with ~ to** a respeito de, com respeito a, relativamente a. ~ful a respeitoso

respectab|le /rɪˈspektəbl/ a respeitável; (passable) passável, aceitável

respective /rɪˈspektɪv/ a respectivo, (P) respetivo. ~ly adv respectivamente, (P) respetivamente

respiration /respəˈreɪʃn/ n respiração f

respite /ˈrespaɪt/ n pausa f, trégua f, folga f

respond /rɪˈspɒnd/ vi responder (**to** a); (react) reagir (**to** a)

response /rɪˈspɒns/ n resposta f; (reaction) reação f

responsib|le /rɪˈspɒnsəbl/ a responsável; ‹job› de responsabilidade. ~lity /-ˈbɪlətɪ/ n responsabilidade f

responsive /rɪˈspɒnsɪv/ a receptivo, (P) recetivo, que reage bem; ~ **to** sensível a

rest[1] /rest/ vt/i descansar, repousar; (lean) apoiar(-se) ● n descanso m, repouso m; (support) suporte m. ~room n Amer banheiro m, (P) toaletes mpl

rest[2] /rest/ vi (remain) ficar; **it ~s with him** cabe a ele ● n (remainder) resto m (of de); **the ~ (of the)** (others) os outros

restaurant /ˈrestrɒnt/ n restaurante m

restful /ˈrestfl/ a sossegado, repousante, tranquilo

restless /ˈrestlɪs/ a agitado, desassossegado

restor|e /rɪˈstɔː(r)/ vt restaurar; (give back) restituir, devolver. ~ation /restəˈreɪʃn/ n restauração f

restrain /rɪˈstreɪn/ vt conter, reprimir; ~ **o.s.** controlar-se; ~ **sb from** impedir alguém de. ~ed a comedido, reservado. ~t n controle m; (moderation) moderação f, comedimento m

restrict /rɪˈstrɪkt/ vt restringir, limitar. ~ion /-ʃn/ n restrição f. ~ive a restritivo

result /rɪˈzʌlt/ n resultado m ● vi resultar (**from** de); ~ **in** resultar em

resum|e /rɪˈzjuːm/ vt/i reatar, retomar; ‹work, travel› recomeçar. ~ption /rɪˈzʌmpʃn/ n reatamento m, retomada f, (of work) recomeço m

résumé /ˈrezjuːmeɪ/ n resumo m, (P) CV m

resurgence /rɪˈsɜːdʒəns/ n reaparecimento m, ressurgimento m

resurrect /rezəˈrekt/ vt ressuscitar. ~ion /-ʃn/ n ressureição f

resuscitat|e /rɪˈsʌsɪteɪt/ vt ressuscitar, reanimar. ~ion /-ˈteɪʃn/ n reanimação f

retail /ˈriːteɪl/ n retalho m ● a & adv a retalho ● vt/i vender(-se) a retalho. ~er n retalhista mf

retain /rɪˈteɪn/ vt reter; (keep) conservar, guardar

retaliat|e /rɪˈtælɪeɪt/ vi retaliar, exercer represálias, desforrar-se. ~ion /-ˈeɪʃn/ n retaliação f, represália f, desforra f

retarded /rɪˈtɑːdɪd/ a retardado, atrasado

retch /retʃ/ vi fazer esforço para vomitar, estar com ânsias de vômito or (P) vómito

retention /rɪˈtenʃn/ n retenção f

reticen|t /ˈretɪsnt/ a reticente. ~ce n reticência f

retina /ˈretɪnə/ n retina f

retinue /ˈretɪnjuː/ n séquito m, comitiva f

retire /rɪˈtaɪə(r)/ vi reformar-se, aposentar-se; (withdraw) retirar-se; (go to bed) ir deitar-se ● vt reformar, aposentar. ~d a reformado, aposentado. ~ment n reforma f, aposentadoria f, (P) aposentação f

retiring /rɪˈtaɪərɪŋ/ a reservado, retraído

retort /rɪˈtɔːt/ vt/i retrucar, retorquir ● n réplica f

retrace /riːˈtreɪs/ vt ~ **one's steps** refazer o mesmo caminho; fig recordar, recapitular

retract /rɪˈtrækt/ vt/i retratar(-se), desdizer(-se); ‹wheels› recolher; ‹claws› encolher, recolher

retreat /rɪˈtriːt/ vi retirar-se; Mil retirar, bater em retirada ● n retirada f; (seclusion) retiro m

retrial /riːˈtraɪəl/ n novo m julgamento

retribution /retrɪˈbjuːʃn/ n castigo (merecido) m; (vengeance) vingança f

retriev|e /rɪˈtriːv/ vt ir buscar; (rescue) salvar; (recover) recuperar; (put right) reparar. ~er n (dog) perdigueiro m, (P) retriever m

retrograde /ˈretrəgreɪd/ a retrógrado ● vt retroceder, recuar

r

retrospect /ˈretrəspekt/ n
in ~ retrospectivamente, (P)
retrospetivamente. **~ive** /-ˈspektɪv/ a
retrospetivo; (of law, payment) retroativo

return /rɪˈtɜːn/ vi voltar; regressar;
retornar (**to a**) ● vt devolver;
‹compliment, visit› retribuir; (put back)
pôr de volta ● n volta f, regresso m,
retorno m; (profit) lucro m, rendimento
m; (restitution) devolução f; **in ~ for** em
troca de; **~ journey** viagem f de volta;
~ match Sport desafio m de desforra;
~ ticket bilhete m de ida e volta; **many
happy ~s (of the day)** muitos parabéns

reunion /riːˈjuːnɪən/ n reunião f

reunite /riːjuːˈnaɪt/ vt reunir

rev /rev/ n Ⓘ Auto rotação f ● vt/i (pt
revved) **~ (up)** Ⓘ Auto acelerar (o
motor)

reveal /rɪˈviːl/ vt revelar; (display) expor.
~ing a revelador

revel /ˈrevl/ vi (pt revelled) divertir-se;
~ in deleitar-se com. **~ry** n festas fpl,
festejos mpl

revelation /revəˈleɪʃn/ n revelação f

revenge /rɪˈvendʒ/ n vingança f; Sport
desforra f ● vt vingar

revenue /ˈrevənjuː/ n receita f,
rendimento m; **Inland R~** Fisco m

reverberate /rɪˈvɜːbəreɪt/ vi ecoar,
repercutir

revere /rɪˈvɪə(r)/ vt reverenciar, venerar

reverend /ˈrevərənd/ a reverendo; **R~**
Reverendo

reveren|t /ˈrevərənt/ a reverente. **~ce**
n reverência f, veneração f

revers|e /rɪˈvɜːs/ a contrário, inverso
● n contrário m; (back) reverso m; (gear)
marcha f à ré or (P) atrás ● vt virar ao
contrário; ‹order› inverter; (turn inside
out) virar do avesso; ‹decision› anular
● vi Auto fazer marcha à ré or (P) atrás.
~al n inversão f, mudança f em sentido
contrário; (of view etc) mudança f

revert /rɪˈvɜːt/ vi **~ to** reverter a

review /rɪˈvjuː/ n (inspection; magazine)
revista f; (of a situation) revisão f;
(critique) crítica f ● vt revistar, passar or
(P) fazer revista em; ‹situation› rever;
‹book, film etc› fazer a crítica de. **~er** n
crítico m

revis|e /rɪˈvaɪz/ vt rever; (amend)
corrigir. **~ion** /-ˈɪʒn/ n revisão f;
(amendment) correção f

reviv|e /rɪˈvaɪv/ vt/i ressuscitar,
reavivar; ‹play› reapresentar; ‹person›
reanimar(-se). **~al** n reflorescimento m,

renascimento m

revoke /rɪˈvəʊk/ vt revogar, anular,
invalidar

revolt /rɪˈvəʊlt/ vt/i revoltar(-se)
● n revolta f

revolting /rɪˈvəʊltɪŋ/ a (disgusting)
repugnante

revolution /revəˈluːʃn/ n revolução
f. **~ary** a & n revolucionário m. **~ize** vt
revolucionar

revolv|e /rɪˈvɒlv/ vi girar; **~ing door**
porta f giratória

revolver /rɪˈvɒlvə(r)/ n revólver m

revulsion /rɪˈvʌlʃn/ n repugnância f,
repulsa f

reward /rɪˈwɔːd/ n prémio m, (P)
prémio m; (for criminal, for lost/
stolen property) recompensa f ● vt
recompensar. **~ing** a compensador;
‹task etc› gratificante

rewind /riːˈwaɪnd/ vt (pt rewound)
rebobinar

rewrite /riːˈraɪt/ vt (pt rewrote, pp
rewritten) reescrever

rhetoric /ˈretərɪk/ n retórica f. **~al**
/rɪˈtɒrɪkl/ a retórico; ‹question› retórico

rheumati|c /ruːˈmætɪk/ a reumático.
~sm /ˈruːmətɪzm/ n reumatismo m

rhinoceros /raɪˈnɒsərəs/ n (pl -oses)
rinoceronte m

rhubarb /ˈruːbɑːb/ n ruibarbo m

rhyme /raɪm/ n rima f; (poem) versos
mpl ● vt/i (fazer) rimar

rhythm /ˈrɪðəm/ n ritmo m. **~ic(al)**
/ˈrɪðmɪk(l)/ a rítmico, compassado

rib /rɪb/ n costela f

ribbon /ˈrɪbən/ n fita f; **in ~s** em tiras

rice /raɪs/ n arroz m

rich /rɪtʃ/ a (-er, -est) rico; ‹food› rico
em açúcar e gordura. **~es** npl riquezas
fpl. **~ly** adv ricamente

rickety /ˈrɪkətɪ/ a (shaky)
desconjuntado

ricochet /ˈrɪkəʃeɪ/ n ricochete m ● vi
(pt ricocheted /-ʃeɪd/) fazer ricochete,
ricochetear

rid /rɪd/ vt (pt rid, pres p ridding)
desembaraçar (**of** de); **get ~ of**
desembaraçar-se de, livrar-se de

riddance /ˈrɪdns/ n **good ~!** que
alívio!, vai com Deus!

ridden /ˈrɪdn/ ▶ RIDE

riddle¹ /ˈrɪdl/ n enigma m; (puzzle)
charada f

riddle² /ˈrɪdl/ vt **~ with** crivar de

ride /raɪd/ vi (pt **rode**, pp **ridden**) andar (de bicicleta, a cavalo, de carro) ● vt ⟨horse⟩ montar; ⟨bicycle⟩ andar de; ⟨distance⟩ percorrer ● n passeio m or volta f (de carro, a cavalo etc); (distance) percurso m. ~r /-ə(r)/ n cavaleiro m, amazona f; (cyclist) ciclista mf; (in document) aditamento m

ridge /rɪdʒ/ n aresta f; (of hill) cume m

ridicule /ˈrɪdɪkjuːl/ n ridículo m ● vt ridicularizar

ridiculous /rɪˈdɪkjʊləs/ a ridículo

riding /ˈraɪdɪŋ/ n equitação f

rife /raɪf/ a be ~ estar espalhado; (of illness) grassar; ~ with cheio de

riff-raff /ˈrɪfræf/ n gentinha f, povinho m, ralé f

rifle /ˈraɪfl/ n espingarda f ● vt revistar e roubar, saquear

rift /rɪft/ n fenda f, brecha f; fig (dissension) desacordo m; desavença f; desentendimento m

rig[1] /rɪg/ vt (pt **rigged**) equipar; ~ out enfarpelar 🔢; ~ up arranjar ● n (for oil) plataforma f de poço de petróleo

rig[2] /rɪg/ vt (pt **rigged**) pej manipular

right /raɪt/ a (correct, moral) certo; correto; (fair) justo; (not left) direito; (suitable) certo, próprio ● n (entitlement) direito m; (not left) direita f; (not evil) o bem; ~ of way Auto prioridade f ● vt ⟨a wrong⟩ reparar; ⟨sth fallen⟩ endireitar ● adv (not left) à direita; (directly) direito; (exactly) mesmo, bem; (completely) completamente; ~ away logo, imediatamente; be ~ ⟨person⟩ ter razão (to em); be in the ~ ter razão; on the ~ à direita; put ~ acertar, corrigir. ~ angle n ângulo reto m; ~-hand a à or de direita; ~-handed a (person) destro; ~-wing a Pol de direita

righteous /ˈraɪtʃəs/ a justo, virtuoso

rightful /ˈraɪtfl/ a legítimo

rightly /ˈraɪtlɪ/ adv devidamente, corretamente; (with reason) justificadamente

rigid /ˈrɪdʒɪd/ a rígido. ~ity /rɪˈdʒɪdətɪ/ n rigidez f

rig|our /ˈrɪɡə(r)/ n rigor m. ~orous a rigoroso

rile /raɪl/ vt 🔢 irritar; exasperar

rim /rɪm/ n borda f; (of wheel) aro m

rind /raɪnd/ n (on cheese, fruit) casca f; (on bacon) pele f

ring[1] /rɪŋ/ n (on finger) anel m; (for napkin, key etc) argola f; (circle) roda f, círculo m; Boxing ringue m; (arena) arena f; (of people) grupo m ● vt rodear, cercar. ~ road n estrada f periférica or perimetral or (P) circular f

ring[2] /rɪŋ/ vt/i (pt **rang**, pp **rung**) tocar; (of words etc) soar ● n toque m; 🔢 (phone call) telefonadela f 🔢; ~ the bell tocar a campainha; ~ back telefonar de volta; ~ off desligar; ~ up telefonar (a). ~tone n toque m, (P) tom de toque m

ringleader /ˈrɪŋliːdə(r)/ n cabeça m, cérebro m

rink /rɪŋk/ n rinque m de patinação or (P) patinagem

rinse /rɪns/ vt enxaguar ● n enxaguada f, (P) enxaguadela f; (hair tint) enxaguada f, (P) enxaguadela f

riot /ˈraɪət/ n distúrbio m, motim m; (of colours) festival m ● vi fazer distúrbios or motins; run ~ desenfrear-se, descontrolar-se; (of plants) crescer em matagal. ~er n desordeiro m

riotous /ˈraɪətəs/ a desenfreado, turbulento, desordeiro

rip /rɪp/ vt/i (pt **ripped**) rasgar(-se) ● n rasgão m; ~ off (defraud) defraudar, enrolar 🔢. ~-off n 🔢 roubalheira f 🔢

ripe /raɪp/ a (-er, -est) maduro. ~ness n madureza f, (P) amadurecimento m

ripen /ˈraɪpən/ vt/i amadurecer

ripple /ˈrɪpl/ n ondulação f leve; (sound) murmúrio m ● vt/i encrespar(-se), agitar(-se), ondular

rise /raɪz/ vi (pt **rose**, pp **risen**) subir, elevar-se; (stand up) erguer-se, levantar-se; ⟨rebel⟩ sublevar-se; ⟨sun⟩ nascer; ⟨curtain, prices⟩ subir ● n (increase) aumento m; (slope) subida f, ladeira f; (origin) origem f; give ~ to originar, causar, dar origem a. ~r /-ə(r)/ n early ~r madrugador m

rising /ˈraɪzɪŋ/ n (revolt) insurreição f ● a ⟨sun⟩ nascente

risk /rɪsk/ n risco m ● vt arriscar; at ~ em risco, em perigo; at one's own ~ por sua conta e risco; ~ doing (venture) arriscar-se a fazer. ~y a arriscado

risqué /ˈriːskeɪ/ a picante

rite /raɪt/ n rito m; last ~s últimos sacramentos mpl

ritual /ˈrɪtʃʊəl/ a & n ritual m

rival /ˈraɪvl/ n & a rival mf; fig concorrente mf; competidor m ● vt (pt **rivalled**) rivalizar com. ~ry n rivalidade f

river /ˈrɪvə(r)/ n rio m ● a fluvial

rivet /ˈrɪvɪt/ n rebite m ● vt (pt **riveted**) rebitar; fig prender; cravar. ~ing a fascinante

road /rəʊd/ n estrada f; (in town) rua f; (small) fig caminho m; ~ **tax** imposto m de circulação. **~block** n barricada f; ~ **map** n mapa m das estradas; ~ **sign** n sinal m, placa f de sinalização; **~works** npl obras fpl (na via)

roadside /ˈrəʊdsaɪd/ n beira f da estrada

roadway /ˈrəʊdweɪ/ n pista f de rolamento, (P) faixa f de rodagem

roadworthy /ˈrəʊdwɜːðɪ/ a em condições de ser utilizado na rua/estrada

roam /rəʊm/ vi errar, andar sem destino ● vt percorrer

roaming /ˈrəʊmɪŋ/ n Telecom roaming m

roar /rɔː(r)/ n berro m, rugido m; (of thunder) ribombo m, troar m; (of sea, wind) bramido m ● vt/i berrar, rugir; (of lion) rugir; (of thunder) ribombar, troar; (of sea, wind) bramir; ~ **with laughter** rir às gargalhadas

roaring /ˈrɔːrɪŋ/ a ‹trade› florescente; ‹success› enorme; ‹fire› com grandes chamas

roast /rəʊst/ vt/i assar ● a & n assado m

rob /rɒb/ vt (pt robbed) roubar (sb of sth algo de/a alguém); ‹bank› assaltar; (deprive) privar (of de). ~**ber** n ladrão m. **~bery** n roubo m; (of bank) assalto m

robe /rəʊb/ n veste f comprida e solta; (dressing gown) robe m

robin /ˈrɒbɪn/ n papo-roxo m, (P) pintarroxo m

robot /ˈrəʊbɒt/ n robô m, (P) robot m, autômato m, (P) autómato m

robust /rəʊˈbʌst/ a robusto

rock¹ /rɒk/ n rocha f; (boulder) penhasco m, rochedo m; (sweet) pirulito m, (P) chupa-chupa m comprido; **on the ~s** 🄸 (of marriage) em crise; 🄸 (of drinks) com gelo. ~ **bottom** n ponto m mais baixo ● a (of prices) baixíssimo 🄸

rock² /rɒk/ vt/i balouçar(-se); (shake) abanar, sacudir; ‹child› embalar ● n Mus rock m. **~ing chair** n cadeira f de balanço, (P) cadeira f de baloiço; **~ing horse** n cavalo m de balanço, (P) cavalo m de baloiço

rocket /ˈrɒkɪt/ n foguete m

rocky /ˈrɒkɪ/ a (-ier, -iest) ‹ground› pedregoso; ‹hill› rochoso; 🄸 (unsteady) instável; 🄸 (shaky) tremido 🄸

rod /rɒd/ n vara f, vareta f; Mech haste f; (for curtains) bastão m, (P) varão m; (for fishing) vara (de pescar) f, (P) cana f de pesca

rode /rəʊd/ ▶ RIDE

rodent /ˈrəʊdnt/ n roedor m

rogue /rəʊg/ n (dishonest) patife m, velhaco m; (mischievous) brincalhão m

role /rəʊl/ n papel m

roll /rəʊl/ vt/i (fazer) rolar; (into ball or cylinder) enrolar(-se); **be ~ing in money** 🄸 nadar em dinheiro 🄸; ~ **over** (turn over) virar-se ao contrário ● n rolo m; (list) rol m, lista f; (bread) pãozinho m; (of ship) balanço m; (of drum) rufar m; (of thunder) ribombo m 🄰 ~ **up** vi 🄸 aparecer ● vt ‹sleeves› arregaçar; ‹umbrella› fechar. **~call** n chamada f; **~ing pin** n rolo m de pastel

roller /ˈrəʊlə(r)/ n cilindro m; (wave) vagalhão m; (for hair) rolo m. ~ **blind** n estore m; ~ **coaster** n montanha f russa; ~ **skate** n patim m de rodas

Roman /ˈrəʊmən/ a & n romano m; ~ **numerals** algarismos mpl romanos. **R~ Catholic** a & n católico

romance /rəʊˈmæns/ n (love affair) romance m, romantismo m

romantic /rəʊˈmæntɪk/ a romântico. **~ism** n romantismo m. **~ize** vi fazer romance ● vt romantizar

Romania /rʊˈmeɪnɪə/ n Romênia f, (P) Roménia f. **~n** a & n romeno m

romp /rɒmp/ vi brincar animadamente ● n brincadeira f animada

roof /ruːf/ n (pl roofs) telhado m; (of car) teto m, (P) capota f; (of mouth) palato m, céu m da boca; **hit the ~** 🄸 ficar furioso ● vt cobrir com telhado. ~ **rack** n porta-bagagem m; **~top** n cimo m do telhado

rook¹ /rʊk/ n (bird) gralha f

rook² /rʊk/ n Chess torre f

room /ruːm/ n quarto m, divisão f; (bedroom) quarto m de dormir; (large hall) sala f; (space) espaço m, lugar m; **~s** (lodgings) apartamento m, cômodo m. **~mate** n companheiro m de quarto. **~y** a espaçoso; ‹clothes› amplo, largo

roost /ruːst/ n poleiro m ● vi empoleirar-se. **~er** n Amer galo m

root¹ /ruːt/ n raiz f; fig origem f; **take ~** criar raízes ● vt/i enraizar(-se), radicar(-se); ~ **out** extirpar, erradicar

root² /ruːt/ vi ~ **about** revolver, remexer; ~ **for** Amer 🅧 torcer por

rope /rəʊp/ n corda f; **know the ~s** estar por dentro (do assunto) ● vt atar; ~ **in** convencer a participar de/em

rose¹ /rəʊz/ n rosa f; (nozzle) ralo m (de regador)

rose² /rəʊz/ ▶ RISE

rosé /'rəʊzeɪ/ n rosé m

roster /'rɒstə(r)/ n lista (de serviço) f, escala (de serviço) f

rostrum /'rɒstrəm/ n tribuna f; (for conductor) estrado m; Sport pódio m

rosy /'rəʊzɪ/ a (-ier, -iest) rosado; fig risonho

rot /rɒt/ vt/i (pt rotted) apodrecer ● n putrefação f, podridão f; 🅱 (nonsense) disparate m; asneiras fpl

rota /'rəʊtə/ n escala f de serviço

rotary /'rəʊtərɪ/ a rotativo, giratório

rotat|e /rəʊ'teɪt/ vt/i (fazer) girar, (fazer) revolver; (change round) alternar. ~ion /-ʃn/ n rotação f

rote /rəʊt/ n by ~ de cor, maquinalmente

rotten /'rɒtn/ a podre; (corrupt) corrupto; 🅱 (bad) mau; ruim; ~ eggs ovos mpl podres; **feel** ~ (ill) não se sentir nada bem

rough /rʌf/ a (-er, -est) rude; (to touch) áspero, rugoso; (of ground) acidentado, irregular; (violent) violento; (of sea) agitado, encapelado; (of weather) tempestuoso; (not perfect) tosco, rudimentar; (of estimate etc) aproximado; ~ paper rascunho m, borrão m ● n (ruffian) rufia m, desordeiro m ● adv (live) ao relento; (play) bruto, (P) à bruta ● vt ~ it viver de modo primitivo, não ter onde morar 🅱; ~ out fazer um esboço preliminar de. ~ly adv asperamente, rudemente; (approximately) aproximadamente. ~ness n rudeza f, aspereza f; (violence) brutalidade f

roughage /'rʌfɪdʒ/ n alimentos mpl fibrosos

roulette /ruː'let/ n roleta f

round /raʊnd/ a (-er, -est) redondo; ~ trip viagem f de ida e volta ● n (circle) círculo m; (slice) fatia f; (postman's) entrega f; (patrol) ronda f; (of drinks) rodada f; (competition) partida f, rodada f, (P) ronda f; Boxing round m; (of talks) ciclo m, série f; ~ of applause salva f de palmas ● prep & adv em volta (de), em torno (de); **come** ~ (into consciousness) voltar a si; **go** or **come** ~ **to** (a friend etc) dar um pulo na casa de, passar pela casa de; ~ about (nearby) por aí; fig mais ou menos; ~ the clock noite e dia sem parar ● vt arredondar; ‹cape, corner› dobrar, virar; ~ off terminar; ~ up (gather) juntar; ‹a figure› arredondar. ~-up n (of cattle) rodeio m; (of suspects) captura f

roundabout /'raʊndəbaʊt/ n carrossel m; (for traffic) rotatória f, (P) rotunda f ● a indireto

rous|e /raʊz/ vt acordar, despertar; **be ~ed** (angry) exaltar-se, inflamar-se, ser provocado. ~ing a ‹speech› inflamado, exaltado; ‹music› vibrante; ‹cheers› frenético

route /ruːt/ n percurso m, itinerário m; Naut, Aviat rota f

routine /ruː'tiːn/ n rotina f; Theat número m; **daily** ~ rotina f diária ● a de rotina, rotineiro

row[1] /rəʊ/ n fila f, fileira f; (in knitting) carreira f; **in a** ~ (consecutive) seguido em fila or (P) a fio

row[2] /rəʊ/ vt/i remar. ~ing n remo m. ~ing boat n barco m a remo

row[3] /raʊ/ n 🅱 (noise) barulho m, bagunça f, banzé m 🅱; 🅱 (quarrel) discussão f, briga f ● vi ~ (with) 🅱 brigar (com), discutir (com)

rowdy /'raʊdɪ/ a (-ier, -iest) desordeiro

royal /'rɔɪəl/ a real

royalty /'rɔɪəltɪ/ n família f real; (payment) direitos (de autor, de patente, etc) mpl

RSI abbr = REPETITIVE STRAIN INJURY

rub /rʌb/ vt/i (pt rubbed) esfregar; (with ointment etc) esfregar, friccionar ● n esfrega f; (with ointment etc) fricção f; ~ it in repisar/insistir em; ~ off on comunicar-se a, transmitir-se a; ~ out (with rubber) apagar

rubber /'rʌbə(r)/ n borracha f; ~ band elástico m; ~ stamp carimbo m

rubbish /'rʌbɪʃ/ n (refuse) lixo m; (nonsense) disparates mpl. ~ dump n lixeira f

rubble /'rʌbl/ n entulho m

ruby /'ruːbɪ/ n rubi m

rucksack /'rʌksæk/ n mochila f

rudder /'rʌdə(r)/ n leme m

ruddy /'rʌdɪ/ a (-ier, -iest) avermelhado; (of cheeks) corado, vermelho; 🅱 (damned) maldito 🅱

rude /ruːd/ a (-er, -est) mal-educado, malcriado, grosseiro. ~ness n má-educação f, má-criação f, grosseria f

rudiment /'ruːdɪmənt/ n rudimento m. ~ary /-'mentrɪ/ a rudimentar

ruffian /'rʌfɪən/ n desordeiro m

ruffle /'rʌfl/ vt ‹feathers› eriçar; ‹hair› despentear; ‹clothes› amarrotar; fig perturbar ● n (frill) franzido m, (P) folho m

r

rug /rʌg/ n tapete m; (covering) manta f

rugged /'rʌgɪd/ a rude, irregular; ‹coast, landscape› acidentado; ‹character› forte; ‹features› marcado

ruin /'ruːɪn/ n ruína f ● vt arruinar; fig estragar

rule /ruːl/ n regra f; (regulation) regulamento m; Pol governo m; **as a ~** regra geral, por via de regra ● vt governar; (master) dominar; Jur decretar; (decide) decidir ● vi governar; **~ out** excluir; **~d paper** papel m pautado. **~r** /-ə(r)/ n (sovereign) soberano m; (leader) governante m; (measure) régua f

ruling /'ruːlɪŋ/ a ‹class› dirigente; Pol no poder ● n decisão f

rum /rʌm/ n rum m

rumble /'rʌmbl/ vi ribombar, ressoar; (of stomach) roncar ● n ribombo m, estrondo m

rummage /'rʌmɪdʒ/ vt revistar, remexer

rumour /'ruːmə(r)/ n boato m, rumor m ● vt **it is ~ed that** corre o boato de que, consta que

rump /rʌmp/ n (of horse etc) garupa f; (of fowl) mitra f. **~ steak** n bife m de alcatra

run /rʌn/ vi (pt **ran**, pp **run**, pres p **running**) correr; (flow) correr; (pass) passar; (function) andar, funcionar; (melt) derreter, pingar; ‹bus etc› circular; ‹play› estar em cartaz; ‹colour› desbotar; (in election) candidatar-se (for a); **~ away** fugir; **~ down** descer correndo; **~ out** esgotar-se; ‹lease› expirar; **I ran out of sugar** o açúcar acabou; **~ over** (of vehicle) atropelar; **~ up** deixar acumular ● vt (manage) dirigir, gerir; ‹a risk› correr; ‹a race› participar em; ‹water› deixar correr; ‹a car› ter, manter; **~ across** encontrar por acaso, dar com; **~ down** (of vehicle) atropelar; (belittle) dizer mal de, denigrir; **be ~ down** estar exausto; **~ in** ‹engine› ligar; **~ into** (meet) encontrar por acaso; (hit) bater em, ir de encontro a ● n corrida f; (excursion) passeio m, ida f; (rush) corrida f, correria f; (in cricket) ponto m; **be on the ~** estar foragido; **have the ~ of** ter à sua disposição; **in the long ~** a longo prazo; **the ~-up to** o período que precede □ **~ off** vt ‹copies› tirar; ‹water› deixar correr ● vi fugir. **~-of-the-mill** a vulgar

runaway /'rʌnəweɪ/ n fugitivo m ● a fugitivo, em fuga; ‹horse› desembestado; ‹vehicle› desvairado; ‹success› grande

rung¹ /rʌŋ/ n (of ladder) degrau m

rung² /rʌŋ/ ▶ RING²

runner /'rʌnə(r)/ n (person) corredor m; (carpet) passadeira f; **~ bean** feijão m verde. **~-up** n segundo classificado m

running /'rʌnɪŋ/ n corrida f; (functioning) funcionamento m; **be in the ~** (competitor) ter probabilidades de êxito ● a consecutivo, seguido; (water) corrente; **four days ~** quatro dias seguidos or a fio; **~ commentary** reportagem f, comentário m

runny /'rʌnɪ/ a derretido

runway /'rʌnweɪ/ n pista f de decolagem, (P) descolagem

rupture /'rʌptʃə(r)/ n ruptura f, (P) rutura f; Med hérnia f ● vt/i romper(-se), rebentar

rural /'ruərəl/ a rural

ruse /ruːz/ n ardil m, estratagema m, manha f

rush¹ /rʌʃ/ n (plant) junco m

rush² /rʌʃ/ vi (move) precipitar-se; (be in a hurry) apressar-se ● vt fazer, mandar etc a toda a pressa; (person) pressionar; Mil tomar de assalto ● n tropel m; (haste) pressa f; **in a ~** a(s) pressa(s); **~ hour** rush m, (P) hora f de ponta

Russia /'rʌʃə/ n Rússia f. **~n** a & n russo m

rust /rʌst/ n (on iron, plants) ferrugem f ● vt/i enferrujar(-se). **~proof** a inoxidável. **~y** a ferrugento, enferrujado; fig enferrujado

rustic /'rʌstɪk/ a rústico

rustle /'rʌsl/ vt/i restolhar, (fazer) farfalhar, Amer (steal) roubar; **~ up** 🅸 ‹food etc› arranjar

rut /rʌt/ n sulco m; fig rotina f; **in a ~** numa vida rotineira

ruthless /'ruːθlɪs/ a implacável

rye /raɪ/ n centeio m

Ss

sabbath /'sæbəθ/ n (Jewish) sábado m; (Christian) domingo m

sabbatical /sə'bætɪkl/ n Univ período m de licença, licença f sabática

sabotage /'sæbətɑːʒ/ n sabotagem f ● vt sabotar. **~ur** /-'tɜː(r)/ n sabotador m

sachet /'sæʃeɪ/ n sachê m, saqueta f

sack /sæk/ n saco m, saca f ● vt 🔲 despedir; **get the ~** 🔲 ser despedido

sacred /'seɪkrɪd/ a sagrado

sacrifice /'sækrɪfaɪs/ n sacrifício m; fig sacrifício m ● vt sacrificar

sacrileg|e /'sækrɪlɪdʒ/ n sacrilégio m. **~ious** /-'lɪdʒəs/ a sacrílego

sad /sæd/ a (**sadder**, **saddest**) ‹person› triste; ‹story, news› triste. **~ly** adv tristemente; (unfortunately) infelizmente. **~ness** n tristeza f

sadden /'sædn/ vt entristecer

saddle /'sædl/ n sela f ● vt ‹horse› selar; **~ sb with** sobrecarregar alguém com

sadis|m /'seɪdɪzəm/ n sadismo m. **~t** /-ɪst/ n sádico m. **~tic** /sə'dɪstɪk/ a sádico

safe /seɪf/ a (**-er**, **-est**) (not dangerous) seguro; (out of danger) fora de perigo; (reliable) confiável; **~ from** salvo de risco de; **~ and sound** são e salvo; **~ conduct** salvo-conduto m; **~ keeping** custódia f, (P) proteção f; **to be on the ~ side** por via das dúvidas ● n cofre m, caixa-forte f. **~ly** adv (arrive etc) em segurança; (keep) seguro

safeguard /'seɪfɡɑːd/ n salvaguarda f ● vt salvaguardar

safety /'seɪftɪ/ n segurança f. **~ belt** n cinto m de segurança; **~ pin** n alfinete m de fralda, (P) alfinete m de ama

sag /sæɡ/ vi (pt **sagged**) afrouxar

saga /'sɑːɡə/ n saga f

sage[1] /seɪdʒ/ n (herb) salva f

sage[2] /seɪdʒ/ a sensato, prudente ● n sábio m

Sagittarius /sædʒɪ'teərɪəs/ n Astrol Sagitário m

said /sed/ ▶ SAY

sail /seɪl/ n vela f; (trip) viagem f em barco à vela ● vi navegar; (leave) partir; Sport velejar ● vt navegar. **~ing** n navegação f à vela. **~ing boat** n barco m à vela

sailor /'seɪlə(r)/ n marinheiro m

saint /seɪnt/ n santo m. **~ly** a santo, santificado

sake /seɪk/ n **for the ~ of** em consideração a; **for my/your/ its own ~** por mim/por você/por isso

salad /'sæləd/ n salada f. **~ dressing** n molho m para salada

salary /'sælərɪ/ n salário m

sale /seɪl/ n venda f; (at reduced prices) liquidação f; **for ~** "vende-se"; **on ~** à venda; **~s assistant**, Amer **~s clerk** vendedor m; **~s department** departamento m de vendas

sales|man /'seɪlzmən/ n (pl **-men**) (in shop) vendedor m; (traveller) caixeiro-viajante m. **~woman** n (pl **-women**) (in shop) vendedora f; (traveller) caixeira-viajante f

saliva /sə'laɪvə/ n saliva f

salmon /'sæmən/ n (pl invar) salmão m

saloon /sə'luːn/ n (on ship) salão m; (bar) botequim m; **~ (car)** sedã m

salt /sɔːlt/ n sal m; **~ water** água f salgada, água f do mar ● a salgado ● vt (season) salgar; (cure) pôr em salmoura. **~ cellar** n saleiro m. **~y** a salgado

salute /sə'luːt/ n saudação f ● vt/i saudar

salvage /'sælvɪdʒ/ n Naut salvamento m; (of waste) reciclagem f ● vt salvar

salvation /sæl'veɪʃn/ n salvação f

same /seɪm/ a mesmo (**as** que); **at the ~ time** (at once) ao mesmo tempo ● pron **the ~** o mesmo ● adv **the ~** o mesmo; **all the ~** (nevertheless) mesmo assim, apesar de tudo

same-sex a ‹couple, marriage› do mesmo sexo

sample /'sɑːmpl/ n amostra f ● vt experimentar, provar

sanatorium /sænə'tɔːrɪəm/ n (pl **-iums**) sanatório m

sanctify /'sæŋktɪfaɪ/ vt santificar

sanctimonious /sæŋktɪ'məʊnɪəs/ a santarrão, carola

sanction /'sæŋkʃn/ n (approval) aprovação f; (penalty) pena f, sanção f ● vt sancionar

sanctuary /'sæŋktʃʊərɪ/ n Relig santuário m; (refuge) refúgio m; (for animals) reserva f

sand /sænd/ n areia f; (beach) praia f ● vt (with sandpaper) lixar

sandal /'sændl/ n sandália f

sandbank /'sændbæŋk/ n banco m de areia

sandcastle /'sændkɑːsl/ n castelo m de areia

sandpaper /'sændpeɪpə(r)/ n lixa f ● vt lixar

sandpit /'sændpɪt/ n caixa f de areia

sandwich /'sænwɪdʒ/ n sanduíche m, (P) sandes f invar ● vt **~ed between** encaixado entre; **~ course** curso m profissionalizante envolvendo estudo teórico e estágio em local de trabalho

sandy /'sændɪ/ a (**-ier**, **-iest**) arenoso; ‹beach› arenoso; ‹hair› ruivo

S

sane /seɪn/ a (-er, -est) (not mad) são m; (sensible) sensato, ajuizado

sang /sæŋ/ ▶ SING

sanitary /'sænɪtrɪ/ a sanitário; (system) sanitário; ~ **towel**, Amer ~ **napkin** toalha f absorvente, (P) penso m higiénico

sanitation /sænɪ'teɪʃn/ n condições fpl sanitárias, saneamento m

sanity /'sænɪtɪ/ n sanidade f

sank /sæŋk/ ▶ SINK

Santa Claus /'sæntəklɔːz/ n Papai m Noel, Pai m Natal

sap /sæp/ n seiva f ● vt (pt sapped) esgotar, minar

sapphire /'sæfaɪə(r)/ n safira f

sarcas|m /'sɑːrkæzəm/ n sarcasmo m. ~**tic** /sɑːr'kæstɪk/ a sarcástico

sardine /sɑː'diːn/ n sardinha f

sash /sæʃ/ n (around waist) cinto m; (over shoulder) faixa f

sat /sæt/ ▶ SIT

satchel /'sætʃl/ n sacola f

satellite /'sætəlaɪt/ n satélite m; ~ **dish** antena f de satélite; ~ **television** televisão f via satélite

satin /'sætɪn/ n cetim m

satir|e /'sætaɪə(r)/ n sátira f. ~**ical** /sə'tɪrɪkl/ a satírico. ~**ist** /'sætərɪst/ n satirista mf. ~**ize** vt satirizar

satisfact|ion /sætɪs'fækʃn/ n satisfação f. ~**ory** /-'fæktərɪ/ a satisfatório

satisfy /'sætɪsfaɪ/ vt satisfazer; (convince) convencer; (fulfil) atender. ~**ing** a satisfatório

saturat|e /'sætʃəreɪt/ vt saturar; fig cansar

Saturday /'sætədɪ/ n sábado m

sauce /sɔːs/ n molho m; 🔟 (cheek) atrevimento m

saucepan /'sɔːspən/ n panela f, (P) caçarola f

saucer /'sɔːsə(r)/ n pires m invar

saucy /'sɔːsɪ/ a (-ier, -iest) picante

Saudi Arabia /saʊdɪə'reɪbɪə/ n Arábia f Saudita

sauna /'sɔːnə/ n sauna f

saunter /'sɔːntə(r)/ vi perambular

sausage /'sɒsɪdʒ/ n salsicha f, linguiça f; (pre-cooked) salsicha f

savage /'sævɪdʒ/ a (wild) selvagem; (fierce) cruel; (brutal) brutal ● n selvagem mf ● vt atacar ferozmente. ~**ry** n selvageria f, ferocidade f

sav|e /seɪv/ vt (rescue) salvar; (keep) guardar; (collect) colecionar; ‹money› economizar, poupar; ‹time› ganhar; (prevent) evitar; impedir (**from** de) ● n Sport salvamento m ● prep salvo, exceto. ~**er** n poupador m. ~**ing** n economia f, poupança f. ~**ings** npl economias fpl, poupanças fpl

saviour /'seɪvɪə(r)/ n salvador m

savour /'seɪvə(r)/ n sabor m ● vt saborear. ~**y** a (tasty) saboroso; (not sweet) salgado

saw[1] /sɔː/ ▶ SEE[1]

saw[2] /sɔː/ n serra f ● vt (pt sawed, pp sawn or sawed) serrar

sawdust /'sɔːdʌst/ n serragem f

saxophone /'sæksəfəʊn/ n saxofone m

say /seɪ/ vt/i (pt said /sed/) dizer, falar ● n have a ~ (**in sth**) ter direito a opinar sobre algo; **have one's** ~ exprimir sua (a) opinião; **I** ~! olhe! ou escute!. ~**ing** n ditado m, provérbio m

scab /skæb/ n casca f, crosta f; 🔟 (blackleg) fura-greve mf invar

scaffold /'skæfəʊld/ n cadafalso m, andaime m. ~**ing** /-əldɪŋ/ n andaime m

scald /skɔːld/ vt escaldar, queimar ● n escaldadura f, queimadura f

scale[1] /skeɪl/ n (of fish etc) escama f

scale[2] /skeɪl/ n (ratio, size) escala f; Mus escala f; (of salaries, charges) tabela f; **on a small/large/etc** ~ numa pequena/grande/etc escala ● vt (climb) escalar; ~ **down** reduzir

scales /skeɪlz/ npl (for weighing) balança f

scallop /'skɒləp/ n Culin concha f de vieira; (shape) concha f de vieira

scalp /skælp/ n couro m cabeludo ● vt escalpar

scalpel /'skælpl/ n bisturi m

scamper /'skæmpə(r)/ vi sair correndo, (P) a correr or à(s) pressa(s)

scampi /'skæmpɪ/ npl camarões mpl fritos

scan /skæn/ vt (pt scanned) (intently) perscrutar, esquadrinhar; (quickly) passar os olhos em; Med examinar; (radar) explorar ● n Med exame m

scandal /'skændl/ n (disgrace) escândalo m; (gossip) fofoca f. ~**ous** a escandaloso

Scandinavia /skændɪ'neɪvɪə/ n Escandinávia f. ~**n** a & n escandinavo m

scanty /'skæntɪ/ a (-ier, -iest) escasso; ‹clothing› sumário

scapegoat /'skeɪpgəʊt/ n bode m expiatório

scar /skɑː(r)/ n cicatriz f ● vt (pt **scarred**) marcar; fig deixar marcas

scarc|e /skeəs/ a (**-er, -est**) escasso, raro; **make o.s. ~e** 𝕀 sumir, dar o fora 𝕀, (P) desaparecer sem deixar rasto. **~ity** n escassez f. **~ely** adv mal, apenas

scare /skeə(r)/ vt assustar, apavorar; **be ~d** estar com medo (**of de**) ● n pavor m, pânico m; **bomb ~** pânico m causado por suspeita de bomba num local

scarecrow /'skeəkrəʊ/ n espantalho m

scarf /skɑːf/ n (pl **scarves**) (oblong) cachecol m; (square) lenço m de cabelo

scarlet /'skɑːlət/ a escarlate m

scary /'skeərɪ/ a (**-ier, -iest**) 𝕀 assustador; apavorante

scathing /'skeɪðɪŋ/ a mordaz

scatter /'skætə(r)/ vt (strew) espalhar; (disperse) dispersar ● vi espalhar-se

scavenge /'skævɪndʒ/ vi procurar comida etc no lixo. **~r** /-ə(r)/ n (person) que procura comida etc no lixo; (animal) que se alimenta de carniça, (P) necrófago

scenario /sɪ'nɑːrɪəʊ/ n (pl **-os**) sinopse f, resumo m detalhado

scene /siːn/ n cena f; (of event) cenário m; (sight) vista f, panorama m; **behind the ~s** nos bastidores; **make a ~** fazer um escândalo

scenery /'siːnərɪ/ n cenário m, paisagem f; Theat cenário m

scenic /'siːnɪk/ a pitoresco, cênico, (P) cénico

scent /sent/ n (perfume) perfume m, fragância f; (trail) rastro m, pista f ● vt (discern) sentir. **~ed** a perfumado, aromático

sceptic /'skeptɪk/ n cético m. **~al** a cético. **~ism** /-sɪzəm/ n ceticismo m

schedule /'ʃedjuːl/ n programa m; (timetable) horário m ● vt marcar, programar; **according to ~** conforme planejado or (P) planeado; **behind ~** atrasado; **on ~** ‹train› na hora, à hora prevista; ‹work› em dia

scheme /skiːm/ n esquema m; (plan of work) plano m; (plot) conspiração f, maquinação f ● vi planejar, (P) planear; pej intrigar; maquinar; tramar

schizophreni|a /skɪtsəʊ'friːnɪə/ n esquizofrenia f. **~c** /-'frenɪk/ a esquizofrênico, (P) esquizofrénico

scholar /'skɒlə(r)/ n erudito m, estudioso m, escolar m. **~ly** a erudito.

~ship n erudição f, saber m; (grant) bolsa f de estudo

school /skuːl/ n escola f; (of university) escola f, faculdade f ● a ‹age, year, holidays› escolar ● vt ensinar; (train) treinar, adestrar. **~ing** n instrução f; (attendance) escolaridade f

school|boy /'skuːlbɔɪ/ n aluno m. **~girl** n aluna f

school|master /'skuːlmɑːstə(r)/, **~mistress**, **~teacher** ns professor m, professora f

scien|ce /'saɪəns/ n ciência f; **~ce fiction** ficção f científica. **~tific** /-'tɪfɪk/ a científico

scientist /'saɪəntɪst/ n cientista mf

scissors /'sɪzəz/ npl (**pair of**) **~** tesoura f

scoff[1] /skɒf/ vi **~ at** zombar de, (P) troçar de

scoff[2] /skɒf/ vt 🗵 (eat) devorar; tragar

scold /skəʊld/ vt ralhar com

scone /skɒn/ n Culin scone m, bolinho m para o chá

scoop /skuːp/ n (for grain, sugar etc) pá f; (ladle) concha f; (news) furo m ● vt **~ out** (hollow out) escavar, tirar com concha or pá; **~ up** (lift) apanhar

scoot /skuːt/ vi 𝕀 fugir, mandar-se 𝕀, (P) pôr-se a milhas 𝕀

scooter /'skuːtə(r)/ n (child's) patinete f, (P) trotinete m; (motor cycle) motoreta f, lambreta f

scope /skəʊp/ n âmbito m; fig (opportunity) oportunidade f

scorch /skɔːtʃ/ vt/i chamuscar(-se), queimar de leve. **~ing** a 𝕀 escaldante; abrasador

score /skɔː(r)/ n Sport contagem f, escore m; Mus partitura f ● vt marcar com corte(s), riscar; ‹a goal› marcar; Mus orquestrar ● vi marcar pontos; (keep score) fazer a contagem; Football marcar um gol or (P) golo; **a ~ (of)** (twenty) uma vintena (de), vinte; **~s** muitos, dezenas; **on that ~** nesse respeito, quanto a isso. **~board** n marcador m. **~r** /-ə(r)/ n (score-keeper) marcador m; (of goals) autor m

scorn /skɔːn/ n desprezo m ● vt desprezar. **~ful** a desdenhoso, escarninho

Scorpio /'skɔːpɪəʊ/ n Astr Escorpião m

scorpion /'skɔːpɪən/ n escorpião m

Scot /skɒt/ n, **~tish** a escocês m

Scotch /skɒtʃ/ a escocês ● n uísque m

Scotland /'skɒtlənd/ n Escócia f

S

Scots /skɒts/ a escocês

Scottish Parliament O Parlamento *i*
Escocês foi estabelecido em
Edimburgo em 1999. Tem competência
legislativa e executiva em assuntos
internos na Escócia e poderes
tributários limitados. Há 129 *MSPs*
(*Members of the Scottish Parliament*),
dos quais 73 são eleitos diretamente
e o restante através do sistema de
representação proporcional.

---

scoundrel /'skaʊndrəl/ n patife m,
canalha m

scour[1] /'skaʊə(r)/ vt (clean) esfregar,
arear. **~er** n esfregão m de palha de aço
or de nylon

scour[2] /'skaʊə(r)/ vt (search) percorrer,
esquadrinhar

scourge /skɜːdʒ/ n açoite m; fig
flagelo m

scout /skaʊt/ n Mil explorador m
● vi **~ about (for)** andar à procura de

Scout /skaʊt/ n escoteiro m, (P)
escuteiro m

scowl /skaʊl/ n carranca f, ar m
carrancudo ● vi fazer um ar carrancudo

scramble /'skræmbl/ vi trepar; (crawl)
avançar de rastros, rastejar, arrastar-se
● vt ‹eggs› mexer ● n luta f, confusão f

scrap[1] /skræp/ n bocadinho m; **~ heap**
monte m de ferro-velho; **~ merchant**
sucateiro m ● vt (pt scrapped) jogar fora,
(P) deitar fora; ‹plan etc› abandonar,
pôr de lado. **~s** npl restos mpl. **~book** n
álbum m de recortes; **~ iron** n ferro m
velho, sucata f; **~ paper** n papel m de
rascunho. **~py** a fragmentário

scrap[2] /skræp/ n 🔟 (fight) briga f;
pancadaria f 🔟; rixa f

scrape /skreɪp/ vt raspar; (graze)
esfolar, arranhar; **~ through** escapar
pela tangente, (P) à tangente or por um
triz; ‹exam› passar pela tangente, (P) à
tangente; **~ together** conseguir juntar
● vi (graze, rub) roçar ● n (act of scraping)
raspagem f; (mark) raspão m, esfoladura
f; fig encrenca f; maus lençóis mpl 🔟

scratch /skrætʃ/ vt/i arranhar(-se); ‹a
line› riscar; (to relieve itching) coçar(-se)
● n arranhão m; (line) risco m; (wound
with claw, nail) unhada f; **start from ~**
começar do princípio; **up to ~** à altura,
ao nível requerido

scrawl /skrɔːl/ n rabisco m, garrancho
m, garatuja f ● vt/i rabiscar, fazer
garranchos, garatujar

scrawny /'skrɔːnɪ/ a (-ier, -iest)
descarnado, ossudo, magricela

scream /skriːm/ vt/i gritar ● n grito
(agudo) m

screech /skriːtʃ/ vi guinchar, gritar;
(of brakes) chiar, guinchar ● n guincho m,
grito m agudo

screen /skriːn/ n écran m, tela f;
(folding) biombo m; fig (protection)
manto m; fig capa f fig ● vt resguardar,
tapar; ‹film› passar; ‹candidates etc›
fazer a triagem de. **~ing** n Med exame
m médico

screw /skruː/ n parafuso m ● vt
aparafusar, atarraxar; **~ up** ‹eyes, face›
franzir; 🔀 (ruin) estragar; **~ up one's
courage** cobrar arranjar coragem

screwdriver /'skruːdraɪvə(r)/ n chave
f de parafusos or de fenda(s)

scribble /'skrɪbl/ vt/i rabiscar, garatujar
● n rabisco m, garatuja f

script /skrɪpt/ n escrita f; (of film)
roteiro m, (P) guião m. **~writer** n Film
roteirista m, (P) autor m do guião,
guionista mf

scroll /skrəʊl/ n rolo (de papel ou
pergaminho) m; Archit voluta f ● vt/i
Comput passar na tela, (P) no ecrã

scrounge /skraʊndʒ/ vt 🔟 (cadge)
filar 🔀, (P) cravar 🔀 ● vi (beg) parasitar,
viver à(s) custa(s) de alguém. **~r** /-ə(r)/ n
parasita mf; filão m 🔀, (P) crava mf 🔀

scrub[1] /skrʌb/ n (land) mato m

scrub[2] /skrʌb/ vt/i (pt scrubbed)
esfregar, lavar com escova e sabão;
🔟 (cancel) cancelar ● n esfrega f

scruff /skrʌf/ n **by the ~ of the neck**
pelo cangote, (P) pelo cachaço

scruffy /'skrʌfɪ/ a (-ier, -iest)
desmazelado; desleixado

scrum /skrʌm/ n rixa f; Rugby placagem f

scruple /'skruːpl/ n escrúpulo m

scrupulous /'skruːpjʊləs/ a
escrupuloso. **~ly** adv escrupulosamente;
~ly clean impecavelmente limpo

scrutin|y /'skruːtɪnɪ/ n averiguação
f, escrutínio m. **~ize** vt examinar em
detalhe

scuffle /'skʌfl/ n tumulto m, briga f

sculpt /skʌlpt/ vt/i esculpir. **~or** n
escultor m. **~ure** /-tʃə(r)/ n escultura f
● vt/i esculpir

scum /skʌm/ n (on liquid) espuma f; pej
(people) gentinha f; escumalha f; ralé f

scurry /'skʌrɪ/ vi dar corridinhas; (hurry)
apressar-se; **~ off** escapulir-se

scuttle[1] /'skʌtl/ n ‹bucket, box› balde m para carvão

scuttle[2] /'skʌtl/ vt (ship) afundar abrindo rombos or as torneiras de fundo, afundar voluntariamente

scuttle[3] /'skʌtl/ vi ~ **away** or **off** fugir, escapulir-se

sea /siː/ n mar m; **at** ~ no alto mar, ao largo; **all at** ~ desnorteado; **by** ~ por mar ● a do mar, marinho, marítimo; ~ **bird** ave f marinha; ~ **horse** cavalo-marinho m, hipocampo m; ~ **level** nível m do mar; ~ **lion** leão-marinho m; ~ **shell** concha f; ~ **water** água f do mar. ~**shore** n litoral m, costa f; (beach) praia f

seafood /'siːfuːd/ n marisco(s) m(pl)

seagull /'siːgʌl/ n gaivota f

seal[1] /siːl/ n (animal) foca f

seal[2] /siːl/ n selo m, sinete m ● vt selar; (with wax) lacrar; ~ **off** ‹area› vedar

seam /siːm/ n (in cloth etc) costura f; (of mineral) veio m, filão m. ~**less** a sem costura

seaman /'siːmən/ n (pl -men) marinheiro m, marítimo m

seance /'seɪɑːns/ n sessão f espírita

search /sɜːtʃ/ vt/i revistar, dar busca (a); ‹one's heart, conscience etc› examinar ● n revista f, busca f; (quest) procura f, busca f; (official) inquérito m; **in** ~ **of** à procura de; ~ **for** procurar. ~ **party** n equipe f or (P) equipa de busca; ~ **warrant** n mandado m de busca. ~**ing** a (of look) penetrante; (of test etc) minucioso

searchlight /'sɜːtʃlaɪt/ n holofote m

seasick /'siːsɪk/ a enjoado. ~**ness** n enjoo m

seaside /'siːsaɪd/ n costa f, praia f, beira-mar f

season /'siːzn/ n (of year) estação f; (proper time) época f; Cricket, Football etc temporada f; **in** ~ na época ● vt temperar; ‹wood› secar. ~**able** a próprio da estação. ~**al** a sazonal. ~**ed** a (of people) experimentado. ~**ing** n tempero m. ~ **ticket** n (train etc) passe m; (theatre etc) assinatura f

seat /siːt/ n assento m; (place) lugar m; (of bicycle) selim m; (of chair) assento m; (of trousers) fundilho m; ~ **of learning** centro m de cultura ● vt sentar; (have seats for) ter lugares sentados para; **be** ~**ed, take a** ~ sentar-se. ~ **belt** n cinto m de segurança

seaweed /'siːwiːd/ n alga f marinha

seaworthy /'siːwɜːðɪ/ a navegável, em condições de navegabilidade

seclu|de /sɪ'kluːd/ vt isolar. ~**ded** a isolado, retirado. ~**sion** /sɪ'kluːʒn/ n isolamento m

second[1] /'sekənd/ a segundo; ~ **thoughts** dúvidas fpl; **on** ~ **thoughts** pensando melhor ● n segundo m; (in duel) testemunha f; ~ **(gear)** Auto segunda (velocidade) f; **the** ~ **of April** dois de Abril; ~**s** (goods) artigos mpl de segunda (categoria) or de refugo ● adv (in race etc) em segundo lugar ● vt secundar. ~**best** a resignado em segundo lugar; ~**class** a de segunda classe; ~**hand** a de segunda mão ● n (on clock) ponteiro m dos segundos; ~**rate** a medíocre, de segunda ordem or categoria. ~**ly** adv segundo, em segundo lugar

second[2] /sɪ'kɒnd/ vt (transfer) destacar (to para)

secondary /'sekəndrɪ/ a secundário; ~ **school** escola f secundária

secrecy /'siːkrəsɪ/ n segredo m

secret /'siːkrɪt/ a secreto ● n segredo m; **in** ~ em segredo. ~ **agent** n agente mf secreto. ~**ly** adv em segredo, secretamente

secretar|y /'sekrətrɪ/ n secretário m, secretária f; **S~y of State** ministro m de Estado, (P) Secretário m de Estado; Amer ministro m dos Negócios Estrangeiros. ~**ial** /-'teərɪəl/ a ‹work, course etc› de secretária

secret|e /sɪ'kriːt/ vt segregar; (hide) esconder. ~**ion** /-ʃn/ n secreção f

secretive /'siːkrətɪv/ a misterioso, reservado

sect /sekt/ n seita f. ~**arian** /-'teərɪən/ a sectário

section /'sekʃn/ n seção f; (of country, community etc) setor m, (P) sector m; (district of town) zona f

sector /'sektə(r)/ n setor m

secular /'sekjʊlə(r)/ a secular, leigo, (P) laico; ‹art, music etc› profano

secure /sɪ'kjʊə(r)/ a seguro, em segurança; ‹firm› seguro, sólido; (in mind) tranquilo ● vt prender bem or com segurança; (obtain) conseguir, arranjar; (ensure) assegurar; ‹windows, doors› fechar bem. ~**ly** adv solidamente; (safely) em segurança

securit|y /sɪ'kjʊərətɪ/ n segurança f; (for loan) fiança f, caução f. ~**ies** npl Finance títulos mpl

S

sedate /sɪ'deɪt/ a sereno, comedido ● vt Med tratar com sedativos

sedation /sɪ'deɪʃn/ n Med sedação f; **under ~** sob o efeito de sedativos

sedative /'sedətɪv/ n Med sedativo m

sediment /'sedɪmənt/ n sedimento m, depósito m

seduce /sɪ'djuːs/ vt seduzir

seduction /sɪ'dʌkʃn/ n sedução f. **~ive** /-tɪv/ a sedutor, aliciante

see[1] /siː/ vt/i (pt saw, pp seen) ver; (escort) acompanhar; **~ about** or **to** tratar de, encarregar-se de; **~ through** ⟨task⟩ levar a cabo; (not be deceived by) não se deixar enganar por; **~ (to it) that** assegurar que, tratar de fazer com que; **~ing that** visto que, uma vez que; **~ you later!** 🔲 até logo! 🔲 □ **~ off** vt (wave goodbye) ir despedir-se de; (chase) acompanhar

see[2] /siː/ n sé f, bispado m

seed /siːd/ n semente f, fig (origin) germe(n) m; Tennis cabeça f de série; (pip) caroço m; **go to ~** produzir sementes; fig desmazelar-se 🔲. **~ling** n planta f brotada a partir da semente

seedy /'siːdɪ/ a (-ier, -iest) (com um ar) gasto, surrado; 🔲 (unwell) abatido; deprimido; em baixo astral 🔲 or (P) em baixo

seek /siːk/ vt (pt sought) procurar; ⟨help etc⟩ pedir

seem /siːm/ vi parecer. **~ingly** adv aparentemente, ao que parece

seen /siːn/ ▶ SEE[1]

seep /siːp/ vi (ooze) filtrar-se; (trickle) pingar, escorrer, passar

see-saw /'siːsɔː/ n gangorra f, (P) balanço m

seethe /siːð/ vi **~ with** ⟨anger⟩ ferver de; ⟨people⟩ fervilhar de

segment /'segmənt/ n segmento m; (of orange) gomo m

segregat|e /'segrɪgeɪt/ vt segregar, separar. **~ion** /-'geɪʃn/ n segregação f

seize /siːz/ vt agarrar, (P) deitar a mão a, (take possession by force) apoderar-se de; (by law) apreender; confiscar; (P) apresar ● vi **~ on** ⟨opportunity⟩ aproveitar; **~ up** ⟨engine etc⟩ grimpar, emperrar; **be ~d with** ⟨fear, illness⟩ ter um ataque de

seizure /'siːʒə(r)/ n Med ataque m, crise f; (law) apreensão f, captura f

seldom /'seldəm/ adv raras vezes, raramente, raro

select /sɪ'lekt/ vt escolher, selecionar ● a seleto. **~ion** /-ʃn/ n seleção f; Comm sortido m

selective /sɪ'lektɪv/ a seletivo

self /self/ n (pl selves) **the ~** o eu, o ego

self- /self/ pref. **~assurance** n segurança f; **~assured** a seguro de si; **~catering** a em que os hóspedes têm condições de cozinhar; **~centred** a egocêntrico; **~confidence** n autoconfiança f, confiança f em si mesmo; **~confident** a que tem confiança em si mesmo; **~conscious** a inibido, constrangido; **~contained** a independente; **~control** n autodomínio m; **~controlled** a senhor de si; **~defence** n legítima defesa f; **~employed** a autónomo, independent; **~esteem** n amor m próprio; **~evident** a evidente; **~indulgent** a que não resiste a tentações; (for ease) comodista; **~interest** n interesse m pessoal; **~portrait** n auto-retrato m; **~possessed** a senhor de si; **~respect** n amor m próprio; **~righteous** a que se tem em boa conta; **~sacrifice** n abnegação f, sacrifício m; **~satisfied** a cheio de si; convencido 🔲; **~seeking** a egoísta; **~service** a auto-serviço, self-service; **~styled** a pretenso; **~sufficient** a auto-suficiente

self-harm n automutilação f

selfish /'selfɪʃ/ a egoísta; ⟨motive⟩ interesseiro. **~ness** n egoísmo m

selfless /'selflɪs/ a desinteressado

sell /sel/ vt/i (pt sold) vender(-se); **~by date** válido até; **~ off** liquidar; **be sold out** estar esgotado. **~out** n ⟨show⟩ sucesso m; 🔲 (betrayal) traição f. **~er** n vendedor m

Sellotape® /'seləʊteɪp/ n fita f adesiva, (P) fita-cola f

semen /'siːmən/ n sêmen m, (P) sémen m, esperma m

semester /sɪ'mestə(r)/ n Univ semestre m

semi- /semɪ/ pref semi-, meio

semibreve /'semɪbriːv/ n Mus semibreve f

semicirc|le /'semɪsɜːkl/ n semicírculo m. **~ular** /-sɜːkjʊlə(r)/ a semicircular

semicolon /semɪ'kəʊlən/ n ponto e vírgula f

semi-detached /semɪdɪ'tætʃt/ a **~ house** casa f geminada

semi-final /semɪ'faɪnl/ n semifinal f, (P) meia-final f

seminar /'semɪnɑː(r)/ n seminário m

semiquaver /'semɪkweɪvə(r)/ n Mus semicolcheia f

semitone /'semɪtəʊn/ n Mus semitom m

senat|e /'senɪt/ n senado m. **~or** /-ətə(r)/ n senador m

send /send/ vt/i (pt sent) enviar, mandar; **~ back** devolver; **~ for** ‹person› chamar, mandar vir; ‹help› pedir; **~ (away** or **off) for** encomendar, mandar vir; **~ up** Ⓘ parodiar. **~off** n despedida f, bota-fora m. **~er** n expedidor m, remetente m

senil|e /'siːnaɪl/ a senil. **~ity** /sɪ'nɪlətɪ/ n senilidade f

senior /'siːnɪə(r)/ a mais velho; mais idoso (to do que); (in rank) superior; (in service) mais antigo; (after surname) sênior, (P) sénior; **~ citizen** pessoa f de idade or da terceira idade, idoso m ● n pessoa f mais velha; Schol finalista mf. **~ity** /-'ɒrɪtɪ/ n (in age) idade f; (in service) antiguidade f

sensation /sen'seɪʃn/ n sensação f. **~al** a sensacional. **~alism** n sensacionalismo m

sense /sens/ n sentido m; (wisdom) bom-senso m; (sensation) sensação f; (mental impression) sentimento m; **~s** (sanity) razão f; **make ~** fazer sentido; **make ~ of** compreender ● vt pressentir. **~less** a disparatado, sem sentido; Med sem sentidos, inconsciente

sensible /'sensəbl/ a sensato, razoável; ‹clothes› prático

sensitiv|e /'sensətɪv/ a sensível (to a); (touchy) susceptível. **~ity** /-'tɪvətɪ/ n sensibilidade f

sensory /'sensərɪ/ a sensorial

sensual /'senʃʊəl/ a sensual. **~ity** /-'ælətɪ/ n sensualidade f

sensuous /'senʃʊəs/ a sensual

sent /sent/ ▶ SEND

sentence /'sentəns/ n frase f; Jur (decision) sentença f; (punishment) pena f ● vt **~ to** condenar a

sentiment /'sentɪmənt/ n sentimento m; (opinion) modo m de ver

sentimental /sentɪ'mentl/ a sentimental; **~ value** valor m estimativo. **~ity** /-men'tælətɪ/ n sentimentalidade f, sentimentalismo m or sentimental

sentry /'sentrɪ/ n sentinela f

separable /'sepərəbl/ a separável

separate¹ /'seprət/ a separado, diferente. **~s** npl ‹clothes› conjuntos mpl. **~ly** adv separadamente, em separado

separat|e² /'sepəreɪt/ vt/i separar(-se). **~ion** /-'reɪʃn/ n separação f

September /sep'tembə(r)/ n setembro m

septic /'septɪk/ a séptico, (P) sético, infetado

sequel /'siːkwəl/ n resultado m, sequela f; (of novel, film) continuação f

sequence /'siːkwəns/ n sequência f

sequin /'siːkwɪn/ n lantejoula f

serenade /serə'neɪd/ n serenata f ● vt fazer uma serenata para or (P) a

seren|e /sɪ'riːn/ a sereno. **~ity** /-'enətɪ/ n serenidade f

sergeant /'sɑːdʒənt/ n sargento m

serial /'sɪərɪəl/ n folhetim m ● a ‹number› de série. **~ize** /-laɪz/ vt publicar em folhetim

series /'sɪərɪːz/ n invar série f

serious /'sɪərɪəs/ a (very bad, critical) grave, sério. **~ly** adv seriamente, gravemente, a sério; **take ~ly** levar a sério. **~ness** n seriedade f, gravidade f

sermon /'sɜːmən/ n sermão m

serpent /'sɜːpənt/ n serpente f

servant /'sɜːvənt/ n criado m, criada f, empregado m, empregada f

serv|e /sɜːv/ vt/i servir; ‹a sentence› cumprir; Jur (a writ) entregar; Mil servir, prestar serviço; ‹apprenticeship› fazer ● n Tennis saque m, (P) serviço m; **~e as/ to** servir de/para; **~e its purpose** servir para o que é Ⓘ, servir os seus fins; **it ~es you/him** etc **right** é bem feito. **~ing** n (portion) dose f, porção f

server /'sɜːvə(r)/ n Comput servidor m

service /'sɜːvɪs/ n serviço m; Relig culto m; Tennis saque m, (P) serviço m; (maintenance) revisão f; **~s** Mil forças fpl armadas; **of ~ to** útil a/para, de utilidade a/para; **~ area** área f de serviço; **~ charge** serviço m; **~ station** posto m de gasolina, (P) posto m de abastecimento ● vt ‹car etc› fazer a revisão de

serviceman /'sɜːvɪsmən/ n (pl -men) militar m

serviette /sɜːvɪ'et/ n guardanapo m

session /'seʃn/ n sessão f; Univ ano m académico, (P) académico; Amer Univ semestre m; **in ~** (sitting) em sessão, reunidos

set /set/ vt (pt set, pres p setting) pôr, colocar; (put down) pousar; ‹limit etc› fixar; ‹watch, clock› regular, acertar; ‹example› dar; ‹exam, task› marcar; (in plaster) engessar; **~ about** or **to**

S

começar a, pôr-se a; ~ **fire to** atear fogo a, (P) deitar fogo a; ~ **free** pôr em liberdade; ~ **off** <*mechanism*> pôr para funcionar, (P) pôr a funcionar; ~ **out** (*state*) expor; (*arrange*) dispor; ~ **sail** partir, içar as velas; ~ **square** esquadro m; ~ **the table** pôr a mesa; ~ **theory** teoria f de conjuntos; ~ **up** (*establish*) fundar, estabelecer ● vi (*sun*) pôr-se; <*jelly*> endurecer, solidificar(-se); ~ **in** <*rain etc*> pegar, (P) vir para ficar; ~ **off** or **out** partir, começar a viajar ● n (*of people*) círculo m, roda f; (*of books*) coleção f; (*of tools, chairs etc*) jogo m; TV, radio aparelho m; (*hair*) mise f; Theat cenário m; Tennis partida f, set m ● a fixo; <*habit*> inveterado; <*jelly*> duro, sólido; <*book*> do programa; <*meal*> a preço fixo; **be** ~ **on doing** estar decidido a fazer; ~ **back** <*plans etc*> atrasar; 🖩 <*cost*> custar. ~**back** n revés m; contratempo m; atraso m 🔢; ~**to** n briga f; ~**up** n (*system*) sistema m, organização f; (*situation*) situação f

settee /se'tiː/ n sofá m

setting /'setɪŋ/ n (*framework*) quadro m; (*of jewel*) engaste m; Typ composição f; Mus arranjo m musical

settle /'setl/ vt (*arrange*) resolver; <*date*> marcar; <*nerves*> acalmar; <*doubts*> esclarecer; <*new country*> colonizar, povoar; <*bill*> pagar ● vi assentar; (*in country*) estabelecer-se; (*in house, chair etc*) instalar-se; <*weather*> estabilizar(-se); ~ **down** acalmar-se; (*become orderly*) assentar; (*sit, rest*) instalar-se; ~ **for** aceitar; ~ **up (with)** fazer contas (com); fig ajustar contas (com). ~**r** /-ə(r)/ n colono m, colonizador m

settlement /'setlmənt/ n (*agreement*) acordo m; (*payment*) pagamento m; (*colony*) colônia f, (P) colónia f; (*colonization*) colonização f

seven /'sevn/ a & n sete m. ~**th** a & n sétimo m

seventeen /sevn'tiːn/ a & n dezessete m, (P) dezassete m. ~**th** a & n décimo sétimo m

sevent|y /'sevntɪ/ a & n setenta m. ~**ieth** a & n septuagésimo m

sever /'sevə(r)/ vt cortar. ~**ance** n corte m

several /'sevrəl/ a & pron vários, diversos

sever|e /sɪ'vɪə(r)/ a (-**er**, -**est**) severo; <*pain*> forte, violento; <*illness*> grave; <*winter*> rigoroso. ~**ely** adv severamente; (*seriously*) gravemente. ~**ity** /sɪ-'verɪtɪ/ n severidade f;

(*seriousness*) gravidade f

sew /səʊ/ vt/i (pt **sewed**, pp **sewn** or **sewed**) coser, costurar. ~**ing** n costura f. ~**ing machine** n máquina f de costura

sewage /'sjuːɪdʒ/ n efluentes mpl dos esgotos, detritos mpl

sewer /'sjuːə(r)/ n cano m de esgoto

sewn /səʊn/ ▶ **sew**

sex /seks/ n sexo m; **have** ~ ter relações sexuais ● a sexual; ~ **maniac** tarado m sexual ▢ ~ **up** vt/i tornar mais apelativo. ~**y** a sexy invar, que tem sex-appeal

sexist /'seksɪst/ a & n sexista mf

sexual /'seksʊəl/ a sexual; ~ **harassment** assédio m sexual; ~ **intercourse** relações fpl sexuais. ~**ity** /-'ælətɪ/ n sexualidade f

shabb|y /'ʃæbɪ/ a (-**ier**, -**iest**) (*clothes, object*) gasto, surrado; (*person*) maltrapilho, mal vestido; (*mean*) miserável. ~**ily** adv miseravelmente

shack /ʃæk/ n cabana f, barraca f

shackles /'ʃæklz/ npl grilhões mpl, algemas fpl

shade /ʃeɪd/ n sombra f; (*of colour*) tom m, matiz m; (*of opinion*) matiz m; (*for lamp*) abat-jour m, quebra-luz m; Amer (*blind*) estore m; **a** ~ **bigger/ etc** ligeiramente maior/etc; **in the** ~ à sombra ● vt resguardar da luz; (*darken*) sombrear

shadow /'ʃædəʊ/ n sombra f ● vt cobrir de sombra; (*follow*) seguir, vigiar; **S~ Cabinet** gabinete m formado pelo partido da oposição. ~**y** a ensombrado, sombreado; fig vago; indistinto

shady /'ʃeɪdɪ/ a (-**ier**, -**iest**) sombreiro, (P) que dá sombra; (*in shade*) à sombra; fig (*dubious*) suspeito; duvidoso

shaft /ʃɑːft/ n (*of arrow, spear*) haste f; (*axle*) eixo m, veio m; (*of mine, lift*) poço m; (*of light*) raio m

shaggy /'ʃægɪ/ a (-**ier**, -**iest**) <*beard*> hirsuto; <*hair*> desgrenhado; <*animal*> peludo, felpudo

shake /ʃeɪk/ vt (pt **shook**, pp **shaken**) abanar, sacudir; <*bottle*> agitar; <*belief, house etc*> abalar ● vi estremecer, tremer; ~ **hands with** apertar a mão de; ~ **off** (get rid of) sacudir, livrar-se de; ~ **one's head** (to say no) fazer que não com a cabeça; ~ **up** agitar ● n (*violent*) abanão m, safanão m; (*light*) sacudidela f. ~**up** n (*upheaval*) reviravolta f

shaky /'ʃeɪkɪ/ a (-**ier**, -**iest**) <*hand, voice*> trêmulo, (P) trémulo; (*unsteady, unsafe*) pouco firme, inseguro; (*weak*) fraco

shall /ʃæl unstressed ʃəl/ v aux **I/we ~ do** (*future*) farei/faremos; **I/you/he ~ do** (*command*) eu hei-de/você há-de/tu hás-de/ele há-de fazer

shallot /ʃə'lɒt/ n cebolinha f, (P) chalota f

shallow /'ʃæləʊ/ a (**-er, -est**) pouco fundo, raso; *fig* superficial

sham /ʃæm/ n fingimento m; ‹*jewel etc*› imitação f; ‹*person*› impostor m, fingido m ● a fingido; (*false*) falso ● vt (*pt* **shammed**) fingir

shambles /'ʃæmblz/ npl ☐ (*mess*) balbúrdia f, trapalhada f

shame /ʃeɪm/ n vergonha f; **it's a ~** é uma pena; **what a ~!** que pena! ● vt (*fazer*) envergonhar. **~ful** a vergonhoso. **~less** a sem vergonha, descarado; (*immodest*) despudorado, desavergonhado

shampoo /ʃæm'puː/ n xampu m, (P) champô m, shampoo m ● vt lavar com xampu, (P) champô or shampoo

shan't /ʃɑːnt/ (= shall not) = SHALL

shanty /'ʃænti/ n barraca f; **~ town** favela f, (P) bairro(s) m(pl) da lata

shape /ʃeɪp/ n forma f ● vt moldar ● vi **~ (up)** andar bem, fazer progressos; **take ~** concretizar-se, avançar. **~less** a informe, sem forma f; (*of body*) deselegante, disforme

shapely /'ʃeɪpli/ a (**-ier, -iest**) ‹*leg, person*› bem feito, elegante

share /ʃeə(r)/ n parte f, porção f; *Comm* ação f ● vt/i partilhar (**with** com **in** de)

shareholder /'ʃeəhəʊldə(r)/ n acionista mf

shark /ʃɑːk/ n tubarão m

sharp /ʃɑːp/ a (**-er, -est**) ‹*knife, pencil etc*› afiado; ‹*pin, point etc*› pontiagudo, aguçado; ‹*words, reply*› áspero; (*of bend*) fechado; (*acute*) agudo; (*sudden*) brusco; (*dishonest*) pouco honesto; (*well-defined*) nítido; (*brisk*) rápido, vigoroso; (*clever*) vivo; **six o'clock ~** seis horas em ponto ● adv (*stop*) de repente ● n *Mus* sustenido m. **~ly** adv (*harshly*) rispidamente; (*suddenly*) de repente

sharpen /'ʃɑːpən/ vt aguçar; ‹*pencil*› fazer a ponta de, (P) afiar; ‹*knife etc*› afiar, amolar. **~er** n afiadeira f; (*for pencil*) apontador m, (P) apara-lápis m, (P) afia-lápis m

shatter /'ʃætə(r)/ vt/i despedaçar(-se), esmigalhar(-se); ‹*hopes*› destruir(-se); ‹*nerves*› abalar(-se). **~ed** a (*upset*) passado; (*exhausted*) estourado ☐

shav|e /ʃeɪv/ vt/i barbear(-se), fazer a barba (de) ● n **have a ~e** barbear-se; **have a close ~e** *fig* escapar por um triz. **~er** n aparelho m de barbear, (P) máquina f de barbear. **~ing brush** n pincel m para a barba; **~ing cream** n creme m de barbear

shaving /'ʃeɪvɪŋ/ n apara f

shawl /ʃɔːl/ n xale m, (P) xaile m

she /ʃiː/ pron ela ● n fêmea f

shear /ʃɪə(r)/ vt (*pp* **shorn** or **sheared**) ‹*sheep etc*› tosquiar

shears /ʃɪəz/ npl tesoura f para jardim

sheath /ʃiːθ/ n (*pl s* /ʃiːðz/) bainha f; (*condom*) preservativo m, camisa de Vénus f

shed[1] /ʃed/ n (*hut*) casinhola f; (*for cows*) estábulo m

shed[2] /ʃed/ (*pres p* **shedding**) perder, deixar cair; (*spread*) espalhar; (*blood, tears*) deitar, derramar; **~ light on** lançar luz sobre

sheep /ʃiːp/ n (*pl invar*) carneiro m, ovelha f. **~dog** n cão m de pastor

sheepish /'ʃiːpɪʃ/ a encabulado

sheepskin /'ʃiːpskɪn/ n pele f de carneiro; (*leather*) carneira f

sheer /ʃɪə(r)/ a mero, simples; (*steep*) íngreme, a pique; ‹*fabric*› diáfano, transparente ● adv a pique, verticalmente

sheet /ʃiːt/ n lençol m; (*of glass, metal*) chapa f, placa f; (*of paper*) folha f

sheikh /ʃeɪk/ n xeque m, sheik m

shelf /ʃelf/ n (*pl* **shelves**) prateleira f

shell /ʃel/ n (*of egg, nut etc*) casca f; (*of mollusc*) concha f; (*of ship, tortoise*) casco m; (*of building*) estrutura f, armação f; (*explosive*) cartucho m ● vt descascar; *Mil* bombardear

shellfish /'ʃelfɪʃ/ n (*pl invar*) crustáceo m; (*as food*) marisco m

shelter /'ʃeltə(r)/ n abrigo m, refúgio m ● vt abrigar; (*protect*) proteger; (*harbour*) dar asilo a ● vi abrigar-se, refugiar-se. **~ed** a ‹*life etc*› protegido; ‹*spot*› abrigado

shelve /ʃelv/ vt pôr em prateleiras; (*fit with shelves*) pôr prateleiras em; *fig* engavetar; pôr de lado

shelving /'ʃelvɪŋ/ n (*shelves*) prateleiras fpl

shepherd /'ʃepəd/ n pastor m; **~'s pie** empadão m de batata e carne moída ● vt guiar

sheriff /'ʃerɪf/ n xerife m

S

sherry /'ʃerɪ/ n Xerez m

shield /ʃiːld/ n (armour, heraldry) escudo m; (screen) anteparo m ● vt proteger (**from** contra, de)

shift /ʃɪft/ vt/i mudar de posição, deslocar(-se); (exchange, alter) mudar de ● n mudança f; (workers, work) turno m; **make ~** arranjar-se

shifty /'ʃɪftɪ/ a (-ier, -iest) velhaco, duvidoso

shimmer /'ʃɪmə(r)/ vi luzir suavemente ● n luzir m

shin /ʃɪn/ n perna f. **~ bone** n tíbia f, canela f; **~ pad** n Football caneleira f

shin|e /ʃaɪn/ vt/i (pt shone) (fazer) brilhar, (fazer) reluzir; ‹shoes› engraxar; **the sun is ~ing** faz sol ● n lustro m; **~e a torch (on)** iluminar com uma lanterna de mão

shingle /'ʃɪŋgl/ n (pebbles) seixos mpl

shingles /'ʃɪŋglz/ npl Med zona f, herpes-zóster f, (P) herpes m

shiny /'ʃaɪnɪ/ a (-ier, -iest) brilhante; (of coat, trousers) lustroso

ship /ʃɪp/ n barco m, navio m ● vt (pt **shipped**) transportar; (send) mandar por via marítima; (load) embarcar. **~ment** n (goods) carregamento m; (shipping) embarque m. **~per** n expedidor m. **~ping** n navegação f; (ships) navios mpl

shipbuilding /'ʃɪpbɪldɪŋ/ n construção f naval

shipshape /'ʃɪpʃeɪp/ adv & a em (perfeita) ordem, impecável

shipwreck /'ʃɪprek/ n naufrágio m. **~ed** a naufragado; **be ~ed** naufragar

shipyard /'ʃɪpjɑːd/ n estaleiro m

shirk /ʃɜːk/ vt fugir a, furtar-se a, (P) baldar-se a ▣

shirt /ʃɜːt/ n camisa f; (of woman) blusa f; **in ~sleeves** em mangas de camisa

shiver /'ʃɪvə(r)/ vi arrepiar-se, tiritar ● n arrepio m

shoal /ʃəʊl/ n (of fish) cardume m

shock /ʃɒk/ n choque m, embate m; Electr choque m elétrico; Med choque m ● a de choque; **~ absorber** Mech amortecedor m ● vt chocar. **~ing** a chocante; ▣ (very bad) horrível

shodd|y /'ʃɒdɪ/ a (-ier, -iest) mal feito, ordinário, de má qualidade. **~ily** adv mal

shoe /ʃuː/ n sapato m; (footwear) calçado m; (horse) ferradura f; (brake) sapata f, (P) calço (de travão) m; **on a ~string** ▣ com/por muito pouco dinheiro, na pindaíba ▣, por uma tuta

e meia ▣ ● vt (pt shod, pres p shoeing) ‹horse› ferrar. **~ polish** n pomada f, (P) graxa f para sapatos; **~ shop** n sapataria f

shoehorn /'ʃuːhɔːn/ n calçadeira f

shoelace /'ʃuːleɪs/ n cordão m de sapato, (P) atacador m

shoemaker /'ʃuːmeɪkə(r)/ n sapateiro m

shone /ʃɒn/ ▶ SHINE

shoo /ʃuː/ vt enxotar ● int xô

shook /ʃʊk/ ▶ SHAKE

shoot /ʃuːt/ vt (pt shot) ‹gun› disparar; ‹glance, missile› lançar; (kill) matar a tiro; (wound) ferir a tiro; (execute) executar, fuzilar; (hunt) caçar; (film) filmar, rodar. **~ down** abater (a tiro) ● vi disparar; atirar (**at** contra, sobre); **~ in/out** (rush) entrar/sair correndo, (P) correr/surgir abruptamente; **~ up** (spurt) jorrar; (grow quickly) crescer a olhos vistos, dar um pulo; ‹prices› subir em disparada or (P) disparar ● n Bot rebento m. **~ing** n (shots) tiroteio m; **~ing star** estrela f cadente. **~ing range** n carreira f de tiro

shop /ʃɒp/ n loja f; (workshop) oficina f; **~ assistant** empregado m, caixeiro m, vendedor m; **~ steward** delegado m sindical; **~ window** vitrina f, (P) montra f; **talk ~** falar de coisas profissionais ● vi (pt shopped) fazer compras; **~ around** procurar, ver o que há nas lojas. **~ floor** n (workers) trabalhadores mpl; **~soiled** Amer **~worn** adjs enxovalhado. **~per** n comprador m

shopkeeper /'ʃɒpkiːpə(r)/ n lojista mf, comerciante mf

shoplift|er /'ʃɒplɪftə(r)/ n gatuno m de lojas. **~ing** n furto m or (P) ladrão m de lojas

shopping /'ʃɒpɪŋ/ n (goods) compras fpl; **go ~** ir às compras; **~ bag** sacola f or (P) saco m de compras; **~ centre** centro m comercial

shore /ʃɔː(r)/ n (of sea) praia f, costa f; (of lake) margem f

short /ʃɔːt/ a (-er, -est) curto; ‹person› baixo; (brief) breve, curto; (curt) seco, brusco; **be ~ of** (lack) ter falta de; **a ~ time** pouco tempo; **he is called Tom for ~** o diminutivo dele é Tom; **in ~** em suma; **~ circuit** Electr curto-circuito m; **~ cut** atalho m; **~ list** pré-seleção f; **~ story** conto m; **~ wave** Radio onda(s) f(pl) curta(s) ● adv (abruptly) bruscamente, de repente; **cut ~** abreviar; (interrupt) interromper ● n Electr curto-circuito m; (film) curta-metragem f, short m;

~s (*trousers*) calção m, (P) calções mpl, short m. **~change** vt (*cheat*) enganar; **~circuit** vt/i Electr fazer or dar um curto-circuito (em); **~lived** a de pouca duração; **~sighted** a míope; **~tempered** a irritadiço

shortage /ˈʃɔːtɪdʒ/ n falta f, escassez f

shortbread /ˈʃɔːtbred/ n shortbread m, biscoito m de massa amanteigada

shortcoming /ˈʃɔːtkʌmɪŋ/ n falha f, imperfeição f

shorten /ˈʃɔːtn/ vt/i encurtar(-se), abreviar(-se), diminuir

shorthand /ˈʃɔːthænd/ n estenografia f; **~ typist** estenodactilógrafa f, (P) estenodatilógrafa f, (P) estenógrafo m

shortly /ˈʃɔːtlɪ/ adv (*soon*) em breve, dentro em pouco

shot /ʃɒt/ ▶ **shoot** n (*firing, bullet*) tiro m; (*person*) atirador m; (*pellets*) chumbo m; (*photograph*) fotografia f; (*injection*) injeção f; (*in golf, billiards*) tacada f; **go like a ~** ir disparado; **have a ~** (**at sth**) experimentar (fazer algo). **~gun** n espingarda f, caçadeira f

should /ʃʊd unstressed ʃəd/ v aux **you ~ help me** você devia me ajudar, (P) devias ajudar-me; **I ~ have stayed** devia ter ficado; **I ~ like to** ; gostaria de or gostava de; **if he ~ come** se ele vier

shoulder /ˈʃəʊldə(r)/ n ombro m ● vt ‹responsibility› tomar, assumir; ‹burden› carregar, arcar com. **~ blade** n Anat omoplata f; **~ pad** n enchimento m de ombro, ombreira f, (P) chumaço m

shout /ʃaʊt/ n grito m, brado m; (*very loud*) berro m ● vt/i gritar (**at** com); (*very loudly*) berrar (**at** com); **~ down** fazer calar com gritos. **~ing** n gritaria f, berraria f

shove /ʃʌv/ n empurrão m ● vt/i empurrar; 1️⃣ (*put*) meter, enfiar; **~ off** 1️⃣ (*depart*) começar or pôr-se a andar 1️⃣, dar o fora 1️⃣, (P) cavar 1️⃣

shovel /ˈʃʌvl/ n pá f; (*machine*) escavadora f ● vt (pt **shovelled**) remover com pá

show /ʃəʊ/ vt (pt **showed**, pp **shown**) mostrar; (*of dial, needle*) marcar; (*put on display*) expor; ‹film› dar, passar; **~ in** mandar entrar ● vi ver-se, aparecer, estar à vista; **~ out** acompanhar à porta ● vi ver-se, aparecer, estar à vista; **~ up** ser claramente visível, ver-se bem; 1️⃣ (*arrive*) aparecer ● n mostra f, demonstração f, manifestação f; (*ostentation*) alarde m, espalhafato m; (*exhibition*) mostra f, exposição f;

Theatre, Cinema espetáculo m, show m; **for ~** para fazer vista, (P) para dar nas vistas; **on ~** exposto, em exposição ▢ **~ off** vt exibir, ostentar ● vi exibir-se, querer fazer figura. **~down** n confrontação f; **~jumping** n concurso m hípico; **~off** n exibicionista m; **~piece** n peça f digna de se expor. **~ing** n (*performance*) atuação f, performance f; Cinema exibição f

shower /ˈʃaʊə(r)/ n (*of rain*) aguaceiro m, chuvarada f; (*of blows etc*) saraivada f; (*in bathroom*) chuveiro m; ducha f; (P) duche m ● vt **~ with** cumular de, encher de ● vi tomar um banho de chuveiro or uma ducha, (P) um duche. **~y** a chuvoso

shown /ʃəʊn/ ▶ **show**

showroom /ˈʃəʊrʊm/ n espaço m de exposição, show-room m; (*for cars*) stand m

showy /ˈʃəʊɪ/ a (**-ier, -iest**) vistoso; (*too bright*) berrante; pej espalhafatoso

shrank /ʃræŋk/ ▶ **shrink**

shred /ʃred/ n tira f, retalho m, farrapo m; fig mínimo m; sombra f ● vt (pt **shredded**) reduzir a tiras, estraçalhar; Culin desfiar. **~der** n trituradora f; (*for paper*) fragmentadora f, (P) trituradora f

shrewd /ʃruːd/ a (**-er, -est**) astucioso, fino, perspicaz. **~ness** n astúcia f, perspicácia f

shriek /ʃriːk/ n grito m agudo, guincho m ● vt/i gritar, guinchar

shrill /ʃrɪl/ a estridente, agudo

shrimp /ʃrɪmp/ n camarão m

shrine /ʃraɪn/ n (*place*) santuário m; (*tomb*) túmulo m; (*casket*) relicário m

shrink /ʃrɪŋk/ vt/i (pt **shrank**, pp **shrunk**) encolher; (*recoil*) encolher-se; **~ from** esquivar-se a, fugir a (+ inf) /de (+ noun), retrair-se de

shrivel /ˈʃrɪvl/ vt/i (pt **shrivelled**) encarquilhar(-se)

Shrove /ʃrəʊv/ n **~ Tuesday** Terça-feira f Gorda or de Carnaval

shrub /ʃrʌb/ n arbusto m. **~bery** n arbustos mpl

shrug /ʃrʌɡ/ vt (pt **shrugged**) **~ one's shoulders** encolher os ombros; **~ off** não dar importância a ● n encolher m de ombros

shrunk /ʃrʌŋk/ ▶ **shrink**

shudder /ˈʃʌdə(r)/ vi arrepiar-se, estremecer, tremer; **I ~ to think** tremo só de pensar ● n arrepio m, tremor m, estremecimento m

S

shuffle /'ʃʌfl/ vt ‹feet› arrastar; ‹cards› embaralhar, (P) baralhar ● vi arrastar os pés ● n marcha f arrastada (P)

shun /ʃʌn/ vt (pt shunned) evitar, fugir de

shunt /ʃʌnt/ vt/i (train) mudar de linha, manobrar

shut /ʃʌt/ vt (pt shut, pres p shutting) fechar; ~ in or up trancar ● vi fechar-se; ‹shop, bank etc› encerrar, fechar; ~ down or up fechar; ~ up! 🔊 cale-se!, cale a boca! □ ~ up vi 🔊 (stop talking) calar-se ● vt 🔊 (silence) mandar calar

shutter /'ʃʌtə(r)/ n taipais mpl, (P) portada f de madeira; (of laths) persiana f; (in shop) taipais mpl; Photo obturador m

shuttle /'ʃʌtl/ n (of spaceship) ônibus m espacial, (P) nave f espacial; ~ service (plane) ponte f aérea; (bus) ônibus m, (P) autocarro m

shuttlecock /'ʃʌtlkɒk/ n volante m

shy /ʃaɪ/ a (-er, -est) tímido, acanhado, envergonhado ● vi ‹horse› espantar-se (at com); fig assustar-se (at or away from com). ~ness n timidez f, acanhamento m, vergonha f

Sicily /'sɪsɪlɪ/ n Sicília f

sick /sɪk/ a doente; ‹humour› negro; be ~ (vomit) vomitar; be ~ of estar farto de; feel ~ estar enjoado. ~bay n enfermaria f; ~ leave n licença f por doença; ~room n quarto m de doente

sicken /'sɪkn/ vt (distress) desesperar; (disgust) repugnar ● vi be ~ing for flu começar a pegar or (P) chocar uma gripe 🔊

sickly /'sɪklɪ/ a (-ier, -iest) ‹person› doentio, achacado; ‹smell› enjoativo; (pale) pálido

sickness /'sɪknɪs/ n doença f; (vomiting) náusea f; vômito m, (P) vómito m

side /saɪd/ n lado m; (of road, river) beira f; (of hill) encosta f; Sport equipe f, (P) equipa f; on the ~ (extra) nas horas vagas; (secretly) pela calada; ~ by ~ lado a lado ● a lateral ● vi ~ with tomar o partido de, alinhar com. ~car n sidecar m; ~effect n efeito m secundário; ~show n espetáculo m suplementar; ~step vt evitar; ~track vt (fazer) desviar dum propósito

sideboard /'saɪdbɔːd/ n aparador m

sideburns /'saɪdbɜːnz/ npl suíças fpl, costeletas fpl, (P) patilhas fpl

sidelight /'saɪdlaɪt/ n Auto luz f lateral, (P) farolim m

sideline /'saɪdlaɪn/ n atividade f secundária; Sport linha f lateral

sidelong /'saɪdlɒŋ/ adv & a de lado

sidewalk /'saɪdwɔːk/ n Amer passeio m

sideways /'saɪdweɪz/ adv & a de lado

siding /'saɪdɪŋ/ n desvio m, ramal m

siege /siːdʒ/ n cerco m

siesta /sɪ'estə/ n sesta f

sieve /sɪv/ n peneira f; (for liquids) coador m ● vt peneirar; ‹liquids› passar, coar

sift /sɪft/ vt peneirar; (sprinkle) polvilhar; ~ through examinar minuciosamente, esquadrinhar

sigh /saɪ/ n suspiro m ● vt/i suspirar

sight /saɪt/ n vista f; (scene) cena f; (on gun) mira f ● vt avistar, ver, divisar; at or on ~ à vista; catch ~ of avistar; in ~ à vista, visível; lose ~ of perder de vista; out of ~ longe dos olhos, longe da vista

sightsee|**ing** /'saɪtsiːɪŋ/ n visita f, turismo m; go ~ing visitar lugares turísticos. ~r /'saɪtsiːə(r)/ n turista mf

sign /saɪn/ n sinal m; (symbol) signo m ● vt (in writing) assinar ● vi (make a sign) fazer sinal; ~ on or up ‹worker› assinar contrato. ~ language n mímica f, linguagem f gestual

signal /'sɪgnəl/ n sinal m ● vi (pt signalled) fazer signal ● vt comunicar (por sinais); ‹person› fazer sinal para

signature /'sɪgnətʃə(r)/ n assinatura f; ~ tune indicativo m musical

significan|**t** /sɪg'nɪfɪkənt/ a importante; (meaningful) significativo. ~ce n importância f; (meaning) significado m

signify /'sɪgnɪfaɪ/ vt significar

signpost /'saɪnpəʊst/ n poste m de sinalização ● vt sinalizar

silence /'saɪləns/ n silêncio m ● vt silenciar, calar

silent /'saɪlənt/ a silencioso; (not speaking) calado; ‹film› mudo. ~ly adv silenciosamente

silhouette /sɪlu'et/ n silhueta f ● vt be ~d against estar em silhueta contra

silicon /'sɪlɪkən/ n silicone m; ~ chip circuito m integrado

silk /sɪlk/ n seda f. ~en, ~y adjs sedoso

sill /sɪl/ n (of window) parapeito m; (of door) soleira f, limiar m

sill|**y** /'sɪlɪ/ a (-ier, -iest) tolo, idiota. ~iness n tolice f, idiotice f

silt /sɪlt/ n aluvião m, sedimento m

silver /'sɪlvə(r)/ n prata f; (*silverware*) prataria f, pratas fpl ● a de prata; ~ **paper** papel m prateado; ~ **wedding** bodas fpl de prata

silversmith /'sɪlvəsmɪθ/ n ourives m

silverware /'sɪlvəweə(r)/ n prataria f, pratas fpl

SIM card /'sɪm kɑːd/ n SIM m, (P) cartão SIM

similar /'sɪmɪlə(r)/ a ~ **(to)** semelhante (a), parecido (com). ~**ity** /-ə'lærətɪ/ n semelhança f

simmer /'sɪmə(r)/ vt/i cozinhar em fogo brando; *fig* (*smoulder*) ferver; fremir; ~ **down** acalmar(-se)

simpl|e /'sɪmpl/ a (-er, -est) simples. ~**e-minded** a simples; (*feeble-minded*) pobre de espírito, tolo. ~**icity** /-'plɪsətɪ/ n simplicidade f. ~**y** adv simplesmente; (*absolutely*) absolutamente, simplesmente

simpleton /'sɪmpltən/ n simplório m

simplif|y /'sɪmplɪfaɪ/ vt simplificar. ~**ication** /-ɪ'keɪʃn/ n simplificação f

simulat|e /'sɪmjʊleɪt/ vt simular, imitar. ~**ion** /-'leɪʃn/ n simulação f, imitação f

simultaneous /sɪml'teɪnɪəs/ a simultâneo, concomitante. ~**ly** adv simultaneamente

sin /sɪn/ n pecado m ● vi (pt **sinned**) pecar

---

since /sɪns/ ● prep

····▸ desde; **I haven't seen him** ~ **Monday** não o vejo desde segunda-feira; **I have been waiting** ~ **yesterday** estou esperando desde ontem; **she had been living in Lisbon** ~ **1985** ela estava vivendo em Lisboa desde 1985

● adv

····▸ desde então; **he hasn't been seen** ~ ninguém o viu desde então

● conj

····▸ (*in time expressions*) desde que; ~ **she's been working here** desde que ela trabalha aqui

····▸ (*because*) como, visto que; ~ **he was ill, he couldn't go** como estava doente, não pôde ir

---

sincer|e /sɪn'sɪə(r)/ a sincero. ~**ely** adv sinceramente. ~**ity** /-'serətɪ/ n sinceridade f

sinful /'sɪnfl/ a (*wicked*) pecaminoso; (*shocking*) escandaloso

sing /sɪŋ/ vt/i (pt **sang**, pp **sung**) cantar. ~**er** n cantor m

singe /sɪndʒ/ vt (pres p **singeing**) chamuscar

single /'sɪŋgl/ a único, só; (*unmarried*) solteiro; ‹bed› de solteiro; ‹room› individual; ‹ticket› de ida, simples; **in** ~ **file** em fila indiana; ~ **parent** pai m solteiro, mãe f solteira ● n (ticket) bilhete m de ida or simples; (record) disco m de 45 r.p.m.; ~**s** Tennis singulares mpl ● vt ~ **out** escolher. ~**handed** a sem ajuda, sozinho; ~**minded** a decidido, aferrado à sua ideia, (P) determinado, tenaz. **singly** adv um a um, um por um

singular /'sɪŋgjʊlə(r)/ n singular m ● a (*uncommon*) *Gramm* singular; (*noun*) no singular

sinister /'sɪnɪstə(r)/ a sinistro

sink /sɪŋk/ vt (pt **sank**, pp **sunk**) ‹ship› afundar, ir a pique; (*well*) abrir; (*invest money*) empatar; (*lose money*) enterrar ● vi afundar-se; (*of ground*) ceder; (*of voice*) baixar; ~ **in** fig ficar gravado, entrar 🄸; ~ **or swim** ou vai ou racha 🄸 ● n pia f, (P) lava-louça f

sinner /'sɪnə(r)/ n pecador m

sip /sɪp/ n gole m ● vt (pt **sipped**) beberricar, beber aos golinhos

siphon /'saɪfn/ n sifão m ● vt ~ **off** extrair por meio de sifão

sir /sɜː(r)/ n senhor m; ~ (title) Sir m; **Dear S~** Exmo Senhor; **excuse me,** ~ desculpe, senhor; **no,** ~ não, senhor

siren /'saɪərən/ n sereia f, sirene f

sister /'sɪstə(r)/ n irmã f; (nun) irmã f, freira f; (nurse) enfermeira-chefe f; ~**in-law** cunhada f

sit /sɪt/ vt/i (pt **sat**, pres p **sitting**) sentar(-se); (of committee etc) reunir-se; ~ **for an exam** fazer um exame, prestar uma prova; **be** ~**ting** estar sentado; ~ **around** não fazer nada; ~ **down** sentar-se; ~ **up** endireitar-se na cadeira; (not go to bed) passar a noite acordado. ~**ting** n reunião f, sessão f; (in restaurant) serviço m. ~**ting room** n sala f de estar

site /saɪt/ n local m; (building) ~ terreno m para construção, lote m ● vt localizar, situar

situat|e /'sɪtʃʊeɪt/ vt situar. **be** ~**ed** estar situado. ~**ion** /-'eɪʃn/ n (position, condition) situação f; (job) emprego m, colocação f

six /sɪks/ a & n seis m. ~**th** a & n sexto m

sixteen /sɪk'stiːn/ a & n dezesseis m, (P) dezasseis m. ~**th** a & n décimo sexto m

S

sixty|y /'sɪkstɪ/ a & n sessenta m. **~ieth** a & n sexagésimo m

size /saɪz/ n tamanho m; (of person, garment etc) tamanho m, medida f, (P) número m; (of shoes) número m; (extent) grandeza f ● vt ~ **up** calcular o tamanho de; **①** (judge) formar um juízo sobre, avaliar. **~able** a bastante grande, considerável

sizzle /'sɪzl/ vi chiar, rechinar

skate[1] /skeɪt/ n (pl invar) (fish) (ar)raia f

skat|e[2] /skeɪt/ n patim m ● vi patinar. **~er** n patinador m. **~ing** n patinação f, (P) patinagem f. **~ing rink** n rinque m de patinação or (P) patinagem f

skateboard /'skeɪtbɔːd/ n skate m

skelet|on /'skelɪtən/ n esqueleto m; (framework) armação f; **~on crew** or **staff** pessoal m reduzido; **~on key** chave f mestra. **~al** a esquelético

sketch /sketʃ/ n esboço m, croqui(s) m; Theat sketch m, peça f curta e humorística; (outline) ideia f or (P) ideia f geral, esboço m ● vt esboçar, delinear ● vi fazer esboços. **~book** n caderno m de desenho

sketchy /'sketʃɪ/ a (-ier, -iest) incompleto, esboçado

skewer /'skjʊə(r)/ n espeto m

ski /skiː/ n (pl -s) esqui m ● vi (pt **ski'd**, or **skied**, pres p **skiing**) esquiar; (go skiing) fazer esqui. **~er** n esquiador m. **~ing** n esqui m

skid /skɪd/ vi (pt **skidded**) derrapar, patinar ● n derrapagem f

skilful /'skɪlfl/ a hábil, habilidoso

skill /skɪl/ n habilidade f, jeito m; (craft) arte f; **~s** aptidões fpl. **~ed** a hábil, habilidoso; (worker) especializado

skim /skɪm/ vt (pt **skimmed**) tirar a espuma de; (milk) desnatar, tirar a nata de; (pass or glide over) deslizar sobre, roçar ● vi ~ **through** ler por alto, passar os olhos por; **~med milk** leite m desnatado

skimp /skɪmp/ vt (use too little) poupar em ● vi ser poupado

skimpy /'skɪmpɪ/ a (-ier, -iest) (clothes) sumário, mínimo; (meal) escasso; racionado fig

skin /skɪn/ n (of person, animal) pele f; (of fruit) casca f ● vt (pt **skinned**) (animal) esfolar, tirar a pele de; (fruit) descascar

skinny /'skɪnɪ/ a (-ier, -iest) magricela, escanzelado

skint /skɪnt/ a ⊠ sem dinheiro; na última lona ⊠, (P) nas lonas ⊠

skip[1] /skɪp/ vi (pt **skipped**) saltar, pular; (jump about) saltitar; (with rope) pular corda, (P) saltar à corda ● vt (page) saltar; (class) faltar a ● n salto m. **~ping rope** n corda f de pular or (P) de saltar

skip[2] /skɪp/ n (container) container m or (P) contentor m grande para entulho

skipper /'skɪpə(r)/ n capitão m

skirmish /'skɜːmɪʃ/ n escaramuça f

skirt /skɜːt/ n saia f ● vt contornar, ladear. **~ing board** n rodapé m

skittle /'skɪtl/ n pino m. **~s** npl boliche m, (P) jogo m da laranjinha

skive /skaɪv/ vi ⊠ eximir-se de um dever; evitar trabalhar, (P) furtar-se ao trabalho ⊠

skull /skʌl/ n caveira f, crânio m

skunk /skʌŋk/ n (animal) gambá m, (P) doninha f

sky /skaɪ/ n céu m. **~-blue** a & n azul-celeste m

skylight /'skaɪlaɪt/ n claraboia f

skyscraper /'skaɪskreɪpə(r)/ n arranha-céus m invar

slab /slæb/ n (of marble) placa f; (of paving stone) laje f; (of metal) chapa f; (of cake) fatia f grossa

slack /slæk/ a (-er, -est) (rope) bambo, frouxo; (person) descuidado, negligente; (business) parado, fraco; (period, season) morto ● n **the ~** (in rope) a parte bamba ● vt/i (be lazy) estar com preguiça; fazer cera fig

slacken /'slækən/ vt/i (speed, activity etc) afrouxar, abrandar

slain /sleɪn/ ▶ **SLAY**

slam /slæm/ vt (pt **slammed**) bater violentamente com; (throw) atirar; ⊠ (criticize) criticar; malhar ● vi (door etc) bater violentamente ● n (noise) bater m, pancada f

slander /'slɑːndə(r)/ n calúnia f, difamação f ● vt caluniar, difamar. **~ous** a calunioso, difamatório

slang /slæŋ/ n calão m, gíria f. **~y** a de calão

slant /slɑːnt/ vt/i inclinar(-se); (news) apresentar de forma tendenciosa ● n inclinação f; (bias) tendência f; (point of view) ângulo m; **be ~ing** ser/estar inclinado or em declive

slap /slæp/ vt (pt **slapped**) (strike) bater, dar uma palmada em; (on face) esbofetear, dar uma bofetada em; (put *forcefully*) atirar com ● *n* palmada *f*, bofetada *f* ● *adv* em cheio. **~up** *a* ▣ (*excellent*) excelente

slapdash /ˈslæpdæʃ/ *a* descuidado; (*impetuous*) precipitado

slapstick /ˈslæpstɪk/ *n* farsa *f* com palhaçadas

slash /slæʃ/ *vt* (*cut*) retalhar, dar golpes em; (*sever*) cortar; ‹*a garment*› golpear; *fig* (*reduce*) reduzir drasticamente; fazer um corte radical em ● *n* corte *m*, golpe *m*

slat /slæt/ *n* (*in blind*) ripa *f*, (*P*) lâmina *f*

slate /sleɪt/ *n* ardósia *f* ● *vt* ▣ (*criticize*) criticar severamente

slaughter /ˈslɔːtə(r)/ *vt* chacinar, massacrar; ‹*animals*› abater ● *n* chacina *f*, massacre *m*, mortandade *f*; (*animals*) abate *m*

slaughterhouse /ˈslɔːtəhaʊs/ *n* matadouro *m*

slave /sleɪv/ *n* escravo *m* ● *vi* mourejar, trabalhar como um escravo. **~driver** *n* *fig* o que obriga os outros a trabalharem como escravos; condutor *m* de escravos. **~ry** /-ərɪ/ *n* escravatura *f*

slay /sleɪ/ *vt* (*pt* slew, *pp* slain) matar

sleazy /ˈsliːzɪ/ *a* (-ier, -iest) ▣ esqualido; sórdido

sledge /sledʒ/ *n* trenó *m*. **~hammer** *n* martelo *m* de forja, marreta *f*

sleek /sliːk/ *a* (-er, -est) liso, macio e lustroso

sleep /sliːp/ *n* sono *m* ● *vi* (*pt* slept) dormir ● *vt* ter lugar para, alojar; **go to ~** ir dormir, adormecer; **put to ~** (*kill*) mandar matar; **~ around** ser promíscuo. **~er** *n* aquele que dorme; *Rail* (*beam*) dormente *m*; (*berth*) couchette *f*. **~ing bag** *n* saco *m* de dormir, (*P*) saco-cama *m*. **~less** *a* insone; (*night*) em claro, insone. **~walker** *n* sonâmbulo *m*

sleepy /ˈsliːpɪ/ *a* (-ier, -iest) sonolento; **be ~y** ter or estar com sono

sleet /sliːt/ *n* geada *f* miúda ● *vi* cair geada miúda

sleeve /sliːv/ *n* manga *f*; (*of record*) capa *f*; **up one's ~** de reserva, escondido, (*P*) na manga. **~less** *a* sem mangas

sleigh /sleɪ/ *n* trenó *m*

sleight /slaɪt/ *n* **~ of hand** prestidigitação *f*, passe *m* de mágica

slender /ˈslendə(r)/ *a* esguio, esbelto; *fig* (*scanty*) escasso

slept /slept/ ▶ SLEEP

sleuth /sluːθ/ *n* ▣ detetive *m*

slew[1] /sluː/ *vi* (*turn*) virar-se

slew[2] /sluː/ ▶ SLAY

slice /slaɪs/ *n* fatia *f* ● *vt* cortar em fatias; *Golf, Tennis* cortar

slick /slɪk/ *a* (*slippery*) escorregadio; (*cunning*) astuto, habilidoso; (*unctuous*) melífluo ● *n* (*oil*) **~** mancha *f* de óleo, (*P*) derrame *m* de petróleo

slid|e /slaɪd/ *vt/i* (*pt* slid) escorregar, deslizar ● *n* escorregadela *f*, escorregão *m*; (*in playground*) escorrega *m*; (*for hair*) prendedor *m*, (*P*) travessa *f*; *Photo* diapositivo *m*, slide *m*. **~ing** *a* ‹*door, panel*› corrediço, de correr; **~ing scale** escala *f* móvel

slight /slaɪt/ *a* (-er, -est) (*slender, frail*) delgado, franzino; (*inconsiderable*) leve, ligeiro; **not in the ~est** em absoluto ● *vt* desconsiderar, desfeitear ● *n* desconsideração *f*, desfeita *f*. **the ~est** *a* o/a menor. **~ly** *adv* ligeiramente, um pouco

slim /slɪm/ *a* (slimmer, slimmest) magro, esbelto; ‹*chance*› pequeno, remoto ● *vi* (*pt* slimmed) emagrecer

slim|e /slaɪm/ *n* lodo *m*. **~y** *a* lodoso; (*slippery*) escorregadio; *fig* (*servile*) servil; bajulador

sling /slɪŋ/ *n* (*weapon*) funda *f*; (*for arm*) tipoia *f* ● *vt* (*pt* slung) atirar, lançar

slip /slɪp/ *vt/i* (*pt* slipped) escorregar; (*move quietly*) mover-se de mansinho; **~ away** esgueirar-se; **~ by** passar sem se dar conta, passar despercebido; **~ into** (*go*) entrar de mansinho, enfiar-se em; ‹*clothes*› enfiar; **~ped disc** disco *m* deslocado; **~ sb's mind** passar pela cabeça de alguém; **~ up** ▣ cometer uma gafe ● *n* escorregadela *f*, escorregão *m*; (*mistake*) engano *m*, lapso *m*; (*petticoat*) combinação *f*; (*of paper*) tira *f* de papel; **give the ~ to** livrar-se de, escapar(-se) de; **~ of the tongue** lapso *m*. **~ road** *n* acesso *m* a autoestrada; **~up** *n* ▣ gafe *f*

slipper /ˈslɪpə(r)/ *n* chinelo *m*

slippery /ˈslɪpərɪ/ *a* escorregadio; *fig* ‹*person*› que não é de confiança; sem escrúpulos

slipshod /ˈslɪpʃɒd/ *a* ‹*person*› desleixado, desmazelado; ‹*work*› feito sem cuidado, desleixado

slit /slɪt/ *n* fenda *f*; (*cut*) corte *m*; (*tear*) rasgão *m* ● *vt* (*pt* slit, *pres p* slitting) fender; (*cut*) fazer um corte em, cortar

slither /ˈslɪðə(r)/ *vi* escorregar, resvalar

sliver /ˈslɪvə(r)/ *n* (*of cheese etc*) fatia *f*; (*splinter*) lasca *f*

S

slog /slɒg/ vt (pt **slogged**) (hit) bater com força ● vi (walk) caminhar com passos pesados e firmes; (work) trabalhar duro ● n (work) trabalheira f; (walk, effort) estafa f

slogan /'sləʊgən/ n slogan m, lema m, palavra f de ordem

slop /slɒp/ vt/i (pt **slopped**) transbordar, entornar. ~s npl (dirty water) água(s) f(pl) suja(s); (liquid refuse) despejos mpl

slope /sləʊp/ vt/i inclinar(-se), formar declive ● n (of mountain) encosta f; (of street) rampa f, ladeira f. ~ing a inclinado, em declive

sloppy /'slɒpɪ/ a (-ier, -iest) ‹ground› molhado, com poças de água; ‹food› aguado; ‹clothes› desleixado; ‹work› descuidado; feito de qualquer jeito or maneira 🔢; ‹person› desmazelado; (maudlin) piegas

slosh /slɒʃ/ vt entornar; 🔢 (splash) esparrinhar, (P) salpicar; 🔢 (hit) bater em; dar (uma) sova em ● vi chapinhar

slot /slɒt/ n ranhura f; (in timetable) horário m; TV espaço m; Aviat slot m ● vt/i (pt **slotted**) enfiar(-se), meter(-se), encaixar(-se). ~ machine n (for stamps, tickets etc) distribuidor m automático; (for gambling) caça-níqueis m, (P) slot machine f

slouch /slaʊtʃ/ vi (stand, move) andar com as costas curvadas; (sit) sentar-se em má postura

slovenly /'slʌvnlɪ/ a desmazelado, desleixado

slow /sləʊ/ a (-er, -est) lento, vagaroso ● adv devagar, lentamente ● vt/i ~ (up or down) diminuir a velocidade, afrouxar; Auto desacelerar; be ~ ‹clock etc› atrasar-se, estar atrasado; in ~ motion em câmara lenta. ~ly adv devagar, lentamente, vagarosamente

slow|coach /'sləʊkəʊtʃ/, ~poke Amer ns lesma m/f; pastelão m fig

sludge /slʌdʒ/ n lama f, lodo m

slug /slʌg/ n lesma f

sluggish /'slʌgɪʃ/ a (slow) lento, moroso; (lazy) indolente, preguiçoso

sluice /sluːs/ n (gate) comporta f; (channel) canal m ● vt lavar com jorros de água

slum /slʌm/ n favela f, (P) bairro m da lata; (building) cortiço m

slumber /'slʌmbə(r)/ n sono m ● vi dormir

slump /slʌmp/ n (in prices) baixa f, descida f; (in demand) quebra f na procura;

Econ depressão f ● vi (fall limply) cair, afundar-se; (of price) baixar bruscamente

slung /slʌŋ/ ▶ SLING

slur /slɜː(r)/ vt/i (pt **slurred**) (speech) pronunciar indistintamente, mastigar ● n (in speech) som m indistinto; (discredit) nódoa f, estigma m

slush /slʌʃ/ n (snow) neve f meio derretida; ~ fund Comm fundo m para subornos, (P) saco m azul. ~y a ‹road› coberto de neve derretida, lamacento

slut /slʌt/ n (dirty woman) porca f, desmazelada f; (immoral woman) desavergonhada f, (P) galdéria f

sly /slaɪ/ a (slyer, slyest) (crafty) manhoso; (secretive) sonso, subreptício ● n on the ~ na calada

smack[1] /smæk/ n palmada f; (on face) bofetada f ● vt dar uma palmada or um tapa em; (on the face) esbofetear, dar uma bofetada em ● adv 🔢 em cheio; direto

smack[2] /smæk/ vi ~ of sth cheirar a algo

small /smɔːl/ a (-er, -est) pequeno; ~ change trocado m, dinheiro m miúdo; ~ talk conversa f fiada, bate-papo m ● n ~ of the back zona f dos rins ● adv (cut etc) em pedaços pequenos, aos bocadinhos

smallpox /'smɔːlpɒks/ n varíola f

smarmy /'smɑːmɪ/ a (-ier, -iest) 🔢 bajulador; puxa-saco 🔢, (P) lambe-botas mf inv

smart /smɑːt/ a (-er, -est) elegante; (clever) esperto, vivo; (brisk) rápido ● vi (sting) arder, picar

smarten /'smɑːtn/ vt/i ~ (up) arranjar(-se), dar um ar mais cuidado a; ~ (o.s.) up embelezar-se, arrumar-se, (P) pôr-se elegante/bonito; (tidy) arranjar-se

smash /smæʃ/ vt/i (to pieces) despedaçar(-se); espatifar(-se) 🔢; ‹a record› quebrar, (P) partir; ‹opponent› esmagar; (ruin) (fazer) falir; (of vehicle) espatifar(-se) ● n (noise) estrondo m; (blow) pancada f forte, golpe m; (collision) colisão f; Tennis smash m

smashing /'smæʃɪŋ/ a 🔢 formidável; estupendo 🔢

smattering /'smætərɪŋ/ n leves noções fpl, conhecimento m superficial

smear /smɪə(r)/ vt (stain; discredit) manchar; (coat) untar, besuntar ● n mancha f, nódoa f; Med esfregaço m

smell /smel/ n cheiro m, odor m; (sense) cheiro m; olfato m ● vt/i (pt **smelt**, or smelled) ~ (of) cheirar (a). ~y a mal-cheiroso

smelt[1] /smelt/ ▶ SMELL

smelt[2] /smelt/ vt (ore) fundir

smil|e /smaɪl/ n sorriso m ● vi sorrir

smirk /smɜːk/ n sorriso m falso or afetado

smock /smɒk/ n guarda-pó m

smog /smɒg/ n mistura f de nevoeiro e fumaça, smog m

smoke /sməʊk/ n fumo m, fumaça f ● vt fumar; ‹bacon etc› fumar, defumar ● vi fumar, fumegar. ~screen n lit & fig cortina f de fumaça or (P) de fumo. ~less a ‹fuel› sem fumo. ~r /-ə(r)/ n (person) fumante mf, (P) fumador m. **smoky** a ‹air› enfumaçado, fumacento, fumoso

smooth /smuːð/ a (-er, -est) liso; (soft) macio; (movement) regular, suave; (manners) lisonjeiro, conciliador, suave ● vt alisar; ~ out fig aplanar, remover

smother /'smʌðə(r)/ vt (stifle) abafar, sufocar; (cover, overwhelm) cobrir (with de); (suppress) abafar, reprimir

smoulder /'sməʊldə(r)/ vi lit & fig arder; abrasar-se

SMS abbr (= Short Message or Messaging Service) mensagem f de texto

smudge /smʌdʒ/ n mancha f, borrão m ● vt/i sujar(-se), manchar(-se), borrar(-se)

smug /smʌg/ a (smugger, smuggest) presunçoso; convencido 🗆

smuggl|e /'smʌgl/ vt contrabandear, fazer contrabando de. ~er n contrabandista mf. ~ing n contrabando m

smut /smʌt/ n fuligem f. ~ty a cheia de fuligem; 🗆 (obscene) indecente; sujo 🗆

snack /snæk/ n refeição f ligeira. ~ bar n lanchonete f, (P) snack(-bar) m

snag /snæg/ n (obstacle) obstáculo m; (drawback) problema m, contra m, contratempo m; (in cloth) rasgão m; (in stocking) fio m puxado, (P) malha f

snail /sneɪl/ n caracol m; at a ~'s pace em passo de tartaruga or (P) caracol

snake /sneɪk/ n serpente f, cobra f

snap /snæp/ vt/i (pt snapped) (whip, fingers) (fazer) estalar; (break) estalar(-se), partir(-se) com um estalo, rebentar; (say) dizer irritadamente ● n estalo m; (photo) instantâneo m, (P) instantânea f; Amer (fastener) mola f ● a súbito, repentino; ~ at (bite) abocanhar, tentar morder; (speak angrily) retrucar or (P) retorquir asperamente; ~ up (buy) comprar rapidamente

snappy /'snæpɪ/ a (-ier, -iest) 🗆 vivo; animado; **make it ~** 🗆 vai rápido!, apresse-se! 🗆

snapshot /'snæpʃɒt/ n instantâneo m, (P) (fotografia f) instantânea f

snare /sneə(r)/ n laço m, cilada f, armadilha f

snarl /snɑːl/ vi rosnar ● n rosnadela f

snatch /snætʃ/ vt (grab) agarrar, apanhar; (steal) roubar; ~ from sb arrancar de/a alguém ● n (theft) roubo m; (bit) bocado m, pedaço m

sneak /sniːk/ vi (slink) esgueirar-se furtivamente; 🗷 (tell tales) fazer queixa(s); delatar ● vt 🗷 (steal) rapinar 🗆 ● n 🗷 dedo-duro m; queixinhas mf 🗷. ~ing a secreto. ~y a sonso

sneer /snɪə(r)/ n sorriso m de desdém ● vi sorrir desdenhosamente

sneeze /sniːz/ n espirro m ● vi espirrar

snide /snaɪd/ a 🗆 sarcástico

sniff /snɪf/ vi fungar ● vt/i ~ (at) (smell) cheirar; (dog) farejar; ~ at fig (in contempt) desprezar ● n fungadela f

snigger /'snɪgə(r)/ n riso m abafado ● vi rir dissimuladamente

snip /snɪp/ vt (pt snipped) cortar com tesoura ● n pedaço m, retalho m; 🗷 (bargain) pechincha f

snipe /snaɪp/ vi dar tiros de emboscada. ~r /-ə(r)/ n franco-atirador m

snivel /'snɪvl/ vi (pt snivelled) choramingar, lamuriar-se

snob /snɒb/ n esnobe mf, (P) snob mf. ~bery n esnobismo m, (P) snobismo m. ~bish a esnobe, (P) snob

snog /snɒg/ Brit vt/i (pres p etc. -gg-) 🗆 beijar apaixonadamente ● n 🗆 longa troca de carícias e beijos f

snooker /'snuːkə(r)/ n snooker m, sinuca f

snoop /snuːp/ vi 🗆 bisbilhotar; meter o nariz em toda a parte; ~ on espiar, espionar

snooty /'snuːtɪ/ a (-ier, -iest) 🗆 convencido; arrogante

snooze /snuːz/ n 🗆 soneca f 🗆 ● vi 🗆 tirar or (P) fazer uma soneca

snore /snɔː(r)/ n ronco m ● vi roncar, (P) ressonar

snorkel /'snɔːkl/ n tubo m de respiração, snorkel m

snort /snɔːt/ n resfôlego m, bufido m ● vi resfolegar, bufar

snout /snaʊt/ n focinho m

s

snow /snəʊ/ n neve f ● vi nevar; **be ~ed under** fig (be overwhelmed) estar sobrecarregado de fig. **~board** n snowboard m; **~drift** n banco m de neve; **~plough** n limpa-neve m. **~y** a nevado, coberto de neve

snowball /'snəʊbɔːl/ n bola f de neve ● vi atirar bolas de neve (em); fig acumular-se; ir num crescendo; aumentar rapidamente

snowdrop /'snəʊdrɒp/ n Bot fura-neve m

snowfall /'snəʊfɔːl/ n nevada f, (P) nevão m

snowflake /'snəʊfleɪk/ n floco m de neve

snowman /'snəʊmæn/ n (pl -men) boneco m de neve

snub /snʌb/ vt (pt snubbed) desdenhar, tratar com desdém ● n desdém m

snuffle /'snʌfl/ vi fungar

snug /snʌg/ a (snugger, snuggest) (cosy) aconchegado; (close-fitting) justo

snuggle /'snʌgl/ vt/i (nestle) aninhar-se, aconchegar-se; (cuddle) aconchegar

so /səʊ/ adv tão, de tal modo; (thus) assim, deste modo ● conj por isso, portanto, por consequinte; **~ am I** eu também; **~ does he** ele também; **that is ~** é isso; **I think ~** acho que sim; **five or ~** uns cinco; **~ as to** de modo a; **~ far** até agora, até aqui; **~ long!** 🔲 até já! 🔲; **~ many** tantos; **~ much** tanto; **~ that** para que, de modo que; **~-and-~** fulano m. **~-called** a pretenso, soi-disant, chamado; **~-so** a & adv assim assim, mais ou menos

soak /səʊk/ vt/i molhar(-se), ensopar(-se), encharcar(-se); **leave to ~** pôr de molho; **~ through** repassar □ **~ in**, **~ up** vt absorver, embeber. **~ing** a ensopado, encharcado

soap /səʊp/ n sabão. m; (toilet) **~** sabonete m ● vt ensaboar; **~ opera** Radio novela f radiofônica, (P) radiofónica; TV telenovela f; **~ flakes** flocos mpl de sabão; **~ powder** sabão m em pó. **~y** a ensaboado

soar /sɔː(r)/ vi voar alto; (go high) elevar-se; (hover) pairar

sob /sɒb/ n soluço m ● vi (pt sobbed) soluçar

sober /'səʊbə(r)/ a (not drunk, calm, of colour) sóbrio; (serious) sério, grave ● vt/i **~ up** (fazer) ficar sóbrio 🔲, (fazer) curar a bebedeira 🔲

soccer /'sɒkə(r)/ n 🔲 futebol m

sociable /'səʊʃəbl/ a sociável

social /'səʊʃl/ a social; (sociable) sociável; (gathering, life) de sociedade; **~ security** previdência f social, (P) segurança f social; (for old age) pensão f, (P) reforma f; **~ worker** assistente mf social ● n reunião f social. **~ media** n mídia m social, (P) meios mpl de comunicação social; **~ networking site** n rede f social. **~ly** adv socialmente; (meet) em sociedade

socialis|t /'səʊʃəlɪst/ n socialista mf. **~m** /-zəm/ n socialismo m

socialize /'səʊʃəlaɪz/ vi socializar(-se), reunir-se em sociedade; **~ with** frequentar, conviver com

society /sə'saɪətɪ/ n sociedade f

sociolog|y /səʊsɪ'ɒlədʒɪ/ n sociologia f. **~ist** n sociólogo m

sock[1] /sɒk/ n meia f curta; (men's) meia f (curta), (P) peúga f; (women's) soquete f

sock[2] /sɒk/ vt ⊠ (hit) esmurrar; dar um murro em 🔲

socket /'sɒkɪt/ n cavidade f; (for lamp) suporte m; Electr tomada f; (of tooth) alvéolo m

soda /'səʊdə/ n soda f; (baking) **~** Culin bicarbonato m de soda; **~(-water)** água f gasosa, soda f limonada, (P) água f gaseificada

sodden /'sɒdn/ a ensopado, empapado

sodium /'səʊdɪəm/ n sódio m

sofa /'səʊfə/ n sofá m

soft /sɒft/ a (-er, -est) (not hard, feeble) mole; (not rough, not firm) macio; (gentle, not loud, not bright) suave; (tender-hearted) sensível; (fruit) sem caroço; (wood) de coníferas; (drink) não-alcoólico; **~ spot** fig fraco m. **~ness** n moleza f; (to touch) maciez f; (gentleness) suavidade f, brandura f

soften /'sɒfn/ vt/i amaciar, amolecer; (tone down, lessen) abrandar

software /'sɒftweə(r)/ n software m

soggy /'sɒgɪ/ a (-ier, -iest) ensopado, empapado

soil[1] /sɔɪl/ n solo m, terra f

soil[2] /sɔɪl/ vt/i sujar(-se). **~ed** a sujo

solace /'sɒlɪs/ n consolo m; (relief) alívio m

solar /'səʊlə(r)/ a solar

sold /səʊld/ ▶ SELL a **~ out** esgotado

soldier /'səʊldʒə(r)/ n soldado m ● vi **~ on** 🔲 perseverar com afinco, batalhar 🔲

sole[1] /səʊl/ n (of foot) planta f, sola f do pé; (of shoe) sola f

sole[2] /səʊl/ n (fish) solha f

sole[3] /səʊl/ a único. **~ly** adv unicamente

solemn /'sɒləm/ a solene

solicit /sə'lɪsɪt/ vt (seek) solicitar ● vi (of prostitute) aproximar-se de homens na rua, angariar clientes

solicitor /sə'lɪsɪtə(r)/ n advogado m

solicitous /sə'lɪsɪtəs/ a solícito

solid /'sɒlɪd/ a sólido; (not hollow) maciço, cheio, compacto; ‹gold etc› maciço; ‹meal› substancial ● n sólido m; **~s** (food) alimentos mpl sólidos

solidarity /sɒlɪ'dærətɪ/ n solidariedade f

solidify /sə'lɪdɪfaɪ/ vt/i solidificar(-se)

solitary /'sɒlɪtrɪ/ a solitário, só; (only one) um único; **~ confinement** prisão f celular, solitária f

solitude /'sɒlɪtjuːd/ n solidão f

solo /'səʊləʊ/ n (pl os) solo m ● a solo; **~ flight** voo m (a) solo. **~ist** n solista mf

soluble /'sɒljʊbl/ a solúvel

solution /sə'luːʃn/ n solução f

solv|e /sɒlv/ vt resolver, solucionar. **~able** a resolúvel, solúvel

solvent /'sɒlvənt/ a (dis)solvente; Comm solvente ● n (dis)solvente m

sombre /'sɒmbə(r)/ a sombrio

some /sʌm/ ● a

••••▶ (unspecified number) uns, umas; **he ate ~ olives** ele comeu umas azeitonas; **have ~ more vegetables** coma mais uns vegetais; (unspecified amount) algum(a); **there's still ~ milk in the fridge** ainda há algum leite no congelador; **I need to buy ~ bread** preciso comprar pão; **would you like ~ coffee?** quer café?

••••▶ (certain, not all) alguns, algumas; **~ people say...** algumas pessoas dizem...; **I like ~ modern writers** gosto de alguns escritores modernos

••••▶ (indefinite) um(a)... qualquer, uns... quaisquer, umas... quaisquer; **~ man came to the house** um homem entrou na casa; **there must be ~ mistake** deve haver um erro qualquer; **for ~ reason** por algum motivo; **~ day next week** algum dia da semana que vem

••••▶ (considerable amount) **we've known each other for ~ time** nos conhecemos há algum tempo

● pron

••••▶ (part of an amount) um pouco; **would you like ~?** quer um pouco?; **if you want sugar, I'll give you ~** se quiser açúcar, lhe dou um pouco

••••▶ (a number of) alguns, algumas; **here are ~ of our suggestions** aqui estão algumas das nossas sugestões; **~ are mine, but ~ aren't** alguns são meus, mas os outros não

● adv

••••▶ (approximately) uns, umas; **~ thirty people attended the funeral** umas trinta pessoas estiveram no funeral

somebody /'sʌmbədɪ/ pron alguém ● n **be a ~** ser alguém

somehow /'sʌmhaʊ/ adv (in some way) de algum modo, de alguma maneira; (for some reason) por alguma razão

someone /'sʌmwʌn/ pron & n = SOMEBODY

somersault /'sʌməsɔːlt/ n cambalhota f; (in the air) salto m mortal ● vi dar uma cambalhota/um salto mortal

something /'sʌmθɪŋ/ pron & n uma/ alguma/qualquer coisa f, algo; **~ good/ etc** uma coisa boa/etc, qualquer coisa de bom/etc; **~ like** um pouco como

sometime /'sʌmtaɪm/ adv a certa altura, um dia ● a (former) antigo; **~ last summer** a certa altura no verão passado; **I'll go ~** hei-de ir um dia

sometimes /'sʌmtaɪmz/ adv às vezes, de vez em quando

somewhat /'sʌmwɒt/ adv um pouco, um tanto (ou quanto)

somewhere /'sʌmweə(r)/ adv (position) em algum lugar; (direction) para algum lugar

son /sʌn/ n filho m. **~-in-law** n (pl **~s-in-law**) genro m

sonata /sə'nɑːtə/ n Mus sonata f

song /sɒŋ/ n canção f

soon /suːn/ adv (-er, -est) em breve, dentro em pouco, daqui a pouco; (early) cedo; **as ~ as possible** o mais rápido possível; **I would ~er stay** preferia ficar; **~ after** pouco depois; **~er or later** mais cedo ou mais tarde

soot /sʊt/ n fuligem f

soothe /suːð/ vt acalmar, suavizar; ‹pain› aliviar. **~ing** a ‹remedy› calmante, suavizante; ‹words› (re)confortante

sophisticated /sə'fɪstɪkeɪtɪd/ a sofisticado, refinado, requintado; ‹machine etc› sofisticado

sopping /'sɒpɪŋ/ a encharcado, ensopado

soppy /'sɒpɪ/ a (-ier, -iest) Ⓘ (sentimental) piegas; Ⓘ (silly) bobo, (P) tonto

soprano /sə'prɑːnəʊ/ n (pl ~s) & a soprano mf

sorbet /'sɔːbeɪ/ n (water ice) sorvete m feito sem leite

sorcerer /'sɔːsərə(r)/ n feiticeiro m

sordid /'sɔːdɪd/ a sórdido

sore /sɔː(r)/ a (-er, -est) dolorido; (vexed) aborrecido (at, with com) ● n ferida f; **have a ~ throat** ter a garganta inflamada, ter dores de garganta

sorely /'sɔːlɪ/ adv fortemente, seriamente

sorry /'sɒrɪ/ a (-ier, -iest) (state, sight etc) triste; **be ~ to/that** (regretful) sentir muito/que, lamentar que; **be ~ about** (repentant) ter pena de, estar arrependido de; **feel ~ for** ter pena de; **~!** desculpe!, perdão!

sort /sɔːt/ n gênero m, (P) género m, espécie f, qualidade f; **of ~s** Ⓘ uma espécie de Ⓘ pej; **out of ~s** indisposto ● vt separar por grupos; (tidy) arrumar; **~ out** ‹problem› resolver; (arrange, separate) separar, distribuir

soufflé /'suːfleɪ/ n Culin suflê m, (P) soufflé m

sought /sɔːt/ ▶ SEEK

soul /səʊl/ n alma f; **the life and ~ of** fig a alma f de fig

soulful /'səʊlfl/ a emotivo, expressivo, cheio de sentimento

sound[1] /saʊnd/ n som m, barulho m, ruído m; **~ barrier** barreira f de/do som ● vt/i soar; (seem) dar a impressão de; parecer (as if que); **~ a horn** tocar uma buzina, buzinar; **~ like** parecer ser, soar como. **~proof** a à prova de som ● vt fazer o isolamento sonoro de, isolar; **~track** n (of film) trilha f sonora, (P) banda f sonora

sound[2] /saʊnd/ a (-er, -est) (healthy) saudável, sadio; (sensible) sensato, acertado; (secure) firme, sólido; **~ asleep** profundamente adormecido. **~ly** adv solidamente

sound[3] /saʊnd/ vt (test) sondar; Med (views) auscultar

soup /suːp/ n sopa f

sour /'saʊə(r)/ a (-er, -est) azedo ● vt/i azedar, envinagrar

source /sɔːs/ n fonte f; (of river) nascente f

south /saʊθ/ n sul m ● a a sul, do sul; (of country, people etc) meridional. **S~ Africa/America** África/América do Sul f ● adv a, ao/para (o) sul. **S~ African/American** a & n sul-africano/ sul-americano m; **~east** n sudeste m; **~west** n sudoeste m. **~erly** /'sʌðəlɪ/ a do sul, meridional. **~ward(s)** adv para (o) sul

southern /'sʌðən/ a do sul, meridional, austral

souvenir /suːvə'nɪə(r)/ n recordação f, lembrança f

sovereign /'sɒvrɪn/ n & a soberano m. **~ty** n soberania f

Soviet /'səʊvɪət/ a soviético; **the ~ Union** a União Soviética

sow[1] /səʊ/ vt (pt sowed, pp sowed or sown) semear

sow[2] /saʊ/ n Zool porca f

soy /sɔɪ/ n ~ **sauce** molho m de soja

soya /'sɔɪə/ n soja f; **~bean** semente f de soja

spa /spɑː/ n termas fpl

space /speɪs/ n espaço m; (room) lugar m; (period) espaço m, período m ● a ‹research etc› espacial ● vt ~ **out** espaçar

space|craft /'speɪskrɑːft/ n (pl invar) **~ship** n nave f espacial

spacious /'speɪʃəs/ a espaçoso

spade /speɪd/ n (gardener's) pá f de ferro; (child's) pá f; **~s** Cards espadas fpl

spaghetti /spə'getɪ/ n espaguete m, (P) esparguete m

Spain /speɪn/ n Espanha f

spam /spæm/ n **Spam®** Culin marca barata de carne de porco enlatada; Comput spam m ● vt (pres p etc. **-mm-**) enviar spam

span[1] /spæn/ n (of arch) vão m; (of wings) envergadura f; (of time) espaço m, duração f; (measure) palmo m ● vt (pt **spanned**) (extend across) transpor; (measure) medir em palmos; (in time) abarcar, abranger, estender-se por

span[2] /spæn/ ▶ SPIN

Spaniard /'spænɪəd/ n espanhol m

Spanish /'spænɪʃ/ a espanhol ● n Lang espanhol m

spank /spæŋk/ vt dar palmadas or chineladas em. **~ing** n (with hand) palmada f; (with slipper) chinelada f

spanner /'spænə(r)/ n (tool) chave f de porcas; (adjustable) chave f inglesa

spar /spɑ:(r)/ vi (pt sparred) jogar boxe, esp para treino; fig (argue) discutir

spare /speə(r)/ vt (not hurt; use with restraint) poupar; (afford to give) dispensar, ceder; **have an hour to ~** dispor de uma hora; **have no time to ~** não ter tempo a perder ● a (in reserve) de reserva, de sobra; ‹tyre› sobressalente; ‹bed› extra; ‹room› de hóspedes ● n (in part) sobressalente m; **~ time** horas fpl vagas, tempo m livre

sparing /'speərɪŋ/ a poupado; **be ~ of** poupar em, ser poupado com. **~ly** adv frugalmente

spark /spɑ:k/ n centelha f, faísca f ● vt lançar faíscas; **~ off** (initiate) desencadear, provocar

sparkle /'spɑ:kl/ vi cintilar, brilhar ● n brilho m, cintilação f

sparkling /'spɑ:klɪŋ/ a ‹wine› espumante

sparrow /'spærəʊ/ n pardal m

sparse /spɑ:s/ a esparso; ‹hair› ralo. **~ly** adv ‹furnished etc› escassamente

spasm /'spæzəm/ n (of muscle) espasmo m; (of coughing, anger etc) ataque m, acesso m

spasmodic /spæz'mɒdɪk/ a espasmódico; (at irregular intervals) intermitente

spastic /'spæstɪk/ n deficiente mf motor

spat /spæt/ ▶ SPIT¹

spate /speɪt/ n (in river) enxurrada f, cheia f; **a ~ of** ‹letters etc› uma avalanche de

spatter /'spætə(r)/ vt salpicar (**with** de, com)

spawn /spɔ:n/ n ovas fpl ● vi desovar ● vt gerar em quantidade

speak /spi:k/ vt/i (pt spoke, pp spoken) falar (**to/with sb about sth** com alguém de/sobre alg coisa); (say) dizer; **~ out/ up** falar abertamente; (louder) falar mais alto; **~ one's mind** dizer o que se pensa; **so to ~** por assim dizer; **English/ Portuguese spoken** fala-se inglês/ português

speaker /'spi:kə(r)/ n (in public) orador m; (loudspeaker) alto-falante m; (of a language) pessoa f de língua nativa, falante mf nativo/a de uma língua

spear /spɪə(r)/ n lança f

spearhead /'spɪəhed/ n ponta f de lança ● vt (lead) estar à frente de,

encabeçar

special /'speʃl/ a especial. **~ity** /-ɪ'ælətɪ/ n especialidade f. **~ly** adv especialmente. **~ty** n especialidade f

specialist /'speʃəlɪst/ n especialista mf

specialize /'speʃəlaɪz/ vi especializar-se (**in** em). **~d** a especializado

species /'spi:ʃi:z/ n (pl invar) espécie f

specific /spə'sɪfɪk/ a específico. **~ally** adv especificamente, explicitamente

specif|y /'spesɪfaɪ/ vt especificar. **~ication** /-ɪ'keɪʃn/ n especificação f. **~ications** npl (of work etc) caderno m de encargos

specimen /'spesɪmɪn/ n espécime(n) m, amostra f

speck /spek/ n (stain) mancha f pequena; (dot) pontinho m, pinta f; (particle) grão m

speckled /'spekld/ a salpicado, manchado

specs /speks/ npl 🄸 óculos mpl

spectacle /'spektəkl/ n espetáculo m; **(pair of) ~s** (par m de) óculos mpl

spectacular /spek'tækjʊlə(r)/ a espetacular

spectator /spek'teɪtə(r)/ n espectador m

spectrum /'spektrəm/ n (pl -tra) espectro m; (of ideas etc) faixa f, gama f, leque m

speculat|e /'spekjʊleɪt/ vi especular; fazer especulações or conjeturas; (P) conjeturas (**about** sobre); Comm especular; fazer especulação (**in** em). **~ion** /-'leɪʃn/ n especulação f, conjetura f; Comm especulação f. **~or** n especulador m

speech /spi:tʃ/ n (faculty) fala f; (diction) elocução f; (dialect) falar m; (address) discurso m. **~less** a mudo; sem fala, (P) sem palavras (**with** com, de)

speed /spi:d/ n velocidade f, rapidez f ● vt/i (pt sped, move) (send) despedir, mandar; (drive too fast) ultrapassar o limite de velocidade; (drive too fast) ultrapassar o limite de velocidade; **~ camera** radar m; **~ limit** limite m de velocidade; **~ up** acelerar(-se). **~ dating** n: forma rápida de conhecer vários possíveis namorados, através de conversas breves; **~ dial** n discagem f rápida, (P) marcação f rápida. **~ing** n excesso m de velocidade

speedometer /spi:'dɒmɪtə(r)/ n velocímetro m

S

speed|y /'spiːdɪ/ a (-ier, -iest) rápido; (*prompt*) pronto. ~ily adv rapidamente; (*promptly*) prontamente

spell¹ /spel/ n (*magic*) sortilégio m

spell² /spel/ vt/i (pt spelled, or spelt) escrever; fig (mean) significar; ter como resultado; ~ out soletrar; fig (explain) explicar claramente. ~ing n ortografia f

spell³ /spel/ n (*short period*) período m curto, breve espaço m de tempo; (*turn*) turno m

spend /spend/ vt (pt spent) <money, energy> gastar (on em); <time, holiday> passar

spendthrift /'spendθrɪft/ n perdulário m, esbanjador m

spent /spent/ ▶ SPEND a (used) gasto

sperm /spɜːm/ n (pl ~s or ~) (semen) esperma m, sêmen m, (P) sémen m; (cell) espermatozóide m

spew /spjuː/ vt/i vomitar, lançar

sphere /sfɪə(r)/ n esfera f

spic|e /spaɪs/ n especiaria f, condimento m; fig picante m ● vt condimentar. ~y a condimentado; fig picante

spider /'spaɪdə(r)/ n aranha f

spik|e /spaɪk/ n (of metal etc) bico m, espigão m, ponta f. ~y a guarnecido de bicos or pontas, pontiagudo

spill /spɪl/ vt/i (pt spilled, or spilt) derramar(-se), entornar(-se), espalhar(-se); ~ over transbordar, extravasar

spin /spɪn/ vt/i (pt spun, pres p spinning) <wool, cotton> fiar; <web> tecer; <turn> (fazer) girar, (fazer) rodopiar; ~ out <money, story> fazer durar; <time> (fazer) parar ● n volta f; Aviat parafuso m; go for a ~ dar uma volta or um giro or (P) um passeio. ~ drier n centrifugadora f para a roupa, secadora f, (P) máquina f de secar (a roupa); ~off n bônus m, (P) bónus m inesperado; (by-product) derivado m

spinach /'spɪnɪdʒ/ n (plant) espinafre m; (as food) espinafres mpl

spindl|e /'spɪndl/ n roca f, fuso m; Mech eixo m. ~y a alto e magro; (of plant) espigado

spine /spaɪn/ n espinha f, coluna f vertebral; (prickle) espinho m, pico m, (of book) lombada f

spineless /'spaɪnlɪs/ a fig (cowardly) covarde; sem fibra fig

spinster /'spɪnstə(r)/ n solteira f; pej solteirona f

spiral /'spaɪərəl/ a (em) espiral; (staircase) em caracol ● n espiral f ● vi (pt spiralled) subir em espiral

spire /'spaɪə(r)/ n agulha f, flecha f

spirit /'spɪrɪt/ n espírito m; (boldness) coragem f, brio m; ~s (morale) moral m; (drink) bebidas fpl alcoólicas; in high ~s alegre ● vt ~ away dar sumiço em, arrebatar

spirited /'spɪrɪtɪd/ a fogoso; <attack, defence> vigoroso, enérgico

spiritual /'spɪrɪtʃʊəl/ a espiritual

spiritualism /'spɪrɪtʃʊəlɪzəm/ n espiritismo m

spit¹ /spɪt/ vt/i (pt spat, or spit, pres p spitting) cuspir; (of rain) chuviscar; (of cat) bufar ● n cuspe m, (P) cuspo m; the ~ting image of o retrato vivo de, a cara chapada de 🆒

spit² /spɪt/ n (for meat) espeto m; (of land) restinga f, (P) língua f de terra

spite /spaɪt/ n má vontade f, despeito m, rancor m ● vt aborrecer, mortificar. in ~ of a despeito de, apesar de. ~ful a rancoroso, maldoso

splash /splæʃ/ vt salpicar, respingar ● vi esparrinhar, salpicar, esparramar-se; ~ (about) chapinhar ● n (act, mark) salpico m; (sound) chape m; (of colour) mancha f; make a ~ (striking display) fazer um vistão, causar furor

splendid /'splendɪd/ a esplêndido, magnífico; (excellent) estupendo 🆒, ótimo

splendour /'splendə(r)/ n esplendor m

splint /splɪnt/ n Med tala f

splinter /'splɪntə(r)/ n lasca f, estilhaço m; (under the skin) farpa f, lasca f ● vi estilhaçar-se, lascar-se; ~ group grupo m dissidente

split /splɪt/ vt/i (pt split, pres p splitting) rachar, fender(-se); (divide, share) dividir; (tear) romper(-se) ● n racha f, fenda f; (share) quinhão m, parte f; Pol cisão f; ~ on 🆒 (inform on) denunciar; ~ one's sides rebentar de riso; ~ up (of couple) separar-se; a ~ second uma fração de segundo; ~ting headache dor f de cabeça forte

splurge /splɜːdʒ/ n 🆒 espalhafato m; estardalhaço m ● vi 🆒 (spend) gastar os tubos, (P) gastar à doida 🆒

splutter /'splʌtə(r)/ vi falar cuspindo; <engine> cuspir; <fat> crepitar

spoil /spɔɪl/ vt (pt spoilt or spoiled) estragar; (pamper) mimar ● n ~(s) (plunder) despojo(s) m(pl), espólios mpl. ~sport n desmancha-prazeres mf invar.

~t a (*pampered*) mimado, estragado com mimos

spoke¹ /spəʊk/ n raio m

spoke² **spoken** /spəʊk, 'spəʊkən/ ▶ SPEAK

spokes|man /'spəʊksmən/ n (pl -men); **~woman** n (pl -women) porta-voz mf

sponge /spʌndʒ/ n esponja f ● vt (*clean*) lavar com esponja; (*wipe*) limpar com esponja ● vi **~ on** 🄸 (*cadge*) viver à(s) custa(s) de. **~ bag** n bolsa f de toalete; **~ cake** n pão de ló m. **~r** /-ə(r)/ n 🄸 parasita mf 🄧

sponsor /'spɒnsə(r)/ n patrocinador m; (*for membership*) (sócio) proponente m ● vt patrocinar; (*for membership*) propor. **~ship** n patrocínio m

spontaneous /spɒn'teɪnɪəs/ a espontâneo

spoof /spuːf/ n 🄸 paródia f

spooky /'spuːkɪ/ a (-ier, -iest) 🄸 fantasmagórico; que dá arrepios

spool /spuːl/ n (*of sewing machine*) bobina f; (*for thread, line*) carretel m, (P) carrinho m

spoon /spuːn/ n colher f. **~feed** vt (pt -fed) alimentar de colher; fig (*help*) dar na bandeja para fig, (P) dar de bandeja a fig. **~ful** n colherada f

sporadic /spə'rædɪk/ a esporádico, acidental

sport /spɔːt/ n esporte m, (P) desporto m; **(good) ~** 🄧 (*person*) gente f fina, (P) bom tipo m, (P) tipo m fixe 🄸; **~s car/ coat** carro m /casaco m esporte or (P) de desporto ● vt (*display*) exibir, ostentar. **~y** a 🄸 esportivo; (P) desportivo

sporting /'spɔːtɪŋ/ a esportivo, (P) desportivo; **a ~ chance** uma certa possibilidade de sucesso, uma boa chance

sports|man n (pl -men); **~woman** (pl women) desportista mf. **~manship** n (*spirit*) espírito m esportivo, (P) desportivo; (*activity*) esportismo m, (P) desportismo m

spot /spɒt/ n (*mark, stain*) mancha f; (*in pattern*) pinta f, bola f; (*drop*) gota f; (*place*) lugar m, ponto m; (*pimple*) borbulha f, espinha f; TV spot m televisivo; **a ~ of** 🄸 um pouco de; **be in a ~** 🄸 estar numa encrenca 🄸, (P) estar metido numa alhada 🄸; **on the ~** no local; (*there and then*) ali mesmo, logo ali ● vt (pt spotted) manchar; 🄸 (*detect*) descobrir; detectar 🄸; **~ check** inspeção f de surpresa;

(*of cars*) fiscalização f de surpresa. **~ on** a 🄸 certo, exacto. **~ted** a manchado; (*with dots*) de pintas, de bolas; (*animal*) malhado. **~ty** a (*with pimples*) com borbulhas

spotless /'spɒtlɪs/ a impecável, imaculado

spotlight /'spɒtlaɪt/ n foco m; Cine, Theat refletor m, holofote m

spouse /spaʊz/ n cônjuge mf, esposo m

spout /spaʊt/ n (*of vessel*) bico m; (*of liquid*) esguicho m, jorro m; (*pipe*) cano m ● vi jorrar, esguichar; **up the ~** 🄧 (*ruined*) liquidado 🄧 (P) acabado

sprain /spreɪn/ n entorse f, mau jeito m ● vt torcer, dar um mau jeito a

sprang /spræŋ/ ▶ SPRING

sprawl /sprɔːl/ vi (*sit*) estirar-se, esparramar-se; (*fall*) estatelar-se; ‹town› estender-se, espraiar-se

spray¹ /spreɪ/ n (*of flowers*) raminho m, ramalhete m

spray² /spreɪ/ n (*water*) borrifo m, salpico m; (*from sea*) borrifo m de espuma; (*device*) bomba f, aerossol m; (*for perfume*) vaporizador m, atomizador m ● vt aspergir, borrifar, pulverizar; (*with insecticide*) pulverizar

spread /spred/ vt/i (pt spread) (*extend, stretch*) estender(-se); ‹news, fear, illness etc› alastrar(-se), espalhar(-se), propagar(-se); ‹butter etc› passar, (P) barrar; ‹wings› abrir ● n (*expanse*) expansão f, extensão f; (*spreading*) propagação f; (*paste*) pasta f para passar no pão, (P) para barrar no pão; 🄸 (*meal*) banquete m. **~sheet** n Comput folha f de cálculo

spree /spriː/ n **go on a ~** 🄸 cair na farra, (P) ir para a farra

sprightly /'spraɪtlɪ/ a (-ier, -iest) vivo, animado

spring /sprɪŋ/ vi (pt sprang, pp sprung) (*arise*) nascer; (*jump*) saltar, pular; **~ up** surgir ● vt (*produce suddenly*) sair-se com; (*a surprise*) fazer (**on sb** a alguém); **~ from** vir de, originar-se de, provir de ● n salto m, pulo m; (*device*) mola f; (*season*) primavera f; (*of water*) fonte f, nascente f; **~ onion** cebolinha f. **~clean** vt fazer limpeza geral

springboard /'sprɪŋbɔːd/ n trampolim m

springtime /'sprɪŋtaɪm/ n primavera f

springy /'sprɪŋɪ/ a (-ier, -iest) elástico

sprinkle /'sprɪŋkl/ vt (*with liquid*) borrifar, salpicar; (*with salt, flour*)

S

polvilhar (**with** de); **~ sand**/etc espalhar areia/etc. **~r** /-ə(r)/ n (in garden) regador m; (for fires) sprinkler m

sprinkling /'sprɪŋklɪŋ/ n (amount) pequena quantidade f; (number) pequeno número m

sprint /sprɪnt/ n Sport corrida f de pequena distância, sprint m ● vi correr em sprint or a toda a velocidade; Sport correr

sprout /spraʊt/ vt/i brotar, germinar; (put forth) deitar ● n (on plant etc) broto m; (**Brussels**) **~s** couves f de Bruxelas

sprung /sprʌŋ/ ▶ SPRING a <mattress etc> de molas

spry /spraɪ/ a (spryer, spryest) vivo, ativo; (nimble) ágil

spud /spʌd/ n 🔲 batata f

spun /spʌn/ ▶ SPIN

spur /spɜː(r)/ n (of rider) espora f; fig (stimulus) aguilhão m; fig espora f fig ● vt (pt spurred) esporear, picar com esporas; fig (incite) aguilhoar; esporear; **on the ~ of the moment** impulsivamente, no calor do momento

spurn /spɜːn/ vt desdenhar, desprezar, rejeitar

spurt /spɜːt/ vi jorrar, esguichar; fig (accelerate) acelerar subitamente; dar um arranco súbito ● n jorro m, esguicho m; (of energy, speed) arranco m, arrancada f, surto m

spy /spaɪ/ n espião m ● vt (make out) avistar, descortinar ● vi **~ (on)** espiar, espionar; **~ out** descobrir. **~ing** n espionagem f

squabble /'skwɒbl/ vi discutir, brigar ● n briga f, disputa f

squad /skwɒd/ n Mil pelotão m; (team) equipe f, (P) equipa f; **firing ~** pelotão m de fuzilamento; **flying ~** brigada f móvel

squadron /'skwɒdrən/ n Mil esquadrão m; Aviat esquadrilha f; Naut esquadra f

squal|id /'skwɒlɪd/ a esquálido, sórdido. **~or** n sordidez f

squall /skwɔːl/ n borrasca f

squander /'skwɒndə(r)/ vt desperdiçar

square /skweə(r)/ n quadrado m; (in town) largo m, praça f, (T-square) régua-tê f; (set square) esquadro m; **go back to ~ one** recomeçar tudo do princípio, voltar à estaca zero ● a (of shape) quadrado; <metre, mile etc> quadrado; (honest) direito, honesto; (of meal) abundante, substancial; **(all) ~** (quits) quite(s); **~ brackets** parênteses

mpl retos ● vt Math elevar ao quadrado; (settle) acertar; **~ up to** enfrentar ● vi (agree) concordar. **~ly** adv diretamente; (fairly) honestamente

squash /skwɒʃ/ vt (crush) esmagar; (squeeze) espremer; (crowd) comprimir, apertar ● n (game) squash m; Amer (marrow) abóbora f; **lemon ~** limonada f; **orange ~** laranjada f. **~y** a mole

squat /skwɒt/ vi (pt squatted) acocorar-se, agachar-se; (be a squatter) ser ocupante ilegal ● a (dumpy) atarracado. **~ter** n ocupante mf ilegal de casa vazia, posseiro m

squawk /skwɔːk/ n grasnido m, crocito m ● vi grasnar, crocitar

squeak /skwiːk/ n guincho m, chio m; (of door, shoes etc) rangido m ● vi guinchar, chiar; (of door, shoes etc) ranger. **~y** a <shoe etc> que range; <voice> esganiçado

squeal /skwiːl/ vi dar gritos agudos, guinchar ● n grito m agudo, guincho m; **~ (on)** 🔲 (inform on) delatar, (P) denunciar

squeamish /'skwiːmɪʃ/ a (nauseated) que enjoa à toa, impressionável, delicado

squeeze /skwiːz/ vt <lemon, sponge etc> espremer; <hand, arm> apertar; (extract) arrancar; extorquir (**from** de) ● vi (force one's way) passar à força, meter-se por ● n aperto m, apertão m; (hug) abraço m; Comm restrições fpl de crédito

squid /skwɪd/ n lula f

squiggle /'skwɪgl/ n rabisco m, floreado m

squint /skwɪnt/ vi ser estrábico or vesgo; (with half-shut eyes) franzir os olhos, (P) semicerrar os olhos ● n Med estrabismo m

squirm /skwɜːm/ vi (re)torcer-se, contorcer-se

squirrel /'skwɪrəl/ n esquilo m

squirt /skwɜːt/ vt/i esguichar ● n esguicho m

stab /stæb/ vt (pt stabbed) apunhalar; (knife) esfaquear ● n punhalada f; (with knife) facada f; (of pain) pontada f; 🔲 (attempt) tentativa f

stabilize /'steɪbɪlaɪz/ vt estabilizar

stab|le[1] /'steɪbl/ a (-er, -est) estável. **~ility** /stə'bɪlətɪ/ n estabilidade f

stable[2] /'steɪbl/ n cavalariça f, estrebaria f

stack /stæk/ n pilha f, montão m; (of hay etc) meda f ● vt ~ **(up)** empilhar, amontoar

stadium /'steɪdɪəm/ n estádio m

staff /stɑːf/ n pessoal m; (in school) professores mpl; Mil estado-maior m; (stick) bordão m, cajado m; (pl **staves**) Mus pauta f ● vt prover de pessoal

stag /stæg/ n veado (macho) m, cervo m. ~ **party** n Ⅱ reunião f masculina; (before wedding) despedida f de solteiro

stage /steɪdʒ/ n Theat palco m; (phase) fase f, ponto m; (platform in hall) estrado m; **go on the ~** seguir a carreira teatral, ir para teatro Ⅱ; ~ **door** entrada f dos artistas ● vt encenar, pôr em cena; fig (organize) organizar. ~**fright** n nervosismo m, medo m do palco

stagger /'stægə(r)/ vi vacilar, cambalear ● vt (shock) atordoar, chocar; <holidays etc> escalonar. ~**ing** a atordoador, chocante

stagnant /'stægnənt/ a estagnado, parado

stagnat|e /stæg'neɪt/ vi estagnar

stain /steɪn/ vt manchar, pôr nódoa em; (colour) tingir, dar cor a ● n mancha f, nódoa f; (colouring) corante m; ~**ed glass window** vitral m; ~**less steel** aço m inoxidável

stair /steə(r)/ n degrau m; ~**s** escada(s) f(pl)

stair|case /'steəkeɪs/, ~**way** /-weɪ/ ns escada(s) f(pl), escadaria f

stake /steɪk/ n (post) estaca f, poste m; (wager) parada f, aposta f; **at ~** em jogo; **have a ~ in** ter interesse em ● vt <area> demarcar, delimitar; (wager) jogar, apostar; ~ **a claim to** reivindicar

stale /steɪl/ a (-er, -est) estragado, velho; <bread> duro, mofado; <smell> rançoso; <air> viciado; <news> velho

stalemate /'steɪlmeɪt/ n (chess) empate m; fig (deadlock) impasse m; beco sem saída m

stalk[1] /stɔːk/ n (of plant) caule m

stalk[2] /stɔːk/ vi andar com um ar empertigado ● vt <prey> perseguir furtivamente, tocaiar

stall /stɔːl/ n (in stable) baia f; (in market) tenda f, barraca f; ~**s** Theat poltronas fpl de orquestra; Cinema plateia f ● vt/i Auto enguiçar, (P) ir abaixo; ~ **(for time)** ganhar tempo, empatar

stalwart /'stɔːlwət/ a forte, rijo; (supporter) fiel

stamina /'stæmɪnə/ n resistência f

stammer /'stæmə(r)/ vt/i gaguejar ● n gagueira f, (P) gaguez f

stamp /stæmp/ vt/i ~ **(one's foot)** bater com o pé (no chão), pisar com força ● vt estampar; <letter> estampilhar, selar; (with rubber stamp) carimbar; ~ **out** <fire, rebellion etc> esmagar; <disease> erradicar ● n estampa f; (for postage) selo m; fig (mark) cunho m; **rubber ~** carimbo m. ~ **collecting** n filatelia f

stampede /stæm'piːd/ n (scattering) debandada f; (of horses, cattle etc) debandada f, fig (rush) corrida f ● vt/i (fazer) debandar; <horses, cattle etc> tresmalhar

stance /stæns/ n posição f, postura f

stand /stænd/ vi (pt **stood**) estar em pé; (keep upright position) ficar em pé; (rise) levantar-se; (be situated) encontrar-se, ficar, situar-se; Pol candidatar-se (for por); ~ **back** recuar; ~ **by** or **around** estar parado sem fazer nada; ~ **by** (be ready) estar a postos; <promise, person> manter-se fiel a; ~ **down** desistir, retirar-se; ~ **out** (be conspicuous) sobressair; ~ **still** estar/ficar imóvel; ~ **still!** não se mexa!, fique, quieto!; ~ **to reason** ser lógico; ~ **up** levantar-se, pôr-se em or de pé ● vt pôr (de pé), colocar; (tolerate) suportar, aguentar; ~ **a chance** ter uma possibilidade; ~ **for** representar, simbolizar; Ⅱ (tolerate) aturar; ~ **in for** substituir; ~ **up for** defender, apoiar; ~ **up to** enfrentar ● n posição f; (support) apoio m; Mil resistência f; (at fair) stand m, pavilhão m; (in street) quiosque m; (for spectators) arquibancada f, (P) bancada f; Amer (witness box) banco m das testemunhas. ~**by** n (for emergency) de reserva; <ticket> de stand-by, (P) de reserva ● n (at airport) stand-by m; **on ~by** Mil de prontidão; Med de plantão; ~**in** n substituto m, suplente mf; ~**offish** a Ⅱ (aloof) reservado, distante

standard /'stændəd/ n norma f, padrão m; (level) nível m; (flag) estandarte m, bandeira f; ~**s** (morals) princípios mpl; ~ **of living** padrão m de vida, (P) nível m de vida ● a regulamentar; (average) standard, normal; ~ **lamp** candeeiro m de pé

standardize /'stændədaɪz/ vt padronizar

standing /'stændɪŋ/ a em pé, de pé invar; <army, committee etc> permanente ● n posição f; (reputation) prestígio m; (duration) duração f; ~ **order** (at bank)

S

ordem f permanente, (P) autorização f de pagamento por transferência bancária

standpoint /'stændpɔɪnt/ n ponto m de vista

standstill /'stændstɪl/ n paralisação f; **at a ~** parado, paralisado; **bring/ come to a ~** (fazer) parar, paralisar(-se), imobilizar(-se)

stank /stæŋk/ ▶ STINK

staple[1] /'steɪpl/ n (for paper) grampo m, (P) agrafo m ● vt <paper> grampear, (P) agrafar. **~r** /-ə(r)/ n grampeador m, (P) agrafador m

staple[2] /'steɪpl/ a principal, básico ● n Comm artigo m básico

star /stɑː(r)/ n estrela f; (cinema) estrela f, vedete f, (P) vedeta f; (celebrity) celebridade f ● vt (pt **starred**) (of film) ter no papel principal, (P) ter como ator principal ● vi **~ in** ser a vedete or (P) vedeta, ter o papel principal em. **~dom** n celebridade f, estrelato m

starch /stɑːtʃ/ n amido m, fécula f; (for clothes) goma f ● vt pôr em goma, engomar. **~y** a (of food) farináceo, feculento; fig (of person) rígido; formal

stare /steə(r)/ vi **~ at** olhar fixamente ● n olhar m fixo

stark /stɑːk/ a (**-er, -est**) (desolate) árido, desolado; (severe) austero, severo; (utter) completo, rematado; <fact etc> brutal ● adv completamente; **~ naked** nu em pelo, (P) em pelota 🔢

starling /'stɑːlɪŋ/ n estorninho m

starry /'stɑːrɪ/ a estrelado. **~-eyed** a 🔢 sonhador; idealista

start /stɑːt/ vt/i começar; <machine> ligar, pôr em andamento; <fashion etc> lançar; (leave) partir; (cause) causar, provocar; (jump) sobressaltar-se, estremecer; (of car) arrancar, partir ● n começo m, início m; (of race) largada f, partida f; (lead) avanço m; (jump) sobressalto m, estremecimento m; **by fits and ~s** aos arrancos, intermitentemente; **for a ~** para começar; **give sb a ~** sobressaltar alguém, pregar um susto a alguém; **~ to do** começar a or pôr-se a fazer. **~er** n Auto arranque m; (competitor) corredor m; Culin entrada f. **~ing point** n ponto m de partida

startl|**e** /'stɑːtl/ vt (make jump) sobressaltar, pregar um susto a; (shock) alarmar, chocar. **~ing** a alarmante; (surprising) surpreendente

starv|**e** /stɑːv/ vi (suffer) passar fome; (die) morrer de fome; **be ~ing** 🔢 (very hungry) ter muita fome, (P) estar esfomeado, morrer de fome ● vt fazer passar fome a; (deprive) privar. **~ation** /-'veɪʃn/ n fome f

stash /stæʃ/ vt 🔀 guardar; esconder; enfurnar 🔢

state /steɪt/ n estado m, condição f; (pomp) pompa f, gala f; Pol Estado m; **in a ~** muito abalado ● a de Estado, do Estado; <school> público; <visit etc> oficial ● vt afirmar (**that** que); <views> exprimir; (fix) marcar, fixar

stately /'steɪtlɪ/ a (**-ier, -iest**) majestoso; **~ home** solar m, palácio m

statement /'steɪtmənt/ n declaração f; (of account) extrato m de conta

---

state school Na Grã-Bretanha, é um colégio federal de educação gratuita, financiado direta ou indiretamente pelo governo. Inclui educação primária e secundária, colégios especializados, comprehensive schools, etc. ⓘ

---

statesman /'steɪtsmən/ n (pl **-men**) homem m de estado, estadista m

static /'stætɪk/ a estático ● n Radio, TV estática f, interferência f

station /'steɪʃn/ n (position) posto m; (rail, bus, radio) estação f; (rank) condição f, posição f social ● vt colocar; **~ed at** or **in** Mil estacionado em. **~ wagon** n perua f, (P) carrinha f

stationary /'steɪʃnrɪ/ a estacionário, parado, imóvel; <vehicle> estacionado, parado

stationer /'steɪʃənə(r)/ n dono m de papelaria; **~'s shop** papelaria f. **~y** n artigos mpl de papelaria; (writing paper) papel m de carta

statistic /stə'tɪstɪk/ n dado m estatístico. **~s** n (as a science) estatística f. **~al** a estatístico

statue /'stætʃuː/ n estátua f

stature /'stætʃə(r)/ n estatura f

status /'steɪtəs/ n (pl **-uses**) situação f, posição f, categoria f; (prestige) prestígio m, importância f, status m; **~ quo** quo m; **~ symbol** símbolo m de status

statut|**e** /'stætjuːt/ n estatuto m, lei f. **~ory** /-ʊtrɪ/ a estatutário, regulamentar; <holiday> legal

staunch /stɔːntʃ/ a (**-er, -est**) <friend> fiel, leal

stave /steɪv/ n Mus pauta f ● vt ~ **off** (keep off) conjurar, evitar; (delay) adiar

stay /steɪ/ vi estar, ficar, permanecer; (dwell temporarily) ficar, alojar-se, hospedar-se; (spend time) demorar-se; ~ **behind** ficar para trás; ~ **in** ficar em casa; ~ **put** ⊞ não se mexer; ~ **up** (late) deitar-se tarde, ficar acordado até tarde ● vt ⟨hunger⟩ enganar ● n estada f, visita f, permanência f. ~**ing power** n resistência f

steadfast /'stedfɑːst/ a firme, constante

stead|y /'stedɪ/ a (-ier, -iest) (stable) estável, firme, seguro; (regular) regular, constante; ⟨hand, voice⟩ firme ● vt firmar, fixar, estabilizar; (calm) acalmar; **go ~y with** ⊞ namorar, ter uma relação estável com. ~**ily** adv firmemente; (regularly) regularmente, de modo constante

steak /steɪk/ n bife m

steal /stiːl/ vt/i (pt **stole**, pp **stolen**) roubar (**from sb** de alguém); ~ **away/ in/**etc sair/entrar/etc furtivamente, esgueirar-se; ~ **the show** pôr os outros na sombra, roubar a atenção de todos

stealth /stelθ/ n **by** ~ furtivamente, na calada, às escondidas. ~**y** a furtivo

steam /stiːm/ n vapor m de água; (on window) condensação f; ~ **iron** ferro m a vapor ● vt (cook) cozinhar a vapor ● vi soltar vapor, fumegar; (move) avançar; ~ **up** ⟨window⟩ embaciar. ~ **engine** n máquina f a vapor; (locomotive) locomotiva f a vapor. ~**y** a (heat) úmido, (P) húmido

steamer /'stiːmə(r)/ n (ship) (barco a) vapor m; Culin utensílio m para cozinhar a vapor

steel /stiːl/ n aço m; ~ **industry** siderurgia f ● a de aço ● vpr ~ **o.s.** endurecer-se, fortalecer-se

steep[1] /stiːp/ vt (soak) mergulhar, pôr de molho; (permeate) passar, impregnar; ~**ed in** fig ⟨vice, misery etc⟩ mergulhado em; fig ⟨knowledge, wisdom etc⟩ impregnado de, repassado de

steep[2] /stiːp/ a (-er, -est) íngreme, escarpado; ⊞ exagerado; exorbitante; **rise ~ly** ⟨slope⟩ subir a pique; ⟨price⟩ disparar

steeple /'stiːpl/ n campanário m, torre f

steeplechase /'stiːpltʃeɪs/ n (race) corrida f de obstáculos

steer /stɪə(r)/ vt/i guiar, conduzir, dirigir; ⟨ship⟩ governar, (P) comandar; fig guiar, orientar; ~ **clear of** evitar passar perto de. ~**ing** n Auto direção f. ~**ing wheel** n Auto volante m

stem[1] /stem/ n caule m, haste f; (of glass) pé m; (of pipe) boquilha f; (of word) radical m ● vi (pt **stemmed**) ~ **from** provir de, vir de

stem[2] /stem/ vt (pt **stemmed**) (check) conter; (stop) estancar

stem cell n célula-tronco f, célula f estaminal

stench /stentʃ/ n mau cheiro m, fedor m

stencil /'stensl/ n estêncil m, (P) stencil m ● vt (pt **stencilled**) ⟨document⟩ policopiar

step /step/ vi (pt **stepped**) ir andar; ~ **down** (resign) demitir-se; ~ **in** (intervene) intervir ● vt ~ **up** aumentar ● n passo m, passada f; (of stair, train) degrau m; (action) medida f, passo m; ~**s** (ladder) escada f; **in** ~ no mesmo passo, a passo certo; fig em conformidade (**with** com). ~**ladder** n escada f portátil; ~**ping stone** n fig (means to an end) ponte f; trampolim m

step|brother /'stepbrʌðə(r)/ n meio-irmão m. ~**daughter** n nora f, (P) enteada f. ~**father** n padrasto m. ~**mother** n madrasta f. ~**sister** n meia-irmã f. ~**son** n genro m, (P) enteado m

stereo /'sterɪəʊ/ n (pl -os) estéreo m; (record player etc) equipamento or sistema m estéreo m ● a estéreo invar. ~**phonic** /-ə'fɒnɪk/ a estereofônico, (P) estereofónico

stereotype /'sterɪətaɪp/ n estereótipo m

sterile /'steraɪl/ a estéril

steriliz|e /'sterəlaɪz/ vt esterilizar. ~**ation** /-'zeɪʃn/ n esterilização f

sterling /'stɜːlɪŋ/ n libra f esterlina ● a esterlino; (silver) de lei; fig excelente; de (primeira) qualidade

stern[1] /stɜːn/ a (-er, -est) severo

stern[2] /stɜːn/ n (of ship) popa f, ré f

stethoscope /'steθəskəʊp/ n estetoscópio m

stew /stjuː/ vt/i estufar, guisar; (fruit) cozer ● n ensopado m; ~**ed fruit** compota f

steward /'stjuəd/ n (of club etc) ecônomo m, (P) ecónomo m; administrador m; (on ship etc) camareiro m (de bordo), (P) comissário m (de bordo). ~**ess** /-'des/ n aeromoça f, (P) assistente f de bordo

stick[1] /stɪk/ n pau m; (for walking) bengala f; (of celery) talo m

stick² /stɪk/ vt (pt **stuck**) ‹glue› colar; (thrust) cravar, espetar; ① (put) enfiar, meter; ⊠ (endure) aguentar, aturar, suportar; **be stuck with sb/sth** ① não conseguir descartar-se or livrar-se de alguém/algo ①; **~ to** ‹promise› ser fiel a ● vi (pt **stuck**) (adhere) colar, aderir; (remain) ficar enfiado or metido; (be jammed) emperrar, ficar engatado; **~ in one's mind** ficar na memória; **~ up for** ① tomar o partido de, defender □ **~ out** vt ‹head› esticar, pôr de fora; ‹tongue etc› mostrar ● vi (protrude) sobressair. **~up** n ⊠ assalto à mão armada m; **~ing plaster** n esparadrapo m, (P) adesivo m

sticker /'stɪkə(r)/ n adesivo m, etiqueta f (adesiva)

sticky /'stɪkɪ/ a (**-ier, -iest**) pegajoso; ‹label, tape› adesivo; ‹weather› abafado, mormacento

stiff /stɪf/ a (**-er, -est**) teso, hirto, rígido; ‹limb, joint› (hard) duro; (unbending) inflexível; ‹price› elevado; puxado ①; ‹penalty› severo; ‹drink› forte; ‹manner› reservado, formal; **be bored/scared ~** ① estar muito aborrecido/com muito medo, ① estar morto de aborrecimento/medo; **~ neck** torcicolo m. **~ness** n rigidez f

stiffen /'stɪfn/ vt/i (harden) endurecer; ‹limb, joint› emperrar

stifl|e /'staɪfl/ vt/i abafar, sufocar. **~ing** a sufocante

stigma /'stɪgmə/ n estigma m. **~tize** vt estigmatizar

stiletto /stɪ'letəʊ/ n (pl **-os**) estilete m. **~ heel** n salto m alto fino

still¹ /stɪl/ a imóvel, quieto; (quiet) sossegado; **~ life** natureza f morta ● n silêncio m, sossego m ● adv ainda; (nevertheless) apesar disso, apesar de tudo; **keep ~!** fique quieto!, não se mexa!

still² /stɪl/ n (apparatus) alambique m

stillborn /'stɪlbɔːn/ a natimorto, (P) nado-morto

stilted /'stɪltɪd/ a afetado, (P) afetado

stilts /stɪlts/ npl pernas fpl de pau, (P) andas fpl

stimul|ate /'stɪmjʊleɪt/ vt estimular. **~ant** n estimulante m. **~ating** a estimulante. **~ation** /-'leɪʃn/ n estimulação f

stimulus /'stɪmjʊləs/ n (pl **-li** /-laɪ/) (spur) estímulo m

sting /stɪŋ/ n picada f; ‹organ› ferrão m ● vt (pt **stung**) picar ● vi picar, arder

stingy /'stɪndʒɪ/ a (**-ier, -iest**) pão-duro m; sovina (**with** com)

stink /stɪŋk/ n fedor m, catinga f, mau cheiro m ● vi (pt **stank** or **stunk**, pp **stunk**) **~ (of)** cheirar (a), tresandar (a) ● vt **~ out** ‹room etc› empestar. **~ing** a malcheiroso; **~ing rich** ⊠ podre de rico ①

stint /stɪnt/ vi **~ on** poupar em, apertar em ● n (work) tarefa f, parte f, quinhão m

stipulat|e /'stɪpjʊleɪt/ vt estipular. **~ion** /-'leɪʃn/ n condição f, estipulação f

stir /stɜːr/ vt/i (pt **stirred**) (move) mexer(-se), mover(-se); (excite) excitar; ‹a liquid› mexer; **~ up** ‹trouble etc› provocar, fomentar ● n agitação f, rebuliço m

stirrup /'stɪrəp/ n estribo m

stitch /stɪtʃ/ n (in sewing) Med ponto m; (in knitting) malha f, ponto m; (pain) pontada f; **in ~es** ① às gargalhadas ① ● vt coser

stock /stɒk/ n Comm estoque m, (P) stock m, provisão f; Finance valores mpl, fundos mpl; (family) família f, estirpe f; Culin caldo m; (flower) goivo m; **in ~** em estoque; **out of ~** esgotado; **take ~** fig fazer um balanço; **~ market** Bolsa (de Valores) f; (de Valores) ● a (goods) corrente, comum; (hackneyed) estereotipado ● vt ‹shop etc› abastecer, fornecer; (sell) vender ● vi **~ up with** abastecer-se de. **~ cube** n cubo m de caldo; **~taking** n Comm inventário m

stockbroker /'stɒkbrəʊkə(r)/ n corretor m da Bolsa

stocking /'stɒkɪŋ/ n meia f

stockist /'stɒkɪst/ n armazenista m

stockpile /'stɒkpaɪl/ n reservas fpl ● vt acumular reservas de, estocar

stocky /'stɒkɪ/ a (**-ier, -iest**) atarracado

stoic /'stəʊɪk/ n estoico m

stoke /stəʊk/ vt ‹boiler, fire› alimentar, carregar

stole¹ /stəʊl/ n (garment) estola m

stole², stolen /stəʊl, stəʊlən/ ▶ **STEAL**

stomach /'stʌmək/ n estômago m; (abdomen) barriga f, ventre m ● vt (put up with) aturar. **~ ache** n dor f de estômago; (abdomen) dores fpl de barriga

ston|e /stəʊn/ n pedra f; (pebble) seixo m; (in fruit) caroço m; (weight) 6,348 kg; Med cálculo m, pedra f ● vt apedrejar; ‹fruit› tirar o caroço de; **within a ~'s throw (of)** muito perto (de). **~e-cold**

a gelado. **~e-deaf** totalmente surdo.
~ed a 🔤 (*drunk*) bebão m 🔤, (P)
bêbado m 🔤; 🔤 (*drugged*) drogado, (P)
pedrado 🔤. **~y** a pedregoso.

stood /stʊd/ ▶ STAND

stool /stuːl/ n banco m, tamborete m

stoop /stuːp/ vi (*bend*) curvar-se,
baixar-se; (*condescend*) condescender,
dignar-se; **~ to sth** rebaixar-se a (fazer)
algo ● n walk with a **~** andar curvado

stop /stɒp/ vt/i (*pt* stopped) parar;
(*prevent*) impedir (**from** de); ‹hole,
leak etc› tapar, vedar; ‹pain, noise etc›
parar; 🔤 (*stay*) ficar; **~ it!** acabe logo
com isso!, (P) para com isso! ● n (*of bus*)
parada f; (P) paragem f; (*full stop*) ponto
m final; **put a ~ to** pôr fim a. **~watch** n
cronômetro m, (P) cronómetro

stopgap /'stɒpɡæp/ n substituto m
provisório; tapa-buracos mpl 🔤 ● a
temporário

stoppage /'stɒpɪdʒ/ n parada f, (P)
paragem f; (*of work*) paralização f de
trabalho; (*of pay*) suspensão f

stopper /'stɒpə(r)/ n rolha f, tampa f

storage /'stɔːrɪdʒ/ n (*of goods, food etc*)
armazenagem f, armazenamento m; **in
cold ~** no frigorífico

store /stɔː(r)/ n reserva f, provisão f;
(*warehouse*) armazém m, entreposto m;
(*shop*) grande armazém m; Amer loja f;
(*in computer*) memória f; **be in ~** estar
guardado; **have in ~ for** reservar para;
set ~ by dar valor a ● vt (*for future*)
pôr de reserva, juntar, fazer provisão
de; (*in warehouse*) armazenar. **~room**
n depósito m, almortarifado m, (P)
armazém m

storey /'stɔːri/ n (*pl* -eys) andar m

stork /stɔːk/ n cegonha f

storm /stɔːm/ n tempestade f; **a ~
in a teacup** uma tempestade num
copo de água ● vt tomar de assalto
● vi enfurecer-se. **~y** a tempestuoso

story /'stɔːri/ n estória f, (P) história f; (*in
press*) artigo m, matéria f; Amer (*storey*)
andar m; 🔤 (*lie*) cascata f, (P) peta f

stout /staʊt/ a (-er, -est) (*fat*) gordo,
corpulento; (*strong, thick*) resistente,
sólido, grosso; (*brave*) resoluto ● n
cerveja f preta forte

stove /staʊv/ n (*for cooking*) fogão (de
cozinha) m

stow /staʊ/ vt **~ (away)** (*put away*)
guardar, arrumar; (*hide*) esconder
● vi **~ away** viajar clandestinamente

stowaway /'stəʊəweɪ/ n passageiro m
clandestino

straggle /'stræɡl/ vi (*lag behind*)
desgarrar-se, ficar para trás; (*spread*)
estender-se desordenadamente. **~r**
/-ə(r)/ n retardatário m

straight /streɪt/ a (-er, -est) direito;
(*tidy*) em ordem; (*frank*) franco; direto;
(*of hair*) liso; (*of drink*) puro; **keep a ~
face** não se desmanchar, manter um ar
sério ● adv (*in straight line*) reto; (*directly*)
direito; direto; diretamente; **~ ahead**
or **on** (sempre) em frente; **~ away**
logo, imediatamente; **go ~** viver
honestamente ● n linha f reta

straighten /'streɪtn/ vt endireitar;
(*tidy*) arrumar, pôr em ordem

straightforward /streɪt'fɔːwəd/ a
franco, sincero; (*easy*) simples

strain¹ /streɪn/ n (*breed*) raça f; (*streak*)
tendência f, veia f

strain² /streɪn/ vt (*rope*) esticar,
puxar; (*tire*) cansar; (*filter*) filtrar,
passar; ‹vegetables, tea etc› coar; Med
distender, torcer; fig forçar; pôr à prova
● vi esforçar-se ● n tensão f; fig (*effort*)
esforço m; Med distensão f; **~s** (*music*)
melodias fpl; **~ one's ears** apurar o
ouvido. **~ed** a forçado; ‹relations› tenso.
~er n coador m, (P) passador m

strait /streɪt/ n estreito m; **~s** estreito m;
fig apuros mpl, dificuldades fpl. **~-
laced** a severo, puritano

strand /strænd/ n (*thread*) fio m; (*lock of
hair*) mecha f, madeixa f

stranded /'strændɪd/ a (*person*)
em dificuldades, deixado para trás,
abandonado

strange /streɪndʒ/ a (-er, -est)
estranho. **~ly** adv estranhamente

stranger /'streɪndʒə(r)/ n estranho m,
desconhecido m

strangle /'stræŋɡl/ vt estrangular,
sufocar

strap /stræp/ n (*of leather etc*) correia
f; (*of dress*) alça f; (*of watch*) pulseira f
com correia ● vt (*pt* strapped) prender
com correia

strapping /'stræpɪŋ/ a robusto,
grande

strata ▶ STRATUM

strategic /strə'tiːdʒɪk/ a estratégico;
(*of weapons*) estratégico de longo
alcance

strategy /'strætədʒɪ/ n estratégia f

stratum /'strɑːtəm/ n (*pl* strata)
estrato m, camada f

S

straw /strɔː/ n palha f; (for drinking) canudo m, (P) palhinha f; **the last ~** a última gota f

strawberry /ˈstrɔːbrɪ/ n (fruit) morango m; (plant) morangueiro m

stray /streɪ/ vi (deviate from path etc) extraviar-se; (desencaminhar-se; afastar-se (**from** de); (lose one's way) perder-se; (wander) vagar, (P) vaguear, errar ● a perdido, extraviado; (isolated) isolado, raro, esporádico ● n animal m perdido or vadio

streak /striːk/ n risca f, lista f; (strain) veia f; (period) período m; **~ of lightning** relâmpago m ● vt listrar, riscar ● vi ir como um raio

stream /striːm/ n riacho m, córrego m, regato m; (current) corrente f; fig (flow) jorro m; torrente f; Schol nível m, grupo m ● vi correr; (of banner, hair) flutuar; (sweat) escorrer, pingar

streamer /ˈstriːmə(r)/ n (of paper) serpentina f, (flag) flâmula f, bandeirola f

streamline /ˈstriːmlaɪn/ vt dar forma aerodinâmica a; fig racionalizar. **~d** a ‹shape› aerodinâmico

street /striːt/ n rua f; **the man in the ~** o homem da rua, (P) o cidadão m comum; **~ lamp** poste m de iluminação

streetcar /ˈstriːtkɑː(r)/ n Amer bonde m, (P) (carro m) elétrico m

strength /streŋθ/ n força f; (of wall) solidez f; (of fabric etc) resistência f; **on the ~ of** à base de, em virtude de

strengthen /ˈstreŋθn/ vt fortificar, fortalecer, reforçar

strenuous /ˈstrenjʊəs/ a enérgico; (arduous) árduo; estrênuo, (P) estrénuo; (tiring) fatigante, esgotante

stress /stres/ n acento m; (pressure) pressão f, tensão f; Med stress m, (P) (e) stress(e) m ● vt acentuar, sublinhar; (sound) acentuar. **~ful** a estressante, (P) (e)stressant(e)

stretch /stretʃ/ vt (pull taut) esticar; ‹arm, leg, neck› estender, esticar; ‹clothes› alargar; ‹truth› forçar, torcer ● vi estender-se; (after sleep etc) espreguiçar-se; (of clothes) alargar-se; **~ one's legs** esticar as pernas ● n extensão f, trecho m; (period) período m; (of road) troço m; **at a ~** sem parar ● a (of fabric) com elasticidade

stretcher /ˈstretʃə(r)/ n maca f, padiola f

strew /struː/ vt (pt strewed, pp strewed, or strewn) (scatter) espalhar; (cover) juncar, cobrir

strict /strɪkt/ a (**-er, -est**) estrito, rigoroso. **~ly** adv estritamente; **~ly speaking** a rigor, (P) em rigor

stride /straɪd/ vi (pt strode, pp stridden) caminhar a passos largos ● n passada f; **make great ~s** fig fazer grandes progressos; **take sth in one's ~** fazer algo sem problemas

strident /ˈstraɪdnt/ a estridente

strife /straɪf/ n conflito m, dissensão f, luta f

strike /straɪk/ vt (pt struck) bater (em); ‹blow› dar; ‹match› riscar, acender; ‹gold etc› descobrir; (of clock) soar, dar, bater (horas); (of lightning) atingir ● vi fazer greve; (attack) atacar; **~ a bargain** fechar negócio; **~ off** or **out** riscar; **~ up** Mus começar a tocar; ‹friendship› travar ● n (of workers) greve f; Mil ataque m; (find) descoberta f; **on ~** em greve

striker /ˈstraɪkə(r)/ n grevista mf

striking /ˈstraɪkɪŋ/ a notável, impressionante; (attractive) atraente

string /strɪŋ/ n corda f, fio m; (of violin, racket etc) corda f; (of pearls) fio m; (of onions, garlic) réstia f; (of lies etc) série f; (row) fila f; **pull ~s** usar pistolão, (P) puxar os cordelinhos ● vt (pt strung) (thread) enfiar; **~ out** espaçar-se. **~ed** a ‹instrument› de cordas. **~y** a filamentoso, fibroso; ‹meat› com nervos

stringent /ˈstrɪndʒənt/ a rigoroso, estrito

strip[1] /strɪp/ vt/i (pt stripped) (undress) despir(-se); ‹machine› desmontar; (deprive) despojar, privar. **~per** n artista mf de strip-tease; (solvent) removedor m, (P) decapante m

strip[2] /strɪp/ n tira f; (of land) faixa f; **comic ~** história f em quadrinhos, (P) banda f desenhada; **~ light** tubo m de luz fluorescente

stripe /straɪp/ n risca f, lista f, barra f. **~d** a listrado, com listras

strive /straɪv/ vi (pt strove, pp striven) esforçar-se (**to** por)

strode /strəʊd/ ▷ STRIDE

stroke[1] /strəʊk/ n golpe m; (of pen) penada f, (P) traço m; (in swimming) braçada f; (in rowing) remada f; Med ataque m, congestão f; **~ of genius** rasgo m de genialidade or de génio; **~ of luck** golpe m de sorte

stroke[2] /strəʊk/ vt (with hand) acariciar, fazer festas em

stroll /strəʊl/ vi passear, dar uma volta; **~ in/etc** entrar/etc tranquilamente ● n

s

volta f, (P) passeio m

strong /strɒŋ/ a (**-er, -est**) forte; ‹shoes, fabric etc› resistente; **be a hundred**/etc~ ser em número de cem/ etc; **~ language** linguagem f grosseira, palavrões mpl. **~room** n casa-forte f. **~ly** adv (greatly) fortemente, grandemente; (with energy) com força; (deeply) profundamente

stronghold /'strɒŋhəʊld/ n fortaleza f; fig baluarte m; bastião m

strove /strəʊv/ ▶ STRIVE

struck /strʌk/ ▶ STRIKE ● a ~ **on** 🅶 apaixonado por, (P) apanhado por 🅶

structur|e /'strʌktʃə(r)/ n estrutura f; (of building etc) edifício m, construção f. **~al** a estrutural, de estrutura, de construção

struggle /'strʌɡl/ vi (to get free) debater-se; (contend) lutar; (strive) esforçar-se (**to, for** por); ~ **to one's feet** levantar-se a custo ● n luta f; (effort) esforço m; **have a ~ to** ter dificuldade em

strum /strʌm/ vt (pt **strummed**) ‹banjo etc› dedilhar

strung /strʌŋ/ ▶ STRING

strut /strʌt/ n (support) suporte m, escora f ● vi (pt **strutted**) (walk) pavonear-se

stub /stʌb/ n (of pencil, cigarette) ponta f; (of tree) cepo m, toco m; (counterfoil) talão m, canhoto m ● vt (pt **stubbed**) ~ **one's toe** dar uma topada; ~ **out** esmagar

stubble /'stʌbl/ n (on chin) barba f por fazer; (of crop) restolho m

stubborn /'stʌbən/ a teimoso, obstinado. **~ness** n teimosia f, obstinação f

stubby /'stʌbɪ/ a (**-ier, -iest**) ‹finger› curto e grosso; ‹person› atarracado

stuck /stʌk/ ▶ STICK² ● a emperrado. **~-up** a 🆒 (snobbish) convencido; esnobe, (P) snob

stud¹ /stʌd/ n tacha f; (for collar) botão m de colarinho ● vt (pt **studded**) enfeitar com tachas; **~ded with** salpicado de

stud² /stʌd/ n (horses) haras m, (P) coudelaria. **~ (farm)** n coudelaria f; **~ (horse)** n garanhão m

student /'stjuːdnt/ n Univ estudante mf, aluno m; Schol aluno m ● a ‹life, residence› universitário

studio /'stjuːdɪəʊ/ n (pl **-os**) estúdio m; **~ flat** estúdio m

studious /'stjuːdɪəs/ a ‹person› estudioso; (deliberate) estudado

study /'stʌdɪ/ n estudo m; (office) escritório m ● vt/i estudar

stuff /stʌf/ n substância f, matéria f; 🆒 (things) coisa(s) f ● vt encher; ‹animal› empalhar; (cram) apinhar, encher ao máximo; Culin rechear; (block up) entupir; (put) enfiar, meter. **~ing** n enchimento m; Culin recheio m

stuffy /'stʌfɪ/ a (**-ier, -iest**) abafado, mal arejado; (dull) enfadonho

stumble /'stʌmbl/ vi tropeçar; **~e across** or **on** dar com, encontrar por acaso, topar com. **~ing block** n obstáculo m

stump /stʌmp/ n (of tree) cepo m, toco m; (of limb) coto m; (of pencil, cigar) ponta f

stumped /stʌmpt/ a 🆒 (baffled) atrapalhado; perplexo

stun /stʌn/ vt (pt **stunned**) aturdir, estontear

stung /stʌŋ/ ▶ STING

stunk /stʌŋk/ ▶ STINK

stunning /'stʌnɪŋ/ a atordoador; 🆒 (delightful) fantástico; sensacional

stunt¹ /stʌnt/ vt ‹growth› atrofiar. **~ed** a atrofiado

stunt² /stʌnt/ n (feat) façanha f, proeza f; (trick) truque m; Aviat acrobacia f aérea. **~ man** n dublê m, (P) duplo m

stupefy /'stjuːpɪfaɪ/ vt estupefazer, (P) estupeficar, espantar

stupendous /stjuː'pendəs/ a estupendo, assombroso, prodigioso

stupid /'stjuːpɪd/ a estúpido, obtuso. **~ity** /-'pɪdətɪ/ n estupidez f. **~ly** adv estupidamente

stupor /'stjuːpə(r)/ n estupor m, torpor m

sturdy /'stɜːdɪ/ a (**-ier, -iest**) robusto, vigoroso, forte

stutter /'stʌtə(r)/ vi gaguejar ● n gagueira f, (P) gaguez f

sty /staɪ/ n (pigsty) pocilga f, chiqueiro m

style /staɪl/ n estilo m; (fashion) moda f; (kind) gênero m, (P) género m; tipo m; (pattern) feitio m, modelo m; **in ~e** (live) em grande estilo; (do things) com classe ● vt (design) desenhar, criar; **~e sb's hair** fazer um penteado em or (P) a alguém. **~ist** n (of hair) cabeleireiro m

stylish /'staɪlɪʃ/ a elegante, na moda

suave /swɑːv/ a polido, de fala mansa, (P) melífluo

subconscious /sʌb'kɒnʃəs/ a & n subconsciente m

subcontract /sʌbkən'trækt/ vt dar de subempreitada, (P) subcontratar

subdivide /sʌbdɪ'vaɪd/ vt subdividir

subdue /səb'djuː/ vt ‹enemy, feeling› dominar, subjugar; ‹sound, voice› abrandar. ~d a ‹weak› submisso; ‹quiet› recolhido; ‹light› velado

subject[1] /'sʌbdʒɪkt/ a ‹state etc› dominado; ~ to sujeito a ● n sujeito m; Schol, Univ disciplina f, matéria f; ‹citizen› súdito m, (P) súbdito m. ~ matter n conteúdo m, tema m, assunto m

subject[2] /səb'dʒekt/ vt submeter

subjective /sʌb'dʒektɪv/ a subjetivo

subjunctive /səb'dʒʌŋktɪv/ a & n subjuntivo m, (P) conjuntivo m

sublime /sə'blaɪm/ a sublime

submarine /sʌbmə'riːn/ n submarino m

submerge /səb'mɜːdʒ/ vt submergir, mergulhar ● vi submergir, mergulhar

submissive /səb'mɪsɪv/ a submisso

submit /səb'mɪt/ vt/i (pt submitted) submeter(-se) (to a); Jur ‹argue› alegar. ~ssion /-'mɪʃn/ n submissão f

subnormal /sʌb'nɔːml/ a subnormal; ‹temperature› abaixo do normal

subordinate[1] /sə'bɔːdɪnət/ a subordinado, subalterno; Gram subordinado ● n subordinado m, subalterno m

subordinate[2] /sə'bɔːdɪneɪt/ vt subordinar (to a)

subscribe /səb'skraɪb/ vt/i subscrever; contribuir (to para); ~ to ‹theory, opinion› subscrever, aceitar; ‹newspaper› assinar. ~r /-ə(r)/ n subscritor m, assinante m

subscription /səb'skrɪpʃn/ n subscrição f; (to newspaper) assinatura f

subsequent /'sʌbsɪkwənt/ a subsequente, posterior. ~ly adv subsequentemente, a seguir, posteriormente

subservient /səb'sɜːvɪənt/ a servil, subserviente

subside /səb'saɪd/ vi ‹flood, noise etc› baixar; ‹land› ceder, afundar; ‹wind, storm, excitement› abrandar, acalmar. ~nce /-əns/ n (of land) afundamento m

subsidiary /səb'sɪdɪərɪ/ a subsidiário ● n Comm filial f, sucursal f

subsidy /'sʌbsədɪ/ n subsídio m, subvenção f. ~ize /-ɪdaɪz/ vt subsidiar, subvencionar

subsist /səb'sɪst/ vi subsistir; ~ on viver de. ~ence n subsistência f; ~ence allowance ajudas fpl de custo

substance /'sʌbstəns/ n substância f

substandard /sʌb'stændəd/ a de qualidade inferior

substantial /səb'stænʃl/ a substancial. ~ly adv substancialmente

substitut|e /'sʌbstɪtjuːt/ n (person) substituto m; suplente mf (for de); (thing) substituto m (for de) ● vt substituir (for por). ~ion /-'tjuːʃn/ n substituição f

subtitle /'sʌbtaɪtl/ n subtítulo m, (P) legenda f

subtle /'sʌtl/ a (-er, -est) sutil, (P) subtil. ~ty n sutileza f, (P) subtileza f

subtotal /'sʌbtəʊtl/ n soma f parcial

subtract /səb'trækt/ vt subtrair, diminuir. ~ion /-kʃn/ n subtração f, diminuição f

suburb /'sʌbɜːb/ n subúrbio m, arredores mpl. ~an /sə'bɜːbən/ a dos subúrbios, suburbano. ~ia /sə'bɜːbɪə/ n pej os arredores, os subúrbios

subvert /səb'vɜːt/ vt subverter. ~sion /-ʃn/ n subversão f. ~sive /-sɪv/ a subversivo

subway /'sʌbweɪ/ n passagem f subterrânea; Amer (underground) metropolitano m, (P) metro m

succeed /sək'siːd/ vi ser bem-sucedido, ter êxito; ~ in doing sth conseguir fazer algo ● vt ‹follow› suceder a. ~ing a seguinte, sucessivo

success /sək'ses/ n sucesso m, êxito m

succession /sək'seʃn/ n sucessão f; (series) série f; in ~ seguidos, consecutivos

successive /sək'sesɪv/ a sucessivo, consecutivo

successor /sək'sesə(r)/ n sucessor m

succinct /sək'sɪŋkt/ a sucinto

succulent /'sʌkjʊlənt/ a suculento

succumb /sə'kʌm/ vi sucumbir

---

such /sʌtʃ/ ● a

····➤ (of that kind) tal, semelhante, assim; ~ a book um tal livro; ~ a person uma tal pessoa; ~ people essas pessoas; there is no ~ thing uma coisa assim não existe

····➤ (so much) tanto; I've got ~ a headache! tenho uma dor de cabeça tão grande!; it was ~ fun! foi tão divertido!

● *adv*

····▸ tão; **~ a big house** uma casa tão grande; **he has ~ lovely blue eyes** ele tem uns olhos azuis tão bonitos; **~ a long time** tanto tempo ····▸ (*in phrases*) **as ~: the new job is not a promotion as ~** o novo emprego não é bem uma promoção; **there is no garden as ~** não existe um jardim no real sentido da palavra; **in ~ a way that** de tal maneira que; **~ as** tal como; **wild flowers ~ as primroses are becoming rare** as flores selvagens, tais como as prímulas, estão ficando raras; **~ as?** por exemplo?; **~ is: ~ is life** assim é a vida

such-and-such a on **~and-~ day in July** em tais e tais dias de julho

suck /sʌk/ *vt* chupar; ‹*breast*› mamar; **~ in** or **up** (*absorb*) absorver, aspirar; (*engulf*) tragar; **~ up to** puxar o saco a 🗌; **~ one's thumb** chuchar no dedo. **~er** *n* 🖾 (*greenhorn*) trouxa *mf* 🗌; *Bot* broto *m*

suction /sʌkʃn/ *n* sucção *f*

sudden /sʌdn/ *a* súbito, repentino; **all of a ~** de repente, de súbito. **~ly** *adv* subitamente, repentinamente

sue /suː/ *vt* (*pres p* suing) processar

suede /sweɪd/ *n* camurça *f*

suet /suːɪt/ *n* sebo *m*

suffer /sʌfə(r)/ *vt/i* sofrer; (*tolerate*) tolerar, suportar. **~er** *n* sofredor *m*, o que sofre; (*patient*) doente *mf*, vítima *f*. **~ing** *n* sofrimento *m*

suffice /səfaɪs/ *vi* bastar, chegar, ser suficiente

sufficien|t /səfɪʃnt/ *a* suficiente, bastante

suffocat|e /sʌfəkeɪt/ *vt/i* sufocar. **~ion** /-keɪʃn/ *n* sufocação *f*, asfixia *f*

sugar /ʃʊɡə(r)/ *n* açúcar *m*; **brown ~** açúcar *m* preto, (*P*) açúcar *m* amarelo ● *vt* adoçar, pôr açúcar em. **~ lump** *n* torrão *m* de açúcar, (*P*) quadradinho *m* de açúcar. **~y** *a* açucarado; *fig* (*too sweet*) delico-doce, (*P*) adocicado

suggest /səˈdʒest/ *vt* sugerir. **~ion** /-tʃn/ *n* sugestão *f*. **~ive** *a* sugestivo; (*improper*) brejeiro, picante; **be ~ive of** sugerir, fazer lembrar

suicid|e /suːɪsaɪd/ *n* suicídio *m*; **commit ~e** suicidar-se. **~ attack** *n* ataque *m* suicida; **~ bomber** *n* terrorista *mf* suicida, (*P*) bombista *mf* suicida. **~al** /-saɪdl/ *a* suicida

suit /suːt/ *n* terno *m*, (*P*) fato *m*; (*woman's*) costume *m*, (*P*) fato *m* de saia e casaco; *Cards* naipe *m*; **follow ~** *fig* seguir o exemplo ● *vt* convir a; (*of garment, style*) ficar bem em or (*P*) a; (*adapt*) adaptar. **~able** *a* conveniente; apropriado (**for** para). **~ably** *adv* convenientemente. **~ed a be ~ed to** ser feito para, servir para; **be well ~ed** (*matched*) combinar-se bem; (*of people*) ser o ideal

suitcase /suːtkeɪs/ *n* mala *f* (de viagem)

suite /swiːt/ *n* (*of rooms; mus*) suíte *f*, (*P*) suite *f*; (*of furniture*) mobília *f*

suitor /suːtə(r)/ *n* pretendente *m*

sulk /sʌlk/ *vi* amuar, ficar emburrado. **~y** *a* amuado; emburrado 🗌

sullen /sʌlən/ *a* carrancudo

sulphur /sʌlfə(r)/ *n* enxofre *m*

sultana /sʌlˈtɑːnə/ *n* (*fruit*) passa *f* branca, (*P*) sultana *f*

sultry /sʌltrɪ/ *a* (**-ier, -iest**) abafado, opressivo; *fig* sensual

sum /sʌm/ *n* soma *f*; (*amount of money*) soma *f*, quantia *f*, importância *f*; (*in arithmetic*) conta *f* ● *vt* (*pt* summed) somar; **~ up** recapitular, resumir; (*assess*) avaliar, medir

summar|y /sʌmərɪ/ *n* sumário *m*, resumo *m* ● *a* sumário. **~ize** *vt* resumir

summer /sʌmə(r)/ *n* verão *m*, estio *m* ● *a* de verão, veranil. **~ time** *n* verão *m*, época *f* de verão. **~y** *a* estival, próprio de verão, veranil

> ┌─────────────────────────────┐
> **summer camp** Nos Estados   *i*
> Unidos, é o acampamento de
> verão, considerado um aspecto
> importante na vida de muitas crianças.
> Praticam-se atividades ao ar livre em
> ambiente natural, como natação,
> montanhismo, sobrevivência ao ar livre.
> Nesses acampamentos, milhares de
> estudantes trabalham como
> supervisores.

summit /sʌmɪt/ *n* cume *m*, cimo *m*; **~ conference** *Pol* conferência *f* de cúpula, (*P*) reunião *f* de) cimeira

summon /sʌmən/ *vt* mandar chamar; (*to meeting*) convocar; **~ up** ‹*strength, courage etc*› chamar a si, fazer apelo a

summons /sʌmənz/ *n* *Jur* citação *f*, intimação *f* ● *vt* citar, intimar

S

sumptuous /'sʌmptʃʊəs/ a suntuoso, (P) sumptuoso, luxuoso

sun /sʌn/ n sol m ● vt (pt sunned) ~ o.s. aquecer-se ao sol. ~glasses npl óculos mpl de sol. ~roof n teto m solar; ~tan n bronzeado m. ~tanned a bronzeado. ~tan oil n óleo m de bronzear

sunbathe /'sʌnbeɪð/ vi tomar um banho de sol

sunburn /'sʌnbɜːn/ n queimadura f solar. ~t a queimado pelo sol

Sunday /'sʌndɪ/ n domingo m; ~ school catecismo m, (P) catequese f

sundr|y /'sʌndrɪ/ a vários, diversos; all and ~y todo o mundo, todo e cada um. ~ies npl artigos mpl diversos

sunflower /'sʌnflaʊə(r)/ n girassol m

sung /sʌŋ/ ▶ SING

sunk /sʌŋk/ ▶ SINK

sunken /'sʌŋkən/ a ‹ship etc› afundado; ‹eyes› fundo

sunlight /'sʌnlaɪt/ n luz f do sol, sol m

sunny /'sʌnɪ/ a (-ier, -iest) ‹room, day etc› ensolarado

sunrise /'sʌnraɪz/ n nascer m do sol

sunset /'sʌnset/ n pôr m do sol

sunshade /'sʌnʃeɪd/ n (awning) toldo m; (parasol) para-sol m, (P) guarda-sol m

sunshine /'sʌnʃaɪn/ n sol m, luz f do sol

sunstroke /'sʌnstrəʊk/ n Med insolação f

super /'suːpə(r)/ a 🔢 (excellent) formidável

superb /suːˈpɜːb/ a soberbo, esplêndido

superficial /suːpəˈfɪʃl/ a superficial

superfluous /suˈpɜːfluəs/ a supérfluo

superhuman /suːpəˈhjuːmən/ a sobre-humano

superimpose /suːpərɪmˈpəʊz/ vt sobrepor (on a)

superintendent /suːpərɪnˈtendənt/ n superintendente m; (of police) comissário m, chefe m de polícia

superior /suːˈpɪərɪə(r)/ a & n superior m. ~ity /-ˈɒrətɪ/ n superioridade f

superlative /suːˈpɜːlətɪv/ a supremo, superlativo ● n Gram superlativo m

supermarket /'suːpəmɑːkɪt/ n supermercado m

supernatural /suːpəˈnætʃrəl/ a sobrenatural

superpower /'suːpəpaʊə(r)/ n superpotência f

supersede /suːpəˈsiːd/ vt suplantar, substituir

superstiti|on /suːpəˈstɪʃn/ n superstição f. ~ous a /-ˈstɪʃəs/ supersticioso

superstore /'suːpəstɔː(r)/ n hipermercado m

supervis|e /'suːpəvaɪz/ vt supervisar, fiscalizar, supervisionar. ~ion /-ˈvɪʒn/ n supervisão f. ~or n supervisor m; (shop) chefe mf de seção or (P) secção; (firm) chefe mf de serviço

supper /'sʌpə(r)/ n jantar m; (late at night) ceia f

supple /'sʌpl/ a flexível, maleável

supplement[1] /'sʌplɪmənt/ n suplemento m. ~ary /-'mentrɪ/ a suplementar

supplement[2] /'sʌplɪment/ vt suplementar

supplier /səˈplaɪə(r)/ n fornecedor m

suppl|y /səˈplaɪ/ vt suprir, prover; Comm fornecer, abastecer ● n provisão f; (of goods, gas etc) fornecimento m, abastecimento m ● a ‹teacher› substituto; ~ies (food) víveres mpl; Mil suprimentos mpl; ~y and demand oferta e procura

support /səˈpɔːt/ vt (hold up, endure) suportar, aguentar; (provide for) sustentar, suster; (back) apoiar, patrocinar; Sport torcer por ● n apoio m; Techn suporte m. ~er n partidário m; Sport torcedor m, (P) adepto m

suppos|e /səˈpəʊz/ vt/i supor; ~e that supondo que, na hipótese de que; he's ~ed to do ele deve fazer; (believed to) consta que ele faz. ~ed a suposto. ~edly /-ɪdlɪ/ adv segundo dizem; (probably) supostamente, em princípio. ~ing conj se. ~ition /sʌpəˈzɪʃn/ n suposição f

suppress /səˈpres/ vt (put an end to) suprimir; (restrain) conter, reprimir; (stifle) abafar, sufocar; Psych recalcar. ~ion /-ʃn/ n supressão f; (restraint) repressão f; Psych recalque m, (P) recalcamento m

suprem|e /suːˈpriːm/ a supremo. ~acy /-eməsɪ/ n supremacia f

surcharge /'sɜːtʃɑːdʒ/ n sobretaxa f; (on stamp) sobrecarga f

sure /ʃʊə(r)/ a (-er, -est) seguro, certo ● adv 🔢 (certainly) deveras; não há dúvida que; de certeza; be ~ about or of ter a certeza de; be ~ to (not fail) não deixar de; he is ~ to find out ele vai descobrir com certeza; **make ~** assegurar. **~ly** adv com certeza, certamente

surf /sɜːf/ n (waves) ressaca f, rebentação f. **~er** n surfista mf. **~ing** n surfe m, (P) surf m, jacaré-na-praia m

surface /'sɜːfɪs/ n superfície f ● a superficial ● vt/i revestir; (rise, become known) emergir; **~ mail** via f marítima

surfboard /'sɜːfbɔːd/ n prancha f de surfe, (P) surf

surge /sɜːdʒ/ vi ‹waves› ondular, encapelar-se; (move forward) avançar ● n (wave) onda f, vaga f; (motion) arremetida f

surgeon /'sɜːdʒən/ n cirurgião m

surg|ery /'sɜːdʒərɪ/ n cirurgia f; (office) consultório m; (session) consulta f; (consulting hours) horas fpl de consulta. **~ical** a cirúrgico

surly /'sɜːlɪ/ a (-ier, -iest) carrancudo, trombudo

surmise /sə'maɪz/ vt imaginar, supor, calcular ● n conjetura f; hipótese f

surmount /sə'maʊnt/ vt sobrepujar, vencer, (P) superar

surname /'sɜːneɪm/ n sobrenome m, (P) apelido m

surpass /sə'pɑːs/ vt superar, ultrapassar, exceder

surplus /'sɜːpləs/ n excedente m, excesso m; Finance saldo m positivo ● a excedente, em excesso

surpris|e /sə'praɪz/ n surpresa f ● vt surpreender. **~ed** a surpreendido; admirado (at com). **~ing** a surpreendente. **~ingly** adv surpreendentemente

surrender /sə'rendə(r)/ vi render-se ● vt (hand over) Mil entregar ● n Mil rendição f; (of rights) renúncia f

surrogate /'sʌrəgeɪt/ n delegado m; **~ mother** mãe f de aluguel, (P) aluguer

surround /sə'raʊnd/ vt rodear, cercar; Mil etc cercar. **~ing** a circundante, vizinho. **~ings** npl arredores mpl, (P) redondezas fpl; (setting) meio m, ambiente m

surveillance /sɜː'veɪləns/ n vigilância f

survey[1] /sə'veɪ/ vt ‹landscape etc› observar; (review) passar em revista; (inquire about) pesquisar; ‹land› fazer o levantamento de; ‹building› vistoriar; inspecionar. **~or** n (of buildings) fiscal m; (of land) agrimensor m

survey[2] /'sɜːveɪ/ n (inspection) vistoria f; inspeção f; (general view) panorâmica f; (inquiry) pesquisa f

survival /sə'vaɪvl/ n sobrevivência f; (relic) relíquia f, vestígio m

surviv|e /sə'vaɪv/ vt/i sobreviver (a). **~or** n sobrevivente mf

suspect[1] /sə'spekt/ vt suspeitar; (doubt, distrust) desconfiar de, suspeitar de

suspect[2] /'sʌspekt/ a & n suspeito m

suspen|d /sə'spend/ vt (hang, stop) suspender; (from duty etc) suspender; **~ded sentence** suspensão f de pena. **~sion** n suspensão f; **~sion bridge** ponte f suspensa or pênsil

suspender /sə'spendə(r)/ n (presilha f de) liga f; **~s** Amer (braces) suspensórios mpl. **~ belt** n cinta-liga f, (P) cinta f de ligas, (P) cinto m de ligas

suspense /sə'spens/ n ansiedade f, incerteza f; (in book etc) suspense m, tensão f

suspicion /sə'spɪʃn/ n suspeita f; (distrust) desconfiança f; (trace) vestígio m, (P) traço m

suspicious /səs'pɪʃəs/ a desconfiado; (causing suspicion) suspeito; **be ~ of** desconfiar de

sustain /sə'steɪn/ vt (support) suster, sustentar; (suffer) sofrer; (keep up) sustentar; Jur (uphold) sancionar; ‹interest, effort› manter; **~ed effort** esforço m contínuo

sustenance /'sʌstɪnəns/ n (food) alimento m, sustento m

SUV abbr (= sport utility vehicle) carro m esporte, (P) veículo m utilitário desportivo

swagger /'swægə(r)/ vi pavonear-se, andar com arrogância

swallow[1] /'swɒləʊ/ vt/i engolir; **~ up** (absorb, engulf) devorar, tragar

swallow[2] /'swɒləʊ/ n (bird) andorinha f

swam /swæm/ ▶ SWIM

swamp /swɒmp/ n pântano m, brejo m ● vt (flood, overwhelm) inundar, submergir

swan /swɒn/ n cisne m

swank /swæŋk/ vi 🄸 (show off) gabar-se; mostrar-se 🄸

swap /swɒp/ vt/i (pt swapped) 🄸 trocar (for por) ● n 🄸 troca f

S

swarm /swɔːm/ n (of insects, people) enxame m ● vi formigar; ~ **into** or **round** invadir

swarthy /'swɔːðɪ/ a (**-ier, -iest**) moreno, trigueiro

swat /swɒt/ vt (pt **swatted**) ‹fly etc› esmagar, esborrachar

sway /sweɪ/ vt/i oscilar, balançar(-se); (influence) mover, influenciar ● n oscilação f, balanceio m; (rule) domínio m, poder m

swear /sweə(r)/ vt/i (pt **swore**, pp **sworn**) jurar; (curse) praguejar; rogar pragas (**at/a** contra); ~ **by** jurar por; [I] (recommend) ter grande fé em. ~ **word** n palavrão m

sweat /swet/ n suor m ● vi suar. ~**y** a suado

sweater /'swetə(r)/ n suéter m, (P) camisola f

sweatshirt /'swetʃɜːt/ n suéter m or (P) camisola f de malha or algodão

Swed|e /swiːd/ n sueco m. ~**en** n Suécia f. ~**ish** a & n sueco m

sweep /swiːp/ vt/i (pt **swept**) varrer; (go majestically) avançar majestosamente; (carry away) arrastar; ‹chimney› limpar ● n (with broom) varredela f; (curve) curva f; (movement) gesto m largo; (chimney-)~ limpa-chaminés m. ~**ing** a ‹gesture› largo; ‹action› de grande alcance; ~**ing statement** generalização f fácil

sweet /swiːt/ a (**-er, -est**) doce; [I] (charming) doce; gracinha, (P) encanto; [I] (pleasant) agradável ● n doce m; ~ **corn** milho m; ~ **pea** ervilha-de-cheiro f; ~ **shop** confeitaria f; **have a** ~ **tooth** gostar de doce, (P) ser guloso. ~**ness** n doçura f

sweeten /'swiːtn/ vt adoçar; fig (mitigate) suavizar. ~**er** n (for tea, coffee) adoçante (artificial) m; [I] (bribe) agrado m, (P) suborno m

sweetheart /'swiːthɑːt/ n namorado m, namorada f; (term of endearment) querido m, querida f, amor m

swell /swel/ vt/i (pt **swelled**, pp **swollen**, or **swelled**) (expand) inchar; (increase) aumentar ● n (of sea) ondulação f ● a [I] (excellent) excelente; [I] (smart) chique. ~**ing** n Med inchação f, inchaço m

swelter /'sweltə(r)/ vi fazer um calor abrasador; (person) abafar (com calor)

swept /swept/ ▶ SWEEP

swerve /swɜːv/ vi desviar-se, dar uma guinada

swift /swɪft/ a (**-er,, -est**) rápido, veloz

swig /swɪg/ vt (pt **swigged**) [I] (drink) emborcar [I]; beber em longos tragos ● n [I] trago m; gole m

swim /swɪm/ vi (pt **swam**, pp **swum**, pres p **swimming**) nadar; ‹room, head› rodar ● vt atravessar a nado; (distance) nadar ● n banho m. ~**mer** n nadador m. ~**ming** n natação f. ~**ming bath**, ~ming **pool** ns piscina f; ~**ming cap** n touca f de banho or (P) de natação; ~**ming costume**, ~**suit** ns maiô m, (P) fato m de banho; ~**ming trunks** npl calção m or (P) calções mpl de banho

swindle /'swɪndl/ vt trapacear, fraudar, (P) vigarizar ● n vigarice f. ~**r** /-ə(r)/ n vigarista mf

swine /swaɪn/ npl (pigs) porcos mpl ● n (pl invar) [I] (person) animal m; canalha m [I]. ~ **flu** n gripe f suína

swing /swɪŋ/ vt/i (pt **swung**) balançar(-se); (turn round) girar ● n (seat) balanço m; (of opinion) reviravolta f; Mus swing m; (rhythm) ritmo m; **in full** ~ no máximo, em plena atividade; ~ **round** (of person) virar-se

swipe /swaɪp/ vt [I] (hit) bater em; dar uma pancada em; [I] (steal) afanar [I]; roubar ● n [I] (hit) pancada f; ~ **card** cartão m magnético

swirl /swɜːl/ vi rodopiar, redemoinhar ● n turbilhão m, redemoinho m

swish /swɪʃ/ vt/i sibilar, zunir, (fazer) cortar o ar; (with brushing sound) roçar ● a [I] chique, fino

Swiss /swɪs/ a & n suíço m

switch /swɪtʃ/ n interruptor m; (change) mudança f ● vt (transfer) transferir; (exchange) trocar ● vi desviar-se; ~ **off** desligar

switchboard /'swɪtʃbɔːd/ n (telephone) PBX m, mesa f telefônica or (P) telefónica

Switzerland /'swɪtsələnd/ n Suíça f

swivel /'swɪvl/ vt/i (pt **swivelled**) (fazer) girar; ~ **chair** cadeira f giratória

swollen /'swəʊlən/ ▶ SWELL a inchado

swoop /swuːp/ vi ‹bird› lançar-se; cair (**down on** sobre); ‹police› dar uma batida policial, (P) fazer uma rusga

sword /sɔːd/ n espada f

swore /swɔː(r)/ ▶ SWEAR

sworn /swɔːn/ ▶ SWEAR a ‹enemy› jurado, declarado; ‹ally› fiel

swot /swɒt/ vt/i (pt **swotted**) [I] (study) estudar muito, (P) marrar ⊠ ● n [I] estudante *m* muito aplicado, (*P*) marrão *m* ☒

swum /swʌm/ ▶ **SWIM**

swung /swʌŋ/ ▶ **SWING**

syllable /ˈsɪləbl/ *n* sílaba *f*

syllabus /ˈsɪləbəs/ *n* (*pl* **-uses**) programa *m*

symbol /ˈsɪmbl/ *n* símbolo *m*. **~ic(al)** /-ˈbɒlɪk(l)/ *a* simbólico. **~ism** *n* simbolismo *m*

symbolize /ˈsɪmbəlaɪz/ *vt* simbolizar

symmetr|y /ˈsɪmətrɪ/ *n* simetria *f*. **~ical** /sɪˈmetrɪkl/ *a* simétrico

sympathize /ˈsɪmpəθaɪz/ *vi* **~ with** ter pena de, condoer-se de; *fig* compartilhar os sentimentos de. **~r** *n* simpatizante *mf*

sympath|y /ˈsɪmpəθɪ/ *n* (*pity*) pena *f*, compaixão *f*; (*solidarity*) solidariedade *f*; (*condolences*) pêsames *mpl*, condolências *fpl*; **be in ~y with** estar de acordo com. **~etic** /-ˈθetɪk/ *a* compreensivo, simpático; (*likeable*) simpático; (*showing pity*) compassivo

symphon|y /ˈsɪmfənɪ/ *n* sinfonia *f* ● *a* sinfônico, (*P*) sinfónico

symptom /ˈsɪmptəm/ *n* sintoma *m*

synagogue /ˈsɪnəgɒg/ *n* sinagoga *f*

synchronize /ˈsɪŋkrənaɪz/ *vt* sincronizar

syndrome /ˈsɪndrəʊm/ *n* *Med* síndrome *f*, (*P*) síndroma *f*

synonym /ˈsɪnənɪm/ *n* sinônimo *m*, (*P*) sinónimo *m*. **~ous** /sɪˈnɒnɪməs/ *a* sinônimo; (*P*) sinónimo (**with** de)

synopsis /sɪˈnɒpsɪs/ *n* (*pl* **-opses** /-siːz/) sinopse *f*, resumo *m*

synthesis /ˈsɪnθəsɪs/ *n* (*pl* **-theses** /-siːz/) síntese *f*

synthetic /sɪnˈθetɪk/ *a* sintético

Syria /ˈsɪrɪə/ *n* Síria *f*

syringe /sɪˈrɪndʒ/ *n* seringa *f* ● *vt* seringar, injetar

syrup /ˈsɪrəp/ *n* (*liquid*) xarope *m*; (*treacle*) calda *f* de açúcar. **~y** *a* *fig* melado; enjoativo

system /ˈsɪstəm/ *n* sistema *m*; (*body*) organismo *m*; (*order*) método *m*. **~atic** /sɪstəˈmætɪk/ *a* sistemático

Tt

tab /tæb/ *n* (*flap*) lingueta *f*; (*for fastening, hanging*) aba *f*; (*label*) etiqueta *f*; (*loop*) argola *f*; *Amer* 🏛 (*bill*) conta *f*; **keep ~s on** 🏛 vigiar

table /ˈteɪbl/ *n* mesa *f*; (*list*) tabela *f*, lista *f*; **at ~** à mesa; **lay** or **set the ~** pôr a mesa; **turn the ~s** inverter as posições; **~ tennis** pingue-pongue *m*; **~ of contents** índice *m* (das matérias) ● *vt* (*submit*) apresentar; (*postpone*) adiar. **~cloth** *n* toalha de mesa *f*

tablespoon /ˈteɪblspuːn/ *n* colher *f* grande de sopa

tablet /ˈtæblɪt/ *n* (*of stone*) lápide *f*, placa *f*; (*drug*) comprimido *m*

tabloid /ˈtæblɔɪd/ *n* tablóide *m*; **~ journalism** *pej* jornalismo *m* sensacionalista, imprensa *f* marrom

taboo /təˈbuː/ *n* & *a* tabu *m*

taciturn /ˈtæsɪtɜːn/ *a* taciturno

tack /tæk/ *n* (*nail*) tacha *f*; (*stitch*) ponto *m* de alinhavo; *Naut* amura *f*; *fig* (*course of action*) rumo *m* ● *vt* (*nail*) pregar com tachas; (*stitch*) alinhavar ● *vi* *Naut* bordejar; **~ on** (*add*) acrescentar, juntar

tackle /ˈtækl/ *n* equipamento *m*, apetrechos *mpl*; *Sport* placagem *f* ● *vt* ‹*problem etc*› atacar; *Sport* placar; ‹*a thief etc*› agarrar-se a

tacky /ˈtækɪ/ *a* (**-ier, -iest**) peganhento, pegajoso

tact /tækt/ *n* tato *m*. **~ful** *a* cheio de tato, diplomático. **~fully** *adv* com tato. **~less** *a* sem tato

tactic /ˈtæktɪk/ *n* (*expedient*) tática *f*. **~s** *n(pl)* (*procedure*) tática *f*. **~al** *a* tático

tadpole /ˈtædpəʊl/ *n* girino *m*

tag /tæg/ *n* (*label*) etiqueta *f*; (*on shoelace*) agulheta *f*; (*phrase*) chavão *m*, clichê *m* ● *vt* (*pt* **tagged**) etiquetar; (*add*) juntar ● *vi* **~ along** 🏛 andar atrás, seguir

tail /teɪl/ *n* cauda *f*, rabo *m*; (*of shirt*) fralda *f*; **~s!** (*tossing coin*) coroa! ● *vt* (*follow*) seguir, vigiar ● *vi* **~ away** or **off** diminuir, baixar. **~back** *n* (*traffic*) fila *f*, (*P*) bicha *f*; **~ light** *n* *Auto* farolete *m* traseiro, (*P*) farolim *m* traseiro

tailor /ˈteɪlə(r)/ *n* alfaiate *m* ● *vt* ‹*garment*› fazer; *fig* (*adapt*) adaptar. **~-made** *a* feito sob medida, (*P*) por medida; **~made for** *fig* feito para, talhado para

take /teɪk/ *vt/i* (*pt* **took**, *pp* **taken**) (*get hold of*) agarrar em, pegar em; (*capture*) tomar; ‹*a seat, a drink, train, bus etc*› tomar; (*carry*) levar (**to** a, para); (*contain, escort*) levar; (*tolerate*) suportar, aguentar; ‹*choice, exam*› fazer; ‹*photo*› tirar; (*require*) exigir; **be ~n by** or **with** ficar encantado com; **be ~n ill** adoecer; **it ~s time to** leva tempo para; **~ after** parecer-se a; **~ away** levar; **~ away from sb/sth** tirar de alguém/de algo; **~ back** aceitar de volta; (*return*) devolver; (*accompany*) acompanhar; (*statement*) retirar, retratar; **~ down** ‹*object*› tirar para baixo; ‹*notes*› tirar, tomar; **~ in** ‹*garment*› meter para dentro; (*include*) incluir; (*cheat*) enganar, levar 🆒; (*grasp*) compreender; (*receive*) receber; **~ it that** supor que; **~ on** ‹*task*› encarregar-se de; ‹*staff*› admitir, contratar; **~ out** tirar; (*on an outing*) levar para sair; **~ part** participar or tomar parte (**in** em); **~ place** ocorrer, suceder; **~ sides** tomar partido; **~ sides with** tomar o partido de; **~ to** gostar de, simpatizar com; ‹*activity*› tomar gosto por, entregar-se a; **~ up** ‹*object*› apanhar, pegar em; ‹*hobby*› dedicar-se a; (*occupy*) ocupar, tomar □ **~ off** *vt* (*remove*) tirar; (*mimic*) imitar, macaquear ● *vi Aviat* decolar, levantar voo, (*P*) descolar. **~ over** *vt* tomar conta de, assumir a direção de ● *vi* tomar o poder; **~ over from** (*relieve*) render, substituir; (*succeed*) suceder a. **~away** *n* (*meal*) comida *f* para levar, take-away *m*; (*shop*) loja *f* que só vende comida para ser consumida em outro lugar; **~off** *n* imitação *f*; *Aviat* decolagem *f*, (*P*) descolagem *f*; **~over** *n Pol* tomada *f* de poder; *Comm* take-over *m*

takings /ˈteɪkɪŋz/ *npl* receita *f*

talcum /ˈtælkəm/ *n* talco *m*; **~ powder** pó *m* (de) talco

tale /teɪl/ *n* conto *m*, história *f*

talent /ˈtælənt/ *n* talento *m*. **~ed** *a* talentoso, bem dotado

talk /tɔːk/ *vt/i* falar; (*chat*) conversar; **~ into doing** convencer a fazer; **~ nonsense** dizer disparates; **~ over** discutir; **~ shop** falar de assuntos profissionais; **~ to o.s.** falar sozinho, falar com os seus botões ● *n* conversa *f*; (*mode of speech*) fala *f*; (*lecture*) palestra *f*; **small ~** conversa *f* banal; **there's ~ of** fala-se de

talkative /ˈtɔːkətɪv/ *a* falador, conversador, tagarela

tall /tɔːl/ *a* (**-er, -est**) alto; **~ story** 🆒 história *f* do arco-da-velha

tally /ˈtælɪ/ *vi* corresponder (**with** a); conferir (**with** com)

tame /teɪm/ *a* (**-er, -est**) manso; (*domesticated*) domesticado; (*dull*) insípido ● *vt* amansar, domesticar

tamper /ˈtæmpə(r)/ *vi* **~ with** mexer indevidamente em; (*text*) alterar

tampon /ˈtæmpən/ *n Med* tampão *m*; (*sanitary towel*) toalha *f* higiénica, (*P*) tampão *m*

tan /tæn/ *vt/i* (*pt* **tanned**) queimar, bronzear; ‹*hide*› curtir ● *n* bronzeado *m* ● *a* castanho amarelado

tandem /ˈtændəm/ *n* (*bicycle*) tandem *m*; **in ~** em tandem, um atrás do outro

tang /tæŋ/ *n* (*taste*) sabor *m* or gosto *m* característico *m*; (*smell*) cheiro *m* característico

tangerine /tændʒəˈriːn/ *n* tangerina *f*

tangible /ˈtændʒəbl/ *a* tangível

tangle /ˈtæŋgl/ *vt* emaranhar, enredar; **become ~d** emaranhar-se, enredar-se ● *n* emaranhado *m*

tank /tæŋk/ *n* tanque *m*, reservatório *m*; (*for petrol*) tanque *m*, (*P*) depósito *m*; (*for fish*) aquário *m*; *Mil* tanque *m*

tanker /ˈtæŋkə(r)/ *n* carro-tanque *m*, camião-cisterna *m*; (*ship*) petroleiro *m*

tantaliz|e /ˈtæntəlaɪz/ *vt* atormentar, tantalizar. **~ing** *a* tentador

tantamount /ˈtæntəmaʊnt/ *a* **be ~ to** equivaler a

tantrum /ˈtæntrəm/ *n* chilique *m*, ataque *m* de mau génio, (*P*) génio *m*, birra *f*

tap[1] /tæp/ *n* (*for water etc*) torneira *f*; **on ~** 🆒 (*available*) disponível ● *vt* (*pt* **tapped**) ‹*resources*› explorar; ‹*telephone*› grampear 🆒, pôr escutas em or colocar sob escuta

tap[2] /tæp/ *vt/i* (*pt* **tapped**) bater levemente. **~ dance** *n* sapateado *m*

tape /teɪp/ *n* (*for dressmaking*) fita *f*; (*sticky*) fita *f* adesiva, (*P*) fita-cola *f*; **(magnetic) ~** fita (magnética) *f* ● *vt* (*tie*) atar, prender; (*stick*) colar; (*record*) gravar. **~ measure** *n* fita *f* métrica; **~ recorder** *n* gravador *m*

taper /ˈteɪpə(r)/ *n* vela *f* comprida e fina ● *vt/i* **~ (off)** estreitar(-se), afilar(-se). **~ed**, **~ing** *adjs* ‹*fingers etc*› afilado; ‹*trousers*› afunilado

tapestry /ˈtæpɪstrɪ/ *n* tapeçaria *f*

tar /tɑ:(r)/ n alcatrão m ● vt (pt **tarred**) alcatroar

target /'tɑ:gɪt/ n alvo m ● vt ter como alvo

tariff /'tærɪf/ n tarifa f; (on import) direitos mpl aduaneiros

Tarmac® /'tɑ:mæk/ n macadame (alcatroado) m, (P) asfalto m; (runway) pista f

tarnish /'tɑ:nɪʃ/ vt/i (fazer) perder o brilho; (stain) manchar

tarpaulin /tɑ:'pɔ:lɪn/ n lona f impermeável (alcatroada or (P) asfaltada or encerada)

tart[1] /tɑ:t/ a (-er, -est) ácido; fig (cutting) mordaz; azedo

tart[2] /tɑ:t/ n Culin torta f de fruta, (P) tarte f; ⊠ (prostitute) prostituta f; mulher f da vida ⊠ ● vt ~ **up** ⊡ embonecar(-se)

tartan /'tɑ:tn/ n tecido m escocês ● a escocês

task /tɑ:sk/ n tarefa f, trabalho m; **take to** ~ repreender, censurar. ~ **force** n Mil força-tarefa f, (P) unidade f especial

tassel /'tæsl/ n borla f

taste /teɪst/ n gosto m; fig (sample) amostra f, have a ~ **of** (experience) provar ● vt (eat, enjoy) saborear; (try) provar; (perceive taste of) sentir o gosto de ● vi ~ **of** or **like** ter o sabor de, saber a. ~**ful** a de bom gosto. ~**less** a insípido, insosso; fig (not in good taste) sem gosto; fig (in bad taste) de mau gosto

tasty /'teɪstɪ/ a (-ier, -iest) saboroso, gostoso

tat /tæt/ ▶ **TIT**[2]

tatter|s /'tætəz/ npl farrapos mpl. ~**ed** /-əd/ a esfarrapado

tattoo /tə'tu:/ vt tatuar ● n tatuagem f

tatty /'tætɪ/ a (-ier, -iest) ⊡ enxovalhado; em mau estado

taught /tɔ:t/ ▶ **TEACH**

taunt /tɔ:nt/ vt escarnecer de, zombar de ● n escárnio m

Taurus /'tɔ:rəs/ n Astr Touro m

taut /tɔ:t/ a esticado, retesado; fig (of nerves) tenso

tawdry /'tɔ:drɪ/ a (-ier, -iest) espalhafatoso e ordinário

tax /tæks/ n taxa f, imposto m; (on income) imposto m de renda, (P) sobre o rendimento; ~ **relief** isenção f de imposto; ~ **return** declaração f do imposto de renda, (P) sobre o rendimento; ~ **year** ano m fiscal ● vt taxar, lançar impostos sobre, tributar; fig

(put to test) pôr à prova. ~**free** a isento de imposto. ~**able** a tributável, passível de imposto. ~**ation** /-'seɪʃn/ n impostos mpl, tributação f. ~**ing** a penoso, difícil

taxi /'tæksɪ/ n (pl -is) táxi m; ~ **rank**, ~ **stand** ponto m de táxis, (P) praça f de táxis ● vi (pt **taxied**, pres p **taxiing**) Aviat rolar na pista, taxiar. ~**cab** n táxi m; ~-**driver** n motorista mf de táxi

taxpayer /'tækspeɪə(r)/ n contribuinte mf

tea /ti:/ n chá m; **high** ~ refeição f leve à noite. ~**bag** n saquinho m de chá; ~-**break** n intervalo m para o chá; ~ **leaf** n folha f de chá; ~ **shop** n salão m or casa f de chá; ~**time** n hora f do chá; ~ **towel** n pano m de prato

teach /ti:tʃ/ vt (pt **taught**) ensinar, dar aulas de, lecionar (**sb sth** alg coisa a alguém) ● vi ensinar, ser professor. ~**er** n professor m. ~**ing** n ensino m; (doctrines) ensinamento(s) m(pl) ● a pedagógico, de ensino; ‹staff› docente

teacup /'ti:kʌp/ n xícara f de chá, (P) chávena f

teak /ti:k/ n teca f

team /ti:m/ n equipe f, (P) equipa f; (of oxen) junta f; (of horses) parelha f ● vi ~ **up** juntar-se, associar-se (**with** a). ~**work** n trabalho m de equipe, (P) equipa

teapot /'ti:pɒt/ n bule m

tear[1] /teə(r)/ vt/i (pt **tore**, pp **torn**) rasgar(-se); (snatch) arrancar, puxar; (rush) lançar-se, ir numa correria; fig dividir ● n rasgão m; ~ **o.s. away** arrancar-se (**from** de)

tear[2] /tɪə(r)/ n lágrima f. ~ **gas** n gases mpl lacrimogênios, (P) gás m lacrimogénio

tearful /'tɪəfl/ a lacrimoso, choroso. ~**ly** adv choroso, com (as) lágrimas nos olhos

tease /ti:z/ vt implicar; (make fun of) caçoar de, (P) fazer troça de

teaspoon /'ti:spu:n/ n colher f de chá

teat /ti:t/ n (of bottle) bico m; (of animal) teta f

technical /'teknɪkl/ a técnico. ~**ity** /-'kælətɪ/ n questão f de ordem técnica. ~**ly** adv tecnicamente

technician /tek'nɪʃn/ n técnico m

technique /tek'ni:k/ n técnica f

technolog|y /tek'nɒlədʒɪ/ n tecnologia f. ~**ical** /-ə'lɒdʒɪkl/ a tecnológico

t

teddy /'tedɪ/ a ~ **(bear)** ursinho m de pelúcia, (P) peluche

tedious /'tiːdɪəs/ a maçante

tedium /'tiːdɪəm/ n tédio m

tee /tiː/ n Golf tee m

teem[1] /tiːm/ vi ~ **(with)** (swarm) pulular (de), fervilhar (de), abundar (em)

teem[2] /tiːm/ vi ~ **(with rain)** chover torrencialmente

teenage /'tiːneɪdʒ/ a juvenil, de/ para adolescente. ~r /-ə(r)/ n jovem mf, adolescente mf

teens /tiːnz/ npl in one's ~ na adolescência, entre os 13 e os 19 anos

teeter /'tiːtə(r)/ vi cambalear

teeth /tiːθ/ ▶ TOOTH

teeth|e /tiːð/ vi começar a ter dentes; ~ing troubles fig problemas mpl iniciais

teetotaller /tiː'təʊtlə(r)/ n abstêmio m, (P) abstémio m

telecommunications /telɪkəmjuːnɪ'keɪʃnz/ npl telecomunicações fpl

telegram /'telɪgræm/ n telegrama m

telepath|y /tɪ'lepəθɪ/ n telepatia f

telephone /'telɪfəʊn/ n telefone m ● vt ‹person› telefonar a; ‹message› telefonar ● vi telefonar; ~ **book** lista f telefónica, (P) telefónica; ~ **box**, ~ **booth** cabine f telefónica, (P) telefónica; ~ **call** chamada f; ~ **directory** lista f telefónica, (P) telefónica, guia m telefónico; ~ **number** número m de telefone

telephoto /telɪ'fəʊtəʊ/ n ~ **lens** teleobjetiva f

telescop|e /'telɪskəʊp/ n telescópio m ● vt/i encaixar(-se). ~**ic** /-'skɒpɪk/ a telescópico

televise /'telɪvaɪz/ vt televisionar, transmitir pela televisão

television /'telɪvɪʒn/ n televisão f; ~ **set** aparelho m de televisão, televisor m

teleworking /'telɪwɜːkɪŋ/ n teletrabalho m

tell /tel/ vt (pt told) dizer (**sb sth** alg coisa a alguém); ‹story› contar; (distinguish) distinguir, diferençar, diferenciar; **I told you so** bem lhe disse; ~ **off** (scold) ralhar com, dar uma bronca em; ~ **tales** mexericar, fofocar ● vi (know) ver-se, saber; ~ **of** falar de; ~ **on** (have effect on) afetar; (inform on) fazer queixa de. ~**tale** n mexeriqueiro m, fofoqueiro m ● a (revealing) revelador

telly /'telɪ/ n TV f

temp /temp/ n empregado m temporário

temper /'tempə(r)/ n humor m, disposição f; (anger) mau humor m ● vt temperar; **keep/lose one's** ~ manter a calma/perder a calma or a cabeça, zangar-se

temperament /'temprəmənt/ n temperamento m. ~**al** /-'mentl/ a caprichoso

temperate /'tempərət/ a moderado, comedido; ‹climate› temperado

temperature /'temprətʃə(r)/ n temperatura f; **have a** ~ estar com or ter febre

tempestuous /tem'pestʃʊəs/ a tempestuoso

template /'templ(e)ɪt/ n molde m

temple[1] /'templ/ n templo m

temple[2] /'templ/ n Anat têmpora f, fonte f

tempo /'tempəʊ/ n (pl -os) Mus tempo m; (pace) ritmo m

temporar|y /'temprərɪ/ a temporário, provisório

tempt /tempt/ vt tentar; ~ **sb to do** tentar alguém a fazer, dar a alguém vontade de fazer. ~**ation** /-'teɪʃn/ n tentação f. ~**ing** a tentador

ten /ten/ a & n dez m

tenac|ious /tɪ'neɪʃəs/ a tenaz. ~**ity** /-æsətɪ/ n tenacidade f

tenant /'tenənt/ n inquilino m, locatário m

tend[1] /tend/ vt tomar conta de, cuidar de

tend[2] /tend/ vi ~ **to** (be apt to) tender a, ter tendência para

tendency /'tendənsɪ/ n tendência f

tender[1] /'tendə(r)/ a (soft, delicate) terno; (sore, painful) sensível, dolorido; (loving) terno, meigo. ~**hearted** a compassivo. ~**ly** adv (lovingly) ternamente, meigamente; (delicately) delicadamente. ~**ness** n (love) ternura f, meiguice f

tender[2] /'tendə(r)/ vt ‹money› oferecer; ‹apologies, resignation› apresentar ● vi ~ **(for)** apresentar orçamento (para) ● n Comm orçamento m; **legal** ~ (money) moeda f corrente

tendon /'tendən/ n tendão m

tenement /'tenəmənt/ n prédio m de apartamentos de renda moderada; Amer (slum) prédio m pobre

tennis /'tenɪs/ n ténis m, (P) ténis m; **~ court** quadra f de tênis, (P) court m de ténis

tenor /'tenə(r)/ n (meaning) teor m; Mus tenor m

tense[1] /tens/ n Gram tempo m

tense[2] /tens/ a (-er, -est) tenso ● vt ‹muscles› retesar

tension /'tenʃn/ n tensão f

tent /tent/ n tenda f, barraca f

tentative /'tentətɪv/ a provisório; (hesitant) hesitante

tenterhooks /'tentəhʊks/ npl **on ~** em suspense

tenth /tenθ/ a & n décimo m

tenuous /'tenjʊəs/ a tênue, (P) ténue

tepid /'tepɪd/ a tépido, morno

term /tɜːm/ n (word) termo m; (limit) prazo m, termo m; Schol etc período m, trimestre m; Amer semestre m; (of imprisonment) (duração de) pena f; **~ of office** Pol mandato m; **come to ~s with** chegar a um acordo com; (become resigned to) resignar-se a; **~s** (conditions) condições fpl; **on good/bad ~s** de boas/más relações; **not on speaking ~s** de relações cortadas ● vt designar, denominar, chamar

terminal /'tɜːmɪnl/ a terminal, final; ‹illness› fatal, mortal ● n (oil, computer) terminal m; Rail estação f terminal; Electr borne m; **(air) ~** terminal m (de avião)

terminat|e /'tɜːmɪneɪt/ vt terminar, pôr termo a ● vi terminar. **~ion** /-'neɪʃn/ n término m, (P) terminação f, termo m

terminology /tɜːmɪ'nɒlədʒɪ/ n terminologia f

terminus /'tɜːmɪnəs/ n (pl **-ni** /-naɪ/) (rail, coach) estação f terminal

terrace /'terəs/ n terraço m; (in cultivation) socalco m; (houses) casas fpl em fileira contínua, lance m de casas; **the ~s** Sport arquibancada f, (P) bancada f (principal); **~d house** casa f ladeada por outras casas

terrain /te'reɪn/ n terreno m

terribl|e /'terəbl/ a terrível. **~y** adv terrivelmente; 🔲 (very) extremamente; espantosamente

terrific /tə'rɪfɪk/ a terrífico, tremendo; 🔲 (excellent; great) tremendo, fantástico. **~ally** adv 🔲 (very) tremendamente 🔲; 🔲 (very well) lindamente; maravilhosamente

terrif|y /'terɪfaɪ/ vt aterrar, aterrorizar; **be ~ied of** ter pavor de

territorial /terɪ'tɔːrɪəl/ a territorial

territory /'terɪtərɪ/ n território m

terror /'terə(r)/ n terror m, pavor m

terrorism /'terərɪzəm/ n terrorismo m

terroris|t /'terərɪst/ n terrorista mf. **~m** /-zəm/ n terrorismo m

terrorize /'terəraɪz/ vt aterrorizar, aterrar

terse /tɜːs/ a conciso, lapidar; (curt) lacônico, (P) lacónico

test /test/ n teste m, exame m, prova f; Schol prova f, teste m; (of goods) controle m; (of machine etc) ensaio m; (of strength) prova f; **put to the ~** pôr à prova; **~ match** jogo m internacional ● vt examinar; (check) controlar; (try) ensaiar; ‹pupil› interrogar, (P) examinar. **~ tube** n proveta f; **~-tube baby** bebê m de proveta, (P) bebé-proveta mf

testament /'testəmənt/ n testamento m; **Old/New T~** Antigo/Novo Testamento m

testicle /'testɪkl/ n testículo m

testify /'testɪfaɪ/ vt/i testificar, testemunhar, depôr

testimonial /testɪ'məʊnɪəl/ n carta f de recomendação

testimony /'testɪmənɪ/ n testemunho m

tetanus /'tetənəs/ n tétano m

tether /'teðə(r)/ vt prender com corda ● n **be at the end of one's ~** estar nas últimas

text /tekst/ n texto m; **~ message** mensagem f escrita or (P) sms m ● vt enviar uma mensagem de texto a

textbook /'tekstbʊk/ n compêndio m, manual m, livro m de texto

textile /'tekstaɪl/ n & a têxtil m

texture /'tekstʃə(r)/ n (of fabric) textura f; (of paper) grão m

Thai /taɪ/ a & n tailandês m. **~land** n Tailândia f

Thames /temz/ n Tâmisa m

than /ðæn unstressed ðən/ conj que, do que; (with numbers) de; **more/less ~ ten** mais/menos de dez

thank /θæŋk/ vt agradecer; **~ you!** obrigado! **~s!** 🔲 obrigado. **~s** npl agradecimentos mpl; **~s to** graças a; **T~sgiving (Day)** Amer Dia m de Ação de Graças

t

thankful /'θæŋkfl/ a grato; agradecido; reconhecido (**for** por). **~ly** adv com gratidão; (happily) felizmente

thankless /'θæŋklɪs/ a ingrato

that /ðæt unstressed ðət/ ● a

····▸ (nearer) esse/essa; **I want ~ drink** quero essa bebida; **give me ~ one** me dê esse; (further away) aquele/aquela; **~ drink over there** aquela bebida lá

● pron

····▸ esse/essa; (indefinite) isso; **what's ~ on your shirt?** o que é isso na sua camiseta?; (further away) aquele/aquela; (indefinite) aquilo; **who's ~?** quem é?; **~'s Peter over there** aquele ali é o Peter; **those are my parents** aqueles são os meus pais; **what's ~ over there on the hill?** o que é aquilo lá na montanha?

● rel pron

····▸ que; **where's the letter ~ came yesterday?** onde está a carta que veio ontem?; **the man ~ stole the car** o homem que roubou o carro

! With a preposition, use o qual, a qual when referring to objects: **the chair that I was sitting on** a cadeira na qual eu estava sentada

! With a preposition, use quem when referring to people: **the people that I've talked about** as pessoas de quem falei; **the girls that I was talking to** as meninas com quem eu estava falando (referring to time) em que; **the year ~ he died** o ano em que ele morreu; **the day ~ we went to the beach** o dia em que fomos para a praia

● adv

····▸ tão, tanto assim; **he's not ~ stupid** ele não é assim tão estúpido; **it isn't ~ cold** não está assim tanto frio

● conj

····▸ que; **I don't think ~ he'll come** não me parece que ele venha; **we know ~ you're right** sabemos que você tem razão

····▸ (in phrases) **~ is (to say)** isto é; **~'s right** é isso mesmo; **like ~** assim; **don't be like ~!** não seja assim!

thatch /θætʃ/ n colmo m. **~ed** a de colmo; **~ed cottage** casa f com telhado de colmo

thaw /θɔː/ vt/i derreter(-se), degelar; ‹food› descongelar ● n degelo m,

derretimento m

the before vowel /ðɪ before consonant ðə stressed ðiː/ ● definite article

····▸ o, a; pl os, as; **~ dog** o cão; **~ tree** a árvore; **go to ~ dentist** ir ao dentista; **in ~ garden** no jardim

! When the articles o and a follow the prepositions a, de, and em, they often contract to form ao, à, do, da and no, na. (+ adjective to form noun) **~ blind** os cegos; **~ unemployed** os desempregados; **~ impossible** o impossível; (+ nationality) **~ French** os franceses; **~ Portuguese** os portugueses; (per) **paid by ~ hour** pago por hora; **sold by ~ dozen** vendido por dúzia

● adv

····▸ **~ more...~ more...** quanto mais...tanto mais...

theatre /'θɪətə(r)/ n teatro m

theatrical /θɪˈætrɪkl/ a teatral

theft /θeft/ n roubo m

their /ðeə(r)/ a deles, delas, seu

theirs /ðeəz/ poss pron o(s) seu(s), a(s) sua(s), o(s) deles, a(s) delas; **it is ~** é (o) deles/delas or o seu

them /ðem unstressed ðəm/ pron os, as; (after prep) eles, elas; **(to) ~** lhes

theme /θiːm/ n tema m; **~ park** parque m temático

themselves /ðəmˈselvz/ pron eles mesmos/próprios, elas mesmas/próprias; (reflexive) se; (after prep) si (mesmos, próprios); **by ~** sozinhos; **with ~** consigo

then /ðen/ adv (at that time) então, nessa altura; (next) depois, em seguida; (in that case) então, nesse caso; (therefore) então, portanto, por conseguinte

theolog|y /θɪˈɒlədʒɪ/ n teologia f. **~ian** /θɪəˈləʊdʒən/ n teólogo m

theor|y /'θɪərɪ/ n teoria f. **~etical** /-ˈretɪkl/ a teórico

therapeutic /θerəˈpjuːtɪk/ a terapêutico

therap|y /'θerəpɪ/ n terapia f. **~ist** n terapeuta mf

there /ðeə(r)/ adv aí, ali, lá; (over there) lá, acolá ● int (triumphant) pronto, aí está; (consoling) então, vamos lá; **he goes ~** ele vai aí or lá; **~ he goes** aí vai ele; **~ is, ~ are** há; **~ you are** (giving) toma; **~ and then** logo ali. **~abouts** adv por aí. **~by** adv desse modo

therefore /'ðeəfɔː(r)/ adv por isso, portanto, por conseguinte

thermal /'θɜːml/ a térmico

thermometer /θə'mɒmɪtə(r)/ n termômetro m, (P) termómetro m

Thermos® /'θɜːməs/ n garrafa f térmica, (P) termo m

thermostat /'θɜːməstæt/ n termostato m

thesaurus /θɪ'sɔːrəs/ n (pl -ri /-raɪ/) dicionário m de sinónimos, (P) sinónimos

these /ðiːz/ ▶ THIS

thesis /'θiːsɪs/ n (pl theses /-siːz/) tese f

they /ðeɪ/ pron eles, elas; ~ say (that)... diz-se ou dizem que

thick /θɪk/ a (-er, -est) espesso, grosso; Ⓘ (stupid) estúpido ● adv = THICKLY ● n in the ~ of no meio de. ~-skinned a insensível. ~ly adv espessamente; (spread) em camada espessa. ~ness n espessura f, grossura f

thicken /'θɪkən/ vt/i engrossar, espessar(-se); the plot ~s o enredo complica-se

thief /θiːf/ n (pl thieves /θiːvz/) ladrão m, gatuno m

thigh /θaɪ/ n coxa f

thimble /'θɪmbl/ n dedal m

thin /θɪn/ a (thinner, thinnest) (slender) estreito, fino, delgado; (lean, not plump) magro; (sparse) ralo, escasso; (flimsy) leve, fino; <soup> aguado; <hair> ralo ● adv = THINLY ● vt/i (pt thinned) (of liquid) diluir(-se); (of fog etc) dissipar(-se); (of hair) rarear; ~ out (in quantity) diminuir, reduzir; <seedlings etc> desbastar. ~ly adv (sparsely) esparsamente. ~ness n (of board, wire etc) finura f; (of person) magreza f

thing /θɪn/ n coisa f; ~s (belongings) pertences mpl; the best ~ is to o melhor é; for one ~ em primeiro lugar; just the ~ exatamente o que era preciso; poor ~ coitado

think /θɪnk/ vt/i (pt thought) pensar (about, of em); (carefully) refletir (about, of em, sobre); I ~ so eu acho que sim; ~ better of it (change one's mind) pensar melhor; ~ nothing of achar natural; ~ of (hold opinion of) pensar de, achar de; ~ over pensar bem em; ~ up inventar. ~ tank n comissão f de peritos

third /θɜːd/ a terceiro; T~ World Terceiro Mundo m; ~-party insurance seguro m contra terceiros ● n terceiro

m; (fraction) terço m. ~-rate a inferior, medíocre. ~ly adv em terceiro lugar

thirst /θɜːst/ n sede f. ~y a sequioso, sedento; be ~y estar com or ter sede

thirteen /θɜː'tiːn/ a & n treze m. ~th a & n décimo terceiro m

thirt|y /'θɜːtɪ/ a & n trinta m. ~ieth a & n trigésimo m

---

this /ðɪs/ (pl these) ● a

••••▶ este, esta; I don't like ~ car não gosto deste carro; ~ morning esta manhã; ~ Wednesday esta quarta-feira; ~ one este, esta; these ones estes, estas; I'll have ~ one, please quero este, por favor

● pron

••••▶ este, esta; (indefinite) isto; what's ~? o que é isto?; what are these? o que são (estes/estas)?; ~ is the kitchen esta é a cozinha; after ~ depois disto

● adv

••••▶ ~ far tão longe; I didn't think we would get ~ far nunca pensei que chegássemos tão longe; ~ high desta altura; it's about ~ high é mais ou menos desta altura

••••▶ (in phrases) like ~ assim, desta forma; do it like ~ faça assim; ~ and that isto e aquilo; 'what did you talk about?'– 'oh, ~ and that' 'de que falaram?'– 'oh, disto e daquilo'

---

thistle /'θɪsl/ n cardo m

thorn /θɔːn/ n espinho m, pico m. ~y a espinhoso; fig bicudo; espinhoso

thorough /'θʌrə/ a consciencioso; (deep) completo, profundo; <cleaning, washing> a fundo. ~ly adv <clean, study etc> completo, a fundo; (very) perfeitamente, muito bem

thoroughbred /'θʌrəbred/ n <horse etc> puro-sangue m invar

those /ðəʊz/ ▶ THAT

though /ðəʊ/ conj se bem que, embora, conquanto ● adv Ⓘ contudo; no entanto

thought /θɔːt/ ▶ THINK ● n pensamento m; ideia f; on second ~s pensando bem

thoughtful /'θɔːtfl/ a pensativo; (considerate) atencioso, solícito. ~ly adv pensativamente; (considerately) com consideração, atenciosamente

thoughtless /'θɔːtlɪs/ a irrefletido; (inconsiderate) pouco atencioso. ~ly

t

adv sem pensar; (*inconsiderately*) sem consideração

thousand /ˈθaʊznd/ a & n mil m; **~s of** milhares de. **~th** a & n milésimo m

thrash /θræʃ/ vt surrar, espancar; (*defeat*) dar uma surra ou sova em; **~ about** debater-se; **~ out** debater a fundo, discutir bem

thread /θred/ n fio m; (*for sewing*) linha f de coser; (*of screw*) rosca f ● vt enfiar; **~ one's way** abrir caminho, furar

threadbare /ˈθredbeə(r)/ a puído, surrado

threat /θret/ n ameaça f

threaten /ˈθretn/ vt/i ameaçar

three /θriː/ a & n três m

thresh /θreʃ/ vt <*corn etc*> malhar, debulhar

threshold /ˈθreʃəʊld/ n limiar m, soleira f; fig limiar m

threw /θruː/ ▶ **THROW**

thrift /θrɪft/ n economia f, poupança f. **~y** a económico, (P) económico, poupado

thrill /θrɪl/ n arrepio m de emoção, frêmito m, (P) frémito m ● vt excitar(-se), emocionar(-se), (fazer) vibrar; **be ~ed** estar/ficar encantado. **~ing** a excitante, emocionante

thriller /ˈθrɪlə(r)/ n livro ou filme de suspense m

thriv|e /θraɪv/ vi (pt **thrived** or **throve**, pp **thrived** or **thriven**) prosperar, florescer; (*grow strong*) dar-se bem (on com). **~ing** a próspero

throat /θrəʊt/ n garganta f; **have a sore ~** ter dores de garganta

throb /θrɒb/ vi (pt **throbbed**) <*wound, head*> latejar; <*heart*> palpitar, bater; <*engine*> also fig vibrar, trepidar ● n (of *pain*) latejo m, espasmo m; (of *heart*) palpitação f, batida f; (of *engine*) vibração f, trepidação f

throes /θrəʊz/ npl **in the ~ of** fig às voltas com, no meio de

throne /θrəʊn/ n trono m

throttle /ˈθrɒtl/ n Auto válvula-borboleta f, estrangulador m, acelerador m de mão ● vt estrangular

through /θruː/ prep através de, por; (*during*) durante; (*by means or way of, out of*) por; (*by reason of*) por, por causa de ● adv através; (*entirely*) completamente, até o fim; **be ~** ter acabado (with com); *Telephone* estar ligado; **come** or **go ~** (*cross, pierce*) atravessar; **get ~** <*exam*> passar; **be**

wet ~ estar ensopado ou encharcado ● a <*train, traffic etc*> direto

throughout /θruːˈaʊt/ prep durante, por todo; **~ the country** por todo o país (afora); **~ the day** durante todo a dia, pelo dia afora ● adv completamente; (*place*) por toda a parte; (*time*) durante todo o tempo

throw /θrəʊ/ vt (pt **threw**, pp **thrown**) atirar, jogar, lançar; I (*baffle*) desconcertar; **~ a party** I dar uma festa; **~ away** jogar fora, (P) deitar fora; **~ off** (*get rid of*) livrar-se de; **~ out** <*person*> expulsar; (*reject*) rejeitar; **~ over** (*desert*) abandonar, deixar; **~ up** <*one's arms*> levantar; (*resign from*) abandonar; I (*vomit*) vomitar ● n lançamento m; (*of dice*) lance m

thrush /θrʌʃ/ n (*bird*) tordo m

thrust /θrʌst/ vt (pt **thrust**) arremeter, empurrar, impelir ● n empurrão m, arremetida f; **~ into** (*put*) enfiar em, mergulhar em; **~ upon** (*force on*) impôr a

thud /θʌd/ n som m surdo, baque m

thug /θʌɡ/ n bandido m, facínora m, malfeitor m

thumb /θʌm/ n polegar m; **under sb's ~** completamente dominado por alguém ● vt <*book*> manusear; **~ a lift** pedir carona, (P) boleia

thumbtack /ˈθʌmtæk/ n Amer percevejo m

thump /θʌmp/ vt/i bater (em), dar pancadas (em); (*with fists*) dar murros (em); <*piano*> martelar (em); (*of heart*) bater com força ● n pancada f; (*thud*) baque m

thunder /ˈθʌndə(r)/ n trovão m, trovoada f; (*loud noise*) estrondo m ● vi (*weather, person*) trovejar; **~ past** passar como um raio. **~y** a <*weather*> tempestuoso

thunderbolt /ˈθʌndəbəʊlt/ n raio m e ribombo m de trovão; fig raio m fulminante fig

thunderstorm /ˈθʌndəstɔːm/ n tempestade f com trovoadas, temporal m

Thursday /ˈθɜːzdɪ/ n quinta-feira f

thus /ðʌs/ adv assim, desta maneira; **~ far** até aqui

thwart /θwɔːt/ vt frustrar, contrariar

thyme /taɪm/ n tomilho m

tick[1] /tɪk/ n (*sound*) tique-taque m; (*mark*) sinal m; I (*moment*) instantinho m ● vi fazer tique-taque ● vt **~ (off)**

marcar com sinal; **~ off** Ⅱ (scold) dar uma bronca em Ⅱ (P) ralhar com; **~ over** ‹engine, factory› funcionar em marcha lenta, (P) em 'ralenti'

tick² /tɪk/ n (insect) carrapato m

ticket /'tɪkɪt/ n bilhete m; (label) etiqueta f; (for traffic offence) aviso m de multa. **~ collector** n (railway) guarda m; **~ office** n bilheteira f

tickle /'tɪkl/ vt fazer cócegas; fig (amuse) divertir ● n cócegas fpl, comichão m

ticklish /'tɪklɪʃ/ a coceguento, sensível a cócegas; fig delicado; melindroso

tidal /'taɪdl/ a de marés, que tem marés; **~ wave** onda f gigantesca; fig onda f de sentimento popular, vaga f de fundo

tide /taɪd/ n maré f; (of events) marcha f, curso m; **high ~** maré f cheia, preia-mar f; **low ~** maré f baixa, baixa-mar f ● vt **~ over** (help temporarily) aguentar

tid|y /'taɪdɪ/ a (-ier, -iest) ‹room› arrumado; ‹appearance, work› asseado, cuidado; (methodical) bem ordenado; Ⅱ ‹amount› belo Ⅱ ● vt arrumar, arranjar. **~iness** n arrumação f, ordem f

tie /taɪ/ vt (pres p tying) atar, amarrar, prender; (link) ligar, vincular; ‹a knot› dar, fazer ● vi Sport empatar ● n fio m, cordel m; (necktie) gravata f; (link) laço m, vínculo m; Sport empate m; **~ in with** estar ligado com, relacionar-se com; **~ up** amarrar, atar; ‹animal› prender; ‹money› imobilizar; (occupy) ocupar

tier /tɪə(r)/ n cada fila f, camada f, prateleira f etc colocada em cima de outra; (in stadium) bancada f; (of cake) andar m; (of society) camada f

tiger /'taɪɡə(r)/ n tigre m

tight /taɪt/ a (-er, -est) ‹clothes› apertado, justo; ‹rope› esticado, tenso; ‹control› rigoroso; ‹knot, schedule, lid› apertado; Ⅱ (drunk) embriagado Ⅱ; **be in a ~ corner** fig estar em apuros or num aperto, (P) estar entalado Ⅱ ● adv = **TIGHTLY**. **~ly** adv bem; (squeeze) com força

tighten /'taɪtn/ vt/i ‹rope› esticar; ‹bolt, control› apertar; **~ up on** apertar o cinto

tightrope /'taɪtrəʊp/ n corda f (de acrobacias) f; **~ walker** funâmbulo m

tights /taɪts/ npl collants mpl, meias-colant fpl

tile /taɪl/ n (on wall, floor) ladrilho m, azulejo m; (on roof) telha f ● vt ladrilhar, pôr azulejos em; (roof) telhar, cobrir com telhas

till¹ /tɪl/ vt ‹land› cultivar

till² /tɪl/ prep & conj = **UNTIL**

till³ /tɪl/ n caixa (registadora) f

tilt /tɪlt/ vt/i inclinar(-se), pender ● n (slope) inclinação f; **(at) full ~** a toda a velocidade

timber /'tɪmbə(r)/ n madeira (de construção) f; (trees) árvores fpl

time /taɪm/ n tempo m; (moment) momento m; (epoch) época f, tempo m; (by clock) horas fpl; (occasion) vez f; (rhythm) compasso m; **~s** (multiplying) vezes; **at ~s** às vezes; **for the ~ being** por agora, por enquanto; **from ~ to ~** de vez em quando; **have a good ~** divertir-se; **have no ~ for** não ter paciência para; **in no ~** num instante; **in ~** a tempo; (eventually) com o tempo; **in two days' ~** daqui a dois dias; **on ~** na hora, (P) a horas; **take your ~** não se apresse; **what's the ~?** que horas são?; **~ bomb** bomba-relógio f; **~ off** tempo m livre; **~ zone** fuso m horário ● vt escolher a hora para; (measure) marcar o tempo de; Sport cronometrar; (regulate) acertar. **~ limit** n prazo m

timeless /'taɪmlɪs/ a intemporal; (unending) eterno

timely /'taɪmlɪ/ a oportuno

timer /'taɪmə(r)/ n Techn relógio m; (with sand) ampulheta f

timetable /'taɪmteɪbl/ n horário m

timid /'tɪmɪd/ a tímido; (fearful) assustadiço, medroso

timing /'taɪmɪŋ/ n (measuring) cronometragem f; (of artist) ritmo m; (moment) cálculo m do tempo, timing m; **good/bad ~** (moment) momento m bem/mal escolhido

tin /tɪn/ n estanho m; (container) lata f; **~ foil** papel m de alumínio; **~ plate** lata f, folha-(-de-Flandres) f ● vt (pt tinned) estanhar; ‹food› enlatar; **~ned foods** conservas fpl. **~ opener** n abridor m de latas, (P) abre-latas m. **~ny** a ‹sound› metálico

tinge /tɪndʒ/ vt **~ (with)** tingir (de); fig dar um toque (de) ● n tom m, matiz m; fig toque m

tingle /'tɪŋɡl/ vi (sting) arder; (prickle) picar ● n ardor m; (prickle) picadela f

tinker /'tɪŋkə(r)/ n latoeiro m ambulante ● vi **~ (with)** mexer (em), tentar consertar

tinkle /'tɪŋkl/ n tinido m, tilintar m ● vt/i tilintar

t

tinsel /'tɪnsl/ n fio m prateado/dourado, enfeites mpl metálicos de Natal; fig falso brilho m; ouropel m

tint /tɪnt/ n tom m, matiz m; (for hair) tintura f, tinta f ● vt tingir, colorir

tiny /'taɪnɪ/ a (-ier, -iest) minúsculo, pequenino

tip¹ /tɪp/ n ponta f; **(have sth) on the ~ of one's tongue** ter algo na ponta da língua

tip² /tɪp/ vt/i (pt tipped) (tilt) inclinar(-se); (overturn) virar(-se); (pour) colocar, (P) deitar; (empty) despejar(-se); **~ off** avisar, prevenir ● n (money) gorjeta f; (advice) sugestão f; dica f ▣; (for rubbish) lixeira f. **~-off** n (warning) aviso m; (information) informação f

tipsy /'tɪpsɪ/ a ligeiramente embriagado, alegre, tocado ▣

tiptoe /'tɪptəʊ/ n on **~** na ponta dos pés

tir|e¹ /'taɪə(r)/ vt/i cansar(-se) (of de). **~eless** a incansável, infatigável. **~ing** a fatigante, cansativo

tire² /'taɪə(r)/ n Amer pneu m

tired /taɪəd/ a cansado, fatigado; **~ of** (sick of) farto de; **~ out** morto de cansaço

tiresome /'taɪəsəm/ a maçador; aborrecido; chato ▣

tissue /'tɪʃuː/ n tecido m; (handkerchief) lenço m de papel. **~ paper** n papel m de seda

tit¹ /tɪt/ n (bird) chapim m, canário-da-terra m

tit² /tɪt/ n give **~ for tat** pagar na mesma moeda

titbit /'tɪtbɪt/ n petisco m

title /'taɪtl/ n título m

to /tuː unstressed tə/ ● prep

····▸ (direction) a; **go ~ the beach** ir para a praia; **go ~ the dentist** ir ao dentista; **go ~ a party** ir a uma festa; **go ~ Portugal** (for a short time) ir a Portugal; (for good) ir para Portugal; **go ~ bed** ir para a cama; **go ~ school/university** ir para a escola/faculdade

❗ The preposition a often contracts with the definite articles o and a to form ao and à.

····▸ (up to) até; **go ~ the end of the street** ir até ao fim da rua; **~ this day** até hoje; **from Monday ~ Friday** de segunda a sexta

····▸ (expressing indirect object) give sth **~ sb** dar algo para alguém; **give the book ~ her** dá o livro para ela; **give it ~ me** me dá isso

····▸ (attitude) para (com); **she was nice ~ him** ela foi simpática para com ele

····▸ (in telling time) para; **it's ten ~ six** são dez para as seis

····▸ (expressing duration) **it lasts three ~ four hours** dura entre três a quatro horas

● infinitive particle

····▸ (forming infinitive) **~ eat** comer

❗ In an infinitive to is not translated: **to sing** cantar; **to go** ir (purpose) para; **I set out ~ buy food** saí para ir buscar comida

····▸ (after be + adjectives) de; **be easy/difficult ~ read** ser fácil/difícil de ler; **it's easy ~ forget** é fácil esquecer

····▸ (in phrases) **go ~ and fro** andar de um lado para o outro.

~-do n [!](fuss) agitação f; **he made a great ~-do about being left off the guest list** causou muita agitação por ter sido excluído da lista de convidados; **~-be** adj her husband-**~-be** o seu futuro marido →For verbal expressions using the infinitive to such as **to tell sb to do sth** and to **help sb to do sth** see entries **tell** and **help**

toad /təʊd/ n sapo m

toady /'təʊdɪ/ n lambe-botas ▣ mf, puxa-saco ▣ m ● vi puxar saco ▣ bajular, ser um(a) lambe-botas

toast /təʊst/ n fatia f de pão torrado, torrada f; (drink) brinde m, saúde f ● vt (bread) torrar; (drink to) brindar, beber à saúde de. **~er** n torradeira f

tobacco /tə'bækəʊ/ n tabaco m

toboggan /tə'bɒgən/ n tobogã m

today /tə'deɪ/ n & adv hoje m

toddler /'tɒdlə(r)/ n criança f que está aprendendo a andar or (P) a aprender a andar

toe /təʊ/ n dedo m do pé; (of shoe, stocking) biqueira f; **on one's ~s** alerta, vigilante ● vt **~ the line** andar na linha. **~nail** n unha f do dedo do pé

TOEFL – Test of English as a Foreign Language Exame que se faz para se candidatar a qualquer universidade americana e que certifica o domínio do inglês dos estudantes que falam outros idiomas como língua materna.

toffee /'tɒfɪ/ n puxa-puxa m, (P) caramelo m. ~ **apple** n maçã f caramelizada

together /tə'geðə(r)/ adv junto, juntamente, juntos; (at the same time) ao mesmo tempo; ~ **with** juntamente com. ~**ness** n camaradagem f, companheirismo m

toil /tɔɪl/ vi labutar ● n labuta f, labor m

toilet /'tɔɪlɪt/ n banheiro m, (P) casa f de banho; (grooming) toalete f; ~ **water** água-de-colônia f, (P) água-de-colónia. ~ **paper** n papel m higiénico or (P) higiénico; ~ **roll** n rolo m de papel higiénico, (P) higiénico

toiletries /'tɔɪlɪtrɪz/ npl artigos mpl de toalete

token /'təʊkən/ n sinal m, prova f; (voucher) cheque m; (coin) ficha f ● a simbólico

told /təʊld/ ▶ TELL ● a **all** ~ (all in all) ao todo

tolerab|le /'tɒlərəbl/ a tolerável; (not bad) sofrível, razoável

toleran|t /'tɒlərənt/ a tolerante (of para com). ~**ce** n tolerância f

tolerate /'tɒləreɪt/ vt tolerar

toll[1] /təʊl/ n pedágio m, (P) portagem f; **death** ~ número m de mortos; **take its** ~ (of age) fazer sentir o seu peso

toll[2] /təʊl/ vt/i (of bell) dobrar

tomato /tə'mɑːtəʊ/ n (pl -oes) tomate m

tomb /tuːm/ n túmulo m, sepultura f

tomboy /'tɒmbɔɪ/ n menina f levada (e masculinizada), (P) maria-rapaz f

tombstone /'tuːmstəʊn/ n lápide f, pedra f tumular

tomorrow /tə'mɒrəʊ/ n & adv amanhã m; ~ **morning/night** amanhã de manhã/à noite

ton /tʌn/ n tonelada f (= 1016 kg); (metric) ~ tonelada f (= 1000 kg); ~**s of** 🄸 montes de 🄸, (P) carradas de 🄸

tone /təʊn/ n tom m; (of radio, telephone etc) sinal m; (colour) tom m, tonalidade f; Med tonicidade f ● vt ~ **down** atenuar ● vi ~ **in** combinar-se, harmonizar-se (with com); ~ up ‹muscles› tonificar. ~**deaf** a sem ouvido musical

tongs /tɒŋz/ n tenaz f; (for sugar) pinça f; (for hair) pinça f

tongue /tʌŋ/ n língua f. ~**in-cheek** a & adv sem ser a sério, com ironia, a brincar. ~**tied** a calado. ~**twister** n trava-língua m

tonic /'tɒnɪk/ n Med tônico m, (P) tónico m; Mus tônica f, (P) tónica f ● a tônico, (P) tónico

tonight /tə'naɪt/ adv & n hoje à noite, logo à noite, esta noite f

tonne /tʌn/ n (metric) tonelada f

tonsil /'tɒnsl/ n amígdala f

tonsillitis /tɒnsɪ'laɪtɪs/ n amigdalite f

too /tuː/ adv demasiado, demais; (also) também, igualmente; 🄸 (very) muito

took /tʊk/ ▶ TAKE

tool /tuːl/ n (carpenter's, plumber's etc) ferramenta f; (gardener's) utensílio m; fig (person) joguete m. ~**bag** n saco m de ferramenta(s)

toot /tuːt/ n toque m de buzina ● vt/i ~ **(the horn)** buzinar

tooth /tuːθ/ n (pl teeth) dente m. ~**less** a desdentado

toothache /'tuːθeɪk/ n dor f de dentes

toothbrush /'tuːθbrʌʃ/ n escova f de dentes

toothpaste /'tuːθpeɪst/ n pasta f de dentes, dentifrício m, (P) dentifrico m

toothpick /'tuːθpɪk/ n palito m

top[1] /tɒp/ n (highest point; upper part) alto m, cimo m, topo m; (of hill; also fig) cume m; (upper surface) cimo m, topo m; (surface of table) tampo m; (lid) tampa f; (of bottle) rolha f; (of list) cabeça f; **from** ~ **to bottom** de alto a baixo; **on** ~ **of** em cima de; fig além de; **on** ~ **of that** ainda por cima ● a ‹shelf etc› de cima, superior; (in rank) primeiro; (best) melhor; (distinguished) eminente; (maximum) máximo; ~ **gear** Auto a velocidade mais alta; ~ **hat** chapéu m alto; ~ **secret** ultrassecreto ● vt (pt topped) (exceed) ultrapassar, ir acima de; ~ **up** encher; (mobiles) recarregar; ~**ped with** coberto de. ~**heavy** a mais pesado na parte de cima

top[2] /tɒp/ n (toy) pião m; **sleep like a** ~ dormir como uma pedra

topic /'tɒpɪk/ n tópico m, assunto m

topical /'tɒpɪkl/ a da atualidade, corrente

topless /'tɒplɪs/ a com o peito nu, topless

topple /'tɒpl/ vt/i (fazer) desabar, (fazer) tombar, (fazer) cair

top-up card n cartão m pré-pago

t

top-up fees *npl*: contribuição complementar às mensalidades da universidade, para fins de matrícula; (*P*) contribuição suplementar acrescida às propinas da universidade

torch /tɔːtʃ/ *n* (*electric*) lanterna *f* elétrica; (*flaming*) archote *m*, facho *m*

tore /tɔː(r)/ ▶ TEAR[1]

torment[1] /'tɔːmənt/ *n* tormento *m*

torment[2] /tɔː'ment/ *vt* atormentar, torturar; (*annoy*) aborrecer, chatear

torn /tɔːn/ ▶ TEAR[1]

tornado /tɔː'neɪdəʊ/ *n* (*pl* -oes) tornado *m*

torpedo /tɔː'piːdəʊ/ *n* (*pl* -oes) torpedo *m* ● *vt* torpedear

torrent /'tɒrənt/ *n* torrente *f*. ~ial /tə'renʃl/ *a* torrencial

torso /'tɔːsəʊ/ *n* (*pl* -os) torso *m*

tortoise /'tɔːtəs/ *n* tartaruga *f*

tortoiseshell /'tɔːtəsʃel/ *n* (*for ornaments etc*) tartaruga *f*

tortuous /'tɔːtʃʊəs/ *a* (*of path etc*) que dá muitas voltas, sinuoso; *fig* tortuoso; retorcido

torture /'tɔːtʃə(r)/ *n* tortura *f*, suplício *m* ● *vt* torturar

Tory /'tɔːrɪ/ *a* & *n* [] conservador *m*

toss /tɒs/ *vt* atirar, jogar, (*P*) deitar; (*shake*) agitar, sacudir ● *vi* agitar-se, debater-se; ~ **a coin**, ~ **up** tirar cara ou coroa

tot[1] /tɒt/ *n* criancinha *f*; [] (*glass*) copinho *m*

tot[2] /tɒt/ *vt/i* (*pt* totted) ~ **up** [] somar

total /'təʊtl/ *a* & *n* total *m* ● *vt* (*pt* totalled) (*find total of*) totalizar; (*amount to*) elevar-se a, montar a. ~**ity** /-'tælətɪ/ *n* totalidade *f*. ~**ly** *adv* totalmente

totalitarian /təʊtælɪ'teərɪən/ *a* totalitário

totter /'tɒtə(r)/ *vi* cambalear, andar aos tombos; (*of tower etc*) oscilar

touch /tʌtʃ/ *vt/i* tocar; (*of ends, gardens etc*) tocar-se; (*tamper with*) mexer em; (*affect*) comover; ~ **down** *Aviat* aterrissar, (*P*) aterrar; ~ **off** disparar; (*cause*) dar início a, desencadear; ~ **on** (*mention*) tocar em; ~ **up** retocar ● *n* (*sense*) tato *m*; (*contact*) toque *m*; (*of colour*) toque *m*, retoque *m*; **a** ~ **of** (*small amount*) um pouco de; **get in** ~ **with** entrar em contato, (*P*) contacto com; **lose** ~ perder contato, (*P*) contacto. ~-**and-go** (*risky*) arriscado; (*uncertain*) duvidoso, incerto; ~**line** *n* linha *f* lateral

touching /'tʌtʃɪŋ/ *a* comovente, comovedor

touchy /'tʌtʃɪ/ *a* melindroso, suscetível, que se ofende facilmente

tough /tʌf/ *a* (**-er, -est**) (*hard, difficult; relentless*) duro; (*strong*) forte, resistente ● *n* ~ (**guy**) valentão *m*, durão *m* []; ~ **luck!** [] pouca sorte!, que azar!

toughen /'tʌfn/ *vt/i* (*person*) endurecer; (*strengthen*) reforçar

tour /tʊə(r)/ *n* viagem *f*; (*visit*) visita *f*; (*by team etc*) tournée *f*; **on** ~ em tournée ● *vt* visitar

tourism /'tʊərɪzəm/ *n* turismo *m*

tourist /'tʊərɪst/ *n* turista *mf* ● *a* turístico; ~ **office** agência *f* de turismo

tournament /'tʊərnəmənt/ *n* torneio *m*

tousle /'taʊzl/ *vt* despentear, esguedelhar

tout /taʊt/ *vi* angariar clientes (**for** para) ● *vt* (*try to sell*) tentar revender ● *n* (*hotel etc*) angariador *m*; (*ticket*) cambista *m*, (*P*) revendedor *m*

tow /təʊ/ *vt* rebocar; ~ **away** ‹*vehicle*› rebocar ● *n* reboque *m*; **on** ~ a reboque. ~**path** *n* caminho *m* de sirga; ~ **rope** *n* cabo *m* de reboque

toward(s) /tə'wɔːd(z)/ *prep* para, em direção a, na direção de; (*of attitude*) para com; (*time*) por volta de

towel /'taʊəl/ *n* toalha *f*; (*tea towel*) pano *m* de prato ● *vt* (*pt* **towelled**) esfregar com a toalha. ~ **rail** *n* toalheiro *m*. ~**ling** *n* atoalhado *m*, (*P*) pano *m* turco

tower /'taʊə(r)/ *n* torre *f*; ~ **block** prédio *m* alto ● *vi* ~ **above** dominar. ~**ing** *a* muito alto; *fig* (*of rage etc*) violento

town /taʊn/ *n* cidade *f*; **go to** ~ [] perder a cabeça []; ~ **council** município *m*; ~ **hall** câmara *f* municipal; ~ **planning** urbanização *f*

toxic /'tɒksɪk/ *a* tóxico

toy /tɔɪ/ *n* brinquedo *m* ● *vi* ~ **with** ‹*object*› brincar com; ‹*idea*› considerar, cogitar

trace /treɪs/ *n* traço *m*, rastro *m*, sinal *m*; (*small quantity*) traço *m*, vestígio *m* ● *vt* seguir or encontrar a pista de; (*draw*) traçar; (*with tracing paper*) decalcar

track /træk/ *n* (*of person etc*) rastro *m*, pista *f*; (*racetrack, of tape*) pista *f*; (*record*) faixa *f*; (*path*) trilho *m*, carreiro *m*; *Rail* via *f* ● *vt* seguir a pista or a trajetória de; **keep** ~ **of** manter-se em contato com; (*keep oneself informed*) seguir; ~ **down**

(*find*) encontrar, descobrir; (*hunt*) seguir a pista de; **~ suit** conjunto *m* de jogging, (*P*) fato *m* de treino

tractor /'træktə(r)/ *n* trator *m*

trade /treɪd/ *n* comércio *m*; (*job*) ofício *m*, profissão *f*; (*swap*) troca *f*; **~ mark** marca *f* de fábrica; **~ union** sindicato *m* ● *vt/i* comerciar (em), negociar (em); **~ on** (*exploit*) tirar partido de, abusar de ● *vt* (*swap*) trocar; **~ in** ‹*used article*› trocar. **~r** /-ə(r)/ *n* negociante *mf*, comerciante *mf*

tradesman /'treɪdzmən/ *n* (*pl* **-men**) comerciante *m*

trading /'treɪdɪŋ/ *n* comércio *m*; **~ estate** zona *f* industrial

tradition /trə'dɪʃn/ *n* tradição *f*. **~al** *a* tradicional

traffic /'træfɪk/ *n* (*trade*) tráfego *m*, tráfico *m*; (*on road*) trânsito *m*, tráfego *m*; *Aviat* tráfego *m*; **~ circle** *Amer* giratória *f*, (*P*) rotunda *f*; **~ island** ilha *f* de pedestres, (*P*) refúgio *m* para peões; **~ jam** engarrafamento *m*; **~ warden** guarda *mf* or (*P*) polícia *mf* de trânsito ● *vi* (*pt* **trafficked**) traficar (**in** em). **~ lights** *npl* sinal *m* luminoso, (*P*) semáforo *m*. **~ker** *n* traficante *mf*

tragedy /'trædʒədɪ/ *n* tragédia *f*.

tragic /'trædʒɪk/ *a* trágico

trail /treɪl/ *vt/i* arrastar(-se), rastejar; (*plant, on ground*) rastejar; (*of plant, over wall*) trepar; (*track*) seguir ● *n* (*of powder, smoke etc*) esteira *f*; rastro *m*, (*P*) rasto *m*; (*track*) pista *f*; (*beaten path*) trilho *m*

trailer /'treɪlə(r)/ *n* reboque *m*; *Amer* (*caravan*) reboque *m*, caravana *f*; trailer *m*; (*film*) trailer *m*, apresentação *f* de filme

train /treɪn/ *n* *Rail* trem *m*, (*P*) comboio *m*; (*procession*) fila *f*; (*of dress*) cauda *f*; (*retinue*) comitiva *f* ● *vt* (*instruct, develop*) educar, formar, treinar; ‹*plant*› guiar; ‹*sportsman, animal*› treinar; ‹*aim*› assestar, apontar ● *vi* estudar, treinar-se. **~ed** *a* (*skilled*) qualificado; ‹*doctor etc*› diplomado. **~er** *n* *Sport* treinador *m*; (*shoe*) tênis *m*, (*P*) ténis *m*. **~ing** *n* treino *m*

trainee /treɪ'niː/ *n* estagiário *m*

trait /treɪ(t)/ *n* traço *m*, característica *f*

traitor /'treɪtə(r)/ *n* traidor *m*

tram /træm/ *n* bonde *m*, (*P*) (carro) elétrico *m*

tramp /træmp/ *vi* marchar (com passo pesado) ● *vt* percorrer, palmilhar ● *n* som *m* de passos pesados; (*vagrant*) vagabundo *m*, andarilho *m*; (*hike*) longa caminhada *f*

trample /'træmpl/ *vt/i* **~ (on)** pisar com força; *fig* menosprezar

trampoline /'træmpəliːn/ *n* (lona *f* usada como) trampolim *m*

trance /trɑːns/ *n* (*hypnotic*) transe *m*; (*ecstasy*) êxtase *m*, arrebatamento *m*; *Med* estupor *m*

tranquil /'træŋkwɪl/ *a* tranquilo, sossegado. **~lity** /-'kwɪlətɪ/ *n* tranquilidade *f*, sossego *m*

tranquillizer /'træŋkwɪlaɪzə(r)/ *n* (*drug*) tranquilizante *m*, calmante *m*

transact /træn'zækt/ *vt* ‹*business*› fazer; efetuar. **~ion** /-kʃn/ *n* transação *f*

transcend /træn'send/ *vt* transcender

transcri|be /træn'skraɪb/ *vt* transcrever. **~pt**, **~ption** /-ɪpʃn/ *ns* transcrição *f*

transfer[1] /træns'fɜː(r)/ *vt* (*pt* **transferred**) transferir; ‹*power, property*› transmitir; **~ the charges** (*telephone*) ligar a cobrar ● *vi* mudar(-se), ser transferido; (*change planes etc*) fazer transferência

transfer[2] /'trænsfɜː(r)/ *n* transferência *f*; (*of power, property*) transmissão *f*; (*image*) decalcomania *f*

transform /træns'fɔːm/ *vt* transformar. **~ation** /-ə'meɪʃn/ *n* transformação *f*. **~er** *n* *Electr* transformador *m*

transfusion /træns'fjuːʒn/ *n* (*of blood*) transfusão *f*

transient /'trænzɪənt/ *a* transitório, transiente, efêmero, (*P*) efémero, passageiro

transistor /træn'zɪstə(r)/ *n* (*device, radio*) transístor *m*

transit /'trænsɪt/ *n* trânsito *m*; **in ~** em trânsito

transition /træn'zɪʃn/ *n* transição *f*. **~al** *a* transitório

transitive /'trænsətɪv/ *a* transitivo

transitory /'trænsɪtərɪ/ *a* transitório

translat|e /trænz'leɪt/ *vt* traduzir. **~ion** /-ʃn/ *n* tradução *f*. **~or** *n* tradutor *m*

transmi|t /trænz'mɪt/ *vt* (*pt* **transmitted**) transmitir. **~ssion** *n* transmissão *f*. **~tter** *n* transmissor *m*

transparen|t /træns'pærənt/ *a* transparente. **~cy** *n* transparência *f*; *Photo* diapositivo *m*

transpire /træn'spaɪə(r)/ *vi* ‹*secret etc*› transpirar, vir a saber-se; (*happen*) suceder, acontecer

t

transplant[1] /trænsˈplɑːnt/ *vt* transplantar

transplant[2] /ˈtrænsplɑːnt/ *n Med* transplantação *f*, (P) transplante *m*

transport[1] /trænˈspɔːt/ *vt* (*carry, delight*) transportar. **~ation** /-ˈteɪʃn/ *n* transporte *m*

transport[2] /ˈtrænspɔːt/ *n* (*of goods, delight etc*) transporte *m*

transpose /trænˈspəʊz/ *vt* transpor

transvestite /trænzˈvestaɪt/ *n* travesti *mf*

trap /træp/ *n* armadilha *f*, ratoeira *f*, cilada *f* ● *vt* (*pt* **trapped**) apanhar na armadilha; (*cut off*) prender, bloquear

trapdoor /træpˈdɔː(r)/ *n* alçapão *m*

trapeze /trəˈpiːz/ *n* trapézio *m*

trash /træʃ/ *n* (*worthless stuff*) porcaria *f*; (*refuse*) lixo *m*; (*nonsense*) disparates *mpl*. **~ can** *n Amer* lata *f* do lixo, (P) caixote *m* do lixo. **~y** *a* que não vale nada, porcaria

trauma /ˈtrɔːmə/ *n* trauma *m*, traumatismo *m*. **~tic** /-ˈmætɪk/ *a* traumático

travel /ˈtrævl/ *vi* (*pt* **travelled**) viajar; (*of vehicle, bullet, sound*) ir ● *vt* percorrer ● *n* viagem *f*; **~ agent** agente *mf* de viagem. **~ler** *n* viajante *mf*; **~ler's cheque** cheque *m* de viagem

travesty /ˈtrævəstɪ/ *n* paródia *f*, caricatura *f*

trawler /ˈtrɔːlə(r)/ *n* traineira *f*, (P) arrastão *m*

tray /treɪ/ *n* tabuleiro *m*, bandeja *f*

treacherous /ˈtretʃərəs/ *a* traiçoeiro

treachery /ˈtretʃərɪ/ *n* traição *f*, perfídia *f*, deslealdade *f*

treacle /ˈtriːkl/ *n* melaço *m*

tread /tred/ *vt/i* (*pt* **trod**, *pp* **trodden**) (*step*) pisar; (*walk*) andar, caminhar; (*walk along*) seguir; **~ sth into** ‹carpet› esmigalhar or pisar algo sobre/em ● *n* passo *m*, maneira *f* de andar; (*of tyre*) trilho *m*

treason /ˈtriːzn/ *n* traição *f*

treasure /ˈtreʒə(r)/ *n* tesouro *m* ● *vt* ter o maior apreço por; (*store*) guardar bem guardado. **~r** *n* tesoureiro *m*

treasury /ˈtreʒərɪ/ *n* (*building*) tesouraria *f*; (*department*) Ministério *m* das Finanças or da Fazenda; *fig* tesouro *m*

treat /triːt/ *vt/i* tratar; **~ sb to sth** convidar alguém para algo ● *n* (*pleasure*) prazer *m*, regalo *m*; (*present*) mimo *m*, gentileza *f*

treatment /ˈtriːtmənt/ *n* tratamento *m*

treaty /ˈtriːtɪ/ *n* (*pact*) tratado *m*

treble /ˈtrebl/ *a* triplo ● *vt/i* triplicar ● *n Mus* (*voice*) soprano *m*

tree /triː/ *n* árvore *f*

trek /trek/ *n* viagem *f* penosa; (*walk*) caminhada *f* ● *vi* (*pt* **trekked**) viajar penosamente; (*walk*) caminhar

trellis /ˈtrelɪs/ *n* grade *f* para trepadeiras, treliça *f*

tremble /ˈtrembl/ *vi* tremer

tremendous /trɪˈmendəs/ *a* (*fearful, huge*) tremendo; 🆒 (*excellent*) fantástico; formidável

tremor /ˈtremə(r)/ *n* tremor *m*, estremecimento *m*; **(earth) ~** abalo (sísmico) *m*, tremor *m* de terra

trench /trentʃ/ *n* fossa *f*, vala *f*; *Mil* trincheira *f*

trend /trend/ *n* tendência *f*; (*fashion*) moda *f*. **~y** *a* 🆒 na (última) moda, (P) na berra 🆒

trepidation /trepɪˈdeɪʃn/ *n* (*fear*) receio *m*, apreensão *f*

trespass /ˈtrespəs/ *vi* entrar ilegalmente (**on** em); **no ~ing** entrada *f* proibida. **~er** *n* intruso *m*

trial /ˈtraɪəl/ *n Jur* julgamento *m*, processo *m*; (*test*) ensaio *m*, experiência *f*, prova *f*; (*ordeal*) provação *f*; **on ~** em julgamento; **~ and error** tentativas *fpl*, (P) tentativa *f* e erro

triangle /ˈtraɪæŋgl/ *n* triângulo *m*. **~ular** /-ˈæŋgjʊlə(r)/ *a* triangular

tribe /traɪb/ *n* tribo *f*. **~al** *a* tribal

tribunal /traɪˈbjuːnl/ *n* tribunal *m*

tributary /ˈtrɪbjʊtərɪ/ *n* afluente *m*, tributário *m*

tribute /ˈtrɪbjuːt/ *n* tributo *m*; **pay ~ to** prestar homenagem a, render tributo a

trick /trɪk/ *n* truque *m*; (*prank*) partida *f*; (*habit*) jeito *m* ● *vt* enganar; **do the ~** 🆒 (*work*) dar resultado

trickle /ˈtrɪkl/ *vi* pingar, gotejar, escorrer ● *n* fio *m* de água *etc*; *fig* (*small number*) punhado *m*

tricky /ˈtrɪkɪ/ *a* (*crafty*) manhoso; ‹problem› delicado, complicado

tricycle /ˈtraɪsɪkl/ *n* triciclo *m*

trifle /ˈtraɪfl/ *n* ninharia *f*, bagatela *f*; (*sweet*) sobremesa *f* feita de pão-de-ló, frutas e creme ● *vi* **~ with** brincar com; **a ~** um pouquinho

trifling /ˈtraɪflɪŋ/ *a* insignificante

trigger /ˈtrɪgə(r)/ *n* (*of gun*) gatilho *m* ● *vt* **~ (off)** (*initiate*) desencadear, despoletar

trim /trɪm/ a (**trimmer**, **trimmest**) bem arranjado, bem cuidado; ‹*figure*› elegante, esbelto ● *vt* (*pt* **trimmed**) (*cut*) aparar; ‹*sails*› orientar, marear; (*ornament*) enfeitar; guarnecer (**with** com) ● *n* (*cut*) aparadela *f*, corte *m* leve; (*decoration*) enfeite *m*; (*on car*) acabamento(s) *m(pl)*, estofado *m*; **in ~** em ordem; (*fit*) em boa forma. **~ming(s)** *n* (*dress*) enfeite *m*; *Culin* guarnição *f*, acompanhamento *m*

trinket /'trɪŋkɪt/ *n* bugiganga *f*; (*jewel*) bijuteria *f*, berloque *m*

trio /'triːəʊ/ *n* (*pl* **-os**) trio *m*

trip /trɪp/ *vi* (*pt* **tripped**) (*stumble*) tropeçar, dar um passo em falso; (*go or dance lightly*) andar/dançar com passos leves ● *vt* **~ (up)** fazer tropeçar, passar uma rasteira a ● *n* (*journey*) viagem *f*; (*outing*) passeio *m*, excursão *f*; (*stumble*) tropeção *m*, passo *m* em falso

tripe /traɪp/ *n* (*food*) dobrada *f*, tripas *fpl*; 🔲 (*nonsense*) disparates *mpl*

triple /'trɪpl/ a triplo, tríplice ● *vt/i* triplicar. **~ts** /-plɪts/ *npl* trigémeos *mpl*, (P) trigémeos *mpl*

triplicate /'trɪplɪkət/ *n* **in ~** em triplicado

tripod /'traɪpɒd/ *n* tripé *m*

trite /traɪt/ a banal, corriqueiro

triumph /'traɪəmf/ *n* triunfo *m* ● *vi* triunfar (**over** sobre); (*exult*) exultar, rejubilar(-se). **~ant** /-'ʌmfənt/ a triunfante

trivial /'trɪvɪəl/ a insignificante

trod, trodden /trɒd, 'trɒdn/ ▶ TREAD

trolley /'trɒlɪ/ *n* carrinho *m*; (**tea-**)**~** carrinho *m* de chá

trombone /trɒm'bəʊn/ *n Mus* trombone *m*

troop /truːp/ *n* bando *m*, grupo *m*; **~s** *Mil* tropas *fpl*; **~ing the colour** a saudação da bandeira ● *vi* **~ in/out** entrar/sair em bando ou grupo

trophy /'trəʊfɪ/ *n* troféu *m*

tropic /'trɒpɪk/ *n* trópico *m*; **~s** trópicos *mpl*. **~al** a tropical

trot /trɒt/ *n* trote *m*; **on the ~** 🔲 a seguir, a fio ● *vi* (*pt* **trotted**) trotar; (*of person*) correr em passos curtos, ir num or a trote 🔲; **~ out** 🔲 (*produce*) exibir; 🔲 (*state*) desfiar

trouble /'trʌbl/ *n* (*difficulty*) dificuldade(s) *f(pl)*, problema(s) *m(pl)*; (*distress*) desgosto(s) *m(pl)*, aborrecimento(s) *m(pl)*; (*pains, effort*) cuidado *m*, trabalho *m*, maçada *f*; (*inconvenience*) transtorno *m*; incômodo *m*, (P) incómodo *m*; *Med* doença *f*; **~(s)** (*unrest*) agitação *f*, conflito(s) *m(pl)*; **be in ~** estar em apuros, estar em dificuldades; **get into ~** meter-se em encrenca/apuros; **it is not worth the ~** não vale a pena ● *vt/i* (*bother*) incomodar(-se), (P) maçar(-se); (*worry*) preocupar(-se); (*agitate*) perturbar. **~maker** *n* desordeiro *m*, provocador *m*; **~shooter** *n* mediador *m*, negociador *m*. **~d** a agitado, perturbado; (*of sleep*) agitado; (*of water*) turvo

troublesome /'trʌblsəm/ a problemático, importuno, (P) maçador

trough /trɒf/ *n* (*drinking*) bebedouro *m*; (*feeding*) comedouro *m*; **~ (of low pressure)** depressão *f*, linha *f* de baixa pressão

trounce /traʊns/ *vt* (*defeat*) esmagar; (*thrash*) espancar

troupe /truːp/ *n Theat* companhia *f*, troupe *f*

trousers /'traʊzəz/ *npl* calça *f*, (P) calças *fpl*; **short ~** calções *mpl*

trousseau /'truːsəʊ/ *n* (*pl* **-s** /-əʊz/) (*of bride*) enxoval *m* de noiva

trout /traʊt/ *n* (*pl invar*) truta *f*

trowel /'traʊəl/ *n* (*garden*) colher *f* de jardineiro; (*for mortar*) trolha *f*

truant /'truːənt/ *n* absenteísta *mf*, (P) absentista *mf*; *Schol* gazeteiro *m*; **play ~t** fazer gazeta. **~cy** *n* absenteísmo *m*, (P) absentismo *m*

truce /truːs/ *n* trégua(s) *f(pl)*, armistício *m*

truck /trʌk/ *n* (*lorry*) caminhão *m*, (P) camião *m*; (*barrow*) carro *m* de bagageiro; (*wagon*) vagão *m* aberto. **~ driver** *n* motorista *mf* de caminhão, (P) camionista *mf*

trudge /trʌdʒ/ *vi* caminhar com dificuldade, caminhar a custo, arrastar-se

true /truː/ a (**-er**, **-est**) verdadeiro; (*accurate*) exato; (*faithful*) fiel; **come ~** (*happen*) realizar-se, concretizar-se; **it is ~** é verdade

truffle /'trʌfl/ *n* trufa *f*

truly /'truːlɪ/ *adv* verdadeiramente; (*faithfully*) fielmente; (*truthfully*) sinceramente

trump /trʌmp/ *n* trunfo *m*; **~ card** carta *f* de trunfo; 🔲 (*valuable resource*) trunfo *m* ● *vt* jogar trunfo, trunfar; **~ up** forjar, inventar

trumpet /'trʌmpɪt/ *n* trombeta *f*

truncheon /'trʌntʃən/ *n* cassetete *m*

t

trunk /trʌŋk/ n (of tree, body) tronco m; (of elephant) tromba f; (box) mala f grande; Amer Auto mala f; **~s** (for swimming) calção m or calções mpl de banho. **~ call** n chamada f interurbana; **~ road** n estrada f nacional

trust /trʌst/ n confiança f; (association) truste m, (P) trust m; consórcio m; (foundation) fundação f; (responsibility) responsabilidade f; Jur fideicomisso m; **in ~** em fideicomisso; **on ~** (without proof) sem verificação prévia; (on credit) a crédito, (P) à confiança ● vt (rely on) ter confiança em, confiar em; (hope) esperar; **~ sb with sth** confiar alguma coisa a alguém ● vi **~ in** or **to** confiar em. **~ed** a <friend etc> de confiança, seguro. **~ful**, **~ing** adjs confiante. **~y** a fiel

trustee /trʌsˈtiː/ n administrador m; Jur fideicomissário m

trustworthy /ˈtrʌstwɜːðɪ/ a (digno) de confiança

truth /truːθ/ n (pl **-s** /truːðz/) verdade f. **~ful** a <account etc> verídico; <person> verdadeiro, que fala verdade

try /traɪ/ vt/i (pt **tried**) tentar, experimentar; (be a strain on) cansar, pôr à prova; Jur julgar; **~ for** <post, scholarship> candidatar-se a; <record> tentar alcançar; **~ on** <clothes> provar; **~ out** experimentar; **~ to do** tentar fazer ● n (attempt) tentativa f, experiência f; <Rugby> ensaio m. **~ing** a difícil

T-shirt /ˈtiːʃɜːt/ n T-shirt f, camiseta f de algodão de mangas curtas

tub /tʌb/ n selha f; Ⅱ (bath) tina f, banheira f

tuba /ˈtjuːbə/ n Mus tuba f

tubby /ˈtʌbɪ/ a (**-ier**, **-iest**) baixote e gorducho

tub|e /tjuːb/ n tubo m; Ⅱ (railway) metrô m, (P) metro m; **inner ~e** câmara f de ar. **~ing** n tubos mpl, tubagem f

tuberculosis /tjuːbɜːkjʊˈləʊsɪs/ n tuberculose f

tubular /ˈtjuːbjʊlə(r)/ a tubular

tuck /tʌk/ n (fold) prega f cosida; (for shortening or ornament) refego m ● vt/i fazer pregas; (put) guardar, meter, enfiar; (hide) esconder; **~ in** or **into** Ⅱ (eat) atacar; **~ in** <shirt> meter as fraldas para dentro; <blanket> prender em; <person> cobrir bem, aconchegar. **~ shop** n School loja f de balas, (P) pastelaria f (junto à escola)

Tuesday /ˈtjuːzdɪ/ n terça-feira f

tuft /tʌft/ n tufo m

tug /tʌg/ vt/i (pt **tugged**) puxar com força; <vessel> rebocar ● n (boat) rebocador m; (pull) puxão m; **~ of war** disputa f cabo-de-guerra

tuition /tjuːˈɪʃn/ n ensino m

tulip /ˈtjuːlɪp/ n tulipa f

tumble /ˈtʌmbl/ vi tombar, baquear, dar um trambolhão ● n tombo m, trambolhão m. **~ drier** n máquina f de secar (roupa)

tumbledown /ˈtʌmbldaʊn/ a em ruínas

tumbler /ˈtʌmblə(r)/ n copo m

tummy /ˈtʌmɪ/ n Ⅱ (stomach) estômago m; Ⅱ (abdomen) barriga f. **~ ache** n Ⅱ dor f de barriga/de estômago

tumour /ˈtjuːmə(r)/ n tumor m

tumult /ˈtjuːmʌlt/ n tumulto m. **~uous** /-ˈmʌltʃʊəs/ a tumultuado, barulhento, agitado

tuna /ˈtjuːnə/ n (pl invar) atum m

tune /tjuːn/ n melodia f ● vt <engine> regular, (P) afinar; <piano etc> afinar ● vi **~ in (to)** Radio, TV ligar (em), (P) sintonizar; **~ up** afinar; **be in ~/out of ~** <instrument> estar afinado/desafinado; <singer> cantar afinado/desafinado. **~ful** a melodioso, harmonioso. **~r** n afinador m; Radio sintonizador m

tunnel /ˈtʌnl/ n túnel m ● vi (pt **tunnelled**) abrir um túnel (**into** em)

turban /ˈtɜːbən/ n turbante m

turbine /ˈtɜːbaɪn/ n turbina f

turbulen|t /ˈtɜːbjʊlənt/ a turbulento. **~ce** n turbulência f

turf /tɜːf/ n (pl **turfs** or **turves**) gramado m, (P) relva f, relvado m; **the ~** (racing) turfe m, hipismo m; **~ accountant** corretor m de apostas ● vt **~ out** Ⅱ jogar fora, (P) deitar fora

Turk /tɜːk/ n turco m. **~ey** n Turquia f. **~ish** a turco m ● n Lang turco m

turkey /ˈtɜːkɪ/ n peru m

turmoil /ˈtɜːmɔɪl/ n agitação f, confusão f, desordem f; **in ~** em ebulição

turn /tɜːn/ vt/i virar(-se), voltar(-se), girar; (change) transformar(-se) (**into** em); (become) ficar, tornar-se; <corner> virar, dobrar; <page> virar, voltar; **~ against** virar-se or voltar-se contra; **~ down** recusar; (fold) dobrar para baixo; (reduce) baixar; **~ in** (hand in) entregar; Ⅱ (go to bed) deitar-se; **~ off** <light etc> apagar; <tap> fechar; <road> virar (para rua transversal); **~ on** <light etc> acender, ligar; <tap> abrir; **~ round**

virar-se, voltar-se ● volta f; (in road) curva f; (of mind, events) mudança f; (occasion, opportunity) vez f; 🔲 ataque m; crise f; 🔲 (shock) susto m; **do a good ~** prestar (um) serviço; **in ~** por sua vez, sucessivamente; **speak out of ~** dizer o que não se deve, cometer uma indiscrição; **take ~s** revezar-se; **~ of the century** virada f or (P) viragem f do século □ **~ away** vi virar-se or voltar-se para o outro lado ● vt (avert) desviar; (reject) recusar; (send back) mandar embora. **~ back** vi (return) devolver; ‹vehicle› dar meia volta, voltar para trás ● vt (fold) dobrar para trás. **~ out** vt ‹light› apagar; (empty) esvaziar, despejar; ‹pocket› virar do avesso; (produce) produzir ● vi (transpire) vir a saber-se, descobrir-se; 🔲 (come) aparecer. **~ up** vi aparecer, chegar; (be found) aparecer ● vt (find) desenterrar; (increase) aumentar; ‹collar› levantar. **~out** n assistência f; **~up** n (of trousers) dobra f

turning /'tɜːnɪŋ/ n rua f transversal; (corner) esquina f. **~ point** n momento m decisivo

turnip /'tɜːnɪp/ n nabo m

turnover /'tɜːnəʊvə(r)/ n (pie, tart) pastel m, empada f; (money) faturamento m, (P) faturação f; (of staff) rotatividade f

turnpike /'tɜːnpaɪk/ n Amer auto-estrada f com pedágio, (P) portagem f

turnstile /'tɜːnstaɪl/ n (gate) torniquete m, borboleta f

turntable /'tɜːnteɪbl/ n (for record) prato m do toca-disco, (P) gira-discos; (record player) toca-disco m, (P) gira-discos m

turquoise /'tɜːkwɔɪz/ a turquesa invar

turret /'tʌrɪt/ n torreão m, torrinha f

turtle /'tɜːtl/ n tartaruga-do-mar f. **~neck** a de gola alta

tusk /tʌsk/ n (tooth) presa f; (elephant's) defesa f, dente m

tutor /'tjuːtə(r)/ n professor m particular; Univ professor m universitário

tutorial /tjuː'tɔːrɪəl/ n Univ seminário m

TV /tiː'viː/ n tevê f, (P) TV

tweet /twiːt/ n pio m, pipilo m ● vi pipilar

tweezers /'twiːzəz/ npl pinça f

twelve /twelv/ a & n doze m; **~ (o'clock)** doze horas. **~fth** a & n décimo segundo m; **T~fth Night** véspera f de Reis

twent|y /'twentɪ/ a & n vinte m. **~ieth** a & n vigésimo m

twice /twaɪs/ adv duas vezes

twiddle /'twɪdl/ vt/i **~ (with)** (fiddle with) torcer, brincar (com); **~ one's thumbs** girar os polegares, não ter nada para fazer

twig /twɪg/ n galho m, graveto m

twilight /'twaɪlaɪt/ n crepúsculo m ● a crepuscular

twin /twɪn/ n & a gêmeo m, (P) gémeo m ● vt (pt twinned) (pair) emparelhar, emparceirar; **~ beds** par m de camas de solteiro

twine /twaɪn/ n guita f, cordel m ● vt/i (weave together) entrançar; (wind) enroscar(-se)

twinge /twɪndʒ/ n dor f aguda e súbita, pontada f; fig pontada f, (P) ferroada f

twinkle /'twɪŋkl/ vi cintilar, brilhar ● n cintilação f, brilho m

twirl /twɜːl/ vt/i (fazer) girar; ‹moustache› torcer

twist /twɪst/ vt torcer; (weave together) entrançar; (roll) enrolar; (distort) torcer, deturpar; **~ sb's arm** forçar alguém ● vi ‹rope etc› torcer-se, enrolar-se; ‹road› dar voltas or curvas, serpentear ● n (act of twisting) torcedura f, (P) torcedela f; (of rope) nó m; (of events) reviravolta f

twit /twɪt/ n 🔲 idiota mf

twitch /twɪtʃ/ vt/i contrair(-se) ● n (tic) tique m; (jerk) puxão m

two /tuː/ a & n dois m; **in or of ~ minds** indeciso; **put ~ and ~ together** tirar conclusões. **~faced** a de duas caras, hipócrita; **~piece** n (garment) duas-peças m invar, (P) fato de duas peças; **~seater** n (car) carro m de dois lugares; **~way** a (of road) mão dupla

twosome /'tuːsəm/ n par m

tycoon /taɪ'kuːn/ n magnata m

tying /'taɪɪŋ/ ▸ TIE

type /taɪp/ n (example, print) tipo m; (kind) tipo m; gênero m, (P) género m; 🔲 (person) cara m, (P) tipo m 🔲 ● vt/i (write) bater à máquina; datilografar, (P) dactilografar

typescript /'taɪpskrɪpt/ n texto m datilografado, (P) dactilografado

typewrit|er /'taɪpraɪtə(r)/ n máquina f de escrever. **~ten** /-ɪtn/ a batido à máquina, datilografado, (P) dactilografado

t

typhoid /ˈtaɪfɔɪd/ n ~ **(fever)** febre f tifóide

typhoon /taɪˈfuːn/ n tufão m

typical /ˈtɪpɪkl/ a típico. ~**ly** adv tipicamente

typify /ˈtɪpɪfaɪ/ vt ser o (protó)tipo de, tipificar, symbolizar

typing /ˈtaɪpɪŋ/ n datilografia f, (P) dactilografia f

typist /ˈtaɪpɪst/ n datilógrafo m, (P) dactilógrafo m

tyrann|y /ˈtɪrənɪ/ n tirania f. ~**ical** /tɪˈrænɪkl/ a tirânico

tyrant /ˈtaɪərənt/ n tirano m

tyre /ˈtaɪə(r)/ n pneu m

....

Uu

....

ubiquitous /juːˈbɪkwɪtəs/ a ubíquo, omnipresente

UFO /ˈjuːfəʊ/ n OVNI m

ugl|y /ˈʌglɪ/ a (**-ier, -iest**) feio. ~**iness** n feiura f, (P) fealdade f

UK abbr ▶ UNITED KINGDOM

ulcer /ˈʌlsə(r)/ n úlcera f

ulterior /ʌlˈtɪərɪə(r)/ a ulterior; ~ **motive** razão f inconfessada, segundas intenções fpl

ultimate /ˈʌltɪmət/ a último, derradeiro; (definitive) definitivo; (maximum) supremo; (basic) fundamental. ~**ly** adv finalmente

ultimatum /ʌltɪˈmeɪtəm/ n (pl **-ums**) ultimato m

ultra- /ˈʌltrə/ pref ultra-, super-

ultraviolet /ʌltrəˈvaɪələt/ a ultravioleta

t umbilical /ʌmˈbɪlɪkl/ a ~ **cord** cordão m umbilical

u umbrella /ʌmˈbrelə/ n guarda-chuva m

umpire /ˈʌmpaɪə(r)/ n Sport árbitro m ● vt arbitrar

umpteen /ˈʌmptiːn/ a 🖾 sem conta; montes de 🆃; **for the ~th time** 🖾 pela centésima or enésima vez

UN abbr (= United Nations) ONU f

un- /ʌn/ pref não, pouco

unable /ʌnˈeɪbl/ a **be ~ to do** ser incapaz de/não poder fazer

unabridged /ʌnəˈbrɪdʒd/ a ‹text› integral

unacceptable /ʌnəkˈseptəbl/ a inaceitável, inadmissível

unaccompanied /ʌnəˈkʌmpənɪd/ a só, desacompanhado

unaccountable /ʌnəˈkaʊntəbl/ a (strange) inexplicável; (not responsible) que não tem que dar contas a alguém or que não pode ser responsabilizado

unaccustomed /ʌnəˈkʌstəmd/ a desacostumado; ~ **to** não acostumado or não habituado a

unadulterated /ʌnəˈdʌltəreɪtɪd/ a (pure, sheer) puro

unaided /ʌnˈeɪdɪd/ a sem ajuda, sozinho, por si só

unanim|ous /juːˈnænɪməs/ a unânime. ~**ously** adv unanimemente, por unanimidade

unarmed /ʌnˈɑːmd/ a desarmado, indefeso

unashamed /ʌnəˈʃeɪmd/ a desavergonhado, sem vergonha. ~**ly** /-ɪdlɪ/ adv sem vergonha

unassuming /ʌnəˈsjuːmɪŋ/ a modesto, despretencioso

unattached /ʌnəˈtætʃt/ a ‹person› livre

unattainable /ʌnəˈteɪnəbl/ a inacessível

unattended /ʌnəˈtendɪd/ a ‹person› desacompanhado; ‹car, luggage› abandonado

unattractive /ʌnəˈtræktɪv/ a sem atrativos; ‹offer› de pouco interesse, pouco apetecível

unauthorized /ʌnˈɔːθəraɪzd/ a não-autorizado, sem autorização

unavoidabl|e /ʌnəˈvɔɪdəbl/ a inevitável. ~**y** adv inevitavelmente

unaware /ʌnəˈweə(r)/ a **be ~ of** desconhecer, ignorar, não ter consciência de. ~**s** /-eəz/ adv (unexpectedly) inesperadamente; **catch sb ~s** apanhar alguém desprevenido or de surpresa

unbalanced /ʌnˈbælənst/ a ‹mind, person› desequilibrado or instável

unbearable /ʌnˈbeərəbl/ a insuportável

unbeat|able /ʌnˈbiːtəbl/ a imbatível. ~**en** a não vencido, invicto; (unsurpassed) insuperado

unbelievable /ʌnbɪˈliːvəbl/ a inacreditável, incrível

unbiased /ʌnˈbaɪəst/ a imparcial

unblock /ʌnˈblɒk/ vt desbloquear, desobstruir; ‹pipe› desentupir

unbreakable /ʌnˈbreɪkəbl/ a inquebrável

unbroken /ʌnˈbrəʊkən/ a (intact) intato, inteiro; (continuous) ininterrupto

unburden /ʌnˈbɜːdn/ vpr ~ o.s. (open one's heart) desabafar (to com)

unbutton /ʌnˈbʌtn/ vt desabotoar

uncalled-for /ʌnˈkɔːldfɔː(r)/ a injustificável, gratuito

uncanny /ʌnˈkænɪ/ a (-ier, -iest) estranho, misterioso

unceasing /ʌnˈsiːsɪŋ/ a incessante

uncertain /ʌnˈsɜːtn/ a incerto; be ~ whether não saber ao certo se, estar indeciso quanto a. **~ty** n incerteza f

unchang|ed /ʌnˈtʃeɪndʒd/ a inalterado, sem modificação. **~ing** a inalterável, imutável

uncivilized /ʌnˈsɪvɪlaɪzd/ a não civilizado, bárbaro

uncle /ˈʌŋkl/ n tio m

uncomfortable /ʌnˈkʌmfətəbl/ a ‹thing› desconfortável; incômodo, (P) incómodo; (unpleasant) desagradável; **feel** or **be ~** (uneasy) sentir-se or estar pouco à vontade

uncommon /ʌnˈkɒmən/ a pouco vulgar, invulgar, fora do comum. **~ly** adv invulgarmente, excepcionalmente

uncompromising /ʌnˈkɒmprəmaɪzɪŋ/ a intransigente

unconcerned /ʌnkənˈsɜːnd/ a (indifferent) indiferente (by a)

unconditional /ʌnkənˈdɪʃənl/ a incondicional

unconscious /ʌnˈkɒnʃəs/ a inconsciente (of de). **~ly** adv inconscientemente

unconventional /ʌnkənˈvenʃənl/ a não convencional, fora do comum

uncooperative /ʌnkəʊˈɒpərətɪv/ a ‹person› pouco cooperativo; do contra 🆃

uncork /ʌnˈkɔːk/ vt desarrolhar, tirar a rolha de

uncouth /ʌnˈkuːθ/ a rude, grosseiro

uncover /ʌnˈkʌvə(r)/ vt descobrir, revelar

undecided /ʌndɪˈsaɪdɪd/ a (irresolute) indeciso; (not settled) por decidir, pendente

undeniable /ʌndɪˈnaɪəbl/ a inegável, incontestável

under /ˈʌndə(r)/ prep debaixo de, sob; (less than) com menos de; (according to) conforme, segundo; **~ age** menor de idade; **~ way** em preparo, (P) em preparação ● adv por baixo, debaixo

under- /ˈʌndə(r)/ pref sub-

undercarriage /ˈʌndəkærɪdʒ/ n Aviat trem m de aterrissagem or (P) de aterragem

underclothes /ˈʌndəkləʊðz/ npl ▶ UNDERWEAR

undercoat /ˈʌndəkəʊt/ n (of paint) primeira mão f, (P) primeira demão f

undercover /ʌndəˈkʌvə(r)/ a ‹agent, operation› secreto

undercurrent /ˈʌndəkʌrənt/ n corrente f subterrânea; fig filão m; fig tendência f oculta

undercut /ʌndəˈkʌt/ vt (pt undercut, pres p undercutting) Comm vender a preços mais baixos do que a concorrência

underdeveloped /ʌndədɪˈveləpt/ a atrofiado; ‹country› em vias de desenvolvimento

underdog /ˈʌndədɒg/ n desprotegido m; o mais fraco

underdone /ˈʌndədʌn/ a (of meat) mal passado

underestimate /ʌndərˈestɪmeɪt/ vt subestimar, não dar o devido valor a

underfed /ʌndəˈfed/ a subalimentado, subnutrido

underfoot /ʌndəˈfʊt/ adv debaixo dos pés; (on the ground) no chão

undergo /ʌndəˈgəʊ/ vt (pt -went, pp -gone) (be subjected to) sofrer; (treatment) ser submetido a

undergraduate /ʌndəˈgrædʒʊət/ n estudante mf universitário

underground¹ /ʌndəˈgraʊnd/ adv debaixo da terra; fig (secretly) clandestinamente

underground² /ˈʌndəgraʊnd/ a subterrâneo; fig (secret) clandestino ● n Rail metro(politano) m, (P) metro m

undergrowth /ˈʌndəgrəʊθ/ n mato m

underhand /ˈʌndəhænd/ a (deceitful) sonso, dissimulado

under|lie /ʌndəˈlaɪ/ vt (pt -lay, pp -lain, pres p -lying) estar por baixo de. **~lying** a subjacente

underline /ʌndəˈlaɪn/ vt sublinhar, ressaltar

undermine /ʌndəˈmaɪn/ vt minar, solapar

u

underneath /ʌndə'niːθ/ *prep* sob, debaixo de, por baixo de ● *adv* abaixo, em baixo, por baixo

underpaid /ʌndə'peɪd/ *a* mal pago

underpants /'ʌndəpænts/ *npl* (*man's*) cuecas *fpl*

underpass /'ʌndəpɑːs/ *n* (*for cars, people*) passagem *f* inferior

underprivileged /ʌndə'prɪvɪlɪdʒd/ *a* desfavorecido

underrate /ʌndə'reɪt/ *vt* subestimar, depreciar

underside /'ʌndəsaɪd/ *n* lado *m* inferior, base *f*

underskirt /'ʌndəskɜːt/ *n* anágua *f*

understand /ʌndə'stænd/ *vt/i* (*pt* **-stood**) compreender, entender. **~able** *a* compreensível. **~ing** *a* compreensivo ● *n* compreensão *f*; (*agreement*) acordo *m*, entendimento *m*

understatement /'ʌndəsteɪtmənt/ *n* versão *f* atenuada da verdade, litotes *f*, eufemismo *m*

understudy /'ʌndəstʌdɪ/ *n* substituto *m*

undertak|e /ʌndə'teɪk/ *vt* (*pt* **-took**, *pp* **-taken**) empreender; (*responsibility*) assumir; **~e to** encarregar-se de. **~ing** *n* (*task*) empreendimento *m*; (*promise*) compromisso *m*

undertaker /'ʌndəteɪkə(r)/ *n* agente *m* funerário; papa-defuntos *m* 🔲, (*P*) coveiro *m*

undertone /'ʌndətəʊn/ *n* **in an ~** a meia voz or em surdina

undervalue /ʌndə'væljuː/ *vt* avaliar por baixo, subestimar

underwater /ʌndə'wɔːtə(r)/ *a* submarino ● *adv* debaixo de água

underwear /'ʌndəweə(r)/ *n* roupa *f* interior or de baixo

underweight /'ʌndəweɪt/ *a* **be ~** estar com o peso abaixo do normal, ter peso a menos

underwent /ʌndə'went/ ▶ **UNDERGO**

underworld /'ʌndəwɜːld/ *n* (*of crime*) submundo *m*, (*P*) bas-fonds *mpl*

underwriter /'ʌndəraɪtə(r)/ *n* segurador *m*, subscritor *m*; (*marine*) underwriter *m*, segurador *m*

undeserved /ʌndɪ'zɜːvd/ *a* imerecido, injusto

undesirable /ʌndɪ'zaɪərəbl/ *a* indesejável, inconveniente

undies /'ʌndɪz/ *npl* 🔲 roupa *f* de baixo or interior

undignified /ʌn'dɪgnɪfaɪd/ *a* pouco digno, sem dignidade

undisputed /ʌndɪ'spjuːtɪd/ *a* incontestado

undo /ʌn'duː/ *vt* (*pt* **-did**, *pp* **-done** /dʌn/) desfazer; (*knot*) desfazer, desatar; (*coat, button*) abrir; **leave ~ne** não fazer, deixar por fazer. **~ing** *n* desgraça *f*, ruína *f*

undoubted /ʌn'daʊtɪd/ *a* indubitável. **~ly** *adv* indubitavelmente

undress /ʌn'dres/ *vt/i* despir(-se); **get ~ed** despir-se

undu|e /ʌn'djuː/ *a* excessivo, indevido. **~ly** *adv* excessivamente, indevidamente

undying /ʌn'daɪɪŋ/ *a* eterno, perene

unearth /ʌn'ɜːθ/ *vt* desenterrar; *fig* descobrir

unearthly /ʌn'ɜːθlɪ/ *a* sobrenatural, misterioso; **~ hour** 🔲 hora *f* absurda or inconveniente

uneasy /ʌn'iːzɪ/ *a* (*ill at ease*) pouco à vontade; (*worried*) preocupado

uneconomic /ʌniːkə'nɒmɪk/ *a* antieconômico

uneducated /ʌn'edʒʊkeɪtɪd/ *a* (*person*) inculto, sem instrução

unemploy|ed /ʌnɪm'plɔɪd/ *a* desempregado. **~ment** *n* desemprego *m*; **~ment benefit** auxílio-desemprego *m*, (*P*) subsídio *m* de desemprego

unending /ʌn'endɪŋ/ *a* interminável, sem fim

unequal /ʌn'iːkwəl/ *a* desigual. **~led** *a* sem igual, inigualável

unequivocal /ʌnɪ'kwɪvəkl/ *a* inequívoco, claro

uneven /ʌn'iːvn/ *a* desigual, irregular

unexpected /ʌnɪk'spektɪd/ *a* inesperado. **~ly** *a* inesperadamente

unfair /ʌn'feə(r)/ *a* injusto (**to** com). **~ness** *n* injustiça *f*

unfaithful /ʌn'feɪθfl/ *a* infiel

unfamiliar /ʌnfə'mɪlɪə(r)/ *a* estranho, desconhecido; **be ~ with** desconhecer, não conhecer, não estar familiarizado com

unfashionable /ʌn'fæʃənəbl/ *a* fora de moda

unfasten /ʌn'fɑːsn/ *vt* (*knot*) desatar, soltar; (*button*) abrir

unfavourable /ʌn'feɪvərəbl/ *a* desfavorável

unfeeling /ʌn'fiːlɪŋ/ *a* insensível

unfit /ʌn'fɪt/ *a* sem preparo físico, (*P*) preparação física, fora de forma;

(*unsuitable*) impróprio (**for** para)

unfold /ʌnˈfəʊld/ vt desdobrar; (*expose*) expor, revelar ● vi desenrolar-se

unforeseen /ʌnfɔːˈsiːn/ a imprevisto, inesperado

unforgettable /ʌnfəˈgetəbl/ a inesquecível

unforgivable /ʌnfəˈgɪvəbl/ a imperdoável, indesculpável

unfortunate /ʌnˈfɔːtʃənət/ a (*unlucky*) infeliz; (*regrettable*) lamentável; **it was very ~ that** foi uma pena/lamentável que. **~ly** adv infelizmente

unfounded /ʌnˈfaʊndɪd/ a ‹*rumour etc*› infundado, sem fundamento

unfriendly /ʌnˈfrendlɪ/ a pouco amável, antipático, frio

unfurnished /ʌnˈfɜːnɪʃt/ a sem mobília

ungainly /ʌnˈgeɪnlɪ/ a desajeitado, deselegante

ungrateful /ʌnˈgreɪtfl/ a ingrato

unhapp|y /ʌnˈhæpɪ/ a (**-ier, -iest**) infeliz, triste; (*not pleased*) descontente; pouco contente (**with** com). **~iness** n infelicidade f, tristeza f

unharmed /ʌnˈhɑːmd/ a incólume, são e salvo, ileso

unhealthy /ʌnˈhelθɪ/ a (**-ier, -iest**) ‹*climate etc*› doentio, insalubre; ‹*person*› adoentado, com pouca saúde

unholy /ʌnˈhəʊlɪ/ a (**-ier, -iest**) ‹*person, act etc*› ímpio; 🇮 (*great*) incrível; espantoso

unhurt /ʌnˈhɜːt/ a ileso, incólume

unicorn /ˈjuːnɪkɔːn/ n unicórnio m

uniform /ˈjuːnɪfɔːm/ n uniforme m ● a uniforme, sempre igual. **~ity** /-ˈfɔːmətɪ/ n uniformidade f. **~ly** adv uniformemente

unif|y /ˈjuːnɪfaɪ/ vt unificar. **~ication** /-ɪˈkeɪʃn/ n unificação f

unilateral /juːnɪˈlætrəl/ a unilateral

unimaginable /ʌnɪˈmædʒɪnəbl/ a inimaginável

unimportant /ʌnɪmˈpɔːtnt/ a sem importância, insignificante

uninhabited /ʌnɪnˈhæbɪtɪd/ a desabitado

unintentional /ʌnɪnˈtenʃənl/ a involuntário, não propositado

uninterest|ed /ʌnˈɪntrəstɪd/ a desinteressado (**in** em), indiferente (**in** a). **~ing** a desinteressante, sem interesse

union /ˈjuːnɪən/ n união f; (*trade union*) sindicato m; **U~ Jack** bandeira f britânica. **~ist** n sindicalista mf; Pol unionista mf

unique /juːˈniːk/ a único, sem igual

unisex /ˈjuːnɪseks/ a unissexo

unison /ˈjuːnɪsn/ n **in ~** em uníssono

unit /ˈjuːnɪt/ n unidade f; (*of furniture*) peça f; unidade f, (P) módulo m

unite /juːˈnaɪt/ vt/i unir(-se). **U~d Kingdom** n Reino m Unido; **U~d Nations (Organization)** n Organização f das Nações Unidas; **U~d States (of America)** Estados mpl Unidos (da América)

unity /ˈjuːnətɪ/ n unidade f; fig (*harmony*) união f

universal /juːnɪˈvɜːsl/ a universal

universe /ˈjuːnɪvɜːs/ n universo m

university /juːnɪˈvɜːsətɪ/ n universidade f ● a universitário; ‹*student, teacher*› universitário, da universidade

unjust /ʌnˈdʒʌst/ a injusto

unkempt /ʌnˈkempt/ a desmazelado, desleixado; (*of hair*) despenteado, desgrenhado

unkind /ʌnˈkaɪnd/ a desagradável, duro

unknowingly /ʌnˈnəʊɪŋlɪ/ adv sem saber, inconscientemente

unknown /ʌnˈnəʊn/ a desconhecido ● n **the ~** o desconhecido

unleaded /ʌnˈledɪd/ a sem chumbo

unless /ʌnˈles/ conj a não ser que, a menos que, salvo se, se não

unlike /ʌnˈlaɪk/ a diferente ● prep ao contrário de

unlikely /ʌnˈlaɪklɪ/ a improvável

unlimited /ʌnˈlɪmɪtɪd/ a ilimitado

unload /ʌnˈləʊd/ vt descarregar

unlock /ʌnˈlɒk/ vt abrir (com chave), (P) destrancar

unluck|y /ʌnˈlʌkɪ/ a (**-ier, -iest**) infeliz, sem sorte; ‹*number*› que dá azar; **be ~y** ter pouca sorte, ter azar. **~ily** adv infelizmente

unmarried /ʌnˈmærɪd/ a solteiro, celibatário

unmask /ʌnˈmɑːsk/ vt desmascarar

unmistakable /ʌnmɪsˈteɪkəbl/ a ‹*voice etc*› inconfundível; (*clear*) claro, inequívoco

unnatural /ʌnˈnætʃrəl/ a que não é natural; (*wicked*) desnaturado

unnecessary /ʌnˈnesəserɪ/ a desnecessário; (*superfluous*) supérfluo, dispensável

u

unnerve /ʌnˈnɜːv/ vt desencorajar, desmoralizar, intimidar

unnoticed /ʌnˈnəʊtɪst/ a go ~ passar despercebido

unobtrusive /ʌnəbˈtruːsɪv/ a discreto

unofficial /ʌnəˈfɪʃl/ a oficioso, que não é oficial; ‹strike› ilegal, não autorizado

unorthodox /ʌnˈɔːθədɒks/ a pouco ortodoxo, não ortodoxo

unpack /ʌnˈpæk/ vt ‹suitcase etc› desfazer; ‹contents› desembalar, desempacotar ● vi desfazer a mala

unpaid /ʌnˈpeɪd/ a não remunerado; ‹bill› a pagar, por pagar

unpalatable /ʌnˈpælətəbl/ a ‹food, fact etc› desagradável, intragável

unparalleled /ʌnˈpærəleld/ a sem paralelo or comparação, incomparável

unpleasant /ʌnˈpleznt/ a desagradável (to com); ‹person› antipático

unplug /ʌnˈplʌɡ/ vt (pt -plugged) Electr desligar a tomada, (P) tirar or desligar a ficha da tomada

unpopular /ʌnˈpɒpjʊlə(r)/ a impopular

unprecedented /ʌnˈpresɪdntɪd/ a sem precedentes, inaudito, nunca visto

unpredictable /ʌnprəˈdɪktəbl/ a imprevisível

unprepared /ʌnprɪˈpeəd/ a sem preparação, improvisado; ‹person› desprevenido

unpretentious /ʌnprɪˈtenʃəs/ a despretencioso, sem pretensões

unprincipled /ʌnˈprɪnsəpld/ a sem princípios, sem escrúpulos

unprofessional /ʌnprəˈfeʃnl/ a ‹work› de amador; ‹conduct› sem consciência profissional, pouco profissional

unprofitable /ʌnˈprɒfɪtəbl/ a não lucrativo

unqualified /ʌnˈkwɒlɪfaɪd/ a sem habilitações; ‹success etc› total, absoluto; be ~ to não estar habilitado or ter qualificações para

unquestionable /ʌnˈkwestʃənəbl/ a incontestável, indiscutível, inquestionável

unravel /ʌnˈrævl/ vt (pt unravelled) desenredar, desemaranhar; ‹knitting› desmanchar

unreal /ʌnˈrɪəl/ a irreal

unreasonable /ʌnˈriːznəbl/ a pouco razoável, disparatado; (excessive) excessivo

unrecognizable /ʌnˈrekəɡnaɪzəbl/ a irreconhecível

unrelated /ʌnrɪˈleɪtɪd/ a ‹facts› desconexo; sem relação (to com); ‹people› não aparentado (to com)

unreliable /ʌnrɪˈlaɪəbl/ a que não é de confiança

unrest /ʌnˈrest/ n agitação f, distúrbios mpl

unrivalled /ʌnˈraɪvld/ a sem igual, incomparável

unroll /ʌnˈrəʊl/ vt desenrolar

unruly /ʌnˈruːlɪ/ a indisciplinado, turbulento

unsafe /ʌnˈseɪf/ a (dangerous) que não é seguro, perigoso; ‹person› em perigo

unsatisfactory /ʌnsætɪsˈfæktərɪ/ a insatisfatório, pouco satisfatório

unsavoury /ʌnˈseɪvərɪ/ a desagradável, repugnante

unscathed /ʌnˈskeɪðd/ a ileso, incólume

unscrew /ʌnˈskruː/ vt desenroscar, desaparafusar

unscrupulous /ʌnˈskruːpjʊləs/ a sem escrúpulos, pouco escrupuloso, sem consciência

unseemly /ʌnˈsiːmlɪ/ a inconveniente, indecoroso, impróprio

unsettle /ʌnˈsetl/ vt perturbar, agitar. ~d a perturbado; ‹weather› instável, variável; ‹bill› não saldado, por pagar

unshakeable /ʌnˈʃeɪkəbl/ a ‹person, belief etc› inabalável

unshaven /ʌnˈʃeɪvn/ a com a barba por fazer, por barbear

unsightly /ʌnˈsaɪtlɪ/ a feio

unskilled /ʌnˈskɪld/ a inexperiente; ‹work, worker› não especializado; ‹labour› mão-de-obra f não especializada

unsociable /ʌnˈsəʊʃəbl/ a insociável, misantropo

unsophisticated /ʌnsəˈfɪstɪkeɪtɪd/ a simples, natural

unsound /ʌnˈsaʊnd/ a pouco sólido; of ~ mind Jur que não está em plena posse das suas faculdades mentais

unspeakable /ʌnˈspiːkəbl/ a indescritível; (bad) inqualificável

unstable /ʌnˈsteɪbl/ a instável

unsteady /ʌnˈstedɪ/ a ‹step› vacilante, incerto; ‹ladder› instável; ‹hand› pouco firme

unstuck /ʌn'stʌk/ a (not stuck) descolado; **come ~** ▣ (fail) falhar

unsubscribe /ˌʌnsəb'skraɪb/ vi descadastrar-se, (P) anular uma inscrição/subscrição

unsuccessful /ʌnsək'sesfl/ a ‹candidate› malsucedido; ‹attempt› malogrado, fracassado; **be ~** não ter êxito

unsuit|able /ʌn's(j)uːtəbl/ a impróprio; pouco apropriado; inadequado (**for** para)

unsure /ʌn'ʃʊə(r)/ a incerto

unsuspecting /ʌnsə'spektɪŋ/ a sem desconfiar de nada, insuspeitado

untangle /ʌn'tæŋgl/ vt desemaranhar, desenredar, desembaraçar

unthinkable /ʌn'θɪŋkəbl/ a impensável, inconcebível

untid|y /ʌn'taɪdɪ/ a (-ier, -iest) ‹room, desk etc› desarrumado; ‹appearance› desleixado, desmazelado; ‹hair› despenteado. **~iness** n desordem f; (of appearance) desmazelo m

untie /ʌn'taɪ/ vt ‹knot, parcel› desatar, desfazer; ‹person› desamarrar

until /ən'tɪl/ prep até. **not ~** não antes de ● conj até que

untimely /ʌn'taɪmlɪ/ a inoportuno, intempestivo; ‹death› prematuro

untold /ʌn'təʊld/ a incalculável

untoward /ʌntə'wɔːd/ a inconveniente, desagradável

untrue /ʌn'truː/ a falso

unused[1] /ʌn'juːzd/ a (new) novo, por usar; (not in use) não utilizado

unused[2] /ʌn'juːst/ a **~ to** não habituado a, não acostumado a

unusual /ʌn'juːʒʊəl/ a insólito, fora do comum

unveil /ʌn'veɪl/ vt descobrir, revelar; ‹statue, portrait etc› desvelar

unwanted /ʌn'wɒntɪd/ a (useless) que já não serve; ‹child› indesejado

unwelcome /ʌn'welkəm/ a desagradável; ‹guest› indesejável

unwell /ʌn'wel/ a indisposto

unwieldy /ʌn'wiːldɪ/ a difícil de manejar, pouco jeitoso

unwilling /ʌn'wɪlɪŋ/ a relutante (**to** em), pouco disposto (**to** a)

unwind /ʌn'waɪnd/ vt/i (pt unwound /ʌn'waʊnd/) desenrolar(-se); ▣ (relax) descontrair(-se)

unwise /ʌn'waɪz/ a imprudente, insensato

unwittingly /ʌn'wɪtɪŋlɪ/ adv sem querer

unworthy /ʌn'wɜːðɪ/ a indigno

unwrap /ʌn'ræp/ vt (pt unwrapped) desembrulhar, abrir, desfazer

unwritten /ʌn'rɪtn/ a ‹agreement› verbal, tácito

up /ʌp/ adv (to higher place) cima, para cima, para o alto; (in higher place) em cima, no alto; (out of bed) acordado, de pé, (P) a pé; (up and dressed) pronto; (finished) acabado; ‹sun› alto; **be ~ against** defrontar, enfrentar; **be ~ in** ▣ saber; **be ~ to** (do) estar fazendo, (P) estar a fazer; (plot) estar tramando, (P) estar a tramar; ‹task› estar à altura de; **come** or **go ~** subir; **feel ~ to doing** (able) sentir-se capaz de fazer; **it is ~ to you** depende só de você, (P) de ti; **walk ~ and down** andar por um lado para o outro or para a frente e para trás ● prep no cimo de, em cima de, no alto de; **~ the street/river/** etc pela rua/pelo rio/etc acima ● vt (pt upped) (increase) aumentar ● npl **have ~s and downs** fig ter (os seus) altos e baixos. **~-and-coming** a prometedor; **~market** a requintado, fino

upbringing /'ʌpbrɪŋɪŋ/ n educação f

update /ʌp'deɪt/ vt atualizar

upheaval /ʌp'hiːvl/ n pandemônio m, (P) pandemónio m, revolução f fig; (social, political) convulsão f

uphill /'ʌphɪl/ a ladeira acima, ascendente; fig (difficult) árduo ● adv /ʌp'hɪl/ **go ~** subir

uphold /ʌp'həʊld/ vt (pt upheld) sustentar, manter, apoiar, defender

upholster /ʌp'həʊlstə(r)/ vt estofar. **~y** n estofados mpl, (P) estofo(s) m(pl)

upkeep /'ʌpkiːp/ n manutenção f

upon /ə'pɒn/ prep sobre

upper /'ʌpə(r)/ a superior ● n (of shoe) gáspea f; **have the ~ hand** estar por cima or em vantagem, estar em posição de superioridade; **~ class** classe f alta

upright /'ʌpraɪt/ a vertical; (honourable) honesto, honrado, (P) reto

uprising /'ʌpraɪzɪŋ/ n insurreição f, sublevação f, levantamento m

uproar /'ʌprɔː(r)/ n tumulto m, alvoroço m

uproot /ʌp'ruːt/ vt desenraizar; fig erradicar; desarraigar

upset[1] /ʌp'set/ vt (pt upset, pres p upsetting) (overturn) entornar, virar; ‹plan› contrariar, transtornar; ‹stomach›

u

desarranjar, (P) indispor; ‹person›
contrariar, transtornar, incomodar
● *a* aborrecido

upset² /ˈʌpset/ *n* transtorno *m*; (*of stomach*) indisposição *f*; (*distress*) choque *m*

upshot /ˈʌpʃɒt/ *n* resultado *m*

upside-down /ʌpsaɪdˈdaʊn/ *adv* lit & fig ao contrário; de pernas para o ar, (P) de pantanas ⚑

upstairs /ʌpˈsteəz/ *adv* (*at/to*) em/ para cima, no/para o andar de cima ● /ˈʌpsteəz/ *a* ‹flat etc› de cima, do andar de cima

upstart /ˈʌpstɑːt/ *n* arrivista *mf*

upstream /ʌpˈstriːm/ *adv* rio acima, contra a corrente

uptake /ˈʌpteɪk/ *n* **be quick on the ~** pegar, (P) apanhar rapidamente as coisas; *fig* ser de compreensão rápida, ser vivo

up-to-date /ˈʌptədeɪt/ *a* moderno, atualizado

upturn /ˈʌptɜːn/ *n* melhoria *f*

upward /ˈʌpwəd/ *a* ascendente, voltado para cima. **~s** *adv* para cima

uranium /jʊˈreɪniəm/ *n* urânio *m*

urban /ˈɜːbən/ *a* urbano

urge /ɜːdʒ/ *vt* aconselhar vivamente (to a); **~ on** (*impel*) incitar (a) ● *n* (*strong desire*) grande vontade *f*

urgen|t /ˈɜːdʒənt/ *a* urgente; **be ~t** urgir, ser insistente. **~cy** *n* urgência *f*

urinal /jʊəˈraɪnl/ *n* urinol *m*

urin|e /ˈjʊərɪn/ *n* urina *f*. **~ate** *vi* urinar

urn /ɜːn/ *n* urna *f*; (*for tea, coffee*) espécie *f* de samovar

us /ʌs/ unstressed əs/ *pron* nos; (*after preps*) nós; **with ~** connosco; **he knows ~** ele nos conhece, (P) ele conhece-nos

US *abbr* (= **United States**) ▶ UNITE

USA *abbr* (= **United States of America**) ▶ UNITE

usable /ˈjuːzəbl/ *a* utilizável

usage /ˈjuːzɪdʒ/ *n* uso *m*

USB *abbr* (= **universal serial bus**) USB. **~ key** *n* pen drive *m*, (P) pen *m*; **~ port** porta *f* USB

USB port /juːesbiːˈpɔːt/ *n* porto *m* USB, (P) entrada *f* USB

use¹ /juːz/ *vt* usar, utilizar, servir-se de; (*exploit*) servir-se de; (*consume*) gastar, usar, consumir; **~ up** esgotar, consumir. **~r** /-ə(r)/ *n* usuário *m*, (P) utente *mf*. **~r-friendly** *a* fácil de usar

use² /juːs/ *n* uso *m*, emprego *m*; **in ~** em uso; **it is no ~ shouting/etc** não serve de nada ou não adianta gritar/etc; **make ~ of** servir-se de; **of ~** útil

used¹ /juːzd/ *a* (*second-hand*) usado

used² /juːst/ *pt* **he ~ to sing** ele costumava ou ele tinha por costume or hábito cantar ● *a* **a ~ to singing** acostumado a or habituado a cantar

use|ful /ˈjuːsfl/ *a* útil. **~less** *a* inútil; ‹person› incompetente

username /ˈjuːzəneɪm/ *n* nome *m* de usuário, (P) nome *m* de utilizador

usher /ˈʌʃə(r)/ *n* lanterninha *m*, (P) arrumador *m* ● *vt* **~ in** mandar ou fazer entrar. **~ette** *n* vaga-lume *f*, (P) arrumadora *f*

USSR *abbr* URSS

usual /ˈjuːʒʊəl/ *a* usual, habitual, normal; **as ~** como de costume, como habitualmente; **at the ~ time** na hora de costume, (P) à(s) hora(s) de costume. **~ly** *adv* habitualmente, normalmente

utensil /juːˈtensl/ *n* utensílio *m*

uterus /ˈjuːtərəs/ *n* útero *m*

utilitarian /juːtɪlɪˈteərɪən/ *a* utilitário

utility /juːˈtɪlətɪ/ *n* utilidade *f*; **(public) ~** serviço *m* público; **~ room** área *f* de serviço (para as máquinas de lavar a roupa e a louça)

utilize /ˈjuːtɪlaɪz/ *vt* utilizar

utmost /ˈʌtməʊst/ *a* (*furthest, most intense*) extremo; **the ~ care/etc** (*greatest*) o maior cuidado/etc ● *n* **do one's ~** fazer todo o possível or tudo, fazer tudo ao alcance de alguém

utter¹ /ˈʌtə(r)/ *a* completo, absoluto. **~ly** *adv* completamente

utter² /ˈʌtə(r)/ *vt* proferir; ‹sigh, shout› dar

U-turn /ˈjuːtɜːn/ *n* retorno *m*, (P) inversão *f* de marcha *fig*, reviravolta *f*

································

Vv

································

vacan|t /ˈveɪkənt/ *a* ‹post, room, look› vago; ‹mind› vazio; ‹seat, space, time› desocupado, livre. **~cy** *n* (*post*) vaga *f*; (*room in hotel*) vago *m*

vacate /vəˈkeɪt/ *vt* vagar, deixar vago

vacation /vəˈkeɪʃn/ *n* férias *fpl*

vaccinat|e /ˈvæksɪneɪt/ *vt* vacinar. **~ion** /-ˈneɪʃn/ *n* vacinação *f*

vaccine /'væksi:n/ n vacina f

vacuum /'vækjʊəm/ n (pl **-cuums**, or **-cua**) vácuo m, vazio m. ~ **cleaner** n aspirador m (de pó)

vagina /və'dʒaɪnə/ n vagina f

vagrant /'veɪgrənt/ n vadio m, vagabundo m

vague /veɪg/ a (**-er**, **-est**) vago; (outline) impreciso; **be ~ about** ser vago acerca de, não precisar. ~**ly** adv vagamente

vain /veɪn/ a (**-er**, **-est**) (conceited) vaidoso; (useless) vão, inútil; (fruitless) infrutífero; **in ~** em vão. ~**ly** adv em vão

valentine /'væləntaɪn/ n (card) cartão m do dia de São Valentim or dia dos Namorados

valiant /'væliənt/ a corajoso, valente

valid /'vælɪd/ a válido. ~**ity** /və-'lɪdəti/ n validade f

validate /'vælɪdeɪt/ vt validar, confirmar, ratificar

valley /'væli/ n vale m

valuable /'væljʊəbl/ a (object) valioso, de valor; <help, time etc> precioso. ~**s** npl objetos mpl de valor

valuation /væljʊ'eɪʃn/ n avaliação f

value /'vælju:/ n valor m ● vt avaliar; (cherish) dar valor a; ~ **added tax** imposto m de valor adicional, (P) acrescentado

valve /vælv/ n Anat, Techn (of car tyre) válvula f; (of bicycle tyre) pipo m; (of radio) lâmpada f, válvula f

vampire /'væmpaɪə(r)/ n vampiro m

van /væn/ n (large) caminhão m; (small) camionete f, comercial m, (P) carrinha f (comercial); (milkman's, baker's etc) camionete f; Rail bagageiro m, (P) furgão m

vandal /'vændl/ n vândalo m. ~**ism** /-əlɪzəm/ n vandalismo m

vandalize /'vændəlaɪz/ vt destruir, estragar, vandalizar

vanilla /və'nɪlə/ n baunilha f

vanish /'vænɪʃ/ vi desaparecer, sumir-se, desvanecer-se

vanity /'vænəti/ n vaidade f. ~ **case** n bolsa f de maquilagem, (P) de maquilhagem

vantage point /'vɑːntɪdʒpɔɪnt/ n (bom) ponto m de observação

vapour /'veɪpə(r)/ n vapor m; (mist) bruma f

vari|able /'veərɪəbl/ a variável. ~**ation** /-'eɪʃn/ n variação f. ~**ed** /-ɪd/ a variado

variance /'veərɪəns/ n **at ~** em desacordo (**with** com)

variant /'veərɪənt/ a diverso, diferente ● n variante f

varicose /'værɪkəʊs/ a ~ **veins** varizes fpl

variety /və'raɪəti/ n variedade f; (entertainment) variedades fpl

various /'veərɪəs/ a vários, diversos, variados

varnish /'vɑːnɪʃ/ n verniz m ● vt envernizar; <nails> pintar

vary /'veərɪ/ vt/i variar

vase /vɑːz/ n vaso m, jarra f

vast /vɑːst/ a vasto, imenso. ~**ly** adv imensamente, infinitamente

vat /væt/ n tonel m, dorna f, cuba f

VAT /viːeɪ'tiː, væt/ abbr ICM m, (P) IVA m

vault[1] /vɔːlt/ n (roof) abóbada f; (in bank) casa-forte f; (tomb) cripta f; (cellar) adega f

vault[2] /vɔːlt/ vt/i saltar ● n salto m

VDU abbr ▶ **VISUAL DISPLAY UNIT**

veal /viːl/ n (meat) vitela f

veer /vɪə(r)/ vi virar, mudar de direção

vegan /'viːgən/ a & n vegetariano m estrito, (P) vegano

vegetable /'vedʒɪtəbl/ n hortaliça f, legume m ● a vegetal

vegetarian /vedʒɪ'teərɪən/ a & n vegetariano m

vegetation /vedʒɪ'teɪʃn/ n vegetação f

vehement /'viːəmənt/ a veemente. ~**ly** adv veementemente

vehicle /'viːɪkl/ n veículo m

veil /veɪl/ n véu m ● vt velar, cobrir com véu; fig esconder; disfarçar

vein /veɪn/ n (in body; mood) veia f; (in rock) veio m, filão m; (of leaf) nervura f

velocity /vɪ'lɒsəti/ n velocidade f

velvet /'velvɪt/ n veludo m

vendetta /ven'detə/ n vendeta f

vending machine /'vendɪŋməʃiːn/ n vendedora f automática, (P) máquina f de distribuição, automática

vendor /'vendə(r)/ n vendedor m; **street ~** vendedor m ambulante

veneer /və'nɪə(r)/ n folheado m; fig fachada f; máscara f

venerable /'venərəbl/ a venerável

Venezuela /venɪz'weɪlə/ n Venezuela f. ~**n** a & n venezuelano m

V

vengeance /'vendʒəns/ n vingança; **with a ~** furiosamente, em excesso, com mais força do que se pretende

venison /'venɪzn/ n carne f de veado

venom /'venəm/ n veneno m. **~ous** /'venəməs/ a venenoso

vent[1] /vent/ n (in coat) abertura f

vent[2] /vent/ n (hole) orifício m, abertura f; (for air) respiradouro m ● vt (anger) descarregar (on para or em cima de); **give ~ to** fig desabafar, dar vazão a

ventilat|e /'ventɪleɪt/ vt ventilar. **~ion** /-'leɪʃn/ n ventilação f. **~or** n ventilador m

ventriloquist /ven'trɪləkwɪst/ n ventríloquo m

venture /'ventʃə(r)/ n empreendimento m arriscado, aventura f ● vt/i arriscar(-se)

venue /'venju:/ n porto m de encontro

veranda /və'rændə/ n varanda f

verb /vɜ:b/ n verbo m

verbal /'vɜ:bl/ a verbal; (literal) literal

verbose /vɜ:'bəʊs/ a palavroso, prolixo

verdict /'vɜ:dɪkt/ n veredito m; (opinion) opinião f

verge /vɜ:dʒ/ n beira f, borda f; **on the ~ of doing** prestes a fazer ● vi **~ on** estar à beira de

verify /'verɪfaɪ/ vt verificar

vermin /'vɜ:mɪn/ n animais mpl nocivos, verme m; (lice, fleas etc) parasitas mpl

vermouth /'vɜ:məθ/ n vermute m

vernacular /və'nækjʊlə(r)/ n vernáculo m; (dialect) dialeto m

versatil|e /'vɜ:sətaɪl/ a versátil; <tool> que serve para vários fins, multiuso. **~ity** /-'tɪlətɪ/ n versatilidade f

verse /vɜ:s/ n (poetry) verso m, poesia f; (stanza) estrofe f; (of Bible) versículo m

version /'vɜ:ʃn/ n versão f

versus /'vɜ:səs/ prep contra

vertical /'vɜ:tɪkl/ a vertical. **~ly** adv verticalmente

vertigo /'vɜ:tɪgəʊ/ n vertigem f

verve /vɜ:v/ n verve f, vivacidade f

very /'verɪ/ adv muito; **the ~ first/ best/**etc (emph) o primeiro/melhor/ etc de todos; **~ much** muito; **~ well** muito bem ● a (actual) mesmo, próprio; (exact) preciso; exato; **at the ~ end** mesmo or precisamente no fim; **the ~ day/**etc o próprio or o mesmo dia/etc

vessel /'vesl/ n vaso m, recipiente m

vest[1] /vest/ n corpete m, (P) camisola f interior; Amer (waistcoat) colete m

vest[2] /vest/ vt conferir (in a); **~ed interests** interesses mpl

vestige /'vestɪdʒ/ n vestígio m

vestry /'vestrɪ/ n sacristia f

vet /vet/ n 🔢 veterinário m ● vt (pt **vetted**) <candidate etc> examinar atentamente, estudar

veteran /'vetərən/ n veterano m; **(war) ~** veterano m de guerra

veterinary /'vetərɪnərɪ/ a veterinário. **~ surgeon** n veterinário m

veto /'vi:təʊ/ n (pl **-oes**) veto m; (right) direito m de veto ● vt vetar, opor o veto a

vex /veks/ vt aborrecer, irritar, contrariar; **~ed question** questão f muito debatida, assunto m controverso

via /'vaɪə/ prep por, via

viab|le /'vaɪəbl/ a viável. **~ility** /-'bɪlətɪ/ n viabilidade f

viaduct /'vaɪədʌkt/ n viaduto m

vibrant /'vaɪbrənt/ a vibrante

vibrat|e /vaɪ'breɪt/ vt/i (fazer) vibrar. **~ion** /-ʃn/ n vibração f

vicar /'vɪkə(r)/ n (Anglican) pastor m; (Catholic) vigário m, pároco m. **~age** n presbitério m, (P) vicariato m

vice[1] /vaɪs/ n (depravity) vício m

vice[2] /vaɪs/ n Techn torno m

vice- /vaɪs/ pref vice-. **~chairman** n vice-presidente m; **~chancellor** n vice-chanceler m; Univ reitor m; **~president** n vice-presidente mf

vice versa /vaɪsɪ'vɜ:sə/ adv vice-versa

vicinity /vɪ'sɪnətɪ/ n vizinhança f, cercania(s) fpl, arredores mpl; **in the ~ of** nos arredores de

vicious /'vɪʃəs/ a (spiteful) mau, maldoso; (violent) brutal, feroz; **~ circle** círculo m vicioso. **~ly** adv maldosamente; (violently) brutalmente, ferozmente

victim /'vɪktɪm/ n vítima f

victimiz|e /'vɪktɪmaɪz/ vt perseguir. **~ation** /-'zeɪʃn/ n perseguição f

victor /'vɪktə(r)/ n vencedor m

victor|y /'vɪktərɪ/ n vitória f. **~ious** /-'tɔ:rɪəs/ a vitorioso

video /'vɪdɪəʊ/ a vídeo ● n (pl **-os**) 🔢 vídeo ● vt (record) gravar em vídeo; **~ cassette** videocassete m, (P) cassete f de vídeo; **~ recorder** (gravador m de) vídeo m, (P) câmara f de vídeo

vie /vaɪ/ vi (pres p **vying**) rivalizar; competir (**with** com)

view /vjuː/ n vista f ● vt ver; (*examine*) examinar; (*consider*) considerar, ver; ‹*a house*› visitar, ver; **in my ~** a meu ver, na minha opinião; **in ~ of** em vista de; **on ~** em exposição, à mostra; (*open to the public*) aberto ao público; **with a ~ to** com a intenção de, com o fim de. **~er** n TV telespectador m; (*for slides*) visor m

viewfinder /ˈvjuːfaɪndə(r)/ n visor m

viewpoint /ˈvjuːpɔɪnt/ n ponto m de vista

vigil /ˈvɪdʒɪl/ n vigília f; (*over corpse*) velório m; Relig vigília f

vigilan|t /ˈvɪdʒɪlənt/ a vigilante. **~ce** n vigilância f. **~te** /vɪdʒɪˈlænti/ n vigilante m

vig|our /ˈvɪgə(r)/ n vigor m. **~orous** /ˈvɪgərəs/ a vigoroso

vile /vaɪl/ a (*base*) infame, vil; ▣ (*bad*) horroroso; péssimo

vilify /ˈvɪlɪfaɪ/ vt difamar

villa /ˈvɪlə/ n vivenda f, vila f; (*country residence*) casa f de campo

village /ˈvɪlɪdʒ/ n aldeia f, povoado m. **~r** n aldeão m, aldeã f

villain /ˈvɪlən/ n patife m, mau-caráter m

vindicat|e /ˈvɪndɪkeɪt/ vt vindicar, justificar. **~ion** /-ˈkeɪʃn/ n justificação f

vindictive /vɪnˈdɪktɪv/ a vingativo

vine /vaɪn/ n (*plant*) vinha f

vinegar /ˈvɪnɪgə(r)/ n vinagre m

vineyard /ˈvɪnjəd/ n vinha f, vinhedo m

vintage /ˈvɪntɪdʒ/ n (*year*) ano m de colheita de qualidade excepcional, ano m vintage ● a ‹*wine*› de colheita excepcional e de um determinado ano; ‹*car*› de museu ▣; fabricado entre 1917 e 1930

viola /vɪˈəʊlə/ n Mus viola f, violeta f

violat|e /ˈvaɪəleɪt/ vt violar. **~ion** /-ˈleɪʃn/ n violação f

violen|t /ˈvaɪələnt/ a violento. **~ce** n violência f. **~tly** adv violentamente, com violência

violet /ˈvaɪələt/ n Bot violeta f; (*colour*) violeta m ● a violeta

violin /vaɪəˈlɪn/ n violino m. **~ist** n violinista mf

VIP /viːaɪˈpiː/ abbr (= **very important person**) VIP m, personalidade f importante

viper /ˈvaɪpə(r)/ n víbora f

virgin /ˈvɜːdʒɪn/ a & n virgem f. **~ity** /vəˈdʒɪnəti/ n virgindade f

Virgo /ˈvɜːgəʊ/ n Astr Virgem f

viril|e /ˈvɪraɪl/ a viril, varonil. **~ity** /vɪˈrɪləti/ n virilidade f

virtual /ˈvɜːtʃʊəl/ a verdadeiro, que é na prática (embora não em teoria); **a ~ failure/**etc praticamente um fracasso/ etc. **~ly** adv praticamente

virtue /ˈvɜːtʃuː/ n (*goodness, chastity*) virtude f; (*merit*) mérito m; **by** or **in ~ of** por or em virtude de

virtuos|o /vɜːtʃʊˈəʊsəʊ/ n (*pl* **-si** /-siː/) virtuoso m

virtuous /ˈvɜːtʃʊəs/ a virtuoso

virus /ˈvaɪərəs/ n (*pl* **-es**) vírus m; ▣ (*disease*) virose f

visa /ˈviːzə/ n visto m

vise /vaɪs/ n Amer (*vice*) torno m

visib|le /ˈvɪzəbl/ a visível. **~ility** /-ˈbɪləti/ n visibilidade f. **~ly** adv visivelmente

vision /ˈvɪʒn/ n (*dream, insight*) visão f; (*seeing, sight*) vista f, visão f

visionary /ˈvɪʒənərɪ/ a visionário; ‹*plan, scheme etc*› fantasista, quimérico ● n visionário m

visit /ˈvɪzɪt/ vt (*pt* **visited**) ‹*person*› visitar, fazer uma visita a; ‹*place*› visitar ● vi estar de visita ● n (*tour, call*) visita f; (*stay*) estada f, visita f. **~or** n visitante mf; (*guest*) visita f

visor /ˈvaɪzə(r)/ n viseira f; (*in vehicle*) visor m

vista /ˈvɪstə/ n vista f, panorama m

visual /ˈvɪʒʊəl/ a visual. **~ display unit** n terminal m de vídeo. **~ly** adv visualmente

visualize /ˈvɪʒʊəlaɪz/ vt visualizar; (*foresee*) imaginar, prever

vital /ˈvaɪtl/ a vital. **~ statistics** npl estatísticas fpl demográficas; ▣ (*of woman*) medidas fpl

vitality /vaɪˈtæləti/ n vitalidade f

vitamin /ˈvɪtəmɪn/ n vitamina f

vivac|ious /vɪˈveɪʃəs/ a cheio de vida, vivo, animado. **~ity** /-ˈvæsəti/ n vivacidade f, animação f

vivid /ˈvɪvɪd/ a vívido; ‹*imagination*› vivo. **~ly** adv vividamente

vixen /ˈvɪksn/ n raposa f fêmea

vocabulary /vəˈkæbjʊlərɪ/ n vocabulário m

vocal /ˈvəʊkl/ a vocal; fig ‹*person*› eloquente; **~ cords** cordas fpl vocais. **~ist** n vocalista mf

vocation /vəˈkeɪʃn/ n vocação f; (*trade*) profissão f. **~al** a vocacional, profissional

vociferous /vəˈsɪfərəs/ a vociferante

vodka /ˈvɒdkə/ n vodka m

V

vogue /vəʊg/ n voga f, moda f, popularidade f; **in ~** em voga, na moda

voice /vɔɪs/ n voz f ● vt (express) exprimir. **~mail** n (system) correio m de voz; (P) caixa f de correio de voz; (message) mensagem f de voz

void /vɔɪd/ a vazio; Jur nulo, sem validade ● n vácuo m, vazio m; **make ~** anular, invalidar; **~ of** sem, destituído de

volatile /ˈvɒlətaɪl/ a ‹substance› volátil; fig (changeable) instável, volúvel

volcano /vɒlˈkeɪnəʊ/ n (pl -oes) vulcão m. **~ic** /-ˈænɪk/ a vulcânico

volition /vəˈlɪʃn/ n **of one's own ~** de sua própria vontade

volley /ˈvɒlɪ/ n (of blows etc) saraivada f; (of gunfire) salva f; Tennis voleio m. **~ball** n voleibol m, vôlei m, (P) vólei m

volt /vəʊlt/ n volt m. **~age** n voltagem f

voluble /ˈvɒljʊbl/ a falante, loquaz

volume /ˈvɒljuːm/ n (book, sound) volume m; (capacity) capacidade f

voluntary /ˈvɒləntərɪ/ a voluntário; (unpaid) não remunerado. **~ily** /-trəlɪ/ adv voluntariamente

volunteer /vɒlənˈtɪə(r)/ n voluntário m ● vi oferecer-se or voluntariar-se (**to do** para fazer); Mil alistar-se como voluntário ● vt oferecer espontaneamente

voluptuous /vəˈlʌptʃʊəs/ a voluptuoso, sensual

vomit /ˈvɒmɪt/ vt/i (pt vomited) vomitar ● n vômito m, (P) vómito m

voodoo /ˈvuːduː/ n vodu m, (P) vudu m

voracious /vəˈreɪʃəs/ a voraz. **~ty** /vəˈræsɪtɪ/ n voracidade f

vote /vəʊt/ n voto m; (right) direito m de voto ● vt/i votar. **~er** n eleitor m

vouch /vaʊtʃ/ vi **~ for** responder por, garantir

voucher /ˈvaʊtʃə(r)/ n (for meal, transport) vale m; (receipt) comprovante m

vow /vaʊ/ n voto m ● vt ‹loyalty etc› jurar (**to** a); **~ to do** jurar fazer

vowel /ˈvaʊəl/ n vogal f

voyage /ˈvɔɪdʒ/ n viagem (por mar) f. **~r** /-ə(r)/ n viajante m

vulgar /ˈvʌlgə(r)/ a ordinário, grosseiro; (in common use) vulgar. **~ity** /-ˈgærətɪ/ n (behaviour) grosseria f, vulgaridade f

vulnerable /ˈvʌlnərəbl/ a vulnerável. **~ility** /-ˈbɪlətɪ/ n vulnerabilidade f

vulture /ˈvʌltʃə(r)/ n urubu m, (P) abutre m

vying /ˈvaɪɪŋ/ ▶ VIE

Ww

wad /wɒd/ n bucha f, tampão m; (bundle) maço m, rolo m

wadding /ˈwɒdɪŋ/ n enchimento m

waddle /ˈwɒdl/ vi bambolear-se, rebolar-se, gingar

wade /weɪd/ vi **~ through** fig avançar a custo por; ‹mud, water› patinhar em

wafer /ˈweɪfə(r)/ n (biscuit) bolacha f de baunilha; Relig hóstia f

waffle[1] /ˈwɒfl/ n ▣ (talk) lenga-lenga f; papo m; conversa f; ▣ (writing) lenga-lenga f ● vi ▣ escrever muito sem dizer nada de importante

waffle[2] /ˈwɒfl/ n Culin waffle m

waft /wɒft/ vi flutuar ● vt espalhar, levar suavemente

wag /wæg/ vt/i (pt wagged) abanar, agitar, sacudir

wage[1] /weɪdʒ/ vt ‹campaign, war› fazer

wage[2] /weɪdʒ/ n **~(s)** (weekly, daily) salário m, ordenado m. **~ earner** n trabalhador m assalariado; **~ freeze** n congelamento m de salários

wager /ˈweɪdʒə(r)/ n (bet) aposta f ● vt apostar (**that** que)

waggle /ˈwægl/ vt/i abanar, agitar, sacudir

wagon /ˈwægən/ n (horse-drawn) carroça f; Rail vagão m de mercadorias

waif /weɪf/ n criança f abandonada

wail /weɪl/ vi lamentar-se, gemer lamentosamente ● n lamentação f, gemido m lamentoso

waist /weɪst/ n cintura f. **~line** n cintura f

waistcoat /ˈweɪskəʊt/ n colete m

wait /weɪt/ vt/i esperar; **~ for** esperar; **~ on** servir; **keep sb ~ing** fazer alguém esperar ● n espera f; **lie in ~ (for)** estar escondido à espera (de), armar uma emboscada (para). **~ing list** n lista f de espera; **~ing room** n sala f de espera

waiter /ˈweɪtə(r)/ n garçon m, (P) empregado m (de mesa). **~ress** n garçonete f, (P) empregada f (de mesa)

waive /weɪv/ vt renunciar a, desistir de

wake[1] /weɪk/ vt/i (pt woke, pp woken) **~ (up)** acordar, despertar ● n (before burial) velório m

wake[2] /weɪk/ n (ship) esteira (de espuma) f; **in the ~ of** (following) atrás de, na sequência de

Wales /weɪlz/ n País m de Gales

walk /wɔːk/ vi andar, caminhar; (not ride) ir a pé; (stroll) passear; ~ **out** (go away) sair; (go on strike) fazer greve; ~ **out on** abandonar ● vt ‹streets› andar por, percorrer; ‹distance› andar, fazer a pé, percorrer; ‹dog› (levar para/a) passear ● n (stroll) passeio m, volta f; (excursion) caminhada f; (gait) passo m, maneira f de andar; (pace) passo m; (path) caminho m; **it's a 5-minute ~** são 5 minutos a pé; **~ of life** meio m, condição f social. **~over** n vitória f fácil

walker /wɔːkə(r)/ n caminhante mf

walkie-talkie /wɔːkɪˈtɔːkɪ/ n walkie-talkie m

walking /wɔːkɪŋ/ n andar (a pé) m, marcha (a pé) f ● a 🔢 ‹dictionary› vivo. ~ **stick** n bengala f

wall /wɔːl/ n parede f; (around land) muro m; (of castle, town; also fig) muralha f; (of stomach etc) parede(s) f(pl); **go to the ~** sucumbir, falir; ‹firm› ir à falência ● vt ‹city› fortificar; ‹property› murar; **up the ~** 🔢 fora de si

wallet /wɒlɪt/ n carteira f

wallflower /wɔːlflaʊə(r)/ n Bot goivo m; **be a ~** fig tomar chá de cadeira, (P) esperar sentado

wallop /wɒləp/ vt (pt walloped) 🔢 espancar 🔢 ● n 🔢 pancada f forte

wallow /wɒləʊ/ vi (in mud) chafurdar; fig regozijar-se

wallpaper /wɔːlpeɪpə(r)/ n papel m de parede ● vt forrar com papel de parede

---

Wall Street Rua, em Manhattan, Nova Iorque, onde se encontram a Bolsa de Valores e as sedes de muitas instituições financeiras. Quando se fala de Wall Street, muitas vezes se está falando dessas instituições.

---

walnut /wɔːlnʌt/ n (nut) noz f; (tree) nogueira f

waltz /wɔːls/ n valsa f ● vi valsar

wand /wɒnd/ n (magic) varinha f mágica or de condão

wander /wɒndə(r)/ vi andar ao acaso, vagar, errar; ‹river› serpentear; ‹mind, speech› divagar; (stray) extraviar-se. **~er** n vagabundo m, andarilho m. **~ing** a errante

wane /weɪn/ vi diminuir; (decline) declinar ● n **on the ~** em declínio; ‹moon› no quarto minguante

wangle /wæŋgl/ vt 🔢 conseguir algo através de pistolão 🔢 (P) conseguir algo através de persuasão ou manipulação

want /wɒnt/ vt querer (**to do** fazer); (need) precisar (de); (ask for) exigir, requerer; **I ~ you to go** eu quero que você vá/que tu vás ● vi ~ **for** ter falta de ● n (need) necessidade f, precisão f; (desire) desejo m; (lack) falta f, carência f; **for ~ of** por falta de. **~ed** a ‹criminal› procurado pela polícia; (in ad) precisa(m)-se

WAP /wæp/ a WAP

war /wɔː(r)/ n guerra f; **at ~** em guerra; **on the ~path** em pé de guerra

warble /wɔːbl/ vt/i gorjear

ward /wɔːd/ n (in hospital) enfermaria f; Jur (minor) pupilo m; Pol círculo m eleitoral ● vt ~ **off** ‹a blow› aparar; ‹anger› desviar; ‹danger› prevenir, evitar

warden /wɔːdn/ n (of institution) diretor m; (of park) guarda m

warder /wɔːdə(r)/ n guarda (de prisão) m, carcereiro m

wardrobe /wɔːdrəʊb/ n (place) armário m; guarda-roupa m, (P) guarda-fato m; (P) roupeiro m; (clothes) guarda-roupa m

warehouse /weəhaʊs/ n (pl **-s** /-haʊzɪz/) armazém m, depósito m de mercadorias

wares /weəz/ npl (goods) mercadorias fpl, artigos mpl

warfare /wɔːfeə(r)/ n guerra f

warlike /wɔːlaɪk/ a marcial, guerreiro; (bellicose) belicoso

warm /wɔːm/ a (-er, -est) quente; (hearty) caloroso, cordial; **be** or **feel** ~ estar com or ter or sentir calor ● vt/i ~ **(up)** aquecer(-se). **~hearted** a afetuoso, com calor humano. **~ly** adv (heartily) calorosamente; **wrap up ~ly** agasalhar-se bem. **~th** n calor m

warn /wɔːn/ vt avisar, prevenir; ~ **sb off sth** (advise against) pôr alguém de prevenção or de pé atrás com algo; (forbid) proibir algo a alguém. **~ing** n aviso m; **~ing light** lâmpada f de advertência; **without ~ing** sem aviso, sem prevenir

warp /wɔːp/ vt/i ‹wood etc› empenar; fig (pervert) torcer; deformar; desvirtuar. **~ed** a fig deturpado; pervertido

warrant /wɒrənt/ n autorização f; (for arrest) mandato (de captura) m; Comm título m de crédito, warrant m ● vt justificar; (guarantee) garantir

W

warranty /'wɒrənti/ n garantia f

warrior /'wɒrɪə(r)/ n guerreiro m

warship /'wɔːʃɪp/ n navio m de guerra

wart /wɔːt/ n verruga f

wartime /'wɔːtaɪm/ n **in ~** em tempo de guerra

wary /'weərɪ/ a (**-ier, -iest**) cauteloso, prudente

was /wɒz unstressed wəz/ ▶ BE

wash /wɒʃ/ vt/i lavar(-se); (flow over) molhar, inundar; **~ one's hands of** lavar as mãos de; **~ out** ‹cup etc› lavar; ‹stain› tirar lavando; **~ up** lavar a louça; Amer (wash oneself) lavar-se ● n lavagem f; (dirty clothes) roupa f para lavar; (of ship) esteira f; (of paint) fina camada f de tinta; **have a ~** lavar-se. **~basin** n pia f, (P) lavatório m; **~cloth** n Amer (facecloth) toalha f de rosto; **~out** n 🔟 fiasco m; **~room** n Amer banheiro m, (P) casa f de banho. **~able** a lavável. **~ing** n (dirty) roupa f suja; (clean) roupa f lavada. **~ing machine** n máquina f de lavar roupa; **~ing powder** n detergente m em pó; **~ing-up** n lavagem f da louça

washed-out /wɒʃt'aʊt/ a (faded) desbotado; (exhausted) exausto

washer /'wɒʃə(r)/ n (machine) máquina f de lavar roupa, louça f; (ring) anilha f

wasp /wɒsp/ n vespa f

waste /weɪst/ vt desperdiçar, esbanjar; ‹time› perder ● vi **~ away** consumir-se ● a (useless) inútil; ‹material› de refugo; **~ paper** papéis mpl velhos ou usados; **~paper basket** cesto m de papéis ● n desperdício m, perda f; (of time) perda f; (rubbish) lixo m; **lay ~** assolar, devastar; **~ (land)** (desolate) região f desolada, ermo m; (unused) (terreno) baldio m; **~disposal unit** triturador m de lixo

wasteful /'weɪstfl/ a dispendioso; ‹person› esbanjador, gastador, perdulário

watch /wɒtʃ/ vt/i ver bem, olhar com atenção, observar; ‹game, TV› ver; (guard, spy on) vigiar; (be careful about) tomar or ter cuidado com; **~ out** (look out) estar à espreita (**for** de); (take care) acautelar-se ● n vigia f, vigilância f; Naut quarto m; (for telling time) relógio m. **~dog** n cão m de guarda; **~tower** n torre f de observação. **~ful** a atento, vigilante

watchmaker /'wɒtʃmeɪkə(r)/ n relojoeiro m

watchman /'wɒtʃmən/ n (pl **-men**) (of building) guarda m; (**night-)~** guarda-noturno m

water /'wɔːtə(r)/ n água f; **~ polo** polo m aquático ● vt regar; **~ down** juntar água a, diluir; ‹milk, wine› aguar, batizar 🔟; fig (tone down) suavizar ● vi (of eyes) lacrimejar, chorar. **~ closet** n WC m, banheiro m, (P) lavabos mpl; **~colour** n aquarela f; **~melon** n melancia f; **~ pistol** n pistola f de água; **~ polo** n polo m aquático; **~skiing** n esqui m aquático

watercress /'wɔːtəkres/ n agrião m

waterfall /'wɔːtəfɔːl/ n queda f de água, cascata f

watering can /'wɔːtərɪŋkæn/ n regador m

waterlogged /'wɔːtəlɒgd/ a saturado de água; ‹land› empapado, alagado; ‹vessel› inundado, alagado

waterproof /'wɔːtəpruːf/ a impermeável; ‹watch› à prova de água

watershed /'wɔːtəʃed/ n fig momento m decisivo; (in affairs) ponto m crítico

watertight /'wɔːtətaɪt/ a à prova de água, hermético; fig ‹argument etc› inequívoco; irrefutável

waterway /'wɔːtəweɪ/ n via f navegável

watery /'wɔːtərɪ/ a ‹colour› pálido; ‹eyes› lacrimoso; ‹soup› aguado; ‹tea› fraco

watt /wɒt/ n watt m

wav|e /weɪv/ n onda f; (in hair) Radio onda f; (sign) aceno m ● vt acenar com; ‹sword› brandir; ‹hair› ondular; **~e goodbye** dizer adeus ● vi acenar (com a mão); ‹hair etc› ondular; ‹flag› tremular. **~elength** n comprimento m de onda. **~y** a ondulado

waver /'weɪvə(r)/ vi vacilar; (hesitate) hesitar

wax[1] /wæks/ n cera f ● vt encerar; ‹car› polir

wax[2] /wæks/ vi (of moon) aumentar, crescer

waxwork /'wækswɜːk/ n (dummy) figura f de cera. **~s** npl (exhibition) museu m de figuras de cera

way /weɪ/ n (road, path) caminho m, estrada f, rua f (**to** para); (distance) percurso m; (direction) (P) direção f; (manner) modo m, maneira f; (means) meios mpl; (respect) respeito m; **~s** (habits) costumes mpl; **be in the ~** atrapalhar; **be on one's** or **the ~** estar a caminho; **by the ~** a propósito; **by ~ of** por, via, através; **get one's own ~** conseguir o que quer; **give ~** (yield) ceder; (*collapse*) desabar; *Auto* dar a preferência or (*P*) a prioridade; **in a ~** de certo modo; **make one's ~** ir; **that ~** dessa maneira; **this ~** desta maneira; **~ in** entrada *f*; **~ out** saída *f* ● *adv* 🔢 consideravelmente; de longe. **~out** a 🔢 excêntrico

waylay /wer'leɪ/ *vt* (*pt* **-laid**) (*assail*) armar uma cilada para; (*stop*) interceptar, (*P*) intercetar

wayward /'weɪwəd/ *a* (*wilful*) teimoso; (*perverse*) caprichoso, difícil

WC /dʌb(ə)lju:'si:/ *n* WC *m*, banheiro *m*, (*P*) casa *f* de banho

we /wi:/ *pron* nós

weak /wi:k/ *a* (**-er, -est**) fraco; (*delicate*) frágil. **~en** *vt/i* enfraquecer; (*give way*) fraquejar. **~ness** *n* fraqueza *f*; (*fault*) ponto *m* fraco; **a ~ness for** (*liking*) um fraco por

weakling /'wi:klɪŋ/ *n* fraco *m*

wealth /welθ/ *n* riqueza *f*; (*riches, resources*) riquezas *fpl*; (*quantity*) abundância *f*

wealthy /'welθɪ/ *a* (**-ier, -iest**) rico

wean /wi:n/ *vt* (*baby*) desmamar; (*from habit etc*) desabituar

weapon /'wepən/ *n* arma *f*

wear /weə(r)/ *vt* (*pt* **wore**, *pp* **worn**) (*have on*) usar, trazer; (*put on*) pôr; (*expression*) ter; (*damage*) gastar; **~ black/red**/*etc* vestir-se de preto/ vermelho/*etc*; **~ down** gastar; (*person*) extenuar; **~ off** passar; **~ on** (*time*) passar lentamente; **~ out** gastar; (*tire*) esgotar ● *vi* (*last*) durar; (*become old, damaged etc*) gastar-se ● *n* (*use*) uso *m*; (*deterioration*) gasto *m*, uso *m*; (*endurance*) resistência *f*; (*clothing*) roupa *f*; **~ and tear** desgaste *m*

wear|y /'wɪərɪ/ *a* (**-ier, -iest**) fatigado, cansado; (*tiring*) fatigante, cansativo ● *vi* **~y of** cansar-se de

weasel /'wi:zl/ *n* doninha *f*

weather /'weðə(r)/ *n* tempo *m*; **under the ~** 🔢 (*ill*) indisposto, achacado ● *a* meteorológico ● *vt* (*survive*) aguentar, resistir a. **~beaten** a curtido pelo tempo; **~ forecast** *n* boletim *m* meteorológico

weav|e[1] /wi:v/ *vt* (*pt* **wove**, *pp* **woven**) (*cloth etc*) tecer; (*plot*) urdir, criar ● *n* (*style*) tipo *m* de tecido. **~er** /-ə(r)/ *n* tecelão *m*, tecelã *f*

weave[2] /wi:v/ *vi* (*move*) serpear; (*through traffic, obstacles*) ziguezaguear

web /web/ *n* (*of spider*) teia *f*; (*fabric*) tecido *m*; *Comput* web *m*, rede *f*; (*on foot*) membrana *f* interdigital. **~bed** a (*foot*) palmado. **~footed** a palmípede; **~log** blog *m*, (*P*) blogue *m*; **to keep/write a ~log** ter um blog or (*P*) blogue; **~ page** *n* página *f* web; **~site** *n* site *m*, sítio *m*

wed /wed/ *vt/i* (*pt* **wedded**) casar(-se)

wedding /'wedɪŋ/ *n* casamento *m*. **~ cake** *n* bolo *m* de noiva; **~ ring** *n* aliança (de casamento) *f*

wedge /wedʒ/ *n* calço *m*, cunha *f*; (*cake*) fatia *f*; (*of lemon*) quarto *m*; (*under wheel etc*) calço *m*, cunha *f* ● *vt* calçar; (*push*) meter or enfiar à força; (*pack in*) entalar

Wednesday /'wenzdɪ/ *n* quarta-feira *f*

weed /wi:d/ *n* erva *f* daninha ● *vt/i* arrancar as ervas, capinar; **~ out** suprimir, arrancar. **~killer** *n* herbicida *m*. **~y** a *fig* (*person*) fraco

week /wi:k/ *n* semana *f*; **a ~ today/ tomorrow** de hoje/de amanhã a oito dias. **~ly** a semanal ● *a & n* (*periodical*) (jornal) semanário *m* ● *adv* semanalmente, todas as semanas

weekday /'wi:kdeɪ/ *n* dia *m* de semana

weekend /'wi:kend/ *n* fim *m* de semana

weep /wi:p/ *vt/i* (*pt* **wept**) chorar (**for sb** por alguém); **~ing willow** (salgueiro-)chorão *m*

weigh /weɪ/ *vt/i* pesar; **~ anchor** levantar âncora or ferro, zarpar; **~ down** (*weight*) sobrecarregar; (*bend*) envergar; *fig* acabrunhar; **~ up** 🔢 (*examine*) pesar

weight /weɪt/ *n* peso *m*; **lose ~** emagrecer; **put on ~** engordar. **~lifter** *n* halterofilista *m*; **~lifting** *n* halterofilia *f*. **~y** a pesado; (*subject etc*) de peso; (*influential*) influente

weir /wɪə(r)/ *n* represa *f*, açude *m*

weird /wɪəd/ *a* (**-er, -est**) misterioso; (*strange*) estranho, bizarro

welcom|e /'welkəm/ *a* agradável; (*timely*) oportuno; **~e to do** livre para fazer ● *int* bem-vindo! ● *n* acolhimento *m* ● *vt* acolher, receber; (*as greeting*) dar as boas vindas a; **be ~e** ser bem-vindo; **you're ~e!** (*after thank you*) não tem de quê!, de nada!. **~ing** a acolhedor

weld /weld/ *vt* soldar ● *n* solda *f*. **~er** *n* soldador *m*

welfare /'welfeə(r)/ *n* bem-estar *m*; (*aid*) assistência *f*, previdência *f* social; **W~ State** Estado-Providência *m*

W

well¹ /wel/ n (for water, oil) poço m; (of stairs) vão m; (of lift) poço m

well² /wel/ adv (**better, best**) bem; **we may as ~ go** é melhor irmos andando; **as ~ as** tão bem como; (in addition) assim como; **be ~** (healthy) ir or passar bem; **do ~** (succeed) sair-se bem, ser bem-sucedido; **very ~** muito bem; **~ done!** bravo!, muito bem! ● a bem invar ● int bem!. **~behaved** a bem-comportado, educado; **~being** n bem-estar m; **~done** a (of meat) bem passado; **~dressed** a bem-vestido; **~heeled** a 🗆 (wealthy) rico; **~informed** a versado, bem informado; **~known** a (bem-)conhecido; **~meaning** a bem-intencionado; **~off** a rico, próspero; **~read** a instruído; **~spoken** a bem-falante; **~timed** a oportuno; **~to-do** a rico; **~wisher** n admirador m, simpatizante mf

wellington /'welɪŋtən/ n (boot) bota f alta de borracha

Welsh /welʃ/ a galês ● n Lang galês m

> **Welsh Assembly** A Assembleia Nacional de Gales começou a funcionar em Cardiff, em 1999. Embora a Assembleia não tenha poderes para criar impostos, ela passou a ter poderes legislativos depois de um referendo em 2011. É formada por 60 membros ou AMs (Assembly Members); 40 são eleitos diretamente e os restantes, das listas regionais, através do sistema de representação proporcional.

went /went/ ▶ GO

wept /wept/ ▶ WEEP

were /wɜː(r) unstressed wə(r)/ ▶ BE

west /west/ n oeste m; **the W~** Pol o Oeste, o Ocidente ● a ocidental, do oeste; **the W~ Indies** as Antilhas ● adv a oeste, para oeste. **~erly** a ocidental, oeste. **~ward(s)** adv para oeste

western /'westən/ a ocidental, do oeste; Pol ocidental ● n (film) filme m de cowboys, bangue-bangue m

westernize /'westənaɪz/ vt ocidentalizar

wet /wet/ a (**wetter, wettest**) molhado; (of weather) chuvoso, de chuva; 🗆 ⟨person⟩ fraco; **get ~** molhar-se; **~ blanket** 🗆 desmancha-prazeres mf invar 🗆; **~ paint** pintado de fresco; **~ suit** roupa f de mergulho ● vt (**wetted**) molhar

whack /wæk/ vt 🗆 bater em ● n 🗆 pancada f. **~ed** a 🗆 morto de cansaço; rebentado 🗆

whale /weɪl/ n baleia f

wharf /wɔːf/ n (pl **wharfs**) cais m

> **what** /wɒt/ ● pron
>
> ····▶ (in questions) o que; **~ is it?** o que é?; **~ do you want?** o que você quer?; **~ is your name?** como você se chama?; **~ is your favourite?** qual é o seu favorito?; **~ happened?** o que aconteceu?; **~?** (say that again) o quê?/como?
>
> ····▶ (introducing clause) o que; **I don't know ~ he wants** não sei o que ele quer; **tell me ~ happened** conte-me o que aconteceu; **I don't agree with ~ you're saying** não concordo com o que diz; **do ~ I tell you** faça o que lhe digo
>
> ····▶ (with prepositions) que; **~ are you thinking about?** em que você está pensando?; **~'s it for?** para o que é isso?
>
> ····▶ (in phrases) **~ about me/him?** e eu/ele?; **~ about a cup of coffee?** que tal uma xícara de café?; **~ if the train is late?** e se o trem se atrasar?; **~ for?** para quê?; **so ~?** e depois?
>
> ● a
>
> ····▶ (in questions) qual; **~ train did you catch?** qual foi o trem que você pegou?; **~ time is it?** que horas são?; **~ colour is it?** que cor é essa?; **~ shoes should I wear?** que sapatos eu uso?; **~ time does it start?** a que horas começa?
>
> ····▶ (in exclamations) que; **~ an ideal** que ideia!; **~ luck!** que sorte!; **~ a huge house!** que casa enorme!

whatever /wɒt'evə(r)/ a **~ book/** etc qualquer livro/etc que seja ● pron (no matter what) qualquer que seja; (anything that) o que quer que, tudo o que; **~ happens** aconteça o que acontecer; **do ~ you like** faça o que quiser; **nothing ~** absolutamente nada

whatsoever /wɒtsəʊ'evə(r)/ a & pron = WHATEVER

wheat /wiːt/ n trigo m

wheel /wiːl/ n roda f; **at the ~** (of vehicle) ao volante; (helm) ao leme ● vt empurrar ● vi rodar, rolar

wheelbarrow /'wiːlbærəʊ/ n carrinho m de mão

wheelchair /'wi:ltʃeə(r)/ n cadeira f de rodas

when /wen/ adv, conj & pron quando; **the day/moment ~** o dia/momento em que

whenever /wen'evə(r)/ conj & adv (at whatever time) quando quer que, quando; (every time that) (de) cada vez que, sempre que

where /weə(r)/ adv, conj & pron onde, aonde; (in which place) em que, onde; (whereas) enquanto que, ao passo que; **~ is he going?** aonde é que ele vai?. **~abouts** adv onde ● n paradeiro m. **~by** adv pelo que. **~upon** adv após o que, depois do que

whereas /weər'æz/ conj enquanto que, ao passo que

wherever /weər'evə(r)/ conj & adv onde quer que; **~ can it be?** onde pode estar?

whether /'weðə(r)/ conj se; **not know ~** não saber se; **~ I go or not** caso eu vá ou não

which /wɪtʃ/ ● a

····➤ (in questions) que, qual; **~ book do you need?** de que/qual livro precisa?; **~ bag is yours?** qual das malas é a sua?; **~ way is the bank/ hospital/supermarket?** como se vai para o banco/hospital/supermercado?

● pron

····➤ (in questions) qual; **~ is yours?** qual é o seu/a sua?; **there are three peaches, ~ do you want?** há três pêssegos, qual você quer?; **~ is the biggest?** qual é a maior?

····➤ (relative) que, o qual/a qual; (pl) os quais/as quais; **the book ~ is on the table** o livro que está em cima da mesa; **she made a serious mistake, ~ was unusual for her** ela fez um erro grave, o que era incomum para ela; **her work about ~ I know nothing** o trabalho dela, do qual nada sei; **the play ~ I took part in** a peça da qual eu participei

❗ Note that if o qual or a qual are preceded by the prepositions em or de, they often contract with them to form no qual, na qual, do qual, da qual.

whichever /wɪtʃ'evə(r)/ a **~ book/etc** qualquer livro/etc que seja; **take ~ book you wish** leve o livro que quiser ● pron qualquer, quaisquer

whiff /wɪf/ n (of fresh air) sopro m, lufada f; (smell) baforada f

while /waɪl/ n (espaço de) tempo m, momento m; **once in a ~** de vez em quando ● conj (when) enquanto; (while) embora; (whereas) enquanto que ● vt **~ away** ‹time› passar

whim /wɪm/ n capricho m

whimper /'wɪmpə(r)/ vi gemer; ‹baby› choramingar ● n gemido m; (baby) choro m

whimsical /'wɪmzɪkl/ a ‹person› caprichoso; (odd) bizarro

whine /waɪn/ vi lamuriar-se, queixar-se; ‹dog› ganir ● n lamúria f, queixume m; (dog) ganido m

whip /wɪp/ n chicote m ● vt (pt whipped) chicotear; Culin bater; **~ up** excitar; (cause) provocar; 🇬🇧 ‹meal› preparar rapidamente; **~ped cream** creme m chantilly ● vi (move) ir a toda a pressa. **~round** n 🇬🇧 coleta f; vaquinha f

whirl /wɜːl/ vt/i (fazer) rodopiar, girar ● n rodopio m

whirlpool /'wɜːlpuːl/ n redemoinho m

whirlwind /'wɜːlwɪnd/ n redemoinho m de vento, turbilhão m

whirr /wɜː(r)/ vi zunir, zumbir

whisk /wɪsk/ vt/i (snatch) levar/tirar bruscamente; Culin bater; ‹flies› sacudir ● n Culin batedeira f; **~ away** (brush away) sacudir

whisker /'wɪskə(r)/ n fio m de barba. **~s** npl (of animal) bigode m; (beard) barba f; (sideboards) suíças fpl

whisky /'wɪskɪ/ n uísque m

whisper /'wɪspə(r)/ vt/i sussurrar, murmurar; (of stream, leaves) sussurrar ● n sussurro m, murmúrio m; **in a ~** baixinho, em voz baixa

whistle /'wɪsl/ n assobio m; (instrument) apito m ● vt/i assobiar; (with instrument) apitar

white /waɪt/ a (-er, -est) branco, alvo; (pale) pálido; **go ~** (turn pale) empalidecer; (of hair) branquear, embranquecer; **~ coffee** café m com leite; **~collar worker** empregado m de escritório; **~ elephant** fig trambolho m, elefante m branco; **~ lie** mentirinha f ● n (colour; of eyes; person) branco m; (of egg) clara (de ovo) f. **~ness** n brancura f

whiten /'waɪtn/ vt/i branquear

Whitsun /'wɪtsn/ n Pentecostes m

whizz /wɪz/ vi (pt whizzed) (through air) zunir, sibilar; (rush) passar a toda a velocidade. **~kid** n 🇬🇧 prodígio m

W

who /hu:/ *interr pron* quem ● *rel pron* que, o(a) qual, os(as) quais

whoever /hu:'eva(r)/ *pron* (*no matter who*) quem quer que, seja quem for; (*the one who*) aquele que

whole /həʊl/ *a* inteiro, todo; (*not broken*) intacto; **the ~ house/***etc* toda a casa/*etc* ● *n* totalidade *f*; (*unit*) todo *m*; **as a ~** no conjunto, como um todo; **on the ~** de um modo geral. **~hearted** *a* de todo o coração; (*person*) dedicado; **~heartedly** *adv* sem reservas, sinceramente

wholefood /'həʊlfu:d/ *n* comida *f* integral

wholemeal /'həʊlmi:l/ *a* **~ bread** pão *m* integral

wholesale /'həʊlseɪl/ *n* venda *f* por grosso or por atacado ● *a* (*firm*) por grosso, por atacado; *fig* sistemático; em massa ● *adv* (*in large quantities*) por atacado; *fig* em massa; em grande escala. **~r** /-ə(r)/ *n* grossista *mf*, atacadista *mf*

wholesome /'həʊlsəm/ *a* sadio, saudável

wholewheat /'həʊlwi:t/ *a* = WHOLEMEAL

wholly /'həʊlɪ/ *adv* inteiramente, completamente

whom /hu:m/ *interr pron* quem ● *rel pron* (*that*) que; (*after prep*) quem, que, o qual

whore /hɔ:(r)/ *n* prostituta *f*

whose /hu:z/ *rel pron & a* cujo, de quem ● *interr pron* de quem; **~ hat is this?**, **~ is this hat?** de quem é este chapéu?; **~ son are you?** de quem é que o senhor é filho?

why /waɪ/ *adv* porque, por que motivo, por que razão, porquê; **she doesn't know ~ he's here** ela não sabe porque or por que motivo ele está aqui; **she doesn't know ~** ela não sabe porquê; **do you know ~?** você sabe porquê? ● *int* (*protest*) ora, ora essa; (*discovery*) oh; **~ yes/***etc* ah, sim

wick /wɪk/ *n* torcida *f*, mecha *f*, pavio *m*

wicked /'wɪkɪd/ *a* mau, malvado; (*mischievous, spiteful*) maldoso

wicker /'wɪkə(r)/ *n* verga *f*, vime *m*

wicket /'wɪkɪt/ *n Cricket* arco *m*

wide /waɪd/ *a* (-er, -est) largo; (*extensive*) vasto, grande, extenso; **two metres ~** com dois metros de largura ● *adv* longe; (*fully*) completamente; **open ~** (*door, window*) abrir(-se) de par em par, escancarar(-se); (*mouth*) abrir bem; **~ awake** (*bem*) desperto, (*bem*) acordado; **far and ~** por toda a parte. **~ly** *adv* largamente; (*travel, spread*) muito; (*generally*) geralmente; (*extremely*) extremamente

widen /'waɪdn/ *vt/i* alargar(-se)

widespread /'waɪdspred/ *a* muito espalhado, difundido, generalizado

widow /'wɪdəʊ/ *n* viúva *f*. **~ed** *a* (*man*) viúvo; (*woman*) viúva; **be ~ed** enviuvar, ficar viúvo or viúva. **~er** *n* viúvo *m*

width /wɪdθ/ *n* largura *f*

wield /wi:ld/ *vt* (*axe etc*) manejar; *fig* (*power*) exercer

wife /waɪf/ *n* (*pl* **wives**) mulher *f*, esposa *f*

wi-fi, Wi-Fi®, wifi /'waɪfaɪ/ *n* wi-fi *m*

wig /wɪg/ *n* cabeleira (postiça) *f*; (*judge's etc*) peruca *f*

wiggle /'wɪgl/ *vt/i* remexer(-se), retorcer(-se), mexer(-se) dum lado para outro

wild /waɪld/ *a* (-er, -est) selvagem; (*of plant*) silvestre; (*mad*) louco; (*enraged*) furioso, violento; **~-goose chase** falsa pista *f*, tentativa *f* inútil, (*P*) caça *f* aos gambozinos ● *adv* a esmo; (*without control*) à solta. **~s** *npl* regiões *fpl* selvagens. **~ly** *adv* violentamente; (*madly*) loucamente

wilderness /'wɪldənɪs/ *n* deserto *m*

wildlife /'waɪldlaɪf/ *n* animais *mpl* selvagens

wilful /'wɪlfl/ *a* (*person*) voluntarioso; (*act*) intencional, propositado

will[1] /wɪl/ *v aux* **you ~ sing/he ~ do/** *etc* tu cantarás or tu vais cantar/ele fará or ele vai fazer/*etc*; (*1st person: future: expressing will or intention*) **I ~ sing/we ~ do/***etc* eu cantarei or eu vou cantar/nós faremos or nós vamos fazer/*etc*; **~ you have a cup of coffee?** quer tomar um cafezinho?; **~ you shut the door?** quer fazer o favor de fechar a porta?

will[2] /wɪl/ *n* vontade *f*; (*document*) testamento *m*; **at ~** à vontade, quando or como se quiser ● *vt* (*wish*) querer; (*bequeath*) deixar em testamento. **~power** *n* força *f* de vontade

willing /'wɪlɪŋ/ *a* pronto, de boa vontade; **~ to** disposto a. **~ly** *adv* (*with pleasure*) de boa vontade, de bom grado; (*not forced*) voluntariamente. **~ness** *n* boa vontade *f*; disposição *f* (**to do** em para fazer)

willow /'wɪləʊ/ *n* salgueiro *m*

willy-nilly /wɪlɪˈnɪlɪ/ adv de bom ou de mau grado, quer queira ou não

wilt /wɪlt/ vi murchar, definhar

wily /ˈwaɪlɪ/ a (**-ier, -iest**) manhoso, matreiro

win /wɪn/ vt/i (pt **won**, pres p **winning**) ganhar ● n vitória f □ ~ **over** vt convencer, conquistar

winc|e /wɪns/ vi estremecer, contrair-se

winch /wɪntʃ/ n guincho m ● vt içar com guincho

wind¹ /wɪnd/ n vento m; (breath) fôlego m; (flatulence) gases mpl; **get ~ of** fig ouvir rumor de; **put the ~ up** assustar; **in the ~** no ar; ~ **farm** central f eólica; ~ **instrument** Mus instrumento m de sopro. **~swept** a varrido pelo vento

wind² /waɪnd/ vt/i (pt **wound**) enrolar(-se), (wrap) envolver, pôr em volta; (of path, river) serpentear; ~ **(up)** <clock etc> dar corda em/a; ~ **up** (end) terminar, acabar; fig <speech etc> concluir; <firm> liquidar; **he'll ~ up in jail** ele vai acabar na cadeia

windfall /ˈwɪndfɔːl/ n fruta f caída; fig (money) sorte f grande

windmill /ˈwɪndmɪl/ n moinho m de vento

window /ˈwɪndəʊ/ n janela f; (of shop) vitrine f, (P) montra f; (counter) guichê m, (P) guichet m; **go ~-shopping** ir ver vitrines/montras. ~ **box** n jardineira f, (P) floreira f; ~ **cleaner** n limpador m de janelas; **~pane** n vidro m, vidraça f; ~ **sill** n peitoril m

windpipe /ˈwɪndpaɪp/ n traqueia f

windscreen /ˈwɪndskriːn/ n para-brisa m, (P) para-brisas m invar. ~ **wiper** /-waɪpə(r)/ n limpador m de para-brisa, (P) limpa m para-brisas

windshield /ˈwɪndʃiːld/ n Amer = WINDSCREEN

windsurf|er /ˈwɪndsɜːfə(r)/ n surfista mf, (P) praticante mf de windsurf. **~ing** n surfe m, (P) windsurf m

windy /ˈwɪndɪ/ a (**-ier, -iest**) ventoso; **It is very ~** está ventando muito, (P) está muito ventoso

wine /waɪn/ n vinho m; ~ **bar** bar m para degustação de vinhos; ~ **waiter** garçon m, (P) empregado m de vinhos. ~ **cellar** n adega f, cave f; ~ **list** n lista f de vinhos; ~ **tasting** n prova f or degustação f de vinhos

wine glass /ˈwaɪnglɑːs/ n copo m de vinho; (with stem) cálice m

wing /wɪŋ/ n asa f; Mil flanco m; Archit ala f; Auto para-lamas m invar, (P) guarda-lamas m invar; **~s** Theat bastidores mpl; **under sb's ~** debaixo das asas de alguém

wink /wɪŋk/ vi piscar o olho; <light, star> cintilar, piscar ● n piscadela f; **not sleep a ~** não pregar olho

winner /ˈwɪnə(r)/ n vencedor m

winning /ˈwɪnɪŋ/ a vencedor, vitorioso; (number) premiado; (smile) encantador, atraente. **~s** npl ganhos mpl

wint|er /ˈwɪntə(r)/ n inverno m ● vi hibernar. **~ry** a de inverno, invernoso; <smile> glacial

wipe /waɪp/ vt limpar; (dry) enxugar, limpar ● n limpadela f; ~ **off** limpar; ~ **out** (destroy) aniquilar, limpar 🠒; (cancel) cancelar; ~ **up** enxugar

wir|e /ˈwaɪə(r)/ n arame m; 🠒 (telegram) telegrama m; (**electric**) **~e** fio elétrico m ● vt <a house> montar a instalação elétrica em; 🠒 (telegraph) telegrafar. **~ing** n Electr instalação f elétrica

wireless /ˈwaɪəlɪs/ n rádio f; (set) rádio m

wisdom /ˈwɪzdəm/ n sagacidade f, sabedoria f; (common sense) bom senso m, sensatez f; ~ **tooth** dente m (do) siso

wise /waɪz/ a (**-er, -est**) <person> sábio, avisado, sensato; <look> entendedor; ~ **guy** 🠒 sabichão m, 🠒 sabe-tudo m 🠒; **none the ~r** sem entender nada

wisecrack /ˈwaɪzkræk/ n 🠒 (boa) piada f

wish /wɪʃ/ n (desire, aspiration) desejo m, vontade f; (request) pedido m; (greeting) desejo m, voto m; **I have no ~ to go** não tenho nenhum desejo or nenhuma vontade de ir; **with best ~es** (formal) (in letter) com os melhores cumprimentos, com saudações cordiais; (on greeting card) com desejos or votos (**for** de) ● vt (desire, bid) desejar; (want) apetecer; ter vontade de; desejar (**to do** fazer); ~ **sb well** desejar felicidades a alguém; **I don't ~ to go** não me apetece ir, não tenho vontade de ir, não desejo ir; **I ~ he'd leave** eu gostaria que ele partisse, quem dera que ele partisse ● vi ~ **for** desejar

wishful /ˈwɪʃfl/ a ~ **thinking** sonhar acordado, impossível de concretizar

wishy-washy /ˈwɪʃwɒʃɪ/ a sem expressão, fraco, inexpressivo

wistful /ˈwɪstfl/ a melancólico, saudoso

wit /wɪt/ n inteligência f; (humour) presença f de espírito, humor m; (person)

W

senso *m or* (P) sentido *m* de humor; **be at one's ~'s** or **~s' end** não saber o que fazer; **keep one's ~s about one** estar alerta; **live by one's ~s** ganhar a vida de maneira suspeita; **scared out of one's ~s** apavorado

witch /wɪtʃ/ *n* feiticeira *f*, bruxa *f*. **~craft** *n* feitiçaria *f*, bruxaria *f*, magia *f*

with /wɪð/ *prep* com; *(having)* de; *(because of)* de; *(at the house of)* em casa de; **the man ~ the beard** o homem de barbas; **fill/etc~** encher/ *etc* de; **laughing/shaking/etc ~** a rir/a tremer/*etc* de; **I'm not ~ you** 🔲 não estou compreendendo-o, (P) não te estou a compreender

withdraw /wɪðˈdrɔː/ *vt/i* (*pt* **withdrew**, *pp* **withdrawn**) retirar(-se); *‹money›* tirar. **~al** *n* retirada *f*; *Med* estado *m* de privação. **~n** *a* *‹person›* retraído, fechado

wither /ˈwɪðə(r)/ *vt/i* murchar, secar. **~ed** *a* *‹person›* mirrado. **~ing** *a* *fig* *(scornful)* desdenhoso

withhold /wɪðˈhəʊld/ *vt* (*pt* **withheld**) negar, recusar; *(retain)* reter; *(conceal, not tell)* esconder (**from** de)

within /wɪˈðɪn/ *prep & adv* dentro (de), por dentro (de); *(in distances)* a menos de; **~ a month** *(before)* dentro de um mês; **~ sight** à vista

without /wɪˈðaʊt/ *prep* sem; **~ fail** sem falta; **go ~ saying** não ser preciso dizer

withstand /wɪðˈstænd/ *vt* (*pt* **withstood**) resistir a, opor-se a

witness /ˈwɪtnɪs/ *n* testemunha *f*; *(evidence)* testemunho *m* ● *vt* testemunhar, presenciar; *‹document›* assinar como testemunha; **bear ~ to** testemunhar, dar testemunho de. **~ box** *n* banco *m* das testemunhas

witticism /ˈwɪtɪsɪzəm/ *n* dito *m* espirituoso

witty /ˈwɪtɪ/ *a* (**-ier,**, **-iest**) espirituoso

wives /waɪvz/ ▶ **WIFE**

wizard /ˈwɪzəd/ *n* feiticeiro *m*; *fig* *(genius)* gênio *m*, (P) génio *m*

wizened /ˈwɪznd/ *a* encarquilhado

wobble /ˈwɒbl/ *vi* *(of jelly, voice, hand)* tremer; *(stagger)* cambalear, vacilar; *(of table, chair)* balançar. **~y** *a* *(trembling)* trêmulo, (P) trémulo; *(staggering)* cambaleante, vacilante; *‹table, chair›* pouco firme

woe /wəʊ/ *n* dor *f*, infortúnio *m*

woke, woken /wəʊk, ˈwəʊkən/ ▶ **WAKE**[1]

wolf /wʊlf/ *n* (*pl* **wolves** /wʊlvz/) lobo *m*; **cry ~** dar alarme falso, (P) falso alarme ● *vt* *‹food›* devorar. **~ whistle** *n* assobio *m* de admiração

woman /ˈwʊmən/ *n* (*pl* **women**) mulher *f*. **~ly** *a* feminino

womb /wuːm/ *n* seio *m*, ventre *m*; *Med* útero *m*; *fig* seio *m*

women /ˈwɪmɪn/ ▶ **WOMAN**; **~'s movement** movimento *m* feminista

won /wʌn/ ▶ **WIN**

wonder /ˈwʌndə(r)/ *n* admiração *f*; *(thing)* maravilha *f* ● *vt* perguntar-se a si mesmo (**if** se) ● *vi* admirar-se (**at** de, com) , ficar admirado (**at** de, com); espantar-se (**at** de, com); *(reflect)* pensar (**about** em); **it is no ~** não admira (**that** que)

wonderful /ˈwʌndəfl/ *a* maravilhoso. **~ly** *adv* maravilhosamente; **it works ~ly** funciona às mil maravilhas

won't /wəʊnt/ (= **will not**) = **WILL**[1]

wood /wʊd/ *n* madeira *f*, pau *m*; *(for burning)* lenha *f*. **~(s)** *n* *(area)* bosque *m*, mata *f*, floresta *f*. **~ed** *a* arborizado. **~en** *a* de or em madeira, de pau; *fig* *(stiff)* rígido; *fig* *(inexpressive)* inexpressivo; de pau

woodcut /ˈwʊdkʌt/ *n* gravura *f* em madeira

woodland /ˈwʊdlənd/ *n* região *f* arborizada, bosque *m*, mata *f*

woodpecker /ˈwʊdpekə(r)/ *n* *(bird)* pica-pau *m*

woodwind /ˈwʊdwɪnd/ *n* *Mus* instrumentos *mpl* de sopro de madeira

woodwork /ˈwʊdwɜːk/ *n* *(of building)* madeiramento *m*; *(carpentry)* carpintaria *f*

woodworm /ˈwʊdwɜːm/ *n* caruncho *m*

wool /wʊl/ *n* lã *f*. **~len** *a* de lã. **~lens** *npl* roupas *fpl* de lã. **~ly** *a* de lã; *(vague)* confuso ● *n* 🔲 *(garment)* roupa *f* de lã

word /wɜːd/ *n* palavra *f*; *(news)* notícia(s) *f(pl)*; *(promise)* palavra *f* ● *vt* exprimir, formular; **by ~ of mouth** de viva voz, por via oral; **have a ~ with** dizer duas palavras a; **in other ~s** em outras palavras, (P) por outras palavras. **~ processor** *n* processador *m* de texto(s). **~ing** *n* termos *mpl*, redação *f*. **~y** *a* prolixo

wore /wɔː(r)/ ▶ **WEAR**

work /wɜːk/ *n* trabalho *m*; *(product, book etc)* obra *f*; *(building etc)* obras *fpl*; **at ~** no trabalho; **out of ~** desempregado ● *vt/i* *(of person)* trabalhar; *Techn* (fazer) funcionar, (fazer) andar; (of drug etc) agir, fazer efeito; ‹farm, mine› explorar; ‹land› lavrar; **~ sb** (make work) fazer alguém trabalhar; **~ in** introduzir, inserir; **~ loose** soltar-se; **~ off** (get rid of) descarregar; **~ed up** ‹person› enervado, transtornado, agitado. **~ out** vt (solve) resolver; (calculate) calcular; (devise) planejar, (P) planear ● vi (succeed) resultar; Sport treinar-se; **~ up** vt criar ● vi (to climax) ir num crescendo. **~s** npl Techn mecanismo m; (factory) fábrica f

workable /ˈwɜːkəbl/ a viável, praticável

workaholic /wɜːkəˈhɒlɪk/ n **be a ~** Ⓘ trabalhar como um possesso, Ⓘ ser viciado em trabalho

worker /ˈwɜːkə(r)/ n trabalhador m, trabalhadora f; (factory) operário m

working /ˈwɜːkɪŋ/ a ‹day, clothes, hypothesis, lunch etc› de trabalho; **the ~ class(es)** a classe operária, a(s) class(es) trabalhadora(s), o proletariado; **~ mother** mãe f que trabalha; **~ party** comissão f consultiva, de estudo etc; **in ~ order** em condições de funcionamento. **~class** a operário, trabalhador. **~s** npl mecanismo m

workman /ˈwɜːkmən/ n (pl **-men**) trabalhador m; (factory) operário m. **~ship** n trabalho m, execução f, mão-de-obra f; (skill) arte f, habilidade f

workshop /ˈwɜːkʃɒp/ n oficina f, (P) workshop m

world /wɜːld/ n mundo m; **a ~ of** muito(s), grande quantidade de, um mundo de ● a mundial. **~wide** a mundial, universal

worldly /ˈwɜːldlɪ/ a terreno; (devoted to the affairs of life) mundano; **~ goods** bens mpl materiais. **~wise** a com experiência do mundo

worm /wɜːm/ n verme m; (earthworm) minhoca f ● vt **~ one's way into** insinuar-se, introduzir-se, enfiar-se

worn /wɔːn/ a usado. **~out** ‹thing› completamente gasto; ‹person› esgotado

worr|y /ˈwʌrɪ/ vt/i preocupar(-se); **don't ~y** fique descansado, não se preocupe ● n preocupação f. **~ied** a preocupado. **~ying** a preocupante, inquietante

worse /wɜːs/ a & adv pior ● n pior m; **get ~** piorar; **from bad to ~** de mal a pior; **~ luck** pouca sorte, pena

worsen /ˈwɜːsn/ vt/i piorar

worship /ˈwɜːʃɪp/ n (reverence) reverência f, veneração f; (religious) culto m; **Your/His W~** Vossa/Sua Excelência f ● vt (pt **worshipped**) adorar, venerar ● vi fazer as suas devoções, praticar o culto

worst /wɜːst/ a & n **(the)** (o/a) pior mf; **if the ~ comes to the ~** se o pior acontecer, na pior das hipóteses; **do one's ~** fazer todo o mal que se quiser; **get the ~ of it** ficar a perder; **the ~ (thing) that** o pior que ● adv pior

worth /wɜːθ/ a **be ~** valer; (deserving) merecer ● n valor m, mérito m; **ten pounds ~ of** dez libras de; **it's ~ it, it's ~ while** vale a pena; **it's not ~ my while** não vale a pena; **it's ~ waiting/etc** vale a pena esperar/etc; **for all one's ~** Ⓘ dando tudo por tudo. **~less** a sem valor

worthwhile /ˈwɜːθwaɪl/ a que vale a pena; ‹cause› louvável, meritório

worthy /ˈwɜːðɪ/ a (**-ier, -iest**) (deserving) digno; merecedor (**of** de); (laudable) meritório, louvável ● n (person) pessoa f ilustre

would /wʊd unstressed wəd/ v aux **he ~ do/you ~ sing/etc** (conditional tense) ele faria/você cantaria/etc; **he ~ have done** ele teria feito; **she ~ come every day** (used to) ela vinha or costumava vir aqui todos os dias; **~ you please come here?** chegue aqui por favor; **~ you like some tea?** você quer um chá?; **he ~n't go** (refused to) ele não queria ir; **~-be author/doctor/etc** aspirante a autor/médico/etc

wound¹ /wuːnd/ n ferida f ● vt ferir; **the ~ed** os feridos mpl

wound² /waʊnd/ ▶ WIND²

wove, woven /wəʊv, ˈwəʊvn/ ▶ WEAVE²

wrangle /ˈræŋgl/ vi disputar, discutir, brigar ● n disputa f, discussão f, briga f

wrap /ræp/ vt (pt **wrapped**) **~ (up)** embrulhar (**in** em); (in cotton wool, mystery etc) envolver (**in** em); **~ped up in** (engrossed) absorto em, mergulhado em ● vi **~ up** (dress warmly) abrigar-se bem, agasalhar-se bem ● n xaile m. **~per** n (of sweet) papel m; (of book) capa f de papel. **~ping** n embalagem f

wrath /rɒθ/ n ira f

wreath /riːθ/ n (pl **-s** /-ðz/) (of flowers, leaves) coroa f, grinalda f

wreck /rek/ n (sinking) naufrágio m; (ship) navio m naufragado; restos mpl de navio; (remains) destroços mpl; (vehicle) veículo m destroçado; **be a nervous**

W

~ estar com os nervos arrasados ● *vt* destruir; ‹*ship*› fazer naufragar, afundar; *fig* ‹*hope*› acabar. **~age** *n* (*pieces*) destroços *mpl*

wren /ren/ *n* (*bird*) carriça *f*

wrench /rentʃ/ *vt* (*pull*) puxar; (*twist*) torcer; (*snatch*) arrancar (*from* a) ● *n* (*pull*) puxão *m*; (*of ankle, wrist*) torcedura *f*; (*tool*) chave *f* inglesa; *fig* dor *f* de separação

wrestl|e /'resl/ *vi* lutar; debater-se (**with** com or contra;). **~er** *n* lutador *m*. **~ing** *n* luta *f*

wretch /retʃ/ *n* desgraçado *m*, miserável *mf*; (*rascal*) miserável *mf*

wretched /'retʃid/ *a* (*pitiful, poor*) miserável; (*bad*) horrível, desgraçado

wriggle /'rɪgl/ *vt/i* remexer(-se), contorcer-se

wring /rɪŋ/ *vt* (*pt* **wrung**) (*twist; clothes*) torcer; **~ out of** (*obtain from*) arrancar a; **~ing wet** encharcado; (*of person*) encharcado até aos ossos

wrinkle /'rɪŋkl/ *n* (*on skin*) ruga *f*; (*crease*) prega *f* ● *vt/i* enrugar(-se)

wrist /rɪst/ *n* pulso *m*. **~watch** *n* relógio *m* de pulso

write /raɪt/ *vt/i* (*pt* **wrote**, *pp* **written**) escrever; **~ back** responder; **~ down** escrever, tomar nota de; **~ off** ‹*debt*› dar por liquidado; ‹*vehicle*› destinar à sucata; **~ out** (*in full*) escrever por extenso; **~ up** (*from notes*) redigir. **~off** *n* perda *f* total; **~up** *n* relato *m*; (*review*) crítica *f*

writer /'raɪtə(r)/ *n* escritor *m*, autor *m*

writhe /raɪð/ *vi* contorcer(-se)

writing /'raɪtɪŋ/ *n* escrita *f*; **~(s)** (*works*) escritos *mpl*, obras *fpl*; **in ~** por escrito. **~ paper** *n* papel *m* de carta

written /'rɪtn/ ▶ **WRITE**

wrong /rɒŋ/ *a* (*incorrect, mistaken*) mal, errado; (*unfair*) injusto; (*wicked*) mau; (*amiss*) que não está bem; *Mus* ‹*note*› falso; ‹*clock*› que não está certo; **what's ~?** qual é o problema?; **what's ~ with it?** (*amiss*) o que é que não está bem?; (*morally*) que mal há nisso?, que mal tem? ● *adv* mal; **go ~** (*err*) desencaminhar-se, correr mal; (*fail*) ir mal; ‹*vehicle*› quebrar ● *n* mal *m*; (*injustice*) injustiça *f*; **he's in the ~** (*his fault*) ele não tem razão ● *vt* (*be unfair to*) ser injusto com; (*do a wrong to*) fazer mal a. **~ly** *adv* mal; (*blame etc*) sem razão, injustamente

wrongful /'rɒŋfl/ *a* injusto, ilegal

wrote /rəʊt/ ▶ **WRITE**

wrung /rʌŋ/ ▶ **WRING**

wry /raɪ/ *a* (**wryer, wryest**) torto; ‹*smile*› forçado; **~ face** careta *f*

Xx

Xmas /'krɪsməs/ *n* ▶ **CHRISTMAS**

X-ray /'eksreɪ/ *n* raio X *m*; (*photograph*) radiografia *f* ● *vt* radiografar; **have an ~** tirar uma radiografia

xylophone /'zaɪləfəʊn/ *n* xilofone *m*

Yy

yacht /jɒt/ *n* iate *m*. **~ing** *n* iatismo *m*, andar *m* de iate; (*racing*) regata *f* de iate

yank /jæŋk/ *vt* 🠗 puxar bruscamente ● *n* 🠗 puxão *m*

Yank /jæŋk/ *n* 🠗 ianque *mf*

yap /jæp/ *vi* (*pt* **yapped**) latir

yard[1] /jɑːd/ *n* (*measure*) jarda *f* (=0,9144 m)

yard[2] /jɑːd/ *n* (*of house*) pátio *m*; *Amer* (*garden*) jardim *m*; (*for storage*) depósito *m*

yardstick /'jɑːdstɪk/ *n* jarda *f*; *fig* bitola *f*; craveira *f*

yarn /jɑːn/ *n* (*thread*) fio *m*; 🠗 (*tale*) longa *f* história

yawn /jɔːn/ *vi* bocejar; (*be wide open*) abrir-se, escancarar-se ● *n* bocejo *m*

year /jɪə(r)/ *n* ano *m*; **school/tax ~** ano *m* escolar/fiscal; **be ten ~s old/***etc* ter dez/*etc* anos de idade. **~book** *n* anuário *m*. **~ly** *a* anual ● *adv* anualmente

yearn /jɜːn/ *vi* **~ for, to** desejar, ansiar por, suspirar por. **~ing** *n* desejo *m*; anseio *m* (**for** de)

yeast /jiːst/ *n* levedura *f*

yell /jel/ *vt/i* gritar, berrar ● *n* grito *m*, berro *m*

yellow /'jeləʊ/ *a* amarelo; 🠗 (*cowardly*) covarde; poltrão ● *n* amarelo *m*

yelp /jelp/ *n* (*of dog etc*) ganido *m* ● *vi* ganir

yes /jes/ *n* & *adv* sim *m*. **~-man** *n* 🠗 lambe-botas *m invar*; puxa-saco *m*

yesterday /'jestədɪ/ n & adv ontem m; **~ morning/afternoon/evening** ontem de manhã/à tarde/à noite; **the day before ~** anteontem; **~ week** há oito dias, há uma semana

yet /jet/ adv ainda; (already) já; **as ~** até agora, por enquanto; **his best book ~** o seu melhor livro até agora ● conj contudo, no entanto

Yiddish /'jɪdɪʃ/ n ídiche m, (P) iídiche m

yield /jiːld/ vt (produce) produzir, dar; ‹profit› render; (surrender) entregar ● vi (give way) ceder or dar prioridade ● n produção f; Comm rendimento m

yoga /'jəʊɡə/ n ioga f

yoghurt /'jɒɡət/ n iogurte m

yoke /jəʊk/ n jugo m, canga f; (of garment) pala f ● vt jungir; (unite) unir, ligar

yolk /jəʊk/ n gema (de ovo) f

yonder /'jɒndə(r)/ adv acolá, além

you /juː/ pron (familiar) tu, você; pl vocês; (polite) vós, o(s) senhor(es), a(s) senhora(s); (object) (familiar) te, lhe; pl vocês; (polite) o(s), a(s), lhes, vós, o(s) senhor(es), a(s) senhora(s); (after prep) ti, si, você; pl vocês; (polite) vós, o senhor, a senhora; pl os senhores, as senhoras; (indefinite) se; (after prep) si, você; **with ~** (familiar) contigo, consigo, com você; pl com vocês; (polite) com o senhor/a senhora; pl convosco, com os senhores/as senhoras; **I know ~** (familiar) eu te conheço, (P) eu conheço-te, eu o/a conheço, (P) eu conheço-o/a; pl eu os/as conheço, (P) eu conheço-os/as; (polite) eu o conheço o senhor/a senhora; pl conheço os senhores/as senhoras; **~ can see the sea** você pode ver o mar, (P) tu podes ver o mar

young /jʌŋ/ a (-er, -est) jovem, novo, moço ● n ‹people› jovens mpl, a juventude f, a mocidade f; (of animals) crias fpl, filhotes mpl

youngster /'jʌŋstə(r)/ n jovem mf, moço m, rapaz m

your /jɔː(r)/ a (familiar) teu, tua, seu, sua; pl teus, tuas, seus, suas; (polite) vosso, vossa, do senhor, da senhora; pl vossos, vossas, dos senhores, das senhoras

yours /jɔːz/ poss pron (familiar) o teu, a tua, o seu, a sua; pl os teus, as tuas, os seus, as suas; (polite) o vosso, a vossa, o/a do senhor, o/a da senhora; pl os vossos, as vossas, os/as do(s) senhor(es), os/as da(s) senhora(s); **a book of ~** um livro seu; **~ sincerely/faithfully** atenciosamente, com os cumprimentos de

yourself /jɔː'self/ (pl **-selves**) pron (familiar) tu mesmo/a, você mesmo/a; pl vocês mesmos/as; (polite) vós mesmo/a, o senhor mesmo, a senhora mesma; pl vós mesmos/as, os senhores mesmos, as senhoras mesmas; (reflexive) (familiar) te; a ti mesmo/a; se; a si mesmo/a; pl a vocês mesmos/as; (polite) ao senhor mesmo, à senhora mesma; pl aos senhores mesmos, às senhoras mesmas; (after prep: familiar) ti mesmo/a, si mesmo/a, você mesmo/a; pl vocês mesmos/as; (after prep: polite) vós mesmo/a, o senhor mesmo, a senhora mesma; pl vós mesmos/as, os senhores mesmos, as senhoras mesmas; **with ~** (familiar) contigo mesmo/a, consigo mesmo/a, com você; pl com vocês; (polite) convosco, com o senhor, com a senhora; pl com os senhores, com as senhoras; **by ~** sozinho

youth /juːθ/ n (pl **-s** /-ðz/) mocidade f, juventude f; (young man) jovem m, moço m; **~ club** centro m de jovens; **~ hostel** albergue m da juventude. **~ful** a juvenil, jovem

yo-yo® /'jəʊjəʊ/ n (pl **-os**) ioiô m

Yugoslav /'juːɡəslɑːv/ a & n iugoslavo m, (P) jugoslavo m. **~ia** /-'slɑːvɪə/ n Iugoslávia f, (P) Jugoslávia f

Zz

zany /'zeɪnɪ/ a -ier, -iest tolo, bobo, pateta

zeal /ziːl/ n zelo m

zealous /'zeləs/ a zeloso

zebra /'zebrə, 'ziːbrə/ n zebra f; **~ crossing** faixa f para pedestres, (P) passagem f para peões, passadeira f

zenith /'zenɪθ/ n zênite m, (P) zénite m, auge m

zero /'zɪərəʊ/ n (pl **-os**) zero m; **~ hour** a hora H; **below ~** abaixo de zero

zest /zest/ n (gusto) entusiasmo m; fig (spice) sabor m especial; (lemon or orange peel) casca f de limão/laranja ralada

zigzag /'zɪɡzæɡ/ n ziguezague m ● a & adv em ziguezague ● vi (pt **zigzagged**) ziguezaguear

zinc /zɪŋk/ n zinco m

zip /zɪp/ n (vigour) energia f, alma f; ~
(fastener) fecho m ecler ● vt (pt zipped)
fechar o fecho ecler de ● vi ir a toda
a velocidade. Z~ code n Amer CEP de
endereçamento postal m, (P) código m
postal

zipper /'zɪpə(r)/ n (= zip(-fastener))
▶ ZIP

zodiac /'zəʊdɪæk/ n zodíaco m

zombie /'zɒmbɪ/ n zumbi m; ⊞ zumbi
m, (P) autómato m, zombie m

zone /zəʊn/ n zona f

zoo /zuː/ n jardim m zoológico

zoolog|y /zəʊ'ɒlədʒɪ/ n zoologia f.
~ical /-ə'lɒdʒɪkl/ a zoológico. ~ist n
zoólogo m

zoom /zuːm/ vi (rush) sair roando; ~ off
or past passar zunindo; ~ lens zum m,
zoom m

zucchini /zuː'kiːnɪ/ n (pl invar) Amer
courgette f

Portuguese verbs

Portuguese verbs can be divided into three categories: regular verbs, those with spelling peculiarities determined by their sound and irregular verbs.

Regular verbs:

in -ar (e.g. **comprar**)

Present: compr|o, ~as, ~a, ~amos, ~ais, ~am
Future: comprar|ei, ~ás, ~á, ~emos, ~eis, ~ão
Imperfect: compr|ava, ~avas, ~ava, ~ávamos, ~áveis, ~avam
Preterite: compr|ei, ~aste, ~ou, ~amos (P: ~ámos), ~astes, ~aram
Pluperfect: compr|ara, ~aras, ~ara, ~áramos, ~áreis, ~aram
Present subjunctive: compr|e, ~es, ~e, ~emos, ~eis, ~em
Imperfect subjunctive: compr|asse, ~asses, ~asse, ~ássemos, ~ásseis, ~assem
Future subjunctive: compr|ar, ~ares, ~ar, ~armos, ~ardes, ~arem
Conditional: comprar|ia, ~ias, ~ia, ~íamos, ~ieis, ~iam
Personal infinitive: comprar, ~es, ~, ~mos, ~des, ~em
Present participle: comprando
Past participle: comprado
Imperative: compra, comprai

in ~er (e.g. **bater**)

Present: bat|o, ~es, ~e, ~emos, ~eis, ~em
Future: bater|ei, ~ás, ~á, ~emos, ~eis, ~ão
Imperfect: bat|ia, ~ias, ~ia, ~íamos, ~íeis, ~iam
Preterite: bat|i, ~este, ~eu, ~emos, ~estes, ~eram

Pluperfect: bat|era, ~eras, ~era, ~êramos, ~êreis, ~eram
Present subjunctive: bat|a, ~as, ~a, ~amos, ~ais, ~am
Imperfect subjunctive: bat|esse, ~esses, ~esse, ~êssemos, ~êsseis, ~essem
Future subjunctive: bat|er, ~eres, ~er, ~ermos, ~erdes, ~erem
Conditional: bater|ia, ~ias, ~ia, ~íamos, ~ieis, ~iam
Personal infinitive: bater, ~es, ~, ~mos, ~des, ~em
Present participle: batendo
Past participle: batido
Imperative: bate, batei

in ~ir (e.g. **admitir**)

Present: admit|o, ~es, ~e, ~imos, ~is, ~em
Future: admitir|ei, ~ás, ~á, ~emos, ~eis, ~ão
Imperfect: admit|ia, ~ias, ~ia, ~íamos, ~ieis, ~iam
Preterite: admit|i, ~iste, ~iu, ~imos, ~istes, ~iram
Pluperfect: admit|ira, ~iras, ~ira, ~iramos, ~ireis, ~iram
Present subjunctive: admit|a, ~as, ~a, ~amos, ~ais, ~am
Imperfect subjunctive: admit|isse, ~isses, ~isse, ~íssemos, ~ísseis, ~issem
Future subjunctive: admit|ir, ~ires, ~ir, ~irmos, ~irdes, ~irem
Conditional: admitir|ia, ~ias, ~ia, ~íamos, ~ieis, ~iam
Personal infinitive: admitir, ~es, ~, ~mos, ~des, ~em
Present participle: admitindo
Past participle: admitido
Imperative: admite, admiti

Regular verbs with spelling changes:

-ar verbs:

in -car (e.g. ficar)

Preterite: fiquei, ficaste, ficou, ficamos (P: ficámos), ficais, ficam
Present subjunctive: fique, fiques, fique, fiquemos, fiqueis, fiquem

in -çar (e.g. abraçar)

Preterite: abracei, abraçaste, abraçou, abraçamos (P: abraçámos), abraçastes, abraçaram
Present subjunctive: abrace, abraces, abrace, abracemos, abraceis, abracem

in -ear (e.g. passear)

Present: passeio, passeias, passeia, passeamos, passeais, passeiam
Present subjunctive: passeie, passeies, passeie, passeemos, passeeis, passeiem
Imperative: passeia, passeai

in -gar (e.g. apagar)

Preterite: apaguei, apagaste, apagou, apagamos (P: apagámos), apagastes, apagaram
Present subjunctive: apague, apagues, apague, apaguemos, apagueis, apaguem

in -oar (e.g. voar)

Present: voo, voas, voa, voamos, voais, voam

averiguar

Preterite: averiguei, averiguaste, averiguou, averiguamos (P: averiguámos), averiguastes, averiguaram
Present subjunctive: averigue, averigues, averigue, averiguemos, averigueis, averiguem

enxaguar

Present: enxaguo, enxaguas, enxagua, enxaguamos, enxaguais, enxaguam
Preterite: enxaguei, enxaguaste, enxaguou, enxaguamos (P: enxaguámos), enxaguastes, enxaguaram
Present subjunctive: enxágue, enxagues, enxague, enxaguemos, enxagueis, enxaguem
Similarly: aguar, desaguar

saudar

Present: saúdo, saúdas, saúda, saudamos, saudais, saúdam
Present subjunctive: saúde, saúdes, saúde, saudemos, saudeis, saúdem
Imperative: saúda, saudai

-er verbs:

in -cer (e.g. tecer)

Present: teço, teces, tece, tecemos, teceis, tecem
Present subjunctive: teça, teças, teça, teçamos, teçais, teçam

in -ger (e.g. proteger)

Present: protejo, proteges, protege, protegemos, protegeis, protegem
Present subjunctive: proteja, protejas, proteja, protejamos, protejais, protejam

in -guer (e.g. erguer)

Present: ergo, ergues, ergue, erguemos, ergueis, erguem
Present subjunctive: erga, ergas, erga, ergamos, ergais, ergam

in -oer (e.g. roer)

Present: roo, róis, rói, roemos, roeis, roem
Imperfect: roía, roías, roía, roíamos, roíeis, roíam
Preterite: roí, roeste, roeu, roemos, roestes, roeram
Past participle: roído
Imperative: rói, roei

-ir verbs:

in -**ir** with -**e**- in stem (e.g. **vestir**)

Present: visto, vestes, veste, vestimos, vestis, vestem

Present subjunctive: vista, vistas, vista, vistamos, vistais, vistam

Similarly: mentir, preferir, refletir, repetir, seguir, sentir, servir

in -**ir** with -**o**- in stem (e.g. **dormir**)

Present: durmo, dormes, dorme, dormimos, dormis, dormem

Present subjunctive: durma, durmas, durma, durmamos, durmais, durmam

Similarly: cobrir, descobrir, tossir

in -**ir** with -**u**- in stem (e.g. **subir**)

Present: subo, sobes, sobe, subimos, subis, sobem

Similarly: consumir, cuspir, fugir, sacudir, sumir

in -**air** (e.g. **sair**)

Present: saio, sais, sai, saímos, saís, saem

Imperfect: saía, saías, saía, saíamos, saíeis, saíam

Preterite: saí, saíste, saiu, saímos, saístes, saíram

Pluperfect: saíra, saíras, saíra, saíramos, saíreis, saíram

Present subjunctive: saia, saias, saia, saiamos, saiais, saiam

Imperfect subjunctive: saísse, saísses, saísse, saíssemos, saísseis, saíssem

Future subjunctive: sair, saíres, sair, sairmos, sairdes, saírem

Personal infinitive: sair, saíres, sair, sairmos, sairdes, saírem

Present participle: saindo

Past participle: saído

Imperative: sai, saí

in -**gir** (e.g. **dirigir**)

Present: dirijo, diriges, dirige, dirigimos, dirigis, dirigem

Present subjunctive: dirija, dirijas, dirija, dirijamos, dirijais, dirijam

in -**guir** (e.g. **distinguir**)

Present: distingo, distingues, distingue, distinguimos, distinguis, distinguem

Present subjunctive: distinga, distingas, distinga, distingamos, distingais, distingam

in -**uir** (e.g. **atribuir**)

Present: atribuo, atribuis, atribui, atribuímos, atribuís, atribuem

Imperfect: atribuía, atribuías, atribuía, atribuíamos, atribuíeis, atribuíam

Preterite: atribuí, atribuíste, atribuiu, atribuímos, atribuístes, atribuíram

Pluperfect: atribuíra, atribuíras, atribuíra, atribuíramos, atribuíreis, atribuíram

Present subjunctive: atribua, atribuas, atribua, atribuamos, atribuais, atribuam

Imperfect subjunctive: atribuísse, atribuísses, atribuísse, atribuíssemos, atribuísseis, atribuíssem

Future subjunctive: atribuir, atribuíres, atribuir, atribuirmos, atribuirdes, atribuírem

Personal infinitive: atribuir, atribuíres, atribuir, atribuirmos, atribuirdes, atribuírem

Present participle: atribuindo

Past participle: atribuído

Imperative: atribui, atribuí

proibir

Present: proíbo, proíbes, proíbe, proibimos, proibis, proíbem

Present subjunctive: proíba, proíbas, proíba, proibamos, proibais, proíbam

Imperative: proíbe, proibi

Similarly: coibir

reunir

Present: reúno, reúnes, reúne, reunimos, reunis, reúnem

Present subjunctive: reúna, reúnas, reúna, reunamos, reunais, reúnam
Imperative: reúne, reuni

in -struir (e.g. **construir**) – like **atribuir** except:

Present: construo, constróis/construis, constrói/construi, construímos, construís, constroem/construem
Imperative: constrói/construi, construí

in -duzir (e.g. **produzir**)

Present: produzo, produzes, produz, produzimos, produzis, produzem
Imperative: produz(e), produzi
Similarly: luzir, reluzir

Irregular verbs

caber

Present: caibo, cabes, cabe, cabemos, cabeis, cabem
Preterite: coube, coubeste, coube, coubemos, coubestes, couberam
Pluperfect: coubera, couberas, coubera, coubéramos, coubéreis, couberam
Present subjunctive: caiba, caibas, caiba, caibamos, caibais, caibam
Imperfect subjunctive: coubesse, coubesses, coubesse, coubéssemos, coubésseis, coubessem
Future subjunctive: couber, couberes, couber, coubermos, couberdes, couberem

dar

Present: dou, dás, dá, damos, dais, dão
Preterite: dei, deste, deu, demos, destes, deram
Pluperfect: dera, deras, dera, déramos, déreis, deram
Present subjunctive: dê, dês, dê, demos, deis, deem
Imperfect subjunctive: desse, desses, desse, déssemos, désseis, dessem
Future subjunctive: der, deres, der, dermos, derdes, derem
Imperative: dá, dai

dizer

Present: digo, dizes, diz, dizemos, dizeis, dizem
Future: direi, dirás, dirá, diremos, direis, dirão
Preterite: disse, disseste, disse, dissemos, dissestes, disseram
Pluperfect: dissera, disseras, dissera, disséramos, disséreis, disseram
Present subjunctive: diga, digas, diga, digamos, digais, digam
Imperfect subjunctive: dissesse, dissesses, dissesse, disséssemos, dissésseis, dissessem
Future subjunctive: disser, disseres, disser, dissermos, disserdes, disserem
Conditional: diria, dirias, diria, diríamos, diríeis, diriam
Present participle: dizendo
Past participle: dito
Imperative: diz, dizei

estar

Present: estou, estás, está, estamos, estais, estão
Preterite: estive, estiveste, esteve, estivemos, estivestes, estiveram
Pluperfect: estivera, estiveras, estivera, estivéramos, estivéreis, estiveram
Present subjunctive: esteja, estejas, esteja, estejamos, estejais, estejam
Imperfect subjunctive: estivesse, estivesses, estivesse, estivéssemos, estivésseis, estivessem
Future subjunctive: estiver, estiveres, estiver, estivermos, estiverdes, estiverem
Imperative: está, estai

fazer

Present: faço, fazes, faz, fazemos, fazeis, fazem
Future: farei, farás, fará, faremos, fareis, farão
Preterite: fiz, fizeste, fez, fizemos, fizestes, fizeram

Pluperfect: fizera, fizeras, fizera, fizéramos, fizéreis, fizeram
Present subjunctive: faça, faças, faça, façamos, façais, façam
Imperfect subjunctive: fizesse, fizesses, fizesse, fizéssemos, fizésseis, fizessem
Future subjunctive: fizer, fizeres, fizer, fizermos, fizerdes, fizerem
Conditional: faria, farias, faria, faríamos, faríeis, fariam
Present participle: fazendo
Past participle: feito
Imperative: faz(e), fazei

frigir

Present: frijo, freges, frege, frigimos, frigis, fregem
Present subjunctive: frija, frijas, frija, frijamos, frijais, frijam
Imperative: frege, frigi

haver

Present: hei, hás, há, hemos/havemos, haveis/heis, hão
Preterite: houve, houveste, houve, houvemos, houvestes, houveram
Pluperfect: houvera, houveras, houvera, houvéramos, houvéreis, houveram
Present subjunctive: haja, hajas, haja, hajamos, hajais, hajam
Imperfect subjunctive: houvesse, houvesses, houvesse, houvéssemos, houvésseis, houvessem
Future subjunctive: houver, houveres, houver, houvermos, houverdes, houverem
Imperative: há, havei

ir

Present: vou, vais, vai, vamos, ides, vão
Imperfect: ia, ias, ia, íamos, íeis, iam
Preterite: fui, foste, foi, fomos, fostes, foram
Pluperfect: fora, foras, fora, fôramos, fôreis, foram
Present subjunctive: vá, vás, vá, vamos, vades, vão

Imperfect subjunctive: fosse, fosses, fosse, fôssemos, fôsseis, fossem
Future subjunctive: for, fores, for, formos, fordes, forem
Present participle: indo
Past participle: ido
Imperative: vai, ide

ler

Present: leio, lês, lê, lemos, ledes, leem
Imperfect: lia, lias, lia, líamos, líeis, liam
Preterite: li, leste, leu, lemos, lestes, leram
Pluperfect: lera, leras, lera, lêramos, lêreis, leram
Present subjunctive: leia, leias, leia, leiamos, leiais, leiam
Imperfect subjunctive: lesse, lesses, lesse, lêssemos, lêsseis, lessem
Future subjunctive: ler, leres, ler, lermos, lerdes, lerem
Present participle: lendo
Past participle: lido
Imperative: lê, lede
Similarly: crer

odiar

Present: odeio, odeias, odeia, odiamos, odiais, odeiam
Present subjunctive: odeie, odeies, odeie, odiemos, odieis, odeiem
Imperative: odeia, odiai
Similarly: incendiar

ouvir

Present: ouço (P also: oiço), ouves, ouve, ouvimos, ouvis, ouvem
Present subjunctive: ouça, ouças, ouça, ouçamos, ouçais, ouçam (P also: oiça, oiças, oiça, oiçamos, oiçais, oiçam)

pedir

Present: peço, pedes, pede, pedimos, pedis, pedem
Present subjunctive: peça, peças, peça, peçamos, peçais, peçam
Similarly: despedir, impedir, medir

. . . .

perder

Present: perco, perdes, perde,
perdemos, perdeis, perdem
Present subjunctive: perca, percas, perca,
percamos, percais, percam

poder

Present: posso, podes, pode, podemos,
podeis, podem
Preterite: pude, pudeste, pôde,
pudemos, pudestes, puderam
Pluperfect: pudera, puderas, pudera,
pudéramos, pudéreis, puderam
Present subjunctive: possa, possas, possa,
possamos, possais, possam
Imperfect subjunctive: pudesse, pudesses,
pudesse, pudéssemos, pudésseis,
pudessem
Future subjunctive: puder, puderes,
puder, pudermos, puderdes,
puderem

polir

Present: pulo, pules, pule, polimos,
polis, pulem
Present subjunctive: pula, pulas, pula,
pulamos, pulais, pulam
Imperative: pule, poli

pôr

Present: ponho, pões, põe, pomos,
pondes, põem
Future: porei, porás, porá, poremos,
poreis, porão
Imperfect: punha, punhas, punha,
púnhamos, púnheis, punham
Preterite: pus, puseste, pôs, pusemos,
pusestes, puseram
Pluperfect: pusera, puseras, pusera,
puséramos, puséreis, puseram
Present subjunctive: ponha, ponhas,
ponha, ponhamos, ponhais, ponham
Imperfect subjunctive: pusesse, pusesses,
pusesse, puséssemos, pusésseis,
pusessem
Future subjunctive: puser, puseres,
puser, pusermos, puserdes, puserem
Conditional: poria, porias, poria,
poríamos, poríeis, poriam

Present participle: pondo
Past participle: posto
Imperative: põe, ponde
Similarly: compor, depor, dispor, opor,
supor etc

prover

Present: provejo, provês, provê,
provemos, provedes, proveem
Present subjunctive: proveja, provejas,
proveja, provejamos, provejais,
provejam
Imperative: provê, provede

querer

Present: quero, queres, quer, queremos,
quereis, querem
Preterite: quis, quiseste, quis, quisemos,
quisestes, quiseram
Pluperfect: quisera, quiseras, quisera,
quiséramos, quiséreis, quiseram
Present subjunctive: queira, queiras,
queira, queiramos, queirais, queiram
Imperfect subjunctive: quisesse,
quisesses, quisesse, quiséssemos,
quisésseis, quisessem
Future subjunctive: quiser, quiseres,
quiser, quisermos, quiserdes,
quiserem
Imperative: quer, querei

requerer

Present: requeiro, requeres, requer,
requeremos, requereis, requerem
Present subjunctive: requeira, requeiras,
requeira, requeiramos, requeirais,
requeiram
Imperative: requer, requerei

rir

Present: rio, ris, ri, rimos, rides, riem
Present subjunctive: ria, rias, ria, riamos,
riais, riam
Imperative: ri, ride
Similarly: sorrir

saber

Present: sei, sabes, sabe, sabemos,
sabeis, sabem

Preterite: soube, soubeste, soube, soubemos, soubestes, souberam

Pluperfect: soubera, souberas, soubera, soubéramos, soubéreis, souberam

Present subjunctive: saiba, saibas, saiba, saibamos, saibais, saibam

Imperfect subjunctive: soubesse, soubesses, soubesse, soubéssemos, soubésseis, soubessem

Future subjunctive: souber, souberes, souber, soubermos, souberdes, souberem

Imperative: sabe, sabei

ser

Present: sou, és, é, somos, sois, são

Imperfect: era, eras, era, éramos, éreis, eram

Preterite: fui, foste, foi, fomos, fostes, foram

Pluperfect: fora, foras, fora, fôramos, fôreis, foram

Present subjunctive: seja, sejas, seja, sejamos, sejais, sejam

Imperfect subjunctive: fosse, fosses, fosse, fôssemos, fôsseis, fossem

Future subjunctive: for, fores, for, formos, fordes, forem

Present participle: sendo

Past participle: sido

Imperative: sê, sede

ter

Present: tenho, tens, tem, temos, tendes, têm

Imperfect: tinha, tinhas, tinha, tínhamos, tínheis, tinham

Preterite: tive, tiveste, teve, tivemos, tivestes, tiveram

Pluperfect: tivera, tiveras, tivera, tivéramos, tivéreis, tiveram

Present subjunctive: tenha, tenhas, tenha, tenhamos, tenhais, tenham

Imperfect subjunctive: tivesse, tivesses, tivesse, tivéssemos, tivésseis, tivessem

Future subjunctive: tiver, tiveres, tiver, tivermos, tiverdes, tiverem

Present participle: tendo

Past participle: tido

Imperative: tem, tende

trazer

Present: trago, trazes, traz, trazemos, trazeis, trazem

Future: trarei, trarás, trará, traremos, trareis, trarão

Preterite: trouxe, trouxeste, trouxe, trouxemos, trouxestes, trouxeram

Pluperfect: trouxera, trouxeras, trouxera, trouxéramos, trouxéreis, trouxeram

Present subjunctive: traga, tragas, traga, tragamos, tragais, tragam

Imperfect subjunctive: trouxesse, trouxesses, trouxesse, trouxéssemos, trouxésseis, trouxessem

Future subjunctive: trouxer, trouxeres, trouxer, trouxermos, trouxerdes, trouxerem

Conditional: traria, trarias, traria, traríamos, traríeis, trariam

Imperative: traze, trazei

valer

Present: valho, vales, vale, valemos, valeis, valem

Present subjunctive: valha, valhas, valha, valhamos, valhais, valham

ver

Present: vejo, vês, vê, vemos, vedes, veem

Imperfect: via, vias, via, víamos, víeis, viam

Preterite: vi, viste, viu, vimos, vistes, viram

Pluperfect: vira, viras, vira, víramos, víreis, viram

Present subjunctive: veja, vejas, veja, vejamos, vejais, vejam

Imperfect subjunctive: visse, visses, visse, víssemos, vísseis, vissem

Future subjunctive: vir, vires, vir, virmos, virdes, virem

Present participle: vendo

Past participle: visto

Imperative: vê, vede

. . . .

vir

Present: venho, vens, vem, vimos, vindes, vêm

Imperfect: vinha, vinhas, vinha, vínhamos, vínheis, vinham

Preterite: vim, vieste, veio, viemos, viestes, vieram

Pluperfect: viera, vieras, viera, viéramos, viéreis, vieram

Present subjunctive: venha, venhas, venha, venhamos, venhais, venham

Imperfect subjunctive: viesse, viesses, viesse, viéssemos, viésseis, viessem

Future subjunctive: vier, vieres, vier, viermos, vierdes, vierem

Present participle: vindo

Past participle: vindo

Imperative: vem, vinde

Verbos irregulares ingleses

Infinitivo	Pretérito	Particípio passado	Infinitivo	Pretérito	Particípio passado
be	was	been	find	found	found
bear	bore	borne	flee	fled	fled
beat	beat	beaten	fly	flew	flown
become	became	become	freeze	froze	frozen
begin	began	begun	get	got	got, gotten US
bend	bent	bent	give	gave	given
bet	bet, betted	bet, betted	go	went	gone
bid	bade, bid	bidden, bid	grow	grew	grown
bind	bound	bound	hang	hung,	hung,
bite	bit	bitten		hanged	hanged
bleed	bled	bled	have	had	had
blow	blew	blown	hear	heard	heard
break	broke	broken	hide	hid	hidden
breed	bred	bred	hit	hit	hit
bring	brought	brought	hold	held	held
build	built	built	hurt	hurt	hurt
burn	burnt,	burnt,	keep	kept	kept
	burned	burned	kneel	knelt	knelt
burst	burst	burst	know	knew	known
buy	bought	bought	lay	laid	laid
catch	caught	caught	lead	led	led
choose	chose	chosen	lean	leaned,	leaned,
cling	clung	clung		leant	leant
come	came	come	learn	learnt,	learnt,
cost	cost,	cost,		learned	learned
	costed (vt)	costed	leave	left	left
cut	cut	cut	lend	lent	lent
deal	dealt	dealt	let	let	let
dig	dug	dug	lie	lay	lain
do	did	done	lose	lost	lost
draw	drew	drawn	make	made	made
dream	dreamt,	dreamt,	mean	meant	meant
	dreamed	dreamed	meet	met	met
drink	drank	drunk	pay	paid	paid
drive	drove	driven	put	put	put
eat	ate	eaten	read	read	read
fall	fell	fallen	ride	rode	ridden
feed	fed	fed	ring	rang	rung
feel	felt	felt	rise	rose	risen
fight	fought	fought	run	ran	run

Verbos irregulares ingleses

Infinitivo	Pretérito	Particípio passado	Infinitivo	Pretérito	Particípio passado
say	said	said	**spread**	spread	spread
see	saw	seen	**spring**	sprang	sprung
seek	sought	sought	**stand**	stood	stood
sell	sold	sold	**steal**	stole	stolen
send	sent	sent	**stick**	stuck	stuck
set	set	set	**sting**	stung	stung
sew	sewed	sewn, sewed	**stride**	strode	stridden
shake	shook	shaken	**strike**	struck	struck
shine	shone	shone	**swear**	swore	sworn
shoe	shod	shod	**sweep**	swept	swept
shoot	shot	shot	**swell**	swelled	swollen, swelled
show	showed	shown			
shut	shut	shut	**swim**	swam	swum
sing	sang	sung	**swing**	swung	swung
sink	sank	sunk	**take**	took	taken
sit	sat	sat	**teach**	taught	taught
sleep	slept	slept	**tear**	tore	torn
sling	slung	slung	**tell**	told	told
smell	smelt, smelled	smelt, smelled	**think**	thought	thought
			throw	threw	thrown
speak	spoke	spoken	**thrust**	thrust	thrust
spell	spelled, spelt	spelled, spelt	**tread**	trod	trodden
			understand	understood	understood
spend	spent	spent	**wake**	woke	woken
spit	spat	spat	**wear**	wore	worn
spoil	spoilt, spoiled	spoilt, spoiled	**win**	won	won
			write	wrote	written